Neuro-Vision Systems

Neuro-Vision Systems
Principles and Applications

Edited by

Madan M. Gupta
University of Saskatchewan

George K. Knopf
University of Western Ontario

A Selected Reprint Volume
IEEE Neural Networks Council, *Sponsor*

The Institute of Electrical and Electronics Engineers, Inc., New York

Library of Congress Cataloging-in-Publication Data

Neuro-vision systems : principles and applications / Madan M. Gupta and George K. Knopf, editors.
    p.   cm.
    Includes bibliographical references and index.
    ISBN 0-7803-1042-X
    1. Neural networks (Computer science) 2. Computer vision.
  I. Gupta, Madan M. II. Knopf, George K.
  QA76.87.N494   1993
  006.3'7—dc20
                                     93-30009
                                          CIP

Contents

Foreword

In 1959, Lettvin, Maturana, McCulloch, and Pitts published their paper, "What the frog's eye tells the frog's brain," in the *Proceedings of the Institute of Radio Engineers* (the forebear of IEEE). This pioneering work was accepted with sensational enthusiasm by engineers because it showed that each animal has its own exquisitely designed and organized neural networks for fulfilling its purposes for living. At the same time, the paper suggested innovative, fresh ideas for information processing. However, two decades later, the main stream of visual information processing has completely immersed itself in high-speed digital processing, which society has uncritically embraced. We now realize the limitations and problems of digital computations for image comprehension, and are forced to renew our understanding of the brain and its neural systems, with their heterogeneous approach to information processing.

In parallel with the evolution of computer science, basic research in the visual sciences carried out in the traditional fields of biology, physiology, and psychology have made enormous progress. During the last two decades, new trends in neuroscience, brain science, computational neuroscience, and cognitive neuroscience have emerged, and tremendous advances in our understanding of lower, middle, and higher visual functions have been achieved. The brain is a meta-network of networks of basic neurons. However, its meta-structure is still covered by a deep veil. Visual function is one of the most important sensory systems in the brain, and its role is "understanding" the external world rather than just "seeing." In other words, we see with our brain, not with our eyes. F. H. C. Crick expressed this well in his *Scientific American* article, "Thinking about the brain":

> Few people realize what an astonishing achievement it is to be able to see at all. The main contribution of the relatively new field of artificial intelligence has

been not so much to solve these problems of information handling as to show what tremendously difficult problems they are. When one reflects on the computations that must have to be carried out before one can recognize even such an everyday scene as another person crossing the street, one is left with a feeling of amazement that such an extraordinary series of detailed operations can be accomplished so effortlessly in such a short space of time.

The visual system incorporates many ingenious mechanisms and functions which are still beyond our ken. However, significant progress in understanding these mechanisms and functions has been achieved, especially in the last decade. The way in which external information is represented internally, integrated into understanding, and the rationale behind the way the brain is organized, although still murky, has become clearer. We continue to face challenging problems in comprehending the structure and function of the Neuro-Vision System whose blueprint continues to elude us; what we have found to date may not be true, or might be a very one-sided view. Science always seeks, indeed requires, innovative interpretations. Creative thinking, unfettered by preconceptions and without the limitations of accepted dogma, is sorely needed.

This IEEE book is a valuable, comprehensive compilation of our current understanding of neuro-vision systems, and a milestone in the history of visual science.

Shiro Usui
Toyohashi University of Technology
Toyohashi, Japan

Preface

He believes that he sees his retinal images: he would have a shock if he could.

—George Humphry

The recent emergence of new and complex robotic systems in space, manufacturing, and the health sciences have created a demand for better vision systems. These vision systems should be able to see and perceive—perhaps as we humans do. This has led to an increased appreciation of the neuronal morphology of biological vision, especially for the human vision system. Scientists from various disciplines, such as neuroanatomy and neurophysiology, are discovering some exciting facts about the visual pathway, which extends from the retina to the visual cortex, through their experimental studies on various biological species. On the other hand, scientists from disciplines such as systems science, computer sciences, and mathematics are formulating the theories of neuronal functions in the visual pathway from mathematical and computational points of view. Thus, these recent studies have led to a better understanding of the neuronal morphology of biological vision, as well as better computational neural structures for the construction of artificial vision systems. Some of these studies have evolved over the last four decades, but recent studies, especially those during the last decade, have provided some interesting neural paradigms, models, computing architectures, and hardware implementations.

This IEEE Press volume is about the principles, applications, architectures, and hardware models of neuro-vision systems—artificial neural machines that can "see" and "perceive" our visual world. There are numerous research publications in the field but they are scattered throughout many scientific journals and conference proceedings. In our own research studies and classroom teaching, we have not found a manageable source to which we can refer our students. We are sure that many other educators and researchers in the field must have faced similar frustrations during their own teaching and research efforts. This frustration has motivated us to develop a book devoted to the field, and here is the birth of this volume on neuro-vision systems.

In designing this book, our goal was to present a pedagogically sound reprint volume on neuro-vision systems that would be useful as a supplementary or even as a main text for graduate students. Additionally, this collection of literature should have conceptual and theoretical information embodying a comprehensive view of the general field of neuronal morphology of biological vision, as well as artificial neuro-vision systems. We hope that our efforts in this volume will stimulate the research interest of the readers. This work will also provide a comprehensive view of the field for practicing engineers, researchers, and students.

In order to meet these objectives, 47 of the most significant articles from over thousands of articles published since 1943 (but mostly in the last decade) were chosen, and we feel that these articles will provide a wide perspective of the field. This collection contains a wide breadth of refereed papers dealing with the philosophical aspects of biological vision, survey papers on computational neural networks, and a variety of current papers dealing specifically with neuro-vision architecture, theoretical models, hardware implementations, and a variety of applications.

This collection thus provides "an instant library" from which students, researchers, and practicing engineers may obtain an overall picture of the early and recent activities in this important field. The authors of these research articles are from some very well known schools distributed over a wide geographical area around the globe.*

The field of neuro-vision made slow progress initially, but it has advanced very rapidly as is evident by the increasing num-

---

*The countrywide distribution of the authors for these papers is as follows:

Canada	(2)	Japan	(4)	United States	(37)
Finland	(1)	Singapore	(1)	USSR (former)	(2)
France	(2)	Taiwan	(2)	Yugoslavia	(2)
Israel	(2)				

ber of publications. It was, therefore, an extremely difficult task for the editors to select relatively few articles from the large amount of candidates. We are keenly aware of the many excellent papers that had to be excluded in order to produce a balanced collection of a manageable size. However, our editorial efforts, consultations with some researchers working in the field, and feedback received from many reviewers have resulted in selecting these papers. Extensive editorial comments and reference material are provided in order to unify the set of papers written by such a diverse group of researchers. This collection of articles, however, does provide different mathematical formulations along with different perspectives that were developed during the continual evolution of the field.

Although we have included introductory material to each part, we have also written an extensive tutorial on neurovision systems, especially with regard to the neuronal morphology of biological vision using simple systems-theory explanations. The neural paradigms are described using block diagrams and uncluttered mathematics.

This work is self-contained, and it is our hope that this volume will provide its readers not only with valuable conceptual and technical information, but also with a comprehensive view of the general field of neuro-vision systems, its problems, accomplishments, and future potentials.*

> *. . . for there is no quality in this world that is not what it is merely by contrast. Nothing exists in itself.*
> —Herman Melville

*Entropy is a measure of *uncertainty*. The process of true learning is always driven by the process of curiosity. This curiosity that arises during the process of learning creates some uncertainty in the mind of the reader. Therefore, an effective process of learning always raises the level of entropy in intelligent minds. We will consider our efforts in this collective work to be successful only if its reading helps to increase the entropy level of the curious reader.

Acknowledgments

The ideas for this volume on neuro-vision systems were conceived during classroom and research discussions; these ideas were nurtured in the warm and fertile atmosphere that exists at the Intelligent Systems Research Laboratory, College of Engineering, University of Saskatchewan. After many learning and adaptive iterations, we were able to produce a set of collective knowledge in the form of this book.

During the editorial phases, we discussed the matter with many of our research colleagues. We started with a long list of potential articles (over 300), and, during the $(n-1)$th iteration, we ended up with an appropriate size of the volume, arranged and divided into a pedagogical style. Because the size of the book (about 90 articles) was unmanageable in a single volume, during the nth iteration we cut down the size of the volume to half (it was a painful process), but we preserved the basic theme and structure of the book. We have appended each part of the volume with an extensive reading list; these reading lists contain papers that we were forced to remove during the various editorial phases.

We are grateful to many research colleagues around the globe who have inspired our own thinking in this emerging field of neuro-vision systems. Also, we are grateful to Mr. Dudley Kay, Director of Book Publishing, who continuously provided useful feedback, and Ms. Karen Miller, Production Editor, IEEE Press, who is responsible for the final physical production of the book.

Indeed, we are very much indebted to our families and wives (M. M. Gupta: Suman; G. K. Knopf: Eirin) who have generously supported this project at each step by letting us use family time during evenings, weekends, and holidays.

Madan M. Gupta
George K. Knopf

Major Current Bibliographical Sources on Computational Neural Networks and Applications

Societies (Neural Networks)

- Neural Information Processing Systems (Natural and Synthetic) (NIPS)
- World Congress on Neural Networks (WCNN)
- IEEE International Conference on Neural Networks (IEEE ICNN)
- International Joint Conference on Neural Networks (IJCNN)
- Japanese Neural Network Society (JNNS)
- International Neural Network Society (INNS)
- European Neural Network Society (ENNS)

Major Journals (Neural Networks)

- *IEEE Transactions on Neural Networks*
- *Neural Networks* (ICNN)
- *Neural Computation*
- *Neurocomputing and Networks*
- *International Journal on Neural and Mass-Parallel Computing and Information Systems* (*Neural Network World*)
- *IEEE Transactions on Fuzzy Systems*
- *Biophysical Journal*
- *Biological Cybernetics*
- *International Journal of Neural Systems*

Neuro-Vision Systems: A Tutorial

MADAN M. GUPTA
UNIVERSITY OF SASKATCHEWAN

GEORGE K. KNOPF
UNIVERSITY OF WESTERN ONTARIO

Abstract—The topic of neuro-vision provides many challenges in both our teaching and research efforts. In this introductory chapter, we attempt to give the basic motivation for studying the subject material and provide our readers with an overview of related topics in the field, such as the basis of biological vision, functional role of visual receptive fields, mathematical foundation of computational neural networks, engineering applications of neuro-vision systems, and hardware implementations. This tutorial is prepared with the intent that it will provide a basic and unified view of the field, and will help the reader to better understand the advanced material—written by some world-renowned researchers in the field—presented in the main part of the volume.

1. PERSPECTIVES ON NEURO-VISION SYSTEMS

Copying the round shape of the universe, they confined the two divine revolutions in a spherical body—the head—which is the divinest part of us and lord over all the rest.

Plato [1]

1.1 Introduction

This volume is about the principles and applications of neuro-vision systems—the artificial neural machines that are designed to see and perceive our visual world. In order to comprehend the recent advances made in the field of neuro-vision systems, readers need some basic understanding of both the neuronal* morphology of biological vision and the various artificial neural paradigms reported in the literature. The former is the inspiration and the latter provides the basic theoretical neural computing tools used in the development of neural-vision processes for machine applications. Both of these subfields, which have evolved over the last several decades, offer challenges to mature readers but frustrations to novices in the field. Challenges exist because reading the material in these areas is very satisfying and it provides motivation for further research studies. They do, however, provide frustrations to novice readers because these subfields are still evolving, and the research contributions are being made by a diverse group of scientists from such academic disciplines as

neurophysiology, computer science, systems science, and mathematics. Naturally, the scientists from different disciplines who have made significant contributions to these subfields have viewed the neuro-vision problem from different angles[1.1].** As a result, they have used the mathematical notations and explanations according to their own disciplines. All of this, no doubt, is of great significance to the evolution of the field of neuro-vision, but a mixture of notations and confusing mathematics can be frustrating to the novice reader. Indeed, it is often difficult for an experienced practitioner of neural-network theory to understand some of the mathematical expressions. Even the editors of this volume have experienced the mixed feelings of "pleasure" and "frustration" during their own studies of the vast amount of research literature that exist in the field, and especially during the assembly of this book, with papers authored by a diverse group of scientists. We have taken this "frustrating state of the field" as a challenge and have attempted to unify this diverse set of journal papers by means of this introductory tutorial. We are pleased to report that this diversification in material has provided numerous opportunities to many other diligent researchers whose works appear in various review papers and workshops.

In this introductory part of the volume, we provide a brief review of two areas: the neuronal morphology of biological vision and the various artificial neural-network paradigms used in the development of neuro-vision systems. Since the work reported in this volume is a collection of papers written by over one hundred researchers from some ten countries, spanning a period of some twenty years, this collection can naturally be considered as a collection of thoughts that were developed during the evolutionary phases of the field. Our attempt in this volume has been to provide some basic pedagogical material for the benefit of the reader. We will introduce the field of neuronal morphology of biological vision using simple schematic diagrams and a systems-theory type of explanation. The neural paradigms are developed using block diagrams and

---

*The terms *neuronal* and *neural* have been used simultaneously in the literature. However, the authors reserve *neuronal* for biological processes and *neural* for artificial processes.

**A boldface reference number refers to an article included in this reprint volume.

1

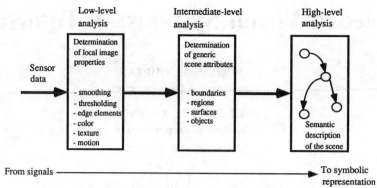

Fig. 1.1 The basic analytical levels of the signals-to-symbols paradigm
for a machine vision system.

mathematics that are uncluttered by super- and subscripts. The basis of our approach, in fact, is the *systems approach*—the field that has the inherent strength of explaining complex phenomena in a simple way using explanatory block diagrams, appropriate mathematics, graphs, and sketches. The editors of the volume are fortunate to have both training and a strong interest in the systems field.

1.2 What Is Neuro-Vision?

The successful operation of any intelligent machine depends on its ability to cope with a variety of unexpected events. Such cognitive machines must independently perceive, memorize, and comprehend the constantly changing real-world environment in which they operate. Vision is considered to be the richest of all the sensory processes because of its diverse informative nature and the remoteness of the vision sensors from the physical scene. Our own visual process is relatively quick, effortless, and highly robust. At present, this sophisticated form of perceptual vision is within the exclusive domain of higher-order biological organisms, such as human beings. These basic attributes are still not found in existing computer-vision algorithms and hardware systems that have been developed over the years for machine-vision applications. In general, machine-vision system designs are still in a very primitive stage, and the present-day technology is unable to support many of the recent theoretical developments in the field.

The science of machine vision largely involves the development of computational strategies that attempt to model certain attributes of human visual perception within the physical constraints of the existing digital computing hardware [**1.4**]. The dominant computational paradigms for vision involve the transformation of raw sensory data into some meaningful scene descriptions by using logical steps that employ progressively more and more abstract representations of the original scene [2]. These sequential transformational steps can be partitioned into three levels: low-level, intermediate-level, and high-level, whereupon each level reflects a progressively more and more complex form of analysis. The low-level scene analysis involves the processing of local image properties, intermediate-level scene analysis uses generic geometric models to determine scene attributes from local image properties,

and high-level scene analysis converts the geometric models into global symbolic representations. These symbolic representations enable the scene to be expressed in a semantic form. The basic processing levels in a typical machine-vision system, called the *signals-to-symbols* paradigm, are illustrated in Fig. 1.1.

On a conventional digital machine, software-based machine-vision systems that use the signals-to-symbols paradigm are not very efficient because the computational power required for processing and extracting features from a typical time-varying visual scene is immense. If only one instruction per pixel is to be performed on a standard digital image containing ¾ million pixels that change at a rate of thirty frames per second, then a software-based vision algorithm implemented on a digital computer would be required to perform approximately 23 million instructions per second. Any realistic vision algorithm, however, involves far more than a single instruction per pixel. Thus, to achieve real-time visual-information-processing capabilities, many machine-vision system designers have proposed using faster and faster digital processors.

This is in sharp contrast to our own visual experience, where we are able to perceive and provide a meaning to a complex time-varying scene in approximately 70 to 200 ms [3] using relatively slow information-processing elements called *neurons;* neurons need about 2 milliseconds to generate a response. Furthermore, many aspects of early biological vision are achieved in only 18 to 46 transformation steps [3], far fewer than the millions of transformation operations required by a sequential algorithm implemented on a conventional digital computer. Therefore, an understanding of the neuronal morphology of biological vision is imperative for designing fast and efficient machine-vision systems. Indeed, many engineers and computer scientists have recently realized the importance of emulating the neuronal computational principles of the biological vision process for designing and developing more robust artificial vision systems.

To achieve a high level of performance, biology employs a computational architecture that is fundamentally different from that of a digital computer. It has been estimated that 60% of the sensory information received by an individual is projected through the visual pathway [**4.3**]. The human visual system may be interpreted, therefore, as the main channel for acquiring perceptual information about the physical environ-

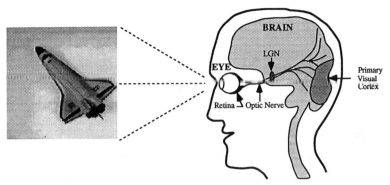

Fig. 1.2 A side view of the human visual pathway, illustrating the primary anatomical regions used for visual information processing and reorganization.

ment. The visual information generated on the photoreceptive layers of the retina undergoes extensive processing and reorganization as it traverses the visual pathway to the visual cortex. The importance placed on vision is further evident by the heavy volume of traffic in electrochemical signals that are being transmitted through the optic nerves. Most nerve fibers that leave the retina as the optic nerve travel along a pathway to the lateral geniculate nucleus (LGN) in the thalamus and then branch out to various areas of the visual cortex, as illustrated in Fig. 1.2. A small percentage of these fibers project onto the superior colliculus, which helps to control eye movement.

The visual pathway can be envisioned as a large ensemble of parallel neuronal channels that transduce, transmit, and process visual information. Each successive anatomical structure along the visual pathway, such as the eye or brain, performs a specific set of computational operations on the incoming visual signals. In essence, biological vision employs not only massively parallel but also a shallow hierarchical information-processing architecture. As visual information flows from the retina to the deeper cortical regions, the visual attributes contained within a scene become progressively more and more abstract [**4.3, 6.2,** 3,4]. The process eventually culminates at certain cortical neurons that respond selectively to complex objects, such as a face or a hand. In other words, different high-level cortical neurons will respond to different faces or positioning of a given face. In this fashion, more global and abstract representations of the visual world can be obtained by accessing information as it travels from the retina toward the cortex.

Although the transformation and reorganization of the detailed visual data into abstract representations in the biological visual process is functionally similar to the signals-to-symbols paradigm of a computer-vision system, the biological visual pathway employs a fundamentally different computational architecture to achieve this task in real time. Each successive anatomical structure along the visual pathway is composed of various neuronal tissue regions, such as the retina or striate cortex, that can be divided into one or more neuronal layers that perform computations in parallel. Furthermore, these densely interconnected neuronal layers perform both spatial

(x–y plane) and temporal (time-dependent) aspects of visual information processing. A schematic diagram illustrating the parallel and hierarchical architecture of the human visual pathway from the retina to the visual cortex is given in Fig. 1.3.

The study of biological vision provides a motivation and a general framework for designing a fast and robust vision system [**1.2**]. From the perspective of a vision-systems engineer, it is not necessary for us to emulate the precise electrophysiological (hardware) aspects of biological vision. Rather, it is desirable to replicate some of the neuronal computational structures found in biological vision that are involved in processing, storing, and interpreting the spatio-temporal visual information [**1.3**]. In this way, the neuronal principles derived from vision physiology may be used to design and develop more effective "engineered" machine-vision systems. The term *neuro-vision* is thus used in this volume to refer to any artificial or machine-vision system that embodies the computational principles of biological neural circuits. The process of designing artificial neuro-vision systems based on biological analogies is more aptly termed *reverse bioengineering* [**3.4,** 3,4] or *inverse biomedical engineering* [5].

1.3 Outline of the Tutorial

The purpose of this volume on neuro-vision systems is to present a broad perspective of the research being undertaken in both the theoretical design and actual implementation of vision systems based on biological analogies. In this context, a wide breadth of classical and contemporary papers dealing with the biological principles of vision, computational neural networks, applications, and hardware implementations of neuro-vision systems are presented. The focus of this volume is to transfer the basic knowledge of visual neuro-biology to the engineering community in order to advance the development of artificial vision algorithms and hardware mechanisms for various applications in robotics, manufacturing, space, and health sciences.

This introduction is organized as follows. Section 2 is a brief overview of the biological vision system from the basic biological computing element—the neuron—to the neuronal tissue of the visual pathway, which includes the retina, the lateral geniculate nucleus (LGN), the primary visual cortex, and

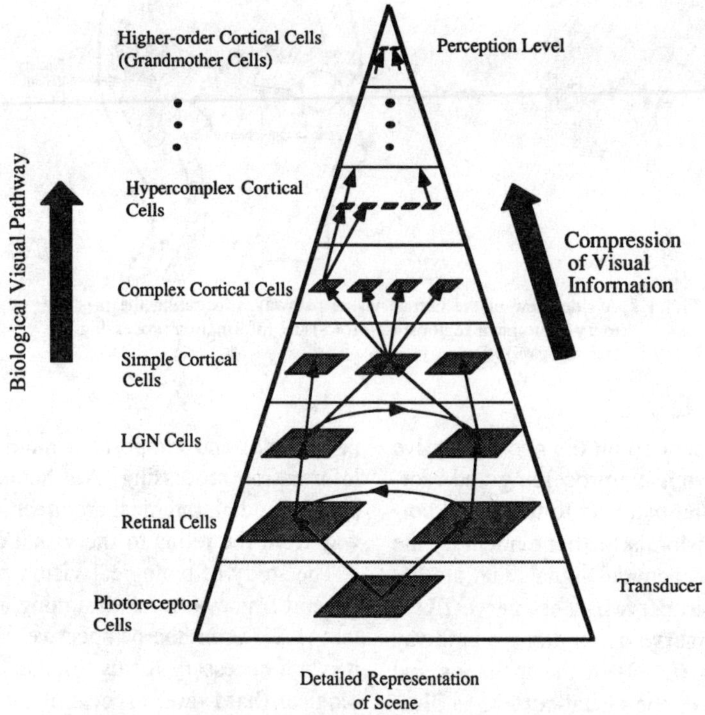

Fig. 1.3 The parallel–hierarchical architecture of the human visual pathway, from the retina (transducer level) to the visual cortex (perception level).

the higher cortical regions of the brain. The functional role of neuronal receptive fields along the visual pathway are described in Section 3. These visual receptive fields can be interpreted as either feature detectors, spatial frequency filters, or Gabor functions. Each of these interpretations has its supporters and detractors.

In Section 4, we present the mathematical foundation of computational neural networks. This section focuses on a simple systems explanation of the computational ability of a single neural-information-processing element and how it can be incorporated within static (feedforward) and dynamic (feedback) neural networks. We have chosen to avoid the numerous labels used to describe specific neural-network models in order to present a unifying picture of neural computing. Specific neural models are described in varying detail in the references and the selected papers included in this volume. Examples of neuro-vision systems for temporal and spatial filtering, image compression, image coding, optical flow, stereo vision correspondence, image segmentation, and invariant shape recognition are briefly described in Section 5. These examples are selected in order to illustrate the versatility of the neuro-vision approach to engineering applications. Section 6 is an overview of the computer-based, electronic, and optical/opto-electronic implementations of neuro-vision systems. Finally, a summary of this introduction and the remaining contents of the volume are presented in Section 7. The references listed in Section 8 will enable the reader to seek out more details on any of these subjects.

2. BIOLOGICAL VISION SYSTEM

A fundamental hypothesis in neuroscience is that all of the computational operations performed by the human nervous system may be explained in terms of the electrical impulses that are being transmitted between individual nerve cells called neurons. The central nervous system (CNS) is viewed as a vast network of neurons arranged in a variety of anatomical structures that have different degrees of complexities in neural interconnectivity. The CNS receives sensory inputs from a vast array of receptors associated with taste, touch, smell, hearing, and sight. These sensory receptors convert stimuli from the external world into some equivalent electrical impulse patterns. These patterns are then communicated to complex multilayer neuronal structures for further processing.

The organized structure of the CNS can be described at several different anatomical scales. Figure 2.1 shows the various scales of the structural organization from the molecular level to the neuron, neuronal layer, neuronal tissue, and system levels [1.1, 6]. As a result, numerous theoretical models have been developed by researchers in order to describe how the CNS, particularly the brain, works. Some researchers have developed models based on a global or systems perspective [7–10], whereas others [3.6, 11] have attempted to explain brain function at the lowest molecular level. The structure of the CNS is conceptually separable at every scale but not detachable in any physical sense because these levels are all highly interrelated [1.1]. Investigations into brain function

4

Spatial scale	Structural level	Examples in biological vision

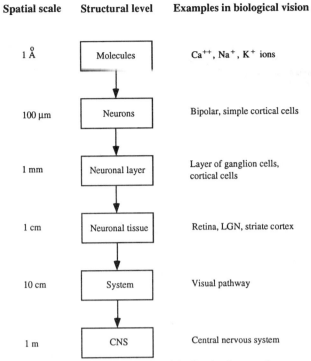

1 Å	Molecules	Ca⁺⁺, Na⁺, K⁺ ions
100 μm	Neurons	Bipolar, simple cortical cells
1 mm	Neuronal layer	Layer of ganglion cells, cortical cells
1 cm	Neuronal tissue	Retina, LGN, striate cortex
10 cm	System	Visual pathway
1 m	CNS	Central nervous system

Fig. 2.1 Different structural levels of organization for the central nervous system (CNS), from molecular level to CNS level at an increasing spatial scale. Examples of the corresponding anatomical components for the biological visual pathway are also given.

and biological vision, therefore, involve examining the neuronal activity generated at several different structural levels.

In terms of biological vision, the molecular level corresponds to the motion of ions such as Na^+ and K^+, the neuronal level to action-potential responses to individual nerve cells, the neuronal-layer level to the behavior of similar cells that function in a coherent fashion, the neuronal-tissue level to anatomical structures such as the retina and striate cortex, and, finally, the systems level to the overall visual pathway. A brief summary of the function of the biological visual pathway, in terms of some of these structural levels, will now be presented.

2.1 The Neuron: The Basic Biological Computing Element

The biological neuron is the basic information-processing and computing element (basic hardware component) in the CNS [2.1, 2.4]. There are typically over 10^{11} neurons in CNS. Figure 2.2 shows a schematic diagram of an ''idealized'' neuron. An individual neuron consists of a cell body, the *soma;* several spinelike extensions that deliver signals to the soma, *dendrites;* and a single output nerve fiber, the *axon,* which branches out from the soma in order to transmit signals to many other neurons. The connections of junction points used to adjoin various neurons are called *synapses.*

Both inside and around the soma are sodium (Na^+), calcium (Ca^{++}), potassium (K^+), and chloride (Cl^-) ions [2.1–2.4, 12, 13]. The Na^+ and K^+ are mainly responsible for generating a train of electrical impulses called *action potentials* in a neuron, Fig. 2.3. The K^+ ions are concentrated inside the neuron,

whereas the Na^+ ions are concentrated outside the cell membrane. If the soma is electrically stimulated by a voltage greater than the threshold, the Na^+ and other ions, such as Ca^{++}, are allowed to pass across its membrane. This movement of ions causes the soma to change its internal electric state. More specifically, the flow of Na^+ into the soma and K^+ out of the soma generates an action potential. The flow of ionic current is triggered by changes in the permeability of the nerve membrane. Before the action potential occurs, the membrane permeability to both Na^+ and K^+ is low, such that there is only a minimal flow of these ionic currents across the membrane. In an unexcited (rest) state, the electrical potential inside of the soma with respect to the outside of the membrane is −70 mV. The action potential is generated when the axon membrane suddenly becomes permeable to Na^+ ions, enabling this positive ion to rush into the soma. Since Na^+ ions have a positive charge, an electrode placed inside the membrane will record an increase in positive charges. After about 0.5 millisecond, the membrane permeability to Na^+ ion decreases, and its permeability to K^+ increases, which causes the K^+ ions to flow out of the membrane fiber. Since a K^+ ion also has a positive charge, the electrode records a decrease in the positive charge inside the axon membrane until the charge returns to its original rest level (−70 mV). The overall process of this ion exchange occurs within a millisecond. In summary, the action potentials can be considered as traveling positive charges generated by the flow of charged ions (Na^+, K^+) across the wall of the soma membrane [2.1]. The action potentials generated at the soma are transmitted along the axon toward other neurons as a train of impulses.

In terms of information processing, each neuron encodes the aggregation of the stimulus signals received by the dendrites into a sequence of frequency-modulated impulses called action potentials. Two important properties of the action potential, as shown in Fig. 2.3(a), are directly related to the frequency-encoding abilities of the soma. The first is the effective rise time, or *latency,* which is defined as the time between the application of the stimulus and the peak of the resulting action potential. This response time is observed to decrease exponentially with the stimulus intensity. The second property is the minimum time required for the axon to generate two consecutive action-potential responses. This minimum time between two action potentials is called the *refractory period.* The inverse of the minimum refractory period indicates the highest frequency of action potential that a neuron (or axon) can achieve. In summary, if a constant stimulus greater than the threshold intensity is applied to an axon, both the latency and refractory period will control the frequency of the train of action potentials. For example, a stimulus with a high intensity will yield a fast rise time and a short refractory period, thereby generating a high pulse frequency. From experimental work, it has been observed that the approximate relationship between the change in stimulus intensity (ΔS) and the change in nerve pulse frequency (Δf) is linear over a limited range and with a saturation characteristic at low and high stimulus levels, as shown in Fig. 2.4. This functional relationship can be modeled by a sigmoidal function.

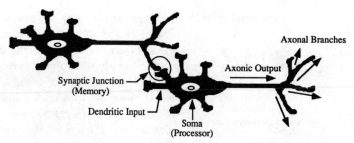

Fig. 2.2 A schematic view of two ideal neurons. Each neuron receives many inputs (on the average, 10^4) through the dendrites, and generates a single neural output along the axon, which branches out to many other neurons. The axon of a neuron is connected to the dendrites of many other neurons by means of synaptic junctions.

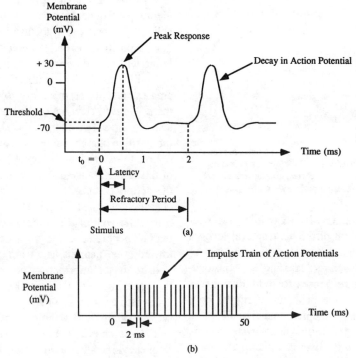

Fig. 2.3 Action potential and a train of action potentials following a stimulus at $t = t_0$. (a)Schematic diagram of two consecutive action potentials. (b) Train of action potential impulses over a long time window.

The axon (or output) from one neuron branches out to other neurons by making connections through the synaptic junctions. This synapse employs a chemical transmitter substance to convey a signal across the boundary of the junction. At the synaptic junction, the axonic action potentials are converted to a voltage potential called the *postsynaptic potential* (PSP). The PSP is proportional to the amount of transmitter substance released, which, in turn, is proportional to the frequency of the axonic action potentials. The PSP becomes saturated for large amounts of transmitter substance. A *temporal summation* occurs because of a large time constant, far greater than the period of the train of action potentials, associated with the synaptic junction. Any new action potentials are simply added to the partially decayed remains of past PSPs. This accumulated effect at the dendrite side of the synapse results in slow amplitude potentials. Thus, the magnitude of this dendritic de-

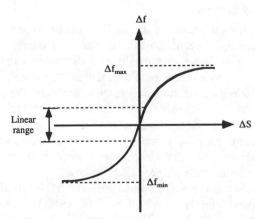

Fig. 2.4 Linear (for small ΔS) and saturation characteristics (for large ΔS) for the change in the frequency of action potentials generated by a typical neuron.

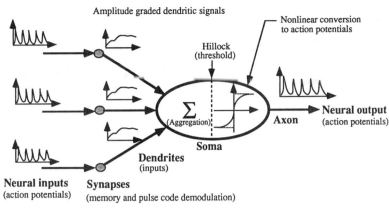

Fig. 2.5 A simplified model of a biological neuron from an information-processing perspective.

polarization is proportional to the average frequency at which the pulses arrive at the synaptic junction. A schematic diagram of the signal-coding characteristics of a biological neuron is shown in Fig. 2.5. From an information-processing perspective, the synapse performs two important functions. One is a crude pulse frequency-to-voltage conversion, and the other is long-term memory (LTM). These synaptic junctions exist between axons and dendrites, but specialized synapses may also exist between axons and axons, dendrites and dendrites, and even axons and cell bodies.

When the action potentials traveling along the axon reach the synaptic junction, the transmitter substance in the synaptic vesicles is released onto the dendrite of the neuron, causing an electrical response. This electrical response can be either excitatory or inhibitory, depending on the type of transmitter released and the nature of the dendrite membrane. The dendritic inputs originating from the excitatory synapses will increase the rate of neural firing, whereas inputs from the inhibitory synapses will decrease this firing rate.

The dendrites transmit numerous slow potentials to the soma of the neuron. On the average, each soma receives about 10^4 excitatory and inhibitory inputs. For example, certain neurons in the cortex receive inputs from thousands of other neurons. The role of the soma is to perform a spatio-temporal weighted aggregation (often assumed to be a summation) of all excitatory and inhibitory PSPs. This weighted aggregation is converted, at the *axon hillock,* into action potentials with an appropriate output frequency, and the action potentials are transmitted along the axon to the other neurons for further processing. The generation of these action potentials depends, therefore, on the interplay of the excitatory ($+$) and inhibitory ($-$) input signals received by the soma.

Experimental studies in neurophysiology have shown that the action-potential response of a neuron is largely a random variable, and only by an ensemble observation of many action potentials is it possible to obtain predictable results [14, 15]. This observed random variability in the response of a neuron is a function of both the uncontrolled extraneous electrical signals that are being received from the activated neurons in other parts of the nervous system and intrinsic fluctuations of the electrical membrane potential within the individual neuron. The only way to achieve fast and efficient neural information processing by using slow (bandwidth of the order of 500 Hz or less) and unpredictable processing elements is to employ large numbers of such neuronal processing elements in order to perform some parallel computation. This is how the CNS as a whole operates. For example, the human brain alone is comprised of approximately 10^{11} neurons, each with an average of 10^4 synaptic interconnections with other neurons. The exact function of each constituent neuron cannot, therefore, be known in precise detail. However, the large connectivity (of the order of 10^5) and parallelism in neuronal morphology are responsible for the robust and fast processing.

In the next section, we will move from the individual neuronal level to the neuronal-layer and system levels of the visual pathway.

2.2 The Visual Pathway

The computational role of the various anatomical structures along the visual pathway may be analyzed in terms of the neuronal interactions [**1.2, 2.4, 4.1–4.3**]. Figure 2.6 is a schematic diagram of the various neuronal layers found along the biological visual pathway. Neurophysiologists have attempted to experimentally determine what patterns of visual stimulation (light patterns), when presented to the eye, will increase the firing of a particular groups of neurons within the neuronal layers of each anatomical structure. The visual pattern that best activates a given layer of nerve cells is called a *trigger feature.* The area of the photoreceptor surface that elicits a strong response for this activated neuronal layer is called the *receptive field* of that neuron. Both the notions of trigger features and receptive fields are being used extensively to explain the computational behavior of the neurons in the various neuronal layers such as the retina, the LGN, the primary visual cortex, and the higher cortical regions of the visual cortex. In this section, we present a brief description of the neuronal morphology of the biological visual pathway with the hope that it will provide some insight to vision-systems scientists and engineers in their theoretical endeavors and design work.

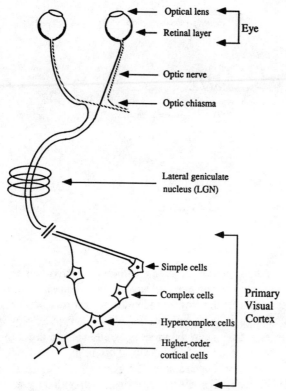

Fig. 2.6 A schematic diagram showing the various anatomical structures of the biological visual pathway. (Compare this figure with those structures given in Figs. 1.2 and 1.3.)

2.2.1 *The retina*

The primary sensory system for biological vision is the retinal layer, shown in Fig. 2.7, located at the back of each eye. The light stimulus from a visual object is initially focused on a layer of photoreceptor cells. The retinal receptors include approximately 120 million rods (long and rod-shaped) and 6 million cones (short and cone-shaped). The cones are sensitive to bright light, whereas the rods are sensitive to dim light. Electrophysiological studies [7] suggest that a rod can respond to a single photon of light, whereas cones respond to a broader range of wavelengths in the electromagnetic spectrum. Thus, rods respond primarily to dim light and are good for night vision, whereas the cones respond to bright light and are good for color vision. These two types of photoreceptors have an uneven distribution in the retinal layer. The receptor density is a function of visual angle, or eccentricity. Cones are most dense in the central part of the retina, called the *fovea*, and the rods dominate the peripheral region of the retina.

Following excitation by the light stimulus, the retinal cells (R, C, H, B, and A) yield graded slow potentials, whereas the ganglion cells (G) generate a train of action potentials. Various intermediate neural layers (H, B, A) that follow the photoreceptor layer feed visual information to the ganglion cells (G), and the axonic outputs of the ganglion cells become the optic nerves that transmit information to the visual cortex for further processing. These intermediate neural layers are comprised of horizontal (H), bipolar (B), and amacrine (A) cells. Certain ganglion cells receive signals directly from the bipolar

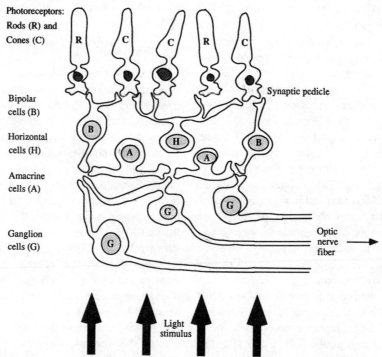

Fig. 2.7 A cross section of the human retina. Retinal information processing largely occurs due to the lateral inhibitory transmission of signals by the horizontal and amacrine cells. Note that the light stimulus passes through the transparent layers of G, A, B, and H cells in order to excite the photoreceptors (R and C) [7].

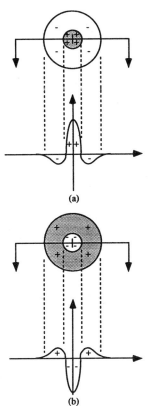

Fig. 2.8 Typical center-surround receptive field characteristics for certain retinal ganglion cells. This type of receptive field organization is able to provide intensity-contrast information about the visual stimulus. (a) On-center (+) off-surround (−) receptive field structure. (b) Off-center (−) on-surround (+) receptive field structure.

cells, while others are driven only by the amacrine cells. The horizontal cells receive signals from many neighboring photoreceptors and transmit them across the retina, enabling different receptors and bipolar cells to communicate. Similarly, the amacrine cells enable the bipolar and ganglion cells to communicate. Most inhibition that arises within the retina is caused by the horizontal and amacrine cells. As a result, most ganglion cells exhibit receptive fields with center-surround organizations as shown in Fig. 2.8.

In terms of information processing, the photoreceptors in the retina act as transducers that convert light energy to an equivalent electrical signal. The horizontal cells pass the information to the bipolar cells in order for these cells to act as spatial (center-surround) comparators for spatial integration. The amacrine cells perform temporal differentiation and rectification. The mode of signal transmission from the photoreceptors to the interactions between the amacrine and ganglion cells involves graded potentials. These neural signals are then converted into a train of action potentials by the ganglion cells, and this train of action potentials is transmitted along the optic nerve. Thus, the ganglion cells function as a pulse-rate encoder for transmitting visual signals over a communication line called the *optic nerve*. Even though about 126 million photoreceptors exist in each retina, there are only one million ganglion axon fibers in the optic nerve, which transmits all the visual information to the visual cortex. Thus, the retina is in-

volved in doing some low-level processing and compression (by a ratio of 126:1) on the visual information.

2.2.2 *The lateral geniculate nucleus (LGN)*

The axons of the ganglion cells form a bundle of optic nerves that transmit the reorganized visual information toward the visual cortex. Before the information from the retina reaches the primary visual cortex in the brain, the axons of the retinal ganglion cells are divided into two groups. These axons meet at the optic chiasma, after which a large number of them pass onto two multilayer neuronal structures called the *lateral geniculate nuclei* (LGN). About half of the ganglion axons from each eye cross over, so that one LGN ends up with fibers from the left half of the visual field, and the other LGN receives information from the right half of the visual field. The precise nature of signal processing being performed in the LGN is not yet known; however, it appears that it acts as a relay station for redirecting information to different parts of the cerebral cortex. These LGN cells have center-surround receptive field organizations similar to the retinal receptive fields, except that they function over a narrower spatial frequency bandwidth than the ganglion cells [4.3]. Some researchers [13] also believe that the LGN cells are used largely for color vision.

2.2.3 *The primary visual cortex*

The signals transmitted from the LGN cells flow into the primary visual cortex (also called the *striate cortex*) located at the rear of the brain [4.4, 4.5]. The neuronal morphology of the primary visual cortex is in the form of columnar structures called *hypercolumns* [4.1, 4.3–4.6]. As shown in Fig. 2.9, this cortex can be modeled as a three-dimensional matrix structure made of columns and rows. This columnar neuronal structure enables certain neurons to respond selectively to specific orientations, movements, and directions of movement in the visual stimulus. Numerous such columns reside side-by-side throughout all of the six layers of the cortex. The neurons within each column are densely interconnected with neurons in the other columns, as well as other parts of the brain. These cortical columns are believed to play a major computational role in the brain.

To better understand the role of the columnar neuronal structure, Fig. 2.9, assume that an electrode is lowered perpendicular to the cortical surface. Three types of orientation-selective nerve cells are encountered. The first type of neuron, called *simple cortical cells,* responds best to bars of light projected onto the retinal surface that have specific orientations. The second type, called *complex cortical cells,* responds strongest to correctly oriented bars of light that move over the entire receptive field. That is, most complex cells will respond to a specific direction of stimuli motion. The third type of cell, called a *hypercomplex cortical cell,* responds only to visual stimuli that are moving lines with specific lengths, moving corners, or moving angles. Although the length of the stimuli has no effect on the response of a complex cell, it does have a direct effect on hypercomplex cells, such that if the stimulus is too long, the nerve cell will not fire.

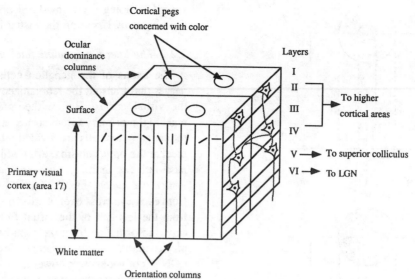

Fig. 2.9 An illustration of the columnar neuronal structure of the primary visual cortex [13].

2.2.4 The higher cortical regions

The visual information from the primary visual cortex flows through a parallel–serial structure of approximately twenty visual areas located in the brain [3]. Some neurophysiologists believe that two main pathways diverge from the primary visual cortex. One pathway transfers information to the inferior temporal areas of the brain. This area is believed to be responsible for color and shape analyses, which are necessary prerequisites for recognizing objects within the visual field. The second pathway transfers information to the inferior parietal areas of the brain, which are believed to be responsible for analyzing the spatial interrelations of objects and how object movement changes these relationships. Furthermore, separate pathways to the temporal lobe and frontal lobe enable visual information to be associated with information derived from the other senses such as auditory, olfactory, and tactile.

At the most advanced levels of the biological visual pathway that has been investigated by neuroscientists, there appear to exist high-level cortical neurons that fire only to very specific visual stimuli patterns. Many of these cells respond to complex stimuli such as a triangle, hand, or face. Their response behavior is seldom affected by the position or size of the stimulus pattern. For example, a particular neuron will respond to a familiar face, but not faces in general. These cells are believed to correspond to the so-called ''grandmother cells.'' Each of these grandmother cells appear to be situated at the highest point of a complex network of information-processing neurons (see Fig. 1.3), perhaps part of a larger computational structure that responds collectively to that object.

3. VISUAL RECEPTIVE FIELD STRUCTURES

The functional role of the neurons along the visual pathway has largely been studied by observing the neural responses generated by electrophysiological experiments and then performing some mathematical analysis. Neurophysiologists have determined that the neurons within the retina, the LGN, the primary visual cortex, and the mid-brain visual system (superior colliculus) exhibit relatively precise receptive field structures that enable them to respond to a narrow group of visual stimuli, as shown in Fig. 3.1. Neighboring nerve cells within a common neuronal layer may have broadly overlapping receptive fields and yet respond to very distinctive visual stimuli. The two-dimensional retinal image is transmitted in a continuous fashion and projected onto the advancing neuronal-tissue regions in the visual pathway. This projection of two-dimensional information is called *retinotopic mapping*. At the higher cortical levels, a transition from a retinotopic to abstract representation of the visual information is believed to occur. These higher-order neuronal cells do not have specific receptive field structures. Rather, they respond selectively to entire complex objects.

The understanding of the biological vision process is related to the understanding of the phenomena of seeing and perceiving. The phenomenon of seeing corresponds to the low- and intermediate-level neuronal processing taking place along the visual pathway from the retina to the striate cortex. This phenomenon is relatively well understood, but the specific functional role of the constituent neurons is a source of continued debate. However, the phenomenon of perception, which takes place at the higher levels of the visual cortex, is not well understood and, therefore, we can only make general hypotheses as to the mechanisms of perception. In the following sections, we will briefly describe three plausible conjectures for the functional roles performed by neurons situated in the early stages of the visual pathway. Although the first two conjectures that visual neural cells act as *feature detectors* and *spatial frequency filters* have strong correlations, they are based on physiological and psychological experimentation, respectively. The third conjecture is based on a strong mathematical expla-

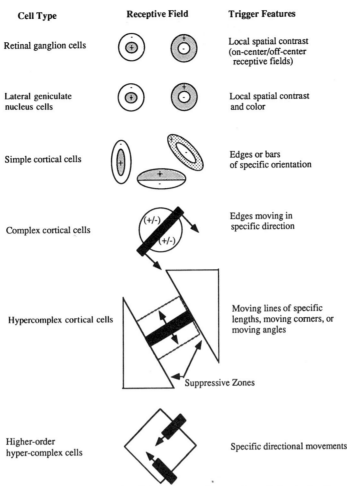

Cell Type	Receptive Field	Trigger Features

Retinal ganglion cells — Local spatial contrast (on-center/off-center receptive fields)

Lateral geniculate nucleus cells — Local spatial contrast and color

Simple cortical cells — Edges or bars of specific orientation

Complex cortical cells — Edges moving in specific direction

Hypercomplex cortical cells — Moving lines of specific lengths, moving corners, or moving angles

Suppressive Zones

Higher-order hyper-complex cells — Specific directional movements

Fig. 3.1 Typical receptive field structures for a variety of visual stimuli that activate specific groups of neurons along the visual pathway [10].

nation using *Gabor functions,* which use the localized frequency structure of neuronal activity.

3.1 Visual Neurons Act as Feature Detectors

The neural cells along the visual pathway are often believed to act as feature detectors [**1.2, 4.1,** 10, 12, 16–18] because experimental studies have found that they respond to specific visual stimulus patterns projected onto the photoreceptors in the retina. As the visual information flows from the retina up the visual pathway, the neural cells require more and more specific stimuli characteristics in order to fire. For example, the ganglion cells respond to the presence of any stimulus contrast, whereas the hypercomplex nerve cells respond only to bars of stimuli moving in a particular direction. This selective nature of cells is even more pronounced in the neuronal layers outside the primary visual cortex. The cortical neural cells in the temporal lobe respond best to faces rather than to any other stimulus pattern.

Although it is possible that certain specialized neurons respond to complex objects such as a face, it is highly unlikely that our perception of visual forms, in general, is based on the firing of individual feature-detector neural cells. The infinite

number of such spatial patterns that exist in the visual world make it virtually impossible to construct such a feature-detector architecture. It is, however, reasonable to assume that the orientation-selective neural cells do play an important role in the perception of simple geometric stimulus patterns such as the orientation of line segments.

3.2 Visual Neurons Act as Spatial Frequency Filters

An alternative conjecture is to view the computational role of neurons along the visual pathway as detectors of spatial frequencies [**4.3, 5.6,** 8–10, 16] and not as mere detectors of geometric features. It is well known in engineering that any spatially distributed pattern can be analyzed as a complex Fourier waveform in a fashion similar to temporal patterns [10, 19, 20]. The visual stimuli incident on the retinal surface can be assumed to be a spatial pattern made up of various sinusoids with different spatial frequencies, amplitudes, and phases. Thus, it is possible to interpret the neural behavior at any location in terms of Fourier mathematics.

The assumption that the input pattern is composed of sinusoids with varied spatial frequencies enables the response of a neuron to be described in terms of sinusoidal grating patterns

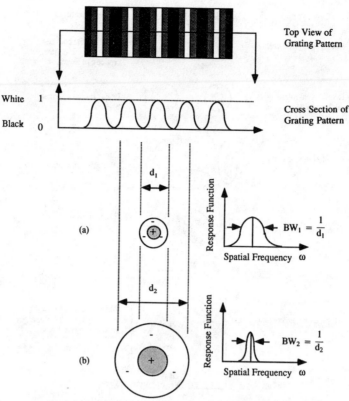

Fig. 3.2 A sketch illustrating the inverse relationship between the receptive field size, d_1 and d_2, and bandwidth, BW_1 and BW_2, for the same sinusoidal grating pattern.

with variable frequencies focused onto the various receptive fields. Using this experimental technique, it is possible to observe which neurons along the visual pathway generate a maximum response to specific spatial frequencies. This range of frequencies can then be used to describe spatial filters with specific frequency selectivity.

In terms of the neurons along the visual pathway, the ganglion cells in the retina have concentric receptive fields with varying geometrical sizes. Above a certain spatial frequency, there is no response by a particular ganglion neuron because the net change in incident illumination over either the center or surround regions is zero. Thus, the smaller the size of the receptive field, the higher the maximum spatial frequency to which the neuron will respond, Fig. 3.2. That is, the bandwidth BW of the spatial filter is inversely proportional to the size d of the receptive field.

Experimental studies have shown that the size of the receptive fields around the foveal region of the retina are concentric. All receptive fields equidistant from the fovea, therefore, have the same tuning properties affiliated with a particular spatial frequency range. Also, all equidistant receptive fields located in the LGN have similar spatial frequency tuning properties. However, both the simple and complex cortical neural cells of the primary visual cortex are believed to be more narrowly tuned to a specific range of spatial frequencies [4.3].

The hypercolumns of the primary visual cortex are believed to analyze various local aspects of the visual stimulus patterns as they respond to a wider range of spatial frequencies. One way that this is achieved in the cortex may be through multiple informational channels. A multichannel system is plausible by assuming that a series of separate Fourier-like analyzers exist for each aggregate neural region of the visual field. If a pattern in the stimuli has a specific frequency "signature" tuned to a particular neuron, then its response could signify the presence of an object in the field of view. This multichannel interpretation of the biological visual pathway has some support in both neurophysiology [**4.3, 5.6,** 21, 22] and psychology [8, 9].

The conjecture that the retinal and cortical cells act as spatial frequency filters is no more definitive than the conjecture that they function as feature detectors. For example, if the visual system did function as a biological spectrum analyzer, then each neuron must be sensitive to the presence of the same narrow band of spatial frequencies, regardless of its location in the visual field. Instead, these neurons possess receptive fields with limited sizes and are experimentally observed to respond to spatial frequencies over a wider range [16]. In essence, the function of a neuron cannot be a global Fourier transformation or any other simple harmonic decomposition scheme because these neurons have spatially dependent characteristics that are inhomogeneous. At best, the neurons along the visual pathway may perform short-range spectral decomposition.

3.3 Visual Neurons Act as Localized Gabor Functions

The localized spatial frequency decomposition due to the receptive fields may be modeled using elementary Gabor functions [23, 24]. The localized time-frequency analysis of arbitrary signals proposed by Gabor is based on the notion that the optimal set of basis functions for analyzing signals consists of the product of sinusoidal and Gaussian functions of time. The sinusoidal component of this function introduces a "waviness," whereas the Gaussian component localizes the signal to a region in time surrounding the "mean" time value of the Gaussian. Gabor showed that the use of such a basis function for a signal of fixed duration will minimize the joint uncertainty associated with the product of the effective time duration of the signal and its effective bandwidth. These Gaussian-weighted sinusoids are termed Gabor functions or *logons*.

The spatial-response profiles of the cortical cells may be mathematically described by a Gabor function given in the direction perpendicular to the optimal orientation of the neural cell. The Gabor function has the property that it minimizes the joint uncertainty in a two-dimensional information space, whereupon the axes of the information space represent spatial (x) frequency (ω) components. There exist an infinite number of Gabor functions that can be used to model time signals. All possible types of logons consist of sine and cosine waveforms with amplitudes modulated by Gaussian functions [**4.3**, 23]. Examples of one-dimensional Gabor functions are shown in Fig. 3.3.

Daugman [**5.1**, 25, 26] developed a two-dimensional version of the Gabor function. A typical two-dimensional logon is constructed by multiplying a sinusoidal grating pattern by a two-dimensional Gaussian function. Daugman further generalized this concept to a two-dimensional Gabor function that consists of a one-dimensional cosine or sine wave that is free to vary both its orientation and period. This wave function is modulated by a bivariate Gaussian. As a result, this function minimizes the joint uncertainty in a four-dimensional information space with axes given by the Cartesian coordinates for space (x, y,) and the corresponding spatial frequency (u, v). Based on neurophysiological evidence [25], Daugman developed a set of universal Gabor functions [24] with the following characteristics that could be used to analyze any arbitrary image. The fundamental characteristics of the generalized Gabor functions are

1. the ratio of the major axes of the Gaussians used to define the Gabor function are fixed at about 8:5;
2. only five or six discrete major axis lengths are required;
3. the direction of oscillation for the sinusoidal gratings are perpendicular to the major axis of the Gaussians;
4. typically 1.5 oscillation cycles are used between the 1 standard deviation of the minor axis of its Gaussian component;

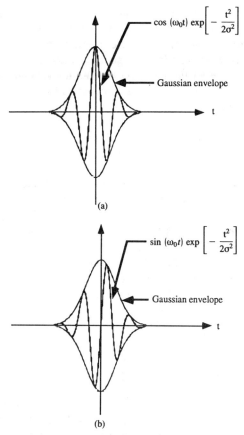

Fig. 3.3 Typical cosine- and sine-type Gabor functions. The variable σ denotes the effective spread of the Gaussian function and ω_0 is the frequency of the sinusoids. In this example, $\sigma = 2$ and $\omega_0 = 2$. (a) Cosine-type Gabor-function envelope. (b) Sine-type Gabor function.

5. the functions are oriented at three to six azimuth angles, distributed evenly over 0° to 360°; and
6. a complete set of functions, containing cosine and sine waves with all orientations and scales, are located at regularly spaced points in the image plane.

In a physiological context, the first steps of information processing along the visual pathway are assumed to be analogous to these Gabor correlation operations. Gabor operations of various orientations and scales are carried out simultaneously over the entire visual field. Subsequent higher-order visual information processing is believed to be performed on the resultant Gabor correlation. The analysis of certain receptive field profiles along the visual pathway show a strong similarity to these two-dimensional Gabor functions [**4.3**, 25]. However, some researchers [27] feel that there is insufficient evidence that the visual cortical cells do perform Gabor-like operations.

The primary result of a Gabor-function representation for the receptive field profiles reflects the principle of economical coding, or minimal representation, by the visual neuronal receptive fields [**4.3**, **5.1**–**5.3**]. The receptive-field profiles of simple neural cells appear to minimize the uncertainty in the four-dimensional space. Furthermore, it appears that no two

13

neural cells in the same neuronal layer perform the exact same function, thereby generating no wasteful redundancy in local computations. Finally, if it were true that the neurons along the pathway act as Gabor functions, then a very efficient method of presenting a complex image for viewing purposes would be to represent it as a combination of such two-dimensional Gabor functions.

4. FOUNDATIONS OF COMPUTATIONAL NEURAL NETWORKS

A brief description of the possible functional roles played by the various neuronal layers along the biological visual pathway was presented in Section 3. From a computational perspective, the individual neuronal layers such as the retina and striate cortex can be conceptualized as one or more two-dimensional arrays (neural networks) of neurons that perform specific operations on the visual signals. The primary structural characteristics of a *computational neural network* (CNN) are an organized morphology containing numerous parallel-distributed neurons, a method of encoding (i.e., learning) information within the synaptic connections found between the individual neurons, and a method of recalling information when presented with a stimulus input pattern.

Although a large number of computational neural-network architectures and learning algorithms are reported in the literature [**3.1–3.6**, 10, 24, 28–33], most of these neural networks have certain features in common with biological neural systems. Incidentally, it is these very features that are absent within the traditional sequential computer paradigm. The primary benefits of CNNs over digital computers can be summarized as follows.

1. The neural-network models have many neurons (the computational processing elements) linked via the adaptive (synaptic) weights arranged in a massive parallel structure. Because of its high parallelism, failures of a few neurons do not greatly affect the overall system performance. This characteristic is called *fault-tolerance*.
2. The main strength of neural-network structures lies in their learning and adaptive abilities. The ability to adapt and learn from the environment means that the neural-network models can deal with imprecise data and ill-defined situations. As a result, a suitably trained network has the ability to generalize inputs, even if they do not appear in the training data.
3. Another significant characteristic of neural networks is their ability to approximate any nonlinear continuous function to the desired degree of accuracy. This ability of neural networks has made them useful to model a variety of nonlinear systems.
4. Neural networks also have many inputs and outputs; therefore, they are easily applicable to modeling multivariable systems.
5. With the advancements in hardware technology, many vendors have recently introduced dedicated very large scale integrated (VLSI) hardware implementations of neural networks. This brings additional speed in neural computing for real-time applications.

A detailed discussion of the various neural-network architectures described in the literature is far beyond the scope of this tutorial. However, to unify this diverse and abundant material, we will now present a generalized interpretation of computational neural mechanisms from a systems-science perspective. It is hoped that this section will simplify the overwhelming volume of research on neural computing for the novice reader. In this context, we will consider only a single neuron and study its intrinsic properties.

4.1 Neural Processing Element: Synaptic and Somatic Operations

A biological neuron consists of synapses (junction points) and a soma—the main body of the neuron. The numerous synapses that adjoin a neuron receive neural inputs from other neurons and transmit modified (weighted) versions of these signals to the soma via the dendrites. Each soma receives, on the average, 10^4 dendritic inputs. The role of the soma is to perform a spatio-temporal weighted aggregation (summation) of all these inputs. If this weighted aggregation is greater than an intrinsic threshold value, then the weighted signal is converted into an action potential yielding a neural output. These action potentials are transmitted along the axon to the other neurons for further processing.

From a signal-processing point of view, the biological neuron has two key elements, the synapse and soma, that are responsible for performing computational tasks such as learning, acquiring knowledge (storage or memory of past experience), and recognizing patterns. Each synapse is a storage element that contains some attribute of the past experience. The synapse learns by continuously adapting its strength (weight) to the new neuronal inputs. The soma combines the weighted inputs such that, if it exceeds a certain threshold value, then the neuron will fire. This axonal (output) signal undergoes a nonlinear transformation prior to leaving the axonic hillock in the soma. Mathematically, the synapses and early stage of the soma provide a confluence operation [35] between the fresh neuronal inputs and stored knowledge (past experience). The latter part of the soma, the nonlinear activation operation, provides a nonlinear bounded mapping to the aggregated signal.

In simple terms, a neuron can be depicted as an information processing element that receives an n-dimensional neural input vector,

$$\mathbf{X}(k) = [x_1(k), x_2(k), \ldots, x_i(k), \ldots, x_n(k)]^{\mathsf{T}} \in \Re^n \quad (4.1)$$

and yields a scalar neural output $y(k) \in \Re^1$ (symbol T represents the vector transpose and $\Re$ is the set of real numbers). The input vector $\mathbf{X}(k) \in \Re^n$ represents the signals being transmitted from the n-neighboring neurons (including self-feedback signal) and/or the outputs (measurements) from the sensory neurons. The continuous time variable (t) is given by $t = k\Delta T$, where ΔT is the fixed sampling period and k is the discrete time variable.

Mathematically, the information-processing ability of a neuron can be represented as a nonlinear mapping operation

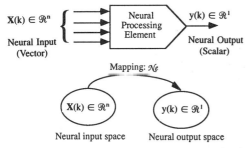

Fig. 4.1 The information-processing ability of a computational neuron processing element, as represented by the nonlinear mapping function $\mathcal{N}e$: $\mathbf{X}(k) \in \mathfrak{R}^n \to y(k) \in \mathfrak{R}^1$.

$\mathcal{N}e$, from the input vector $\mathbf{X}(k) \in \mathfrak{R}^n$ to the scalar output $y(k) \in \mathfrak{R}^1$; that is,

$$\mathcal{N}e: \mathbf{X}(k) \in \mathfrak{R}^n \to y(k) \in \mathfrak{R}^1 \qquad (4.2)$$

The nonlinear mapping operator $\mathcal{N}e$, from the n-dimensional input space to the one-dimensional output space, is shown in Fig. 4.1.

Alternatively, we can rewrite 4.2 as

$$y(k) = \mathcal{N}e\,[\mathbf{X}(k) \in \mathfrak{R}^n] \in \mathfrak{R}^1 \qquad (4.3)$$

A summary of the mathematical operations given by 4.1 to 4.3 for a typical neuron is illustrated in Fig. 4.2. In the neural-network literature, these computational neurons are interchangeably called neuronal processing elements (PEs), neural populations, nodes, or threshold logic units.

Mathematically, the neuronal nonlinear mapping function $\mathcal{N}e$ can be divided into two parts: *confluence* and *nonlinear activation* operations. The confluence operation provides weighting, aggregation, and thresholding operations to the neural inputs. In order to account for the thresholding operation, we will define the augmented vectors of the neural inputs and synaptic weights as follows:

$$\mathbf{X}_a(k) = [x_0(k), x_1(k), \ldots, x_i(k), \ldots, x_n(k)]^{\mathsf{T}} \qquad (4.4a)$$
$$\in \mathfrak{R}^{n+1}, \quad x_0(k) = 1$$

and

$$\mathbf{W}_a(k) = [w_0(k), w_1(k), \ldots, w_i(k), \ldots, w_n(k)]^{\mathsf{T}} \qquad (4.4b)$$
$$\in \mathfrak{R}^{n+1}$$

where the elements $x_0(k)$ and $w_0(k)$ introduce a thresholding (bias) term in the confluence operation. This confluence operation, ©, essentially provides a measure of similarity between the augmented neural-input vector $\mathbf{X}_a(k)$ (new information) and the augmented synaptic-weight vector $\mathbf{W}_a(k)$ (accumulated knowledge base). The nonlinear activation operation then performs a nonlinear mapping on the similarity measure. These two basic mathematical operations of a computational neuron, Fig. 4.3, will now be described in greater detail.

4.1.1 Confluence operation: measure of similarity

From a biological perspective, the confluence operation represents the weighting of the input signals $\mathbf{X}_a(k) \in \mathfrak{R}^{n+1}$

with the accumulated knowledge stored at the synapses $\mathbf{W}_a(k)$, and the aggregation of these weighted inputs as performed by the soma. This confluence operation [35] assigns a relative weight to each incoming signal component $x_i(k)$ according to an attribute of the past experience (knowledge or memory) stored in synaptic weight $w_i(k)$, $i = 0, 1, \ldots, n$.

One can mathematically view this confluence operation as a linear weighted mapping from the $(n+1)$-dimensional neural input space $\mathbf{X}_a(k) \in \mathfrak{R}^{n+1}$ to the one-dimensional space $u(k) \in \mathfrak{R}^1$. The synaptic (weighting) and somatic (aggregation and thresholding) linear mapping can thus be defined as

$$u(k) = \mathbf{W}_a(k) © \mathbf{X}_a(k) \qquad (4.5)$$

where © is a confluence operation.* Equation (4.5) represents a measure of the similarity between $\mathbf{X}_a(k)$ (input vector) and $\mathbf{W}_a(k)$ (synaptic weight vector). Two common types of similarity measures are: (a) the scalar product of the vectors $\mathbf{X}_a(k)$ and $\mathbf{W}_a(k)$, and (b) the Euclidean distance between vectors $\mathbf{X}_a(k)$ and $\mathbf{W}_a(k)$. The computational neurons of most neural networks described in the literature assume a confluence operation given by the scalar product. A popular exception to this is the radial basis function (RFB) network that uses the distance measure for describing the confluence between the inputs and weights [30, 34]. These two models of the confluence operations will now be described in detail.

Scalar product of $\mathbf{X}_a(k)$ and $\mathbf{W}_a(k)$. The projection of the neural inputs $\mathbf{X}_a(k)$ (new information) onto the synaptic weights $\mathbf{W}_a(k)$ (the accumulated knowledge) in the vector space is given by the scalar product of the two vectors, and is graphically illustrated in Fig. 4.4. That is,

$$u(k) = \mathbf{W}_a(k)^{\mathsf{T}}\mathbf{X}_a(k) = \sum_{i=0}^{n} w_i(k)\,x_i(k) \qquad (4.6)$$

where $\mathbf{X}_a(k)$ and $\mathbf{W}_a(k)$ are defined in (4.4).

Euclidean distance measure between $\mathbf{X}_a(k)$ and $\mathbf{W}_a(k)$. An alternative approach for measuring the similarity between the vectors $\mathbf{X}_a(k)$ and $\mathbf{W}_a(k)$ is to use the distance measure shown in Fig. 4.5. The Euclidean distance between the new neural information $\mathbf{X}_a(k)$ and the accumulated knowledge $\mathbf{W}_a(k)$ is given by

$$\frac{D}{\beta} = \sqrt{[\mathbf{W}_a(k) - \mathbf{X}_a(k)]^{\mathsf{T}}[\mathbf{W}_a(k) - \mathbf{X}_a(k)]} \in \mathfrak{R}^1 \qquad (4.7)$$

where β is a normalization constant such that $0 \leq D \leq 1$. The measure of similarity between $\mathbf{X}_a(k)$ and $\mathbf{W}_a(k)$ may then be defined as

$$u(k) = [1 - D] \qquad (4.8)$$

4.1.2 Somatic nonlinear activation function

The somatic nonlinear activation function $f[\cdot]$ maps the confluence value $u(k) \in [-\infty, \infty]$ to a bounded neural output.

---

*The confluence operation defined in (4.5) is a combination of the synaptic weighting, somatic aggregation, and somatic thresholding operations. This linear weighted mapping yields a scalar output $u(k)$ that is a measure of the similarity between the augmented neural input vector $\mathbf{X}_a(k)$ and the accumulated knowledge stored in the augmented synaptic weight vector $\mathbf{W}_a(k)$.

Gupta and Knopf

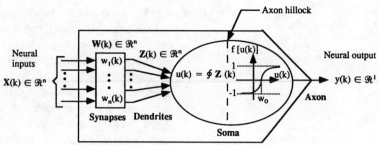

Fig. 4.2 Summary of the computational structure of a neuron: $\mathbf{X}(k) \in \Re^n$, neuronal input vector (from sensors or other neurons); $\mathbf{W}(k) \in \Re^n$, synaptic weight vector (storage of past experience); $\mathbf{Z}(k) \in \Re^n$, dendritic input vector; ϕ, somatic aggregation operator; $f[u(k)]$, nonlinear activation operator; and w_0, somatic threshold.

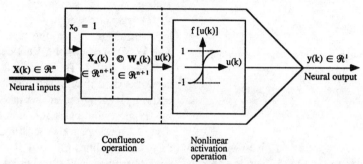

Fig. 4.3 A block-diagram representation of a generalized neuron. The confluence operation © compares new information $\mathbf{X}_a(k)$ with the past experience $\mathbf{W}_a(k)$, and the nonlinear activation operation $f[.]$ provides a bounded scalar neural output $y(k)$. For illustrative purposes, the thick arrows in the block diagram represent vectors and the thin arrows represent scalars. This graphical notation will be used throughout the remainder of this paper.

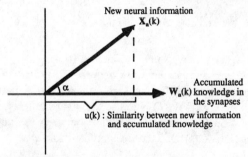

Fig. 4.4 A measure of similarity based on the projection (scalar product) of the augmented neural input vector $\mathbf{X}_a(k)$ onto the augmented synaptic weight vector $\mathbf{W}_a(k)$. Note that, if angle $\alpha = 0°$ in the vector space, then $u(k)$ becomes a maximum value. Alternatively, if $\alpha = 90°$ then the two vectors are orthogonal and the similarity measure is $u(k) = 0$.

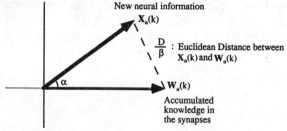

Fig. 4.5 Euclidean distance measure of similarity between the new neural information and the previously accumulated synaptic knowledge. Note that, if $D = 0$, then $\mathbf{X}_a(k)$ has a lot in common with $\mathbf{W}_a(k)$, and $u(k) = 1.0$. Conversely, if $D = 1$, then $\mathbf{X}_a(k)$ and $\mathbf{W}_a(k)$ have zero commonality, yielding $u(k) = 0$.

In general, the neural output is in the range of [0,1] for unipolar signals, and [−1, 1] for bipolar signals.

Mathematically, the nonlinear activation operator transforms the aggregate $u(k)$ into a bounded neural output $y(k)$ by

$$y(k) = f[u(k)] \tag{4.9a}$$
$$= f[\mathbf{W}_a(k) © \mathbf{X}_a(k)] \tag{4.9b}$$

Many different forms of mathematical functions can be used to model the nonlinear activation function. Some of the possible geometric shapes are given in Table 1. The sigmoidal form is a widely used activation function. However, the selection of a nonlinear function in neuronal models needs more careful study than what is presently given in the neural-network paradigms.

4.1.3 Learning: adapting the knowledge base

The weighting and spatio-temporal aggregation operations performed by the synapses and soma, respectively, provide a similarity measure between the input vector $\mathbf{X}_a(k)$ (new neural

16

TABLE 1 Examples of typical nonlinear activation operators $f[\cdot]$

Type	Equation	Functional Form
Linear	$f[u(k)] = vu(k)$ ($v > 0$, *activation gain*)	
Unipolar hard limiter	$f[u(k)] = \begin{cases} 1 & \text{if } u(k) > 0 \\ 0 & \text{otherwise} \end{cases}$	
Unipolar sigmoidal	$f[u(k)] = \dfrac{1}{1 + \exp(-vu(k))}$ ($v > 0$, activation gain)	
Bipolar hard limiter	$f[u(k)] = sgn\,[u(k)]$	

information) and the synaptic weight vector $\mathbf{W}_a(k)$ (accumulated knowledge base). With some initial random weights, a small measure of similarity may exist between the knowledge base and any new neural input pattern. As the neural network "learns" this new pattern, the similarity between the new information and accumulated knowledge increases. In other words, the process of learning can be interpreted as making the synaptic weight vector $\mathbf{W}_a(k)$ as similar to a given input pattern $\mathbf{X}_a(k)$ as possible.

The learning rules reported in the CNN literature use different methodologies. Figure 4.6 is a flow diagram illustrating some of the learning algorithms that are normally used. As shown in this diagram, the learning algorithms may be broadly categorized as either supervised or unsupervised. Nearly all the neural networks incorporate one of these two rules or a variation thereof. Some CNNs, however, have fixed weights and operate by changing only the activity levels of the neurons (i.e., no changes in the synaptic weights) [5.4, 6.1, 36].

17

TABLE 1 (continued)

Type	Equation	Functional Form
Piecewise linear	$f[u(k)] = \begin{cases} +1 & \text{if } \nu u(k) > +1 \\ \nu\, u(k) & \text{if } |\nu u(k)| \leq 1 \\ -1 & \text{if } \nu u(k) < -1 \end{cases}$ $(\nu > 0,\ \text{activation gain})$	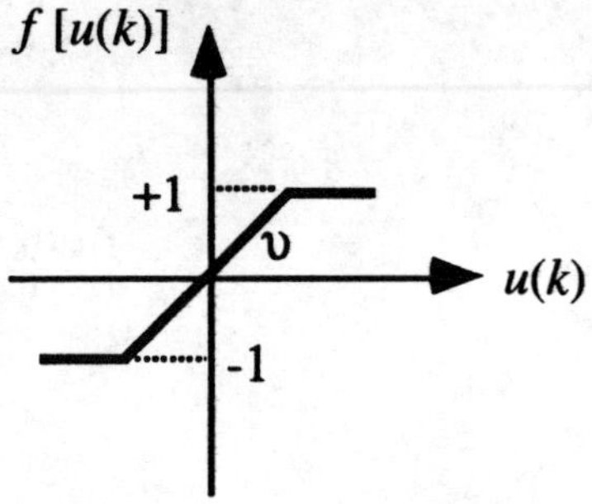
Bipolar sigmoidal	$f[u(k)] = \tanh(\nu u(k))$ $(\nu > 0,\ \text{activation gain})$	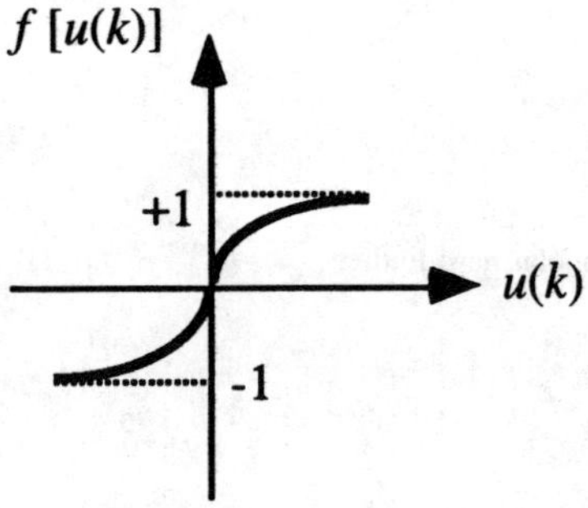
Multimodal	$f[u(k)] =$ $\frac{1}{2}\left[1 + \frac{1}{M}\sum_{m=1}^{M} \tanh\left(\nu_m\left(u(k) - w_{0_m}(k)\right)\right)\right]$ $(\nu_m > 0,\ \text{activation gain})$	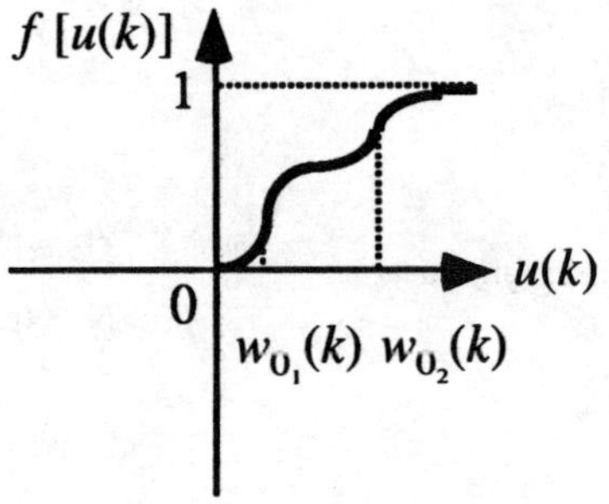
Gaussian	$f[u(k)] = \exp\left[\dfrac{-u(k)}{2\sigma^2}\right]$ where $u(k) = \sum_{i=0}^{n} (w_i(k) - x_i(k))^2$	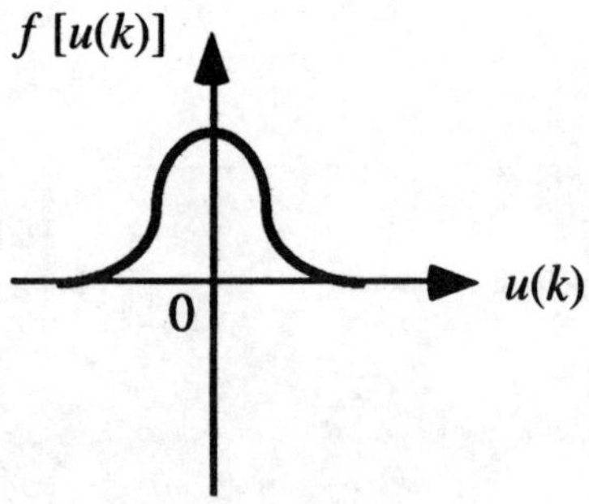

A supervised (error-based) learning algorithm employs an external reference signal (teacher) and generates an error signal by comparing the reference signal with the neural response. Based on the error signal, a learning algorithm modifies the synaptic connections of the neural network to improve the system performance. In this scheme, also known as *off-line learning*, it is always assumed that the desired response is known *a priori*. A schematic of the supervised learning procedure is shown in Fig. 4.7

A general equation for the supervised (error-based) learning algorithm is

$$w_i(k + 1) = w_i(k) + \Delta w_i(k) \tag{4.10a}$$

where

$$\Delta w_i(k) = \mu\, x_i(k)\, e(k) = \mu\, x_i(k)\, [y_d(k) - y(k)] \tag{4.10b}$$

and $w_i(k)$ is the synaptic weight corresponding to the input $x_i(k)$, $\Delta w_i(k)$ is the change in synaptic weight $w_i(k)$, μ is the

Neural Network Learning Algorithms

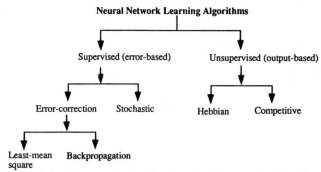

Fig. 4.6 A flow diagram of various learning algorithms employed by different computational neural networks to adapt the synaptic weight vector $\mathbf{W}_a(k)$.

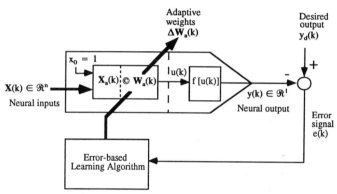

Fig. 4.7 A supervised (error-based) learning scheme where the learning process is guided by the error signal $e(k)$.

learning rate, $y_d(k)$ is the desired neural output, and $y(k)$ is the actual neural response. The proper selection of μ is of critical importance in these learning rules. A very small value of μ will result in an extremely slow learning process. On the other hand, a large value of μ will make learning faster, but it may also result in oscillations or make the system unstable.

Alternatively, stochastic learning algorithms make random changes to the synaptic weights and then determine the resultant "energy" created by this change. The changes in the weights are retained if the energy relationship for the neural network is lowered. However, to escape local energy minima, it is often necessary to accept some random changes that do not result in lower energy. An additional criterion that employs a predefined probability distribution may be used to accept the weight change, even if energy is not lowered.

In contrast, unsupervised (output-based) learning algorithms do not incorporate a reference signal, and generally involve self-organization principles that rely only on local information and internal control mechanisms in order to discover emergent collective neural properties. An important form of unsupervised learning is called *Hebbian learning*. Hebbian learning [24, 34, 37], Fig. 4.8, involves the adjustment of a synaptic weight according to the correlation between the neural input and output. A simple Hebbian learning rule used to describe the correlation of the input $x_i(k)$ with the neuron output $y(k)$ is

$$\Delta w_i(k) = \mu \, x_i(k) \, y(k) \qquad (4.11)$$

where $\Delta w_i(k)$ represents the change in the synaptic weight $w_i(k)$ and μ is the learning rate. A large number of variations of this simple learning law are described in the neural-network literature [5, 24, 29, 34].

4.2 Computational Neural-Network Structures

After having provided a brief description of the neural mathematics for a simple computational neuron, we will now extend these notions to complex neural-network structures. Computational neural networks can be partitioned into two basic categories: *static* (feedforward) and *dynamic* (feedback) networks. The outputs of a static neural network are only a function of present inputs and, therefore, these networks have no dynamic memory or feedback because the neural response activity is not based on the past input or output behavior. These static neural networks are described by purely algebraic equations. Alternatively, a dynamic neural network has inherent local memory due to feedback within the system. These dynamic neural networks are typically described by difference or differential equations. A detailed description of these structures is beyond the scope of this introduction. However, we will now attempt to provide some of the basic static and dynamic neural-network concepts used in vision applications.

4.2.1 Static (feedforward) neural networks

Although the single neuron described in Fig. 4.3 can perform various simple pattern-detection tasks, the power of neural computing comes from the collective action of a large number of neurons interconnected in a multilayer structure. Arranging neurons within layers, or stages, mimics the layered structures found along the biological visual pathway. These multilayer networks have capabilities far beyond those of the single layer. The most commonly used neural-network architecture for image-processing, pattern-recognition, and control applications is the multilayer feedforward neural network (MNN). A typical MNN composed of an input layer, an output layer, and one hidden layer of neurons is shown in Fig. 4.9. A simplified block-diagram representation of the MNN is given in Fig. 4.10

The input-output mapping of the three-layer MNN shown in Fig. 4.10 can be mathematically represented by

$$\mathbf{Y}(k) = \mathcal{N}_3 \left[\mathcal{N}_2 \big[\mathcal{N}_1[\mathbf{X}(k) \in \mathfrak{R}^n] \big] \right] \in \mathfrak{R}^m \qquad (4.12)$$

In terms of the confluence and nonlinear activation operators described in Sections 4.1.1 and 4.1.2, (4.12) can be rewritten as

$$\mathbf{Y}(k) = f \left[\mathbf{W}_a^3(k) \, \copyright \, f \left[\mathbf{W}_a^2(k) \, \copyright \, f \left[\mathbf{W}_a^1(k) \, \copyright \, \mathbf{X}_a(k) \right] \right] \right] \qquad (4.13)$$

where $f[\cdot]$ is the nonlinear activation function (Table 1), $\copyright$ is the confluence operator (scalar product or distance measure), and $\mathbf{W}_a^1(k)$, $\mathbf{W}_a^2(k)$, and $\mathbf{W}_a^3(k)$ are the augmented synaptic weight vectors for the input, hidden, and output layers, respectively.

19

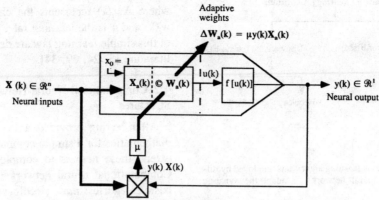

Fig. 4.8 An unsupervised (output-based) learning scheme (*Hebbian learning*) is guided by the neural output (rather than the output error, as in supervised learning).

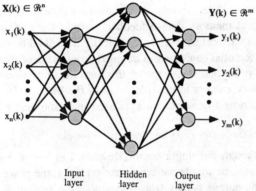

Fig. 4.9 The generalized topology of a densely interconnected three-layer static neural network. Each node (shaded circle) represents the neuron shown in Fig. 4.3. This neural network consists of an input layer (stage) with neural inputs $\mathbf{X}(k) = [x_1(k), \ldots, x_i(k), \ldots, x_n(k)]^T \in \Re^n$ and an output layer with neural outputs $\mathbf{Y}(k) = [y_1(k), \ldots, y_i(k), \ldots, y_m(k)]^T \in \Re^m$. Layers between the input and output layers are normally referred to as hidden (intermediate) layers. To keep the diagram uncluttered, the bias input $x_0(k)$ applied to each node is not shown.

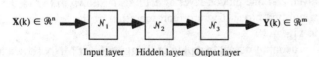

Fig. 4.10 A block-diagram representation of a three-layer static neural network (MNN) with the input vector $\mathbf{X}(k) \in \Re^n$ and output vector $\mathbf{Y}(k) \in \Re^m$. The information-processing ability of each neural layer is represented as a nonlinear mapping $\mathcal{N}_i$ (*where* $i = 1, 2$, and 3) from a multidimensional input space to a multidimensional output space. The dimension of the output space for each neural layer is equal to the number of neurons in that layer.

The information is stored in the synaptic weights of the feedforward neural network. During the learning process, the elements of the synaptic matrices $\mathbf{W}_a^1(k)$, $\mathbf{W}_a^2(k)$, and $\mathbf{W}_a^3(k)$ are continuously updated to the new information. Supervised learning algorithms based on an error-correction procedure are often used to determine $\Delta\mathbf{W}_a^1(k)$, $\Delta\mathbf{W}_a^2(k)$, and $\Delta\mathbf{W}_a^3(k)$. One method to adapt the feedforward weights of the neurons in

a static neural network is to minimize the least-mean square (LMS) error [**6.5**, 37–29] between the computed and desired outputs for each neuron in the network. The feedforward connections of static networks can also be updated using a gradient descent error-correction algorithm that is usually called the *backpropagation method* [34]. Certain static neural networks employ a basis function to produce localized response behavior to the stimulus. The feedforward weights of these networks are modified by an unsupervised K-means clustering algorithm [31]. Another unsupervised learning technique can be used by a static neural network if the feedforward weights are adapted using the Hebbian learning rule [34, 37].

4.2.2 Dynamic (feedback) neural networks

The second fundamental class of CNNs are called dynamic (feedback) neural networks. Unlike the static neural networks briefly described above, a dynamic neural network employs extensive feedback between the neurons of a layer. This feedback implies that the network has local memory characteristics. Typically, a dynamic neural network uses both feedforward and feedback inputs, as shown in Fig. 4.11. Mathematically, this neural layer can be described in discrete time as

$$\mathbf{Y}(k+1) = f\left[\mathbf{W}_a^1(k) \copyright \mathbf{X}_a(k) + \mathbf{W}_a^2(k) \copyright \mathbf{Y}_a(k)\right] \quad (4.14)$$

where $\copyright$ is the confluence operator (dot product or distance measure), k is the discrete time instant, $f[\cdot]$ is the nonlinear activation operator (Table 1), $\mathbf{X}(k) \in \Re^n$ is the neural input vector, $\mathbf{Y}_a(k) = [1, y_1(k), \ldots, y_j(k), \ldots, y_m(k)]^T \in \Re^{m+1}$ is the augmented output vector, $\mathbf{W}_a^1(k) \in \Re^{(n+1)\times(m+1)}$ is the feedforward synaptic weight matrix, and $\mathbf{W}_a^2(k) \in \Re^{(m+1)\times(m+1)}$ is the feedback synaptic weight matrix. The generalized topology of a dynamic neural network is illustrated in Fig. 4.12

4.3 Summary of Computational Neural-Network Structures

Several basic structural and computational differences can be used to categorize the various CNN structures described in

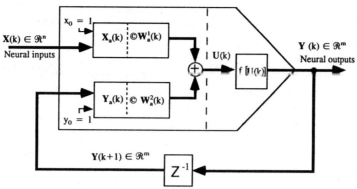

Fig. 4.11 An example of a dynamic neural network with feedforward inputs $\mathbf{W}_a^1(k) \copyright \mathbf{X}_a(k)$ and output feedback $\mathbf{W}_a^2(k) \copyright \mathbf{Y}_a(k)$. The term Z^{-1} is the unit time-delay operator.

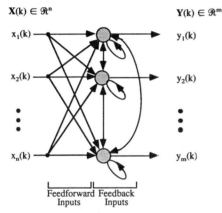

Fig. 4.12 The generalized topology of a dynamic neural network with extensive feedforward and feedback inputs. The feedforward inputs arise from a source outside the neural layer, whereas the feedback inputs are a result of dense lateral and recurrent connections between the neurons in the layer. This representation of the dynamic neural network is equivalent to Fig. 4.11

the literature. Simpson [34] describes over 27 different neural-network paradigms based on structural and computational differences. From a structural point of view, the method of recalling information by the neurons can be either static or dynamic. Furthermore, the organized topology of the neural-network architectures are classified as either single layer or multiple layer. Computational differences in the various neural-network paradigms arise from the different types of synaptic connections between the neurons. These synaptic connections can be strictly interlayer feedforward, intralayer feedback via lateral and recurrent connections, topologically ordered connections, interlayer feedforward/feedback, and a mixture of several different connective structures (called a *hybrid* network). A flow graph illustrating the interrelationship of these CNN structures is shown in Fig. 4.13. The applications of these neural networks are categorized into four classes: [A] pattern recognition and classification, [B] image processing and vision, [C] system identification and control, and [D] signal processing. The letters in brackets under each neural-network structure in this figure indicate some of the

tasks that the particular neural network has been applied to. In the next section, we will give several examples of various neural morphologies used in vision systems.

5. NEURO-VISION SYSTEM APPLICATIONS: SELECTED EXAMPLES

In the previous section, we gave a brief description of feedforward (static) and feedback (dynamic) neural structures. We will now summarize various applications of neuro-vision systems. Detailed journal articles describing a variety of neurovision system architectures for preattentive vision [6.1, 6.2], visual perception [6.3, 6.4], object recognition [6.5–6.8], color vision [6.9, 6.10], stereo vision [6.11, 6.12], and image restoration [6.13] are included in this reprint volume. It is important to realize, however, that no single neural-network structure described in the previous section can perform all tasks related to vision. Rather, vision arises from the processing and reorganizing of spatio-temporal information as it is being projected through various neuronal layers along the visual pathway. The neurons in each neuronal layer will perform only a small number of computational operations on the incoming signals. Although the neurons within a layer function in parallel, each layer must wait to receive inputs from other neural layers along the visual pathway. This final characteristic of visual information processing imposes a serial component to the computational architecture of the eye-brain system.

The parallel-serial architecture of the visual pathway enables numerous diverse computational operations to be executed at the same time. The advantages of both parallel and serial information processing can be combined in order to optimize both time and storage requirements. In this fashion, the information extracted from localized regions in the field of view can be successively merged in order to obtain more and more global representations. That is, very complex visual information-processing tasks can be performed by cascading simpler parallel processes.

Artificial vision systems often require temporal and spatial filtering, image compression, image coding, optical flow, stereo vision correspondence, image segmentation, and invari-

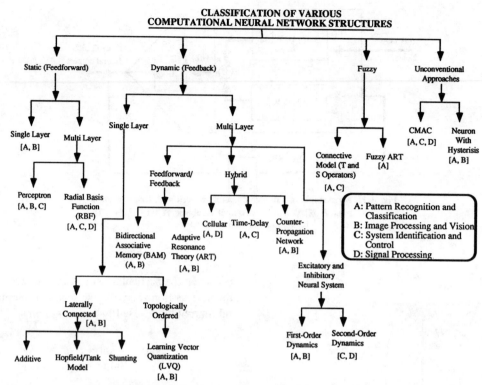

Fig. 4.13 Flow chart of common neural-network structures and their possible applications.

ant shape recognition. Each of these visual information-processing tasks, shown in Fig. 5.1, will now be realized by the static and dynamic neural networks described in Section 4. Neither of these tasks nor the neuro-vision system architectures used in these examples are comprehensive. Rather, they represent selected examples that are used to illustrate the versatility of the neural-network approach to engineering applications.

5.1 Spatial and Temporal Filtering

An important role of low-level vision is to preprocess the sensor data in an effort to suppress temporal and spatial noise that may arise from the data acquisition system, and enhance information in the scene. A variety of static and dynamic neural networks can be programmed to perform as adaptive filters [**6.5**, 24, 34, 38, 39]. For illustration purposes, an adaptive neuro-vision filter design based on a simple static neural network that can achieve near-optimum noise-removal characteristics in either temporal or spatial domains will now be described.

5.1.1 Temporal filter

The basic goal of removing temporal noise by adaptive filtering is to interpolate the middle input signal value $x(k-(n/2))$ of $(n + 1)$ sampled inputs taken from a contiguous time series signal. In other words, the static neural network receives as its input a time series of discretely sampled data values, $\mathbf{X}(k) = [x(k), x(k-1), \ldots, x(k-n)]^T \in \Re^{n+1}$, and then estimates the central value where

$$y(k) \approx x\left(k - \frac{n}{2}\right) \qquad (5.1)$$

The neural output $y(k)$ is assumed to correspond to the uncontaminated signal component in the time-sampled inputs.

The basic neuron shown in Fig. 4.3 can function as an adaptive filter by computing the scalar product of the augmented input vector $\mathbf{X}_a(k)$ and augmented synaptic weight vector $\mathbf{W}_a(k)$. The elements of the synaptic weight vector $\mathbf{W}_a(k)$ are modified by the LMS error learning algorithm [**6.5**, 38,39]. This adaptive filter design, seen in Fig. 5.2, is trained using noise-contaminated samples for which the correct uncontaminated signal values $y_d(k)$ are known. In other words, the desired neural output is known for each input sample.

This basic static neural structure can be used to either amplify or attenuate each of the frequency components of the incoming time-series $\mathbf{X}(k)$ [39]. This approach will do a near-perfect job if the desired signal and noise do not overlap in frequency. However, if the signal and noise do overlap in frequency, then the process will also tend to filter out the signal. In other words, this structure will significantly degrade the system performance.

5.1.2 Spatial filter

The static neural network described earlier for adaptive temporal filtering can easily be extended to a two-dimensional spatial filter where the neural inputs are taken from a small region in the digital image, as shown in Fig. 5.3. A neural network acting as a spatial filter multiplies each neural input within the spatial region by a weight and then sums them to-

Biological Visual Pathway

Neuro-Vision System Application

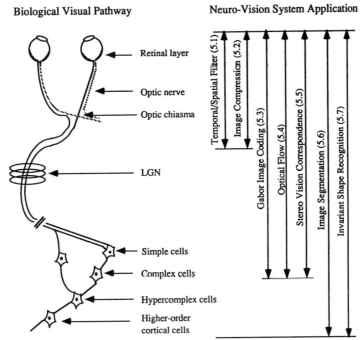

Fig. 5.1 A schematic diagram of the neuronal tissue regions of the visual pathway, and the corresponding neuro-vision system (neural-network) architectures that can realize certain visual information-processing attributes of these tissue regions. The numbers given in brackets refer to the sections that follow.

gether. A separate neuron can be applied to the spatial region surrounding each pixel in the original input image. Thus, the total number of neurons required by the static neural network to perform adaptive spatial filtering is equal to the number of pixels in the input image. The spatial filter performs mathematical operations similar to the receptive fields of the ganglion cells in the retina (see Section 2.2.1).

5.2 Image Compression

The process of coding images in order to reduce the volume of data that must be transmitted over a communication channel is called *image compression*. Image compression is possible because neighboring pixels in an image are often highly correlated, thereby enabling local statistical relationships to be exploited for efficient coding.

One technique for compressing image data [24] is to use a static (feedforward) neural network, Fig. 5.4, with a back-propagation learning algorithm. The goal of this approach is to force the neural network to learn a set of feedforward weight vectors (called *feature vectors*) for representing the input image data without throwing away any essential information. The neural layer A at the transmission end has fewer neurons than the number of pixels of the image region that is to be compressed. This squeezing action forces the network to generate a near-optimal set of weights for this neural layer. These weights define combinations of input values that contain statistically meaningful information necessary to reconstruct the input image. The pixels of the compressed image are then transmitted and, at the receiving end, the image is reconstructed by another neural layer B. The number of neurons in layer B is equal to the number of pixels in the original image.

By training the weights of layer B, all the essential features of the image can be recovered.

To illustrate this image-compression technique, assume that an input image is sampled over an (8×8) pixel block in order to create an input vector $\mathbf{X}^A(k)$ with 64 elements. The first layer of the static neural network uses 16 neurons to compress the 64 inputs $\mathbf{X}^A(k)$. In other words, the neurons in layer A are responsible for taking the $(8 \times 8 = 64)$ pixel image and re-expressing them as a $(4 \times 4 = 16)$ pixel image. Layer B then attempts to reconstruct the $(8 \times 8 = 64)$ pixel image from the compressed set of $(4 \times 4 = 16)$ inputs.

During learning, the (8×8) blocks of pixels for each image are entered into the neuro-vision system architecture, beginning at the upper-left-hand corner and moving right one pixel at a time. In this fashion, a single high-resolution image provides hundreds of thousands of training patterns for adjusting the feedforward weights of layers A and B. As a training pattern is generated, it is entered in the neurons of transmission layer A and used to correct the output at receiver layer B. The training process continues until the error is stabilized. The error is measured with respect to the input patterns that are not used during the learning procedure.

Once learning is complete, the system is ready for actual operation. The blocks of image pixels used as inputs are usually chosen so that they do not overlap. For the previous example, the pixel blocks are selected at 8-pixel intervals. Each block of data is entered into the network, and the corresponding 16-byte signal is generated by layer A and transmitted over the communication channel. At the receiving end, layer B attempts to reconstruct the block of data. This block of data is then reinserted into the received image array at the proper lo-

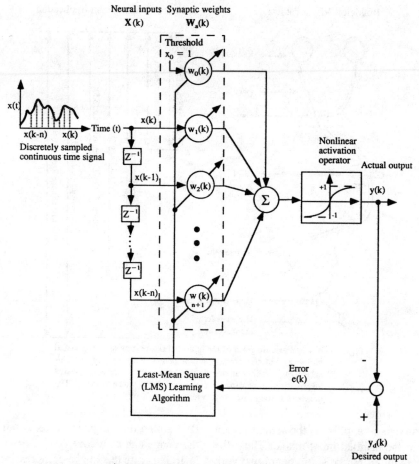

Fig. 5.2 An adaptive filter design based on a static neural-network architecture for removing temporal noise. The feedforward weights $\mathbf{W}_a(k)$ in this network are adjusted according to the LMS learning algorithm [**6.5**, 38,39].

cation. With this image-compression scheme, the number of bits required for transmission is reduced by a factor of 4; that is, data is reduced from (64×8) bits to (16×8) bits.

5.3 Gabor Image Coding

Extensive processing and reorganization occurs along the biological visual pathway. Even at the retinal level, the rate of information flow is reduced by a factor of 100 [**4.3**]. Obviously, the visual pathway employs some form of data coding and compression. One mechanism for this may be that the visual cells perform Garbor-like operations (see Section 3.3).

Recently, Daugman [**5.1**, 25, 26] developed a universal set of two-dimensional functions (Gabor functions or logons) that could be used for coding, compressing, and analyzing images. In terms of image coding and compression, it is possible to approximate an input image by means of a linear sum of two-dimensional Gabor functions $\mathcal{G} = [\mathbf{G}_1, \mathbf{G}_2, \ldots, \mathbf{G}_l, \ldots, \mathbf{G}_L]^T \in \mathfrak{R}^{L(I \times J)}$. Each function $\mathbf{G}_l \in \mathfrak{R}^{I \times J}$ is a two-dimensional $(I \times J)$ matrix with individual elements that represent spatially sampled values of a two-dimensional sinusoidal function multiplied by a Gaussian envelope. An important characteristic of this Gabor function is that all pixels with significant amplitudes are located within one standard deviation (1σ) of the ellipsoid generated by the Gaussian envelope.

All amplitudes outside this 1σ Gaussian ellipsoid can, therefore, be assumed to be zero. Thus, this Gaussian ellipsoid determines the size, aspect ratio, and orientation of the particular Gabor function $\mathbf{G}_l$. Note that ellipsoids of identical shape, aspect ratios, and orientation but different spatial locations represent different Gabor functions. From a signal-processing perspective, the Gabor function $\mathbf{G}_l$ can be envisioned as a discretely sampled image with an amplitude value assigned to each pixel. The dot product of the Gabor function and input image is the sum of the pixel-by-pixel products of $\mathbf{G}_l \in \mathfrak{R}^{I \times J}$ and the image $\mathbf{X}(k) \in \mathfrak{R}^{I \times J}$, as shown in Fig. 5.5.

For a fixed set of Gabor functions $\mathcal{G}$, it is possible to code the image $\mathbf{X}(k)$ by determining the proper weight vector $\mathbf{W}(k)$,

$$\mathbf{W}(k) = [w_1(k), \ldots, w_l(k), \ldots, w_l(k)]^T \in \mathfrak{R}^L \qquad (5.2)$$

In mathematical terms, Gabor-function image analysis involves determining the weighting (coefficient) vector $\mathbf{W}(k)$ such that

$$\mathbf{Y}(k) \approx \mathbf{X}(k) \qquad (5.3a)$$

$$= \sum_{l=1}^{L} w_l(k) \, \mathbf{G}_l \qquad (5.3b)$$

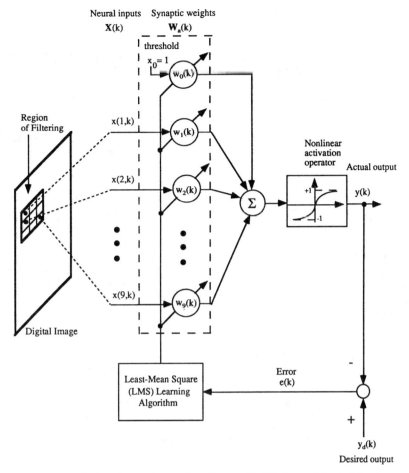

Fig. 5.3 A static neural-network architecture for filtering spatial noise. A (3 × 3) 9-element regional window is used in this example. The feedforward connections are modified using the LMS learning algorithm.

where L is the total number of functions in set $\mathcal{G}$, $w_l(k)$ is the weight (coefficient) assigned to $\mathbf{G}_l$, and $\mathbf{W}(k)$ is the weight vector.

One method of determining the weights for a particular input image is to employ the neuro-vision system architecture shown in Fig. 5.6. For mathematical convenience, assume that the input image and Gabor functions are represented by column vectors; that is, $\mathbf{X}(k) \in \mathfrak{R}^n$ and $\mathbf{G}_l \in \mathfrak{R}^n$, where $n = (\text{I} \times \text{J})$. The feedforward synaptic weights of the network are adjusted by using an LMS error learning rule to minimize the error between $\mathbf{X}(k)$ and $\mathbf{Y}(k)$ for all pixels.

The neural architecture shown in Fig. 5.6 can be used for a variety of image-compression applications if the image to be transmitted over the communication channel is expressed as the sum of elementary Gabor functions. The weight vector $\mathbf{W}(k)$ can then be coded, transmitted, and used at the receiving end to reconstruct an approximation $\mathbf{Y}(k)$ of the original input image $\mathbf{X}(k)$. Daugman [5.1] demonstrated that a near-perfect reconstruction of an 8-bit gray-scale image is possible with a data-compression ratio of 3. Furthermore, he achieved compression ratios of up to 8 with only minor degradations. The presumed compatibility with the human visual system as described in Section 3.3 makes the Gabor image analysis ap-

proach a natural choice for image compression [5.1, 5.2] and texture classification [5.1, 5.3, 40].

5.4 Optical Flow

The perception of motion information is another essential role of vision. Many vision researchers believe that an intrinsic flow function, called *optical flow*, is first extracted from time-varying imagery. Optical flow can be mathematically modeled as a vector flow field that records the point-wise instantaneous velocity of the moving brightness patterns. Under ideal circumstances, the optical flow will correspond to the motion field generated by the objects in a scene. However, this ideal is seldom the case because of the noise from the sensors and constant changes in the illuminating source.

One approach to obtain an optical flow field from time-varying digital images is based on changes in local intensities [5.5, 41, 42]. This intensity-based approach relies on the assumption that the changes in brightness of a scene are due solely to the object motion. Spatial and temporal differences in intensity value can, therefore, be used to compute the optical flow at each pixel location on an image. At any instant in time, the velocity associated with each point on the object is projected onto the image plane as a motion vector. The optical

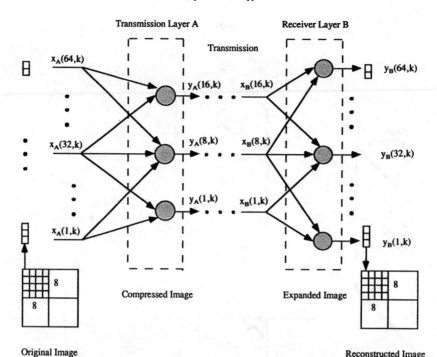

Fig. 5.4 A two-layer static (feedforward) neural network [24] for image-compression tasks. This image-compression technique uses a backpropagation algorithm to learn a near-optimal set of weights for layer *A*. These weights are necessary for compressing the input image prior to transmission over a communication channel. Layer *B* uses the outputs of layer *A* to attempt to reconstruct the original input. Each node (shaded circle) in the diagram represents a neuron of the type described in Fig. 4.3.

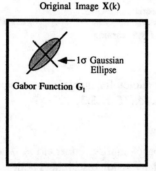

Fig. 5.5 A schematic diagram illustrating the dot product of a two-dimensional Gabor function $\mathbf{G}_l$ and the image $\mathbf{X}(k)$. The pixel intensities of $\mathbf{G}_l$ are multiplied by those of $\mathbf{X}(k)$ to yield $\mathbf{G}_l \cdot \mathbf{X}(k)$ [24].

flow vector at spatial coordinate (i,j) of a two-dimensional image is defined as

$$\Delta i(k + 1) = i(k + 1) - i(k) \qquad (5.4a)$$

and

$$\Delta j(k + 1) = j(k + 1) - j(k) \qquad (5.4b)$$

where $(i(k), j(k))$ and $(i(k + 1), j(k + 1))$ are the positions of the brightness pattern at time k and $k + 1$, respectively. Optical flow, therefore, is simplified as the computation of the displacements $(\Delta i(k + 1), \Delta j(k + 1))$ of the brightness pattern.

Optical flow is determined by using measurement primitives that calculate conjugate points by checking every pixel within a spatial neighborhood of two uniformly sampled consecutive image frames. The maximum search range (or displacement) is a function of the maximum possible speed of the objects in the scene. If the velocity component of each pixel is subsampled over one time interval by a displacement bin of size D (a real number less than 1), then the number of neurons necessary for each pixel in the original image plane is $n = (1/D + 1)^2$. The total number of neurons required, therefore, for an image with N_r rows and N_c columns is $\{N_r \times N_c \times (1/D + 1)^2\}$. Since the intensities of no two objects can occupy the same pixel at one time, only one velocity value can be assigned to each pixel location. Thus, only one neuron within the total $(1/D + 1)^2$ for each pixel can be in an active state for a given input image. The velocity value associated with this neuron is determined by its direction selectivity. The neuro-vision system architecture [42] can be envisioned as a two-dimensional grid (see Fig. 5.7), with spatially distributed blocks that are equal to the number of pixels in the original image. Furthermore, each pixel block is a two-dimensional subarray containing $(1/D + 1)^2$ neurons that represent the possible velocity values for a pixel at the spatial location.

The input from the external world applied to each neuron in the dynamic (feedback) neural network (Fig. 5.8) is given in the form of the initial state value [**6.13**, 42]; that is, $\mathbf{Y}(0) = \mathbf{X}(0)$. This initial state is based on several different types of measurement primitives that are related to intensities,

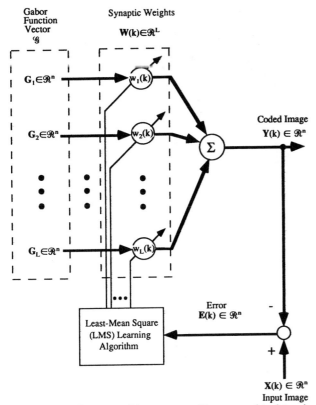

Fig 5.6 A simplified neuro-vision system architecture used to determine the expansion weights (coefficients) $\mathbf{W}(k)$ for a gray-level image $\mathbf{X}(k)$. Different images will generate different sets of weights. Note that the thick arrows in the diagram represent vectors and the thin arrows represent scalars.

edges, and corners. The neurons with similar velocity-selective characteristics in the neighboring pixel blocks will affect each other's dynamic behavior through mutual lateral interconnections. Finally, an individual neuron also receives recurrent inputs from itself and other similarly selective neurons within the neighboring pixel blocks. Mathematically, the multidimensional neural network for optical flow calculation is described by

$$\mathbf{Y}(k+1) = f\left[\mathbf{W}_a(k) \, \copyright \, \mathbf{Y}_a(k)\right] \qquad (5.5)$$

where the initial state is $\mathbf{Y}(0) = \mathbf{X}(0)$ and $f[\cdot]$ is the nonlinear activation operator (Table 1). After numerous iterations, the neuron with maximum excitation in the $(1/D + 1)^2 \times (1/D + 1)^2$ pixel block remains active and all others are set to zero. For example, if the (m,l)th neuron in the (i,j)th block remains active, then the velocities calculated in the m and l directions at pixel location (i,j) are $(m\,D)$ and $(l\,D)$, respectively.

5.5 Stereo Vision Correspondence

Physiological studies of vertebrate binocular vision systems have shown that the distance perceived by the eyes depends upon the *retinal disparity*. The retinal disparity is the difference between the location of the retinal-image points in the two eyes. As a result of the slightly different views generated in two eyes, the retinal points nearer to the observer will have a larger disparity than the retinal points associated with ob-

jects that are farther away from the observer. The separate retinal images are fused together in the visual cortex in order to produce a perception of a single three-dimensional image.

Stereopsis is a technique that determines the depth of an object in a scene by means of comparing two offset images. Based on the geometry of stereopsis, it is possible to determine depth d given the focal length f and the separation b, as shown in Fig. 5.9 [41]. Critical to stereopsis is the correspondence process that attempts to establish a linkage between similar areas found in the left and right images. Two basic approaches are used to solve the correspondence problem: (a) match every point in the left and right images, and (b) extract distinct features from each image and try to match them [42]. It is not certain whether the human visual pathway performs stereo fusion cooperatively in a point-to-point manner or by using distinct features.

Finding the corresponding feature points between two images is very difficult, especially when the feature points in one image are not visible in the second, due to object occlusion or shading caused by indirect illumination. As a result, only a small number of points found in the left image may have a correct match in the right image, and vice versa. However, the best solution for any match should satisfy the uniqueness constraint; that is, each feature point in the left image should have a unique match in the right image.

One approach to obtaining an optimal solution is to use parallel-matching techniques where compatibility measures between matched features are used to find the "best" solution. In terms of neural networks, this correspondence problem can be formulated as minimizing a cost function by a distributed dynamic neural network [6.12]. Each neuron in the network represents a possible match between the feature in the left and right images. Correspondence is achieved by initializing each neuron that represents a possible match and then allowing the neurons in the network to evolve to a stable state. The network uses the initial points (initial states) and compatibility measures (synaptic weights) between matched feature points to find a solution (stable state).

The first step of this neuro-vision approach is to extract features (points of interest related to corners, etc.) from both left and right images. A feature-selection operator that finds the variance in the horizontal, vertical, and both diagonal directions for each pixel in the image can be used [6.12]. The minimum of these values is then chosen as the variance for that pixel location. A two-dimensional dynamic (feedback) network, similar to the one shown in Fig. 5.8, is used to find the correspondence between the features in the left and right images. The network is represented as a $N_L \times N_R$ array of neurons, Fig. 5.10, where N_L and N_R are the total number of selected features in the left and right images, respectively. The state of each binary bipolar neuron in the network represents a possible match of a feature in the left image with one in the right image.

The objective of this approach is to find the degree of compatibility of a match between a pair of feature points (i,j) in the left image and a pair of feature points (m,l) in the right image. To achieve this task, i is selected randomly from all the fea-

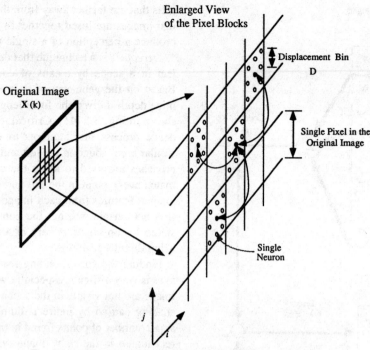

Fig. 5.7 A schematic diagram showing the two-dimensional topology for calculating optical flow using a dynamic (feedback) neural network. The external input **X**(0) becomes the initial state **Y**(0) of the constituent neurons. Each neuron receives inputs from itself and other neurons that have similar selective characteristics located at the neighboring pixel blocks. The state activity evolves such that only one neuron within the pixel block remains active. The location of the active neuron in the pixel subarray corresponds to the velocity value associated with the pixel.

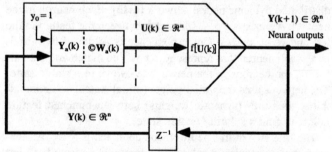

Fig. 5.8 A block diagram of the state feedback dynamic neural network that is used to calculate optical flow. The initial state of the neurons is equal to the external input; that is, **Y**(0) = **X**(0). The activity of the neurons evolve such that only one neuron in each pixel block will remain active (firing) under steady-state conditions.

tures in the left image. The neighboring feature points within a window (say, of size 40×40) opened around feature i are taken as j's for that comparison; all other features are assumed to have zero compatibility contributions because they are too far apart and probably belong to another object in the scene. Each feature m is also chosen randomly out of a window (40×40) opened around i's (x,y) locations offset by an estimated disparity in the right image. The window is used to eliminate the possibility of choosing m points that have no chance of being a candidate for a match.

5.6 Image Segmentation: Boundary Contour System

The Boundary Contour System (BCS) developed by Grossberg, Mingolla, and Todorovic [**6.1**] is a complex multilevel neuro-vision system architecture used for image segmentation. An important feature of the BCS is its ability to connect edge segments that may be separated by a distance of several pixels. The architecture of the BCS is based on the neurophysiology of the mammalian vision system and can mimic a number of phenomena observed in visual psychophysics. This neuro-vision system architecture illustrates how different levels of information processing can be interconnected in order to solve an overall complex vision problem.

The key element of the BCS is feedforward, feedback, and lateral interactions between the neurons of the dynamic neural network, similar to the model shown in Fig. 4.11. The lateral synaptic connections between the neurons of a common neural layer are specifically designed such that the excitatory (cooperative) and inhibitory (competitive) synaptic weights balance each other in some predefined fashion. During operation, a stimulus excites certain neurons, which, in turn, transmit excitatory (positive) signals to neurons whose activations will strengthen their own response behavior. In addition, the excited neurons send out inhibitory (negative) signals to those neurons whose activations would interfere or compete with their own response activity. This network enables certain neurons to selectively strengthen their response activity to a

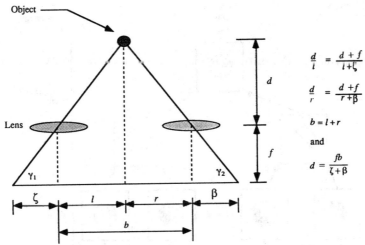

Fig. 5.9 The geometry of stereopsis used to fuse two disparate images. The separation of the two lenses is *b*, the distance of the left lens from center is *l*, the distance of the right lens from center is *r*, the displacement pair is (ζ, β), the focal length is *f*, and the distance of the object from the lenses is *d*.

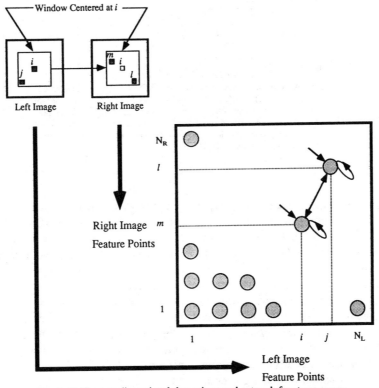

Fig. 5.10 The two-dimensional dynamic neural network for stereo correspondence. For simplicity, only the connections to two neurons are shown. Each node, or shaded circle, represents the neuron shown in Fig. 4.3. The initial state of the neurons is equal to the external input; that is, $\mathbf{Y}(0) = \mathbf{X}(0)$. The activity of the neurons evolves such that only one neuron will remain active (firing) after a period of time (see Fig. 5.8).

particular stimulus, and to decrease the activity of the neighboring neurons that exhibit a lesser response to the same stimulus. As a result, this dynamic neural network is able to sharpen the input-intensity contrast when different neurons are simultaneously excited by the same stimulus intensity.

The dynamic (cooperative-competitive) neural network is used by all neural layers at levels 2, 3, and 4 of the Boundary Contour System shown in Fig. 5.11. The number of neurons in each neural layer is the same. The synaptic connections between the neurons in the BCS are fixed and, therefore, the sys-

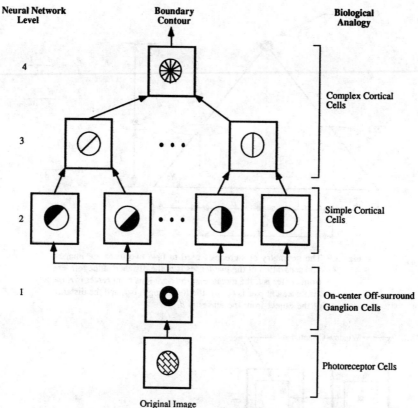

Neural Network Level   Boundary Contour   Biological Analogy

Complex Cortical Cells

Simple Cortical Cells

On-center Off-surround Ganglion Cells

Photoreceptor Cells

Original Image

Fig. 5.11 A simplified block diagram of the BCS used for image segmentation. The BCS consists of four levels that contain cooperative-competitive neural layers. Each neural layer performs a specialized task. The BCS is a subsystem of an overall complex neuro-vision system architecture developed to emulate preattentive vision [6.1].

tem does not exhibit learning capabilities. Each neural layer within the BCS is designed to perform a unique task.

Each neuron in the neural layer of the first level generates an on-center and off-surround response based on the neighborhood stimuli originating from the original input image. The on-center and off-surround response is generated by excitatory (positive) recurrent and inhibitory (negative) lateral connections. These neurons mimic the behavior of the ganglion cells found in the retina (Section 2.2.1). The neurons of the various neural layers that make up level 2 are programmed to emulate the simple cells found in the primary visual (striate) cortex (Section 2.2.3). This level of information processing is composed of 12 different neural layers, whereupon the neurons within each layer are tuned to a particular orientation and direction of contrast in the inputs received from the neurons in level 1. Any neuron that becomes activated in level 2 will transmit a positive response to (i.e., cooperate with) similar neurons in the other neural layers that share the same retinal position and orientation, but respond to different directions-of-contrast. These cooperative interactions produce the inputs for the neurons situated in the neural layers of level 3, which are sensitive to the same orientation and position, but are insensitive to the direction-of-contrast. Thus, if 12 neural layers are used in level 2 to store 12 different orientation and

direction-of-contrast activations, then only six layers are required by level 3 of the BCS.

The activated neurons in level 3 perform two types of short-range competitive (negative) interactions. First, an active neuron will inhibit neighboring neurons that respond to the same orientation. This process results in the thinning and sharpening of edge information. Second, the neurons that are sensitive to different types of orientation will inhibit each other. This process prevents the boundary edges from extending beyond the region that originally generated them. Finally, the neurons of the neural layer in level 4 combine the thresholded outputs from all the orientation-specific neural layers in level 3, and employ a long-range form of cooperation (positive) interaction in order to obtain a complete thinned boundary contour. This long-range cooperation between neurons with similar orientations enables the boundaries to override small gaps that might otherwise produce disjointed contours. In addition, active neurons in the layers of level 4 send a positive feedback to the neurons in level 2 that have similar orientations. The competition between neurons at this level keeps the edge information from spreading. The combined action of the neurons in levels 3 and 4 is believed to correspond to the signal-processing operations taking place by the complex cells in the primary visual (striate) cortex.

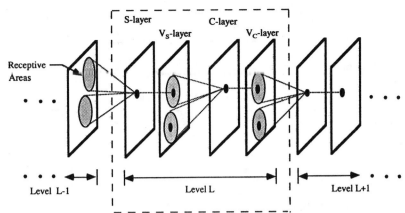

Fig. 5.12 The computational architecture of the Neocognitron. Each level consists of four layers (cell planes) with distinct types of neurons (cells). The S-cells are feature-extraction neurons and the C-cells are neurons that assist in position-invariant object recognition. The V_s-cells and V_c-cells provide linkages between the S-cells and C-cells.

5.7 Invariant Shape Recognition: Neocognitron

The Neocognitron developed by Fukushima [**6.6**, 43–45] is a biologically motivated neuro-vision system architecture for pattern-recognition applications. Similar to the Boundary Contour System described in the previous section, the Neocognitron attempts to emulate certain attributes of the mammalian visual system. However, unlike the BCS the Neocognitron utilizes the same neural structure at each information-processing level of the neuro-vision system architecture. This reflects a fundamental goal of the Neocognitron design to employ a common neural-computing structure that performs the same function throughout the entire architecture, but at continually higher levels of abstraction.

The Neocognitron is organized into a hierarchical series of neural-network levels. Each level has the same basic computational structure. Each constituent level contains four different types of neurons (called *cells* by Fukushima) that are organized into separate neural layers (*cell planes*). The Neocognitron is able to perform position-, rotation-, and scale-invariant pattern-recognition tasks because it interlaces layers of feature-selection neurons with layers of neurons that respond to the same feature but at different positions in the input array. The organization of the levels and neural layers in the Neocognitron are shown in Fig. 5.12. These neural layers are comprised of S-cells, V_s-cells, C-cells, and V_c-cells. The S-cells are used specifically for feature extraction, the C-cells assist in position-invariant object recognition, and the V_s- and V_c-cells provide linkages between S- and C-cells.

The S-cells and C-cells, at a particular level, are divided into various different neural layers based on the number of features used for recognition purposes. All neurons in a single neural layer will respond to the same feature but centered at different spatial locations on the layer surface. Each C-cell receives signals from a group of S-cells that extract the same features, but with slight variations in position. In this fashion, the C-cells generate a position-invariant response to a specific feature stimulus. Finally, layers of V_s- and V_c-cells at each level provide inhibitory connections that enable the S-cells to respond only to the particular feature it has learned to recognize.

The feedforward connections from the C-cells to each S-cell are modified by a learning algorithm, and each layer of S-cells learns to respond to a different feature. A C-cell is activated if at least one of its connecting S-cells is active. The output from a C-cell is projected to many different S-cell layers in the next level. Each of these advancing S-cell layers will attempt to recognize a new higher-order feature. In this fashion, local features at the earlier levels are gradually integrated into more and more global (abstract) forms that are position-independent.

The topmost level in the hierarchical architecture is a C-cell layer that is able to recognize a particular pattern through the progressive generation of more and more abstract features by the advancing levels. The interlacing of S-cell layers and C-cell layers enables complex patterns to be easily recognized because the positional error is tolerated a little bit at each stage.

The Neocognitron can be programmed by either supervised or unsupervised learning algorithms. In both situations, all connections are fixed except the feedforward connections from the C-cells of one level to the S-cells of the next level. In supervised learning, the teacher assigns certain features to the different neural layers. For unsupervised learning, the S-cells undergo a neural-layer variation of the winner-take-all Hebbian learning rule (Section 4.1.3). The active connections to the winning cell undergo the greatest amount of adaptation. In addition, all other cells that share the same neural layer learn to respond to the same feature. That is, all S-cells in a neural layer have input connections of the same spatial distribution as the winning cell. However, each S-cell learns to respond to the feature in a slightly different position on the input layer.

There are two issues to be considered when constructing a Neocognitron. First, the number of neural layers in each level must be sufficient to recognize enough features in order to carry out recognition tasks. The number of neural layers necessary is not easily specified because the architecture is self-organizing. However, the number of neural layers needs to be

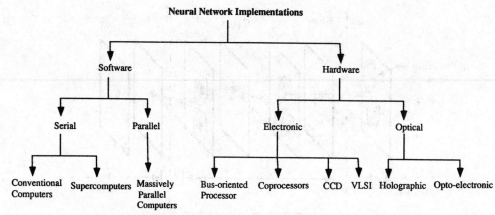

Fig. 6.1 Flow chart of various classes and subclasses for neural-network implementations.

increased when the number of pattern classes are increased. At minimum, the number of neural layers in the topmost level must be equal to the number of classes to be recognized. Second, in order to achieve good characteristics, the Neocognitron must be designed with a high degree of overlap between adjacent regions of input. It has been estimated [33] that a Neocognitron architecture with about 15 levels is necessary for shift-invariant object recognition in a (128 × 128) pixel image.

6. NEURO-VISION SYSTEM IMPLEMENTATIONS

A large number of software- and hardware-based neuro-vision system implementations have been developed in recent years that attempt to streamline the number of computations and take advantage of the inherent parallelism found within computational neural-network structures. In general, these neural-network implementations have three key characteristics. First, they are computationally intensive. That is, the output of each neuron in a layer is the summation of several products. Every synaptic connection in the neural layer requires a separate multiplication operation. Second, these neural layers employ massive parallelism. Each neuron of the layer can be treated as a local processor acting in parallel with the other neurons. As a result, the network computational speed is dependent on the number of mathematical operations performed by each neuron and not the overall number of neurons. Third, the neural layers require immense memory. Individual neurons in the layer have many synaptic connections, where each synaptic connection has an associated weight that must be stored. This situation becomes a serious problem as the size of the network increases. For example, doubling the number of neurons will result in a factor-of-four increase in the number of synaptic connections. As we have shown in the previous section, vision requires large numbers of neurons to be distributed in two-dimensional arrays. In order for neural networks to be useful for vision applications, it is therefore necessary that they have an adequate amount of storage.

The three broad areas of neural-network implementation are computer-based software, electronic hardware, and optical/opto-electronic hardware. The various classes and subclasses of neural-network implementations are shown in Fig. 6.1. Computer implementations are largely software-based algorithms that utilize existing computing machines that were not designed explicitly for neural-network processing. Supercomputers, massively parallel computers, and the conventional digital computers are examples of hardware computing systems that can be programmed by adequate software to simulate neural-network functions for neuro-vision applications. Electronic neural-network implementations involve bus-oriented processors, coprocessors [7.2, 7.4], CCD [7.6, 46], and very large scale integrated (VLSI) circuit designs [7.1–7.5, 47–52]. In general, this includes any electronic hardware that is designed specifically for neural-network implementations. Finally, optical/opto-electronic implementations are neural networks that involve either optical [7.7, 7,8] or a mixture of optical and electronic components in their hardware in order to achieve real-time parallel processing [53].

7. SUMMARY

The general focus of this volume on neuro-vision systems is to transfer the basic knowledge of visual neuro-biology toward the development of artificial vision algorithms and hardware mechanisms. The biological foundation, computational architectures, and software/hardware implementations of neuro-vision systems were briefly summarized in this introductory tutorial. It is impossible to address all related theoretical issues, mathematical models, and computational paradigms in such a short presentation. Rather, it was the objective of the authors to present a *holistic* view of neuro-vision research in an effort to stress the interdisciplinary relationship between biological and artificial vision paradigms.

The remaining parts of this book are collected papers that follow the basic outline presented in this introduction. The first part of the volume introduces the reader to various perspectives about the field of neuro-vision systems. These papers provide some philosophical and physiological aspects of biological vision and motivation for the subject by directing the reader toward the computational aspects of vision. The second part gives a broad view of biological neuronal morphology, which is the foundation of biological vision. The objective of the Part 3 is to present an introduction to biological and artificial neurocomputing systems. An overview of some important research in the field of visual neurophysiology is presented in the fourth part of the volume. These papers deal with information-processing aspects of the various neuronal layers such as the retina, the LGN, the primary visual cortex, and the higher cortical regions of the brain. Some mathematical models that help us understand how visual images are processed in the retina and visual cortex are presented in Part 5. The sixth part of the volume contains a set of papers that deal with various neuro-vision system architectures for solving engineering problems. Finally, the seventh part gives an overview of the different hardware implementations of neurovision systems. The key features of these articles and how they relate to neuro-vision research is described by an introduction to each part of this book. A bibliography of related books, journal articles, and conference papers is included with the introduction to each section.

References*

[1] C. Blakemore, *Mechanics of the Mind*. Cambridge: Cambridge University Press, 1977.

[2] M. A. Fischler and O. Firschein, *Intelligence: The Eye, the Brain and the Computer*. Reading, MA: Addison-Wesley, 1987.

[3] L. Uhr, "Highly parallel, hierarchical, recognition cone perceptual structures," in *Parallel Computer Vision*, L. Uhr, Ed., New York: Academic Press, pp. 249–292, 1987.

[4] L. Uhr, "Psychological motivation and underlying concepts," in *Structured Computer Vision*, S. Tanimoto and A. Klinger, Ed., New York: Academic Press, pp. 1–30, 1980.

[5] M. M. Gupta, "Biological basis for computer vision: Some perspectives," *SPIE's Advances in Intelligent Robotics*, vol. 1192, pp. 811–823, 1989.

[6] P. S. Churchland and T. J. Sejnowski, *The Computational Brain*. Cambridge, MA: MIT Press, 1992.

[7] E. B. Goldstein, *Sensation and Perception*. Belmont, CA: Wadsworth, 1989.

[8] N. Graham, "Spatial-frequency channels in human vision: Detecting edges without edge detectors," in *Visual Coding and Adaptability*, C. S. Harris, Ed., Hillsdale, NJ: Lawrence Erlbaum, pp. 215–262, 1980.

[9] C. F. Hall and E. L. Hall, "Nonlinear model for the spatial characteristics of the human visual system," *IEEE Trans. Syst., Man, Cybern.*, vol. 7, no. 3, pp. 161–170, 1977.

[10] M. D. Levine, *Vision in Man and Machine*. New York: McGraw-Hill, 1985.

[11] F. Crick, "Memory and molecular turnover," *Nature*, vol. 312, p. 101, 1984.

[12] D. H. Hubel, *Eye, Brain and Vision*. New York: W. H. Freeman, 1988.

[13] E. R. Kandel and J. H. Schwartz, *Principles of Neural Science*. New York: North-Holland, 1985.

[14] R. J. MacGregor and E. R. Lewis, *Neural Modeling: Electrical Signal Processing in the Nervous System*. New York: Plenum Press, 1977.

[15] H. R. Wilson and J. D. Cowan, "A mathematical theory of the functional dynamics of cortical and thalamic nervous tissue," *Kybernetik*, vol. 13, pp. 55–80, 1973.

[16] V. Bruce and P. Green, *Visual Perception: Physiology, Psychology and Ecology*. London: Lawrence Erlbaum Assoc., 1985.

[17] D. Marr, *Vision*. San Francisco: W. H. Freeman, 1982.

[18] D. M. Marr and E. Hildreth, "Theory of edge detection," *Proc. Roy. Soc. Lond.*, vol. B 207, pp. 187–217, 1980.

[19] K. R. Castleman, *Digital Image Processing*. Englewood Cliffs, NJ: Prentice-Hall, 1979.

[20] R. C. Gonzalez and R. E. Woods, *Digital Image Processing*. Reading, MA: Addison-Wesley, 1992.

[21] J. R. Bergen, H. R. Wilson, and J. D. Cowan, "Further evidence for four mechanisms mediating vision at threshold: Sensitivities to complex gratings and aperiodic stimuli," *J. Opt. Soc. Amer.*, vol. 69, no. 11, pp. 1580–1587, 1979.

[22] H. R. Wilson and J. R. Bergen, "A four mechanism model for threshold spatial vision," *Vision Res.*, vol. 19, pp. 19–22, 1979.

[23] D. Gabor, "Theory of communication," *J. IEE*, vol. 93, pp. 429–457, 1946.

[24] R. Hecht-Nielson, *Neurocomputing*. Reading, MA: Addison-Wesley, 1990.

[25] J. G. Daugman, "An information-theoretic view of analog representation in the striate cortex," in *Computational Neuroscience*, E. L. Schwartz, Ed., Cambridge, MA: MIT Press, pp. 403–423, 1990.

[26] J. G. Daugman, "Six formal properties of two-dimensional visual filters: Structural principles and frequency/orientation selectivity," *IEEE Trans. Syst., Man, Cybern.*, vol. 13, no. 5, pp. 882–887, 1983.

[27] D. G. Stork and H. R. Wilson, "Do Gabor functions provide appropriate descriptions of visual cortical receptive fields?" *J. Opt. Soc. Amer.*, vol. 7, no. 8, pp. 1362–1337, 1990.

[28] M. A. Arbib, *Brains, Machines and Mathematics*. New York: Springer-Verlag, 1987.

[29] S. Grossberg, "Nonlinear neural networks: Principles, mechanisms, and architectures," *Neural Networks*, vol. 1, pp. 17–61, 1988.

[30] D. R. Hush and B. G. Horne, "Progress in supervised neural networks," *IEEE Signal Process. Mag.*, Jan., pp. 8–39, 1993.

[31] T. Kohonen, *Self-Organization and Associative Memory*. Berlin: Springer-Verlag, 1984.

[32] R. P. Lippmann, "An introduction to computing with neural nets," *IEEE ASSP Mag.*, April, pp. 4–22, 1987.

[33] A. J. Maren, C. T. Harston, and R. M. Pap, *Handbook of Neural Computing*. San Diego: Academic Press, 1990.

[34] P. K. Simpson, *Artificial Neural Systems*. New York: Pergamon Press, 1990.

[35] M. M. Gupta, *Introduction to Neuro-Computational Systems with Applications to Control and Vision*. Tutorial Notes, University of Saskatchewan, 1993.

[36] G. K. Knopf and M. M. Gupta, "Design of a multitask neurovision processor," *J. Math. Imaging Vision*, vol. 2, pp. 233–250, 1992.

[37] D. Hebb, *Organization of Behavior: A Neuropsychological Theory*. New York: John Wiley, 1949.

[38] B. Widrow and M. A. Lehr, "30 Years of adaptive neural networks: Perceptron, Madaline and backpropagation," *Proc. IEEE*, vol. 78, no. 9, pp. 1415–1442, 1990.

[39] B. Widrow and R. Winter, "Neural nets for adaptive filtering and adaptive pattern recognition," *IEEE Computer*, March, pp. 25–39, 1988.

[40] M. Porat and Y. Y. Zeevi, "The generalized Gabor scheme of image representation in biological and machine vision," *IEEE Trans. Pattern Anal. Machine Intell.*, vol. 10, no. 4, pp. 452–468, 1988.

[41] H. Wechsler, *Computational Vision*. Boston: Academic Press, 1990.

[42] Y. -T. Zhou and R. Chellappa, *Artificial Neural Networks for Computer Vision*. New York: Springer-Verlag, 1992.

[43] K. Fukushima, "Neocognitron: A hierarchical network for visual pattern recognition," in *Fuzzy Computing*, M. M. Gupta and T. Yamakawa, Eds., Amsterdam: North-Holland, pp. 53–69, 1988.

[44] K. Fukushima, "Selective attention in pattern recognition and associative recall," in *Fuzzy Computing*, M. M. Gupta and T. Yamakawa, Eds., Amsterdam: North-Holland, pp. 71–88, 1988.

[45] K. Fukushima, "A feature extractor for curvilinear patterns: A design suggested by the mammalian visual system," *Kybernetik*, vol. 7, pp. 153–160, 1970.

[46] S. Kemeny, H. Torbey, H. Meadows, R. Bredthauer, M. La Shell, and E. Fossum, "CCD focal-plane image reorganization processors for lossless image compression," *IEEE J. Solid-State Circuits*, vol. 27, pp. 398–405, 1992.

*A boldface reference number in the text refers to an article included in this reprint volume.

[47] B. E. Boser, E. Sackinger, J. Bromley, Y. Le Cun, and L. D. Jackel, "An analog neural network processor with programmable topology," *IEEE J. Solid-State Circuits*, vol. 26, no. 12, pp. 2017–2025, 1991.

[48] H. P. Graf, L. D. Jackel, and W. E. Hubbard, "VLSI implementation of a neural network model," *IEEE Computer*, vol. 21, no. 3, pp. 41–49, 1988.

[49] J. Hutchinson, C. Koch, J. Luo, and C. Mead, "Computing motion using analog and binary resistive networks," *IEEE Computer*, vol. 21, pp. 52–64, 1981.

[50] H. Li and C. H. Chen, "Simulating a function of visual peripheral processes with an analog VLSI network," *IEEE Micro*, vol. 11, pp. 8–15, 1991.

[51] M. A. Maher, S. P. Deweerth, M. A. Mahowald, and C. A. Mead, "Implementing neural architectures using analog VLSI Circuits," *IEEE Trans. Circuits Syst.*, vol. 36, no. 5, pp. 643–653, 1989.

[52] M. A. Mahowald and C. Mead, "The silicon retina," *Sci. Amer.*, pp. 76–82, 1991.

[53] D. Casasent, "Multifunctional hybrid neural net," *Neural Networks*, vol. 5, pp. 361–370, 1992.

Part 1
Neuro-Vision Systems:
Some Perspectives

Man has always dreamed of creating a portrait of himself. The neuro-vision system is an attempt to recapitulate some of the attributes of human vision in a machine.

HUMANS, like many other biological species, are endowed with very rich neurosensory systems, flexible neuro-control mechanisms, and a mysterious carbon-based organ for perception and cognition—the *brain*. The basic sensory, control, and perception abilities are innate within the organism, while the advanced faculty of cognition evolves through the process of learning.

The richest human sense—*vision* (the subject of this volume)—and its cognitive faculty—the *brain*—have always intrigued philosophers, physiologists, neurophysiologists, mathematicians, computer scientists, and engineers. An understanding of the phenomena of *sight* and *perception* still remain some of the deepest challenges confronted by scientists. Numerous researchers around the world that work in the various allied fields have accepted the challenge of understanding the mysteries of biological vision in order to develop the field of artificial (machine) vision systems. The understanding of biological vision and the development of a vision machine fall under the general category of neuro-vision systems. One of the driving forces behind the vast number of studies being undertaken by various research groups around the globe is the desire to emulate certain computational aspects of biological vision in an effort to design and develop robust neuro-vision sensors and systems for applications to such diverse areas as robotics in space, manufacturing, and health sciences. The term *neuro-vision systems* used in the present book means an artificial (machine) vision system that embodies the basic computational principles found in biological neural processes. The basic mechanism for realizing all these complex biological processes and computations is the *neuron*. The subject of neurobiology has been intensely studied for over 150 years; however, the field of neuro-vision is only about 15 years old. Over this short period of time, many intense studies, ranging from some theoretical ones to simple architectures and implementations, have appeared. We can safely say, however, that the field of neuro-vision systems is still in its primitive stages.

Though several theoretical advances have been made, implementations have been hindered by the limitations in computational technology. Emerging computational technologies based upon very large scale integration (VLSI), opto-electronics, and molecular computing promise to provide a great impetus to both computational and applications aspects.

In Part One of this volume, we introduce the reader to various perspectives about the field of neuro-vision systems. This part contains four recently published articles written by some well-known researchers in the field. These researchers are involved in studying perception, cognition, visual models, biological vision, and computational aspects of vision processes. Although these representative articles do not provide a complete historical perspective of neuro-vision systems, they do provide some philosophical and physiological aspects of biological vision and motivation for the subject by directing the reader toward the computational aspects of vision.

We must add that though a considerable amount of effort has gone into the areas of brain and vision research over the past 150 years or so, it is only in recent years that the computational and engineering aspects have been studied. These studies were inspired by a desire to recreate in a machine some attributes of the brain and human vision system. The next decade of research in this field, combined with the new computational tools that are being presently developed, promises to advance this research to the point that, not too far in the future, robots in space, manufacturing, and medicine will be able to see—albeit not with the same perfection and fineness that humans do.

Patricia S. Churchland of the Department of Philosophy, University of California at San Diego, and Terrence J. Sejnowski of the Salk Institute and the Department of Biology, University of California at San Diego, have made many seminal contributions to the neuroscience field. In article (1.1), they pose some questions on how it is that we can perceive, learn, and be aware of the world. Neuroscience and cognitive science share the goal of trying to understand how the mind-brain works. In the past, discoveries at the neuronal level and explanations at the cognitive level were so far apart that each discipline often seemed to be only remotely related to the other. To bring these disciplines closer together, the authors propose that research and development in cognitive neuroscience should employ a coevolutionary strategy, where research at one level provided constraints, corrections, and inspirations for further developments at the other levels. Indeed, the development of new techniques for studying neural activity in the brain, together with insights from computational modeling and a better understanding of cognitive processes, have opened the door for collaborative research that could lead to major advances in our understanding of the brain.

The purpose of studying neuro-vision is to develop a theoretical understanding of biological vision and provide some computational aspects for its implementation on a machine. In article (1.2), T. J. Sejnowski, C. Koch, and P. S. Churchland provide several classes of brain models. The ultimate aim of computational neuroscience is to explain how electrical and chemical signals are used in the brain to represent and process information. Although this goal in not new, more has been learned in the last decade about the brain because of recent advances in neuroscience. These advances, combined with increased computing power, enable researchers to simulate more realistic brain models. However, neuronal morphology is very complex. Neurons interact at various levels and this interaction yields many interesting phenomena. For example, rhythmic pattern generation in some neural circuits is a property of neural interactions and not that of isolated pacemaker neurons. This article, therefore, provides some interesting insights into the computational aspects of the brain. The models presented in this article may be considered provisional, but they do promise to provide directions for further experimental and theoretical advances.

Human visual behavior is very complex and it would be interesting to understand and implement some of these functions on a machine for various image-processing applications. In article (1.3), D. J. Granrath provides an engineer's insight into the mechanisms by which the human eye forms a neural image. The visual scene information is first focused on the back of the retina where photoreceptor cells transform these light intensities into equivalent electrical impulses. Through a complex network of inter-retinal neural layers, these images are then encoded into neural signals that are to be carried by the optic nerve to the visual cortex. Information from the original visual scene, and the eye-retinal system can be viewed as a system for image encoding and bandwidth compression. Some mathematical models of these neural mechanisms that can be exploited for engineering applications, such as image bandwidth compression, image quality assessment, and image enhancement, are discussed by the author. Furthermore, this article provides some interesting insight into the low-level retinal process and its adaptivity to various light intensities. Such studies may, indeed, lead to the development of an intelligent image processor.

A. Rosenfeld, who is with the Center for Automation Research at the University of Maryland, has studied various aspects of computer vision for many years. In article (1.4), Rosenfeld reviews some basic computer vision techniques and speculates about their possible relevance to the modeling of human visual processes. Special emphasis is given to image segmentation techniques and their relationship to the process of visual organization. Segmentation is a basic step in most neuro-vision applications, and Rosenfeld has given a sketch of a class of pyramid-based segmentation techniques. The purpose of including this brief article in this volume is to introduce our readers to the vision segmentation process. It would be of interest to investigate whether such segmentation techniques may be used to understand the biological visual processes, and thus advance the field of neuro-vision systems.

Further Reading

[1] S. M. Anstis, "The perception of apparent movement," *Phil. Trans. Roy. Soc. London*, vol. B 290, pp. 153–168, 1980.

[2] R. Arnheim, *Visual Thinking*. Berkeley: University of California Press, 1969.

[3] H. B. Barlow, "The absolute efficiency of perceptual decisions," *Phil. Trans. Roy. Soc. London*, vol. B 290, pp. 71–82, 1980.

[4] M. Bertero, T. A. Poggio, and V. Torre, "Ill-posed problems in early vision," *Proc. IEEE*, vol. 76, no. 8, pp. 869–889, 1988.

[5] C. Blakemore, *Mechanics of the Mind*. Cambridge: Cambridge University Press, 1977.

[6] V. Bruce and P. Green, *Visual Perception: Physiology, Psychology and Ecology*. London: Lawrence Erlbaum, 1985.

[7] P. S. Churchland and T. J. Sejnowski, *The Computational Brain*. Cambridge MA: MIT Press, 1992.

[8] M. Coltheart, "The persistences of vision," *Phil. Trans. Roy. Soc. London*, vol. B 290, pp. 57–69, 1980.

[9] S. Coren and J. S. Girgus, *Seeing is Deceiving: The Psychology of Visual Illusions*. Hillsdale N.J.: Lawrence Erlbaum, 1978.

[10] F. Crick, "The recent excitement about neural networks," *Nature*, vol. 337, pp. 129–132, 1989.

[11] M. J. B. Duff, "The limits of computing in arrays of processors," in *Pixels to Features*. J. C. Simon, Ed., Amsterdam: Elsevier Science, pp. 403–413, 1989.

[12] M.-T. Evangelia, "Neural aspects of vision and related technological advances," *Proc. IEEE*, vol. 76, no. 9, pp. 1130–1142, 1988.

[13] J. A. Feldman, "Connectionist models and parallelism in high level models," *Comput. Vision, Graphics, Image Process.*, vol. 31, pp. 178–200, 1985.

[14] M. A. Fischler and O. Firschein, *Intelligence: The Eye, The Brain and the Firschein Computer*. Reading, MA: Addison-Wesley, 1987.

[15] W. J. Freeman, "Why neural networks don't yet fly: Inquiry into neurodynamics of biological intelligence," *Proc. IEEE Conf. Neural Networks*, San Diego, CA, vol. 2, pp. 1–7, 1988.

[16] E. B. Goldstein, *Sensation and Perception*. Belmont CA: Wadsworth, 1989.

[17] R. L. Gregory, "Perceptions as hypotheses," *Phil. Trans. Roy. Soc. London.*, vol. B 290, pp. 181–197, 1980.

[18] J. Hochberg, "Machines should not see as people do, but must know how people see," *Comput. Vision, Graphics Image Process.*, vol. 37, pp. 221–237, 1987.

[19] D. Jameson and L. M. Hurvich, "From contrast to assimilation: In art and in the eye," in *Vision and Artifact*. M. Henle, Ed., New York: Springer, pp. 49–64, 1976.

[20] D. N. Lee, "The optic flow field: The foundation of vision," *Phil. Trans. Roy. Soc. London*, vol. B 290, pp. 169–179, 1980.

[21] D. Marr, "Visual information processing: The structure and creation of visual representations," *Phil. Trans. Roy. Soc. London*, vol. B 290, pp. 199–218, 1980.

[22] M.J. Morgan, "Analogue models of motion perception", *Phil. Trans. Roy. Soc. London,* vol. B 290, pp. 117–135, 1980.

[23] G. Nagy, "Neural networks—Then and now," *IEEE Trans. Neural Networks,* vol. 2, no. 2, pp. 316–318, 1991.

[24] T. Poggio, "Early vision. From computational structure to algorithms and parallel hardware," *Comput. Vision, Graphics, Image Process.,* vol. 31, pp. 139–155, 1985.

[25] C. A. Skarda and W. J. Freeman, "How brains make chaos in order to make sense of the world," *Behavioral Brain Sci.,* vol. 10, pp. 161–195, 1987.

[26] J. G. Taylor, "Can neural networks ever be made to think," *Neural Networks World,* vol. 1, pp. 4–12, 1991.

[27] L. Uhr, "Psychological motivation and underlying concepts," in *Structured Computer Vision.* S. Tanimoto and A. Klinger, Eds., New York: Academic Press, pp. 1–30, 1980.

[28] L. Uhr, "Highly parallel, hierarchical, recognition cone perceptual structures," in *Parallel Computer Vision.* L. Uhr, Ed., New York: Academic Press, pp. 249–292, 1987.

[29] H. Wechsler, *Computational Vision.* Boston: Academic Press, 1990.

Perspectives on Cognitive Neuroscience

Patricia S. Churchland and Terrence J. Sejnowski

How is it that we can perceive, learn and be aware of the world? The development of new techniques for studying large-scale brain activity, together with insights from computational modeling and a better understanding of cognitive processes, have opened the door for collaborative research that could lead to major advances in our understanding of ourselves.

NEUROSCIENCE AND COGNITIVE SCIENCE SHARE THE GOAL of trying to understand how the mind-brain works. In the past, discoveries at the neuronal level and explanations at the cognitive level were so distant that each often seemed of merely academic significance to the other. Symbol processing models based on the digital computer have been unpromising as a means to bridge the gap between neuroscience and cognitive science, because they did not relate to what was known about nervous systems at the level of signal processing. However, there is now a gathering conviction among scientists that the time is right for a fruitful convergence of research from hitherto isolated fields. The research strategy developing in cognitive neuroscience is neither exclusively from the top down, nor exclusively from the bottom up. Rather, it is a coevolutionary strategy, typified by interaction among research domains, where research at one level provides constraints, corrections, and inspiration for research at other levels (1).

Levels

There are in circulation at least three different notions of the term "levels," as it is used to describe scientific research, each notion carving the landscape in a different way—levels of analysis, levels of organization, and levels of processing.

Levels of analysis concern the conceptual division of a phenomenon in terms of different classes of questions that can be asked about it. A framework articulated by Marr and Poggio (2) drew upon the conception of levels in computer science and identified three levels: (i) the computational level of abstract problem analysis, decomposing the task into its main constituents (for example, determination of the three-dimensional structure of a moving object from successive views); (ii) the level of the algorithm, specifying a formal

P. S. Churchland is in the Department of Philosophy at the University of California at San Diego, La Jolla, CA 92093. T. J. Sejnowski is at The Salk Institute, La Jolla, CA 92093, and in the Department of Biology, University of California at San Diego, La Jolla, CA 92093.

procedure to perform the task by providing the correct output for a given input; and (iii) the level of physical implementation. Marr (3) maintained that computational problems of the highest level could be analyzed independently of understanding the algorithm that performs the computation. Similarly, he thought the algorithmic problem of the second level was solvable independently of understanding its physical implementation.

Some investigators have used the doctrine of independence to conclude that neuroscience is irrelevant to understanding cognition. However, the independence that Marr emphasized pertained only to the formal properties of algorithms, not to how they might be discovered (4). Computational theory tells us that algorithms can be run on different machines and in that sense, and that sense alone, the algorithm is independent of the implementation. The formal point is straightforward: since an algorithm is formal, no specific physical parameters (for example, vacuum tubes or Ca^{2+}) are part of the algorithm. That said, it is important to see that the purely formal point cannot speak to the issue of how best to discover the algorithm used by a given machine, nor how best to arrive at the neurobiologically adequate task analysis. Certainly it cannot tell us

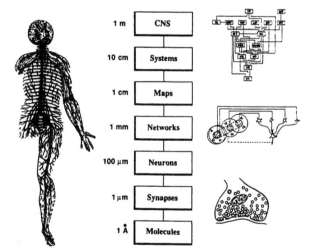

Fig. 1. Structural levels of organization in the nervous system. The spatial scale at which anatomical organizations can be identified varies over many orders of magnitude. (**Left**) Drawing by Vesalius (33) of the human brain, the spinal column, and the peripheral nerves. (**Right**) Schematic diagrams illustrate (top) a processing hierarchy of visual areas in monkey visual vortex (34); (center) a small network model for the synthesis of oriented receptive fields of simple cells in visual cortex (35); and (bottom) the structure of a chemical synapse (36). Relatively little is known about the properties at the network level in comparison with the detailed knowledge we have of synapses and the general organization of pathways in sensory and motor system.

Reprinted with permission from *Science*, P. S. Churchland and T. J. Sejnowski, ''Perspectives on Cognitive Neuroscience,'' vol. 242, pp. 741–745, Nov. 1988. © AAAS.

that the discovery of the algorithms relevant to cognitive functions will be independent of a detailed understanding of the nervous system. Moreover, different implementations display enormous differences in speed, size, efficiency, and elegance. The formal independence of algorithm from architecture is something we can exploit to build other machines once we know how the brain works, but it is not a guide to discovery when we do not yet know how the brain works. Knowledge of brain architecture also can be the essential basis and invaluable catalyst for devising likely and powerful algorithms—algorithms that might explain how in fact the brain does its job.

Levels of organization. How do the three levels of analysis map onto the nervous system? There is organized structure at different scales: molecules, synapses, neurons, networks, layers, maps, and systems (5) (Fig. 1). The range of structural organization implies, therefore, that there are many levels of implementation and that each has its companion task description. But if there are as many types of task description as there are levels of structural organization, this diversity will be reflected in a multiplicity of algorithms that characterize how the tasks are accomplished. This in turn means that the notion of *the* algorithmic level is as oversimplified as the notion of *the* implementation level. Structure at every scale in the nervous system—molecules, synapses, neurons, networks, layers, maps, and systems (Fig. 1)—is separable conceptually but not detachable physically. Psychological phenomena may be associated with a variety of levels. Some perceptual states such as the "raw" pain of a toothache might be a low-level effect, whereas attention may depend on a variety of mechanisms, some of which can be found at the level of local neural networks and others at the level of larger neural systems that reside in many different locations in the brain.

Levels of processing. This concept could be described as follows: The greater the distance from cells responding to sensory input, the higher the degree of information processing. Thus the level assigned is a function of synaptic distance from the periphery. On this measure, cells in the primary visual area of the neocortex that respond to oriented bars of light are at a higher level than cells in the lateral geniculate nucleus (LGN), which in turn are at a higher level than retinal ganglion cells.

Once the sensory information reaches the cerebral cortex it fans out through cortico-cortical projections into a multitude of parallel streams of processing. In the primate visual system 24 visual areas have been identified (6). Many (perhaps all) forward projections are accompanied by a back projection, and there are even massive feedback projections from primary visual cortex to the LGN. Given these reciprocal projections, it might seem that the processing levels do not really form a hierarchy, but there is a way to order the information flow by examining the layer of cortex into which fibers project. Forward projections generally terminate in the middle layers of cortex and feedback projections usually terminate in the upper and lower layers (7). However, we do not yet understand the function of these feedback pathways. If higher areas can affect the flow of information through lower areas, then the concept of sequential processing must be modified.

The hierarchical organization typical of earlier sensory areas is not adhered to everywhere. On the contrary, the anatomy of association areas and prefrontal cortex suggests a more "democratic" organization, and processing appears to take place in webs of strongly interacting networks (8). Decisions to act and the execution of plans and choices could be the outcome of a system with distributed control rather than a single control center. Coming to grips with systems having distributed control will require both new experimental techniques and new conceptual advances. Perhaps more appropriate metaphors for this type of processing will emerge from studying models of interacting networks of neurons.

Color Vision: A Case Study

As an illustration of fruitful interactions between psychology and physiology on a problem in perception, we have chosen several examples from color vision. Similar examples can also be found in the areas of learning and addiction (9) and sensory-motor integration (10, 11). Newton's ingenious prism experiment demonstrated that white light can be decomposed into a mixture of wavelengths and recombined to recover the white light. This physical description of color, however, did not satisfy artists, who were well aware that the perception of color involved complex spatial and temporal effects. As Goethe pointed out in *Zur Farbenlehre*, dark shadows often appear blue. The physical description of color and the psychological description of color perception are at two different levels: The link between them is at the heart of the problem of relating brain to cognition. Three examples will be given to illustrate how such links are being made in color vision.

The knowledge that mixtures of only three wavelengths of light are needed to match any color led Young to propose in 1802 (12) that there are only three types of photoreceptors. Quite a different theory of color vision was later proposed by Hering, who suggested that color perception was based on a system of color opponents, one for yellow versus blue, one for red versus green, and a separate system for black versus white (13). Convincing experiments and impressive arguments were marshaled by supporters of these two rival theories for nearly a century. The debate was finally settled by physiological studies proving that both theories were right—in different parts of the brain. In the retina three different types of color-sensitive photoreceptors were found, as predicted by Young, and the genes for the three cone photopigments have been sequenced (14). In the thalamus and visual cortex there are neurons that respond to Hering's color opponents (15). Evidently, even at this early stage of visual processing the complexity of the brain may lead to puzzles that can only be settled by knowing how the brain is constructed (16).

Recent progress in solving the problem of color constancy is a second example of converging physiological and psychological research. Red apples look red under a wide range of illumination even though the physical wavelengths impinging on the retina vary dramatically from daylight to interior lighting. Insights into color constancy have come from artists, who manipulate color contrasts in paintings, psychophysicists, who have quantified simultaneous contrast effects (17), and theorists, who have modeled them (18). Color constancy depends on being able to compute the intrinsic reflectance of a surface independently of the incident light. The reflectance of a patch of surface can be approximately computed by comparing the energy in wavelength bands coming from the patch of surface to the average energy in these bands from neighboring and distant regions of the visual field. The signature of a color-sensitive neuron that was performing this computation would be a long-range suppressive influence from regions of the visual field outside the conventional receptive field. Neurons with such color-selective surrounds have been reported in visual cortex area V4 (19); the first nonclassical

Fig. 2. Schematic diagram of anatomical connections and response selectivities of neurons in early visual areas of the macaque monkey. Visual information from the retina is split into two parallel streams at the level of the lateral geniculate nucleus (LGN), the parvocellular and magnocellular divisions. The parvocellular stream projects to two divisions of primary visual cortex (V1): the cytochrome oxidase–rich regions (Blob) and cytochrome oxidase–poor regions surrounding the blobs (Interblob). The magnocellular stream projects to layer 4B of V1. These three divisions of V1 project into

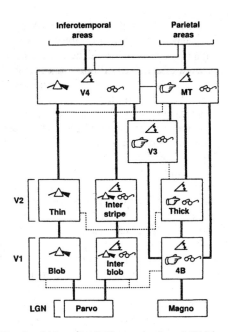

corresponding areas of V2: the "thin stripe," "interstripe," and "thick stripes" of cytochrome oxidase–rich and –poor regions in V2. These areas in turn project to visual areas V3, V4, and MT (middle temporal area, also called V5). Heavy lines indicate robust primary connections, and thin lines indicate weaker, more variable connections. Dotted lines indicate connections that require additional verification. Not all projections from these areas to other brain areas are represented. The neurons in each visual area respond preferentially to particular properties of visual stimuli as indicated by the icons: Prism, tuned or opponent wavelength selectivity; Angle, orientation selectivity; Spectacles, binocular disparity selectivity or strong binocular interactions; Pointing hand, direction of motion selectivity. [Reprinted with permission from (6)]

surrounds were found for motion-selective cells in area MT (20). If these neurons are necessary for color constancy then their loss should result in impairments of color vision. Bilateral lesions of certain extrastriate visual areas in man do produce achromatopsia—a total loss of color perception (21)—although this condition is usually found with other deficits and the damaged areas may not be homologous with area V4 in monkeys.

The third example of a link between brain and cognition comes from research on how form, motion, and color information are processed in the visual system. If different parts of the system are specialized for different tasks, for example, for motion or color, then there should be conditions under which these specializations are revealed. Suppose the "color system" is good at distinguishing colors, but not much else, and, in particular, is poor at determining shape, depth, and motion, whereas the "shape system" is not sensitive to color differences but to brightness differences. When boundaries are marked only by color differences—all differences in brightness are experimentally removed—shape detection should be impaired. Psychophysical research has shown that this is indeed the case. The perceived motion of equiluminant contours is degraded (22); form cues such as shape-from-shading are difficult to interpret (23), and perceived depth in random-dot stereograms collapses (24). Physiological and anatomical research has begun to uncover a possible explanation for these phenomena (25). The separate processing streams in cerebral cortex mentioned earlier carry visual information about different properties of objects (6, 26). In particular the predominant pathway for color information diverges from those carrying information on motion and depth (Fig. 2). The

separation is not perfect, however, but equiluminant stimuli provide physiologists with a visual "scalpel" for tracking down the correlates of perceptual coherence in different visual areas.

The lessons learned from color perception may have significance for studying other cognitive domains. So far as we know only a small fraction of the neurons in the visual system respond in a way that corresponds to our perceptual report of color. The locations in the brain where links between physiological states and perceptual states can be found vary from the retina to deep in the visual system for different aspects of color perception (27). New experimental techniques will be needed to study these links when the information is encoded in a large population of interacting neurons (10, 28).

Techniques and Research Strategies

Color vision is a problem that has been studied for hundreds of years; we know much less about the biological basis of other perceptual and cognitive states. Fortunately, new techniques, such as regional blood flow analysis with positron emission tomography (PET) and magnetic resonance imaging (MRI) are becoming available for noninvasively measuring brain activity in humans. With these techniques the large-scale pattern of what is happening where and when in the brain can be determined; later, as techniques with higher resolution are developed they can be focused on the relevant areas to ask how the processing is accomplished.

A useful way to get an overview of the assorted techniques is to graph them with respect to temporal and spatial resolution. This permits us to identify areas where there do not yet exist techniques to get access to levels of organization at those spatio-temporal resolutions and to compare their strengths and weaknesses (Fig. 3). For example, it is apparent that we lack detailed information about processing in neural networks within cortical layers and columns over a wide range of time scales, from milliseconds to hours. There is also a pressing need for experimental techniques designed to address the dendritic and synaptic level of investigation in cerebral cortex. Without these data it will not be possible to develop realistic models of information processing in cortical circuits.

Although we need experimental data concerning the properties of neurons and behavioral data about psychological capacities, we also need to find models that explain how patterns of activity in neurons represent surfaces, optical flow, and objects; how networks develop and learn, store, and retrieve information; and how networks accomplish sensorimotor and other types of integration. Ideally, modeling and experimental research will have a symbiotic relationship, such that each informs, corrects, and inspires the other.

Although many diverse kinds of things are presented as models for some part of the nervous system, it is useful to distinguish between realistic models, which are genuinely and strongly predictive of some aspect of nervous system dynamics or anatomy, and simplifying models, which though not so predictive, demonstrate that the nervous system could be governed by specific principles. Connectionist network models (29), which are simplifying models, are typically motivated by cognitive phenomena and are governed primarily by computational constraints, while honoring very general neurobiological constraints such as number of processing units and time required to perform a task. Accordingly, they are more properly considered demonstrations of what could be possible and sometimes what is not possible. Realistic models of actual neural networks, by contrast, are primarily motivated by biological constraints, such as the physiological and anatomical properties of specific cell types (30). Despite their different origins and sources of dominant constraints, simplifying models and realistic neural models are both based on the mathematics of nonlinear dynamical systems in high-dimensional spaces (31). The common conceptual and technical tools used in these models should provide links between two rich sources of experimental data, and consequently, connectionist and neural models have the potential to coevolve toward an integrated, coherent account of information processing in the mind-brain.

The ultimate goal of a unified account does not require that it be a single model that spans all the levels of organization. Instead the integration will probably consist of a chain of models linking adjacent levels. When one level is explained in terms of a lower level, this does not mean that the higher level theory is useless or that the high-level phenomena no longer exist. On the contrary, explanations will coexist at all levels, as they do in chemistry and physics, genetics, and embryology.

Conclusions

It would be convenient if we could understand the nature of cognition without understanding the nature of the brain itself. Unfortunately, it is difficult if not impossible to theorize effectively on these matters in the absence of neurobiological constraints. The primary reason is that computational space is consummately vast, and there are many conceivable solutions to the problem of how a cognitive operation could be accomplished. Neurobiological data provide essential constraints on computational theories, and they consequently provide an efficient means for narrowing the search space. Equally important, the data are also richly suggestive in hints concerning what might really be going on and what computational strategies evolution might have chanced upon. Moreover, it is by no means settled what exactly are the functional categories at the cognitive levels, and theories of lower level function may well be crucial to the discovery of the nature of higher level organization. Accordingly, despite the fact that the brain is experimentally demanding, basic neurobiology is indispensable in the task of discovering the theories that explain how we perform such activities as seeing, thinking, and being aware.

On the other hand, the possibility that cognition will be an open book once we understand the details of each and every neuron and its development, connectivity, and response properties is likewise misconceived. Even if we could simulate, synapse for synapse, our entire nervous system, that accomplishment, by itself, would not be the same as understanding how it works. The simulation might be just as much of a mystery as the function of the brain currently is, for it may reveal nothing about the network and systems properties that hold the key to cognitive effects. Even simulations of small network models have capabilities that are difficult to understand (32).

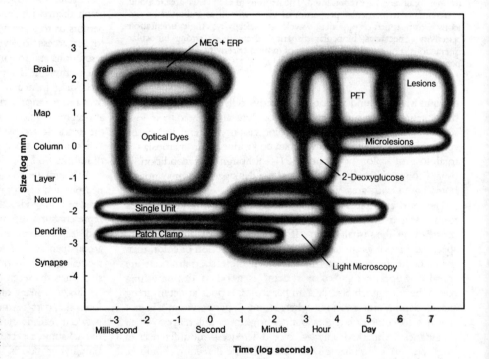

Fig. 3. Schematic illustration of the ranges of spatial and temporal resolution of various experimental techniques for studying the function of the brain. The vertical axis represents the spatial extent of the technique, with the boundaries indicating the largest and smallest sizes of the region from which the technique can provide useful information. Thus, single-unit recording can only provide information from a small region of space, typically 10 to 50 μm on a side. The horizontal axis represents the minimum and maximum time intervals over which information can be collected with the technique. Thus, action potentials from a single neuron can be recorded with millisecond accuracy over many hours. Patch-clamp recording allows the ionic currents through single ionic channels to be measured. Optical and fluorescent dyes that can reveal membrane potential, ionic concentrations, and intracellular structure have been used with high resolution in tissue culture, where it is possible to obtain a clear view of single cells (37, 38). However, recordings from the central nervous system are limited in resolution by the optical properties of nervous tissue and only about 0.1-mm resolution has been achieved (39). Confocal microscopy is a recent development in light microscopy that could be used for improving the resolution of the technique for three-dimensional specimens (40). ERP (evoked response potential) and MEG (magnetoencephalography) record the average electrical and magnetic activity over large brain regions and are limited to events that take place over about 1 s (41). The temporal resolution of PET (positron emission tomography) depends on the lifetime of the isotope being used, which ranges from minutes to an hour. It may be possible to achieve a temporal resolution of seconds with ^{15}O to study fast changes in blood flow by using temporal binning of the gamma ray events (equivalent to the poststimulus time histogram for action potentials) (42). The 2-deoxyglucose (2-DG) technique has a time resolution of about 45 min and a spatial resolution of 0.1 mm with large pieces of tissue and 1 μm with small pieces of tissue (43). The 2-DG technique can also be applied to humans with PET (44). Lesions allow the interruption of function to be studied immediately after ablation of the tissue and for a long period of time after the ablation (21, 45). Microlesion techniques make selective modifications with substances such as ibotenic acid, which destroys neurons but not fibers of passage, and 4-amino-phosphonobutyric acid, which selectively and reversibly blocks a class of glutamate receptors (46). Video-enhanced light microscopy has opened a window onto dynamical activity within neurons, such as the recent visualization of axonal transport of organelles on microtubules (37, 47). All of the boundaries drawn show rough regions of the spatio-temporal plane where these techniques have been used and are not meant to indicate fundamental limitations.

Genuine theorizing about the nature of neurocomputation is therefore essential.

Many major questions remain to be answered. Although some problems in vision, learning, attention, and sensorimotor control are yielding, this will be harder to achieve for more complex psychological phenomena such as reasoning and language. Nonetheless, once we understand some fundamental principles of brain function, we may see how to reformulate the outstanding problems and address them in ways that are impossible now to predict. Whatever the outcome, the results are likely to surprise us.

REFERENCES AND NOTES

1. P. S. Churchland, *Neurophilosophy: Toward a Unified Science of the Mind-Brain* (MIT Press, Cambridge, MA, 1986); J. LeDoux and W. Hirst, *Mind and Brain: Dialogues in Cognitive Neuroscience* (Cambridge Univ. Press, Cambridge, 1986); S. M. Kosslyn, *Science* 240, 1621 (1988).
2. The original conception of levels of analysis can be found in D. Marr and T. Poggio [*Neurosci. Res. Program Bull.* 15, 470 (1977)]. Although Marr (3) emphasized the importance of the computational level, the notion of a hierarchy of levels grew out of earlier work by W. Reichardt and T. Poggio [*Q. Rev. Biophys.* 9, 311 (1976)] on the visual control of orientation in the fly. In a sense, the current view on the interaction between levels is not so much a departure from the earlier views as a return to the practice that was previously established by Reichardt, Poggio, and even by Marr himself, who published a series of papers on neural network models of the cerebellar cortex and cerebral cortex. See, for example, D. Marr, *J. Physiol. (London)* 202, 437 (1969); *Proc. R. Soc. London B* 176, 161 (1970). The emphasis on the computational level has nonetheless had an important influence on the problems and issues that concern the current generation of neural and connectionist models [T. J. Sejnowski, C. Koch, P. S. Churchland, *Science* 241, 1299 (1988)].
3. D. Marr, *Vision* (Freeman, San Francisco, 1982).
4. P. M. Churchland, *Dialogue* 21, 223 (1982).
5. F. H. C. Crick, *Sci. Am.* 241, 219 (September 1979); P. S. Churchland and T. J. Sejnowski, in *Neural Connections and Mental Computation*, L. Nadel, Ed. (MIT Press, Cambridge, MA, 1988); G. M. Shepherd, *Yale J. Biol. Med.* 45, 584 (1972); P. Grobstein, *Brain Behav. Evol.* 31, 34 (1988).
6. E. A. DeYoe and D. C. Van Essen, *Trends Neurosci.* 11, 219 (1988).
7. J. H. R. Maunsell and D. C. Van Essen, *J. Neurosci.* 3, 2563 (1983).
8. P. S. Goldman-Rakic, *Annu. Rev. Neurosci.* 11, 137 (1988); V. B. Mountcastle, *Trends Neurosci.* 9, 505 (1986).
9. T. H. Brown, P. Chapman, E. W. Kairiss, C. L. Keenan, *Science* 242, 724 (1988); G. F. Koob and F. E. Bloom, *ibid.*, p. 715; L. R. Squire, *Memory and Brain* (Oxford Univ. Press, Oxford, 1987); E. R. Kandel *et al.*, in *Synaptic Function*, G. M. Edelman, W. E. Gall, W. M. Cowan, Eds. (Wiley, New York, 1987), pp. 471–518; M. Mishkin and T. Appenzeller, *Sci. Am.* 256, 80 (June 1987).
10. S. P. Wise and R. Desimone, *Science* 242, 736 (1988).
11. S. G. Lisberger, *ibid.*, p. 728.
12. T. Young, *Philos. Trans. R. Soc. London* 92, 12 (1802).
13. E. Hering, *Zur Lehre vom Lichtsinn* (Berlin, 1878).
14. J. Nathans, T. P. Piantanida, R. L. Eddy, T. B. Shows, D. S. Hogness, *Science* 232, 203 (1986).
15. The possibility of a two-stage analysis for color vision was suggested as early as 1881, but no progress was made until physiological techniques became available for testing the hypothesis. There are still some issues that have not yet been fully resolved by this theory.
16. H. B. Barlow, *Q. J. Exp. Psychol.* 37, 121 (1985).
17. D. Jameson and L. M. Hurvich, *J. Opt. Soc. Am.* 51, 46 (1961).
18. E. H. Land, *Proc. Natl. Acad. Sci. U.S.A.* 83, 3078 (1986); A. Hurlbert and T. Poggio, *Science* 239, 482 (1988).
19. S. Zeki, *Neuroscience* 9, 741 (1983); R. Desimone, S. J. Schein, L. G. Ungerleider, *Vision Res.* 25, 441 (1985).
20. J. Allman, F. Miezin, E. McGuiness, *Annu. Rev. Neurosci.* 8, 407 (1985).
21. A. R. Damasio, in *Principles of Behavioral Neurology*, M. M. Mesulam, Ed. (Davis, Philadelphia, 1985), pp. 259–288; O. Sacks, R. L. Wasserman, S. Zeki, R. M. Siegel, *Soc. Neurosci. Abstr.* 14, 1251 (1988).
22. V. S. Ramachandran and R. L. Gregory, *Nature* 275, 55 (1978).
23. P. Cavanagh and Y. Leclerc, *Invest. Ophthalmol. Suppl.* 26, 282 (1985).
24. C. Lu and D. H. Fender, *ibid.* 11, 482 (1972).
25. M. S. Livingstone and D. H. Hubel, *Science* 240, 740 (1988).
26. S. Zeki, *Nature* 335, 311 (1988).
27. D. Y. Teller and E. N. Pugh, Jr., in *Color Vision: Physiology and Psychophysics*, J. D. Mollon and L. T. Sharpe, Eds. (Academic Press, New York, 1983).
28. T. J. Sejnowski, *Nature* 332, 308 (1988).
29. T. Kohonen, *Self-Organization and Associative Memory* (Springer-Verlag, New York, 1984); J. J. Hopfield and D. W. Tank, *Science* 233, 625 (1986); S. Grossberg and M. Kuperstien, *Neural Dynamics of Adaptive Sensory-Motor Control* (North-Holland, Amsterdam, 1986); M. A. Arbib, *Brains, Machines and Mathematics* (McGraw-Hill, New York, ed. 2, 1987); D. E. Rumelhart and J. L. McClelland, *Parallel Distributed Processing: Explorations in the Microstructure of Cognition* (MIT Press, Cambridge, MA, 1986).
30. T. J. Sejnowski, C. Koch, P. S. Churchland, *Science* 241, 1299 (1988); C. Koch and I. Segev, *Methods in Neuronal Modeling: From Synapse to Networks* (MIT Press, Cambridge, MA, in press).
31. R. F. Abraham and C. D. Shaw, *Dynamics, the Geometry of Behavior* (Aerial Press, Santa Cruz, CA, 1982).
32. G. Edelman, *Neural Darwinism* (Basic Books, New York, 1987); R. A. Andersen and D. Zipser, *Can. J. Physiol. Pharmacol.* 66, 488 (1988); S. R. Lehky and T. J. Sejnowski, *Nature* 333, 452 (1988).
33. A. Vesalius, *De Humani Corporis* (Brussels, 1543).
34. J. H. R. Maunsell and W. T. Newsome, *Annu. Rev. Neurosci.* 10, 363 (1987).
35. D. H. Hubel and T. N. Wiesel, *J. Physiol. (London)* 160, 106 (1962).
36. E. Kandel and J. Schwartz, *Principles of Neural Science* (Elsevier, New York, ed 2, 1984).
37. S. J Smith, *Science* 242, 708 (1988).
38. J. Dodd and T. M. Jessell, *ibid.* 242, 692 (1988); A. L. Harrelson and C. S. Goodman, *ibid.*, p. 692.
39. G. G. Blasdel and G. Salama, *Nature* 321, 579 (1986); A. Grinvald, E. Lieke, R. D. Frostig, C. D. Gilbert, T. N. Wiesel, *ibid.* 324, 361 (1986).
40. A. Fine, W. B. Amos, R. M. Durbin, P. A. McNaughton, *Trends Neurosci.* 11, 346 (1988).
41. S. J. Williamson, G. L. Romani, L. Kaufman, I. Modena, *Biomagnetism: An Interdisciplinary Approach* (Plenum, New York, 1983); 2-DG: S. A. Hillyard and T. W. Picton, in *Handbook of Physiology*, section 1, *Neurophysiology*, F. Plum, Ed. (American Physiological Society, New York, 1987), pp. 519–584.
42. M. E. Raichle, *Trends Neurosci.* 9, 525 (1986); M. I. Posner, S. E. Petersen, P. T. Fox, M. E. Raichle, *Science* 240, 1627 (1988).
43. L. Sokoloff, *Metabolic Probes of Central Nervous System Activity in Experimental Animals and Man* (Sinauer, Sunderland, MA, 1984).
44. M. E. Phelps and J. C. Mazziotta, *Science* 228, 799 (1985).
45. M. M. Mesulam, in *Principles of Behavioral Neurology*, M. M. Mesulam, Ed. (Davis, Philadelphia, 1985), pp. 125–168; B. Milner, in *Amnesia*, C. W. M. Whitty and O. Zangwill, Eds. (Butterworth, London, 1966), pp. 109–133; R. W. Sperry and M. Gazzaniga; in *Brain Mechanisms Underlying Speech and Language*, C. Millikan and F. Darley, Eds. (Grune and Stratton, New York, 1967), pp. 108–115; E. H. Land, D. H. Hubel, M. S. Livingstone, S. H. Perry, M. M. Burns, *Nature* 303, 616 (1983); S. M. Kosslyn, J. D. Holtzman, M. S. Gazzaniga, M. J. Farrah, *J. Exp. Psychol. General* 114, 311 (1985).
46. P. Schiller, *Nature* 297, 580 (1982); J. C. Horton and H. Sherk, *J. Neurosci.* 4, 374 (1984).
47. B. J. Schnapp and T. S. Reese, *Trends Neurosci.* 9, 155 (1986).
48. We thank F. Crick whose insights as well as critical judgments were a major resource in writing this article. We also thank P. Churchland, R. Cone, C. Koch, and D. MacLeod for helpful suggestions. T.J.S. is supported by a grants from the National Science Foundation, the Seaver Institute, the Air Force Office of Scientific Research, the Office of Naval Research, and the General Electric Corporation; P.S.C. is supported by grants from the National Science Foundation and the James S. McDonnell Foundation. Portions of this article are based on our chapter in *Foundations of Cognitive Science* [P. S. Churchland and T. J. Sejnowski, in *Foundations of Cognitive Science*, M. Posner, Ed. (MIT Press, Cambridge, in press)].

Computational Neuroscience

TERRENCE J. SEJNOWSKI, CHRISTOF KOCH, PATRICIA S. CHURCHLAND

The ultimate aim of computational neuroscience is to explain how electrical and chemical signals are used in the brain to represent and process information. This goal is not new, but much has changed in the last decade. More is known now about the brain because of advances in neuroscience, more computing power is available for performing realistic simulations of neural systems, and new insights are available from the study of simplifying models of large networks of neurons. Brain models are being used to connect the microscopic level accessible by molecular and cellular techniques with the systems level accessible by the study of behavior.

UNDERSTANDING THE BRAIN IS A CHALLENGE THAT IS attracting a growing number of scientists from many disciplines. Although there has been an explosion of discoveries over the last several decades concerning the structure of the brain at the cellular and molecular levels, we do not yet understand how the nervous system enables us to see and hear, to learn skills and remember events, to plan actions and make choices. Simple reflex systems have served as useful preparations for studying the generation and modification of behavior at the cellular level (1). In mammals, however, the relation between perception and the activity of single neurons is more difficult to study because the sensory capacities assessed with psychophysical techniques are the result of activity in many neurons from many parts of the brain. In humans, the higher brain functions such as reasoning and language are even further removed from the properties of single neurons. Moreover, even relatively simple behaviors, such as stereotyped eye movements, involve complex interactions among large numbers of neurons distributed in many different brain areas (2–4).

Explaining higher functions is difficult, in part, because nervous systems have many levels of organization between the molecular and systems levels, each with its own important functions. Neurons are organized in local circuits, columns, laminae, and topographic maps for purposes that we are just beginning to understand (5–8). Properties not found in components of a lower level can emerge from the organization and interaction of these components at a higher level. For example, rhythmic pattern generation in some neural circuits is a property of the circuit, not of isolated pacemaker neurons (9, 10). Higher brain functions such as perception and attention may depend on temporally coherent functional units distributed through several different maps and nuclei (4, 8). The sources of such network properties are not accessible by the use of methods suited to investigating single neurons.

Assuming that there are emergent properties of networks, it is difficult to imagine a major advance in our understanding of brain function without a concomitant development in direct, efficient techniques for probing the mechanisms of distributed processing. New experimental techniques currently being developed include methods for simultaneously recording from multiple single units, optical recording of columnar organization in cortex with voltage- and ion-sensitive dyes, and large-scale measurements of brain structure and activity with positron emission tomography (PET), magnetoencephalogram (MEG), 2-deoxyglucose (2-DG), and magnetic resonance imaging (MRI) (11). Statistical methods are also being developed for analyzing and interpreting the information that will be collected (12, 13). Though valuable, each of these new techniques has severe limitations on its spatial or temporal resolution, and new approaches to understanding distributed processing are needed (14).

Modeling promises to be an important adjunct to these experimental techniques and is essential in addressing the conceptual issues that arise when one studies information-processing in the brain (15–17). The advantages of brain models are varied. (i) A model can make the consequences of a complex, nonlinear brain system with many interacting components more accessible. (ii) New phenomena may be discovered by comparing the predictions of simulation to experimental results and new experiments can be designed based on these predictions. (iii) Experiments that are difficult or even impossible to perform in living tissue, such as the selective lesion of particular channels, synapses, neurons, or pathways, can be simulated by the use of a model.

What kind of a computer is the brain? Mechanical and causal explanations of chemical and electrical signals in the brain are different from computational explanations (18). The chief difference is that a computational explanation refers to the information content of the physical signals and how they are used to accomplish a task. This difference is easiest to see in simpler physical systems that compute. For example, a mechanical explanation for the operation of a slide rule includes the observations that certain marks are lined up, the slider is moved, and a result is read. A computational explanation states that a slide rule computes products because the marks on the sliding wood rules correspond to logarithms, and adding two logarithms is equivalent to multiplying the corresponding pair of numbers. Thus, the physical system carries out a computation by virtue of its relation to a more abstract algorithm (19). One of the major research objectives of computational neuroscience is to discover the algorithms used in the brain.

T. Sejnowski is in the Department of Biophysics at the Johns Hopkins University, Baltimore, MD 21218. C. Koch is with the Computation and Neural Systems Program at the California Institute of Technology, Pasadena, CA 91125. P. S. Churchland is in the Department of Philosophy at the University of California at San Diego, La Jolla, CA 92093.

Reprinted with permission from *Science*, T. J. Sejnowski, C. Koch, and P. S. Churchland, ''Computational Neuroscience,'' vol. 241, pp. 1299–1306, Sept. 1988. © AAAS.

Unlike a digital computer, which is general purpose and can be programmed to run any algorithm, the brain appears to be a collection of special purpose systems that are very efficient at performing their tasks, but are limited in their flexibility. The architecture of an efficient, dedicated system like a slide rule, or a brain system, constrains the algorithm it implements in a fashion that does not occur in digital computer (20). The clues from structure are particularly valuable because the nervous system is a product of evolution, not engineering design. The computational solutions evolved by nature may be unlike those that humans would invent, if only because evolutionary changes are always made within the context of a design and architecture that already is in place (21).

Classes of Brain Models

Realistic brain models. One modeling strategy consists of a very large scale simulation that tries to incorporate as much of the cellular detail as is available. We call these realistic brain models. While this approach to simulation can be very useful, the realism of the model is both a weakness and a strength. As the model is made increasingly realistic by adding more variables and more parameters, the danger is that the simulation ends up as poorly understood as the nervous system itself. Equally worrisome, since we do not yet know all the cellular details, is that there may be important features that are being inadvertently left out, thus invalidating the results. Finally, realistic simulations are highly computation-intensive. Present constraints limit simulations to tiny nervous systems or small components of more complex systems. Only recently has sufficient computer power been available to go beyond the simplest models.

An example of a realistic model at the level of a single neuron is the Hodgkin-Huxley model (22) of the action potential in the squid giant axon. The action potential is a stereotyped, transient, electrical event that propagates along an axon and is used for communicating information over long distances. The action potential is a result of the voltage- and time-dependent properties of several types of membrane channels. The dynamics of the membrane channels were modeled by a set of coupled, nonlinear differential equations that were solved numerically. The velocity of the action potential predicted by Hodgkin and Huxley agreed to within 10 percent of the measured value. Two important lessons can be learned from this example. First, the model was the culmination of a large number of experiments. In general, realistic models with a large number of parameters require a correspondingly large number of measurements to fit the parameters. Second, the voltage-dependent membrane channels postulated to account for the data were verified only much later with the introduction of single-channel recording techniques (23). In general, we should expect to make hypotheses that go beyond the immediate data.

An example of a realistic model at the network level is the Hartline-Ratliff model of the *Limulus* lateral eye (24). The photoreceptors in the retina have lateral inhibitory synaptic interactions with neighboring photoreceptors, and as a consequence the contrast in the firing rates at light intensity borders is enhanced. Because the interactions are approximately linear, a model of the network can be mathematically analyzed in great detail. Once all of the parameters are determined from experimental measurements, the model can accurately predict the firing rates of all the fibers in the optic nerve stimulated by an arbitrary spatiotemporal pattern of light falling on the retina. Models of networks that are nonlinear and have feedback connections are much more difficult to analyze, so that only a

qualitative mathematical analysis is possible and simulations of their behavior are essential. It is worth emphasizing again the necessity of collecting a nearly complete set of experimental measurements before a realistic model can be attempted.

Simplifying brain models. Because even the most successful realistic brain models may fail to reveal the function of the tissue, computational neuroscience needs to develop simplifying models that capture important principles. Textbook examples in physics that admit exact solutions are typically unrealistic, but they are valuable because they illustrate physical principles. Minimal models that reproduce the essential properties of physical systems, such as phase transitions, are even more valuable. The study of simplifying models of the brain can provide a conceptual framework for isolating the basic computational problems and understanding the computational constraints that govern the design of the nervous system.

The class of models that is currently being investigated under the general headings of connectionist models, parallel distributed processing models, and "neural networks" is of this second type, which we shall hereafter refer to as simplifying brain models. These models abstract from the complexity of individual neurons and the patterns of connectivity in exchange for analytical tractability (25). Independent of their use as brain models, they are being investigated as prototypes of new computer architectures (26, 27) and as models for psychological phenomena (28–30). Some of the lessons learned from these models can be applied to the brain.

One of the best studied models is the class of layered feed-forward networks. In this architecture, information is coded as a pattern of activity in an input layer of model neurons and is transformed by successive layers receiving converging synaptic inputs from preceding layers. The following three findings are of significance for the brain. (i) Even systems with only a few intermediate layers have enormous power in representing complex nonlinear functions (31, 32). (ii) The performance of a network in specific problem domains (such as visual and speech processing) depends critically on how the incoming information is represented by the neurons (such as the type of preprocessing) and the symmetries in the pattern of connections. (iii) For difficult problems, the processing units in the middle or "hidden" layers generally encode many different combinations of input variables by the use of a semidistributed type of representation (33). By combining the power of these models with further constraints from neurophysiology and neuroanatomy it may be possible to interpret some of the properties that have been observed from single-unit recordings, as we illustrate in the next section (34–36).

These simplifying brain models also make an important bridge to computer science and other disciplines that study information processing. Issues such as convergence of the network to a stable solution, the amount of time needed for the network to achieve a solution, and the capacity of networks to store information are being investigated in simplifying models in ways that are not at present feasible with realistic models (37). The scaling of these properties with the size of the network is crucially important for practical applications and for the plausibility of the model as a brain model (38–39). Many of the current models do not scale well without additional constraints on the architecture, such as restricting the connectivity to local neighborhoods.

Technology for brain modeling. Computational brain models are almost always simulated on digital computers. Computers are getting faster, but they must perform the many parallel operations of the brain one at a time and are many orders of magnitude too slow. Parallel computers with thousands of processors are being developed, but are still inadequate (40). A new approach toward simulating biological circuitry is being pioneered by Mead (20), who is constructing hardware devices that have components that directly mimic the circuits in the brain. Fast hardware can deliver the computing power necessary to evaluate the performance of a model in real time. Furthermore, the physical restrictions on the density of wires and the cost of communications imposed by the spatial layout of the electronic circuits are similar to the constraints imposed on biological circuits. This approach may lead to a "synthetic neurobiology" (20).

Mead uses analog subthreshold complementary metal oxide semiconductor VLSI (very large scale integrated) circuit technology. Several chips that implement simplifying models of visual information processing have already been produced that are highly efficient. A "retina" chip computes the spatial and temporal derivative of arbitrary images projected onto an hexagonal array of 48 by 48 phototransistors, which are approximately logarithmic over five orders of magnitude of light amplitude, coupled by means of a horizontal resistive grid and injecting current into model "amacrine" cells that compute a temporal derivative (41). Similar circuits can be designed for computing optical flow in real time (42–43).

These VLSI chips and new techniques in optical information processing may lead to a new computing technology, sometimes called artificial neural systems, or neurocomputing (44, 45). This technology for performing massively parallel computations could have a major influence on the next generation of research in computational neuroscience. For example, an analog VLSI model of a neuron that included conductance mechanisms, synaptic apparatus, and dendritic geometry could be produced in great quantities. These chips could be used as coprocessors in a conventional digital computer to greatly increase the speed of realistic simulations. If this technology is developed now, it should be possible to simulate our visual system in real time by the 21st century (40).

Specific Examples of Brain Models

We will discuss several different models that show the great variety of different levels of structure, analysis, and measurement existing in contemporary computational neuroscience. It is impossible to discuss in this article even a small fraction of the models in the literature that address a particular problem in neurobiology, so we will limit ourselves to a few examples from the invertebrate and vertebrate vision literature. This choice reflects the idiosyncrasies and research interests of the authors and in no way implies that other areas within neurobiology have not developed equally relevant models (46).

The modeling of learning and memory is an important area not covered here. Evidence for neural plasticity is accumulating at the cellular and molecular levels in a variety of systems (47–51). The conditions for plasticity can be incorporated onto large-scale network models that have properties that can be explored in simulations of realistic models (46, 52, 53) and analytically for simplifying models (54, 57). A separate review would be required to summarize all the interesting models of learning and memory in brain circuits that are now being explored (58–60).

Detecting and computing motion. Visual motion is a fundamental source of information about the world (61, 62), and motion detection is the first stage of motion processing. Reichardt's motion detection scheme was first proposed 30 years ago. Behavioral data, gained on the basis of open- and closed-loop experiments performed on beetles and flies (63, 64), indicated that a sequence of two light

stimuli impinging on adjacent photoreceptors is the elementary event evoking an optomotor response. The relation between stimulus input to these two photoreceptors and the strength of the optomotor output follows the rule of algebraic sign multiplication (65, 66).

The correlation model of motion detection follows from these observations (63). The output of one photoreceptor is multiplied by a low-pass filtered signal from a neighboring receptor (Fig. 1A). The product is then integrated in time, which is equivalent to the autocorrelation of the visual input (67). Since the low-pass filter can be thought of as a delay, this direction-selective subunit (Fig. 1A) will respond with a positive signal in one direction and with a negative response in the opposite direction. This theoretical model has a number of nontrivial properties, such as phase invariance and dependence on contrast frequency (67), that have been confirmed experimentally. In humans, the psychophysical evidence favors a slight modification of the original correlation model (68, 69). Thus, the correlation model for motion detection is consistent with psychophysics in several different species. It is a realistic model at the systems level.

Motion detection has also been explored at the cellular level. Barlow and Levick (70) systematically studied the rabbit retina by recording extracellularly from the output cells of the retina. About 20 percent of all ganglion cells responded vigorously to the motion of both black and white spots in one direction but were silent when the spots moved in the opposite direction. Barlow and Levick's two principal conclusions were that inhibition is crucial for direction discrimination and that this discrimination must occur at many different sites within the receptive field. They proposed that direction selectivity is based on a scheme whereby the response in the null direction is vetoed or inhibited by appropriate neighboring inputs (Fig. 1B); directionality is achieved by a delay between the excitatory and inhibitory channels (extending from photoreceptors to ganglion cells). This proposal is a cellular level version of Reichardt's correlation detector.

Techniques are being developed to study motion detection at the biophysical level. The key experimental finding is that lateral inhibition is induced in ganglion cells for all directions of movement except for the preferred direction (71). This inhibition could be generated by mechanisms presynaptic to the ganglion cell (72). Werblin et al. (73) have found evidence in the retina of the tiger salamander for movement-gated lateral inhibition generated by interactions among amacrine and bipolar cells. This mechanism for motion detection has not yet been integrated into a model of directional selectivity. Another possible mechanism for motion detection is through postsynaptic interaction in the ganglion cell dendrite between an excitatory synapse and a delayed inhibitory synapse with a reversal potential close to the resting potential of the cell (shunting or silent inhibition), as shown in Fig. 1C (74, 76). The latter mechanism has been proven feasible with modeling studies, though a direct experimental test has not yet been performed in the retina.

Visual motion detection has many different uses. Reichardt and his group (77, 80) have studied the use of motion information for pattern discrimination in the house fly, *Musca domestica*. Pattern discrimination here is a special case of the more general problem of figure-ground segregation, where the figure is one pattern and the ground is the other. The fly can distinguish relative motion between two moving objects, even if both objects have a similar texture, such as random dot patterns. The cellular basis of this behavior was explored by use of a combination of exacting behavioral studies,

46

electrophysiology, and systems analysis. The model circuitry (Fig. 1D) gives a satisfactory account of how the fly behaves under different conditions of relative motion (for example, a small figure oscillating on a background) and also explains the observed inde-

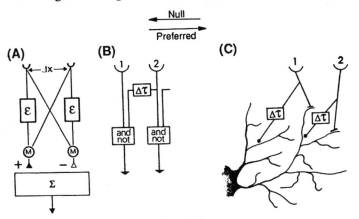

Fig. 1. Movement detection and figure-ground segregation. (**A**) The correlation model (63, 64). In its essential form, the two outputs from two neighboring photoreceptors are multiplied after one signal is delayed with respect to the second. If the product is averaged in time and subtracted from the time-averaged product from the other branch, the overall operation is equivalent to cross correlating the intensity on the retina. The model is symmetrical from an anatomical point of view, but is functionally antisymmetrical. The correlation model was proposed on the basis of behavioral experiments carried out in insects (65). (**B**) The scheme proposed by Barlow and Levick (70) to account for direction-selective ganglion cells in the rabbit retina. The output of one channel is gated in the null direction by a signal from a neighboring channel. In the preferred direction, the delayed signal from the neighboring receptor arrives too late to veto the excitatory signal. (**C**) A detailed cellular implementation of Barlow and Levick's scheme of direction selectivity (76), based on the proposal (75) that the nonlinear interaction between excitatory and inhibitory synaptic induced conductance changes of the silent or shunting type can approximate a multiplication. Detailed computer simulations of the cable properties of dendrites show that shunting inhibition (solid circles) can effectively veto excitation (bars) as long as the inhibitory synapses are close to the excitatory synapses or between excitation and the cell body (76). (**D**) The neural circuitry underlying pattern discrimination in the visual system of the house fly *Musca domestica*, as proposed by Reichardt and his group (77, 80). In each eye, two overlapping sets of retinotopic arrays of elementary movement detectors of the correlation type (63) respond selectively to either front-to-back (+) or back-to-front (−) motion. All movement detectors feed into two pool neurons (S_R and S_L). One of these cells (pr) is excited by motion in the front-to-back direction, while the second is excited by the opposite motion (▶— indicates excitatory synapses and ▷— indicates hyperpolarizing inhibitory synapses). The pool cells are also coupled with their homologues in the contralateral hemisphere. The output of both pool neurons shunts (▷—) the output of the movement detectors (the inhibitory synaptic reversal potential is close to the resting potential of the cell) before they either excite (▶●—) or inhibit (▷○—) the two output cells (X_R and X_L). The final motor output is controlled by the X cells. The key elements of this model (X and S cells) have been identified with neurons in the third optic ganglion of the fly (79, 80). Abbreviations: L, left; R, right; T, a channel that computes the running average of the output from the X cells. [Courtesy of W. Reichardt]

pendence of the behavioral optomotor response from the spatial extent of motion—that is, the size of the moving object. Although the key neurons in the model (Fig. 1D) have been identified in the third optic ganglion of the fly (79) (Fig. 2), the proposed synaptic interactions are still under investigation.

What has been learned about visual processing from the fly? An engineer might have designed a motion system that first extracted pure velocity information. However, in the fly visual system, motion detection is accomplished by use of the same neurons that process local pattern information. The models of motion detection and motion processing have shown how populations of neurons with mixed pattern and motion signals can accomplish figure-ground segregation. We can begin to see how the fly uses time-varying visual information to control its behavior in ways that were not intuitively obvious. Models were used at the systems, network, cellular, and biophysical levels to generate hypotheses and help guide experimental work.

Orientation selectivity in visual cortex. Our second example is taken from the mammalian visual system. In an influential study, Hubel and Wiesel (81) showed that most cells in the cat striate cortex optimally respond to elongated bar stimuli, oriented in a specified

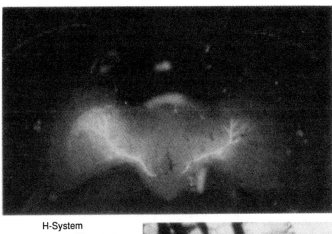

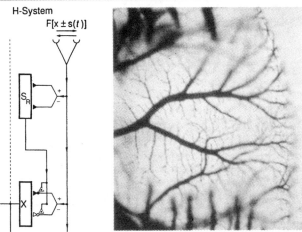

Fig. 2. Visual motion detecting system in the house fly. Two Lucifer yellow–filled horizontal cells are shown in the third optic ganglia (top) and a horizontal cell is shown at higher magnification with cobalt fill (right bottom). This cell is a possible correlate of the output x cell in the model (bottom left) that is involved in the generation of yaw torque. Additional cells controlling, for example, pitch, roll, lift, and thrust are likely to exist as well. The components of the network model are described in Fig. 1D. [Courtesy of K. Hausen and W. Reichardt].

direction. The receptive field of a simple cell is divided into several elongated subregions (Fig. 3A). Illumination of part or all of an excitatory region increased the cellular response, whereas such stimuli suppressed the response if projected onto inhibitory regions. The input to striate cortex from cells in the lateral geniculate nucleus also possesses such excitatory and inhibitory subdivisions but is organized in a concentric fashion (Fig. 3A). Hubel and Wiesel postulated that the orientation selectivity of simple cells was generated by a row of appropriately aligned excitatory geniculate cells converging on their cortical target neuron (Fig. 3B). The firing threshold of this cortical cell at its cell body is such that only simultaneous input from a large number of geniculate cells triggers a burst of action potentials. According to this hypothesis, the arrangement of the receptive fields of presynaptic inputs is sufficient to produce orientation selectivity (81).

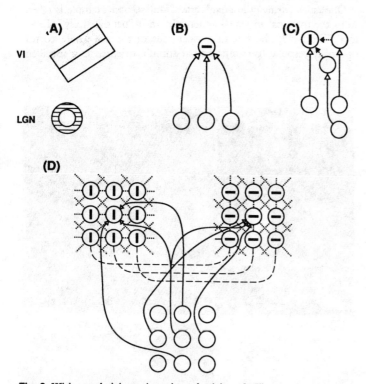

Fig. 3. Wiring underlying orientation selectivity. (**A**) The concentric center-surround receptive field of geniculate cells contrasts with the elongated receptive fields of their cortical target cells. (**B**) The excitatory-only model put forth by Hubel and Wiesel (81). A row of appropriately located geniculate cells excites the oriented cortical cell. A number of geniculate cells whose receptive fields are located along a given axis monosynaptically excite the cortical cell (open arrows). The firing threshold of the simple cell determines the degree of orientation tuning. Here and in the following, only the excitatory centers of the geniculate cells is drawn. (**C**) One instance of an inhibitory-only model (82, 84–86, 100). Nonoriented cortical inhibitory (filled arrows) interneurons sculpture the orientation tuning of their target cell by suppressing its response at nonoptimal orientations. For example, a horizontal bar will lead to activation of the interneuron, which will inhibit the vertically oriented cortical cell. (**D**) "Eclectic" model combining features of all models (88, 89). An excitatory Hubel-and-Wiesel–type of presynaptic arrangement is superimposed on two inhibitory ones: reciprocal inhibition among similarly oriented cortical cells with spatially nonoverlapping receptive fields (dotted lines) and cross-orientation inhibition among orthogonal oriented cells (dashed lines). Because of the massive feedback among the participating cortical neurons [the model can be formulated as an associative network (101)], each neuron acquires orientation selection by means of a collective computation. Abbreviations: LGN, lateral geniculate nucleus; VI, visual cortex area VI.

Blockage of cortical inhibition by pharmacological agents leads to a partial loss of orientation selectivity in some neurons (82, 83). This observation leads to a different set of models for orientation selectivity that use intracortical inhibition (82, 84–86). In the version shown in Fig. 3C, nonoriented cortical interneurons suppress the response of the oriented simple cell to nonoptimal oriented stimuli by synaptically mediated inhibition. However, the nonoriented inhibitory interneurons postulated by this model have not been found in the cat striate cortex. Alternatively, intracortical inhibition from oriented cells could suppress firing of cells to stimuli with orthogonal orientations [cross-orientation inhibition (87)].

More recently, an "eclectic" model has been proposed that accounts for most of the experimental data by conferring orientation selectivity on all cells through massive feedback connections among cortical neurons (86, 88, 89). It assumes a Hubel-and-Wiesel–type of excitatory presynaptic arrangement superimposed on two inhibitory systems: (i) inhibition among similarly oriented cells but with spatially nonoverlapping receptive fields and (ii) cross-orientation inhibition among cells with spatially overlapping receptive fields but differing orientation. Intracellular recordings of simple cells support the existence of at least the first two systems (90).

It is a sign of the complexity of the brain that such a seemingly simple question—what is the circuitry underlying orientation selectivity—has not been satisfactorily answered 25 years after it was first posed. Realistic models of cortical processing could be used to test the strengths and weakness of the various proposals (91). A simulation of a realistic model that includes massive inhibitory cortical interactions is presented in Fig. 4. In addition to verifying the consistency of the model with experimental measurements, the simulation also makes interesting predictions for the gain control of responses to visual stimuli of varying contrasts (91).

These models of orientation tuning for simple cells in the visual cortex provide explanations for how the response properties of neurons are generated. The question remains as to what these properties contribute to visual processing. It is believed that because simple cells respond best to bars of light, they are used to detect the presence of an edge or line at a particular orientation and position in the visual field. However, the same neurons also respond to spatial frequency gratings and textured patterns, so it is not clear how to infer their actual function. The problem of inferring function from response properties applies to neurons throughout the nervous system. One way to test a functional hypothesis is to construct a network model with processing units having the same response properties as those found in the nervous system and to show that the network does perform the desired computation (92). Although a working model can help generate hypotheses, and rule some out, it cannot prove that the brain necessarily solves the problem in the same way.

Using this approach, Lehky and Sejnowski (36) have constructed a small layered feed-forward network that takes as input a small patch of shaded image, as transformed by the retina and lateral geniculate nucleus, and computes the principal curvatures and orientation of the surface from which the image was derived. The resulting network can compute surface curvatures regardless of the direction of illumination, a computational problem in which the shape of a surface is recovered from the shading in the image (93, 94). The construction of the network model was made possible by recent advances in network learning algorithms that allow complex networks with many thousands of connections to be synthesized from an input-output level description of the problem (95, 96). The network is trained by presenting images to the input layer and comparing the firing rates of the units on the output layer with the desired values. The error signals are used to correct the synaptic weights between the processing units. The learning algorithm was used solely as a technique to create the network and not as a model for learning in the brain, nor as a model for how orientation tuning actually develops. Models of development have been proposed that use unsupervised learning algorithms (53, 97).

The surprising finding was that most of the cells on the hidden layer, which received the geniculate input directly, had responses when probed with simulated spots or bars of light that were similar to those of the simple cells in the visual cortex (Fig. 5B; see also Fig. 3A). These properties emerged through the learning procedure as the appropriate ones for extracting information about the principal curvatures, and were not put into the network directly. Curvatures were represented on the output layer by units having tuning curves for curvature magnitudes and orientations (Fig. 5A). When probed with bars of light, the output units have receptive field properties similar to complex cells in the visual cortex that are end-stopped. [The response was reduced when the end of a bar of light was extended into an inhibitory region (98).]

A finding of general significance was that the function of the model neurons in the network could not be understood solely by examination of their receptive field properties. For example, some cells with simple receptive fields were responsible not for signaling orientation to the output layer, but rather were providing information about the convexity or concavity of the surface. Examining the outputs of a simple cell, called its "projective" field by analogy with the input receptive field, was critical in uncovering its function in the network. Thus, the very same simple cells can be engaged in several functions—on one hand detecting edges, on the other hand participating in the computation of curvature from

shading information—depending on the circuits to which the cell projects (36). Determining what was required for understanding the function of cells in this network model has consequences for the more difficult task of determining the function of real neurons.

This simplifying network model of shape-from-shading has generated several hypotheses about cortical processing without directly simulating the detailed connectivity of the cortex, which is not yet known. The prediction that end-stopped cells should be selectively tuned for the surface curvature can be tested by use of shaded images as stimuli along with bars of light. The model can also evolve toward a realistic model that incorporates lateral interactions between circuits at neighboring patches of the visual field and interactions with circuits that use other cues for computing shape.

Conclusions

A scientific field is defined primarily by its problem space and its successful large-scale theories. Until there are such theories in computational neuroscience, the field is defined most by the problems it seeks to solve, and the general methodology and specific techniques it hopes will yield successful theories. Models of brain function driven primarily by functional considerations can provide only the most general guidance about what might be happening in the brain; conversely, models driven primarily by signal measurements and anatomy can easily miss those aspects of the signals that are relevant for information-processing. In this review we have presented several examples of models that attempt to combine insights from the functional and the implementational levels of analysis. More examples can be found in other areas of neurobiology where models are being used to explore information-processing by

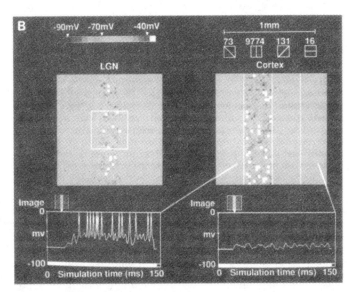

Fig. 4. Results from a realistic simulation of a 2° × 2° patch of the early visual pathway of the adult cat. (**A**) Diagram of the divergence and convergence between the lateral geniculate nucleus (LGN) and striate cortex (cortex). A hexagonal grid of retinal X–type ganglion cells with on-center, off-surround receptive fields, modeled by differences of two Gaussian curves, project in the ratio of 1:4 to the LGN cells. A single LGN cell (small yellow square in the left central rectangle) projects to 220 cells in layer IVc of striate cortex (small yellow squares in cortex) within a disk having an area of 0.72 mm², in agreement with anatomical data. A typical cortical neuron (small red square indicated by white arrow in cortex) is innervated by 40 cells in the LGN (small orange cells surrounded by circular receptive fields in blue) and has a "simple-cell"–like receptive field. The cells in cortex are arranged according to their orientation preference into vertical strips, as indicated in

the box beneath each "column". Inhibition between neighboring cortical cells in Fig. 3D is not shown. (**B**) Response of cells in the LGN and cortex to a presentation of vertical light bars to the retina, starting at 20 ms. The small squares representing neurons in the LGN and cortex are color coded by their membrane potentials at 140 ms (see calibration bar for color scheme). Simulated intracellular recordings from two cortical cells are shown in the bottom panels, one preferring a vertical orientation (left) and one preferring a horizontal orientation (right). Many cells in the vertical cortical "column" are highly excited, and these suppress the firing of cells in adjacent columns (numbers above the columns are the integrated spike counts for all of the neurons in the orientation column). Cross-orientation inhibition is of the shunting type.

49

brain mechanisms at many different levels of structural organization (46).

Realistic and simplifying brain models have been distinguished to reveal their separate strengths and weakness. Neither type of model should be used uncritically. Realistic models require a substantial empirical database; it is all too easy to make a complex model fit a limited subset of the data. Simplifying models are essential but are also dangerously seductive; a model can become an end in itself and lose touch with nature. Ideally these two types of models should complement each other. For example, the same mathematical tools and techniques that are developed for studying a simplifying model could well be applied to analyzing a realistic model, or even the brain itself. More accurately, the two types of models are really end points of a continuum, and any given model may have features of both. Thus, we expect future brain models to be intermediate types that combine the advantages of both realistic and simplifying models.

It may be premature to predict how computational models will develop within neuroscience over the next decade, but several

general features are already emerging. First, in view of the many different structural levels of organization in the brain, and the realization that models rarely span more than two levels, we expect that many different types of models will be needed. It will be especially difficult to find a chain of models to cross the gap of at least three identified levels between the cellular and systems levels of investigation. Second, a model of an intermediate level of organization will necessarily simplify with respect to the structural properties of lower level elements, though it ought to try to incorporate as many of that level's functional properties as actually figure in the higher level's computational tasks. Thus, a model of a large network of neurons will necessarily simplify the molecular level within a single neuron.

At this stage in our understanding of the brain, it may be fruitful to concentrate on models that suggest new and promising lines of experimentation, at all levels of organization. In this spirit, a model should be considered a provisional framework for organizing possible ways of thinking about the nervous system. The model may not be able to generate a full range of predictions owing to incompleteness, some assumptions may be unrealistic simplifications, and some details may even be demonstrably wrong (99). Nevertheless, if the computational model is firmly based on the available experimental data, it can evolve along with the experimental program and help to guide future research directions.

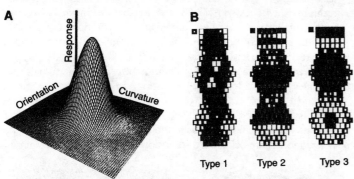

Fig. 5. Properties of model neurons in a network model that computes surface curvatures from shaded images of surfaces (36). (**A**) Representation of the tuning curve for one of the output cells in the network. Each cell is trained to respond jointly to one of the two principal curvatures and to the orientation of the long axis of the curved surface. The response of a single cell is broadly tuned and nonmonotonic. The 24 output cells have different preferred combinations of orientation and curvature with overlapping tuning curves. The pattern of responses in the population of output cells uniquely represents the curvatures and orientation. When probed with simulated bars of light these cells show some properties of end-stopped complex cells in the visual cortex. (**B**) Representative examples of three types of cells in the middle layer of a network that receive geniculate inputs and project to the output units. The hexagonal region at the bottom represents an array of inputs to the unit from on-center geniculate cells, and the hexagonal region above it are inputs from off-center geniculate cells. The white squares represent excitatory influences and the black squares represent inhibitory influences, and the area of each square is proportional to the magnitude of the synaptic strength. The patterns in the synaptic weights accurately predict the response of a cell when stimulated with simulated patterns of light and can be interpreted as the receptive field of the cell. The rectangle at the top represents the values of the weights from the cell to the 24 output cells that represent the curvature. All the cells in each column have a different preferred orientation, and each row is tuned to a different curvature, as indicated in (A). The isolated square in the upper left corner is a constant bias on the cell (negative of the threshold). Three types of cells were found in the hidden layer after training the network to produce the correct pattern on the output layer for each image. Type 1 and type 2 cells have oriented receptive fields and behave like simple cells when probed with bars of light (compare to the wiring diagram in Fig. 3A). However, the type 2 cell provides information to the output layer not about orientation, but about the convexity of the surface, as determined by pattern of projection to the cells on the output layer. The type 3 cell has a circularly symmetric receptive field and is sensitive to the ratio of the two principal curvatures.

REFERENCES AND NOTES

1. See, for example, work on stretch reflexes of the spinal cord [J. C. Houk and W. Z. Rymer, in *Handbook of Physiology*, section I, *The Nervous System*, vol. 2, *Motor Control*, V. B. Brooks, Ed. (American Physiological Society, Bethesda, MD, 1981), pp. 257–323], the jamming-avoidance response in the electric fish [W. J. Heiligenberg, *J. Comp. Physiol.* A161, 621 (1987)], and the gill-withdrawal reflex of the sea slug [E. R. Kandel *et al.*, in *Synaptic Function*, G. M. Edelman, W. E. Gall, W. M. Cowan, Eds. (Wiley, New York, 1987), pp. 471–518.]
2. S. G. Lisberger, E. J. Morris, L. Tychsen, *Annu. Rev. Neurosci.* **10**, 97 (1987).
3. C. Lee, W. H. Rohrer, D. L. Sparks, *Nature* **332**, 357 (1988).
4. P. S. Goldman-Rakic, *Annu. Rev. Neurosci.* **11**, 137 (1988).
5. E. I. Knudsen, S. du Lac, S. D. Esterly, *ibid.* **10**, 41 (1987).
6. H. B. Barlow, *Vision Res.* **26**, 81 (1986).
7. E. Schwartz *ibid.* **20**, 645 (1980).
8. V. B. Mountcastle, in *The Neurosciences*, G. Adelman and B. H. Smith, Eds. (MIT Press, Cambridge, MA, 1979), pp. 21–42.
9. A. I. Selverston, J. P. Miller, M. Wadepuhl, *IEEE Trans. Sys. Man Cybern.* SMC-13, 749 (1983).
10. P. A. Getting, *J. Neurophysiol.* **49**, 1017 (1983).
11. Multielectrode recording: H. J. P. Reitboeck, *IEEE Trans. Sys. Man Cybern.* SMC-13, 676 (1983); R. R. Llinas, in *Gap Junctions*, M. E. L. Bennett and D. C. Spray, Eds. (Cold Spring Harbor Laboratory, Cold Spring Harbor, NY, 1985), pp. 337–353. Voltage- and ion-dependent dyes: A. Grinvald, *Annu. Rev. Neurosci.* **8**, 263 (1985); R. Y. Tsien and M. Poenie, *Trends Bio. Sci.* **11**, 450 (1986). PET: M. E. Raichle, *Trends Neurosci.* **9**, 525 (1986). MEG: S. J. Williamson, G. L. Romani, L. Kaufman, I. Modena, *Biomagnetism: An Interdisciplinary Approach* (Plenum, New York, 1983). 2-DG: L. Sokoloff, *Metabolic Probes of Central Nervous System Activity in Experimental Animals and Man* (Sinauer, Sunderland, MA, 1984). MRI: R. Bachus, E. Mueller, H. Koenig, G. Braeckle, H. Weber, in *Functional Studies Using NMR*, V. R. McCready, M. Leach, P. J. Ell, Eds. (Springer-Verlag, New York, 1987), pp. 43–60. New York, 1987), pp. 43–60.
12. G. L. Gerstein and A. M. H. J. Aertsen, *J. Neurophysiol.* **54**, 1513 (1985).
13. M. Abeles, *Local Cortical Circuits* (Springer-Verlag, New York, 1982).
14. T. J. Sejnowski and P. S. Churchland, in *Foundations of Cognitive Science*, M. I. Posner, Ed. (MIT Press, Cambridge, MA, in press).
15. W. E. Reichardt and T. Poggio, *Theoretical Approaches in Neurobiology* (MIT Press, Cambridge, MA, 1981); F. H. C. Crick, *Sci. Am.* **241**, 219 (September 1979).
16. M. Arbib, in *Computational Neuroscience*, E. Schwartz, Ed. (MIT Press, Cambridge, MA, in press).
17. J. D. Cowan and D. H. Sharp, *Daedalus (Boston)* **117**, 85 (1988).
18. Marr and Poggio [D. Marr and T. Poggio, *Science* **194**, 283 (1976); D. Marr, *Vision* (Freeman, San Francisco, CA, 1982)] have emphasized the importance of this level of analysis.
19. P. S. Churchland, C. Koch, T. J. Sejnowski, in *Computational Neuroscience*, E. Schwartz, Ed. (MIT Press, Cambridge, MA, 1988).
20. C. Mead, *Analog VLSI and Neural Systems* (Addison-Wesley, Reading, MA, 1988).

21. F. Jacob, *The Possible and the Actual* (Univ. of Washington Press, Seattle, WA, 1982).
22. A. K. Hodgkin and A. F. Huxley, *J. Physiol.* **116**, 449 (1952).
23. A. L. Hodgkin, *ibid.* **263**, 1 (1976).
24. F. Ratliff, *Studies on Excitation and Inhibition in the Retina* (Rockefeller Univ. Press, New York, 1974).
25. J. J. Hopfield and D. W. Tank, *Science* **233**, 625 (1986).
26. J. A. Feldman and D. H. Ballard, *Cognitive Sci.* **6**, 205 (1982).
27. T. Kohonen, *Neural Networks* **1**, 3 (1988).
28. G. E. Hinton and J. A. Anderson, *Parallel Models of Associative Memory* (Erlbaum, Hillsdale, NJ, 1981).
29. J. L. Rumelhart and J. L. McClelland, *Parallel Distributed Processing: Explorations in the Microstructure of Cognition* (MIT Press, Cambridge, MA, 1986).
30. S. Grossberg and G. Carpenter, *Neural Networks* **1**, 17 (1988).
31. R. P. Lippmann, *IEEE Acous. Speech Signal Process. Mag.* **4**, 4 (1987).
32. A. Lapedes and R. Farber, in *Neural Information Processing Systems*, D. V. Anderson, Ed. (American Institute of Physics, New York, 1988), pp. 442–456.
33. T. J. Sejnowski and C. R. Rosenberg, *Complex Sys.* **1**, 145 (1987).
34. D. Zipser and R. Andersen, *Nature* **331**, 679 (1988).
35. A. C. Hurlbert and T. A. Poggio, *Science* **239**, 482 (1988).
36. S. R. Lehky and T. J. Sejnowski, *Nature* **333**, 452 (1988).
37. G. J. Mitchison and R. M. Durbin, *King's College Res. Center, Cambridge, U.K., Tech. Rep.* (1988).
38. Y. S. Abu-Mostafa, *IEEE Trans. Inf. Theory* **IT-32**, 513 (1986).
39. G. Tesauro and B. Janssens, *Complex Sys.* **2**, 39 (1988).
40. T. J. Sejnowski, *J. Math. Psychol.* **31**, 203 (1987).
41. M. Sivilotti, M. Mahowald, C. Mead, in *Stanford VLSI Conference*, P. Losleben, Ed. (MIT Press, Cambridge, MA, 1987), pp. 295–312.
42. J. Tanner and C. Mead, in *VLSI Signal Processing II*, S. Y. Kung, R. Owen, G. Nash, Eds. (IEEE Press, New York, 1986), pp. 59–76.
43. J. Hutchinson, C. Koch, J. Luo, C. Mead, *Computer*, **21**, 52 (March 1988).
44. Y. S. Abu-Mostafa and D. Psaltis, *Sci. Am.* **256**, 88 (March 1987).
45. Special issue on artificial neural systems, B. D. Shriver, *Computer* (March 1988).
46. Models in motor control and vision: F. Crick, *Proc. Natl. Acad. Sci. U.S.A.* **81**, 4586 (1984); E. C. Hildreth and J. M. Holerbach, in *Handbook of Physiology*, F. Plum, Ed. (American Physiological Society, Bethesda, MD, 1987); S. Ullman, *Annu. Rev. Neurosci.* **9**, 1 (1986). Models of olfaction: W. J. Freeman, *Mass Action in the Nervous System* (Academic Press, New York, 1975); G. Lynch, in *Perspectives in Memory Research and Training*, M. S. Gazzaniga, Ed. (MIT Press, Cambridge, MA, in press), M. Wilson and J. M. Bower, in *Neural Information Processing Systems*, D. V. Anderson, Ed. (American Institute of Physics, New York, 1988), pp. 114–126. Models of sensory-motor integration: D. A. Robinson, *Annu. Rev. Neurosci.* **4**, 463 (1981); M. A. Arbib, *Behav. Brain Sci.* **10**, 407 (1987); A. Pellionisz and R. Llinas, *Neuroscience* **16**, 245 (1985); S. Grossberg and M. Kuperstein, *Neural Dynamics of Adaptive Sensory-Motor Control* (North-Holland, Amsterdam, 1986).
47. E. R. Kandel *et al.*, in *Synaptic Function*, G. M. Edelman, W. E. Gall, W. M. Cowan, Eds. (Wiley, New York, 1987), pp. 471–518.
48. D. L. Alkon, *Memory Traces in the Brain* (Cambridge Univ. Press, New York, 1987).
49. R. F. Thompson, *Science* **233**, 941 (1986).
50. T. H. Brown, A. H. Ganong, E. W. Kariss, C. L. Keenan, S. R. Kelso, in *Neural Models of Plasticity*, J. H. Byrne and W. O. Berry, Eds. (Academic Press, New York, 1988).
51. M. M. Merzenich, and J. H. Kaas, *Trends Neurosci.* **5**, 434 (1982).
52. R. D. Traub, R. Miles, R. K. S. Wong, *J. Neurophysiol.* **58**, 752 (1987).
53. L. H. Finkel and G. M. Edelman, in *Synaptic Function*, G. M. Edelman, W. E. Gall, W. M. Cowan, Eds. (Wiley, New York, 1987), pp. 711–757; J. C. Pearson, L. H. Finkel, G. M. Edelman, *J. Neurosci.* **7**, 4209 (1987).
54. J. J. Hopfield, *Proc. Natl. Acad. Sci. U.S.A.* **79**, 2554 (1982).
55. T. Kohonen, *Self-Organization and Associative Memory* (Springer-Verlag, New York, 1984).
56. G. Palm, *Neural Assemblies: An Alternative Approach to Artificial Intelligence* (Springer-Verlag, New York, 1982).
57. S. Amari, *IEEE Trans. Sys. Man Cybern.* **SMC-13**, 741 (1983).
58. T. J. Sejnowski and G. Tesauro, in *Brain Organization and Memory*, J. L. McGaugh, N. M. Weinberger, G. Lynch, Eds. (Oxford Univ. Press, New York, in press).
59. B. L. McNaughton and R. G. Morris, *Trends Neurosci.* **10**, 408 (1987).
60. N. H. Donegan, M. A. Gluck, R. F. Thompson, in *Psychology of Learning and Motivation*, G. H. Bower, Ed. (Academic Press, San Diego, CA, in press).
61. E. Hildreth and C. Koch, *Annu. Rev. Neurosci.* **10**, 477 (1987).
62. K. Nakayama, *Vision Res.* **25**, 625 (1985).
63. B. Hassenstein and W. Reichardt, *Z. Naturforsch.* **11b**, 513 (1956).
64. W. Reichardt, *ibid.* **12b**, 448 (1957).
65. D. Varju and W. Reichardt, *ibid.* **22b**, 1343 (1967).
66. A fly eye contains about 24,000 visual receptors [N. Franceschini, *Neurosci. Res. Suppl.* **2**, S17 (1985)], and four layers of neurons between the photoreceptors at the input level and motoneurons at the output level [K. Hausen and R. Hengstenberg, *Annu. Meet. Soc. Neurosci. Abstr.* **17**, 295 (1987)].
67. W. Reichardt, in *Sensory Communication*, W. A. Rosenbluth, Ed. (MIT Press, Cambridge, MA, 1961), pp. 303–318.
68. J. P. H. van Santen, and G. Sperling, *J. Opt. Soc. Am.* **A1**, 451 (1984).
69. K. Gotz, *Kybernetik* **2**, 215 (1964).
70. H. B. Barlow and W. R. Levick, *J. Physiol.* **178**, 477 (1965).
71. H. J. Wyatt and N. W. Daw, *Science* **191**, 204 (1976).
72. N. M. Grzywacz and C. Koch, *Synapse* **1**, 417 (1987).
73. F. Werblin, G. Maguire, P. Lukasiewicz, S. Eliasof, S. Wu, *Neurobio. Group Univ. CA. Berkeley, Tech. Rep.* (1988).
74. W. Rall, in *Neuronal Theory and Modeling*, R. F. Reiss, Ed. (Stanford Univ. Press, Palo Alto, CA, 1964), pp. 73–97.
75. V. Torre and T. Poggio, *Proc. R. Soc. London Ser. B* **202**, 409 (1978).
76. C. Koch, T. Poggio, V. Torre, *Philos. Trans. R. Soc. London* **298**, 227 (1982).
77. W. Reichardt and T. Poggio, *Biol. Cybern.* **35**, 81 (1979).
78. ———, K. Hausen, *Biol. Cybern. Suppl.* **46**, 1 (1983).
79. M. Egelhaaf, *Biol. Cybern.* **52**, 195 (1985).
80. W. Reichardt and A. Guo, *ibid.* **53**, 285 (1986); W. Reichardt, R. W. Shloegel, M. Egelhaaf, *Naturwissenschaften*, **75**, 313 (1988); M. Egelhaaf, K. Hausen, W. Reichardt, C. Wehrhahan, *Trends Neurosci.* **11**, 351 (1988).
81. D. H. Hubel and T. N. Wiesel, *J. Physiol. (London)* **160**, 106 (1962).
82. A. M. Sillito, *ibid.* **250**, 305 (1975).
83. A. M. Sillito *et al.*, *Brain Res.* **194**, 517 (1980).
84. L. A. Benevento, O. D. Creutzfeldt, H. Kuhnt, *Nature New Biol.* **238**, 124 (1972).
85. P. Heggelund, *Exp. Brain Res.* **42**, 89 (1981).
86. G. A. Orban, *Neuronal Operations in the Visual Cortex* (Springer-Verlag, New York, 1984).
87. N. C. Morrone, D. C. Burr, L. Massei, *Proc. R. Soc. London Ser. B* **216**, 335 (1982); V. Braitenberg and C. Braitenberg, *Biol. Cybern.* **33**, 179 (1979).
88. C. Koch, *Ophthalmol. Vis. Sci.* **28**, (suppl. 3), 126 (1987).
89. D. Ferster and C. Koch, *Trends Neurosci.* **10**, 487 (1987).
90. D. Ferster, *J. Neurosci.* **6**, 1284 (1986).
91. U. Wehmeier, D. Dong, C. Koch, in *Methods in Neuronal Modeling*, C. Koch and I. Segev, Eds. (MIT Press, Cambridge, MA, in press).
92. T. J. Sejnowski, in (29), vol. 2, pp. 372–389.
93. ———, P. K. Kienker, G. E. Hinton, *Physica* **22D**, 260 (1986).
94. D. E. Rumelhart, G. E. Hinton, R. J. Williams, *Nature* **323**, 533 (1986).
95. K. Ikeuchi and B. K. P. Horn, *Artif. Intell.* **17**, 141 (1981).
96. A. P. Pentland, *IEEE Trans. Pattern Anal. Mach. Intell.* **6**, 170 (1984).
97. For models of cortical plasticity see M. F. Bear, L. N. Cooper, F. F. Ebner, *Science* **237**, 42 (1987); R. Linsker, *Proc. Natl. Acad. Sci. U.S.A.* **83**, 8779 (1986); C. von der Malsburg and D. Willshaw, *Trends Neurosci.* **4**, 80 (1981).
98. Network models can also be constructed that extract one-dimensional curvature of lines in a plane [A. Dobbins, S. W. Zucker, M. S. Cynader, *Nature* **329**, 438 (1987); H. R. Wilson and W. A. Richards, *J. Opt. Soc. Am.*, in press].
99. An example of an imperfect, but useful model from physics is the Bohr model of the hydrogen atom. This model served an essential role as a bridge between classical physics and quantum physics.
100. P. O. Bishop, J. S. Coombs, G. H. Henry, *J. Physiol. (London)* **219**, 659 (1971).
101. J. J. Hopfield, *Proc. Natl. Acad. Sci. U.S.A.* **81**, 3088 (1984).
102. We are grateful to R. Cone, F. Crick, T. Poggio, G. Tesauro, and W. Reichardt for helpful comments on this article. T.J.S. is supported by an NSF Presidential Young Investigator Award and grants from the Sloan Foundation, Seaver Institute, the Lounsbery Foundation, the Air Force Office of Scientific Research, the Office of Naval Research, and the General Electric Corporation; C.K. is supported by an NSF Presidential Young Investigator Award and grants from the Office of Naval Research, the Advanced Engineering program at the National Foundation, the Sloan Foundation, and by the Powell Lee Foundation; P.S.C. is supported by a grant from the NSF.

The Role of Human Visual Models in Image Processing

DOUGLAS J. GRANRATH

Invited Paper

Abstract—The mechanisms are discussed by which the human eye forms a neural image of the outside world for transmission along the optic nerve. Mathematical models of these mechanisms which can be exploited for engineering purposes are presented and their usefulness and limitations are discussed. Three areas in which human vision models have been successfully applied are image bandwidth compression, image quality assessment, and image enhancement; results from these areas are summarized and some example results are given. Some future directions are suggested.

I. INTRODUCTION

AS THE FIELD of digital image processing advanced due to technical progress in its hardware and in its processing algorithms, the performance of increasingly more complex image transformation tasks became possible. In its earliest beginnings some sixty years ago [1], digital image transmission was of a highly mechanical nature, and without the aid of modern electronics the transmission and reproduction of a picture was truly a remarkable achievement. The advent of the digital computer supplied image transmission with a brain, but at first the image processing it performed was solely to correct for erroneous or distorted data introduced in the image-forming and image-transmitting equipment itself [2], [3]. As work in the allied area of picture coding, or image bandwidth compression, progressed, it became recognized that the research could be better understood, if not unified, upon the basis of an understanding of human vision [4]. During this same period the study of human vision was also becoming important to the study of image fidelity [5], where the research objective became one of finding a computable fidelity measure that would correspond to the way human vision itself assessed image fidelity. The study of human vision was then recognized to be of central importance in the design of image processing systems [6] and was no longer an area to be studied after the fact. As image processing capabilities have grown in recent years, so has the complexity of human visual models which have been incorporated into the processing. This, in turn, has had a positive impact upon the study of human visual behavior and has resulted in a significant increase in our understanding of the complexities of the human visual process. Thus, a symbiotic relationship has developed between the study of digital image processing and of the human visual system that holds much promise for the advancement of both areas.

Although some modern day models of human vision are quite elaborate, major differences still exist between the behaviors that these models can emulate and the actual behavior of human vision. These differences are indicative of our current state of ignorance about the mechanisms of vision and mark some of the present-day limitations on the visual behavior that can be simulated. A primary characteristic of human vision is its ability to adapt to a wide variety of ambient scene conditions. We are able to see under scene illumination conditions spanning nine orders of magnitude [7], and our retinas are able to respond simultaneously to three orders of intensity magnitude in a given scene [8]. In addition to the adaptation of visual sensitivity in the retina proper, the coded visual information which is transmitted along the optic nerve to the brain adapts to certain scene characteristics which remain stable over time so that stimulus variations primarily are transmitted [9]. These adaptive behaviors present a fundamental difficulty in the analysis and modeling of vision. Namely, the sensing of an image by the retina as well as its neural encoding are highly signal dependent by nature, and models of these behaviors which are largely linear can only approximate the adaptive behavior within certain limits.

This paper will begin by discussing specific human visual behaviors along with how they are normally modeled. Where the behavior is adaptive in nature, the assumptions and restrictions necessary before using its model will be described also. Overall models of human vision will then be described which piece together some of these elemental models and which are able to be programmed on a digital computer. The usefulness of these computerized models will be explored in the following section where the models will be seen in three roles, in image bandwidth compression, in image quality assessment, and in image enhancement. Two related questions will be addressed here: How can human vision be modeled on a computer? And, how can such models be exploited to solve image processing problems?

II. THE MODELING OF HUMAN VISUAL BEHAVIOR

Most visual behaviors in man can be attributed to a level of origin in our visual anatomy. Roughly speaking, visual perception increases in complexity as one follows the progression of an image from the retina through the optic nerve, the optical chiasm, the lateral geniculate nuclei, and the cerebral cortex [10]. A line needs to be drawn for present purposes to separate that part of the human visual system which can be modeled to the point of actually being able to process images on a computer. Although such a demarkation is somewhat artificial, a convenient line can conceptually be drawn across the optic nerve. This line separates the eye-retina system from the higher visual centers and limits the discussion to the formation of neural images for transmission along the optic nerve. How the brain interprets this information in the visual cortex is ignored here, but this subject has been extensively studied in the fields of image understanding and pattern recognition.

Manuscript received April 2, 1980; revised November 3, 1980.
The author is with the Science Applications, Inc., 5055 East Broadway, Suite A-214, Tucson, AZ 85711.

Reprinted from *Proc. IEEE*, vol. 69, no. 5, pp. 552–561, May 1981.

Fig. 1. Generic model of neural image formation.

The models of human vision presented in this paper will then actually be models of neural image formation, as depicted by Fig. 1. Scene information in the form of light intensity comes to us a function of position in the scene $\bar{p}$ of time t and of the radiation's wavelength λ. Refraction by our cornea, intraocular fluids, and lens focuses some of this information on our retina forming a retinal intensity image as a function of retinal position, time, and wavelength. Receptor cells at the back of the retina sense these intensities and, through a complex network of interconnecting cells, encode the image into neural signals to be carried by the optic nerve [11]. Information from the original scene, and the eye/retina system can be viewed as a bandwidth compression system as well as a system for neural encoding. As a bandwidth compression device the retina extracts visual information which is important to us for survival; its job is to extract just the information necessary for discriminations to be made about objects in the outside world without actually making those discriminations. It is noteworthy that in animals which are prey rather than predator many of these discriminations are made in the retina proper. This enables such animals to react more quickly to avoid attacks by their predators, and their retinas exhibit a great deal more neural interconnections than ours as a result. As a predator, man has had the luxury of being able to think about his visual world.

A. Retinal Image Formation

The eye's optics, especially their adaptive nature, present the first challenge in developing a model of human visual function. Perhaps the most commonly known adaptive visual behavior is the pupillary response of the iris. The diameter of the iris can increase from approximately 2 to 8 mm in response to a decrease in ambient illumination. This increases the amount of light reaching the retina by a factor of 16 and compensates temporarily for the light loss, but compensation is made at the expense of retinal image quality. If sufficient light remains, the photoreceptors in the retina will increase their sensitivity through chemical adaptation and the iris's diameter will contract substantially. The reason that the iris tries to maintain itself in a "stopped-down" position is that our visual optics have large amounts of spherical and chromatic aberrations which must be kept under control [12], [13]. Anyone who has come out of his optometrist's office during the day with dilated pupils has a personal understanding of just how bad these aberrations can be.

In our generic model (Fig. 1), the retinal image shown is a function of position, time, wavelength, and of overall illumination which itself is a function of time $I_0(t)$. If the level of scene radiance is relatively unchanging over some minutes of time, then the iris diameter will become fixed and the retinal image will be a linear function of just position, time and wavelength $\Re(\bar{p}, t, \lambda)$. As such, the visual optics can be modeled as a linear, spatially-varying optical system. How does the retinal image vary with wavelength? As mentioned, chromatic abberation of the retinal image is pronounced. Along the optical axis, blue light is focused some 1.5 diopters closer to the front of the eye than red light. Curiously, chromatic aberration decreases with age, and it is believed to

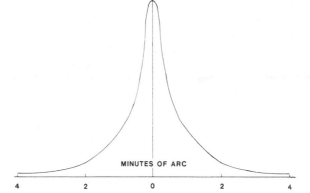

Fig. 2. Optical linespread function of the human eye for a pupil diameter of 2.4 mm (from Campbell and Gubish [17]).

be of less importance to visual acuity than spherical and paraxial distortions [14]. The question may then be asked: which wavelength is focused on our retina? The answer depends upon whether we are looking at something near or far: for a distant object the wavelength in focus is 675 nm and for a near object the wavelength is on the order of 475 nm. It has been suggested that our vision actually uses chromatic aberration to extend the range over which we can accommodate or focus, our eyes [14]. Chromatic aberration is believed to have little or no affect on visual perception; our retinas have a very good ability to maintain a consistent perception of color under conditions which shift the image's dominant wavelength. This phenomenon of color constancy will be discussed in a later section.

Given that our perception of the retinal image is relatively independent of wavelength, we can model the visual optics by a linear, spatially varying image formation system which is characterized by a point-spread or a line-spread function that varies in shape and size from one retinal location to another [15], [16]. Under some additional restrictions we can simplify our model an important further step, and use a spatially invariant model for retinal image formation; this will enable us to use a transfer-function representation in later discussions. Measurements of the line-spread function as formed on the retina have been made [17], and have revealed a back-to-back exponential function for large pupil diameters (5 mm and greater) and a central Gaussian with exponential tails for the smaller pupil sizes. As the pupil diameter decreases the central Gaussian more closely approximates the line-spread function of a diffraction limited optical system. An optically optimum pupil diameter occurs at about 2.4 mm. At this diameter the line-spread function is Gaussian down to its half-width point and exponential below (see Fig. 2). The smallest half-width occurs at the 2.4 mm pupil diameter since at greater pupil diameters the exponential spread is larger due to optical defects of the eye and at small diameters the Gaussian spread is larger due to greater pupil diffraction. Recall that this gives the best image as formed on the retina, and that neural processing then comes into play. In fact, when visual acuity is measured by psychophysical means which includes the neural processing, acuity remains relatively constant over a range of 2 to 5 mm in pupil diameter.

B. Neural Image Sensing

As light is focused by a camera onto its film plane, so the eye focuses light onto its light sensitive medium, the retina. Except perhaps for the fact that they both sense light by photon-induced chemical changes, the retina is quite unlike photographic film. Whereas a particular piece of film has one level of sensitivity, the retina can adapt its overall sensitivity to some 9 orders of magnitude in light intensity. It covers this vast range by chemical adaptation within its receptors and by the use of two separate receptor systems, involving specialized low light-level receptors called rods and high light-level receptors called cones. The retina can also adapt to local variations across a single image by neurally changing the sensitivity threshold of individual receptor cells. Film, of course, responds to all image locations in an equivalent manner. When it comes to representing color the retina is remarkable in its ability to adapt to spectral shifts in the scene illumination and to reproduce object colors in a highly consistent manner. When one uses outdoor color film to photograph an indoor scene under tungsten illumination, it becomes apparent that film has very little color adaptability.

The retinal image begins its transformation into a neural image by initiating a series of chemical reactions in the receptor cells [18]. A single photon can initiate such a response, and at the lowest visual light levels the rods operate at a quantum efficiency of 10 percent, responding to one out of ten photons on the average [19]. At higher levels of light, a chemical equilibrium is attained in rods between available photochemicals being bleached by photons and those which have previously been bleached and are being regenerated into a photoreceptive state. This means that the photoreceptors' response to additional light depends upon the intensity of the background and that response saturation occurs at varying levels. A first-order differential equation model of this equilibrium [20] yields a result consistent with an empirically derived result by Naka and Rushton [21], namely that

$$\frac{R}{R_{max}} = \frac{I}{I + c_2/c_1}.$$ (1)

Equation (1) gives the rod response ratio relative to its maximum response as a function of the total light intensity I, the regeneration rate of the bleached photoreceptors c_2, and the photosensitivity constant c_1. The ratio c_2/c_1 is known as the semisaturation constant, but it is a true constant only for rods and remains constant only for brief test flashes when cones are observed.

A well-known experimental result is that while the rods can be saturated by a steady, strong background light, the cones effectively cannot [22]. In order to observe saturation in cone responses the background light must be flashed as well as the test light [23]. It is believed that neural adaptive mechanisms in addition to the chemical mechanism of sensitivity adaptation accounts for this [24]. Shevell [25] has a model for cone response which accounts for the non-saturation of a steady background in addition to modeling correctly the saturation of flashed background and test lights. He accomplishes this by expressing the fraction of unbleached photochemical p in a dynamic equation involving the strength of the background field θ. The fraction p modulates the quantum catch of the test intensity I as well as the background and results in the following response equation:

$$N = \frac{Ip}{Ip + \sigma} \cdot \frac{\theta_D}{\theta + \theta_D}$$ (2)

where θ_D is a constant which represents receptor noise known as the "eigengrau," σ is now the semisaturation constant, and N is the cone's neural response. The dynamic saturation of (2)

occurs when a bright enough background flash bleaches essentially all of the photochemical and the test light is flashed before enough photochemical returns to the unbleached state to be able to record a test response. If $\log I$ is plotted versus $\log \theta$ for a constant threshold sensation N_c then between the saturation and the eigengrau regions a linear operating region exists in which

$$\log I = \log \theta + \log\left(\frac{I_0}{\theta_D}\right)$$ (3)

where I_0 is the absolute intensity test threshold.

Sensing of the retinal image intensities and transducing them into neural correlates is thus highly nonlinear in nature. The question then arises as to how one incorporates this nonlinearity into a model of vision. The typical answer is to transform the image at some stage of the model in a point-by-point fashion by a simple nonlinear function. The logarithm or the cube-root function is typically used for this. Choice of the logarithm is theoretically satisfying due to the Weber–Fechner relationship from classical psychophysics theory [26]. The cube-root relationship is more satisfying to the modern psychophysicists [27], [28], and has been shown empirically to be the better choice in a particular vision model [29]. Neither relationship, however, models either an eigengrau or a saturation level, which can be important if the image intensity ranges over three orders of magnitude. In an actual application, if the image is represented in some absolute intensity measure with a limited dynamic range, then there is little qualitative difference between the two relationships. A more important issue is the proper location of the nonlinearity within the visual model.

An extensive experimental examination of human visual response to light flashes was reported by Mansfield [30]. He reported his results in terms of exponents in power-law form

$$N = kI^\beta$$ (4)

where k is a scaling constant. Using psychophysical methods his subjects reported on observed brightness for stimuli which differed in size, color, retinal location, and presentation time. The results indicate that there are at least two power laws, one with an exponent of $\frac{1}{2}$ for transient stimuli and one with an exponent of $\frac{1}{3}$ for steady stimuli (several seconds or longer). This was consistently found to be the case for all stimuli except for the smallest target (0.05 degree) which had a transient exponent of 1 and a steady-state exponent of 0.5. Mansfield's results corroborate results from the electrophysiological measurement of retinal cells that there are two distinct nonlinear stages in the transduction of light intensity within the retina. One occurs in the photoreceptors themselves, while the second one occurs in the interconnecting retinal cells just beyond. It is thus of importance to the validity of a visual model whether it describes the viewing of still or of moving images.

It is well known from personal experience that night vision is largely achromatic while day vision provides us with a rich spectral view of the world. Our color sensation is made possible by differential spectral sensitivities in the photochemicals of the photopic (cone) system in the retina [31]. Three spectral "bands" are involved, and the three corresponding types of cones are commonly known as the red, green, and blue cones. A model of color vision in man must then begin with three spectral sensitivity function $S_R(\lambda)$, $S_G(\lambda)$, $S_B(\lambda)$, which are used to describe a cone's response to the spectral

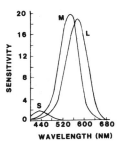

Fig. 3. Effective spectral sensitivity functions; *L*—long wavelength (red) cone; *M*—medium wavelength (green) cone; and *S*—short wavelength (blue) cone. Sensitivity is expressed as a percentage of incident quanta absorbed by the visual pigment.

composition of the retinal image

$$C(\bar{p}) = \int R(\bar{p}, \lambda) \cdot S(\lambda) \, d\lambda. \qquad (5)$$

When the absorptions of the photopigments are measured directly as a function of the wavelength of the incident light, three absorption spectra are obtained with peaks at 440 nm, 535 nm, and 565 nm. All of the curves overlap to some degree, and there is considerable overlap between the medium wavelength (green) and long wavelength (red) curves. Perhaps a better set of spectral absorption curves for modeling purposes come from measurements by Wald [32], who included the spectral absorption effects of the eye's optics and of the pigmentation in the central portion of the retina. These curves are reproduced in Fig. 3, where in addition to the spectral overlap it is significant that the short wavelength (blue) curve is a factor of 10 less sensitive than the medium and long wavelength curves. As will be seen in the next section other evidence exists which points to the relative greater importance of the red and green receptors over the blue receptors.

C. Neural Image Coding

Although image color coding is actually begun in the receptors themselves considerably more image coding takes place in the retina, including the coding of the image's spatial and temporal as well as spectral characteristics. This coding is accomplished by an intricate network of retinal neurons which cross-connect the receptor cells, connect to the ganglion cells which make up the optic nerve, and cross-connect the ganglion cells as well [33], [34]. The primary purpose of this network is to adapt retinal sensation of the visual world to be invariant to changes in scene illumination so that visual information concerning actual objects in the scene is faithfully transmitted to the brain to be acted upon. Since the optic nerve has a limited channel capacity the retina can be viewed as performing bandwidth compression of the retinal image. This viewpoint will be exploited in the bandwidth compression of digital images by using a human visual model for that purpose. To the extent that the retina extracts certain image features at the expense of others, it can be viewed as weighting the importance of certain features over others. Visual models can thus be used as a means of assessing image quality, either for its own end or for the purpose of image enhancement.

In addition to retinal adaptation to the overall image light level, the retina adapts the sensitivity of its receptors across the image in a local fashion as well. Rather than a purely chemical adaptation, this phenomenon is one of neural adaptation which is effected by laterally connecting cells, primarily by the horizontal cells with perhaps the aid of the amacrine

cells [35]. Evidence from a variety of sources indicates a pervasive two-channel organization of spatial information in the neural representation of imagery [36]. One of these channels is spatially low pass in nature and contains information about the local brightness average across the image. It provides feedback to the receptor cells which then respond relative to their local brightnesses. This enables the receptors a relatively fast means of adapting their sensitivity and extends their dynamic range roughly from one to three orders of magnitude in intensity. The receptor cell response with the low frequencies removed then forms the other channel which has overall a bandpass spatial frequency character. Whereas the lowpass channel carries information about the degree of contrast across the image, the bandpass channel carries the line and edge information from the image. It is this edge information which is important to us for discriminating objects in the outside world and which the retina extracts for use by the higher visual centers of the brain.

The post-receptor neurons in the retina also perform adaptive coding of the spectral characteristics of the image. Involving most likely the amacrine cell network [11], retinal color coding strives to produce a color code which is invariant to the spectral composition of the illuminating light. The retina achieves such color constancy by coding color in a relative fashion, comparing the response from two neighboring cones with different spectral responses and transmitting their differential response rather than their absolute responses. Evidence points to red–green differential coding as being the primary color dimension with yellow–blue differential coding of secondary importance [37]-[39]. In addition, an achromatic channel is formed which involves response signals from all three types of cones. Models of color image coding thus involve, as we shall see, three channels, one achromatic and two chromatic in nature.

Given that there are three neural channels for color coding and two spatial frequency channels, the question of how they are combined arises. For instance, is each of the three color channels composed of two spatial channels yielding six neural channels altogether? Or, are there two achromatic channels, one spatially low-pass and one spatially bandpass, and two chromatic channels each spatially bandpass in nature? This issue remains largely unresolved, although some experimental work has been done in its regard. The existence of a spatial bandpass response to light modulated only in color (and not in luminance) is a subject of some controversy. Although some claim that such color Mach bands do occur [40], others have found them difficult, if not impossible, to observe in a psychophysical type of experiment [41]. Electrophysiological experimentation [42], which has clearly demonstrated bandpass responses for stimuli modulated in luminance, has thus far been unable to show a similar response to color modulated signals. In one view of why color Mach bands do not occur [43] there is just one type of horizontal cell which connects to all three spectral types of cones. This produces just one low spatial frequency channel which is achromatic and which imparts a bandpass spatial response to each cone before opponent color coding occurs. Such a viewpoint must be taken as only a tentative one until more conclusive experimental evidence has been published.

As discussed in the context of adaptation, the retina has temporal response characteristics as well as spatial and spectral ones. If the relatively slow chemical adaptation of retinal photochemicals is ignored, the temporal characteristics of the

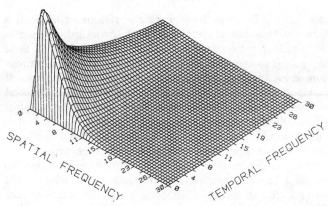

Fig. 4. Human visual system response surface (from Kenderink *et al.* [45]).

Fig. 5. The Hall and Hall [45] model of human achromatic vision.

retina's neural network can be modeled by a transfer function just as the spatial characteristics [44]. When considered one-dimensionally, the temporal frequency transfer function is bandpass in form with a peak sensitivity of about 5 Hz and a high-frequency cutoff around 30 Hz. This high-frequency cut-off is closely related to the critical flicker frequency (CFF) beyond which the temporal variations are too fast for the retina to follow. The CFF has been extensively studied [7] and depends upon a number of variables including light level, contrast, and target size. The temporal transfer function has been expressed analytically by Koenderink *et al.* [45], in a two-dimensional format along with the spatial transfer function. Two of these response surfaces are necessary, one for stimuli which are spatio-temporally modulated in intensity and one modulated in color (see Fig. 4). Whereas the intensity-modulated surface has a bandpass characteristic in both dimensions (space and time), the color-modulated surface is low-pass in both dimensions. The chromatic response curve is at its maximum for sustained colors (zero temporal frequency) at all spatial frequencies, while the intensity response curve theoretically goes to zero for a sustained intensity image. In actual practice the retinal image is never perfectly stationary due to continual jitter of the eyeball, but when the retinal image is artifically stabilized in the laboratory all of the image's lines and edges disappear along with all the sharply defined forms in the image. Most of the models in the next section ignore the retina's temporal response and as such are most appropriate for the processing and viewing of still images.

D. Models of Human Vision

Specific models of human vision will now be discussed which encompass some of the visual behaviors discussed in the previous sections. That one all-encompassing model is not given instead can be attributed to the complexity such a model implies and to the subsequent amount of computation which would be involved in any implementation of the model. Each model given here will, however, emulate enough visual behavior to be of significant value in engineering applications. There are other models of human vision, but they are either subsumed within or have been superceded by one of the four models given here.

The first model we consider is an achromatic, one-channel model by Charles Hall and Ernest Hall [46]. Their model has a simple in-line structure (Fig. 5) composed of three subsystems: a linear low-pass filter representing the formation of the retinal image by the eye's optics, a point-wise logarithmic transform representing image sensing, and a linear high-pass

filter representing neural image formation. Derived from published measurements of the eye's optical line-spread function, their low-pass filter is of the form

$$H_1(\omega) = \frac{2\alpha}{\alpha^2 + \omega^2} \qquad (6)$$

and with ω expressed in cycles per degree they set $\alpha = 0.7$ in correspondence with a pupil diameter of 3 mm. For their high-pass filter Hall and Hall chose a continuous analog to a discrete model of neural interaction in the retina [10]. They assumed that there is inhibitory feedback from neighboring photoreceptors which decreases exponentially with distance and derived the following filter:

$$H_2(\omega) = \frac{a^2 + \omega^2}{2a_0 a + (1 - a_0)(a^2 + \omega^2)}. \qquad (7)$$

By comparing their filter's reponse with actual data from psychophysical experiments, they arrived at the values $a = 0.01$ and $a_0 = 0.2$. Thus the Hall and Hall model is primarily concerned with the spatial frequency response of the human visual system to still images, including some of vision's adaptive response in the form of the log transformation. It makes the simplifying assumptions of rotational invariance (or, isotropy), of shift invariance, of temporal homogeneity, and of continuity of the retinal mosaic. In spite of these limitations the model has been successfully applied to the reduction of image bandwidth and to the assessment of image quality [47], and is theoretically important due to the structural validity of its three components to the actual processing of images in the human visual system.

The next model we consider includes the dimension of color by forming three channels, two of which carry chromatic information while the other carries purely achromatic information. Published by Faugeras [48], the block diagram in Fig. 6 shows the model's main structure. The color intensity image at the retina $R(x, y, \lambda)$, is first separated into three signals by being integrated with the spectral sensitivity functions of the three cone types as in (5). This image sensing stage is followed by a log transformation to model the retina's primary nonlinearity as done in the previous model. Next, the three log-transformed cone signals are combined into an achromatic channel involving all three, a chromatic channel composed of the red minus the green signals, and a second chromatic channel of the red minus the blue signals. This chromatic mixing of the cone signals is governed by a set of coefficients as follows:

$$\begin{bmatrix} A \\ C_1 \\ C_2 \end{bmatrix} = \begin{bmatrix} a\alpha & a\beta & a\gamma \\ u_1 & -u_1 & 0 \\ u_2 & 0 & -u_2 \end{bmatrix} \begin{bmatrix} L^* \\ M^* \\ S^* \end{bmatrix}. \qquad (8)$$

Faugeras used $\alpha = 0.612$, $\beta = 0.369$, and $\gamma = 0.019$ to form his achromatic channel, and set a, u_1, and u_2 so that a just noticeable difference in the perception of brightness or color is represented by a sphere of radius one in the $A \times C_1 \times C_2$ space. Finally, the spatial frequencies of the three channels

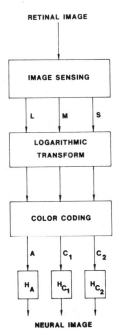

Fig. 6. The Faugeras [47] model of human chromatic vision.

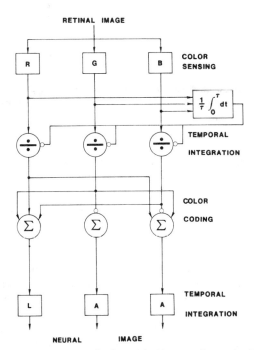

Fig. 7. The Koenderink [44] model of human chromatic vision.

are linearly filtered by the bandpass filters H, H_1, and H_2. In the case of black-and-white imagery the two chromatic channels C_1 and C_2, become zero and the model reduces to a single channel composed of the log transform and the achromatic bandpass filter; this corresponds exactly to the achromatic visual model proposed by Stockham [6]. Faugeras demonstrated the usefulness of his model in enhancing the brightness and the chromaticity of an image, as well as in image coding and in image quality assessment.

There are human vision models which incorporate temporal response characteristics in addition to spatial and color characteristics, but these models are currently of more theoretical than practical interest due to their increased complexity. As shown in Fig. 7 the model of Koenderink et al. [45] uses temporal integrators at two distinct levels, the receptor cell and the amacrine/ganglion cell level. The "leaky" integrator at the receptor level models horizontal cell behavior and feeds back a time-averaged, spatially local response to the receptors. Chromatic mixing then produces an achromatic channel composed of all three cone signals, a red–green channel, and a red+green–blue or yellow–blue channel. The achromatic signal is then acted upon by an "L" detector which fires a signal whenever the short-term variation in the channel exceeds a threshold distance above or below the long-term average of the channel. Simple temporal integration occurs in both of the chromatic channels and serves to make these channels slower to respond than the achromatic channel, allowing for a slow adaptation to occur. By performing a slow integration of the chromatic signals and allowing rapid firing of the achromatic signal the model's output is separated into sustained and transient channels in accordance with experimental observation of ganglion cell responses [49]. A one-dimensional computer simulation of their model has demonstrated such emulation of experimental results.

Another largely theoretical model by Buffart [50] describes the formation of a neural image in the retina as it occurs simultaneously in space and time. The model first transforms the retinal intensity image by a local nonlinearity of the following form:

$$R(\vec{r}, t) = \frac{L(\vec{r}, t) - \tau}{L(\vec{r}, t) - \tau + \delta} \tag{9}$$

where τ and δ are constants expressed in the same luminance units as the input image L. A linear shift-invariant system in two spatial and one temporal variables then constitutes the remainder of the model. Thus far Buffart's model is very similar to the previous ones, but he imposes a neural causality condition and makes an important assumption regarding the retina's output signal which lead to a unique and an interesting retinal model. His neural causality condition arises from the fact that neural signals travel across and through the retina at limited velocities so that signal simultaneity or propinquity at a post-receptor level depends upon the onset times and locations of the component signals at the receptor level. His output signal assumption is that first-order temporal changes in the retinal signal constitute all that is transmitted via the optic nerve. This assumption is largely valid since the majority of cells at the ganglion level and higher are of the transient type, but a fraction of the observed cells are, in fact, sustained in nature [44]. Buffart assumes a rotationally symmetric impulse response function which is "turned on" by a step function in accordance with the causality condition

$$h(\vec{r}, t) = \text{step}\left(t - \left[\frac{\vec{r}^2 + a}{c^2}\right]^{1/2}\right) \cdot s(\vec{r}, t). \tag{10}$$

Here c is the retinal conduction velocity, a is a constant which models retinal depth, and s in the noncausal impulse response function. This leads to a model of neural image formation as follows:

$$N(\vec{r}, t) = \iint_{-\infty}^{\infty} \int_{-\infty}^{t'} h(\vec{r} - \vec{\rho}, t - \tau) \cdot \frac{\partial}{\partial \tau} R(\vec{\rho}, \tau) \, d\tau \, d\vec{\rho} \tag{11a}$$

and

$$t' = t - \left[\frac{(\vec{r} - \vec{\rho})^2 + a}{c^2} \right]^{1/2} \qquad (11b)$$

In order to be able to compare his model with psychovisual experimental results, Buffart assumes that his impulse response function is separable in space and time

$$h(\vec{r}, t) = h_1(\vec{r}) \cdot h_2(t). \qquad (12)$$

He notes that $h_2(t)$ is a low or a bandpass filter, and he postulates a spatial filter $h_1(\vec{r})$, which in one spatial dimension is given by

$$h_1(x) = \frac{1}{\pi} \frac{\alpha}{(\alpha^2 + x^2)} + \frac{\beta}{\pi} \frac{\alpha(\alpha^2 - x^2)}{(\alpha^2 + x^2)^2}. \qquad (13)$$

This produces a point response composed of a high narrow central peak surrounded by a pair of broad negative sidelobes, and results in a bandpass filter characteristic. For measurements made within the fovea, the parameter α is varied to match the spread of the observed point response as manifested in the peak frequency response of the data, and the parameter β is adjusted to match the relative strength of the inhibitory component via a determination of the zero-frequency response level. Although these parameters vary from one individual to another, Buffart gives a nominal value of 33 for β and $0.13/2\pi$ cycles/degree for α in retinal distance units.

III. Applications of Human Vision Models

Given that we have a valid model of human visual behavior which can be implemented on a digital computer, we would like to use the model to help us solve some image processing problems. The exact form of the model's implementation will vary according to its application, but this will be the result of taking different viewpoints of the same model. In bandwidth compression applications the idea is to code just that image information which is important in viewing the image, while in image quality assessment the idea is to measure the degree of distortion one can see in the displayed image. In an image enhancement application we predistort an image before display according to our vision model so as to maximize some aspect of perceived image quality.

A. Image Bandwidth Compression

The basic paradigm used in subjective image bandwidth compression is to transform the image with a vision model, to apply a coding algorithm, and then after transmission or storage to decode and invert the image from the perceptual domain back into the intensity domain (see Fig. 8). From our earlier viewpoint of human visual modeling, this corresponds to coding the image in the form it would be in at the optic nerve level. That the retina also performs image compression is apparent when one considers that the image is sensed by approximately 7-million cones in daylight and 100-million rods at night, but that the neural image must be transmitted over the 1-million fibers of the optic nerve [33]. Although the image compression desired normally is greater than the implied 7:1 retinal compression in daylight, the additional distortion to the image due to further compression is equalized better when coding takes place in the perceptual domain. Which form of image coding is best to use for this purpose? If one takes the straightforward approach and simply quantizes the vision model's output, the resulting quantization

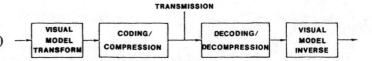

Fig. 8. Paradigm for image bandwidth compression with a vision model.

noise will produce pseudo-edges in the image which will limit the degree of compression [51]. One answer is to dither the signal [52], to break these edges up, but more commonly the answer is to choose a coding algorithm that will spatially decorrelate the quantization noise. Coding in the Fourier domain is a common means of accomplishing this.

Subjective image coding results are quite good down to an average rate of 1 bit/pel and are acceptable, depending upon the coding scheme, down to 0.1 bit/pel. Probably the simplest subjective image coder is a logarithmic transform of the intensity-valued pels; this permits an 8- to 6-bit reduction in image representation without any noticeable loss [10]. By using a model which includes the spatial and chromatic aspects of the retina much better results can be achieved. Hall [47] has demonstrated that an achromatic vision model can improve the compression of still images by almost a factor of 10 when used in conjunction with Fourier domain coding techniques. Color images are typically represented with 8 bits per color primary (red, green, and blue) per pel. By coding the Fourier coefficients at the output of his color vision model, Faugeras [48] demonstrated good compression results with a total average rate of 1 bit/pel distributed by 0.7 bit/pel for the brightness channel, 0.2 bit/pel for the red–green channel, and 0.1 bit/pel for the yellow–blue channel. Hall [47] achieved similar results with his color vision model, finding that an image is virtually indistinguishable from its original at 1 bit/pel of compression and that acceptable images can be obtained down to 0.5 and even 0.25 bit/pel. In addition to the increase in compression a vision model preprocessor gives to image coding, there is evidence that vision model coding may be more resistant to outside sources of noise for achromatic images [6], as well as for color [53].

B. Image Quality Assessment

When an image is distorted from processing, the error between it and its original is typically measured by taking the average across the image of the squared pel differences, known as the mean-squared error. Although this measure has a good physical and theoretical basis, it often correlates poorly with the subjectively judged distortion of the image. Much of the reason for this is due to the fact that the human visual system does not process the image in a point-by-point fashion but extracts certain spatial, temporal, and chromatic features for neural coding. Image quality assessment can be viewed as the search for a metric which will reflect these subjective properties of the image and provide the engineer with an objective criteria he can use in the design of image-processing systems [54].

If the assumption is made that the neural image produced by the retina is transmitted on the optic nerve with uniform emphasis in its perceptual dimensions, then human vision models can be used to assess image quality in a straightforward fashion by applying error measures to the image after transformation to the perceptual domain. An error metric applied in this manner could, at least theoretically, properly weight such image characteristics as edge fidelity, image contrast, color fidelity, and so on. The success of the resulting image quality measure would then depend on the validity of the vision model, and which metric was used in the perceptual domain. If the image were transformed to a truly uniform perceptual domain so that a unit change is equivalent on any range and in any perceptual dimension, then an absolute deviation measure would be appropriate. That some experimental results indicate a squared deviation measure is better [55] implies that the perceptual domain used placed greater emphasis on larger deviations. It is generally true, however, that choice of the error metric is less important than choice of the vision model. Faugeras [48] has shown experimentally that images do not change in their relative rankings for three different metrics: the maximum absolute deviation, the mean absolute deviation, and the root-mean-squared deviation.

Experimental results from studies which compare perceptual domain error metrics with image quality judgments made by human viewers have been encouraging. In each case, the subjective ratings were made by the viewer comparing global image quality between an original and a degraded image, while the objective measure was computed between the two images in digital form. Viewers were allowed to base their judgments on whatever image features they wished and were, thus, in a nontasked environment. Hall [47] performed such evaluations with color as well as with monochromatic images and found good correlation between subjective rankings and perceptual domain quality metrics. In the achromatic case he transformed an original image and twelve degraded versions with the Mannos and Sakrison vision model [29], and then applied the mean-square error between each degraded image and the original to yield the image quality measure. With additive Gaussian noise as well as blocking errors in the image, correlation between these image quality measures and an average subjective ranking of the images was 0.92. This is significantly better than the 0.84 correlation between the conventional normalized mean-square error and the subjective rankings. Hall found a comparable correlation of 0.94 for a color image quality metric based on his color vision model, but the conventional mean-square error in this case was 0.96 and performed slightly better. That this would be the case for a different data set or different viewers is unclear, but the perceptual domain measure is likely more robust to changes than the conventional measure. In a smaller experiment involving five distorted versions of an original image, Faugeras [48] found that three different distortion metrics (root-mean-square error, maximum absolute deviation, and mean absolute deviation) applied in the perceptual domain of his color vision model yielded three sets of image quality measurements which were entirely consistent with the average subjective ranking of the distorted images.

Image quality assessment by the calculation of error in the perceptual domain of a vision model is limited, as mentioned earlier, by the validity of the model. It is also limited by the scope of the model. The vision models discussed in this paper have been concerned with image processing in the early stages of vision up to optic nerve transmission and ignore subsequent "processing" of the imagery at higher neural levels. Thus much additional precognitive image processing and all of the cognitive image processing is beyond the scope of these vision models, and the visual behaviors associated with these levels are not reflected in the image quality measure. For example, when the subject in an image quality viewing experiment makes his judgment he does so by scanning the images not in a uniform fashion, but in a selective fashion according to decisions he is making on a cognitive level. He chooses specific image areas to make his judgments upon and, in essence, weights these areas more heavily than the rest of the image. Since different viewers may choose different image areas to look at and since a single viewer may vary his area weights from one judgment to the next, it is not surprising that the correlation between viewer experiments and perceptual domain metrics is not higher.

C. Image Enhancement

Another role human vision models can play is in the enhancement of images for display. The image either lacks the overall quality to be displayed in its present form, or there is some subjective quality of the image which needs to be emphasized relative to other qualities. An example of this is histogram hyperbolization [56], in which just the image's contrast is enhanced. This technique works in a pel-by-pel manner and transforms the image histogram into a hyperbolic form which upon viewing results in a uniform pel distribution due to the receptor cell's nonlinearity. The intrinsic vision model used here is simply the log or cube-root mapping, but it suffices to enhance the quality of interest.

The predominant spatial quality of interest concerns the edges in the image. As discussed in Section II, the retina acts to extract and emphasize the edges from the scene by subtracting the low spatial frequency variations and by amplifying the resulting signal to fill the dynamic range of the optic nerve. A technique which is often used to produce edge enhancement is that of unsharp masking [57]. In unsharp masking a low-passed version of the original image is formed and then a proportionate amount of it is subtracted from the original. When it is viewed the resulting image is more strongly represented in the retina's bandpass spatial channel, and the image's apparent sharpness is increased. Unsharp masking thus uses a human vision model in an inherent fashion. Another image enhancement technique which exploits the spatial frequency qualities of an image is that of homomorphic image processing [6], [58], [59]. This technique assumes that the radiance from a scene is the product of a low spatial frequency illumination component and a high spatial frequency reflectance component from the objects in the scene. The image is first log transformed, is then sent through a high-pass spatial filter which suppresses the illumination component and enhances the reflectance, and is finally exponentially transformed back into intensity space. The resulting displayed image has its contrast subjectively equalized so that the contrast of an object depends upon the reflectance of its background and does not depend upon whether it is fully illuminated or is in the shade. And although this technique is based on physical rather than on physiological reasoning, it is successful because it exploits the same type of enhancement which occurs in the retina.

Models of color vision in humans lead to the possibility of color image enhancement. Since virtually all color vision models are three channel by nature with one achromatic and two chromatic channels, it is possible to enhance achromatic and chromatic image characteristics separately. For instance, a high-pass filter can be applied to the achromatic channel to produce homorphic enhancement on a color image just as well as on a black and white image. By high-pass filtering the chromatic channels in addition to the achromatic channel of a transformed image, Faugeras [48] has demonstrated a chromatic version of homomorphic enhancement. The resulting enhanced image has better color balance than the original and, in particular, an overall yellowish tint in the original is removed. There have been few, if any, other investigations into chromatic image enhancement which make explicit use of human vision models. There are, however, a couple of enhancement techniques which owe their success to the exploitation of some property of color vision. Pseudocolor takes an achromatic image and maps it into a tristimulus color space [56, p. 336] in which different original pel values have different colors upon display. The utility of such a mapping varies in an ad hoc manner with the application and will often depend upon the compatability of the mapping with our previous experience. For example, if a thermal scan of a patient is displayed with the warmer regions depicted in the red end of the visual spectrum and the cooler regions in the blue end, there will be good compatability between the displayed image and our psychological notion regarding "warm" and "cool" colors. An enhancement technique used successfully in multispectral imagery involves displaying an image which is the pel-by-pel ratio of the same image in two spectral bands [60]. This technique largely removes the illumination component and displays primarily the spectral variations between the two imaging bands. As we have seen, the retina uses a nearly identical technique to take an image which is sensed in three spectral "bands" by the photoreceptors and represent it as the ratio or log difference of these bands in the optic nerve.

IV. CONCLUSION

We have seen that many of the complexities of human visual behavior can be mathematically modeled in sufficient quantitative detail to permit them to be represented by programs on a digital computer. Whether represented in mathematical or in digital form, such human visual models provide us with a unifying basis for our understanding of the visual process itself as well as for the application of this knowledge to the processing of images. In this role, human visual models can provide feedback to those investigating human visual behavior and, in particularly, can aid our understanding of large-scale phenomena by using a computer to model the complexities involved. In the role of concern in this paper, human visual models find direct application to the processing of images which someone will look at in the end. As we have seen, a human visual model can be exploited in image bandwidth compression to yield a final image whose perceived distortion is minimized. In a more passive role the model can be used to assess the perceived distortion or quality of a previously processed image and thereby save the image processing system designer from extensive image viewing experiments. To the display designer or the image analyst a human visual model can be used in an image enhancement role to bypass display limitations and/or to enhance those image qualities of primary interest. Aside from the direct results such applications bring, human visual modeling aids our understanding of image processing problems by providing us with valuable analogies. Nature has evolved our visual system in a long series of trials and failures spanning many millions of years. The laws of physics governing image formation and detection have presumably been the same over this span of time, and the evolution of vision had to work under these laws just as the image-processing engineer does today. By taking this view we should not be surprised that an image-processing algorithm based on human vision often will provide a good physical solution to the problem as well. Rather, we should expect it to.

Our success at exploiting these analogies is limited by our knowledge of how the visual system is constructed and of how this structure works to produce our visual experience. Retina modeling, in particular, is currently limited by our inexact knowledge of how the various types of retinal cells are interconnected. Better knowledge in this area will lead to a more complete understanding of the role each cell type takes in the formation of the neural image, with the interesting prospect of being able to perform computer simulations of neural image formation at different stages within the retina. Another limitation, as we have seen, is our difficulty in modeling adaptive behaviors. Here we are more limited by our ability to model the behaviors rather than by our ability to study them in the laboratory. The various nonlinearities implied by visual adaptation can be mathematically modeled in an independent fashion, but their lack of tractability makes it difficult to combine them into an overall model. This difficulty can be circumvented to an extent by using computer models incorporating the nonlinearities, but then the problem becomes one of validating the resulting model in some fashion.

As our knowledge of the human visual process grows, more of its complexity and its adaptive nature will surely be modeled. This will lead to the development of more "intelligent" image processors which will be able to consistently extract and process desired image information under a wide range of image-forming conditions. At the higher levels of vision in the brain an increased understanding of the processes of visual perception and visual thought will eventually lead to the design of truely interactive image processors. Such systems will use the human operator's higher level visual perceptions and judgments as a controller of the image processing computer, whose superior speed and precision will be exploited to transform the imagery. The resulting system of man and machine will be a synthesis of the best qualities of both and will be a significant extension of man's visual abilities alone.

REFERENCES

[1] M. D. McFarlane, "Digital pictures fifty years ago," *Proc. IEEE*, vol. 60, pp. 768–770, July 1972.
[2] T. C. Rindfleisch, J. A. Dunne, H. J. Frieden, W. D. Stromberg, and R. M. Ruiz, "Digital processing of the Mariner 6 and 7," *J. Geophys. Res.*, vol. 76, pp. 394–417, Jan. 1971.
[3] D. A. O'Handley and W. B. Green, "Recent developments in digital image processing at the Jet Propulsion Laboratory," *Proc. IEEE*, vol. 60, pp. 821–828, July 1972.
[4] W. F. Schreiber, "Picture coding," *Proc. IEEE*, vol. 55, no. 3, pp. 320–330, Mar. 1967.
[5] Z. L. Budrikis, "Visual fidelity criterion and modeling," *Proc. IEEE*, vol. 60, pp. 771–779, July 1972.
[6] T. G. Stockham, Jr., "Image processing in the context of a visual models," *Proc. IEEE*, vol. 60, pp. 828–842, July 1972.
[7] H. Graham, Ed., *Vision and Visual Perception*. New York: Wiley, 1965.
[8] F. S. Werblin, "The control of sensitivity in the retina," *Scientific Amer.*, May 1968.
[9] W. R. Uttal, *The Psychobiology of Sensory Coding*. New York: Harper and Row, 1973.
[10] T. N. Cornsweet, *Visual Perception*. New York: Academic Press, 1970.
[11] H. Davson, Ed., *The Eye*, Volume 2A: *Visual Function in Man*. New York: Academic Press, 1976.
[12] G. Westheimer, "Optical properties of vertibrate eyes," in *Handbook of Sensory Physiology*, vol. VII/2, M.G.F. Fuortes, Ed. New York: Springer-Verlag, 1972.
[13] F. W. Campbell and D. G. Green, "Optical and retinal factors affecting visual resolution," *J. Physiology*, vol. 181, no. 3, pp. 576–593, Dec. 1965.
[14] M. Millodot, "Effect of the abberations of the eye on visual perception," in *Visual Psychophysics and Physiology*, J. C. Armington, J. Krauskopf, and B. R. Wooten, Eds. New York: Academic Press, 1978, ch. 35, pp. 441–452.

[15] M. Hines, "Line spread function variation near the fovea," *Vision Res.*, vol. 16, pp. 567–572, 1976.

[16] J. O. Limb and C. B. Rubinstein, "A model of threshold vision incorporating inhomogeneity of the visual field," *Vision Res.*, vol. 17, pp. 571–584, 1977.

[17] F. W. Campbell and R. W. Gubisch, "Optical quality of the human eye," *J. Physiol.*, vol. 186, no. 3, pp. 558–578, Oct. 1966.

[18] C. T. Morgan, *Physiological Psychology*. New York: McGraw-Hill, 1965.

[19] A. Rose, *Vision: Human and Electronic*. New York: Plenum Press, 1973.

[20] T. P. Williams and J. G. Gale, "Compression of retinal responsivity: V-log I functions and increment thresholds," *Vision Res.*, vol. 18, pp. 587–590, 1978.

[21] K. Naka and W. A. H. Rushton, "S-potentials from color units in the retina of fish (Cyprinidae)," *J. Physiology*, vol. 185, pp. 536–558, 1966.

[22] W. S. Stiles, "Increment thresholds and the mechanisms of color vision," *Documenta Opthal.*, vol. 3, pp. 138–163, 1949.

[23] M. Alpern, F. Maaseidvaag, and N. Ohla, "The kinetics of cone visual pigments in man," *Vision Res.*, vol. 11, pp. 539–549, 1971.

[24] R. A. Normann and F. S. Werblin, "Control of retinal sensitivity, I. Light and dark adaptation of vertibrate rods and cones," *J. Gen. Physiol.*, vol. 63, pp. 37–61, 1974.

[25] S. K. Shevell, "Saturation in human cones," *Vision Res.*, vol. 17, pp. 427–434, 1977.

[26] C. G. Boring, *A History of Experimental Psychology*. New York: Appleton-Century-Crofts, 1950, ch. 14, pp. 275–296.

[27] S. S. Stevens, "The psychophysics of sensory function," *Amer. Scientist*, vol. 48, pp. 226–253, 1960.

[28] D. Jameson and L. M. Hurvich, Eds., *Visual Psychophysics*, vol. 4 of the *Handbook of Sensory Physiology*. Berlin, Germany: Springer-Verlag, 1972.

[29] J. L. Mannos and D. J. Sakrison, "The effects of a visual fidelity criterion on the encoding of images," *IEEE Trans. Inform. Theory*, vol. IT-20, pp. 525–536, July 1974.

[30] R. J. W. Mansfield, "Visual adaptation: Retinal transduction, brightness and sensitivity," *Vision Res.*, vol. 16, pp. 679–690, 1976.

[31] D. A. Burkhardt and G. Hassin, "Retinal mechanisms of color vision," in *Visual Psychophysics and Physiology*, J. C. Armington, J. Krauskopf, and B. R. Wooten, Eds. New York: Academic Press, 1978, ch. 2, pp. 25–34.

[32] G. Wald, "The receptors of human color vision," *Science*, vol. 145, pp. 1007–1017, Sept. 4, 1964.

[33] S. L. Polyak, *The Retina*. Chicago, IL: Univ. Chicago Press, 1941.

[34] B. B. Boycott and J. E. Dowling, "Organization of the primate retina: Light microscopy," *Phil. Trans. Royal Soc. B*, vol. 255, pp. 109–184, 1969.

[35] F. Ratliff, *Mach Bands: Quantitative Studies on Neural Networks in the Retina*. San Francisco, CA: Holden-Day, 1965.

[36] D. Granrath and B. R. Hunt, "A two-channel model of image processing in the human retina," in *Proc. SPIE*, vol. 199, pp. 126–133, Aug. 1979.

[37] T. N. Wiesel and D. H. Hubel, "Spatial and chromatic interactions in the lateral geniculate body of the rhesus monkey," *J. Neurophysiol.*, vol. 29, pp. 1115–1156, 1966.

[38] D. G. Green and M. B. Fast, "On the appearance of mach bands in gradients of varying color," *Vision Res.*, vol. 11, pp. 1147–1155, 1971.

[39] A. Eisner and P. I. A. MacLeod, "Blue-sensitive cones do not contribute to luminance as defined by flicker photometry," *J. Opt. Soc. Amer.*, vol. 70, no. 1, pp. 121–123, Jan. 1980.

[40] E. L. Hall, *Computer Image Processing and Recognition*. New York: Academic Press, 1979, ch. 2.

[41] G. J. C. Van Der Horst, C. M. M. DeWeert, and M. A. Bouman, "Transfer of spatial chromaticity-contrast at threshold in the human eye," *J. Opt. Soc. Amer.*, vol. 67, no. 10, pp. 1260–1266, Oct. 1967.

[42] R. L. DeValois and P. L. Pease, "Contours and contrast: Responses of monkey lateral geniculate nucleus cells to luminance and color figures," *Science*, vol. 171, pp. 694–696, Feb. 19, 1971.

[43] J. J. Koenderink, W. A. Van De Grind, and M. A. Bouman, "Foveal information processing at photopic luminances," vol. 8, no. 4, pp. 128–144, 1971.

[44] K. Motokawa, *Physiology of Color and Pattern Vision*. Tokyo, Japan: Igaku Shoin Ltd., 1970, ch. 11.

[45] J. J. Koenderink, W. A. Van De Grind, and M. A. Bouman, "Opponent color coding: A mechanistic model and a new metric for color space," *Kybernetik*, vol. 10, no. 2, pp. 78–98, 1972.

[46] C. F. Hall and E. L. Hall, "A nonlinear model for the spatial characteristics of the human visual system," *IEEE Trans. Syst., Man, Cybern.*, vol. SMC-7, pp. 161–170, Mar. 1977.

[47] C. F. Hall, "Digital color image compression in a perceptual space," USC Image Processing Inst. Rep. 790, Feb. 1978.

[48] O. D. Faugeras, "Digital color image processing within the framework of a human visual model," *IEEE Trans. Acoust., Speech, Signal Processing*, vol. ASSP-27, pp. 380–393, Aug. 1979.

[49] G. E. Legge, "Sustained and transient mechanisms in human vision: Temporal and spatial properties," *Vision Res.*, vol. 18, pp. 69–81, 1978.

[50] H. F. J. M. Buffart, "Brightness and contrast," in *Formal Theories of Visual Perception*, E. Leeuwenberg and H. Buffart, Eds. New York: Wiley, 1978, ch. 8, pp. 171–182.

[51] D. J. Granrath, "Models of human vision in digital image bandwidth compression," Ph.D. dissertation, Univ. Arizona, Tucson, 1979.

[52] L. G. Roberts, "Picture coding using pseudorandom noise," *IRE Trans. Inform. Theory*, vol. IT-18, pp. 145–154, Feb. 1962.

[53] R. J. Rom, "Image transmission and coding based on human vision," Ph.D. dissertation, Univ. California, Berkeley, Dec. 1972.

[54] W. A. Pearlman, "A visual system model and a new distortion measure in the context of image processing," *J. Opt. Soc. Amer.*, vol. 68, no. 3, pp. 374–386, Mar. 1978.

[55] J. O. Limb, "Distortion criteria of the human viewer," *IEEE Trans. Syst., Man, Cybern.*, vol. SMC-9, pp. 778–793, Dec. 1979.

[56] W. K. Pratt, *Digital Image Processing*. New York: Wiley, 1978, p. 316.

[57] W. F. Schreiber, "Wirephoto quality improvement by unsharp masking," *J. Pattern Recognition* (Pergamon Press, London), vol. 2, pp. 121–171, 1970.

[58] A. V. Oppenheim and R. W. Schafer, *Digital Signal Processing*. Englewood Cliffs, NJ: Prentice-Hall, 1975, ch. 10, pp. 487–490.

[59] A. V. Oppenheim, R. W. Schafer, and T. G. Stockham, Jr., "Nonlinear filtering of multiplied and convolved signals," *Proc. IEEE*, vol. 56, pp. 1264–1291, Aug. 1968.

[60] G. S. Robinson and W. Frei, "Final research report on computer processing of ERTS images," Univ. Southern California, Image Processing Institute, Report USCIPI 640, Sept. 1975.

Computer Vision: A Source of Models for Biological Visual Processes?

AZRIEL ROSENFELD, FELLOW, IEEE

(*Invited Paper*)

Abstract—This paper reviews some basic computer vision techniques and speculates about their possible relevance to the modeling of human visual processes. Special emphasis is given to image segmentation techniques and how they relate to processes of perceptual organization, such as those embodied in the Gestalt "laws."

I. INTRODUCTION

VISION is a valuable sense; it provides high-resolution, high-precision measurements of the light that reaches an organism from its surroundings. Humans and animals are able to extract many types of useful information about their surroundings from these measurements. The goal of computer vision research is to provide computers with analogous abilities.

The designers of computer vision systems are not trying to model biological vision. They need to solve many of the same computational problems that biological visual systems solve, but they are not constrained to use the same methods. Most of their methods, in fact, have been developed without taking into account what is known about biological vision, and many of them do not have natural implementations in neural hardware. Nevertheless, those who study human and animal vision may find at least some computer vision techniques of interest as a potential source of computational models for biological visual processes.

We will not attempt in this paper to present a comprehensive survey of computer vision techniques and their possible biological relevance. Rather, we will deal almost entirely with a particular class of techniques that seem to play a key role in the early stages of the visual process—namely, techniques for segmenting the image into distinctive parts. For simplicity, we will deal only with the processing of a single, static, grayscale image; we will not consider color, stereopsis, or time sequences of images.

General overviews of computer vision can be found in the textbooks and collections [1]–[9]. Several of these, notably [4] and [9], give particular emphasis to the relationships between biological and computer vision, and one of them [5] is primarily devoted to a computational model of human vision (but does not deal with the problem of segmentation).

Manuscript received January 18, 1988.
The author is with the Center for Automation Research, University of Maryland, College Park, MD 20742.
IEEE Log Number 8824420.

II. SEGMENTATION TECHNIQUES

When we look at a scene, we do not perceive an array of brightnesses; usually, we see a collection of regions separated by more or less well-defined edges. In computer vision, processes that decompose a scene into parts are called segmentation techniques. In this section, we briefly summarize the basic techniques that can be used to segment images, and speculate on their possible biological relevance.

A. Thresholding

If a scene contains bright objects on a dark background (or vice versa), the objects can be segmented from the background by "thresholding," i.e., finding a brightness value t such that nearly all image points belonging to the objects have brightnesses greater than t, and nearly all those belonging to the background have brightnesses less than t. To find t, we measure the brightness at every point, and count how often each brightness value occurs; the graph of these values is called the image's *histogram*. The points belonging to the background should give rise to a peak in this graph since there are many of them, and similarly for the points belonging to the objects, whereas between these peaks there should be a valley since points of intermediate brightness should be rare. (A histogram that contains two peaks separated by a valley is called *bimodal*.) Thus, we can choose t by plotting the image's histogram, finding the peaks, and taking t (say) at the bottom of the valley between the peaks.

Thresholding is psychologically plausible, in the sense that when we look at a scene containing bright objects on a dark background, we do indeed perceive it as consisting of two types of regions, whose points lie in two different brightness ranges. But it does not seem likely that biological visual systems explicitly compute histograms of brightnesses and analyze them. In the next section, we will present some speculations about a method of detecting bimodality of brightness, without the need for histogram computation.

B. Edge (or Feature) Detection

An edge is an abrupt change in brightness; thus, brightness differences have high (absolute) values at points that lie on edges. Many dozens of edge detection operators have been defined in the computer vision literature. We

Reprinted from *IEEE Trans. Biomed. Eng.*, vol. 36, no. 1, pp. 93–96, Jan, 1989.

62

will not attempt to describe them here; suffice it to say that most of them detect edges as maxima of first differences of brightness, or as zero crossings of second differences. The differences are typically computed at each point of the image by subtracting weighted local averages of brightness, taken over various neighborhoods of the point.

Similar remarks apply to the detection of other types of brightness discontinuities, such as lines (or, more generally, bars), line ends, and spots. Such "features" are commonly detected by computing appropriate types of brightness differences in the vicinity of each point. For example, suppose we compute a weighted average of the brightness in an elongated neighborhood of a point, and subtract from it a weighted average of the brightness in a pair of flanking elongated neighborhoods; then the result will have a high value if there is a bright bar through the point, oriented in the direction of elongation.

It is well known that difference operators of these types are in fact computed by many biological visual systems, so there is no question about their biological plausibility. However, it should be realized that such operations in themselves do not yield a segmentation off the image. They detect edges or lines *locally*, i.e., they provide evidence that an edge or line passes through a given point; but they do not explicitly link these local features into "global" region boundaries or curves. Conventionally, such global features are extracted by sequential "tracking" of the features from point to point. Such tracking is biologically plausible, but it is slow; it does not account for our ability to perceive long curves and edges "at a glance." In the next section, we will suggest a fast approach to global feature extraction that might conceivably have a biological realization.

C. Region Growing

Thresholding segments an image into bright and dark regions without regard to how complex the shapes of the regions are; in fact, they need not be connected, but can be composed of arbitrary sets of points. A more refined approach to segmentation is to divide the image into connected regions, each of which has approximately constant brightness. Many algorithms have been developed to do this; for example, one can "grow" a connected bright region by starting from a bright point, and successively incorporating bright points into the growing region if they are adjacent to points already incorporated. As in the case of global edge or curve tracking, this sequential approach is slow; it does not suffice to account for the human ability to perceive large connected regions "at a glance." On the other hand, this ability is not equally effective for regions of arbitrary shapes. Complex or elongated regions can be distinguished at a glance, but if an image contains two complex "interlocked" regions (e.g., two interlocked spirals), it is hard to tell that there are two of them (rather than one that doubles back on itself). In the next section, we will suggest a possible basis for the fast segmentation of regions of simple shapes.

D. Textural Segmentation

The segmentation techniques described up to now assume that the image consists of regions (or sets of points) having approximately constant brightnesses, separated by brightness discontinuities ("edges"). More generally, one often wants to segment an image into regions of uniform "texture," i.e., regions in which the local spatial *variations* in brightness are approximately stationary.

There are many standard approaches to the textural analysis of images. One of the simplest is based on the trick of converting textural differences into brightness differences by computing a set of suitably defined local properties at each point of the image. If a given type of textured region contains many repetitions of a certain local pattern, we compute a local property at each point for which that pattern yields a high value; in the resulting array of local property values, the region now contains many high-valued points, while regions that are texturally dissimilar to it do not. In principle, this trick allows us to segment an image into differently textured regions by computing local property arrays and then applying thresholding, edge detection, or region growing to them. Thus, if we can define biologically plausible techniques for segmenting images based on (approximate) constancy of gray level, it should in principle be possible to generalize these techniques to segment images based on (approximate) stationarity of texture.

III. Fast Segmentation

In this section, we briefly describe a class of fast image segmentation techniques that could conceivably provide ideas for modeling biological visual processes. Specifically, we describe techniques for bimodality detection, global edge or curve extraction, and blob or ribbon extraction. More detailed descriptions of these techniques can be found in [10] and in the references cited therein.

The techniques described here are designed for implementation on an exponentially tapering "pyramid" of processing elements. A pyramid is a stack of arrays, each (say) half the size of the one below it. Each processor (for brevity: "node") is connected to its neighbors on its own level of the stack, and also to a small block of "children" on the level below it. The image is input to the bottom level, (say) one pixel per mode.

The basic idea of the algorithms in this section is that the nodes at successively higher levels obtain information about successively bigger blocks of the image by combining the information provided by their children. The nodes at each level do this in parallel; each of them does only a bounded amount of computation since it has only a small block of children. After k stages of this process, the nodes at level k have obtained information about large blocks of the image, e.g., of size $2^k \times 2^k$. Thus, this approach allows us to obtain global information about an image in a relatively small number of computational steps.

A. Biomodality Detection

Suppose that each node on the first level (the level above the bottom) examines the pixels input to its children and finds the "best" partition of these pixels into two disjoint brightness ranges ("best" in the sense that the ranges are narrowest and farthest apart). The node stores the endpoints of the two ranges and the number of pixels in each of them. Each node on the second level examines the pairs of ranges computed by its children and finds the "best" combination of them into a single pair of ranges. (It may no longer be possible for these two ranges to be disjoint, but the node finds the "best" pair in the sense of smallest overlap.) This process is repeated on the third, fourth, · · · , levels. If the two ranges computed in this way by the node at the top of the pyramid have a sufficiently small overlap, we can conclude that the image is bimodal. (If desired, the means of the ranges can also be computed by each node based on the information provided by its children.)

The computation just described may seem unusual from the standpoint of biological implementation. Conventional neural computations typically involve linear combinations of inputs, rather than comparisons. But there is no fundamental reason why such computations could not be performed by small assemblies of neurons.

Bimodality detection can serve as a basis for an important type of texture-based segmentation known as "similarity grouping." Suppose an image contains two types of local patterns of brightness—for example, horizontal streaks and vertical streaks. By computing an appropriate local property at each point of the image—for example, a property that has high values at points lying on horizontal streaks—we obtain a derived image that has a bimodal distribution of values. The local property can be computed in parallel at the bottom level of the pyramid (using the connections between neighboring nodes), and the bimodality can then be detected as described above.

B. Edge (or Curve) Extraction

To extract edges or curves using a pyramid of nodes, we begin by performing local edge (or curve) detection at the bottom level of the pyramid, using the neighbor connections. Each node on the first level now examines the edge elements in its block of the image and groups them into smoothly connected edges. (Since the block is small and contains only a few edge elements, this requires only a limited amount of computation.) The node stores the endpoint positions (and slopes) of these edges. Each node on the second level now examines its children's sets of edges and, when possible, combines them into longer smoothly connected edges. This process is repeated on successively higher levels. If desired, the nodes can also store properties of the curves, such as arc length, average curvature, etc. Thus, if the image contains only a few connected edges, the node at the top of the pyramid can compute their properties in a small number of steps. [If the image contains many small edge fragments, it would be computationally expensive for the nodes at high levels to keep track of them; instead, they can be discarded, or if desired, the nodes can keep only statistical information about them (e.g., their average lengths, curvatures, etc.).]

Here again, the computations (comparing endpoint coordinates, etc.) are not of the conventional "neural" types, but there is no reason why they could not be carried out by small networks of neurons. The process of linking edge or curve elements into smoothly connected global edges or curves can be regarded as a computational implementation of "good continuation" grouping.

C. Blob (or Ribbon) Detection

If each node at each successive level of a pyramid simply computes a weighted average of its children's values, we obtain at each level a reduced-resolution version of the input image. (In fact, it can be shown that for a wide range of choices of the weights given to the children, the weighted averages (of large image blocks) obtained at high levels have weights that very closely approximate a Gaussian.) This uses a pyramid to efficiently perform a very conventional "neural" type of computation.

When we reduce the resolution of the image, blobs (i.e., compact regions) of all sizes become progressively smaller, and at some level of the pyramid (before disappearing entirely) they become spots, which are detectable by a suitable local operation (e.g., compare the value at each point with the values at its neighbors) that can be carried out using the neighbor connections. Similarly, thick streaks become progressively thinner, and at some level (before disappearing entirely) they become thin curves, which are detectable locally. Thus, bloblike and ribbon-like regions in the image that contrast with their surroundings can be detected by using the pyramid to construct reduced-resolution versions of the image and then applying suitable local operations at every level of the pyramid.

This method immediately generalizes to the detection of bloblike or ribbonlike regions that differ texturally from their surroundings. As before, we simply compute a suitable local property at each point of the image, using the neighbor connections at the bottom level of the pyramid, and thereby convert the textural difference into a difference in average "brightness." Segmentation of compact or elongated (= bloblike or ribbonlike) regions that differ texturally from their surrounds can be regarded as a form of "proximity grouping."

An alternative method of detecting blobs or ribbons is to first extract connected edges from the image, as described in Section III-B. At each level of the pyramid, we then look for points that are locally surrounded by edges (facing away from each other) on two sides or on all sides. In the former case, we have detected a ribbon; in the latter case, a blob. This edge-based method of detecting such regions can be regarded as an implementation of "closure" grouping.

IV. Concluding Remarks

Segmentation is a basic step in most computer vision applications, but many of the standard segmentation techniques involve biologically "unnatural" computations. In this paper, we have sketched a class of pyramid-based segmentation techniques that have properties and limitations that in some ways resemble those of human perception. It would be of interest to investigate whether techniques of this type might be implemented in biological visual systems.

References

[1] D. H. Ballard and C. M. Brown, *Computer Vision*. Englewood Cliffs, NJ: Prentice-Hall, 1982.

[2] J. M. Brady, Ed., *Computer Vision*. Amsterdam: North-Holland, 1981.

[3] B. K. P. Horn, *Robot Vision*. Cambridge, MA: M.I.T. Press, and New York: McGraw-Hill, 1986.

[4] M. D. Levine, *Vision in Man and Machine*. New York: McGraw-Hill, 1985.

[5] D. Marr, *Vision*. San Francisco: Freeman, 1982.

[6] R. Nevatia, *Machine Perception*. Englewood Cliffs, NJ: Prentice-Hall, 1982.

[7] T. Pavlidis, *Structural Pattern Recognition*. Berlin: Springer, 1977.

[8] A. Rosenfeld and A. C. Kak, *Digital Picture Processing*, 2nd ed. New York: Academic, 1982.

[9] P. H. Winston, Ed., *The Psychology of Computer Vision*. New York: McGraw-Hill, 1975.

[10] A. Rosenfeld, "Pyramid algorithms for efficient vision," in *Vision: Coding and Efficiency*, C. Blakemore, Ed. Cambridge: Cambridge Univ. Press, 1988.

Part 2
Neuronal Morphology
of Biological Systems

Understanding the morphology of biological neural systems is a challenge, and scientists from many disciplines are thriving on this challenge.

THE carbon-based cognitive faculty, the brain, has a very complex morphology. All our actions, from simple to complex, are controlled by this mysterious organ. The brain enables us to see, perceive, think, and learn. We are able to write and recite poetry. We can compose music and play musical instruments. We enjoy the beauty of snow peaks and that of the blue sky. Some events make us happy and we laugh, while others make us unhappy and we cry or get angry. We are able to devise mechanisms for solving complex problems by recalling what we know, and incorporating new concepts. Intuition tells us that the organ responsible for doing all these wonderful things must be complex. Indeed, the brain is too complex to understand. It is wrong to call it a computer because, unlike a computer, it does things beyond numerical computation, such as cognition and perception. Nature has given this cognitive faculty a marvelous morphology that is, unfortunately, beyond the understanding of our human minds. Yet we know that it is composed of a large number of nerve cells (neurons) with a high degree of interconnectivity. There are over 10^{11} (one hundred billion) nerve cells, and each neuron, on the average, receives information from about 10^4 neighboring neurons. Thus, there are typically over 10^{15} connections (synapses) in the brain. The anatomical morphology of these neurons and their connections are what make the brain so complex, and yet it is very effective in conducting various cognitive tasks.

The objective of Part Two of this volume is to give a broad view of biological neural morphology, which is the foundation of our further investigation into neuro-vision processes. Let us look at our own visual experience. When we write and read these lines, the photonic energy emitting from these lines strikes the photoreceptors—125 million rods and 5 million cones—in each retina. Complex biochemical reactions occur in the photoreceptors that change the photonic energy into equivalent electrical impulses. The task of the retina and the rest of the brain is not only to coordinate the function of our hands (in writing) and eyes (in reading), but also to think and extract useful cognitive information from the messages written in these lines. It would be wonderful if we could explain this phenomenon of neural computing in our retina and brain. In spite of tremendous progress in neurophysiology, our knowledge of biological neural computing is largely shrouded by ignorance. However, over the last decade or so, scientists and engineers have embarked on the creation of an artificial neural computing machine.

In this part, we introduce readers to a collection of four basic tutorial articles, all written by experts in the field and taken from the journal *Scientific American*. The first article, (2.1), by C. F. Stevens, provides a very good description of the biological neurons as the building blocks of the brain. E. R. Kandel explains how small sets (systems) of neurons can form some intricate functions of the brain, such as learning and memory, in article (2.2). The author draws on his own studies of the large snail *Aplysia* to illustrate how such systems are the elementary units for performing mental functions. The understanding of such small-scale morphology is very important for creating artificial neural systems for vision and control.

In article (2.3), we learn from R. E. Kalil how the synaptic connections are formed in the mammalian brain as it develops. It is remarkable that the complex structure of the brain evolves from a single collection of immature and undifferentiated cells. The formation of synaptic connections explains many phenomena, such as learning and memory.

These three articles represent merely a small sample of articles taken from a large volume of literature that exists in the area of neuronal morphology of biological systems. Hopefully, this sample, along with the cited references, will provide new directions to readers for further work in the field. The next part of this volume contains articles related to artificial neural systems.

Further Reading

[1] C. Aoki and P. Siekevitz, "Plasticity in brain development," *Sci. Amer.*, Dec., vol. 259, No. 6, pp. 56–64, 1988.

[2] B. G. Cragg and H. N. V. Temperley, "Memory: The analogy with ferromagnetic hysteresis," *Brain*, vol. 78, pp. 304–316, 1955.

[3] F. Crick, "Memory and molecular turnover," *Nature*, vol. 312, p. 101, 1984.

[4] W. J. Freeman, *Mass Action in the Nervous System*. New York: Academic Press, 1975.

[5] W. J. Freeman, "The physiological basis of mental images," *Biol. Psych.*, vol. 18, no. 10, pp. 1107–1125, 1983.

[6] J. M. Fuster and G. E. Alexander, "Neuron activity related to short-term memory," *Science*, vol. 173, pp. 652–654, 1971.

[7] D. O. Hebb, *The organization of behavior: A neuropsychological theory*, New York: John Wiley & Sons, 1949.

[8] D. H. Hubel, *Eye, Brain and Vision*. New York: W. H. Freeman and Co., 1988.

[9] D. H. Hubel, "The brain," *Sci. Amer.*, vol. 241, no. 3, pp. 45–53, 1979.

[10] L. L. Iverson, "The chemistry of the brain," *Sci. Amer.*, vol. 241, no. 3, pp. 134–149, 1979.

[11] E. R. Kandel and J. H. Schwartz, *Principles of Neural Science*. New York: North-Holland, 1985.

[12] R. J. MacGregor and E. R. Lewis, *Neural Modeling: Electrical Signal Processing in the Nervous System*. New York: Plenum Press, 1977.

[13] R. F. Schmidt, Ed., *Fundamentals of Sensory Physiology*. New York: Springer-Verlag, 1981.

[14] G. Schoner and J. A. S. Kelso, "Dynamic pattern generation in behavioral and neural systems," *Science*, vol. 239, pp. 1513–1520, 1988.

[15] A. C. Scott, *Neurophysics*. New York: John Wiley & Sons, 1977.

The Neuron

*It is the individual nerve cell, the building block of the brain.
It transmits nerve impulses over a single long fiber (the axon)
and receives them over numerous short fibers (the dendrites)*

by Charles F. Stevens

Neurons, or nerve cells, are the building blocks of the brain. Although they have the same genes, the same general organization and the same biochemical apparatus as other cells, they also have unique features that make the brain function in a very different way from, say, the liver. The important specializations of the neuron include a distinctive cell shape, an outer membrane capable of generating nerve impulses, and a unique structure, the synapse, for transferring information from one neuron to the next.

The human brain is thought to consist of 10^{11} neurons, about the same number as the stars in our galaxy. No two neurons are identical in form. Nevertheless, their forms generally fall into only a few broad categories, and most neurons share certain structural features that make it possible to distinguish three regions of the cell: the cell body, the dendrites and the axon. The cell body contains the nucleus of the neuron and the biochemical machinery for synthesizing enzymes and other molecules essential to the life of the cell. Usually the cell body is roughly spherical or pyramid-shaped. The dendrites are delicate tube-like extensions that tend to branch repeatedly and form a bushy tree around the cell body. They provide the main physical surface on which the neuron receives incoming signals. The axon extends away from the cell body and provides the pathway over which signals can travel from the cell body for long distances to other parts of the brain and the nervous system. The axon differs from the dendrites both in structure and in the properties of its outer membrane. Most axons are longer and thinner than dendrites and exhibit a different branching pattern: whereas the branches of dendrites tend to cluster near the cell body, the branches of axons tend to arise at the end of the fiber where the axon communicates with other neurons.

The functioning of the brain depends on the flow of information through elaborate circuits consisting of networks of neurons. Information is transferred from one cell to another at specialized points of contact: the synapses. A typical neuron may have anywhere from 1,000 to 10,000 synapses and may receive information from something like 1,000 other neurons. Although synapses are most often made between the axon of one cell and the dendrite of another, there are other kinds of synaptic junction: between axon and axon, between dendrite and dendrite and between axon and cell body.

At a synapse the axon usually enlarges to form a terminal button, which is the information-delivering part of the junction. The terminal button contains tiny spherical structures called synaptic vesicles, each of which can hold several thousand molecules of chemical transmitter. On the arrival of a nerve impulse at the terminal button, some of the vesicles discharge their contents into the narrow cleft that separates the button from the membrane of another cell's dendrite, which is designed to receive the chemical message. Hence information is relayed from one neuron to another by means of a transmitter. The "firing" of a neuron—the generation of nerve impulses—reflects the activation of hundreds of synapses by impinging neurons. Some synapses are excitatory in that they tend to promote firing, whereas others are inhibitory and so are capable of canceling signals that otherwise would excite a neuron to fire.

Although neurons are the building blocks of the brain, they are not the only kind of cell in it. For example, oxygen and nutrients are supplied by a dense network of blood vessels. There is also a need for connective tissue, particularly at the surface of the brain. A major class of cells in the central nervous system is the glial cells, or glia. The glia occupy essentially all the space in the nervous system not taken up by the neurons themselves. Although the function of the glia is not fully understood, they provide structural and metabolic support for the delicate meshwork of the neurons.

One other kind of cell, the Schwann cell, is ubiquitous in the nervous system. All axons appear to be jacketed by Schwann cells. In some cases the Schwann cells simply enclose the axon in a thin layer. In many cases, however, the Schwann cell wraps itself around the axon in the course of embryonic development, giving rise to the multiple dense layers of insulation known as myelin. The myelin sheath is interrupted every millimeter or so along the axon by narrow gaps called the nodes of Ranvier. In axons that are sheathed in this way the nerve impulse travels by jumping from node to node, where the extracellular fluid can make direct contact with the cell membrane. The myelin sheath seems to have evolved as a means of conserving the neuron's metabolic energy. In general myelinated nerve fibers conduct nerve impulses faster than unmyelinated fibers.

Neurons can work as they do because their outer membranes have special

NEURON FROM A CAT'S VISUAL CORTEX has been labeled in the photomicrograph on the opposite page by injection with the enzyme horseradish peroxidase. The cell bodies in the background are counterstained with a magenta dye. All the fibers extending from the cell body are dendrites, which receive information from other neurons. The fiber that transmits information, the axon, is much finer and not readily visible at this magnification. The thickest fiber, extending vertically upward, is known as the apical dendrite, only a small portion of which falls within this section. At this magnification (about 500 diameters) the complete apical dendrite would be about 75 centimeters long. (It can be traced through adjacent sections.) The activity of this particular cell was recorded in the living animal and was found to respond optimally to a light-dark border rotated about 60 degrees from the vertical. The neuron is classified as a pyramidal cell because of its form. It is one of two major types in cortex of mammals. Micrograph was made by Charles Gilbert and Torsten N. Wiesel of Harvard Medical School.

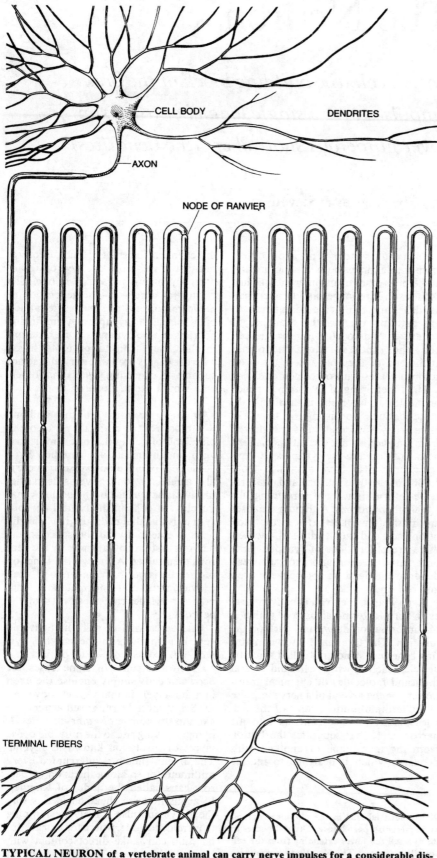

CELL BODY

DENDRITES

AXON

NODE OF RANVIER

TERMINAL FIBERS

TYPICAL NEURON of a vertebrate animal can carry nerve impulses for a considerable distance. The neuron depicted here, with its various parts drawn to scale, is enlarged 250 times. The nerve impulses originate in the cell body and are propagated along the axon, which may have one or more branches. This axon, which is folded for diagrammatic purposes, would be a centimeter long at actual size. Some axons are more than a meter long. The axon's terminal branches form synapses with as many as 1,000 other neurons. Most synapses join the axon terminals of one neuron with the dendrites forming a "tree" around the cell body of another neuron. Thus the dendrites surrounding the neuron in the diagram might receive incoming signals from tens, hundreds or even thousands of other neurons. Many axons, such as this one, are insulated by a myelin sheath interrupted at intervals by the regions known as nodes of Ranvier.

properties. Along the axon the membrane is specialized to propagate an electrical impulse. At the terminal of the axon the membrane releases transmitters, and on the dendrites it reponds to transmitters. In addition the membrane mediates the recognition of other cells in embryonic development, so that each cell finds its proper place in the network of 10^{11} cells. Much recent investigation therefore focuses on the membrane properties responsible for the nerve impulse, for synaptic transmission, for cell-cell recognition and for structural contacts between cells.

The neuron membrane, like the outer membrane of all cells, is about five nanometers thick and consists of two layers of lipid molecules arranged with their hydrophilic ends pointing toward the water on the inside and outside of the cell and with their hydrophobic ends pointing away from the water to form the interior of the membrane. The lipid parts of the membrane are about the same for all kinds of cells. What makes one cell membrane different from another are various specific proteins that are associated with the membrane in one way or another. Proteins that are actually embedded in the lipid bilayer are termed intrinsic proteins. Other proteins, the peripheral membrane proteins, are attached to the membrane surface but do not form an integral part of its structure. Because the membrane lipid is fluid even the intrinsic proteins are often free to move by diffusion from place to place. In some instances, however, the proteins are firmly fastened down by a substructure.

The membrane proteins of all cells fall into five classes: pumps, channels, receptors, enzymes and structural proteins. Pumps expend metabolic energy to move ions and other molecules against concentration gradients in order to maintain appropriate concentrations of these molecules within the cell. Because charged molecules do not pass through the lipid bilayer itself cells have evolved channel proteins that provide selective pathways through which specific ions can diffuse. Cell membranes must recognize and attach many types of molecules. Receptor proteins fulfill these functions by providing binding sites with great specificity and high affinity. Enzymes are placed in or on the membrane to facilitate chemical reactions at the membrane surface. Finally, structural proteins both interconnect cells to form organs and help to maintain subcellular structure. These five classes of membrane proteins are not necessarily mutually exclusive. For example, a particular protein might simultaneously be a receptor, an enzyme and a pump.

Membrane proteins are the key to understanding neuron function and therefore brain function. Because they play such a central role in modern views of the neuron, I shall organize my discussion around a description of an ion pump, various types of channel and some other proteins that taken together endow neurons with their unique properties. The general idea will be to summarize the important characteristics of the membrane proteins and to explain how these characteristics account for the nerve impulse and other complex features of neuron function.

Like all cells the neuron is able to maintain within itself a fluid whose composition differs markedly from that of the fluid outside it. The difference is particularly striking with regard to the concentration of the ions of sodium and potassium. The external medium is about 10 times richer in sodium than the internal one, and the internal medium is about 10 times richer in potassium than the external one. Both sodium and potassium leak through pores in the cell membrane, so that a pump must operate continuously to exchange sodium ions that have entered the cell for potassium ions outside it. The pumping is accomplished by an intrinsic membrane protein called the sodium-potassium adenosine triphosphatase pump, or more often simply the sodium pump.

The protein molecule (or complex of protein subunits) of the sodium pump has a molecular weight of about 275,000 daltons and measures roughly six by eight nanometers, or slightly more than the thickness of the cell membrane. Each sodium pump can harness the energy stored in the phosphate bond of adenosine triphosphate (ATP) to exchange three sodium ions on the inside of the cell for two potassium ions on the outside. Operating at the maximum rate, each pump can transport across the membrane some 200 sodium ions and 130 potassium ions per second. The actual rate, however, is adjusted to meet the needs of the cell. Most neurons have between 100 and 200 sodium pumps per square micrometer of membrane surface, but in some parts of their surface the density is as much as 10 times higher. A typical small neuron has perhaps a million sodium pumps with a capacity to move about 200 million sodium ions per second. It is the transmembrane gradients of sodium and potassium ions that enable the neuron to propagate nerve impulses.

Membrane proteins that serve as channels are essential for many aspects of neuron function, particularly for the nerve impulse and synaptic transmission. As an introduction to the role played by channels in the electrical activity of the brain I shall briefly describe the mechanism of the nerve impulse and then return to a more systematic survey of channel properties.

Since the concentration of sodium and potassium ions on one side of the cell membrane differs from that on the

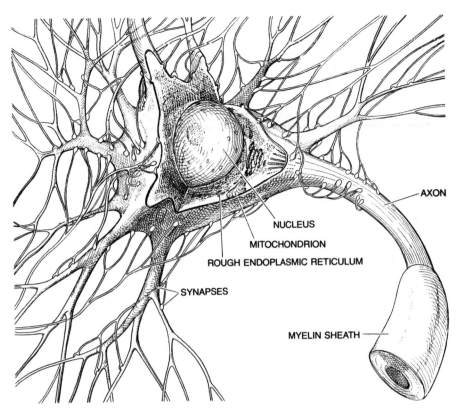

CELL BODY OF A NEURON incorporates the genetic material and complex metabolic apparatus common to all cells. Unlike most other cells, however, neurons do not divide after embryonic development; an organism's original supply must serve a lifetime. Projecting from the cell body are several dendrites and a single axon. The cell body and dendrites are covered by synapses, knoblike structures where information is received from other neurons. Mitochondria provide the cell with energy. Proteins are synthesized on the endoplasmic reticulum. A transport system moves proteins and other substances from cell body to sites where they are needed.

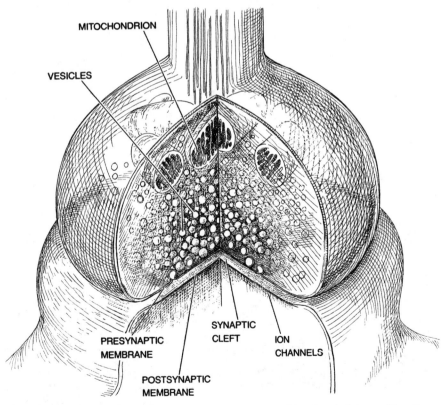

SYNAPSE is the relay point where information is conveyed by chemical transmitters from neuron to neuron. A synapse consists of two parts: the knoblike tip of an axon terminal and the receptor region on the surface of another neuron. The membranes are separated by a synaptic cleft some 200 nanometers across. Molecules of chemical transmitter, stored in vesicles in the axon terminal, are released into the cleft by arriving nerve impulses. Transmitter changes electrical state of the receiving neuron, making it either more likely or less likely to fire an impulse.

other side, the interior of the axon is about 70 millivolts negative with respect to the exterior. In their classic studies of nerve-impulse transmission in the giant axon of the squid a quarter of a century ago, A. L. Hodgkin, A. F. Huxley and Bernhard Katz of Britain demonstrated that the propagation of the nerve impulse coincides with sudden changes in the permeability of the axon membrane to sodium and potassium ions. When a nerve impulse starts at the origin of the axon, having been triggered in most cases by the cell body in response to dendritic synapses, the voltage difference across the axon membrane is locally lowered. Immediately ahead of the electrically altered region (in the direction in which the nerve impulse is propagated) channels in the membrane open and let sodium ions pour into the axon.

The process is self-reinforcing: the flow of sodium ions through the membrane opens more channels and makes it easier for other ions to follow. The sodium ions that enter change the internal potential of the membrane from negative to positive. Soon after the sodium channels open they close, and another group of channels open that let potassium ions flow out. This outflow restores the voltage inside the axon to its resting value of −70 millivolts. The sharp positive and then negative charge, which shows up as a "spike" on an oscilloscope, is known as the action potential and is the electrical manifestation of the nerve impulse. The wave of voltage sweeps along until it reaches the end of the axon much as a flame travels along the fuse of a firecracker.

This brief description of the nerve impulse illustrates the importance of channels for the electrical activity of neurons and underscores two fundamental properties of channels: selectivity and gating. I shall discuss these two properties in turn. Channels are selectively permeable and selectivities vary widely. For example, one type of channel lets sodium ions pass through and largely excludes potassium ions, whereas another type of channel does the reverse. The selectivity, however, is seldom absolute. One type of channel that is fairly nonselective allows the passage of about 85 sodium ions for every 100 potassium ions; another more selective type passes only about seven sodium ions for every 100 potassium ions. The first type, known as the acetylcholine-activated channel, has a pore about .8 nanometer in diameter that is filled with water. The second type, known as the potassium channel, has a much smaller opening and contains less water.

The sodium ion is about 30 percent smaller than the potassium ion. The exact molecular structure that enables the larger ion to pass through the cell membrane more readily than the smaller one is not known. The general principles that underlie the discrimination, however, are understood. They involve interactions between ions and parts of the channel structure in conjunction with a particular ordering of water molecules within the pore.

The gating mechanism that regulates the opening and closing of membrane channels takes two main forms. One type of channel, mentioned above in the description of the nerve impulse, opens and closes in response to voltage differences across the cell membrane; it is therefore said to be voltage-gated. A second type of channel is chemically gated. Such channels respond only slightly if at all to voltage changes but open when a particular molecule—a transmitter—binds to a receptor region

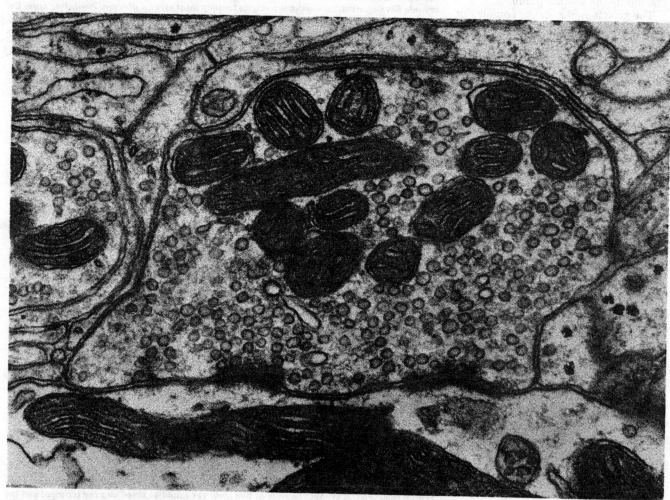

SYNAPTIC TERMINAL occupies most of this electron micrograph made by John E. Heuser of the University of California School of Medicine in San Francisco and Thomas S. Reese of the National Institutes of Health. The cleft separating the presynaptic membrane from the postsynaptic one undulates across the lower part of the picture. The large dark structures are mitochondria. The many round bodies are vesicles that hold transmitter. The fuzzy dark thickenings along the cleft are thought to be principal sites of transmitter release.

on the channel protein. Chemically gated channels are found in the receptive membranes of synapses and are responsible for translating the chemical signals produced by axon terminals into ion permeability changes during synaptic transmission. It is customary to name chemically gated channels according to their normal transmitter. Hence one speaks of acetylcholine-activated channels or GABA-activated channels. (GABA is gamma-aminobutyric acid.) Voltage-gated channels are generally named for the ion that passes through the channel most readily.

Proteins commonly change their shape as they function. Such alterations in shape, known as conformational changes, are dramatic for the contractile proteins responsible for cell motion, but they are no less important in many enzymes and other proteins. Conformational changes in channel proteins form the basis for gating as they serve to open and close the channel by slight movements of critically placed portions of the molecule that unblock and block the pore.

When either voltage-gated or chemically gated channels open and allow ions to pass, one can measure the resulting electric current. Quite recently it has become possible in a few instances to record the current flowing through a single channel, so that the opening and closing can be directly detected. One finds that the length of time a channel stays open varies randomly because the opening and closing of the channel represents a change in the conformation of the protein molecule embedded in the membrane. The random nature of the gating process arises from the haphazard collision of water molecules and other molecules with the structural elements of the channel.

In addition to ion pumps and channels neurons depend on other classes of membrane proteins for carrying out essential nervous-system functions. One of the important proteins is the enzyme adenylate cyclase, which helps to regulate the intracellular substance cyclic adenosine monophosphate (cyclic AMP). Cyclic nucleotides such as cyclic AMP take part in cell functions whose mechanisms are not yet understood in detail. The membrane enzyme adenylate cyclase appears to have two chief subunits, one catalytic and the other regulatory. The catalytic subunit promotes the formation of cyclic AMP. Various regulatory subunits, which are thought to be physically distinct from the catalytic one, can bind specific molecules (including transmitters that open and close channels) in order to control intracellular levels of cyclic AMP. The various types of regulatory subunit are named according to the molecule that normally binds to them; one, for example, is called serotonin-activated ade-

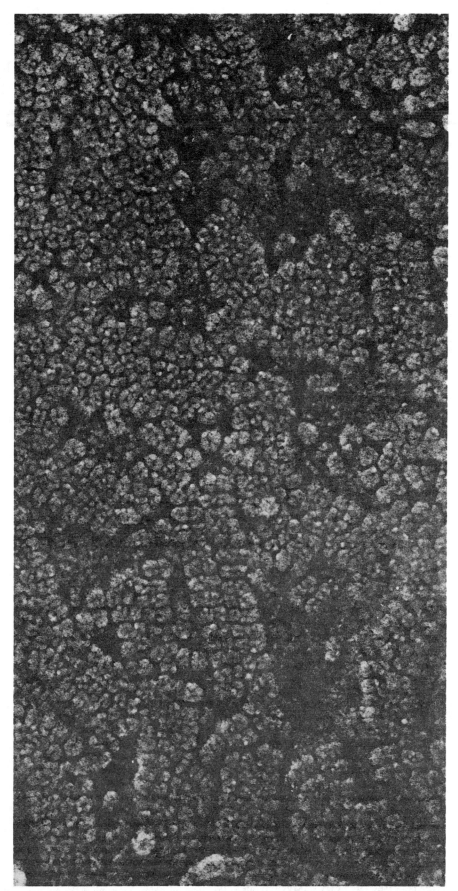

ACETYLCHOLINE-ACTIVATED CHANNELS are densely packed in the postsynaptic membrane of a cell in the electric organ of a torpedo, a fish that can administer an electric shock. This electron micrograph shows the platinum-plated replica of a membrane that had been frozen and etched. The size of the platinum particles limits the resolution to features larger than about two nanometers. According to recent evidence the channel protein molecule, which measures 8.5 nanometers across, consists of five subunits surrounding a channel whose narrowest dimension is .8 nanometer. The micrograph was made by Heuser and S. R. Salpeter.

73

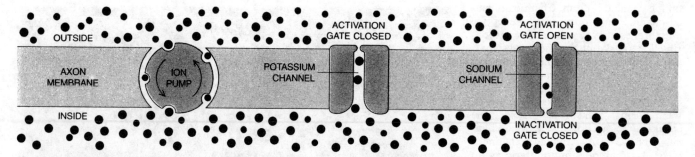

AXON MEMBRANE separates fluids that differ greatly in their content of sodium ions (*light dots*) and potassium ions (*black dots*). The exterior fluid is about 10 times richer in sodium ions than in potassium ions; in the interior fluid the ratio is the reverse. The membrane is penetrated by proteins that act as selective channels for preferentially passing either sodium or potassium ions. In the resting state, when no nerve impulse is being transmitted, the two types of channel are closed and an ion pump maintains the ionic disequilibrium by pumping out sodium ions in exchange for potassium ions. The interior of the axon is normally about 70 millivolts negative with respect to the exterior. If this voltage difference is reduced by the arrival of a nerve impulse, the sodium channel opens, allowing sodium ions to flow into the axon. An instant later the sodium channel closes and the potassium channel opens, allowing an outflow of potassium ions. The sequential opening and closing of the two kinds of channel effects the propagation of the nerve impulse, which is illustrated below.

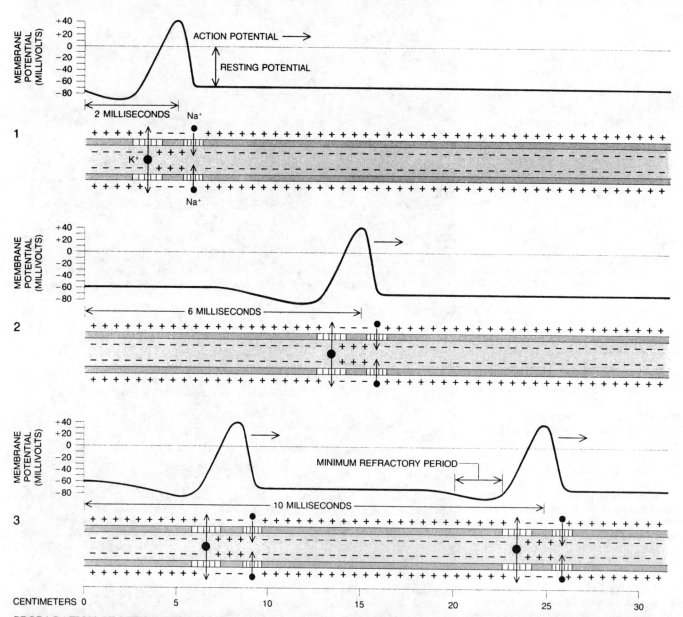

PROPAGATION OF NERVE IMPULSE along the axon coincides with a localized inflow of sodium ions (Na^+) followed by an outflow of potassium ions (K^+) through channels that are "gated," or controlled, by voltage changes across the axon membrane. The electrical event that sends a nerve impulse traveling down the axon normally originates in the cell body. The impulse begins with a slight depolarization, or reduction in the negative potential, across the membrane of the axon where it leaves the cell body. The slight voltage shift opens some of the sodium channels, shifting the voltage still further. The inflow of sodium ions accelerates until the inner surface of the membrane is locally positive. The voltage reversal closes the sodium channel and opens the potassium channel. The outflow of potassium ions quickly restores the negative potential. The voltage reversal, known as the action potential, propagates itself down the axon (*1, 2*). After a brief refractory period a second impulse can follow (*3*). The impulse-propagation speed is that measured in the giant axon of the squid.

nylate cyclase. Adenylate cyclase and related membrane enzymes are known to serve a number of regulatory functions in neurons, and the precise mechanisms of these actions are now under active investigation.

In the course of the embryonic development of the nervous system a cell must be able to recognize other cells so that the growth of each cell will proceed in the right direction and give rise to the right connections. The process of cell-cell recognition and the maintenance of the structure arrived at by such recognition depend on special classes of membrane proteins that are associated with unusual carbohydrates. The study of the protein-carbohydrate complexes associated with cell recognition is still at an early stage.

The intrinsic membrane proteins I have been describing are neither distributed uniformly over the cell surface nor all present in equal amounts in each neuron. The density and the type of protein are governed by the needs of the cell and differ among types of neuron and from one region of a neuron to another. Thus the density of channels of a particular type ranges from zero up to about 10,000 per square micrometer. Axons generally have no chemically gated channels, whereas in postsynaptic membranes the density of such channels is limited only by the packing of the channel molecules. Similarly, dendritic membranes typically have few voltage-gated channels, whereas in axon membranes the density can reach 1,000 channels per square micrometer in certain locations.

The intrinsic membrane proteins are synthesized primarily in the body of the neuron and are stored in the membrane in small vesicles. Neurons have a special transport system for moving such vesicles from their site of synthesis to their site of function. The transport system seems to move the vesicles along in small jumps with the aid of contractile proteins. On reaching their destination the proteins are inserted into the surface membrane, where they function until they are removed and degraded within the cell. Precisely how the cell decides where to put which membrane protein is not known. Equally unknown is the mechanism that regulates the synthesis, insertion and destruction of the membrane proteins. The metabolism of membrane proteins constitutes one of cell biology's central problems.

How do the properties of the various membrane proteins I have been discussing relate to neuron function? To approach this question let us now return to the nerve impulse and examine more closely the molecular properties that underlie its triggering and propagation. As we have seen, the interior of the neuron is about 70 millivolts negative with respect to the exterior. This "resting po-

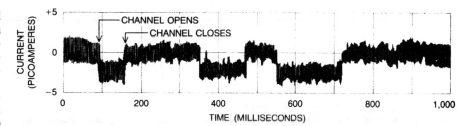

RESPONSE OF A SINGLE MEMBRANE CHANNEL to the transmitter compound acetylcholine is revealed by a recently developed technique that has been applied by Erwin Neher and Joseph H. Steinbach of the Yale University School of Medicine. Acetylcholine-activated channels, which are present in postsynaptic membranes, allow the passage of roughly equal numbers of sodium and potassium ions. The record shows the flow of current through a single channel in the postsynaptic membrane of a frog muscle activated by the compound suberyldicholine, which mimics action of acetylcholine but keeps channels open longer. Experiment shows that channels open on an all-or-none basis and stay open for random lengths of time.

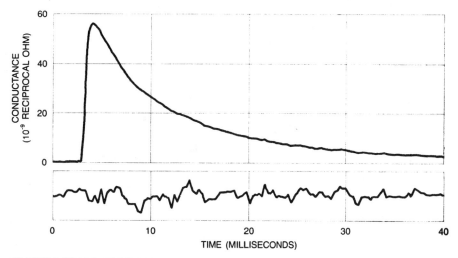

SODIUM CHANNELS IN AN AXON also operate in simple open-or-shut manner as well as independently of one another, according to investigations conducted by Frederick J. Sigworth of the Yale University School of Medicine. During the propagation of a nerve impulse about 10,000 channels normally open in a myelin-free region of the axon membrane, namely a node of Ranvier. The upper trace depicts the sodium permeability at such a node as a function of time. The lower trace, recorded at a 12-fold amplification of the upper one, shows fluctuations in permeability around the average due to the random opening and closing of channels.

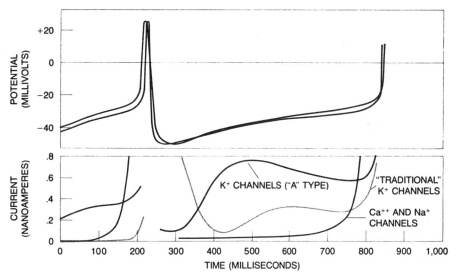

NERVE IMPULSES IN BODIES OF NEURONS require the coordinated opening and closing of five types of channel permeable to various kinds of ion (sodium, potassium or calcium). The contribution of the different channels to the nerve impulse can be represented by simultaneous nonlinear differential equations. The upper pair of curves represent an actual recording of voltage changes as a function of time in the body of a neuron (*black*) and changes computed from equations (*light*). The lower curves depict the current carried by the principal types of channel as a function of time. A complicated interaction of channel types is required to achieve a train of nerve impulses. The study on which curves are based was carried out by John A. Connor at the University of Illinois and by the author at the Yale University School of Medicine.

75

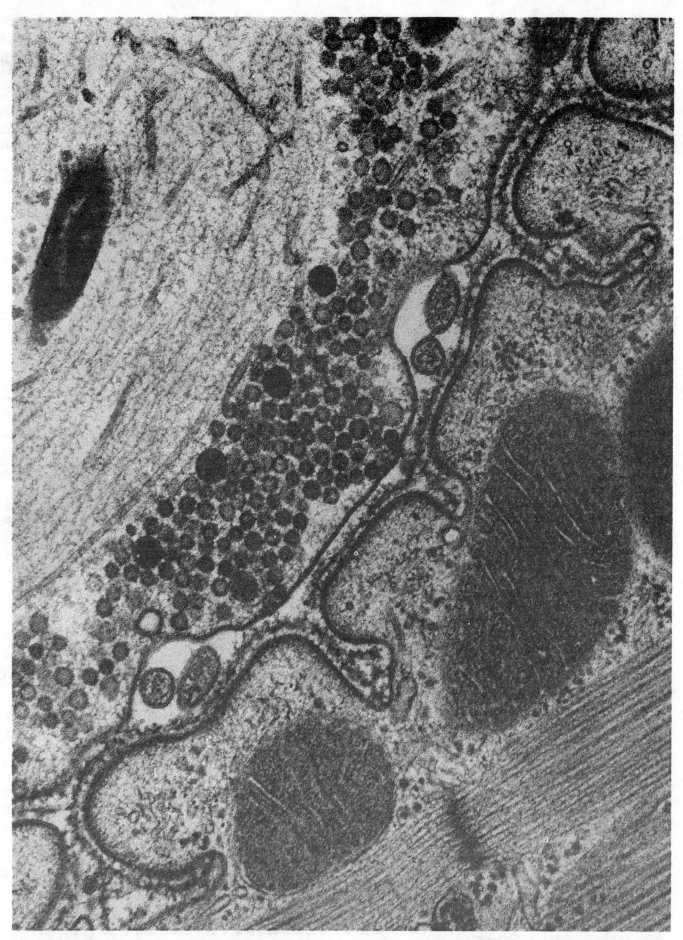

FROG NEUROMUSCULAR JUNCTION appears in this electron micrograph made by Heuser. The synaptic cleft separates the axon at the upper left from the muscle cell at the lower right. Synaptic vesicles cluster along the presynaptic membrane, with two synaptic contacts visible near the center. Postsynaptic membrane of the muscle cell exhibits a feature that is not seen at other synapses: the membrane forms postjunctional folds opposite each contact. Freeze-fracture replicas of presynaptic membrane are shown on opposite page.

tential" is a consequence of the ionic disequilibrium brought about by the sodium pump and by the presence in the cell membrane of a class of permanently open channels selectively permeable to potassium ions. The pump ejects sodium ions in exchange for potassium ions, making the inside of the cell about 10 times richer in potassium ions than the outside. The potassium channels in the membrane allow the potassium ions immediately adjacent to the membrane to flow outward quite freely. The permeability of the membrane to sodium ions is low in the resting condition, so that there is almost no counterflow of sodium ions from the exterior to the interior even though the external medium is tenfold richer in sodium ions than the internal medium. The potassium flow therefore gives rise to a net deficit of positive charges on the inner surface of the cell membrane and an excess of positive charges on the outer surface. The result is the voltage difference of 70 millivolts, with the interior being negative.

The propagation of the nerve impulse depends on the presence in the neuron membrane of voltage-gated sodium channels whose opening and closing is responsible for the action potential. What are the characteristics of these important channel molecules? Although the sodium channel has not yet been well characterized chemically, it is a protein with a molecular weight probably in the range of 250,000 to 300,000 daltons. The pore of the channel measures about .4 by .6 nanometer, a space through which sodium ions can pass in association with a water molecule. The channel has many charged groups critically placed on its surface. These charges give the channel a large electric dipole moment that varies in direction and magnitude when the molecular conformation of the channel changes as the channel goes from a closed state to an open one.

Because the surface membrane of the cell is so thin the difference of 70 millivolts across the resting membrane gives rise to a large electric field, on the order of 100 kilovolts per centimeter. In the same way that magnetic dipoles tend to align themselves with the lines of force in a magnetic field, the electric dipoles in the sodium-channel protein tend to align themselves with the membrane electric field. Changes in the strength of the membrane field can therefore drive the channel from the closed conformation to the open one. As the inner surface of the membrane is made more positive by the entering vanguard of sodium ions the sodium channels tend to spend an increasing fraction of their time in the open conformation. The process in which the channels are opened by a change in the membrane voltage is known as sodium-channel activation.

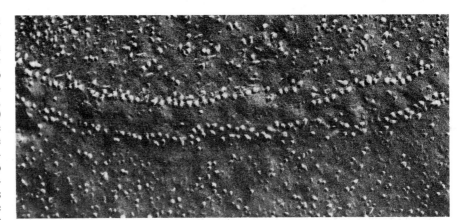

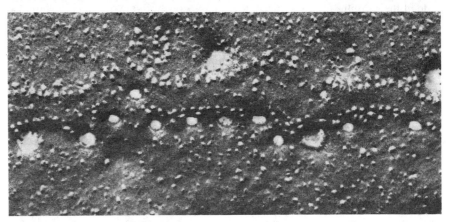

FREEZE-FRACTURE REPLICAS of the presynaptic membrane of the frog neuromuscular junction were made by Heuser. The upper micrograph shows the membrane three milliseconds after the muscle had been stimulated. Running across the axon membrane is a double row of particles: membrane proteins that may be calcium channels or structural proteins to which vesicles attach. The lower micrograph shows the membrane five milliseconds after stimulation. The stimulation has caused synaptic vesicles to fuse with presynaptic membrane and form pits.

The process is terminated by a phenomenon called sodium inactivation. Voltage differences across the membrane that cause sodium channels to open also drive them into a special closed conformation different from the conformation characteristic of the channel's resting state. The second closed conformation, called the inactivated state, develops more slowly than the activation process, so that channels remain open briefly before they are closed by inactivation. The channels remain in the inactivated state for some milliseconds and then return to the normal resting state.

The complete cycle of activation and inactivation normally involves the opening and closing of thousands of sodium channels. How can one tell whether the increase in overall membrane permeability reflects the opening and closing of a number of channels in an all-or-none manner or whether it reflects the operation of channels that have individually graded permeabilities? The question has been partly answered by a new technique that relates fluctuations in membrane permeability to the inherently probabilistic nature of conformational changes in the channel proteins. One can trigger repeated episodes of channel opening and calculate the average permeability at a particular time and also the exact permeability on a given trial. The exact permeability fluctuates 10 percent or so around a mean value. Analysis of the fluctuations shows that the sodium channels open in an all-or-none manner and that each channel opening increases the conductance of the membrane by 8×10^{-12} reciprocal ohms. One of the principal challenges in understanding the neuron is the development of a complete theory that will describe the behavior of the sodium channels and relate it to the molecular structure of the channel protein.

As I noted briefly above, axons also have voltage-gated potassium channels that help to terminate the nerve impulse by letting potassium ions flow out of the axon, thereby counteracting the inward flow of sodium ions. In the cell body of the neuron the situation is still more complex, because there the membrane is traversed by five types of channel. The different channels open at different rates, stay open for various intervals and are preferentially permeable to different species of ions (sodium, potassium or calcium).

The presence of the five types of channel in the cell body of the neuron, compared with only two in the axon, gives rise to a more complex mode of nerve-impulse generation. If an axon is presented with a maintained stimulus, it generates only a single impulse at the onset of the stimulus. Cell bodies, however, generate a train of impulses with a frequency that reflects the intensity of the stimulus.

Neurons are able to generate nerve impulses over a wide range of frequencies, from one or fewer per second to several hundred per second. All nerve impulses have the same amplitude, so that the information they carry is represented by the number of impulses generated per unit of time, a system known as frequency coding. The larger the magnitude of the stimulus to be conveyed, the faster the rate of firing.

When a nerve impulse has traveled the length of the axon and has arrived at a terminal button, one of a variety of transmitters is released from the presynaptic membrane. The transmitter diffuses to the postsynaptic membrane, where it induces the opening of chemically gated channels. Ions flowing through the open channels bring about the voltage changes known as postsynaptic potentials.

Most of what is known about synaptic mechanisms comes from experiments on a particular synapse: the neuromuscular junction that controls the contraction of muscles in the frog. The axon of the frog neuron runs for several hundred micrometers along the surface of the muscle cell, making several hundred synaptic contacts spaced about a micrometer apart. At each presynaptic region the characteristic synaptic vesicles can be recognized readily.

Each of the synaptic vesicles contains some 10,000 molecules of the transmitter acetylcholine. When a nerve impulse reaches the synapse, a train of events is set in motion that culminates in the fusion of a vesicle with the presynaptic membrane and the resulting release of acetylcholine into the cleft between the presynaptic and the postsynaptic membranes, a process termed exocytosis. The fused vesicle is subsequently reclaimed from the presynaptic membrane and is quickly refilled with acetylcholine for future release.

Many details of the events leading to exocytosis have recently been elucidated. The fusion of vesicles to the presynaptic membrane is evidently triggered by a rapid but transient increase in the concentration of calcium in the terminal button of the axon. The arrival of a nerve impulse at the terminal opens calcium channels that are voltage-gated and allows calcium to flow into the terminal. The subsequent rise in calcium concentration is brief, however, because the terminal contains a special apparatus that rapidly sequesters free calcium and returns its concentration to the normal very low level. The brief spike in the free-calcium level leads to the fusion of transmitter-filled vesicles with the presynaptic membrane, but the precise mechanism of this important process is not yet known.

Interesting details of the structure of the terminal membrane have been revealed by the freeze-fracture technique, a method that splits the layers of the bilayer membrane and exposes the intrinsic membrane proteins for examination by electron microscopy. In the frog neuromuscular junction a double row of large membrane proteins runs the width of each synapse. Synaptic vesicles become attached on or near the proteins. Only these vesicles then fuse to the membrane and release their transmitter; other vesicles seem to be held in reserve some distance away. The fusion of vesicles is a random process and occurs independently for each vesicle.

In less than 100 microseconds acetylcholine released from fused vesicles diffuses across the synaptic cleft and binds to the acetylcholine receptor: an intrinsic membrane protein embedded in the postsynaptic membrane. The receptor is also a channel protein that is chemically gated by the presence of acetylcholine. When two acetylcholine molecules attach themselves to the channel, they lower the energy state of the open conformation of the protein and thereby increase the probability that the channel will open. The open state of the channel is a random event with an average lifetime of about a millisecond. Each packet of 10,000 acetylcholine molecules effects the opening of some 2,000 channels.

During the brief period that a channel is open about 20,000 sodium ions and a roughly equal number of potassium ions pass through it. As a result of this ionic flow the voltage difference between the two sides of the membrane tends to approach zero. How close it approaches to zero depends on how many channels open and how long they stay open. The acetylcholine released by a typical nerve impulse produces a postsynaptic potential, or voltage change, that lasts for only about five milliseconds. Because postsynaptic potentials are produced by chemically gated chan-

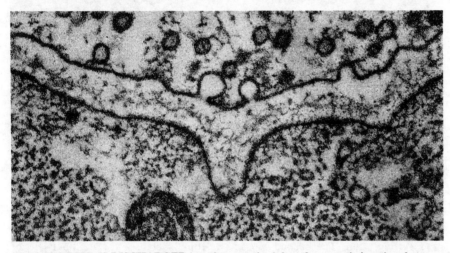

TRANSMITTER IS DISCHARGED into the synaptic cleft at the synaptic junctions between neurons by vesicles that open up after they fuse with the axon's presynaptic membrane, a process called exocytosis. This electron micrograph made by Heuser has caught the vesicles in the terminal of an axon in the act of discharging acetylcholine into the neuromuscular junction of a frog. The structures that appear in the micrograph are enlarged some 115,000 diameters.

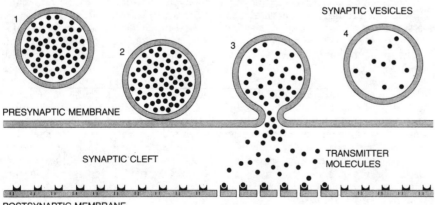

SYNAPTIC VESICLES are clustered near the presynaptic membrane. The diagram shows the probable steps in exocytosis. Filled vesicles move up to synaptic cleft, fuse with the membrane, discharge their contents and are reclaimed, re-formed and refilled with transmitter.

nels rather than by voltage-gated ones they have properties quite different from those of the nerve impulse. They are usually smaller in amplitude, longer in duration and graded in size depending on the quantity of transmitter released and hence on the number of channels that open.

Different types of chemically gated channels exhibit different selectivities. Some resemble the acetylcholine channel, which passes sodium and potassium ions with little selectivity. Others are highly selective. The voltage change that results at a particular synapse depends on the selectivity of the channels that are opened. If positive ions move into the cell, the voltage change is in the positive direction. Such positive-going voltage channels tend to open voltage-gated channels and to generate nerve impulses, and so they are known as excitatory postsynaptic potentials. If positive ions (usually potassium) move out of the cell, the voltage change is in the negative direction, which tends to close voltage-gated channels. Such postsynaptic potentials oppose the production of nerve impulses, and so they are termed inhibitory. Excitatory and inhibitory postsynaptic potentials are both common in the brain.

Brain synapses differ from neuromuscular-junction synapses in several ways. Whereas at the neuromuscular junction the action of acetylcholine is always excitatory, in the brain the action of the same substance is excitatory at some synapses and inhibitory at others. And whereas acetylcholine is the usual transmitter at neuromuscular junctions, the brain synapses have channels gated by a large variety of transmitters. A particular synaptic ending, however, releases only one type of transmitter, and channels gated by that transmitter are present in the corresponding postsynaptic membrane. In contrast with neuromuscular channels activated by acetylcholine, which stay open for about a millisecond, some types of brain synapses have channels that stay open for less than a millisecond and others have channels that remain open for hundreds of milliseconds. A final major difference is that whereas the axon makes hundreds of synaptic contacts with the muscle cell at the frog's neuromuscular junction, axons in the brain usually make only one or two synaptic contacts on a given neuron. As might be expected, such different functional properties are correlated with significant differences in structure.

As we have seen, the intensity of a stimulus is coded in the frequency of nerve impulses. Decoding at the synapse is accomplished by two processes: temporal summation and spatial summation. In temporal summation each postsynaptic potential adds to the cumulative total of its predecessors to yield a

voltage change whose average amplitude reflects the frequency of incoming nerve impulses. In other words, a neuron that is firing rapidly releases more transmitter molecules at its terminal junctions than a neuron that is firing less rapidly. The more transmitter molecules that are released in a given time, the more channels that are opened in the postsynaptic membrane and therefore the larger the postsynaptic potential is. Spatial summation is an equivalent process except that it reflects the integration of nerve impulses arriving from all the neurons that may be in synaptic contact with a given neuron. The grand voltage change derived from temporal and spatial summation is encoded as nerve-impulse frequency for transmission to other cells "downstream" in the nerve network.

I have described what is usually regarded as the normal flow of information in neural circuits, in which postsynaptic voltage changes are encoded as nerve-impulse frequency and transmitted over the axon to other neurons. In recent years, however, a number of instances have been discovered where a postsynaptic potential is not converted into a nerve impulse. For example, the voltage change due to a postsynaptic potential can directly cause the release of transmitter from a neighboring site that lacks a nerve impulse. Such direct influences are thought to come into play in synapses between dendrites and also in certain reciprocal circuits where one dendrite makes a synaptic contact on a second dendrite, which in turn makes a synaptic contact back on the first dendrite. Such direct feedback seems to be quite common in the brain, but its implications for information processing remain to be worked out.

Much current investigation of the neuron focuses on the membrane proteins that endow the cell's bilayer membrane, which is otherwise featureless, with the special properties brain function depends on. With regard to channel proteins there are many unanswered questions about the mechanisms of gating, selectivity and regulation. Within the next five or 10 years it should be possible to relate the physical processes of gating and selectivity to the molecular structure of the channels. The basis of channel regulation is less well understood but is now coming under intensive investigation. It seems that hormones and other substances play a role in channel regulation that is now becoming appreciated. The central problems at synaptic junctions involve exocytosis and other activities related to the metabolism and release of transmitters. One can expect increasing attention to be focused on the role of the surface membrane in the growth and development of neurons and their synaptic connections, the remarkable process that establishes the integration of the nervous system.

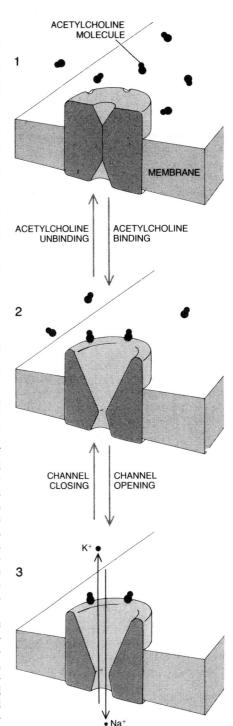

ACETYLCHOLINE CHANNEL in a postsynaptic membrane is opened by acetylcholine molecules' discharging into the synaptic cleft. The drawing shows the acetylcholine receptor at the frog neuromuscular junction. Two acetylcholine molecules bind rapidly to the resting closed channel to form a receptor-acetylcholine complex (1, 2). The complex undergoes a change in its conformation that opens the channel to the passage of sodium and potassium ions (3). The time required for conformational change in the complex limits the speed of the reaction. The channel remains open for about a millisecond on the average and then reverts to the receptor-acetylcholine complex. While it is open the channel passes about 20,000 sodium ions and an equal number of potassium ions. The acetylcholine rapidly dissociates and is destroyed by the enzyme acetylcholine esterase. Acetylcholine receptor appears in micrograph on page 73.

Small Systems of Neurons

Such systems are the elementary units of mental function. Studies

of simple animals such as the large snail Aplysia show that small

systems of neurons are capable of forms of learning and memory

by Eric R. Kandel

Many neurobiologists believe that the unique character of individual human beings, their disposition to feel, think, learn and remember, will ultimately be shown to reside in the precise patterns of synaptic interconnections between the neurons of the brain. Since it is difficult to examine patterns of interconnections in the human brain, a major concern of neurobiology has been to develop animal models that are useful for studying how interacting systems of neurons give rise to behavior. Networks of neurons that mediate complete behavioral acts allow one to explore a hierarchy of interrelated questions: To what degree do the properties of different neurons vary? What determines the patterns of interconnections between neurons? How do different patterns of interconnections generate different forms of behavior? Can the interconnected neurons that control a certain kind of behavior be modified by learning? If they can, what are the mechanisms whereby memory is stored?

Among the many functions that emerge from the interactions of neurons, the most interesting are the functions concerned with learning (the ability to modify behavior in response to experience) and with memory (the ability to store that modification over a period of time). Learning and memory are perhaps the most distinctive features of the mental processes of advanced animals, and these features reach their highest form in man. In fact, human beings are what they are in good measure because of what they have learned. It is therefore of theoretical importance, for the understanding of learning and for the study of behavioral evolution, to determine at what phylogenetic level of neuronal and behavioral organization one can begin to recognize aspects of the learning and

memory processes that characterize human behavior. This determination is also of practical importance. The difficulty in studying the cellular mechanisms of memory in the brain of man or other mammals arises because such brains are immensely complex. For the human brain ethical issues also preclude this kind of study. It would therefore be congenial scientifically to be able to examine these processes effectively in simple systems.

It could be argued that the study of memory and learning as it relates to man cannot be pursued effectively in simple neuronal systems. The organization of the human brain seems so complex that trying to study human learning in a reduced form in simple neuronal systems is bound to fail. Man has intellectual abilities, a highly developed language and an ability for abstract thinking, which are not found in simpler animals and may require qualitatively different types of neuronal organization. Although such arguments have value, the critical question is not whether there is something special about the human brain. There clearly is. The question is rather what the human brain and human behavior have in common with the brain and the behavior of simpler animals. Where there are points of similarity they may involve common principles of brain organization that could profitably be studied in simple neural systems.

The answer to the question of similarity is clear. Ethologists such as Konrad Lorenz, Nikolaas Tinbergen and Karl von Frisch have shown that human beings share many common behavioral patterns with simpler animals, including elementary perception and motor coordination. The capacity to learn, in particular, is widespread; it has evolved in many invertebrate animals and in all

vertebrates. The similarity of some of the learning processes suggests that the neuronal mechanisms for a given learning process may have features in common across phylogeny. For example, there appear to be no fundamental differences in structure, chemistry or function between the neurons and synapses in man and those of a squid, a snail or a leech. Consequently a complete and rigorous analysis of learning in such an invertebrate is likely to reveal mechanisms of general significance.

Simple invertebrates are attractive for such investigation because their nervous systems consist of between 10,000 and 100,000 cells, compared with the many billions in more complex animals. The cells are collected into the discrete groups called ganglia, and each ganglion usually consists of between 500 and 1,500 neurons. This numerical simplification has made it possible to relate the function of individual cells directly to behavior. The result is a number of important findings that lead to a new way of looking at the relation between the brain and behavior.

The first major question that students of simple systems of neurons might examine is whether the various neurons of a region of the nervous system differ from one another. This question, which is central to an understanding of how behavior is mediated by the nervous system, was in dispute until recently. Some neurobiologists argued that the neurons of a brain are sufficiently similar in their properties to be regarded as identical units having interconnections of roughly equal value.

These arguments have now been strongly challenged, particularly by studies of invertebrates showing that many neurons can be individually identified and are invariant in every member of the species. The concept that neurons are unique was proposed as early as 1912 by the German biologist Richard Goldschmidt on the basis of his study of the nervous system of a primitive worm, the intestinal parasite *Ascaris*. The brain

GROUP OF NEURONS appears in the photomicrograph on the opposite page, which shows the dorsal surface of the abdominal ganglion of the snail *Aplysia*. The magnification is 100 diameters. A particularly large, dark brown neuron can be seen at the right side of the micrograph. It is the cell identified as R2 in the map of the abdominal ganglion of *Aplysia* on page 81.

of this worm consists of several ganglia. When Goldschmidt examined the ganglia, he found they contained exactly 162 cells. The number never varied from animal to animal, and each cell always occupied a characteristic position. In spite of this clear-cut result Goldschmidt's work went largely unheeded.

More than 50 years later two groups at the Harvard Medical School returned to the problem independently. Masanori Otsuka, Edward A. Kravitz and David D. Potter, working with the lobster, and Wesley T. Frazier, Irving Kupfermann, Rafiq M. Waziri, Richard E. Coggeshall and I, working with the large marine snail *Aplysia,* found a similar but less complete invariance in the more complex nervous systems of these higher invertebrates. A comparable invariance was soon found in a variety of invertebrates, including the leech, the crayfish, the locust, the cricket and a number of snails. Here I shall limit myself to considering studies of *Aplysia,* particularly studies of a single ganglion: the abdominal ganglion. Similar findings have also emerged from the studies of other invertebrates.

In the abdominal ganglion of *Aplysia* neurons vary in size, position, shape, pigmentation, firing patterns and the chemical substances by which they transmit information to other cells. On the basis of such differences it is possible to recognize and name specific cells (R 1, L1, R15 and so on). The firing patterns illustrate some of the differences. Certain cells are normally "silent" and others are spontaneously active. Among the active ones some fire regular action potentials, or nerve impulses, and others fire in recurrent brief bursts or trains. The different firing patterns have now

been shown to result from differences in the types of ionic currents generated by the membrane of the cell body of the neurons. The cell-body membrane is quite different from the membrane of the axon, the long fiber of the neuron. When the membrane of the axon is active, it typically produces only an inflow of sodium ions and a delayed outflow of potassium ions, whereas the membrane of the cell body can produce six or seven distinct ionic currents that can flow in various combinations.

Whether or not most cells in the mammalian nervous system are also unique individuals is not yet known. The studies in the sensory systems of mammals reviewed by David Hubel and Torsten Wiesel in this issue, however, have revealed fascinating and important differences between neighboring neurons [see "Brain Mechanisms of Vision," by David H. Hubel and Torsten N. Wiesel, page 130]. Studies of the development of the vertebrate brain reviewed by Maxwell Cowan lead to a similar conclusion [see "The Development of the Brain," by W. Maxwell Cowan, page 106].

The finding that neurons are invariant leads to further questions. Are the synaptic connections between cells also invariant? Does a given identified cell always connect to exactly the same follower cell and not to others? A number of investigators have examined these questions in invertebrate animals and have found that cells indeed always make the same kinds of connections to other cells. The invariance applies not only to the connections but also to the "sign," or functional expression, of the connections, that is, whether they are excitatory or inhibitory.

Therefore Frazier, James E. Blan-

kenship, Howard Wachtel and I next worked with identified cells to examine the rules that determine the functional expression of connections between cells. A single neuron has many branches and makes many connections. We asked: Are all the connections of a neuron specialized for inhibition or excitation, or can the firing of a neuron produce different actions at different branches? What determines whether a connection is excitatory or inhibitory? Is the sign of the synaptic action determined by the chemical structure of the transmitter substance released by the presynaptic neuron, or is the nature of the postsynaptic receptor the determining factor? Does the neuron release the same transmitter from all its terminals?

One way to explore these questions is to look at the different connections made by a cell. The first cell we examined gave a clear answer: it mediated different actions through its various connections. The cell excited some follower cells, inhibited others and (perhaps most unexpectedly) made a dual connection, which was both excitatory and inhibitory, to a third kind of cell. Moreover, it always excited precisely the same cells, always inhibited another specific group of cells and always made a dual connection with a third group. Its synaptic action could be accounted for by one transmitter substance: acetylcholine. The reaction of this substance with different types of receptors on the various follower cells determined whether the synaptic action would be excitatory or inhibitory.

The receptors determined the sign of the synaptic action by controlling different ionic channels in the membrane: primarily sodium for excitation and chloride for inhibition. The cells that received the dual connection had two types of receptor for the same transmitter, one receptor that controlled a sodium channel and another that controlled a chloride channel. The functional expression of chemical synaptic transmission is therefore determined by the types of receptor the follower cell has at a given postsynaptic site. (Similar results have been obtained by JacSue Kehoe of the École Normale in Paris, who has gone on to analyze in detail the properties of the various species of receptors to acetylcholine.) Thus, as was first suggested by Ladislav Tauc and Hersch Gerschenfeld of the Institute Marey in Paris, the chemical transmitter is only permissive; the instructive component of synaptic transmission is the nature of the receptor and the ionic channels it interacts with. This principle has proved to be fairly general. It applies to the neurons of vertebrates and invertebrates and to neurons utilizing various transmitters: acetylcholine, gamma-aminobutyric acid (GABA), serotonin, dopamine and histamine. (The principle

GILL-WITHDRAWAL REFLEX of *Aplysia* results when the siphon or the mantle shelf is somehow stimulated. The animal then retracts the gill to the position that is indicated in *dark.*

SIPHON

MANTLE SHELF

GILL

also applies to the actions of certain peptide hormones on neurons, a subject to which I shall return.)

The discovery in invertebrate ganglia of identifiable cells that make precise connections with one another has led to the working out of the "wiring diagram" of various behavioral circuits and has therefore made possible an exact study of the causal relation of specific neurons to behavior. The term behavior refers to the observable actions of an organism. These range from complex acts such as talking or walking to simple acts such as the movement of a body part or a change in heart rate. Types of behavior that have been at least partly worked out in leeches, crayfishes and snails include feeding, various locomotor patterns and a variety of escape and defensive reactions.

The first finding to emerge from these studies is that individual cells exert a control over behavior that is specific and sometimes surprisingly powerful. The point can be illustrated by comparing the neural control of the heart in *Aplysia* with that in human beings.

The human heart beats spontaneously. Its intrinsic rhythm is neuronally modulated by the inhibitory action of cholinergic neurons (acetylcholine is the transmitter substance) with their axons in the vagus nerve and the excitatory action of noradrenergic neurons with their axons in the accelerator nerve. The modulation involves several thousand neurons. In *Aplysia* the heart also beats spontaneously; it is neuronally modulated by the inhibitory action of cholinergic neurons and the excitatory action of serotonergic neurons, but the modulation is accomplished by only four cells! Two cells excite the heart (only the "major excitor" cell is really important) and two inhibit it. Three other cells give rise to a constriction of the blood vessels and thereby control the animal's blood pressure.

Since individual cells connect invariably to the same follower cells and can mediate actions that have a different sign, certain cells at a critical point in the nervous system are in a position to control an entire behavioral sequence. As early as 1938 C. A. G. Wiersma, working with the crayfish at the California Institute of Technology, had appreciated the importance of single cells in behavior and had called them "command cells." Such cells have now been found in a variety of animals. A few of them have proved to be dual-action neurons. Hence John Koester, Earl M. Mayeri and I, working with *Aplysia* at the New York University School of Medicine, found that the dual-action neuron described above is a command cell for the neural circuit controlling the circulation. This one cell increases the rate and output of the heart by exciting the

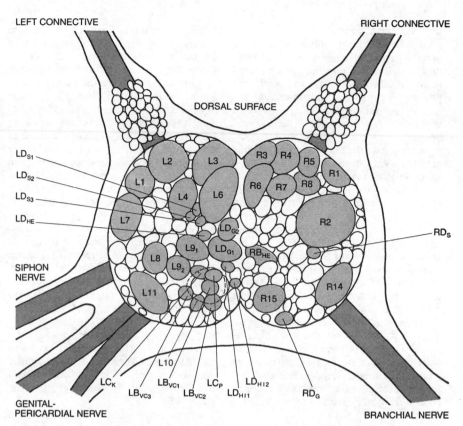

MAP OF ABDOMINAL GANGLION in *Aplysia californica* shows the location of the identified neurons, which have been labeled L or R (for left or right hemiganglion) and assigned a number. Neurons that are members of a cluster, consisting of cells with similar properties, are further identified by a cluster letter (LD) and a subscript representing the behavioral function of the neuron, such as HE for heart excitor and G1 and G2 for two gill motor neurons.

major cell that excites the heart while inhibiting the cells that inhibit the heart and the cells that constrict the major blood vessels. As a result of the increased activity of this one cell the heart beats faster and pumps more blood.

This is only a simple example of the behavioral functions of a command cell. In the crayfish and even in a more complex animal, the goldfish, a single impulse in a single command neuron causes the animal to flee from threatened danger. Recently Vernon Mountcastle of the Johns Hopkins University School of Medicine has suggested in this context that small groups of cells may serve similar command functions in the primate brain to control purposeful voluntary movements.

Hence a functional purpose of dual-action cells is to bring about a constellation of different physiological effects. A similar constellation can be achieved by the action of neuroendocrine cells, neurons that release hormones (the chemical substances that are usually carried in the bloodstream to act at distant sites). The abdominal ganglion of *Aplysia* contains two clusters of neuroendocrine cells, which are called bag cells because each cluster is bag-shaped. Kupfermann, working in our division at the Columbia University College of Physicians and Surgeons, has shown, as have

Stephen Arch of Reed College and Felix Strumwasser and his colleagues at Cal Tech, that the bag cells release a polypeptide hormone that controls egg laying. Mayeri has found that this hormone has long-lasting actions on various cells in the abdominal ganglion, exciting some and inhibiting others.

One of the cells excited by this hormone is the dual-action command cell that controls the heart rate. As a result the heart speeds up to provide the extra flow of blood to the tissues that the animal requires during egg laying. Thus superimposed on a precise pattern of connections that provide short-range interaction of neurons is an equally precise pattern of long-range interactions achieved by the hormones released by neuroendocrine cells. The precise effect of each hormone seems to be determined, as synaptic effects are, by the nature of the receptors on the target cells.

The finding that behavior is mediated by invariant cells interconnecting in precise and invariant ways might suggest that simple animals differ from more complex ones in having stereotyped and fixed repertories of activity. It is not so. Studies in different invertebrates have shown that behavior in simple animals is quite capable of being modified by learning.

We have explored this subject most

fully in one of *Aplysia*'s simplest kinds of behavior: a defensive reflex action in which the gill is withdrawn after a stimulus. The gill is in a respiratory chamber called the mantle cavity. The chamber is covered by a protective sheet, the mantle shelf, that terminates in a fleshy spout, the siphon. When a weak or a moderately intense stimulus is applied to the siphon, the gill contracts and withdraws into the mantle cavity. This reflex is analogous to the withdrawal responses found in almost all higher animals, such as the one in which a human being jerks a hand away from a hot object. *Aplysia* and the other animals exhibit two forms of learning with such reflexes: habituation and sensitization.

Habituation is a decrease in the strength of a behavioral response that occurs when an initially novel stimulus is presented repeatedly. When an animal is presented with a novel stimulus, it at first responds with a combination of orienting and defensive reflexes. With repeated stimulation the animal readily learns to recognize the stimulus. If the stimulus proves to be unrewarding or innocuous, the animal will reduce and ultimately suppress its responses to it. Although habituation is remarkably simple, it is probably the most widespread of all forms of learning. Through habituation animals, including human beings, learn to ignore stimuli that have lost novelty or meaning; habituation frees them to attend to stimuli that are rewarding or significant for survival. Habituation is thought to be the first learning process to emerge in human infants and is commonly utilized to study the development of intellectual processes such as attention, perception and memory.

An interesting aspect of habituation in vertebrates is that it gives rise to both short- and long-term memory and has therefore been employed to explore the relation between the two. Thomas J. Carew, Harold M. Pinsker and I found that a similar relation holds for *Aplysia*. After a single training session of from 10 to 15 tactile stimuli to the siphon the withdrawal reflex habituates. The memory for the stimulus is short-lived; partial recovery can be detected within an hour and almost complete recovery generally occurs within a day. Recovery in this type of learning is equivalent to forgetting. As with the repetition of more complex learning tasks, however, four repeated training sessions of only 10 stimuli each produce profound habituation and a memory for the stimulus that lasts for weeks.

The first question that Vincent Castellucci, Kupfermann, Pinsker and I asked was: What are the loci and mechanisms of short-term habituation? The neural circuit controlling gill withdrawal is quite simple. A stimulus to the skin of the siphon activates the 24 sensory neurons there; they make direct connections to six motor cells in the gill, and the motor cells connect directly to the muscle. The sensory neurons also excite several interneurons, which are interposed neurons.

By examining these cells during habituation we found that short-term habituation involved a change in the strength of the connection made by the sensory neurons on their central target cells: the interneurons and the motor neurons. This localization was most fortunate, because now we could examine what happened during habituation simply by analyzing the changes in two cells, the presynaptic sensory neuron and the postsynaptic motor neuron, and in the single set of connections between them.

The strength of a connection can be studied by recording the synaptic action produced in the motor cells by an individual sensory neuron. It is possible to simulate the habituation training session of from 10 to 15 stimuli by stimulating a sensory neuron following the exact time sequence used for the intact animal. The stimulus can be adjusted so that it generates a single action potential. The first time the neuron is caused to fire an action potential it produces a highly effective synaptic action, which is manifested as a large excitatory postsynaptic potential in the motor cell. The subsequent action potentials initiated in the sensory neuron during a training session give rise to progressively smaller excitatory postsynaptic potentials. This depression in the effectiveness of the connection parallels and accounts for the behavioral habituation. As with the behavior, the synaptic depression resulting from a single training session persists for more than an hour. Following a second training session there is a more pronounced depression of the synaptic potential, and further training sessions can depress the synaptic potential completely.

What causes the changes in the strength of the synaptic connection? Do they involve a change in the presynaptic sensory neuron, reflecting a decrease in the release of the transmitter substance, or a change in the postsynaptic cell, reflecting a decrease in the sensitivity of the receptors to the chemical transmitter? The questions can be answered by analyzing changes in the amplitude of the synaptic potential in terms of its quantal components.

As was first shown by José del Castillo and Bernhard Katz at University College London, transmitter is released not as single molecules but as "quanta," or multimolecular packets. Each packet contains roughly the same amount

R2

|← 10 SECONDS →|

R3

|← 10 SECONDS →|

R15

|← 10 SECONDS →|

L10

|← 50 SECONDS →|

FIRING PATTERNS of identified neurons in *Aplysia*'s abdominal ganglion are portrayed. R2 is normally silent, R3 has a regular beating rhythm, R15 a regular bursting rhythm and L10 an irregular bursting rhythm. L10 is a command cell that controls other cells in the system.

a

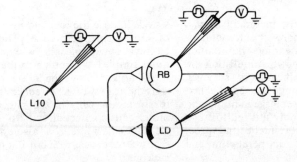

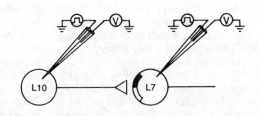

b

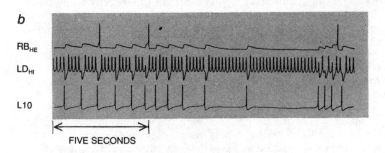

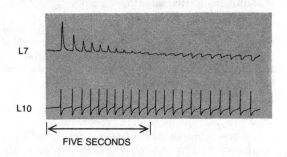

c

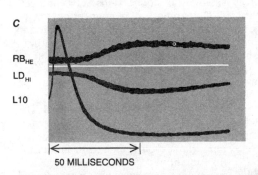

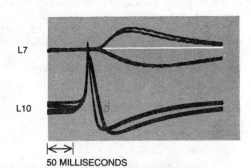

INVARIANCE OF CONNECTIONS between cell L10 and some of its follower cells was ascertained (*a*) by an arrangement in which double-barrel microelectrodes for recording and passing current were inserted in L10, which is a presynaptic neuron, and three of its follower cells. L10 produces excitation (*white*) in RB, inhibition (*black*) in LD and both excitation and inhibition in L7. The respective firing patterns are shown at *b*. Several superposed sweeps (*at the left in* c) illustrate the brief but constant latency between an impulse in the presynaptic neuron and the response of two follower cells. Superposed traces from L10 and L7 (*at the right in* c) show that effect is excitatory when L10 fires initially, as indicated by tall and narrow impulses, and inhibitory when it fires repeatedly, as shown by short and broad impulses.

of transmitter (several thousand molecules). The quanta are thought to be stored in subcellular organelles called synaptic vesicles that are seen in abundance at synaptic endings examined with the electron microscope. Since the number of transmitter molecules in each quantum does not ordinarily change, the number of quanta released by each action potential is a fairly reliable index of the total amount of transmitter released. Each quantum in turn produces a miniature excitatory postsynaptic potential of characteristic size in the postsynaptic cell. The size is an indication of how sensitive the postsynaptic receptors are to the several thousand molecules of transmitter released by each packet.

Castellucci and I, working with *Aplysia,* found that the decrease in the amplitude of the synaptic action potential with habituation was paralleled by a decrease in the number of chemical quanta released. In contrast, the size of the miniature postsynaptic potential did not change, indicating that there was no

change in the sensitivity of the postsynaptic receptor. The results show that the site of short-term habituation is the presynaptic terminals of the sensory neurons and that the mechanism of habituation is a progressive decrease in the amount of transmitter released by the sensory-neuron terminals onto their central target cells. Studies in the crayfish by Robert S. Zucker of the University of California at Berkeley and by Franklin B. Krasne of the University of California at Los Angeles and in the cat by Paul B. Farel and Richard F. Thompson of the University of California at Irvine indicate that this mechanism may be quite general.

What is responsible for the decrease in the number of quanta released by each action potential? The number is largely determined by the concentration of free calcium in the presynaptic terminal. Calcium is one of three kinds of ion involved in the generation of each action potential in the terminal. The depolarizing upstroke of the action potential is produced mainly by the inflow of so-

dium ions into the terminal, but it also involves a lesser and delayed flow of calcium ions. The repolarizing downstroke is largely produced by the outflow of potassium ions. The inflow of calcium is essential for the release of transmitter. Calcium is thought to enable the synaptic vesicles to bind to release sites in the presynaptic terminals. This binding is a critical step preliminary to the release of transmitter from the vesicles (the process termed exocytosis). It therefore seems possible that the amount of calcium coming into the terminals with each action potential is not fixed but is variable and that the amount might be modulated by habituation.

The best way to examine changes in the flow of calcium into terminals would be to record from the terminals directly. We have been unable to do so because the terminals are very small. Because the properties of the calcium channels of the cell body resemble those of the terminals, however, one of our graduate students, Marc Klein, set about examining the change in the calcium current of

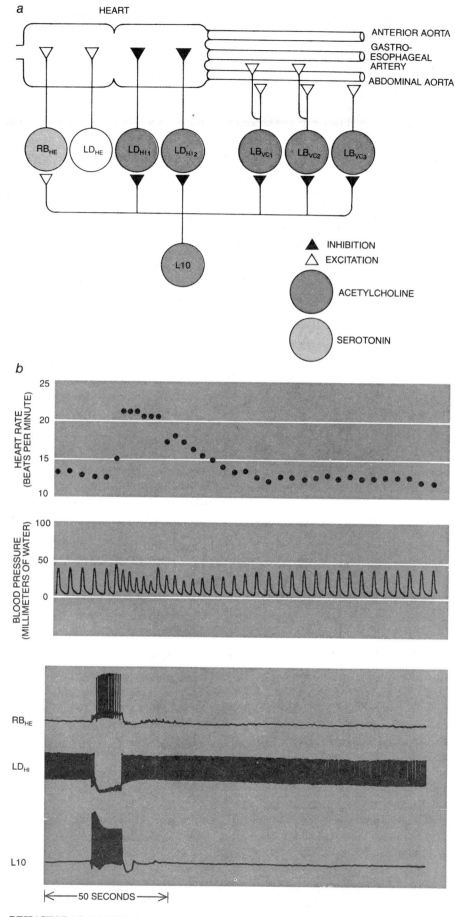

a

HEART

ANTERIOR AORTA
GASTRO-ESOPHAGEAL ARTERY
ABDOMINAL AORTA

RB_{HE} LD_{HE} LD_{HI1} LD_{HI2} LB_{VC1} LB_{VC2} LB_{VC3}

L10

▲ INHIBITION
△ EXCITATION

● ACETYLCHOLINE

● SEROTONIN

b

HEART RATE (BEATS PER MINUTE)

25
20
15
10

BLOOD PRESSURE (MILLIMETERS OF WATER)

100
50
0

RB_{HE}

LD_{HI}

L10

|← 50 SECONDS →|

BEHAVIORAL CONTROL exerted by the single neuron L10 is shown by its effect on cardiovascular motor neurons of *Aplysia*. L10 is known to make synaptic connections (a) with six of the cells (LD_{HE} has not yet been examined for this synaptic connection); the color of each cell indicates what chemical transmitter it utilizes. It can be seen (b) that activity in L10 increases the animal's heart rate and blood pressure by exciting RB_{HE} and inhibiting LD_{HI}.

the cell body that accompanies the synaptic depression.

The calcium current turns on slowly during the action potential and so is normally overlapped by the potassium current. To unmask the calcium current we exposed the ganglion to tetraethylammonium (TEA), an agent that selectively blocks some of the delayed potassium current. By blocking the repolarizing action of the potassium current the agent produces a significant increase in the duration of the action potential. Much of this prolongation is due to the unopposed action of the calcium current. The duration of the action potential prolonged by TEA is a good assay for changes in calcium current.

We next examined the release of transmitter by the terminals of the sensory neurons, as measured by the size of the synaptic potential in the motor cell, and the changes recorded simultaneously in the calcium current, as measured by the duration of the action potential. We found that repeated stimulation of the sensory neuron at rates that produce habituation led to a progressive decrease in the duration of the calcium component of the action potential that paralleled the decrease in the release of transmitter. Spontaneous recovery of the synaptic potential and of the behavior were accompanied by an increase in the calcium current.

What we have learned so far about the mechanisms of short-term habituation indicates that this type of learning involves a modulation in the strength of a previously existing synaptic connection. The strength of the connection is determined by the amount of transmitter released, which is in turn controlled by the degree to which an action potential in the presynaptic terminal can activate the calcium current. The storage of the memory for short-term habituation therefore resides in the persistence, over minutes and hours, of the depression in the calcium current in the presynaptic terminal.

What are the limits of this change? How much can the effectiveness of a given synapse change as a result of learning, and how long can such changes endure? I have mentioned that repeated training sessions can completely depress the synaptic connections between the sensory and the motor cells. Can this condition be maintained? Can long-term habituation give rise to a complete and prolonged inactivation of a previously functioning synapse?

These questions bear on the longstanding debate among students of learning about the relation of short- and long-term memory. The commonly accepted idea is that the two kinds of memory involve different memory processes. This idea is based, however, on rather indirect evidence.

Castellucci, Carew and I set out to

examine the hypothesis more directly by comparing the effectiveness of the connections made by the population of sensory neurons on an identified gill motor cell, L7, in four groups of *Aplysia:* untrained animals that served as controls, and groups examined respectively one day, one week and three weeks after long-term habituation training. We found that in the control animals about 90 percent of the sensory neurons made extremely effective connections to L7, whereas in the animals examined one day and one week after long-term habituation the figure was 30 percent. Even in the three-week group only about 60 percent of the cells made detectable connections to L7. Here, then, are previously effective synaptic connections that become inactive and remain that way for more than a week as a result of a simple learning experience.

Hence whereas short-term habitua-tion involves a transient decrease in synaptic efficacy, long-term habituation produces a more prolonged and profound change, leading to a functional disruption of most of the previously effective connections. The data are interesting for three reasons: (1) they provide direct evidence that a specific instance of long-term memory can be explained by a long-term change in synaptic effectiveness; (2) they show that surprisingly little training is needed to produce a profound change in synaptic transmission at synapses critically involved in learning, and (3) they make clear that short- and long-term habituation can share a common neuronal locus, namely the synapses the sensory neurons make on the motor neurons. Short- and long-term habituation also involve aspects of the same cellular mechanism: a depression of excitatory transmission. One now needs to determine whether the long-term synaptic depression is presynaptic and whether it involves an inactivation of the calcium current. If it does, it would support on a more fundamental level the notion that short- and long-term memory can involve a single memory trace.

Sensitization is a slightly more complex form of learning that can be seen in the gill-withdrawal reflex. It is the prolonged enhancement of an animal's preexisting response to a stimulus as a result of the presentation of a second stimulus that is noxious. Whereas habituation requires an animal to learn to ignore a particular stimulus because its consequences are trivial, sensitization requires the animal to learn to attend to a stimulus because it is accompanied by potentially painful or dangerous consequences. Therefore when an *Aplysia* is presented with a noxious stimulus

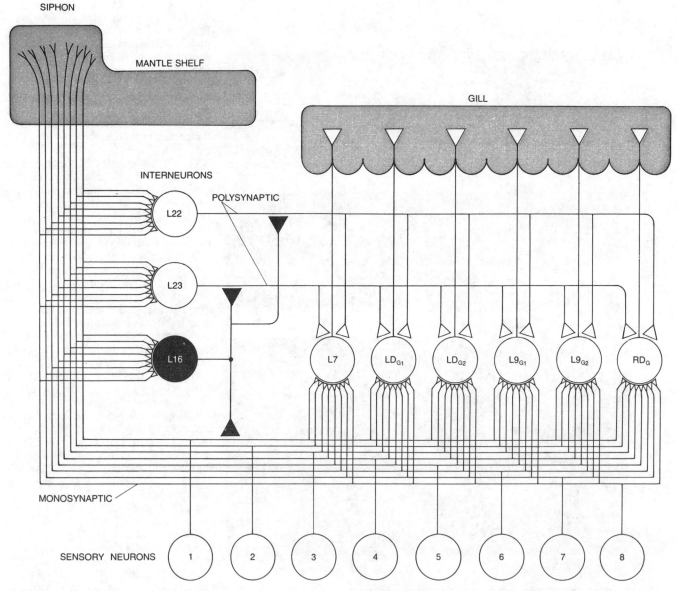

NEURAL CIRCUITRY of a behavioral reflex of *Aplysia,* the gill-withdrawal reflex, is depicted schematically. In the reflex action the animal withdraws its gill when a fleshy spout (the siphon) on a protective sheet (the mantle shelf) is stimulated in some way. The skin of the siphon is innervated by about 24 sensory neurons; the diagram has been simplified to focus on only eight of them. The sensory neurons make monosynaptic, or direct, connections to six identified gill motor neurons, which are shown in the row beginning with L7, and to at least one inhibitory cell (L16) and two interposed excitatory interneurons (L22 and L23), which make synapses with motor neurons.

to the head, the gill-withdrawal reflex response to a repeated stimulus to the siphon is greatly enhanced. As with habituation, sensitization can last from minutes to days and weeks, depending on the amount of training. Here I shall focus only on the short-term form.

Castellucci and I found that sensitization entails an alteration of synaptic transmission at the same locus that is involved in habituation: the synapses made by the sensory neurons on their central target cells. Our physiological studies and subsequent morphological studies by Craig Bailey, Mary C. Chen and Robert Hawkins indicate that the neurons mediating sensitization end near the synaptic terminals of the sensory neurons and enhance the release of transmitter by increasing the number of quanta turned loose by each action potential in the sensory neuron. The process is therefore called presynaptic facilitation. It is interesting because it illustrates (as does the earlier finding of presynaptic inhibition in another system by Joseph Dudel and Stephen Kuffler of the Harvard Medical School) that neurons have receptors to transmitters at two quite different sites. Receptors on the cell body and on the dendrites determine whether a cell should fire an action potential, and receptors on the synaptic terminals determine how much transmitter each action potential will release.

The same locus—the presynaptic terminals of the sensory neurons—can therefore be regulated in opposite ways by opposing forms of learning. It can be depressed as a result of the intrinsic activity within the neuron that occurs with habituation, and it can be facilitated by sensitization as a result of the activity of other neurons that synapse on the terminals. These findings at the level of the single cell support the observation at the behavioral level that habituation and sensitization are independent and opposing forms of learning.

This finding raises an interesting question. Sensitization can enhance a normal reflex response, but can it counteract the profound depression in the reflex produced by long-term habituation? If it can, does it restore the completely inactivated synaptic connections produced by long-term habituation? Carew, Castellucci and I examined this question and found that sensitization reversed the depressed behavior. Moreover, the synapses that were functionally inactivated (and would have remained so for weeks) were restored within an hour by a sensitizing stimulus to the head.

Hence there are synaptic pathways in the brain that are determined by developmental processes but that, being predisposed to learning, can be functionally inactivated and reactivated by experience! In fact, at these modifiable synapses a rather modest amount of training or experience is necessary to produce profound changes. If the finding were applicable to the human brain, it would imply that even during simple social experiences, as when two people speak with each other, the action of the neuronal machinery in one person's brain is capable of having a direct and perhaps long-lasting effect on the modifiable synaptic connections in the brain of the other.

Short-term sensitization is particularly attractive from an experimental point of view because it promises to be amenable to biochemical analysis. As a first step Hawkins, Castellucci and I have identified specific cells in the abdominal ganglion of *Aplysia* that produce presynaptic facilitation. By injecting an electron-dense marker substance to fill the cell and label its synaptic endings we found that the endings contain vesicles resembling those found in *Aplysia* by Ludmiela Shkolnik and James H. Schwartz in a neuron whose transmitter had previously been established to be serotonin. Consistent with the possible serotonergic nature of this cell, Marcel-

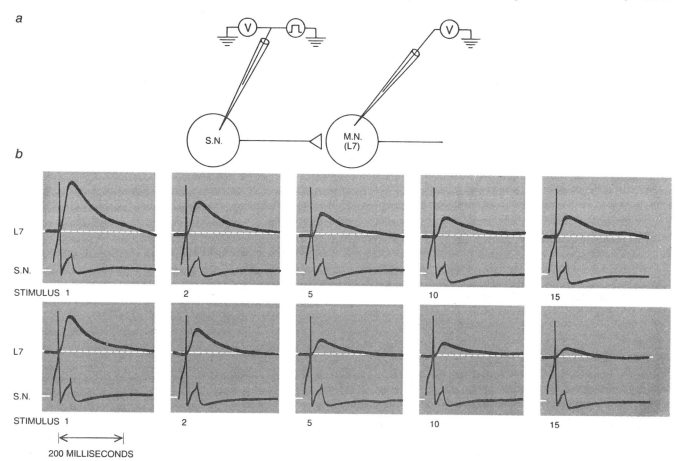

HABITUATION PROCESS, in which an animal's response to a stimulus gradually declines if the stimulus proves to be unimportant, is an elementary form of learning and memory that can be seen at the level of the single motor neuron. Here a sensory neuron (*S.N.*) from *Aplysia* **that synapses on motor neuron L7 has been set up (*a*) so that the sensory neuron can be stimulated every 10 seconds. Selected records from two consecutive training sessions of 15 stimuli, separated by 15 minutes, show that the response of L7 declines and vanishes.**

lo Brunelli, Castellucci, Tom Tomosky-Sykes and I found that serotonin enhanced the monosynaptic connection between the sensory neuron and the motor cell L7, whereas other likely transmitters did not.

We next uncovered an interesting link between serotonin and the intracellular messenger cyclic adenosine monophosphate (cyclic AMP). It has been known since the classic work of Earl W. Sutherland, Jr., and his colleagues at Vanderbilt University that most peptide hormones do not enter the target cell but instead act on a receptor on the cell surface to stimulate an enzyme called adenylate cyclase that catalyzes the conversion in the cell of adenosine triphosphate (ATP) into cyclic AMP, which then acts as a "second messenger" (the hormone is the first messenger) at several points inside the cell to initiate a set of appropriate changes in function.

Howard Cedar, Schwartz and I found that strong and prolonged stimulation of the pathway from the head that mediates sensitization in *Aplysia* gave rise to a synaptically mediated increase in cyclic AMP in the entire ganglion. Cedar and Schwartz and Irwin Levitan and Samuel Barondes also found that they could generate a prolonged increase in cyclic AMP by incubating the ganglion with serotonin. To explore the relation between serotonin and cyclic AMP, Brunelli, Castellucci and I injected cyclic AMP intracellularly into the cell body of the sensory neuron and found that it also produced presynaptic facilitation, whereas injection of 5'-AMP (the breakdown product of cyclic AMP) or still another second messenger, cyclic GMP, did not.

Since habituation involves a decrease in calcium current, it was attractive to think that cyclic AMP might exert its facilitating actions by increasing the calcium current. As I have mentioned, the calcium current is normally masked by the potassium current. Klein and I therefore examined action potentials in the sensory neurons with the potassium current reduced by TEA. Stimulating the pathway from the head that mediates sensitization or a single facilitating neuron enhanced the calcium current, as was evident in the increased duration of the action potential in TEA, and the enhancement persisted for 15 minutes or longer. The increase in calcium current paralleled the enhanced transmitter release, and both synaptic changes in turn paralleled the increase in the reflex response to a sensitizing stimulus.

The enhancement of the calcium current, as it is seen in the prolongation of the calcium component of the action potential after stimulation of the sensitizing pathway, could be produced by extracellular application of either serotonin or two substances that increase the intracellular level of cyclic AMP by in-

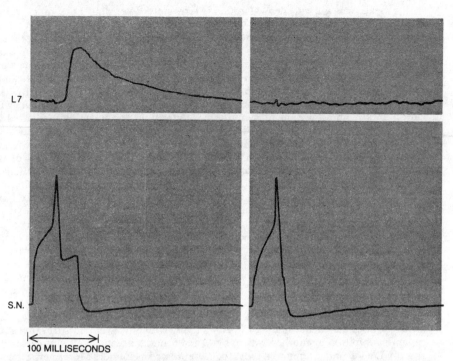

100 MILLISECONDS

LONG-TERM HABITUATION is revealed in a comparison of synaptic connections between a sensory neuron (*S.N.*) and the motor neuron L7 in untrained *Aplysia* (*left*), which served as controls, and in *Aplysia* that had received long-term habituation training (*right*). In the control animals an impulse in the sensory neuron is followed by a large excitatory synaptic response from the motor neuron. In the trained animals the synaptic connection is almost undetectable.

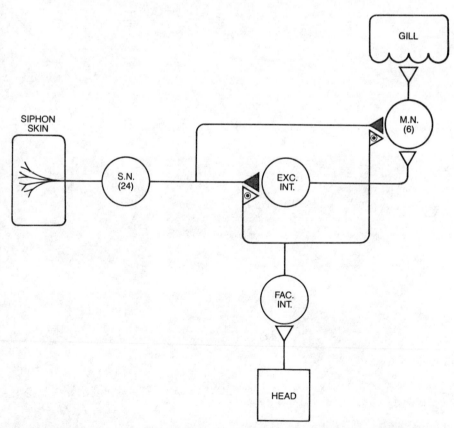

SENSITIZATION is a form of learning and memory in which the response to a stimulus is enhanced because of another and more noxious stimulus. Here gill-withdrawal reflex of *Aplysia* is intensified because of a noxious stimulus to the head. This stimulus activates neurons that excite facilitating interneurons, which end on the synaptic terminals of the sensory neurons. Those neurons are plastic, that is, capable of changing the effectiveness of their synapse. The transmitter of the facilitating interneurons, thought to be serotonin (*circled dots*), modulates the release of sensory-neuron transmitter to the excitatory interneurons and motor neurons.

hibiting phosphodiesterase, the enzyme that breaks down cyclic AMP. Similar effects were observed after direct intracellular injection of cyclic AMP, but not of 5'-AMP.

On the basis of these results Klein and I have proposed that stimulation of the facilitating neurons of the sensitizing pathway leads to the release of serotonin, which activates a serotonin-sensitive enzyme (adenylate cyclase) in the membrane of the sensory-neuron terminal. The resulting increase in cyclic AMP in the terminal leads to a greater activation of the calcium current either directly by activation of the calcium channel or indirectly by a decrease in an opposing potassium current. With each action potential the influx of calcium rises and more transmitter is released.

The availability of large cells whose electrical properties and interconnections can be thoroughly studied was the major initial attraction for using *Aplysia* to study behavior. The size of these cells might now prove to be an even greater advantage for exploring the subcellular and biochemical mechanisms of learning on the one hand and possible changes in membrane structure on the other. For example, it will be interesting to see more precisely how the increase in the level of cyclic AMP during sensitization is linked to the activation of a calcium current, because the linkage could provide the first step toward a molecular understanding of this simple form of short-term learning.

A number of mechanisms come to mind. The channels through which ions traverse the neuronal membranes are thought to consist of protein molecules. An obvious possibility is therefore that cyclic AMP activates one or more protein kinases, enzymes that Paul Greengard of the Yale University School of Medicine has suggested may provide a common molecular mechanism for mediating the various actions of cyclic AMP within the cell. Protein kinases are enzymes that phosphorylate proteins, that is, they link a phosphoryl group to a side chain of the amino acids serine or threonine in the protein molecule, thereby changing the charge and configuration of proteins and altering their function, activating some and inactivating others. Phosphorylation could serve as an effective mechanism for the regulation of memory. One way sensitization might work is that the calcium-channel protein becomes activated (or the opposing potassium-channel protein becomes inactivated) when it is phosphorylated by a protein kinase that is dependent on cyclic AMP.

Sensitization holds an interesting position in the hierarchy of learning. It is frequently considered to be a precursor form of classical conditioning. In both sensitization and classical conditioning a reflex response to a stimulus is enhanced as a result of the activation of another pathway. Sensitization differs from conditioning in being nonassociative; the sensitizing stimulus is effective in enhancing reflex responsiveness whether or not it is paired in time with the reflex stimulus. Several types of associative learning have now been demonstrated in mollusks by Alan Gelperin of Princeton University, by George Mpitsos and Stephen Collins of Case Western Reserve University and by Terry Crow and Daniel L. Alkon of the National Institutes of Health. Recently Terry Walters, Carew and I have obtained evidence for associative conditioning in *Aplysia*. We may therefore soon be in a position to analyze precisely how the mechanisms of sensitization relate to those of associative learning.

Another direction that research can now take is to examine the relation between the initial development of the neural circuit in the embryo and its later modification by learning. Both development and learning involve functional changes in the nervous system: changes in the effectiveness of synapses and in other properties of neurons. How are such changes related? Are the mechanisms of learning based on those of developmental plasticity, or do completely new processes specialized for learning emerge later?

Whatever the answers to these intriguing questions may be, the surprising and heartening thing that has emerged from the study of invertebrate animals is that one can now pinpoint and observe at the cellular level, and perhaps ultimately at the molecular level, simple aspects of memory and learning. Although certain higher mental activities are characteristic of the complex brains of higher animals, it is now clear that elementary aspects of what are regarded as mental processes can be found in the activity of just a very few neurons. It will therefore be interesting both philosophically and technically to see to what degree complex forms of mentation can be explained in terms of simpler components and mechanisms. To the extent that such reductionist explanations are possible it will also be important to determine how the units of this elementary alphabet of mentation are combined to yield the language of much more complex mental processes.

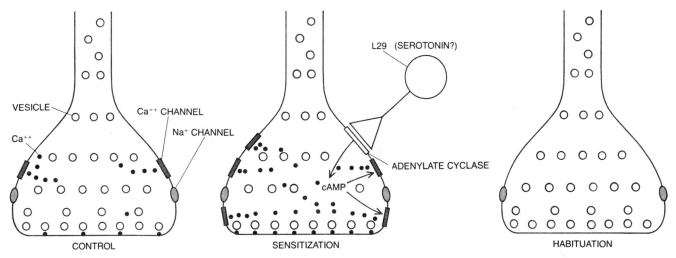

SHORT-TERM SENSITIZATION AND HABITUATION at the level of the single sensory neuron are modeled, beginning with what happens in a control situation (*left*) in which a cell fires before either sensitization or habituation has set in. A nerve impulse in the terminal membrane of the neuron opens up a number of channels for calcium ions (Ca^{++}) in parallel with the sodium channels (Na^+). Sensitization is produced by cell group L29 (perhaps more) that are believed to release the transmitter serotonin. It acts on an adenylate cyclase, an enzyme that catalyzes the synthesis of cyclic adenosine monophosphate (cyclic AMP) in the neuron terminals. The cyclic AMP increases the influx of calcium ions, perhaps by making more calcium channels available. The calcium causes a greater binding of transmitter-bearing vesicles to release sites, increasing the probability that the neuron will release transmitter. In habituation repeated impulses in the terminals could decrease the number of open calcium channels, depressing the calcium influx and inactivating the synapse.

Synapse Formation in the Developing Brain

As the brain develops, existing synapses between nerve cells are refined and new connections are made. The changes are not automatic; they depend in part on the young neurons generating impulses

by Ronald E. Kalil

The development of the mammalian brain is an extraordinary achievement. From a single collection of immature, undifferentiated cells emerges an organ so structurally complex that most other natural or human-crafted systems seem simple by comparison. In spite of such intricacy, neurobiologists have managed in the past century to learn a great deal about how the brain's electrical circuitry is formed and refined in the course of embryonic and postnatal development.

Most investigators would agree that genes determine which neurons are initially wired together to establish the basic circuits of the brain. Yet for years there was much disagreement over whether genes control every aspect of neuronal maturation. Many workers suspected that experience—in particular, the flow through neuronal circuits of impulses known as action potentials—helps to control such details as the number, distribution and efficiency of synapses, which are the sites of communication between neurons.

In the past 25 years a host of studies have shown that atypical activity in the immature brain can certainly give rise to abnormal wiring. What is perhaps more intriguing, recent work

RONALD E. KALIL was educated at Harvard College and the Massachusetts Institute of Technology. In 1973 he joined the faculty of the University of Wisconsin-Madison, where he is now professor of ophthalmology and Director of the Center for Neuroscience. In addition to studying the role of experience in directing the formation of synaptic connections in the brain, Kalil is interested in the mechanisms by which the brain's visual circuits recover from injury.

has demonstrated that brain activity does not merely influence synaptic development; action potentials are, in fact, essential to several aspects of such development. For example, my colleagues and I at the University of Wisconsin at Madison and at the University of Colorado at Boulder have shown that when young neurons are prevented from generating action potentials, their synapse-forming structures known as axon terminal bulbs become "frozen" in an immature state: they fail to grow, to form new synapses and to change in a variety of other important ways.

The cessation of change is actually desirable at some point in many brain systems—in a major sensory pathway that has fully matured, for example. Indeed, certain pathways established during gestation remain plastic for only a limited time after birth, during which their wiring is fine-tuned. (The timing of these so-called critical periods varies from one part of the brain to another.) Once such honing is complete, however, the pathways essentially lose their ability to change, which ensures that a mature system will respond in a consistent way to a given stimulus (such as a flash of light).

On the other hand, in some brain systems the ongoing ability to alter the wiring of neurons is crucial. For instance, the systems responsible for learning presumably remain plastic indefinitely; otherwise, new knowledge could not be stored.

Studies of how plasticity is maintained by the learning centers of the brain are yielding what may be important clues to some of the molecular events mediating the effects of brain activity on synaptic development. Certain of the findings suggest that critical periods may simply be epochs in

which young neurons in widespread areas of the brain temporarily share the molecular characteristics that enable the learning centers to perpetually alter their neuronal connections. There is even some reason to suppose that closely related mechanisms may help mediate the effect of brain activity on synapse strength, control the timing of critical periods and enable learning to continue throughout life.

Although the brains of various mammals differ in size, shape and detail, all are built on a common plan and share a similar history during growth and maturation. Early in gestation, a number of cells aggregate to form the neural tube, which then gives rise to discernible layers and clusters of cells; these groupings will later become the specialized parts of the mature brain.

Once the cells are organized into groups, they differentiate by extending projections: a single axon and many dendrites. The axon, which can grow to be tens of centimeters long, typically transmits signals, whereas the dendrites, which usually are shorter, generally receive signals.

Growing axons are thought to make their way to specific parts of the rudimentary brain by following a chemical trail whose production is probably determined genetically. After the leading tip of an axon reaches its destination, it elaborates an arbor of branches, each of which has a bulbous terminal. The bulbs, in turn, make synapses with dendrites or other receptive regions on selected target cells. Most synapses consist of a specialized region on a presynaptic axon bulb, a receptive region on a postsynaptic dendrite and a narrow cleft between the two regions. (An axon can make contact with a number of cells, each of

Reprinted with permission from *Bio Systems*, vol. 23, pp. 297–303, 1990.

which may receive input not only from that particular axon but also from many others.)

Once synapses are established, signals can be passed from neuron to neuron. Transmissions in most places in the mammalian brain take place chemically. The presynaptic bulb releases a neurotransmitter, which diffuses across the synaptic cleft and binds to receptor molecules in the cell membrane of the postsynaptic cell. The binding causes the receptors to change their shape and thus activate channels through which selected ions flow into or out of the cell.

The net change of ions in the cell body (which can receive many signals at once) determines whether a neuron will be inhibited or else stimulated to generate an action potential, or nerve

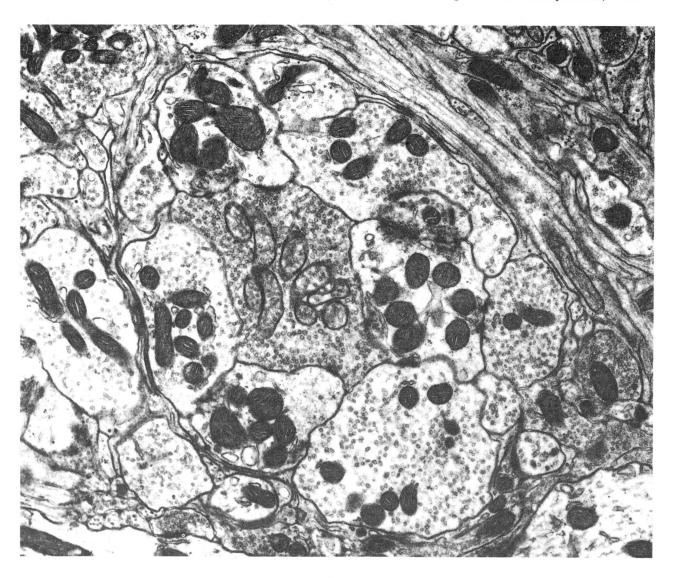

COMPLEX SYNAPTIC ZONE in the part of the brain known as the lateral geniculate nucleus is one of many such zones that normally form during the first eight weeks of a cat's life. In the center is a terminal *(center on map)* of an axon (a long, signal-transmitting projection) that extends from a ganglion cell in the retina of the eye. At birth such terminals, which are bulbous, are about half their mature size and have already formed some synapses (sites of communication) with the dendrites (relatively short projections) of what are called geniculate relay cells *(please see map)*. During the next eight weeks the bulbs grow and also form synapses with F profiles *(blue on map)*, specialized appendages of the dendrites of the geniculate cells known as interneurons. The bulbs and their surrounding dendrites then become enclosed in a capsule *(edge of map)* that defines the complex synaptic zone. The author has found that all of this anatomical development in the first eight weeks of life depends on the generation of nerve impulses known as action potentials. The zone shown in the electron micrograph is magnified some 18,000 diameters.

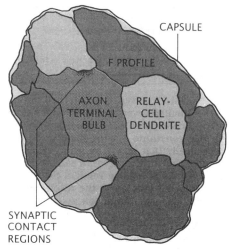

CAPSULE

F PROFILE

AXON TERMINAL BULB

RELAY-CELL DENDRITE

SYNAPTIC CONTACT REGIONS

impulse. These impulses propagate down the length of the cell's axon and, if many of them are fired, can trigger the release of the cell's own neurotransmitter molecules, which then act on a new set of neurons.

What exactly is an action potential? Such impulses, which last less than a thousandth of a second, are essentially momentary, self-limiting reversals of the transmembrane potential—the difference between the charge inside and along the external surface of the cell. In a resting cell the transmembrane potential is 70 millivolts (.07 volt), with the inside of the cell negative relative to the outside. Action potentials arise in a resting cell after the net ionic flux (the average of all inputs from the presynaptic cells) increases the positive charge in the cell body enough to reduce the transmembrane potential by about 40 millivolts.

When that voltage threshold is attained, the cell membrane in a specialized region known as the axon hillock (where the axon joins the cell body) becomes extremely permeable to sodium ions, which are positively charged. These flood into the cell and for an instant make the charge of the interior positive relative to that of the exterior; a concomitant outflow of other positive ions restores the resting voltage almost immediately, as the action potential continues to travel down the axon.

The suspicion that action potentials might be critical to brain development grew to a great extent out of several studies done in the 1960's and 1970's, mainly involving the visual system of the cat. This system is much studied, in part because a great deal of its maturation is delayed until the first two months after birth, which makes the last stages of development relatively easy to examine and manipulate.

The cat's neuronal pathways for vision begin with the ganglion cells in the retina. These cells convey information received from the retina's photoreceptors to way stations known as lateral geniculate nuclei in the thalamus of the brain. As is true for many mammals, the ganglion cells in the right side of each eye (which receive input from the left side of the visual field) send axons to the lateral geniculate nucleus in the right hemisphere of the brain; the ganglion cells in the left side of each eye send axons to the nucleus in the left hemisphere [see illustration on opposite page]. So-called relay cells of the lateral geniculate nucleus, in turn, transmit the information to the visual cortex in the same hemisphere for processing.

Carla J. Shatz, David W. Sretavan and Marla B. Luskin of the Stanford University School of Medicine have uncovered much of what is known about the prenatal development of these pathways. The embryonic axons from the retinal ganglion cells normally arrive at the lateral geniculate nuclei about midway through gestation, which in the cat lasts for a total of about 63 days. At this point, each lateral geniculate nucleus consists of a cluster of randomly arranged cells.

The nuclei are transformed greatly during the second half of gestation. Their constituent cells become organized into layers, each of which will eventually be sensitive to signals from only one eye. This specialization of the layers is accomplished by the gradual stratification of the retinogeniculate axons coming into the thalamus from

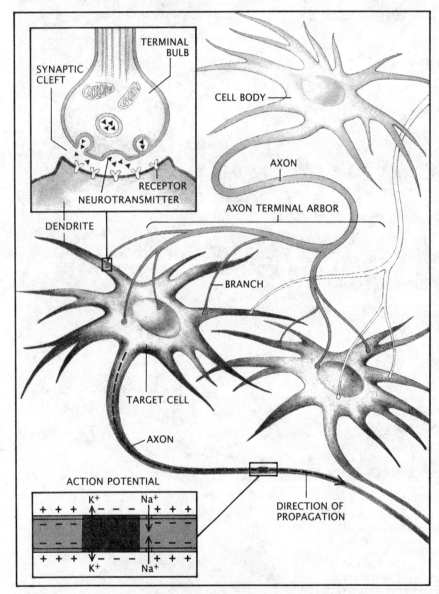

EXCITATORY SIGNALS received by a target cell can give rise to an action potential—a momentary, self-limited reversal of the charges along the inside and outside of the cell membrane. Action potentials propagate down the length of a cell's axon (*broken arrow*) and thus constitute a nerve impulse. Signals are generally passed across synapses chemically (*top detail*): an axon terminal bulb from one cell releases a neurotransmitter that diffuses across a narrow cleft and binds to receptor molecules on the target cell. Such binding renders the postsynaptic cell membrane locally permeable to selected ions. When the result (*bottom detail*) is a sufficiently large influx of sodium ions (Na⁺), an action potential *(upper right)* is generated. Then the interior of the cell, which is normally negative relative to the exterior, becomes positive, and the exterior becomes negative—for an instant. A concomitant outflow of potassium ions (K⁺) helps to restore the original charges almost immediately.

the retinal ganglion cells. Axons receiving input from the right eye ultimately terminate in specific layers of geniculate cells, whereas the axons receiving input from the left eye terminate in adjacent layers.

About 10 days before the cat is born, axons from the relay cells of the lateral geniculate nucleus enter the visual cortex. These geniculocortical axons end primarily in the fourth of six primitive layers there. At first, axons associated with the right eye overlap with axons receiving input from the left eye; the axons often terminate on the same cells, which means that the target cells can be stimulated by activity in either eye.

That state of affairs is temporary, however. Simon D. LeVay, Michael P. Stryker and Shatz showed while they were at Harvard Medical School that during the second month after the cat's birth, the geniculocortical axons become segregated by eye. They appear to retract some of their terminal branches, so that individual cortical cells remain in contact with geniculate cells responsive only to the left or only to the right eye. (Presumably the axons also increase the strength, or efficiency, of the remaining synapses, although this has not yet been proved.)

The net result of the segregation is the establishment of alternating, similarly proportioned ocular-dominance columns in the cortex: some columns of cortical cells respond only to signals from the right eye, whereas the alternating columns respond only to signals from the left eye.

Several of the most important studies showing that normal visual experience is critical to such developmental changes were done in the 1960's by Torsten N. Wiesel and David H. Hubel of Harvard Medical School. These early studies involved suturing closed the lid of one eye in newborn cats. The studies demonstrated that limiting the activity of one eye in this way severely interferes with the development of ocular-dominance columns. Measurements of electrical activity in the fourth layer of the visual cortex revealed that virtually all of the cells there responded exclusively to signals from the open eye.

Much of the explanation for the cortical abnormality rests with the axons extending from the lateral geniculate nuclei. By staining these axons, Shatz and Stryker showed in cats, and Hubel, Wiesel and LeVay showed in monkeys, that the geniculocortical axons of animals raised for many weeks with one eye closed do not segregate into the

usual eye-specific domains. Instead those axons associated with the open eye elaborate new terminal branches, thereby expanding their territory in the cortex and crowding out axon terminals carrying information from the deprived eye.

Once it became clear that atypical neuronal activity during brain development could distort the usual wiring of the visual system, attention turned to the issue of whether neuronal activity is necessary for wiring to proceed. The possibility existed that some amount of synaptic development could occur even in the absence of action potentials, which would mean that some aspects of the development were under genetic control.

The only way to resolve the issue was to eliminate action potentials. Investigators initially attempted to do

that by raising cats in complete darkness from birth. The suturing of both eyes closed would have been insufficient because some light would have entered the eyes through the closed lids. (The absence of visual stimulation does not seem to disturb kittens: they remain vigorous and playful, and they grow at a normal rate.)

The visual system of dark-reared subjects developed abnormally but did develop somewhat. In contrast to the ocular-dominance columns of normal animals, those of the dark-reared cats were imprecisely defined, and the spacing between adjacent patches of the columns was often uneven. In other words, the postnatal eye-specific segregation of geniculocortical axons must have begun but was incomplete.

Initially the finding that some development took place seemed to imply

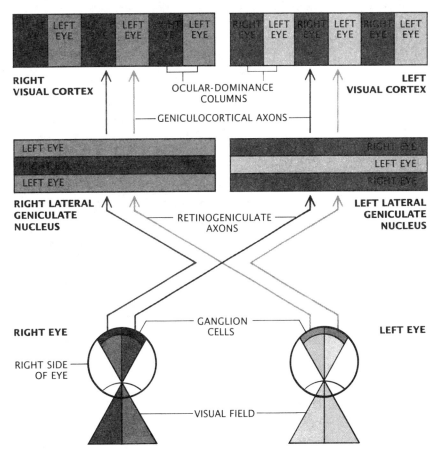

NEURONAL PATHWAYS important for vision in the cat resemble those of other mammals that have forward-facing eyes. Retinal ganglion cells in the right side of both retinas transmit visual information to the lateral geniculate nucleus in the right hemisphere of the brain; the axons from the right eye terminate on cells in the middle layer of the nucleus, and axons from the left eye terminate on cells above or below that layer. Similarly, ganglion cells in the left side of both retinas project to the lateral geniculate nucleus of the left hemisphere, again with the axons segregated into eye-specific layers. Relay cells in each lateral geniculate nucleus, in turn, convey visual signals to the visual cortex of the same hemisphere. In each hemisphere the axons associated with the right eye terminate on specific columns of cortical cells, and the axons associated with the left eye end on the alternating columns. Such segregation gives rise to what are called ocular-dominance columns in the cortex.

that maturation could proceed at least partially even in the absence of activity in the visual pathway. Other work showed, however, that action potentials had not been fully eliminated, which meant that alternative explanations were possible. For example, William Burke and William R. Hayhow of the University of Sydney showed that a total lack of visual stimulation does not completely silence retinal ganglion cells; the cells discharge action potentials spontaneously even in the absence of light. In addition, Robert W. Rodieck and P. S. Smith, while at the University of Sydney, and David N. Mastronarde of the University of Colorado at Boulder separately showed that ganglion cells in one eye often discharge spontaneously at about the same time, but the activity of ganglion cells in one eye is not correlated with the activity of cells in the other eye.

Collectively these results suggested that the correlated, spontaneous firing of impulses by ganglion cells within each eye might have accounted for the observed development. In particular, it seemed reasonable to suspect that the distinct patterns of spontaneous ganglion-cell activity in the right and left eye could have acted as signatures that enabled developing geniculocortical axons to be sorted into rudimentary ocular-dominance columns.

The failure of dark-rearing to block action potentials made it imperative to find a different approach to determine whether action potentials are necessary for synaptic development. Fortunately nature has provided a toxin, tetrodotoxin, that is perfectly suited for the task. The substance, which is found in the ovaries of the Japanese puffer fish and also in a newt common in California, prevents action potentials from arising but does not destroy nerve tissue. It works by binding to voltage-sensitive sodium ion channels and thereby blocking the crucial ion's entry into the cells. Unfortunately the circulation in the blood of just a few millionths of a gram of tetrodotoxin per kilogram of body weight is lethal for most mammals, and so until recently the substance was not an appropriate research tool. (The drug rapidly arrests such nerve-dependent functions as breathing.)

About 10 years ago methods were developed for injecting the toxin into the eye so that it would essentially remain confined there, unable to circulate. A painless injection every two or three days is enough to prevent retinal ganglion cells from generating action potentials.

With the new method Stryker, who had moved to the University of California at San Francisco, and William A.

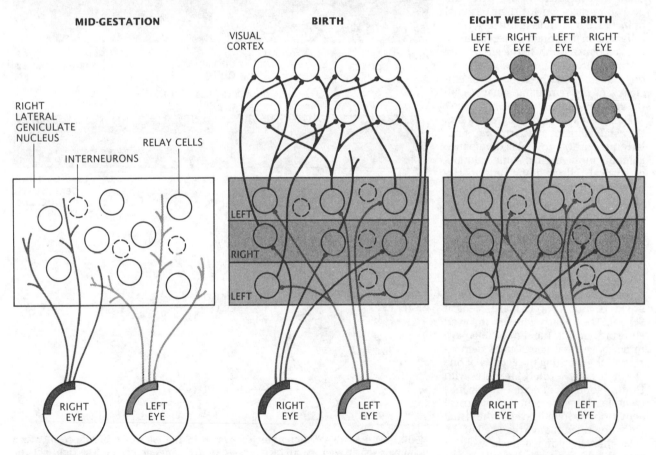

DEVELOPMENT of the cat's visual pathways normally follows a standard course. Axons growing from the retinal ganglion cells arrive at the lateral geniculate nucleus about midway through gestation. Initially the axons are too immature to form synapses with the geniculate cells, which are randomly arranged in the nucleus. By the time the cat is born the geniculate cells have been parceled into layers, and the entering retinogeniculate axons have been segregated, so that each geniculate layer receives input from only the right eye *(very dark)* or the left *(very light)*. The retinogeniculate axons have begun to establish synapses with relay cells, but synapses with interneurons have not yet been formed. At this point, too, axons from many relay cells have made synapses with cells in the visual cortex. These axons overlap, however: those conveying information from the right eye *(very dark)* often terminate on the same cortical cells as axons from the left eye *(very light)*. By the end of the first eight weeks of life, the retinogeniculate axons have made synapses with both relay cells and interneurons; the geniculocortical axons have become segregated by eye, and ocular-dominance columns can be identified.

Harris of the San Diego campus were able to eliminate the ambiguity of the dark-rearing results. By treating both eyes of newborn cats with tetrodotoxin until the cats were six weeks old, they blocked the formation of ocular-dominance columns in the visual cortex. They thereby demonstrated that action potentials are needed for the columns to arise.

By staining geniculocortical axons associated with each eye, Stryker and Harris further showed that, as might be expected, the stalled cortical development derived from a failure of the geniculocortical axons extending into layer four of the visual cortex to segregate into eye-specific patches; instead axons representing the right or the left eye often made synaptic contact with the same cells. As a result, when the toxin wore off, most cortical cells responded almost equally to input from both eyes. These properties are typical of the visual cortex of neonatal kittens but are unusual for animals that are six weeks old.

At about the same time as Stryker and Harris were doing their studies, Mark W. Dubin, Louisa A. Stark and Steven M. Archer of the University of Colorado at Boulder examined the neurophysiological effects of ganglion-cell blockade on the lateral geniculate nucleus. They injected tetrodotoxin into one eye of a group of cats for the first two months of life and then recorded the electrical activity in geniculate cells a few days after the drug wore off.

Their recordings showed that eliminating action potentials in ganglion cells during that period prevents an important change from taking place in the lateral geniculate neurons. Normally by the end of a cat's second month of life, its geniculate neurons not only have been parceled into eye-specific layers but also have become specialized in another way: some cells fire action potentials only when a spot of light at the center of their receptive field flashes on, whereas some cells fire only when the spot disappears. (The receptive field is the part of the visual field about which a cell receives information.) This specialization results from the segregation of retinogeniculate axons in such a way that the axons of ganglion cells responsive to the flashing on of light end on different geniculate cells than do the axons of ganglion cells responsive to the light's disappearance.

In the treated animals, however, most of the geniculate cells associated with the treated eye could be excited by both the turning on and the turning

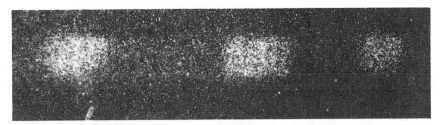

SEGMENT OF VISUAL CORTEX in a normal eight-week-old cat is strikingly different from a comparable segment in a cat of the same age in whom input from one eye was eliminated experimentally during development. In the normal cat (*top*) the presence of ocular-dominance columns is revealed by the alternation of white and black patches. (The white patches were produced by radioactive tracers that traveled to the cortex after being injected into one eye.) In contrast, a corresponding stretch of cortex in the treated cat has no such patches (*bottom*); the bright band indicates that the region is sensitive throughout to inputs from the eye that received visual information (*solid white band*). Clearly, a flow of impulses through the visual pathways from both eyes is needed if ocular-dominance columns are to develop.

off of a spot of light. The cells were unable to distinguish between the two conditions.

This group of studies exploiting tetrodotoxin, then, enabled investigators to gather strong evidence that when action potentials in the visual system are silenced, synaptic development does not proceed normally: geniculocortical axons do not segregate into eye-specific domains, and the on-off segregation of retinogeniculate axons does not proceed properly in the lateral geniculate nucleus. Yet these studies could say nothing conclusive about what was happening structurally at the level of the synapse. For instance, it was unclear whether eliminating action potentials in ganglion cells interfered with the anatomical development of their axon terminal bulbs.

Direct evidence relating to this problem could be obtained only with electron microscopy, and so I undertook such studies with Dubin, Stark and Grayson L. Scott, a colleague of mine at Wisconsin. This effort was facilitated by earlier work Scott and I had done, in which we identified many aspects of normal retinogeniculate synaptic development.

The earlier work had demonstrated that the terminal bulbs of retinal ganglion cells normally change in several specific ways in the two months after a cat is born. For instance, their cross-

sectional size typically doubles, and the length of the regions specialized for synaptic contact shrinks by about a third. (The shrinkage may help focus the flow of released neurotransmitter molecules.)

We also had learned that beginning about the third week after birth the bulbs begin to increase the number of contacts they make with the dendrites in the lateral geniculate nucleus. The bulbs retain any existing contacts they have established with the dendrites of the geniculate relay cells and also form new synapses with specialized appendages (called F profiles) of the dendrites of cells known as interneurons. Interneurons, which emit inhibitory messages in the lateral geniculate nucleus, are important in fine-tuning the behavior of the relay cells.

Another change generally occurs by the end of the second month. At that point about 30 percent of all retinogeniculate terminal bulbs are situated in what are called complex synaptic zones, which typically consist of the bulb surrounded by a cluster of dendrites and F profiles. Each complex synaptic zone is encapsulated by protoplasmic extensions from what are called glial cells, which help to give the brain its structure. Although the function of the complex zones is not understood precisely, they may help to isolate the internal synaptic connections from external influences.

When we injected one eye of a group

of cats with tetrodotoxin for the first eight weeks of life, we found that the synaptic connections made by ganglion cells in the treated eye remained identical to those found in cats at birth. Development had been stopped completely. In the absence of action potentials, the bulbs did not grow in size, did not exhibit a decrease in the length of their contact regions and did not make synaptic contacts with F profiles. Essentially all synapses were made with the dendrites of relay cells, and virtually no complex synaptic zones could be found.

Although our studies demonstrated that the elimination of action potentials halts the maturation of the axon bulbs in ganglion cells, the results did not exclude the possibility that retinal blockade simply produces a moratorium on development that can be undone if neuronal activity is restored. The results also did not indicate whether development can proceed in the usual way if a newborn kitten is given normal stimulation for some amount of time before action potentials are blocked. We tried to settle these issues with two additional sets of experiments.

In the first set we blocked action potentials in the retinal ganglion cells of one eye for the first four or 10 weeks after birth; then we discontinued the drug to allow for several months of normal activity. If we found that retinogeniculate connections developed normally even with belated activity, we could conclude that action potentials, although necessary for development, need not be present during a specific period.

In the second set of experiments, we allowed the animals to have normal visual experiences until the third or fifth postnatal week before we initiated the tetrodotoxin injections. If we found that retinogeniculate connections developed normally, we could conclude that action potentials are required to initiate synaptic development but not to sustain it.

Under none of these conditions did retinogeniculate connections develop properly. We saw the closest approximation to normal development in the first set of experiments, when retinal blockade was discontinued earliest (after the first four weeks of treatment). Then the size of the axon terminals and the number of synapses they formed were close to normal (75 percent of normal), but the number of complex synaptic zones was markedly decreased.

The second set of experiments demonstrated that early visual experience prior to the onset of retinal blockade cannot initiate the usual synaptic development. Even when action potentials are allowed to occur throughout the first postnatal month, retinogeniculate connections look almost the same as they do at birth. Our combined results show, then, that action potentials are required throughout the first two months of life (and particularly in the second month) if ganglion-cell terminal bulbs are to mature and establish new synaptic connections. If action potentials are blocked at any time during this period, normal development will be prevented.

The problem of mechanism remains. By what sequence of molecular events might the flow of impulses from neuron to neuron during brain development trigger the maturation of axonal terminal bulbs or alter the distribution or strength of synaptic connections? These questions still await answers.

Theoretical and experimental work on learning may, however, illuminate the issue of synaptic strength. Studies of learning are potentially applicable to development because learning, in common with development, involves assembling and strengthening some synaptic connections and weakening and eliminating others. A prescient assault on the problem of how synaptic connections might be altered by activity was made by Donald O. Hebb of McGill University in 1949. He suggested that when one cell "repeatedly or persistently" succeeds in activating another, metabolic or structural changes in one cell or both of them increase the efficiency of the connection between the cells. (Random or occasional activity, then, would not be sufficient to strengthen synapses.)

Hebb's ideas could not be tested at

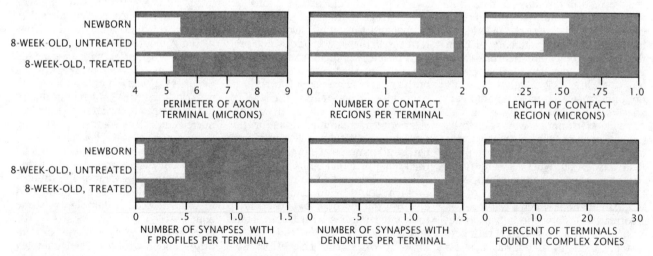

GRAPHS summarize much of the data demonstrating that retinal ganglion cells have to generate action potentials if their axon terminal bulbs are to mature. Electron micrographs were made of single cross sections through the lateral geniculate nucleus of newborn cats, normal eight-week-olds and "treated" eight-week-olds in whom ganglion-cell action potentials were silenced in one eye from birth. The collected images revealed that the axon terminal bulbs of the silenced ganglion cells in the treated eight-week-olds were virtually identical with those of the newborns. Compared with the bulbs of normal (untreated) eight-week-olds, those of the newborns and of the treated cats were smaller, made fewer synaptic contacts and had longer contact regions (regions specialized for the release of neurotransmitter); they also made essentially no synapses with F profiles. Virtually none of the axon terminal bulbs of the newborns or the treated animals were in complex synaptic zones, whereas approximately 30 percent of the terminal bulbs of the normal, mature cats were in such complex zones.

the time. More recently, though, studies of the molecular basis of a phenomenon known as long-term potentiation have suggested a mechanism by which extensive activity across synapses might strengthen them. Long-term potentiation, which was first described by Terje Lømo of the University of Oslo in 1966, is the increasing of synaptic efficiency for days, or even indefinitely, in response to controlled bursts of stimulation. In mammals long-term potentiation occurs most readily in the hippocampus, a part of the brain that is critical to learning and memory.

Exposure of a neuron in the hippocampus to a particular pattern of excitatory stimulation—brief, high-frequency electric currents—can within seconds produce a long-lasting increase in synaptic efficiency. For many years no one understood how that critical pattern achieved long-term potentiation, but an important clue was gained when a molecule known as the NMDA (N-methyl-D-aspartate) receptor was found to be activated specifically by that pattern. The receptor acts as a gate, regulating the activity of a channel through which calcium (a ubiquitous intracellular messenger) enters the cell. The receptor's name derives from the fact that the associated channel, which normally is voltage sensitive, can be opened under experimental conditions when it is exposed to NMDA; presumably the effect is mediated by the binding of NMDA to the gating molecule.

The brief, high-frequency stimulation of a postsynaptic cell in the hippocampus gives rise to an inflow of positively charged ions and, in turn, lowers the membrane potential below a set threshold. This change activates NMDA receptors, causing their associated calcium channels to open. Calcium ions then flood into the cell through the open channels and activate intracellular enzymes, probably including enzymes that are major constituents of the part of the postsynaptic membrane specialized to receive transmissions. The events that follow have not been identified in detail, but the enzymes may effect a reorganization of membrane proteins, leading to a subsequent improvement in the efficiency with which the postsynaptic cell responds to specific patterns of stimulation [see "Memory Storage and Neural Systems," by Daniel L. Alkon; SCIENTIFIC AMERICAN, July].

It is tempting to suppose that a similar mechanism may also participate in the strengthening of synapses during the development of the brain.

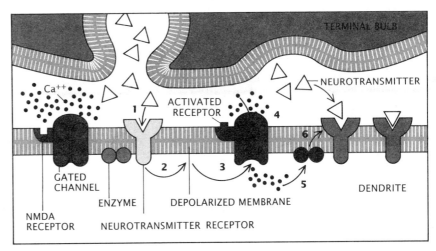

MECHANISM by which NMDA receptors might effect long-term potentiation—a persistent change in the strength of synaptic connections—in the hippocampus of the brain has been partially deciphered. When input from a presynaptic cell is patterned and timed appropriately (1), the stimulation depolarizes the cell membrane (2) enough to activate NMDA receptors, causing them to open NMDA-receptor-gated channels permeable to calcium ions (3). As the ions flow into the cell (4), they activate various enzymes (5), presumably including some that help to reorganize the membrane's proteins in a way that improves the efficiency of the synapse (6). The systematic activation of one neuron by another in the developing brain may well strengthen synapses by a mechanism similar to the one described here.

For instance, the repeated activation of cortical cells by geniculocortical axons associated with one eye might be detected by a voltage-sensitive receptor, such as the NMDA receptor. The detection of the change could then trigger a calcium-mediated reorganization of the postsynaptic membrane, which would lead to the strengthening and ultimate stabilization of the active synapses.

This mechanism is particularly attractive because it suggests a fairly simple model for the control of the beginning and end of critical periods for activity-dependent development in different brain systems. The timing of the periods could be efficiently controlled in given groups of neurons if their biochemical machinery were genetically instructed when to start and stop synthesizing molecules that, like the NMDA receptor, are sensitive to particular patterns of incoming stimulation. Such a model seems plausible because the inclusion of the start and stop commands in the genes would not require very much coding.

An added advantage of the model is that it can also account for protracted plasticity in other parts of the brain. All that would be required is that neurons be genetically programmed to produce NMDA receptors or functionally related molecules indefinitely instead of halting production at some specified time. Thus, variation on a single biochemical theme could ac-

count for relatively brief periods of activity-dependent plasticity, such as is found in the developing visual cortex, as well as for the apparently lifelong plasticity found in other parts of the brain, such as the hippocampus.

FURTHER READING

THE FIRST STAGE OF PERCEPTION: GROWTH OF THE ASSEMBLY. The Organization of Behavior: A Neuropsychological Theory. Donald O. Hebb. John Wiley & Sons, Inc., 1949.

BINOCULAR IMPULSE BLOCKADE PREVENTS THE FORMATION OF OCULAR DOMINANCE COLUMNS IN CAT VISUAL CORTEX. Michael P. Stryker and William A. Harris in Journal of Neuroscience, Vol. 6, No. 8, pages 2117–2133; August, 1986.

ELIMINATION OF ACTION POTENTIALS BLOCKS THE STRUCTURAL DEVELOPMENT OF RETINOGENICULATE SYNAPSES. Ronald E. Kalil, Mark W. Dubin, Grayson Scott and Louisa A. Stark in Nature, Vol. 323, No. 6084, pages 156–158; September 11, 1986.

THE ROLE OF ACTION POTENTIALS IN THE MORPHOLOGICAL DEVELOPMENT OF RETINOGENICULATE CONNECTIONS IN THE CAT. Ronald E. Kalil and Mark W. Dubin in Cellular Thalamic Mechanisms. Edited by Marina Bentivoglio and Roberto Spreafico. Elsevier Science Publishers, 1988.

THE ROLE OF FUNCTION IN THE PRENATAL DEVELOPMENT OF RETINOGENICULATE CONNECTIONS. Carla J. Shatz in Cellular Thalamic Mechanisms. Edited by Marina Bentivoglio and Roberto Spreafico. Elsevier Science Publishers, 1988.

Part 3
Computational Neural Systems: Foundations

Early research in the field of neurophysiology and more recent studies on the neuronal morphology of biological vision have inspired mathematicians, computer scientists, and engineers. Our recent studies have replicated some of the neuronal functions for the development of a new class of computing systems—computational neural systems or computational neural networks (CNN).

ALTHOUGH the subject of neurophysiology is relatively old, it is only within the last decade that we started thinking in terms of artificial neural computing systems. Since 1985, the field has faced an exponential growth, giving rise to a large volume of literature in the form of books, scientific journals, and international scientific conferences and symposia sponsored by some major scientific societies. At the same time, the field of neural computing has generated a large amount of commercial interest, which has resulted in many major computer-oriented companies becoming involved in the development of new neural hardware and software. Interestingly, at the same time, this development gave birth to many new commercial enterprises around the globe, and caused keen competition among them. Some of them have survived and are doing well, while others experienced an untimely demise.

In Part Three of this volume, we present an introduction to neurocomputing systems. We have assembled six representative articles written during recent years (1983–1993) by various experts in the field. In the first tutorial article (3.1), J. A. Anderson provides a neurobiological explanation of parallelism, distributiveness, and associate attributes in the brain. Several simple neural models based on experimental evidence are presented in order to illustrate how distributed parallel associative models can be used for cognitive computation.

S. I. Amari, a pioneer in the field of neural networks, proposes a unified field theory as a mathematical method for analyzing learning and self-organizing neural networks in article (3.2). This theory suggests that fine structures of the brain, such as signal detecting cells, are formed by self-organization. The process of self-organization ensures that the brain cells are compatible with the environment from which the animal receives sensory signals. It is believed that self-organization is responsible for refining the pre-existing retino-tectal connections into an accurate topographic map with fine resolution.

This theory may help to construct a topological cognitive machine with abilities such as learning and perception.

A brief survey of the motivations, fundamentals, detailed analytical theory, and applications of neural computing systems are presented in the tutorial article (3.3) by T. Kohonen. Important issues discussed by Kohonen include the nature of neural computing, what biological neural networks can and cannot do, and applications of artificial neural computers.

J. J. Hopfield and D. W. Tank were the first to suggest the use of dynamic neural networks for complex computing purposes. In article (3.4), Hopfield and Tank show how a simple dynamic neural network can solve an optimization problem. They relate their model to the behavior of biological neural circuits.

In the fifth article, G. Toulouse, S. Dehaene, and J. Changeux describe a neuronal learning mechanism that is formally related to statistical mechanics. Networks with symmetric interactions have been shown to function as content-addressable memories. The approach proposed by the authors includes four biologically relevant aspects: initial state before learning, synaptic sign changes, hierarchical categorization of stored patterns, and the synaptic learning rules. This brief, but interesting, article provides a theory for describing memory storage during the early development of a child and adulthood. The spin-glass model treated in this article provides an additional bridge between statistical mechanics and theoretical biology.

Finally, we have also included an article authored by D. Koruga. In this article, the author provides a new approach to the research in the field of neural networks. This research is based on molecular networks within a biological neuron. A few fundamental concepts of molecular computing based on cytoskeleton networks and feedback control theory are presented. Some research in the field suggests that molecular computing based on nanoelectronics and organic and biological polymers will be possible in the near future.

In the next part of this volume, we will make use of these various neural models to examine neuro-vision problems in closer detail.

Further Reading

[1] S. Amari, "Mathematical foundation of neurocomputing," *Proc. IEEE,* vol. 78, no. 9, pp. 1443–1463, 1990.

[2] S. Amari and K. Maginu, "Statistical neurodynamics of associative memory," *Neural Networks,* vol. 1, pp. 63–73, 1988.

[3] S. Amari, "Characteristics of random nets of analog neuron-like elements," *IEEE Trans. Syst., Man, Cybern.,* vol. 2, no. 5, pp. 643–657, 1972.

[4] J. A. Anderson, "A simple neural network generating an interactive memory," *Math. Biosci.,* vol. 14, pp. 197–220, 1972.

[5] J. A. Anderson and E. Rosenfeld, Eds., *Neurocomputing: Foundations of Research.* Cambridge MA: MIT Press, 1988.

[6] P. A. Anninos, "Mathematical model of memory trace and forgetfulness," *Kybernetik,* vol. 10, no. 3, pp. 165–167, 1972.

[7] P. A. Anninos, B. Beek, T. J. Csermely, E. M. Harth, and G. Pertile, "Dynamics of neural structures," *J. Theoret. Biol.,* vol. 26, pp. 121–148, 1970.

[8] M. A. Arbib and J. A. Robinson, Eds., *Natural and Artificial Parallel Computation.* Cambridge, MA: MIT Press, 1990.

[9] S. Chen, C. F. N. Cowan, and P. M. Grant, "Orthogonal least squares learning algorithm for radial basis function networks," *IEEE Trans. Neural Networks,* vol. 2, no. 2, pp. 302–309, 1991.

[10] M. A. Cohen and S. Grossberg, "Absolute stability of global pattern formulation and parallel memory storage by competitive neural networks," *IEEE Trans. Syst., Man, Cybern.,* vol. 13, no. 5, pp. 815–826, 1983.

[11] S. Grossberg, "Nonlinear neural networks: Principles, mechanisms, and architectures," *Neural Networks,* vol. 1, pp. 17–61, 1988.

[12] S. Grossberg, Ed., *The Adaptive Brain I.* Amsterdam: North-Holland, 1987.

[13] S. Grossberg, Ed., *The Adaptive Brain II.* Amsterdam: North-Holland, 1987.

[14] E. Harth, "Order and chaos in neural systems: An approach to the dynamics of higher brain functions," *IEEE Trans. Syst., Man, Cybern.,* vol. SMC-13, no. 5, pp. 782–789, 1983.

[15] R. Hecht-Nielson, *Neurocomputing.* Reading MA: Addison-Wesley, 1990.

[16] G. W. Hoffmann, "A neural network model based on the analogy with the immune system," *J. Theoret. Biol.,* vol. 122, pp. 33–67, 1986.

[17] G. W. Hoffmann, M. W. Benson, G. M. Bree, and P. E. Kinahan, "A teachable neural network based on an unorthodox neuron," *Physica 22D,* pp. 233–246, 1986.

[18] J. J. Hopfield, "Neural networks and physical systems with emergent collective computation abilities," *Proc. Nat. Acad. Sci. U.S. (Biophysics),* vol. 79, pp. 2554–2558, 1982.

[19] J. J. Hopfield, "Neurons with graded response have collective computational properties like those of two-state neurons," *Proc. Nat. Acad. Sci. U.S. (Biophysics),* vol. 81, pp. 3088–3092, 1984.

[20] D. R. Hush and B. G. Horne, "Progress in supervised neural networks," *IEEE Signal Process. Mag.,* vol. 10, no. 1, January, pp. 8–39, 1993.

[21] T. Kohonen, *Self-Organization and Associative Memory.* Berlin: Springer-Verlag, 1984.

[22] B. Kosko, "Bidirectional associative memories," *IEEE Trans. Syst., Man, Cybern.,* vol. 18, no. 1, pp. 49–60, 1988.

[23] D. S. Levine, "Neural population modeling and psychology: A review," *Math. Biosci.,* vol. 66, pp. 1–86, 1983.

[24] R. P. Lippmann, "An introduction to computing with neural nets," *IEEE ASSP Mag.,* April, vol. 4, no. 2, pp. 4–22, 1987.

[25] R. Linsker, "Self-organization in a perceptual network," *IEEE Computer,* March, vol. 21, no. 3, pp. 105–117, 1988.

[26] W. S. McCulloch and W. Pitts, "A logical calculus of the ideas immanent in nervous activity," *Bull. Math. Biophys.,* vol. 5, pp. 115–133, 1943.

[27] B. Nabet and R. B. Pinter, *Sensory Neural Networks: Lateral Inhibition.* Boca Raton, FL: CRC Press, 1991.

[28] K. Nakano, "Associatron—A model of associative memory," *IEEE Trans. Syst., Man, Cybern.,* vol. 2, no. 3, pp. 380–388, 1972.

[29] G. N. Reeke, O. Sporns, and G. M. Edelman, "Synthetic neural modeling: The "Darwin" series of recognition automata," *Proc. IEEE,* vol. 78, no. 9, pp. 1498–1530, 1990.

[30] F. Rosenblatt, "The Perceptron: A probabilistic model for information storage and organization in the brain," *Psychol. Rev.,* vol. 65, pp. 386–408, 1958.

[31] D. E. Rumelhart and D. Zipser, "Feature discovery by competitive learning," *Cognitive Sci.,* vol. 9, pp. 75–112, 1985.

[32] E. L. Schwartz, Ed., *Computational Neuroscience.* Cambridge, MA: MIT Press, 1990.

[33] P. K. Simpson, *Artificial Neural Systems.* New York: Pergamon Press, 1990.

[34] B. Widrow and M. A. Lehr, "30 Years of adaptive neural networks: Perceptron, Madaline, and backpropagation," *Proc. IEEE,* vol. 78, no. 9, pp. 1415–1441, 1990.

[35] H. R. Wilson and J. D. Cowan, "Excitatory and inhibitory interactions in localized populations of model neurons," *Biophys. J.,* vol. 12, pp. 1–24, 1972.

[36] H. R. Wilson and J. D. Cowan, "A mathematical theory of the functional dynamics of cortical and thalamic nervous tissue," *Kybernetik* (Springer-Verlag) vol. 13, no. 2, pp. 55–80, 1973.

Cognitive and Psychological Computation with Neural Models

JAMES A. ANDERSON

Abstract—Biological support exists for the idea that large-scale models of the brain should be parallel, distributed, and associative. Some of this neurobiology is reviewed. It is then assumed that state vectors, large patterns of activity of groups of individual somewhat selective neurons, are the appropriate elementary entities to use for cognitive computation. Simple neural models using this approach are presented that will associate and will respond to prototypes of sets of related inputs. Some experimental evidence supporting the latter model is discussed. A model for categorization is then discussed. Educating the resulting systems and the use of error correcting techniques are discussed, and an example is presented of the behavior of the system when diffuse damage occurs to the memory, with and without compensatory learning. Finally, a simulation is presented which can learn partial information, integrate it with other material, and use that information to reconstruct missing information.

The object of science is the connection of phenomena; but the theories are like dry leaves which fall away when they have ceased to be the lungs of the tree of science.

Ernst Mach (1872)

I. INTRODUCTION

THE DESIRE to build artificial systems that do the kinds of interesting things that we do has long existed. From mechanical automata in past centuries to electronic devices now, we have tried to make hardware and software that acts like us, or at least some significant part of us. Much of the current work in this tradition now tries to model with computers various aspects of human cognition. The things that make us most interesting to each other and which seem to be the most highly developed in humans as opposed to other animals are the faculties that are usually called cognitive, that is, our abilities to speak, to perceive, to reason, and to speculate.

There are many ways to understand cognition, in particular, to understand it well enough to mimic it with models or gadgets. We have access to a number of examples of a cognizing organism (i.e., us). We can study us in detail, both in terms of our system performance (psychology) and in terms of our hardware (neuroscience). We can also study us in the abstract, asking essentially, how we would (prefer-ably from first principles) build a system that performs the cognitive functions that we can. The result of such a design process may bear little or no relationship to the system that nature has evolved, though it has been claimed that there are powerful constraints on intelligence, so that all systems that can do the same intelligent things are somehow related since they have solved the same problems.

My own bias, however, based more on faith than concrete accomplishment, is that the best approach to understanding and constructing intelligent devices is to study carefully the one that we know works. The limitations of this approach are obvious: birds fly. Airplanes are neither feathered nor flap their wings. Studying flying from first principles might have given rise to hot air balloons and rockets, but it is unlikely that studying birds in order to fly would have done so.

This paper will discuss some of the hardware of real nervous systems. We will then develop some simple neural models for cognition that try to work within the constraints that nature has had to work with. At the end of this paper we show the beginnings of an approach to cognitive computation: that is, how it is possible to use these distributed parallel associative models to compute and what they can be used for.

II. BIOLOGICAL ASSUMPTIONS

State Vectors

Our claim is that biology places severe restrictions on the kinds of computations done by our brains. A great deal is currently known about neuroscience that bears on this point. A particularly good introduction to neuroscience for nonbiologists is an issue of *Scientific American* now available as a book [16]. An excellent textbook has also recently appeared [55].

Two key conclusions must be mentioned. First, neurons are analog devices. That is, they take their synaptic inputs, perform a computation on these inputs, and generate an output which is almost always a continuous valued firing frequency, represented as the time between discrete pulses called action potentials. A weighted integration of the synaptic inputs over a brief period of time is an oversimplified but useful first approximation of a neuron model. The neuron typically does not act like a digital device such as a McCulloch–Pitts neural logic element, but as a pulse-code modulation system.

Manuscript received August 1, 1982; revised April 4, 1983. This work was supported in part by the National Science Foundation under Grants BNS-79-23900 and BNS-82-14728, administered by the Memory and Cognitive Processes section, in part by the Alfred P. Sloan Foundation, in part by the Digital Equipment Corporation, and in part by Contract N-00014-81-K-0136 from the U.S. Office of Naval Research.

The author is with the Department of Psychology and Center for Neural Science, Brown University, Providence, RI 02912.

Reprinted from *IEEE Trans. Syst. Man, Cybern.*, vol. SMC-13, no. 5, pp. 799–815, Sept./Oct. 1983.

Second, ten billion or more individual neurons exist in the mammalian nervous system. This means that the computational strategies used by the nervous system can take advantage of the presence of very large numbers of elements. However, since neurons are slow devices, operating with integration times in the millisecond or tens of milliseconds range, no time exists for the long strings of elementary computations that characterize digital computers. A highly parallel strategy is employed. The brain's "machine operations" must be of a very powerful kind since not many of them will have time to execute during a single "program."

When a stimulus of any complexity is presented, many neurons respond. (Not all of them, but not a single one either.) When a motor action of any significant kind is made, many motor neurons respond. Therefore, a pattern of activity of many neurons represents response to the input and many neurons respond as the output of the system. Internal communication between brain areas has the same many-to-many architecture. Therefore, we become interested in elementary operations involving the simultaneous activities of many individual neurons which give rise to the activities of many neurons. In the models to be presented, we represent·these activities as state vectors of simultaneous neuron activities, and we claim that elementary operations involving transformations of state vectors form a useful approach to nervous system models.

This approximation is one way of avoiding the "homunculus" problem. No internal CPU (a high-tech homunculus) abstractly processes information. Activity pattern may follow activity pattern in lawful sequence, but information is not represented in a form other than as neuron activities or as connection strengths between neurons.

Neurons

Large state vectors are a biologically justifiable way to represent information in the human nervous system. The elements of these vectors correspond with something of the size and properties of single neurons.

At the lowest level, single neurons devote great care to analyzing what is important to the organism. In primary visual cortex, many cells analyze orientation, binocular interactions, movement, color, spatial frequency, and spatial location. Less or no analysis is made of absolute light intensity, large areas with no change in intensity, and stationary stimuli in general. The implication of this is that interesting things potentially affect a number of cells strongly though only a small number are actually excited or inhibited by a stimulus. The cells not affected are also contributing information of a kind. Interesting aspects of the stimulus are "richly coded" in that they may make profound effects on potentially very many elements of the state vectors.

As one example, higher mammals are born with what are apparently inbuilt orientation detectors in their visual system whose properties can be modified (usually for the worse) by environmental manipulation. However, these orientation selective units are also affected by other physical aspects of the stimulus such as binocularity, spatial frequency, wavelength, or movement. The biological approach taken seems to be to have many cells responding somewhat selectively to important aspects of the environment. An alternative design would be to have a few high-quality feature detectors, but this design does not seem to be used by mammals, though it is by invertebrates and perhaps by some nonmammalian vertebrates. The equivalents of the exquisitely selective neural responses to pheromones, say, or to particular patterns and frequencies of sound found in invertebrate species may also exist in mammals, but they seem to be outnumbered by less selective cells, where the emphasis has shifted to developing processing selectivity at the group level.

The question of specificity and distribution in the nervous system is important for neuroscientists and for theoreticians as well. As a recent example, Feldman and Ballard [18] have suggested that information is represented in the nervous system by a very small number of active neurons. Each potential value of a stimulus parameter (say size, brightness, color) is represented by a single neuron. Combinations of parameters may be represented by single cells also, though Feldman and Ballard devote some time to discussing ways of avoiding the obvious combinatorial explosion of the required number of units. They develop the nice idea of "winner take all" networks where only one of a number of contending values is excited and the rest are inhibited. The final representation is that stable coalitions are formed: they give as an example of a stable coalition one containing three active units.

Interestingly, Barlow [8], a neurophysiologist, suggested a similar idea: very selective cells ("on the order of selectivity of a word") are present in the nervous system, and most cells are quiet most of the time. However, Barlow came to the same conclusion as Feldman and Ballard that, to represent information of any complexity, more than one active cell was necessary. Barlow concluded there were no "pontifical" cells, but there was a distributed "college of cardinals."

The physiology supports a degree of selectivity in neural coding. Suppose one percent of cells were active in a complex concept or perception. This would correspond to many millions of cells, yet a microelectrode would reveal very little electrical activity in such a brain. The conclusions that representation of information in the nervous system is contained in simultaneous discharge of a number of neurons and that information is distributed in this sense are difficult to avoid.

Cerebral Cortex

The cerebral cortex is a flat thin two-dimensional structure on the order of a fifth of a square meter in area [12]. It is extensively folded in higher mammals to fit inside a skull of reasonable size. The neocortex is relatively homogeneous; the similarities of cell type and circuitry between different areas are more striking than the differences. (See the collection of essays on cortical organization edited by

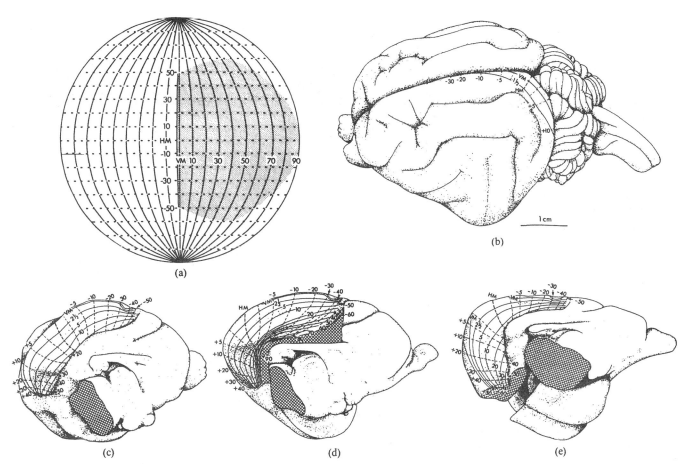

Fig. 1. Diagram of representation of visual field in area 17 (primary visual cortex) of cat. (a) Perimeter chart showing extent of visual field represented in area 17. (b)–(e) Location of visual field in area 17 of cat brain. From Tusa *et al.* [60], reprinted by permission.

Schmitt *et al.* [52]). The already two-dimensional cortex is strongly layered. There are numerous subareas (perhaps 50 or so) of cerebral cortex, which seem to be functional areas, though details of organization and function are often quite obscure. Thus Area 17 (located in humans at the back of the head) is the primary cortical receiving area for visual inputs. Area 3 receives somatic sensory inputs (skin senses). The cortex is exquisitely structured. Areas associated with a sensory system have topographic organization, that is, the visual field in area 17 is represented as a distorted map of visual space. Fig. 1 shows a diagram of the topography of the map of visual space onto the surface of cortex. If the location of a cell is known, its general area of maximum visual responsiveness can be inferred. The body surface is represented in the somatosensory areas, frequency is loosely plotted on the surface of the auditory cortex, and so on. Although the overall outlines of the map are lawful in the large, individual cells may show local variability.

The maps show striking distortions. The human retina has an area of greatest optical quality called the fovea. The fovea has a higher receptor density than other regions of the retina and is correspondingly overrepresented in the cortex. It is possible to get a good first impression of the relative importance of a structure in the life of a mammal by looking at its cortical map: in our own somatosensory system we have a very large cortical area devoted to our fingers and a small area devoted to the toes. A rhesus

monkey has more equal representation of toes and fingers. Any model of the cortex must be consistent with this "more is better" philosophy because it is not immediately obvious why it should be so. The brain could have simply paid more attention to input signals from the fovea, for example and not had more of them. Nervous tissue is very costly in terms of its biological overhead: it consumes enormous amounts of energy, it is very sensitive mechanically and biochemically and is generally more of a burden than other tissue types. Therefore, if it physically expands to the extent it has in us, it must earn its keep in enhanced processing power. Whatever organizational scheme is used in the cortex must be such as to add on power by expansion in a simple way, without requiring too much in the way of detailed interconnection specifications.

Connections between sensory receptors and cortex, and between one cortical area and another are physically parallel. One sheet of cells projects to another, with very many fibers and considerable convergence and divergence in the projections. This striking parallelism in the anatomy has led to interest in parallel models for brain function over the past decades, from the Perceptron onward.

These points are worth briefly mentioning here, because I feel that our minds are much less of a general purpose cognitive device than we might like to think. What we seem to be is a somewhat flexible analog processor with enormous memory capacity, which is good at performing a class of tasks that interest us as a species and which are important for our success in our particular world. Our attempts at general purpose computation (logic, say, or even language) are often inconsistent. They are unnatural. Far more complex tasks that are biologically relevant (throwing a ball, recognizing a face, understanding speech) are so effortless that we do not realize how hard they are until we try to make a machine do them. On the other hand, the pitiful mess most humans make of formal logical reasoning or arithmetic would embarrass a $10 pocket calculator. Yet we can recognize a face with speed and accuracy no computer can match.

William James made this point 90 years ago.

In the main, if a phenomenon is important for our welfare, it interests and excites us the first time we come into its presence. Dangerous things fill us with involuntary fear; poisonous things with distaste; indispensible things with appetite. Mind and world in short have been evolved together, and in consequence are something of a mutual fit [27, p. 17].

III. Associative Models

Several sections of this paper will contain reviews of previously published material. Several general references have been published for this area. Kohonen's book [30] is essential. A recent collection of papers [26] contains some related and alternate approaches. The Perceptron of Rosenblatt and related models in the late 1950's and early 1960's pioneered the use of models for cognition inspired by parallel nervous system architecture. Nilsson [42] summarizes this literature. Minsky and Papert [40] pointed out the considerable limitations in processing ability of simple Perceptrons. (We argue later that limitations in ability are to be expected from brainlike models and allow the strongest experimental tests of such models.) McCulloch and Pitts, after their immensely influential paper on neurons as discrete logical devices [38], published a paper [44] proposing a parallel model for eye movements using continuous mathematics and based on the topographic organization of the superior colliculus.

A recent paper by Sutton and Barto [57] contains a fine review of work in the area along with an application of a learning model to psychological classical conditioning. A specifically parallel model using state vectors and tensors to model the cerebellum has been described by Pellionisz and Llinas [43]. Papers by Bienenstock *et al.* [9] and by Cooper [13] deal with application of the learning rule used in this paper and extensions of it to plasticity in the visual cortex, with careful fitting of neurophysiological data to theoretical predictions.

A somewhat different approach to cognitive questions is taken by Grossberg [21] but with significant similarities in direction. Arbib's book [6] and his work with Szentagothai [59] contain many valuable insights and interesting material. These sources will provide more detailed references to the journal literature, as will many of the papers in this journal. The visual system lends itself in a very obvious way to parallel analysis. The well-known work of Marr [36] discusses in detail the kind of parallel computation, tied closely to physiology, that may be used in the early stages of visual information processing. Marr's early work on cerebellum [34] and neocortex [35] assumes highly parallel architecture combined with simple conjunctional learning rules.

Minsky [39] has proposed a distributed model with centralized elements where information is represented in states of many low-level agents whose activities constitute a "mental state." Memory is the reconstruction of a past state. Some powerful and selective elements (K-lines) control states of many agents and can reconstruct past states. The agents are not specifically neurons, but they communicate by means of excitation and inhibition, and the mental state notion is similar to the state vectors used in this paper. The model is a hybrid of localized and distributed computation.

These models as a group involve massive parallelism of many* simple elements and often have simple rules for modifying strengths of connections between elements. Variations between them come in specifying the assumed rules and operations. The details of wiring can be specifically brainlike or much more abstract.

In this paper, we will adhere less closely to the details of the neuroscience than some would like. We will focus our attention on the implications for cognition of models which seem to us to capture the appropriate parallel, distributed essence of most of the models proposed to date, yet which are simple enough to analyze and simulate in some detail. This means we will start with a linear model which demonstrates how associative learning can arise naturally in parallel neural models. We will show that even this simple, rather unrealistic model is capable of some striking psychological predictions. Then we will introduce simple nonlinearities as we need them to make a first step at curing some of the obvious defects of the linear model, always hoping that each increase in complexity pays for itself in explaining a new psychological phenomenon or giving us more cognitive computing power. Such successive refinement seems to us to be one valid way of approaching a system with the complexity of the brain.

Synaptic Connectivity

Neurons talk to one another. The connections between neurons are called synapses. We have argued that many neurons talk to many neurons. The connectivity of cortical neurons is extensive; a single large cortical pyramidal cell is estimated to have thousands of synapses. The exact value is a function of the type and location of the cell. Although competing hypotheses have been seriously considered, almost every neuroscientist believes that changes in synaptic strength are the location of memory. In some cases, it has been possible to demonstrate convincingly that synaptic changes occur in learning-related contexts: the best studied example of this is the marine mollusk *Aplysia* which has been studied by Kandel and coworkers for a number of years [28].

One might first think that learning is simply a matter of strengthening synapses by use: the more a synapse is used (or not used) the stronger (or weaker) it gets. Indeed, the *Aplysia* has an inverted version of this in the habituation paradigm, where recurrent stimulation causes a diminution (habituation) of the resulting response. However, this kind of learning, though interesting, present, and important, seems to be inadequate for most complex and cognitively interesting kinds of learning. For millenia, since Aristotle, those interested in memory recognized its associative aspect. That is, events tended to become linked together because, "... one (event) is of a nature to occur after another." [7, p. 54]. Association of a sufficiently flexible kind seems not to be possible with a simple stimulus directed change-by-use rule such as habituation. A close connection with the response is required.

The rule that seems to be the starting point for virtually every recent model of associative memory seems to have first been formulated by Hebb [22]. Hebb's proposal for cellular learning was

> When an axon of cell A is near enough to excite a cell B and repeatedly or persistently takes part in firing it, some growth process or metabolic change takes place in one or both cells such that A's efficiency as one of the cells firing B, is increased [22, p. 62].

This rule suggests that a correlation between pre- and postsynaptic cell will develop, and such a synapse is called a correlational synapse. Such a rule is indeed adequate to build an associative memory that does a number of quite interesting things. The rest of this paper will be devoted to exploring some of the specifically psychological and cognitive implications of networks using correlational synapses.

Simple Association

The basic system that we shall discuss in one variant or another throughout this review is shown in Fig. 2. We assume one set of simple model neurons projects to another set (or to the same set, a special case). This architecture is specifically inspired by projection systems in the brain, where one set of elements projects to another over highly parallel pathways.

Suppose we have two sets of N neurons, called alpha and beta, where every neuron in beta projects to every neuron in alpha. A neuron j in alpha is connected to neuron i in beta by way of a modifiable synapses with strength $A(i, j)$, forming an $N \times N$ connectivity matrix A. We are interested in the set of simultaneous individual neuron activities in a group of neurons. We represent these large patterns as state vectors. We assume these components can have positive or negative values. This could occur if we build inhibition as well as excitation into the system and if we assume that the nervous system is concerned with deviations from spontaneous level, positive as well as negative.

If pattern f occurs in alpha and pattern g occurs in beta, we can associate these two patterns using a simple learning

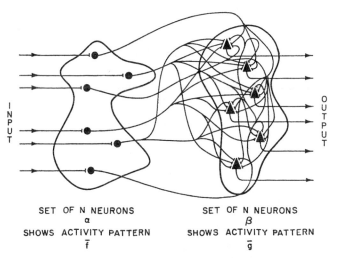

Fig. 2. Models assume two sets of N neurons, alpha projecting to beta. Every neuron in alpha projects to every neuron in beta. This drawing has $N = 6$. From Anderson *et al.* [4], reprinted by permission.

rule, a generalization of a Hebb synapse. We need to change the connectivity matrix according to the rule,

$$\Delta A(i, j) = \eta f(j)g(i).$$

We have introduced a learning parameter η. Note that this is information locally available to the junction: it is proportional to the product of pre- and postsynaptic activity. This defines the matrix ΔA to be of the form

$$\Delta A = \eta g f^T.$$

This matrix now acts like an associator. Consider the simplest case: Initially, $A = 0$, $\eta = 1$, and f and g are normalized. If now

$$A = g f^T,$$

we have established connections between the first and second set of neurons. Now, if an input pattern of activation is impressed on f, a pattern will appear on g. If we assume as an initial approximation a simple linear integrator model for the way neurons respond to their inputs, we can calculate the output pattern as the product of the connectivity matrix A, and the input pattern. Suppose the pattern is f. Then the output pattern will be g, since

$$g = g f^T f.$$

The classic neural system showing simple linearity of this kind is the Limulus eye, where the approximation is quite accurate [10], [11]. Other systems show various nonlinearities, but often (referring to communication from one neuron to another) a simple linear model is quite good as a first approximation. Sensory transduction of the physical stimulus can be quite nonlinear, however, masking what may be a simpler relationship at the neuron level. Linearity is an adequate approximation only up to a point. The relationship of linearity and the nervous system is a complex one; see Anderson and Silverstein [5] for a few examples and caveats. For a fuller discussion of this issue in the visual system, see Ratliff [47].

In general, we want to couple more than one set of patterns. Suppose we have a set of associations that we wish to teach the system $(f_1, g_1), (f_2, g_2), \cdots, (f_k, g_k)$. Suppose we teach our matrix these pairs of patterns with each pair having associated with it an incremental matrix of the form

$$\Delta A_i = g_i f_i^{T}.$$

Let us then assume that the overall synaptic connectivity matrix is given by the sum of all the incremental matrices so that

$$A = \sum_i g_i f_i^{T}.$$

Single matrix elements (synaptic contacts) can do multiple duty in that they may participate in storing information about associations between any pairs of statea vectors. This means information may not be localized or localizable, and the joint operation of many synapses is required for function. Information is distributed in the state vectors (since the simultaneous pattern of many cells is required for meaning) and also in the actual locus of memory. This is a holographic property, though these models are not Fourier transform holograms.

Suppose that the input vectors are orthonormal. Then, if one of the stored items is impressed on alpha, we have

$$(\text{pattern on beta}) = A f_i$$
$$= g f_i^{T} f_i + g \left(\sum_{i \neq j} f_j^{T} f_i \right)$$
$$= g.$$

This means that vector g_i can be generated at the output if vector f_i is presented at the input. Note that the state vectors are large, and if components are statistically independent, then the resulting vectors will be close to orthogonal. We assume as a fundamental coding assumption that stimuli very different from each other have uncorrelated state vectors, that is, orthogonal to each other on the average.

Many intriguing properties emerge from the interaction between learned vectors. Two recent psychological papers [41], [17] use a vector approach similar to the foregoing to explain a good many psychological phenomena. The model they both use stores associations by a convolution operation and retrieves them by correlation, extensions of a model of Liepa [31]. The memory vectors are "superimposed in a composite memory trace" [17, p. 627]. Murdock and Eich discuss, simulate, and suggest explanations for some classic list learning experiments, some short-term memory phenomena, the qualitative effects found during the learning of lists of associations, and prototype formation. Many of the most interesting effects in their model arise because "... the events stored in such a memory combine and interfere with one another ..." [17, p. 657]. As Eich comments, "... it is precisely because CHARM [Eich's model] transforms and combines events that the model is psychologically interesting" [17, p. 654].

General Properties

Matrix and vector associative models have some pronounced strengths and limitations. Their strengths are, first, that they are intrinsically parallel. Second, they are very tolerant of noise and partial connectivity. Since they contain correlational and averaging elements, the resulting systems are often optimal or close to optimal in a signal processing sense. (See the section on error correction.) They tend to be computationally robust. Third, they work better in the sense of better discrimination and signal-to-noise ratio as the state vectors increase in size. Since the models are parallel, this can be done with no increase in processing time if the hardware is also parallel.

Their primary limitation is their limited storage capacity relative to the size of the system. Clearly, only N orthogonal vectors can exist. Second, they can generate noise and inappropriate behavior of an unpredictable nature since things mix together in storage. (This can be a virtue or a problem, depending on context.) Third, they are poorly suited to rapid computation using traditional digital computers. Fourth, they tend to be rather ponderous and inflexible. Fifth, as linear models, they are subject to a host of essential limitations. As Sejnowski comments, "The matrix model resembles memory in the way a toy glider resembles a bird. It does fly, in a rigid sort of way, but it lacks dynamics and grace" [53, p. 203]. However, if it flies even crudely, let us see if it takes us anywhere interesting.

III. CATEGORIZATION

Concepts and Prototypes

The nervous system is faced with the problem of using information from many moderately selective analyzers. Another problem is intrinsic to the functions of a cognitive system: analysis of the world cannot be too precise. It is necessary to form equivalence classes of events and things of a convenient size. For example, many real things are described by the words "dog" or "bird." Not only are particular individuals different from each other, but the same individual at different times is quite different in its exact physical description. A simple change in lighting can cause great changes in the physical properties of the reflections from the object. We are constructed to ignore these differences, a photocell is not. This process is so basic that we are often not aware of its operation.

A malfunction of this mechanism described in the psychological literature is the subject burdened with an exceptional memory described by Luria [32]. Luria's mnemonist had difficulty recognizing people because, as Luria commented:

S. often complained that he had a poor memory for faces: "They're so changeable," he had said. "A person's expression depends on his mood and on the circumstances under which you happen to meet him. People's faces are constantly changing; it's the different shades of expression that confuse me and make it so hard to remember faces." [32, p. 64]

We are faced with the problem of forming equivalence classes in a natural way. A tremendous amount of biology is involved in this. We discriminate what we are built to be good at discriminating.

In cognitive science and cognitive psychology, the equivalence classes that result are usually called concepts. The study of concepts is difficult because different kinds exists and because concepts, by their nature, are not consistent or totally stable entities. Good introductions to the modern study of concepts are contained in books by Rosch and Lloyd [50] and by Smith and Medin [56]. One idea supported by a good deal of evidence is that humans will normally operate at a "natural" level of concept complexity, often related to sensory aspects of the stimulus. We will say in normal speech, "Look at that bird on the lawn," as opposed to, "Look at that organism on the flat area of Kentucky bluegrass, clover, and creeping red fescue." We can say the last, but a default level exists which seems to correspond to a natural concept level. The second sentence is both too general and too specific.

We will be concerned in the next sections with two particular aspects of simple concept formation: prototypes and categories. We make the fundamental assumption that items that belong in the same natural categories will have similar neural codings. Their state vectors will be correlated in terms of our models. The study of natural psychological categories does suggest this: many familiar birds look and behave similarly to each other; birds that do not (penguins or ostriches) are often handled as concepts by themselves. One will say, "There is a bird on the lawn," if the bird is a sparrow, pigeon, or robin but, "There is a penguin on the lawn." This observation is related to the model of concepts usually associated with the work of Rosch, which holds that many natural concepts (dogs, birds, vegetables, etc.) are represented by prototypical members, i.e., best examples of the class. People agree on how close objects are to the prototype. There are "good" birds (robins, sparrows, etc.) and birds which are not good examples, such as turkeys, ostriches, and buzzards. To use one of Rosch's more picturesque examples, one would not be bothered in the least by the occurrence in a novel of a sentence such as, "Twenty or so birds often perch on the telephone wires outside my window and twitter in the morning" [49, p. 39] until one replaces the word "birds" with "turkeys."

Prototype Formation in a Neural Model

Suppose we have a number of examples of a category. Suppose we call the category name the state vector g and the different example vectors $f_1, f_2, \cdots, f_k$. Each incremental matrix is generated as before, and we arrive at an overall connectivity matrix given by

$$A = g \sum_i f_i^T.$$

This expression contains the sum of the f's. This term acts like an average response computer. The central tendency of the f's will emerge. The amplitude of response to

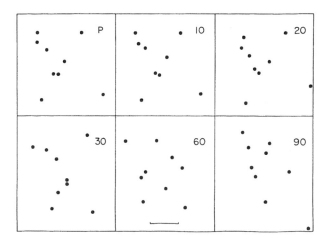

Fig. 3. Prototype dot pattern (P), followed by five examples at various degrees of distortion. Dots were generated on 512×512 array and presented to subjects on CRT screen. Number refers to average number of locations moved on the array. Distance of 100 array locations is indicated. In experiments distortions of about 24 units were used. From Knapp and Anderson [29], reprinted by permission.

a new state vector will give a measure of distance from the central tendency. (See [2,], [17], [29] for further discussions of this effect and its implications from a psychological perspective.)

Posner–Keele Experiments

Psychologists Posner and Keele have demonstrated what might be a simple example of this process [45], [46]. These experiments, extensions of them, and a theoretical discussion, of which the following is a summary, can be found in Knapp and Anderson [29].

A pattern of nine random dots is generated on an oscilloscope screen. These initial patterns are denoted "prototypes." Then examples of the prototypes are made by moving the dots random directions and distances. Fig. 3 shows a prototype and different examples of the prototype, as the average distance a dot moved is increased. Subjects classify examples of a prototype together in the learning phase of the experiment by pressing one of several buttons, each button associated arbitrarily with distortions of a particular prototype by the experimenter. After the response, they are told whether their classification was correct. They do not see the prototype. They are then given a test where they are asked to classify a set of patterns. Classification is correct if a new example is associated with the same response as old distortions of the same prototype. In the testing phase, they can be given 1) the examples they saw, 2) the prototypes, and 3) new examples of the prototypes. Depending on experimental conditions, the prototype (which subjects never saw) may be the best classified, both in terms of reaction time, percent correct classification, and confidence the pattern had been seen before.

In our experiments, patterns of nine random dots were used. Distortions were generated in such a way as to ensure the prototype was extremely unlikely to occur as a stimulus, yet the prototype was often categorized most accurately. This is a common result in the concept literature.

RESPONSE TO A DOT

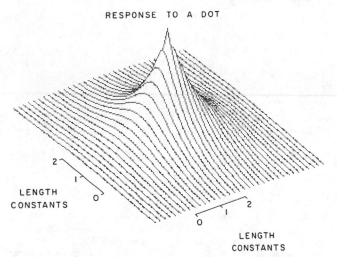

Fig. 4. Activity pattern on hypothetical cortex from single dot in the real world. This is exponential falloff of activity from a single location. From Knapp and Anderson [29], reprinted by permission.

MEMORY FORMATION

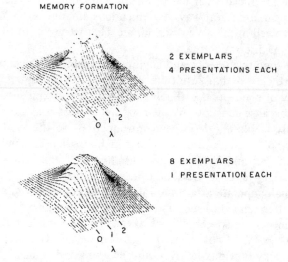

2 EXEMPLARS
4 PRESENTATIONS EACH

8 EXEMPLARS
1 PRESENTATION EACH

Fig. 5. Sum of eight activity patterns. In one case, two exemplars (presented four times each) form memory; in other case, eight different exemplars are used. In both cases, significant representation is seen at prototype location, but in two exemplar case is also stronger representation of patterns actually seen ("old" patterns). From Knapp and Anderson [29], reprinted by permission.

Application of our concept abstraction model is straightforward. Suppose the neural representation of a dot in the visual system is somewhat localized. (The spectacular map of the visual field shown in Fig. 1 would certainly suggest this.) Suppose that the amount of activity in a two-dimensional representation of visual space falls off exponentially from a central location on the topographic map. Fig. 4 shows the activity pattern due to a single dot on a hypothetical flat cortex. The model predicts that we should sum activities due to different examples of the same prototype, since they are associated with the same response. Fig. 5 shows activity patterns of a single dot in eight patterns when added together. In one case, there were eight different dot locations, in the other only two different dot locations. Note that the first case has "averaged out," few irregularities appear on the resulting summed activity; the second case has strong representations at the locations of the two presented examples. Both have strong representations at the location of the prototype, even though the prototype had never actually been seen.

It is convenient to simplify our calculations. Since we do not know and are not really interested in the details of the output of the system, we want to compute interactions between the stimuli (the vector f's). These will be the coefficients multiplying the g's in the vector model. We assume the output pattern with the largest coefficient will be the categorization made. This is a nonlinear decision rule.

Ultimately, we could use a nonlinear classification model to generate a model response directly, but for initial studies this seemed premature. We want to know the strength of response to different patterns given a memory constructed from the activities. These will be given by dot products of the stored vectors with the input vectors, that is, if similarity of f_1 and f_2 are to be judged.

$$(\text{output strength}) = f_1^T f_2.$$

These are interactions at the level of the rows of the connectivity matrix. A memory composed of K items,

$f_1 \cdots f_K$ associated with the same response would have, in response to input f,

$$(\text{output strength}) = \sum_i f_i^T f.$$

A series of experiments was done to collect similarities between dot patterns generated with different degrees of distortion. The prediction is that subjective similarity should be proportional to the inner product between one pattern of activity and the other pattern. The fit using the model, assuming an exponential falloff of activity as shown in Fig. 4, is quite good (0.97 correlation between theory and prediction) and allows determination of the spatial falloff length constant of the activity.

We can see that a number of different examples learned and average displacement of examples from prototype should be powerful determiners of the classification ability of the system. One experimental manipulation was to change the number of different examples learned and study the resulting behavior.

The experimental results are shown in Fig. 6 for an experiment where prototypes were formed from nine random dots presented on a CRT screen. One, six, and 24 different examples were learned. In any given experiment three different prototypes were used. Results show a pronounced change in behavior. If 24 examples are used, pronounced prototype enhancement occurs. With one example, the example presented gives the largest correct classification as would be expected. Of course, a one-example category does not, strictly speaking, show prototype averaging but similarity between one pattern and a different one, since the resulting memory representation will be a multiple of activity at a single dot location.

A direct computer simulation of this experiment using the model presented is possible using this length constant determined from the similarity experiment. The resulting

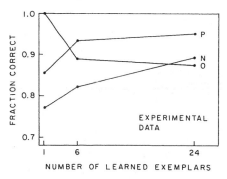

Fig. 6. Experimental results from categorization experiment using dot patterns like those in Fig. 3. Subjects received during learning part same total number of patterns, but generated from one, six, or 24 different exemplars. Three prototypes were used during each experiment. Subjects were taught to classify distortions of given prototype together. During test phase, percent correct categorization was measured for old, new, and prototype patterns. From Knapp and Anderson [29], reprinted by permission.

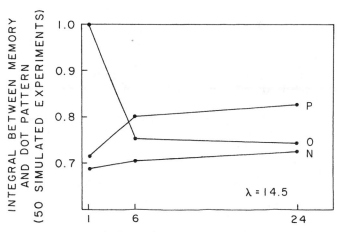

Fig. 7. Simulation of experimental results for prototype experiments. Dot patterns were generated exactly as in experiment, length constant of exponential falloff was measured in similarity judgment experiment, and model computed integral between resulting memory and input pattern (old, new, or prototype, as in experiments). Simulation was repeated 50 times; averages are plotted. Percent correct does not map directly into this integral, but qualitative agreement is quite good. From Knapp and Anderson [29], reprinted by permission.

activity patterns for all conditions of the experiment are generated, summed, and theoretical similarities between memory and the prototype, new examples, and old examples, are computed. These computations are shown in Fig. 7. A very strong qualitative similarity exists between the two figures. There is not necessarily a simple relationship between computed similarity and percent correct classification, but we should expect relative relationships to be maintained. Since we have accounted for the similarity data with the same constants and model, we find that a reasonably powerful model for actual data can be evolved essentially from the first principles of the associative model.

Teaching Methods

Cognitively oriented neural models become problems in teaching. We assume that when an input state vector is presented, an output state vector appears. The problem is how to arrange synaptic interactions to ensure that the output state vector is the one we want. Many of the difficult problems in distribution systems arise in a context that can only be called educational. Putting information into the system is tricky. Once the system works correctly, however, information retrieval is easy, since only simple operations need be performed independent of what other or how much information has been put into the system. Since the system is parallel, everything is searched at once. The combinatorially growing search trees, common in some information retrieval methods, do not occur.

This leads to a difficult problem for distributed systems: how to debug an incorrectly functioning system. In a complex computer program that malfunctions there is faith that the cause is reasonable, discoverable, and correctable. In a distributed system, the error is also distributed and is no more localizable than the correct information. There are some ways around this problem; the error correction procedures discussed next are one example. In general, this is a major difficulty for distributed systems because stored information interacts in so many unpredictable and subtle ways. This problem will not yield to a quick fix—first,

since it is fundamental, and second, since some of the more desirable features of distributed systems (such as inference, prototype extraction, and concept formation) are due to the same interactions in a constructive role.

Error Correction

The state vector models presented up to now can learn arbitrary associations in a few favorable cases. Correct operation of the system consists of generating the proper output paired with the input during learning. Suppose due to the nonorthogonality of the learned inputs, or noise, the correct output does not appear. That is, if g is the correct association, what can be done if Af does not equal g?

We have described a classical statistical problem. Because of the correlational nature of the synaptic modification scheme we have assumed, it has been pointed out [30], [19], [20] that the associative model discussed and simple variants are often optimal in the least mean squares sense: the output is often the best linear estimator of what the completely correct response pattern would be, and many useful neural models realize known statistical techniques.

How can we modify our system to converge to the correct, or nearly correct, association? As Sutton and Barto [57] have pointed out, a slight modification of the association model implements the well-known Widrow–Hoff procedure (see, for example, Duda and Hart [15]). Suppose that, instead of incrementing the connectivity matrix with the outer product gf^T, we use the error signal

$$\Delta A = \eta(g - Af)f^T.$$

Here, we learn the difference between what the output of the system ought to be (g) and what it actually is (Af). We assume the learning system has access to both patterns: trying to match a pronunciation during foreign language learning could be one example of such a situation.

This algorithm is computationally robust and converges well for many situations. It can be shown in many cases to converge to the best mean square error approximation possible for a linear system. We can see immediately that the system can be stable if there is no error since there is then no learning.

Dynamic error correction procedures have an additional interesting property: they contain a kind of short-term memory. This approach has been applied with success by Heath [23], who has shown that some psychological reaction time data can be quantitatively modeled by assuming a rapid adaptive process in memory that acts like an error correction procedure.

The short-term memory aspect arises in the following way. If we consider the foregoing formula when a sequence of associated inputs and outputs that are not orthogonal are learned, the immediately last pair learned will (with appropriate parameters) have small or no error. As more pairs are learned, pairs further in the past will develop an error because of the later material stored in the system. In situations where perfect association does not occur, the system gives its most accurate response to items presented in the immediate past: a recency effect. Fig. 8 shows a computational example of this as a demonstration. Interestingly, the amount of recency is powerfully affected by the nature of the learned vectors. The top trace is the correlation between desired and actual output vectors for random vectors as the last presentation of the pair recedes into the past. The bottom trace plots the same thing for a highly structured set of vectors generated for a cognitive example, where a number of the input vectors were highly correlated in parts, causing interference between associations. The qualitative prediction is that a correlated group of inputs should be more difficult to keep straight in short-term memory and should show a relatively stronger recency effect than uncorrelated inputs. This is consistent with much psychological data.

A Nonlinear Algorithm for Categorization

Throughout this review, the emphasis has been on state vectors; nothing is analysed or represented, but one state vector is transformed into another, eventually to become a pattern of motor neuron discharges. When psychologists or linguists describe the component parts of a complex stimulus, the word most frequently used is "feature." To claim the existence of "feature detectors" in the nervous system (single elements) that respond to psychological or linguistic features is then only a small step.

Neurons, though selective, do not show this kind of extreme selectivity. Features, a very useful concept, must correspond to more complex and abstract aspects of the stimulus. We have argued elsewhere [4] that it is possible to discriminate two different kinds of featurelike entities in a way that seems consistent with single neuron properties. We differentiate microfeatures (selective single units) and macrofeatures (vector valued activity patterns that act in a featurelike manner).

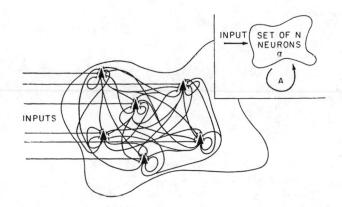

1. SET OF N NEURONS, α
2. EVERY NEURON IN α IS CONNECTED TO EVERY OTHER NEURON IN α THROUGH LEARNING MATRIX OF SYNAPTIC CONNECTIVITIES A

Fig. 8. Set of neurons projects to itself through synapses. Used as basis of nonlinear categorization model. From Anderson *et al.* [4], reprinted by permission.

The engineering literature on features sometimes defines features as vector valued quantities: the chapter in [63] on feature extraction was influential in developing the categorization model described next. Having features to be more than single elements in the vectors (i.e., selective single neurons) is neither the terminology or the tradition in psychology or neuroscience, hence the attempt on our part to emphasize this distinction with the microfeature versus macrofeature dichotomy.

We can develop a vector feature model quite easily if we assume a kind of connection known to exist in the cerebral cortex. The cortex contains an extensive set of collateral connections so that one pyramidal cell can influence another over a distance of millimeters. These collateral connections are not inhibitory (i.e., they are not "lateral inhibition," though this exists also) but probably excitatory, as indicated by the shape of the neurotransmitter containing vesicles in the collateral synapses. (For more details of the relevant anatomy see Szentagothai [58] or Shepherd [54].) Note that the system of extensive lateral interconnections forces the system to become closely related to many relaxation type models, models which give a generally good account of themselves on the types of problems that concern us here [48], [24].

Feedback Models

Let us assume that we have a single set of neurons and that this set of neurons projects to itself over a set of modifiable synapses. This anatomy is shown in Fig. 9. Let us assume that this set of lateral interconnections shows the same kind of Hebbian modification discussed earlier. When a pattern of activity learns itself, the synaptic incremental matrix is given by

$$A(i, j) = f(i)f(j).$$

The form of the resulting matrix is essentially that of the sample covariance matrix. This means that the kinds of

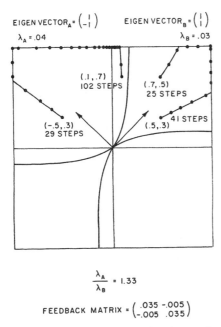

EIGEN VECTOR$_A$ = $\begin{pmatrix} 1 \\ -1 \end{pmatrix}$ EIGEN VECTOR$_B$ = $\begin{pmatrix} 1 \\ 1 \end{pmatrix}$

$\lambda_A = .04$ $\lambda_B = .03$

(.1, .7)
102 STEPS

(.7, .5)
25 STEPS

41 STEPS

(-.5, .3)
29 STEPS

(.5, .3)

$\dfrac{\lambda_A}{\lambda_B} = 1.33$

FEEDBACK MATRIX = $\begin{pmatrix} .035 & -.005 \\ -.005 & .035 \end{pmatrix}$

Fig. 9. Simple example of two-dimensional brain-state-in-a-box model. x and y axes correspond to activities in two-neuron system. Feedback is applied through feedback matrix, which has eigenvectors pointing toward corners and eigenvalues as shown. Curved lines passing through origin are boundaries of equivalence regions corresponding to one or another corner. Dots are placed on trajectories every five iterations, and total number of steps required to reach corner is placed next to starting point. From Anderson and Silverstein [5], reprinted by permission.

results obtained in principal component analysis (factor analysis) hold, and the eigenvectors, with the largest positive eigenvectors of the resulting matrix, contain the largest amount of the variance of the system. This is another example of the correlation synapse giving us a statistically useful result. The cognitive importance of these eigenvectors is that if we wish to discriminate members of a stimulus set, these particular eigenvectors are the ones to use.

However, this is also a feedback system. The coefficient of feedback of a pattern corresponding to an eigenvector is a function of the eigenvalue of that eigenvector. This positive feedback will cause a relative enhancement of eigenvectors with large positive eigenvalue over the others. We have created a system with differential weighting of a useful set of eigenvectors. This looks something like feature analysis (representation is a better word), but at no point was the stimulus actually analyzed into its component parts.

Nonlinearities

We should discriminate two aspects of this model: learning and performance. Feedback, eigenvector enhancement, takes place in real time. Learning takes place on a different time scale and may or may not affect feedback, depending on the learning time constant.

Let us consider a particular example of such a system. Suppose we have a feedback system which has generated a feedback matrix A. An input $x(0)$ is presented to the system. Suppose decay of activity is quite long (i.e., the

membrane time constants are long, say). Left to itself, the activity pattern would be unchanged. When feedback through the matrix enters the system, then we have, assuming linear addition of activities again, after t time periods,

$$x(t+1) = x(t) + Ax(t)$$
$$= (I + A)x(t)$$

as a convenient discrete representation of the underlying continuous system.

This is positive feedback system, and any nonzero eigenvector with a positive eigenvalue will increase its activity without bound. Such instability is undesirable and untypical of the nervous system which is normally exceedingly stable under almost all conditions. The simplest (traditional) way of stabilizing the system is simply to put limits on element activity. This is quite consistent with physiology where cells can fire no slower than zero or faster than a limiting rate. This has the effect of putting the state vector in a hypercube, leading to the nickname for this model of the "brain-state-in-a-box."

Qualitative Dynamics

Once the system has learned, the qualitative dynamics of this nonlinear system are quite intuitive (and easy to simulate on a computer). If we start with an activity pattern inside the box, it receives positive feedback on certain components which have the effect of forcing it outward. When its elements start to limit (i.e., when it hits the walls of the box), it moves into a corner of the box where it remains for eternity. The corners then become particularly salient aspects of the system, and the elements take on a hybrid aspect, being partially continuous (when within the box) and partly discrete (when limited).

Fig. 10 shows a simple two-dimensional system of this kind. The connectivity matrix has two eigenvectors pointing toward corners. The box becomes divided into regions, where the final state of every point in the region is the same corner. This system forms a categorizer in a strict sense. All information about the starting point is lost, and the final state only contains the category information.

This is a classification algorithm. Its novelty is that it actually constructs the classification rather than represents the classification. We have suggested that such a system might perform a useful function as a preprocessor of noisy data, since moderate noise in the starting point is supressed in the final state.

Simulations

We have done a large number of simulations of this system over the past few years, experimenting with parameters, learning assumptions, etc. As might be expected, because of powerful feedback coupled with a limiting nonlinearity, the system is robust, and most variants work similarly. (A detailed analysis of a simulation is given in [3] and another in [2].)

A typical simulation would start with a set of vectors to be discriminated, say codings of letters, or whatever. This

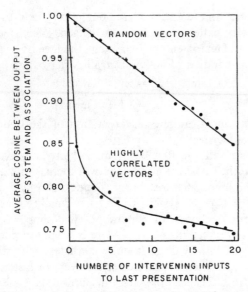

Fig. 10. Short-term changes in response can be seen when error correction techniques is used. Here input is presented, and as additional inputs from set are learned in error correction procedure, response to first input becomes less and less accurate as last presentation recedes in time. Loss of accuracy with time is function of nature of input set. Random, nearly orthogonal vectors gradually lose accuracy; highly correlated input set shows more rapid dropoff.

starting state vector $x(t)$ would change under the influence of feedback according to the rule given earlier, so that

$$x(t + 1) = (I + A)x(t).$$

After seven iterations (seven is chosen arbitrarily as being large enough to approximate a continuous system and small enough to compute quickly), the process is stopped. The final state is then learned according to the rule

$$\Delta A = \eta xx^{T}.$$

The main technical problem is making learning "turn off" when the synapses have learned enough. The simplest assumption is that no synapse associated with a cell learns when the cell limits. (This means the corresponding row and column of the incremental matrix are set to zero.) Limitation rules related to error correction models work somewhat better. The matrix is no longer the sample covariance matrix, but often is closely related to it, sufficiently enough to have many of the same desirable properties.

In the first few presentations very few elements saturate, and the matrix learns rapidly. Typically, all members of the input set finish in the same corner if the matrix is allowed to operate until all elements are limited. As learning goes on, members of the input set start to separate, so different final states emerge. When learning has ceased (i.e., all elements of the input vector saturate in seven iterations) all or almost all of the input set have separate corners.

This model has several psychologically interesting aspects. The first is its categorization behavior. Anderson et al. [4] pointed out that this model duplicates some of the qualitative properties of categorical perception in speech perception. Second, the model tends to work both faster

and better as it learns. The most common aspects of the stimulus set are learned first. Third, the macrofeatures that the model develops are indeed satisfactory in representing the input set (see Anderson and Mozer [3]). Fourth, the model has been used to give a quantitative account of a classical effect in statistical learning theory called "probability matching." Fifth, it can be used to generate concepts and compute with conceptlike elements in cognitive applications, as we discuss next.

Brain Damage

One of the properties claimed for distributed models is that they are damage resistant. If function is spread over many elements, loss of a few will not do much harm. Wood [62] has done simulations on the neural model presented here studying the effect of selective "ablations" of matrix elements. The effects are more complex than at first might be thought. Although the statistical predictions are clearcut, removing some elements may be harmful for particular associations, giving a mixed picture of distribution of function (sometimes) and localization (sometimes). Also, real brains have topographic representations of sensory and motor areas, and localized lesions there will often give rise to very specific deficits, no matter how distributed is the rest of the system.

We have also performed ablation studies on a brain-state-in-a-box simulation, confirming Wood's observations [1]. We used a 50-dimensional system, presented with an input set of vectors representing 26 letters, using oriented line segments to represent the letters. (Details are available in Anderson and Mozer [3].) After a few thousand learning trials, a very stable set of final categories was formed, so that all input vectors representing different letters were either in corners by themselves or with a small number of other letters. (The codings used by design contained some very difficult discriminations with highly correlated input vectors.) Initially, the connectivity matrix was 90-percent connected; that is, ten percent of the matrix elements were permanently zero. After 45 000 more learning trials, no significant changes occurred in the final corners. The matrix at 5000 learning trials was used for the ablation. Small numbers of elements were randomly set to zero, and categorization behavior of the system was observed. Physiologically, this corresponds to loss of synapses rather than neurons. The connectivity was changed in four-percent decrements to a final value of ten percent. Fig. 11 shows the average value of correlation between corners at 90 percent and corners at intermediate stages. Essentially, no change in categorization occurred until 20 percent of the matrix elements had been removed. It was possible to see an increase in the number of iterations required to reach a corner before the change in categorization.

Ablation studies in animals usually show that slow damage is much less harmful than rapid damage. The brain, like most organs, is powerfully homeostatic and will resist change. Suppose we allow learning between ablations. When the matrix was allowed to learn for 1000 trials

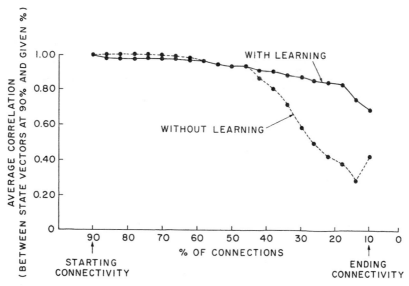

Fig. 11. Computer ablation study. Set of codings designed to represent letters was categorized by brain-state-in-a-box model with 90-percent connectivity. Connections were removed, four percent at time, and resulting categorizations were observed. With learning, system was allowed to learn for 1000 presentations of letters between each ablation. From Anderson [1], reprinted with permission.

between each four-percent ablation, we saw similar behavior in the simulation. As can be seen from Fig. 11, learning maintained the category structure of the system in the face of significantly larger amounts of diffuse damage.

IV. AN EXAMPLE OF A COGNITIVE COMPUTATION

Let us give an example of a simple cognitive computation. We have discussed simple models for association, abstraction, and feature analysis, as well as a few of the biological constraints that our models must fulfill. One way to proceed is to use these models as tools to build complex structures to perform the kinds of operations that we perform. This allows us to see if our models are computationally adequate.

An important cognitive function is the following: can the models make use of partial information to generalize or infer facts not specifically presented? Humans are extremely good at this. A successful model for distributed inference using state vectors is given in [25]. Hinton's elements were somewhat more intelligent than the model neurons we used, but the distributed representation of information is similar. See also [14] for an example of a parallel system which can perform mathematical conjecture, studying many examples of numerical behavior and inferring regularities from its experience. McClelland and Rumelhart [37], [51] have described a distributed word and letter recognition simulation which uses a network of lateral and hierarchical connections between elements. Their model does an impressive job of accounting for many effects found in the psychological literature on the perception of words and letters, and its reconstructive behavior acts similarly to the model to be described

Suppose we have some information we want to represent in a small nervous system: specifically, we have several words. These words represent entities in the real world. Because of computer limitations and for ease in presentation, we will arrange our state vectors in a convenient way. We use a 50-dimensional system. Individual words are sets of 16 nonzero elements. We use our general assumption about neural coding: things that are different in the world are different in their neural codes. The coding is sufficiently rich so that different things will have orthogonal codings for their state vectors. We assume the state vectors are partitioned so that elements 1–16 contain names (Socrates, Alcibiades, Plato, Zeus, Apollo, Diana), elements 17–32 contain supernatural status (man or god), and elements 33–48 contain life span (immortal or mortal). Elements 49–50 were not used in this simulation and were initially set to zero. We assumed that all state vectors were orthogonal and values could only be +1 or −1, represented by + and − in the figures. Other elements were set to zero, with "." representing zero.

Orthogonality in this system can be achieved in two ways. Members of groups (i.e., Zeus and Socrates) use the same neurons but have orthogonal codings (in this case, Walsh functions). Members of different groups (i.e., Zeus and immortal) use different neurons entirely. This structure conforms to the psychological truth that antonyms (black–white or mortal–immortal) are actually very similar, since they make use of the same set of features in different ways, often differing from one another along a single dimension. Things dissimilar (shoes–sealing wax or cabbages–kings) share no or very few common conceptual elements. The convenient partition of the state vector is artificial. A more realistic simulation would take the active elements, mix them together arbitrarily, and add in several hundred zero elements to represent nonresponding cells. The ten different word vectors used are presented in Fig. 12.

```
Name              Species          Life span          Title
+++++++---------  ...............  ...............  .. Socrates
----+++----++++   ...............  ...............  .. Alcibiades
+-+-+-+-+-+-+-+-  ...............  ...............  .. Plato
--++--++--++--++  ...............  ...............  .. Zeus
++++--------++++  ...............  ...............  .. Apollo
+--++--++--++--+  ...............  ...............  .. Diana

...............  +-+-+-+-+-+-+-+-  ...............  .. Man
...............  --++--++--++--++  ...............  .. God

...............  ...............  +--++--++--++--+ .. Mortal
...............  ...............  -------++++++++  .. Immortal
```

Fig. 12. Fifty-dimensional state vectors learned by system for inference simulation. Plus is value of +1, minus is −1, and "." corresponds to zero. These small 16-dimensional vectors were words that matrix learned first.

Teaching the Matrix

We wish our system to be able to infer missing bits of information when appropriate. We will use the brain-state-in-a-box model to do the learning. The essence of this model is that it is an automatic classification algorithm, that generates an output state vector from an input one, driven by the synaptic connectivity matrix. It is a categorizer with only a discrete number of final states and thus can perfectly reconstruct missing vector information in appropriate situations. Again, we emphasize the importance of this behavior to the nervous system: the nervous system is not trying to analyze anything, it is trying to generate appropriate behavior. It is action oriented, as Arbib has said, and its output is a suitable set of neuron discharges.

We use a partially connected matrix (from 50 to 75 percent in this simulation). Zeros appear along the main diagonal, for aesthetic reasons. Feedback of a neuron on itself exists in the nervous system but is almost always "special" in some way, often serving an inhibitory gain control or gating function. Renshaw cells which feedback on and gate by inhibition spinal motor neurons provides one example. A small amount of Gaussian noise is present, for realism.

First the system is taught the words. The developing matrix was presented the words randomly for 500 learning trials. Second, since we wish to test ability to regenerate missing information, we will teach the matrix pairs of words. We present "Socrates mortal," "Socrates man," "Zeus immortal," and "Zeus god," for example, randomly for 1000 trials. The complete set of assertions learned is give in Fig. 13.

The entire teaching process given here takes about 5 min of CPU time on a VAX 11/780. A number of parameters exist, but exact values are not critical. After a few false starts getting the parameters in the right range, the matrix learned satisfactorily three times in a row using different initial conditions. The critical variable was to ensure that there was sufficient synaptic flexibility to learn the new information being presented. This was achieved most directly by learning the words with 50-percent connectivity and then learning the pairs of words with 75-percent connectivity, ensuring 25 percent uninstructed synapses.

```
Name              Species          Life span          Title
+++++++---------  ...............  +--++--++--++--+ .. Socrates mortal
----+++----++++   ...............  +--++--++--++--+ .. Alcibiades mortal
+-+-+-+-+-+-+-+-  ...............  +--++--++--++--+ .. Plato mortal

+++++++---------  +-+-+-+-+-+-+-+-  ...............  .. Socrates man
----+++----++++   +-+-+-+-+-+-+-+-  ...............  .. Alcibiades man
+-+-+-+-+-+-+-+-  +-+-+-+-+-+-+-+-  ...............  .. Plato man

--++--++--++--++  ...............  -------++++++++  .. Zeus immortal
++++--------++++  ...............  -------++++++++  .. Apollo immortal
+--++--++--++--+  ...............  -------++++++++  .. Diana immortal

--++--++--++--++  --++--++--++--++  ...............  .. Zeus god
++++--------++++  --++--++--++--++  ...............  .. Apollo god
+--++--++--++--+  --++--++--++--++  ...............  .. Diana god

...............  +-+-+-+-+-+-+-+-  +--++--++--++--+ .. Man mortal
...............  --++--++--++--++  -------++++++++  .. God immortal
```

Fig. 13. Fifty-dimensional state vectors representing associations between pairs of words. After learning words, system next learned pairs of words.

```
Name              Species          Life span          Title
-+++++++----+---  +-+-+-+-+-+-+-+-  +--++--++--++--+ -- Socrates mortal
----++++----++++  +-+-+-+-+-+-+-+-  +--++--++--++--+ -- Alcibiades mortal
+-+-+-+-+-+-+-+-  +-+-+-+-+-+-+-+-  +--++--++--++--+ -- Plato mortal

-+++++++---------  +-+-+-+-+-+-+-+-  +--++--++--++--+ -- Socrates man
----++++----++++  +-+-+-+-+-+-+-+-  +--++--++--++--+ -- Alcibiades man
+-+-+-+-+-+-+-+-  +-+-+-+-+-+-+-+-  +--++--++--++--+ -- Plato man

--+----++--++  --++--++--++--++  -------++++++++  -- Zeus immortal
++++--------++++  --++--++--++--++  -------++++++++  -- Apollo immortal
+--++--++--++--+  --++--++--++--++  -------++++++++  -- Diana immortal

---++----++--++  --++--++--++--++  -------++++++++  -- Zeus god
++++---+----+++-  --++--++--++--++  -------++++++++  -- Apollo god
+--++--++--++--+  --++--++--++--++  -------++++++++  -- Diana god

+-+-+-++++--+++  +-+-+-+-+-+-+-+-  +--++--++--++--+ -- Man mortal
--++--+--++--++  --++--++--++--++  -------++++++++  -- God immortal
```

Fig. 14. Fifty-dimensional state vectors corresponding to final states of system after learning. Limits of box were set at 1.5, so plus now corresponds to 1.5, and minus to −1.5. Note that system has filled in missing parts of input state vectors (Fig. 13) in way consistent with what it has learned.

Operation of the System

Having learned that Socrates is a man and that men are mortal, we would like to generate the triple, "Socrates is a man and mortal." This would be a satisfactory output from the program. Given a new person, say, Herb, who is also a man, if we present "Herb is a man," we would like to retrieve at the output "Herb is a man and mortal." The matrix we have generated will do this. Fig. 14 shows responses to the pairs of words the system originally learned.

The system supplies the missing information in all the cases the system learned. The system was never actually presented with a triple, but with pairs of words. In every pair containing a name, the missing information is filled in correctly. For names, the output pattern is not exactly the same as the input for the name but may have changed in one or another sign; the pattern of signs for the second and third word locations were identical to those actually learned in the case presented here, but this is not always the case. If the correct triples are presented, the final states are exactly those presented here as the final states for incomplete information. It would be possible to force the system

114

to a desired final state using a correction procedure as described earlier if this was felt to be necessary.

Two pairs do not contain a name: "man mortal" and "god immortal." In the first case, the final state contains nonsense in the name location (a pattern which does not correspond to any name the system saw). In the second case, the final state reads "Zeus god immortal." If we present only the pattern "god," we obtain this triple. Zeus has become the prototypical god, whereas the prototypical man was not one of those actually learned. Further analysis seemed unpropitious.

If we present a new example of a man, say Herb, with a state vector orthogonal to those learned, then the final state corresponds to "Herb man mortal," but the name location contains several unsaturated elements, corresponding to long reaction time (time to reach a corner) and what might be interpreted as uncertainty. Vector Frank, not orthogonal to the other names, is transmuted in the memory process to be close to Plato. Odin, also not orthogonal, ends near to Zeus, suggesting Odin and Zeus are different names for the same thing. Statements the system saw or which conform to the information presented reach corners rapidly. If we deliberately present a state vector containing an error, the system can respond in several ways. Fig. 15 give examples of system responses to different test vectors which contain partial or erroneous information.

If we present "Socrates immortal," then the final state contains "god immortal" but a nonsense pattern containing an unsaturated element in the name location. If we present "Plato god immortal," then the system ends up containing "god immortal," but the name location contains nonsense with three unsaturated elements. If we present "Zeus man immortal," then we get nonsense in both the name and "man" location. "Zeus man mortal" generates several errors in the name location.

Conclusion

We have produced a system which can generate missing information. This could easily be considered to be inference, under one interpretation, since presentation of partial information generated a consistent whole. It is also similar to what is called "property inheritance," another interpretation. This is because partial information automatically brings in and presents associated information.

Relations to Formal Logic

The reason this particular set of names was used was obviously that it conforms in structure to the most famous of the classic syllogisms: "Socrates is a man, men are mortal, therefore Socrates is mortal." Clearly, our system is not doing formal logic. It is not clear that humans do formal logic, either. Logic is extremely difficult for most humans, and we need machines, diagrams, and extensive use of memory to work with formal logic. Human reasoning and logic is highly memory-oriented, using analogy, probabalistic inference, and a very effective but nonlogical set of strategies to infer information about a real, not an

abstract, world. Our model has more similarities to human logic than formal logic.

```
              Test Stimuli -- Inference Program

Name            Species         Life span           Title

Learned Patterns - Mortals:

-+++++++----+--- +-+-+-+-+-+-+- +--++--++--++--+ --  Socrates
----++++----++++ +-+-+-+-+-+-+- +--++--++--++--+ --  Alcibiades
+-+-+-+-+-+-+- +-+-+-+-+-.+-+- +--++--++--++--+ --    Plato

New mortals:

--.+++++--.,--+ +-+-+-+-+-+-+- +--++--++--++--+ --   Herb
-.,+++++--,-,--+ +-+-+-+-+-+-+- +--++--++--++--+ -    Herb man
-,++++++--,-,--+ +-+-+-+-+-+-+- +--++--++--++--+ --   Herb mortal
+-+-+-+-+-+-+- +-+-+-+-+-+-+- +--++--++--++--+ --     Frank man

Learned patterns - Gods:

---+---+--++--++ --++--++--++--++ --------+++++++++ --  Zeus
++++---+----+++- --++--++--++--++ --------+++++++++ --  Apollo
+--++--++--++--+ --++--++--++--++ --------+++++++++ --  Diana

New god:

--.+---+--++--++ --++--++--++--++ --------+++++++++ --  Odin immortal

Learned patterns:

+-+-+-+^+---+-++ +-+-+-+-+-+-+- +--++--++--++--+ --   Man
---+---+--++--++ --++--++--++--++ --------+++++++++ --  God
+-+-+-+++---+-++ +-+-+-+-+-+-+- +--++--++--++--+ --    Mortal
---+---+--++--++ --++--++--++--++ --------+++++++++ --  Immortal

Deliberate errors:

+-+----++--++--++ +-+-+-+-+-+-++ --------+++++++++ --  Man immortal
+.+++.++---+--. --++--++--++--+- +--++--++--++--+ --   God mortal

-+-+++-+---.++-- --++--++--++--++ --------+++++++++ --  Socrates immortal
-+-+++-+---.++-- --++--++--++--++ --------+++++++++ --  Socrates god

+--.,---+-+++.+- --++--++--++--++ --------+++++++++ --  Plato god immortal
+---+-+-+-+-+-+- +-+-+-+-+-+-+-+. --------+++++++++ --  Plato man immortal

--++---+--++--++ +-+-+-+-+-+-++ --------+++++++++ --   Zeus man immortal
--+-.-++.-+---++ +-+-+-+-+-+-+- +--++--++--++--+ --    Zeus man mortal
```

Fig. 15. Fifty-dimensional state vectors used to test stimuli after learning. These special, partial, or erroneous stimuli were used to check different aspects of resulting inference system (see text). Limits of box were set at 1.5 as in Fig. 14. "." now means that element did not reach limit in 50 interations.

V. Summary

We have used vectorlike quantities as elementary entities in all these models. We have showed that these entities can be used to perform operations reminscent of simplified version of a few psychological abilities of humans. Using state vectors in this way may not be the most effective or efficient way to do the computation. The resulting systems have serious trouble with logic and accuracy and have problems with unpredictable errors. However, in return, they provide properties like abstraction, concepts, and possibly inference that looks somewhat like ours. Use of systems like these is a constraint forced on us, I feel, by nervous system organization. Perhaps the virtues of the approach for certain kinds of computations make their drawbacks worthwhile.

Acknowledgment

Some of this work has appeared in more detail elsewhere. My collaborators Jack Silverstein, Stephen Ritz, Randall Jones, Andrew Knapp, and Michael Mozer have had a major part in the development of these ideas. I would like to acknowledge my debt to Geoffrey Hinton who suggested to me that it was indeed feasible to do computations with parallel systems. I would also like to express special thanks to Teuvo Kohonen and his collaborators whose pioneering work in the field of parallel, associative models has benefited us all. At Brown I have learned a great deal from discussions with Stuart Geman, Barry Davis, Gregory Murphy, and Richard Heath. A summer at U.S.C.D. allowed me to talk with Geoffrey Hinton. Donald Norman, David Rumelhart, and Jay McClelland and suggested a host of new problems to think about. Leon Cooper and the Center for Neural Science have provided immense help over the past few years. Computer simulations described here were performed on the VAX 11/780 of the Center for Cognitive Science, Richard Millward, Director.

REFERENCES

[1] J. A. Anderson, "Neural models and a little about language," in *Biological Bases of Language*, D. Caplan, A. Smith, and A. Roche-Lecour, Eds. Cambridge, MA: MIT Press (to appear).
[2] _____, "Neural models with cognitive implications," in *Basic Processes in Reading*, D. LaBerge and S. J. Samuels, Eds. Hillsdale, NJ: Erlbaum, 1977.
[3] J. A. Anderson and M. Mozer, "Categorization and selective neurons," in *Parallel Models of Associative Memory*, G. Hinton and J. A. Anderson, Eds. Hillsdale, NJ: Erlbaum, 1981.
[4] J. A. Anderson, J. W. Silverstein, S. A. Ritz, and R. S. Jones, "Distinctive features, categorical perception, and probability learning: Some applications of a neural model," *Psychol. Rev.*, vol. 84, pp. 413–451, 1977.
[5] J. A. Anderson and J. W. Silverstein, "Reply to Grossberg," *Psychol. Rev.*, vol. 85, pp. 597–603, 1978.
[6] M. A. Arbib, *The Metaphorical Brain*. New York: Wiley, 1972.
[7] R. Sorabji, tr., *Aristotle on Memory*. Providence, RI: Brown Univ. Press, 1972.
[8] H. B. Barlow, "Single units and sensation," *Perception*, vol. 1, pp. 371–394, 1972.
[9] E. L. Bienenstock, L. N. Cooper, and P. W. Monro, "A theory for the development of neuron selectivity: Orientation selectivity and binocular interactions in visual cortex," *J. Neurosci.*, vol. 2, pp. 32–48, 1982.
[10] S. E. Brodie, B. W. Knight, and F. Ratliff, "The responses of the Limulus retina to moving stimuli: Prediction by Fourier synthesis," *J. General Physiol.*, vol. 72, pp. 129–166, 1978.
[11] _____, "The spatio-temporal transfer function of the Limulus lateral eye," *J. Gen. Physiol.*, vol. 72, pp. 167–202, 1978.
[12] M. Colonnier, "The electron-microscopic analysis of the neuronal organization of the cerebral cortex," in *The Organization of the Cerebral Cortex*, F. O. Schmitt, F. G. Worden, G. Adelman, and S. G. Dennis, Eds. Cambridge, MA: MIT Press, 1981.
[13] L. N. Cooper, "Distributed memory in the central nervous system: Possible test of assumptions in visual cortex," in *The Organization of the Cerebral Cortex*, F. O. Schmitt, F. G. Worden, G. Adelman, and S. G. Dennis, Eds. Cambridge, MA: MIT Press, 1981.
[14] B. Davis, "A neurobiological approach to machine intelligence," Ph.D. thesis, Div. of Appl. Math., Brown Univ., Providence, RI, June 1982.
[15] R. O. Duda and P. E. Hart, *Pattern Classification and Scene Analysis*. New York: Wiley, 1973.
[16] Editors of *Scientific American*, *The Brain*. San Francisco, CA: Freeman, 1979.
[17] J. M. Eich, "A composite holographic associative recall model," *Psychol. Rev.*, vol. 89, pp. 627–661, 1982.
[18] J. A. Feldman and D. H. Ballard, "Connectionist models and their properties," *Cognitive Sci.*, vol. 6, pp. 205–254, 1982.
[19] S. Geman, "Application of stochastic averaging to learning systems," *Brain Theory Newsletter*, vol. 3, pp. 69–71, 1978.
[20] S. Geman, "The law of large numbers in neural modelling," *SIAM-AMS Proc.*, vol. 13, pp. 91–105, 1981.
[21] S. Grossberg, "How does the brain build a cognitive code?," *Psychol. Rev.*, vol. 87, pp. 1–51, 1980.
[22] D. O. Hebb, *The Organization of Behavior*. New York: Wiley, 1949.
[23] R. A. Heath, "A model for signal detection based on an adaptive filter," *Biol. Cybern.*, in press.
[24] G. E. Hinton, "Relaxation and its role in vision," Ph.D. dissertation, Univ. of Edinburgh, 1976.
[25] _____, "Implementing semantic networks in parallel hardware," in *Parallel Models of Associative Memory*, G. E. Hinton and J. A. Anderson, Ed. Hillsdale, NJ: Erlbaum, 1981.
[26] G. Hinton and J. A. Anderson, Eds., *Parallel Models of Associative Memory*. Hillsdale, NJ: Erlbaum, 1981.
[27] W. James, *Psychology (Briefer Course)*. New York: Collier, 1962 (originally published 1890).
[28] E. Kandel, "Small systems of neurons," in *The Brain*, Editors of *Scientific American*, Eds. San Francisco, CA: Freeman, 1979.
[29] A. Knapp and J. A. Anderson, "A signal averaging model for concept formation," *J. Exp. Psychol.*, *Learning, Memory, and Cognition*, submitted.
[30] T. Kohonen, *Associative Memory: A System Theoretic Approach*. Berlin, Germany: Springer-Verlag, 1977.
[31] P. Liepa, "Models of content addressable distributed associative memory (CADAM)," unpublished manuscript, Univ. of Toronto, Toronto, ON, Canada, 1977.
[32] A. R. Luria, *The Mind of a Mnemonist*. New York: Basic Books, 1968.
[33] E. Mach, "Ernst Mach," in *Dictionary of Scientific Bibgraphy*, vol. VIII, C. C. Gillespie, Ed. New York: Scribners, 1973.
[34] D. Marr, "A theory of cerebellar cortex," *J. Physiol.*, vol. 202, pp. 437–470 1969.
[35] _____, "A theory for cerebral neocortex," *Proc. Roy. Soc.*, Ser. B, vol. 176, pp. 161–234, 1970.
[36] _____, *Vision*. San Francisco, CA: Freeman, 1982.
[37] J. L. McClelland, and D. E. Rumelhart, "An interactive activation model of context effects in letter perception: Part 1. An account of basic findings," *Psychol. Rev.*, vol. 88, pp. 375–497, 1981.
[38] W. S. McCulloch and W. Pitts, "A logical calculus of the ideas immanent in nervous activity," *Bull. Math. Biophys.*, vol. 5, pp. 115–133, 1943.
[39] M. Minsky, "K-lines: A theory of memory," *Cognitive Sci.*, vol. 4, pp. 117–133, 1980.
[40] M. Minsky and S. Papert, *Perceptrons*. Cambridge, MA: MIT Press, 1969.
[41] B. B. Murdock, Jr., "A theory for the storage and retrieval of item and associative information," *Psychol. Rev.*, pp. 609–626, 1982.
[42] N. J. Nilsson, *Learning Machines*. New York: McGraw-Hill, 1965.
[43] A. Pellionisz and R. Llinas, "Brain modelling by tensor network theory and computer simulation. The Cerebellum: Distributed processor for predictive coordination," *Neurosci.*, vol. 4, pp. 323–348, 1979.
[44] W. Pitts and W. S. McCulloch, "How we know universals: The perception of auditory and visual forms," *Bull. Math. Biophys.*, vol. 9, pp. 127–147, 1947.
[45] M. I. Posner and S. W. Keele, "On the genesis of abstract ideas," *J. Exp. Psychol.*, vol. 77, pp. 353–363, 1968.
[46] _____, "Retention of abstract ideas," *J. Exp. Psychol.*, vol. 83, pp. 304–308, 1970.
[47] F. Ratliff, "Form and function: Linear and nonlinear analyses of neural networks in the visual system," in *Neural Mechanisms in Behavior*, D. McFadden, Ed. New York: Springer, 1980.
[48] A. Rosenfeld, "Iterative methods in image analysis," *Pattern Recognition*, vol. 10, pp. 181–187, 1978.
[49] E. Rosch, "Principles of categorization," in *Cognition and Categorization*, E. Rosch and B. B. Lloyd, Eds. Hillsdale, NJ: Erlbaum, 1978.
[50] E. Rosch and B. B. Lloyd, Eds., *Cognition and Categorization*. Hillsdale, NJ: Erlbaum, 1978.
[51] D. E. Rumelhart and J. L. McClelland, "An interactive activation model of context effects in letter perception: Part 2. The contextual enhancement effect and some tests and extensions of the model," *Psychol. Rev.*, vol. 89, pp. 60–94, 1982.
[52] F. O. Schmitt, F. G. Worden, G. Adelman, and S. G. Dennis, *The Organization of the Cerebral Cortex*. Cambridge, MA: MIT Press, 1981.
[53] T. J. Sejnowski, "Skeleton filters in the brain," in *Parallel Models of*

Associative Memory, G. E. Hinton and J. A. Anderson, Eds. Hillsdale, NJ: Erlbaum, 1981.

[54] G. Shepherd, *The Synaptic Organization of the Brain*, 2nd ed. New York: Oxford Univ. Press, 1979.

[55] ____, *Neurobiology*. New York: Oxford Univ. Press, 1983.

[56] E. E. Smith and D. L. Medin, *Categories and Concepts*. Cambridge, MA: Harvard Univ. Press, 1981.

[57] R. S. Sutton and A. G. Barto, "Toward a modern theory of adaptive networks: expectation and prediction," *Psychol. Rev.*, vol. 88, pp. 135–170, 1981.

[58] J. Szentagothai, "Specificity versus (quasi) randomness in cortical connectivity," in *Architectonics of the Cerebral Cortex*, M. A. B. Brazier and H. Petsche, Eds. New York: Raven Press, 1978.

[59] J. Szentagothai and M. Arbib, "Conceptual models of neural organization," *Neurosci. Res. Program Bull.*, vol. 12, pp. 307–510, 1974.

[60] R. J. Tusa, L. A. Palmer, and A. C. Rosenquist, "The retinotopic organization of area 17 (Striate Cortex) in the cat," *J. Comp. Neurol.*, vol. 177, pp. 213–235, 1978.

[61] C. Wood, "Variations on a theme by Lashley: Lesion experiments on the neural models of Anderson, Silverstein, Ritz, and Jones," *Psychol. Rev.*, vol. 85, 582–591, 1978.

[62] ____, "Implications of simulated lesion experiments for the interpretation of lesions in real nervous systems," in *Neural Models of Language Processes*, M. A. Arbib, D. Caplan, and J. C. Marshall, Eds. New York: Academic, 1983.

[63] T. Y. Young and T. W. Calvert, *Classification, Estimation, and Pattern Recognition*. New York: American Elsevier, 1974.

Field Theory of Self-Organizing Neural Nets

SHUN-ICHI AMARI, MEMBER, IEEE

Abstract—A field theory is proposed as a mathematical method for analyzing learning and self-organizing nerve nets and systems in a unified manner. It is shown by the use of the theory that a nerve net has an ability of automatically forming categorizers or signal detecting cells for the signals which the net receives from its environment. Moreover, when the set of signals has a topological structure, the detectors of these signals are arranged in the nerve system (or field) to preserve the topology, so that the topographical structure is introduced in the nerve system by self-organization.

I. INTRODUCTION

THE BRAIN has strong ability of self-organization. Its characteristics are modified according to the nature of the environment from which signals are obtained, so that it adapts to the information structures of the environment. The brain is widely believed to self-organize by modifying the synaptic weights of connections between neurons. A vast amount of direct and indirect evidence has been found concerning the plasticity of the nerve system. This evidence includes, for example, the automatic formation of feature-detecting cells in the striate cortex guided by visual experiences of young kittens (e.g., [1], [2]), the automatic formation of topographic arrangements of cells in the nerve field [3], [4], etc. This suggests that fine structures of the brain are formed by self-organization to be compatible with the outer world from which the animal receives signals.

Many mathematical or computer models of learning and self-organizing neural nets have been proposed (cf, for example, perceptron [5], [6]; associative memory [7]–[10]). A computer model of automatic formation of feature or category detecting cells was proposed by Malsburg [11], and its versions are treated by many investigators [12]–[14]. Models of topographic organization of nerve fields have also been studied from the viewpoint of self-organization [15]–[19].

Although these models work very well in some situations, obtaining the whole characteristics of these models is difficult, because no general methods exist for analyzing them mathematically. Based on the author's endeavors to construct a mathematical theory of nerve systems [8], [14],

[17], [18], [20]–[28], the present paper proposes a field theory of self-organization by which various models of learning and self-organizing nets are treated in a unified manner. The dynamical behavior of self-organization is described by a field differential equation on the signal space. By the use of this theory, characteristics of formation of signal detecting cells are analyzed in a simple and revised nerve net models. Self-organization of nerve fields is also analyzed, and it is shown that signal detecting cells are automatically arranged to be compatible with the natural topology of the signals in the outer world. Thus self-organization is shown to be responsible for the formation of topographic maps in the neural fields.

However, much of global topological organization is genetically determined in the brain. Self-organization plays an important role in modifying the fine structures of the connectivities in the brain such that they fit well in the structures of signals in the environment. In the case of formation of a topographic map in the retino-tectal connections, self-organization can only refine the already existing rough connections into an accurate map with fine resolution. When some part of the retina and/or tectum is broken, self-organization accounts for reformation of the map. However, a rough map is necessary before self-organization takes place. An initial rough map seems to be developed by another mechanism which takes place at an early stage of development. The present paper proposes a unified field theory approach to the problems of self-organization which seems to play an important role in refining the neural structures. These results unify recent theoretical results on self-organization [14], [17], [18], [24].

II. SELF-ORGANIZATION OF NEURONS

A. Behavior of Model Neuron

A neuron receives a large number of input signals, processes them, and emits an output signal. Let $x_1, x_2, \cdots, x_n$ be the input signals, and let z be the output signal. In general, these signals take analog values, representing pulse rates in the nerve axons. They change with time t. Let $s_1, \cdots, s_n$ be the synaptic weights of the signals $x_1, \cdots, x_n$, respectively. It is convenient to use the vector notation

Manuscript received August 1, 1982; revised April 1, 1983. This work was supported in part by the Japanese Ministry of Education under Grant-in-Aid for Special Project Research #56121006.

The author is with the Department of Mathematical Engineering and Instrumentation Physics, Faculty of Engineering, University of Tokyo, Tokyo, 113 Japan.

Reprinted from *IEEE Trans. Syst. Man, Cybern.*, vol. SMC-13, no. 5, pp. 741–748, Sept./Oct. 1983.

$$x = (x_1, x_2, \cdots, x_n),$$
$$s = (s_1, s_2, \cdots, s_n),$$

so that the total input stimulation S to the neuron is given by the inner product

$$S = s \cdot x = \sum s_i x_i.$$

Let $u(t)$ be a quantity representing the state of the neuron at time t. It may be regarded as the short-time average of the membrane potential of the neuron. It increases in proportion to the total input stimulation $s \cdot x$, while it decreases toward the resting potential $-h$. Hence the behavior of the model neuron is described by the differential equation

$$\tau' \dot{u}(t) = -u(t) + s \cdot x(t) - h, \qquad (1)$$

where τ' is a time constant and the dot above the variable denotes the time derivative d/dt. The output pulse rate $z(t)$ at time t of the neuron is determined by the potential $u(t)$ as

$$z(t) = f[u(t)], \qquad (2)$$

where f is a nonlinear function having a saturation characteristic. The output function f is assumed to be a monotonically nondecreasing function satisfying $0 \leq f \leq 1$, with $f(u) = 0$ for $u \leq 0$. When the input vector signal x is kept constant for a while, the potential converges to $u = s \cdot x - h$ and the output becomes

$$z = f(s \cdot x - h).$$

The neuron is believed to have the ability to modify its synaptic weight vector s depending on the input signals and the output signals (and in some cases also on extra teacher signals when they exist). A simple generalized Hebbian law without teacher signals is used in the present paper: a synaptic weight s_i increases in proportion to the input x_i when some condition is satisfied and decays slowly. The equation of synaptic modification is written as

$$\tau \dot{s}_i(t) = -s_i(t) + c r(t) x_i(t), \qquad (3)$$

where τ and c are constants and $r(t)$ specifies the condition on which the synaptic modification takes place. In the present paper, $r(t)$ is assumed to be equal to the output $z(t)$ of the neuron. Various types of learning rules can be obtained by choosing appropriate $r(t)$ which may depend on extra teacher signals. For example, perceptron learning, associative memory learning, etc., can be formulated in similar manners (see [8], [14], [24]). Hence the learning equation in the present case is written as

$$\tau \dot{s}(t) = -s(t) + c f[u(t)] x(t) \qquad (4)$$

in the vector notation.

B. Information Source and Averaged Learning Equation

A neuron self-organizes by receiving signals from the environment to adapt to it. Let us consider an information source I which includes many signals x and which emits one of them at a time, according to the prescribed probability or relative frequency $p(x)$. This probability distribution $p(x)$ represents the structure of the environment to which a neuron is to adapt its behavior. Hence the information source I is identified with a space of signals x with a probability measure $p(x)$. It chooses a signal x randomly with probability $p(x)$ and emits it for a short time Δt, and then it chooses another signal x' independently of the previous signals and emits it for the same time duration Δt, repeating these processes. It thus produces an ergodic time series $x(t)$ of the input signal, such that any typical sequence $x(t)$ includes signals x with the relative frequency $p(x)$. Thus the environment is modeled by an information source I.

The learning equation (4) is a stochastic differential equation driven by a stochastic input $x(t)$ from I. Since I is ergodic, it is expected that the synaptic weight vector $s(t)$ converges in some sense to a value reflecting stochastic properties of the environment I for almost all input sequences $x(t)$ from I. It is assumed that the duration Δt is sufficiently large compared with the time constant τ' of neural dynamics but sufficiently small compared with the time constant τ of the dynamics of synaptic modification. When a signal x is chosen, the output z quickly converges to $z = f(s \cdot x - h)$, because τ' is small.

Let $\langle \cdot \rangle$ be the average of a function of x over all $x \in I$ with probability $p(x)$, e.g.,

$$\langle f(s \cdot x - h)x \rangle = \int f(s \cdot x - h) x p(x)\, dx,$$

where $p(x)$ is the probability density function. (When I includes only a finite number of signals, the integration is replaced by summation.) Since many independent signals x are emitted for a period of order τ, the learning equation can be approximated by the averaged one

$$\tau \dot{s}(t) = -s(t) + c \langle f(s \cdot x - h)x \rangle, \qquad (5)$$

which is a deterministic equation in $s(t)$. This is called the averaged learning equation [14], [24]. The solution of (4) is proved to converge to that of the averaged equation (5) in probability, when τ becomes large. See, for example, Geman [29] for mathematical treatment of the averaged processes.

C. Receptive Region

A neuron fires by receiving a signal x, when $f(s \cdot x - h) > 0$ or the function

$$U(x; s) = s \cdot x - h \qquad (6)$$

is positive. The function $U(x; s)$ is useful for knowing the behavior of the neuron with the synaptic weight vector s. For example, we can define the subset $R(s)$ of the signal space I by

$$R(s) = \{x | U(x; s) > 0\}, \qquad (7)$$

which is called the receptive region of the neuron with weight s. The neuron fires by receiving any signals belonging to its receptive region R. The function $U(x; s)$ can be regarded as the potential of excitability of x and is positive for $x \in R$. The potential $U(x)$, and hence the receptive region R, changes as the synaptic weight vector s is modified by self-organization. Hence it depends on time t through $s(t)$.

By substituting (5) in $U(x; s) = s \cdot x$, the following equation is derived,

$$\tau \dot{U}(x; s) = -U - h + c \langle f(s \cdot x' - h)x' \rangle \cdot x$$
$$= -U - h + c \int x \cdot x' f[U(x')] \, p(x') \, dx.$$

Hence, by putting $c(x, x') = cx \cdot x'$, it is rewritten as

$$\tau \dot{U}(x) = -U - h + c(x, x') * f[U(x')], \qquad (8)$$

where s in U is omitted and $*$ is the integral operator over I with respect to the measure $p(x)$, e.g.,

$$c(x, x') * f[U(x')] = \int c(x, x') f[U(x')] \, p(x') \, dx'. \qquad (9)$$

This is the dynamical equation describing the change in the receptive region R or the potential distribution $U(x)$ of a neuron. It is a field equation over the signal space I, where $c(x, x')$ denotes the intensity of interactions between two signal points x and x' in I.

III. Field Equations of Self-Organizing Nerve Systems and Fields

A. Self-Organization of Neural Systems

The self-organization of a neural system is more complex than that of a single neuron because of the dynamical interactions among the component neurons. We cannot treat the synaptic modification of one neuron independently of the others. Let us consider a neuron net consisting of m mutually connected neurons. All of the neurons receive the same input vector signals x from a common information source I. These signals are assumed to be excitatory, and the neurons receive a common inhibitory input of intensity x_0. Let u_i be the average membrane potential of the ith neuron. Let w_{ij} be the synaptic weight of the recurrent connection from the jth neuron to the ith neuron. Moreover, let s_i be the synaptic weight vector of the ith neuron receiving vector input x, and let s_{0i} be the synaptic weight of the ith neuron for the inhibitory input x_0. Then the dynamical equation of excitation is written as

$$\tau' \dot{u}_i = -u_i + \sum_j w_{ij} f(u_j) + s_i \cdot x - s_0 x_0 - h \qquad (10)$$

when an input x is applied to the system. Equation (10) is assumed to be monostable and the potentials $u_i(t)$ to converge quickly to the stable equilibrium state $U_i(x)$, which is the solution of the equation

$$U_i(x) = \sum w_{ij} f(U_j) + s_i \cdot x - s_0 x_0 - h \qquad (11)$$

obtained by putting $\dot{u}_i = 0$.

The function $U_i(x)$ depends on all of the synaptic weight vectors $s_1, s_2, \cdots, s_m, s_{0i}, \cdots, s_{0m}$ of the system so that it may be written as

$$U_i(x; s_1, s_2, \cdots, s_m; s_{01}, \cdots, s_{0m}).$$

The set

$$R_i = \{ x | U_i(x) > 0 \} \qquad (12)$$

represents the receptive region of the ith neuron. The ith neuron is excited when the system receives an input signal x belonging to R_i. When the synaptic weights change by self-organization, the functions $U_i(x)$ or the receptive regions R_i are also modified.

The equation of synaptic modification is written as

$$\tau \dot{s}_i = -s_i + cf[u_i(t)] x(t). \qquad (13)$$
$$\tau \dot{s}_{0i} = -s_{0i} + c' f[u_i(t)] x_0, \qquad (14)$$

where the same rule is applied to the modification of inhibitory synapses but with different constant c'. For simplicity, the synaptic weights w_{ij} of the recurrent connections are assumed not to be modifiable but fixed. Since $u_i(t)$ converges quickly to the equilibrium $U_i(x)$ when x is applied, we can replace $u_i(t)$ in (13), (14) by $U_i[x(t)]$ because of the relation $\tau' \ll \Delta t \ll \tau$. This is a kind of adiabatic approximation or slaving principle (cf [24], [25], [30]) in which the difference in the orders of the time constants τ and τ' is taken into account. By taking the average over the signal space I with respect to $p(x)$, the averaged learning equations of the neural system is obtained as

$$\tau \dot{s}_i = -s_i + c \langle f[U_i(x; s_1, \cdots, s_m)] x \rangle, \qquad (15)$$
$$\tau \dot{s}_{0i} = -s_{0i} + c' \langle f[U_i(x)] x_0 \rangle. \qquad (16)$$

In order to convert these equations to the field equations of self-organization, new quantities V_i are introduced by

$$V_i(x) = U_i(x) - \sum w_{ij} f[U_j(x)]$$
$$= s_i \cdot x - s_{0i} x_0 - h. \qquad (17)$$

The field equations are then obtained by differentiating V_i with respect to time t and by substituting (15) and (16) in it,

$$\tau \dot{V}_i(x) = -V_i(x) - h + c(x, x') * f[U_i(x')], \qquad (18)$$

where the term $c(x, x')$ is given by

$$c(x, x') = cx \cdot x' - c' x_0^2 \qquad (19)$$

in the present case. The equilibrium state $\bar{U}_i(x)$ of self-organization should satisfy $\dot{V}_i(x) = 0$, or

$$\overline{U}_i(x) = \sum w_{ij} f\left[\overline{U}_j(x)\right] - h + c(x, x') * f\left[\overline{U}_i(x')\right]. \quad (20)$$

The above equations show that the receptive fields R_i of the component neurons are determined, not independently to one another, but subject to the mutual interactions via the term $\sum w_{ij} f[U_j(x)]$. Extending the model such that some of the recurrent connections w_{ij} are also subject to synaptic modification (some of the neurons have different self-organizing characteristics, etc.), is easy.

B. Self-Organization of Nerve Fields

When neurons are arranged in a sheet to form a neural field, the system can be treated as a neural continuum or neural field. Self-organization of nerve fields is treated to explain the mechanism of topographic arrangements of nerve field in a later section. Let ξ be the spatical coordinate system introduced in a neural field Ξ. Let $u(\xi, t)$ be the average of the membrane potentials of neurons located at around position ξ at time t. Let $w(\xi, \xi')$ be the average synaptic weight of recurrent connections within the field from the neurons at position ξ' to those at ξ. When the field is homogeneous, $w(\xi, \xi')$ depends only on the difference $\xi - \xi'$. Let $S(\xi, t)$ be the total stimulation by the inputs given to the neurons at position ξ at time t from the outside. Then the dynamical equation of neural excitations is written as

$$\tau' \frac{\partial u(\xi, t)}{\partial t} =$$
$$-u(\xi, t) + w(\xi, \xi') \circ f\left[u(\xi', t)\right] + S(\xi, t) \quad (21)$$

where $\circ$ denotes the convolution or spatial integration,

$$w(\xi, \xi') \circ f\left[u(\xi', t)\right] = \int w(\xi, \xi') f\left[u(\xi', t)\right] d\xi',$$

which represents the total effect of recurrent connections since the output of the neurons at ξ' is $f[u(\xi', t)]$.

When excitatory inputs x are applied from a common information source I and an inhibitory input x_0 is applied at the same time from an inhibitory neuron pool, the total stimulus given to the neurons at ξ is

$$S(\xi, t) = s(\xi) \cdot x(t) - s_0(\xi) x_0 - h, \quad (22)$$

where $s(\xi)$ is the synaptic weight vector of the neurons at ξ for the vector input x and $s_0(\xi)$ is the inhibitory synaptic weight of the neurons at ξ.

Again, (21) is assumed to be monostable for a constant input x. The equilibrium state of the equation when x is input is denoted by $U(\xi, x)$, which is the solution of the equation

$$U(\xi, x) = w(\xi, \xi') \circ f\left[U(\xi', x)\right]$$
$$+ s(\xi) \cdot x - s_0(\xi) x_0 - h. \quad (23)$$

Obviously, the receptive region of the neurons at ξ is given by

$$R(\xi) = \{ x | U(\xi, x) > 0 \}.$$

The function $U(\xi, x)$ defines a potential distribution on the direct product $\Xi \times I$ of the neural field Ξ and the signal space I. The set

$$E(x) = \{ \xi | U(\xi, x) > 0 \}$$

consists of the positions of the neurons which are excited by receiving a common input x in the equilibrium. The function $U(\xi, x)$ summarizes the behavior of the neural field Ξ in the equilibrium. The function depends on the synaptic weights $s(\xi)$ and $s_0(\xi)$ so that it changes by self-organization.

The averaged learning equations are written as

$$\tau \frac{\partial s(\xi, t)}{\partial t} = -s(\xi, t) + c\langle f\left[U(\xi, x)\right] x \rangle, \quad (24)$$

$$\tau \frac{\partial s_0(\xi, t)}{\partial t} = -s_0(\xi, t) + c'\langle f\left[U(\xi, x)\right] x_0 \rangle, \quad (25)$$

where the slaving principle is used and the recurrent connections $w(\xi, \xi')$ are assumed to be fixed.

By introducing the function

$$V(\xi, x) = U(\xi, x) - w(\xi, \xi') \circ f\left[U(\xi', x)\right] \quad (26)$$

the field equation of self-organization is derived as

$$\tau \frac{\partial V(\xi, x, t)}{\partial t} = -V(\xi, x, t) - h$$
$$+ c(x, x') \circ f\left[U(\xi, x', t)\right]. \quad (27)$$

The equilibrium state $\overline{U}(\xi, x)$ is obtained by solving

$$\overline{U}(\xi, x) = w \circ f[\overline{U}] + c * f(\overline{U}) - h \quad (28)$$

in which the term of the positional convolution $\circ$ represents the interactions between the neurons of different positions and the term of the signal convolution $*$ represents the interactions among the signals included in the information source I.

IV. AUTOMATIC FORMATION OF CATEGORIZORS AND FEATURE EXTRACTORS

A. Primitive Model

A self-organizing system has an ability of forming categorizors, detectors or feature extractors for the signals which the system receives. A neuron is said to be a detector of a set A of signals, when the neuron is excited, responsive to any signals belonging to A but no signals outside A. By using a simple model we show that the model system automatically forms detectors of various clusters of signals, thus categorizing them automatically. By receiving the same signals from I, the neurons in the system differentiate and become detectors of different sets of signals. Therefore, a number of different detectors are formed in the system, so that the system as a whole can categorize the signals of I.

The primitive model considered here consists of a pool of neurons, in which no mutual connections exist, so that

121

each neuron self-organizes independently. The dynamical equation of self-organization is obtained by putting $w_{ij} = 0$ in (17) and (18). Hence the field equation is

$$\tau \dot{U}(x) = -U(x) + c * f[U], \qquad (29)$$

where we put $h = 0$ for simplicity. The equation is the same for all the neurons, so that the suffix i is omitted.

The equilibrium $\overline{U}(x)$ of the foregoing equation satisfies

$$\overline{U}(x) = c * f[\overline{U}]. \qquad (30)$$

The receptive region R corresponding to $\overline{U}(x)$ is called the equilibrium receptive region under I and is given by $R = \{x | \overline{U}(x) > 0\}$. Equation (29) is in general multistable so that several equilibrium solutions exist. The receptive region of a neuron in the system eventually converges to one of the equilibrium solutions by self-organization. For R determined by $\overline{U}(x)$, we define

$$p_R = \langle f[\overline{U}(x)] \rangle. \qquad (31)$$

$$x_R = \langle xf[\overline{U}(x)] \rangle / p_R, \qquad (32)$$

which latter may be called the center of R. By substituting (31) and (32) in (30), the equilibrium $\overline{U}(x)$ can be reconstructed from p_R and x_R by (30)

$$\overline{U}(x) = p_R(cx_R \cdot x - c'x_0^2). \qquad (33)$$

Let $\bar{s}$ and $-\bar{s}_0$ be the synaptic weights of the neuron whose receptive region is R. Then, by comparing (33) with (11),

$$\bar{s} = cp_R x_R \qquad \bar{s}_0 = c'p_R x_0$$

are obtained.

Since $\overline{U}(x)$ should be positive for $x \in R$ and negative for $x \notin R$, by putting $\lambda = c'x_0^2/c$, x_R satisfies $x_R \cdot x > \lambda$ for $x \in R$ and $x_R \cdot x < \lambda$ for $x \notin R$ or, equivalently,

$$\inf_{x \in R} x_R \cdot x > \lambda > \sup_{x \notin R} x_R \cdot x. \qquad (34)$$

On the other hand, if a vector x_R satisfies (34), the function $\overline{U}(x)$ constructed from this x_R by (33) is an equilibrium solution of (30). Hence a set R is an equilibrium receptive region if and only if it satisfies (34). This is a generalization of the theorem proved by Amari and Takeuchi [14].

This result demonstrates what kinds of signal detectors or categorizors are formed by self-organization. In general, a number of equilibrium receptive regions R satisfy (34). Every neuron eventually becomes a detector of one of these R. In order to study the property of the categorizors formed from self-organization, let us consider an information source I which includes only a finite number of signals $x_1, \cdots, x_k$ with probabilities $p_1, \cdots, p_k$, respectively. We further assume that every signal is normalized, $|x_i|^2 = 1$, and that $x_i \cdot x_j < b$ $(i \neq j)$ holds for some $b < 1$. Let R_i be a set of signals which includes x_i but no other x_j $(j \neq i)$. If such an R_i is an equilibrium receptive region, x_i-detectors, which are responsive for x_i but not responsive for x_j $(j \neq i)$, can be formed by self-organization. We look for

the condition which guarantees that x_i-detectors $\overline{\text{can be}}$ formed for every x_i. Since

$$p_{Ri} = p_i f[\overline{U}(x_i)] \qquad x_{Ri} = x_i$$

hold for R_i, the relation (34) reduces in this case to

$$1 > \lambda > b. \qquad (35)$$

Therefore, when and only when the constant λ satisfies (35), x_i-detectors for every x_i are automatically formed by self-organization.

The constant λ designates the degree of resolution of the receptive regions to be formed. When $x_i \cdot x_j > \lambda$ for some x_i and x_j, neither x_i-detectors nor x_j-detectors can be formed. In this case, an equilibrium receptive region exists which includes both x_i and x_j. Hence x_i and x_j are categorized into the same class and their common detectors are formed.

The resolution of the detectors can be shown more clearly from the following example in which the probability measure of I is uniform on the set $|x| = 1$, i.e., the probability measure is distributed uniformly on the unit sphere S in the first quadrangle of the signal space. Since $\overline{U}(x)$ is linear in x, the corresponding R is a portion of the sphere S cut by the hyperplane $\overline{U}(x) = 0$. Let $x_R = ax_0$ be the center of R, where $x_0 \in S$ is a unit vector (i.e., $|x_0| = 1$). The constant a is determined from

$$ax_0 = x_R = \langle xf[\overline{U}(x)] \rangle / p_R.$$

The hyperplane $\overline{U}(x) = x_R \cdot x - \lambda = 0$ intersects S only when $\lambda < 1$. Hence the nonzero equilibrium solutions exist only when $\lambda < 1$. For an $x_0 \in S$, an equilibrium receptive region R exists whose center is $x_R = ax_0$, when

$$\inf_{x \in R} x_R \cdot x > \lambda > \sup_{x \notin R} x_R \cdot x$$

is satisfied for $x \subset S$. The boundary of R is indeed given by $x_R \cdot x = \lambda$ or

$$x_0 \cdot x = \lambda/a, \qquad x \in S, \qquad (36)$$

where a is determined depending on λ. When $\lambda < 1$, an equilibrium R is found for any $x_0 \in S$, provided the hyperplane $x_R \cdot x = \lambda$ intersects S in the first quadrangle. This shows that an equilibrium stable region R exists around any $x_0 \in S$. Hence an infinite number of equilibrium solutions exists. The size of R becomes small, when λ tends to one.

It can also be shown that, when the probability measure distributed on S is not uniform but has a number of peaks, equilibrium stable regions R are formed only around these peaks. Hence detectors are formed for sets of signals around the peaks of the probability distributions.

B. Revised Model

Even the simple primitive model has an ability of forming categorizors or detectors of signals. However, since each neuron behaves independently in it, it might occur that a large number of neurons become detectors of one signal while only a few neurons become detectors of another signal. This shortcoming is overcome by introducing mutual interactions among the neurons. We consider a simple revised model in which every neuron is recurrently connected with inhibitory synapses of constant weight, $w_{ij} = -w, i, j = 1, 2, \cdots, m$. Let R_i be the equilibrium receptive region of the ith neuron corresponding to the equilibrium solution $\overline{U}_i(x)$. By the use of the quantities

$$p_{Ri} = \langle f[\overline{U}_i(x)]\rangle,$$

$$x_{Ri} = \langle xf[\overline{U}_i(x)]\rangle / p_{Ri},$$

we have from (20)

$$\overline{U}_i(x) = -wg(x) + p_i(cx_{Ri} \cdot x - c'x_0^2), \quad (37)$$

where

$$g(x) = \sum_{i=1}^{m} f[\overline{U}_i(x)]. \quad (38)$$

This shows that all $\overline{U}_i(x)$ or R_i ($i = 1, 2, \cdots, m$) are mutually related.

The equilibrium solution $\overline{U}_i(x)$ is not linear in x in this case. The nonlinear term $g(x)$ is given rise to by the mutual interactions. When the union $\cup R_i$ of the receptive regions do not include a point x, $g(x) = 0$ at this point, and hence $\overline{U}_i(x)$ reduces to (33). Hence an equilibrium receptive region R of the primitive model is also an equilibrium region of at least one neuron of the revised model, provided the receptive regions of the other neurons do not cover this R. When the receptive regions of some neurons cover R, $g(x) > 0$ on this region, so that the value of $\overline{U}_i(x)$ decreases around R, preventing some neurons from becoming detectors of R. This helps balanced formation of detectors, in the sense that a reasonable number of detectors are formed for every cluster of signals in I.

Let us consider again an information source I including k signals $x_1, \cdots, x_k$, $|x_i|^2 = 1$, $x_i \cdot x_j < b$ ($i \neq j$). When the constant λ satisfies $1 > \lambda > b$, for every signal $x_i \in I$, at least one detector can be formed in the equilibrium. Let N_i be the number of the detectors for signal x_i. When the i'th neuron is a detector of signal x_i, we have

$$p_{Ri'} = p_i f[U_{i'}(\bar{x}_i)], \qquad x_{Ri'} = x_i,$$

and

$$g(x_i) = \sum_j f[U_j(x_i)] = N_i f[\overline{U}_{i'}(x_i)]. \quad (39)$$

Hence the equilibrium solution $\overline{U}_j(x)$ can be written as

$$\overline{U}_{i'}(x) = -wg(x) + cp_i f[\overline{U}_{i'}(x_i)](x_i \cdot x - \lambda). \quad (40)$$

Since the i'th neuron is responsive for x_i but not for x_j ($j \neq i$), the solution $\overline{U}_{i'}(x)$ satisfies

$$\overline{U}_{i'}(x_i) > 0 \qquad \overline{U}_{i'}(x_j) < 0, \qquad j \neq i.$$

These relations are written, respectively, as

$$N_i < \frac{c(1 - \lambda)}{w} p_i,$$

$$N_j > \frac{c}{w}(b - \lambda) p_i f[\overline{U}_{i'}(x_i)] / f[\overline{U}_{j'}(x_j)],$$

which latter is always satisfied because of $b > \lambda$. The former inequality shows that the maximum number of x_i-detectors is limited by $(1/w)c(1 - \lambda)p_i$, which increases in proportion to the relative frequency p_i of signal x_i. This shows an interesting property of the revised model that detectors of a signal are formed in number in proportion to the frequency of that signal.

V. FORMATION OF TOPOGRAPHIC MAPS IN NEURAL FIELDS

A. Topology of Input Signals

The probability measure of an information source I is sometimes concentrated on a certain subset T of the space of signals. The subset T is, for example, a circle imbedded in the signal space, a two-dimensional submanifold, or a complex linear graph, etc., having a certain topological structure. When a neural field Ξ self-organizes by receiving the signals in T, the neurons are arranged in the field to have topographic organization compatible with the topology of the input signals.

Let us label a point of T by τ, and let $x(\tau) \in T$ be a signal labeled by τ. Let $p(\tau)$ be the probability density of signal $x(\tau)$. Then the information source I is specified by the set $T = \{x(\tau)\}$ and the probability measure $p(\tau)$ on T.

We consider, for example, a case in which input signals x are firing patterns of another two-dimensional neural field (say, the retina). Moreover, only bars of various orientations are given to the center of the retina. Let τ be the angle of a bar, $x(\tau)$ denoting the firing pattern of the bar of orientation τ. The signals of the bars $T = \{x(\tau)\}$, $0 \leq \tau < \pi$, forms a circle in the space of signals. Hence it has the one-dimensional topology. The visual cortex is known to be organized in such a manner that detectors of various orientations of bars are arranged continuously in the order of τ so that their topographic arrangements are compatible with the topology of T [31].

Let us define

$$\overline{U}(\xi, \tau) = \overline{U}[\xi, x(\tau)],$$

$$R(\xi) = \{\tau | \tau \in T, \overline{U}(\xi, \tau) > 0\},$$

$$E(\tau) = \{\xi | \xi \in \Xi, \overline{U}(\xi, \tau) > 0\}.$$

Obviously, $R(\xi)$ is a subset of T such that the neurons at $\xi \in \Xi$ are excited by receiving signals $x(\tau) \in R(\xi)$. Hence $R(\xi)$ is the equilibrium receptive region defined on T. Conversely, $E(\tau)$ is a subset of the neural field Ξ such that, when a signal $x(\tau)$ is input, the neurons belonging to $E(\tau)$ are excited. Hence $E(\tau)$ is the set of detectors of signal $x(\tau)$. The set T is hence projected to the family of sets $\{E(\tau)\}$ on the neural field Ξ. When the $E(\tau)$'s are arranged in the field, preserving the topological structure of T in some sense, the topographic organization may be said to be compatible with the topology of T. We show that self-organization gives rise to a topographic organization of a neural field compatible with the topology of input signals. This provides a mathematical justification of Zeeman's idea on neural learning of topology [32].

We call the quantity

$$k(\tau, \tau') = c[x(\tau), x(\tau')]$$
$$= cx(\tau) \cdot x(\tau') - c'x_0^2 \quad (41)$$

the correlation function of signals in T. Equation (28) of the equilibrium solution can be rewritten in terms of $U(\xi, \tau)$ and $k(\tau, \tau')$ as

$$\overline{U}(\xi, \tau) = w \circ f[\overline{U}] + k * f[\overline{U}], \quad (42)$$

where we put $h = 0$ and

$$k * f[\overline{U}] = \int k(\tau, \tau') p(\tau') f[\overline{U}(\xi, \tau')] \, d\tau'. \quad (43)$$

The characteristics of the topographic organization are obtained from the above integral equation.

B. Topographic Organization of Nerve Fields

We treat self-organization of a neural system consisting of two neural fields, in which the fields are unilaterally connected such that the postsynaptic field self-organizes by receiving inputs from the presynaptic field. We will show that a continuous projection is formed between them by self-organization. Let η be two-dimensional coordinates of the presynaptic field. Its firing pattern x is shown by a function $x = x(\eta)$ instead of a vector $x = (x_i)$, where $x(\eta)$ is the firing rate of the neurons at around position η. The synaptic weight vector $s(\xi)$ is also replaced by a function $s(\xi, \eta)$, which denotes the weight of the connections from the neurons at η of the presynaptic field to the neurons at ξ of the postsynaptic field. The inner product $s(\xi) \cdot x$ is naturally replaced by the integral $\int s(\xi, \eta) x(\eta) \, d\eta$.

An excitation pattern x of the presynaptic field is called a localized excitation, when the support of x is confined to a small region, i.e., $x(\eta)$ is zero outside this small region. We assume that only local excitations are output from the presynaptic field. Let $x(\tau)$ be a local excitation aroused at position τ of the presynaptic field. When the waveform of every local excitation is identical, the local excitation aroused at position τ is represented by

$$x(\tau) = x(\eta - \tau),$$

which is a parallel shift of $x(\eta)$ by τ.

The set $T = \{x(\tau)\}$ of all the local excitations labeled by positions τ forms a two-dimensional submanifold homeomorphic to the presynaptic field. This T together with the probability density $p(\tau)$ specifies the information source I. The correlation function $k(\tau, \tau')$ is obtained as

$$k(\tau, \tau') = c \int x(\eta - \tau) x(\eta - \tau') \, d\eta - c'x_0^2, \quad (44)$$

which depends only on the difference $\tau - \tau'$, so that it is denoted by $k(\tau - \tau')$.

The two fields are connected topographically, when $E(\tau)$ are arranged in the same manner as points τ are arranged in T. Let $m(\tau)$ be the center of the region $E(\tau)$. Then the mapping $m: T \to \Xi$ projects T on Ξ, and the topological structure of T is reproduced in Ξ when m is topology-preserving. Let $a(\tau)$ be the area of the region $E(\tau)$. When $a(\tau)$ is small, the representation of T on Ξ is accurate. Since a small region $\Delta\tau$ around a point $\tau \in T$ is mapped on a small region of area $|m'(\tau)|\Delta\tau$ around $m(\tau) \in \Xi$, where $|m'(\tau)|$ is the Jacobian of the mapping m, the quantity

$$r(\tau) = |m'(\tau)|/a(\tau) \quad (45)$$

represents the degree of resolution of the projection m from the presynaptic to the postsynaptic fields. When $a(\tau)$ is kept nearly constant, the mapping m has fine resolution at τ, when $|m'(\tau)|$ is large. In this case, the projection m expands this part of presynaptic field so that its map occupies a large part in Ξ.

It is in general difficult to obtain the exact solutions of the field equations of self-organization. However, the results of computer simulations [15], [33], [34] show that topographic maps can be obtained by self-organization. However, it seems difficult, not to say impossible, to obtain a topographic map starting from completely random initial connections. It might be plausible that two stages of mechanisms are involved in forming a topographic map. A rough and inaccurate map is quickly formed at the first stage by one mechanism (cf [16], [19]). The rough map is slowly modified at the second stage to have fine resolution and to be compatible with the topology of T by self-organization.

Amari [17] analyzed a one-dimensional case in which k assumes a special form. It has been proved by mathematical analysis that the field equation really has a topographic solution and that the resolution $r(\tau)$ of the resultant map is proportional to the relative frequency $p(\tau)$ of signals. This predicts the amplification property that, when a part in T is stimulated frequently, the part eventually occupies a wide area in the map on the postsynaptic field. In other words, the signals in that part get finer resolution.

C. Stability of Topographic Organization

Let us consider a homogeneous case in which the presynaptic field (or signal space T) and the postsynaptic field have the same topology. We assume that their shapes are the same. When both fields are homogeneous and when $p(\tau)$ is constant for all τ, the field equation is expected to admit the identical maps $\xi = m(\tau) = \tau$ in the equilibrium, if the coordinates ξ and τ are suitably chosen. In this case, the equilibrium solution can be written as

$$\overline{U}(\xi, \tau) = b(\xi - \tau),$$

because the fields are homogeneous, where $b(\xi - \tau)$ is positive only for small $|\xi - \tau|$.

Takeuchi and Amari [18] have analyzed the stability of this kind of continuous homogeneous solution and have shown that the solution is unstable under a certain condition. In this case, spatially nonhomogeneous solutions exist, and hence pattern formation takes place in a homogeneous field. When the homogeneous solution is unstable, both the presynaptic and postsynaptic fields are divided into a number of small homogeneous blocks, and a topographic correspondence is observed between the blocks of the two fields. In other words, the discrete microstructures are automatically formed in the fields, and the topographic map preserves the arrangements of these blocks or microstructures, as is seen in the columnar microstructures in the cerebral cortex.

Treating the stability of self-organization within the framework of the field theory of self-organization is possible. Since the dynamical equations (26) and (27) reduce to

$$\tau \frac{\partial V(\xi, \tau, t)}{\partial t} = -V + k * f[U] \qquad (46)$$

$$V(\xi, \tau, t) = U(\xi, \tau, t) - w \circ f[U] \qquad (47)$$

in the present case, the variational equation for $U(\xi, \tau, t)$ $= \bar{U}(\xi, \tau) + \delta U(\xi, \tau, t)$ around the homogeneous solution $\bar{U}(\xi, \tau) = b(\xi - \tau)$ is given by

$$\tau (I - W \circ)^{-1} \frac{\partial \delta U}{\partial t} = -\delta U + (K * + W \circ) \delta U, \qquad (48)$$

where I is the identity operator and

$$W \circ \delta U = \int w(\xi - \xi') f'[b(\xi' - \tau)] \delta U(\xi', \tau) \, d\xi' \qquad (49)$$

$$K * \delta U = \int k(\tau - \tau') f'[b(\xi - \tau')] \delta U(\xi, \tau') \, d\tau'. \qquad (50)$$

Hence the homogeneous solution is stable when the real parts of all the eigenvalues of the linear operator $K * + W \circ$ are smaller than one and is unstable when at least one of the eigenvalues has real part larger than one.

VI. Conclusion

We have proposed a nonlinear field equation of self-organization on the signal space and on the neural field. The equilibrium solutions of the equation are obtained in some special cases. They can explain the mechanism and property of the formation of neural categorizors and of the fine topographic organization of neural fields in a unified manner. The equation has an interesting property of biological pattern formation on a homogeneous neural structure. The property of the field equation should further be studied in detail, not only from the mathematical viewpoint, but also from the neural modeling viewpoint.

References

[1] C. Blakemore and R. C. van Sluysters, "Development of the brain depends on the visual environment," *Nature*, vol. 28, pp. 477–478, 1970.

[2] H. V. B. Hirsch and D. N. Spinelli, "Visual experience modifies distribution of horizontally and vertically oriented receptive fields in cats," *Science*, vol. 168, pp. 869–871, 1970.

[3] R. M. Gaze, *The Formation of Nerve Connections*. London: Academic, 1970.

[4] M. Yoon, "Reorganization of retinotectal projection following surgical operations on the optic tectum in goldfish," *Expl. Neurol.*, vol. 33, pp. 395–411, 1971.

[5] F. Rosenblatt, *Principles of Neurodynamics*. Washington, DC: Spartan, 1961.

[6] D. Marr, "A theory of cerebellar cortex," *J. Physiol.*, vol. 202, pp. 437–470, 1969.

[7] T. Kohonen, *Associative Memory*. Berlin, Germany: Springer, 1977.

[8] S. Amari, "Learning patterns and pattern sequences by self-organizing nets of threshold elements," *IEEE Trans. Comput.*, vol. C-21, pp. 1197–1206, 1972.

[9] K. Nakano, "Associatron—a model of associative memory," *IEEE Trans. Syst., Man., Cybern.*, vol. SMC-2, pp. 381–388, 1972.

[10] J. A. Anderson, "A simple neural network generating interactive memory," *Math. Biosci.*, vol. 14, pp. 197–220, 1972.

[11] Ch. von der Malsburg, "Self-organization of orientation sensitive cells in the striate cortex," *Kybernetik*, vol. 14, pp. 85–100, 1973.

[12] M. M. Nass and L. N. Cooper, "A theory for the development of feature detecting cells in the visual cortex," *Biol. Cybern.*, vol. 19, pp. 1–18, 1975.

[13] S. Grossberg, "Adaptive pattern classification and universal recording: I," *Biol. Cybern.*, vol. 23, pp. 121–134, 1976.

[14] S. Amari and A. Takeuchi, "Mathematical theory on formation of category detecting nerve cells," *Biol. Cybern.*, vol. 29, pp. 127–136, 1978.

[15] D. J. Willshaw and C. von der Malsburg, "A marker induction mechanism for the establishment of ordered neural mapping: Its application to the retinotectal connections," *Phil. Trans. Proc. R. Soc. Lond.*, B, vol. 287, pp. 203–243, 1979.

[16] R. A. Hope and B. J. Hammond, "The arrow model—Retinotectal specificity and map formation in the goldfish visual system," *Proc. R. Soc.*, vol. B-194, pp. 447–466, 1976.

[17] S. Amari, "Topographic organization of nerve fields," *Bull. Math. Biology*, vol. 42, pp. 339–364, 1980.

[18] A. Takeuchi and S. Amari, "Formation of topographic maps and columnar microstructures," *Biol. Cybern.*, vol. 35, pp. 63–72, 1979.

[19] K. J. Overton and M. S. Arbib, "Systems matching and topographic maps: The branch-arrow model (BAM)," in *Competition and Cooperation in Neural Nets*, S. Amari and M. A. Arbib, Eds., *Lecture Notes in Biomathematics*, vol. 45. Berlin, Germany: Springer, 1982.

[20] S. Amari, "Characteristics of randomly connected threshold element networks and network systems," *Proc. IEEE*, vol. 59, pp. 35–47, 1971.

[21] _____, "Characteristics of random nets of analog neuron-like elements," *IEEE Trans. Syst., Man, Cybern.*, vol. SMC-2, pp. 643–657, 1972.

[22] _____, "A method of statistical neurodynamics," *Kybernetik*, vol. 14, pp. 201–125, 1974.

[23] _____, "Dynamics of pattern formation in lateral-inhibition type neural fields," *Biol. Cybern.*, vol. 27, pp. 77–87, 1977.

[24] _____, "Neural theory of association and concept-formation," *Biol. Cybern.*, vol. 26, pp. 175–185, 1977.

[25] _____, "A mathematical theory of self-organizing nerve systems," in *Biomathematics: Current Status and Perspectives*, L. M. Ricciardi and A. Scott, Eds. Amsterdam, The Netherlands: North-Holland, 1982, pp. 159–197.

[26] S. Amari and M. A. Arbib, "Competition and cooperation in neural nets," in *Systems Neurosciences*, J. Metzler, Ed. New York: Academic, 1977, pp. 119–165.

[27] S. Amari, K. Yoshida, and K. Kanatani, "A mathematical foundation for statistical neurodynamics," *SIAM J. Appl. Math.*, vol. 33, pp. 95–126, 1977.

[28] K. Kishimoto and S. Amari, "Existence and stability of local excitations in neural fields," *J. Math. Biol.*, vol. 7, pp. 303–318, 1979.

[29] S. Geman, "Some averaging and stability results for random differential equations," *SIAM J. App. Math.*, vol. 36, pp. 86–105, 1979.

[30] H. Haken, *Synergetics, An Introduction*, 2nd enlarged ed. Berlin, Germany: Springer, 1979.

[31] D. H. Hubel and T. N. Wiesel, "Receptive fields of single neurones in the cat's striate cortex," *J. Physiol.*, vol. 148, pp. 574–591, 1959.

[32] C. Zeeman, "The topology of the brain and visual perception," in *Topology of 3-Manifolds and Related Topics*, M. K. Fort, Ed. Englewood Cliffs, NJ: Prentice-Hall, 1962, pp. 240–256.

[33] T. Kohonen, "Self-organized formation of topologically correct feature maps," *Biol. Cybern.*, vol. 43, pp. 59–69, 1982.

[34] T. Kohonen, "A simple paradigm for the self-organized formation of structured feature maps," in *Competition and Cooperation in Neural Nets*, S. Amari and M. A. Arbib, Eds., *Lecture Notes in Biomathematics*, vol. 45. Berlin, Germany: Springer-Verlag, 1982.

Article 3.3

An Introduction to Neural Computing

Teuvo Kohonen

Helsinki University of Technology

(*Received and accepted* 28 *September* 1987)

Abstract—*This article contains a brief survey of the motivations, fundamentals, and applications of artificial neural networks, as well as some detailed analytical expressions for their theory.*

Keywords—Neural computing, Neural networks, Adaptive systems, Learning machines, Pattern recognition.

1. HISTORICAL OVERVIEW

Theoretical explanations of the brain and thinking processes were first suggested by some ancient Greek philosophers, such as Plato (427–347 B.C.) and Aristotle (384–322 B.C.). Rather physical views of mental processes were held by Descartes (1596–1650) and the 18th century empiricist philosophers.

The class of so-called cybernetic machines to which the "neural computers" belong have a much longer history than generally believed: Heron the Alexandrian built hydraulic automata around 100 B.C. Among the numerous animal models, which have been built to demonstrate need-driven behavior in variable living conditions, one may mention the "Protozoon" of Lux from 1920, the "dogs" of Philips from 1920 to 1930, the "Homeostat" of Ashby from 1948, the "Machina Speculatrix" and "Machina Docilis" of Walter from 1950, the "ladybird" of Szeged from 1950, the "squirrel" of Squee from 1951, the "tortoise" of Eichler from 1956, and many versions of a "mouse in the labyrinth" (Nemes, 1969).

Abstract, conceptual information processing operations were performed by mechanical devices a couple of centuries ago, for example, the slide rule for the demonstration of syllogisms by Ch. Stanhope (1753–1816), and many mechanisms for set-theoretic and logic operations devised in the 19th century.

Analytical neural modeling has usually been pursued in connection with psychological theories and neurophysiological research. The first theorists to conceive the fundamentals of *neural computing* were W. S. McCulloch and W. A. Pitts (1943) from Chicago, who launched this research in the early 1940s. Models for adaptive stimulus-response relations in random networks were set up by Farley and Clark (1954). These theories were further elaborated by Rosenblatt (1958), Widrow and Hoff (1960), Caianiello (1961), and Steinbuch (1961). Many implementations of "neural computers" were realized in the 1960s.

It is difficult to describe in detail what happened in the subsequent 25 years or so in neural modeling. There were many scientists who made rigorous works on the biophysics of neural networks and psychophysical studies of the sensory systems. It has been estimated that the number of papers on vision alone is at least on the order of 10,000. The number of papers on general neural modeling amounts perhaps to a few thousand.

2. ON THE NATURE OF NEURAL COMPUTING

The primary purpose of all neural systems is *centralized control* of various biological functions. Some of them are responsible for energy supply; the corresponding neural systems are connected with metabolism, cardiovascular control, and respiration. There are neural mechanisms for biological rhythms, emergency functions, etc. The above functions are common to most animals, and in the biological neural structures it is even possible to discern various "sediments" from different phases of evolution. In the higher animals, on the other hand, the major capacity of the central nervous system is connected with *behavior*, that is, control of the state of the organism with respect to its environment, which encompasses many different tasks ranging from elementary actions to complicated social behavior. When talking of "neural computing," however, one usually only has in mind the *sensory and motor functions*, as well as some kind of "internal processing,"

Requests for reprints should be sent to Teuvo Kohonen, Helsinki University of Technology, Laboratory of Computer and Information Science, Rakentajanaukio 2C, SF-02150 Espoo, Finland.

loosely called *thinking.* All of these functions are mutually dependent in one way or another, but it may be possible to conceptualize some of them in idealized forms.

In the development of information technology there now seems to exist a new phase whereby the aim is to replicate many of these "neural" functions artificially. Nonetheless, it is not always clear which ones of the above aspects are meant. A central motive seems to be to develop new types of computers. For instance, one may aim at the implementation of *artificial sensory functions,* in order to make the machines "see" or "hear"; this is an extension of the more traditional instrumentation techniques. Analysis of, say, satellite data may in itself comprise a practical task which has to be automated in one way or another. Then there exist needs to develop "intelligent robots" whose *motor control and other actions* must be integrated with the sensory systems; some kind of internal "neural computer" is° needed to coordinate these actions. It further seems that certain expectations are held of new types of "thinking machines," which have no sensors or actuators, but which are capable of answering complex queries and solving abstract problems. The science-fiction robots, of course, are doing all of this. Although the potential of the Artificial Intelligence methods by which these problems were earlier approached has been known for about 25 years, it is still hoped that new avenues to Artificial Intelligence could be opened when massive parallelism of the computing circuits, and new technologies (eventually, optical computing) are developed whereby the computing capacity is increased by orders of magnitude. Before that, however, it will be necessary to find out *what* to compute. There is at least one new dimension of computation visible which has been very difficult to reach by the digital computers, namely, to take into account all the high-order statistical relationships in stochastic data. Apparently the biological brain always has to deal with stochastic signals, whereas even in the best "intelligent" machines developed so far, all data occur in discrete form. In other words, the knowledge they handle is usually of the linguistic type, and the pieces of information inputted to the machines have always been prepared carefully by human beings. One intriguing objective would therefore be to leave such a preprocessing to the machines.

Since the concepts of (artificial) "neural networks" and "neural computers" appear widely in publicity nowadays, it may be necessary to specify their exact meaning. Briefly, in relation to the above motives, we may give the following definition:

"Artificial neural networks" are massively parallel interconnected networks of simple (usually adaptive) elements and their hierarchical organizations which are intended to interact with the objects of the real world in the same way as biological nervous systems do.

It is necessary to note that such "neural computers" do not execute typical machine instructions of digital computers, unless they are made to *emulate* the behavior of physical neural networks. In principle, the basic processing operation performed by every processing element is an *analog operation,* or *transformation* of its input signals.

In biological neural networks, the neural cells (*neurons*), or tightly interacting groups of them correspond to the above processing elements. The interconnections are made by the outgoing branches, the *axons,* which make variable connections, *synapses,* with other neurons (or perhaps with other parts like muscles and glands). Neural networks are thus systems of simple, tightly interconnected processing elements. The elementary function of the latter is to act as selective, "tuned" filters to particular signal patterns. The complex operation of neural networks results from abundant feedback loops which, together with nonlinearities of the processing elements and adaptive changes of their parameters, can define even very complicated dynamic phenomena.

One peculiarity of biological neural networks is their size: in the whole human central nervous system there are on the order of 10^{11} neurons, but the number of their interconnections is still higher, probably up to the order of 10^{15}. It does not seem possible to *program* the function of such a system according to a prior plan, not even by genetic information; consider, too, that the size and structure of the network is changing radically during and after childhood, when it is already in use.

It is true that certain textural features of the network are inherited, and during ontogenesis, the neural projections (certain axon bundles) grow approximately to those places in which they are later needed. In other words, a rough allocation of the resources, and the main communication paths are formed according to a genetic plan, whereas the rest of the "programming," especially the content of *memory,* must be acquired postnatally. Programming of such a network can then only mean two things: (a) The *structures* of interconnections between the cells are altered; and (b) The *strengths,* or "signal transmittances" of these interconnections are changed. It seems that there exist rather clear strategies of how to change the strengths in the right direction, whereas changes in the interconnectivities are more difficult to define, because they usually have radical effects on the network behavior, especially concerning sequential operation and hierarchical functions.

It is indeed very difficult to imagine how such an enormous network could be "programmed" at all. One possibility, especially relating to the sensory subsystems could be that the system structure, or the dynamical process defined by it, in some way directly tends to *image* the sensory experiences or other occurrences. One does not thereby mean any photographic models, static representations of the environment, or metrically faithful copies of signals; "imaging" must be understood in a more general and abstract sense, for example, that certain feature dimensions of the observations are imaged, or that there appear events in the behavior of the network, the temporal, or logic relationships of which can be put to correspond to similar relationships between some events of the exterior world or its history. This is the "internal representation" in the most general sense, as it apparently occurs in mental images, too. It may be understandable that some kind of images of experiences are formed in the primary sensory areas of the brain, and that memory, whatever its realization, stores copies of experiences and their relations. The latter are then logically faithful, although physically reduced images of the exterior events. The imaging property of memory is needed to complement, correct, and extrapolate (predict) the primary sensory information.

Another important function of the nervous systems is to define *actions* which are part of behavior, and control the state of the organism relative to the environment or circumstances. While the internal representations on which thinking is based can be derived from inputs in a rather straightforward way, definition of the output actions must be based on completely different strategies. In fact, there hardly seems to exist any other possibility to program the actions than to apply the principle of reward and punishment in order to alter the mechanisms which are responsible for them; some kind of *backpropagation* of information is then needed. The meaning and "quality" of the actions, on the other hand, must be judged, not from the immediate movements, but from some performance criterion which takes into account the wanted result, sometimes rather indirectly. Often the actions are only correct if they are made in a certain sequence, whereby the motor mechanisms must contain circuits that define such sequences, and which are changed in relation to the learning results. It will be clear that programming the actions is a much more indirect process than programming the internal representations; random trials may not be avoided.

Programming input and output functions, however, only leads to a "behavioristic" operation in which the stimuli and the responses are considered most relevant. Certainly it is possible to implement rather complex automata and need-driven behavior that way. It seems, however, that some expectations are held about neural networks being able to act as *computers* for abstract problems, too, whereby this computation takes place in the internal state of the network. We shall revert to the problem of *searching from knowledge data bases* (memory) in Section 4.2. Instead, let it be mentioned briefly at this point that one category of problems which is sometimes believed to be amenable to "neural computing" consists of various *optimization tasks*. They can be very simple and concrete, such as optimal allocation of the organism's own resources, or more abstract like the well-known "traveling-salesman problem" (Hopfield & Tank, 1986). In setting up such problems, the neural network is directly regarded to constitute a static or dynamic *analogy* of the problem structure; for instance, if the purpose is to minimize a loss function where the total cost is built up of interdependent cost elements, then it may be possible to put these elements to correspond to the connection strengths in a network; the network structure itself then represents the different combinatorial alternatives of the problem "graphically." The activities in different parts of the network shall isomorphically stand for values of corresponding variables of the problem. When the network, by relaxation of its activity due to its feedback loops converges to certain optimal states, then this state, by isomorphism, is also assumed to define the solution to the original problem. The main problem seems to be who shall program such a network.

One could also interpret the interest in "neural computers" in a slightly different way. The new technologies, such as optical processing of information, high-density semiconductor networks, and eventually new materials like the "spin glasses" offer an unforeseen capacity for computation. On the other hand, their elementary operations may not be perfect. The question is then how it would be possible to utilize this vast, although slightly unreliable capacity. Obviously the brain has an answer to this, and so the new computer technology has been motivated by the biological brain research. Obviously, too, such networks must be highly *adaptable*. This consideration then leads to the next problem: *What component and system properties of the network underlie such a high degree of adaptation that the system, in a complex way, becomes able to exhibit the wanted behavior?* Apparently, if such a property exists, it must also be possible to dress it into analytical *training or learning strategies, and algorithms.* This is the crucial problem of the neural network theory.

3. WHAT THE BIOLOGICAL NEURAL NETWORKS ARE NOT

In order to understand the real potential of neural computing, it will be necessary to make a clear distinction between neural and digital computers. Below are some assertions followed by their argumentation.

The biological neural systems do not apply principles of digital or logic circuits.

A digital computing principle must be either asynchronous or synchronous. If it were asynchronous, the duration of the neural impulses would have to be variable in order to hold one of the binary values for indefinite periods of time, which is not the case. If the principle were synchronous, one would need a global clock to which the pulses are synchronized. This is not the case either. The neurons cannot be threshold-logic circuits, because there are thousands of variable inputs at most neurons, and the "threshold" is time-variable, being affected by arousal, attention, etc.; the accuracy and stability of such circuits is not sufficient then, to define any Boolean functions. The collective processes which are centrally important in neural computing are not implementable by logic circuits. Accordingly, the brain must be an *analog* computer.

Neither the neurons, nor the synapses are bistable memory elements.

All physiological facts speak in favor of neurons acting as (nonlinear) analog integrators, and the efficacies of the synapses change gradually. At least they do not flip back-and-forth.

No machine instructions or control codes occur in neural computing.

Due to stability problems discussed above, the format of such codes cannot be maintained for any significant periods of time, in particular during the growth processes.

The brain circuits do not implement recursive computation, and are thus not algorithmic.

Due to the stability problems, the neural circuits are not stable enough for recursive definition of functions like in digital computing. An algorithm, by definition, defines a function recursively.

Even on the highest level, the nature of information processing is different in the brain and in digital computers.

In order to emulate each other, at least on some level of abstraction, the internal states of two computing systems must be equally accessible. Such an equivalence does not exist between the brain and the programming systems. Artificial computers can neither acquire nor interpret all the human experiences on which the assessment of values is based.

4. APPLICATIONS OF NEURAL COMPUTERS

This section describes more closely those application areas for which neural computers have been suggested, and the particular problems thereby encountered.

4.1. Pattern Recognition

The term "pattern recognition" was introduced in the early 1960s, and it originally meant detection of simple forms such as handwritten characters, weather maps, and speech spectra. A more ambitious objective, of course, has all the time been to implement *artificial perception,* that is, to imitate the functions of the biological sensory systems in their most complete forms. The first experiments around 1960 were indeed based on elementary "neural networks," known by names like Perceptron (Rosenblatt, 1958), Adaline (Widrow & Hoff, 1960), and Learning Matrix (Steinbuch, 1961), respectively. The first steps, as always, were easy, but it was soon realized that the performance of the biological sensory systems is very difficult to reach. Even high computing capacity, achievable by parallel computing circuits, did not solve the problems, and especially in image analysis there exist requirements which are very difficult to fulfill: (a) *invariance* of detection with respect to translation, rotation, scale, perspective, partial occlusion, and modest marring of the objects, especially under widely varying illumination conditions; and (b) relation of observations to various *contexts* at different levels of abstraction, in order to distinguish the events more selectively.

Notice that animals are capable of paying *attention* to individual objects in a scene, for each of which the invariance of perception must separately be valid. This ought to show that the easy tricks such as preprocessing of the complete scene by the Fourier, or Mellin transformations with subsequent application of "template matching" cannot constitute the whole solution.

What was obviously also ignored is that even the most developed biological sensory systems do not operate autonomously; sensory perception is always closely associated with global *cognitive processes.* For the replication of the sensory functions, it is then not enough to imitate the sensory system, but one has to replicate the whole brain with all its thinking capabilities, and refine the recognition accuracy by high-level learning.

It would, of course, be unreasonable to wait for the solution of all these problems before proceeding with possible applications. In engineering, the problems are usually simplified. Take for example locomotion: it is difficult to implement coordinated limb movements, but a more straightforward method is to apply wheels and to modify the terrain, building roads. Similarly there exist plenty of applications for which artificial, nonnatural solutions may even be more effective than the biological ones. The development of pattern recognition (especially computer vision) took this course in the mid-1960s. Notice that the spatial acuity of the mammalian vision varies by a factor of twenty when comparing the foveal and peripheral areas of the retina, and the eyeball is in continual saccadic or nystagmic motion. Nonetheless, by some delicate sampling and reconstruction of the visual information, a steady and clear visual perception becomes possible. Nothing comparable has been achieved or even tried in computer vision, where the image field, first of all, is discretized into a regular array of picture elements (pixels) which are then scanned and grouped into homogeneous areas (segmented), their contours are analyzed, and their geometric and topological relationships are described by "picture grammars." It is self-evident that it is possible to achieve certain types of invariance with respect to picture signals, if only topological relations of such parts are taken into account in recognition. Effective as these methods may be, however, they have very little in common with the principles of operation of the biological sensory functions, and thus leave the basic problem of "neural computing" in perception open.

If now artificial "neural network" methods are being developed for the same purpose, it will be necessary to redevelop the "pattern recognition" methods starting from scratch, thereby letting the circuits themselves learn the elementary features and functions, and to become self-organized without heuristic programming.

The most important *application areas* for "neural pattern recognition" could be the same as those for which conventional, heuristic methods have been developed during the past thirty years: (a) remote sensing, (b) medical image analysis, (c) industrial computer vision (especially for robotics), and (d) input devices for computers.

More concrete tasks for which special computer equipment has already been developed are: (a) segmentation and classification of regions from images, (b) recognition of handwritten characters and text, (c) recognition of speech, and (d) processing, especially restoration of noisy pictures.

On a more ambitious level, one may wish to achieve the capabilities of: (a) image analysis (referring to different thematic levels of abstraction, such as monitoring of land use on the basis of satellite pictures), (b) image understanding (interpretation of scenes), and (c) speech understanding (parsing and interpretation of spoken sentences).

To implement these tasks, certain basic problems still call for better understanding, for instance, those concerning the *intrinsic properties* (features) of input information, such as: (a) the most natural pattern primitives (lines, their curvatures and end points, edges, statistics of point groups), (b) visual information which describes the surface curvature and cusps, (c) texture, and (d) phonological invariants in speech.

On the other hand, integration of these functions into a high-level cognitive system is an objective which is orders of magnitude more elaborate than generally believed. There thus seems to exist plenty of potential applications but also unsolved problems. It does not seem reasonable to continue the development of sophisticated heuristic methods: it is estimated that over 30,000 papers and a couple hundred textbooks have already been written on technical pattern recognition and computer vision during the past 30 years (cf. Young

& Calvert, 1974), and if the solutions would have been achievable in that way, they were already visible.

4.2. Knowledge Data Bases for Stochastic Information

A large memory capacity, and readiness to recall relevant items from it are often held as signs of intelligence. A mental storage for a large number of relations is similarly imagined to form the knowledge base for thinking and problem solving. The notion that human memory operates according to associative principles is in fact very old: Aristotle published some theoretical treatises on memory and reminiscence where these laws were qualitatively expounded.

Although it may be clear that most objects of the exterior world are distinct and discrete, and their occurrences can be described by logic relations, the primary information obtained from them in the form of sensory signals is stochastic, fuzzy, and very seldom expressible in terms of distinctive features. If the description of the exterior world can be made *verbally*, these relations, of course, can readily be expressed in a concise and discrete way, but such an operation is not possible without *a thinking and understanding subject*. For those who are used to defining problems by formal logic or other discrete formalisms like Artificial Intelligence techniques, it seems difficult to realize how much is actually required from an artificial system before it is able to automatically form concepts, distinct attributes, and other discrete abstract representations from the fuzzy, nondistinctive, and stochastic sensory signals. However, this phase is indispensable before one can talk of *genuine* "neural networks" or "neural computers."

If, nonetheless, one could *tentatively* assume that the preanalysis and selection of semantic items and their relations had already been made, their storage is then most effectively made in *spatially separate memory locations.* (A node in a semantic network also corresponds to a location.) To find an item quickly on the basis of its content, there exist classical solutions, based on both software (*hash-coding*) and hardware (*content-addressable memory, CAM*) which have been known since 1955 (for a review, see Kohonen, 1987).

Let us consider the logic of searching in somewhat more detail. *Semantic information* usually consists of data items and their links (relations, "associations") to subsets of other items. The *knowledge* acquired in such a data base can be managed through long chains of such links, which are realized when the associations are made to overlap. It is perhaps illustrative to compare a data base and the searching process with a system of mathematical equations and their solution. When we present a query, we in fact set up one or more "equations" which contain unknown variables: For instance, we may specify a number of partial relations in which some of the members are unknown, and the system has to find from memory all the relations that match with the "equations" in their specified parts, whereby a number of solutions for the unknown variables become known.

The above discussed the so-called *relational data bases* which are widely used for business data. Searching of information from them calls for the following elementary operations: (a) parallel or otherwise very fast matching of a number of search arguments (such as known members in the above relations) with all the elementary items stored in memory, and their provisional marking, and (b) analysis of the markings and sequential readout of the results that satisfy all conditions.

In order to find a solution to a searching task which is defined in terms of several simultaneous incomplete queries, as the case in formal problem solving tasks usually is, it is thus not sufficient to implement a content-addressable (or autoassociative) memory, but the partial searching results must somehow be buffered and studied sequentially. This, of course, is completely expedient for a digital computer, which can store the candidates as lists and study them by a program code; in a neural network, however, tasks like holding a number of candidates in temporary storage, and investigation of their "markings" would be very cumbersome.

In artificial neural networks, the searching arguments are usually imposed as initial conditions to the network, and solution for the "answers" results when the activity state of the network relaxes to some kind of "energetic minimum." One has to note the following facts that are characteristic of these devices: (a) Their network elements are *analog devices,* whereby representation of numerical variables, and their matching can only be defined with relatively low accuracy. This, however, may be sufficient for prescreening purposes which is most time-consuming; (b) A vast number of relations in memory which only approximately match with the search argument can be activated. On the other hand, since the "conflicts" then cannot be totally resolved but only minimized, the state of the neural network to which it converges in the process represents some kind of *optimal* answer (usually, however, only in the sense of Euclidean metric); and (c) The "answer," or the asymptotic state which represents the searching result has *no alternatives.* Accordingly, it is not possible, except in some rather weird constructs, to find the complete set of solutions, or even a number of the best candidates for them. It is not sure that the system will converge to the *global* optimum; it is more usual that the answer corresponds to one of the local optima which, however, may be an acceptable solution in practice.

4.3. Optimization Computations

In general, the objective in optimization is to allocate a limited amount of resources to a set of certain partial tasks such that some *objective* or *cost function* is minimized (or maximized). A great number of variables usually enter the problem, and to evaluate and minimize the objective function, a combinatorial problem has to be solved. In large-scale problems such as optimization of economic or business operations, the systems of equations are usually static, although nonlinear, and if conventional computers are used, the solutions must be found in a great many iterative steps.

Another category of complex optimization tasks is met in systems and control problems which deal with physical variables and space- and time-continuous processes. Their interrelations (the restricting conditions) are usually expressed as systems of partial differential equations, whereas the objective function is usually an integral-type functional. Mathematically these problems often call for methods of variational calculus. Although the number of variables then may be orders of magnitude smaller than in the first category of problems, exact mathematical treatment of the functionals again creates the need of rather large computing power.

It may come as a surprise that "massively parallel" computers for both of the above categories of problems existed in the 1950s. The *differential analyzers,* based on either analog or digital computing principles and components, were set up as direct analogies for the systems to be studied whereby plenty of interconnections (feedbacks) were involved. For details of these systems and the many problems already solved by them, see Korn and Korn (1964), Aoki (1967), and Tsypkin (1968).

It may then also be obvious that if the "massively parallel computers" such as the "neural networks" are intended to solve optimization problems, they must, in principle at least, operate as analog devices; the dynamics of their processing elements must be definable with sufficient accuracy and individually for each element, and the interconnectivities must be specifically configurable.

4.4. Robot Control

There are two main categories of robots: *trajectory-programmed* ones, and so-called *intelligent robots.* To program the former, a human operator first controls their movements and actions in the desired way, whereby the sequences of coordinates and commands are stored in memory. During subsequent use, identical trajectories and commands are defined by the memorized information. The "intelligent" robots are supposed to plan their own actions; typical applications for them are assembly tasks whereby the components have to be located and fetched from random places, or the robots may be moving freely in the natural environment, at the same time performing non-programmed tasks.

The "intelligence" exhibited by the robots has so far been implemented by AI programs, which means

131

that the strategies have to be invented and programmed heuristically by a human being. It is often desirable to have a higher degree of learning in such robots, which then calls for "neural computers." For instance, learning of locomotion in an unknown environment is a task which hardly can be formalized by logic programming, and coordination of complex sensory functions with the motor ones cannot be solved in analytical form. Some computer simulations have already been performed which have demonstrated such autonomous learning capabilities (e.g., Barto, Sutton, & Anderson, 1983).

4.5. Decision Making

A more abstract and complex version of behavior which nonetheless belongs to the same category as the robot operation is the non-rule-based decision making, eventually connected with playing games. In the conventional AI implementations, the conditions and actions entering the problem are described as a decision tree, the evaluation of which is a combinatorial problem, and for the solution of which the branches have to be studied up to a certain depth. This, however, is not exactly the way in which a natural object thinks. He may make similar formal analyses in order to avoid bad decisions, but when it comes to the final strategy, then other reasons, based on hunches and intuitive insight into the situation become more important. These capabilities, however, may also result in sufficiently large artificial learning systems which operate according to "neural computing" principles. The performance criterion thereby applied is more complex, although implicit, and it will be learned automatically from examples as some kind of high-order statistical description. It may then be said that such strategies are also stored in the form of rules, whereas these rules are established automatically, and they only exist in implicit form, as the collective states of the adaptive interconnections.

5. THE FORMAL NEURON

The logic circuits are building blocks of digital computers. For historical reasons, because the first computers were conceptualized simultaneously with the first steps made in neural computing, it is still often believed that the operation of neural networks could also be described in terms of *threshold-logic units*. Assume a processing element depicted in Figure 1 which is then imagined to describe a biological neuron.

Each of the continuous-valued input signals ξ_j, $j = 1, 2, \ldots, n$ shall represent the electrical *activity* on the corresponding input line, or alternatively, the momentary frequency of neural impulses delivered by another neuron to this input. In the simplest formal model, the output frequency η is often approximated by a function

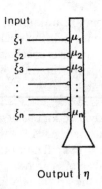

FIGURE 1. The formal neuron.

$$\eta = \text{const. } \mathbf{1}(\sum_{j=1}^{n} \mu_j \xi_j - \theta) \qquad (1)$$

where $\mathbf{1}(\cdot)$ is the *Heaviside function* ($=1$ for positive argument, $=0$ for negative and zero argument), the μ_j are called *synaptic efficacies* or *weights*, and θ is a *threshold*. Thus η is here restricted to binary values (zero and high activity, respectively). If the ξ_j similarly assume only binary values, then, after scaling all signals to $\{0, 1\}$, it can be shown that an arbitrary Boolean function is implementable by a suitable selection of (positive and negative) weights μ_j and the threshold.

In reality, however, the neural cell acts as some kind of nonlinear "leaky integrator" of input. If all the biophysical and chemical phenomena taking place at the cell membrane were taken into account, we would have to describe the triggering cycle of the neuron using a couple of dozen state variables. For the basic processing element in neural computing, however, we need a much simpler, although realistic mathematical operator. This author has recently pointed out (Kohonen, 1988) that a rather influential modeling law for a formal neuron is the following which qualitatively complies with the real biophysical process. Let the output η be a continuous-valued nonnegative activity variable. In accordance with the operation of the biological neuron, η is described by a dynamic system equation which is written

$$d\eta/dt = I - \gamma(\eta). \qquad (2)$$

Here I is the integrated effect of all input currents to the cell membrane, and thus triggering frequency, whereas $\gamma(\eta)$ is a nonlinear loss term which opposes this effect.

It is still unclear how accurately the input term I can be approximated by a linear function of the input signals; there is some evidence for nonlinear interactions between the synapses (cf. Rall & Segev, in press; Shepherd, in press). For artificial neural networks, however, we are free to assume that I can be expressed like in equation (1),

$$I = \sum_{j=1}^{n} \mu_j \xi_j. \qquad (3)$$

If now the input signals are held steady or are changing slowly, η approaches the asymptotic equilibrium whereby $d\eta/dt = 0$, and then η can be solved from equations (2) and (3) yielding

$$\eta = \gamma^{-1}(I), \qquad (4)$$

where γ^{-1} is the inverse function of γ. In reality, saturation effects are always encountered at high activity which means that the loss term $\gamma(\eta)$ must be a progressively increasing function of activity η. On the other hand, remembering that η cannot become negative, it is possible to deduce that $\eta = \eta(I)$ then indeed coarsely resembles the Heaviside function.

6. ADAPTIVE FORMATION OF FEATURE-SENSITIVE UNITS

Although the threshold-logic operations would already define many information processing functions, the discussion becomes still more interesting if the μ_j are time-variable. In most neural models, the assumption is made that *the synaptic efficacies, or the weights μ_j change in proportion to the product of input and output signals;* this is the famous hypothesis of Hebb (1949) dressed in analytical form. However, since all activities must be nonnegative, the changes would always be unidirectional, which is not possible in the long run. Therefore, some kind of *forgetting* or other similar effect must be introduced which makes the changes reversible. This author is of the opinion that the "forgetting" effect must be proportional to activity η, that is, that the forgetting is "active," which is a biologically motivated assumption. Then the *law of adaptation* would read

$$d\mu_j/dt = \alpha\eta\xi_j - \beta(\eta) \cdot \mu_j \qquad (5)$$

where α is a "plasticity parameter," and $\beta(\eta)$ is some positive function of η. In order to implement the interesting phenomena discussed later, it seems necessary that in the Taylor expansion of $\beta(\eta)$ the constant term is zero. This assumption sounds natural, too, because at zero activity, no changes may be made in the cell structure. Then, for a rather general selection of the functional law, the following rule seems to be valid (cf. Sec. 4.3 of Kohonen, 1988). Let us first denote $\mathbf{x} = [\xi_1, \xi_2, \ldots, \xi_n]^T$ and $\mathbf{m} = [\mu_1, \mu_2, \ldots, \mu_n]^T$ where we have used matrix notations, and T means the transpose. Let $\mathbf{C}_{xx}$ be the correlation matrix of $\mathbf{x}$.

Proposition: If the ξ_j are stochastic variables with stationary statistical properties, then the μ_j, according to equation (5), converge to asymptotic values such that $\mathbf{m}$ then represents the largest-eigenvalue eigenvector of $\mathbf{C}_{xx}$.

In other words, the neuron then becomes most sensitive to a particular type of statistical input "feature" which describes certain fundamental properties of input $\mathbf{x}$. This result actually needs a mathematically rigorous

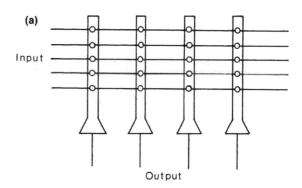

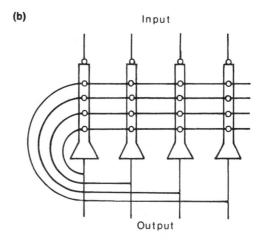

FIGURE 2. Basic network structures.

proof, which for several case examples has been presented in Kohonen (1988).

7. NETWORK STRUCTURES

The basic structure in most neural networks formed of elementary processing elements is the *crossbar switch* (Figure 2a). The next step towards more complex functions results from inclusion of *lateral feedback* (Figure 2b). This kind of connectivity has for a long time been known in neuroanatomy; we applied it to modeling in the early 1970s (cf. a rather late publication on neural associative memory Kohonen, Lehtiö, & Rovamo, 1974, and another series of publications on the "novelty filter" based on it, e.g., Kohonen, 1976).

In an attempt to devise complete *operational modules* for neural systems, it is useful to define the basic network structure containing adaptive crossbars, for input as well as for feedback (Figure 3).

The most natural topology of the network is two-dimensional (Figures 2 and 3 only show a one-dimensional section of it for simplicity), and the distribution of lateral feedbacks within this subsystem, in the first approximation, could be the same around every neuron; however, the distribution of the interconnections could strongly depend on the distance between two points in the network. Within an artificial module, all units ("neurons") could receive the same set of input

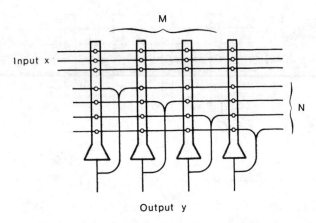

M

Input x

N

Output y

FIGURE 3. Operational module for neural systems.

signals in parallel. None of these assumptions is unnatural, even when relating to biological structures.

If more complex systems have to be defined, an arbitrary new organization can then be implemented by interconnecting such operational modules, each one perhaps with somewhat different internal structure and/or parameters. This would then correspond to the "compartmental" approximation frequently made in the description of other physiological functions.

We may now write the system equations for one module in the following general way:

$$dy/dt = f(\mathbf{x}, \mathbf{y}, \mathbf{M}, \mathbf{N}), \qquad (6a)$$

$$d\mathbf{M}/dt = g(\mathbf{x}, \mathbf{y}, \mathbf{M}), \qquad (6b)$$

$$d\mathbf{N}/dt = h(\mathbf{y}, \mathbf{N}). \qquad (6c)$$

Here x is the vector of all external inputs to the module, y the vector of all output activities, and M and N two (adaptive) connectivity matrices, respectively. In biological systems, equation (6a) might be called the *relaxation equation,* and its time constants are small, of the order of ten milliseconds; y describes electrical activities, and among other things involves the effect of diffusion of light ions. Equations (6b) and (6c) have much larger time constants, say, weeks, because M and N describe changes in proteins and anatomical structures. Both of these equations are *adaptation equations;* equation (6c) further seems to describe the basic function of *associative* or *content-addressable memory.*

8. PATTERN RECOGNITION BY LEARNED RESPONSES

Fundamentally, pattern recognition is a *decision process* for which the only and ultimate criterion is minimization of the average number of misclassifications. Accordingly, the theory of the *average conditional loss in decision making* which stems from the Bayes theory of probability (Kohonen, 1988) constitutes the best theoretical setting. It comes perhaps as a surprise that there already exists a neural network which has a similar performance (cf. Section 9); nonetheless we shall

commence with certain other methods which enjoy a doctrinal status nowadays. For certain tasks such as adaptive control, they may even be optimal.

In a simple approach to pattern recognition, the neural network operates as a "black box" which receives a set of observation signals constituting the input vector x, and produces a response η_i on one of its output ports i, each port being assigned to a different class of observed items. A straightforward idea followed in neural network theory has been to stipulate that the output must be $\eta_i = 1$ if x belongs to class i, and $\eta_j = 0$ for $j \neq i$. This may work in certain very nonlinear discriminator systems which are designed by heuristic methods. A physical network, however, usually has a continuous transfer function such that

$$\eta_i = f_i(\mathbf{x}, \mathbf{m}) \qquad (7)$$

where m is the vector of *internal parameters* of the network. If the system is stimulated by input x, it is then thought that x belongs to class i if for all $j \neq i$, $\eta_i > \eta_j$. The theoretical problem is to devise an adaptive process such that given a set of pairs of input and output ($\mathbf{x}^{(k)}$, $\eta_i^{(k)}$) one finally hopes to have

$$\forall (i, k), \eta_i^{(k)} = f_i(\mathbf{x}^{(k)}, \mathbf{m}). \qquad (8)$$

In all practical applications the statistical density functions of the different classes overlap whereby only optimal approximate solutions to equation (8) can be found. In a traditional statistical approach one defines the least-square functional J,

$$J = \sum_i E\{(\eta_i - f_i(\mathbf{x}, \mathbf{m}))^2\} \qquad (9)$$

where $E\{\cdot\}$ is the mathematical expectation. For the determination of the parameter vector m one must then minimize J requiring that

$$\text{grad}_{\mathbf{m}}(J) = 0, \qquad (10)$$

where the left side means gradient of J in the parameter space. This is the general formulation of the problem; it is then even not necessary that the neural network consists of a single layer of processing elements, or is layered at all. The network may even contain internal, delayed feedback paths, in which case it may be assumed that the $\eta_i = f_i(\mathbf{x}, \mathbf{m})$ represent asymptotic equilibrium values for a steady input x, after the transient phenomena have died out, like in the feedback structures of Figures 2 and 3.

Important special cases are the Perceptron and the Adaline which have one layer of adaptive units between input and output and in which there is a separate parametric vector $\mathbf{m}_i$ associated with each output. In particular, in the Adaline, there are *linear outputs* $\eta_i = \mathbf{m}_i^T \mathbf{x} - \theta_i$ which may be converted into *digital outputs* by discriminator elements. If then the input and output samples ($\mathbf{x}^{(k)}$, $\eta_i^{(k)}$) are applied sequentially, $k = 1, 2, \ldots$, an iterative solution of equation (10), in which all terms in the sum over i can be minimized independently, can be dressed into the form of the familiar *Widrow-Hoff equation* (Widrow & Hoff, 1960). If, for analytical simplicity, θ_i is regarded as the $(n + 1)$th component of the $\mathbf{m}_i$ vector, whereby the $(n + 1)$th component of $\mathbf{x}$ is -1, respectively, we can write (using these so-called augmented vectors) $\eta_i = \mathbf{m}_i^T \mathbf{x}$, whereby

$$\mathbf{m}_i^{(k+1)} = \mathbf{m}_i^{(k)} + \alpha^{(k)}[\eta_i^{(k)} - \mathbf{m}_i^{(k)T}\mathbf{x}^{(k)}]\mathbf{x}^{(k)}, \quad (11)$$

with $\{\alpha^{(k)}\}$ another decreasing sequence of "gain parameters"; a possible choice is $\alpha^{(k)} = \text{const.}/k$. After a great many steps, the $\mathbf{m}_i^{(k)}$ then converge to the optimal values. This process is identical with the mathematical method called *stochastic approximation,* which was earlier developed by Robbins and Monro (1951), as well as Kiefer and Wolfowitz (1952) for regression problems.

For a random network configuration, it is difficult to find a similar theoretically justified optimal recursive expression; however, it is always possible to optimize the internal parameters directly from equation (10). For instance, randomly selected internal parameters (components of the $\mathbf{m}$ vector) can be adjusted iteratively in such a direction that J always decreases. A similar idea is applied in the so-called "Boltzmann machines" (Hinton & Sejnowski, 1984). This process, however, is computationally formidably slow, as can be imagined. Therefore there exists considerable interest in methods by which faster training of, say, multilevel networks becomes possible. The solution, however, usually remains suboptimal. In the principle of *backpropagation of errors,* originally invented by Werbos (1975, 1982), the differences $\eta_i^{(k)} - f_i(\mathbf{x}^{(k)}, \mathbf{m})$ are converted into hypothetical signals which are then propagated through the network in the opposite direction, thereby adjusting the internal parameters in proportion to them, like in the Widrow-Hoff scheme. The correction signals thus pass several layers, not only the last one like in the classical constructs, and all the corrections can be made in parallel by special hardware.

While it is possible to demonstrate many interesting learned stimulus-response relationships in networks of the above kinds, like conversion of pieces of text into phonetic transcriptions (which can then be synthesized into speech by standard methods) (Sejnowski & Rosenberg, 1986), one has to emphasize that in difficult pattern recognition tasks such as recognition of natural speech, none of these principles works particularly well; for instance, the recognition of phonemes from continuous speech by the optimal "learned response" method defined above has only succeeded with an accuracy of 65%, whereas the theoretically optimal Bayes classifier has an accuracy exceeding 80%. (Using auxiliary syntactic methods which take into account the coarticulation effects (Kohonen, 1986a), we have in fact transcribed continuous speech into text with an accuracy of 90 to 95%.) As stated earlier, and explained in the next section, *an accuracy comparable to that of the Bayes classifier is achievable by another simple network which is based on decision-controlled learning.* The main reason for the failure of the learned-response method in difficult recognition tasks seems to be that the "learning" criterion always tries to define a correct *amplitude* to each response, independent of the fact whether the sample is inside or at the border of the class, which is an unnecessarily strong condition, whereas this principle does not pay any attention to the exact location of the *decision surfaces* between the classes. In decision-theoretic classifiers, however, the decision surfaces (which define misclassifications) are directly optimized. Further it seems to be advantageous, as in the following method, to have several outputs for each class.

9. THE LEARNING VECTOR QUANTIZATION (LVQ)

This is a new method (Kohonen, 1986b, 1988) which, nonetheless, has already found its way to practical speech recognition (Kohonen, Torkkola, Shozakai, Kangas, & Ventä, 1987). If it is described in an algorithmic form, then it is not even necessary to define any network topology for it. A more general form of it, called "topology-preserving maps" (Kohonen, 1988, 1982a, 1982b; Kohonen, Mäkisara, & Saramäki, 1984) cannot be discussed here.

Assume a predetermined number of processing elements, each one provided with a parametric vector $\mathbf{m}_i$. Their number may be a multiple (say, ten times) of the number of classes considered. The vectors $\mathbf{m}_i$ are allocated to different classes, as explained below, and labeled correspondingly. The same input vector $\mathbf{x}$ shall then be broadcast to all elements, and it is assumed that each element is somehow able to evaluate the *similarity* of $\mathbf{x}$ and its $\mathbf{m}_i$. The most similar $\mathbf{m}_i$ then defines the classification of $\mathbf{x}$. This method, explained in more detail below, works with almost arbitrary similarity measures, some of which may be biologically more correct than the others. For simplicity, it is now assumed that the norms of the differences $\|\mathbf{x} - \mathbf{m}_i\|$ can be evaluated by the processing elements. (The "neural" justification of this approximation has been presented in Kohonen, 1988.) Further it will be necessary to assume that these results can be compared mutually. This comparison seems to be implementable by certain collective phenomena in a laterally interconnected "neural network" (Kohonen, 1988), although we shall not consider physical implementations here. Let the best-matching processing element have index c and be called the "winner."

The following simple algorithm is a supervised method, like learning in stimulus-response networks usually is. Consider a sequence of *training inputs* $\{\mathbf{x}^{(k)}\}$, *each one with a known classification. Let the* $\mathbf{m}_i$, $i = 1$,

..., K be *initialized* in the following way. First of all we have to know the a priori probability of occurrences of various classes among the input samples, and a corresponding fraction of the available processing elements is then allocated to each class and *labeled* in accordance with that class. For the initial values of the various m_i, values of the first samples of $x^{(k)}$ with known classification can often be taken; the processing elements are labeled correspondingly. (It is sometimes safer to initialize the m_i by values which are averages of their due classes, with a small random noise component superimposed on them.)

New inputs $x^{(k)}$ are thereafter compared with all the m_i in parallel, and the "winner," indexed by c, is found at each step. The m_i are then updated recursively according to the following rule, whereby $m_i^{(k)}$ means the value of m_i at step k:

$$m_c^{(k+1)} = m_c^{(k)} + \alpha^{(k)}(x^{(k)} - m_c^{(k)}),$$

if the classes of $x^{(k)}$ and $m_c^{(k)}$ agree

$$m_c^{(k+1)} = m_c^{(k)} - \alpha^{(k)}(x^{(k)} - m_c^{(k)}),$$

if the classes of $x^{(k)}$ and $m_c^{(k)}$ disagree

$$m_i^{(k+1)} = m_i^{(k)} \quad \text{for } i \neq c. \tag{12}$$

Here $\{\alpha^{(k)}\}$ is a similar decreasing sequence of "gain parameters" as in stochastic approximation, equation (11); however, it has turned out that over a finite training interval, $\alpha^{(k)}$ could decrease to zero linearly with k, starting with a small value, say, .1 or .2. The recommended number of training steps could be, for example, 500 to 5000 times the number of processing elements. This may sound large, but since the algorithm is computationally extremely light, the convergence is reasonably fast. Special parallel (or array processor) hardware is readily developed for this method (Kohonen *et al.*, 1987).

Naturally one may not be able to collect such a large number of samples in a real application. A smaller training set may then be recycled, preferably with random permutation of its members.

After training, the m_i will have acquired such values that classification by the "nearest neighbor" principle, by comparison of x with the m_i, very closely complies with that of the Bayes classifier. Figure 4 represents an illustrative example whereby x was two-dimensional, and its probability density functions overlapped seriously. The decision surface defined by this "*learning vector quantization*" (LVQ) classifier seems to be near-optimal, although piecewise linear, and the classification accuracy even in this rather difficult example is very close the same as with the Bayes classifier, within a fraction of a percent.

10. LEARNED RESPONSES FOR MOTOR CONTROL AND OTHER ACTIONS

It may have become clear from the previous section that pattern recognition represents a typical decision

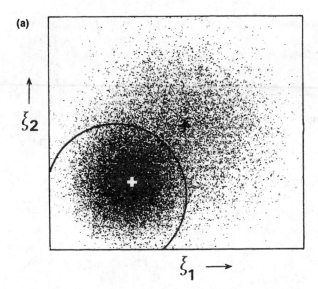

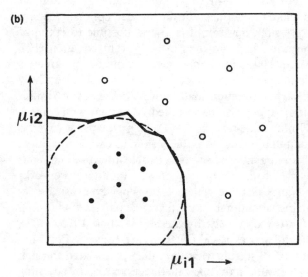

FIGURE 4. (a) The probability density function of $x = [\xi_1, \xi_2]^T$ is represented here by its samples, the small dots. The superposition of two symmetric Gaussian density functions corresponding to two different classes C_1 and C_2, with their centroids shown by the white and the dark cross, respectively, is shown. Solid curve: the theoretically optimal Bayes decision surface. (b) Large black dots: reference vectors of class C_1. Open circles: reference vectors of class C_2. Solid curve: decision surface in the learning vector quantization. Broken curve: Bayes decision surface.

process which has to be optimized according to misclassifications. A problem of completely different nature is to define proper output actions in response to a particular input, such as the motor reactions usually are; then each response is equally important, because no classes for the inputs are defined at all, and the optimization of the internal parameters by any of the methods discussed in the previous section is completely expedient; the J functional represents the only applicable criterion.

One aspect, as pointed out by Pellionisz (1986), is that for the input–output relation in systems which contain interdependent mechanisms, transformation of signals in curvilinear coordinates must be considered carefully.

11. THE LATERALLY INTERCONNECTED NETWORKS AS MEMORIES

Certain widely known neural network structures whose processing elements are even simpler than those discussed in Sections 5 and 6 may only briefly be delineated here. Consider, for instance, the network of Figure 3 whereby we first neglect the input crossbar, and have a unit delay in the feedback. Anderson, Silverstein, Ritz, and Jones (1977) have studied system equations of the type

$$\mathbf{y}^{(t+1)} = S[\mathbf{y}^{(t)} + \mathbf{N}\mathbf{y}^{(t)}], \qquad (13)$$

where $\mathbf{N}$ is the feedback matrix (cf. Figure 3), $t = 0, 1, 2 \ldots$, the notation $S[\cdot]$ means a "linearized sigmoidal function" on all vector components, that is, for a scalar x, $S(x) = x$ for $|x| \leq F$, $S(x) = +F$ for $x \geq F$, and $S(x) = -F$ for $x \leq -F$, and F is thereby the saturation limit. Anderson *et al.* have shown that if $\mathbf{N}$ can somehow be defined as the correlation matrix $\mathbf{C}_{xx}$ of input $\mathbf{x}$, then $\mathbf{y}$ will converge to "eigenvectors," which often closely approximate the eigenvectors of $\mathbf{C}_{xx}$, at least correlating with the large and small components of it. In particular, if $\mathbf{C}_{xx}$ is formed of vectors $\mathbf{x}^{(k)}$ which are fewer in number than the rank of $\mathbf{C}_{xx}$, then, starting with the initial state of $\mathbf{y}^{(0)}$ which is an incomplete version of a binary $\mathbf{x}^{(k)}$, the output state $\mathbf{y}$ will converge to the latter. This is in effect an *autoassociative memory* operation. Hopfield (1982) has later demonstrated a similar result.

Another interesting property of the feedback network has been pointed out by the present author (Kohonen, 1988, 1974). Assume for simplicity that the $\mathbf{M}$ matrix of Figure 3 is an identity matrix, that is, the inputs are like in Figure 2 b, and a sequence of inputs $\{\mathbf{x}^{(k)}\}$ is applied such that each input vector $\mathbf{x}^{(k)}$ is held steady, until it is switched into a new one. Assume that equation (6c) can be written

$$d\mathbf{N}/dt = -\alpha \mathbf{y}\mathbf{y}^T, \quad \text{where}$$
$$\mathbf{y} = \mathbf{x} + \mathbf{N}\mathbf{y}, \qquad (14)$$

and one should notice the minus sign in front of the right side of the upper equation. Then, with continued, iterative application of the sequence $\{\mathbf{x}^{(k)}\}$, the system is relaxed to an asymptotic state such that the overall input–output transfer operator of the network converges to an *orthogonal projection operator*. In other words, if later an arbitrary input vector $\mathbf{x}$ is applied, then the output $\mathbf{y}$ in response to $\mathbf{x}$ only contains that contribution in $\mathbf{x}$ which is "maximally new," that is, which is not expandable in terms of a linear combination of the $\mathbf{x}^{(k)}$. Then $\mathbf{y}$ is orthogonal to the space spanned by the $\mathbf{x}^{(k)}$. This output $\mathbf{y}$ is called the "novelty component," and in general it suppresses nonimportant fea-

tures of the input, and enhances the relevant ones. This "novelty filter" can also act as an autoassociative memory; if the input $\mathbf{x}$ is an incomplete version of a memorized pattern $\mathbf{x}^{(k)}$, the latter, superposed on $\mathbf{x}$, appears at the output as the negative $-\mathbf{x}^{(k)}$.

Notice that the adaptive "novelty filter" has here been described as a genuine continuous-time adaptive physical system, not involving any precomputed memories like in many other "neural" models. On the other hand, a word of caution may be necessary: the elements of the $\mathbf{N}$ matrix may become very large (in principle, infinite). Therefore, a forgetting effect like in equation (5), or a "sigmoidal function" like in equation (13) must be employed. The transfer operator of the system is then no longer an ideal orthogonal projection operator, although with high dimensionality of the variables, it may be a rather good approximation of it.

12. IS THERE ANY PLACE FOR MENTAL IMAGES IN NEURAL COMPUTING?

There is nothing as primary and concrete in the psychic experiences as mental images. They occur as operands in thinking, and it is apparent that they are caused by memory effects, although their stereotype forms have resulted from dropping unessential details, and averaging over the more common characteristics. However, it would not be sufficient to say that the mental images are structured recollections from an (auto)associative memory. The main problem is that there exists no "projection screen" in the brain; there is no place where, say, recollections of retinal projection images are reconstructed. It has sometimes been said that the brain is "blind," it has no secondary "mental eye." (Notice that if it had it, we would also need a "mental mind," "mental mind's eye," and so on to infinity.) This paradox is familiar, but it has usually been dodged in scientific discussion. It would neither be correct to identify the mental images or mental items with *logic concepts*. The latter are actually only defined as the set of their characteristics or attributes, and the logic concepts, to be exact, were originally introduced only to define *languages*. The mental images, on the other hand, are direct copies, although possibly simplified and statistically averaged ones, of real experiences; in philosophy they are called *psychic concepts* for distinction.

Most "connectionist" neural networks, especially those intended for the handling of linguistic or other abstract information structures, define a concept either as a hypothetical singular representation (node or point), or as a set of attributes. A neural computer which deals with such discrete variables is then not dissimilar from any digital computer in principle. In the field of Artificial Intelligence it is hardly ever considered that our thinking in fact proceeds in a totally different way than logic reasoning. Therefore, if we talk of the theory of "neural networks," at least then the essence of the mental items should somehow be made clear. It seems that the only reasonable way to explain them is to resort to a concept which is called *virtual image* in physics. Consider a mirror or lens, or perhaps a hologram which transmits optic wavefronts to the eye. The virtual image is that imaginary source of wavefronts which is sensed real, although it does not exist at all. This concept is now generalized.

For the present discussion, it is even not necessary to know how the neural signals are interpreted mentally; for instance, nobody thinks of such a thing when discussing optical imaging. On the other hand, in the reductionistic view (sometimes also called the psychophysical parallelism theory of Spinoza or W. James) it is assumed that a certain perception corresponds to a certain neurophysiological state. Re-establishing the latter would then evoke the former. Notice that the optical virtual images are in fact explained by the same principle: for the creation of an illusion, it will suffice to reconstruct the optic wavefronts, which are only approximate replicas of the original ones.

Consider now Figure 5 which depicts a network, consisting of two divisions, A and B. It is not necessary that one of the networks belongs to a lower hierarchical level and the other to the higher one; the division line can be abstract, imaginary, and different from case to case. The two divisions can even be intermingled. What is necessary to assume is that in this particular case, the result of perception is mainly formed by components of subsystem B, based on its input signal vector $y = f(x, M)$ where x is the signal vector which stimulates system A, and M is a parametric state of system A (equivalent to its transmittance). System B cannot know what there is inside A; so it assumes that A is always the same. Let the *unperturbed* state of system A ("empty memory") be denoted by M_0. Then, if the signals transmitted by system A leave "memory traces" in it, the *perturbed* system state is denoted by $M = M_0 + \Delta M$. In Figure 5b the same signal vector y is also assumed to be explainable by an "*empty memory*" and *effective input excitation* which contains an extra component, the *virtual image* Δx. In other words, y shall be expressible in two alternative ways:

$$y = f(x, M_0 + \Delta M) = f(x + \Delta x, M_0). \quad (15)$$

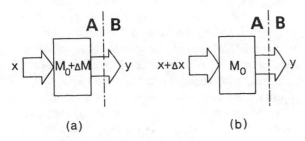

FIGURE 5. Illustration of the principle of virtual images.

If the law by which ΔM is formed has certain properties (like in holography, or if the adaptive changes depend on signals as discussed in Section 6), and the transfer function f has a simple analytical form, then Δx can be solved (accurately or approximately, i.e., in the sense of least squares). Computer simulations of this principle in neural networks with partly random structure have been reported in Kohonen (1971) and Kohonen (1973).

Explanations for many intriguing phenomena discussed in experimental psychology become now readily available: for example, hallucinations, so-called phantom effects in amputated limbs, and geometric illusions. Without the principle of virtual images, on the other hand, the neural networks or computers are only "behavioristic" machines, and at least it can be said that they then do not reflect the most important phenomenological features of thinking.

13. VISTAS TO NEUROCOMPUTER SYSTEMS

More complicated architectures for neurocomputers can be implemented by interconnecting several modules of the above types. For instance, Grossberg (1982) and Carpenter and Grossberg (in press) have suggested circuits for the interaction of different subsystems in the brain.

In engineering systems, the neurocomputers ought to be understood as special-purpose models or coprocessors which are operating under the control of a more conventional host computer. The latter defines a program code on the application level and schedules the application operations, while the "neurocomputer" implements various bulk tasks, such as preprocessing natural input information like images or speech, or acts as a "neural expert system," answering queries in a statistically optimal fashion.

A more complete view to neurocomputer architectures can be obtained from the books edited by McClelland and Rumelhard (1986), from the SPIE (The Society of Photo-Optical Instrumentation Engineers) Advanced Institutes proceedings (1987), as well as special issues published by Applied Optics (1986, 1987).

REFERENCES

Anderson, J. A., Silverstein, J. W., Ritz, S. A., & Jones, R. S. (1977). Distinctive features, categorical perception, and probability learning: Some applications of a neural model. *Psychological Review, 84*, 413–451.

Aoki, M. (1967). *Optimization of stochastic systems—Topics in discrete-time systems*. New York: Academic Press.

Applied Optics (1986, September 15). 25(18).

Applied Optics (1987, May 15). 26(10).

Barto, A. G., Sutton, R. S., & Anderson, C. W. (1983). Neuronlike adaptive elements that can solve difficult learning control problems. *Institute of Electrical and Electronics Engineers Transactions, SMC-13*, 834–846.

Caianiello, E. R. (1961). Outline of a theory of thought-processes and thinking machines. *Journal of Theoretical Biology, 2*, 204–235.

Carpenter, G. A., & Grossberg, S. (in press). A massively parallel architecture for a self-organizing neural pattern recognition machine. In *Computer vision, graphics, and image processing.*

Farley, B. G., & Clark, W. A. (1954). Simulation of self-organizing systems by digital computer. *Institute of Radio Engineers— Transactions of Professional Group of Information Theory,* **PGIT-4**, 76–84.

Grossberg, S. (1982). *Studies of mind and brain: Neural principles of learning, perception, development, cognition, and motor control.* Amsterdam: Reidel Press.

Hebb, D. (1949). *Organization of behavior.* New York: Wiley.

Hinton, G. E., Sejnowski, T. J., & Ackley, D. H. (1984). *Boltzmann machines: Constraint satisfaction networks that learn.* (Tech. Rep. No. CMU-CS-84-119). Pittsburgh, PA: Carnegie Mellon University.

Hopfield, J. J. (1982). Neural networks and physical systems with emergent collective computational abilities. Proceedings of the National Academy of Sciences of the United States of America, **79**, 2554–2558.

Hopfield, J. J., & Tank, D. W. (1986). Computing with neural circuits: A model. *Science, 233*, 625–633.

Kiefer, J., & Wolfowitz, J. (1952). Stochastic estimation of the maximum of a regression function. *Annals of Mathematical Statistics, 23*, 462–466.

Kohonen, T. (1971). Introduction of the principle of virtual images in associative memories. *Acta Polytechnica Scandinavica,* **El. 29.**

Kohonen, T. (1973). A new model for randomly organized associative memory. *International Journal of Neuroscience, 5*, 27–29.

Kohonen, T. (1982a) A simple paradigm for the self-organized formation of structured feature maps. In S. Amari & M. A. Arbib (Eds.), *Competition and cooperation in neural nets,* Lecture Notes in Biomathematics (Vol. 45, pp. 248–266). Berlin: Springer-Verlag.

Kohonen, T. (1982b). Clustering, taxonomy, and topological maps of patterns. In *Proceedings of the Sixth International Conference on Pattern Recognition* (pp. 114–128). Silver Spring, MD: IEEE Computer Society.

Kohonen, T. (1986a). Dynamically expanding context, with application to the correction of symbol strings in the recognition of continuous speech. In *Proceedings of the Eighth International Conference on Pattern Recognition* (pp. 1148–1151). Washington, DC: IEEE Computer Society.

Kohonen, T. (1986b). *Learning vector quantization for pattern recognition.* (Tech. Rep. No. TKK-F-A601). Finland: Helsinki University of Technology.

Kohonen, T. (1987a). *Content-addressable memories* (2nd ed.). Berlin: Springer-Verlag.

Kohonen, T. (1988). *Self-organization and associative memory* (2nd ed.). Berlin: Springer-Verlag.

Kohonen, T., Lehtiö, P., & Rovamo, J. (1974). *Annales Academiae Scientarum, Fennicae, Series A. V Medica, 167.*

Kohonen, T., Mäkisara, K., & Saramäki, T. (1984). Phonotopic maps—Insightful representation of phonological features for speech recognition. In *Proceedings of the Seventh International Conference on Pattern Recognition* (pp. 182–185). Silver Spring, MD: IEEE Computer Society.

Kohonen, T., & Oja, E. (1976). Fast adaptive formation of orthogonalizing filters and associative memory in recurrent networks of neuron-like elements. *Biological Cybernetics,* **21**, 85–95.

Kohonen, T., Torkkola, K., Shozakai, M., Kangas, J., & Ventä, O. (1987). Microprocessor implementation of a large vocabulary speech recognizer and phonetic typewriter for Finnish and Japanese. In J. A. Laver & M. A. Jack (Eds.), *Proceedings of European Conference on Speech Technology* (pp. 377–380). Edinburgh: CEP Consultants Ltd.

Korn, G. A., & Korn, T. M. (1964). *Electronic analog and hybrid computers.* New York: McGraw-Hill.

McClelland, J. L., Rumelhard, D. E., & PDP Research Group. (1986). *Parallel distributed processing.* Cambridge, MA: MIT Press.

McCulloch, W. S., & Pitts, W. A. (1943). A logical calculus of the ideas immanent in nervous activity. *Bulletin of Mathematics and Biophysics, 5*, 115–133.

Nemes, T. N. (1969). *Kibernetikai Gepek (Cybernetic Machines).* Budapest: Akademiai Kiado.

Optical and Hybrid Computing. (1987). H. H. Szu, R. F. Potter (Eds.), *SPIE* (Vol. 634). Washington: SPIE.

Pellionisz, A. J. (1986). Tensor network theory of the central nervous system and sensorimotor modeling. In G. Palm & A. Aertsen (Eds.), *Brain theory* (pp. 121–145). Berlin: Springer-Verlag.

Rall, W., & Segev, I. (in press). Excitable dendritic spine clusters: Nonlinear synaptic processing. In R. Cotterill (Ed.), *Proceedings of Conference on Computer Simulation in Brain Science.* Cambridge University Press.

Robbins, H., & Monro, S. (1951). A stochastic approximation method. *Annals of Mathematical Statistics, 22*, 400–407.

Rosenblatt, F. (1958). The perceptron: A probabilisitic model for information storage and organization in the brain. *Psychoanalytic Review, 65*, 386–408.

Sejnowski, T. J., & Rosenberg, C. R. (1986). *NETtalk: A parallel network that learns to read aloud.* (Tech. Rep. No. JHU/EECS-86/01). Baltimore, MD: Johns Hopkins University.

Shepherd, G. M. (in press). The significance of axon collaterals and distal dendrites in brain circuits. In R. Cotterill (Ed.), *Proceedings of Conference on Computer Simulation in Brain Science.* Cambridge University Press.

Steinbuch, K. (1961). Die Lernmatrix. *Kybernetik, 1*, 36–45.

Tsypkin, Y. A. (1968). *Adaptation and learning in cybernetic systems.* Moscow: Nauka.

Werbos, P. (1975). *Beyond regression: New tools for prediction and analysis in behavioral sciences.* (Doctoral thesis and published report). Cambridge, MA: Harvard University.

Werbos, P. (1982). Applications of advances in nonlinear sensitivity analysis. In R. Drenick & F. Kozin (Eds.), *Systems modeling and optimization: Proceedings of the International Federation for Information Processing.* (pp. 762–770). New York: Springer-Verlag.

Widrow, B., & Hoff, M. E. (1960). Adaptive Switching Circuits. 1960 WESCON Convention, Record Part IV, pp. 96–104.

Young, T. Y., & Calvert, T. W. (1974). *Classification, estimation, and pattern recognition.* New York: Elsevier.

Computing with Neural Circuits: A Model

John J. Hopfield and David W. Tank

A new conceptual framework and a minimization principle together provide an understanding of computation in model neural circuits. The circuits consist of nonlinear graded-response model neurons organized into networks with effectively symmetric synaptic connections. The neurons represent an approximation to biological neurons in which a simplified set of important computational properties is retained. Complex circuits solving problems similar to those essential in biology can be analyzed and understood without the need to follow the circuit dynamics in detail. Implementation of the model with electronic devices will provide a class of electronic circuits of novel form and function.

A COMPLETE UNDERSTANDING OF HOW A NERVOUS SYSTEM computes requires comprehension at several different levels. Marr (1) noted that the computational problem the system is attempting to solve (the problem of stereopsis in vision, for example) must be characterized. An understanding at this level requires determining the input data, the solution, and the transformations necessary to compute the desired solution from the input. The goal of computational neurobiology is to understand what these transformations are and how they take place. Intermediate computational results are represented in a pattern of neural activity. These representations are a second, and system-specific, level of understanding. It is important to understand how algorithms—transformations between representations—can be carried out by neural hardware. This understanding requires that one comprehend how the properties of individual neurons, their synaptic connections, and the dynamics of a neural circuit result in the implementation of a particular algorithm. Recent theoretical and experimental work attempting to model computation in neural circuits has provided insight into how algorithms can be implemented. Here we define and review one class of network models—nonlinear graded-response neurons organized into networks with effectively symmetric synaptic connections—and illustrate how they can implement algorithms for an interesting class of problems (2).

Early attempts to understand biological computation were stimulated by McCulloch and Pitts, who described (3) a "logical calculus of the ideas immanent in nervous activity." In these early theoretical studies, biological neurons were modeled as logical decision elements described by a two-valued state variable (on-off), which were organized into logical decision networks that could compute simple Boolean functions. The timing of the logical operations was controlled by a system clock. In studies of the "perceptron" by Rosenblatt (4), simple pattern recognition problems were solved by logical decision networks that used a system of feed-forward synaptic connectivity and a simple learning algorithm. Several reviews of McCulloch and Pitts and perceptron work are available (5). More recent studies have used model neurons having less contrived

properties, with continuous dynamics and without the computerlike clocked dynamics. For example, Hartline et al. (6) showed that simple linear models with continuous variables could explain how lateral inhibition between adjacent photoreceptor cells enhanced the detection of edges in the compound eye of *Limulus*. Continuous variables and dynamics have been widely used in simulating membrane currents and synaptic integration in single neurons (7) and in simulating biological circuits, including central pattern generators (8) and cortical structures (9). Both two-state (10, 11) and continuous-valued nonlinear models (12) have been extensively studied in networks organized to implement algorithms for associative memories and associative tasks (13).

The recent work being reviewed here has been directed toward an understanding of how particular computations can be performed by selecting appropriate patterns of synaptic connectivity in a simple dynamical model system. Circuits can be designed to provide solutions to a rich repertoire of problems. Early work (10) was designed to examine the computational power of a model system of two-state neurons operating with organized symmetric connections. The inclusion of feedback connectivity in these networks distinguished them from perceptron-like networks, which emphasized feed-forward connectivity. Graded-response neurons described by continuous dynamics were combined with the synaptic organization described by earlier work to generate a more biologically accurate model (14) whose computational properties include those of the earlier model. General principles for designing circuits to solve specific optimization problems were subsequently developed (15–17). These networks demonstrated the power and speed of circuits that were based on the graded-response model. Unexpectedly, new computational properties resulted (15) from the use of nonlinear graded-response neurons instead of the two-state neurons of the earlier models. The problems that could be posed and solved on these neural circuits included signal decision and decoding problems, pattern recognition problems, and other optimization problems having combinatorial complexity (15–20).

One lesson learned from the study of these model circuits is that a detailed description of synaptic connectivity or a random sampling of neural activity is generally insufficient to determine how the circuit computes and what it is computing. As an introduction to the circuits we review, this analysis problem is illustrated on a simple and well-understood model neural circuit. We next define and discuss the simple dynamical model system and the underlying assumptions and simplifications that relate this model to biological neural circuits. A conceptual framework and minimization principle applied to the model provide an understanding of how these circuits compute, specifically, how they compute solutions to optimization problems. The design and architecture of circuits for two specific problems are presented, including the formerly enigmatic circuit used earlier to illustrate the analysis problem.

J. J. Hopfield is with the Divisions of Chemistry and Biology, California Institute of Technology, Pasadena, CA 91125. D. W. Tank and J. J. Hopfield are with the Molecular Biophysics Research Department, AT&T Bell Laboratories, Murray Hill, NJ 07974.

Reprinted with permission from *Science*, J. J. Hopfield and D. W. Tank, "Computing with Neural Circuits: A Model," vol. 233, pp. 625–633, 1986.

Understanding Computation in a Simple Neural Circuit

Let us analyze the hypothetical neural circuit shown in Fig. 1 with simulation experiments based on the tools and methods of neurophysiology and anatomy. The analysis will show that the usual available neurobiological measures and descriptions are insufficient to explain how even small circuits of modest complexity compute. The seven-neuron circuit in Fig. 1 is designed to compute in a specific way that will later be described. From a neurobiological viewpoint, the basic anatomy of the circuit contains four principal neurons (21), identified in the drawing as P_0, P_1, P_2, and P_3. Each neuron has an axon leaving the circuit near the bottom of the figure. The computational results of the circuit must be evident in the activity of these neurons. The one input pathway, from a neuron external to the circuit, is provided by axon Q. Neurons IN_1, IN_2, and IN_3 are intrinsic interneurons in the circuit.

In attempting to understand the circuit's operation, we simultaneously monitor the activity (computer simulated) in each of the seven neurons while providing for a controllable level of impulse activity in the input axon Q. Results from this experiment on the hypothetical circuit for several fixed levels of input activity are shown in Fig. 2A. The top trace represents our controlled activity in Q. In each time epoch this activity is progressively larger, as illustrated by the increasing number of action potentials per unit time. Although the activity of IN_3 is steadily rising as the activity in Q increases, the activities of the other neurons in the circuit are not simply related to this input. From these results we know what the output patterns of activity on the principal neurons are for specific

levels of impulse activity on the input axon Q, but we cannot explain what computation the circuit is computing. Furthermore, we do not know how the structure and organization of the circuit has provided these particular patterns of neural activities for the different input intensities.

Study of the synaptic organization of the connections between the neurons by electrophysiological or ultrastructural techniques could provide the numerical description of synaptic strengths shown in Table 1. The results of these experiments would show that each individual principal neuron P_i inhibits the other three principal neurons (P_j). There is either monosynaptic inhibition from P_i to P_j or polysynaptic inhibition by an excitatory synapse from P_i to an interneuron (IN_k), which then forms an inhibitory synapse with P_j (for example, the P_1-to-P_2 pathway in Fig. 1). This synaptic organization provides an "effective" inhibitory synapse between any two principal neurons; an action potential elicited in one principal neuron always contributes to inhibition of each of the others. Similar experiments measuring the strengths of the synaptic connections between the input axon Q and the P_i would show effective excitatory connections (Table 1). While the organization between principal neurons could be described classically as "lateral inhibition," the output patterns of activity in the P_i, shown in Fig. 2A for different input intensities, cannot be explained by this qualitative description.

Given the synaptic strengths in Table 1 and an appropriate mathematical description of the neurons, we can simulate the model neural circuit and produce the output activity patterns for the different inputs. Such detailed simulations can also be done for real neural circuits if the required parameters are known. In general, an ability to correctly predict a complex result that relies solely on simulation of the system provides a test of the simulation model, but does not provide an understanding of the result. Thus, despite our classical analysis of the simple neural circuit in Fig. 1, we still have no understanding of *why* these particular synaptic strengths (Table 1) provide these particular relations between input and output activity. Computation in the circuit shown in Fig. 1 can, however, be defined and understood within the conceptual framework provided by an analysis of dynamics in the simple neural circuit model we now discuss.

The Model Circuits and Their Relation to Biology

Neurons are continuous, dynamical systems, and neuron models must be able to describe smooth, continuous quantities such as graded transmitter release and time-averaged pulse intensity. In McCulloch-Pitts models, neurons were logical decision elements described by a two-valued state variable (on-off) and received synaptic input from a small number of other neurons. In general, McCulloch-Pitts models do not capture two important aspects of biological neurons and circuits: analog processing and high interconnectivity. While avoiding these limitations, we still want to model individual neurons simply. In the absence of appropriate simplifications, the complexities of the individual neurons will loom so large that it will be impossible to see the effects of organized synaptic interactions. A simplified model must describe a neuron's effective output, input, internal state, and the relation between its input and output.

In the face of the staggering diversity of neuronal properties, the goal of compressing their complicated characteristics is especially difficult. For the present, let us consider a prototypical biological neuron having inputs onto its dendritic arborization from other neurons and outputs to other neurons from synapses on its axon.

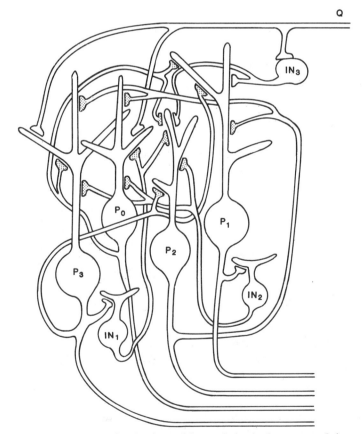

Fig. 1. "Anatomy" of a simple model neural circuit. Input axon Q has excitatory synapses (direct or effective) on each of the principal neurons P_0 through P_3. Each of these principal neurons has inhibitory synapses (direct or indirect) with all other principal neurons. Inhibitory synapses are shaded. IN_1 to IN_3, intrinsic interneurons.

Action potentials initiate near the soma and propagate along the axon, activating synapses. Although we *could* model the detailed synaptic, integrative, and spike-initiating biophysics of this neuron, following, for example, the ideas of Rall (7), the first simplification we make in our description of the neuron is to neglect electrical effects attributable to the shape of dendrites and axon. (The axon and dendrite space-constants are assumed to be very large.) Our model neuron has the capacitances and conductances of the arborization added directly to those of the soma. The input currents from all synaptic channels are simply additive; more complex interactions between input currents are ignored. Membrane potential changes are assumed to arrive at the presynaptic side of synapses at the same time as they are initated at the soma. The second simplification is to deal only with "fast" synaptic events. When a potential fluctuation occurs in the presynaptic terminal of a chemical synapse, a change in the concentration of neurotransmitter is followed (with a slight delay) by a current in the postsynaptic cell. In our model neurons we presume this delay is much shorter than the membrane time constant of the neuron.

These two suppositions on time scale mean that when a change in potential is initiated at the soma of cell j, it introduces an effectively instantaneous conductance change in a postsynaptic cell i. The amount of the conductance change depends on the nature and strength of the synapse from cell j to cell i.

Biological neurons that produce action potentials do so (in steady state) at a rate determined by the net synaptic input current. This current acts indirectly by charging the soma and changing the cell potential. A characteristic charging or discharging time constant is determined by the cell capacitance C and membrane resistance R. The input current is "integrated" by the cell RC time constant to determine a value of an effective "input-potential," u. Conceptually, this potential u is the cell membrane potential after deletion of the action potentials. Action potentials (and postsynaptic responses in follower cells) are then generated at a rate dependent on the value of u. Dependencies of firing rates on input currents (and hence u) vary greatly, but have a generally sigmoid and monotonic form (Fig. 3A), rising continuously between zero and some maximum value (22). The firing rate of cell i can be described by the function $f_i(u_i)$. For processing in which individual action potentials are not synchronized or highly significant, a model that suppresses the details of action potentials should be adequate. In such a limiting case, two variables describe the state of neuron i: the effective input potential u_i and the output firing rate $f_i(u_i)$. The strength of the synaptic current into a postsynaptic neuron j due to a presynaptic neuron i is proportional to the product of the presynaptic cell's output $[f_i(u_i)]$

Table 1. Effective synaptic strengths for the circuit in Fig. 1.

Post-synaptic neuron	Presynaptic neuron				
	P_0	P_1	P_2	P_3	Q
P_0		−2	−4	−8	+1
P_1	−2		−8	−16	+2
P_2	−4	−8		−32	+4
P_3	−8	−16	−32		+8

and the strength of the synapse from i to j. In our model, the strength of this synapse is represented by the parameter T_{ij}, so that the postsynaptic current is given by $T_{ij} f_j(u_j)$. The net result of our description is that action potentials have their effects represented by continuous variables, just as the usual equations describing the behavior of electrical circuits replace discrete electrons by continuous charge and current variables.

Many neurons, both central and peripheral, show a graded response and do not normally produce action potentials (23). The presynaptic terminals of these graded-response neurons secrete neurotransmitters, and hence induce postsynaptic currents, at a rate dependent on the presynaptic cell potential. The effective output of such cells is also a monotonic sigmoid function of the net synaptic input. Thus the model treats both neurons with graded responses and those exhibiting action potentials with the same mathematics.

We can now describe the dynamics of an interacting system of N neurons. The following set of coupled nonlinear differential equations results from our simplifications and describes how the state variables of the neurons (u_i; $i = 1, \ldots, N$) will change with time under the influence of synaptic currents from other neurons in the circuit.

$$C_i \frac{du_i}{dt} = \sum_{j=1}^{N} T_{i,j} f_j(u_j) - \frac{u_i}{R_i} + I_i \qquad (i = 1, \ldots, N) \qquad (1)$$

These equations might be thought of as a description of "classical" neurodynamics (12, 14). They express the net input current charging the input capacitance C_i of neuron i to potential u_i as the sum of three sources: (i) postsynaptic currents induced in i by presynaptic activity in neuron j, (ii) leakage current due to the finite input resistance R_i of neuron i, and (iii) input currents I_i from other neurons external to the circuit. The time evolution of any hypothetical circuit, defined by specific values of T_{ij}, I_i, f_i, C_i, and R_i, can be simulated by numerical integration of these equations.

Some intuitive feeling for how a model neural circuit might behave can be provided by considering the electrical circuit shown in Fig. 3B, which obeys the same differential equation (Eq. 1). The "neurons" consist of amplifiers in conjunction with feedback circuits composed of wires, resistors, and capacitors organized to represent axons, dendritic arborization, and synapses connecting the neurons. The firing rate function of our model neurons $[f_i(u_i)]$ is replaced in the circuit by the output voltage V_i of amplifier i. This output is $V_i = V_i^{max} g_i(u_i)$, where the dimensionless function $g_i(u_i)$ has the same sigmoid monotonic shape (Fig. 3A) as $f_i(u_i)$ and a maximum value of 1. V_i^{max} is the electrical circuit equivalent of the maximum firing rate of cell i. The input impedance of our model neuron is represented in the circuit by an equivalent resistor ρ_j and an input capacitor C_j connected in parallel from the amplifier input to ground. These components define the time constants of the neurons and provide for the integrative analog summation of the synaptic input currents from other neurons in the network. To provide for both excitatory and inhibitory synaptic connections between neurons while using conventional electrical components, each amplifier is given two outputs—a normal (+) output and an inverted (−) output of the same magnitude but opposite in sign. A synapse

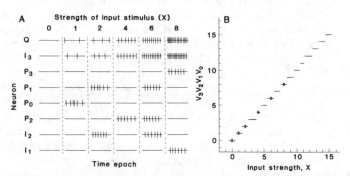

Fig. 2. (A) Results of an experiment in which the activity in each neuron in the circuit of Fig. 1 was simultaneously recorded (by simulation) as a function of the strength of the input stimulus on axon Q. The strength of the input stimulus is indicated by the numbers above each time epoch. (B) A selective rearrangement of the data in (A) illustrating the analog-binary computation being performed by the circuit. The digital word $V_3 V_2 V_1 V_0$ is calculated from the records.

between two neurons is defined by a conductance T_{ij}, which connects one of the two outputs of amplifier j to the input of amplifier i. This connection is made with a resistor of value $R_{ij} = 1/|T_{ij}|$. If the synapse is excitatory ($T_{ij} > 0$), this resistor is connected to the normal (+) output of amplifier j. For an inhibitory synapse ($T_{ij} < 0$), it is connected to the inverted (−) output of amplifier j. Thus, the normal and inverted outputs for each neuron allow for the construction of both excitatory and inhibitory connections through the use of normal (positive valued) resistors. The circuits include a wire providing an externally supplied input current I_i for each neuron (Fig. 3B). These inputs can be used to set the general level of excitability of the network through constant biases, which effectively shift the input-output relation along the u_i axis, or to provide direct parallel inputs to drive specific neurons. As in Eq. 1, the net input current to any neuron is the sum of the synaptic currents (flowing through the set of resistors connecting its input to the outputs of the other neurons), externally provided currents, and leakage current.

In the model represented by Eq. 1 and Fig. 3, the properties of individual model neurons have been oversimplified, in comparison with biological neurons, to obtain a simple system and set of equations. However, essential features that have been retained include the idea of a neuron as transducer of input to output, with a smooth sigmoid response up to a maximum level of output; the integrative behavior of the cell membrane; large numbers of excitatory and inhibitory connections; the reentrant or feedback nature of the connections; and the ability to work with both graded-response neurons and neurons that produce action potentials. None of these features was the *result* of approximations. Their inclusion in a simplified model emphasizes features of the biological system we believe important for computation. The model retains the two important aspects for computation: dynamics and nonlinearity.

The model of Eq. 1 and Fig. 3 has immense computing power, achieved through organized synaptic interactions between the neurons. The model neurons lack many complex features that give biological neurons, taken individually, greater computational capabilities. It seems an appropriate model for the study of how the cooperative effects of neuronal interactions can achieve computational power.

A New Concept for Understanding the Dynamics of Neural Circuitry

A specific circuit of the general form described by Eq. 1 and Fig. 3 is defined by the values of the synapses (T_{ij}) and input currents (I_i). Given this architecture, the state of the system of neurons is defined by the values of the outputs V_i (or, equivalently, the inputs u_i) of each neuron. The circuit computes by changing this state with time. In a geometric space with a Cartesian axis for each neural output V_i, the instantaneous state of the system is represented by a point. A given circuit has dynamics that can be pictured as a time history or motion in this state space. For a circuit having arbitrarily chosen values for the synaptic connections, these motions can be very complex, and no simplifying description has been found. A broad class of simplified circuits, however, has a unifying principle of behavior while remaining capable of powerful computation. These circuits are literally or effectively symmetric.

A symmetric circuit is defined as having synaptic strength and sign (excitation or inhibition) of the connection from neuron i to j the same as from j to i. The two neurons need not, however, have the same input-output relation, threshold, or capacitance. Our model circuit (Fig. 3B) is symmetric if, for all i and j, T_{ij} is equal to T_{ji}. This symmetry refers only to connections between neurons in the circuit. It specifically excludes the input connections (represented in Fig. 3B as the input currents I_i) and any output connections from the circuit.

Symmetry of the connections results in a powerful theorem about the behavior of the system. The only additional conditions necessary are that the input-output relation of the model neurons be monotonic and bounded and that the external inputs I_i (if any) should change only slowly over the time of the computation. The theorem shows that a mathematical quantity E, which might be thought of as the "computational energy," decreases during the change in neural state with time described by Eq. 1. Started in any initial state, the system will move in a generally "downhill" direction of the E function, reach a state in which E is a local minimum, and stop changing with time. The system cannot oscillate. This concept can be illustrated graphically by a flow map in a state-space diagram. Each line corresponds to a possible time-history of the system, with

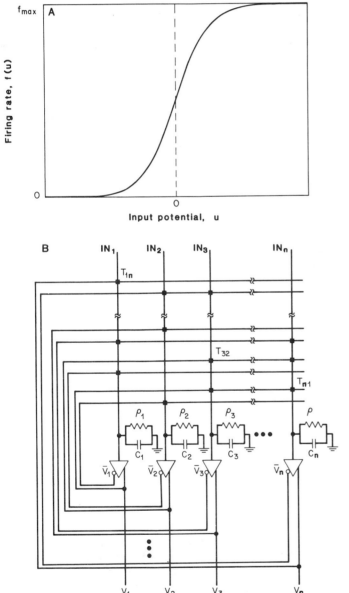

Fig. 3. (A) The sigmoid monotonic input-output relation used for the model neurons. (B) The model neural circuit in electrical components. The output of any neuron can potentially be connected to the input of any other neuron. Black squares at intersections represent resistive connections (with conductance T_{ij}) between outputs and inputs. Connections between inverted outputs (represented by the circles on the amplifiers) and inputs represent negative (inhibitory) connections.

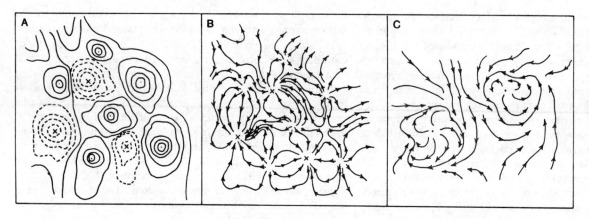

Fig. 4. (A) Energy-terrain contour map for the flow map shown in (B). (B) Typical flow map of neural dynamics for the circuit of Fig. 3 for symmetric connections ($T_{ij} = T_{ji}$). (C) More complicated dynamics that can occur for unrestricted (T_{ij}). Limit cycles are possible.

arrows showing the direction of motion. The structure imposed on the flow map for a circuit with symmetry is illustrated for a two-dimensional state space in Fig. 4. With symmetric connections, the flow map of the neural dynamics resembles Fig. 4B. Such a flow, in which each trajectory goes to stable points and stops, results from always going "downhill" on an "energy-terrain," coming to the bottom of a local valley, and stopping. The contour map of an E function that matches the flow in Fig. 4B is shown in Fig. 4A; it shows separated hills and valleys. The valleys are located where the trajectories in Fig. 4B stop. For a nonsymmetric circuit, the complications illustrated in the flow map in Fig. 4C can occur. This flow map has trajectories corresponding to complicated oscillatory behaviors. Such trajectories are undoubtedly important in neural computations, but as yet we lack the mathematical tools to manipulate and understand them at a computational level. The motion of a neural circuit comprising N neurons must be pictured in a space of N dimensions rather than the two dimensions of Fig. 4, but the qualitative picture of the effects of symmetric synaptic strengths is exactly the same.

The computational energy is a global quantity not felt by an individual neuron. The states of individual neurons simply obey the neural equations of motion (Eq. 1). The computational energy is our way of understanding why the system behaves as it does. A similar situation occurs in the concept of entropy in a simple gas. We understand that when a nonequilibrium state is set up with all the air molecules in one corner of the room, a uniform distribution will rapidly result. We explain that fact by the tendency of the entropy of isolated systems to increase whenever possible, but the individual molecules know nothing of entropy. They simply follow their Newtonian equations of motion.

Symmetric chemical synapses are observed in neural systems (24). Nonrectifying electrical synapses are intrinsically symmetric synapses of positive sign (25). Lateral inhibition in the visual system of *Limulus* is implemented with symmetric inhibitory synapses (6). An asymmetric network can also behave as though it were symmetric. In the olfactory bulb, the local circuit of mitral cell to granule cell to mitral cell provides an equivalent symmetric inhibitory connection between the pair of mitral cells (26). A similar situation occurs in the circuit shown in Fig. 1, where a direct equivalence between a neural circuit which is manifestly not symmetric and one which is effectively symmetric can be made if the inhibitory interneurons (IN_1, IN_2) are faster than other neurons.

The requirement of symmetry for this theorem can also be weakened. We have proven stability for a wide class of circuits having organized asymmetry between two sets of neurons with different time constants (16). (A neurobiological example would be the existence, in mammalian systems, of fast inhibitory interneurons that could provide effective symmetric inhibitory connections between neurons that are otherwise excitatory.) In one potentially

useful example (16), stability could be guaranteed even though the sign of T_{ij} was always opposite that of T_{ji}. Also, there is a family of transformations by which a broader class of synaptic organizations can be made equivalent to symmetric ones (27). From an empirical viewpoint, moderate disorganized asymmetry (for example, having a random set of connections missing in an otherwise symmetric associative memory circuit) has little experimental effect on dynamic stability (28). Because the general features of symmetric circuits persist in circuits that are only equivalently symmetric, and real neural circuits can often be so viewed (except for inputs and outputs), the behavior of symmetric circuit models should be of direct use in trying to understand how neural computation is done in biology.

In general, systems having organized asymmetry can exhibit oscillation and chaos (29). In some neural systems like central pattern generators (8), coordinated oscillation *is* the desired computation of the circuit. Processing in the olfactory bulb also seems to make explicit use of oscillatory patterns (30). In such a case, proper combinations of symmetric synapses can enforce chosen phase relationships between different oscillators, an effect similar to those presented above.

Hard Problems Naturally Solved by Model Neural Circuits

In thinking about how difficult computational problems can be done on such networks, it is useful to recall the simple problem of associative memory, which these networks implement in a "natural" fashion (10, 13). This naturalness has two aspects. (i) The symmetry of the networks is natural because, in simple associations, if A is associated with B, B is symmetrically associated with A. (ii) If the desired memories can be made the stable states of a network, the desired computation (given partial information as input, find the memory that most resembles it) can be directly visualized as a motion toward the nearest stable state whose position is the recalled memory. Finally, the way the connection strengths must be chosen for a given set of memories can be easily implemented by learning rules (13) such as the one proposed by Hebb (31).

To what extent can more difficult computations—for example, those relevant to object recognition or speech perception—be carried out naturally on these model neural circuits? One of the characteristics of such computations seems to be a combinatorial explosion—the huge number of possible answers that must be considered. The desired computation (for example, matching a set of words to a sound pattern) can often be stated as an optimization. Although it is not yet known how to map most biological problems onto model circuits, it is now possible to design model circuits to solve nonbiological problems having combinatorial complexity.

Because well-defined problems have been used, the effectiveness of the neural circuit computation can be quantified. We will review two circuit examples.

The idea of most algorithms or procedures for optimization is to move in a space of possible configurations representing solutions, progress in a direction that tends to decrease the cost function being minimized, and hope that the space and method of moving are smooth enough that a good solution will ultimately be reached. Such ideas lie behind conventional computer optimization algorithms and the recent work in simulated annealing (*32*) and Bayesian image analysis (*33*). In our approach (*15–17*), the optimization problem is mapped onto a neural network in such a way that the network configurations correspond to possible solutions to the problem. An E function appropriate to the problem is then constructed. The form of the E function is chosen so that at configurations representing possible solutions, E is proportional to the cost function of the problem. Since, in general, E is minimized as the circuit computes, the dynamics produce a path through the space that tends to minimize the energy and therefore the cost function. Eventually, a stable-state configuration is reached that corresponds to a local minimum in the E function. The solution to the problem is then decoded from this configuration.

It is particularly easy to construct appropriate E functions when the sigmoid input-output relation is steep, because in this "high-gain" limit, each neuron will be either very near 0 output or very near its maximal output when the system is in a low E stable state (*14*). In the high-gain case, the energy function is

$$E = -\frac{1}{2} \sum_{i,j} T_{ij} V_i V_j - \sum_j I_j V_j \quad (2)$$

When lower gain is considered, terms containing the function $g_i(u_i)$ must be included in E (*14*). The following two examples make use of this high-gain limit.

The simple seven-neuron circuit described in Fig. 1 was designed according to this conceptual framework to be a four-bit analog-to-binary (A-B) converter. Given an analog input to the circuit represented by the time-averaged impulse activity in the input axon Q, the neural circuit is organized to adjust the firing rates in the principal neurons so that they can be interpreted as the binary number numerically equal to the time-averaged input activity. Reorganization of the data in Fig. 2A will illustrate this computation. In each time epoch in Fig. 2A, assign the value 0 or 1 to the variable V_i representing the output of P_i; if P_i is firing strongly, $V_i = 1$; if it is quiescent, $V_i = 0$. Represent the activity in axon Q by a continuous variable X. The value of the binary word interpreted from the ordered list of numbers $(V_3 V_2 V_1 V_0)$ is plotted in Fig. 2B for each of the different values of input strength X. The data points (asterisks) lie on a staircase function (dotted line) characteristic of an A-B converter. (Although not shown, the outputs computed for any other input would also lie on this curve.)

Through the consideration of a specific energy function in the high-gain limit and the synaptic strengths and inputs listed in Table 1, the behavior of the neural circuit can be predicted and understood. We decide in advance that outputs $V_3 V_2 V_1 V_0$ of P_3 through P_0 are interpreted as a computed binary word. The problem to be solved is stated as an optimization: Given analog input X, which binary word (set of outputs) best represents the numerical value of X? The solution is provided when the following E is minimized (*16*):

$$E = -\frac{1}{2} \left(X - \sum_{j=0}^{3} 2^j V_j\right)^2 + \sum_{j=0}^{3} (2^{2j-1}) [V_j(1 - V_j)] \quad (3)$$

The second term in E is minimized (and numerically equal to 0) when all V_j are either close to 0 or close to 1. Since E is minimized as

the circuit converges, stable states having the correct "syntax" tend to develop. Since the first term in E is a minimum when the expression in the parentheses vanishes, this term biases the circuit towards the states closest, in the least-squares sense, to the analog value of X. The E in Eq. 3 is like that in Eq. 2, a quadratic in the V_i. Rearranging Eq. 3 and comparing it with this general form yields values for T_{ij} and I_i for a circuit of the form in Fig. 3B that can be deduced within a common scale factor as

$$T_{ij} = -2^{(i+j)}; \quad I_i = (-2^{(2i-1)} + 2^i X) \quad (4)$$

The coefficient of X in I_i is the synaptic strength from the input axon Q to the principal neurons. These specific values are equal to the strengths of the "effective" synapses tabulated in Table 1. Knowledge that E is minimized as the circuit computes provides an *understanding* of how this synaptic organization both enforces the necessary syntax and biases the network to choose the optimum solution.

Our second example is a neural circuit that computes solutions to the traveling salesman problem (TSP) (*15*). In this frequently studied optimization problem (*34*), a salesman is required to visit in some sequence each of n cities; the problem is to determine the shortest closed tour in which every city is visited only once. Specific problems are defined by the distances (d_{ij}) between pairs of cities (i, j). Assigning letters to the cities in a TSP permits a solution to be specified by an ordered list of letters. For example, the list *CAFGB* is interpreted as "visit C, then A, then F, then G, then B, and finally return to C." For an n-city TSP, this list can be decoded from the outputs of $N = n^2$ neurons if we let a single neuron correspond to the hypothesis that one of the n cities is in a particular one of the n possible positions in the final tour list. This rule suggests the arrangement illustrated in Fig. 5 for displaying the neural output states. The output of a neuron (V_i) is graphically illustrated by shading; a filled square represents a neuron which is "on" and firing strongly. An empty square represents a neuron that is not firing. The output states of the n neurons in each row are interpreted as information about the location of a particular city in the tour solution. The output states of the n neurons in each column are interpreted as information about what cities are to be associated with a particular position in the tour. If the neuron from column 5 in row C is "on," the hypothesis that city C is in position 5 in the final tour solution is true.

Hypothetically, each of the n cities could indicate its position in any one of the n possible tour locations. Therefore, 2^N possible "neural states" could conceivably be represented by these outputs. However, only a subset of these actually correspond to valid solutions to the TSP (valid tours): a city must be in one, and only one, position in a valid tour, and any position must be filled by one and only one city. This constraint implies that only output states in which only one neuron is "on" in every row and in every column are of the correct "syntax" to represent valid solutions to the TSP. A TSP circuit that is to operate correctly must have synapses favoring this subset of states. Simple lateral inhibition between neurons within each row and column will provide this bias. For example, if $V_{B,2}$ (representing city B in position 2) is "on," all other neurons in row B and column 2 should be inhibited. This can be provided by the inhibitory connections from neuron $V_{B,2}$ drawn in Fig. 5 (red lines). Similar row and column inhibitory connections are drawn for neuron $V_{D,5}$. A complex "topology" of syntax-enforcing connections is generated. We can also think of these connections as contributing a term to the E function for the circuit. For example, a term $+A\ V_{X,i}\ V_{Y,i}$ in E makes a contribution $-A$ to the synaptic strength $T_{X,i;Y,i}$ and represents a mutual lateral inhibition between neurons (X,i) and (Y,i). The term is positive (higher E) when both of these neurons are "on," but contributes nothing if only one of the two is "on." The proper combination of similar terms in an E function can specify the synapses that coordinate correct syntax.

In a syntactically correct state representing a valid solution (tour), if neurons $V_{X,i}$ and $V_{Y,i+1}$ are both "on," the salesman travels from city X directly to city Y. Therefore, the distance $d_{X,Y}$ between these two cities is included in the total tour length for that solution. A term of the form $+d_{X,Y} V_{X,i} V_{Y,i+1}$ in the E function provides a "distance" contribution of d_{xy} to the value of E when these neurons are "on." Similar terms, properly summed, will add to E a value equal to the length of the tour. Since the circuit minimizes E, the final state will be biased toward those valid solutions representing short tours. Such inhibitory connections are drawn in Fig. 5 with blue lines for neurons $V_{B,2}$ and $V_{D,5}$. In TSP and in the earlier example, the rules of syntax are expressed in inhibitory connections. It seems easier to define what these systems should not do (by inhibitory connections), and to define what they should do by default, rather than to define what they should do by writing syntax in excitatory connections.

The inhibitory synapses define the computational connections for the TSP circuit. With a common sigmoid gain curve, R, and C for each neuron, the description of the circuit is complete. The gain curve is chosen so that with zero input, a neuron has a nonzero but modest output. This circuit can rapidly compute good solutions to a TSP problem (15). When started from an initial "noise" state favoring no particular tour, the network rapidly converges to a steady state describing a very short tour. The state of the circuit at several time points in a typical convergence is illustrated in Fig. 6. In a 30-city problem, there are about 10^{30} possible tours—the combinatorial problem has gotten completely out of hand. But the circuit of 900 neurons can find one of the best 10^7 solutions in a single

convergence—a few time constants of the circuit. It selects good answers and rejects bad ones by a factor of 10^{23}.

The continuous response characteristic of the analog neurons in the TSP circuit represents partial knowledge or belief. A value for $V_{X,j}$ between 0 and 1 represents the "strength" of the hypothesis that city X is in position j of the tour. During an analog convergence, several conflicting solutions or propositions can be simultaneously considered through the continuous variables. It is as though the logical operations of a calculation could be given continuous values between "true" and "false" and evolve toward certainty only near the end of the calculation. This is evident during the TSP convergence process (Fig. 6) and is important for finding good solutions to this problem (15). If the gain is greatly increased, the output of any given neuron will usually be either 1 or 0, and the potential analog character of the network will not be utilized. When operated in this mode, the paths found are little better than random. The analog nature of the neural response is in this problem essential to its computational effectiveness. This use of a continuous variable between true and false is similar to the theory of fuzzy sets (35) and to the use of evidence voting for the truth of competing propositions in Bayesian inference and connectionist modeling in cognitive psychology (36). Two-state neurons do not capture this computational feature.

Discussion

The work reviewed here has shown that a simple model of nonlinear neurons organized into networks with effectively symmetric connections has a "natural" capacity for solving optimization problems. The general behavior can be readily adapted to particular problems by appropriately selecting the synaptic connections. Optimization problems are ubiquitous where goals are attempted in the presence of conflicting constraints, and they arise in problems of perception (What three-dimensional shape "best" describes a given shading pattern in a two-dimensional image?), behavioral choice, and motor control (What is the optimum trajectory to move an appendage to minimize internal stresses?). Hence circuits consistent with this model could efficiently solve problems important in biological information processing.

Biologically relevant problems in vision have already been formulated in terms of optimization problems. Edge-detection, stereopsis, and motion detection can be described as "ill-posed" problems, and solutions can be found by minimizing appropriate quadratic functionals (37). The emphasis in these formulations has been simple convex problems with a single minimum in the energy. Networks solving these problems can be implemented by linear circuits having local connections. The nonlinear circuits described here can implement solutions to much more complex problems and have recently been used to solve the object-discontinuity problem in early vision (18).

The concept of an energy function and its use in circuit design provide an understanding of *how* model neural circuits rapidly compute solutions to optimization problems. The state of each neuron changes in time in a simple way determined by the state of neurons to which it is connected, but the organization of the synapses results in collective dynamics that minimize an E function relevant to the optimization problem. Knowledge of this E function helps us understand the collective dynamics. The two circuit examples reviewed here, the A-B converter and TSP circuit, were "forward-engineered." Given the optimization problem, a representation of hypothetical solutions to the problem as a particular set of neural states was constructed. Synaptic connections in the operating circuit move the neural state toward these solution states and bias

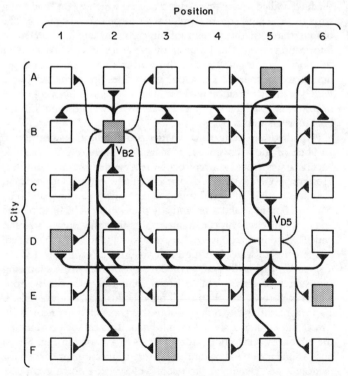

Fig. 5. A stylized picture of the syntax and connections of the TSP neural circuit. Each neuron is symbolically indicated by a square. The neurons are arranged in an n by n array. Each city is associated with n neurons in a row, and each position in the final tour is associated with n neurons in a column. A given neuron ($V_{X,j}$) represents the hypothesis that city X is in position j in the solution. The patterns of synaptic connection for two different neurons are indicated.

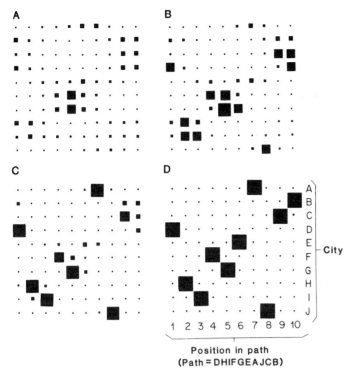

Fig. 6. The convergence of a ten-city analog circuit to a tour. The linear dimension of each square is proportional to the value of $V_{X,i}$. (A to C) Intermediate times. (D) The final state. Indices illustrate how the final state is decoded into a tour (solution of the TSP).

this motion toward the best solution. The values of these synaptic strengths were summarized in the single algebraic statement of the E function. [The two problems illustrate different ways in which "data" modulate the circuit parameters: as input currents in the A-B converter or as changes in the connection strengths in the TSP circuit (17).] Forward-engineered examples of model neural circuits add to the known repertoire of computational circuits that seem neurobiologically plausible. The general problem of neurobiology is "reverse engineering"—to understand the operation of a complex biological circuit with unknown design principles and internal representations. In general, the set of neural circuits whose functioning is understood provides an information base for hypothesizing function in biological neural circuits in the same way that the study of understood electrical circuits aids the attempt to understand or reverse engineer an unfamiliar electrical circuit diagram.

When a problem falls naturally onto a neural circuit, its convergence to a collective analog decision in a few time constants represents immense computation for the amount of hardware involved. For example, the 30-city TSP can be done on a network of 900 neurons. When that kind of combinatorial problem occurs in perception and pattern recognition, the input to the system will occur in parallel and take little time. A biological neural network of this structure would converge to an answer in a few neural time constants, thus in about 0.1 second. An electronic circuit of the same structure would converge in about 1 μsec. A comparably good solution to this problem, with conventional algorithms used for the TSP, can be found in about 0.1 second on a typical microcomputer having 10^4 times as many devices. The effectiveness of the neural system on the basis of computations per device per time constant is great in comparison with the usual general-purpose digital machine. The ability of the model networks to compute effectively is based on large connectivity, analog response, and reciprocal or reentrant connections. The computations are qualitatively different from those performed by Boolean logic.

Other specific circuit designs have been studied. Many problems in signal processing can be described as the attempt to detect the presence or absence of a waveform having a known stereotyped shape in the presence of other waveforms and noise. (The recognition of phonemes in a stream of speech is conceptually similar, but fraught with large problems of variability from the stereotype form.) We have described the general organization of neural circuits that could solve this task (16). Energy functions have been described for other combinatorial optimization problems, including graph coloring (17), the Euclidean-match problem (17), and the transposition code problem (15). Circuits that relax the restriction on a symmetric connection matrix (as biology does) have also been studied. A circuit designed to provide solutions to linear programming problems (16) functions without oscillation when the characteristic times of these elements are properly specified, even though its computing elements have antisymmetric connection strengths. The associative memory originally discussed (10) and used in a model of learning in a simple invertebrate (38) can be described as an optimization problem (15). The same conceptual framework can seemingly be applied to a large number of different problems.

Because the basic idea of the model neural circuit can be expressed as an electrical circuit, there have been efforts to build such hardware. Associative memories of 32 neurons (amplifiers) have been built in conventional electrical circuit technology (39). A 22-neuron circuit has been successfully microfabricated on a single silicon chip (40). Shrinking this kind of network to a compact size seems possible (41). The most compact and useful form of such a device would involve an electrically writable resistance change in a two-terminal device, which would function approximately as a Hebbian (31) synapse. Examples of such material fabrications exist (42). A 32-neuron system has been fabricated that uses optics to implement connections (43). Technological questions have so far focused chiefly on associative memory. Similar circuits could be used to solve problems in signal detection and analysis, such as artificial visual systems, in which there tends to be immense data overload and where concurrent distributed processing is desired.

In both biological neural systems and man-made computing structures, hierarchy and rhythmic or timed behaviors are important. The addition of rhythms, adaptation, and timing provides a mechanism for moving from one aspect of a computation to another and for dealing with time-dependent inputs and will lead to new computational abilities even in small networks. Hierarchy is necessary to keep the number of synaptic connections to a reasonable level. To extend the present ideas from neural circuit to neural system, such notions will be essential.

REFERENCES AND NOTES

1. D. Marr, *Vision* (Freeman, San Francisco, 1982).
2. Implementations different from those reviewed here are discussed in: T. Poggio and C. Koch, *Artificial Intelligence Lab. Memo 773* (Massachusetts Institute of Technology, Cambridge, 1984); S. E. Fahlman, G. E. Hinton, T. J. Sejnowski, *Proceedings of National Conference on Artificial Intelligence* (1983), p. 109; S. Geman and D. Geman, *IEEE Trans. Pattern Anal. Mech. Intell.* 6, 721 (1984).
3. W. S. McCulloch and W. Pitts, *Bull. Math. Biophys.* 5, 115 (1943).
4. F. Rosenblatt, *Principles of Neurodynamics* (Spartan, Washington, DC, 1961).
5. W. S. McCulloch, *Embodiments of Mind* (MIT Press, Cambridge, MA, 1965); M. Minsky and S. Papert, *Perceptrons* (MIT Press, Cambridge, MA, 1969); A. C. Scott, *J. Math. Psychol.* 15, 1 (1977).
6. H. K. Hartline, H. G. Wagner, F. Ratliff, *J. Gen. Physiol.* 39, 651 (1956).
7. For a summary of appropriate mathematical methods, see D. Noble, J. J. B. Jack, and R. Tsien [*Electric Current Flow in Excitable Cells* (Clarendon, Oxford, 1974)].
8. D. K. Hartline, *Biol. Cybern.* 33, 223 (1979); D. H. Perkel and B. Mulloney, *Science* 185, 181 (1974); A. I. Selverston, *Behav. Brain Sci.* 3, 535 (1980); W. O. Freisen and G. S. Stent, *Biol. Cybern.* 28, 27 (1977).
9. See, for example: R. D. Traub and R. K. S. Wong, *Science* 216, 745 (1982).
10. J. J. Hopfield, *Proc. Natl. Acad. Sci. U.S.A.* 79, 2554 (1982).
11. While space does not permit the review of modern developments using two-state neurons, the following references provide an introduction to this literature: W. A. Little, *Math. Biosci.* 19, 101 (1974); ——— and G. L. Shaw, *ibid.* 39, 281 (1978);

G. L. Shaw, D. J. Silverman, J. C. Pearson, *Proc. Natl. Acad. Sci. U.S.A.* **82**, 3364 (1985); M. Y. Choi and B. A. Huberman, *Phys. Rev. A* **28**, 1204 (1983); T. Hogg and B. A. Huberman, *Proc. Natl. Acad. Sci. U.S.A.* **81**, 6871 (1984); M. A. Cohen and S. Grossberg, *IEEE Trans. Syst. Man Cybern.* **SMC-13**, 815 (1983); K. Nakano, *ibid.* **SMC-2** (no. 3) (1972). For recent work on stochastic models applied to two states, see G. E. Hinton, T. J. Sejnowski, and D. H. Ackley [*Technical Report CMU-CS-84-119* (Carnegie-Mellon University, Pittsburgh, 1984)].

12. We refer to the dynamics as "classical" because we are ignoring propagation time delays and the quantal nature of action potentials, in analogy to classical mechanics. Similar equations have been described: T. J. Sejnowski, in *Parallel Models of Associative Memory*, G. E. Hinton and J. A. Anderson, Eds. (Erlbaum, Hillsdale, NJ, 1981), p. 189.

13. T. Kohonen, *Self-Organization and Associative Memory* (Springer-Verlag, Berlin, 1984); T. Kohonen *et al.*, *Neuroscience* **2**, 1065 (1977); T. Kohonen, *Biol. Cybern.* **43**, 59 (1982); L. N. Cooper, F. Liberman, E. Oja, *ibid.* **33**, 9 (1979); D. Ackley, G. E. Hinton, T. J. Sejnowski, *Cognit. Sci.* **9**, 147 (1985); D. d'Humieres and B. A. Huberman, *J. Stat. Phys.* **34**, 361 (1984); K. Fukushima, *Biol. Cybern.* **36**, 193 (1980); A. G. Barto, R. S. Sutton, P. S. Brouwer, *ibid.* **40**, 201 (1981); *Parallel Models of Associative Memory*, G. E. Hinton and J. A. Anderson, Eds. (Erlbaum, Hillsdale, NJ, 1981). The capacity of associative memories constructed from networks of two-state neurons is discussed by P. Peretto [*Biol. Cybern.* **50**, 51 (1984)], D. J. Amit, H. Gutfreund, H. Sompolinsky [*Phys. Rev. Lett.* **55**, 1530 (1985)], R. J. McEliece and E. C. Posner [*JPL Telecommunications and Data Acquisition Progress Report 42-83* (1985), p. 209], Y.-S. Abu-Mostafa and J. St. Jacques [*IEEE Trans. Inf. Theory* **IT-31**, 461 (1985)], and L. Personnaz, I. Guyon, and G. Dreyfus [*J. Physique Lett.* **46**, L-359 (1985)].

14. J. J. Hopfield, *Proc. Natl. Acad. Sci. U.S.A.* **81**, 3088 (1984).

15. _____ and D. W. Tank, *Biol. Cybern.* **52**, 141 (1985).

16. D. W. Tank and J. J. Hopfield, *IEEE Circuits Syst.* **CAS-33**, 533 (1986).

17. J. J. Hopfield and D. W. Tank, in *Disordered Systems and Biological Organization* (Springer-Verlag, Berlin, 1986).

18. C. Koch, J. Marroquin, A. Yuille, *Proc. Natl. Acad. Sci. U.S.A.* **83**, 4263 (1986).

19. E. Mjolsness, *CalTech Computer Science Dept. Publication 5153:DF* (1984).

20. T. J. Sejnowski and G. E. Hinton, in *Vision, Brain, and Cooperative Computation*, M. Arbib and A. R. Hanson, Eds. (MIT Press, Cambridge, MA, 1985).

21. G. M. Shepherd, *The Synaptic Organization of the Brain* (Oxford Univ. Press, New York, 1979), p. 3.

22. For a review of observed input-output relations and their ionic basis, see W. E Crill and P. C. Schwindt [*Trends NeuroSci* **6**, 236 (1983)].

23. K. G. Pearson, in *Simpler Networks and Behavior*, J. C. Fentress, Ed. (Sinauer, Sunderland, MA, 1976).

24. J. McCarragher and R. Chase, *J. Neurosci* **16**, 69 (1985).

25. M. V. L. Bennett and D. A. Goodenough, *Neurosci. Res. Program Bull.* **16**, 371 (1978).

26. W. Rall and G. M. Shepherd, *J. Neurophysiol.* **31**, 884 (1968).

27. C. Koch and A. Yuille, personal communication.

28. J. Platt, personal communication.

29. E. Harth, *IEEE Trans. Syst. Man Cybern.* **SMC-13**, 782 (1983).

30. W. J. Freeman, *Mass Action in the Nervous System* (Academic Press, New York, 1975).

31. D. O. Hebb, *The Organization of Behavior* (Wiley, New York, 1949).

32. S. Kirkpatrick, C. D. Gelatt, M. P. Vecchi, *Science* **220**, 671 (1983).

33. S. Geeman and D. Geeman, *IEEE Trans. Pattern Anal.* **6**, 721 (1984).

34. M. R. Garey and D. S. Johnson, *Computers and Intractability* (Freeman, New York, 1979).

35. L. A. Zadeh, *IEEE Trans. Syst. Man Cybern.* **SMC-3**, 38 (1974).

36. D. H. Ballard, *Pattern Recognition* **13**, 111 (1981); J. A. Feldman and D. H. Ballard, *Cognit. Sci.* **6**, 205 (1982); D. L. Waltz and J. B. Pollack, *ibid.* **9**, 51 (1985); J. B. Pollack and D. L. Pollack, *Byte Magazine* **11** (no. 2), 189 (1986).

37. T. Poggio, V. Torre and C. Koch, *Nature (London)* **317**, 314 (1985).

38. A. E. Gelperin, J. J. Hopfield, D. W. Tank, in *Model Neural. Networks and Behavior*, A. Selverston, Ed. (Plenum, New York, 1985).

39. J. Lambe, A. Moopenn, A. P. Thakoor, *Proceedings of the AIAA: Fifth Conference on Computers in Space*, in press; J. Lambe, A. Moopenn, A. P. Thakoor, *Jet Propulsion Lab Publication 85-69* (Jet Propulsion Laboratory, Pasadena, CA, 1985).

40. M. Sivilotti, M. Emmerling, C. Mead, *1985 Conference on Very Large Scale Integration*, H. Fuchs, Ed. (Computer Science, Rockville, MD, 1985), p. 329.

41. L. D. Jackel, R. E. Howard, H. P. Graf, B. Straughn, J. S. Denker, *J. Vac. Sci. Tech.*, in press.

42. A. E. Owen, P. G. Le Comber, G. Sarrabayrouse, W. E. Spear, *IEE Proc.* **129** (part 1, no. 2), 51 (1982).

43. D. Psaltis and N. Farhat, *Optics Lett.* **10**, 98 (1985).

44. Supported in part by NSF grant PCM-8406049.

Spin glass model of learning by selection

(Darwinism/categorization/Hebb synapse/ultrametricity/frustration)

Gérard Toulouse, Stanislas Dehaene, and Jean-Pierre Changeux

Unité de Neurobiologie Moléculaire and Laboratoire Associé au Centre National de la Recherche Scientifique, no. 270, Interactions Moléculaires et Cellulaires, Institut Pasteur, 25 rue du Docteur Roux, 75724 Paris Cédex 15, France

Contributed by Jean-Pierre Changeux, October 31, 1985

ABSTRACT   A model of learning by selection is described at the level of neuronal networks. It is formally related to statistical mechanics with the aim to describe memory storage during development and in the adult. Networks with symmetric interactions have been shown to function as content-addressable memories, but the present approach differs from previous instructive models. Four biologically relevant aspects are treated—initial state before learning, synaptic sign changes, hierarchical categorization of stored patterns, and synaptic learning rule. Several of the hypotheses are tested numerically. Starting from the limit case of random connections (spin glass), selection is viewed as pruning of a complex tree of states generated with maximal parsimony of genetic information.

Aside from the inneist, or preformist, point of view, according to which experience does not cause any significant increase of order in an already highly structured brain organization, two main classes of learning theories have been proposed and discussed (for review see ref. 1). On the empiricist side, the initial state is considered as a *tabula rasa*, and the whole internal organization results from direct instructive prints by the environment. Alternatively, selectionist theories postulate that the increase of internal order associated with experience is indirect (2–8). The organism generates, spontaneously, variable patterns of connections (3) at the sensitive period of development, referred to as "transient redundancy" (6), or variable patterns of activity named prerepresentations (7, 8) in the adult. Interaction with the environment merely selects or selectively stabilizes the preexisting patterns of connections and/or firings that fit with the external input, a step named "resonance" (7, 8). As a correlate of learning, connections between neurons are eliminated and/or the number of accessible firing patterns is reduced.

Several attempts to model learning at the level of large ensembles or "assemblies" of interconnected neurons have been made in quantitative terms mostly with the help of statistical mechanics (9, 10). Their revival is largely due to the introduction by Hopfield (10) of the conceptual simplification that (*i*) if one restricts the interactions between neurons only to symmetric ones, this allows for the introduction of an energy function and, as a consequence, the dynamics of neuronal networks can be viewed as a downhill motion in an energy landscape and (*ii*) then, the reallowance for dissymmetric interactions does not discontinuously upset the picture.

On the other hand, such models still belonged to the empiricist mode of learning with the initial state taken as a flat energy landscape (*tabula rasa*) that becomes progressively structured and complex by direct instructions from the environment.

The aim of this communication is to propose a model of learning by selection based on an advance in the statistical mechanics of disordered systems—namely, the theory of spin glasses (11–13). In contrast to the empiricist approach, the initial state is viewed as a complex energy landscape with an abundance of valleys typical of spin glasses with learning consisting of the progressive smoothening and gardening of this landscape. The paper also contains a biological critique of the standard instructive version of the Hopfield model, referred to here in short as the instructive model. The main proposals for a selectionist model of learning are outlined and preliminary numerical results are reported and discussed.

The Activity of Neuronal Networks Described by Statistical Mechanics

The all-or-none firing of a neuron is represented by a spin that can take two values: $S = +1$ (firing), $S = -1$ (rest). A pattern of activity, α, of a network of N neurons is represented by a spin configuration (S_i^α), $i = 1, \ldots, N$, that lies at one of the corners of a hypercube in N-dimensional configuration space. Two patterns of activity, α and β, may then be compared through their overlap, which is an index of proximity or matching in configuration space:

$$q^{\alpha\beta} = \frac{1}{N} \sum_{i=1}^{N} S_i^\alpha S_i^\beta. \qquad [1]$$

The neurons interact via binary synapses of synaptic strength, T_{ij}. With the assumption (5) of symmetric interactions $T_{ji} = T_{ij}$, an energy function can be written as follows:

$$E = -\frac{1}{2} \sum_{i \neq j} T_{ij} S_i S_j - \sum_i h_i S_i, \qquad [2]$$

where h_i is a local field acting on spin S_i and is often used to represent an external input (yielding an apparent shift of the firing threshold of a neuron). The neuron dynamics is such that, in the absence of probabilistic effects leading to random spontaneous activity, each spin tends to decrease its energy. A stable configuration is, therefore, a local minimum of the energy E. On the other hand, probabilistic effects can be described by introducing a finite temperature (14).

Synaptic modifications have been hitherto often expressed by the learning rule:

$$\Delta T_{ij} \sim \langle S_i S_j \rangle, \qquad [3]$$

where the brackets mean some time average. This expression, referred to as the "generalized Hebb rule," differs from the original Hebb rule (15), which may be written as

$$\Delta T_{ij} \sim \left\langle \left(\frac{S_i + 1}{2} \right) \left(\frac{S_j + 1}{2} \right) \right\rangle, \qquad [4]$$

and exclusively takes into account reinforcements of excitatory synapses. Rule **3** has attractive features—it is local and formally natural—but it also has undesirable ones—for instance, when neuron *i* makes inhibitory synapses with neuron

---

Reprinted with permission from *Proc. Natl. Acad. Sci. USA*, vol. 83, no. 6, pp. 1695–1698, 1986.

j, rule **3** would predict a modification of synaptic strength T_{ij} and eventually a reversal from inhibitory to excitatory, if none of the neurons is firing and the synapses are silent.

Instructive Models of Learning

Instructive models of learning (10) postulate that, in the initial state, the interactions between neurons are vanishingly small and the energy landscape is flat (*tabula rasa*). Storage into memory of an activity pattern α, where $S_i = \mu_i^\alpha$, results from the following synaptic modification,

$$\Delta T_{ij} = \frac{1}{N} \mu_i^\alpha \mu_j^\alpha, \qquad [5]$$

and the network is said to have learned M patterns, $\alpha = 1$, ..., M, when the interactions have been set to

$$T_{ij} = \frac{1}{N} \sum_{\alpha=1}^{M} \mu_i^\alpha \mu_j^\alpha, \qquad [6]$$

as a consequence of the successive prints of the M input patterns. With such interactions **6**, the network functions as a distributed, fault-tolerant, content-addressable memory. Starting from any input data, the network configuration rapidly converges toward a local minimum and recognizes the closest stored memory pattern (provided M is not too large and no confusion takes place) (10).

Assuming that the learned patterns are random and uncorrelated, Hopfield (10) has suggested that the maximal storage capacity is $M_c = \gamma N$ (with $\gamma < 1/2$, since each pattern corresponds to N bits of information, and the information is stored in the interactions, with $N^2/2$ of them) and further has shown that loss of recall occurred around $\gamma = 0.15$, an estimate that has been confirmed by subsequent analytical calculations (16, 17).

Such instructive mode of learning, if legitimate and useful for artificial intelligence, does not hold for the brain for the following reasons.

(*i*) As more and more patterns are stored, according to formula **6**, the synaptic patterns keep changing sign. As was already stressed by Hopfield (10), it is the signs of the interactions T_{ij} together with their absolute values that are responsible for the proper shaping of the energy landscape. Thus, storing a new memory amounts largely to reversing the signs of a particular set of synaptic strengths. Yet, no physiological evidence exists of synaptic sign reversal, such as a shift of postsynaptic response from excitatory to inhibitory, as a cellular correlate of learning (1).

(*ii*) Up to now, the ultimate organization of stored patterns in memory space has been viewed as a configuration-space-filling *jardin à la française*, with a regular distribution of the basins of attraction corresponding to the various stored patterns (18). A more hierarchical distribution less prone to confusions, with categorization properties and correlations between stored patterns, appears more appropriate for higher brain functions, even if it is wasteful of configuration space.

(*iii*) The hypothesis of an initial state with vanishing interactions does not take into account the existence of an already connected and functional neuronal network at the moment learning occurs.

Spin Glasses

Spin glasses, by definition, consist of networks of spins with symmetric random (positive and negative) interactions. The energy is simply given by

$$E = -\frac{1}{2} \sum_{i \neq j} T_{ij} S_i S_j. \qquad [7]$$

The mean field theory of spin glasses (valid for a fully connected network and a number of spins N large) is intricate

but yields a simple physical picture for the energy landscape. The total number of local minima in configuration space is exponential in N. However, the dominant valleys (their importance is weighed by the Boltzmann factor, which favors low-energy valleys) have positive mutual overlaps. More precisely, to any spin state, time-reversal symmetry associates another state with all spins flipped and the same energy, so that the previous statement holds for each half of the valleys separately. In geometric terms, the dominant valleys of a spin glass lie within a cone, centered at the origin and of right angle in configuration space (one-half of the valleys within one sector of the cone, the other half within the opposite sector). Such a right-angle cone spans a very small fraction of configuration space, which is another way of stating that the dominant valleys are strongly intercorrelated.

Furthermore, the distribution of these valleys possesses an ultrametric structure (11)—i.e., a hierarchical organization of clusters within clusters—in configuration space. A similar ultrametric distribution occurs in taxonomy when species are classified, for instance, according to protein sequence homologies (19).

The spin glass energy landscape thus exhibits, spontaneously, a categorized organization. The appearance of ultrametricity for large heterogeneous assemblies is a remarkable feature, which may be partly understood by realizing that there are fewer bonds ($N^2/2$) than possible spin configurations (2^N), and thus that the energy states have to exhibit some form of correlation. Indeed, if ever random multiple-spin (ternary, quaternary, etc.) interactions are introduced, since they occur in larger combinatorial number than ordinary binary interactions, the energy landscape tends to become more and more rough, and the notion of hills, passes, and valleys eventually disappears (20).

Spin Glass Model of Learning by Selection

The proposal we make here is that the theory and formalism of spin glasses appear particularly adequate to model learning by selection. As discussed (7), selection has been postulated to operate during development on a variable connective organization (3, 6) or, in the adult, on variable patterns of activity named prerepresentations (7, 8). In both cases, a significant (though limited) randomness characterizes the initial state. This legitimizes the modeling of this "fringe" state by a network of N neurons with randomly connected excitatory and inhibitory synapses that would behave as a spin glass.

In brief, a spin glass has an energy landscape with: (*i*) an abundance of valleys and (*ii*) dominant valleys strongly intercorrelated (positive mutual overlaps) in a tree-like fashion.

Item (*i*) gives to this network the property of a "generator of internal diversity" (7, 21)—that is, each valley corresponds to a particular set of active neurons and plays the role of a prerepresentation. Item (*ii*) further indicates a spontaneous categorization of the prerepresentations.

Learning with very small synaptic changes is both advantageous and possible. It is advantageous because it tends to preserve ultrametricity—i.e., the spontaneous hierarchical categorization of the prerepresentations. It is possible because learning by selection involves the stabilization of preexisting valleys instead of creation of new ones. The foremost constraint is interdiction of synaptic sign reversals. Other proposals for the learning rule fall into two categories. The rule should remain local but avoid the inconsistencies mentioned above. In addition, a weighted factor is introduced and contributes to the selection of the input patterns that match the prerepresentations (resonance). This selective factor enters naturally as a time average, if one assumes that the synaptic changes occur during a relaxation time of the configuration initiated by the input pattern. More coherent synaptic modifications will favor input patterns that match with preexisting valleys.

In summary, learning by selection may occur as follows: An input pattern sets an initial configuration that converges toward an attractor of the dynamics (bottom of a valley, i.e., a prerepresentation). The energy of this selected valley is lowered by synaptic modifications (particularly if the learning time is longer than the relaxation time), and its basin of attraction is shifted and enlarged at the expense of other valleys. Starting from a hierarchical distribution of valleys, the learning process can be viewed as pruning of a tree, analogous to that occurring in the course of phylogenesis. As a consequence the whole energy landscape evolves during the learning process, the already stored information influencing the prerepresentations available for the next learning event. Moreover, the constraints on the synaptic modifications give internal rigidity to the system. Not every external stimulus can equally be stored. Selection by the external stimuli among internal prerepresentations has its counterpart in selection by the internal network among external inputs. In a parallel assembly of such networks, one may further speculate that an input pattern will select its memory location, the place where it fits, if any.

A prerequisite of learning by selection is the existence of a nontrivial valley structure prior to the interaction with the outside world. There are only two ways whereby a neuronal network with symmetric binary connections can exhibit such a structure.

One way is via frustration (22). The frustration function $\Phi(c)$ of a closed loop (c) of interacting spins is the product of the interactions around the loop:

$$\Phi(c) = \prod_{(c)} T_{ij}. \qquad [8]$$

If $\Phi(c) > 0$, it is possible to find a spin configuration around the loop such that each bond is satisfied. If $\Phi(c) < 0$, this is not possible, and the spin configurations can be at best partially satisfactory. In this latter case, the loop is said to be frustrated. Frustration is a source of metastability and degeneracy. By definition, an unfrustrated network, where all loops are unfrustrated, has only two minima, related by time-reversal symmetry.

The other way to get multiplicity of valleys is via disconnection. A network, broken into p disconnected unfrustrated clusters, has 2^p minima.

The rich valley structure of a long-range, fully connected spin glass stems from frustration. It differs sharply from the valley structure of a set of disconnected clusters, although intermediate cases are conceivable. Indeed, if all the neurons are decoupled, the storage capacity is in some sense maximal, but all the useful properties of a distributed, associative memory are lost.

Any realistic neuronal network model for biological learning by selection should include both frustration and disconnection. Not only is the initial connectivity in central nervous systems far from maximal (see for instance, the anatomical evidence for columns) but the occurrence of synaptic elimination during development is well documented (6, 23). The constrained learning rules, introduced above, preserve frustration because they forbid sign reversals and allow for synaptic elimination.

Numerical Implementations and Results

Our model contains a set of hypotheses that are precise enough to be tested numerically, and we have begun a systematic investigation of their consequences. Some salient results, for small network sizes ranging from $N = 30$ to $N = 200$, are reported. A more elaborate discussion will be presented elsewhere. For the sake of clarity, we have studied separately the effects of each of our basic hypotheses and compared them with the instructive model.

The *Tabula Rasa* Withdrawn. In the initial state, the synapses are set with random signs and an average strength S. It is known from spin glass theory that partial learning of an arbitrary pattern can be obtained with synaptic increments of order $S/\sqrt{N}$ for a complete graph of N neurons. Keeping unchanged the form of the generalized Hebb rule, for the sake of comparison,

$$\Delta T_{ij} = \frac{\varepsilon S}{\sqrt{N}} \, \mu_i^\alpha \, \mu_j^\alpha, \qquad [9]$$

we have checked that retrieval quality [more precisely, in notations defined below, a normalized index $R = (q_a - q_b)/(1 - q_b)$] is a function of ε, independent of network size N. Furthermore, for $\varepsilon \gtrsim 2.5$, retrieval quality was found to be practically perfect.

As more and more patterns are stored, the strength of a given synapse undergoes a random walk, with steps of length $\varepsilon S/\sqrt{N}$ starting from the initial values $+S$ or $-S$. Whenever the strength of a synapse hits the value zero (an occurrence possible after learning $p \sim \sqrt{N}/\varepsilon$ patterns) it is prevented from changing sign. Two subsequent rules are conceivable, and both have been examined. Either the synapse is altogether eliminated, which is a strong form of the constraint, or its strength is temporarily blocked at zero until it eventually receives an increment of the correct sign, which obviously constitutes a weaker constraint.

In the case of the strong constraint, ruin theory (24) predicts that the fraction of surviving synapses will decay as $1/\sqrt{p}$, for p large (where p is the number of memorized patterns). With the weaker constraint, the fraction of nonvanishing synapses tends toward a constant.

We have defined a global learning index G and studied its variation as a function of p. This learning index is the difference between retrieval overlaps (a retrieval overlap is the overlap between an input pattern and its attractor) measured after learning and before learning, summed over all p patterns. Note that learning an additional pattern modifies the retrieval of previously stored patterns. Thus, the global index has to be completely recalculated after each learning event.

For p small, $G(p)$ is linear in p; for $\varepsilon \gtrsim 2.5$, the slope is the same for the *tabula rasa* condition or the non*tabula rasa* condition. Both curves are also asymptotically linear for p large (with smaller slope) and superimposed, showing a regime where the influence of the initial state has been lost. In the intermediate regime, the two curves differ. In addition, there is a difference between the cases with sign constraints (under weak or strong form) and the case without, which is clearly observed even on the smaller samples ($N = 30$).

Learning Strength and Selectivity. For comparison with previous studies, the values of ε chosen above were so large as to "burn a hole" in the energy landscape, for any input pattern. Such storage is clearly unselective. We have plotted the statistics of retrieval-overlap-after-learning q_a versus retrieval-overlap-before-learning q_b for various values of ε. Starting from $\varepsilon = 0$, for which the curve is obviously along the diagonal $q_a = q_b$, there is a range of values of ε for which marked fluctuations in retrieval quality are observed, before the hole burning regime sets in, with $q_a = 1$.

These results prove the existence of a diversity and an incipient selectivity. Note that, in these simulations as in earlier studies (10, 14, 16, 17), the learned configurations are the input patterns, because no relaxation effects are taken into account. The selectivity in the learning process, resulting from the existence of an initial structured energy landscape, will be enhanced by averaging over time. A learned configuration will then be intermediate between an input pattern

151

and its attractor, and the total amount of synaptic modification will be larger for a matching pattern than for a nonmatching one.

Alternatives to the "Generalized Hebb Rule"

Consistent with current models of regulation of synapse efficacy inspired from the allosteric properties of the acetylcholine receptor (25), one may express the change in the efficacy of a synapse between neurons i and j as a function of the activities of the other neurons k afferent on j, as

$$\Delta T_{ij} \sim \sum_k C_{ji}^k \langle S_i S_k \rangle, \qquad [10]$$

the coefficient C_{ji}^k being determined by chemical and geometrical factors, such as the relative positions of the synapses (i, j) and (k, j) on the dendrites of neuron j. Such a general expression points to the possibility that the printing process does not stabilize with exact precision a given imposed pattern but rather introduces a shift between an input and its trace. However, at this stage, we limit ourselves to a modification of the generalized Hebb rule 3, which eliminates its most obvious flaws while keeping symmetric interactions. A simple way consists in replacing rule 5 by

$$\Delta T_{ij} = \frac{1}{4N} [3 \, \mu_i^\alpha \mu_j^\alpha + (\mu_i^\alpha + \mu_j^\alpha) - 1]. \qquad [11]$$

Then, no synaptic modification occurs if $\mu_i = \mu_j = -1$, as desired. Consequently, every neuron will not be equally stabilized after the storage of one pattern and any stored pattern will have some labile spots.

As a first step, we have looked at the consequences of learning rule 11 in comparison with the generalized Hebb rule 5, within the instructive model. The new rule has been found to affect the retrieval quality of the Hopfield model significantly. The reduction of the performances is comparable in magnitude to the effect of withdrawing the *tabula rasa* hypothesis (with generalized Hebb rule and without synaptic sign constraints) as described above.

Conclusions

Learning by selection is a generalization to the development of neuronal networks (3, 6) and to higher brain functions (4, 5, 8) of the selectionist (or Darwinist) mechanisms that have already been successfully applied to the evolution of species and antibody biosynthesis (2, 19). The spin glass model described here creates an additional bridge between statistical mechanics and theoretical biology and may offer original theoretical "tools" to quantitatively treat the neuronal bases of highly integrated brain processes. At this stage the model contains a severe restriction in scope due to its limitation to static memory patterns (time sequences and synchronicity effects are beyond present investigation).

One major neurobiological outcome of our model is the description of a memory with a hierarchical, ultrametric, structure which offers possibilities of "categorization" (11) on a rather simple basis—an initial "fringe" state of random synapses yielding a spin glass-like energy landscape and strong learning constraints at the storage level. This does not preclude, but rather complements, a hierarchical categorization at the encoding level (26) that originates, for instance, from a more innate organization of the sensory analyzers at the cortical level with multiple entries of the inputs into a

layered architecture. In this framework, our study considers the less genetically determined layers that would then receive partially precategorized inputs.

In conclusion, this learning process can be epitomized as pruning (by selection) instead of packing (by instruction). It is too early yet to predict what will be the most fruitful implementation of this model, but two ideas appear profound and worth stressing. The first idea for the physicist is that selection, par excellence, is pruning of a tree and that the spin glass supplies the tree with parsimony of genetic information. The second idea for the biologist is that random synapses in a neuronal network cannot be equated with a *tabula rasa*.

We acknowledge valuable discussions with D. Amit, E. Bienenstock, J. J. Hopfield, H. Sompolinsky, and M. Virasoro. G.T. thanks the Aspen Center for Physics where part of this work was carried out. Computations were performed on the IBM 4341 of the Centre de Calcul de l'Ecole Normale Supérieure.

1. Marler, P. & Terrace, H., eds. (1984) *The Biology of Learning* (Springer, Berlin).
2. Jerne, N. (1967) in *The Neurosciences: A Study Program*, eds. Quarton, G., Melnechuk, T. & Schmitt, F. O. (The Rockefeller Univ. Press, New York), pp. 200–208.
3. Changeux, J. P., Courrège, P. & Danchin, A. (1973) *Proc. Natl. Acad. Sci. USA* 70, 2974–2978.
4. Edelman, G. (1978) *The Mindful Brain* (MIT Press, Cambridge, MA).
5. Finkel, L. & Edelman, G. (1985) *Proc. Natl. Acad. Sci. USA* 82, 1291–1295.
6. Changeux, J. P. & Danchin, A. (1976) *Nature (London)* 264, 705–712.
7. Changeux, J. P., Heidmann, T. & Patte, P. (1984) in *The Biology of Learning*, eds. Marler, P. & Terrace, H. (Springer, Berlin), pp. 115–133.
8. Heidmann, A., Heidmann, T. & Changeux, J. P. (1984) *C.R. Acad. Sci. Ser. 2*, 299, 839–844.
9. Little, W. & Shaw, G. (1978) *Math. Biosci.* 39, 281–290.
10. Hopfield, J. J. (1982) *Proc. Natl. Acad. Sci. USA* 79, 2554–2558.
11. Mézard, M., Parisi, G., Sourlas, N., Toulouse, G. & Virasoro, M. (1984) *Phys. Rev. Lett.* 52, 1156–1159.
12. Toulouse, G. (1984) *Helv. Phys. Acta* 57, 459–469.
13. Mézard, M. & Virasoro, M. (1985) *J. Phys. (Les Ulis, Fr.)* 46, 1293–1307.
14. Peretto, P. (1984) *Biol. Cybern.* 50, 51–62.
15. Hebb, D. (1949) *The Organization of Behavior* (Wiley, New York).
16. Amit, D. J., Gutfreund, H. & Sompolinsky, H. (1985) *Phys. Rev. A* 32, 1007–1018.
17. Amit, D. J., Gutfreund, H. & Sompolinsky, H. (1985) *Phys. Rev. Lett.* 55, 1530–1533.
18. Hopfield, J. J., Feinstein, D. I. & Palmer, R. G. (1983) *Nature (London)* 304, 158–159.
19. Ninio, J. (1983) *Molecular Approaches to Evolution* (Princeton Univ. Press, Princeton, NJ).
20. Derrida, B. (1980) *Phys. Rev. Lett.* 45, 79–82.
21. Stein, D. L. & Anderson, P. W. (1984) *Proc. Natl. Acad. Sci. USA* 81, 1751–1753.
22. Toulouse, G. (1977) *Commun. Phys.* 2, 115–119.
23. Cowan, W., Fawcett, J., O'Leary, D. & Stanfield, B. (1984) *Science* 225, 1258–1265.
24. Feller, W. (1957) *An Introduction to Probability Theory and Its Applications* (Wiley, New York).
25. Heidmann, T. & Changeux, J. P. (1982) *C.R. Acad. Sci. Ser. 2* 295, 665–670.
26. Virasoro, M. (1985) in *Disordered Systems and Biological Organization*, eds. Bienenstock, E., Fogelman, F. & Weisbuch, G. (Springer, Berlin), in press.

Article 3.6

Molecular networks as a sub-neural factor of neural networks

Djuro Koruga

Molecular Machines Research Center, Faculty of Machine Engineering, University of Belgrade, 27 Marta 80, 11000 Belgrade (Yugoslavia)

(Received May 31st, 1989)
(Revision received October 4th, 1989)

We describe a new approach in the research of neural networks. This research is based on molecular networks in the neuron. If we use molecular networks as a sub-neuron factor of neural networks, it is a more realistic approach than today's concepts in this new computer technology field, because the artificial neural activity profile is similar to the profile of the action potential in the natural neuron. The molecular networks approach can be used in three technologies: neurocomputer, neurochip and molecular chip. This means that molecular networks open new fields of science and engineering called molecular-like machines and molecular machines.

Keywords: Molecular networks; Cytoskeleton; Control model; Coding.

1. Introduction

The three fields of technology, micro-electronics, advanced biotechnology and computer technology, are prime candidates to establish a new field of science and technology called information biotechnology. The first step is done in the field of computer science. Today there are a few types of neurocomputers based on artificial neural networks. The second step has already been accomplished in the research and the development of the neurochip, in laboratory conditions, on the basis of VLSI technology. The first research results in the field of molecular networks point out that the application of this approach in neural networks is possible (Koruga, 1988). Some research indicates that artificial molecular networks based on nanoelectronics, organic and biological polymers will be possible in the beginning of the 21st century (Hong, 1989, in press). In this way the third step will be accomplished with the construction of molecular machines.

During the past 30 years, interest in neural networks has generated a number of different models: binary (McCulloch-Pitts, Cianiello, Rosenblatts, . . .), linear (Widrow, Kohonen . . .), and non-linear (Hartline-Ratliff, Hodgkin-Huxley, Grossberg, Wilson-Cowan . . .) (Grossberg, 1988). The main point in our research is sub-neural activities on a molecular level in cytoskeletal networks. We consider such neuron control networks in which the neuron response depends on input signals, sub-neural activities and its interactions with other neurons. We have made a link between subneuron networks based on cytoskeleton and the control model based on the theory of automatic control (Ogata, 1970). This approach showed that the sub-neuron network based on cytoskeleton plays an important role in the control mechanism of the neural network. This first step indicates that it is necessary in the future to research neurotransmitters, second messengers (cAMP and cGMP) and cytoskeleton as a sub-neural factor of the neural network.

2. Cytoskeleton

Cytoskeletal lattices include protein polymers microtubules (MT), actin, intermediate filaments and more than 15 other proteins. The major neuron architectural elements of MT are cylindrical polymers, which also comprise cilia, mitotic spindles and other organelles. MT are intimately involved in dynamic biological activities, but mechanisms of "real time" regulation and control by MT or other cytoskeletal filaments are still completely unknown.

Of all the biological structures that participate in bioinformation molecular processes, only a small number work on such a principle that can be applied to the computer sciences. One of these rare biological structures are microtubules, self-organized organelles usually consisting of 13 subunits. These cytological structures create a network of protofilaments in the cell (neuron), similar to the way in which the neurons create a network in the brain (Figs. 1 and 2).

MT are organelles present in nearly all eucaryotic cells, composed of equimolar amounts of the two globular ($\sim 50,000$ Da) subunits, α and β tubulin, each having similar amino acid composition and a similar globular (sphere) shape.

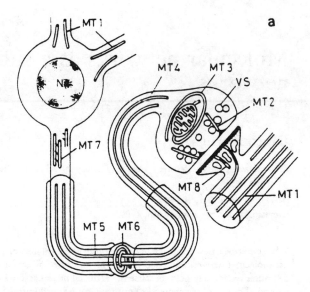

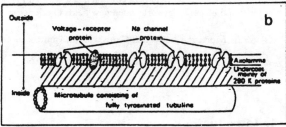

Fig. 2. Network in the neuron and its role in generating ion currents. (a) Variety of MT in neurons. MT 1, dendritic MT; MT 2, presynaptic MT, demonstrated by fixation in the presence of albumin, and contacting the synaptic membrane (VS synaptic vesicle); MT 3, helical MT surrounding a mitochondrion in a synaptic ending, mainly observed after incubation in Locke's liquid (artifact?, compared to the spiral MT of blood platelets); MT 4, axonal MT, in a non-myelinated region; MT 5, axonal MT, in a myelinated axon; MT 6, helix of MT observed in Ranvier's nodes (perhaps artifactual); MT 7, MT, close to the cell body, displaying thick inter-tubular "bridges"; MT 8, post-synaptic MT. (b) The axonal undercoat and cytoskeletal structures play a role in generating Na currents in the neuron membrane. The undercoat is constituted mainly of 260 K proteins and possibly of actins. Among cytoskeletal components of microtubules and neurofilaments, microtubules are essential in functioning Na channels. (After: Matsumoto, G., 1984, J. Theor. Biol. 107, 657.)

The subunits of tubulin molecules are assembled into long tubular structures with an average exterior diameter of ~ 24 nm, capable of changes of length by self-assembly or disassembly of their subunits; sensitive to cold, high hydrostatic pressure and several specific chemicals, such as colch-

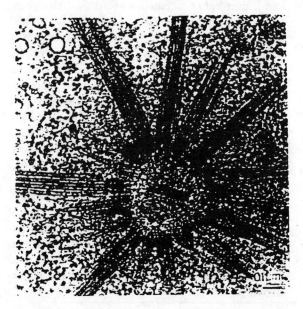

Fig. 1. MT sub-neuron network in the cell (neuron).

icine, vinblastine etc. The stable form of tubulin, both in vivo and in vitro is a dimer, and the functional unit in MT assembly is the α-β hetero-dimer. MT build with other proteins complex assemblies, such as the mitotic spindle, centrioles, cilia and flagella, axonemes and neurotubules, and they intervene in the cell shape, the motility and the mitosis, and some part of the cell functional information processing.

3. The information system of microtubules

Microtubules participate in intracellular transport, addressing, growth form and many other dynamic activities (Dustin, 1978). Some experimental results link tubulin and microtubules to bioinformation processes such as memory and learning (Mileusnić, 1980; Rose, 1977). They are remarkable because they play two distinct and separable roles: as structural materials (cytoskeleton) and as dynamic machines that operate on a molecular level. They are carbon based 3D intelligent machines which function on the nanometer size scale. Frohlich has shown that non-linear dipole excitations among molecular subunits of membranes and proteins of high dielectric strength will result in coherent oscillations (10^{-10} to 10^{-11} s fluctuations), lower frequency meta-stable states, coherent polarization waves and long-range order (Frohlich, 1968, 1970, 1975). Coherent oscillations of MT and other cytoskeletal lattice subunits may derive from intrinsic oscillations dependent on a high dipole moment and dielectric strength across the MT wall (Stebbings and Hunt, 1982; Del Guidice et al., 1982) or coupling to oscillations in membranes (Fig. 2b). Del Guidice et al. (1982) have suggested that MT and other cytoskeletal filaments entrain and focus depolarization waves by non-linear waveguide behavior.

Protein conformational coupling to coherent dipole excitation among individual subunits in biomolecular arrays conceptually resembles non-linear propagation and would apparently depend on genetic and environmental biochemical factors as well as neighbour interactions. Protein polymer neighbour interactions can be mediated by factors which include electrostatic dipole interactions, conformational states, binding of water, ions, MAPs, phosphate nucleotides and associated proteins, intrinsic subunit factors. Net effects of these influences could alter oscillatory phases of particular subunits in coherent biomolecular arrays, possibly resulting in dynamic patterns, polarization waves and long-range order. Dynamic and stable patterns of dipole excitation and conformational states in MT could have direct, profound effects on regulation and organization of cellular processes. Self-organizing patterns and information processing based on neighbour interactions at discrete time intervals among lattice subunit states have been described and are defined as cellular automata (von Neumann, 1966; Gardner, 1971; Hameroff, 1987). Coherent oscillations in tubulin dimer subunits whose phases at discrete time intervals depend on lattice neighbour interactions may be considered as a molecular information machine model of dynamic biological organization. If MT are primary information processors, then their subunits should be arranged in lattice by sphere packing derived from information coding laws.

Symmetry properties of Oh ($\bar{6}/4$) group was used as a starting point of investigation. This symmetry group possesses both cubic and hexagonal packing characteristics. In this symmetry group there are divided information coding laws which might be explained by a 48-dimensional space where face-centered-packing is realized (Leech, 1964, 1971). Hexagonal packing of protein monomers independent of the Oh ($\bar{6}/4$) symmetry group has been used to explain the form patterns of viruses, flagella, and MT (Erickson, 1973). Since hexagonal packing and face-centered-cubic packing have equal density, we use both to explain MT organization as a molecular information system.

Let face-centered-cubic packing of spheres be in the volume of a 48-dimensional sphere of unit radius, and let the normalized packing density depend on the packing dimension (Sloane, 1984). In that case, the normalized density is $D = \log_2 D + n(24 - n)/96$. Figure 3 shows the value of D for laminated lattice packing. Hexagonal packing may

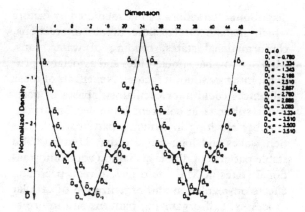

Fig. 3. The value of normalized density (D) of the packing depends on the dimension in which the packing is done. Since packing is constructed from codes for the digital transmission of information, dimensions 11, 12 and 13 are optimal for information processing.

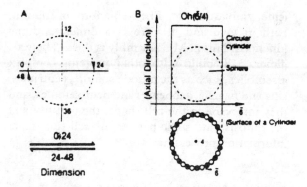

Fig. 4. (A) The distribution dimensions on the circumference of the circle leads to the symmetry (0-24, 24-28) as in Fig. 3. (B) Symmetry group Oh ($\bar{6}/4$) is self-dual because it possesses cubic and hexagonal properties.

be used under fixing conditions. This is possible if centers of spheres lie on the surface of a cylinder (with radius equal to the 48-dimensional unit sphere) and if (and only if) the sphere value in the axial direction (lattice) of the cylinder is by order of sphere packing the same as the dimension in which the face-centered-cubic packing is done. Thus each sphere on the circumference of the cylindrical circle will represent one dimension of space in which the face-centered-cubic packing was done.

Under these conditions packing on the cylindrical surface is hexagonal. Because the $\bar{6}$-fold symmetry axis of Oh group is inverse, there must be two kinds of spheres ("white" and "black") on the cylinder surface, linked so that they have the dimension value ("b" − "w" = n) in which the face-centered-cubic packing is done. Hexagonal packing on the cylinder surface leads to "screw symmetry". Figure 5 shows solution for packing of 13 spheres (Koruga, 1986).

Maximal normalized density ($\bar{D}$) has 11, 12 or 13 spheres (Fig. 3). Since these packings are constructed from codes for the digital transmission of information, this means that this number of spheres whose centers lie on the circumference of a circle is optimal for information processing (Fig. 4). Although the number of spheres 11 and 13 are optimal, microtubules can

contain from 8 to 18 protofilaments. This is possible because by the symmetry theory, this number of spheres maximize the value of normalized density (Fig. 3).

Further, Fig. 5 shows that if 13 spheres are on the surface of a circular cylinder, the distance between the spheres in order of packing will be 5. Sphere indexes in the axial direction of dimers ("white" and "black") must be 13 because each dimer represents the dimension of face-centered-cubic packing. Having the information theory in

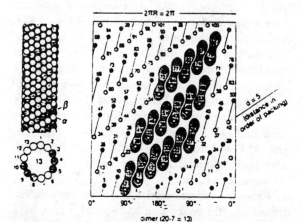

Fig. 5. The sphere indices are results of hexagonal packing of 13 spheres on the surface of the circular cylinder. The protofilament as a cylinder can be from 100 nm to 1 m long in nerves. Thus the protofilaments (left) make sub-neural networks in neurons create a network in the brain like neurons.

156

mind, this means that arrangement of "white" and "black" spheres corresponds to the binary code of length $n = 13$ and distance $d = 5$.

MT are comprised of α ("white") and β ("black") tubulin subunits which constitute from 8 to 16 protofilaments with screw symmetry. Screw symmetry in hexagonal packing determines distances among spheres and implies that MT possess all elements of a coding system. From the coding theory it is known that a code of length $n = 13$ and distance $d = 5$ is one of the best known binary error-correcting codes with 64 codewords (MacWilliams and Sloane, 1977). The latent bioinformation K code has been identified (Koruga, 1986) and in that way shows that microtubules possess capabilities of the molecular information machine.

With hexagonal packing, seven different sphere packing arrangements of 13 subunits are possible (Erickson, 1973). However, the face-centered-cubic packing allows only three different packing arrangements of 13 subunits. By Oh $(\overline{6}/4)$ symmetry group and the information theory, some microtubules of 13 subunits possess information properties but others do not. K_1 packing is one of three packing arrangements of 13 subunits which possess information properties.

Code K_1 is a result of the hexagonal property of the Oh $(\overline{6}/4)$ symmetry group but its cubic property has also been used in the information theory. Since the density of packing in the 48-dimensional space is symmetrical (Figs. 3,4) the analagous symmetry group which derives the same law of a dense packing of spheres is 24-dimensional. This means that on the surface of a circular cylinder in axial direction, there must be a code of length 24 monomer subunits (12 dimers). The coding theory states that binary information must be transformed into a new code more fit for transmission. If the coding efficiency is used as a criterion of transmission, then 6-binary dimers of the K_1 code must be coded to give a 4-dimer ternary sequence of the K_1^* code (Catchpole, 1975). As the K_1^* code should have length $n = 24$ in the axial direction of the circular cylinder, from Fig. 5 it is possible to write K_1^* [24,3^4,13]. This code may result from interaction between 24 tubulin monomers and HMW proteins. Under the influence of Ca^{2+}-calmodulin binary dimers of the K_1 code give dimers ternary sequence of the K_1 code. In this way, K_1 and K_1^* codes which result from the property of the Oh $(\overline{6}/4)$ symmetry group lead to a K_1^{**} (B^6T^4) transmission code which may combine with ATP, GTP, cAMP, cGMP and ions for intelligent intracellular dynamic and organizational activities.

4. Microtubules as a sub-neural factor of neural network

Having in mind that we have found that the microtubules' structure is optimal for information processing on a sub-neural level, we believe that non-linear control networks in which the neuron response depends on input signal, sub-neural activities, and its interactions with other neurons. Thus microtubules play an important role in neural networks as a sub-neuron factor of neuron activities, such as memory and learning. Here we note that such a control model has already been used for response analysis of the vertebrate retina (Oguztoreli, 1982, 1986), but we believe that it is a better example for explanation of the molecular network in the neuron.

Having this in mind, the neural control networks model based on microtubules may exist in the form:

$$a_{i0}^{-1}\dot{X}(t) + X_i(t) = NL\left\{f_i + \sum_{j=1}^{n} C_{ij}X_j(t - \sigma_{ij})\right.$$
$$\left. + \sum_{k=1}^{m} b_{ij}\int_{0}^{t} X_i(\tau)e^{-a_{ik}(t-\tau)}d\tau\right\}$$

where t = time, n = the number of neurons in the network, m = the number of MT in the sub-neuron network, f_i = the external input to the ith neuron at time t, $X_i(t)$ = the activity function, a_{i0} = the constant rate characterized by the fact that the stop charge input to the ith neuron produced an exponential approach from the initial value $X_i(0)$ to a steady-state firing rate X_i with a rate constant a_{i0}, b_{ik} = inhibition factor for the ith MT in case $b_{ik} < 0$, excitation factor for the ith MT in case $b_{ik} > 0$, C_{ik} = the interaction coeffi-

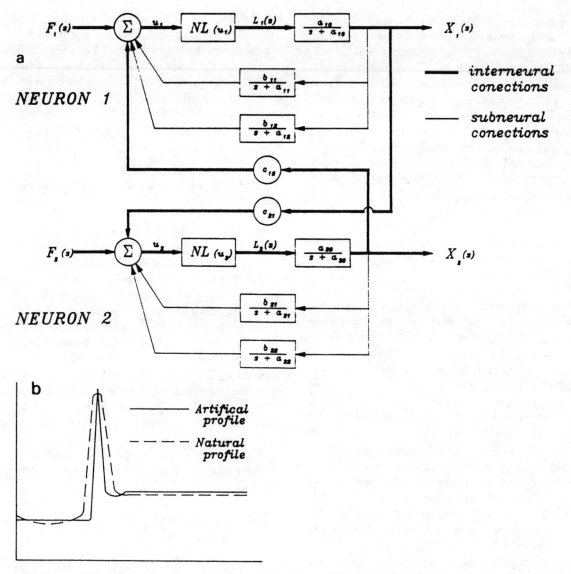

a

NEURON 1

interneural conections

subneural conections

NEURON 2

b

— Artifical profile

- - - Natural profile

Fig. 6. Neural activity profile with underdamped response of a first order neuron whose structure is characterized by $a_{io} = 100$, $a_{i1} = 10$, $b_{i1} = -315.62$. For $f_{io} = 4.926$ it is $\xi_{io} = 0.2$ and $g_i = 0.16$ (Oguztoreli, 1986). This profile is very similar to the neural activity of the ion's current where MT play an important role (see Fig. 2b).

cient ith neuron jth neuron, $\sigma_{ij} =$ the time lag occurring in the transfer of the activity of the jth neuron to the ith neuron, and NL is the non-linear element $1/(1 + e^{-u})$.

From the control theory point of view (Ogata, 1970) it is possible to find transfer functions from this equation. The frequency analysis in this case shows that the system which represents this model is most sensitive to resonant frequency ω_r

(Oguztoreli, 1986). The equation ω_r for $m = 2$ is:

$$\omega_r = \frac{a_{i0}a_{i1}a_{i2} + qa_{i0}(a_{i1}b_{i2} + a_{i2}b_{i1})^{1/2}}{a_{i0} + a_{i1} + a_{i2}}$$

As we can see in this equation there are coefficients b_{i1} and b_{i2} which in our molecular network represents MT. This means that MT play a role in the control frequency of neural networks at the

158

same time the neural activity profile (Fig. 6) depends on coefficients b_{ik}. This profile is very similar to the ion current profile in neurobiology. As MT play a direct role in generating ion currents (Fig. 2b) that means that our model of molecular networks based on MT (Koruga, 1984) as a sub-neural factor of neural networks opens a biophysical and engineering approach to the research of neural networks.

5. Conclusion

(1) The symmetry theory and MT structure lead to the conclusion that the packing of tubulin subunits is equal to information coding. This means that MT possess code systems which can provide in the neuron dynamic information activities.

(2) If we use the sub-neuron network based on MT as part of the neuron network it is a more realistic approach to functions such as learning and intelligence than if we use today's concept of neuron networks.

(3) If we put into the neural network model a sub-neuron factor of neuron activities based on MT, the neural activity profile is similar to the profile of action potential. The sub-neuron factor also plays an important role in the control mechanism of neural networks in this case.

(4) From these investigations emerge that MT activities are strongly cooperative with action potential in the neuron.

(5) The molecular networks approach opens new fields of science and engineering called molecular-like machines and molecular machines.

References

Catchpole, R.J., 1975, Efficient ternary transmission codes. Electron. Lett. 11, 482—484.

Del Guidice, E., Doglia, S. and Milani, M., 1982, Self-focusing of Frohlich waves and cytoskeletal dynamics. Phys. Lett. 90A, 104.

Dustin, P., 1978, Microtubules (Springer-Verlag, Berlin, New York).

Erickson, R.O., 1973, Tubular packing of spheres in biological fine structure. Science 181, 705—716.

Frohlich, H., 1968, Long range coherence and energy storage in biological systems. Int. J. Quant. Chem. II, 641.

Frohlich, H., 1970, Long-range coherence and the action of enzymes. Nature 228, 1093.

Frohlich, H., 1975, The extraordinary dielectric properties of biological materials and the action of enzymes. Proc. Natl. Acad. Sci. 72, 4211.

Gardner, M., 1971, Mathematical games. Sci. Am. 224, 112.

Grossberg, S., 1988, Nonlinear neural networks: principles, mechanisms and architectures. Neural Networks 1, 17—61.

Hameroff, S.R., 1987, Ultimate Computing: Biomolecular Consciousness and Nanotechnology (North-Holland, Amsterdam).

Hong, F., 1989, Molecular Electronics and Biocomputers (Pergamon Press), in press.

Koruga, D.J., 1984, Qi Engineering (Poslovna politka, Beograd) (in Serbo-Croation).

Koruga, D.J., 1986, Microtubular screw symmetry: packing of spheres as a latent bioinformation code. Ann. NY Acad. Sci. 466, 953.

Koruga, D.J., 1988, Sub-neural learning networks. Neural Networks 1, 263.

Leech, J., 1964, Some sphere packing in higher space. Can. J. Math. 16, 657—682.

Leech, J. and Sloane, N.J.A., 1971, Sphere packings and error-correcting codes. Can. J. Math. 4, 718—745.

MacWilliams, F.J. and Sloane, N.J., 1977, The Theory of Error-Correcting Codes: 674 (North-Holland, Amsterdam).

Mileusnić, R., et al., 1980, Learning and chick brain tubulin. J. Neurochem. 34, 1007.

Ogata, K., 1970, Modern Control Engineering (Prentice Hall, Englewood Cliffs, NJ).

Oguztoreli, M.N., 1982, Response analysis of vertebrate retina. Biol. Cybernet. 44, 1—8.

Oguztoreli, M.N., Steil, G.M. and Caelli, T.M., 1986, Control mechanisms of a neural network. Biol. Cybernet. 54, 21.

Rose, S.P.R., 1977, Early visual experience, learning and neurochemical plasticity in the rat and the chick. Philos. Trans. R. Soc. London B. 278—307.

Sloane, N.J.A., 1984, The packing of spheres. Sci. Am. 250, 116—125.

Stebbings, H. and Hunt, C., 1982, The nature of the clear zone around microtubules. Cell Tissue Res. 227—609.

von Neumann, J., 1966, Collected Works, A.H. Tareb (ed.), 5, 288.

Wolfram, S., 1982, Statistical mechanics in cellular automata. Caltech preprint Calt, 68—915.

Part 4
Visual Neurophysiology: Models and Motivations

Recent advances in the understanding of the mammalian visual physiology have motivated computer scientists and systems engineers to develop new mathematical models and architectures of artificial vision for applications to robotic systems in space, manufacturing, and health sciences.

OVER the past few decades, advances in the physiology of biological vision has spurred the interest of computer scientists and system engineers to explore the field of neurovision. Biology has provided the basic motivation in the field. Recent mathematical models and architectures of neuro-vision systems are, therefore, nothing but the simplification, extension, and generalization of what is found in mammalian visual systems.

In Part Four, we present six articles that have appeared in the literature over the last decade and a half, which provide an overview of some important research in the field of visual neurophysiology. This work deals with the information processing aspects of the various neuronal layers in a biological visual pathway: retina, lateral geniculate nucleus (LGN), primary visual cortex, and high cortical regions in the brain. The general focus of these research articles is to enable the reader to develop a basic understanding of the visual neurophysiology. This introduction will lead us toward the development of the mathematical morphology and computational architectures used by the neuro-vision systems described in the following parts. Advances in the field of visual neurophysiology and morphology of biological vision stand at an exciting threshold, analogous, perhaps, to that occupied by physics at the turn of the century. These articles provide unprecedented motivation and insights into visual functions from the retina to the visual cortex.

The first three articles deal with the general aspects of the biological vision system. In article (4.1), D. Hubel and T. Wiesel postulate a functional architecture that may underlie the processing of sensory information in the cortex. In article (4.2), M. Livingstone and D. Hubel provide some physiological perspectives on the perception of form, color, and movement. R. E. Kronauer and Y. Y. Zeevi provide an insight into the extensive processing and reorganization of visual information as it flows through the early stages of the visual

pathway prior to the higher stages of pattern recognition, in article (4.3).

In the second group of articles, we present three articles that deal with the processing of images in the primary visual cortex and the high cortical regions in the brain. In particular, article (4.4), authored by I. A. Rybak, N. A. Shevtsova, L. N. Podladchikova, and A. V. Golovan of the Institute of Neurocybernetics at Rostov State University in the former USSR, shows the development of a neuronal model of an iso-orientation domain of the visual cortex. The simulation studies of this neuronal model seem to compare well with that of neurophysiological evidence obtained by the authors. This article provides some basic neurophysiological understanding and potential methodology for building a neuronal model of the visual cortex.

In article (4.5), by F. Alexandre, F. Guyot, J.-P. Haton, and Y. Burnod, a neuronal model of the cortical column in the visual cortex is presented. The authors use this model in tasks such as character recognition and speech recognition.

Finally, A. B. Watson and A. J. Ahumada present their views about the representation of visual information as it moves from the retina to the primary visual cortex, in article (4.6). Although we lack comprehensive knowledge about the biological visual system, it has been observed that in the early stages of visual information processing (that is, at the retinal level) the receptive fields are homogenous and, in frequency terms, provide a broad bandwidth for the visual information received from the photoreceptors. In the cortex, the receptive fields are narrow-band and direction-oriented. These cortical receptive fields may differ markedly from one another in their orientation, size, bandwidth, and peak frequency. This structure implies that the retina has a homogenous and simple representation, whereas the cortex has multiple representations generated by distinct neural populations that respond to differences in orientation and spatial frequency.

This collection of articles will provide the readers with some appreciation for the biological visual pathway from the retina to the cortex. In the next part, we discuss some of the mathematical morphology of biological vision processes.

Further Reading

[1] M. A. Arbib, *The Metaphorical Brain*. New York: John Wiley & Sons, 1972.

[2] M. A. Arbib and A. R. Hanson, Eds., *Vision, Brain, and Cooperative Computation*. Cambridge, MA: MIT Press, 1987.

[3] J. R. Bergen, H. R. Wilson, and J. D. Cowan, "Further evidence for four mechanisms mediating vision at threshold: Sensitivities to complex gratings and aperiodic stimuli," *J. Op. Soc. Amer.*, vol. 69, no. 11, pp. 1580–1587, 1979.

[4] C. Blakemore, R. H. S. Carpenter, and M. A. Georgeson, "Lateral inhibition between orientation detectors in the human visual system," *Nature*, vol. 228, pp. 37–39, 1970.

[5] O. J. Braddik, "Low-level and high-level processes in apparent motion," *Phil. Trans. Roy. Soc. London*, vol. B 290, pp. 137–151, 1980.

[6] V. Braitenberg and C. Braitenberg, "Geometry of orientation columns in the visual cortex," *Biol. Cybern.*, vol. 33, pp. 179–186, 1979.

[7] F. W. Campbell, "The human eye as an optical filter," *Proc. IEEE*, vol. 56, no. 6, pp. 1009–1014, 1968.

[8] J. Curlander and V. Marmarelis, "Processing of visual information in the distal neurons of the vertebrate retina," *IEEE Trans. Syst., Man, Cybern.*, vol. 13, no. 5, pp. 934–943, 1983.

[9] H. Davson, *Physiology of the Eye*. New York: Academic Press, 1980.

[10] D. C. Deno, E. L. Keller, and W. F. Crandall, "Dynamical neural network organization of the visual pursuit system," *IEEE Trans. Biomed. Engi.*, vol. 36, no. 1, pp. 85–92, 1989.

[11] A. Gottschalk and G. Buchsbaum, "Information theoretic aspects of color signal processing in the visual system," *IEEE Trans. Syst., Man, Cybern.*, vol. SMC-13, no. 5, pp. 864–873, 1983.

[12] L. H. Hurvich, *Colour Vision*. Sunderland, MA: Sinauer Assoc., 1981.

[13] M. E. Jernigan and R. W. Wardell, "Does the eye contain optimal edge detection mechanisms?" *IEEE Trans. Syst., Man, Cybern.*, vol. 11, no. 6, pp. 441–444, 1981.

[14] G. Krone, H. Mallot, G. Palm, and A. Schuz, "Spatio-temporal receptive fields: A dynamical model derived from cortical architectonics," *Proc. Roy. Soc. London*, vol. B 226, pp. 421–444, 1986.

[15] P. Lennie, "Perceptual signs of parallel pathways," *Phil. Trans. Roy. Soc. London*, vol. B 290, pp. 23–57, 1980.

[16] J. Y. Lettvin, H. R. Maturana, W. S. McCulloch, and W. H. Pitts, "What the frog's eye tells the frog's brain," *Proc. IRE* Oct., pp. 1940–1951, 1959.

[17] M. D. Levine, *Vision in Man and Machine*. New York: McGraw-Hill, 1985.

[18] A. J. Maren, C. T. Harston, and R. M. Pap, *Handbook of Neural Computing*. San Diego: Academic Press, 1990.

[19] D. Marr, *Vision*. San Francisco: W.H. Freeman and Co., 1982.

[20] R. H. Masland, "The functional architecture of the retina," *Sci. Amer.*, vol. 255, no. 6, pp. 102–111, 1986.

[21] T. Nagano and S. Miyajima, "A neural network model for the development process of hypercomplex cells," *IEEE Trans. Syst., Man, Cybern.*, vol. SMC-13, no. 5, pp. 847–850, 1983.

[22] M. N. Oguztoreli, "Modeling and simulation of vertebrate primary visual system: Basic network," *IEEE Trans. Syst., Man, Cybern.*, vol. SMC-13, no. 5, pp. 766–781, 1983.

[23] M. A. Paradiso, "A theory for the use of visual orientation information which exploits the columnar structure of striate cortex," *Biol. Cybern.*, vol. 58, pp. 35–49, 1988.

[24] W. Pitts and W. S. McCulloch, "How we know universals: The perception of auditory and visual forms," *Bull. Math. Biophys.*, vol. 9, pp. 127–147, 1947.

[25] J. Richter and S. Ullman, "Non-linearities in cortical simple cells and the possible detection of zero crossings," *Biol. Cybern.*, vol. 53, pp. 195–202, 1986.

[26] J. Richter and S. Ullman, "A model for the temporal organization of X- and Y-type receptive fields in the primate retina," *Biol. Cybern.*, vol. 43, pp. 127–145, 1982.

[27] E. L. Schwartz, "A quantitative model of the functional architecture of human striate cortex with application to visual illusion and cortical texture analysis," *Biol. Cybern.*, vol. 37, pp. 63–76, 1980.

[28] R. Siminoff, "Systems analysis of an analog model of the vertebrate cone retina," *IEEE Trans. Syst., Man, Cybern.*, vol. SMC-13, no. 5, pp. 1021–1028, 1983.

[29] R. Siminoff, "A cybernetic model of the vertebrate cone retina," *Vision Res.*, vol. 21, pp. 1537–1539, 1981.

[30] A. Takeuchi and S. Amari, "Formation of topographic maps and columnar microstructures in nerve fields," *Biol. Cybern.*, vol. 35, pp. 63–72, 1979.

[31] V. Torre and T. Poggio, "A synaptic mechanism possibly underlying directional selectivity to motion," *Proc. Roy. Soc. London*, vol. B 202, pp. 409–416, 1978.

[32] F. L. van Nes, J. J. Koenderink, H. Nas, and M. A. Bouman, "Spatiotemporal modulation transfer in the human eye," *J. Opt. Soc. Amer.*, vol. 57, no. 9, pp. 1082–1088, 1959.

[33] C. von der Malsburg and J. D. Cowan, "Outline of a theory for the ontogenesis of iso-orientation domains in visual cortex," *Biol. Cybern.*, vol. 45, pp. 49–56, 1982.

[34] C. von der Malsburg, "Self-organization of orientation sensitive cells in the striate cortex," *Kybernetik*, vol. 14, pp. 85–100, 1973.

[35] A. B. Watson, "The cortex transform: Rapid computation of simulated neural images," *Comput. Vision, Graphics, Image Process.*, vol. 39, pp. 311–327, 1987.

[36] H. R. Wilson and J. R. Bergen, "A four mechanism model for threshold spatial vision," *Vision Res.*, vol. 19, pp. 19–32, 1979.

Brain Mechanisms of Vision

A functional architecture that may underlie processing of sensory information in the cortex is revealed by studies of the activity and the organization in space of neurons in the primary visual cortex

by David H. Hubel and Torsten N. Wiesel

Viewed as a kind of invention by evolution, the cerebral cortex must be one of the great success stories in the history of living things. In vertebrates lower than mammals the cerebral cortex is minuscule, if it can be said to exist at all. Suddenly impressive in the lowest mammals, it begins to dominate the brain in carnivores, and it increases explosively in primates; in man it almost completely envelops the rest of the brain, tending to obscure the other parts. The degree to which an animal depends on an organ is an index of the organ's importance that is even more convincing than size, and dependence on the cortex has increased rapidly as mammals have evolved. A mouse without a cortex appears fairly normal, at least to casual inspection; a man without a cortex is almost a vegetable, speechless, sightless, senseless.

Understanding of this large and indispensable organ is still woefully deficient. This is partly because it is very complex, not only structurally but also in its functions, and partly because neurobiologists' intuitions about the functions have so often been wrong. The outlook is changing, however, as techniques improve and as investigators learn how to deal with the huge numbers of intricately connected neurons that are the basic elements of the cortex, with the impulses they carry and with the synapses that connect them. In this article we hope to sketch the present state of knowledge of one subdivision of the cortex: the primary visual cortex (also known as the striate cortex or area 17), the most elementary of the cortical regions concerned with vision. That will necessarily lead us into the related subject of visual perception, since the workings of an organ cannot easily be separated from its biological purpose.

The cerebral cortex, a highly folded plate of neural tissue about two mil-limeters thick, is an outermost crust wrapped over the top of, and to some extent tucked under, the cerebral hemispheres. In man its total area, if it were spread out, would be about 1.5 square feet. (In a 1963 article in *Scientific American* one of us gave the area as 20 square feet and was quickly corrected by a neuroanatomist friend in Toronto, who said he thought it was 1.5 square feet—"at least that is what Canadians have.") The folding is presumably mainly the result of such an unlikely structure's having to be packed into a box the size of the skull.

A casual glance at cortical tissue under a microscope shows vast numbers of neurons: about 10^5 (100,000) for each square millimeter of surface, suggesting that the cortex as a whole has some 10^{10} (10 billion) neurons. The cell bodies are arranged in half a dozen layers that are alternately cell-sparse and cell-rich. In contrast to these marked changes in cell density in successive layers at different depths in the cortex there is marked uniformity from place to place in the plane of any given layer and in any direction within that plane. The cortex is morphologically rather uniform in two of its dimensions.

One of the first great insights about cortical organization came late in the 19th century, when it was gradually realized that this rather uniform plate of tissue is subdivided into a number of different regions that have very different functions. The evidence came from clinical, physiological and anatomical sources. It was noted that a brain injury, depending on its location, could cause paralysis or blindness or numbness or speech loss; the blindness could be total or limited to half or less of the visual world, and the numbness could involve one limb or a few fingers. The consistency of the relation between a given defect and the location of the lesion gradually led to a charting of the most obvious of these specialized regions, the visual, auditory, somatic sensory (body sensation), speech and motor regions.

In many cases a close look with a microscope at cortex stained for cell bodies showed that in spite of the relative uniformity there were structural variations, particularly in the layering pattern, that correlated well with the clinically defined subdivisions. Additional confirmation came from observations of the location (at the surface of the brain) of the electrical brain waves produced when an animal was stimulated by touching the body, sounding clicks or tones in the ear or flashing light in the eye. Similarly, motor areas could be mapped by stimulating the cortex electrically and noting what part of the animal's body moved.

This systematic mapping of the cortex soon led to a fundamental realization: most of the sensory and motor areas contained systematic two-dimensional maps of the world they represented. Destroying a particular small region of cortex could lead to paralysis of one arm; a similar lesion in another small region led to numbness of one hand or of the upper lip, or blindness in one small part of the visual world; if electrodes were placed on an animal's cortex, touching one limb produced a correspondingly localized series of electric potentials. Clearly the body was systematically mapped onto the somatic sensory and motor areas; the visual world was mapped onto the primary visual cortex, an area on the occipital lobe that in man and in the macaque monkey (the animal in which our investigations have mainly been conducted) covers about 15 square centimeters.

In the primary visual cortex the map is uncomplicated by breaks and discontinuities except for the remarkable split of the visual world down the exact middle, with the left half projected to the right cerebral cortex and the right half

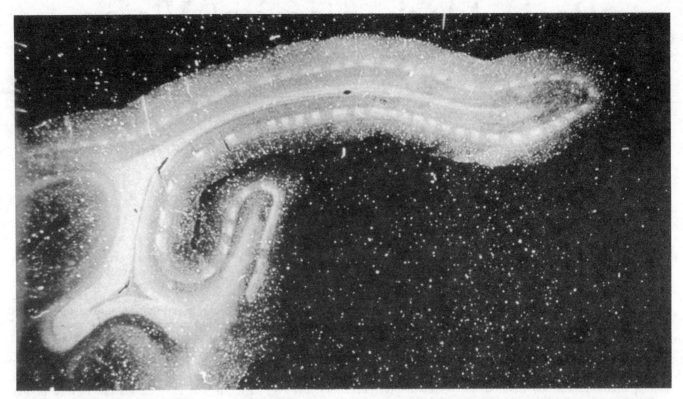

OCULAR-DOMINANCE COLUMNS, one of the two major systems that characterize the functional architecture of the primary visual cortex, are revealed as periodic bright patches in this dark-field autoradiograph of a section of macaque monkey cortex. The columns (actually curving slabs of cortex, seen here in cross section in a brain slice cut perpendicularly to the surface) are regions in which all neurons respond more actively to the right eye than to the left one; dark regions separating the bright patches are columns of left-eye prefer- ence. The autoradiograph was made by injecting a radioactively labeled amino acid into the right eye of an anesthetized animal. The amino acid was taken up by cell bodies in the retina and transported via the lateral geniculate nucleus, a way station in the brain, to cells in the cortex. A brain slice was coated with a photographic emulsion, which was exposed for several months and then developed. Exposed silver grains overlying the regions of radioactivity form the light-scattering patches that represent ocular-dominance columns.

projected to the left cortex. The map of the body is more complicated and is still perhaps not completely understood. It is nonetheless systematic, and it is similarly crossed, with the right side of the body projecting to the left hemisphere and the left side projecting to the right hemisphere. (It is worth remarking that no one has the remotest idea why there should be this amazing tendency for nervous-system pathways to cross.)

An important feature of cortical maps is their distortion. The scale of the maps varies as it does in a Mercator projection, the rule for the cortex being that the regions of highest discrimination or delicacy of function occupy relatively more cortical area. For the body surface, a millimeter of surface on the fingers, the lips or the tongue projects to more cortex than a millimeter of trunk, buttocks or back; in vision the central part of the retina has a representation some 35 times more detailed than the far peripheral part.

Important as the advances in mapping cortical projections were, they tended for some time to divert thought from the real problem of just how the brain analyzes information. It was as though the representation could be an end in itself

instead of serving a more subtle purpose—as though what the cortex did was to cater to some little green man who sat inside the head and surveyed images playing across the cortex. In the course of this article we shall show that, for vision at least, the world is represented in a far more distorted way; any little green man trying to glean information from the cortical projection would be puzzled indeed.

The first major insight into cortical organization was nonetheless the recognition of this subdivision into areas having widely different functions, with a tendency to ordered mapping. Just how many such areas there are has been a subject of wide speculation. Anatomists' estimates have on the whole been rather high—up to several hundred areas, depending on the individual worker's sensitivity to fine differences in microscopic patterns and sometimes also on his ability to fool himself. Physiologists began with lower estimates, but lately, with more powerful mapping methods, they have been revising their estimates upward. The important basic notion is that information on any given modality such as sight or sound is transmitted first to a primary cortical area and from there,

either directly or via the thalamus, to successions of higher areas. A modern guess as to the number of cortical areas might be between 50 and 100.

The second major insight into cortical organization came from the work of the anatomist Santiago Ramón y Cajal and his pupil Rafael Lorente de Nó. This was the realization that the operations the cortex performs on the information it receives are local. What that means can best be understood by considering the wiring diagram that emerged from the Golgi method used by Cajal and Lorente de Nó. In essence the wiring is simple. Sets of fibers bring information to the cortex; by the time several synapses have been traversed the influence of the input has spread vertically to all cell layers; finally several other sets of fibers carry modified messages out of the area. The detailed connections between inputs and outputs differ from one area to the next, but within a given area they seem to be rather stereotyped. What is common to all regions is the local nature of the wiring. The information carried into the cortex by a single fiber can in principle make itself felt through the entire thickness in

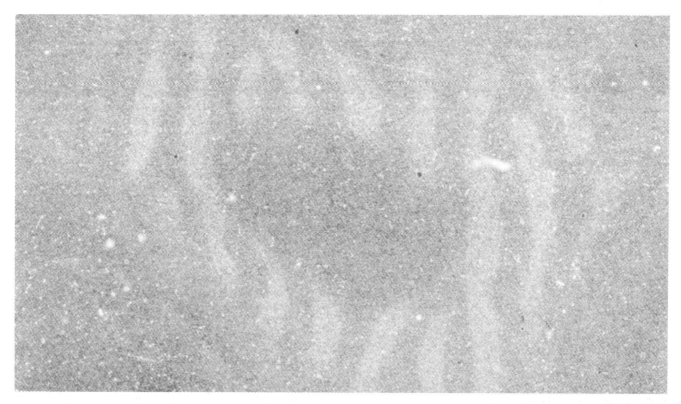

DOMINANCE PATTERN is seen face on in an axonal-transport autoradiograph of a brain section parallel, rather than perpendicular, to the surface of the primary visual cortex. As can be seen in the autoradiograph at the top of the page, the label is brightest in one layer of the folded cortex, layer IV. This is the level at which the axons bringing visual information to the cortex terminate and where the label therefore accumulates. This section was cut in a plane tangential to the dome-shaped surface of the cortex and just below layer IV, which therefore appears as a ring of roughly parallel bright bands. These are the radioactively labeled ocular-dominance regions, which are now seen from above instead of edge on. The actual width of the ocular-dominance regions is typically about .4 millimeter.

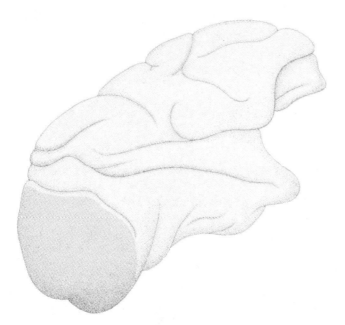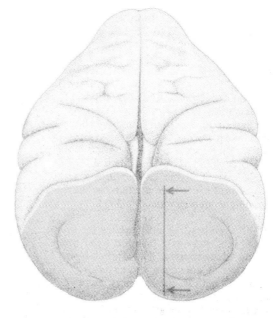

PRIMARY VISUAL CORTEX, also known as the striate cortex or area 17, is a region of the cerebral cortex: a layered plate of neurons that envelops the primate brain. In the macaque brain, seen here from the side (left) and from above and behind (right), the primary visual cortex (darker areas) occupies most of the exposed surface of the two occipital lobes. It also curves around the medial surface between the two cerebral hemispheres. It continues in a complex fold underneath the convex outer surface, as is shown in a parasagittal section (see top illustration on opposite page) that was cut along the colored line and is viewed in the direction indicated by the arrows.

165

about three or four synapses, whereas the lateral spread, produced by branching trees of axons and dendrites, is limited for all practical purposes to a few millimeters, a small proportion of the vast extent of the cortex.

The implications of this are far-reaching. Whatever any given region of the cortex does, it does locally. At stages where there is any kind of detailed, systematic topographical mapping the analysis must be piecemeal. For example, in the somatic sensory cortex the messages concerning one finger can be combined and compared with an input from elsewhere on that same finger or with input from a neighboring finger, but they can hardly be combined with the influence from the trunk or from a foot. The same applies to the visual world. Given the detailed order of the input to the primary visual cortex, there is no likelihood that the region will do anything to correlate information coming in from both far above and far below the horizon, or from both the left and the right part of the visual scene. It follows that this cannot by any stretch of the imagination be the place where actual perception is enshrined. Whatever these cortical areas are doing, it must be some kind of local analysis of the sensory world. One can only assume that as the information on vision or touch or sound is relayed from one cortical area to the next the map becomes progressively more blurred and the information carried more abstract.

Even though the Golgi-method studies of the early 1900's made it clear that the cortex must perform local analyses, it was half a century before physiologists had the least inkling of just what the analysis was in any area of the cortex. The first understanding came in the primary visual area, which is now the best-understood of any cortical region and is still the only one where the analysis and consequent transformations of information are known in any detail. After describing the main transformations that take place in the primary visual cortex we shall go on to show how increasing understanding of these cortical functions has revealed an entire world of architectural order that is otherwise inaccessible to observation.

We can best begin by tracing the visual path in a primate from the retina to the cortex. The output from each eye is conveyed to the brain by about a million nerve fibers bundled together in the optic nerve. These fibers are the axons of the ganglion cells of the retina. The messages from the light-sensitive elements, the rods and cones, have already traversed from two to four synapses and have involved four other types of retinal cells before they arrive at the ganglion cells, and a certain amount of sophisticated analysis of the information has already taken place.

A large fraction of the optic-nerve fibers pass uninterrupted to two nests of cells deep in the brain called the lateral geniculate nuclei, where they make synapses. The lateral geniculate cells in turn send their axons directly to the primary visual cortex. From there, after several synapses, the messages are sent to a number of further destinations: neighboring cortical areas and also several targets deep in the brain. One contingent even projects back to the lateral geniculate bodies; the function of this feedback path is not known. The main point for the moment is that the primary visual cortex is in no sense the end of the visual path. It is just one stage, probably an early one in terms of the degree of abstraction of the information it handles.

As a result of the partial crossing of the optic nerves in the optic chiasm, the geniculate and the cortex on the left side are connected to the two left half retinas and are therefore concerned with the right half of the visual scene, and the converse is the case for the right geniculate and the right cortex. Each geniculate and each cortex receives input from both eyes, and each is concerned with the opposite half of the visual world.

To examine the workings of this visual pathway our strategy since the late 1950's has been (in principle) simple. Beginning, say, with the fibers of the optic nerve, we record with microelectrodes from a single nerve fiber and try to find out how we can most effectively influence the firing by stimulating the retina with light. For this one can use patterns of light of every conceivable size, shape and color, bright on a dark background or the reverse, and stationary or moving. It may take a long time, but sooner or later we satisfy ourselves that we have found the best stimulus for

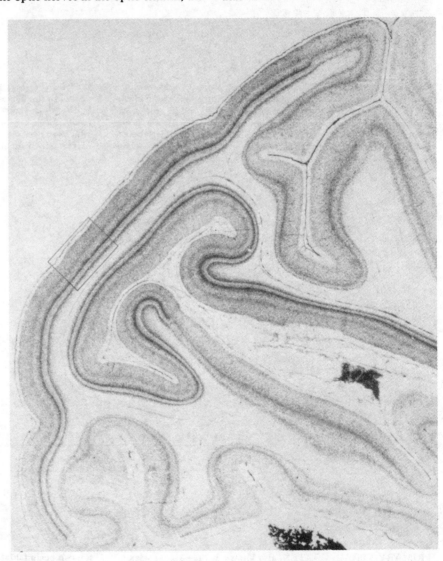

SECTION OF VISUAL CORTEX along the colored line in the illustration on the opposite page was stained by the Nissl method, which makes cell bodies but not fibers visible. The visual cortex is seen to be a continuous layered sheet of neurons about two millimeters thick. The black rectangle outlines a section like the one that is further enlarged in the illustration below.

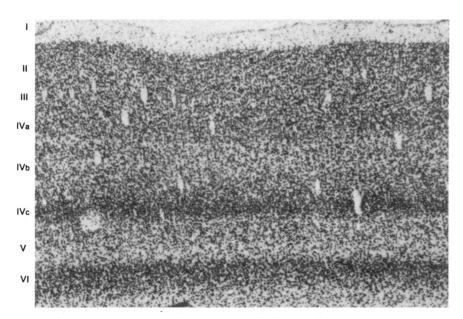

CROSS SECTION OF PRIMARY VISUAL CORTEX in the macaque, stained here by the Nissl method and enlarged about 35 diameters, shows the layered structure and gives the conventional designations of the six layers (*left*). The white gaps are sectioned blood vessels.

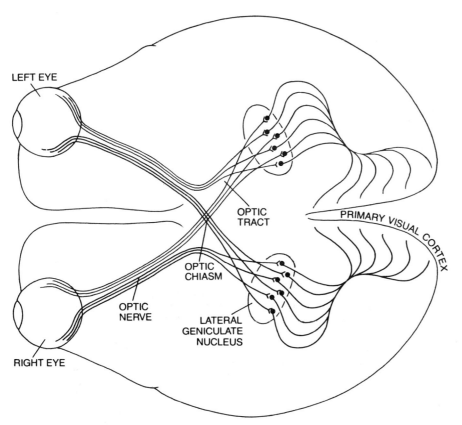

VISUAL PATHWAY is traced schematically in the human brain, seen here from below. The output from the retina is conveyed, by ganglion-cell axons bundled in the optic nerves, to the lateral geniculate nuclei; about half of the axons cross over to the opposite side of the brain, so that a representation of each half of the visual scene is projected on the geniculate of the opposite hemisphere. Neurons in the geniculates send their axons to the primary visual cortex.

the cell being tested, in this case a ganglion cell of the retina. (Sometimes we are wrong!) We note the results and then go on to another fiber. After studying a few hundred cells we may find that new types become rare. Satisfied that we know roughly how the neurons at this stage work, we proceed to the next stage (in this case the geniculate) and repeat the process. Comparison of the two sets of results can tell us something about what the geniculate does. We then go on to the next stage, the primary cortex, and repeat the procedure.

Working in this way, one finds that both a retinal ganglion cell and a geniculate cell respond best to a roughly circular spot of light of a particular size in a particular part of the visual field. The size is critical because each cell's receptive field (the patch of retinal receptor cells supplying the cell) is divided, with an excitatory center and an inhibitory surround (an "on center" cell) or exactly the reverse configuration (an "off center" cell). This is the center-surround configuration first described by Stephen W. Kuffler at the Johns Hopkins University School of Medicine in 1953. A spot exactly filling the center of an on-center cell is therefore a more effective stimulus than a larger spot that invades the inhibitory area, or than diffuse light. A line stimulus (a bar of light) is effective if it covers a large part of the center region and only a small part of the surround. Because these cells have circular symmetry they respond well to such a line stimulus whatever its orientation. To sum up, the retinal ganglion cells and the cells of the lateral geniculate—the cells supplying the input to the visual cortex—are cells with concentric, center-surround receptive fields. They are primarily concerned not with assessing levels of illumination but rather with making a comparison between the light level in one small area of the visual scene and the average illumination of the immediate surround.

The first of the two major transformations accomplished by the visual cortex is the rearrangement of incoming information so that most of its cells respond not to spots of light but to specifically oriented line segments. There is a wide variety of cell types in the cortex, some simpler and some more complex in their response properties, and one soon gains an impression of a kind of hierarchy, with simpler cells feeding more complex ones. In the monkey there is first of all a large group of cells that behave (as far as is known) just like geniculate cells: they have circularly symmetrical fields. These cells are all in the lower part of one layer, called layer IV, which is precisely the layer that receives the lion's share of the geniculate input. It makes sense that these least sophisticated cortical cells should be the ones most immediately connected to the input.

Cells outside layer IV all respond best to specifically oriented line segments. A typical cell responds only when light falls in a particular part of the visual world, but illuminating that area diffusely has little effect or none, and small spots of light are not much better. The best response is obtained when a line that has just the right tilt is flashed in the region or, in some cells, is swept across the region. The most effective orientation varies from cell to cell and is usually defined sharply enough so that a change of 10 or 20 degrees clockwise or counterclockwise reduces the response markedly or abolishes it. (It is hard to convey the precision of this discrimination. If 10 to 20 degrees sounds like a wide range, one should remember that the angle between 12 o'clock and one o'clock is 30 degrees.) A line at 90 degrees to the best orientation almost never evokes any response.

Depending on the particular cell, the stimulus may be a bright line on a dark background or the reverse, or it may be a boundary between light and dark regions. If it is a line, the thickness is likely to be important; increasing it beyond some optimal width reduces the response, just as increasing the diameter of a spot does in the case of ganglion and geniculate cells. Indeed, for a particular part of the visual field the geniculate receptive-field centers and the optimal cortical line widths are comparable.

Neurons with orientation specificity vary in their complexity. The simplest, which we call "simple" cells, behave as though they received their input directly from several cells with center-surround, circularly symmetrical fields—the type of cells found in layer IV. The response properties of these simple cells, which respond to an optimally oriented line in a narrowly defined location, can most easily be accounted for by requiring that the centers of the incoming center-surround fields all be excitatory or all be inhibitory, and that they lie along a straight line. At present we have no direct evidence for this scheme, but it is attractive because of its simplicity and because certain kinds of indirect evidence support it. According to the work of Jennifer S. Lund of the University of Washington School of Medicine, who in the past few years has done more than anyone else to advance the Golgi-stain anatomy of this cortical area, the cells in layer IV project to the layers just above, which is roughly where the simple cells are found.

The second major group of orientation-specific neurons are the far more numerous "complex" cells. They come in a number of subcategories, but their main feature is that they are less particular about the exact position of a line. Complex cells behave as though they received their input from a number of simple cells, all with the same receptive-field orientation but differing slightly in the exact location of their fields. This scheme readily explains the strong steady firing evoked in a complex cell as a line is kept in the optimal orientation and is swept across the receptive field. With the line optimally oriented many cells prefer one direction of movement to the opposite direction. Several possible circuits have been proposed to explain this behavior, but the exact mechanism is still not known.

Although there is no direct evidence that orientation-sensitive cells have anything to do with visual perception, it is certainly tempting to think they represent some early stage in the brain's analysis of visual forms. It is worth asking which cells at this early stage would be expected to be turned on by some very simple visual form, say a dark blob on a light background. Any cell whose receptive field is entirely inside or outside the boundaries of such an image will be completely unaffected by the figure's presence because cortical cells effectively ignore diffuse changes in the illumination of their entire receptive fields.

The only cells to be affected will be those whose field is cut by the borders. For the circularly symmetrical cells the ones most strongly influenced will be those whose center is grazed by a boundary (because for them the excitatory and inhibitory subdivisions are most unequally illuminated). For the orientation-specific cells the only ones to be activated will be those whose optimal orientation happens to coincide with the prevailing direction of the border. And among these the simple cells will be much more exacting than the complex ones, responding optimally only when the border falls along a line separating an excitatory and an inhibitory region. It is important to realize that this part of the cortex is operating only locally, on bits of the form; how the entire form is analyzed or handled by the brain—how this information is worked on and synthesized at later stages, if indeed it is—is still not known.

The second major function of the monkey visual cortex is to combine the inputs from the two eyes. In the lateral geniculate nuclei a neuron may respond to stimulation of the left eye or of the right one, but no cell responds to stimulation of both eyes. This may seem surprising, since each geniculate receives inputs from both eyes, but the fact is that the geniculates are constructed in a way that keeps inputs from the two eyes segregated. Each geniculate body is divided into six layers, three left-eye layers interdigitated with three right-eye ones. The opposite-side half of the visual world is mapped onto each layer (with the six maps in precise register, so that in a radial pathway traversing the six layers the receptive fields of all the cells encountered have virtually identical positions in the visual field). Since any one layer has input from only one eye, the individual cells of that layer must be monocular.

Even in the visual cortex the neurons to which the geniculate cells project directly, the circularly symmetrical cells in layer IV, are all (as far as we can tell) strictly monocular; so are all the simple cells. Only at the level of the complex cells do the paths from the two eyes converge, and even there the blending of information is incomplete and takes a special form. About half of the complex cells are monocular, in the sense that any one cell can be activated only by stimulating one eye. The rest of the cells can be influenced independently by both eyes.

If one maps the right-eye and left-eye receptive fields of a binocular cell (by stimulating first through one eye and then through the other) and compares the two fields, the fields turn out to have identical positions, levels of complexity, orientation and directional preference; everything one learns about the cell by stimulating one eye is confirmed through the other eye. There is only one exception: if first one eye and then the other are tested with identical stimuli, the two responses are usually not quantitatively identical; in many cases one eye is dominant, consistently producing a higher frequency of firing than the other eye.

From cell to cell all degrees of ocular dominance can be found, from complete monopoly by one eye through equality to exclusive control by the other eye. In the monkey the cells with a marked eye preference are somewhat commoner than the cells in which the two eyes make about equal contributions. Apparently a binocular cell in the primary visual cortex has connections to the two eyes that are qualitatively virtually identical, but the density of the two sets of connections is not necessarily the same.

It is remarkable enough that the elaborate sets of wiring that produce specificity of orientation and of direction of movement and other special properties should be present in two duplicate copies. It is perhaps even more surpris-

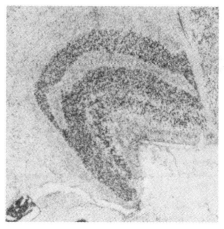

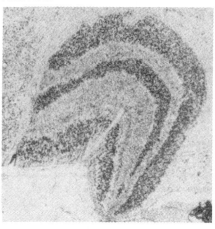

RIGHT EYE   LEFT EYE   RIGHT EYE

LATERAL GENICULATE NUCLEUS of a normal monkey (*left*) is a layered structure in which cells in layers 1, 4 and 6 (numbered from bottom to top) receive their input from the eye on the opposite side and those in layers 2, 3 and 5 receive information from the eye on the same side. The maps are in register, so that the neurons along any radius (*black line*) receive signals from the same part of the visual scene. **The layered nature of the input is demonstrated in the two geniculates of an animal that had vision in the left eye only (*two micrographs at right*): in each geniculate cells in the three layers with input from right eye have atrophied. Geniculates are enlarged 10 diameters.**

ing that all of this can be observed in a newborn animal. The wiring is mostly innate, and it presumably is genetically determined. (In one particular respect, however, some maturation of binocular wiring does take place mostly after birth.)

We now turn to a consideration of the way these cells are grouped in the cortex. Are cells with similar characteristics—complexity, receptive-field position, orientation and ocular dominance—grouped together or scattered at random? From the description so far it will be obvious that cells of like complexity tend to be grouped in layers, with the circularly symmetrical cells low in layer IV, the simple cells just above

them and the complex cells in layers II, III, V and VI. Complex cells can be further subcategorized, and the ones found in each layer are in a number of ways very different.

These differences from layer to layer take on added interest in view of the important discovery, confirmed by several physiologists and anatomists during the past few decades, that fibers projecting from particular layers of the cortex have particular destinations. For example, in the visual cortex the deepest layer, layer VI, projects mainly (perhaps only) back to the lateral geniculate body; layer V projects to the superior colliculus, a visual station in the midbrain; layers II and III send their projections to other parts of the cortex.

This relation between layer and projection site probably deserves to be ranked as a third major insight into cortical organization.

The next stimulus variable to be considered is the position of the receptive field in the visual field. In describing the lateral geniculate nucleus we pointed out that in each layer the opposite-half visual field forms an ordered topographical map. In the projection from lateral geniculate to primary visual cortex this order is preserved, producing a cortical map of the visual field. Given this ordered map it is no surprise that neighboring cells in this part of the cortex always have receptive fields that are close together; usually, in fact, they overlap. If one plunges a microelectrode

a

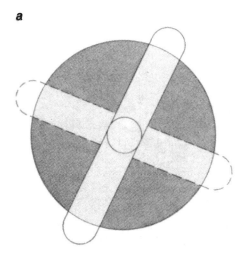

b

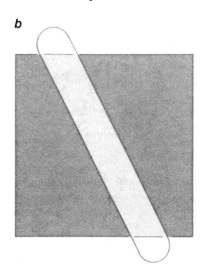

c

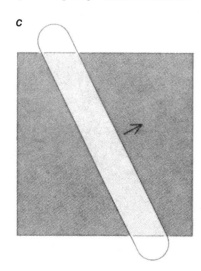

RECEPTIVE FIELDS of various cells in the visual pathway are compared. Retinal ganglion cells and neurons in the lateral geniculate nucleus have circular fields with either an excitatory center and an inhibitory surround (*a*) or the opposite arrangement. A spot of light falling on the center stimulates a response from such a cell; so does a bar of light falling on the field in any orientation, provided it falls on the center. In the visual cortex there is a hierarchy of neurons with in- **creasingly complex response properties. The cortical cells that receive signals directly from the geniculate have circularly symmetrical fields. Cortical cells farther along the pathway, however, respond only to a line stimulus in a particular orientation. A "simple" cell (*b*) responds to such a line stimulus only in a particular part of its field. A "complex" cell (*c*) responds to a precisely oriented line regardless of where it is in its field and also to one moving in a particular direction (*arrow*).**

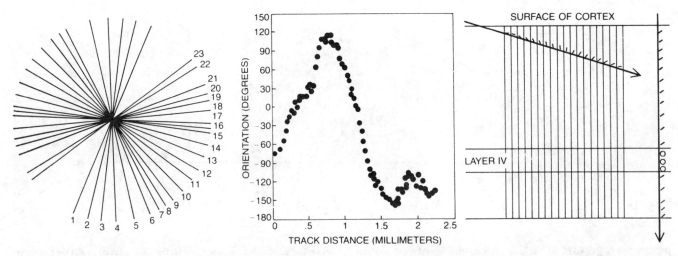

into the cortex at a right angle to the surface and records from cell after cell (as many as 100 or 200 of them) in successively deeper layers, again the receptive fields mostly overlap, with each new field heaped on all the others. The extent of the entire pile of fields is usually several times the size of any one typical field.

There is some variation in the size of these receptive fields. Some of the variation is tied to the layering: the largest fields in any penetration tend to be in layers III, V and VI. The most important variation, however, is linked to eccentricity, or the distance of a cell's receptive field from the center of gaze. The size of the fields and the extent of the associated scatter in the part of the cortex that maps the center of gaze are tiny compared to the size and amount of scatter in the part that maps the far periphery. We call the pile of superimposed fields that are mapped in a penetration beginning at any point on the cortex the "aggregate field" of that point. The size of the aggregate field is obviously a function of eccentricity.

If the electrode penetrates in an oblique direction, almost parallel to the surface, the scatter in field position from cell to cell is again evident, but now there is superimposed on the scatter

POSITIONS OF RECEPTIVE FIELDS (*numbered from 1 to 9*) of cortical neurons mapped by an electrode penetrating at roughly a right angle to the surface are essentially the same (*left*), although the fields are different sizes and there is some scatter. In an oblique penetration (*right*) from two to four cells were recorded, at .1-millimeter intervals, at each of four sites (*numbered from 1 to 4*) one millimeter apart. Each group includes various sizes and some scatter, but now there is also a systematic drift: fields of each successive group of cells are somewhat displaced.

ORIENTATION PREFERENCES of 23 neurons encountered as a microelectrode penetrated the cortex obliquely are charted (*left*); the most effective tilt of the stimulus changed steadily in a counterclockwise direction. The results of a similar experiment are plotted (*center*); in this case, however, there were several reversals in direction of rotation. The results of a large number of such experiments, together with the observation that a microelectrode penetrating the cortex perpendicularly encounters only cells that prefer the same orientation (apart from the circularly symmetrical cells in layer IV, which have no preferred orientation), suggested that the cortex is subdivided into roughly parallel slabs of tissue, with each slab, called an orientation column, containing neurons with like orientation specificity (*right*).

170

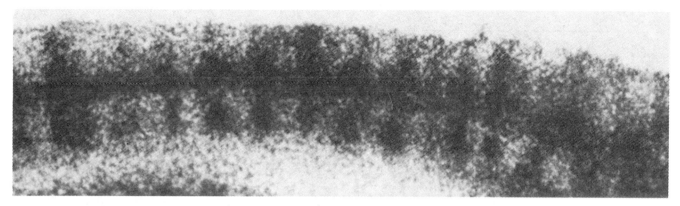

ORIENTATION COLUMNS are visualized as anatomical structures in a deoxyglucose autoradiograph made by the authors and Michael P. Stryker. Radioactively labeled deoxyglucose was injected into a monkey; it was taken up primarily by active neurons, and an early metabolite accumulated in the cells. Immediately after the in- jection the animal was stimulated with a pattern of vertical stripes, so that cells responding to vertical lines were most active and became most radioactive. In this section perpendicular to surface active-cell regions are narrow bands about .5 millimeter apart. Layer IV (with no orientation preference) is, as expected, uniformly radioactive.

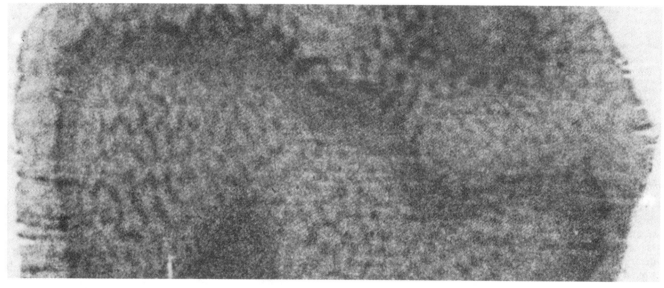

ORIENTATION PATTERN, seen face on, is unexpectedly complex. This deoxyglucose autoradiograph is of a section tangential to the somewhat curved layers of the cortex. The darker regions repre- sent continuously labeled layer IV. In the other layers the orientation regions are intricately curved bands, something like the walls of a maze seen from above, but distance from one band to next is uniform.

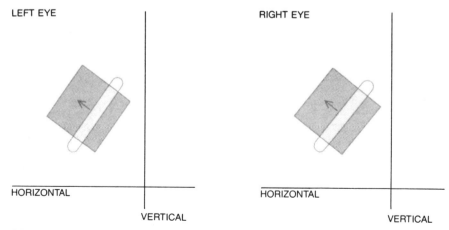

BINOCULAR CELL in the cortex can be influenced independently by both eyes or more strongly by both eyes together. Here the left-eye and right-eye fields are mapped for a complex cell whose receptive field is in the upper left quadrant of the visual field. (The lines represent the horizontal and vertical meridians of the field, intersecting at the point of fixation.) The two receptive fields are identical, but the amount of response may differ depending on whether the left eye or the right eye is stimulated. Preference for one eye is called ocular dominance.

a consistent drift in field position, its direction dictated by the topographical map of the visual fields. And an interesting regularity is revealed: it turns out that moving the electrode about one or two millimeters always produces a displacement in visual field that is roughly enough to take one into an entirely new region. The movement in the visual field, in short, is about the same as the size of the aggregate receptive field. For the primary visual cortex this holds wherever the recording is made. At the center of gaze the fields and their associated scatter are tiny, but so is the displacement corresponding to a one-millimeter movement along the cortex. With increasing eccentricity (farther out in the visual field) both the field and scatter and the displacement become larger, in parallel fashion. It seems that every-

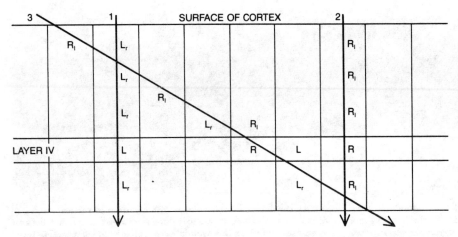

GROUPING OF CELLS according to ocular dominance was revealed by physiological studies. In one typical vertical penetration of the cortex (*1*) a microelectrode encounters only cells that respond preferentially to the left eye (L_r) and, in layer IV, cells that respond only to the left eye (*L*); in another vertical penetration (*2*) the cells all have right-eye dominance (R_l) or, in layer IV, are driven exclusively by the right eye (*R*). In an oblique penetration (*3*) there is a regular alternation of dominance by one eye or the other eye. Repeated penetrations suggest that the cortex is subdivided into regions with a cross-sectional width of about .4 millimeter and with walls perpendicular to the cortical surface and layers: the ocular-dominance columns.

where a block of cortex about one or two millimeters in size is what is needed to take care of a region of the visual world equivalent to the size of an aggregate field.

These observations suggest the way the visual cortex solves a basic problem: how to analyze the visual scene in detail in the central part and much more crudely in the periphery. In the retina, which has the same problem, for obvious optical reasons the number of millimeters corresponding to a degree of visual field is constant. The retina handles the central areas in great detail by having huge numbers of ganglion cells, each subserving a tiny area of central visual field; the layer of ganglion cells in the central part of the retina is thick, whereas in the outlying parts of the retina it is very thin. The cortex, in contrast, seems to want to be uniform in thickness everywhere. Here there are none of the optical constraints imposed on the retina, and so area is simply allotted in amounts corresponding to the problem at hand.

The machinery in any square millimeter of cortex is presumably about the same as in any other. A few thousand geniculate fibers enter such a region, the cortex does its thing and perhaps 50,000 fibers leave—whether a small part of the visual world is represented in great detail or a larger part in correspondingly less detail. The uniformity of the cortex is suggested, as we indicated at the outset, by the appearance of stained sections. It is compellingly confirmed when we examine the architecture further, looking specifically at orientation and at ocular dominance.

For orientation we inquire about groupings of cells just as we did with field position, looking first at two cells sitting side by side. Two such cells almost invariably have the same optimal stimulus orientation. If the electrode is inserted in a direction perpendicular to the surface, all the cells along the path of penetration have identical or almost identical orientations (except for the cells deep in layer IV, which have no optimal orientation at all). In two perpendicular penetrations a millimeter or so apart, however, the two orientations observed are usually different. The cortex must therefore be subdivided by some kind of vertical partitioning into regions of constant receptive-field orientation. When we came on this system almost 20 years ago, it intrigued us because it fitted so well with the hierarchical schemes we had proposed to explain how complex cells are supplied by inputs from simple cells: the circuit diagrams involve connections between cells whose fields cover the same part of the visual world and that respond to the same line orientation. It seemed eminently reasonable that strongly interconnected cells should be grouped together.

If the cortex is diced up into small regions of constant receptive-field orientation, can one say anything more about the three-dimensional shape of the regions than that their walls are perpendicular to the surface? Are neighboring regions related in any systematic way or are regions subserving all the possible orientations scattered over the cortex at random? We began to study these questions simply by penetrating the cortex

obliquely or parallel to the surface. When we first did this experiment in about 1961, the result was so surprising that we could hardly believe it. Instead of a random assortment of successive orientations there was an amazing orderliness. Each time the electrode moved forward as little as 25 or 50 micrometers (thousandths of a millimeter) the optimal orientation changed by a small step, about 10 degrees on the average; the steps continued in the same direction, clockwise or counterclockwise, through a total angle of anywhere from 90 to 270 degrees. Occasionally such a sequence would reverse direction suddenly, from a clockwise progression to a counterclockwise one or vice versa. These reversals were unpredictable, usually coming after steady progressions of from 90 to 270 degrees.

Since making this first observation we have seen similar order in almost every monkey. Either there is a steady progression in orientation or, less frequently, there are stretches in which orientation stays constant. The successive changes in orientation are small enough so that it is hard to be sure that the regions of constant orientation are finite in size; it could be that the optimal orientation changes in some sense continuously as the electrode moves along the cortex.

We became increasingly interested in the three-dimensional shape of these regional subdivisions. From considerations of geometry alone the existence of small or zero changes in every direction during a horizontal or tangential penetration points to parallel slabs of tissue containing cells with like orientation specificity, with each slab perpendicular to the surface. The slabs would not necessarily be planar, like slices of bread; seen from above they might well have the form of swirls, which could easily explain the reversals in the direction of orientation changes. Recording large numbers of cells in several parallel electrode penetrations seemed to confirm this prediction, but it was hard to examine more than a tiny region of brain with the microelectrode.

Fortunately an ideal anatomical method was invented at just the right time for us. This was the 2-deoxyglucose technique for assessing brain activity, devised by Louis Sokoloff and his group at the National Institute of Mental Health and described elsewhere in this issue [see "The Chemistry of the Brain," by Leslie L. Iversen, page 118]. The method capitalizes on the fact that brain cells depend mainly on glucose as a source of metabolic energy and that the closely similar compound 2-deoxyglucose can to some extent masquerade as glucose. If deoxyglucose is injected into an animal, it is taken up actively by neurons as though it were glucose; the more active the neuron, the greater the uptake. The compound begins to be metabolized, but for reasons best known to biochemists the sequence stops with a metabolite that cannot cross the cell wall and therefore accumulates within the cell.

The Sokoloff procedure is to inject an animal with deoxyglucose that has been labeled with the radioactive isotope carbon 14, stimulate the animal in a way calculated to activate certain neurons and then immediately examine the brain for radioactivity, which reveals active areas where cells will have taken up more deoxyglucose than those in quiescent areas. The usual way of examining the brain for this purpose is to cut very thin slices of it (as one would for microscopic examination) and press them against a photographic plate sensitive to the radioactive particles. When the film is developed, any areas that were in contact with radioactive material are seen as dark masses of developed silver grains. Together with Michael P. Stryker we adapted the Sokoloff method to our problem, injecting an anesthetized animal with deoxyglucose and then moving a pattern of black and white vertical stripes back and forth 1.5 meters in front of the animal for 45 minutes. We then cut the brain into slices, either perpendicular to the surface of the cortex or parallel to it.

The autoradiographs quickly confirmed the physiological results. Sections cut perpendicular to the surface showed narrow bands of radioactivity about every 570 micrometers (roughly half a millimeter), extending through the full thickness of the cortex. Evidently these were the regions containing cells responsive to vertical lines. The deep part of layer IV was uniformly radioactive, as was expected from the fact that the cells in the layer have circularly symmetrical receptive fields and show no orientation selectivity.

Sections cut parallel to the surface showed an unexpectedly complex set of periodically spaced bands, often swirling, frequently branching and rejoining, only here and there forming regular parallel slabs. What was particularly striking was the uniformity of the distance from one band to the next over the entire cortex. This fitted perfectly with the idea of a uniform cortex. Moreover, the distance between stripes fitted well with the idea that the cortical machinery must repeat itself at least every millimeter. If the distance were, for example, 10 millimeters from vertical through 180 degrees and back to vertical, sizable parts of the visual field would lack cells sensitive to any given orientation, making for a sketchy and extremely bizarre representation of the visual scene.

The final variable whose associated architecture needs to be considered is eye preference. In microelectrode studies neighboring cells proved almost invariably to prefer the same eye. If in vertical penetrations the first cell we encountered preferred the right eye, then so did all the cells, right down to the bottom of layer VI; if the first cell preferred the left eye, so did all the rest. Any penetration favored one eye or the other with equal probability. (Since the cells of layer IV are monocular, there it was a matter not of eye preference but of eye monopoly.) If the penetration was oblique or horizontal, there was an alternation of left and right preferences, with a rather abrupt switchover about every half millimeter. The cortex thus

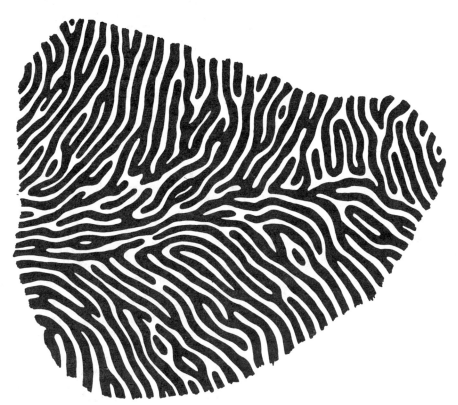

ANATOMICAL CONFIRMATION of ocular-dominance columns came from various staining methods and from axonal-transport autoradiographs such as those shown in color on page 131. This composite autoradiograph visualizing the pattern over an area some 10 millimeters wide was made by cutting out and pasting together the regions representing layer IV in a number of parallel sections: the one in bottom illustration on page 131 and others at different depths.

RECONSTRUCTION of the ocular-dominance pattern over the entire exposed part of the right primary visual cortex was made by the authors and Simon LeVay from a series of sections stained by a reduced-silver method he developed. The left-hand margin is at the medial edge of occipital lobe, where cortex folds downward; pattern is enlarged about six diameters.

proved to be diced up into a second set of regions separated by vertical walls that extend through the full cortical thickness. The ocular-dominance system was apparently quite independent of the orientation system, because in oblique or tangential penetrations the two sequences had no apparent relation to each other.

The basis of these ocular-dominance columns, as they have come to be called, seems to be quite simple. The terminals of geniculate fibers, some subserving the left eye and others the right, group themselves as they enter the cortex so that in layer IV there is no mixing. This produces left-eye and right-eye patches at roughly half-millimeter intervals. A neuron above or below layer IV receives connections from that layer from up to about a millimeter away in every direction. Probably the strongest connections are from the region of layer IV closest to the neuron, so that it is presumably dominated by whichever eye feeds that region.

Again we were most curious to learn what these left-eye and right-eye regions might look like in three dimensions; any

of several geometries could lead to the cross-sectional appearance the physiology had suggested. The answer first came from studies with the silver-degeneration method for mapping connections, devised by Walle J. H. Nauta of the Massachusetts Institute of Technology. Since then we have found three other independent anatomical methods for demonstrating these columns.

A particularly effective method (because it enables one to observe in a single animal the arrangement of columns over the entire primary visual cortex) is based on the phenomenon of axonal transport. The procedure is to inject a radioactively labeled amino acid into an area of nervous tissue. A cell body takes up the amino acid, presumably incorporates it into a protein and then transports it along the axon to its terminals. When we injected the material into one eye of a monkey, the retinal ganglion cells took it up and transported it along their axons, the optic-nerve fibers. We could then examine the destinations of these fibers in the lateral geniculate nuclei by coating tissue slices with a silver emulsion and developing the emulsion; the

radioactive label showed up clearly in the three complementary layers of the geniculate on each side.

This method does not ordinarily trace a path from one axon terminal across a synapse to the next neuron and its terminals, however, and we wanted to follow the path all the way to the cortex. In 1971 Bernice Grafstein of the Cornell University Medical College discovered that after a large enough injection in the eye of a mouse some of the radioactive material escaped from the optic-nerve terminals and was taken up by the cells in the geniculate and transported along their axons to the cortex. We had the thought that a similarly large injection in a monkey, combined with autoradiography, might demonstrate the geniculate terminals from one eye in layer IV of the visual cortex.

Our first attempt yielded dismayingly negative results, with only faint hints of a few silver grains visible in layer IV. It was only after several weeks that we realized that by resorting to dark-field microscopy we could take advantage of the light-scattering properties of silver grains and so increase the sensitivity of the method. We borrowed a dark-field condenser, and when we looked at our first slide under the microscope, there shining in all their glory were the periodic patches of label in layer IV [*see top illustration on page 131*].

The next step was to try to see the pattern face on by sectioning the cortex parallel to its surface. The monkey cortex is dome-shaped, and so a section parallel to the surface and tangent to layer IV shows that layer as a circle or an oval, while a section below layer IV shows it as a ring. By assembling a series of such ovals and rings from a set of sections one can reconstruct the pattern over a wide expanse of cortex.

From the reconstructions it was immediately obvious that the main overall pattern is one of parallel stripes representing terminals belonging to the injected eye, separated by gaps representing the other eye. The striping pattern is not regular like wallpaper. (We remind ourselves occasionally that this is, after all, biology!) Here and there a stripe representing one eye branches into two stripes, or else it ends blindly at a point where a stripe from the other eye branches. The irregularities are commonest near the center of gaze and along the line that maps the horizon. The stripes always seem to be perpendicular to the border between the primary visual cortex and its neighbor, area 18, and here the regularity is greatest. Such general rules seem to apply to all macaque brains, although the details of the pattern vary from one individual to the next and even from one hemi-

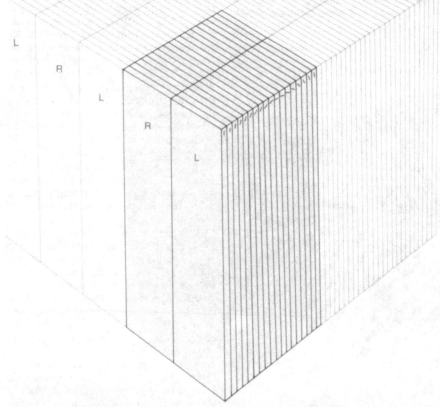

BLOCK OF CORTEX about a millimeter square and two millimeters deep (*light color*) can be considered an elementary unit of the primary visual cortex. It contains one set of orientation slabs subserving all orientations and one set of ocular-dominance slabs subserving both eyes. The pattern is reiterated throughout the primary visual area. The placing of the boundaries (at the right or the left eye, at a vertical, horizontal or oblique orientation) is arbitrary; representation of the slabs as flat planes intersecting at right angles is an oversimplification.

sphere to the other in the same monkey.

The width of a set of two stripes is constant, about .8 millimeter, over the entire primary visual cortex, once more emphasizing the uniformity of the cortex. Again the widths fit perfectly with the idea that all of the apparatus needed to look after an area the size of an aggregate field must be contained within any square millimeter of cortex. The two techniques, deoxyglucose labeling and amino acid transport, have the great advantage of being mutually compatible, so that we have been able to apply both together, one to mark orientation lines and the other to see the ocular-dominance columns. The number of brains examined so far is too small to justify any final conclusions, but the two systems appear to be quite independent, neither parallel nor at right angles but intersecting at random.

The function served by ocular-dominance columns is still a mystery. We know there are neurons with all grades of eye preference throughout the entire binocular part of the visual fields, and it may be that a regular, patterned system of converging inputs guarantees that the distribution will be uniform, with neither eye favored by accident in any one place. Why there should be all these grades of eye preference everywhere is itself not clear, but our guess is that it has something to do with stereoscopic depth perception.

Given what has been learned about the primary visual cortex, it is clear that one can consider an elementary piece of cortex to be a block about a millimeter square and two millimeters deep. To know the organization of this chunk of tissue is to know the organization for all of area 17; the whole must be mainly an iterated version of this elementary unit. Of course the elementary unit should not be thought of as a discrete, separable block. Whether the set of orientation slabs begins with a slab representing a vertical orientation, an oblique one or a horizontal one is completely arbitrary; so too is whether an ocular-dominance sequence begins with a left-plus-right pair of dominance slabs or a right-plus-left pair. The same thing is true for a unit crystal of sodium chloride or for any complex repetitive pattern such as is found in wallpaper.

What, then, does the visual scene really look like as it is projected onto the visual cortex? Suppose an animal fixes its gaze on some point and the only object in the visual field is a straight line above and a bit to the left of the point where the gaze is riveted. If each active cell were to light up, and if one could stand above the cortex and look down at it, what would the pattern be? To make the problem more interesting, suppose

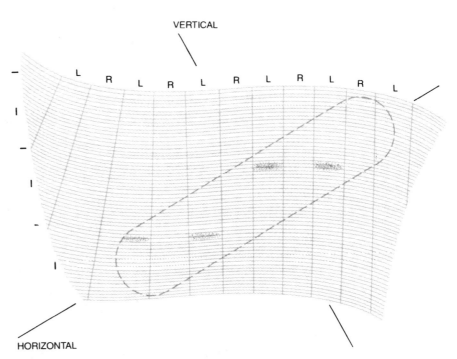

HYPOTHETICAL PATTERN OF CORTICAL ACTIVITY that might result from stimulation of the left eye with a single short horizontal line, placed in the upper left quadrant of the visual field, is shown by the colored patches on a diagram of an area of the right cortex, seen face on. The area receiving input from the object in the visual field is indicated by the broken black line. If ocular-dominance and orientation columns are arrayed as shown, activated cells will be those that respond optimally to approximately horizontal stimuli from the left eye.

the pattern is seen by one eye only. In view of the architecture just described the pattern turns out to be not a line but merely a set of regularly spaced patches [see illustration above]. The reasoning can be checked directly by exposing a monkey with one eye closed to a set of vertical stripes and making a deoxyglucose autoradiograph. The resulting pattern should not be a great surprise: it is a set of regularly spaced patches, which simply represents the intersection of the two sets of column systems. Imagine the surprise and bewilderment of a little green man looking at such a version of the outside world!

Why evolution has gone to the trouble of designing such an elaborate architecture is a question that continues to fascinate us. Perhaps the most plausible notion is that the column systems are a solution to the problem of portraying more than two dimensions on a two-dimensional surface. The cortex is dealing with at least four sets of values: two for the x and y position variables in the visual field, one for orientation and one for the different degrees of eye preference. The two surface coordinates are used up in designating field position; the other two variables are accommodated by dicing up the cortex with subdivisions so fine that one can run through a complete set of orientations or eye preferences and meanwhile have a shift in visual-field position that is small with respect to the resolution in that part of the visual world.

The strategy of subdividing the cortex with small vertical partitions is certainly not limited to the primary visual area. Such subdivisions were first seen in the somatic sensory area by Vernon B. Mountcastle of the Johns Hopkins University School of Medicine about 10 years before our work in the visual area. In the somatic sensory area, as we pointed out above, the basic topography is a map of the opposite half of the body, but superimposed on that there is a twofold system of subdivisions, with some areas where neurons respond to the movement of the joints or pressure on the skin and other areas where they respond to touch or the bending of hairs. As in the case of the visual columns, a complete set here (one area for each kind of neuron) occupies a distance of about a millimeter. These subdivisions are analogous to ocular-dominance columns in that they are determined in the first instance by inputs to the cortex (from either the left or the right eye and from either deep receptors or receptors in the upper skin layers) rather than by connections within the cortex, such as those that determine orientation selectivity and the associated system of orientation regions.

The columnar subdivisions associated with the visual and somatic sensory systems are the best-understood ones, but there are indications of similar vertical subdivisions in some other areas: several higher visual areas, sensory parietal regions recently studied by Mountcastle

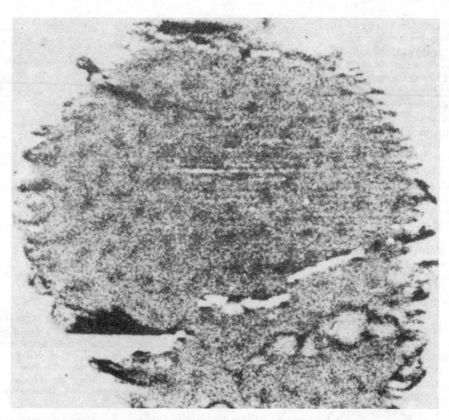

ACTUAL PATTERN of cortical activity was elicited by exposing only the left eye to a set of vertical stripes. The deoxyglucose autoradiograph is of a tangential section in the outer layers of the cortex. The pattern of regularly spaced dark patches of radioactivity represents intersection of ocular-dominance and orientation systems. Magnification is about eight diameters.

and the auditory region, where Thomas J. Imig, H. O. Adrián and John F. Brugge of the University of Wisconsin Medical School and their colleagues have found subdivisions in which the two ears seem alternately to add their information or to compete.

For most of these physiologically defined systems (except the visual ones) there are so far no anatomical correlates. On the other hand, in the past few years several anatomists, notably Edward G. Jones of the Washington University School of Medicine and Nauta and Patricia Goldman at M.I.T., have shown that connections from one region of the cortex to another (for example from the somatic sensory area on one side to the corresponding area on the other side) terminate in patches that have a regular periodicity of about a millimeter. Here the columns are evident morphologically, but one has no idea of the physiological interpretation. It is clear, however, that fine periodic subdivisions are a very general feature of the cerebral cortex. Indeed, Mount-castle's original observation of that feature may be said to supply a fourth profound insight into cortical organization.

It would surely be wrong to assume that this account of the visual cortex in any way exhausts the subject. Color, movement and stereoscopic depth are probably all dealt with in the cortex, but to what extent or how is still not clear. There are indications from work we and others have done on depth and from work on color by Semir Zeki of University College London that higher cortical visual areas to which the primary area projects directly or indirectly may be specialized to handle these variables, but we are a long way from knowing what the handling involves.

What happens beyond the primary visual area, and how is the information on orientation exploited at later stages? Is one to imagine ultimately finding a cell that responds specifically to some very particular item? (Usually one's grandmother is selected as the particular item, for reasons that escape us.) Our answer is that we doubt there is such a cell, but we have no good alternative to offer. To speculate broadly on how the brain may work is fortunately not the only course open to investigators. To explore the brain is more fun and seems to be more profitable.

There was a time, not so long ago, when one looked at the millions of neurons in the various layers of the cortex and wondered if anyone would ever have any idea of their function. Did they all work in parallel, like the cells of the liver or the kidney, achieving their objectives by pure bulk, or were they each doing something special? For the visual cortex the answer seems now to be known in broad outline: Particular stimuli turn neurons on or off; groups of neurons do indeed perform particular transformations. It seems reasonable to think that if the secrets of a few regions such as this one can be unlocked, other regions will also in time give up their secrets.

Article 4.2

Segregation of Form, Color, Movement, and Depth: Anatomy, Physiology, and Perception

MARGARET LIVINGSTONE AND DAVID HUBEL

Anatomical and physiological observations in monkeys indicate that the primate visual system consists of several separate and independent subdivisions that analyze different aspects of the same retinal image: cells in cortical visual areas 1 and 2 and higher visual areas are segregated into three interdigitating subdivisions that differ in their selectivity for color, stereopsis, movement, and orientation. The pathways selective for form and color seem to be derived mainly from the parvocellular geniculate subdivisions, the depth- and movement-selective components from the magnocellular. At lower levels, in the retina and in the geniculate, cells in these two subdivisions differ in their color selectivity, contrast sensitivity, temporal properties, and spatial resolution. These major differences in the properties of cells at lower levels in each of the subdivisions led to the prediction that different visual functions, such as color, depth, movement, and form perception, should exhibit corresponding differences. Human perceptual experiments are remarkably consistent with these predictions. Moreover, perceptual experiments can be designed to ask which subdivisions of the system are responsible for particular visual abilities, such as figure/ground discrimination or perception of depth from perspective or relative movement—functions that might be difficult to deduce from single-cell response properties.

PEOPLE WITH NORMAL COLOR VISION WILL PROBABLY FIND the left illustration in Fig. 1 less clear and three-dimensional than the one on the right. But it springs forth if you look at it through a blue filter, such as a piece of colored glass or cellophane. In the left version the gray and yellow are equally bright, or luminant, for the average person, whereas the right version has luminance-contrast information. The ability to infer distance and three-dimensional shape from a two-dimensional image is an example of a visual function that can use luminance but not color differences. Depth from perspective and color perception are thus aspects of vision that seem to be handled by entirely separate channels in our nervous system.

Even though intuition suggests that our vision can plausibly be subdivided into several components—color, depth, movement, form, and texture perception—our perception of any scene usually seems well unified. Despite this apparent wholeness, studies of anatomy, physiology, and human perception are converging toward the conclusion that our visual system is subdivided into several

The authors are members of the faculty, Department of Neurobiology, Harvard Medical School, Boston, MA 02115.

Reprinted with permission from *Science*, M. Livingstone and D. Hubel, "Segregation of Form, Color, Movement, and Depth: Anatomy, Physiology, and Perception," vol. 240, pp. 740–749, May 6, 1988. © AAAS.

separate parts whose functions are quite distinct. In this article we summarize some of these anatomical, physiological, and human-perceptual observations.

Physiological and Anatomical Studies

Occasionally people with strokes suffer surprisingly specific visual losses—for example, loss of color discrimination without impairment of form perception, loss of motion perception without loss of color or form perception, or loss of face recognition without loss of the ability to recognize most other categories of objects or loss of color or depth perception (*1*). Such selectivity seems to indicate that the visual pathway is functionally subdivided at a fairly gross level.

Anatomical and physiological studies in monkeys also support this idea of functional divergence within the visual pathway. They reveal major anatomical subdivisions at the earliest peripheral stages in the visual system as well as segregation of function at the highest known cortical stages, but until recently there was little information about corresponding subdivisions in the intermediate levels, the first and second cortical visual areas.

Subdivisions at early stages in the visual pathway. It has been known for a century that the nerve fibers leaving the eyes diverge to provide input both to the lateral geniculate bodies and to the superior colliculi. The colliculus seems to be relatively more important in lower mammals than it is in primates, in which its main role is probably orientation toward targets of interest; here we will be

Fig. 1. The same image at equiluminance (left) and non-equiluminance (right). Depth from perspective, spatial organization, and figure/ground segregation are diminished in the equiluminant version. To convince yourself that the left version does indeed contain the same information as the other, look at it through a piece of blue cellophane or glass. These two colors may not be close enough to your equiluminance point to be effective. Changing the light source may help.

Fig. 2. The primate lateral geniculate body. This six-layered structure is the first stage in the visual system after the retina, and it consists of two distinct subdivisions, the ventral two magnocellular layers and the dorsal four parvocellular layers. The two eyes project to different layers in the interdigitating fashion shown: c indicates layers that are innervated by the contralateral eye; i indicates layers with input from the ipsilateral eye.

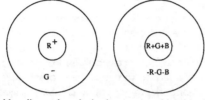

Fig. 3. Receptive fields for **(left)** typical color-opponent parvocellular geniculate neuron, excited over a small region by red light and inhibited over a larger region by green light and **(right)** typical broadband magnocellular neuron, excited by all wavelengths in the center and inhibited by all wavelengths in its surround.

concerned exclusively with the geniculo-cortical part of the visual system, which seems to be directly concerned with visual perception (2)—what we think of as seeing.

The primate lateral geniculate body is a six-layered structure, with two obviously different subdivisions: the four dorsal, small-cell (parvocellular) layers and the two ventral, large-cell (magnocellular) layers; these two subdivisions differ both anatomically and physiologically. In 1920 Minkowski (3) discovered that each eye projects to three of the six layers in the peculiar alternating fashion shown in Fig. 2: each half-retina is mapped three times onto one geniculate body, twice to the parvocellular layers and once to the magnocellular, and all six topographic maps of the visual field are in precise register (4).

The four parvocellular layers seem to be very similar, if not identical, anatomically and physiologically. But the magno- and parvocellular divisions are profoundly different, implying a major split in the visual pathway. This division is most obvious, and was first recognized, in the geniculate, but it does not originate there; the two geniculate subdivisions receive input from two intermixed but anatomically distinct types of retinal ganglion cells: type A cells are larger and project to the magnocellular division, and the smaller type B cells project to the parvocellular division (5). These two subdivisions of the visual pathway, which we will refer to as magno and parvo, are distinguishable both anatomically and physiologically. Whether this duality in the visual path arises even earlier, at the bipolar or horizontal cells in the retina, is not known. We can at least be reasonably certain that the two components must both derive their inputs from the same rods and cones and that the marked differences in response properties must therefore depend on the way the photoreceptor inputs are combined.

Though they differ significantly in their response characteristics, the magno and parvo systems do share some basic physiological properties. Their receptive fields (the regions of retina over which their impulse activity can be influenced) are all circularly symmetrical, and about 90% show center-surround opponency (6, 7); some cells are excited (impulse rate speeded up) by illumination of a small

retinal region and inhibited (impulse rate slowed down) by illumination of a larger surrounding region, whereas others are the reverse, inhibited from the center and excited from the surround. Because of the antagonism between center and surround, large uniform spots produce feeble responses or none. This center-surround arrangement is found also at earlier levels, starting with the retinal bipolar cells. Clearly these cells are wired up so as to convert the information from the photoreceptors into information about spatial discontinuities in light patterns. This should not be surprising, since we ourselves are very poor in judging overall levels of illumination, as anyone who tries doing photography without a light meter well knows—we are lucky if we can come within an *f* stop (a factor of 2) of the right exposure. On the other hand we can detect a spot that is as little as a few percent brighter or darker than its immediate surround.

The magno and parvo divisions nevertheless differ physiologically in four major ways—color, acuity, speed, and contrast sensitivity (7–10).

Color. About 90% of the cells in the parvocellular layers of the geniculate are strikingly sensitive to differences in wavelength, whereas cells in the magnocellular layers are not. The three types of cones in the primate retina have broad, overlapping spectral sensitivities and can be loosely termed red-, green-, and blue-sensitive, to indicate that their peak sensitivities are in the long-, middle-, and short-wavelength regions of the spectrum. Parvo cells are wavelength selective because they combine these cone inputs so as in effect to subtract them (Fig. 3, left). A typical parvo cell may, for example, receive excitatory inputs to its receptive field center from red cones only, and inhibitory inputs to its receptive field surround from green cones only. Such a cell will be excited by long wavelengths (reds), inhibited by short wavelengths (blues and greens), and be unresponsive to some intermediate wavelength (yellow). Besides such red–on center, green–off surround cells, most of the other possibilities also occur, most commonly red cones antagonized by green, and blue versus the sum of red and green (that is, yellow). In contrast to the color selectivity of most parvo cells, magno cells (and also the remaining 10% of the parvo cells) sum the inputs of the three cone types, so that the spectral sensitivity curves are broad, and the response to a change in illumination is of the same type, either on or off, at all wavelengths (Fig. 3, right) (11). The magno system is thus in effect color-blind: as in black-and-white photography, two different colors, such as red and green, at some relative brightness will be indistinguishable.

Acuity. The second difference between magno and parvo cells is the size of their field centers. For both systems the average size of the receptive field center increases with distance from the fovea, consistent with the differences in acuity between foveal and peripheral vision. Yet at any given eccentricity, magno cells have larger receptive field centers than parvo cells, by a factor of 2 or 3.

Speed. Magno cells respond faster and more transiently than parvo cells. This sensitivity to the temporal aspects of a visual stimulus suggests that the magno system may play a special role in detecting movement. Many cells at higher levels in this pathway are selective for direction of movement.

Contrast. Shapley *et al.* (10) found that magno cells are much more sensitive than parvo cells to low-contrast stimuli. Both begin to respond when the center and surround brightnesses differ by only 1 or 2%, but with increasing contrast magno responses increase rapidly and level off at about 10 to 15% contrast, whereas parvo responses increase more slowly, and saturate at far higher contrasts.

These four major differences between the two subdivisions, in color, acuity, quickness, and contrast sensitivity, imply that they contribute to different aspects of vision. Exactly what aspects have become clearer recently, with new anatomical techniques that have made it possible to follow these subdivisions farther into the central nervous system and to correlate them with the response selectivity of cells at later stages in each subdivision for more abstract stimulus features.

Continuation of the magno and parvo subdivisions in visual area 1. The segregation of the two pathways is perpetuated in the primary visual cortex (*12*) (Fig. 4). Cells in the magnocellular geniculate layers project to layer 4Cα, which projects in turn to layer 4B, which then projects to visual area 2 and to cortical area MT. Parvo cells project to layer 4Cβ, and from there the connections go to layers 2 and 3, and from there to visual area 2. The parvocellular division splits to form an additional subdivision in the upper layers of visual area 1. The first evidence for this further subdivision came in 1978 when Wong-Riley (*13*) stained visual area 1 for the mitochondrial enzyme cytochrome oxidase and saw alternating regions of light and dark staining. The dark regions are round or oval in sections cut parallel to the surface; they are most prominent in the upper layers (2 and 3) but are also faintly visible in layers 5 and 6. They turned out to represent pillar-like structures about 0.2 mm in diameter, spaced 0.5 mm apart (*14*). We term these structures blobs because of their three-dimensional shape. Blobs are found only in the primary visual cortex; they occur in all primates that have been looked at, and in the prosimian *Galago*, but have not been found in other prosimians or any lower mammals (*15*).

Since layers 2 and 3 receive most of their inputs from parvo-recipient layer 4Cβ, both the blobs and the interblobs could be considered continuations of the parvo subdivision. Nevertheless the blobs should probably be thought of as a separate subdivision, because they have somewhat different inputs and very different response properties from the interblobs (*16–18*). The visual response properties of cells in the blobs suggest that they may also receive magnocellular input (*17, 18*).

Thus by the output stage of visual area 1 the magno system remains segregated, and the parvo system seems to have split into two branches. All three subdivisions, magno→4Cα→4B, parvo→4Cβ→ interblob, and parvo(+magno?)→4Cβ→blob, then project to visual area 2.

These anatomically defined subdivisions in the primary visual cortex differ from each other in the kinds of visual information they carry (*18*), as in earlier stages.

In the magno pathway, cells in layer 4B are orientation selective; that is, they respond best to lines of a particular orientation, and most of them also show selectivity for the direction of movement (*18, 19*)—for example, a cell preferring horizontal lines may respond when an edge is moved upward but not when it moves downward. Like magnocellular geniculate cells, cells in 4B lack color selectivity.

In the interblobs, most, perhaps all, cells are also orientation selective. Unlike cells in layer 4B, most are not direction selective; 10 to 20% are end-stopped, responding to short but not long line or edge stimuli. The receptive fields are small, and the optimum line thickness is similar to the optimum spot size of cells in the geniculate parvocellular layers at the same eccentricity. This system may therefore be responsible for high-resolution form perception. Although anatomical evidence indicates that the interblob system receives its major input from the color-coded parvocellular geniculate layers, most of the interblob cells are not explicitly color-coded: they show no color opponency and respond well to achromatic luminance contrast borders. Nevertheless, many of them respond to an appropriately oriented color-contrast edge regardless of the colors forming the edge or the relative brightness of the two colors. Similarly, they usually respond to lines or borders of any brightness contrast (light-on-dark or dark-on-light), even though the antecedent geniculate cells are either on-center or off-center but not both. This suggests that much of the color-coded parvocellular input is pooled in such a way that color contrast can be used to identify borders but that the information about the colors (including black versus white) forming the border is lost (*20*).

Blob cells are not orientation selective but are either color or brightness selective. The blob system thus seems to carry information complementary to the information carried by the interblob system. The brightness-selective (non–color-coded or broadband) blob cells have larger receptive field centers than the broadband geniculate cells but are otherwise similar—they are either excited or inhibited by small spots of light, and they respond less well to large spots, indicating surround inhibition. These broadband blob cells could receive input from either the magnocellular geniculate cells or from the broadband parvo cells, but the physiological properties of many of them would be more consistent with input from the magno system (*17, 18*). We assume that the color-opponent blob cells receive input from the color-opponent parvocellular geniculate cells,

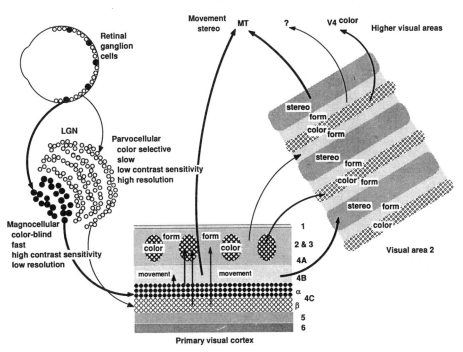

Fig. 4. Diagram of the functional segregation of the primate visual system. MT, middle temporal lobe; V4, visual area 4; LGN, lateral geniculate body.

179

Fig. 5. Section parallel to the surface through visual areas 1 and 2 of a squirrel monkey, stained for cytochrome oxidase. Visual area 1 is on the left; the blobs appear as small round dots. In Visual area 2 the cytochrome-oxidase stain reveals a pattern of alternating thin, thick, and pale stripes.

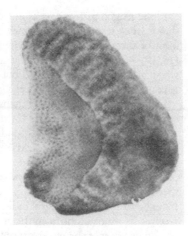

though they differ from them in that their receptive field centers are larger and their color coding is doubly opponent—they give opposite responses to different parts of the spectrum in the center (say, on to red and off to green), and both types of center response are reduced when the spot is made larger.

The blob and interblob systems thus work in entirely different and complementary ways. Blob cells are explicitly color-coded, excited by colors in one region of the spectrum and inhibited by others, and not selective for stimulus orientation. Interblob cells are selective for stimulus orientation but mostly are not color selective, responding to a line or edge of the correct orientation regardless of its color. The strategy of carrying orientation information in a system that mostly pools color information and color-contrast information in a separate system that does not carry orientation information is probably more efficient than having single cells selective for both the orientation and color of a border. Nevertheless, as emphasized earlier, although most of the interblob cells are not overtly color selective, they probably receive their inputs from explicitly color-coded parvocellular geniculate cells and are most likely not color-blind in the sense that the cells in the magno system probably are. Most interblob cells, even though they lose the information about the colors that form a border or the sign of the contrast of the border, should respond to color-contrast borders in which the two colors are equally bright; such borders would be invisible to magno cells.

Visual area 2. The main target of visual area 1 is visual area 2 (Brodmann's area 18), which shows an equally intriguing pattern when stained for cytochrome oxidase (Fig. 5) (16, 21). Instead of small round dots, tangential sections show a pattern of stripes, much coarser than the blobs of visual area 1; these alternately dark and light stripes are several millimeters wide and run perpendicular to the border between visual areas 1 and 2, probably extending over the entire 8- to 10-mm width of visual area 2. The dark stripes are themselves of two types, thick and thin. The regularity of this pattern of thick, thin, and pale stripes varies from animal to animal and is clearer in New World monkeys than in Old World ones, at least partly because in Old World monkeys visual area 2 is buried in the lunate sulcus. Given three histologically defined regions in visual area 2 and the fact that visual area 1 has three kinds of subdivisions that project to other cortical areas, it was natural to ask if they were related. And indeed, from tracer injections into the three kinds of stripes in visual area 2, we found that the blobs are reciprocally connected to the thin stripes, the interblob regions to the pale stripes, and layer 4B to the thick stripes (Fig. 4) (18, 22).

The next step was to record from cells in visual area 2, to learn whether the three subdivisions carry different types of visual information. We did indeed find marked differences, which were consist-

ent with the properties of cells in the antecedent subdivisions of visual area 1 (18, 23).

Cells in the thin stripes showed no orientation selectivity, and over half were color-coded, just as we had found in the blobs. As in the blobs, most of the color-coded cells were doubly opponent, with two antagonistic inputs to their centers, and surround antagonism for both of these center inputs. About half of the thin-stripe cells, both broadband and color opponent, exhibited an additional property not seen in the blob cells: the receptive field centers were bigger, yet optimum spot sizes were about the same. A typical cell might respond best, say, to a 0.5° diameter spot, give no response at all to 2° or 4° spots (indicating surround antagonism), and yet respond actively to the 0.5° spot anywhere within an area about 4° in diameter. These cells can be broadband or color opponent. Several years ago Baizer, Robinson, and Dow (24) described this kind of broadband cell, which they called "spot cells," in visual area 2.

Cells in the pale stripes are orientation selective but not direction selective. At least half of them are end-stopped; this represents a dramatic increase in the proportion of end-stopping over what is seen in visual area 1. We have argued that end-stopping, like center-surround antagonism, is an efficient way of encoding information about shape (23). Like cells in the interblobs, pale-stripe cells are not explicitly color-coded, and we expect that they would respond to color-contrast borders at all relative brightnesses, though we have not yet tested this.

In the thick stripes the great majority of cells likewise show orientation selectivity, but are seldom end-stopped. The most consistent response selectivity we see in the thick stripes is for stereoscopic depth—most cells respond poorly to stimulation of either eye alone but vigorously when both eyes are stimulated together, and for most cells the responses are extremely sensitive to variations in the relative horizontal positions of the stimuli in the two eyes (retinal disparity). Poggio and Fischer (25) had seen similar disparity-tuned cells in visual area 1 in alert monkeys, predominantly in layer 4B, the layer that projects to the thick stripes of visual area 2. In the thick stripes we find the same three basic

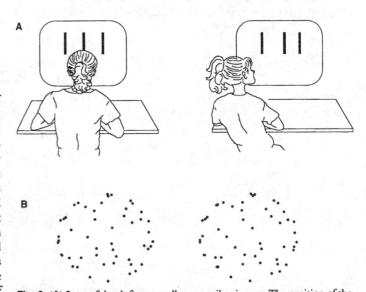

Fig. 6. (A) Loss of depth from parallax at equiluminance. The position of the middle bar is made to vary with the observer's head position. In this case, the center bar appears to lie in front of the reference bars, except when the bars are made equiluminant with the background. (B) Two frames of a movie in which the movement of dots generates the sensation of a three-dimensional object. The dots appear to lie on the surface of a sphere (which you can see by stereo-viewing these two frames). All sensation of depth is lost when the dots are equiluminant with the background.

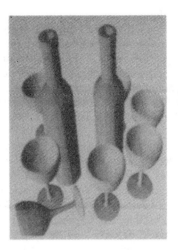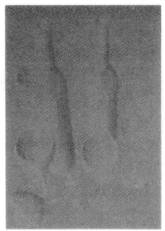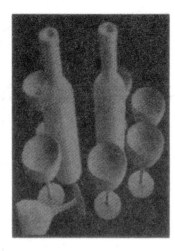

Fig. 7. Computer-generated images in which shape is generated by shading. In the middle image the two colors are equiluminant, and the three-dimensional shape is harder to discern than in the other two images, which have luminance-contrast.

classes of cells described by Poggio and Fischer—cells selective for near stimuli, far stimuli, or stimuli falling on exactly corresponding retinal points. Like cells in the pale stripes, these cells show no color selectivity; moreover, we would predict that these cells would be like their magnocellular predecessors and would not respond to color-contrast borders when the colors are equally bright, though we have not yet tested responses to equiluminant color-contrast borders either in layer 4B of visual area 1 or in the thick stripes of visual area 2.

Other studies (26, 27) have not reported such a clean segregation of cells with different physiological properties in visual area 2, or as clear a correlation of physiological subtypes with the three types of stripes. How clear the functional segregation is in visual area 2 remains to be resolved, but we suspect that these differences are due to choice of classification criteria (23).

Higher visual areas. Meanwhile, explorations of visual areas beyond 1 and 2 are helping close the gap between the functions suggested by electrophysiological studies and what clinical observations imply about the segregation of various functions in the human visual system. The response properties of cells at levels beyond visual area 2 suggest that the segregation of functions begun at the earliest levels is perpetuated at the highest levels so far studied. Indeed, the segregation seems to become more and more pronounced at each successive level, so that subdivisions that are interdigitated in visual areas 1 and 2 become segregated into entirely separate areas at still higher levels. One higher visual area in the middle temporal lobe, MT, seems to be specialized for the analysis of movement and stereoscopic depth (28). It receives input not only from layer 4B in visual area 1 (29), which is also rich in directionality and disparity selectivity, but also from the thick stripes in visual area 2 (26, 30), which, as already described, contain many cells selective for binocular disparity (23). Another higher visual area, visual area 4, has been reported to contain a preponderance of color-selective cells (31), but just how specialized visual area 4 is for color is still unclear since many of the cells show some selectivity for orientation. Visual area 4 receives input from the color-coded thin stripes in visual area 2 and possibly from the pale stripes (26, 30, 32). The notion that there is a higher visual area devoted largely to the processing of color information is consistent with the clinical observation that patients with strokes in the posterior inferior occipital lobe (perhaps in a region homologous to visual area 4) can lose color perception without impairment of form or movement perception.

There are strong suggestions that these channels remain segregated through still higher levels in the brain (33). From lesion studies Pohl (34) and Ungerleider and Mishkin (35) have defined two

functionally distinct divisions of visual association areas: the temporal-occipital region, necessary for learning to identify objects by their appearance, and the parieto-occipital region, needed for tasks involving the positions of objects, a distinction they refer to as "where" versus "what." Visual area 4 preferentially projects to the temporal division and MT primarily to parietal cortex (36). Thus the temporal visual areas may represent the continuation of the parvo system, and the parietal areas the continuation of the magno pathway. There can be little doubt that in the next few years work on the dozen or so areas north of the striate cortex will greatly enhance our understanding of vision in general.

Human Perception

Despite many gaps, the picture beginning to emerge from the anatomical and electrophysiological studies summarized above is that the segregation begun in the eye gives rise to separate and independent parallel pathways. At early levels, where there are two major subdivisions, the cells in these two subdivisions exhibit at least four basic differences—color selectivity, speed, acuity, and contrast sensitivity. At higher stages the continuations of these pathways are selective for quite different aspects of vision (form, color, movement, and stereopsis), thus generating the counterintuitive prediction that different kinds of visual tasks should differ in their color, temporal, acuity, and contrast characteristics. To test this prediction, we asked whether the differences seen in the geniculate can be detected in conscious human visual perception by comparing the color, temporal, spatial, and contrast sensitivities of different visual functions. Many of these questions, not surprisingly, have already been asked, and the answers are wonderfully consistent with the anatomy and physiology. For several decades psychologists have accumulated evidence for two channels in human vision, one chromatic and the other achromatic, by showing that different tasks can have very different sensitivities to color and brightness contrast. Given what we know now about the electrophysiology and the anatomy of the subdivisions of the primate visual system, we can begin to try to correlate the perceptual observations with these subdivisions (37). Though at higher cortical levels there seem to be three subdivisions, possibly with some mixing of magno and parvo inputs to the blob system, the most important distinction is probably between the magno system (magno→4Cα→4B→MT) and the parvo-derived subdivisions (parvo→4Cβ→interblobs→pale stripes→ visual area 4?) and [parvo(+magno?)→4Cβ→blobs→thin stripes→visual area 4]. In our discussion of human perception we will, therefore, stress the distinctions between functions that seem to

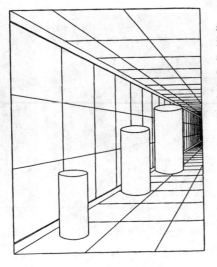

Fig. 8. Gibson's corridor illusion. [From (*47*) with permission, copyright 1950, Houghton Mifflin] At equiluminance the image no longer appears to recede into the distance, and the cylinders all appear to be the same size, as indeed they actually are.

be carried exclusively by the magno system and those that seem to be carried by the parvo-derived pathways.

From the fact that the magno system is color-blind and is faster than the parvo system, we can predict that discrimination of color and discrimination of brightness should have different temporal properties. This is indeed so: in 1923 Ives (*38*) showed that people can follow brightness alternations at much faster rates than pure color alternations.

The high incidence of movement and direction selectivity in MT suggests that this area may be particularly concerned with movement perception. Because anatomically MT receives its major inputs from layer 4B of the primary visual cortex and from the thick stripes of visual area 2, both part of the magno pathway, one would predict that human movement perception should somehow reflect magno characteristics: color blindness, quickness, high contrast sensitivity, and low acuity. Perceptual experiments indicate that movement perception does indeed have these characteristics. First, it is impaired for patterns made up of equiluminant colors: Cavanagh, Tyler, and Favreau (*39*) found that if they generated moving red and green sinewave stripes, "the perceived velocity of equiluminous gratings is substantially slowed . . . the gratings often appear to stop even though their bars are clearly resolved . . . the motion is appreciated only because it is occasionally noticed that the bars are at some new position" (*39*, p. 897; *40*). Second, movement perception is impaired at high spatial frequencies, consistent with the lower acuity of the magno system. Campbell and Maffei (*41*) viewed slowly rotating gratings and found a loss of motion perception at the highest resolvable frequencies, "At a spatial frequency of 16 and 32 cycles/deg a strange phenomenon was experienced, the grating was perceived as rotating extremely slowly and most of the time it actually appeared stationary. Of course, the subject could call upon his memory and deduce that the grating must be moving for he was aware that some seconds before the grating had been at a particular 'clock-face position.' Even with this additional information that the grating must be rotating the illusion of 'stopped motion' persisted" (*41*, p. 714). What is most surprising about the perception of both the equiluminant stripes and the very fine stripes is that even though the sensation of movement is entirely, or almost entirely, lost, the stripes themselves are still clearly visible—they are clear enough that changes in their position can be seen, even though they do not seem to be moving. Last, movement can be vividly perceived with very rapidly alternating or very low contrast images (*37, 41*). Thus, as summarized in Table 1, the properties of human movement perception are remarkably consistent with the properties of the magno system.

Finding cells in the thick stripes of visual area 2 and in MT that are tuned to retinal disparity suggests that the magno system is also involved in stereoscopic depth perception. Consistent with this, Lu and Fender (*42*) found that subjects could not see depth in equiluminant color-contrast random-dot stereograms even though the dots making up the stereogram remained perfectly clear (*43*). This finding has been disputed, but we found that differences in results can arise from variations in subjects' equiluminance points with eccentricity, which make it difficult to achieve equiluminance across the visual field. Like movement perception, stereopsis fails for stereograms containing only high, but resolvable, spatial frequencies, but it is not diminished for rapidly alternating or very low contrast stereograms (*37*) (Table 1).

Deduction of further magno or parvo functions from perceptual tests. Since the functions that electrophysiological studies had suggested should be carried by the magno system did indeed show all four distinguishing characteristics of that system, we decided to ask whether other visual functions, ones not predicted by single-cell response properties, might also manifest some or all of these properties.

If a particular magno cell sums red and green inputs, there will be a red : green ratio at which the red and green will be equally effective in stimulating the cell. This need not imply that every magno cell has the same ratio of red to green inputs and therefore necessarily the same equiluminance point. Nevertheless, the fact that movement and stereopsis fail at equiluminance implies that, for a given observer, the null ratio must be very similar for the majority of his cells responsible for that function. Krüger (*44*) found that of 33 magnocellular geniculate cells studied in two monkeys, 75% were unresponsive to a moving color-contrast border at a particular relative brightness—a brightness ratio that was very close to a human observer's equiluminant point. Thus not only do individual cells in the magno system seem to be color-blind, but the properties of stereopsis and movement perception indicate that the magno system as a whole is color-blind. [There is, however, currently some disagreement about whether the magno system is inactive at equiluminance (*45*).] People with the most common forms of color

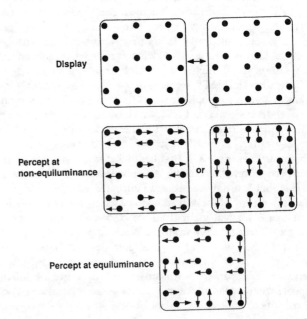

Fig. 9. Linking by movement is lost at equiluminance. All nine of the ambiguous motion squares appear to move in synchrony, even though any one seen alone could be seen moving either horizontally or vertically. This linking disappears at equiluminance, and the dots move every which way.

182

blindness, due to the lack of one of the three cone pigments, are not nearly as color-blind as the magno system appears to be. They still have two cone types to compare, and so they confuse only a small fraction of possible color pairs and can differentiate most color pairs at all relative brightnesses.

Since both motion perception and stereoscopic depth perception are lost at equiluminance, we suspected that the ability to use relative motion as a depth cue might also be lost. Relative motion is a very powerful depth cue: when an observer moves his head back and forth or moves around in his environment, the relative motion of objects provides information about their distance. In the experiment shown in Fig. 6A, the position of the middle bar was coupled to head movement, and the middle bar appeared to be either behind or in front of the reference bars, depending on whether its movement was the same as, or contrary to, the head movement. When the bars were made equiluminant with the background, all sensation of depth disappeared (37).

Relative movement of different parts of a three-dimensional object is also a powerful depth cue. Figure 6B shows two frames of a movie in which random dots move, some to the right and some to the left, as if they were pasted on a rotating spherical surface. The movie gives a powerful sensation of a rotating spherical surface—unless the dots are equiluminant with the background, and then all sensation of depth is lost (37), and the dots seem to dance aimlessly. Thus depth from motion, both from viewer parallax and from object motion, seems also to depend on luminance contrast and could well be a function of the magno system. Consistent with this idea, we could see depth from motion at very low levels of luminance contrast (37).

The retinal image is of course two-dimensional, and to capture the three-dimensional relationships of objects the visual systems uses many kinds of cues besides stereopsis and relative motion—perspective, gradients of texture, shading, occlusion, and relative position in the image. We wondered whether the sensation of depth from any of these other cues might also exhibit magno characteristics. It seemed especially likely that the ability to perceive depth from shading might be carried by an achromatic system, because shading is almost by definition purely luminance-contrast information; that is, under natural lighting conditions a shaded region of an object has the same hue as the unshaded parts, simply darker. But in biology just because something could, or seemingly even should, be done in a certain way does not mean that it will be. Nevertheless, Cavanagh and Leclerc (46) found that the perception of three-dimensional shape from shading indeed depends solely on luminance contrast. That is, in order to produce a sensation of depth and three-dimensionality, shadows can be any hue as long as they are darker than unshaded regions of the same surface. Many artists seem to have been aware of this; for example, in some of the self-portraits of Van Gogh and Matisse the shadows on their faces are green or blue, but they still convey a normally shaped face. Black-and-white photographs of these paintings (taken with film that has approximately the same spectral sensitivity as humans) confirm that the shadows are actually darker than the unshaded parts. The converse can be seen in Fig. 7; here the green shadows do not convey a sensation of depth and shape when they are the same brightness as the blue but do when they are darker (when the blue is darker, the blue parts are interpreted as shadowed).

Perspective was well known to artists by the time of the Renaissance and is a powerful indicator of depth. Converging lines or gradients of texture are automatically interpreted by the visual system as indicating increasing distance from the observer; thus the image in Fig. 8 (47) looks like a corridor receding into the distance despite the conflicting information from other depth cues, the absence of stereopsis or relative motion, which tells us we are looking at a flat surface. The perception of depth from perspective probably underlies many illusions: the two cylinders in Fig. 8 are the same size (and they each cover the same area on your retina), but are perceived by most people as being unequal.

We found that when images with strong perspective are rendered in equiluminant colors instead of black and white, the depth

Table 1. Summary of the correlations between human psychophysical results and the physiological properties of the three subdivisions of the primate geniculo-cortical visual system. A check indicates that the psychophysical results are consistent with the physiology, and a blank indicates that such an experiment has not been done.

Magno System

Physiology	Color selectivity — no	Contrast sensitivity — high	Temporal resolution — fast	Spatial resolution — low
Human perception				
Movement perception				
Movement detection	√	√	√	√
Apparent movement	√	√	√	√
Depth cues				
Stereopsis	√	√	√	√
Interocular rivalry	√			√
Parallax	√			
Depth from motion	√	√		
Shading	√	√		
Contour lines	√			√
Occlusion	√			
Perspective	√	√	√	
Linking properties				
Linking by movement	√	√		
Linking by collinearity (illusory borders)	√	√	√	√
Figure/ground discrimination	√			

Parvo System

Parvo → Interblob pathway

Physiology	Color selectivity — yes	Contrast sensitivity — low	Temporal resolution — slow	Spatial resolution — high
Human perception				
Shape discrimination				
Orientation discrimination	√	√	√	√
Shape discrimination	√	√	√	√

Parvo + (Magno?) → Blob pathway

Physiology	Color selectivity — yes	Contrast sensitivity — high	Temporal resolution — slow	Spatial resolution — low
Human perception				
Color perception				
Color determination	√		√	√
Flicker photometry	√		√	

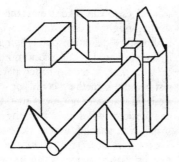

Fig. 10. Linking by collinearity. It is clear which edges are part of the same object, even when occluded by another object. At equiluminance this linking disappears, and it looks like a jumble of lines instead of a pile of blocks. After (49).

Fig. 11. Illusory borders, which disappear at equiluminance. Redrawn from (52).

sensation is lost or greatly diminished (37). Illusions of size are likewise lost at equiluminance—the cylinders in Fig. 8 are then all correctly perceived as being the same size. As with movement and stereopsis, the most startling aspect of this phenomenon is that even though the sensation of depth and the illusory distortions due to inappropriate scale all disappear at equiluminance, the lines defining the perspective and the individual elements in the image are nevertheless still clearly visible. This seems to us to rule out high-level, cognitive explanations for depth from perspective and the illusions of perspective; if you see depth because you merely know that converging lines mean increasing distance, you should be able to perceive the depth from the converging lines at equiluminance. Thus at a relatively low level in the visual system some simple interactions must initiate the automatic interpretation of a two-dimensional image into three-dimensional information; moreover, these operations seem to be performed only in the achromatic magno system, not in the parvo system.

Why should the depth and movement functions described above all be carried by the magno system and not by the parvo system? We at first assumed that it was because they might all be performed best by a system with the special characteristics of the magno system. But later we wondered if these various functions might be more related than they seemed at first—whether they could all be parts of a more global function. We were struck by the similarity between the list of functions we had ascribed to the magno system and the Gestalt psychologists' list of features used to discriminate objects from each other and from the background—figure/ground discrimination (48). Most scenes contain a huge amount of visual information, information about light intensity and color at every point on the retina and the presence and orientation of discontinuities in the light pattern. The Gestalt psychologists recognized that one important step in making sense of an image must be to correlate related pieces of visual information; that is, to decide whether a series of light/dark discontinuities forms a single edge, whether adjacent edges belong to the same object, whether two parts of an occluded edge are related, and so on. They determined that several kinds of cues are used in this way and to organize the visual elements in a scene into

discrete objects, to distinguish them from each other and from the background. Barlow (49) has called these "linking features" because they are used to link or join related elements. These linking features include: common movement (objects move against a stationary background; contours moving in the same direction and velocity are likely to belong to the same object, even if they are different in orientation or not contiguous); common depth (contours at different distances from the observer are unlikely to belong to the same object); collinearity (if a straight or continuously curved contour is interrupted by being occluded by another object, it is still seen as a single contour); and common color or lightness. The results described below suggest, however, that only luminance contrast, and not color differences, is used to link parts together.

Ramachandran and Anstis (50) discovered a powerful example of linking by movement. If two dots on a diagonal are alternated with two other dots, in mirror-image positions, an observer sees apparent movement, which can be either horizontal or vertical. The direction of the observed alternating movement is completely ambiguous; observers usually see one direction for a few seconds, and then flip to the other. With a display of several such ambiguous-motion squares in an array (Fig. 9) all the squares are perceived as moving in the same direction, like Rockettes, either all horizontally or all vertically (even though any one of them viewed alone is equally likely to be perceived as moving in either direction), and when one flips its apparent direction of movement, they all flip. When the dots are made equiluminant with the background the synchrony breaks down and they all seem to move independently (37).

Linking by collinearity (Fig. 10) also breaks down when the lines are equiluminant with the background; the figure then just looks like a jumble of lines instead of a pile of blocks. Linking by collinearity is seen in the phenomenon of illusory contours (51, 52), figures that produce a vivid perception of an edge in the absence of any real discontinuity (Fig. 11). When these figures are drawn in equiluminant colors, the illusory borders disappear, even though the elements defining them (the pacmen, the spokes, the lines, or the circles) remain perfectly visible. Because the perception of illusory borders also manifests fast temporal resolution, high contrast sensitivity, and low spatial resolution, we suspect that it too may represent a magno function. Illusory borders have been called "cognitive contours" because of the suggestion that the perception of the border is due to a high-level deduction that there must be an object occluding a partially visible figure (53). We suspect that this is not the case because the illusory borders disappear at equiluminance, even though the real parts of the figure are still perfectly visible.

Fifty years ago the Gestalt psychologists observed that figure/ground discrimination and the ability to organize the elements in a scene decrease at equiluminance. Equiluminant figures have been described as "jazzy," "unstable," "jelly-like," or "disorganized" (43, 54). Koffka (55) pointed out that luminance differences are strikingly more important than color differences for figure/ground segregation: "Thus two greys which look very similar will give a perfectly stable organization if one is used for the figure and the other for the ground, whereas a deeply saturated blue and a grey of the same luminosity which look very different indeed will produce practically no such organization" (54, p. 127). Edgar Rubin's popular demonstration of the problem of figure/ground discrimination is the vase/faces (Fig. 12). At non-equiluminance the percept is bistable, so that one sees either the faces or the vase, but usually not both at the same time. At equiluminance the two percepts reverse rapidly, and one can occasionally see both the vase and the faces simultaneously. The distinction between figure and ground thus gets weaker or even disappears entirely.

Color contrast versus color bleeding. At any point in the visual field, cells in the blobs have receptive field centers that are two to four

Fig. 12. Rubin's demonstration of figure/ground discrimination [after (*48*)]. In a luminance-contrast image like this you see either the vase or the faces but not both. At equiluminance you can see both simultaneously, or they alternate very rapidly.

times larger than those in the interblobs (*18*). Since only the blobs seem to retain information about the sign of color contrast, we suspect that they are responsible for the perception of the actual colors of objects, as opposed to the ability to use color or luminance contrast to perceive the borders of objects. This implies that color perception should have lower spatial resolution than form perception. This difference in spatial resolution may explain a phenomenon of color perception described by Chevreul (*56*) in 1839 and by von Bezold (*57*) in 1876, the phenomenon of bleeding. The way two adjacent colors can affect each other depends on their geometrical arrangement. When two large regions of color abut, their apparent colors and lightnesses repel each other, each making the other look more like its complement, a phenomenon consistent with the center/surround antagonism in the blob system. For example, a gray spot surrounded by red will look slightly greenish, and the same gray surrounded by green will appear slightly reddish; surrounding the gray by white will make it appear dark, and surrounding it by black will make it seem lighter. This is called simultaneous contrast and can be seen in Fig. 13. Two colors can have exactly the opposite effect on each other if their geometrical arrangement is such that one forms a very fine pattern, such as fine stripes or dots, with the other as a background. In the lower half of Fig. 13, the mortar seems to bleed into the surrounding gray; the white mortar makes the gray look lighter, and the black mortar makes the same gray look darker. We suspect that bleeding occurs when a pattern is too fine to be resolved by the low acuity color system but not too fine for the higher-resolution form system. Thus you see a pattern, but the colors do not seem to conform to the pattern. We think that the interblob system and the magno system can both define shape, and we cannot predict whether one or the other is more important in defining the borders to which the color is assigned. Some observations, however, suggest that the magno system can influence the spreading of color: color bleeding can be contained by illusory borders or by borders defined only by stereopsis; also, stationary patches of color can seem to move with moving luminance-contrast stimuli (*58*).

Of course a pattern can be too fine to be seen by either system, as in the microscopic dots used in magazine illustrations. In this case the individual dots cannot be seen, and the colors simply blend. Many artists of the Impressionist period were aware of the way the colors in a resolvable pattern can bleed; they often made dots or dabs of paint large enough to be seen, but small enough that their colors blended (*59*). The television industry takes advantage of these differences in spatial resolution by broadcasting the color part of the image at a lower resolution than the black and white part, thus reducing the amount of information to be carried.

Why should the visual system be subdivided? Electrophysiological studies suggest that the magno system is responsible for carrying information about movement and depth. We extended our ideas about the possible functions of the magno system with perceptual studies and concluded that the magno system may have a more global function of interpreting spatial organization. Magno func-

tions may include deciding which visual elements, such as edges and discontinuities, belong to and define individual objects in the scene, as well as determining the overall three-dimensional organization of the scene and the positions of objects in space and movements of objects.

If the magno system covers such a broad range of functions, then what is the function of the tenfold more massive parvo system? The color selectivity of the parvo system should enable us to see borders using color information alone and thus borders that might be camouflaged to the color-blind magno system. But defeating camouflage may be only a small part of what the parvo system is specialized for. Experiments with fading of low contrast images (*37*) indicate that the magno system is not capable of sustained scrutiny, since images that can be seen by only the magno system disappear after a few seconds of voluntary fixation. Thus while the magno system is sensitive primarily to moving objects and carries information about the overall organization of the visual world, the parvo system seems to be important for analyzing the scene in much greater and more leisurely detail. These postulated functions would be consistent with the evolutionary relation of the two systems: the magno system seems to be more primitive than the parvo system (*60*) and is possibly homologous to the entire visual system of nonprimate mammals. If so, it should not be surprising that the magno system is capable of what seem to be the essential functions of vision for an animal that uses vision to navigate in its environment, catch prey, and avoid predators. The parvo system, which is well developed only in primates, seems to have added the ability to scrutinize in much more detail the shape, color, and surface properties of objects, creating the possibility of assigning multiple visual attributes to a single object and correlating its parts. Indeed, if the magno system needs to use the various visual attributes of an object in order to link its parts together, this could preclude its being able to analyze the attributes independently. It thus seems reasonable to us that the parvo→ →temporal lobe system might be especially suited for visual identification and association.

Is the existence of separate pathways an accident of evolution or a useful design principle? Segregating the processing of different types of information into separate pathways might facilitate the interactions between cells carrying the same type of information. It might also allow each system to develop functions particularly suited to its specialization. If the parvo system did evolve after the magno system, by duplication of previously existing structures, it should not be surprising to find some redundancy in the properties of the two systems. Indeed, both seem to carry information about orienta-

Fig. 13. Simultaneous contrast versus bleeding. This phenomenon is shown for black and white, but it is also true for colors. When a spot is surrounded by another color or brightness, the apparent color of the spot tends toward the opposite, or complement, of the surround. The exact opposite happens when one color forms a fine pattern on the other; then the colors bleed.

tion, and perceptual experiments indicate that both systems can be used to determine shape.

We have summarized the anatomical, physiological, and psychological evidence for segregation of function in the primate visual system. By comparing our own perceptual abilities with the electrophysiological properties of neurons in different subdivisions of the visual system, we may be able to deduce functions of particular visual areas, functions that might not have been obvious from electrophysiological observations alone. We can now go back to physiological experiments to test some of the ideas raised by the perceptual experiments.

REFERENCES AND NOTES

1. H. Lissauer, *Arch. Psychiatr. Nervenkr.* **21**, 22 (1890); J. Bodamer, *ibid.* **179**, 6 (1947); A. R. Damasio, T. Yamada, H. Damasio, J. Corbett, J. McKee, *Neurology* **30**, 1064 (1980); A. L. Pearlman, J. Birch, J. C. Meadows, *Ann. Neurol.* **5**, 253 (1979); D. Verrey, *Arch. Ophthalmol. (Paris)* **8**, 289 (1888); R. Balint, *Monatsschr. Psychiatr. Neurol.* **25**, 51 (1909); J. Zihl, D. Von Cramon, N. Mai, *Brain* **106**, 313 (1983). Cortical loss of color perception and loss of face recognition usually occur together, but each can occur independently.
2. H. Munk, *Centralbl. Prakt. Augenheilk.* **3**, 255 (1879).
3. M. Minkowski, *Arch. Neurol. Psychiatr.* **6**, 201 (1920).
4. W. E. Le Gros Clark and G. G. Penman, *Proc. R. Soc. Lond. Ser. B* **114**, 291 (1934); S. Brody, *Proc. Kon. Ned. Akad. Wet.* **37**, 724 (1934); J. G. Malpeli and F. H. Baker, *J. Comp. Neurol.* **161**, 569 (1975).
5. A. G. Leventhal, R. W. Rodieck, B. Dreher, *Science* **213**, 1139 (1981).
6. S. W. Kuffler, *J. Neurophysiol.* **16**, 37 (1953).
7. T. N. Wiesel and D. H. Hubel *ibid.* **29**, 1115 (1966); P. H. Schiller and J. G. Malpeli, *ibid.* **41**, 788 (1978).
8. R. L. De Valois, E. Abramov, G. H. Jacobs, *J. Opt. Soc. Am.* **56**, 966 (1966); R. L. De Valois, D. M. Snodderly, Jr., E. W. Yund, N. K. Hepler, *Sens. Process.* **1**, 244 (1977); A. M. Derrington, J. Krauskopf, P. Lennie, *J. Physiol. (London)* **357**, 241 (1984); E. Kaplan and R. M. Shapley, *ibid.* **330**, 125 (1982); *Proc. Natl. Acad. Sci. U.S.A.* **83**, 2755 (1986); B. Dreher, Y. Fukada, R. W. Rodieck, *J. Physiol. (London)* **258**, 433 (1976); T. P. Hicks, B. B. Lee, T. R. Vidyasagar, *ibid.* **337**, 183 (1983); P. Gouras, *ibid.* **199**, 533 (1968); *ibid.* **204**, 407 (1969); F. deMonasterio and P. Gouras, *ibid.* **251**, 167 (1975).
9. A. M. Derrington and P. Lennie, *J. Physiol. (London)* **357**, 219 (1984).
10. R. Shapley, E. Kaplan, R. Soodak, *Nature (London)* **292**, 543 (1981).
11. The magno system clearly combines the inputs from the red and the green cones, but the contribution from the blue cones is so small that it is not clear whether the magno system receives any input at all from the blue cones. Also, magno cells are not completely broadband, in that their receptive field surrounds are often weighted toward the red (7).
12. D. H. Hubel and T. N. Wiesel, *J. Comp. Neurol.* **146**, 421 (1972); J. S. Lund, *ibid.* **147**, 455 (1973); ———— and R. G. Boothe, *ibid.* **159**, 305 (1975).
13. M. Wong-Riley, personal communication.
14. A. E. Hendrickson, S. P. Hunt, and J.-Y. Wu, *Nature (London)* **292**, 605 (1981); J. C. Horton and D. H. Hubel, *ibid.*, p. 762.
15. J. C. Horton, *Philos. Trans. R. Soc. London* **304**, 199 (1984); E. McGuinness, C. MacDonald, M. Sereno, J. Allman, *Soc. Neurosci. Abstr.* **12**, 130 (1986).
16. M. S. Livingstone and D. H. Hubel, *Proc. Natl. Acad. Sci. U.S.A.* **79**, 6098 (1982).
17. C. R. Michael, *Soc. Neurosci. Abstr.* **13**, 2 (1987); D. Fitzpatrick, K. Itoh, I. T. Diamond, *J. Neurosci.* **3**, 673 (1983); R. B. H. Tootell, S. L. Hamilton, E. Switkes, R. L. De Valois, *Invest. Ophthalmol. Visual Sci.* (suppl.) **26**, 8 (1985).
18. M. S. Livingstone and D. H. Hubel, *J. Neurosci.* **4**, 2830 (1984).
19. B. Dow, *J. Neurophysiol.* **37**, 927 (1974).
20. P. Gouras and J. Krüger, *ibid.* **42**, 850 (1979).
21. R. B. H. Tootell *et al.*, *Science* **220**, 737 (1983).
22. M. S. Livingstone and D. H. Hubel, *J. Neurosci.* **7**, 3371 (1987).
23. D. H. Hubel and M. S. Livingstone, *ibid.*, p. 3378.
24. J. S. Baizer, D. L. Robinson, B. M. Dow, *J. Neurophysiol.* **40**, 1024 (1977).
25. G. F. Poggio and B. Fischer, *ibid.*, p. 1392; G. F. Poggio, in *Dynamic Aspects of Neocortical Functions* G. M. Edelman, W. E. Gall, W. M. Cowan, Eds. (Wiley, New York, 1984), pp. 631–632.
26. E. A. DeYoe and D. C. Van Essen, *Nature (London)* **317**, 58 (1985).
27. A. Burkhalter and D. C. Van Essen, *J. Neurosci.* **6**, 2327 (1986).
28. R. Dubner and S. M. Zeki, *Brain Res.* **35**, 528 (1971); J. H. R. Maunsell and D. C. Van Essen, *J. Neurophysiol.* **49**, 1148 (1983).
29. J. S. Lund, R. D. Lund, A. E. Hendrickson, A. H. Bunt, A. F. Fuchs, *J. Comp. Neurol.* **164**, 287 (1975); W. B. Spatz, *Brain Res* **92**, 450 (1975); L. G. Ungerlieder and M. Mishkin, *J. Comp. Neurol.* **188**, 347 (1979).
30. S. Shipp and S. Zeki, *Nature (London)* **315**, 322 (1985).
31. S. Zeki, *ibid.* **284**, 412 (1980).
32. References (26) and (30) are in agreement that the thick stripes project to MT and that the thin stripes project to visual area 4, but only (26) reports that the pale stripes project to visual area 4.
33. For a review, J. H. R. Maunsell, *Matters of Intelligence*, L. M. Vaina, Ed. (Kluwer Academic, Norwell, MA, 1987), pp. 59–87.
34. W. Pohl, *J. Comp. Physiol. Psychol.* **82**, 227 (1973).
35. L. G. Ungerleider and M. Mishkin, in *Analysis of Visual Behavior*, D. J. Ingle, M. A. Goodale, R. J. W. Mansfield, Eds. (MIT Press, Cambridge, MA, 1982), pp. 549–586.
36. K. S. Rockland and D. N. Pandya, *Brain Res.* **179**, 3 (1979); R. Desimone, J. Fleming, C. G. Gross, *ibid.* **184**, 41 (1980); J. H. R. Maunsell and D. C. Van Essen, *J. Neurosci.* **3**, 2563 (1983).
37. M. S. Livingstone and D. H. Hubel, *J. Neurosci.* **7**, 3416 (1987).
38. H. E. Ives, *J. Opt. Soc. Am. Rev. Sci. Instr.* **7**, 363 (1923).
39. P. Cavanagh, C. W. Tyler, O. E. Favreau, *J. Opt. Soc. Am.* **8**, 893 (1984).
40. We found (37) that apparent movement as well as real movement disappeared at equiluminance. This result is controversial, but we suspect that different findings may be due to difficulties in achieving equiluminance across the visual field.
41. F. W. Campbell and L. Maffei, *Vision Res.* **21**, 713 (1981).
42. C. Lu and D. H. Fender, *Invest. Ophthalmol.* **11**, 482 (1972).
43. R. L. Gregory, *Perception* **6**, 113 (1977).
44. J. Krüger, *Exp. Brain Res.* **30**, 297 (1979).
45. Derrington and Lennie (9) have reported that magnocellular neurons are less responsive than parvocellular neurons at equiluminance, but are not unresponsive. P. H. Schiller and C. L. Colby [*Vision Res.* **23**, 1631 (1983)] and A. C. Hurlbert, N. K. Logothetis, E. R. Charles, and P. H. Schiller [*Soc. Neurosci. Abstr.* **13**, 204 (1987)] have reported that cells in the parvo system, not the magno system, become unresponsive at equiluminance. This issue clearly remains to be resolved and is discussed in (37).
46. P. Cavanagh and Y. Leclerc, *Invest. Ophthalmol. Visual Sci.* (suppl.) **26**, 282 (1985).
47. J. J. Gibson, *The Perception of the Visual World*, L. Carmichael, Ed. (Houghton Mifflin, Boston, 1950).
48. E. Rubin, *Synsoplevede Figurer* (Glydendalska, Copenhagen, 1915).
49. H. B. Barlow, *Proc. R. Soc. London* **212**, 1 (1981).
50. V. S. Ramachandran and S. A. Anstis, *Perception* **14**, 135 (1985).
51. F. Schumann, *Z. Psychol.* **23**, 1 (1900).
52. G. Kanizsa, *Riv. Psicologia* **49**, 7 (1955).
53. R. L. Gregory, *Nature (London)* **238**, 51 (1972).
54. S. Liebmann, *Psychol. Forsch.* **9**, 300 (1926).
55. K. Koffka, *Principles of Gestalt Psychology* (Harcourt Brace, New York, 1935).
56. M. E. Chevreul, *De la Loi du Contraste Simultané des Couleurs* (Pitios-Levrault, Paris, 1839).
57. W. von Bezold, *The Theory of Color*, S. R. Koehler, Transl. (Prang, Boston, 1876).
58. H. F. J. M. van Tuijl, *Acta Psychol.* **39**, 441 (1975); K. Nakayama and S. Shimojo, personal communication; V. S. Ramachandran, *Nature (London)* **328**, 645 (1987).
59. M. S. Livingstone, *Sci. Am.* **258**, 78 (January 1988).
60. R. W. Guillery, *Prog. Brain Res.* **51**, 403 (1979); S. M. Sherman, *Prog. Psychobiol. Physiol. Psychol.* **2**, 233 (1985).

Article 4.3

Reorganization and Diversification of Signals in Vision

RICHARD E. KRONAUER AND YEHOSHUA Y. ZEEVI

Abstract—Extensive processing and reorganization of information is required as retinally generated signals flow centrally. Insight into some principles of the reorganization and transformations that occur in the early stages of the visual pathway, prior to the higher stages of pattern recognition, is provided by analysis of receptive fields and cell counts. The rate of information flow is reduced by a retinal position-dependent (inhomogeneous) spatial sampling scheme about 100-fold. This principle of specialization, or nonuniform processing, is further elaborated in the retino-cortical mapping. In the central fovea, where the retinal spatial sampling rate is the highest and processing function is uniform, there are about 4000 striate cortical neurons receiving information from each cone. This number, which provides a measure of function multiplicity, drops to about 200 over the range of the near periphery. In the peripheral field beyond eight degrees, where information is compressed at the retina, the functional multiplicity stays approximately constant at 200. As it seems that no two cells perform exactly the same operation, it is concluded that the striate cortex performs many simultaneous functional mappings. Only a partial description of these various schemes of signal processing is deducible from present data, thus highlighting the challenge associated with understanding how the central nervous system constructs a meaningful representation of the visual world.

INTRODUCTION

THE VISUAL system is the main channel for intake of perceptual information. This is well reflected in the heavy signal traffic carried along the optic nerve, that accounts for about half of the total number of nerve fibers streaming into the primate brain. It is estimated that over 60 percent of the input sensory information is funneled through the visual system. The order of magnitude of channel capacity for the optic nerve is at least 10^8 bits/s (Zeevi and Kronauer [1]), although the actual rate of signal flow may be considerably lower, especially if only mean spike rate coding exists (Bruckstein and Zeevi, [2]). Whatever this number, it is certainly much higher than the rate of information intake at the perceptual level of decisionmaking, which is estimated to be only tens of bits/s (Cherry [3]). This indicates that the information generated in the primate retinal mosaic of photoreceptors must undergo extensive processing and reorganization as it flows centrally along the visual pathway. Perhaps intrinsic redundancy is used to make the processing very reliable in spite of the fact that the cellular components exhibit devia-

tions from strict regularity (though the better we understand the system, the more regular it appears), and signals at the cellular level appear to have major random constituents.

We are dealing here with a system that has evolved to transduce, transmit, and process information through a large ensemble ensemble of parallel channels, operating over an enormous range of light intensity ($> 10^{10}$) with very high sensitivity—absolute sensitivity being limited by the quantal nature of light (Pirenne [4]). It is most natural to adopt, therefore, a communications approach, whereby the behavior of the numerous parallel channels can reasonably be treated only in terms of some general defining characteristics. The factors describing the performance of the visual communication system are the intensity input–output relationship (described as either lightness or brightness), the spatio-temporal frequency response characterized in terms of contrast sensitivity functions (CSF), and the signal-to-noise ratio. These factors can be studied both physiologically and psychophysically and the results can be correlated.

Understanding the organization of visual systems is obviously of great interest to brain scientists and engineers alike; it poses an intellectual challenge to those who have mastered engineering concepts and techniques so useful in organizing and interrelating a vast amount of data. It is also of great importance to the engineer because of its potential use in the design of technological systems. By matching image presentations with the known performance of the visual system, more meaningful and efficient communication can be achieved (Zeevi and Daugman [6]). After all, most information generated for human use is communicated with the visual system as the final receiver. In yet another way, image processing modeled after the visual system may prove to be important in machine vision. And of course, if visual prosthetics are to become a workable reality, this understanding is essential.

The purpose of this paper is to analyze the organization of the early stages of the visual pathway and the coding or transformations of signals achieved therein, relating this as much as possible to overall perceptual performance measures. The emphasis is on preprocessing and transformations that occur prior to processes of pattern recognition, and thus there is no reference to any symbolic language that may subsequently encode the sensory information into a higher order representation of our visual environment.

Manuscript received November 22, 1983; revised August 29, 1984. This work was supported by AFOSR Contract F49620-81-K-0016.

R. E. Kronauer is with the Division of Applied Sciences, Harvard University, Cambridge, MA 02138.

Y. Y. Zeevi is with the Department of Electrical Engineering, Technion —Israel Institute of Technology, Haifa, 32-000, Israel.

Reprinted from *IEEE Trans. Syst. Man, Cybern.*, vol. SMC-15, no. 1, pp. 91–101, Jan./Feb. 1985.

We focus on basic issues related to both the large and small scale of retinal and cortical maps. Summarizing existing data on cell counts and receptive field sizes at different levels, we find it useful to introduce new concepts to better describe such matters as the extent of cortical "hardware" devoted to the processing of signals arising ultimately from a single retinal cone. We evaluate how functional multiplicity, which reflects the variety of operations performed on each of the spatially quantized retinal signals, varies with retinal eccentricity. This highlights the challenges associated with understanding retino-cortical mapping and the various transformations taking place therein.

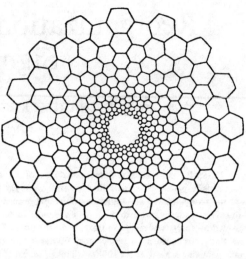

Fig. 1. A schematic representation of "information-density" extracted by the extra-foveal retina (5°–50° of eccentricity). Each of the hexagonal units represents the same number of sample points and contains about 200 ganglion cells in macaque monkey. The "sunflower-heart" is adopted from Koenderink and vanDoorn [13].

PHOTORECEPTORS AND THE RETINA

Many important characteristics of the visual system are ultimately limited by properties of photoreceptors and by photoreceptor distribution across the retina. The evolution of photoreceptors has achieved the theoretical limit of signal detection, since retinal rods can respond to the capture of a single photon (Pirenne [4]; Baylor et al. [5]). However, electrophysiological studies suggest that the probability with which an absorbed photon gives rise to an electrical response is only 0.5 [5]. Other attenuating factors, such as absorption in and dispersion by the ocular media, contribute to a considerably smaller overall quantal efficiency of order 0.1.

As a consequence of the optimal design, photon noise induces signal variability. In fact, many investigators have proposed that this may be the main origin of noisy signals in vision at some light intensities (Rose [7]; Barlow [8]; Barlow and Levick [9]; Zeevi and Mangoubi [10]). Since the energy of a visible photon is far less than that of any appreciable bioelectric signal, an intermediate process of amplification is necessarily incorporated into photoreceptor design, introducing thereby an internal source of noise (Baylor et al. [11]; Simon et al. [12]; Baylor et al. [5]). In addition, there are in subsequent processes various other sources of neural noise. The interplay of all of these sources determines the detection thresholds. Theoretical analysis indicates that, due to the compressive-type photoreceptor nonlinearity, quantal noise is the main limiting factor of incremental intensity sensitivity over only a limited intermediate range of light intensities. At very low and moderately high intensities, receptor internal noise or neural noise determines the bound on sensitivity (Zeevi and Mangoubi [10]).

An important characteristic of the human retina (and of primate retinas in general) is its inhomogeneous distribution of photoreceptors. Considering the cone system (which is responsible for high-quality chromatic image processing), the highest receptor density is in the center of the fovea and decreases with eccentricity according to a power law. (See cone density plot in Fig. 8.) This position-dependent spatial scheme reduces the rate of information flow by about one hundred fold, i.e., to achieve the sampling rate of the central fovea ($\sim$ 7 cones per min^2 of arc) over the entire visual field of one eye ($\sim$ 7500 deg^2) would require about 2×10^8 cones, or about 100 times the number of cones that actually exist. As the cone density decreases the image processing capability decreases, but this actually matches the degradation of the optical image due to spherical aberrations and the nonplanar contour of the retina. The price paid is gradual degradation of the retinal image, and considerable loss of form and color information as a function of eccentricity. Most properties of the retina and of the entire visual system depend on eccentricity, and the "information density" (as measured by sampling density) extracted by the retina outside of the fovea may be represented schematically as shown in Fig. 1. For example, if a test stimulus composed of a finite patch of a counterphase flickering sinusoidal grating is used to measure spatio-temporal contrast sensitivity at various eccentricities, scaling all aspects of the stimulus with eccentricity (approximately the first power) leads to identical thresholds (Koenderink and vanDoorn [13]).

Retinal cones are often seen to be arranged in remarkably regular patterns (deMonesterio et al. [14]; Hirsch and Hylton [15]; foveal cones begin close-packed hexagonal, with only a very gradual distortion of the pattern axes. Patterns of retinal illumination with spatial frequencies higher than the cone Nyquist frequency are perceived as patterns with spatial frequencies lower than Nyquist due to the well-known phenomenon of aliasing (Yellott [16]). As we shall demonstrate below, in primates foveal cones communicate to the brain through individual channels (private lines) so that regularity in the cones patterning can be reflected in cortical processing (Hirsch and Hylton [17]).

The primate retina can be thought of as having three processing regions: 1) the central fovea, up to an eccentricity of about 0.5°, which has the best optical image, maximum receptor density and uniform processing function; 2) an intermediate region up to about 8° of eccentricity in which cone density declines but where the spatial informa-

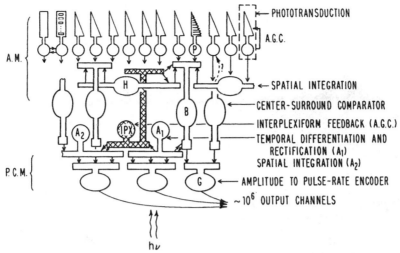

Fig. 2. A schematic diagram of signal flow in the mammalian retina. The "through" pathways extend from the photoreceptors, P, via the bipolar cells, B, to the ganglion cells, G, whose output axons constitute the optic nerve. The "across" processes (lateral interactions) are mediated first by horizontal cells, H, and second by amacrine cells, A. The signal form is amplitude modulation (AM) as far as the amarcine/ganglion cell interactions, at which stage it is converted to pulse code modulation (PCM) for transmission over the relatively long path to the brain. The interplexiform cells (IPX) represent a feedback path for automatic gain control (AGC).

tion generated by the cones is fully transmitted to the cortex; and 3) a peripheral region in which information is compressed before transmission (note transition into ganglion cell limiting regime in Fig. 8), and where the character of the processing emphasizes transients with large spatial scale. What we will be discussing here are the central and intermediate processing functions.

To discuss briefly a simplified linear approximation of signal processing characteristic of one population of retinal channels (the so-called X-type ganglion cells), we first restrict our analysis to the "through" and "across" pathways (Fig. 2). To a first approximation, the through pathway is formed by the chain photoreceptor-bipolar-ganglion cell. The through pathway is modified by across pathways of lateral influences mediated by horizontal and amacrine cells. The receptive field of an X-type ganglion cell, described in Cartesian coordinates centered with respect to the cell position, can be conveniently approximated by the difference of the two Gaussians (Fig. 3).

$$g_X(x, y) = \frac{1}{2\pi d_e^2} \exp\left[-(x^2 + y^2)/2d_e^2\right]$$
$$- \frac{1}{2\pi d_i^2} \exp\left[-(x^2 + y^2)/2d_i^2\right]$$
$$= G_e(x, y) - G_i(x, y), \qquad d_i > d_e \quad (1)$$

where d_e and d_i, respectively, denote the effective widths, or spread functions, of the excitatory center and inhibitory surround of the "Mexican-hat shaped" receptive field. Note that each of the Gaussian functions has properties which make its application to receptive field description so desirable and convenient. First, it remains Gaussian when Fourier transformed to the two-dimensional spatial fre-

quency domain; we denote this by

$$G(x, y) \underset{-2_{\mathscr{F}}}{\overset{2_{\mathscr{F}}}{\rightleftarrows}} \underline{G}(\omega_x, \omega_y). \quad (2)$$

Second, it is separable into a product of functions of x and y in the space domain and into a product of one-dimensional frequency functions in the Fourier transform domain. Of course, the sum of Gaussians is not product separable.

The receptive field described in (1) is defined and experimentally measured as an impulse response in which the measurement coordinates (the position of the cell) are fixed, and the impulse position (the independent variable) varies. Now suppose that in any layer the cell bodies are sufficiently small and densely (though irregularly) packed, compared to stimulus and receptive field dimensions (an assumption that implies extensive overlap of dendritic fields), that we may consider an approximately continuous version of the cellular array. Denoting an X-cell's location by (x, y), and the argument of the stimulus, e, by (x', y'), the output cells' array response $r(x, y)$ can be written as the integral

$$r(x, y) = \iint g(x, x', y, y') e(x', y') \, dx' \, dy' \quad (3)$$

where g denotes the ganglion cell population response kernel. If for the sake of the present argument we assume local position invariant characteristics (or local stationarity) so that

$$g(x, x', y, y') = g(x - x', y - y') \quad (4)$$

then the above described integral becomes a convolution

$$r(x, y) = g * e. \quad (5)$$

189

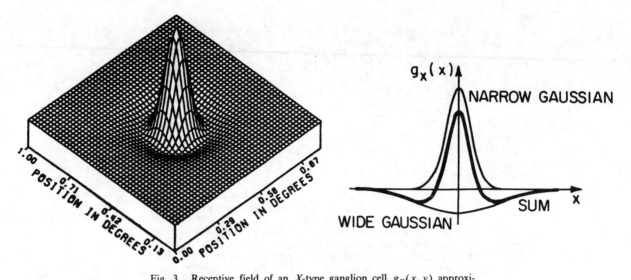

Fig. 3. Receptive field of an X-type ganglion cell $g_X(x, y)$ approximated by the difference of two Gaussians (Rodieck [55]); a narrow Gaussian represents the excitatory center, and a wide one the inhibitory surround. Note that $\iint g_X(x, y)\,dx\,dy = 0$ implies perfect cancellation of response to uniform illumination (spatial dc).

The population response kernel $g(x, y)$ is the mirror image of the receptive field function $g_X(x, y)$ described in (1)

$$g(x, y) = g_X(-x, -y). \qquad (6)$$

For the given symmetrical Mexican-hat function, the two become identical. However, of these two, only g_X can be measured experimentally. Since, as written in (1), both G_e and G_i have a unitary integral over the x, y plane, their difference g_X has an integral which is zero. The transform of g_X is consequently zero at the origin ($\omega_x = 0 = \omega_y$) and furthermore, the transform approaches zero as $\omega_x, \omega_y \to \infty$. Thus, the model of the retinal X-type cell passes spatial frequencies only in an annular band that is defined by $(1.2d_i)^{-2} < \omega_x^2 + \omega_y^2 < (1.2d_e)^{-2}$. For a specific fixed ratio of $d_i/d_e \cong 3.5$, the kernel g_X resembles quite closely the function $-\nabla^2 G_e/2 = G_e[1-(x^2 + y^2)/4d_e^2]$, where $\nabla^2\{\cdot\}$ is the Laplacian operator. This somewhat restrictive approximation has been extensively used by the Massachusetts Institute of Technology artificial intelligence group (Marr [18]).

The linear approximation described so far provides an adequate representation of retinal input–output relations for small signals (low contrasts) modulating a fixed mean luminance. The functional relationship between the input (luminance) and the physiological output r, or the corresponding psychophysical output can, under these conditions, be approximated by a fixed gain. Such fixed gain models cannot describe adaptation phenomena, nor can they approximate the dependency of visual spatio-temporal transfer characteristics on the mean luminance level (Kelly [19]).

To account for adaptation, one has to recognize structural and functional feedback pathways and analyze retinal

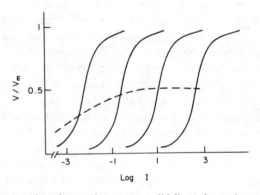

Fig. 4. A series of operating curves (solid lines) for various adapting intensities. The dashed curve represents adaptation conditions. Its intersection with each solid curve corresponds to paired values of imposed adaptation intensity and resulting output voltage.

behavior in the nonlinear regime (Sperling and Sondhi [20]; Zeevi and Shefer [21]). A major portion of retinal gain (sensitivity) control may be accomplished by a cone adaptation mechanism, which tends to keep cone output close to the center of its useful voltage range (Werblin [22]; Normann and Perlman [23]). The steady-state (fully adapted) receptor voltage v_a is related to the adapting light intensity I_a by a highly compressive-type function (Normann and Perlman [23]; Boynton and Whitten [24]). This is shown by the dashed line in Fig. 4. At high intensities, $v_a \cong v_{\max}/2$, where $v_{\max}$ is the maximum attainable level of hyperpolarization. The adaption curve can be represented by

$$v_a/v_{\max} \cong \left(1 + f(I_a)\right)^{-1}, \qquad f \geqslant 1 \qquad (7)$$

where $f(I_a) \to 1$ as $I_a \to \infty$. This compressive type of receptive nonlinearity plays an important role in the suppression of quantal and receptor internal noise (Zeevi and Magnoubi [10]).

For rapid transient changes in I about the adapting level, the receptor voltage is well represented by a simple saturation function

$$v/v_{\max} = I/(I + k(I_a)) \qquad (8)$$

where k is the intensity value for which $v = v_{\max}/2$. A family of such transient operating curves, which are simple translations of one another in the coordinate $\log I$, are shown in Fig. 4. When I_a is very high, so that v_a is very close to $v_{\max}/2$, then $k(I_a) \cong I_a$. For small increments about the adapting conditions, we can define the receptor gain as

$$\mu = dv/dI = v_{\max}/(I_a + k(I_a)). \qquad (9)$$

This form is similar to that describing automatic gain control (AGC) in communications systems. A second level of AGC, so crucial for automatic adjustments of spatio-temporal transfer characteristics, may be mediated within the retina by the large and relatively sparse interplexiform (IPX) cells (Zeevi and Shefer [21]). The input to the IPX cells is exclusively in the inner plexiform layer, whereas in the out plexiform layer the IPX cells are exclusively pre-synaptic; they form synapses on horizontal cells and bipolar dendrites (Dowling [25]; Dowling *et al.* [26]). These cells thus appear to provide a feedback pathway for signal flow from the inner to outer plexiform layer, as shown in Fig. 2.

FROM RETINA TO CORTEX

Under ordinary photopic levels of illumination, the photoreceptors (cones) are the discrete originators of visual information in analog form (graded potentials). The X-type ganglion cells are the retinal output cells transmitting detailed information to the brain in pulse code modulation (PCM) form, or simply by pulse rate, for the relatively long transmission path. (The ganglion cells of other classes, Y-type and W-type, together comprise less than ten percent of all ganglion cells.) Surprisingly, careful cell counts (Rolls and Cowey [27]) show that in primates the number of ganglion cells in the central retina (eccentricity $< 8°$) matches or slightly exceeds the number of photoreceptors (Fig. 8). Thus, while there may be a transformation of the form in which central field information is conveyed, there is probably no significant reduction in it.

The ganglion cells are generally arranged in such a way that the individual cells are spatially coincident in retinal coordinates with the photoreceptors which drive them. The exception to this rule is the central fovea, where the ganglion cells and other neural tissue are displaced into a parafoveal annulus so that the intermediate processing cells do not cause any degeneration of the most critical optical image (Polyak [28]). (In cats, where the resolution is only about one third that of primates and humans, there is no displacement of central ganglion cells.)

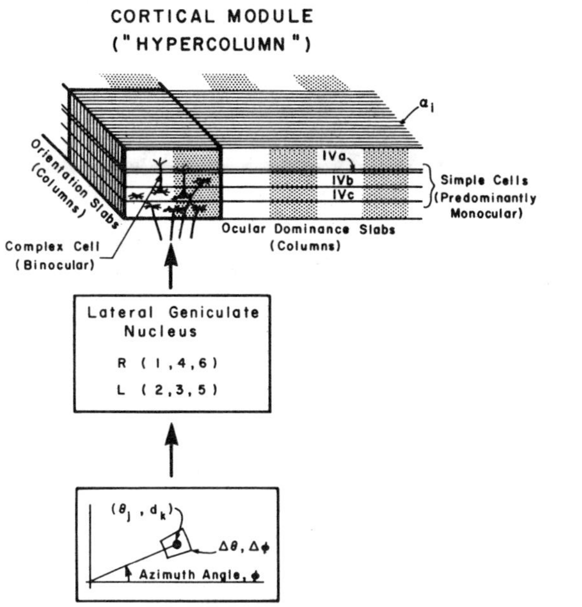

Fig. 5. A schematic representation of signal flow from retina to cortex via the Lateral Geniculate Nuclei (LGN). The six layers of the LGN are segregated, by right (R) and left (L) eye, according to the numbers indicated parenthetically. Processes from the LGN impinge primarily on cortical layer IVc.

Transmission from retina to cortex takes place through two layered structures, called lateral geniculate nuclei (LGN), one in each cerebral hemisphere. In these nuclei, the signals from the left and right eyes are intermixed in the sense that they are assigned to separate, noninteracting cell layers (ipsilateral optic nerve fibers terminate in layers 2, 3, and 5, contralateral fibers in layers 1, 4, and 6). However, the visual field is separated into right and left halves on vertical lines through the foveas, with each half visual field being represented in one of the nuclei (Fig. 5). The cells in each of the nuclei are arranged in the six layers in a retinotopic projection—i.e., their relative positions correspond to the positions of the photoreceptors through which they are stimulated. Precisely what signal processing takes place in the LGN is not entirely clear. The receptive fields of LGN cells have the same center-surround organization as the retinal ganglion cells, and so the LGN has been described as a relay station. It appears that LGN cells have narrower spatial-frequency bandwidths than ganglion cells (smaller ratio of surround to center diameters), and therefore it is likely that a greater variety of preferred spatial frequencies are found at any single retinal location.

The LGN axons impinge on the striate cortex (area 17 of the visual cortex). This cortex contains six morphologically distinct layers (numbered from the outer surface inward (Fig. 5)). The cortex is about 2 mm thick in primates (2.5 mm in humans), and layer IV is subdivided into three laminae (IVa, b, c), each of which is about as thick (about 250 μm) as the other five layers. The LGN afferents certainly excite the cells in IVc and, to a lesser extent, cells in other outer layers. Cell morphology suggests that signals flow from layer IVc to both lower and higher numbered

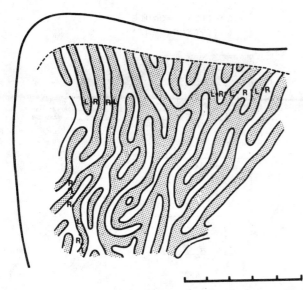

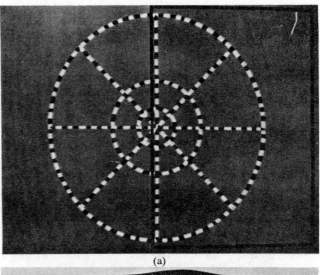

(a)

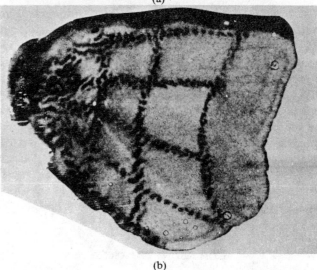

(b)

Fig. 6. Reconstruction of the pattern of ocular dominance stripes in area 17 of the macaque monkey, made from a series of sections tangential to the cortical surface, stained with a reduced-silver technique (LeVay *et al.* [29]). The scale is 5 mm total length.

Fig. 7. (a) The cat retina, when it is excited by the ring-and-ray illumination pattern. (b) The cells in cortical area 17 that are strongly stimulated lie on a distorted grid pattern. Only half of the visual field (in the rectangular box of (a)) is represented in this half of the cortex. The central area of (a) lies to the left in (b) and the innermost semicircle of (a) corresponds to the left-most of the three vertical bands in (b). The blackened (radioactively labeled) segments in (b) correspond to portions of ocular dominance bands. The scale in (b) is 1 cm. From Tootell *et al.* [31].

layers. It is a reasonable approximation to assume that cortical cell somas (cell bodies) are spaced about 30 μm apart in all directions. This means that there are about 7×10^4 cells per mm^2 of cortical surface. In the cortex, signals from the two eyes converge on individual cells, but not with equal strength. This leads to the concept of ocular dominance (OD), denoting that one eye has the greater influence on a particular cell. Experiments in which only one eye is visually excited, and in which a radioactively labeled metabolite is injected into the cortex, demarcate the cells that are strongly driven by the stimulated eye (LeVay *et al.* [29]). The resulting pattern of OD in monkeys is shown in Fig. 6. Note that the pattern shows OD bands that have a repeat interval of about 0.8 mm (repeat interval includes both left (L) and right (R) dominance). Thus, a distinction between the left and right eyes, which is manifested in the LGN as noninteracting laminae, is transformed in the cortex to bands spaced out over the surface —a functional distinction, which is merely one of degree, rather than exclusivity. Because these bands extend through all cortical layers, they have been called OD "columns," but a better description is OD "slabs."

Like the LGN, the cortex is laid out in a kind of overall retinotopic mapping, but it differs from the retina on both large and small scales. The large scale differences come from the fact that on the retina the ganglion cells are packed more densely at the fovea than in the periphery, while in the cortex the cells have a uniform packing density. Thus, to allocate a fixed amount of cortical processing per spatial sample, the representation of the fovea occupies far more of the cortex than it does of the retina. It was suggested by Schwartz [30] that the retina-cortex mapping might be conformal with circular and radial lines in the retina being represented as a rectangular grid in the cortex (complex logarithmic mapping). Tootell *et al.* [31] tested

this directly with just such a retinal image, using a radioactive metabolite in the cortex (Fig. 7). The cortical map bears a crude resemblance to Schwartz's idealization, but differs significantly in detail.

To understand the small scale differences between the retinal and cortical maps, it is important to consider the concept of retinal-cortical magnification factor, M, introduced by Daniel and Whitteridge [32]. M is the ratio between a small displacement, in millimeters over the cortical surface, and the corresponding displacement, in degrees of visual angle, over the retinal surface. At any point the mapping is isotropic, i.e., M is approximately the same for any direction of the displacement vector. In primates M is approximately 30 mm/deg in the central fovea and then declines with increasing eccentricity (Daniel and Whitteridge [32]; Rolls and Cowey [27]; Hubel and

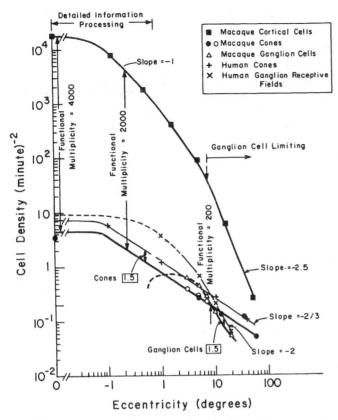

Fig. 8. Distribution of cells over the visual field in primates. The distribution of human cones (+) is from the review of Osterberg's data by Steinberg *et al.* [50] (●), and from Rolls and Cowey [27] (○). The total number of ganglion cells is approximately equal to the total number of cones for an eccentricity of 8°. The actual distribution of macaque ganglion cells (Δ) is from Rolls and Cowey [27]. The distribution of human ganglion cell receptive fields x is taken from Drasdo [35]. Comparing the two species, both cone and ganglion cell densities are in the ratio of 1.5, reflecting the slightly larger optical focal length in humans. The distribution of macaque cortical cells is calculated from the cortical magnification factors given by Dow *et al.* [34]. The ratio of cortical cell density to cone density is the functional multiplicity, which is highest for the central fovea.

Wiesel [33]). Relating functions to structure, it is interesting to observe that the visual acuity is, in turn, inversely proportional to the magnification factor. Knowing M and the cortical cell density, it is easy to calculate the number of cortical cells that are processing the information impinging upon a small unit area of the retina. The result of such a calculation, using the M data of Dow *et al.* [34] for the macaque monkey, is shown as the top curve in Fig. 8. A most instructive comparison is afforded by the photoreceptor density, which is the middle curve of this figure. In the central fovea there are about 4000 cortical neurons for each cone. This number drops to 1000 at an eccentricity of 0.8°, with 2000 being a representative figure for the central fovea as a whole. We call the ratio of cortical cells to photoreceptors the functional multiplicity (FM) of area 17 of the visual cortex, which is a lower bound of how many different operations are performed on each of the spatially quantized retinal inputs.

Also shown in Fig. 8 is the density of retinal ganglion cells in the monkey retina. These data demonstrate the absence of ganglion cells from the central fovea, and that

the counts are approximately the same as for cones up to 8° eccentricity. Thereafter they are fewer in number than cones, showing a convergence of neural processes (information compression) within the retina itself. For eccentricities beyond 8° the ganglion cells should therefore be taken as the basic measure of retinal information density; we call this the ganglion cell limiting regime. We note that the ratio of cortical cells to ganglion cells, which now defines FM at these eccentricities, is approximately constant at 200. Thus, out to quite large angles, there is an indicated uniformity of the cortical processing schema, but one that is significantly less diverse than in the fovea.

The human retina is much the same as the macaque retina. The cones are of equal size and packing, but because of a 22 percent larger focal length the density measured in terms of angular subtend is 1.5 times larger for humans (Fig. 8). The relationship between ganglion cells and cones in humans is virtually identical to that in monkey. Drasdo [35] has taken the data on human ganglion cell density and transformed it to ganglion receptive field density—i.e., shifted the ganglion cells in the parafoveal annulus to the fovea where the receptive fields are located. The result of this somewhat imprecise operation is also shown in Fig. 8. Note that for eccentricities greater than 8° where no transformation of density is required, the human and monkey ganglion cell densities have the same ratio of 1.5 as the cones do. Thus, except for a fixed scale factor, the macaque monkey retina is an excellent model of the human retina.

The challenge associated with understanding area 17 is to determine what the 4000 or so different processes are, and then how they are ordered in the tissue volume. The major discoveries in this regard have been by Hubel and Wiesel [36]. They first showed that area 17 cells are preferentially responsive to oriented lines or edges (i.e., they are tuned to orientation with a tuning width on the order of ±15°). They next showed that the preferred orientations are arranged in discrete sequences, with incremental orientations being in the range of 5° to 12° in primates, and with some random scatter as well. This finding emphasizes the fact that cells, being discrete entities, should be expected to perform discretely catagorized processing operations. Further evidence for discrete processing operations is provided by the finding of Pollen and Ronner [51] that adjacent cells of matching orientation respond to periodic stimuli (gratings) with a 90° shift of their relative phase. This phase quantization is discussed below.

Hubel and Wiesel also showed that a penetration of the cortex normal to its surface sampled cells of the same preferred stimulus orientation—leading to the description "orientation columns." While tangential penetrations would lead in some instances to sequential monotonic increments of orientation angle on a cell-to-cell basis, other tangential penetrations sometimes yield long sequences of cells of almost the same orientation. All this leads to the concept of orientation "slabs," one cell in thickness, within which the cells have the same preferred stimulus orientation, with adjacent slabs having a preferred orientation one discrete

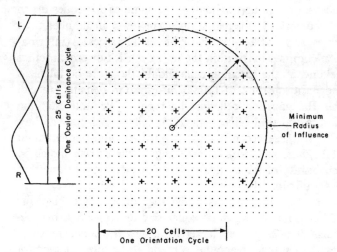

Fig. 9. An idealized representation of cells on the retinal visual field. The crosses represent *X*-type ganglion cells while the dots represent cortical cells. Due to the 2-mm thickness of the cortex, each dot corresponds to a column of 65 cortical cells. The cycle of successive orientations and the cycle of ocular dominance are assumed to be orthogonal. The circular arc centered on a particular cortical cell corresponds in area to the smallest observed fields and embraces about 25 ganglion cells.

step removed (Fig. 4). A total of about 20 different orientations are required to span the full 180° range. If one assumes that the various subdivisions of processing function are independent, so that the overall multiplicity is a product of the multiplicities of the individual functions, then after allowing for orientation multiplicity the residual for foveal processing is 4000/20 = 200. It is seen that orientation accounts for only part of what is available.

Orientation and ocular dominance (OD) are two functional attributes that are known to be arranged in slablike format (i.e., columnar, or invariant normal to the cortical surface). It is convenient to assume for the sake of clarity that the directions in which these functional attributes change are not only parallel to the surface but are approximately orthogonal, although this has not been convincingly demonstrated and, most likely, is not the case. Fig. 9 shows an idealized matrix of regularly and closely spaced cortical cells viewed in plan-form (viewing normal to the surface). Each one of the indicated cells would correspond to some 65 cells arranged in a column normal to the figure plane (2-mm cortical depth). Following conventional practice, the directions of orientation change and OD are shown orthogonally. The number of cells represented by one full cycle of each function are 20 and 25, respectively. This 20 × 25 cell rectangle was given the name "hypercolumn" by Hubel and Wiesel [33], [36], and it contains some 30 000 cells. Since the cortex in this viewing direction is a retinotopic projection, we may in a purely formal way overlay the cortical cell matrix with the corresponding ganglion cells (from a single eye). These are spaced about five cortical cell spacings apart, so that one ganglion cell corresponds to approximately 1600 cortical cells (FM = 1600).

Dow *et al.* [34] have reported the sizes of various foveal receptive fields found for cortical cells in monkeys, while Hubel and Wiesel [33] give representative field sizes at eccentricities between 1° and 20°. The smallest foveal fields are about 3 mm in size (area$^{1/2}$), which means that they contain about 25 cones or ganglion cells. This finding is illustrated graphically, in Fig. 9, by a circle whose diameter is about 30 cortical cell spacings. At the center of this circle is the designated cortical cell presumed to be receiving the inputs from the ganglion cells within the circle. Generally the cortical cells, which are driven by this collection of ganglion cells, cannot all be located centrally. If we use "radius of influence" to denote the distance over which communication between a cortical cell and its associated ganglion cells must be effected, we find that the radius of influence cannot be less than 15 cortical cell spacings (~ 0.5 mm), and will more likely be 20–30 spacings (~ 0.6–1 mm).

An estimate of radius of influence can be made in another way. If, corresponding to any retinal location, all orientations are represented, a single ganglion cell must connect to all orientation slabs. This implies that the radius of influence can never be less than ten cortical cell spacings and, more likely, 20–30 spacings. Not only are these two estimates mutually consistent, but they also correspond to the dimension over which OD is organized and to the half-thickness of the cortex itself. Thus, 1 mm represents the minimum characteristic dimension over which input–output communication is effected in cortical processing, and corresponds to the minimum "jitter" in position between the retinotopic organization of the cortex and the ganglion cells that drive them. The data of Dow *et al.* show that the range of foveal field sizes at any position in the cortex is about 10 : 1. This means that the largest receptive fields have inputs over a range of ten hypercolumns in cortical extent (i.e., the radius of influence is 150 cortical cell spacings, or about 5 mm).

As discussed earlier, after accounting for the 20 different orientations, a factor of 200 in FM remains to be explained. A factor of 2 can be ascribed to OD, but this still leaves 100. There are several candidates for remaining functions, such as a range of field sizes, binocular disparity (for depth perception), color coding (in primates but not in cats), etc. Presumably, any such functional would have to be represented by an ordered array of cells (analogous to orientation and OD), but no orderly variation has yet been discerned in single cell studies.

SPATIAL FREQUENCY INTERPRETATION

The original classification of cortical visual cells (suggested by Hubel and Wiesel) into simple and complex cells has survived the scrutiny of various investigators. Its interpretation in the spatial domain as a feature detection scheme (in the nonlinear sense), hierarchically organized for pattern recognition, with simple cells being local line- and edge-detectors, appears to be simplistic. A search for an alternative interpretation, in the spatial-frequency domain, was motivated by psychophysical findings (Campbell and Robson [37]; Campbell [38]; Zacks *et al.* [39]) and theoretical considerations (Kabrisky [40]) suggesting that there may exist a cortical scheme of visual signal decomposition into harmonic spatial-frequency components or, more generally, a set of spatial-frequency selective channels. This was further generalized recently to a model of analysis in the spatio-temporal domain accounting for the fact that visual signals projected on the retina are dynamic (Gafni and Zeevi [41], [42]).

The operation in question obviously cannot be a global Fourier transformation or, for that matter, any simple harmonic decomposition scheme, since we are dealing with a space(position)-dependent system whose characteristics are inhomogeneous. At best, therefore, we may consider a possible scheme of "short-distance" spectral decomposition analogous to the time-frequency domain spectrogram so widely used in speech analysis (Flanagan [43]).

Consider a region of retina centered on the coordinates (θ, ϕ), where θ is eccentricity, and ϕ is azimuth angle, both measured in degrees (Fig. 5). Consider further a particular preferred stimulus orientation α_i, and let the spatial coordinate normal to this orientation be $l_{\alpha i}$, as in Fig. 10. If the extent of this coordinate is chosen to be S (measured in degrees of visual angle over the retina), and if the representation of the visual stimulus over this extent is limited to a spatial frequency bandwidth of W (measured in cycles/deg), then the representation has a total of $2SW + 1$ degrees of freedom (first shown by Nyquist [44], generalized by Hartley [45], and further elaborated by Gabor [46] and Shannon [47]). The actual realization can be effected in many different ways. For example, if the passband is low-pass (extending from zero to W), the set of basis functions, which are identical except for translation, $\{\sin \pi(2Wl - n)/\pi(2Wl - n)\}$, can be used. Cortical representation does indeed have the character of spatially translated similar functions (Tootell et al. [31]; Daniel and Whitteridge [32]; Drasdo [35]; Hubel and Wiesel [36]). The best documented example of this is the orientation sequence regularity, with its repetition in primates (on the average) every 20 orientation slabs. Another well-documented example is the ocular dominance, with regular alternation, of left-right OD columns. It has been suggested that similar sequence regularity of spatially translated functions may exist with respect to other variables, such as (central) spatial frequency of cells tuned to different bands.

Functions that possess finite spread either in space or spatial frequency, or both, can be appraised by measures of their "effective" spread. One such measure is the rms spread about the mean (i.e., about the center frequency, in the case of spatial frequency). If rms spread is used, it can be shown that the frequency bandwidth Δf_l and the spatial spread Δl are constrained by an inequality

$$\Delta l \cdot \Delta f_l \geq (4\pi)^{-1} \qquad (10)$$

which constitutes a kind of uncertainty relation. The optimal representation minimizing the uncertainty product is obtained by using Gabor's [46] elementary Gaussian functions, described by

$$g(l) = e^{-\pi(l/\lambda)^2} e^{-j(2\pi f_c \cdot l + \psi)} \qquad (11)$$

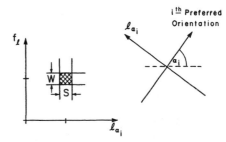

Fig. 10. A simple cell at any retinal location has a preferred stimulus orientation α_i, and $l_{\alpha i}$ is the retinal coordinate normal to that orientation (measured in degrees of visual angle). The Fourier transform variable corresponding to $l_{\alpha i}$ is f_l, while S and W represent the stimulus widths in these paired variables.

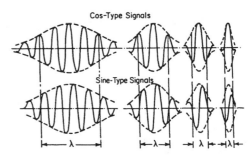

Fig. 11. Cos-type and sine-type Gabor elementary functions progressively increasing in bandwidth from left to right. λ denotes the effective spread of the elementary functions (Gabor [46]).

for central frequency f_c, spatial extent λ, and phase Ψ (Fig. 11), whose Fourier transform $G(f)$ is of the same form

$$G(f) = e^{-\pi[\lambda(f - f_c)]^2} e^{-j\Psi}. \qquad (12)$$

The effective spread in frequency and position becomes in this case

$$\Delta f_l = \frac{1}{\lambda \sqrt{4\pi}}$$

and

$$\Delta l = \frac{\lambda}{\sqrt{4\pi}}. \qquad (13)$$

It is important to comment that while the Gaussian envelope function is extremely convenient as well as optimal, other functions that qualitatively resemble the Gaussian (such as the raised cosine) lead to $\Delta f_l \cdot \Delta l$ products that are not far from optimal.

Thus, as every engineer well knows, sharpening up the spatial resolution results in a spread of the spatial-frequency characteristics, and vice versa. Does this conclusion, based on pure communication theory considerations, bear any relevance to better understanding of cortical engineering design and signal processing in the visual system? Recent studies indicate that, in fact, cortical neurons in area 17 respond in a way that is localized both in space and in spatial frequency (Maffei and Fiorentini [48]; Andrews and Pollen [49]; Tootell et al. [31]; Movshon et al. [50]), in the sense that a cell's stimulus domain exists in a certain well-defined region of visual space (the so-called receptive field) and is also localized in spatial-frequency to a limited

SIMPLE CELL RECEPTIVE FIELD PROFILES

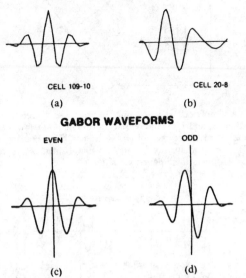

CELL 109-10   CELL 20-8

(a)   (b)

GABOR WAVEFORMS

EVEN   ODD

(c)   (d)

Fig. 12. (a) Receptive field of a simple cell with an even symmetry profile constructed by Andrews and Pollen [51]. (b) With an odd-symmetry profile constructed by Andrews and Pollen [51]. (c) Compared with cos-type (C) Gabor elementary functions [58]. (d) Compared with sine-type Gabor elementary functions [58].

range of luminance-periodicity-modulation. Proceeding from photoreceptors through ganglion- and LGN-cells to cortical simple cells, one finds a progressive loss in localizability of positional information (at the single cell level of operation) and a decrease in spatial frequency bandwidth. The response characteristics of a cortical simple cell can conveniently be described in terms of a receptive field profile (the cell's kernel) that specifies its excitatory and inhibitory substructures. Typically there appear to be two major subclasses of simple-cell receptive field profiles: bipartite ("edge" type) and tripartite. Careful analysis of the receptive fields, reconstructed from spatial-frequency selectivity measurements, indicates additional "ringing" reminiscent of Gabor's elementary function (Fig. 12) (Andrews and Pollen [49]). Most interesting, however, is the finding that pairs of simple cells that are adjacent in the cortical tissue and have the same preferred orientation are tuned to the same spatial frequency and respond to drifting sine wave gratings 90° out of phase, spatially (Pollen and Ronner [51]). Thus, the fact that cortical neurons balance the position frequency trade-off by possessing both some spatial retinotopic localization and, at the same time, a spatial frequency bandwidth of about one octave with matched sine and cosine (phase quadrature) cell pairs, suggests that important kinds of visual processing are going on in both domains (Zeevi and Daugman [6]).

Some recent theoretical studies have emphasized the principle of economical coding (minimal representation) for the cortex (e.g., Sakitt and Barlow [52]). In view of the high-functional multiplicity found in the cortex, this emphasis seems misplaced. Yet, it is true that, from several viewpoints, the processing is economical. The receptive field patterns of simple cells come very close to minimizing

uncertainty in the four-dimensional space comprised of two spatial and two frequency coordinates (Daugman [53], [54]). Moreover, it seems that no two cells perform the same function, so there is no wasteful redundancy in the simple sense. In summary, then, area 17 of the cortex performs many simultaneous transformations of retinal data, yet each such representation is produced in a highly efficient way. At present we have only a partial description of the various representations, and one of the major research challenges is to make this description more complete. Further challenges exist in ascertaining how these representations are processed in subsequent cortical areas (van Essen [57]).

ACKNOWLEDGMENT

The authors wish to thank Dr. J. G. Daugman and the two reviewers for their valuable comments.

REFERENCES

[1] Y. Y. Zeevi and R. E. Kronauer, "Signal preprocessing in visual systems and its relevance to pattern recognition," in *Signal Analysis and Pattern Recognition in Biomedical Engineering*, G. F. Inbar, Ed. New York: Wiley, 1975, pp. 261–274.

[2] A. M. Bruckstein and Y. Y. Zeevi, "Analysis of 'integrate-to-threshold' neural coding schemes," *Biol. Cybern.*, vol. 28, pp. 41–47, 1979.

[3] C. Cherry, *On Human Communication*. Cambridge, MA: MIT Press, 1957.

[4] M. H. Pirenne, *Vision and The Eye*. London: Chapman and Hall, 1967.

[5] D. A. Baylor, T. D. Lamb, and K. W. Yau, "Response of retinal rods to single photons," *J. Physiol.*, vol. 288, pp. 613–634, 1979.

[6] Y. Y. Zeevi and J. G. Daugman, "Some psychophysical aspects of visual processing of displayed information," in *Proc. Image II Conf.*, Phoenix, AZ, 1981.

[7] A. Rose, *Vision, Human and Electronics*. New York: Plenum, 1974.

[8] H. B. Barlow, "Incremental thresholds at low intensities considered as signal/noise discriminations," *J. Physiol.*, vol. 136, pp. 469–488, 1957.

[9] H. B. Barlow and W. R. Levick, "Three factors limiting the reliable detection of light by retinal ganglion cells of the cat," *J. Physiol.*, vol. 200, pp. 1–26, 1969.

[10] Y. Y. Zeevi and S. S. Mangoubi, "Noise suppression in photoreceptors and its relevance to incremental intensity thresholds," *J. Opt. Soc. Am.*, vol. 68, pp. 1772–1776, 1978.

[11] D. A. Baylor, A. L Hodgkin, and T. D. Lamb, "The electrical response of turtle cones to flashes and steps of light," *J. Physiol.*, vol. 242, pp. 685–727, 1974.

[12] E. J. Simon, T. D. Lamb, and A. L. Hodgkin, "Spontaneous voltage fluctuations in retinal cones and bipolar cells," *Nature*, vol. 256, pp. 661–662, 1975.

[13] J. J. Koenderink and A. J. vanDoorn, "Visual detection of spatial contrast: Influence of location in the visual field, target extent, and illuminance level," *Biol. Cybern.*, vol. 30, pp. 157–167, 1978.

[14] F. M. deMonesterio, S. J. Schein, and E. P. McCrane, "Staining of blue-sensitive cones of the macaque retina by a fluorescent dye," *Science*, vol. 213, p. 1278, 1981.

[15] J. Hirsch and R. Hylton, "Quality of the primate photoreceptor lattice and limits of spatial vision," *Vision Res.*, vol. 24, pp. 347–355, 1984.

[16] J. I. Yellott, "Image sampling properties of photoreceptors: A reply to Miller and Bernard," *Vision Res.*, vol. 24, pp. 281–282, 1984.

[17] J. Hirsch and R. Hylton, "Orientation dependence of visual hyperacuity contains components of hexagonal symmetry," *J. Opt. Soc. Am. A*, vol. 1, pp. 300–308, 1984.

[18] D. Marr, *Vision*. San Francisco: Freeman, 1982.

[19] D. H. Kelly, "Visual contrast sensitivity," *Optica Acta*, vol. 24, pp.

107–129, 1977.

[20] G. Sperling and M. M. Sondhi, "Model for visual luminance discrimination and flicker detection," *J. Opt. Soc. Am.*, vol. 58, pp. 1133–1145, 1968.

[21] Y. Y. Zeevi and M. Shefer, "AGC of signal processing in vision," *J. Opt. Soc. Am.*, vol. 71, p. 1556, 1981.

[22] F. S. Werblin, "Adaptation in a vertebrate retina: Intracellular recordings in Necturus," *J. Neurophysiol.*, vol. 34, pp. 228–241, 1971.

[23] R. A. Normann and I. Perlman, "The effects of background illumination on the photoresponses of red and green cones," *J. Physiol.*, vol. 286, pp. 491–507, 1979.

[24] R. M. Boynton and D. N. Whitten, "Visual adaptation in monkey cones: Recordings of late receptor potentials," *Science*, vol. 170, pp. 1423–1426, 1970.

[25] J. E. Dowling, "Information processing by local circuits: The vertebrate retina as a model system," in *Neurosciences*, Fourth Study Program, F. O. Schmitt and F. G. Worden, Eds. Cambridge, MA: MIT Press, 1979, pp. 163–181.

[26] J. E. Dowling, B. Ehinger, and W. Holden, "The interplexiform cell: A new type of retinal neuron," *Invest. Ophthalmol.*, vol. 15, pp. 916–926, 1976.

[27] E. T. Rolls and A. Cowey, "Topography of the retina and striate cortex and its relationship to visual acuity in rhesus and squirrel monkeys," *Exp. Brain Res.*, vol. 10, pp. 298–310, 1970.

[28] S. Polyak, *The Vertebrate Visual System*. Chicago, IL: Univ. of Chicago Press, 1957.

[29] S. Levay, D. H. Hubel, and N. T. Wiesel, "The pattern of ocular dominance columns in macaque visual cortex revealed by reduced silver stain," *J. Comp. Neurol.*, vol. 159, pp. 559–576, 1975.

[30] E. L. Schwartz, "Spatial mapping in the visual system," *J. Opt. Soc. Am.*, vol. 68, pp. 1371–1376, 1978.

[31] R. B. H. Tootell, M. S. Silverman, E. Switkes, and R. L. DeValois, "Deoxyslucose analysis of retinotopic organization in primate striate cortex," *Science*, vol. 218, pp. 902–904, 1982.

[32] P. M. Daniel and D. Whitteridge, "The representation of the visual field on the cerebral cortex in monkeys," *J. Physiol.*, vol. 159, pp. 302–321, 1961.

[33] D. M. Hubel and T. N. Wiesel, "Uniformity of monkey striate cortex: A parallel relationship between field size, scatter, and magnification factor," *J. Comp. Neurol.*, vol. 158, pp. 295–305, 1974.

[34] B. M. Dow, A. Z. Snyder, R. G. Vautin, and R. Bauer, "Magnification factor and receptive field size in foveal striate cortex of the monkey," *Exp. Brain Res.*, vol. 44, pp. 213–228, 1981.

[35] N. Drasdo, "The neural representation of visual space," *Nature*, vol. 266, pp. 554–556, 1977.

[36] D. M. Hubel, and T. N. Wiesel, "Receptive fields, binocular interaction and function architecture in the cat's visual cortex," *J. Physiol.*, vol. 160, pp. 106–154, 1962.

[37] F. W. Campbell and J. G. Robson, "Application of Fourier analysis to the modulation response of the eye," *J. Opt. Soc. Am.*, vol. 54, p. 581, 1964.

[38] F. W. Campbell, "The transmission of spatial information through the visual system," in *Neurosciences*, vol. III, F. O. Schmitt and F. G. Worden, Eds. Cambridge, MA: MIT Press, 1972, pp. 95–103.

[39] M. B. Zachs, J. Nachmias, and J. G. Robson, "Spatial frequency channels in human vision," *J. Opt. Soc. Am.*, vol. 61, pp. 1176–1186, 1971.

[40] M. Kabrisky, "A proposed model for visual information processing in the brain," in *Models for the Perception of Speech and Visual Form*, W. Whem-Dunn, Ed. Cambridge, MA: MIT Press, 1965.

[41] H. Gafni and Y. Y. Zeevi, "A model for separation of spatial and temporal information," *Biol. Cybern.*, vol. 28, pp. 73–82, 1977.

[42] _____, "A model for processing of movement in the visual system," *Biol. Cybern.*, vol. 32, pp. 165–173, 1979.

[43] J. L. Flanagan, *Speech Analysis Synthesis and Perception*. New York: Academic, 1965.

[44] H. Nyquist, "Certain factors affecting telegraph speed," *Bell Syst. Tech. J.*, vol. 3, pp. 429–445, 1924.

[45] R. V. L. Hartley, "Transmission of information," *Bell Syst. Tech. J.*, vol. 7, pp. 535–563, 1928.

[46] D. Gabor, "Theory of communication," *J. Inst. Elect. Eng.*, vol. 93, pp. 429–457, 1946.

[47] C. E. Shannon, "Communication in the presence of noise," *Proc. IRE*, vol. 37, pp. 10–21, 1949.

[48] L. Maffei and A. Fiorentini, "The visual cortex as a spatial frequency analyzer," *Vision Res.*, vol. 13, pp. 1255–1267, 1973.

[49] B. W. Andrews and D. A. Pollen, "Relationship between spatial frequency selectivity and receptive field profile of simple cells," *J. Physiol.*, vol. 287, pp. 163–176, 1979.

[50] J. A. Movshon, I. D. Thompson, and D. J. Tolhurst, "Spatial summation in the receptive fields of simple cells in the cat's striate cortex," *J. Physiol.*, vol. 283, pp. 53–77, 1978.

[51] D. A. Pollen and S. F. Ronner, "Phase relationships between adjacent simple cells in the visual cortex," *Science*, vol. 212, pp. 1409–1411, 1981.

[52] B. Sakitt and H. B. Barlow, "A model for the economical encoding of the visual image in cerebral cortex," *Biol. Cybern.*, vol. 43, p. 97, 1982.

[53] J. G. Daugman, "Two-dimensional spectral analysis of cortical receptive field profiles," *Vision Res.*, vol. 20, pp. 847–856, 1980.

[54] _____, "Uncertainty relation for resolution in space, spatial frequency, and orientation optimized by two-dimensional visual cortical filters," (submitted to *J. Opt. Soc. Am.*), 1982.

[55] R. W. Rodieck, "Quantitative analysis of cat retinal ganglion cell responses to visual stimuli," *Vision Res.*, vol. 5, pp. 583–601, 1965.

[56] R. M. Steinberg, M. Reid, and P. L. Lacy, "The distribution of rods and cones in the retina of the cat," *J. Com. Neur.*, vol. 148, pp. 229–248, 1973.

[57] D. C. Van Essen, "Visual areas of the mammalian cerebral cortex," *Ann. Rev. Neurosci.*, vol. 2, pp. 227–263, 1979.

[58] D. A. Pollen and S. F. Ronner, "Visual cortical neurons as localized spatial frequency filters," *IEEE Trans. Syst., Man, Cybern.*, vol. 13, pp. 907–916, 1983.

197

A Visual Cortex Domain Model and Its Use for Visual Information Processing

Ilya A. Rybak, Natalia A. Shevtsova, Lubov N. Podladchikova, and Alexander V. Golovan

Institute of Neurocybernetics at Rostov State University, USSR

(*Received 8 May* 1989; *revised and accepted 9 August* 1990)

Abstract—*A model of an iso-orientation domain in the visual cortex is developed. The iso-orientation domain is represented as a neural network with retinotopically organized afferent inputs and anisotropic lateral inhibition formed by feedbacks via inhibitory interneurons. Temporal dynamics of neuron responses to oriented stimuli is studied. The results of computer simulations are compared with those of neurophysiological experiments. It is shown that the later phase of neuron response has a more sharp orientation tuning than the initial one. It is suggested that the initial phase of neuron response encodes intensity parameters of visual stimulus, whereas the later phase encodes its orientation. The design of the neural network preprocessor and the architecture of the system for visual information processing, based on the idea of parallel-sequential processing, are proposed. The example of a test image processing is presented.*

Keywords—Visual cortex, Neural network, Lateral inhibition, Iso-orientation domain, Feature extraction, Orientation filtration, Multiresolution image processing.

1. INTRODUCTION

Image recognition research is focused mainly on two problems: 1) elaboration of effective algorithms of image analysis and description, and 2) investigation of the visual system mechanisms. It is still unclear whether these two problems should be distinguished. Some researchers assume that structure and mechanisms used by natural visual system cannot be applied to computer vision. On the contrary, others think that it is necessary to elucidate subtle mechanisms of visual perception to develop new computer vision system architectures. Nevertheless, most researchers come to the conclusion that the von-Neuman architecture does not allow to create computer vision systems comparable with human visual systems in effectiveness (Levialdi, 1983).

It is well known that when images are analyzed with the help of conventional computers of sequential type, most of the time is spent on preliminary processing of bulky input information. Parallel preprocessing and initial data compressing are the main means of reduction of the time of visual information processing. In recent years, a trend manifested itself to create parallel-type systems for visual information analysis with multiprocessor architecture. However, parallel processing cannot solve all the problems of computer vision. Minsky (1975) contends that parallelism is effective at lower levels of information processing dealing with feature extraction, whereas its useful effects have serious limitations at higher levels. Not even high computational efficiency achievable by parallel computing circuits can solve such problems as invariance of feature detection and estimation of contexts at different levels of abstraction (Kohonen, 1988).

It is now a widely-held view that visual perception is based on two interrelated processes: parallel processing of visual information carried out automatically by mechanisms determined by neuronal organization of the retina, lateral geniculate nucleus, and visual cortex; and sequential processing related to image recognition mechanisms and controlled by attention (Julesz, 1975; Neisser, 1967; Shiffrin & Schneider, 1977). In the first process, detector properties of single neurons and local neuron nets are of primary importance. In the second process, eye movements are considered to be an essential factor.

Acknowledgements: The authors thank Vladislav M. Sandler and Tatjana M. Bogatyreva for their participation in discussions, valuable assistance in the preparation of the manuscript and illustrations.

Requests for reprints should be sent to Ilya A. Rybak, Institute of Neurocybernetics, Rostov State University, 194/1 Stachka Ave., Rostov-on-Don 344104, USSR.

As a result of these movements, the most informative parts of the image are sequentially projected onto the fovea for fine processing (Burt, 1988; Yarbus, 1965). During the second process, a tuning of detector properties of low-level neurons can be controlled by high-level structures. Thus, the purposeful feature extraction for image recognition is provided.

Therefore, the adequate computer system for the processing and analysis of visual information should include a preprocessor with a neural network architecture, simulating parallel information processing at low levels of the visual system, and a sequential type computer tuning the preprocessor to obtain necessary information for image recognition.

The development of the neural network preprocessor should be preceded by a study on neuronal organization of low-level structures of the visual system and their mathematical modelling and computer simulation. As noted above, these structures primarily accomplish a preliminary processing of information, including filtration and encoding of image features. However, it is not obvious what features are encoded by neurons of these structures and what mechanisms underlie the encoding. Orientation of edges and contour elements of an image is considered to be one of the main features detected by neurons of the primary visual cortex (Hubel & Wiesel, 1962, 1974). Orientation-selective properties of these neurons make it possible to encode orientations of image elements and to compress initial information (Kunt, Ikonomopoulos, & Kocher, 1985).

2. ISO-ORIENTATION DOMAIN IN THE VISUAL CORTEX

It is well known that neighbor neurons in the visual cortex have a similar orientation tuning and form an orientation-selective column, or an iso-orientation domain. A set of orientation columns with a common receptive field forms a topical module of the cortex— a hypercolumn (Hubel & Wiesel, 1962, 1974). Besides, visual cortex afferents are organized retinitopically (Talbot & Marshall, 1941) and it is believed that in addition to global mapping, there are retinotopically-organized projections of the common receptive field of a hypercolumn onto each iso-orientation domain (Schwartz, 1980).

To date, there are several assumptions about the mechanisms of orientation selectivity in the visual cortex (Baxter & Dow, 1989; Braitenberg & Braitenberg, 1979; Finette, Harth, & Csermely, 1978; Hubel & Wiesel, 1962, 1974; Linsker, 1986a, 1986b; Malsburg, 1973; Malsburg & Cowan, 1982; Paradiso, 1988; Sillito, 1984; Vidyasagar, 1987). Evidently, the mechanism of orientation selectivity of cortical neurons is related to anisotropic distribution of some fibers. The first explanation of this mechanism was based on the idea of anisotropic distribution of afferent fibers forming specifically-elongated receptive fields of cortical neurons (Hubel & Wiesel, 1962). Another idea supposed anisotropic lateral excitation in an iso-orientation domain (Finette, Harth, & Csermely, 1978). However, experiments of Sillito (1975, 1984) showed that orientation selectivity of cortical neurons decreased or disappeared when intracortical inhibition had been blocked by bicuculline. This fact supports the idea that the anisotropy of lateral inhibitory connections may be the primary mechanism of orientation selectivity (Benevento, Creutzfeldt, & Kuhnt, 1972; Creutzfeldt, Kuhnt, & Benevento, 1974).

An abundance of neuroscience data indicate that afferent fibers form only excitatory synaptic contacts in the cortex and inhibition is mediated via intracortical connections of inhibitory interneurons (Benevento, Creutzfeldt, & Kuhnt, 1972; Ferster & Lindstrom, 1983; Garey & Powell, 1971; Hess, Negishi, & Creutzfeldt, 1975; Ito, 1970; Stefanis & Jasper, 1964; Watanabe, Konishi, & Creutzfeldt, 1966). Lateral inhibition may be of direct type when afferent fibers have excitatory synaptic contacts with inhibitory neurons or backward type when inhibitory interneurons are activated by axon collaterals from cells excited by afferent inputs (Eccles, 1969; Supin, 1970). In some studies, evidence of backward character of lateral inhibition in the visual cortex was revealed (Hayashi, 1969; Supin, 1970; Watanabe, Kohishi, & Creutzfeldt, 1966).

Thus, an iso-orientation domain of the visual cortex may be regarded as a neural structure with retinotopically-organized afferent inputs and anisotropic lateral inhibition formed by feedbacks via inhibitory interneurons.

3. THE MODEL OF AN ISO-ORIENTATION DOMAIN OF THE VISUAL CORTEX

A great number of models of neural structures with lateral inhibition were elaborated (Amari, 1977, 1982; Wilson & Cowan, 1972, 1973 and many others). However, anisotropy of connections and dynamics of responses to oriented stimuli were not considered in these studies. On the other hand, in most studies devoted to modelling of orientation selectivity of cortical neurons, the mechanism of selectivity is suggested to be a result of either spatial organization of input afferent fibers or anisotropy of lateral intracortical excitatory connections (Finette, Harth, & Csermely, 1978; Grossberg, Mingolla, & Todorovic, 1989; Linsker, 1986a, 1986b; Malsburg, 1973; Malsburg & Cowan, 1987). The development of neural structure with anisotropy of lateral inhibition and examination of its responses to oriented stimuli was the goal of the current study.

As an element of such a structure, we used a model of a neuron described by

$$T_i \frac{d}{dt} U_i(t) = -U_i(t) + \sum_j q_{ij} Z_j(t)$$

$$+ q_i^s Z_i^s(t) + S_i - h_i; \quad (1)$$

$$Z_i(t) = f[U_i(t)], \quad (2)$$

where $U_i(t)$ is membrane potential of the i-th neuron; $Z_i(t)$ is its output variable (frequency of impulses); h_i is threshold ($h_i > 0$); q_{ij} is synaptic weight of the j-th input to the i-th neuron; q_i^s is synaptic weight of the external input; $Z_i^s(t)$ is test input influence; S_i is uncontrollable input influence which determines the initial level of membrane potential; T_i is time constant; t is time variable; f is nonlinear function

$$f[U] = \begin{cases} kU & \text{if } U \geq 0; \\ 0 & \text{if } U < 0, \end{cases} \quad (3)$$

where $k > 0$.

The system under consideration included a two-dimensional neural structure and a flat receptor layer of $N \times N$ elements (S-layer). For convenience, the neural structure was subdivided into two flat layers of $N \times N$ elements: a layer of excitatory elements (E-layer), and a layer of inhibitory interneurons (I-layer) (Figure 1). Each element in E-layer had an excitatory input from the corresponding element in S-layer and eight excitatory inputs from its neighbors in E-layer. The former input provided a topical mapping $S \rightarrow E$ and the latter inputs resulted in isotropy of lateral excitation within E-layer. Besides, each E-layer element was inhibited by the corresponding interneuron in I-layer (Figure 1a). Each I-layer element had an excitatory input from the corresponding E-layer element and excitatory inputs from some other E-layer elements. The former input provided self-inhibition of E-layer element, the latter inputs resulted in anisotropic backward inhibition (Figure 1b).

The structure under consideration is described as follows:

$$\begin{cases} T_E \frac{d}{dt} U_{ij}^E(t) = -U_{ij}^E(t) + q^{EE} \\ \quad \times \sum_{k=i-1}^{i+1} \sum_{l=j-1}^{j+1} Z_{kl}^E(t) - q^{IE} Z_{ij}^I(t) \\ \quad\quad {\scriptstyle (k,l) \neq (i,j)} \\ \quad + q^{SE} Z_{ij}^S(t) + S_E - h_E; \\ T_I \frac{d}{dt} U_{ij}^I(t) = -U_{ij}^I(t) + q_0^{EI} Z_{ij}^E(t) + q^{EI} \\ \quad \times \sum_{\substack{k,l \in \Omega_{ij}(\varphi) \\ (k,l) \neq (i,j)}} Z_{kl}^E(t) + S_I - h_I; \\ Z_{ij}^E(t) = f[U_{ij}^E(t)]; \\ Z_{ij}^I(t) = f[U_{ij}^I(t)]; \quad i,j = 1, \ldots, N, \quad (4) \end{cases}$$

where indices "E" and "I" at neuron parameters and variables indicate that given neuron belongs to E or I-layer; indices "EE", "IE", "EI", "SE" refer

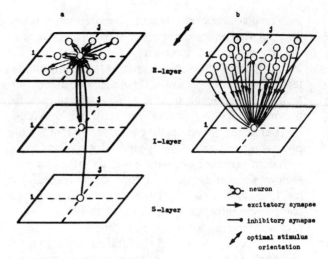

FIGURE 1. Model of the iso-orientation domain in the visual cortex: a) connections of a E-layer neuron; b) connections of a I-layer neuron.

to weights of synaptic connections: the first letter here stands for the layer position of the postsynaptic neuron, while the second letter stands for that of the presynaptic neuron. The shape of area $\Omega_{ij}(\varphi)$ of E-layer elements, forming the excitatory inputs to the (i,j)-th I-layer neuron, determines anisotropy of lateral inhibition corresponding to orientation φ. Examples of the areas $\Omega_{ij}(\varphi)$ are schematically depicted in Figures 2b–e. Figure 2a shows an interneuron with anisotropically ramificated dendritic tree capable to produce anisotropic lateral inhibition. The inhibition like that may be provided also by anisotropic distribution of recurrent collaterals of excitatory cells.

Earlier, simple neural network being elementary parts of the considered structure were studied analytically (Rybak, 1988; Rybak, Shevtsova, Podladchikova, Golovan, & Markarov, 1987). On the basis of these studies, synaptic weights q^{EI}, q_0^{EI}, q^{EI}, q^{EE} were chosen under the conditions

$$\beta > \beta_0 + 1 + \alpha;$$

$$\alpha < 1, \quad (5)$$

where

$$\beta_0 = q_0^{EI} q^{IE} k^2;$$

$$\beta = q^{EI} q^{IE} k^2;$$

$$\alpha = 8 q^{EE} k. \quad (6)$$

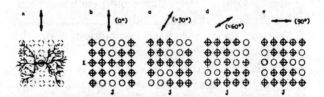

FIGURE 2. Anisotropy of lateral connections; a) inhibitory interneuron with anisotropic dendritic tree; b–e) shapes of areas $\Omega_{ij}(\varphi)$ for different optimal stimulus orientations. The cross mark indicates E-layer neurons which innervate the (i,j)-th interneuron. The stimulus optimal orientations are shown by arrows for each φ.

It is generally agreed that time constants of inhibitory neurons are greater than those of excitatory neurons

$$T_I > T_E. \tag{7}$$

Besides, all neurons were supposed to be on the brink of excitation

$$\begin{cases} S_E - h_E = 0; \\ S_I - h_I = 0. \end{cases} \tag{8}$$

The dynamics of neuron responses to oriented input stimuli was studied in computer simulations. The system of equations (4) was solved by the Runge-Kutta algorithm. Stimuli, switched on at $t = 0$, were presented as a configuration of S-layer excited elements. At $t \geq 0$, $Z_{ij}^S(t) = Z_m$ for excited elements, and $Z_{ij}^S(t) = 0$ for others. Strips of 5×1 excited S-layer elements of different orientations were considered as bar stimuli. Sets of excited S-layer elements belonging to half-planes with different oriented boundaries served as edge stimuli. Excitation of 3×3 S-layer elements was considered as a diffuse stimulus. Stimuli which were orthogonal to the strongest inhibition direction were considered to be optimally oriented. Figure 3 displays responses of E-layer neurons which receive projections from centers of each stimuli.

The analysis of neuron responses in our computer simulations revealed the following:

(1) Neuron responses to optimally oriented stimuli had sustained or biphase character. Neuron responses to otherwise oriented stimuli were transient and monophase.

(2) The later phases of neuron responses were much more sensitive to the stimulus orientation than the initial phases.

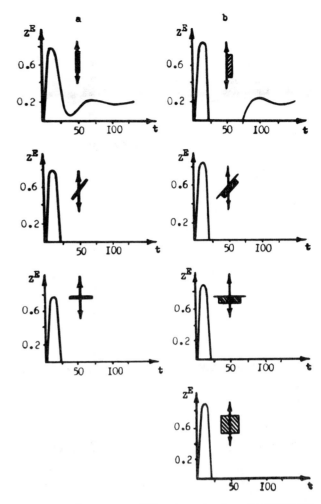

FIGURE 3. Responses of E-layer neurons to optimally (at the top), non-optimally (in the middle) oriented bars (a) and edges (b) and to diffuse stimulation (at the bottom). The curves correspond to the following values of parameters: $N = 16$; $k = 1$; $q^{EE} = 0.1$; $q^{IE} = 1$; $q^{SE} = 1$; $q_0^{EI} = 1.5$; $q^{EI} = 5$; $T_E = 10$; $T_I = 40$; $Z_m = 1$.

4. NEUROPHYSIOLOGICAL RESULTS

Neurophysiological experiments were carried out (Rybak, 1988; Rybak, Shevtsova, Podladchikova, Golovan, & Markarov, 1987) to study response dynamics and orientation sensitivity of neurons of the guinea-pig visual cortex (area 17). Light bars of different orientations were presented for 1 sec. Only on-responses of registered neurons were analyzed here. Figures 4 and 5 illustrate response histograms of some visual cortex neurons and diagrams of their tuning to stimulus orientation depicted for the overall response and for its separate phases.

The results of experiments supported (1) and (2). The analysis of the experimental findings showed that 73% of all orientation-selective neurons, or 85% of those which had later phases in their responses, displayed responses in which later phases had a more sharp tuning to stimulus orientation than initial ones.

Comparison of these results with the known data on orientation selectivity in the visual cortex is rather difficult for several reasons. In particular, the ori-

entation tuning was often estimated over the entire response without its subdivision into phases. Besides, most of the authors used either moving stimuli or stimuli presented for a short time (less 100 ms). However, when moving oriented stimulus is presented, response dynamics depends also on directional properties of cortical and subcortical neurons. When short-time stimulus is presented, the later phase of on-response may be reduced and mixed with off-response. Nevertheless, Creutzfeldt and Ito (1968) revealed a presence of initial phases in responses to nonoptimal stimuli. Moreover, Supin (1974) assumed that many stimulus parameters had a much stronger effect upon the later temporal component of response than upon the initial one. Our findings also resemble data of Pubols and Leroy (1977) on orientation selectivity of somatosensory cortex neurons.

Results of our study indicate that there is the temporal discrimination of image features in the visual cortex. The initial phase of response of an iso-ori-

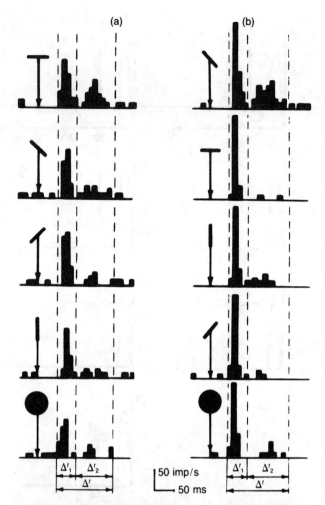

FIGURE 4. Histograms of responses of two neurons (a,b) in the guinea-pig visual cortex to optimally (at the top) and non-optimally (in the middle) oriented light bars and a diffuse stimulus (at the bottom). Onset of stimulation is indicated by the vertical arrow; Δt, Δt_1, Δt_2,—assumed durations of the overall response and its initial and later phases, respectively. Vertically plotted lines separate the phases of responses.

entation domain may encode appearance of a stimulus in the receptive field of the hypercolumn, whereas the later phase of the response may encode existence of contrast or contour image elements oriented in accordance with the domain orientation tuning.

5. SCREEN-TYPE NEURON-LIKE STRUCTURE AS A FUNCTIONAL UNIT OF THE MODEL OF THE NEURAL VISUAL PREPROCESSOR

A model of screen-type neuron-like structure (SNS) was developed on the basis of the model of the iso-orientation domain described above. It was assumed that the SNS had the same function in the preprocessor as the iso-orientation domain (orientation-selective column) had in the visual cortex. The SNS model consisted of 25 (5 × 5) neuron-like elements arranged in a flat layer (Figure 6). Each SNS transformed an 5 × 5 input signal matrix $S = \|S_{ij}\|$ into an output matrix $Z = \|Z_{ij}\|$ of the same size. The

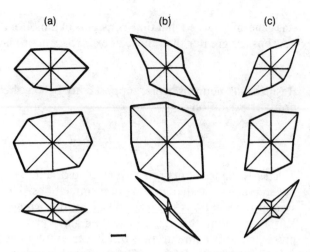

FIGURE 5. Diagrams of orientation tuning of three neurons (a,b,c) estimated on mean number of impulses over the entire response (at the top), over the initial phase (in the middle) and over the later phase (at the bottom). The scale mark corresponds to 10 impulses in the top row and five impulses in the others.

central 3 × 3 elements in matrix Z formed the operation area, while boundary elements served to eliminate possible edge distortion in data processing. The signals from the operation area passed into an output block which encoded information contained in the central 3 × 3 area of input matrix S. Each neuron-like element of the SNS was equivalent to a pair of neurons (E-layer neuron and corresponding I-layer neuron) (Figure 7). In order to reduce processing time, and taking into account (7), we put $T_E = 0$ and assumed E-layer neuron to be an inertialess threshold summarizing element. Input signals X_{ij}^S to each (i, j)-th element of the SNS passed through the F^S-block which performed spatial convolution with the input matrix S on the analogy of on-center/off-surround receptive field.

$$X_{ij}^S = S_{ij} - b_{ij}^S \sum_{k=\max(i-2;1)}^{\min(i+2;5)} \sum_{l=\max(j-2;1)}^{\min(j+2;5)} a_{k-i+3,l-j+3}^S S_{kl}, \quad (9)$$

where

$$b_{ij}^S = \left[\sum_{k=\max(i-2;1)}^{\min(i+2;5)} \sum_{l=\max(j-2;1)}^{\min(j+2;5)} a_{k-i+3,l-j+3}^S \right]^{-1}, \quad (10)$$

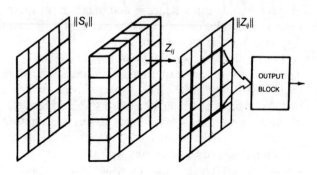

FIGURE 6. Screen-type neuron-like structure (SNS).

202

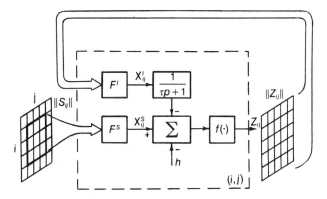

FIGURE 7. The (i,j)-th neuron-like element of the SNS.

where a_{pq}^S is element of matrix $A^S = \|a_{pq}^S\|$:

$$A^S = \|a_{pq}^S\| = \begin{Vmatrix} 0 & 0 & 0 & 0 & 0 \\ 0 & 1 & 1 & 1 & 0 \\ 0 & 1 & 0 & 1 & 0 \\ 0 & 1 & 1 & 1 & 0 \\ 0 & 0 & 0 & 0 & 0 \end{Vmatrix}. \quad (11)$$

According to (9)–(11), $X_{ij} > 0$ if S_{ij} exceeds the mean intensity level in the vicinity of the point (i,j).

Inertial backward inhibition affected the (i,j)-th element of the SNS through the block F^i which performed spatial convolution with the output matrix Z. Coefficients of the convolution matrix determined anisotropy of lateral inhibition.

$$X_{ij}^I = b^I \sum_{k=\max(i-2;1)}^{\min(i+2;5)} \sum_{l=\max(j-2;1)}^{\min(j+2;5)} a_{k-l+3,l-j+3}^I(\varphi) Z_{kl}, \quad (12)$$

where b^I is weight coefficient characterizing backward inhibition. It is similar to β in (6) and is chosen so that $b^I > 1$. $a_{pq}^I(\varphi)$ is element of coefficient matrix $A_\varphi^I = \|a_{pq}^I\|_\varphi$ which provides the orientation tuning of the SNS at an angle φ:

$$A_{\varphi=0}^I o = \|a_{pq}^I\|_{\varphi=0} o = \begin{Vmatrix} 1 & 0 & 0 & 0 & 1 \\ 1 & 1 & 0 & 1 & 1 \\ 1 & 1 & 0 & 1 & 1 \\ 1 & 1 & 0 & 1 & 1 \\ 1 & 0 & 0 & 0 & 1 \end{Vmatrix};$$

$$A_{\varphi=90}^I o = (A_{\varphi=0}^I o)^T;$$

$$A_{\varphi\cong30}^I o = \|a_{pq}^I\|_{\varphi\cong30} o = \begin{Vmatrix} 1 & 1 & 1 & 0 & 0 \\ 1 & 1 & 0 & 0 & 1 \\ 1 & 1 & 0 & 1 & 1 \\ 1 & 0 & 0 & 1 & 1 \\ 0 & 0 & 1 & 1 & 1 \end{Vmatrix};$$

$$A_{\varphi\cong60}^I o = (A_{\varphi\cong30}^I o)^T;$$

$$A_{\varphi\cong120}^I o = \|a_{pq}^I\|_{\varphi\cong120} o = \begin{Vmatrix} 0 & 1 & 1 & 1 & 1 \\ 0 & 0 & 1 & 1 & 1 \\ 1 & 0 & 0 & 0 & 1 \\ 1 & 1 & 1 & 0 & 0 \\ 1 & 1 & 1 & 0 & 0 \end{Vmatrix};$$

$$A_{\varphi\cong150}^I o = (A_{\varphi\cong120}^I o)^T. \quad (13)$$

. Let input signal matrix S be presented to the SNS input at the moment t_o. Then dynamics of SNS elements at $t > t_o$ is defined by partial solution of following system of differential equations:

$$\tau \frac{d}{dt} U_{ij} = -U_{ij} + X_{ij}^S - X_{ij}^I - h;$$

$$Z_{ij} = f[U_{ij}]; \qquad i, j = 1, \ldots, 5, \quad (14)$$

under initial conditions

$$U_{ij}(t_o) = X_{ij}^S - h; \qquad i, j = 1, \ldots, 5, \quad (15)$$

where τ is time constant of inertial block and h is threshold of summarizing element.

Each (i,j)-th element of the SNS displays either monophase (Figure 8a) or biphase (Figure 8b) responses. The intensities of initial and later phases have been estimated by values Z_{ij} at moments t_o and t_1, respectively. Here, t_o is the initial moment of stimulation. The moment t_1 is chosen experimentally to be the same for all elements of the SNS and for all parameters of stimuli presented ($t_1 \cong t_o + 5\tau$).

Let us consider the SNS tuned to vertical stimulus orientation (Figures 8c–f). Output of the SNS $Z = \|Z_{ij}\|$ at time moments t_o and t_1 depends on input

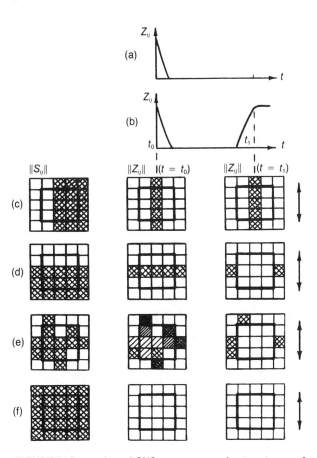

FIGURE 8. Dynamics of SNS responses: a,b—two types of dynamic responses of SNS elements; c–f—output SNS responses to different input stimuli; density of shading reflects intensities of S_{ij} and Z_{ij}.

matrix $S = \|S_{ij}\|$. At t_o, the operation area of output matrix Z contains some excited elements only if intensity differences between S_{ij} are greater than the threshold h (Figures 8c–e). At t_1, the operation area of Z contains three excited elements only if there is an optimally oriented edge in S (Figure 8c). Otherwise, at t_1, the number of excited elements in Z is less (Figures 8d–f).

Thus, each SNS is at first a detector of suprathreshold intensity differences and then it is a detector of the edge of certain orientation.

6. MULTIRESOLUTION CONTOUR FEATURE ENCODING AND PARALLEL-SEQUENTIAL ANALYSIS OF VISUAL INFORMATION

Trying to achieve likeness, an artist usually follows the way which may be called "coarse-to-fine." Throughout this process, he draws a number of auxiliary line segments of different lengths being the elements of more generalized contours of objects depicted. Spatial relationships between the elements of generalized contours play a very important role in making a true picture of the object. The estimation of spatial relations between the elements of coarser and finer contours are also important. Moreover, it should be noted that the artist achieves expressiveness and likeness by omitting some details of the picture and concentrating on its most informative parts.

It is tempting to assume that the artist intuitively employs the algorithms of visual perception, including sequential eye fixations. It is well known (Yarbus, 1965) that when a man is viewing an object, he performs certain eye movements and fixes his gaze on the most informative image fragments (Figure 9). During eye fixations these fragments are projected onto the fovea which has hyperrepresentation in the visual cortex (Talbot & Marshall, 1941; Yarbus, 1965).

Due to such organization of the projections, these fragments may be processed at the highest resolution level. Besides, in the course of consecutive eye fixations, the same parts of the image are repeatedly projected onto the retina at different distances from its center and are processed in the cortex at various levels of resolution. Evidently, the set of iso-orientation domains in different parts of the visual cortex may encode orientations of contour elements of various degrees of generalization. Encoding spatial relationships between coarser elements, as well as between those and finer contour elements, leads to formation of a set of primary features for the invariant shape representation. A substantial reduction of information may be achieved due to omitting a higher resolution level processing of fragments which are less significant for object recognition.

Taking into account the above mentioned, it is reasonable to suggest that two phases of responses of a set of iso-orientation domains (hypercolumn), processing a fragment of an image in a parallel way, transmit different information to higher level of the visual system. The initial phases contain the information about the presence of brightness relief in the fragment and may be used by the oculomotor system in sequential procedure of image viewing. On the other hand, the later phases contain the information about a set of orientations of contour and edge elements in the fragment.

7. NEURAL PREPROCESSOR IN THE SYSTEM OF IMAGE ANALYSIS

The proposed model of image processing is based on image features extraction at different levels of resolution. The method of multiresolution image processing in computer vision has several advantages (Burt, 1988; Levialdi, 1983; Rosenfeldt, 1984). For instance, this method allows the extraction of global features of images by local operators applied at lower resolution levels and to represent images by a set of

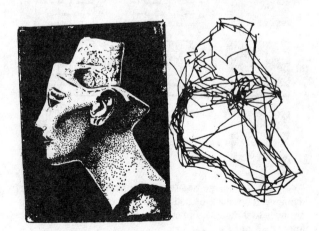

FIGURE 9. Trajectory of eye movements and gaze fixations during recognition of image by man (Yarbus, 1965).

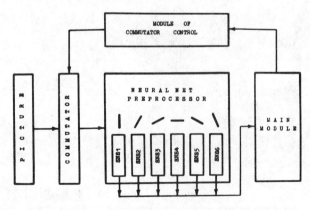

FIGURE 10. Block diagram of the system of image analysis.

FIGURE 11. Test image.

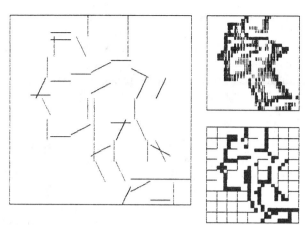

LEVEL=3 coordinates: 14, 14 region: 9X 9

FIGURE 12. Visualized results of sequential processing of the test image at the third level of resolution (on the left). The results of sequential processing of fragments at initial moments t_0 are shown in the top right-hand corner. Summarized results of sequential processing of fragments by all SNSs at later moments t_1 are shown in the bottom right-hand corner.

boundary segments of different scales (Neveu, Dyer, & Chin, 1985; Schneier, 1984).

Figure 10 shows a block diagram of the proposed system of image analysis. The test image was presented in the maximal resolution raster of 243 × 243 pixels. The commutator module, directing the preprocessor to process the part of the image, played the role of the oculomotor system. The module of commutator control set the resolution level, size of the processed image part and its position in the raster. The raster of each resolution level contained $3^n \times 3^n$ pixels, where n was the resolution level number ($n = 1, \ldots, 5$). Stimulus intensity in each point of the raster of the lower resolution level was defined by averaging the intensity over nine (3 × 3) corresponding points of the higher resolution level raster.

Hereby

$$S_{ij}(n) = \tfrac{1}{9} \sum_{k=3i-2}^{3i} \sum_{l=3j-2}^{3j} S_{kl}(n + 1),$$

$$n = 1, 2, 3, 4. \quad (16)$$

At each step of sequential processing, a fragment of 5 × 5 elements was presented to the input of the neural network preprocessor. The preprocessor consisted of six SNSs tuned to different orientations in range from 0° to 180°. At the initial moment, the SNSs provided information about intensity differences in the fragment, and then they performed discrimination and encoding contour element orientations within the fragment. On the basis of information from the preprocessor, the data on the fragment position in the raster and on the resolution level, the

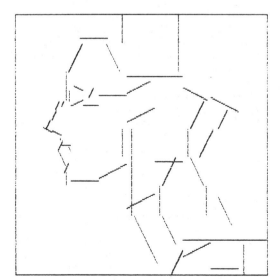

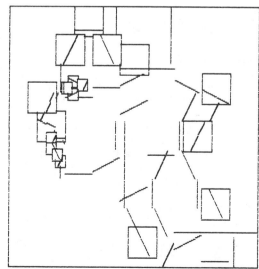

FIGURE 13. Visualized results of test image processing at the third resolution level and additional processing of some fragments at the third and fourth resolution levels. On the right, additionally processed fragments are framed.

main module may compute spatial relationships between contour elements extracted at the present step and elements detected at other steps. By the comparison of the processing results with the template information, the main module should determine the strategy of future steps of the sequential image analysis.

Figure 12 shows the results of sequential processing of the test image of Nefertiti's head (Figure 11) at the third level of resolution. Figure 13 represents the result of processing of the whole image at the third level with additional processing of some fragments at the third and fourth resolution levles. Visualized results of processing presented here seem to be quite sufficient for recognition of test image. Our future efforts will be focused on the following problems:

1. Segmentation of extracted image elements;
2. Development of strategy of sequential image processing;
3. Realization of higher level algorythms for the main module of the system.

REFERENCES

Amari, S. (1977). Dynamics of pattern formation in lateral-inhibition type neural fields. *Biological Cybernetics*, **27**, 77–87.

Amari, S. (1982). Competitive and cooperative aspects in dynamics of neural excitation and self-organization. *Lecture Notes in Biomathematics*, **45**, 1–28.

Baxter, W. T., & Dow, B. M. (1989). Horizontal organization of orientation-sensitive cells in primate visual cortex. *Biological Cybernetics*, **61**, 171–182.

Benevento, L. A., Creutzfeldt, O. D., & Kuhnt, U. (1972). Significance of intracortical inhibition in the visual cortex. *Nature*, **238**, 124–126.

Braitenberg, V., & Braitenberg, C. (1979). Geometry of orientation columns in the visual cortex. *Biological Cybernetics*, **33**, 179–186.

Burt, P. J. (1988). Smart sensing within a pyramidal vision machine. *Proceedings of the IEEE*, **76**, 970–981.

Creutzfeldt, O., & Ito, M. (1968). Functional synaptic organization of primary visual cortex neurones in the cat. *Experimental Brain Research*, **6**, 324–352.

Creutzfeldt, O., Kuhnt, U., & Benevento, L. A. (1974). An intracellular analysis of visual cortical neurones to moving stimuli: responses in a cooperative neuronal network. *Experimental Brain Research*, **21**, 251–274.

Eccles, J. C. (1969). *The inhibitory pathways of the central nervous system*. Liverpool, UK: Liverpool University Press.

Ferster, D., & Lindstrom, S. (1983). An intracellular analysis of geniculo-cortical connectivity in area 17 of the cat. *Journal of Physiology*, **342**, 181–215.

Finette, S., Harth, E., & Csermely, T. J. (1978). Anisotropic connectivity and cooperative phenomena as a basis for orientation sensitivity in the visual cortex. *Biological Cybernetics*, **30**, 231–240.

Garey, L. G., & Powell, T. P. S. (1971). An experimental study of the termination of the lateral geniculo-cortical pathway in the cat and monkey. *Proceedings of the Royal Society of London, Series B*, **119**, 41–63.

Grossberg, S., Mingolla, E., & Todorovic, D. (1989). A neural network architecture for preattentive vision. *IEEE Transaction on Biomedical Engineering*, **36**, 65–84.

Hayashi, Y. (1969). Recurrent collateral inhibition of visual cortical cells projecting to superior colliculus in cats. *Vision Research*, **9**, 1367–1380.

Hess, R., Negishi, K., & Creutzfeldt, O. (1975). The horizontal spread of intracortical inhibition in the visual cortex. *Experimental Brain Research*, **22**, 415–419.

Hubel, D. H., & Wiesel, T. N. (1962). Receptive fields, binocular integration and functional architecture in the cat's visual cortex. *Journal of Physiology*, **160**, 106–154.

Hubel, D. H., & Wiesel, T. N. (1974). Sequence, regularity and geometry of orientation columns in the monkey striate cortex. *Journal of Comparative Neurology*, **158**, 267–293.

Ito, M. (1970). Neuronal linkage in the cat visual cortex. *Journal of Physiological Society of Japan*, **32**, 550–551.

Julesz, B. (1975). Experiments in the visual perception of texture. *Scientific American*, **232**, 34–43.

Kohonen, T. (1988). An introduction to neural computing. *Neural Networks*, **1**, 3–16.

Kunt, M., Ikonomopoulos, A., & Kocher, M. (1985). Second-generation image coding techniques. *Proceedings of the IEEE*, **73**, 549–574.

Levialdi, S. (1983). Neighbourhood operators: an outlook. In Pictorial Data Analysis. *Proceedings of NATO Advanced Study Institute* (F4 pp. 1–14), West Berlin.

Linsker, R. (1986a). From basic network principles to neural architrecture: emergence of orientation-selective sells. *Proceedings of the National Academy of Sciences*, **83**, 8390–8394.

Linsker, R. (1986b). From basic network principles to neural architrecture: emergence of orientation columns. *Proceedings of the National Academy of Sciences*, **83**, 8779–8783.

Malsburg, Chr. von der (1973). Self-organization of orientation sensitive cells in the striate cortex. *Kybernetik*, **14**, 85–100.

Malsburg, Chr. von der & Cowan J. D. (1982). Outline of a theory for the ontogenesis of iso-orientation domains in the visual cortex. *Biological Cybernetics*, **45**, 49–56.

Minsky, M. (1975). A framework for representing knowledge. In P. H. Winston (Ed.) *The Psychology of Computer Vision* (pp. 211–277), New York: McGraw-Hill.

Neisser, V. (1967). *Cognitive psychology*. New York: Appleton.

Neveu, C. G., Dyer, C. R., & Chin, R. T. (1985). Object recognition using Hough pyramids. *In Proceedings of the Computer Society Conference on Computer Vision and Pattern Recognition* (pp. 328–333), San Francisco.

Paradiso, M. A. (1988). A theory for the use of visual orientation information which exploits the columnar structure of striate cortex. *Biological Cybernetics*, **58**, 35–49.

Pubols, L. M., & Leroy, R. F. (1977). Orientation detectors in the primary somatosensory neocortex of the raccoon. *Brain Research*, **129**, 61–74.

Rosenfeldt, A. (Ed.). (1984). *Multiresolution image processing and analysis*. New York: Springer-Verlag.

Rybak, I. A. (1988). *Study of response dynamics and orientation selectivity of visual cortex neurons by methods of mathematical modelling and neurophisiological experiment*. Doctoral thesis, Rostov-on-Don, USSR (in Russian).

Rybak, I. A., Shevtsova, N. A., Podladchikova, L. N., Golovan, A. V., & Markarov, V. G. (1987). Modelling and study of response dynamics and mechanisms of the preprocessing of sensory information in the screen-type neural structures. In All-Union Institute for Scientific and Technical Information. USSR, N 1657-B87 (in Russian).

Schwartz, F. L. (1980). A quantitative model of the functional architecture of human striate cortex with application to visual illusion and cortical texture analysis. *Biological Cybernetics*, **37**, 63–76.

Shiffrin, R. M., & Schneider, W. (1977). Controlled and automatic human information processing. 2. Perceptual learning, automatic attending, and a general theory. *Psychological Review*, **84**, 127–190.

Shneier, M. (1984). Multiresolution feature encodings. In A. Rosenfeldt (Ed.) *Multiresolution Image Processing and Analysis* (pp. 190–199), New York: Springer-Verlag.

Sillito, A. M. (1975). The contribution of inhibitory mechanisms to the receptive field properties of neurones in striate cortex of the cat. *Journal of Physiology*, **250**, 305–329.

Sillito, A. M. (1984). Functional considerations of the operation of GABAergic inhibitory processes in the visual cortex. In *Cerebral Cortex* (Vol. 2, pp. 91–117), New York, London: Plenum Press.

Stefanis, C., & Jasper, H. (1964). Recurrent collateral inhibition in pyramidal tract neurons. *Journal of Neurophysiology*, **27**, 855–877.

Supin, A. J. (1970). Feedback excitation and inhibition in the visual cortex. *Neurophisiologia*, **2**, 418–422 (in Russian).

Supin, A. J. (1974). Possible functional significance of different components of cortical unit responses to patterned visual stimuli. *Sechenov Physiological Journal of the USSR*, **60**, 1634–1640 (in Russian).

Talbot, S. A., & Marshall, W. H. (1941). Physiological studies on neural mechanisms of visual localization and discrimination. *American Journal of Physiology*, **24**, 1255–1263.

Vidyasagar, T. R. (1987). A model of striate response properties based on geniculate anisotropies. *Biological Cybernetics*, **57**, 11–23.

Watanabe, S., Konishi, M., & Creutzfeldt, O. D. (1966). Postsynaptic potentials in the cat's visual cortex following electrical stimulation of afferent volleys. *Experimental Brain Research*, **1**, 272–283.

Wilson, H. R., & Cowan, J. D. (1972). Excitatory and inhibitory interactions in localized populations of model neurons. *Biophysical Journal*, **12**, 1–24.

Wilson, H. R., & Cowan, J. D. (1973). A mathematical theory of the functional dynamics of cortical and thalamic nervous tissue. *Kybernetik*, **13**, 55–80.

Yarbus, A. L. (1965). *The role of eye movements in vision process.* Moscow, USSR: Nauka (in Russian).

NOMENCLATURE

t: time variable.

t_0: initial moment of stimulation in the SNS model. Intensities of initial phases of SNS element responses have been estimated at the same moment.

t_1: moment of time. Intensities of SNS element later phases have been estimated at this moment.

$\Delta t, \Delta t_1, \Delta t_2$: assumed durations of the overall response of neuron and its initial and later phases respectively (in experimental research).

T_i: time constant of the i-th neuron.

T_E, T_I: time constants of neurons in E- and I-layers respectively.

τ: time constant of the inertial block of the SNS.

U_i: membrane potential of the i-th neuron.

U_{ij}^E, U_{ij}^I: membrane potentials of the (i,j)-th neurons in E- and I-layers respectively.

Z_i: output variable (frequency of impulses) of the i-th neuron.

Z_{ij}^E, Z_{ij}^I: output variables of the (i,j)-th neurons in E- and I-layers respectively.

Z_{ij}^S: test input influence on the (i,j)-th neuron.

Z_m: value of $Z_{ij}^S(t)$ at $t \geq 0$.

Z_{ij}: element of output SNS matrix $Z = \|Z_{ij}\|$.

Z: output SNS matrix.

S_i: uncontrollable input influence on the i-th neuron.

S_E, S_I: uncontrollable input influences on neurons in E- and I-layers respectively.

S_{ij}: element of input SNS matrix $S = \|S_{ij}\|$.

S: input SNS matrix.

h_i: threshold of the i-th neuron.

h_E, h_I: thresholds of neurons in E- and I-layers, respectively.

h: threshold of SNS element.

q_{ij}: synaptic weight of the j-th input to the i-th neuron.

q_i^S: synaptic weight of the external input to the i-th neuron.

$q^{EE}, q^{IE}, q_0^{EI}, q^{EI}, q$: weights of synaptic connections between different layer neurons: the first index letter stands for layer position of the postsynaptic neuron, the second index letter stands for that of presynaptic neuron.

X_{ij}^S: input signal to the (i,j)-th SNS element.

X_{ij}^I: inertial backward inhibition to the (i,j)-th SNS element.

φ: optimal stimulus orientation.

$\Omega_{ij}(\varphi)$: area of E-layer elements forming the excitatory inputs to the (i,j)-th I-layer neuron. It determines anisotropy of lateral inhibition corresponding to orientation φ.

a_{pq}^S: element of matrix $A^S = \|a_{pq}^S\|$.

$a_{pq}^I(\varphi)$: element of matrix $A_\varphi^I = \|a_{pq}^I\|\varphi$.

$A^S, A_{\varphi=\varphi_i}^I$: matrices.

$\alpha, \beta_0, \beta, b_{ij}^S, b^I, k$: parameters.

N: $N \times N$ is the number of elements in each layer of the iso-orientation domain model.

n: number of resolution level.

i, j, k, l, p, q: indices.

$\dfrac{d}{dt}$: sign of derivative.

$f[\ ]$: sign of nonlinear function.

Σ: sign of summation.

$\max[a, b]$: sign of maximum of two values.

$A = \|a_{ij}\| = \begin{Vmatrix} a_{11} \cdots a_{1n} \\ \cdots\cdots\cdots \\ a_{n1} \cdots a_{nn} \end{Vmatrix}$: sign of matrix.

$(A)^T$: sign of matrix transposition.

208

The Cortical Column: A New Processing Unit for Multilayered Networks

FRÉDÉRIC ALEXANDRE, FRÉDÉRIC GUYOT, AND JEAN-PAUL HATON

CRIN/INRIA

YVES BURNOD

Institut des Neurosciences, Paris V

(Received 22 August 1989; revised and accepted 3 May 1990)

Abstract—*We propose in this paper a new connectionist unit that matches a biological model of the cortical column. The architectural and functional characteristics of this unit have been designed in the simplest manner in order to simulate human-like reasoning, and to be as similar as possible to the main known features of real intracortical networks. We use a new type of learning rule which can easily take into account goal-oriented combinations of actions in behavioral programs. These learning rules are both simple and biologically plausible. We show in this paper that such units can be used in multilayered networks to perform pattern recognition, with feedback connections effecting an attentive gating of sensory information flow. Computer simulations were performed to assess the ability of a multilayered network made of these biologically inspired units to perform standard speech and visual recognition. Such simulations show levels of performance equivalent to the best currently available connectionist networks for typical human-like problems, with very fast learning and recognition processes. Furthermore, this type of "cortical" unit can be used in more general multilayered networks with units controlling different types of external processing, in order to learn programs of actions which may be included in the process of recognition.*

1. INTRODUCTION

During the past ten years, both artificial intelligence researchers and neuroscientists have been paying increasing attention to connectionist networks (Rumelhart & McClelland, 1986). As a general rule, such networks are built with neuron-like interconnected units, with connective efficiencies that change according to locally available signals. The whole network learns to produce adaptive functions such as recognition, with some similarities to certain brain properties such as associative memories (Rumelhart & McClelland, 1986).

Connectionist models based upon mathematical formalisms share common features with real neural networks. For instance, both have associative properties and content-addressable memories (Minsky & Papert, 1969; Kohonen, 1984), adaptive matching between external inputs, and internal "attractors" in recursive networks (Hopfield, 1982). Multilayered networks could correspond to the successive cortical maps which process sensory information, with learning rules which enable them to learn any type of input–output transformations using an error signal (back-propagation; Fogelman Soulie et al., 1989), or selective attention with top-down feedback control (neocognition, Fukushima, 1980; ART; Grossberg, 1988).

Human processing abilities are mainly due to the cerebral cortex. Direct modeling of the neuronal circuit in this complex structure is difficult: at the cellular level, the cortical tissue includes different neuronal types, each with a defined pattern of connectivity, and different input–output functions due to a variety of transmitters and ionic channels. Consequently, models that attempt to simulate the cortex at the single-neuron level tend to become too complex to be implemented and mathematically controlled.

The basic idea presented in this paper is to progressively shape a processing unit formed by a small group of neurons corresponding to a morphofunctional substrate; in the cortex, this multicellular unit has been defined as the cortical column (Mountcas-

---

Requests for reprints should be sent to Yevs Burnod, Department of Neuroscience de la Vision, Institut des Neurosciences, Bat. C 6éme étage, 9, Quai St. Bernard, Paris 5éme, France.

tle, 1978; Hubel & Wiesel, 1977; Szentagothai, 1975) which is a repetitive circuit perpendicular to the cortical surface.

We thus describe a new connectionist approach, with a processing unit which does not correspond to a neuron but to a cortical column (Burnod, 1988). The main problem is to determine which mathematical operations could model in a simple way the basic functions of such a multicellular unit (Shaw, 1988). Two sources of inspiration are relevant.

The first one is neurobiological; the model has to be biologically plausible: its architectural and functional characteristics have been determined in the light of neurobiological considerations (see justifications in section 2). Even if the cortex is far from being understood, it is possible to use general principles to define the main types of inputs, outputs, and interactions.

The second problem is cognitive; the processing unit combines essential features for human-like data processing, but with parallel and distributed representations.

Consequently, the proposed unit will be interpreted both in terms of neuronal activity and in terms of data processing.

In this paper, we attempt to model this basic cortical function via a minimal set of rules, which nevertheless perform more elaborate functions than individual neurons.

A formal network is developed, inspired from biological findings on the cerebral cortex (Burnod, 1988); this unit can be used to build large multilayered networks for general artificial intelligence (AI) tasks such as pattern recognition (Alexandre et al., 1989) or reasoning.

2. BIOLOGICAL INSPIRATION

The processing unit is designed to be in direct correspondance with the "cortical column," a stereotyped interneuronal circuit (about 100 μm wide) whose main characteristics are repeated throughout the cortex (Mountcastle, 1978; Szentagothai, 1975). These clusters of interconnected cells are not defined by anatomical boundaries, but rather from their homogeneous activities: when the firing frequency of cortical neurons is recorded in response to specific stimuli (Mountcastle, 1978; Hubel & Wiesel, 1977), or during stereotyped behaviour (Evarts & Tanji, 1974), homogeneous activities reveal sets of cells arranged in vertical clusters or columns. It is thus possible to delimit groups of highly interconnected cells sharing the same set of inputs and outputs (Szentagothai, 1975; Jones, 1981). The lateral width of this basic unit is determined by the functional homogeneity of component pyramidal neurons, in general due to the intersection between subsets of connective stripes (Hubel & Wiesel, 1977).

Behavioral tasks, such as pattern recognition, can be conceived as involving several sets of laterally interconnected columns working in parallel (like cortical maps), which effect serial processing on information originating from the environment.

2.1. Architecture

The cortex (and thus, the column) has a six-layered organization. We, like others (Ballard, 1986), have chosen to group these six layers into three major input–output divisions. The model unit thus has three divisions in direct correspondance with the three major input–output divisions of real cortical columns (Mountcastle, 1978; Jones, 1981):

1. The pyramidal neurons of upper layers (layers 2 and 3) are specialized in cortico–cortical connections that form direct or indirect connections between any two columns (Szentagothai, 1975; Jones, 1981); the upper division of the unit will provide a similar set of connections. These connections will be named *internal input* and *internal output* (see, for example, Figure 1).

2. The intermediate layer (layer 4) receives the main sensory inputs, from two different sources:

    either directly from the thalamus which provides information from the "external world";

    or from other cortical areas involved in earlier stages of sensory processing; connectivity upon this division produces a progressive integration of sensory information, by a divergence–convergence resulting in a progressive increase in the size of the receptive fields (Van Essen & Maunsell, 1983; Zeki & Shipp, 1988).

    The intermediate division of the model will also have an external input which includes feed-forward connections.

3. The pyramidal neurons of the lower layers (layer 5 and 6) are more specialized to effect "actions" toward the external world or controls upon the information it produces (Zeki & Shipp, 1988; Van Essen & Maunsell, 1983):

    they project to subcortical structures and command different levels of actions and behavioural adaptations, and

    they participate in the feedback projection to previous cortical areas and can thus effect selective control of this sensory information flow.

    The lower division of the unit will also provide an *external* output which also includes feedback connections.

210

Within each area, a column is connected from both upper and lower layers to neighboring columns of the same "primary indice" (as defined in Ballard, 1986; e.g., in area 17, the same retinotopic position), and to more distant columns sharing similar functional properties, with the same "secondary indice" (e.g., in area 17, the same orientation; Ballard, 1986; Gilbert & Wiesel, 1981).

The three divisions of our unit will thus respect major outlines of the cortical connectivity between columns. Its connections can be used to produce a multilayered network (like a multilayered perceptron) but with feedback pathways (like recursive networks; e.g., Hopfield nets). As columns, the units are not fully interconnected; a column is connected to a limited and rather constant number of cortical columns (Mountcastle, 1978; Szentagothai, 1975).

The general organization of the columns in the cortex displays cytoarchitectonical variations, such as the relative thicknesses of the six layers. These variations are introduced in the unit, which has similar parameters; for example, increasing the width of layer IV (thalamic input) in receptive areas is taken into account by changing the weights of the external input of the unit (see Figure 1).

2.2. Levels of Activity

In the cortex it is necessary to consider different states of activity to describe with minimal complexity several important features, such as selective attention, anticipation, or output actions which result in reentrant feedback inputs. Considering all-or-none activity, like in Hopfield nets (Hopfield, 1982), is insufficient in the case of the cortex. In our unit, we will distinguish three states of activity in correspondance with three cortical functional states (see Figure 1):

1. The low level, that we will call $E1$ in the unit, represents moderate neuronal activities (action potential frequencies in the range of 10 spikes/ sec) which are insufficient to result in output actions; however, such activity, mostly intracortical, can reflect active processes during selective attention, as seen for example in parietal areas when stimuli do not match ongoing behaviour (Mountcastle, Andersen, & Motter, 1981), and also anticipation, as seen for example in frontal areas during waiting for a go signal (Fuster, 1977).

2. A higher level of activation, which we term $E2$ (action potential frequencies with a greater magnitude, 50–100 Hz), models activities observed during sensorimotor interactions with the external world, for stimuli matching intrinsic cortical filtering functions (in receptive areas; Hubel &

Wiesel, 1977), or linked with ongoing behavior (in associative areas; Mountcastle, Andersen, & Motter, 1981), or resulting in command of a movement (in motor areas; Evarts & Tanji, 1974).

3. Finally, we include a nul activity state ($E0$), which describes the effects of inhibitory processes.

2.3. Activation Rules

Activation rules of the unit will model input–output transformations performed by a column using these three activity levels; they are summarized in Figure 1 which details activities of the two output divisions (internal and external for respectively upper and lower layers) depending upon activity levels of the two main inputs (internal and external, respectively to upper and intermediate layers) and the previous state of the column. Such activation rules will match the following three important features of cortical physiology.

- *Conditional inhibitions.* Strong lateral inhibitions are observed in the cortex when produced by focal, well-patterned stimuli although there are also direct corticocortical excitatory connections (Mountcastle, 1978; Hubel & Wiesel, 1977). In a cortical column, inhibitory and excitatory interneurons are branched in parallel on the direct connections between cortical and thalamic inputs

	Inputs Internal	External	prior state	Outputs Internal	External	Comments	Depends upon:
1	E0	E0	E0,E1	E0	E0	Inactivity	
2	E0	E2	E0,E1	E0	E0	Motor	Map
				E1	E0	Associative	
				E2	E2	Sensory	
3	E1	E0	E0,E1	E0	E0	Inhibition	Learning
				E1	E0	Gating	
				E2	E2	Triggering	
4	E1	E2	E0,E1	E2	E2	Amplification	
5	E2	E0,E2	E0,E1	E0	E0	Inhibition	
				E1	E0		
6	E2	E0,E2	E2	E2	E2	Reactivation	

FIGURE 1. Activation rules for a simple model of the cortical column. An in–out table imposes the state of activation of the two outputs (OI$_i'$, OE$_i'$, in the right part) when the activities of internal and external (II$_i'$, IE$_i$) inputs, as well as the prior state of the unit, are known (left part of the table). Three activity levels are considered: $E0$, inhibition (or FALSE); $E1$, low level (or PERHAPS); $E2$, high level (or TRUE). The six lines of the table display the different possible combinations, and are ordered by the intensity of the internal inputs (see text for detailed description). When more than one internal input is active, each potential level of activation is evaluated; the more numerous is selected to be the real level of activation. In case of equality, the unit is set to the uncertain state $E1$. After learning, this case tends to disappear.

onto pyramidal neurons (Szentagothai, 1975; Jones, 1981); the relation between columns is controlled in parallel by excitatory and inhibitory interneurons, which tend to produce nonlinear effects, with a spatiotemporal selectivity depending upon branching patterns and channels of interneurons. The combination performed by the unit (line 5 of Figure 1) will be qualitatively different for different levels of activity; an increasing level of activity can result initially in excitation (for a low level) followed by inhibition (for a high level). Consequently, a strong activity level will inhibit related units with a lower activity.

- *Gating and amplification.* Moderate cortical inputs have a gating effect on other inputs, for example, on thalamic inputs (Connors, Gutnick, & Prince, 1982; Asanuma, Waters, & Yumina, 1982). Consequently, in the unit (line 3 of Figure 1), an internal input alone will have a weak influence (at level $E1$), but the coactivation of two inputs will generate a strong nonlinear increase of activity ($E2$).

- *Selective filtering of inputs.* As described in the cortex, the operation upon the exernal and feedforward inputs will be modelled by a spatial filtering process, with a central positive region and a peripheral negative one. This type of filtering is similar to the transfer function assumed to produce orientation selectivity in visual areas from thalamic inputs (Hubel & Wiesel, 1977).

Combining these rules results in a prediction: cortical activity will spread in the cortico–cortical network (via the upper layers) for a moderate activity, with no output outside the cortex. In contrast, a strong local pattern of activation will have a strong inhibitory effect on less-activated columns and will produce a precise combination of output actions (via lower-pyramidal neurons). Such a model gives an interpretation of neuronal activities within the cortex and their behavioral correlates: a higher level of well-patterned activity corresponds to reaching a goal, whereas lower activity levels correspond to a searching process (propagation of activity) or an attentive state.

2.4. Learning Rules

Local learning rules, such as the Hebb rule or the delta rule, enable neural nets to learn global in–out functions; mathematical generalization of these rules for multilayered networks was provided with backpropagation algorithms. Such algorithms have been used to model the transformations performed by cortical areas (Zipser & Andersen, 1988). But generalization of learning rules such as the backpropagation algorithm is based upon mathematical

properties and has no simple physiological correlates at the neuronal level.

It is possible, however, to define learning rules which match the following features of the cortical network, both at the global and local levels.

- The global logic of the learning rules corresponds to operant conditioning: if a strongly active column participates in an action outside the cortex, and if this external action reactivates the inputs of this column (equivalent to a "reward," or more generally, to a "goal"), this input will gain by learning a new influence: when it has a low activation (corresponding to a "drive"), it selectively activates columns whose actions were previously efficient in satisfying the drive state.

- Local learning rules correspond mostly to activity-dependent plasticity of cortico–cortical pathways: these pathways are mediated by glutamate and involve receptors with potentiating properties (Barrionuevo & Brown, 1983). This plasticity occurs when a strong depolarization of the cell (upper-pyramidal neurons) is followed by a strong reactivation of its inputs (due to glutamate release). Long-term changes in the efficacy of this pathway will increase the influence of moderate cortico–cortical inputs (gating properties), but will not influence the other combinations, particularly with higher inputs.

- Consequently, we will differentiate four stages of learning that can be easily interpreted as activity-dependent changes in the different types of cortical interneurons. The prediction made by considering this unit as a model of the cortical column is that different types of interneurons can modify their transmission efficiencies for specific activation patterns which depend upon the specific input–output connectivities of each type of cell.

The learning rules of the unit (Figure 2) summarize the overall long-term activity-dependent changes of neural transmissions within and between columns, mainly by their global effects on the input–output roles. We do not take into account synaptic weights from neuron to neuron, but transmission coefficients between input and output divisions of the units. Figure 2 (in the right-hand side) shows how a moderate internal input (from a unit A, "presynaptic") can produce four different effects on the target unit (B, which is the learning unit), depending upon previous patterns of activities. Critical features for learning (left part of Figure 3) are time coupling and states of activity, measured by two "repetition factors" called $P2$ and $P0$: $P2$ represents the probability that the learning unit B is active (in state $E2$)

Repetition Factor		Outputs of i when: External input = E0 Internal input = E1		
$P0_i^j$	$P2_i^j$	Internal	External	
-	-	E0,E1	E0	Random
1	0	E0	E0	Inhibition
<1	>0	E1	E0	Gating
0	1	E2	E2	Triggering

FIGURE 2. Learning rules. This table shows the functional consequences (right part of the table) of the long-term changes of transmission produced by two patterns of activities (repetition factor, in the left part of the table): $P0_i^j$ is the conditional probability that the unit i receives a strong internal input j when it was previously inhibited; $P2_i^j$ is the conditional probability that a strong internal activation ($E2$) occurs when the unit i is already strongly active ($E2$). The four lines describe the four learning stages and the four possible resulting states of connections (detailed in the text).

before a strong input (state $E2$) from unit A; conversely, $P0$ measures the inactive state of the learning unit B, before similar strong input from A. Consequences of learning (in the right-hand side of Figure 2) are only visible upon moderate inputs ($E1$). The four learning cases can be interpreted as follows:

1. *Random*: Before learning, a moderate input has weak and random effects.

2. *Inhibition*: If the unit is always inactive before a strong activation of a cortical input ($P0 = 1$), this input will gain by learning an inhibitory anticipatory effect. Behavioral interpretation of this rule is an increased inhibitory influence of possible goals toward actions that happened to be always inhibited before a success. The prediction for cortical physiology is that inhibitory interneurons can be modified like pyramidal neurons: when they are first strongly active (no action is made) and then when they are reactivated by cortico–cortical inputs (success).

3. *Gating*: When the unit is sometimes strongly active (and sometimes inactive) before a strong cortical input, there will be an increase in the gating effect of this input, when moderate; however, another coactive input will still be needed to produce a strong output. The behavioral interpretation is an increase of the gating influence of possible goals toward units which sometimes were efficient in reaching such goals. Prediction is an increased efficacy of the excitatory neurons, mainly upper-pyramidal neurons, as described in the preceding paragraph; such neurons are branched in parallel upon the direct pathway between cortico–cortical inputs and lower-layer output cells. Stabilization of gating could come from the competitive changes in excitatory and inhibitory vertically oriented interneurons which can control the coupling between upper and lower layers of the column.

4. Triggering: If the unit is always strongly active before a strong input ($P2 = 1$), this input, when moderate, will gain a very strong triggering effect that will result in a strong output. The behavioral interpretation is that possible goals can directly trigger actions which were always effective. This learning stage corresponds to the connective logic of vertically oriented disinhibitory interneurons.

• The learning logic of this model is somewhat different from other connectionist models and gives a possible interpretation of the activity in the cerebral cortex.

Within this framework, every strong cortical activation of a cortical column can be viewed as a logical equilibrium state (a goal), due to lateral inhibition; for example, recognition corresponds to well-patterned activity ($E2$ or $E0$) in a cortical region. Conversely, a moderate level of activity which persists represents possible goals and thus an attentive state before recognition (a specific subset of competitive stable states are possible); in this case, activation rules result in a continuous search (or waiting) for cortical actions, adapted to the environment (match between cortical and thalamic inputs), which can result in attaining an equilibrium state, defining for example a full recognition ($E2$–$E0$). Furthermore, the learning rules enable intracortical connections to learn context-dependent combinations of cortical actions which are efficient in reaching this equilibrium.

At the local level, activity-dependent changes occur for in–out combinations which do not have the same temporal sequence as Hebb rules: the cell is first depolarized and then reactivated by its inputs. Such temporal sequences are more compatible with the known physiology of glutamate receptors. This type of learning is not competitive with other mechanisms closer to Hebb rules which could provide a more sensitive adjustment between inputs and outputs.

3. INFORMATION-PROCESSING MODELIZATION

The processing unit that we propose has been interpreted in terms of neuronal activity; we give now a complementary interpretation in terms of data processing.

We propose a realization with six main features, sufficient to specify a connectionist network (Rumelhart & McClelland, 1986). A description and a data-processing interpretation are given for each characteristic.

3.1. Architecture

In human-like functions, at least three types of information can be distinguished: stimuli, actions, and concepts. They are separately expressed in the network:

- stimuli come from the external world via specific receptors,

- external outputs toward the external world will trigger specific actions,

- concepts are represented by distributed activities in the network and interact by internal input–output relations.

Inputs and outputs of a processing unit i are thus divided into an internal component (for concepts) and an external one (for stimuli and actions), as shown in Figure 1; they are denoted by $II_i^j(t)$, $IE_i^k(t)$,

$OI_i(t)$, $OE_i(t)$, where j and k represent the connected units and t stands for the time.

This distinction corresponds to the upper layers of the cortex for internal relations, to the lower layers for external outputs, and to the intermediate one for external inputs.

3.2. Connectivity

The network is not fully interconnected; a unit is connected to a limited and rather constant number of other units in four linking ways that take into account the two types of input–output, as illustrated in Figure 3:

- A unit has $n1$ internal input–output connections with neighboring units in the same map.

- $n2$ internal input-output connections with other maps,

- each unit has an external output which is either a feedback or a response outside the network,

- the external input is either a stimulus or a feed-forward input from other maps. These external connections (both input and output) are organized in continuous overlapping receptive fields.

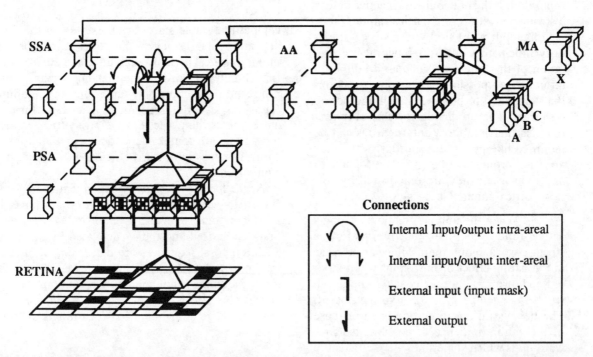

FIGURE 3. Organization and connectivity of the processing layers (modelling cortical areas) used in the simulation. This network for visual recognition has five layers of processing units connected as expected from biological principles. Thick arrows show feed-forward and feedback internal connections between input structures ("retina"), primary, and secondary sensory areas. Transfer functions of units in the primary sensory area are illustrated by oriented patterns (feature extraction) in overlapping receptive fields (illustrated by thick frames in the "retina"). Thin arrows depict internal connections of processing units in associative area, both extra- and intra-areal.

The internal neighboring connections can be regarded as potential pathways between concepts where information propagates step by step.

3.3. Activity Levels

A three-valued logic is a minimal modelization of human-like processing, in order to take into account anticipatory and attentive behaviours. Moreover, the three values directly correspond to the three states of activity described in the neurobiological model ($E0$, $E1$, $E2$):

- $E2$ stands for the "TRUE" value: depending upon its localization, it can be interpreted as a "sure" stimulus, action, or concept.

- $E0$ stands for the "FALSE" value: in the neurobiological model, it is often due to an inhibition.

- $E1$ stands for "PERHAPS": it can be interpreted as a hypothesis. Generally, when a hypothesis is emitted, the system will search to validate it; transition from $E1$ to $E2$ stands for the validation of such a hypothesis, that is a decision.

The intermediate state of activity can propagate in the network; this propagation allows a limited number of connections between units. The communication between distant units can be performed by spread of activity from one unit to the next. Propagation of state $E1$ is thus interpreted as propagation of hypothesis, that is, an active search.

3.4. Activation Rules

The unit has to compute its outputs (internal and external) as a function of its inputs, of its prior state, and of previous learning. The two following functions have to be defined:

$$\mathrm{OI}_i(t) = f(\mathrm{II}_i^j(t), \mathrm{IE}_i^k(t), \mathrm{OE}_i(t-1), P0_i^j, P2_i^j),$$

$$\mathrm{OE}_i(t) = g(\mathrm{II}_i^j(t), \mathrm{IE}_i^k(t), \mathrm{OE}_i(t-1), P0_i^j, P2_i^j),$$

where $j = 1, .., n1 + n2$; k indexes the external receptive field and P_i^j measure previous learning, as described below.

At time t, for each unit i, a global external input, denoted by IE_i, is computed as a function of the $\mathrm{IE}_i^k(t)$. It measures the correspondance between the input mask of a unit i, defined a priori without learning, and its external inputs IE_i^k; IE_i is set either to $E2$ (exact correspondance) or $E0$ (too much difference).

We then compute local outputs (OE_i^j, OI_i^j) for each internal input II_i^j modulated by IE_i thanks to the truth table shown in Figure 1.

Finally, it is necessary to define a rule to combine several synchronous internal inputs at time t for a unit i.

If the event "internal output j of a unit i at time t in state Ex" is denoted by $\mathrm{OI}_i^j x(t)$, and the "number of event $\mathrm{OI}_i^j x(t)$ for $j = 1$ to $n1 + n2$" is denoted by nx, then $\mathrm{OI}_i(t) = Ex$ if $\max(n0, n1, n2) = nx$. In case of equality, the unit is set to $E1$, uncertain state.

The global external output is computed in the same way.

This truth table (Figure 1) is built from the neurobiological data and is a model of neuronal interactions in a cortical column. Moreover, in the light of previous interpretations, the table corresponds to a logical data-processing mechanism. Only the cases which modify the outputs of the unit are taken into account.

- Line 5 illustrates the inhibition mechanism, that selectively limits the number of active units. Validation of a hypothesis (decision) results in a suppression of competitive hypothesis.

- By contrast, in line 6, two different decisions, when successive, are not competitive; furthermore, this temporal relation will result in learning.

- Line 3 is learning dependent, according to the coefficients $P0_i^j$ and $P2_i^j$ (see "learning rules"). When a hypothesis is emitted, its influence depends upon previous experiences as described in the learning rules section. It can suppress other possibilities ($E0$), emit a new hypothesis ($E1$) or trigger a decision ($E2$).

- Line 4 shows how a hypothesis is validated when it matches an external stimulus.

- In line 2, three different kinds of topologic maps are distinguished in the network, each kind devoted to a specific step in the information analysis. A stimulus will imply a certitude in "sensory maps," a hypothesis in "associative maps," but cannot directly trigger an action in "motor maps."

3.5. Learning Rules

Like activation rules, learning rules are both consistent with neurobiological data (see Section 2) and with a data-processing interpretation. As in standard neural nets, learning is locally computed. Figure 2 shows how an internal input j (from a unit $A_{i'}$) can produce four different effects on the target unit A_i (right part of the table), depending upon the probability of their coactivation expressed by the repetition factors $P2_i^j$ and $P0_i^j$. If $N(e)$ measures the number of occurrences of the event e from $t0$ up to current time, then

$$P0_i^j = \frac{N(\mathrm{II}_i^j 2(t) \text{ .and. } \mathrm{OI}_i 0(t-dt))}{N(\mathrm{II}_i^j 2(t))}$$

and

$$P2_i^j = \frac{N(\mathrm{II}_i^j 2(t) \text{ .and. } \mathrm{OI}_i 2(t-dt))}{N(\mathrm{II}_i^j 2(t))}$$

where dt stands for a little delay.

The four cases may be interpreted as follow:

- Before learning, propagation of hypothesis is random.

- During learning, if a concept (A_i in state $E0$) never participates to the validation of another concept (A_j, $E2$), the latter will gain an anticipatory inhibitory effect ($P0_i^j = 1$).

- But if the concept A_i is sometimes linked with the validation of the concept A_j, learning will result in a selective propagation of hypothesis A_j toward A_i ($0 < P0_i^j < 1$, $0 < P2_i^j < 1$).

- Finally, if the coactivation pattern is always observed, a hypothesis from A_j will directly trigger a decision of A_i, even in absence of external confirmation ($P2_i^j = 1$).

4. THE COMPUTATIONAL NETWORK

This theory, consisent with neurobiological data, provides autonomous basic units, each computing an output as a function of its inputs, modulated by its internal features which can change with learning. An implementation consists of building a network of units and simulating the inherent parallel processing.

The network was used to recognize alphabetical patterns (vision) and isolated words (speech recognition). These two sensory functions require the same global architecture shown in Figure 3, summarized by a signification map (SM) where activity represents the state of recognition, a sensory map I (SMI), a sensory map II (SMII) and an associative map (AM) (all chosen to coincide with cortical areas which participate in a specific behavioural or cognitive task).

Since each unit behaves autonomously, the network is efficiently specified by the connectivity pattern of each map:

- The only disparity between auditory and visual networks involves the initial encoding: a 8×8 grid where the letters are digitalized for visual recognition, and for auditory recognition, a 32×50 grid which receives spectrograms over 32 frequency ranges from 0 to 8000 Hz, and from 10 to 50 frames allocated to the word.

- Connections between initial encoding and SMI are unidirectional and retinotopically (or tonotopically) organized. In SMI, units respond to the input, selectively oriented (Hubel & Wiesel, 1977) into local 3×3 overlapping receptive fields, as illustrated in Figure 3. Similarly, in the auditory case, units are specialized for time and frequency range.

- As illustrated in Figure 3, each unit in SMI receives its "external" 3×3 inputs from a field of SMI (feed-forward), sends back its actions to SMI, exchanges symetrically its internal inputs and outputs with its neighbors in SMII, and is connected with a group of adjacent units in AM.

- In the associative map AM, each unit carries out a coactivation test between two neighborhoods taken from SMII and SM, and has reciprocal links with adjacent units in AM (internal relation).

- The map SM contains either a set of 26 units for visual recognition of letters (see Figure 3) or 10 units for number recognition in speech processing; these units are reciprocally connected and receive inputs from groups of adjacent units in AM.

4.1. Processing

Initially, every coefficient in the network is undetermined and requires no a priori choice. In a typical learning session, a given pattern (a character or a spectrogram) is presented to the receptor and all the units in SM are inhibited ($E0$), except the one corresponding to the solution which is forced to $E2$ (stable state). Information propagates and interferes in the whole network, from these two external inputs, according to the connectivity scheme and the functioning rules. Eight evaluations are necessary for the network to come back to a stable state. During the learning phase, each unit reaching the stable state ($E2$) brings its relations with other connected units up to date (coefficients $P0$ and $P2$), following the learning rules. After learning, these coefficients delimit new functional sets of units which correspond to invariant characteristics of the external world.

During the recognition process, an unknown pattern is presented to the receptor and all the units in SM are set to $E1$ (unstable state, desired goal), in order to trigger parallel analysis. The network evolves until one unit in SM reaches the stable state $E2$ (reached goal, solution). The middle set of units AM allows association, through its connectivity, between the invariant characteristics in the two sensorimotor fields (visual or audio and significative). AM changes the activity distribution in SMI and SMII. From an unstable state ($E1$) in all units of SM, the network converges toward a learned distribution (pattern) in SMI and SMII, and a stable state in SM, that is a subset of highly active units ($E2$), inhibiting ($E0$) all the other units in this area.

4.2. Character Recognition

For the first session, the learning corpus is constituted of 26 upper-case characters, binary digitized on a 8 × 8 grid. During learning, each letter is presented twice to the network. As described in previous studies (Fogelman et al., 1989), the test corpus has been built up from the initial letters by randomly inverting n pixels (n varying from 1 to 25) in each image. For the second session, the network trains with noisy letters, each being presented with 6, 9, and 12 randomly inverted pixels (Fogelman Soulie et al., 1989). The recognition rate is reported in Figure 4a as a function of noise. The performances are rather close, whatever the learning corpus. The slight difference between the two graphs in Figure 4a reveals the innate and implicit generalization abilities of the network. Let us mention here that during noisy character recognition, most of the errors were also committed by the human subject, owing to the ratio between the number of randomly inverted pixels and the number of pixels differentiating one letter from an other (confusion between a noisy E and F, or a noisy O and Q . . .)

4.3. Speech Recognition

The learning and the test sets were prepared as follows. Thirty speakers recorded four versions of the 10 numbers. The recordings were made with no particular precaution (background noise, no starting synchronization, no constant rate of speech . . .). A Fast-Fourier transform (FFT) was carried out over 8-ms frames. As a result, each token was represented as a set of 10–50 frames each containing 32 positive values representing the 32 linear frequency ranges from 0 to 8000 Hz. In order to reduce the variation of the number of frames for a same number (beginning of each token not located, pronounciation duration . . .), a temporal compression of the spectrogram eliminates every frame too close to the preceding one and then transforms the 32 linear frequency ranges into 16 physiological frequency ranges. This array of (16 × n) values (n varying from 10 to 25 after compression) is proposed as an initial encoding to sensory map I.

For a speaker-dependent trial, the learning was done only once for each of the 40 spectrograms

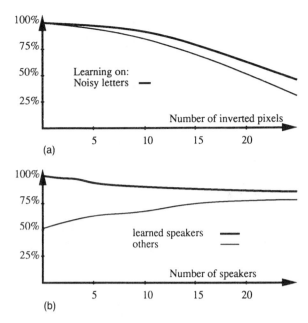

FIGURE 4. Visual and auditory performances of the network. Figure 4a: *The visual case* (upper diagram). This figure shows the recognition rate as a function of noise level. The network was trained on the whole alphabet, with or without noise, and gave very close performances for the recognition of noisy letters. Let us mention here that the system needs only 10 sec to learn the whole alphabet. Figure 4b: *The auditory case* (lower diagram). This shows the recognition rate as a function of the number of speakers in the learning set. In both cases, the network was trained on the 10 numbers and was tested either with the learned speakers, or with unknown speakers. If only one speaker is learned, the network recognizes him or her perfectly but often fails (50%) with another speaker. When more speakers are learned, the performances slightly decrease for the learned speakers (85% for 20 learned speakers), as the number of tokens correctly labeled for unknown people increases up to a similar rate (80%), and toward a supposed common limit for the two curves.

(4 × 10). The network always recognized the learned tokens, and made an average of 3% errors for the test tokens (Elman & Zipser, 1988).

For a speaker-independent trial, the network was trained on the 40 spectrograms from 2 to 20 people. The network's responses were tested either with learned subjects or with unknown subjects (Peeling, Moore, & Tomlinson, 1986). The recognition rate for subjects included in the learned set is reported in Figure 4b. It starts from a maximum rate for one speaker, and becomes stable to an average rate of 85% for many speakers. Regarding the recognition rate for unknown people, it grows from 50% for one learned speaker, up to 80% when the learning set contains many speakers. An unknown speaker may have all versions of a number refused, because of his particular pronunciation. Isolated errors are often due to confusion between two fricatives or two vowels.

Figure 5 illustrates the internal representation of learning through probabilistic coefficients.

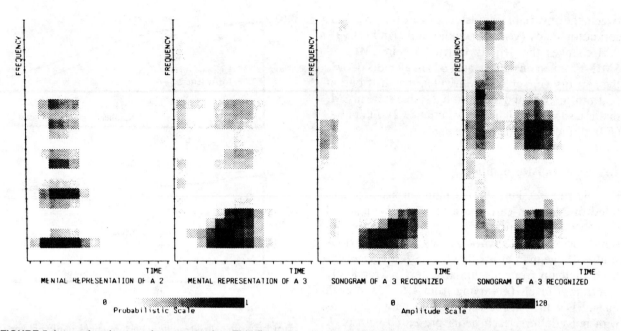

FIGURE 5. Internal and external representation. This figure represents configurations in the network for recognition of isolated words, in order to illustrate the basis on which the matching operation is effected. The two pictures on the left show the memorized coefficients between units of AA and two different units of SA recognizing a "2" (first picture) or a "3" (second picture). This "mental representation" is obtained after learning 20 × 4 occurrences of the digits. By contrast, the two pictures on the right represent the initial encodings for two spectrograms, both corresponding to the digit "3," and produced by two different speakers (note their disparity). These occurrences are recognized by the stored coefficients of the mental representation of "3" (second picture).

4.4. Spatiotemporal Complexity

For vision, the network has 1200 units with 6 connections per unit; for speech recognition the network's size was increased to 4000 units because of the bigger size of the input information flow; the number of connections per unit is identical. The simulations reported here were run on a Sun 3/50. The learning is very fast, so the network needs 15 s to learn the 40 spectrograms of one speaker, and 10 s to learn the 26 letters. Recognition requires in both cases about 0.5 s.

5. CONCLUSION

Several simulations of the processing effected by the cortical areas have been proposed using multilayered neuronal networks and back-propagation algorithms (Zipser & Andersen, 1988; Lehky & Sejnowsky, 1988). But the principles of these algorithms are far from biological mechanisms. Our approach is quite different: we propose a general processing unit which is based upon neuronal properties in the cerebral cortex and fits experimental data; furthermore, this unit is common to all cortical areas and could be used for a variety of adaptative and cognitive functions. Simulations show the ability of the cortical column to effect associative recognition, which is an adaptative function of biological systems commonly implemented by artificial neural networks. Figure 4

demonstrates levels of performance comparable to the best available algorithms; moreover, learning speed is much faster than in algorithms used in other multilayered networks (for example, back-propagation). This work illustrates the fact that it is possible to elaborate models integrating three basic properties: (i) the basic rules and the construction of the network are physiologically plausible; (ii) the rules are simple (in–out tables); and (iii) the network performs rapid pattern recognition with an efficient learning as shown here for both visual and auditory inputs. A promising direction is the capacity of such models to result in sophisticated behaviors (Burnod, 1988), as we shall attempt to illustrate in on-going and future work. This includes (i) construction of functional networks with goals and subgoals to generate planning, (ii) progressive learning of symbolic reasoning, (iii) combination of networks which include several information pathways with specific external inputs and outputs for the different sensory-motor fields (Guyot, Alexandre, & Haton, 1989), and (iv) integration of time (Guyot et al., 1989).

REFERENCES

Alexandre, F., Burnod, Y., Guyot, F., & Haton, J. P. (1989). La colonne corticale, unité de base pour des réseaux multi-couches. *Compte Rendu à l'Académie des Sciences, Paris,* **309**(III), 259–264.

Asanuma, H., Waters, R. S., & Yumina, H. (1982). Physiological properties of neurons projecting from area 3a to area 4 of feline cerebral cortex. *Journal of Neurophysiology*, **48**(4), 1048–1057.

Ballard, D. H. (1986). Cortical Connections and parallel processing: Structure and function. *The Behavioral and Brain Sciences*, **9**, 67–120.

Barrionuevo, G., & Brown, T. H. (1983). Associative long-term potentiation in hippocampal slices. *Proceedings of the National Academy of Sciences, Neurobiology*, **80**, 7347–7351.

Burnod, Y. (1988). *An adaptive neural network: The cerebral cortex.* Paris: Masson.

Connors, B. W., Gutnick, M. J., & Prince, D. A. (1982). Electrophysiological properties of neocortical neurons in vitro. *Journal of Neurophysiology*, **48**(6), 1302–1320.

Elman, J. L., & Zipser, D. (1988). Learning the hidden structure of speech. *Journal of Acoustical Society of America*, **83**(4), 1615–1626.

Evarts, E. V., & Tanji, J. (1974). Gating of motor cortex reflexes by prior instruction. *Brain Research*, **71**, 479–494.

Fogelman Soulie, F., Gallinari, P., Le Cun, Y., & Thiria, S. (1989). Network learning. In Y. Kodratoff & R. Michalski (Eds.), *Machine learning* (Vol. 3). San Mateo, CA: Morgan Kaufmann.

Fukushima, K. (1980). Neocognitron: A self-organizing neural network for a mechanism of pattern recognition unaffected by shift in position. *Biological Cybernetics*, **36**, 193–202.

Fuster, J. M. (1977). Unit activity in the prefrontal cortex during delayed response performance: Neuronal correlates of short-term memory. *Journal of Neurophysiology*, **36**, 61–78.

Gilbert, C. D., & Wiesel, T. N. (1981). Laminar specialization and intracortical connections in cat primary visual cortex. In F. Schmitt et al. (Eds.), *The organization of the cerebral cortex.* Cambridge, MA: MIT Press.

Grossberg, S. (1988). Nonlinear neural networks: Principles, mechanisms, and architectures. *Neural Networks*, **1**, 17–61.

Guyot, F., Alexandre, F., & Haton, J. P. (1989). Toward a continuous model of the cortical column: Application to speech recognition. In *Proceedings of the International Congress of Acoustic and Speech Processing, Glasgow.* New York: IEEE.

Guyot, F., Alexandre F., Haton, J. P., & Burnod, Y. (1989). A potentially powerful connectionist unit: The cortical column. *NATO Advanced Research Workshop on Neuro Computing, Les Arcs.* Heidelberg: Springer-Verlag.

Hopfield, J. J. (1982). Neural network and physical systems with emergent collective computational abilities. *Proceedings of the National Academy of Sciences*, **79**, 2554–2558.

Hubel, D. H., & Wiesel, T. N. (1977). Functional architectures of macaque monkey visual cortex, Ferrier Lecture. *Proceedings of the Royal Society of London B*, **198**, 1–59.

Jones, E. G. (1981). Identification and classification of intrinsic circuit elements in the neocortex. In G. M. Edelman, E. Gall, & W. M. Cowan (Eds), *Dynamic aspects of neocortical functions.* New York: John Wiley & Sons.

Kohonen, T. (1984). *Self-organization and associative memory.* New York: Springer-Verlag.

Lehky, S. R., & Sejnowsky, T. J. (1988). Network model of shape-from-shading: Neural function arises from both receptive and projective fields. *Nature*, **333**, 452–455.

Minsky, M., & Papert, S. (1969). *Perceptrons.* Cambridge MA: MIT Press.

Mountcastle, V. B. (1978). *An organizing principle for cerebral function. The unit module and the distributed system, The mindful brain.* Cambridge, MA: MIT Press.

Mountcastle, V. B., Andersen, R. A., & Motter, B. C. (1981). The influence of attentive fixation upon the excitability of the light-sensitive neurons of the posterior parietal cortex. *Journal of Neurosciences*, **1**, 1218–1235.

Peeling, S. M., Moore, R. K., & Tomlinson, M. J. (1986). The multi-layer perceptron as a tool for speech pattern processing research. In *Proceedings of the IOA Autumn Conferences on Speech and Hearing.* London: Controller HMSO.

Rumelhart, D. E., & McClelland, J. L. (1986). *Parallel distributed processing.* Cambridge, MA: MIT Press.

Shaw, G. L., Silverman, F. J., & Pearson, J. C. (1988). Trion model of cortical organization and the search of the code of short-term memory and of information processing. In J. Delacour & J. C. S. Levy (Eds.), *Systems with learning and memory abilities.* Elsevier, North-Holland.

Szentagothai, J. (1975). The "module concept" in cerebral cortex architecture. *Brain Research*, **95**, 475–496.

Van Essen, D. C., & Maunsell, J. H. R. (1983). Hierarchical organization and functional streams in the visual cortex. *Trends in Neurosciences*, **6**, 9, 370–375.

Zeki, S., & Shipp, S. (1988). The functional logic of cortical connections. *Nature* **335**, 311–316.

Zipser, D., & Andersen, R. A. (1988). A back-propagation programmed nework that simulates responses properties of a subset of posterior parietal neurons. *Nature* **331**, 679–684.

Article 4.6

A Hexagonal Orthogonal-Oriented Pyramid as a Model of Image Representation in Visual Cortex

ANDREW B. WATSON AND ALBERT J. AHUMADA, JR.

Abstract—Retinal ganglion cells represent the visual image with a spatial code, in which each cell conveys information about a small region in the image. In contrast, cells of primary visual cortex employ a hybrid space-frequency code in which each cell conveys information about a region that is local in space, spatial frequency, and orientation. Despite the presumable importance of this transformation, we lack any comprehensive notion of how it occurs. Here we describe a mathematical model for this transformation. The hexagonal orthogonal-oriented quadrature pyramid (HOP) transform, which operates on a hexagonal input lattice, employs basis functions that are orthogonal, self-similar, and localized in space, spatial frequency, orientation, and phase. The basis functions, which are generated from seven basic types through a recursive process, form an image code of the pyramid type. The seven basis functions, six bandpass and one low-pass, occupy a point and a hexagon of six nearest neighbors on a hexagonal sample lattice. The six bandpass basis functions consist of three with even symmetry, and three with odd symmetry. The three even kernels are rotations of 0, 60, and 120° of a common kernel; likewise for the three odd kernels. At the lowest level, the inputs are image samples. At each higher level, the input lattice is provided by the low-pass coefficients computed at the previous level. At each level, the output is subsampled in such a way as to yield a new hexagonal lattice with a spacing $\sqrt{7}$ larger than the previous level, so that the number of coefficients is reduced by a factor of seven at each level. In the biological model, the input lattice is the retinal ganglion cell array. The resulting scheme provides a compact, efficient code of the image and generates receptive fields that resemble those of the primary visual cortex.

INTRODUCTION

VARIOUS roles have been proposed for the neurons of primary visual cortex. A prominent idea, stated most clearly by Barlow [1], is that each cell is a *detector* of a specific image feature. A more recent, and perhaps less exciting view, is that each cell has little meaning on its own, but that the ensemble of cells serves to *represent* the visual image. However, there are on the order of a billion cells in human primary visual cortex [2], and it seems odd to devote this number to a job done quite well by the two million or so ganglion cells of the retina, so this simple representational view must be tempered by the presumption that the particular representation employed by the cortex, or by a particular cortical area [3], has some functional advantage. In this paper, we describe some of the fundamental properties of the cortical representation

of visual imagery, and present a particular mathematical image transform that also exhibits many of these properties. This mathematical formulation may help in understanding the construction and utility of the representation used by primary visual cortex.

As we move from retina to primary visual cortex, a fundamental change takes place in the nature of the representation of visual information. In the retina, each ganglion cell effectively represents a small region in the image. While the receptive field surround plays an important role in adaptive gain control, it is the narrow center, often receiving input from only one cone, that effectively samples the image. In frequency terms, each cell has a broad bandwidth that is essentially equal to that of the organism as a whole. In the cortex, things are strikingly different. Receptive fields are narrow-band and oriented, and may differ markedly from one another in their orientation, size, and peak frequency. This means that we have gone from a single representation by relatively homogeneous cells, to multiple representations by distinct populations of cells differing in orientation and spatial frequency.

Despite the presumable importance of these transformations, we lack any comprehensive notion of how they occur. Here we will describe a particular scheme for achieving this sort of transformation which exhibits many of the properties of the true cortical transform. First we review in more detail the properties of cortical neurons.

ASPECTS OF STRIATE CORTEX

After capture by the receptors of the eye, the visual image undergoes a sequence of transformations in the retina and visual brain. These transformations take place in distinct sets of cells. Certain sets lie in a serial arrangement, so that all the cells of one set receive their input from those of the other set, in which case we may speak of a *stream*. The pathway from retina to brain, and among the various brain areas, is made up of several such streams. In the primate, one important stream is the so-called *P stream* [3], which proceeds from the β retinal ganglion cells, to the parvocellular layers of the lateral geniculate nucleus, and from there primarily to layers $4c\beta$ and $4a$ of the striate cortex.

At each stage of this stream, recordings have been made which characterize the relation between the light image

Manuscript received April 21. 1988: revised July 20. 1988.
The authors are with Vision Group, NASA Ames Research Center. Moffett Field, CA 94035.
IEEE Log Number 8824421.

Reprinted from *IEEE Trans. Biomed. Eng.*, vol. 36, no. 1, pp. 97–106, Jan. 1989.

and the response of the cell, typically in the form of a receptive field. In the cortex, one observes many different varieties of spatial receptive field. This suggests a branching into many streams, each specialized for some particular analysis. However, there is one large population of cells with relatively homogeneous properties. These are the oriented simple cells of V1 [4].

The receptive fields of these cells have a number of interesting properties. First, they exhibit linear spatial summation [5]. They are local in space, in that the receptive field covers a small, compact region of the complete visual field [6]. Since each cell captures only a small region, we suspect that the complete set includes enough cells to capture the complete visual field. The receptive fields are also local in two-dimensional (2-D) spatial frequency [7], [8]. This means that the Fourier transform of the receptive field (the *spectral receptive field*) occupies a small, compact region of the complete *spectral visual field* (the visible portion of the 2-D frequency plane). This localization in 2-D frequency means that the cell responds to a small band of radial spatial frequencies and a small band of orientations. As in the case of spatial localization, it suggests that the complete set includes enough different types to cover the entire spectral visual field. Indeed, since each different type of spectral receptive field captures a different type of information, this suggests that there must be enough *of each type* to cover the spatial visual field.

The different types of spectral receptive fields may be divided along several dimensions. The first is orientation. Each cell responds vigorously only to a range of about 45° [9], which would suggest a minimum of four different orientations. Each cell also responds only within a limited frequency bandwidth. From cell to cell, this bandwidth is most nearly constant when expressed on a logarithmic scale, with a mean value of about 1.5 octaves [7]. This constancy indicates an approximate self-similarity of the various types of receptive field, in the sense that all receptive fields are approximately magnified and rotated versions of a single canonical form. This is not exactly true, as there are rather broad distributions of both orientation and octave bandwidths, but is a useful working approximation.

Some evidence also suggests that the simple cells exist as quadrature pairs, that is, with phases 90° apart [10]. One example of a quadrature pair are cells with even and odd symmetry about a central axis of the receptive field. Quadrature pairs have proven quite useful in modeling the behavior of direction selective cells [11], [12].

In our effort to understand these biological transformations of the visual image, we have made use of concepts from the mathematics of image coding. Some of these concepts are reviewed in the following section.

IMAGE CODES

The discipline of image coding provides some useful examples of image transforms that resemble biological image transforms in various ways. In a digital image transform, the set of pixel values are converted into a set of coefficients. In the biological analog, the response of a single cell corresponds to a single coefficient. Likewise the receptive field is analogous to the kernel of weights that specify how pixel values are combined to form coefficients.

Tanimoto and Pavlidis [13] introduced the notion of an *image pyramid*. In this sort of transform, the image is filtered into several bands of resolution, and then each band is subsampled in proportion to resolution. At the bottom of the pyramid is a high-resolution image with many coefficients, and at the top is a low resolution image with few coefficients. While Tanimoto and Pavlidis used simple averaging of adjacent pixels to reduce resolution, Burt introduced a more "biological" Gaussian filter between each level of the pyramid [14], [15], and Watson [16] proposed ideal low-pass filtering between each level. All three of the preceding transforms are constructed in such a way that they are complete (are invertible and thus permit exact reconstruction of the image), but in each there are 4/3 more coefficients than pixels. All three produce "receptive fields" that are approximately bandpass and self-similar. None, however, partition the image by orientation.

An oriented pyramid called the CORTEX transform was introduced by Watson [17]. The receptive fields have bandwidths of 1 octave in frequency and 45° in orientation. The transform is complete, but expands the image code by 16/3. A later version provides almost exact reconstruction, and expands the code by only 4/3 [18].

Another set of codes that partition by orientation are quadrature mirror filter (QMF) codes [19]–[22]. These codes adopt special constraints on the sampling functions (receptive fields) and reconstruction functions to ensure that sampling artifacts generated in one band are canceled by those in the others. They are complete and produce a code the same size as the image. However, they have the distinctly nonbiological feature of partitioning orientation into three bands, horizontals, verticals, and both diagonals (oblique right and oblique left). More recently, Adelson, Simoncelli, and Hingorani [23] have derived a QMF pyramid based on a hexagonal lattice which partitions orientations into three bands of 60°.

The Gabor transform, in which each receptive field is the product of a Gaussian and a sinusoid, is a popular candidate for biological models [24]–[26], in part because its receptive fields resemble those of the cortex [27], [28], [6]. However, in its exact version it does not lead to self-similarity. Self-similiar, pyramid-style Gabor transforms could presumably be derived.

GOAL OF THE PRESENT WORK

Our goal here is an image transform that is both mathematically coherent and consistent with the properties of primary visual cortex. Specifically, the transform should have the following properties:

pyramid structure
complete (invertible)

basis functions that are:
    local in 2-D space
    local in 2-D frequency
    self-similar
    odd and even (quadrature pairing)
built from known physiological elements
hexagonal lattice
efficient.

We are interested in transforms that are efficient in the sense of having a small number of coefficients. We are also interested in codes that can be easily constructed from the known elements of the striate pathway. In particular, this means that we must build our cortical receptive fields from the receptive fields of retinal ganglion cells. Near to the fovea, ganglion cell receptive fields form an approximately hexagonal lattice. Therefore, we also seek a transform that operates on a hexagonal lattice.

TWO STAGES

The transform we shall describe is most conveniently thought of as occurring in two stages: the first implemented by the retinal ganglion cells, and the second, a transform of the "neural image" supplied by the retinal ganglion cell output. The second stage can be described as a straightforward digital image transform on a hexagonal sample raster, and it may have applications independent of its role as a biological model [29], [30]. For these reasons we shall derive it first, and later explore its utility as a biological model in conjunction with the ganglion cell transformation.

HEXAGONAL ORTHOGONAL-ORIENTED QUADRATURE PYRAMID

We consider transformations in which each new coefficient is a linear combination of input samples. The linear combination can be defined by a kernel of weights specifying the spatial topography of the linear combination. Here we consider kernels that occupy a point and the hexagon of six nearest neighbors on a hexagonal lattice.

We derive a set of kernels under the following constraints:

1) The kernels are expressed on a hexagonal sample lattice.
2) There are seven mutually orthogonal kernels, six high-pass and one low-pass.
3) Each kernel has seven weights corresponding to a point and its six nearest neighbors in the hexagonal lattice.
4) The low-pass kernel has seven equal weights.
5) Two high-pass kernels have an axis of symmetry running through the center sample and between samples on the outer ring (at an angle of 30°).
6) Of these two kernels, one is even about the axis of symmetry, the other is odd.
7) The remaining four high-pass kernels are obtained by rotating the odd and even kernels by 60 and 120°.
8) Each kernel has a norm (square root of sum of squares of weights) of one.

Some of these constraints are suggested by the biological results cited above. For example, 1), 3), 6), and 7) induce a hexagonal structure, spatial localization, quadrature pairs, and rotational self-similarity. Orthogonality 2) is adopted to make the transform easily invertible. Constraint 8) is attractive mathematically and is irrelevant with respect to the physiological comparison. With respect to constraint 5), we have determined that there is no solution when the common axis of symmetry is at 0° (on the sample lattice of the outer ring). Note also that constraints 2) and 4) oblige the even kernels, as well as the odd, to have zero dc response (the weights sum to 0), which is approximately true of primate simple cells. Under the symmetry constraints, the kernel coefficients can be written as shown in Fig. 1.

One even and one odd kernel are shown, along with the low-pass kernel which has seven equal weights h. The variables a–g express the symmetry constraints expressed above. Note that there are two additional even kernels that are not shown, produced by rotations of 60 and 120° of the even kernel. Likewise, there are two additional odd kernels, so that there are a total of seven distinct kernels, six high-pass and one low-pass.

The remaining constraints of orthogonality and unit norm are expressed in a set of eight equations in the eight unknowns a–h. They are

$$7h^2 = 1 \qquad \text{(low-pass unit norm)} \qquad (1)$$

$$a^2 + 2b^2 + 2c^2 + 2d^2 = 1$$
$$\text{(even unit norm)} \qquad (2)$$

$$2e^2 + 2f^2 + 2g^2 = 1$$
$$\text{(odd unit norm)} \qquad (3)$$

$$a + 2b + 2c + 2d = 0$$
$$\text{(even} \perp \text{to low-pass)} \qquad (4)$$

$$a^2 + b^2 + d^2 + 2bc + 2cd = 0$$
$$\text{(even} \perp \text{to 30° self-rotation)} \qquad (5)$$

$$a^2 + 2bc + 2bd + 2cd = 0$$
$$\text{(even} \perp \text{to 60° self-rotation)} \qquad (6)$$

$$e^2 + g^2 - 2ef - 2fg = 0$$
$$\text{(odd} \perp \text{to 60° self-rotation)} \qquad (7)$$

$$2eg - 2ef - 2fg = 0$$
$$\text{(odd} \perp \text{to 120° self-rotation)}. \qquad (8)$$

The value of each coefficient h in the low-pass kernel is given directly by the unit norm constraint (1)

$$h = 1/\sqrt{7}. \qquad (9)$$

Subtracting (5) and (6), and (7) and (8), shows that

$$b = d \qquad (10)$$

$$e = g. \qquad (11)$$

222

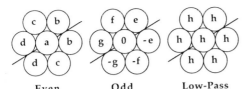

Even   Odd   Low-Pass

Fig. 1. Even and odd high-pass kernels, and lowpass kernel. The oblique line indicates the assumed symmetry axis at 30°.

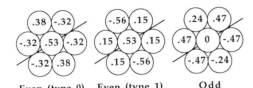

Even (type 0)   Even (type 1)   Odd

Fig. 2. Values for the two types of even kernel and the odd kernel.

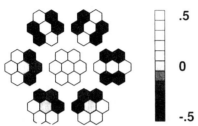

Fig. 3. Seven kernels represented by graylevels. The low-pass kernel is at the center, the three even kernels are in the upper right, and the three odd are to the lower left.

Thus, while not explicitly assumed, we see that both odd and even filters must also be symmetrical about the 120° axis.

Further simplifications lead to the following solution for the coefficients of the odd filter:

$$f = \frac{1}{3\sqrt{2}} \tag{12}$$

$$e = 2f = \sqrt{2}/3. \tag{13}$$

For the even filter, we find

$$a = \sqrt{2}h = \sqrt{2/7}. \tag{14}$$

But two solutions emerge for b and c:

$$b = -(1 + h)f = \frac{-(1 + 1/\sqrt{7})}{3\sqrt{2}} \tag{15}$$

$$c = (2 - h)f = \frac{(2 - 1/\sqrt{7})}{3\sqrt{2}} \tag{16}$$

and

$$b = (1 - h)f = \frac{(1 - 1/\sqrt{7})}{3\sqrt{2}} \tag{17}$$

$$c = -(2 + h)f = \frac{-(2 + 1/\sqrt{7})}{3\sqrt{2}}. \tag{18}$$

We will call the first solution the even filter of type 0, and

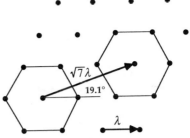

Fig. 4. Tiling the image with hexagonal neighborhoods. Two neighborhoods are shown. This tiling scheme produces a new hexagonal sample lattice that is $\sqrt{7}$ larger, and rotated by 19.1° from the original sample lattice.

the second solution, type 1. The three high-pass kernels are shown in Fig. 2. A complete set of kernels (using even type 0) is shown in Fig. 3. The high-pass kernels are arranged about the low-pass kernel at the center.

SUBSAMPLING

Application of the seven kernels to a neighborhood of seven pixels will yield seven coefficients. Since the kernels are orthogonal, the seven coefficients are a complete representation of the seven pixel image neighborhood. By tiling the plane with hexagonal neighborhoods, a complete image can be transformed. The coefficients produced by each distinct type of kernel may be regarded as a subimage, and each of the seven subimages may also be regarded as a filtered and subsampled version of the original image. Since each kernel consumes seven pixels and yields one coefficient, each subimage has one seventh the number of pixels in the original image. The manner in which the image may be tiled and subsampled is illustrated in Fig. 4.

THE PYRAMID

One virtue of the scheme we have described is that it leads directly to a pyramid structure. The hexagonal image sample lattice is tiled with hexagons with unit sides. Each of the seven kernels is applied in each hexagon, yielding seven subimages, six high-pass and one low-pass, each with one seventh as many samples as the original. The six high-pass subimages form level 0 of the pyramid. The next level is created by applying the seven kernels to the low-pass subimage. This yields seven new subimages, six high-pass and one low-pass, each a factor of seven smaller than the subimages at level 0. This process is repeated until a level is reached at which each subimage has one sample.

This recursive process is illustrated in Fig. 5. The vertices and centers of the smallest hexagons define the input sample lattice. These smallest hexagons show a tiling of the image by the level 0 kernels. Their centers locate the samples of the level 0 subimages. The next larger hexagons tile the level 0 subimages, and their centers define the sample locations for the level 1 subimages. Their vertices (and centers) show where the weights are applied to recursively transform each low-pass subimage. Higher levels are represented by still larger hexagons.

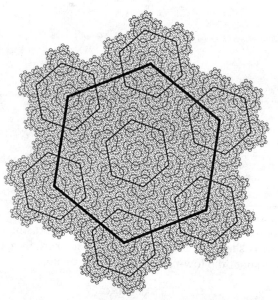

Fig. 5. Construction of the hexagonal pyramid. The image sample lattice is given by the vertices and centers of the smallest hexagons. The hexagons indicate the pooling neighborhoods for the next level. This hexagonal fractal was constructed by first creating the largest hexagon, then placing at each of its vertices a hexagon rotated by $\tan^{-1}(\sqrt{3}/5) \approx 19.1°$ and scaled by $1/\sqrt{7}$. The same procedure is then applied to each of the smaller hexagons, down to some terminating level. The image sample lattice is then a finite-extent periodic sequence with a hexagonal sample lattice defined by the vertices of the smallest hexagons. The sample lattice has 7^6 points, the same as a rectangular lattice of 343^2. The perimeter of this "Gosper flake" is a "Koch curve" with a fractal dimension of $\log 3 / \log \sqrt{7} \approx 1.19$ [31]. The program used to create this image is given in Appendix 1.

While an image shape like that in Fig. 5 is very natural for this code, any shape that is one period of a hexagonally periodic sequence can be exactly encoded if the number of samples is equal to a power of seven. This includes, for example, a parallelogram with sides whose length in samples is a power of seven. Below we show how the code may be applied to a conventional rectangular image.

PYRAMID KERNELS

While we have described the construction of the levels of the pyramid as a recursive transformation of the low-pass subimage, we can also view each subimage as the result of direct application of a kernel to the image at appropriate sample points. As we move higher in the pyramid, the kernels are constructed from the low-pass kernels of the previous level. This yields the kernels shown in Fig. 6.

KERNEL SPECTRA

One of our objectives was to create receptive fields that were local in frequency, that is, somewhat narrow-band and oriented. As continuous functions, the kernel spectra are easily derived. Each kernel consists of a central impulse at the origin, surrounded by three pairs of symmetric (or antisymmetric) impulses at angles of 0, 60, and 120°. Each pair of symmetric impulses transforms into a sinusoid oriented at the angle of the impulse pair, while the impulse at the center transforms into a constant. The complete transform is thus a constant plus three sinusoids at angles of 0, 60, and 120°. The constant is the value of the central coefficient, while each sinusoid has an amplitude twice that of the corresponding coefficient. For the even kernels, the sinusoids are in cosine phase; for the odd kernels, they are in sine phase.

To picture the spectra for the discrete, finite extent case we show the discrete Fourier transform (DFT) of the kernels in Fig. 6. This was done by computing each kernel in a square image, regarded as skewed coordinates of a hexagonal raster, computing the DFT of this image, and appropriately deskewing the DFT. As shown in Fig. 7, the spectra computed in this way are oriented and bandpass, as desired.

AXES OF SYMMETRY AND ORIENTATION

We can define the *orientation* of a kernel as the orientation of the peak of the frequency spectrum, that is, the orientation of a sinusoidal input at which the kernel gives the largest response. An interesting feature of the resulting kernels is that while the axis of symmetry was fixed at 30°, the orientation of the type 0 even kernel (shown in Fig. 7) is actually orthogonal to this axis at 120°. This places its orientation axis on the hexagonal lattice. In contrast, the orientation of the type 1 even kernel and the odd kernel are equal to the initial axis of symmetry at 30°. Thus, if it is desired to have quadrature pairs with equal orientation, the type 1 even kernel must be used.

SAMPLING MATRICES

The subsampling at each level can be formalized as follows (see [32] for a general discussion of nonrectangular sampling). The original hexagonal sampling lattice can be represented by a sampling matrix H:

$$H = \begin{bmatrix} 1 & 1/2 \\ 0 & \sqrt{3}/2 \end{bmatrix}. \tag{19}$$

The column vectors of this matrix map from sample to sample, and the location of any sample can be expressed as $x = (x, y)$,

$$x = Hr \tag{20}$$

where r is an integer vector. Let S_n be the sampling matrix at level n. Since the samples at each level must be a subset of those at the previous level, the column vectors of S_{n+1} must be integer linear combinations of the column vectors of S_n. Thus,

$$S_{n+1} = S_n M \tag{21}$$

where M is an integer matrix. Furthermore, the columns of S_{n+1} must be $\sqrt{7}$ longer than the columns of S_n (corresponding to the increasing radii of the hexagons at each successive level). And finally, because the determinant of a sampling matrix determines the factor by which the density of samples is reduced, we know that

$$\det(M) = 7. \tag{22}$$

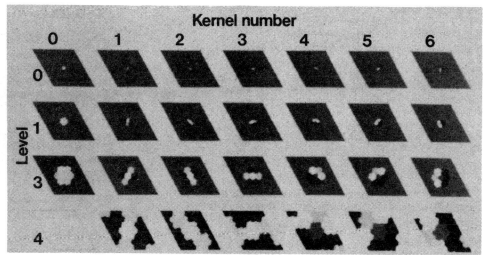

Fig. 6. Pyramid kernels. The seven kernels are numbered 0 (low-pass), 1–3 (even high-pass) and 4–6 (odd high-pass). For this figure, the kernels were first computed on a 49 × 49 pixel square, regarded as skewed coordinates of a hexagonal lattice. The square was then deskewed into a parallelogram, which is an alternate tiling of a hexagonally periodic image (see below). Even kernels are of type 0. Bright regions are positive, dark regions are negative, and gray corresponds to 0. The central kernel is shown for each type and level. At level 4 there is only one kernel of each type and it wraps around to fill the entire image.

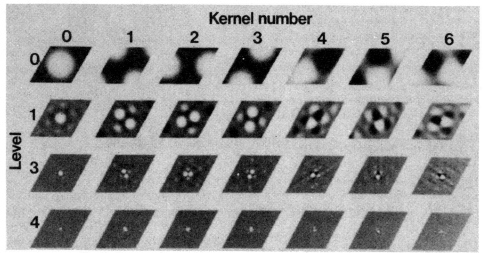

Fig. 7. Spectra of pyramid kernels. The origin is at the center of each figure. Bright regions are positive, dark regions are negative, and gray corresponds to 0.

Two matrices which satisfy these conditions are

$$M_0 = \begin{bmatrix} 2 & -1 \\ 1 & 3 \end{bmatrix} \qquad (23)$$

$$M_1 = \begin{bmatrix} 1 & -2 \\ 2 & 3 \end{bmatrix}. \qquad (24)$$

These generate the only two possible subsamplings from one level to the next. Then S_n can be constructed in various ways, the three most obvious being

$$S_n = HM_0^n \qquad (25)$$

and

$$S_n = HM_1^n \qquad (26)$$

and

$$S_n = HM_0 M_1 M_0 M_1 \cdots (n \text{ terms}). \qquad (27)$$

The first scheme (used in Fig. 5) causes a rotation of $\tan^{-1}(\sqrt{3}/5) \approx 19.1°$ in the sample lattice at each level, as does the second scheme, while the third scheme alternates between rotations of 19.1 and $-19.1°$.

Skewed Coordinates

It is well known that hexagonal samples on a Cartesian plane can also be viewed as rectangular coordinates on a coordinate frame in which one axis is skewed by 60° [Fig. 8(a)] [33], [34]. In this coordinate scheme, the sampling matrices are even simpler. They are the same as above

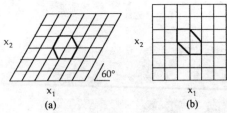

Fig. 8. (a) Hexagonal lattice represented as skewed rectangular coordinates. (b) Deskewed rectangular coordinates. The hexagon is distorted into an oblique lozenge.

[(25)–(27)] except that we drop the matrix H from each expression.

This leads to a natural method for application of this coding scheme to conventional rectangular images. When the skewed coordinates are "deskewed" [Fig. 8(b)], the hexagon is distorted into an oblique lozenge. The orthogonal pyramid may then be constructed using these lozenges as the shape for each kernel. The kernels will no longer be rotationally symmetric, but for some purposes this may be unimportant. As before, exact coding will be possible so long as the sides of the rectangle are a power of seven.

Reconstruction of an image from the transform coefficients is straightforward and is the inverse of the operations used to create the transform. First, the highest level of the pyramid (level n) is inverse transformed. Each coefficient is replaced by a set of seven pixels, produced by multiplying the coefficient and the corresponding kernel. The subimages created in this way from each of the seven subimages are added together to form a low-pass subimage at level $n - 1$. This process is then repeated for each level until the image pixels are produced.

The left side of Fig. 9 shows an original image of $7^3 \times 7^3 = 343^2$ pixels, with zero-order entropy of 7.45 bits/pixel. This image has been transformed by the preceding scheme. The coefficients of each transform subimage have been quantized using a nonlinear quantizer that exploits the masking property of human vision [18]. The severity of quantization decreases with level in the pyramid (high-spatial frequencies are more severely quantized). The image is then reconstructed from the quantized coefficients as described above. The right side of Fig. 8 shows the result when quantization is set so as to yield a coefficient entropy of 0.96 bits/pixel.

A detailed discussion of the coding efficiency and computational complexity of this transform is beyond the scope of this paper, but we note that the recursive computation of the transform is about $6N/7$ faster than direct application of the equivalent kernels where N is the number of layers, and the number of image pixels is 7^N.

BIOLOGICAL IMAGE CODING

As noted earlier, the transformation from image to cortical representation may be partitioned into two stages: the first between image and retinal ganglion cell response array, and the second between this retinal neural image and the cortical neural image. In the preceding sections we developed the second stage, here we add the first stage.

ORIGINAL

7.45 bits/pix

CODED

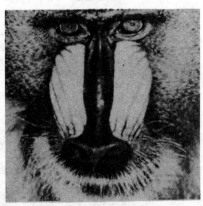

0.96 bits/pix

Fig. 9. Original image and image coded using the hexagonal orthogonal oriented quadrature pyramid.

Retinal ganglion cell receptive fields have a center-surround arrangement, and are described well by a difference-of-Gaussians (DOG) [35]. Near to the fovea, the center is evidently driven by a single cone. Since the cones are in an approximately hexagonal lattice, this means that ganglion cell receptive fields also form a hexagonal lattice. Each retinal ganglion cell may be represented by a DOG function with a center radius of w. The receptive fields are arranged in a hexagonal lattice with sample spacing of λ. Here we assume $w = \lambda$ (Fig. 10), which is approximately true of retinal cells [36]. The output of this hexagonal ganglion cell lattice provides the input to the orthogonal transform described above. The coefficients of the resulting transform then represent the responses of hypothetical cortical cells.

The receptive fields of the complete transform are linear combinations of the retinal DOG receptive fields. At level 0, they are produced by simply weighting each of the seven DOG's in the minimal neighborhood by the weights in the appropriate kernel. An example receptive field is shown in Fig. 11. It is a patch of elongated parallel antagonistic regions, resembling the receptive fields of striate simple cells.

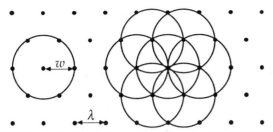

Fig. 10. Hexagonal lattice with spacing λ. Each circle represents the center Gaussian of a retinal ganglion cell receptive field. On the right, a neighborhood of seven cells is shown.

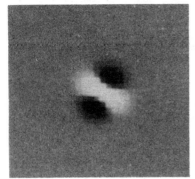

Fig. 11. Cortical receptive field produced by linear combination of seven retinal ganglion cell receptive fields.

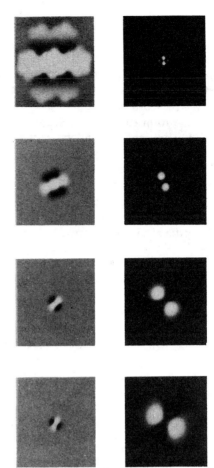

Fig. 12. Spatial and spectral receptive fields of even type 0 cells at four levels of the pyramid.

In general, the receptive field at any level is produced by convolving the corresponding kernel (Fig. 6) with the DOG function. In the frequency domain, this corresponds to multiplying each kernel spectrum (Fig. 7) by the DOG spectrum. Examples of receptive fields and spectra are shown in Fig. 12. As we move up in the pyramid, the spatial receptive field becomes larger and the spectral receptive field smaller. Each spectral receptive field approximates a pair of blobs on either side of the origin, in agreement with the spectral receptive fields of oriented cortical simple cells. The orientation bandwidth of each receptive field is 60°, and the frequency bandwidth is about 1.5 octaves, in rough agreement with biological values.

DISCUSSION

At this point we review our progress in attaining the goals set out at the start of this paper. We have derived an image transform which produces coefficients that are compact and local in 2-D space and in 2-D spatial frequency, with approximately correct frequency and orientation bandwidths. The receptive fields come in various sizes and orientations, and have approximate self-similarity (the self-similarity is exact in the second stage transform). The receptive fields have both odd and even forms. Because the second stage transform is orthogonal, the coefficients are a complete representation of the image provided by the retinal ganglion cells. The representation is efficient in the sense that the number of coefficients is at its theoretical minimum. And the coefficients form a pyramid structure. We have therefore satisfied all of our goals, but we conclude by noting certain defects of this scheme as a model of cortical image coding.

First, the frequency tuning functions of our filters are oriented in the sense of having a strongest response at one orientation, but they have a second, smaller lobe of response (of opposite sign) at the orthogonal orientation. Two-dimensional frequency tuning functions in cortical cells occasionally show such secondary lobes [9], but they do not appear to be common. Second, the units we describe change in size by $\sqrt{7}$ at each level, which might yield rather fewer different scales than are commonly supposed. Third, the 19.1° rotation of the axis of orientation at each scale reduces the degree of rotation invariance of the code, although rotational invariance is not known to hold for the cortical code. Fourth, the tuning functions produced by our scheme are broader in orientation than in spatial frequency, while cortical cells appear to have narrower tuning in orientation than in frequency [37], [6]. Fifth, tangential penetrations of striate cortex sometimes produce long sequences of cells whose orientations increase monotonically in steps considerably smaller than the 60° suggested by the present scheme [38]. Many of the apparent defects of the present scheme may be remedied by relatively minor modifications, such as larger and nonorthogonal kernels [30], which we hope to explore in the future.

Finally, the precise crystalline structure of this code is clearly different from the biological heterogeneity of visual cortex. Nonetheless, the cortex is highly regular, and a scheme like ours may be the canonical form from which the actual cortex is a developmental perturbation. These issues are discussed at greater length elsewhere [30]. Perhaps the best summary is that while this scheme may not describe exactly the cortical encoding architecture, it is an example of the form such an architecture might take. It is a means of expressing our understanding of the system, and bring into focus those aspects of the system about which we are ignorant. The particular structure we have proposed greatly simplifies the computation of the code and its inversion, providing an efficient method of image compression, progressive transmission, and a cortex-like processor for artificial vision systems.

APPENDIX

The following is a program in the Postscript language to draw the pyramid in Fig. 5. The number of levels drawn is determined by the variable *maxdepth*. On an Apple laser printer, a *maxdepth* of three takes about 2 min to print. Each greater depth will take a factor of seven longer.

REFERENCES

[1] H. B. Barlow, "Single units and sensation: A neurone doctrine for perceptual psychology?" *Perception*, vol. 1, pp. 371–394, 1972.

[2] M. Colonnier and J. O'Kusky, "Le nombre de neurones et de synapses dans le cortex visuel de differentes especes," *Rev. Can Biol.*, vol. 40, pp. 91–99, 1981.

[3] E. A. De Yoe and D. C. Van Essen, "Concurrent processing streams in monkey visual cortex," *Trends Neurosci.*, vol. 11, pp. 219–226, 1988.

[4] D. H. Hubel and T. N. Wiesel, "Receptive fields and functional architecture of monkey striate cortex," *J. Physiol. (London)*, vol. 195, pp. 215–243, 1968.

[5] J. A. Movshon, I. D. Thompson, and D. J. Tolhurst, "Spatial summation in the receptive fields of simple cells in the cat's striate cortex," *J. Physiol.*, vol. 283, pp. 53–77, 1978.

[6] J. P. Jones and L. A. Palmer, "The two-dimensional spatial structure of simple receptive fields in cat striate cortex," *J. Neurophysiol.*, vol. 58, pp. 1187–1211, 1987.

[7] R. L. De Valois, D. G. Albrecht, and L. G. Thorell, "Spatial frequency selectivity of cells in macaque visual cortex," *Vision Res.*, vol. 22, pp. 545–559, 1982.

[8] J. P. Jones, A. Stepnoski, and L. A. Palmer, "The two-dimensional spectral structure of simple receptive fields in cat striate cortex," *J. Neurophysiol.*, vol. 58, pp. 1212–1232, 1987.

[9] R. L. De Valois, E. W. Yund, and H. Hepler, "The orientation and

```
/depth 0 def
/maxdepth 3 def                              % maximum levels
/latticeRot 3 sqrt 5 atan def                % lattice rotation angle
/root7 1 7 sqrt div def                      % scale change between levels
/negrot {/latticeRot latticeRot neg def} def
/down {/depth depth 1 add def} def           % increments depth
/up {/depth depth 1 sub def} def             % decrements depth
/inch {72 mul} def                           % scale to inches

/hexside {60 rotate 1 0 lineto currentpoint translate}   % draw one side of a hexagon
   def

/drawhex                                     % draw unit hexagon
{gsave
-60 rotate 1 0 moveto 60 rotate currentpoint translate   % move to first vertex
5 { hexside } repeat                         % draw 5 sides
closepath stroke                             % draw sixth side
grestore } def

/vertex     % angle is on stack     % go to vertex at angle, draw hexagon pyramid
{/angle exch def
gsave
angle rotate 1 0 translate angle neg rotate
fracthex
grestore
} def
/fracthex                                    % draw hexagon pyramid
{gsave
root7 dup scale                              % reduce scale by root 7
2 72 div setlinewidth
down negrot latticeRot rotate drawhex        % move down one level, rotate
                                             lattice, draw hex
depth maxdepth le                            % test if at max level
    {fracthex                                % recursive call to fracthex
    0 60 300 { vertex } for                  % call vertex at each vertex
    } if
up negrot grestore
} def

gsave                                        % main program
4.25 inch 5.5 inch moveto currentpoint translate   % set origin
6 inch 6 inch scale                          % set global scale
latticeRot neg rotate                        % set initial orientation
1 setlinejoin
fracthex                                      % do it
grestore
1 inch 1 inch moveto
/Palatino-Roman findfont 34 scalefont setfont
(Chexagon Pyramid) show                      % label
showpage
```

direction selectivity of cells in macaque visual cortex," *Vision Res.*, vol. 22, pp. 531–544, 1982.

[10] D. A. Pollen and S. F. Ronner, "Phase relationship between adjacent simple cells in the visual cortex," *Science*, vol. 212, pp. 1409–1411, 1981.

[11] A. B. Watson and A. J. Ahumada, Jr., "A look at motion in the frequency domain," NASA Tech. Memorandum 84352, 1983.

[12] ——, "Model of human visual-motion sensing," *J. Opt. Soc. Amer.*, vol. 2, pp. 322–342, 1985.

[13] S. Tanimoto and T. Pavlidis, "A hierarchical data structure for picture processing," *Comput. Graph. Image Proc.*, vol. 4, pp. 104–119, 1975.

[14] P. J. Burt, "Fast filter transforms for image processing," *Comput. Graph. Image Proc.*, vol. 16, pp. 20–51, 1981.

[15] P. J. Burt and E. H. Adelson, "The Laplacian pyramid as a compact image code," *IEEE Trans. Commun.*, vol. COM-31, pp. 532–540, Apr. 1983.

[16] A. B. Watson, "Ideal shrinking and expansion of discrete sequences," NASA Tech. Memorandum 88202, Jan. 1986.

[17] ——, "The cortex transform: Rapid computation of simulated neural images," *Comput. Vision, Graph., Image Proc.*, vol. 39, pp. 311–327, 1987.

[18] ——, "Efficiency of an image code based on human vision," *J. Opt. Soc. Amer.*, vol. 4, pp. 2401–2417, 1987.

[19] M. Vetterli, "Multidimensional sub-band coding: Some theory and algorithms," *Signal Proc.*, vol. 6, pp. 97–112, 1984.

[20] J. W. Woods and S. D. O'Neil, "Subband coding of images," *IEEE Trans. Acoust., Speech, Signal Proc.*, vol. ASSP-34, pp. 1278–1288, 1986.

[21] H. Gharavi and A. Tabatabai, "Sub-band coding of digital images using two-dimensional quadrature mirror filtering," *SPIE Proc. Visual Commun. Image Proc.*, vol. 707, pp. 51–61, 1986.

[22] S. G. Mallat, "A theory for multiresolution signal decomposition: The wavelet representation," GRASP Lab Tech. Memo MS-CIS-87-22, Dep. Comput. Inform. Sci., Univ. Penn., 1987.

[23] E. H. Adelson, E. Simoncelli, and R. Hingorani, "Orthogonal pyramid transforms for image coding," *Proc. SPIE, Visual Commun. Image Proc. II*, 1988.

[24] A. B. Watson, "Detection and recognition of simple spatial forms, *Physical and Biological Processing of Images*, O. J. Braddick and A. C. Sleigh, Eds. Berlin: Springer-Verlag, 1983.

[25] J. G. Daugman, "Uncertainty relation for resolution in space, spatial frequency, and orientation optimized by two-dimensional visual cortex filters," *J. Opt. Soc. Amer.*, vol. 2, pp. 1160–1169, 1985.

[26] D. J. Field, "Relations between the statistics of natural images and the response properties of cortical cells," *J. Opt. Soc. Amer.*, vol. 4, pp. 2379–2394, 1987.

[27] S. Marcelia, "Mathematical description of the responses of simple cortical cells," *J. Opt. Soc. Amer.*, vol. 70, pp. 1297–1300, 1980.

[28] D. J. Field and D. J. Tolhurst, "The structure and symmetry of simple-cell receptive-field profiles in the cat's visual cortex," *Proc. Roy. Soc. London*, vol. 228, pp. 379–400, 1986.

[29] A. B. Watson and A. J. Ahumada, Jr., "An orthogonal oriented quadrature hexagonal image pyramid," NASA Tech. Memorandum 100054, 1987.

[30] A. B. Watson, "Cortical algotecture," in *Vision: Coding and Efficiency*, C. B. Blakemore, Ed. Cambridge, England: Cambridge Univ., 1988.

[31] B. B. Mandelbrot, *The Fractal Geometry of Nature*. New York: Freeman, 1983.

[32] D. A. Dudgeon and R. M. Mersereau, *Multidimensional Digital Signal Processing*. Englewood Cliffs, NJ: Prentice-Hall, 1984.

[33] D. P. Petersen and D. Middleton, "Sampling and reconstruction of wave-number limited functions in *N* dimensional Euclidean spaces," *Inform. Contr.*, vol. 5, pp. 279–323, 1962.

[34] R. M. Mersereau, "The processing of hexagonally sampled two-dimensional signals," *Proc. IEEE*, vol. 67, pp. 930–949, 1979.

[35] C. Enroth-Cugell and J. G. Robson, "The contrast sensitivity of retinal ganglion cells of the cat," *J. Physiol.*, vol. 187, pp. 517–552, 1966.

[36] V. H. Perry and A. Cowey, "The ganglion cell and cone distributions in the monkey's retina: Implications for central magnification factors," *Vision Res.*, vol. 25, pp. 1795–1810, 1985.

[37] M. A. Webster and R. L. De Valois, "Relationship between spatial-frequency and orientation tuning of striate-cortex cells," *J. Opt. Soc. Amer.*, vol. 2, pp. 1124–1132, 1985.

[38] D. H. Hubel and T. N. Wiesel, "Sequence regularity and geometry of orientation columns in the monkey striate cortex," *J. Comp. Neurol.*, vol. 158, pp. 267–294, 1974.

Part 5
Mathematical Morphology of Biological Vision: Tools and Models

Extensive research in the field of neuroscience suggests that the mathematical morphology of the biological vision process is distributed throughout the visual pathway into several discrete anatomical modules—each module performs a variety of specific mathematical functions. This mathematical study has created considerable excitement among vision scientists.

IN the previous part of this book, we presented some models of the biological visual process. These models enable us to develop some basic understanding of how visual images are processed in the retina and visual cortex. In this part, we address some specific issues regarding the mathematical morphology of biological vision. One of the concepts often used in modeling the vision morphology is the receptive field—a notion introduced by Hart in the early forties that is still being used extensively today. The Gabor functions and their generalization—the *wavelets*—are the main mathematical tools being used to model retinal and cortical receptive fields. A brief summary of how Gabor functions can be used as mathematical tools to model receptive fields is presented in the first set of articles (5.1–5.3).

In the first article, J. Daugman describes a three-layer neural network used to transform two-dimensional discrete signals into generalized nonorthogonal two-dimensional Gabor functions. He employs this neural network architecture for image representation, segmentation, and data compression. This work is supported by some impressive theoretical developments and simulation studies.

S. Mallat presents the mathematical properties of image decomposition and wavelet transformation using wavelet orthogonal basis functions in article (5.2). This article is included within this part because it provides a generalized view of wavelet transforms and their application to vision system problems. A mathematical representation of textures using the finite set of Gabor elementary functions is presented in article (5.3) by M. Porat and Y. Zeevi. The authors introduce a method for texture discrimination and image features based on the Gabor approach. This method is invariant under rotation and translation, and is robust with respect to noisy conditions.

Several models of biological vision systems for various applications are presented in the next three articles. In article (5.4), M. M. Gupta and G. K. Knopf present a positive–negative (PN) neural architecture for a programmable multitask

visual information processor. The computational aspects of the PN neural architecture are motivated by the functional dynamics of certain nervous tissues in the cortical and thalamic regions of the brain. The PN neural processor architecture is a generalized neuronal morphology that can be used to perform various spatio-temporal tasks such as filtering, pulse-frequency encoding and decoding of images, image stabilization, and short-term and long-term visual memory. This morphology can be extended to develop a generalized neuro-vision system.

Motion perception is an important aspect of biological vision. S. Ullman provides an explanation how visual motion is analyzed in biological visual systems and how such a motion detection system can be implemented on a computer in article (5.5). This article is about the computational problems that are fundamental to the analysis of time-varying imagery. The computational problems of motion perception fall into two broad categories: 1) motion detection and measurement and 2) interpretation of visual motion.

In the final article, D. Pollen and S. Ronner employ a spatial-frequency approach to mathematically interpret the receptive field profiles in the visual cortex. This description is based on observations of simple and complex cells.

The various models and tools used to describe the mathematical morphology of biological vision will lead us to the numerous computational architectures and applications. Several neuro-vision system architectures and their applications are described in the next part of the volume.

Further Reading

[1] M. A. Arbib, *Brains, Machines and Mathematics*. New York: Springer-Verlag, 1987.

[2] J. G. Daugman, "An information-theoretic view of analog representation in the striate cortex," in *Computational Neuroscience*, E. L. Schwartz, Ed., Cambridge MA: MIT Press, pp. 403–423, 1990.

[3] J. G. Daugman, "Entropy reduction and decorrelation in visual coding by oriented neural receptive fields," *IEEE Trans. Biomed. Eng.*, vol. 36, no. 1, pp. 107–114, 1989.

[4] J. G. Daugman, "Six formal properties of two-dimensional visual filters: Structural principles and frequency/orientation selectivity," *IEEE Trans. Syst. Man, Cybern.*, vol. 13, no. 5, pp. 882–887, 1983.

[5] O. D. Faugeras, "Digital color image processing within the framework of a human visual model," *IEEE Trans. Acous., Speech, Signal Process.*, vol. 27, no. 4, pp. 380–393, 1979.

[6] D. Gabor, "Theory of communication," *J. IEE*, vol. 93, pp. 429–457, 1946.

[7] M. A. Georgeson, "Spatial frequency analysis in early visual processing," *Phil. Trans. Roy. Soc. London*, vol. B 290, pp. 11–22, 1980.

[8] N. Graham, "Spatial-frequency channels in human vision: Detecting edges without edge detectors," in *Visual Coding and Adaptability*, C. S. Harris, Ed., Hillsdale N.J.: Lawrence Erlbaum, 1980, pp. 215–262, 1980.

[9] C. F. Hall and E. L. Hall, "Nonlinear model for the spatial characteristics of the human visual system," *IEEE Trans. Syst., Man, Cybern.*, vol. 7, no. 3, pp. 161–170, 1977.

[10] G. Hartmann, "Motion induced transformations of spatial representations: Mapping 3D information onto 2D," *Neural Networks*, vol. 5, pp. 823–834, 1992.

[11] G. K. Knopf and M. M. Gupta, "Design of a multitask neurovision processor," *J. Math. Imaging Vision*, vol. 2, pp. 233–250, 1992.

[12] G. K. Knopf, "Theoretical studies of a dynamic neuro-vision processor with a biologically motivated design," Ph.D. dissertation, University of Saskatchewan, Canada, 1991.

[13] E. H. Land, "The retinex theory of color vision," *Sci. Amer.*, vol. 237, no. 6, pp. 108–128, Dec. 1977.

[14] E. H. Land, "Experiments in color vision," *Sci. Amer.*, vol. 200, no. 5, pp. 84–99, May 1959.

[15] D. M. Marr and E. Hildreth, "Theory of edge detection," *Proc. Roy. Soc. London*, vol. B 207, pp. 187–217, 1980.

[16] D. Marr, "Early processing of visual information," *Phil. Trans. Roy. Soc. London*, vol. B 275, pp. 483–519, 1976.

[17] T. Poggio and C. Koch, "Ill-posed problems in early vision: From computational theory to analogue networks," *Proc. Roy. Soc. London*, vol. B 226, pp. 303–323, 1985.

[18] M. Porat and Y. Y. Zeevi, "The generalized Gabor scheme of image representation in biological and machine vision," *IEEE Trans. Pattern Anal. Machine Intell.*, vol. 10, no. 4, pp. 452–468, 1988.

[19] T. G. Stockham, "Image processing in the context of a visual model," *Proc. IEEE*, vol. 60, no. 7, pp. 828–842, 1972.

[20] D. G. Stork and H. R. Wilson, "Do Gabor functions provide appropriate descriptions of visual cortical receptive fields?" *J. Opt. Soc. Amer.*, vol. 7, no. 8, pp. 1362–1373, 1990.

[21] A. J. van Doorn and J. J. Koenderink, "The structure of the human motion detection system," *IEEE Trans. Syst., Man, Cybern.*, vol. 13, no. 5 pp. 916–922, 1983.

[22] H. Yan and J. C. Gore, "Weight adjustment rule of neural networks for computing discrete 2-D Gabor transforms," *IEEE Trans. Acous., Speech, Signal Process.*, vol. 38, no. 9, pp. 1654–1656, 1990.

[23] Q. Zhang and A. Benveniste, "Wavelet networks," *IEEE Trans. Neural Networks*, vol. 3, no. 6, pp. 889–898, 1992.

Article 5.1

Complete Discrete 2-D Gabor Transforms by Neural Networks for Image Analysis and Compression

JOHN G. DAUGMAN

(Invited Paper)

Abstract—A three-layered neural network is described for transforming two-dimensional discrete signals into generalized nonorthogonal 2-D "Gabor" representations for image analysis, segmentation, and compression. These transforms are conjoint spatial/spectral representations [10], [15], which provide a complete image description in terms of locally windowed 2-D spectral coordinates embedded within global 2-D spatial coordinates. Because intrinsic redundancies within images are extracted, the resulting image codes can be very compact. However, these conjoint transforms are inherently difficult to compute because the elementary expansion functions are not orthogonal. One orthogonalizing approach developed for 1-D signals by Bastiaans [8], based on biorthonormal expansions, is restricted by constraints on the conjoint sampling rates and invariance of the windowing function, as well as by the fact that the auxiliary orthogonalizing functions are nonlocal infinite series. In the present "neural network" approach, based upon interlaminar interactions involving two layers with fixed weights and one layer with adjustable weights, the network finds coefficients for complete conjoint 2-D Gabor transforms without these restrictive conditions. For arbitrary noncomplete transforms, in which the coefficients might be interpreted simply as signifying the presence of certain features in the image, the network finds *optimal* coefficients in the sense of minimal mean-squared-error in representing the image. In one algebraically complete scheme permitting exact reconstruction, the network finds expansion coefficients that reduce entropy from 7.57 in the pixel representation to 2.55 in the complete 2-D Gabor transform. In "wavelet" expansions based on a biologically inspired log-polar ensemble of dilations, rotations, and translations of a single underlying 2-D Gabor wavelet template, image compression is illustrated with ratios up to 20 : 1. Also demonstrated is image segmentation based on the clustering of coefficients in the complete 2-D Gabor transform. This coefficient-finding network for implementing useful nonorthogonal image transforms may also have neuroscientific relevance, because the network layers with fixed weights use empirical 2-D receptive field profiles obtained from orientation-selective neurons in cat visual cortex as the weighting functions, and the resulting transform mimics the biological visual strategy of embedding angular and spectral analysis within global spatial coordinates.

I. INTRODUCTION

SEVERAL broad classes of problems for which neural networks appear to show promise involve the extraction or exploitation of redundancy. Examples include content addressable memory [1], pattern classification and learning [2], signal reconstruction from partial informa-

tion [3], separation of signals from noise [4], cooperative and fault-tolerant processing [5], estimation and prediction [6], and data compression. The last of these is perhaps both the simplest and the most generic example because it most directly depends upon the exploitation of redundancy. In principle, data compression is possible for a nonrandom signal by virtue of the fact that its value at some points can be predicted from its values at other, possibly remote, points or sequences. Correlation structure in a signal can take many forms and can involve different statistical orders, but in information-theoretic terms [7], its existence implies that the entropy or statistical complexity of the source is less than the entropy of the channel, as determined by its resolution (e.g., 8 bits/pixel). Whenever this situation exists, compression of the signal to a lower bound specified by the elimination of redundancy is in principle possible, without loss of information (cf. Theorems 4.5.1 and 4.5.2 of [7]).

Ordinary images are examples of signals having high degrees of self-correlation. Fundamentally, mutual information arises within an image because of the fact that physical objects and scenes tend to have internal morphological consistency, including first-order correlations (locally similar luminance values), second-order or dipole correlations (e.g., oriented edge continuation), as well as higher-order correlations (e.g., homogeneity of textural signature). These correlations are attributes which distinguish real images from random noise, a distinction that is not exploited in the standard pixel-by-pixel image representation. The analysis, communication, and storage of image information would benefit from an efficient means to encode image structure in ways that extracted and exploited these correlations.

A second typical goal in signal processing is to find a representation in which certain attributes of the signal are made explicit. Often this involves transformations into representations in which the attributes or features sought for in the signal are used as the expansion functions. But it is only for certain transforms that the coefficients for projecting the signal onto that chosen set of functions can be easily obtained. If the desired elementary functions are not orthogonal, for example, then simply computing their inner products with the signal will not produce the correct coefficients. A further problem may be that the primitive functions of interest for extracting certain kinds of signal

Manuscript received December 17, 1987. This work was supported by an NSF Presidential Young Investigator Award and by AFOSR U.R.I. Contract F49620-87-C-0018.

The author is with the Departments of Psychology and Electrical, Computer, and Systems Engineering, 950 William James Hall, Harvard University, Cambridge, MA 02138.

IEEE Log Number 8821369.

Reprinted from *IEEE Trans. Acoust., Speech, Signal Processing*, vol. 36, no. 7, pp. 1169–1179, July 1988.

structure may not constitute a complete basis, or it may be difficult to establish whether or not they do except under strong constraints.

One conjoint transform which illustrates the desirability of obtaining the expansion coefficients on a set of overlapping *non*orthogonal, yet complete, elementary functions is portrayed by Figs. 1 and 2. Displayed in Fig. 1 is a pixel histogram of the 8-bit "Lena" picture commonly used in image processing research. This gray-scale distribution of 65 536 pixels has an entropy of $S = 7.57$, where entropy is defined as average self-information of the pixel ensemble

$$S = -\sum_{i=1}^{n} P_i \log_2 P_i \qquad (1)$$

given that

$$\sum_{i=1}^{n} P_i = 1 \qquad (2)$$

where the P_i are the relative rates of occurrence of each of the n (in this case 256) gray levels in the picture. Characteristically, the pixel histogram is broad and multimodal, with large entropy. (Uncorrelated 8-bit white noise would have only slightly more entropy, namely, $S = 8$.) But when the Lena picture is transformed into a *complete, discrete, 2-D Gabor* representation (to be defined later), the coefficient values in the transform have the far more compact distribution shown in Fig. 2. Quantized again to 8-bit resolution, the set of 65 536 complete 2-D Gabor coefficients has an entropy of only 2.55, while capturing all of the image structure in the original picture and permitting its exact reconstruction. (The reconstruction may be seen in Fig. 8.) For data compression purposes, one consequence of this observation is that the information cost per pixel for transmitting or storing this 8-bit image could be reduced dramatically without any loss of information. By constructing a code whose word length varies inversely with the frequency distribution shown in Fig. 2, such images could in principle be encoded with a compression factor amounting to 5 fewer bits per pixel. This conjoint 2-D Gabor transform is also useful for image analysis and segmentation, since it extracts locally windowed 2-D spectral information concerning form and texture without sacrificing information about 2-D location or more global spatial relationships, as does a Fourier transform.

The problem is that the overlapping elementary functions which form the projection vectors for this transform are not orthogonal, and so finding their coefficients is difficult. In research to date, it has only been possible to find these coefficients under limiting restrictions on the relationships between the conjoint sampling rate parameters of the elementary functions, and through the use of auxiliary biorthogonal functions [8] expressed as nonlocal infinite series. The main purpose of this paper is to describe a simple neural network architecture for finding optimal coefficient values in arbitrary two-dimensional signal

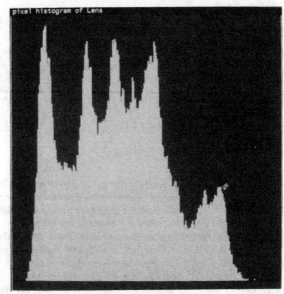

Fig. 1. Pixel histogram of the Lena image, comprising 65 536 8-bit pixels. The entropy of this pixel ensemble is 7.57, only slightly smaller than the entropy of random 8-bit noise with uniform density (namely, 8). Representing images by ensembles of independent pixels does not exploit their intrinsic correlation structure.

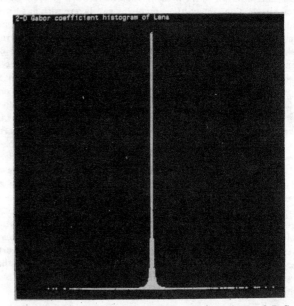

Fig. 2. Histogram of 65 536 coefficients in a complete discrete 2-D Gabor transform, quantized to 8 bits each as was the pixel histogram of Fig. 1 but obviously far more compactly distributed. The entropy of this ensemble of 2-D Gabor coefficients is only 2.55 bits, yet they completely capture the Lena image and allow its exact reconstruction (as shown in Fig. 8). The 2-D Gabor transform itself is shown in Fig. 7.

transforms which in general might be neither complete nor orthogonal. The application of this coefficient-finding scheme to generalized two-dimensional signal transforms is useful for purposes such as image analysis, feature extraction, and data compression. It also leads to an interpretation of the biologically measured two-dimensional anisotropic visual neural receptive field profiles, which have to a large extent motivated the development of the 2-D Gabor transform [10], [15].

II. Neural Network for Finding Projection Coefficients

The general neural network architecture for finding the coefficients in (possibly nonorthogonal and noncomplete) signal transforms is shown in Fig. 3. We shall deal with some discrete two-dimensional signal $I[x, y]$, say, an image supported on $[256 \times 256]$ pixels in $[x, y]$, which we wish to analyze or compress by representing it as a set of expansion coefficients $\{a_i\}$ on some set of two-dimensional elementary functions $\{G_i[x, y]\}$. We may regard a given image $I[x, y]$ as a vector in a 65 536-dimensional vector space, and different representations of the image based on complete orthonormal expansions constitute different bases of this vector space. For example, the conventional pixel representation projects the image onto a set of unit basis vectors, one for each pixel, with coefficients representing lightness values. At the other extreme from the unit basis, each of the linearly independent orthonormal basis vectors might be a 2-D Fourier component, with the associated coefficient being the inner product projection of the image onto this basis vector. More generally, for certain purposes such as feature extraction, we might also wish to represent $I[x, y]$ on a set of linearly *dependent* vectors, which may or may not completely span the vector space; even if they are neither orthogonal nor complete, we can still find *optimal* projections of the image onto each one by satisfying global optimization criteria.

Thus, we wish to represent $I[x, y]$ either exactly or in some optimal sense by projecting it onto a chosen set of vectors $G_i[x, y]$. This requires finding projection coefficients $\{a_i\}$ such that the resultant vector $H[x, y]$

$$H[x, y] = \sum_{i=1}^{n} a_i G_i[x, y] \qquad (3)$$

is either identical to $I[x, y]$ (the complete case) or generates a difference-vector $I[x, y] - H[x, y]$ of minimal length (the optimization case). If the elementary functions $\{G_i[x, y]\}$ form a complete orthogonal set, then the representation in $H[x, y]$ is exact (the difference-vector is zero) and the solution for $\{a_i\}$ is simple:

$$a_i = \frac{\sum_{x, y} \left(G_i[x, y]\, I[x, y] \right)}{\sum_{x, y} G_i^2[x, y]}. \qquad (4)$$

If they do not, however, then in general the representation $H[x, y]$ will be inexact and the desired set of coefficients $\{a_i\}$ must be determined by an optimization criterion, such as minimizing the squared norm of the difference-vector:

$$E = \left\| I[x, y] - H[x, y] \right\|^2$$
$$= \sum_{x, y} \left(I[x, y] - H[x, y] \right)^2. \qquad (5)$$

The norm E will be minimized only when its partial derivatives with respect to all of the n coefficients $\{a_i\}$ equal zero:

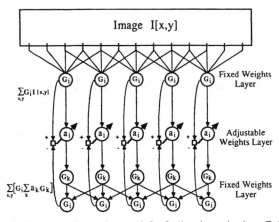

Fig. 3. A three-layered neural network for finding the optimal coefficients in arbitrary image transforms which in general may be neither orthogonal nor complete, nor limited by constraints on sampling uniformity. The first and third layers have fixed weights (in the present work taken to be 2-D Gabor elementary functions as seen in Fig. 4), while the middle layer has weights which are adjusted by interlaminar interactions. In the stable state when equilibrium is reached [see (6) and (9)], the cost function E is minimized and the weight values of the middle layer correspond to the desired transform coefficients.

$$\forall_i, \quad \frac{\partial E}{\partial a_i} = -2 \sum_{x, y} \left(I[x, y]\, G_i[x, y] \right)$$
$$+ \sum_{x, y} \left[2 \left(\sum_{k=1}^{n} a_k G_k[x, y] \right) G_i[x, y] \right] = 0. \qquad (6)$$

Satisfying this condition for each of the a_i then generates a system of n simultaneous equations in n unknowns:

$$\left| \sum_{x, y} \left(I[x, y]\, G_i[x, y] \right) \right.$$
$$= \left. \sum_{x, y} \left[\left(\sum_{k=1}^{n} a_k G_k[x, y] \right) G_i[x, y] \right] \right|. \qquad (7)$$

Thus, the solution which minimizes the squared norm of the difference-vector [(5)] amounts to finding the set of coefficients $\{a_i\}$ such that the inner product of each vector $G_i[x, y]$ with the entire linear combination of vectors $\sum a_k G_k[x, y]$ is the same as its inner product with the original image $I[x, y]$. It should be noted that in the case when the $\{G_i[x, y]\}$ form a set of orthogonal vectors, then the inner products in the right-hand side of (7) are nonzero only for $k = i$, and so each of the n equations then has only a single unknown, and it is immediately apparent that the minimal-difference-vector solution for each a_i is identical to that given earlier in (4) as the familiar orthogonal case.

Even in the nonorthogonal case, the system of n equations [(7)] could still be exactly solved in principle by algebraic means to find the set of optimal coefficients $\{a_i\}$. But unless the enormous (65 536 × 65 536) matrix generated by (7) is very sparse (requiring strictly compact support for the members of $\{G_i[x, y]\}$), it would be completely impractical to solve this huge system of simultaneous equations by algebraic methods such as matrix manipulation, since the complexity of such methods grows factorially with the number of simultaneous equations. (Using Stirling's approximation for the factorial, the general matrix solution for the system of equations in (7) would require $2.5 \times 10^{287\,157}$ floating-point multiplications to find.) Methods based upon iterative improvement are far faster for such large n, although they converge on an exact solution only as a limit, and can become trapped in local minima. Fortunately, the difference-vector cost function (5) is quadratic in each member of $\{a_i\}$, and so a unique global minimum for E exists. The neural network architecture shown in Fig. 3 converges through iteration upon the desired image representation $\{a_i\}$ by implementing gradient descent along the $E(a_i)$ surface, which expresses the quadratic cost function's dependency on all of the $\{a_i\}$ coefficients.

A common feature of neural network architectures is the combination of layers of neurons having adjustable (or adaptive) synaptic weights, and layers with fixed weights. The present scheme begins with a layer of fixed connection strengths which are specified by an arbitrary set of (generally nonorthogonal) elementary functions $\{G_i[x, y]\}$; by summing the different image pixels through these weights, the output of the ith neuron in this layer is simply the inner product of the ith elementary function, $G_i[x, y]$, with the input image $I[x, y]$ in that region. This is precisely the neurophysiological concept of a (linear) neuron's "receptive field profile," which refers to the spatial weighting function by which a local region of the retinal image is multiplied and integrated to generate that neuron's response strength. The second layer contains adjustable weights for multiplying each of these outputs, according to a control signal which arises from interlaminar interactions. The third layer is identical to the first layer and stores the same fixed set of elementary functions. The adjustable weights of the middle layer constitute the transformed image representation as the set of coefficients $\{a_i\}$. The adaptive control signal adjusts each of the weights by an amount Δ_i, given by the difference between a feedforward signal and a feedback signal. The feedforward signal is the level of activity of the neuron from the first layer, and the feedback signal is the inner product of the weighting function of the corresponding neuron in the third layer with the weighted sum of all the other neighboring neurons in that layer with which it is connected. Thus, the weight adjustment is

$$\Delta_i = \sum_{x,y} \left(G_i[x, y]\, I[x, y] \right)$$
$$- \sum_{x,y} \left[G_i[x, y] \left(\sum_{k=1}^{n} a_k G_k[x, y] \right) \right] \quad (8)$$

and the iterative rule for adjusting the value of each coefficient is $a_i \Rightarrow a_i + \Delta_i$. It should be noted that the network does not require a "teacher" that generates the weight adjustment signal by comparing the current representation with a separate copy of the desired pattern. Rather, the adaptive control signal Δ_i arises only from interlaminar network interactions.

It can be seen by inspecting [6] and [8] that the weight adjustment rule is equivalent to

$$\Delta_i = -\frac{1}{2} \frac{\partial E}{\partial a_i}.$$

It should be noted that the minus sign implies that the weight adjustment is always in the downhill direction of the cost surface $E(a_i)$, and that the adjustment is proportional to the slope of the cost surface at this point. A fuller discussion of gradient descent methods may be found in [4, ch. 4]. The equilibrium state of the network that is reached when all $\Delta_i = 0$ is the state in which the cost function E representing the difference-vector squared norm $\| I[x, y] - H[x, y] \|^2$ has reached its minimum; this is the point at which the partial derivative of E with respect to all of the adjustable weights is nil:

$$\forall_i, \qquad \Delta_i = 0 \Leftrightarrow \frac{\partial E}{\partial a_i} = 0. \quad (9)$$

Thus, in the stable state, the middle layer of the network has weights which represent the optimal coefficients $\{a_i\}$ for the projection of the signal $I[x, y]$ onto any set of elementary functions $\{G_i[x, y]\}$ which, as noted earlier, need be neither orthogonal nor complete.

III. 2-D GABOR ELEMENTARY FUNCTIONS AND BIOLOGICAL VISION

The particular choice of nonorthogonal elementary functions which will be used in the remainder of this paper for the fixed-weight layers of the network are taken from actual neurophysiological measurements of the two-dimensional anisotropic receptive field profiles describing single neurons in mammalian visual cortex [9], [10], [15]. A scientific topic of great interest to neural network researchers is the investigation of the properties and functioning of "real" (biological) neural networks. In the case of the mammalian visual nervous system, a great deal is now known about neural signal processing strategies for the extraction and representation of image structure, at least in the earlier levels of visual processing (retina, lateral geniculate, and primary visual cortex). Among the many questions which can fruitfully be studied regarding signal processing strategies in biological visual systems are the following: how image structure is encoded at various levels; the efficiency of these codes in terms such as dynamic range compression, entropy, noise characteristics, and invariances; the interweaving of multiple coding dimensions within single channel firing rates and across separate channels; the roles of spatiotemporal filtering and of nonlinear operations; and the transformations of image information which support higher level visual cognition. For all of these questions, a potential dialogue between neural network theory, signal processing theory, and experimental neurobiology is an exciting prospect, and the potential mutual benefits for all three disciplines could be high.

The several cortical visual areas of mammals contain

many populations of neurons, some linear and many non-linear, with selectivities for a variety of stimulus attributes. These include location in 2-D visual space, orientation, motion, color, stereoscopic depth, size or spatial frequency, symmetry, and others [11]. In the primary visual cortex (Area 17), perhaps the most striking of these is orientation selectivity [12], which imparts to individual neurons a pronounced dependency between their firing rate and the planar orientation of a stimulus such as an edge or bar. Moreover, assemblies of neurons are organized into "columns" which share the same orientation preference, and on a larger scale, these columns reveal a functional "sequence regularity" of systematic shifts in their preferred orientation [13]. The sequence regularity of columnar orientation preference is one of the most crystalline features of visual cortical architecture now known, and it clearly plays a crucial role, although an as yet unspecified role from a signal processing viewpoint, in the logic of the brain's representation of the visual world. A second striking feature, although true only of the linear class of neurons (so-called "simple cells"), is their pairing by symmetry into quadrature phase pairs: adjacent simple cells have spatial receptive field profiles which share the same location in space and the same orientation preference but differ by 90° in their phase [14]. This quadrature phase relation in neural receptive field pairs is suggestive of a kind of local harmonic expansion of image structure.

One suitable model of the two-dimensional receptive field profiles encountered experimentally in cortical simple cells, which captures their salient tuning properties of spatial localization, orientation selectivity, spatial frequency selectivity, and quadrature phase relationship, is the parameterized family of "2-D Gabor filters," as seen in Fig. 4. This neural model was originally proposed in 1980 simultaneously by Daugman [15] in two-dimensional form and by Marcelja [16] in one-dimensional form. The 2-D form has the virtue of capturing explicitly the critical neurobiological variables of a given neuron's orientation and spatial frequency preference, the tuning bandwidths for these variables, the receptive field dimensions, and the relationships among all of these parameters as captured by generalized uncertainty relationships [10] which the 2-D filter family (in complex form) optimizes.

The general functional form of the 2-D Gabor filter family is specified in (10) and (11), in terms of the space-domain impulse response function $G(x, y)$ and its associated 2-D Fourier transform $F(u, v)$:

$$G(x, y) = \exp\left(-\pi\left[(x - x_o)^2\alpha^2 + (y - y_o)^2\beta^2\right]\right)$$
$$\cdot \exp\left(-2\pi i\left[u_o(x - x_o) + v_o(y - y_o)\right]\right)$$
$$(10)$$

$$F(u, v) = \exp\left(-\pi\left[\frac{(u - u_o)^2}{\alpha^2} + \frac{(v - v_o)^2}{\beta^2}\right]\right)$$
$$\cdot \exp\left(-2\pi i\left[x_o(u - u_o) + y_o(v - v_o)\right]\right).$$
$$(11)$$

SPATIAL FILTER PROFILE

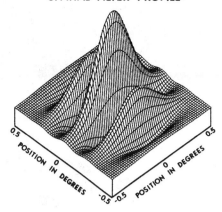

FREQUENCY RESPONSE

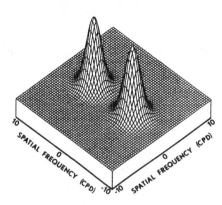

Fig. 4. Example of a 2-D Gabor elementary function (real part) and its 2-D Fourier transform, as originally proposed by Daugman in 1980 [15]. These functions have optimally compact support in conjoint 2-D spatial/2-D spectral representation, and they achieve the lower bound in the general uncertainty relation (12). In the present network (Fig. 3), they provide the weighting functions $\{G_i[x, y]\}$ for the first and third layers.

This family of 2-D elementary functions constitutes a generalization of the 1-D elementary functions proposed in 1946 by Gabor [17] in his famous monograph, "Theory of communication." It should be noted that the 2-D Gabor filter impulse response function $G(x, y)$ and its 2-D Fourier transform $F(u, v)$ have identical functional form; the 2-D Fourier transform theorems for shift, similarity, and modulation are reflected in the position parameters (x_o, y_o), the modulation parameters (u_o, v_o), and the two scale parameters (α, β). If $\alpha \neq \beta$, then a further degree of freedom [for simplicity not included in (10) and (11)] is coordinate rotation of (x, y) out of the principal axes corresponding to (α, β), which in the Fourier domain results in the same coordinate rotation of (u, v). These "noncanonical" members of the 2-D Gabor family simply have additional cross terms in xy in (10) and in uv in (11).

An important property of the family of 2-D Gabor filters is their achievement of the theoretical lower bound of joint uncertainty in the two conjoint domains of (x, y) visual space and (u, v) spatial frequency variables. Defining uncertainty in each of the four variables by the nor-

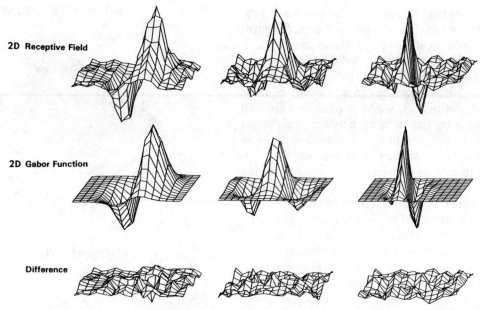

2D Receptive Field

2D Gabor Function

Difference

Fig. 5. Top row: illustrations of empirical 2-D receptive field profiles measured by J. P. Jones and L. A. Palmer (personal communication) in simple cells of the cat visual cortex. Middle row: best-fitting 2-D Gabor elementary function for each neuron, described by (10). Bottom row: residual error of the fit, indistinguishable from random error in the Chi-squared sense for 97 percent of the cells studied.

malized second moments (Δx), (Δy), (Δu), (Δv) about the principle axes (see Daugman [10] for details), it may be shown that a fundamental uncertainty principle exists:

$$(\Delta x)(\Delta y)(\Delta u)(\Delta v) \geq 1/16\pi^2 \qquad (12)$$

and that the lower bound of the inequality is achieved by the family of 2-D Gabor filters [(10) and (11)]. In this sense, these filters achieve the maximal possible joint resolution in the conjoint 2-D visual space and 2-D Fourier domains. These elementary functions also can be regarded as forming a continuum between the opposite extremes of either Kronecker delta functions in the space domain (inherent in the pixel representation of an image) or Kronecker delta functions in the frequency domain (inherent in the 2-D Fourier representation of an image). These limiting cases arise when the parameters (α, β) in (10) and (11) become either very large or very small; in the mixed case when one is very large and the other very small, the representation corresponds to taking 1-D Fourier transforms on each raster line in a rastered image. In general, we will work with intermediate values of (α, β) in self-similar conjoint representations, because this situation appears to have great neurobiological significance.

It is interesting that the great majority of mammalian cortical simple cells (97 percent in the studies described in [9] and [10]) have 2-D receptive field profiles which can be well fit, in the sense of satisfying statistical chi-squared tests, by members of the family of 2-D Gabor elementary functions. Three examples of such empirical studies by J. Jones and L. Palmer (personal communication) are presented in Fig. 5. The top row shows the empirical 2-D receptive field profiles measured with small

spots of light spanning a (16×16) position grid, plotted as the excitatory or inhibitory effect of the stimulus on the neuron's firing rate. The middle row shows the best-fitting 2-D Gabor elementary function for each cell; and the bottom row shows the residual error of the fit. Extensive discussions of the experimental and analytic methods are provided in [9].

Clearly, the parameters in the 2-D Gabor family of elementary functions directly capture the chief neurophysiological properties of localization in visual space (x_o, y_o), spatial dimensions (α, β), preferred orientation and spatial frequency (captured by converting the Cartesian (u_o, v_o) parameters into polar coordinates), and the tuning bandwidths for orientation and spatial frequency (determined jointly by u_o, v_o, α, and β). To this extent, because the neural receptive field profiles $G(x, y)$ are localized *both* in (x, y) visual space *and* in (u, v) 2-D spectral coordinates, we can describe the biological early visual cortical analysis of image structure as forming a conjoint spatial/spatial frequency signal representation with optimized joint resolution, subject to the 4-D uncertainty principle of (12). Roughly speaking, such a representation facilitates the extraction of local 2-D spectral information (texture, scale, axes of modulation) without sacrificing concurrent extraction of information about 2-D location and metrical relationships. For example, the textural structure of a given image region can be separated into its identifying 2-D spectral constituents, while in the same representation, the global spatial structure of the image can be separated into the distinct regions in which a given 2-D spectral structure appears. This scheme of image representation might be considered analogous to a speech spectrogram, generalized to four dimensions; separate signal components having conjoint support in one domain can be given disjoint support in the other domain, a strategy of proven utility in statistical pattern recognition [19]. Further discussion about conjoint 2-D/2-D anisotropic filter representations and neurobiological mechanisms may be found in [10], [15], and [18].

IV. COMPLETE DISCRETE 2-D GABOR TRANSFORMS

For machine vision, the utility of representing image structure in terms of 2-D Gabor elementary functions is complicated by the fact that they do not constitute an orthogonal basis. The inner product of two members of the set specified by (10), in the same location (x_o, y_o) but parameterized differently by i and j, is nonzero:

$$\langle G_i(x, y); G_j(x, y) \rangle$$
$$= \exp\left(-\pi\left[\frac{(u_i - u_j)^2}{(\alpha_i^2 + \alpha_j^2)} + \frac{(v_i - v_j)^2}{(\beta_i^2 + \beta_j^2)}\right]\right). \quad (13)$$

One solution to this problem, developed by Bastiaans [8], is to introduce an auxiliary biorthogonal function $\gamma[x, y]$ which allows one to find the correct coefficients by the usual inner product rule for projecting the signal onto the elementary functions. Thus, in the discrete case, if the elementary functions $\{G_i[x, y]\}$ form a complete but nonorthogonal set on which the image $I[x, y]$ can be exactly represented as

$$I[x, y] = \sum_{i=1}^{n} a_i G_i[x, y], \quad (14)$$

then it may be possible under specific restrictions on $\{G_i[x, y]\}$ to find an auxiliary function $\gamma[x, y]$ such that the desired coefficients $\{a_i\}$ can be found directly by the rule

$$a_i = \sum_{x, y} \gamma[x - x_i, y - y_i]$$
$$\cdot \exp\left[-2\pi i(u_i x + v_i y)\right] I[x, y]. \quad (15)$$

Thus, Bastiaans' auxiliary function $\gamma[x, y]$ is biorthogonal to the (invariant) Gaussian window of the chosen elementary functions $\{G_i[x, y]\}$, and it is derived by demanding that the Kronecker delta inner product rule for orthogonal basis functions be satisfied. Although Bastiaans' 1-D solution can be readily generalized to the 2-D case as a Cartesian product, it is expressed only as an infinite series [8], and so in practice an approximation must be found. More importantly, its derivation depends upon certain severe restrictions on the elementary functions $\{G_i[x, y]\}$; in particular, they must all share the same windowing function. This entails that the spatial frequency bandwidths (in octave terms) and orientation bandwidths of the elementary functions will both be inversely proportional to their center frequencies. We would prefer to relax this requirement, in part because the biological 2-D receptive field profiles tend to have a roughly invariant template shape across scales as illustrated by the

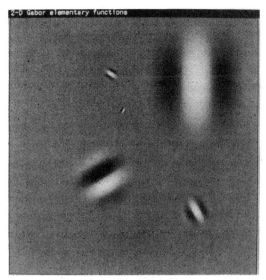

Fig. 6. Five examples of 2-D Gabor elementary functions displayed as luminance primitives. These biologically modeled "wavelets" can all be generated from a single complex member by dilations, rotations, and translations, as specified by (22).

luminance profiles in Fig. 6, lending them constant log-polar bandwidths, rather than having a window of constant size which would entail constant linear bandwidths. A further motivation for averting the requirements of the Bastiaans' biorthogonal approach is that we would also like to be able to find optimal conjoint coefficients $\{a_i\}$ even when the elementary functions do *not* form a complete set, as arises from irregular sampling rules. In these cases, the auxiliary $\gamma[x, y]$ biorthogonal function approach to obtaining the coefficients is not helpful, but the approach based on the neural network architecture illustrated in Fig. 3 is.

Before applying the network to the general (nonorthogonal *and* noncomplete) case, we first demonstrate its ability to accomplish the same goal as the Bastiaans method for regular sampling with invariant window function (the nonorthogonal yet complete case). Here the 2-D Gabor elementary functions are parameterized for an invariant Gaussian window which is positioned on (fully overlapping) Cartesian lattice locations

$$\{x_m, y_n\} = \{mM, nN\} \quad (16)$$

for integers (m, n) and corresponding lattice cell dimensions M, N. The complex exponentials which modulate these overlapping Gaussians are accordingly parameterized for a Cartesian lattice of 2-D spatial frequencies $\{u_r, v_s\}$ appropriate to the M, N spatial lattice:

$$\{u_r, v_s\} = \left\{\frac{r}{M}, \frac{s}{N}\right\} \quad (17)$$

for integer increments of (r, s) spanning $\{-(M - 1/2), (M - 1/2)\}$ and $\{-(N - 1/2), (N - 1/2)\}$, respectively. Thus, for the neural network shown in Fig. 3, we use for the fixed weighting functions of the first and third layers the 2-D Gabor elementary functions

$$G_{mnrs}[x, y] = \exp\left(-\pi\alpha^2[(x - mM)^2 + (y - nN)^2]\right)$$

$$\cdot \exp\left(-2\pi i\left[r\frac{x}{M} + s\frac{y}{N}\right]\right) \quad (18)$$

and allow the network to converge to its stable state, when (9) is satisfied, at which point we may read out the desired coefficients a_{mnrs} from the adjustable weights of the middle layer.

These obtained coefficients a_{mnrs} constitute a complete 2-D Gabor transform of the input image. Each coefficient is complex, but because the input image is real, there is conjugate symmetry among the coefficients: over both parameters r and s, the real part of a_{mnrs} has even symmetry and its imaginary part has odd symmetry. Fig. 7 displays the nonredundant halves of the complete set of real and imaginary coefficients a_{mnrs} as a (256×256) image, giving a complete 2-D Gabor transform of the Lena picture. It is noteworthy that the fundamental uncertainty principle expressed in (12) is implicit in the space/spectral sampling rules expressed in (16) and (17). The larger the size of each spatial lattice cell M or N, which means the fewer the number of spatial sampling positions, the larger is the number of spatial frequency components required in each patch in the corresponding dimension, as expressed above by the ranges of the indexes r and s. Thus, the product of the ranges of the four indexes m, n, r, s is a constant, and in the complete case, is equal to the number of pixels in the image.

The (m, n) lattice that was used in constructing the complete 2-D Gabor transform shown in Fig. 7 is apparent by the periodic clusters of points, which correspond to the centers of the overlapping Gaussian envelopes. Although the size of each $(M \times N)$ lattice cell here was (16×16) pixels, each of the overlapping elementary functions in this transform is fully supported on (32×32) pixels, with Gaussian space constant $(1/\alpha\sqrt{\pi})$ equal to ± 9 pixels at the $1/e$ points; thus, the value at which the overlapping Gaussians are finally truncated and equated to zero is 0.05. Although the value of the Gaussian scale constant α in (18) is arbitrary from the standpoint of completeness and only affects the amount of effective overlap of the 2-D elementary functions across neighboring m, n lattice locations, it does determine the required support size (number of pixels) of each elementary function so that the truncation of the Gaussian tails is negligible. Since the degree of effective overlap of the Gaussians is a free parameter, as was the particular tradeoff between the m, n spatial sampling density and the number of r, s spatial frequency components per patch, these can be manipulated in a signal-dependent fashion without affecting the completeness of the representation. These are signal-dependent flexibilities of the present neural network approach, which are not possible in the biorthogonalizing approach that requires uniform sampling rules and an invariant Gaussian window throughout the image.

Within each of the (m, n) lattice cells apparent in Fig.

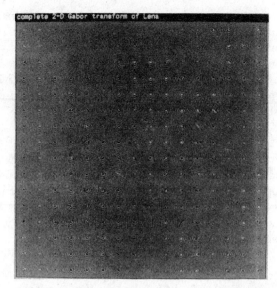

Fig. 7. Complete 2-D Gabor transform of Lena computed by the network of Fig. 3. The amplitude coefficients $\{a_{m,n,r,s}\}$ are quantized to 8-bits and plotted as pixel values (gray being zero), with the spatial center positions m, n of the overlapping elementary functions constituting the global (16×16) lattice centers, and with their 2-D spectral parameters r, s mapped out within each of these local lattice regions. Coefficient histogram shown in Fig. 2; complete reconstruction of Lena from this transform shown in Fig. 8.

7 are embedded the coefficient values a_{mnrs} as (r, s) span their ranges. Thus, the conjoint character of the 2-D Gabor transform is made clear by the way in which local *spectral* variables (r, s) are embedded within the global *spatial* image variables (m, n), for representing the image as the set of coefficients a_{mnrs} on the overlapping, nonorthogonal, elementary functions $G_{mnrs}[x, y]$.

Finally, the completeness of the representation found by the neural network is demonstrated in Fig. 8, which shows the exact reconstruction of the Lena picture from the 2-D Gabor transform of Fig. 7. Each of the transform coefficients was quantized to 8 bits (as in the original pixel image), and the reconstructed picture in Fig. 8 was simply created by the sum of all of the 2-D Gabor elementary functions weighted by their coefficients:

$$H[x, y] = \sum_{m,n,r,s} a_{mnrs} G_{mnrs}[x, y]. \quad (19)$$

The dark points specify the (m, n) lattice locations, and the mean-squared-error of the recovered image is close to zero. Recalling the original entropy comparisons of Figs. 1 and 2, it is striking that all of the image structure seen in Fig. 8 was recovered from the seemingly very impoverished image in Fig. 7, whose histogram has an entropy of only 2.55 bits. Indeed, with the complete 2-D Gabor transform of Fig. 7 quantized to 8 bits, so that each coefficient becomes an integer between -127 and $+128$, about 75 percent of all the coefficients fall within 3 bins of zero. (See Fig. 2.) This means that nearly all the image structure that was recovered in Fig. 8 was contained in just a small subset of the complete 2-D Gabor transform coefficients. For this reason, dramatic factors of data compression are possible by representing images in terms

Fig. 8. Reconstruction of the Lena picture from the complete 2-D Gabor transform displayed in Fig. 7, at only 2.55 bits/pixel. Dark points represent lattice centers for the overlapping 2-D Gabor elementary functions.

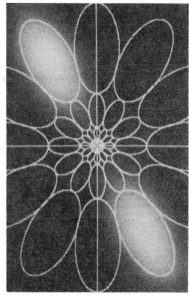

Fig. 9. 2-D Fourier transforms of the Gabor elementary functions employed in one log-polar radial octave "wavelet" scheme. Following physiological data [9], [10], these primitives have logarithmically dispersed center frequencies, $\pm 15°$ orientation bandwidths, 1.5 octave spatial frequency bandwidths, and hence a constant template shape and a 2 : 1 bandwidth aspect ratio.

of these nonorthogonal elementary functions, whose coefficients can be found by the neural network.

V. IMAGE REPRESENTATION IN SELF-SIMILAR 2-D GABOR "WAVELET" SETS

By eliminating degrees of freedom in the family of 2-D Gabor elementary functions so that they all are dilations, rotations, and translations of each other, with the spectral parameters of the set distributed in a 2-D log-polar lattice, it is possible to represent images on a sparse self-similar family of primitives with advantageous reductions in complexity. In this more biologically inspired scheme as was illustrated in Fig. 6, the different 2-D Gabor elementary functions $G_{mnrs}[x, y]$ have sizes distributed in octave steps (and hence, preferred frequencies also changing in octave steps). In (10), this corresponds to setting α and β proportional to u_o and v_o, thus eliminating two degrees of freedom which correspond to orientation bandwidth and spatial frequency bandwidth. (See [10, Fig. 2] for clarification.) The orientations of the elementary functions, given by

$$\theta_o = \tan^{-1}\left(\frac{v_o}{u_o}\right), \qquad (20)$$

are chosen from a fixed set of angles (e.g., six distinct orientations differing in 30° steps). The spectral characteristics of one such set of *log-polar* parameterized 2-D Gabor elementary functions are illustrated in Fig. 9. All the elementary functions in this example have spectral envelopes with a 2 : 1 aspect ratio (a reflection of their 30° orientation bandwidth and 1.5-octave spatial frequency bandwidth), with center frequencies distributed on a log-polar radial octave grid (the defining 2-D spectra sampling rule), and with self-similarity across all scales, reflecting the invariant shape of the image-domain templates.

In certain of these respects, this set of elementary functions resembles the "wavelet" expansions developed recently by Meyer, Daubechies, Grossmann, Morlet, and Mallat (see [20]–[25]) for analyzing 1-D signals into a self-similar family of wavelets, all of which can be generated by dilations and shifts of a single basic wavelet. Families of wavelets have been recently developed which have strictly compact support and which constitute complete orthonormal bases for $L^2(\mathbf{R})$ functions ([20]). All wavelet schemes, including the present nonorthogonal one, are parameterized by a geometric scale parameter m and position parameter n which relate members of the family to each other:

$$\Psi_{mn}(x) = 2^{-m/2}\Psi(2^{-m}x - n). \qquad (21)$$

Generalizing to two dimensions and incorporating discrete rotations θ into the generating function (21) together with shifts p, q and dilations m, the present 2-D Gabor "wavelet" set can be generated from any given member by

$$\Psi_{mpq\theta}(x, y) = 2^{-m}\Psi(x', y') \qquad (22)$$

where

$$x' = 2^{-m}[x \cos(\theta) + y \sin(\theta)] - p \qquad (23)$$

$$y' = 2^{-m}[-x \sin(\theta) + y \cos(\theta)] - q. \qquad (24)$$

By using the network of Fig. 3 to find optimal coefficients on this self-similar multiresolution wavelet scheme in which 2-D Gabor elementary functions serve as the $\Psi_{mpq\theta}(x, y)$, significant further factors of code compression may be achieved as illustrated in Fig. 10. Each column of Fig. 10 corresponds to a different choice for the number of distinct orientations in the wavelet set, and the

Fig. 10. Image compression achieved by the 2-D Gabor "wavelet" transform. Columns: different numbers of distinct wavelet orientations, ranging from six to two. Rows: different quantization depths for each Gabor coefficient, ranging from 8 bits to 5 bits. Overall bit/pixel rates as indicated.

different rows reflect different degrees of quantization of the computed coefficients ranging from 8 bits to 5 bits per coefficient, with the coarsest level always having 2 bits higher quantization accuracy than the finest level. There are 6 distinct values of the scale parameter m of (22)–(24) employed in each decomposition scheme, producing a five-octave range of resolution scales in one-octave steps. Thus, for example, the image in Fig. 10, marked "3 orientations, 1.03 bit/pixel" was reconstructed from 2-D Gabor wavelets present in 3 orientations (changing in 60° steps), 2 quadrature phases, and a total of 2610 positions spanning 5 levels of resolution with variable quantization depth. It is remarkable that rather high image quality is achieved here at only 1 bit/pixel using the coefficients found by the network, even though as few as 3 distinct orientations are represented by the elementary function wavelets.

VI. IMAGE SEGMENTATION

Finally, by examining the distributions of the 2-D Gabor coefficients found by the network in different image regions, it is possible to achieve image segmentation on the basis of spectral signature [26] as demonstrated in Fig. 11. Here the input image to the network (top left panel) is texture consisting of a collage of anisotropically filtered white noise fields, with the noise in different regions of the image having different 2-D bandpass principal orien-

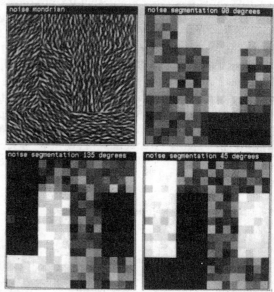

Fig. 11. Image segmentation of anisotropic white noise texture collage (upper left), by the dipole clustering of coefficients in the complete 2-D Gabor transform displayed in Fig. 12.

tations. The complete 2-D Gabor transform of this texture image is displayed in Fig. 12. Close inspection of the transform reveals that associated with each local image region, the 2-D Gabor coefficients a_{mnrs} have significant amplitudes that tend to form dipoles of distinct orienta-

242

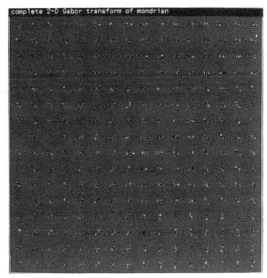

Fig. 12. Complete 2-D Gabor transform of the anisotropic white noise mondrian displayed in Fig. 11. Different local spectral dipoles are apparent in regions of the transform corresponding to regions of the image described by different anisotropic texture moments.

tions. These orientations correspond to the predominant anisotropic texture moment in that region of the image. On this basis, the original textured image was segmented into distinct regions characterized by a certain spectral signature, as demonstrated in the other three panels. Since the 2-D Gabor coefficients which the network generated as shown in Fig. 12 constitute a conjoint space-spectral representation, spectral information remains localized in the image; hence, it can be associated with particular regions of the image having a given textural signature. Many studies [26]–[33] have confirmed the utility of deriving such regional spectral measures for various signal processing applications. We have seen that the neural network of Fig. 3 for computing the transform coefficients on nonorthogonal 2-D Gabor elementary functions can also be used for texture-based image segmentations.

References

[1] T. Kohonen, *Associative Memory—A System-Theoretical Approach.* New York: Springer-Verlag, 1977.
[2] K. Fukushima, S. Miyake, and T. Ito, "Neocognitron: A neural network model for a mechanism of visual pattern recognition," *IEEE Trans. Syst., Man, Cybern.*, vol. SMC-13, pp. 826–834, 1983.
[3] D. Psaltis and N. Farhat, "Optical information processing based on an associative-memory model of neural nets with thresholding and feedback," *Opt. Lett.*, vol. 10, pp. 98–100, 1985.
[4] B. Widrow and S. Stearns, *Adaptive Signal Processing.* Englewood Cliffs, NJ: Prentice-Hall, 1985.
[5] J. Hopfield, "Neural networks and physical systems with emergent collective computational abilities," in *Proc. Nat. Acad. Sci. USA*, vol. 79, pp. 2554–2558, 1982.
[6] A. Lapedes and R. Farber, "Nonlinear signal processing using neural networks: Prediction and system modelling," Los Alamos Nat. Lab.,

preprint LA-UR-87-2662, 1987. (Submitted to *Proc. IEEE.*)
[7] R. Gallager, *Information Theory and Reliable Communication.* New York: Wiley, 1968.
[8] M. Bastiaans, "Gabor's expansion of a signal into Gaussian elementary signals," *Proc. IEEE*, vol. 68, pp. 538–539, 1980.
[9] J. Jones and L. Palmer, "An evaluation of the two-dimensional Gabor filter model of simple receptive fields in cat striate cortex," *J. Neurophysiol.*, vol. 58, pp. 1233–1258, 1987.
[10] J. Daugman, "Uncertainty relation for resolution in space, spatial frequency, and orientation optimized by two-dimensional visual cortical filters," *J. Opt. Soc. Amer.*, vol. 2, no. 7, pp. 1160–1169, 1985.
[11] D. Van Essen, "Hierarchical organization and functional streams in the visual cortex," *Annu. Rev. Neurosci.*, vol. 2, pp. 227–263, 1979.
[12] D. Hubel and T. Wiesel, "Receptive fields, binocular interaction, and functional architecture in the cat's visual cortex," *J. Physiol. (London)*, vol. 160, pp. 106–154, 1962.
[13] ——, "Sequence regularity and geometry of orientation columns in the monkey striate cortex," *J. Comput. Neurol.*, vol. 158, pp. 267–293, 1974.
[14] D. Pollen and S. Ronner, "Phase relationships between adjacent simple cells in the visual cortex," *Science*, vol. 212, pp. 1409–1411, 1981.
[15] J. Daugman, "Two-dimensional spectral analysis of cortical receptive field profiles," *Vis. Res.*, vol. 20, pp. 847–856, 1980.
[16] S. Marcelja, "Mathematical description of the responses of simple cortical cells," *J. Opt. Soc. Amer.*, vol. 70, pp. 1297–1300, 1980.
[17] D. Gabor, "Theory of communication," *J. Inst. Elec. Eng.*, vol. 93, pp. 429–457, 1946.
[18] J. Daugman, "Six formal properties of two-dimensional anisotropic visual filters: Structural principles and frequency/orientation selectivity," *IEEE Trans. Syst., Man, Cybern.*, vol. 13, pp. 882–887, 1983.
[19] R. Duda and P. Hart, *Pattern Classification and Scene Analysis.* New York: Wiley, 1973.
[20] Y. Meyer, "Principe d'incertitude, bases hilbertiennes, et algebres d'operateurs," Seminaire Bourbaki, 1985–1986, no. 662.
[21] J. Morlet, G. Arens, I. Fourgeau, and D. Giard, "Wave propagation and sampling theory," *Geophysics*, vol. 47, pp. 203–236, 1982.
[22] A. Grossman and J. Morlet, "Decomposition of Hardy functions into square integrable wavelets of constant shape," *SIAM J. Math. Anal.*, vol. 15, pp. 723–736, 1984.
[23] A. Grossman, J. Morlet, and T. Paul, "Transforms associated to square integrable group representations. I. General results," *J. Math. Phys.*, vol. 26, pp. 2473–2479, 1985.
[24] I. Daubechies, A. Grossmann, and Y. Meyer, "Painless nonorthogonal expansions," *J. Math. Phys.*, vol. 27, pp. 1271–1283, 1986.
[25] S. Mallat, "A theory for multiresolution signal decomposition: The wavelet representation," *IEEE Trans. Pattern Anal., Machine Intell.*, vol. 10, 1988, in press. (Univ. Pennsylvania GRASP LAB 103, MS-CIS-87-22.)
[26] J. Daugman, "Image analysis by local 2-D spectral signatures," *J. Opt. Soc. Amer. (A)*, vol. 2, p. P74, 1985.
[27] Y. Zeevi and M. Porat, "Combined frequency-position scheme of image representation in vision," *J. Opt. Soc. Amer. (A)*, vol. 1, p. 1248, 1984.
[28] M. Turner, "Texture discrimination by Gabor functions," *Biol. Cybern.*, vol. 55, pp. 71–82, 1986.
[29] M. Clark, A. Bovik, and W. Geisler, "Texture segmentation using a class of narrowband filters," in *Proc. Int. Conf. Acoust., Speech, Signal Processing 87*, 1987, pp. 571–574.
[30] R. Hecht-Nielsen, "Nearest matched filter classification of spatio-temporal patterns," *Appl. Opt.*, vol. 26, pp. 1892–1899, 1987.
[31] R. Haralick, K. Shanmugam, and I. Dinstein, "Textural features for image classification," *IEEE Trans. Syst., Man, Cybern.*, vol. SMC-3, pp. 610–621, 1973.
[32] H. Szu, "Two-dimensional optical processing of one-dimensional acoustic data," *Opt. Eng.*, vol. 21, no. 5, pp. 804–813, 1982.
[33] H. Szu and H. Caulfield, "The mutual time-frequency content of two signals," *Proc. IEEE*, vol. 72, pp. 902–908, 1984.

Multifrequency Channel Decompositions of Images and Wavelet Models

STEPHANE G. MALLAT

Abstract—In this paper we review recent multichannel models developed in psychophysiology, computer vision, and image processing. In psychophysiology, multichannel models have been particularly successful in explaining some low-level processing in the visual cortex. The expansion of a function into several frequency channels provides a representation which is intermediate between a spatial and a Fourier representation. We describe the mathematical properties of such decompositions and introduce the wavelet transform. We review the classical multiresolution pyramidal transforms developed in computer vision and show how they relate to the decomposition of an image into a wavelet orthonormal basis. In the last section we discuss the properties of the zero crossings of multifrequency channels. Zero-crossings representations are particularly well adapted for pattern recognition in computer vision.

I. INTRODUCTION

WITHIN the last 10 years, multifrequency channel decompositions have found many applications in image processing. In the psychophysiology of human vision, multichannel models have also been particularly successful in explaining some low-level biological processes. The expansion of a function into several frequency channels provides a representation which is intermediate between a spatial and a Fourier representation. In harmonic analysis, this kind of transform appeared in the work of Littlewood and Payley in the 1930's. More research has recently been focused on this domain with the modeling of a new decomposition called the wavelet transform. In this paper we review the recent multichannel models developed in psychophysiology, computer vision, and image processing. We describe the motivations of the models within each of these disciplines and show how they relate to the wavelet transform.

In psychophysics and the physiology of human vision, evidence has been gathered showing that the retinal image is decomposed into several spatially oriented frequency channels. In the first section of this paper, we describe the experimental motivations for this model. Biological studies of human vision have always been a source of ideas for computer vision and image processing research. Indeed, the human visual system is generally considered to be an optimal image processor. The goal is not to imitate the processings implemented in the human brain, but rather to understand the motivations of such processings

and analyze their application to computer vision problems. From this point of view, the recent experimental findings in psychophysics and physiology open challenging questions. In order to get a better understanding of multichannel decompositions, we review the main mathematical results in this domain. The best-known decomposition which is intermediate between a spatial and a frequency representation is the window Fourier transform. The window Fourier transform is used in signal processing for coding and pattern detection [47]. We describe its properties but also show why it is not a convenient decomposition for image analysis. The wavelet transform was introduced by Morlet to overcome the shortcomings of the window Fourier transform. It is computed by expanding the signal into a family of functions which are the dilations and translations of a unique function $\psi(x)$. Grossmann and Morlet [20] have shown that any function in $L^2(R)$ can be characterized from its decomposition on the wavelet family $(\sqrt{s}\,\psi(s(x-u)))_{(s,u) \in R^2}$. A wavelet transform can be interpreted as a decomposition into a set of frequency channels having the same bandwidth on a logarithmic scale. We review the most important properties of a wavelet transform and describe its discretization as studied by Daubechies [11]. A very important particular case of discrete wavelet transform was found by Meyer [45] and Stromberg [55]. They proved that there exist some wavelets $\psi(x)$ such that $(\sqrt{2^j}\psi(2^j(x-2^{-j}n)))_{(j,n) \in Z^2}$ is an orthonormal basis of $L^2(R)$. Wavelet orthonormal bases provide an important new tool in functional analysis. Indeed, it was believed that we could not build simple orthonormal bases of $L^2(R)$ whose elements have a good localization both in the spatial and Fourier domains. These bases have already found many applications in pure and applied mathematics [27], [33], [57], in quantum mechanics [15], [48], and in signal processing [30].

In computer vision, multifrequency channel decompositions are interpreted through the concept of multiresolution. Generally, the structures that we want to recognize have very different sizes. Hence, it is not possible to define *a priori* an optimal resolution for analyzing images. Several researchers [22], [42], [52] have developed pattern matching algorithms which process the image at different resolutions. Some pyramidal implementations have been developed for computing these decompositions [4], [10], [50]. A multiresolution transform also decomposes the signal into a set of frequency channels of constant

Manuscript received March 17, 1989. This work was supported by NSF Grant IRI-8903331.

The author is with the Computer Science Department, Courant Institute of Mathematical Sciences, New York University, New York, NY 10012.

IEEE Log Number 8931327.

Reprinted from *IEEE Trans. Acoust., Speech, Signal Processing*, vol. 37, no. 12, pp. 2091–2110, Dec. 1989.

bandwidth on a logarithmic scale. It can be interpreted as a discrete wavelet transform. We review the wavelet multiresolution model [38] which provides a mathematical interpretation of the concept of resolution. We see in particular that a large class of wavelet orthonormal bases can be computed from quadrature mirror filters [39].

Multifrequency channel decompositions are well adapted for data compression in image coding. We show that this efficiency is due to the intrinsic statistical properties of images and to the ability of such representations to match the sensitivity of human vision. For pattern recognition applications, it is also necessary to build a signal representation which translates when the signal translates. Indeed, the representation of a pattern should not depend upon its position. When a pattern is translated, its representation should be translated without being modified. The pyramidal multiresolution representations as well as discrete wavelet transforms do not have this translation property. In the last section, we study the properties of representations based on zero crossings of multifrequency channels. These representations do translate, and for a particular class of band-pass filters, the zero crossings provide the location of the signal edges. It remains to show that a zero-crossing representation can provide a complete and stable signal decomposition. We review previous results on zero-crossings properties and explain how the problem can be expressed through the wavelet model.

II. Multichannel Models in Psychophysics and Physiology of Vision

In this section, we summarize some experimental results showing that a multifrequency channel decomposition seems to be taking place in the human visual cortex. For further details, we refer to tutorials by Georgeson [18] and Levine [34]. Over the past 20 years, a large effort has been devoted in psychophysics and physiology to analyze the response of the human visual system to stimuli having particular orientation and frequency tunings. Linear models have been partly successful in explaining some experimental data. The simplest, which was first developed in psychophysiology, approximates the human visual system with a linear filter. Fig. 1 illustrates the anatomical pathway in the human visual system. Photoreceptors in the eyes measure the light input intensity. This information is processed by bipolar and ganglion cells in the retina and is transmitted through the optic nerve. The optic nerve ends in a relay station (the lateral geniculate nucleus) whose axons extend to the visual cortex.

Replacing these different stages by a global linear filter is clearly an extremely simplified model, but it gives some insights about the visual system sensitivity. Given this hypothesis, Campbell and Green [6] tried to measure the global transfer function of the visual system. In their experiments, the visual stimuli shown to the observer were vertical sinusoidal gratings of different spatial frequencies (see Fig. 2).

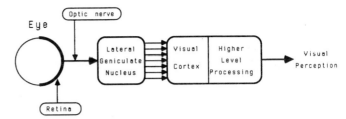

Fig. 1. Illustration of the anatomical visual pathway. The higher level processes are the least understood and are difficult to evaluate in psychophysical experiments.

Fig. 2. This image is a typical visual stimulus used in psychological experiments for computing the transfer function of the visual system. It consists of a sinusoidal grating whose frequency varies during the experiment. In order to evaluate the sensitivity to orientation, these gratings are rotated.

In psychophysics, frequencies are measured in cycles per degree of visual angle subtended on the eye. The transfer function $H(\omega)$ of the visual system is defined as the ratio of the contrast perceived by the observer to the real contrast of the stimulus for sinusoidal gratings of frequency ω. The contrast is given by

$$C = \frac{L_{\max} - L_{\min}}{L_{\max} + L_{\min}},$$

where $L_{\max}$ and $L_{\min}$ are the maximum and minimum luminance of the stimuli. In order to estimate this transfer function, a solution which is widely adopted is to measure the *Contrast Sensitivity Function*. At each frequency ω, we measure the minimum contrast $C_t(\omega)$ necessary to distinguish the sinusoidal gratings from a uniform background. This contrast is called the contrast threshold. The contrast sensitivity function is then defined by

$$CSF(\omega) = \frac{1}{C_t(\omega)}, \quad \text{and} \quad H(\omega) = CSF(\omega).$$

Many experiments [5], [6], [31] have been performed to measure the function $CSF(\omega)$ and they agree approximately with the function shown in Fig. 3. Although this linear model is clearly oversimplified, it shows qualitatively the sensitivity of the human system to stimuli of different frequencies.

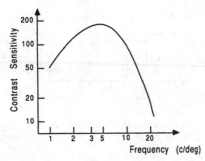

Fig. 3. Contrast Sensitivity Function (redrawn from Kulikowski and King-Smith [31]). The visual system has the maximum sensitivity to contrast when the frequency of the stimulus is around 5 cycles/deg.

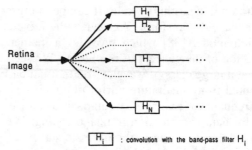

H_i : convolution with the band-pass filter H_i

Fig. 4. Multichannel model. The retinal image is supposed to be filtered by independent band-pass filters. These filters have approximately the same bandwidth on a logarithmic scale and have a spatial orientation selectivity.

With further experiments, Campbell and Robson [8] have shown that the retinal image is likely to be processed in separate frequency channels. These experiments were based on adaptation techniques. If a stimulus is shown to an observer for a long time, the visual sensitivity for the same kind of stimuli decreases. This behavior is called an adaptation process. Campbell and Robson [8] have shown that if the visual system adapts to a sinusoidal grating of a given frequency ω_0, the sensitivity decreases for any stimuli whose frequency is in a frequency band around ω_0. However, outside this frequency band, the sensitivity is not affected. These experiments indicate that at some stage, the visual information in different frequency bands is processed separately. Researchers in psychophysics have tried to measure the width of these bands. In order to simplify the analysis of the problem, Campbell and Robson supposed that the retinal image is decomposed through independent band-pass linear filters as shown in Fig. 4. Their first estimate of the frequency bandwidth of these filters was very narrow. However, other experiments by Georgeson [17] and Nachmias [46] have since contradicted their results. They showed that the frequency bandwidth of these filters is more likely to be around one octave. In other words, the retina image seems to be decomposed in several frequency bands having approximately the same width on a logarithmic scale.

Other psychophysical experiments have shown that the visual sensitivity to a sinusoidal grating also depends upon its spatial orientation. The results of Campbell and Kulikowski [7] show that the human visual system has a maximum sensitivity when the signal has an orientation of 0° or 90°. In between, the sensitivity decreases monotonically reaching a minimum at 45°. The filters of the model shown in Fig. 4 must therefore have a spatial orientation selectivity.

This filter bank model only provides a qualitative description of some low-level processing of the visual system. In particular, it does not take into account the nonlinearities of the biological processes. However, recent physiological experiments support such approaches. Cell recordings are generally performed on cats and monkeys which have a visual cortex similar to the human one. In the cat's visual cortex, Hubel and Wiesel [23] discovered

a class of cells whose response depends upon the frequency and orientation of the visual stimuli. These cells are called simple cells. Maffei and Fiorentini [35] have shown that their response is reasonably linear and that they can be modeled with linear filters. Several groups of researchers have recorded the impulse responses of simple cells [2], [36], [59]. These studies showed that the bandwidths of simple cells range from 0.6 to 2.0 octaves with an average value of 1.3 octaves. The response of simple cells also depends upon the spatial orientation of the stimuli. Fig. 5 shows the two-dimensional impulse response of simple cells measured by Webster and De Valois [61]. These impulse responses have been modeled by Daugmann [12], [13] with Gaussians modulated by sinusoidal waves. As explained in the next section, these functions generate a particular window Fourier transform called the Gabor transform. Fig. 5 shows the comparison between the impulse response of a simple cell and the corresponding Gabor function model. These graphs clearly show that a simple cell behaves like a band-pass filter with a spatial orientation tuning. The support of the impulse response of a cell is called the receptive field. It corresponds to the domain of the retina where the input light influences the cell firings. Simple cells have a receptive field of varying size depending on their frequency tuning [49].

Much evidence has now been gathered about this multifrequency channel modeling of the low-level visual cortex processing. However, we do not know what type of information is extracted from this decomposition and how it relates to further processing by complex and hypercomplex cells [49]. Since the human visual cortex is an excellent image processor, this low-level biological model raises important questions from an image processing point of view. What is the advantage of decomposing a signal into several frequency channels? Is it related to the intrinsic statistical properties of images? Does it lead to a better reorganization of the image information? If we do accept that such a decomposition offers a useful representation of images, it remains to find out how to process these different frequency channels. What type of information do we want to extract? Should we process each channel independently or compare the values of the signal from band to band? In the following sections, we show that some

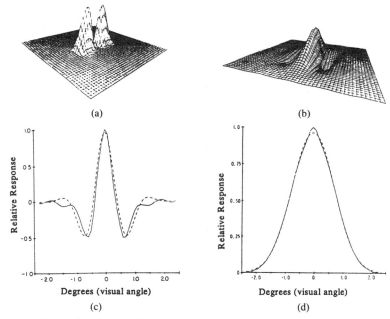

(a)   (b)

(c)   (d)

Fig. 5. (Reprint from Webster and De Valois [61].) (a) This surface is the
two-dimensional transfer function of a simple cell. It is a band-pass oriented filter. Its bandwidth is 0.94 octaves. (b) Impulse response computed by taking the inverse Fourier transform of (a). (c) and (d) Cross
sections of the impulse response respectively along the x and y axes. The
dashed lines give the best fitting Gabor functions.

results in mathematics, computer vision, and image coding give elements of answers to these questions. Our primary goal is not to build a model of the human visual
cortex but rather to justify the use of such decompositions
in image processing.

III. MATHEMATICAL ANALYSIS OF MULTICHANNEL MODELS

In this section we review the mathematical properties
of multifrequency channel decompositions. We do believe that a good mathematical understanding of these decompositions is necessary in order to evaluate their range
of applications in image processing. We summarize the
most relevant mathematical results in this domain. No
proof is written, but references to original works are
given. Most results are first introduced for one-dimensional functions and then generalized to two dimensions
if needed. We review the properties of the window Fourier transform which is the most well-known intermediate
decomposition between spatial and Fourier representations. This decomposition has already found many applications in signal coding and pattern detection [47]. We
describe the drawbacks of the window Fourier transform
for analyzing signals like images. The wavelet transform
is then introduced and compared to the window Fourier
transform. More details can be found in a complete article
by Daubechies [11] and an advanced functional analysis
book by Meyer [44].

Notation: $\boldsymbol{Z}$, $\boldsymbol{R}$, and $\boldsymbol{R}^+$ denote, respectively, the sets
of integers, real numbers, and positive real numbers.
$\boldsymbol{L}^2(\boldsymbol{R})$ denotes the Hilbert space of measurable, square-

integrable one-dimensional functions $f(x)$. We suppose
that our signals are finite energy functions $f(x) \in \boldsymbol{L}^2(\boldsymbol{R})$.
For a pair of functions $f(x) \in \boldsymbol{L}^2(\boldsymbol{R})$, $g(x) \in \boldsymbol{L}^2(\boldsymbol{R})$, the
inner product of $f(x)$ with $g(x)$ is written

$$\langle g(x), f(x) \rangle = \int_{-\infty}^{+\infty} g(x)\overline{f(x)}\, dx, \qquad (1)$$

where $\overline{f(x)}$ is the complete conjugate of $f(x)$. The norm
of $f(x)$ in $\boldsymbol{L}^2(\boldsymbol{R})$ is given by

$$\|f\|^2 = \int_{-\infty}^{+\infty} |f(x)|^2\, dx. \qquad (2)$$

We denote the convolution of two functions $f(x) \in \boldsymbol{L}^2(\boldsymbol{R})$
and $g(x) \in \boldsymbol{L}^2(\boldsymbol{R})$ by

$$f * g(u) = \int_{-\infty}^{+\infty} f(x)g(u-x)\, dx. \qquad (3)$$

The dilation of a function $f(x) \in \boldsymbol{L}^2(\boldsymbol{R})$ by a scaling factor s is written

$$f_s(x) = \sqrt{s}\, f(sx). \qquad (4)$$

The reflection of $f(x)$ about 0 is written

$$\tilde{f}(x) = f(-x). \qquad (5)$$

The Fourier transform of $f(x) \in \boldsymbol{L}^2(\boldsymbol{R})$ is written $\hat{f}(\omega)$
and is defined by

$$\hat{f}(\omega) = \int_{-\infty}^{+\infty} f(x)e^{-i\omega x}\, dx. \qquad (6)$$

A. Definition of a Window Fourier Transform

From the Fourier transform of a function $f(x)$, we get a measure of the irregularities (high frequencies) but this information is not spatially localized. Indeed, the Fourier transform $\hat{f}(\omega)$ is defined through an integral which covers the whole spatial domain. It is therefore difficult to find the position of the irregularities. In order to localize the information provided by the Fourier transform, Gabor [16] defined a new decomposition using a spatial window $g(x)$ in the Fourier integral. This window is translated along the spatial axis in order to cover the whole signal. At a position u and for a frequency ω, the window Fourier transform of a function $f(x) \in L^2(R)$ is defined by

$$Gf(\omega, u) = \int_{-\infty}^{+\infty} e^{-i\omega x} g(x - u) f(x) \, dx. \quad (7)$$

It measures locally, around the point u, the amplitude of the sinusoidal wave component of frequency ω. In the original Gabor transform, the window function $g(x)$ is a Gaussian. It has since been generalized for any type of window function and is called a window Fourier transform [28]. The window function is generally a real even function and the energy of its Fourier transform is concentrated in the low frequencies (see Fig. 6). It can be viewed as the impulse response of a low-pass filter. For normalization purposes, we suppose that the energy of $g(x)$ is equal to 1:

$$\|g\|^2 = \int_{-\infty}^{+\infty} |g(x)|^2 \, dx = 1.$$

Let us denote

$$g_{\omega_0, u_0}(x) = e^{i\omega_0 x} g(x - u_0).$$

A window Fourier transform can also be interpreted as the inner products of the function $f(x)$ with the family of functions $(g_{\omega, u}(x))_{(\omega, u) \in R^2}$:

$$Gf(\omega, u) = \langle f(x), g_{\omega, u}(x) \rangle. \quad (8)$$

In quantum physics, such a family of functions is called a family of coherent states. The Fourier transform $g_{\omega, u_0}(x)$ is given by

$$\hat{g}_{\omega_0, u_0}(\omega) = e^{-iu_0\omega} \hat{g}(\omega - \omega_0), \quad (9)$$

where $\hat{g}(\omega)$ is the Fourier transform of $g(x)$. A family of coherent states thus corresponds to a translation in the spatial domain (parameter u) and in the frequency domain (parameter ω) of the function $g(x)$ (see Fig. 6). This double translation is represented in a phase-space where one axis corresponds to the spatial parameter u and the other to the frequency parameter ω (see Fig. 7). Families of coherent states have found many applications in quantum physics because they make it possible to analyze simultaneously a physical phenomena in both the spatial and frequency domains.

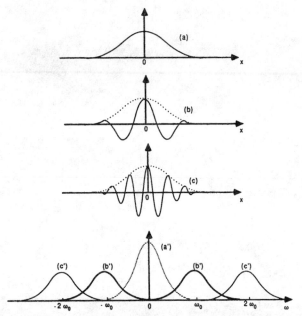

Fig. 6. (a) Window function $g(x)$. (b) Graph of $g(x) \cos(\omega_0 x)$. (c) Graph of $g(x) \cos(2\omega_0 x)$. All these curves have the same support but the number of cycles varies with the frequency of the sinusoidal modulation. The curves (a'), (b'), (c') are, respectively, the Fourier transform of $g(x)$, $g(x) \cos(\omega_0 x)$, and $g(x) \cos(2\omega_0 x)$. They have the same bandwidth but different positions on the frequency axis.

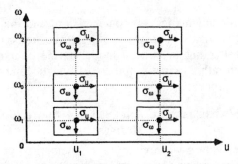

Fig. 7. Phase-space representation. The vertical axis gives the frequency ω whereas the horizontal axis gives the spatial position u. A window Fourier coefficient $Gf(\omega_0, u_0)$ provides a description of $f(x)$ within the resolution cell of $[u_0 - \sigma_u, u_0 + \sigma_u] \times [\omega_0 - \sigma_\omega, \omega_0 + \sigma_\omega]$.

Let us now describe how a window Fourier transform relates to a spatial or a frequency representation. Let σ_u be the standard deviation of $g(x)$

$$\sigma_u^2 = \int_{-\infty}^{+\infty} x^2 |g(x)|^2 \, dx. \quad (10)$$

Let σ_ω be the standard deviation of the Fourier transform of $g(x)$

$$\sigma_\omega^2 = \int_{-\infty}^{+\infty} \omega^2 |\hat{g}(\omega)|^2 \, d\omega. \quad (11)$$

The function $g_{\omega_0, u_0}(x)$ is centered in u_0 and has a standard deviation σ_u in the spatial domain. Its Fourier transform given by (9) is centered in ω_0 and has a standard deviation

σ_ω. By applying the Parseval theorem on (8), we get

$$Gf(\omega_0, u_0) = \int_{-\infty}^{+\infty} f(x) \overline{g_{\omega_0, u_0}(x)} \, dx$$

$$= \int_{-\infty}^{+\infty} \hat{f}(\omega) \overline{\hat{g}_{\omega_0, u_0}(\omega)} \, d\omega. \qquad (12)$$

The first integral shows that in the spatial domain, $Gf(\omega_0, u_0)$ essentially depends upon the values of $f(x)$ for $x \in [u_0 - \sigma_u, u_0 + \sigma_u]$. The second integral proves that in the frequency domain, $Gf(\omega_0, u_0)$ depends upon the values of $\hat{f}(\omega)$ for $\omega \in [\omega_0 - \sigma_\omega, \omega_0 + \sigma_\omega]$. The spatio-frequency domain which is covered by $Gf(\omega_0, u_0)$ can thus be represented in the phase-space by the resolution cell $[u_0 - \sigma_u, u_0 + \sigma_u] \times [\omega_0 - \sigma_\omega, \omega_0 + \sigma_\omega]$ as shown in Fig. 7. The surface and shape of the resolution cell is independent from u_0 and ω_0. The uncertainty principle applied to the function $g(x)$ implies that

$$\sigma_u^2 \sigma_\omega^2 \geq \frac{\pi}{2}. \qquad (13)$$

The resolution cell can therefore not be smaller than $2\sqrt{2\pi}$. The uncertainty inequality reaches its upper limit if and only if $g(x)$ is a Gaussian. Hence, the resolution in the phase-space is maximized when the window function is a Gaussian as in the Gabor transform.

B. Properties of a Window Fourier Transform

A window Fourier transform is an isometry (to a proportionality coefficient) from $L^2(R)$ into $L^2(R^2)$

$$\int_{-\infty}^{+\infty} |f(x)|^2 \, dx = \frac{1}{2\pi} \int_{-\infty}^{+\infty} \int_{-\infty}^{+\infty} |Gf(\omega, u)|^2 \, d\omega \, du. \qquad (14)$$

The function $f(x)$ is reconstructed from $Gf(\omega, u)$ with the formula

$$f(x) = \frac{1}{2\pi} \int_{-\infty}^{+\infty} \int_{-\infty}^{+\infty} Gf(\omega, u) g(u - x) e^{i\omega x} \, d\omega \, du. \qquad (15)$$

Equations (14) and (15) are proved by applying the Parseval theorem and using the definition of $Gf(\omega, x)$ given in (7).

A window Fourier transform is a redundant representation. If instead of computing $Gf(\omega, u)$ for all values $(\omega, u) \in R^2$ we sample uniformly both ω and u, the representation can still be complete and stable. Let u_0 and ω_0 be the sampling intervals in both domains. A discrete Fourier transform is defined by

$$\forall n \in Z, \quad \forall m \in Z \quad G_d f(m, n) = Gf(m\omega_0, nu_0)$$

$$= \int_{-\infty}^{+\infty} e^{-im\omega_0 x} g(x - nu_0) f(x) \, dx. \qquad (16)$$

This discretization corresponds to a uniform sampling of the phase-space as shown in Fig. 8. A discrete window

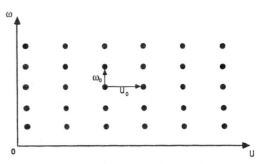

Fig. 8. Sampling pattern of a discrete window Fourier transform in the phase-space. Since the resolution cells are identical everywhere in the phase-space, the sampling is uniform.

Fourier transform is equivalent to a division of the frequency axis into intervals separated by ω_0 (see Fig. 6). In each of these intervals, the signal is sampled at a rate $1/u_0$. Daubechies [11] made a thorough study of the completeness and stability of a discrete window Fourier transform. Intuitively, the sampling intervals u_0 and ω_0 must be chosen in order to cover the whole phase-space with the resolution cells shown in Fig. 7. Formally, to reconstruct any function $f(x) \in L^2(R)$ from the set of sample $(G_d f(n, m))_{(n,m) \in Z^2}$, the operator

$$L^2(R) \xrightarrow{G_d} l^2(Z^2)$$

must be invertible on its range and have a bounded inverse. Each sample $G_d f(n, m)$ can also be expressed as an inner product in $L^2(R)$

$$G_d f(m, n) = \langle f(x), e^{im\omega_0 x} g(x - nu_0) \rangle$$

$$= \langle f(x), g_{m\omega_0, nu_0}(x) \rangle. \qquad (17)$$

The properties of a discrete Fourier transform thus depend upon the family of functions $(g_{m\omega_0, nu_0}(x))_{(n,m) \in Z^2}$. In order to invert G_d, Daubechies [11] has shown that ω_0 and u_0 must verify

$$\omega_0 u_0 < 2\pi.$$

When $\omega_0 u_0 = 2\pi$, we reach the Nyquist frequency limit and G_d does not have a bounded inverse. When $\omega_0 u_0 < 2\pi$, the range of G_d has a complicated structure.

Although several researchers have tried to model the impulse response of simple cells with Gabor functions, it is unlikely that the human visual cortex implements some type of window Fourier transform. Indeed, we saw that a window Fourier transform decomposes a function into a set of frequency intervals having the same size. On the other hand, experimental data indicate that the retinal image is decomposed into a set of frequency channels having approximately a constant bandwidth on a logarithmic scale (octave). The measured impulse responses of simple cells do not have an increasing number of cycles for a constant envelope as in a window Fourier transform (see Fig. 6). Rather, they have a support (receptive field) of varying size.

Although some researchers [58] have been using the Gabor transform in computer vision, this decomposition has several drawbacks when applied to image analysis.

We saw that the spatial and frequency resolution of a window Fourier transform is constant. In the spatial domain, the information provided by this decomposition is therefore unlocalized within intervals of size σ_u. The standard deviation σ_u of $g(x)$ defines a resolution of reference. If the signal has a discontinuity such as an edge, with a window Fourier transform, it is difficult to locate this edge with a precision better than σ_u (see Fig. 9). This localization limit is generally not acceptable. If the signal has important features of very different sizes, we cannot define an optimal resolution for analyzing the signal. This is typically the case with images. For example, in the image of a house, the pattern we want to analyze might range from the overall structure of the house to the details on one of the window curtains. With a given window size, it is difficult to analyze both the fine and the large structures. This fixed resolution also introduces misleading high frequencies when decomposing local features. Let $e(x)$ be an edge as shown in Fig. 9, and suppose that

$$e(x) = \begin{cases} 0 & \text{if } x \le x_0 - \dfrac{\Delta x}{2} \\ \dfrac{1}{2} + \dfrac{1}{2} \sin\left(\dfrac{\pi}{\Delta x}(x - x_0)\right) \\ & \text{if } x_0 - \dfrac{\Delta x}{2} < x < x_0 + \dfrac{\Delta x}{2} \\ 1 & \text{if } x \ge x_0 + \dfrac{\Delta x}{2}. \end{cases}$$

Let us denote $\omega_0 = \pi / \Delta x$. One would expect that at the point x_0, the decomposition coefficients $Ge(\omega, x_0) = \langle e(x), e^{i\omega x} g(x - x_0) \rangle$ decrease very quickly when ω gets larger than ω_0. Indeed, in the neighborhood of x_0, the edge $e(x)$ is a sinusoidal wave of frequency ω_0. In reality, this property does not hold because the edge is very localized and has only half of the sinusoidal wave period. As a consequence, when the frequency ω is large with respect to ω_0, the modulus of the coefficients $Ge(x_0, \omega)$ decreases slowly. Although the signal $e(x)$ is locally a pure sinusoidal wave of frequency ω_0, at a frequency $2\omega_0$, the window Fourier coefficient $|Ge(x_0, 2\omega_0)|$ is still about half the value of $|Ge(x_0, \omega_0)|$. This numerical property makes it hard to interpret the window Fourier coefficients when the features are very localized with respect to the size of the support of $g(x)$. More details about this property can be found in the article of Daubechies [11]. A window Fourier transform is better suited for analyzing signals where all the patterns appear approximately at the same scale.

In order to avoid the inconvenience of a transform having a fixed resolution in the spatial and frequency domains, Morlet defined a decomposition based on dilations. In the next section, we describe the properties of this decomposition which is called the wavelet transform.

C. Definition of a Wavelet Transform

Morlet [20] defined the wavelet transform by decomposing the signal into a family of functions which are the translation and dilation of a unique function $\psi(x)$. The

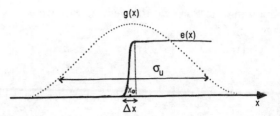

Fig. 9. With a window Fourier transform, a local feature such as an edge $e(x)$ cannot be located with a precision better than the variance σ_u of the window function $g(x)$. Since the variation step Δx of the edge $e(x)$ is small with respect to σ_u, in the neighborhood of x_0, the window Fourier transform of $e(x)$ decreases slowly when the frequency ω gets larger than $\omega_0 = \pi / \Delta x$.

function $\psi(x)$ is called a wavelet and the corresponding wavelet family is given by $(\sqrt{s}\,\psi(s(x - u)))_{(s,u) \in R^2}$. The wavelet transform of a function $f(x) \in L^2(R)$ is defined by

$$Wf(s, u) = \int_{-\infty}^{+\infty} f(x)\sqrt{s}\,\psi(s(x - u))\,dx. \quad (19)$$

The idea behind the wavelet decomposition is not new. It is very much related to some other types of spatial-frequency decompositions such as the Wigner–Ville transform. Some versions of the wavelet transform have been studied independently under other names such as the scale-space decomposition of Witkin [62], and in mathematics its origin can be traced back to be beginning of the century. However, the formalization effort of Morlet and Grossmann [20] opened a broader field of applications and has led to important new mathematical results. Let us denote the dilation of $\psi(x)$ with a factor s by

$$\psi_s(x) = \sqrt{s}\,\psi(sx). \quad (20)$$

A wavelet transform can be rewritten as inner products in $L^2(R)$

$$Wf(s, u) = \langle f(x), \psi_s(x - u) \rangle.$$

It thus corresponds to a decomposition of $f(x)$ on the family of functions $(\psi_s(x - u))_{(s,u) \in R^2}$. As shown in Fig. 10, the functions $\psi_s(x)$ have the same type as $\psi(x)$, but have a support s times smaller. In the following, we suppose that the wavelet $\psi(x)$ and the signal $f(x)$ have real values. As explained later, in order to reconstruct $f(x)$ from its wavelet transform, the Fourier transform $\hat{\psi}(\omega)$ of $\psi(x)$ must satisfy

$$C_\psi = \int_0^{+\infty} \frac{|\hat{\psi}(\omega)|^2}{\omega}\,d\omega < +\infty. \quad (21)$$

This condition implies that $\hat{\psi}(0) = 0$, and that $\hat{\psi}(\omega)$ is small enough in the neighborhood of $\omega = 0$. The function $\psi(x)$ can be interpreted as the impulse response of a bandpass filter. For normalization purposes, we suppose that the energy of $\psi(x)$ is equal to 1. Let us denote $\tilde{\psi}_s(x) = \psi_s(-x)$. We can rewrite the wavelet transform at a point u and a scale s as a convolution product with $\tilde{\psi}_s(x)$

$$Wf(s, u) = f * \tilde{\psi}_s(u). \quad (22)$$

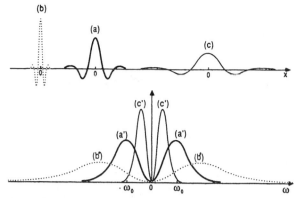

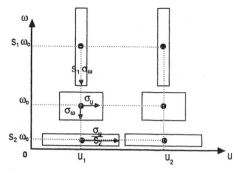

Fig. 11. In the phase-space, the shape of a wavelet resolution cell depends upon the scale. When the scale increases, the resolution increases in the spatial domain and decreases in the frequency domain. The surface of all the resolution cells is the same.

Fig. 10. (a) Graph of a wavelet $\psi(x)$. (b) Graph of $\psi_{s_1}(x)$ for $s_1 > 1$. (c) Graph of $\psi_{s_2}(x)$ for $s_2 < 1$. The curves (a'), (b'), and (c') are, respectively, the Fourier transform of the function shown in (a), (b), and (c). They have the same rms bandwidth on a logarithmic scale.

A wavelet transform can therefore be viewed as a filtering of $f(x)$ with a band-pass filter whose impulse response is $\tilde{\psi}_s(x)$. From (20), we derive that the Fourier transform of $\psi_s(x)$ is given by

$$\hat{\psi}_s(\omega) = \frac{1}{\sqrt{s}} \hat{\psi}\left(\frac{\omega}{s}\right).$$

In opposition to a window Fourier transform which has a fixed resolution in the spatial and frequency domain, the resolution of a wavelet transform varies with the scale parameter s. Since $\psi(x)$ is real, $|\hat{\psi}(\omega)| = |\hat{\psi}(-\omega)|$. Let ω_0 be the center of the passing band of $\hat{\psi}(\omega)$

$$\int_0^{+\infty} (\omega - \omega_0) |\hat{\psi}(\omega)|^2 \, d\omega = 0.$$

Let σ_ω be the rms bandwidth around ω_0

$$\sigma_\omega^2 = \int_0^{+\infty} (\omega - \omega_0)^2 |\hat{\psi}(\omega)|^2 \, d\omega.$$

It is clear that the center of the passing band of $\hat{\psi}_s(\omega)$ is $s\omega_0$ and that its rms bandwidth is $s\sigma_\omega$. On a logarithmic scale, the rms bandwidth of $\hat{\psi}_s(\omega)$ is the same for all $s \in R^+$. Hence, a wavelet transform decomposes the signal into a set of frequency bands having a constant size on a logarithmic scale (see Fig. 10).

Let σ_u be the standard deviation of $|\psi(x)|^2$ around zero. One can also show easily that the wavelet $\psi_s(x - u_0)$ has an energy concentrated around u_0 within a standard deviation σ_u/s. In the frequency domain, we saw that its energy is concentrated around $s\omega_0$ within a standard deviation $s\sigma_\omega$. In the phase-space, the resolution cell of this wavelet is therefore equal to $[u_0 - (\sigma_u/s), u_0 + (\sigma_u/s)] \times [s\omega_0 - s\sigma_\omega, s\omega_0 + s\sigma_\omega]$. As opposed to a window Fourier transform, the shape of the resolution cell varies with the scale s. This is illustrated in Fig. 11. When the scale s is small, the resolution is coarse in the spatial domain and fine in the frequency domain. If the scale s increases, the resolution increases in the spatial domain and decreases in the frequency domain (see Fig. 11). In the next section, we show that this variation of resolution en-

ables the wavelet transform to zoom into the irregularities of the signal and characterize them locally.

For some applications, it can be useful to use a complex wavelet $\psi(s)$ in order to separate a phase and modulus component from the wavelet transform. For this purpose, Morlet and Grossmann are using wavelets whose Fourier transform $\hat{\psi}(\omega)$ is equal to zero for $\omega < 0$ [20]. Such functions are called Hardy functions. The wavelet transform $Wf(s, u)$ is then a complex number. When the scale s is fixed and u varies, the function $Wf(s, u)$ is also a Hardy function. The phase and the modulus of the wavelet transform can easily be separated for any given scale s and position u. Separating the phase and energy component of the wavelet transform signal has found some applications in speech processing [30].

Remark: There is a common misunderstanding in the psychophysiological and computer vision literature around Gabor and wavelet transforms. A Gabor function is a Gaussian modulated by a sinusoidal wave. A Gabor function satisfies the condition (21) and is therefore an admissible wavelet. If we build a transform based on a dilation of this function, it will be a wavelet transform and not a Gabor transform (window Fourier transform). Indeed, in order to define a Gabor transform, we must modify the frequency of the sinusoidal modulation without changing the size of the window function. This is much more than a terminology problem since the properties of a wavelet transform and a Gabor transform are very different.

D. Properties of a Wavelet Transform

Morlet and Grossmann [20] have shown that the wavelet transform is an isometry (to a proportionality coefficient) from $L^2(R)$ into $L^2(R^+ \times R)$

$$\int_{-\infty}^{+\infty} \int_0^{+\infty} |Wf(s, u)|^2 \, ds \, du = C_\psi \int_{-\infty}^{+\infty} |f(x)|^2 \, dx.$$

$$(23)$$

The constant C_ψ is defined by

$$C_\psi = \int_0^{+\infty} \frac{|\hat{\psi}(s\omega)|^2}{s} \, ds = \int_0^{+\infty} \frac{|\hat{\psi}(\omega)|^2}{\omega} \, d\omega < +\infty.$$

Equation (23) is proved by applying the Parseval theorem and using the definition of $Wf(s, u)$ given in (19). Similarly, we can derive that the reconstruction of $f(x)$ from $Wf(s, u)$ is given by

$$f(x) = \frac{1}{C_\psi} \int_{-\infty}^{+\infty} \int_{0}^{+\infty} Wf(s, u)\psi_s(x - u) \, ds \, du. \quad (24)$$

Like a window Fourier transform, a wavelet transform is redundant. In other words, the value of $Wf(s', u')$ depends upon the values of $Wf(s, u)$ for $s \neq s'$ and $u \neq u'$. By inserting (24) in the definition (19) of a wavelet transform, one can show that the function $Wf(s, u)$ satisfies the following reproducing kernel equation [21]:

$$\forall (s', u') \in R^+ \times R, \quad Wf(s', u')$$

$$= \int_{-\infty}^{+\infty} \int_{0}^{+\infty} Wf(s, u)K(s, s', u, u') \, ds \, du, \quad (25)$$

where

$$K(s, s', u, u') = \frac{1}{C_\psi} \int_{-\infty}^{+\infty} \psi_s(x - u)\psi_{s'}(x - u') \, dx.$$

$K(s, s', u, u')$ is called a reproducing kernel. It expresses the redundancy between $Wf(s, u)$ and $Wf(s', u')$ for any two pairs of points (s, u) and (s', u'). Equation (25) shows that, *a priori*, any function $F(s, u) \in L^2(R^+ \times R)$ is not the wavelet transform of some function $f(x) \in L^2(R)$. One can easily prove that there exists a function $f(x) \in L^2(R)$ such that $F(s, u) = Wf(s, u)$, if and only if

$$\forall (s', u') \in R^+ \times R, \quad F(s', u')$$

$$= \int_{-\infty}^{+\infty} \int_{0}^{+\infty} F(s, u)K(s, s', u, u') \, ds \, du. \quad (26)$$

The function $f(x)$ is then given by

$$f(x) = \frac{1}{C_\psi} \int_{-\infty}^{+\infty} \int_{0}^{+\infty} F(s, u)\psi_s(x - u) \, dx \, du. \quad (27)$$

The reproducing kernel equation is an important characterization of a wavelet transform that we use later.

The wavelet transform can be discretized by sampling both the scale parameter s and the translation parameter u. In order to build a complete representation, we must cover the phase-space with the resolution cells shown in Fig. 11. This can be done with an exponential sampling of the scale parameter. We first select a sequence of scales $(\alpha^j)_{j \in Z}$, where α is the elementary dilation step. We saw in (22) that the wavelet transform $Wf(\alpha^j, u)$ can be rewritten

$$Wf(\alpha^j, u) = f * \bar{\psi}_{\alpha^j}(u). \quad (28)$$

For each scale α^j, $\bar{\psi}_{\alpha^j}(x)$ has a Fourier transform centered in $\alpha^j \omega_0$ with an rms bandwidth of $\alpha^j \sigma_\omega$. Equation (28) can therefore be interpreted as a decomposition of $f(x)$ in a set of frequency channels centered in $\alpha^j \omega_0$ and whose rms bandwidth is $\alpha^j \sigma_\omega$. In order to characterize the decom-

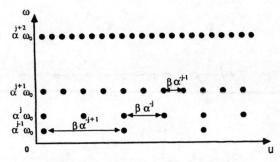

Fig. 12. Sampling of the phase-space corresponding to a discrete wavelet transform (adapted from Daubechies [11]). Each sample corresponds to an inner product with a particular wavelet. This sampling pattern is adapted to the shape of the wavelet resolution cells at the different scales (see Fig. 11).

posed signal in each channel, we must sample it uniformly at a rate proportional to α^j. Let α^j/β be the sampling rate at the scale α^j. The discrete wavelet transformed is defined by

$$W_d f(j, n) = Wf\left(\alpha^j, \frac{n\beta}{\alpha^j}\right) = \int_{-\infty}^{+\infty} f(x)\psi_{\alpha^j}\left(x - \frac{n\beta}{\alpha^j}\right) dx$$

$$= f * \bar{\psi}_{\alpha^j}\left(\frac{n\beta}{\alpha^j}\right). \quad (29)$$

Fig. 12 illustrates this sampling pattern in the phase-space. When the scale increases, the density of samples increases.

It is not possible to understand the properties of this transform by using the Nyquist theorem since the Fourier transform of $\psi(x)$ does not have a compact support (it is not strictly band-limited). With an approach similar to her study of the discrete window Fourier transform, Daubechies [11] analyzed the main properties of a discrete wavelet transform. She made a clear comparison of these two types of multichannel decompositions from a mathematical point of view. In order to reconstruct a function $f(x)$ from the discrete wavelet transform $(W_d f(j, n))_{(n, j) \in Z^2}$, the operator

$$L^2(R) \xrightarrow{W_d} I^2(Z^2) \quad (30)$$

must be invertible on its range and have a bounded inverse. Since

$$W_d(j, n) = \left\langle f(x), \psi_{\alpha^j}\left(x - \frac{n\beta}{\alpha^j}\right)\right\rangle, \quad (31)$$

the properties of the operator W_d depend upon the family of functions $(\psi_{\alpha^j}(x - (n\beta/\alpha^j)))_{(n, j) \in Z^2}$. Daubechies [11] studied the properties of this family of functions and gave some necessary and sufficient conditions on α, β, and $\psi(x)$ so that the operator W_d admits a bounded inverse.

A very important class of discrete wavelet transform was found independently by Meyer [45] and Stromberg [55]. They showed that there exist some wavelets $\psi(x) \in L^2(R)$ such that $(\psi_{2^j}(x - (n/2^j)))_{(n, j) \in Z^2}$ is an orthonormal basis of $L^2(R)$. These particular wavelets are called *orthogonal wavelets*. A wavelet orthonormal basis corresponds to a discrete wavelet transform for $\alpha = 2$ and

252

$\beta = 1$. Wavelet orthonormal bases can be built for sequences of scales other than $(2^j)_{j \in Z}$, but we will concentrate on dyadic scales which lead to simpler decomposition algorithms. These new orthonormal bases had a striking impact in functional analysis. It was indeed believed that one could not find simple orthonormal bases whose elements have a good localization both in the spatial and frequency domains. Any function can be reconstructed from its decomposition into a wavelet orthonormal basis with the classical expansion formula of a vector into an orthonormal basis

$$f(x) = \sum_{j \in Z} \sum_{n \in Z} \left\langle f(u), \psi_{2^j}(u - n2^{-j}) \right\rangle \psi_{2^j}(x - n2^{-j}).$$

$$(32)$$

The Haar basis is a well-known particular case of wavelet orthonormal basis. The orthogonal wavelet corresponding to the Haar basis is given by

$$\psi(x) = \begin{cases} 1 & \text{if } 0 \le x < \frac{1}{2} \\ -1 & \text{if } \frac{1}{2} \le x < 1 \\ 0 & \text{otherwise.} \end{cases} \quad (33)$$

The Haar wavelet is not continuous, which is a major inconvenience for many applications. Meyer [45] showed that we can find some orthogonal wavelets $\psi(x)$ which are infinitely continuously differentiable and whose decay at infinity are faster then any power x^{-n}, $n > 0$. In Section IV-A, we show that the Fourier transform of a large class of orthogonal wavelets can be expressed from the transfer function of a quadrature mirror filter [38]. The decomposition of a function in such a wavelet orthonormal basis can be computed with a quadrature mirror filter bank. Fig. 13 gives the graph of a particular orthogonal wavelet and its Fourier transform. This wavelet is a cubic spline studied independently by Lemarie [32] and Battle [3].

An important property of a wavelet transform is to easily characterize the local regularity of a function. This can have a particularly interesting application for discriminating image textures. In mathematics, it leads to a simple characterization of the classical functional spaces such as the $L^p(R)$ spaces, the Sobolev spaces, the Holder spaces, etc. Let us give an example. One way to measure the local regularity of a function is to measure the lipschitz exponent. A function $f(x)$ is lipschitz α in the neighborhood of a point x_0, if and only if, for any point x in a neighborhood of x_0,

$$\left| f(x) - f(x_0) \right| = O(|x - x_0|^\alpha). \quad (34)$$

A function which is differentiable in x_0 is lipschitz 1. The larger the lipschitz coefficient α, the smoother the function is in the neighborhood of x_0. Let us now suppose that the wavelet $\psi(x)$ is continuously differentiable. We also assume that our signal $f(x)$ is continuous and that there exist $\epsilon > 0$ such that $f(x)$ is lipschitz ϵ everywhere. Jaffard [26] proved that for any $\alpha > 0$, one can find whether

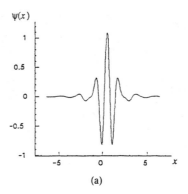

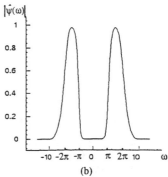

Fig. 13. (a) Example of orthogonal wavelet $\psi(x)$. (b) Modulus of its Fourier transform. The wavelet $\psi(x)$ can be interpreted as the impulse response of a band-pass filter. This particular wavelet is a cubic spline.

$f(x)$ is lipschitz α at x_0 by measuring the decay of wavelet coefficients in the neighborhood of x_0. More precisely, $f(x)$ is lipschitz α at x_0 if and only if

$$\exists C > 0, \quad \forall n \in Z, \quad \left| \left\langle f(x), \psi_{2^j}(x - n2^{-j}) \right\rangle \right|$$
$$\le C2^{-j(1/2 + \alpha)} \left(1 + \left| 2^j x_0 - n \right| \right). \quad (35)$$

The regularity of a function at a point x_0 thus depends upon the decay rate of the wavelet coefficients in neighborhood of x_0, when the scale increases. Other kinds of regularity, such as the derivability at any order (in the sense of Sobolev), can be derived similarly [33]. These results show that it is necessary to combine the information at different scales in order to analyze the local properties of a function. In the next section, we describe the extension of the wavelet model to two-dimensional signals. We come back to orthonormal wavelets in Section IV-A to explain their relation to the concept of multiresolution in computer vision.

E. Wavelet Transform in Two Dimensions

The wavelet transform can be generalized in R^n, but we only consider the two-dimensional case for image processing applications. The model can first be extended without distinguishing any spatial orientation. Let $\Psi(x, y) \in L^2(R^2)$ be a function whose Fourier transform $\hat{\Psi}(\omega_x, \omega_y)$ satisfies

$$\forall (\omega_x, \omega_y) \in R^2 \int_0^{+\infty} \frac{\left| \hat{\Psi}(s\omega_x, s\omega_y) \right|^2}{s} \, ds = C_\Psi < +\infty.$$

$$(36)$$

The value of the integral (36) must be finite and constant for all $(\omega_x, \omega_y) \in R^2$. For example, this property is satisfied for a wavelet $\Psi(x, y)$ which is isotropic ($\Psi(x, y) = \rho(\sqrt{x^2 + y^2})$) and whose Fourier transform is null at the origin ($\hat{\Psi}(0, 0) = 0$). For normalization purposes, we suppose that $\|\Psi\| = 1$. The function $\Psi(x, y)$ can be interpreted as the impulse response of a band-pass filter having no preferential spatial orientation. The wavelet transform of a function $f(x, y) \in L^2(R^2)$ at the scale s and a point (u, v) is defined by

$$
Wf(s, (u, v))
$$
$$
= \int_{-\infty}^{+\infty} \int_{-\infty}^{+\infty} f(x, y) s \Psi(s(x - u), s(y - v)) \, dx \, dy.
$$
$$(37)$$

Let $\Psi_s(x, y) = s\Psi(sx, sy)$ and $\tilde{\Psi}_s(x, y) = \Psi_s(-x, -y)$. The wavelet transform of $f(x, y)$ at the scale s and a point (u, v) can be rewritten as a convolution product

$$
Wf(s, (u, v)) = f * \tilde{\Psi}_s(u, v). \qquad (38)
$$

It can be interpreted as a two-dimensional band-pass filtering with no orientation selectivity. The wavelet transform in two dimensions has the same properties as a one-dimensional wavelet transform. There is an energy conservation equation

$$
\int_{-\infty}^{+\infty} \int_{-\infty}^{+\infty} \int_0^{+\infty} \left| Wf(s, (u, v)) \right|^2 s \, ds \, du \, dv
$$
$$
= C_\Psi \int_{-\infty}^{+\infty} \int_{-\infty}^{+\infty} \left| f(x, y) \right|^2 dx \, dy. \qquad (39)
$$

As in the one-dimensional case, this equation is proved with the Parseval theorem. We can also reconstruct a function $f(x, y)$ from its wavelet transform with a simple two-dimensional extension of (24):

$$
f(x, y) = \frac{1}{C_\Psi} \int_{-\infty}^{+\infty} \int_{-\infty}^{+\infty} \int_0^{+\infty} Wf(s, (u, v))
$$
$$
\cdot \Psi_s(x - u, y - v) s \, ds \, du \, dv. \qquad (40)
$$

In two dimensions, a wavelet transform also satisfies a reproducing kernel equation similar to (25).

For image recognition applications, it is often necessary to have a decomposition which differentiates the local orientation of the image features. Let us define N wavelet functions $\Psi^i(x, y)$ ($1 \leq i \leq N$) whose Fourier transform $\hat{\Psi}^i(\omega_x, \omega_y)$ satisfies

$$
\sum_{i=1}^{N} \left| \hat{\Psi}^i(\omega_s, \omega_y) \right|^2 = \left| \hat{\Psi}(\omega_s, \omega_y) \right|^2. \qquad (41)
$$

Fig. 14 shows an example of decomposition of $\hat{\Psi}(\omega_x, \omega_y)$ into the different functions $\hat{\Psi}^i(\omega_x, \omega_y)$. In the example shown in Fig. 14, the decomposition is symmetrical, but this is not a constraint of the model. Each function $\Psi^i(x, y)$ can be viewed as the impulse response of a band-pass filter having a particular orientation tuning. The wavelet

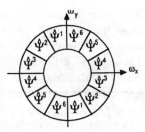

Fig. 14. Decomposition in the Fourier domain of the support of $\hat{\Psi}(\omega_x, \omega_y)$ into 6 wavelets $\hat{\Psi}^i(\omega_x, \omega_y)$ ($1 \leq i \leq 6$) having different orientation selectivities. In this example, the supports of the functions $\hat{\Psi}^i(\omega_x, \omega_y)$ are symmetrical about 0 and are rotated from one another.

transform within the orientation i is defined by

$$
W^i f(s, (u, v))
$$
$$
= \int_{-\infty}^{+\infty} \int_{-\infty}^{+\infty} f(x, y) s \Psi^i(s(x - u), s(y - v)) \, dx \, dy.
$$
$$(42)$$

Let $\Psi_s^i(x, y) = s\Psi^i(sx, sy)$ and $\tilde{\Psi}_s^i(x, y) = \Psi_s^i(-x, -y)$. The wavelet transform of $f(x, y)$ at the scale s and a point (u, v), within the orientation i, can be rewritten

$$
W^i f(s, (u, v)) = f * \tilde{\Psi}_s^i(u, v). \qquad (43)
$$

It can thus be interpreted as a filtering of $f(x, y)$ with a band-pass filter having an orientation selectivity. Similar to (37), the wavelet decomposition in several orientations defines an isometry from $L^2(R^2)$ into $L^2(R^+ \times R^2)$

$$
\sum_{i=1}^{N} \int_{-\infty}^{+\infty} \int_{-\infty}^{+\infty} \int_0^{+\infty} \left| W^i f(s, (u, v)) \right|^2 s \, ds \, du \, dv
$$
$$
= C_\Psi \int_{-\infty}^{+\infty} \int_{-\infty}^{+\infty} \left| f(x, y) \right|^2 dx \, dy. \qquad (44)
$$

We can also reconstruct a function $f(x, y)$ from its wavelet transform decomposed into several directions

$$
f(x, y) = \frac{1}{C_\Psi} \sum_{i=1}^{N} \int_{-\infty}^{+\infty} \int_{-\infty}^{+\infty} \int_0^{+\infty} Wf^i(s, (u, v))
$$
$$
\cdot \Psi_s^i(x - u, y - v) s \, ds \, du \, dv.
$$

The discretization of a wavelet transform in two dimensions is similar to the discretization in one dimension. We choose a sequence of scales $(\alpha^j)_{j \in Z}$ where α is the elementary dilation step. For each scale α^j, the translation vector (u, v) is uniformly sampled on a two-dimensional grid at a rate proportional to α^j. In the next section, we study the two-dimensional extension of the orthonormal wavelet decomposition and its implementation.

IV. COMPUTER VISION AND MULTIRESOLUTION DECOMPOSITION

Let us now analyze the multiresolution approach to image interpretation. A multiresolution decomposition is also an image decomposition in frequency channels of constant bandwidth on a logarithmic scale. It provides a different perspective on this kind of transform. We describe the classical pyramidal implementation of multiresolution transforms and show how it relates to a discrete wavelet decomposition.

Multiresolution transforms have been thoroughly studied in computer vision since the work of Rosenfeld and Thurston [51] on multiscale edge detection, and the Marr theory of low-level vision [40]. At different resolutions, the details of an image generally characterize different types of physical structures. For example, a coarse resolution satellite image of a coast gives a description of only the overall shape of the coast. When the resolution of the image is increased, we are able to successively distinguish the local relief of the region, and if the resolution gets even finer, we can recognize the different types of local vegetation. In order to process these different structures separately, researchers in computer vision have tried to extract the difference of information between the approximation of an image at two different resolutions. Given a sequence of increasing resolutions $(r_j)_{j \in Z}$, the details of $f(x)$ at the resolution r_j are defined as the difference of information between the approximation of $f(x)$ at the resolution r_{j+1} and the approximation at the resolution r_j.

A multiresolution representation also provides a simple hierarchical framework for interpreting the image information [29]. In some sense, the details of the image at a coarse resolution provide the "context" of the image, whereas the finer details correspond to the particular "modalities." For example, it is difficult to recognize that a small rectangle inside an image is the window of a house if we did not previously recognize the house "context." It is therefore natural to first analyze the image details at a coarse resolution and then increase the resolution. This is called a coarse-to-fine processing strategy. At a coarse resolution, the image details are characterized by very few samples. Hence, the coarse information processing can be performed quickly. The finer details are characterized by more samples, but the prior information, derived from the context, constrains and thus speeds up the computations. With a coarse-to-fine strategy, we process the minimum amount of details which are necessary to perform a recognition task. Indeed, if we can recognize an object from a coarse description, we do not need to analyze the finer details. For example, in order to distinguish a car from a house, the coarse details of the image should be enough. Such a strategy is efficient for pattern recognition algorithms. It has already been widely studied for low-level image processing tasks such as stereo matching and template matching [19], [22].

A. Pyramidal Multiresolution Decompositions

The approximation of a signal $f(x)$ at a resolution r is defined as an estimate of $f(x)$ derived from r measurements per unit length. These measurements are computed by uniformly sampling at a rate r the function $f(x)$ smoothed by a low-pass filter whose bandwidth is proportional to r. In order to be consistent when the resolution varies, these low-pass filters are derived from a unique function $\theta(x)$ which is dilated by the resolution

factor r: $\theta_r = \sqrt{r}\theta(rx)$. The set of measurements $A_r f = (f * \theta_r(n/r))_{n \in Z}$ is called a discrete approximation of $f(x)$ at the resolution r. In the following, we study the approximation of a function on a dyadic sequence of resolutions $(2^j)_{j \in Z}$. The discrete approximation of a function $f(x)$ at the resolution 2^j is thus given by

$$A_{2^j} f = \left(f * \theta_{2^j}\left(\frac{n}{2^j}\right) \right)_{n \in Z}. \tag{45}$$

Tanimoto and Pavlidis [56], Burt [4], and Crowley [10] have developed efficient algorithms to compute the approximation of a function at different resolutions. We first describe these decompositions and then explain the Burt and Crowley algorithms for computing the details at different resolutions. The details are regrouped in a pyramid data structure called a Laplacian pyramid. This simple and elegant algorithm does not define the details from the difference of information between $A_{2^{j+1}} f$ and $A_{2^j} f$. At different resolutions, the details computed with this algorithm are correlated. It is thus difficult to know whether a similarity between the image details at different resolutions is due to a property of the image itself or to the intrinsic redundancy of the representation. We review the multiresolution wavelet model which shows that the difference of information between two successive resolutions can be computed by decomposing the signal in a wavelet orthonormal basis.

In pyramidal multiresolution algorithms, the low-pass filter function $\theta(x)$ is chosen such that its Fourier transform can be written

$$\hat{\theta}(\omega) = \prod_{p=1}^{+\infty} U(e^{-i2^{-p}\omega}), \tag{46}$$

where $U(e^{-i\omega})$ is the transfer function of a low-pass discrete filter $U = (u_n)_{n \in Z}$. Daubechies [11] studied the regularity and decay at infinity of the function $\theta(x)$ depending upon the properties of the filter $U(e^{-i\omega})$. In general, we want to have a function $\theta(x)$ which is as smooth as possible and which is well concentrated around 0 in the spatial domain.

Let us suppose that we have already computed the discrete approximation of a function $f(x) \in L^2(R)$ at the resolution 2^{j+1}: $A_{2^{j+1}} f = (f * \theta_{2^{j+1}}(n/2^{j+1}))_{n \in Z}$. One can show [4], [11], [38] that the discrete approximation of $f(x)$ at a resolution 2^j is calculated by filtering $A_{2^{j+1}} f$ with the discrete low-pass filter $U = (u_n)_{n \in Z}$ and keeping every other sample of the convolution product. Let $\Lambda = (\lambda_n)_{n \in Z}$ be such that

$$\Lambda = A_{2^{j+1}} f * U, \tag{47}$$

then

$$A_{2^j} f = (\lambda_{2n})_{n \in Z}. \tag{48}$$

A measuring device provides the approximation of an input signal at a finite resolution. Let us suppose for normalization purposes that this resolution is equal to one. The approximation of this signal at any resolution 2^{-J}, J

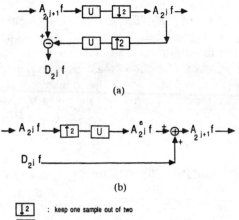

(a)

(b)

$\boxed{\downarrow 2}$: keep one sample out of two

$\boxed{\uparrow 2}$: put a zero between each sample

$\boxed{U}$: convolution with the discrete filter U

Fig. 15. (a) Decomposition of $A_{2^{j+1}}f$ into $A_{2^j}f$ and $D_{2^j}f$ when computing a Laplacian pyramid. (b) Reconstruction of $A_{2^{j+1}}f$ from $A_{2^j}f$ and $D_{2^j}f$ when reconstructing the original signal from a Laplacian pyramid.

> 0, can be computed by iterating on (47) and (48), and j varying between 0 and $J + 1$. This pyramidal algorithm is illustrated in Fig. 15(a). The set of discrete approximations $(A_{2^j}f)_{0 \geq j \geq -J}$ was called a Gaussian pyramid by Burt [4].

We now describe the algorithm of Burt [4] and Crowley [10] in order to extract the details of $f(x)$ which appear in $A_{2^{j+1}}f$ but not in $A_{2^j}f$. The discrete approximation $A_{2^{j+1}}f$ has twice as many samples as $A_{2^j}f$, so we first expand $A_{2^j}f$ by a factor of two. This is performed with a classical interpolation procedure [9]. We put a zero between each sample of $A_{2^j}f$ and filter the resulting signal with a low-pass filter. In this algorithm, the low-pass filter is the filter U defined previously. Let $A^e_{2^j}f$ be the expanded discrete signal. The details $D_{2^j}f$ at the resolution 2^j are then computed by subtracting $A^e_{2^j}f$ from $A_{2^{j+1}}f$

$$D_{2^j}f = A_{2^{j+1}}f - A^e_{2^j}f. \qquad (49)$$

This algorithm decomposes a discrete approximation $A_1 f$ at a resolution of 1 into an approximation $A_{2^{-J}}f$ at a coarse resolution 2^{-J} and the successive detail signals $(D_{2^j}f)_{0 < j \leq -J}$. If the signal $A_1 f$ has N nonzero samples, each detail signal $D_{2^j}f$ has $2^{j+1}N$ samples, whereas the coarse signal $A_{2^{-J}}f$ has $2^{-j}N$ samples. Hence, the total number of samples of this representation is approximately $2N$. The signals $\{A_{2^{-J}}f, (D_{2^j}f)_{0 < j \leq -J}\}$ are regrouped in a data structure called a Laplacian pyramid [4].

The original signal can easily be reconstructed from such a decomposition. At each resolution, we compute $A_{2^{j+1}}f$ by expanding $A_{2^j}f$ by a factor two and adding the details $D_{2^j}f$. By repeating this algorithm when j is varying between $-J$ and 0, we reconstruct $A_1 f$. The reconstruction algorithm is illustrated by a block diagram in Fig. 15(b).

In two dimensions, the discrete approximation of a signal $f(x, y) \in L^2(R^2)$ at the resolution 2^j is similarly defined by

$$A_{2^j}f = (f * \Theta_{2^j}(2^{-j}n, 2^{-j}m))_{(n,m) \in Z^2}, \qquad (50)$$

where $\Theta(x, y)$ is a two-dimensional low-pass filter, and $\Theta_{2^j}(x, y) = 2^j \Theta(2^j x, 2^j y)$. For image processing, the pyramidal algorithm is extended with separable convolutions along the rows and columns of the image [4]. The low-pass filter $\Theta(x, y)$ is chosen such that its Fourier transform can be written

$$\hat{\Theta}(\omega_x, \omega_y) = \prod_{p=1}^{+\infty} U(e^{-i2^{-p}\omega_x}) U(e^{-i2^{-p}\omega_y}).$$

Let us suppose that the video camera provides an image approximated at the resolution 1: $A_1 f = (f * \Theta(n, m))_{(n,m) \in Z^2}$. With a separable extension of the algorithm described in (47) and (48), we can compute the approximation of an image at any resolutions 2^j, ($j < 0$). Fig. 16 shows an image approximated at the resolution 2^j for $0 \geq j \geq -3$ (Gaussian pyramid). The detail signals $(D_{2^j}f)_{0 < j \leq -3}$ can also be computed with a straightforward extension of the one-dimensional algorithm. Fig. 17 shows the Laplacian pyramid of the image given in Fig. 16. If the original image has N^2 pixels, each detail image $D_{2^j}f$ has $2^{j+1}N^2$ pixels and $A_{2^{-J}}f$ has $2^{-J}N^2$ pixels. Hence, the total number of pixels of this representation is approximately $\frac{4}{3}N^2$.

In a Laplacian pyramid, the signals $D_{2^j}f$ do not correspond to the difference of information between $A_{2^{j+1}}f$ and $A_{2^j}f$. If they did, the total number of pixels representing the signal would be the same as in the original signal. We saw that the number of samples representing the signal is increased by a factor of 2 in one dimension and by a factor of $\frac{4}{3}$ in two dimensions. This is due to the correlation between the detail signals $D_{2^j}f$ at different resolutions. The correlation can be understood and suppressed with the multiresolution wavelet model described in [39] and [38]. It is indeed possible to extract exactly the difference of information between $A_{2^{j+1}}f$ and $A_{2^j}f$ by decomposing the signal into a wavelet orthonormal basis.

Let us first explain the multiresolution wavelet model in one dimension. We saw in (45) that the discrete approximation of a function $f(x)$ at the resolution 2^j is defined by $A_{2^j}f = (f * \theta_{2^j}(2^{-j}n))_{n \in Z}$. Let us denote $\tilde{\theta}_{2^j}(x) = \theta_{2^j}(-x)$. Each convolution product in a point can be rewritten as an inner product in $L^2(R)$

$$A_{2^j}f = (\langle f(x), \tilde{\theta}_{2^j}(x - 2^{-j}n) \rangle)_{n \in Z}. \qquad (51)$$

Let us call the *continuous approximation* of $f(x)$ at the resolution of 2^j the best estimate of $f(x)$ given the sequence of inner products $A_{2^j}f$. By "best" we mean as close as possible to $f(x)$ with respect to the $L^2(R)$ distance (mean square distance). One can easily derive from the projection theorem that this best estimate is equal to the orthogonal projection of $f(x)$ on the vector space V_{2^j} generated by the family of functions $(\tilde{\theta}_{2^j}(x - 2^{-j}n))_{n \in Z}$. The vector space V_{2^j} can be viewed as the set of all possible approximations of functions at the resolution 2^j. The sequence of vector spaces $(V_{2^j})_{j \in Z}$ is called a *multiresolution approximation* of $L^2(R)$. The proper-

Fig. 16. Gaussian pyramid. The image is approximated at the resolutions $1, \frac{1}{2}, \frac{1}{4}$, and $\frac{1}{8}$. As the resolution decreases, higher resolution details are lost and the image is characterized by fewer pixels.

Fig. 17. Laplacian pyramid. This figure shows the detail images at the resolution $\frac{1}{2}, \frac{1}{4}, \frac{1}{8}$ and the coarse image approximated at the resolution $\frac{1}{8}$. At each resolution, the pixels of the detail image have a large amplitude when the original image is not "smooth" at the corresponding location.

ties of the vector space V_{2^j} are further studied in [38] and [39]. For any function $f(x) \in L^2(R)$, the continuous approximation of $f(x)$ at the resolution 2^j is thus given by the orthogonal projection of $f(x)$ on V_{2^j}. In order to compute this approximation, we need an orthonormal basis of V_{2^j}. One can show [39] that we can build such an orthonormal basis by dilating and translating a particular function $\phi(x)$ called a *scaling function*. For any resolution 2^j, let us denote $\phi_{2^j}(x) = \sqrt{2^j}\phi(2^j x)$. The family of functions $(\phi_{2^j}(x - 2^{-j}n))_{n \in Z}$ is then an orthonormal basis of V_{2^j}. The Fourier transform of $\phi(x)$ is characterized by

$$\hat{\phi}(\omega) = \prod_{p=1}^{+\infty} H(e^{-i2^{-p}\omega}), \qquad (52)$$

where $H(e^{-i\omega})$ is the transfer function of a discrete filter [39]. One can show that $H(e^{-i\omega})$ satisfies the condition

$$\left| H(e^{-i\omega}) \right|^2 + \left| H(-e^{-i\omega}) \right|^2 = 1. \qquad (53)$$

The discrete filters $H = (h_n)_{n \in Z}$ whose transfer function satisfy (53) are called *quadrature mirror* filters [14].

The orthogonal projection of a function $f(x) \in L^2(R)$ on V_{2^j} can now be computed by decomposing $f(x)$ into the orthonormal basis $(\phi_{2^j}(x - 2^{-j}n))_{n \in Z}$. Let $P_{V_{2^j}}$ be

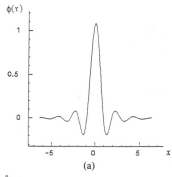

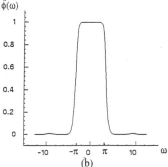

Fig. 18. (a) Example of scaling function $\phi(x)$. (b) Fourier transform $\hat{\phi}(\omega)$. A scaling function can be interpreted as the impulse response of a low-pass filter. The computation of this particular function is described in [38]. The corresponding orthogonal wavelet is shown in Fig. 13.

the orthogonal projection operator on V_{2^j}:

$$P_{V_{2^j}}(f)(x)$$
$$= \sum_{n \in Z} \langle f(u), \phi_{2^j}(u - 2^{-j}n) \rangle \phi_{2^j}(x - 2^{-j}n). \qquad (54)$$

Let us denote $\tilde{\phi}(x) = \phi(-x)$. Since $\phi(x)$ is a low-pass filter, we can redefine the discrete approximation $A_{2^j}f$ with the function $\tilde{\phi}(x)$ instead of $\theta(x)$

$$A_{2^j}f = \left(f * \tilde{\phi}_{2^j}(2^{-j}n) \right)_{n \in Z}$$
$$= \left(\langle f(x), \phi_{2^j}(x - 2^{-j}n) \rangle \right)_{n \in Z}. \qquad (55)$$

The best estimate of $f(x)$ can easily be derived from this discrete approximation by using (54). Let $\tilde{H}$ be the discrete filter whose impulse response is $(h_{-n})_{n \in Z}$. From (52) and (55), one can show [38] that the discrete approximations, $A_{2^j}f$, are computed with the same pyramidal algorithm described in (47) and (48), by using the discrete filter $\tilde{H}$ instead of U. Fig. 18 gives the graph of a scaling function $\phi(x)$.

Let us now explain how to extract exactly the difference of information between the approximations of a function at the resolutions 2^j and 2^{j+1}. The approximations of a function $f(x) \in L^2(R)$ at the resolutions 2^j and 2^{j+1} are given by the orthogonal projection of $f(x)$ on the vector spaces V_{2^j} and $V_{2^{j+1}}$, respectively. Intuitively, the approximation at the resolution 2^{j+1} must give a better estimate of $f(x)$ than the approximation at the resolution 2^j. Hence, the vector spaces V_{2^j} and $V_{2^{j+1}}$ should satisfy

$$V_{2^j} \subset V_{2^{j+1}}. \qquad (56)$$

The difference of information between the approximations at the resolutions 2^j and 2^{j+1} is therefore equal to the orthogonal projection of $f(x)$ on the orthogonal complement of V_{2^j} in $V_{2^{j+1}}$. Let O_{2^j} be this orthogonal complement. The vector space O_{2^j} is orthogonal to V_{2^j} and satisfies

$$O_{2^j} \oplus V_{2^j} = V_{2^{j+1}}.$$

To compute the orthogonal projection of a function $f(x)$ on O_{2^j}, we need to find an orthonormal basis of O_{2^j}. One can show [39] that such an orthonormal basis can be built by dilating and translating a particular wavelet $\psi(x)$. For any resolution 2^j, let us denote $\psi_{2^j}(x) = \sqrt{2^j}\psi(2^j x)$. The family of functions $(\psi_{2^j}(x - 2^{-j}n))_{n \in Z}$ is then an orthonormal basis of O_{2^j}. The Fourier transform of $\psi(x)$ is given by

$$\hat{\psi}(2\omega) = G(e^{-i\omega})\hat{\phi}(\omega)$$
$$\text{with } G(e^{-i\omega}) = e^{-i\omega}\overline{H(e^{-i\omega})}. \quad (57)$$

$G(e^{-i\omega})$ is the transfer function of a discrete filter $G = (g_n)_{n \in Z}$. The filters G and H make a pair of quadrature mirror filters [54].

When the resolution 2^j varies between 0 and $+\infty$, the family of functions $(\psi_{2^j}(x - 2^{-j}n))_{(n,j) \in Z^2}$ constitutes a wavelet orthonormal basis of $L^2(R)$ [39]. This shows that the multiresolution concept and quadrature mirror filters are directly related to wavelet orthonormal bases.

Let $P_{O_{2^j}}f(x)$ be the orthonormal projection of a function $f(x) \in L^2(R)$ on the vector space O_{2^j}. $P_{O_{2^j}}f(x)$ gives the difference of information between the approximations of $f(x)$ at the resolutions of 2^j and 2^{j+1}. It can be computed by expanding $f(x)$ in the orthonormal basis of O_{2^j}

$$P_{O_{2^j}}f(x)$$
$$= \sum_{n \in Z} \langle f(u), \psi_{2^j}(u - 2^{-j}n) \rangle \psi_{2^j}(x - 2^{-j}n). \quad (58)$$

This difference of information is characterized by the set of inner products

$$D_{2^j}f = (\langle f(x), \psi_{2^j}(x - 2^{-j}n) \rangle)_{n \in Z}. \quad (59)$$

Let $\tilde{G}$ be the filter whose impulse response is given by $\tilde{G} = (g_{-n})_{n \in Z}$. From (55), (57), and (59), one can derive that $D_{2^j}f$ is computed by filtering $A_{2^j}f$ with $\tilde{G}$ and keeping every other sample of the convolution product [38]. This algorithm is illustrated by the block diagram shown in Fig. 19(a); it is essentially similar to a quadrature mirror filter bank decomposition [14].

Let us now describe a simple two-dimensional extension of the one-dimensional multiresolution wavelet model. We saw that a separable multiresolution representation is computed by filtering the signal with a low-pass filter $\Theta(x, y) = \theta(x)\theta(y)$ [(50)]. Let $\tilde{\Theta}(x, y) = \Theta(-x, -y)$. The discrete approximation of a function $f(x, y) \in L^2(R^2)$ at the resolution 2^j can also be rewritten

$$A_{2^j}f = (\langle f(x, y),$$
$$\tilde{\Theta}_{2^j}(x - 2^{-j}n, y - 2^{-j}m) \rangle)_{(n,m) \in Z^2}. \quad (60)$$

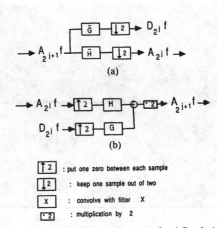

$\boxed{\uparrow 2}$: put one zero between each sample

$\boxed{\downarrow 2}$: keep one sample out of two

$\boxed{X}$: convolve with filter X

$\boxed{\cdot 2}$: multiplication by 2

Fig. 19. (a) Decomposition of $A_{2^{j+1}}f$ into $A_{2^j}f$ and $D_{2^j}f$ when computing an orthogonal wavelet representation. The filters H and G make a pair of quadrature mirror filters. (b) Reconstruction of $A_{2^{j+1}}f$ from $A_{2^j}f$ and $D_{2^j}f$ when reconstructing the original signal from an orthogonal wavelet representation.

The extension of the one-dimensional model is straightforward. The best estimate of $f(x, y)$ given the inner products of $A_{2^j}f$ is equal to the orthogonal projection of $f(x, y)$ on the vector space V_{2^j} generated by the family of functions

$$(\tilde{\Theta}_{2^j}(x - 2^{-j}n, y - 2^{-j}m))_{(n,m) \in Z^2}. \quad (61)$$

The sequence of vector spaces $(V_{2^j})_{j \in Z}$ is called a multiresolution approximation of $L^2(R^2)$. Similarly to the one-dimensional model, the difference of information between the approximation of a signal $f(x, y)$ at the resolutions 2^j and 2^{j+1} is equal to the orthogonal projection of $f(x, y)$ on the orthogonal complement O_{2^j} of V_{2^j} in $V_{2^{j+1}}$. We can build [45] an orthonormal basis of O_{2^j} by scaling and translating three wavelets: $\Psi^1(x, y)$, $\Psi^2(x, y)$, and $\Psi^3(x, y)$. Let us denote $\Psi^i_{2^j}(x, y) = 2^j\Psi^i(2^j x, 2^j y)$ for $1 \le i \le 3$. The family of functions

$$\begin{cases} 2^{-j}\Psi^1_{2^j}(x - 2^{-j}n, y - 2^{-j}m) \\ 2^{-j}\Psi^2_{2^j}(x - 2^{-j}n, y - 2^{-j}m) \\ 2^{-j}\Psi^3_{2^j}(x - 2^{-j}n, y - 2^{-j}m) \end{cases}_{(n,m) \in Z^2} \quad (62)$$

is an orthonormal basis of O_{2^j}. When the resolution 2^j varies between 0 and $+\infty$, the family of functions

$$\begin{cases} 2^{-j}\Psi^1_{2^j}(x - 2^{-j}n, y - 2^{-j}m) \\ 2^{-j}\Psi^2_{2^j}(x - 2^{-j}n, y - 2^{-j}m) \\ 2^{-j}\Psi^3_{2^j}(x - 2^{-j}n, y - 2^{-j}m) \end{cases}_{(n,m,j) \in Z^3} \quad (63)$$

is a wavelet orthonormal basis of $L^2(R^2)$. Fig. 20 shows approximately the frequency support of the three wavelets $\Psi^1(x, y)$, $\Psi^2(x, y)$, $\Psi^3(x, y)$. Each wavelet $\Psi^i(x, y)$ can be interpreted as the impulse response of a band-pass filter having a specific orientation selectivity. This corresponds to a particular case of oriented two-dimensional discrete wavelet transform.

In two dimensions, the difference of information between the approximations $A_{2^{j+1}}f$ and $A_{2^j}f$ is therefore

258

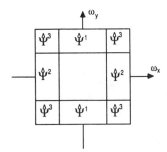

Fig. 20. Approximate repartition of the frequency support of $\hat{\Psi}^1(\omega_x, \omega_y)$, $\hat{\Psi}^2(\omega_x, \omega_y)$, and $\hat{\Psi}^3(\omega_x, \omega_y)$ in the frequency plane.

characterized by the sequences of inner products

$$D_{2^j}^1 f = \left(\left\langle f(x, y),\right.\right.$$
$$\left.\left.\Psi_{2^j}^1(x - 2^{-j}n, y - 2^{-j}m)\right\rangle\right)_{(n,m)\in\mathbf{Z}^2},$$

$$D_{2^j}^2 f = \left(\left\langle f(x, y),\right.\right.$$
$$\left.\left.\Psi_{2^j}^2(x - 2^{-j}n, y - 2^{-j}m)\right\rangle\right)_{(n,m)\in\mathbf{Z}^2},$$

$$D_{2^j}^3 f = \left(\left\langle f(x, y),\right.\right.$$
$$\left.\left.\Psi_{2^j}^3(x - 2^{-j}n, y - 2^{-j}m)\right\rangle\right)_{(n,m)\in\mathbf{Z}^2}.$$

Each of these sequences of inner products can be considered as an image. $D_{2^j}^1 f$ gives the vertical higher frequencies (horizontal edges), $D_{2^j}^2 f$ gives the horizontal higher frequencies (vertical edges), and $D_{2^j}^3 f$ gives the higher frequencies in both directions (corners) (see Fig. 21). Let us suppose that initially we have an image $A_1 f$ measured at the resolution 1. For any $J > 0$, this discrete image can be decomposed between the resolutions 1 and 2^{-J}, and completely represented by the $3J + 1$ discrete images

$$\left(A_{2^{-J}} f, (D_{2^j}^1 f)_{-J \le j \le -1}, (D_{2^j}^2 f)_{-J \le j \le -1},\right.$$
$$\left.(D_{2^j}^3 f)_{-J \le j \le -1}\right).$$

This set of images is called an *orthogonal wavelet representation* in two dimensions [38]. The image $A_{2^{-J}} f$ is a coarse approximation, and the images $D_{2^j}^i f$ give the image details for different orientations and resolutions. If the original image has N^2 pixels, each image $A_{2^j} f$, $D_{2^j}^1 f$, $D_{2^j}^2 f$, $D_{2^j}^3 f$ has $2^j \cdot N^2$ pixels ($j < 0$). The total number of pixels of an orthogonal wavelet representation is therefore equal to N^2. It does not increase the volume of data. This is due to the orthogonality of the representation.

A wavelet representation can be computed with a separable extension of the algorithm illustrated in Fig. 19(a) [38]. This extension corresponds to a separable quadrature mirror filter decomposition as described by Woods [63]. Fig. 21(b) gives the wavelet representation of the image in Fig. 16. From this representation, we can reconstruct the original image with a two-dimensional separable extension of the algorithm illustrated in Fig. 19(b) [38]. Fig. 21(c) is the reconstructed image from the wavelet representation shown in Fig. 21(b). The reconstruction is numerically stable. It enables us to use this type of rep-

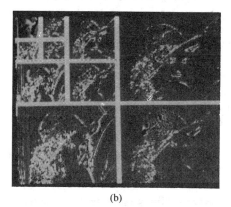

(a)

(b)

(c)

Fig. 21. (a) Labeling of the detail images shown in the wavelet representation. (b) Orthogonal wavelet representation of the lady image for $J = 3$. At a given resolution, each detail image corresponds to a particular spatial orientation tuning. (c) Reconstruction of the original image from the orthogonal wavelet representation. The reconstruction is numerically stable.

resentation for image coding. A more general nonseparable extension of the wavelet model was studied by Meyer [43]. Such extensions are, however, more difficult to implement and are computationally more expensive.

B. Applications of Multiresolution Transforms

The wavelet model gives a precise understanding of the concept of multiresolution by introducing the sequence of vector spaces $(V_{2^j})_{j\in\mathbf{Z}}$. A noncorrelated multiresolution representation can be built by decomposing the signal into a wavelet orthonormal basis. A difficult problem when using a multiresolution representation for analyzing a scene is to relate the details appearing at different resolutions. Many ad hoc techniques have been developed for this purpose. We saw in Section III-D that the local regularity of a function is provided by the decay rate of the wavelet coefficients when the resolution increases. These theorems give a first approach for comparing the value of the decomposition at different resolutions.

Multiband image decompositions are also well adapted for coding images because it is possible to match the human visual system sensitivity and take advantage of the intrinsic statistical properties of images. The contrast sensitivity function (Fig. 3) shows that the sensitivity of human vision depends upon the frequency of the stimulus. We want to quantize each frequency band with the minimum number of bits, and at the same time try to reconstruct the best possible image for the human visual perception. For this purpose, we adapt the quantization noise to the human sensitivity along each frequency band. The more sensitive the human system, the less quantization noise is introduced. This enables us to introduce a minimum amount of perceivable distortion in the reconstructed image. Watson has done some particularly detailed psychophysical experiments to test this type of approach for image coding [60].

The statistical properties of images give another reason for using multiband decompositions in image coding. It is well known that the intensity of images is locally correlated. Predictive codings have been particularly successful to compress the number of bits used in coding an image. The wavelet coefficients give a measure of the local contrast at different scales. Since the image intensity is locally correlated, these local contrasts generally have a small amplitude [38]. We can take advantage of this property for coding the wavelet coefficients on fewer bits without introducing any noticeable distortion. As explained in the previous section, a wavelet orthogonal representation can also be imterpreted as a decomposition into a quadrature mirror filter bank. Several studies in image processing have already shown the efficiency of these filter banks for data compression [1], [63].

In order to use a multiresolution representation for pattern recognition applications, we must be able to build models of patterns within the multiresolution representation. The patterns might be located anywhere in the image. Hence, the models must be independent from the pattern location. When a pattern is translated, its model should only be translated but not modified. Let us show that a multiresolution representation does not verify this translation property. To simplify the explanation, we consider the particular case of a one-dimensional orthogonal wavelet decomposition. At the resolution 2^j, the details of a signal $f(x) \in L^2(R)$ are defined by

$$D_{2^j} f = \left(\langle f(x), \Psi_{2^j}(x - 2^{-j}n) \rangle \right)_{n \in Z}.$$

$D_{2^j} f$ can be expressed as a uniform sampling of the wavelet transform at the scale 2^j

$$D_{2^j} f = \left(Wf(2^j, 2^{-j}n) \right)_{n \in Z}.$$

Let $g(x) = f(x - \tau)$ be a translation of $f(x)$ by τ. Since a wavelet transform can be written as a convolution product [(22)], it is shift invariant

$$Wg(2^j, u) = Wf(2^j, u - \tau).$$

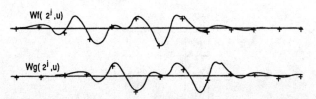

Fig. 22. This drawing shows that the sampling of a wavelet transform (given by the crosses) can be very different after translating the signal. The wavelet transform is translated but the sampling does not translate if the translation is not proportional to the sampling interval (adapted from [37]).

However, the sampling of $Wg(2^j, u)$ does not correspond to a translation of the sampling of $Wf(2^j, u)$ unless $\tau = k2^{-j}$, $k \in Z$ (see Fig. 22).

This distortion through translation implies that the wavelet coefficients of a pattern at the resolution 2^j depend upon the position of the pattern modulo 2^{-j}. This property is inherent to the notion of resolution. Indeed, at the resolution 2^j, we cannot measure anything smaller than 2^{-j} so we cannot represent a displacement smaller than 2^{-j}. One can find the same problem in all the pyramidal multiresolution representations and any uniform sampling of a wavelet transform.

A first solution to this translation problem is to sample the wavelet transform $Wf(2^j, u)$ at a rate much larger than 2^j. The samples then translate approximately when the signal translates. However, this solution considerably increases the redundancy of the representation and the translation is still not perfect. This technique is often adopted for pattern recognition algorithms based on pyramid decompositions. A second solution consists of defining a representation based on an adaptive sampling of the functions $Wf(2^j, u)$ which translates when the signal translates.

V. Zero Crossings of Multifrequency Channels

In the previous sections we studied the properties of the decomposition of a function into multifrequency channels of constant size on a logarithmic scale. We saw that such a decomposition can be interpreted as a wavelet transform. We then described the properties and applications of a discrete wavelet transform built from a uniform sampling of the continuous wavelet transform. However, we showed that such a discretization is difficult to use for pattern recognition applications because it is not invariant through translation. Here, we review the characterization of a signal from the zero crossings of a wavelet transform. Such a characterization defines a discrete representation which translates when the signal translates.

If a function $f(x)$ is translated, for each scale s, the function $Wf(s, u)$ is translated along the parameter u. Hence, the zero crossings of $Wf(s, u)$ are translated as well. Let us suppose that $\psi(x)$ is equal to the second derivative of a smoothing function $\xi(x)$

$$\psi(x) = \xi''(x).$$

A smoothing function is a function which can be interpreted as the impulse response of a low-pass filter. Any zero crossing of $Wf(s, u)$ corresponds to a point of abrupt change in the function $f(x)$ smoothed by $\xi_s(x) = \sqrt{s}\,\xi(sx)$. Indeed, if $\psi(x) = \xi''(x)$

$$Wf(s, u) = f * \bar{\psi}_s(u) = s^2(f * \xi_s)''(u).$$

Hence, a zero crossing of $Wf(s, u)$ is an inflection point of the function $f(x)$ smoothed by $\xi_s(x)$. Fig. 23 illustrates this on a straight edge. This zero-crossing detection is a standard edge finding operation in computer vision [41].

Let us now study the completeness of stability of such a representation. Is it possible to reconstruct $f(x)$ from the zero crossings of $Wf(s, u)$? We know that a wavelet transform $Wf(s, u)$ defines a stable and complete representation of $f(x)$. It is therefore equivalent to study the reconstruction of $Wf(s, u)$ from its own zero crossings. If the function $Wf(s, u)$ was *a priori* any function of $L^2(R^+ \times R)$, it is clear that such a reconstruction would not be possible. Indeed, for a given set of zero crossings, there is an infinite number of functions in $L^2(R^+ \times R)$ whose zero crossings correspond to this set. However, we saw that a wavelet transform $Wf(s, u)$ is not any function of $L^2(R^+ \times R)$. It verifies the constraint of the reproducing kernel [(25)]. We must therefore study whether the constraint of the reproducing kernel plus the information on the zero-crossing positions is enough to have a stable characterization of $Wf(s, u)$.

An interesting particular case of wavelet transform consists of choosing a wavelet equal to the Laplacian of a Gaussian. Since a Gaussian is a smoothing function, the zero crossings of such a wavelet transform can also be interpreted as signal edges [41]. In this particular case, the intrinsic redundancy of the wavelet transform $Wf(s, u)$ can be expressed with the differential equation of heat diffusion [29]. By applying the maximum principles to the solutions of the heat differential equation, Hummel [24] proved that a function $f(x)$ is indeed characterized by the zero crossings of $Wf(s, u)$. However, Hummel also showed that this characterization is not stable. So a slight perturbation of the zero crossings may correspond a substantial perturbation of the high frequencies of the reconstructed function. Reconstruction algorithms have been developed on images by Sanz and Huang [53] as well as Zeevi and Rotem [64]. These reconstruction algorithms are iterative. They were not able to reconstruct the image perfectly in both cases. Hummel and Moniot [25] tried to stabilize the zero-crossings representation by also recording the value of the gradient of $Wf(s, u)$ along each zero crossing. By adding the gradient information, they have shown experimentally that one can then compute a stable reconstruction of $f(x)$ from the zero crossings of $Wf(s, u)$. In this algorithm, the position of the zero crossings and the value of the gradients are kept along a uniform sequence of scales: $(j\alpha)_{j \in Z}$ with $\alpha > 0$. Such a sequence is much more dense than the dyadic sequences $(2^j)_{j \in Z}$ used when we discretized the wavelet transform.

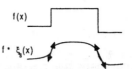

Fig. 23. The zero crossings of a wavelet transform provide the location of the inflection points (edges) of $f * \xi_s(x)$ (adapted from [37]).

Another way to stabilize a zero-crossing representation is to record the energy of $Wf(s, u)$ between two consecutive zero crossings appearing at the same scale [37]. This energy preserves an $L^2(R)$ structure to the zero-crossing representation. In particular, we can then define an $L^2(R)$ distance for pattern recognition applications. By keeping the position of the zero crossings of $Wf(s, u)$ and the local energies only along a dyadic sequence of scales $(2^j)_{j \in Z}$, we showed that the original signal can be reconstructed exactly in few iterations [37]. The reconstruction uses the reproducing kernel equation which is valid for any type of wavelet transform. We believe that the mathematical tools developed within the wavelet model give a simpler approach for analyzing the zero-crossing problem. From a practical point of view, the reconstruction algorithm developed from the reproducing kernel is simple to implement in both one and two dimensions and converges quickly (about 10 iterations).

Representations based on zero crossings of multifrequency channels are still not well understood. They are built with a nonlinear transform which is difficult to model. However, they have very good potential for pattern characterization. They characterize the position of the signal edges and are translation invariant.

VI. CONCLUSION

In this paper, we reviewed the application of multifrequency decompositions to image processing from several viewpoints. We covered some psychophysical and physiological data showing that such a decomposition seems to be implemented in the human visual cortex. We then described the mathematical properties of these decompositions. We first reviewed the properties of a window Fourier transform and explained why this decomposition is not convenient for analyzing signals such as images. We then introduced the wavelet transform and described its most important properties. Although the goal of this paper was not to build any psychophysiological model of the human visual system, it would be interesting to further investigate the relevance of the wavelet model to some low-level processes in the visual cortex.

In computer vision, multifrequency channel decompositions are interpreted through the concept of multiresolution. We described the classical pyramidal multiresolution algorithms and the wavelet approach to multiresolution decompositions. This model shows that the difference of information between the approximation of a function at two different resolutions is computed by decomposing the function into a wavelet orthonormal basis. We also explained the relationship between orthonormal wavelets and quadrature mirror filters. We can compute the decomposition of a function into a wavelet orthonormal basis with a quadrature mirror filter bank. A third motivation for using multiband decomposition is due to the intrinsic statistical properties of images. Images have a relatively simple decomposition into frequency subbands. These bands can be coded on fewer bits with no visible distortions.

A uniform sampling of each multifrequency channel defines a representation which is not translation invariant. It is therefore difficult to build pattern recognition algorithms from such decompositions. We reviewed the properties of zero crossing in multiband decompositions. This adaptive sampling is translation invariant but is much more difficult to analyze. We described some previous results and gave the wavelet formalization of this problem through the reproducing kernel equation.

ACKNOWLEDGMENT

I would like to thank particularly R. Bajcsy for her advice on the writing of this paper, and N. Treil for helping me draw the figures.

REFERENCES

[1] E. Adelson and E. Simoncelli, "Orthogonal pyramid transform for image coding," in *Proc. SPIE, Visual Commun. and Image Processing*, 1987.
[2] B. Andrew and D. Pollen, "Relationship between spatial frequency selectivity and receptive field profile of simple cells," *J. Physiol.*, vol. 287, pp. 163–176, 1979.
[3] G. Battle, "A block spin construction of ondelettes, Part 1: Lemarie functions," *Commun. Math. Phys.*, vol. 110, pp. 601–615, 1987.
[4] P. J. Burt and E. H. Adelson, "The Laplacian pyramid as a compact image code," *IEEE Trans. Commun.*, vol. COM-31, pp. 532–540, Apr. 1983.
[5] F. Campbell, R. Carpenter, and J. Levinson, "Visibility of aperiodic patterns compared with cortical cells compared with sinusoidal gratings," *J. Physiol.*, vol. 204, pp. 283–298, 1969.
[6] F. Campbell and D. Green, "Optical and retina factors affecting visual resolution," *J. Physiol.*, vol. 181, pp. 576–593, 1965.
[7] F. Campbell and J. Kulikowski, "Orientation selectivity of the human visual system," *J. Physiol.*, vol. 197, pp. 437–441, 1966.
[8] F. Campbell and J. Robson, "Application of Fourier analysis to the visibility of gratings," *J. Physiol.*, vol. 197, pp. 551–566, 1968.
[9] R. C. Crochiere and L. R. Rabiner, "Interpolation and decimation in signal processing," *Proc. IEEE*, vol. 69, Mar. 1981.
[10] J. Crowley, "A representation for visual information," Tech. Rep. CMU-RI-TR-82-7, Robotic Inst., Carnegie-Mellon Univ., 1987.
[11] I. Daubechies, "Orthonormal bases of compactly supported wavelets," *Commun. Pure Appl. Math.*, vol. 41, pp. 909–996, Nov. 1988.
[12] J. G. Daugmann, "Two-dimensional spectral analysis of cortical receptive field profile," *Vis. Res.*, vol. 20, pp. 847–856, 1980.
[13] ——, "Six formal properties of two dimensional anisotropic visual filter. Structural principles and frequency/orientation selectivity," *IEEE Trans. Syst., Man, Cybern.*, vol. SMC-13, Sept. 1983.
[14] D. Esteban and C. Galand, "Applications of quadrature mirror filters to split band voice coding schemes," in *Proc. Int. Conf. Acoust., Speech, Signal Processing*, May 1977.
[15] P. Federbush, "Quantum field theory in ninety minutes," *Bull. Amer. Math. Soc.*, 1987.
[16] D. Gabor, "Theory of communication," *J. Inst. Elec. Eng.*, London, vol. 93, pp. 429–457, 1946.
[17] M. Georgeson, "Mechanisms of visual image processing: studies of pattern interaction and selective channels in human vision," Ph.D. dissertation, Univ. Sussex, Brighton, England, 1975.
[18] ——, "Spatial Fourier analysis and human vision," in *Tutorial Essays in Psychology, A Guide to Recent Advances*. N. Sutherland, Ed. Hillsdale, NJ: Lawrence Erlbaum Associates, 1979.
[19] W. Grimson, "Computational experiments with a feature based stereo algorithm," *IEEE Trans. Pattern Anal. Machine Intell.*, vol. PAMI-7, pp. 17–34, Jan. 1985.
[20] A. Grossmann and J. Morlet, "Decomposition of Hardy functions into square integrable wavelets of constant shape," *SIAM J. Math.*, vol. 15, pp. 723–736, 1984.
[21] A. Grossmann, J. Morlet, and T. Paul, "Transforms associated to square integrable group representations," *Int. J. Math. Phys.*, vol. 26, pp. 2473–2479, 1986.
[22] E. Hall, J. Rouge, and R. Wong, "Hierarchical search for image matching," in *Proc. Conf. Decision Contr.*, 1976, pp. 791–796.
[23] D. Hubel and T. Wiesel, "Receptive fields, binocular interaction and functional architecture in the cat's visual cortex," *J. Physiol.*, vol. 160, 1962.
[24] R. Hummel, "Representations based on zero-crossings in scale-space," Tech. Rep. 225, Courant Inst. Dep. Comput. Sci., June 1986.
[25] R. Hummel and R. Moniot, "A network approach to reconstruction from zero-crossings," in *Proc. IEEE Workshop Comput. Vis.*, Dec. 1987.
[26] S. Jaffard, "Estimations Holderiennes ponctuelles des fonctions au moyen des coefficients d'ondelettes," *Notes au Compte-Rendu de l'Academie Des Sciences*, France, 1989.
[27] S. Jaffard and Y. Meyer, "Bases d'ondelettes dans des ouverts de Rn," *J. Mathematiques Pures et Appliquees*, 1987.
[28] J. Klauder and B. Skagerstam, in *Coherent States*. Singapore: World Scientific, 1985.
[29] J. Koenderink, "The structure of images," in *Biological Cybernetics*. New York: Springer-Verlag, 1984.
[30] R. Kronland-Martinet, J. Morlet, and A. Grossmann, "Analysis of sound patterns through wavelet transform," *Int. J. Pattern Recogn. Artificial Intell.*, 1988.
[31] J. Kulikowski and P. King-Smith, "Orientation selectivity of grating and line detectors in human vision," *Vis. Res.*, vol. 13, pp. 1455–1478, 1973.
[32] P. G. Lemarie, "Ondelettes a localisation exponentielles," *J. Math. Pures et Appliquees*, 1988.
[33] P. G. Lemarie and Y. Meyer, "Ondelettes et bases Hilbertiennes," *Revista Matematica Ibero Americana*, vol. 2, 1986.
[34] M. D. Levine, *Vision in Man and Machine*. New York: McGraw-Hill, 1985.
[35] L. Maffei and A. Fiorentini, "The unresponsive regions of visula cortical receptive fields," *Vis. Res.*, vol. 16, pp. 1131–1139, 1976.
[36] L. Maffei, C. Morrone, M. Pirchio, and G. Sandini, *J. Physiol.*, vol. 296, pp. 24–47, 1979.
[37] S. Mallat, "Dyadic wavelets energy zero-crossings," Tech. Rep. MS-CIS-88-30, U. Penn., 1988.
[38] ——, "A theory for multiresolution signal decomposition: The wavelet representation," *IEEE Trans. Pattern Anal. Machine Intell.*, vol. 11, pp. 674–693, July 1989.
[39] ——, "Multiresolution approximation and wavelet orthonormal bases of L2," *Trans. Amer. Math. Soc.*, vol. 3-15, pp. 69–87, Sept. 1989.
[40] D. Marr, in *Vision*. San Francisco, CA: Freeman, 1982.
[41] D. Marr and E. Hildreth, "Theory of edge detection," *Proc. Roy. Soc. London*, vol. 207, pp. 187–217, 1980.
[42] D. Marr and T. Poggio, "A theory of human stereo vision," *Proc. Roy. Soc. London*, vol. B 204, pp. 301–328, 1979.
[43] Y. Meyer, "Ondelettes et fonctions splines," presented at the Seminaire Equations aux Derivees Partielles, Ecole Polytechnique, Paris, France, Dec. 1986.
[44] ——, in *Ondelettes et Operateurs*. Paris, France: Hermann, 1988.
[45] ——, "Principe d'incertitude, bases hilbertiennes et algebres d'operateurs," presented at the Bourbaki seminar, 1985–1986, Paper 662.
[46] J. Nachmais and A. Weber, "Discrimination of simple and complex gratings," *Vis. Res.*, vol. 15, pp. 217–223, 1975.
[47] J. Oppenheim and J. Lim, in *Advanced Topics in Signal Processing*, Signal Processings Series. Englewood Cliffs, NJ: Prentice-Hall, 1988, pp. 289–336.
[48] T. Paul, "Affine coherent states and the radial Schrodinger equation. Radial harmonic oscillator and hydrogen atom," preprint.
[49] D. A. Pollen and S. F. Ronner, "Visual corical neurons as localized spatial frequency filter," *IEEE Trans. Syst., Man, Cybern.*, vol. SMC-13, Sept. 1983.
[50] A. Rosenfeld, *Multiresolution Image Processing and Analysis*. New York: Springer-Verlag, 1982.
[51] A. Rosenfeld and M. Thurston, "Edge and curve detection for visual scene analysis," *IEEE Trans. Comput.*, vol. C-20, 1971.

[52] A. Rosenfeld and G. J. Vanderburg, "Coarse-fine template matching," *IEEE Trans. Syst., Man, Cybern.*, vol. SMC-7, pp. 104–107, 1977.

[53] J. Sanz and T. Huang, "Theorem and experiments on image reconstruction from zero-crossings," IBM, Res. Rep. RJ5460.

[54] M. J. Smith and T. P. Barnwell, "Exact reconstruction techniques for tree-structured subband coders," *IEEE Trans. Acoust., Speech, Signal Processing*, vol. ASSP-34, June 1986.

[55] J. Stromberg, "A modified Franklin system and higher-order systems of Rn as unconditional bases for Hardy spaces," in *Proc. Conf. Harmonic Anal. Honor of a. Zygmund*, vol. 2, Wadsworth Math Series, pp. 475–493.

[56] S. Tanimoto and T. Pavlidis. "A hierarchical data structure for image processing," *Comput. Graphics Image Processing*, vol. 4, pp. 104–119, 1975.

[57] P. Tchamitchian, "Biorthogonalite et theorie des operateurs," *Revista Matematica Ibero Americana*, vol. 2, 1986.

[58] M. Turner, "Texture discrimination by Gabor functions," *Biological Cybern.*, vol. 55, pp. 71–82, 1986.

[59] K. De Valois, R. De Valois, and E. Yund, *J. Physiol.*, vol. 291, pp. 483–505, 1979.

[60] A. Watson, "Efficiency of a model human image code," *J. Opt. Soc. Amer.*, vol. 4, pp. 2401–2417, Dec. 1987.

[61] M. Webster and R. De Valois, "Relationship between spatial-frequency and orientation tuning of striate-cortex cells," *J. Opt. Soc. Amer.*, July 1985.

[62] A. Witkin, "Scale space filtering," in *Proc. Int. Joint Conf. Artificial Intell.*, 1983.

[63] J. W. Woods and S. D. O'Neil, "Subband coding of images," *IEEE Trans. Acoust., Speech, Signal Processing*, vol. ASSP-34, Oct. 1986.

[64] Y. Zeevi and D. Rotem, "Image reconstruction from zero crossings," *IEEE Trans. Acoust., Speech, Signal Processing*, vol. ASSP-34, pp. 1269–1277, Oct. 1986.

Article 5.3

Localized Texture Processing in Vision: Analysis and Synthesis in the Gaborian Space

MOSHE PORAT, MEMBER, IEEE, AND YEHOSHUA Y. ZEEVI, MEMBER, IEEE

Abstract—Recent studies of cortical simple cell function suggest that the primitives of image representation in vision have a wavelet form similar to Gabor elementary functions (EF's). It is shown that textures and fully-textured images can be practically decomposed into, and synthesized from, a finite set of EF's. Textured-images can be synthesized from a set of EF's using image coefficient library. Alternatively, texturing of contoured (cartoon-like) images is analogous to adding chromaticity information to contoured images.

A method for texture discrimination and image segmentation using local features based on the Gabor approach is introduced. Features related to the EF's parameters provide efficient means for texture discrimination and classification. This method is invariant under rotation and translation. The performance of the classification appears to be robust with respect to noisy conditions. The results show an insensitivity of the discrimination to relatively high noise levels, comparable to the performances of the human observer.

I. INTRODUCTION

ONE of the main tasks of a visual system (biological or machine vision) is to separate the image into discrete entities or segments in order to understand the scene. This segmentation is based mainly on the detection of differences between the regions, defining the edges between them.

By generalizing the commonly-used definition of texture, known as "property of physical surfaces" to include color and/or intensity of the surface (illumination-dependent-features), one can conclude that the generalized texture discrimination is one of the most important aspects of image segmentation.

Global approaches to texture discrimination are most valuable for characterizing textures according to their spatial frequencies or moments (average, variance, etc.) [1]–[3]. However, both are unable to give reasonable results when the image, like most natural images, consists of more than one type of texture. Furthermore, changes in the brightness along the spatial axes, or contrast changes due to conditions of nonuniform illumination may hinder classification when global features are used, even in the case of one-texture image.

Manuscript received May 18, 1988; revised July 26, 1988. This work was supported by the Fund for the Promotion of Research at the Technion, the Vice President Research Funds 052-529 and 050-0633, E. and J. Bishop Research Fund, and the Foundation for Research in Electronics, Computers, and Communication, administered by the Israel Academy of Science and Humanities.

The authors are with the Department of Electrical Engineering, Technion-Israel Institute of Technology, Haifa 32000, Israel.

IEEE Log Number 8824423.

In this paper, we present a new approach to a generalized texture analysis and synthesis based on biological principles of image representation at the level of the primary visual cortex [4]–[13]. Traditionally, two complementary approaches to the analysis of visual mechanisms progressed separately and somewhat antagonistically. On the one hand, both retinal and cortical cells have been characterized as having receptive field size of limited extent, and as such described as local feature extractors [7], [14], [15]. Cortical simple cells have accordingly been described as bar or edge detectors. Yet other investigators stressed the importance of spatial frequency analysis in vision [16]–[18], and the fact that the spatial frequency bandwidth characterizing cells along the visual pathway, becomes narrower as one progresses from photoreceptors to the cortical cells [19]. More recently it has been realized that the intrinsic duality of image representation in the spatial and spatial frequency domains is very important and relevant to the understanding of biological vision. The relevance of image representation in the combined position-frequency space, to biological vision is supported by physiological [4], [5], [11]–[13], [20], [21] and psychophysical [22], [23] findings, as well as by mathematical and informational aspects of image representation using such elementary functions, considered from an engineering viewpoint [10], [24].

Careful analysis of cortical cells' tuning characteristics indicates that the receptive fields of simple cells are confined in both of their spatial extent and spatial frequency bandwidth. Cowan [21] proposed already in 1977 that since visual channels (mechanisms) are indeed effectively bandlimited and localized in space, Gabor elementary functions (EF's) [25] may be suitable for their representation. More recently, Marcelja [4] and Kulikowski *et al.* [5] observed that the receptive field organization of simple cells resembles the profile of Gabor EF's. Furthermore, Pollen and Ronner reported that pairs of cells have quadrature Gabor-phase relation [8]. The elaborative physiological research reported by Jones and Palmer and Jones *et al.* provides quantitative data based on recordings from many cells [11]–[13]. These studies assert that Gabor EF's well represent the characteristics of simple cells and present a viable model.

Adopting psychophysical approach, the Gaborian hypothesis was considered by Watson *et al.* [22] and Bennett and Banks [23]. Investigating "what does the eye see best?," Watson *et al.* showed that the pattern of two-di-

Reprinted from *IEEE Trans. Biomed. Eng.*, vol. 36, no. 1, pp. 115–129, Jan. 1989.

mensional Gabor functions is optimal. Bennett and Banks demonstrated the importance of localized phase of the receptive field by analyzing the sensitivity to phase in both foveal and peripheral vision. Engineering aspects of image representation in the combined space are dealt with in [10], [24], [26]. These studies establish that indeed an image can be represented by a set of two-dimensional Gabor EF's in a transform sense.

The basic primitives of images are accordingly described in this paper as localized two-dimensional frequency signatures resembling the form of Gabor elementary functions. Local features are extracted instead of the global ones. The resultant features are position-dependent and, as such, enable the detection of continuity of a feature as well as the edges between different regions. Due to the localized nature of the extraction, illumination differences are compensated by a local expansion of the image into full dynamic range prior to the feature extraction. Multiresolution image segmentation [27] is enabled using different sizes for the basic areas of extraction, and as such establishes a formalism and technique for multilevel segmentation as demonstrated by the results. The proposed algorithm is discussed with regard to rotation, translation, and scaling of textures. The effect of noise performance is also tested and results are presented.

II. The Gaborian Approach to Image Representation in Biological Vision

The Gabor approach [10], [25] is most suitable for localized analysis and synthesis of images since the Gabor EF's are by their very nature localized. These localized operators are also well suited for a pyramidal scheme of multiresolution [27] which appears to be characteristic of vision, and can also serve as oriented-edge operators [20] and in pattern recognition tasks [28]. Another property, the completeness of the Gabor scheme in the mathematical sense [29] lends itself to various interesting possibilities of image representation [10] and computer generated imagery (CGI) [26].

The Gabor scheme was introduced as a discrete set of EF's by means of which signals can be represented [25]. As has been stressed the main advantage of these functions is in achieving the lowest bound on the joint entropy, defined as the product of effective spatial extent and frequency bandwidth. Hence, representation of a signal by these functions provides the best spectral information for every point along the signal variation. In the case of vision and texture discrimination where global analysis of the entire image space is neither desirable nor practical, there is an advantage in using this representation over global transforms such as Fourier.

Because the EF's are not necessarily orthogonal, an analytical method suitable for determination of the expansion coefficients had to be introduced before application to formal image analysis became possible. An analytical method limited to the one-dimensional case was first presented in 1980 [30] and extended to two dimensions more recently [24], paving the way for further research.

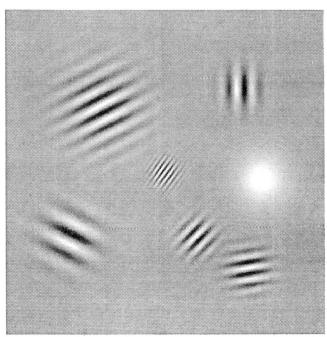

Fig. 1. Examples of the real part of Gabor elementary functions of various frequency numbers (n_x, n_y), position numbers (m_x, m_y), and effective sizes.

According to the Gabor approach, an image $\phi(x, y)$ can be represented as a linear combination of EF's according to [10]

$$\phi(x, y) = \sum_{m_x n_x m_y n_y} a_{m_x n_x m_y n_y} \cdot f_{m_x n_x m_y n_y}(x, y) \quad (1)$$

where $f_{m_x n_x m_y n_y}$ is the EF of the order $(m_x n_x m_y n_y)$

$$f_{m_x n_x m_y n_y}(x, y) = g(x - m_x D_x, y - m_y D_y)$$
$$\cdot \exp(i n_x W_x + i n_y W_y y) \quad (2)$$

and $g(\cdot, \cdot)$ is a two-dimensional normalized window function.

This function $f_{m_x n_x m_y n_y}(x, y)$ is situated at the point $(x = m_x D_x, y = m_y D_y)$ of the Gabor lattice and has a spatial frequency of $(\omega_x = n_x W_x, \omega_y = n_y W_y)$. The constants D_x, D_y and W_x, W_y are the basic sampling intervals along the spatial and the spatial-frequency axes[1] respectively. $a_{m_x n_x m_y n_y}$ is the coefficient of the order $(m_x n_x m_y n_y)$, representing the relative weight of the respective EF in the image $\phi(x, y)$.

When a Gaussian window function is employed as $g(\cdot, \cdot)$, the Gabor EF's (Fig. 1) are not orthogonal and thus the coefficients $\{a_{m_x n_x m_y n_y}\}$ are calculated using an auxiliary function $\gamma(\cdot, \cdot)$ which is biorthogonal [29] in a certain sense to the window function $g(\cdot, \cdot)$:

$$a_{m_x n_x m_y n_y} = \iint \phi(x, y) \gamma^*(x - m_x D_x, y - m_y D_y)$$
$$\cdot \exp(-i n_x W_x x - i n_y W_y y) \, dx \, dy. \quad (3)$$

Theoretically, an infinite number of Gabor coefficients are

[1]In this paper we use equal sampling intervals along the x and the y axes in both spatial and spatial-frequency, i.e., $D_x = D_y = D$, $W_x = W_y = W$.

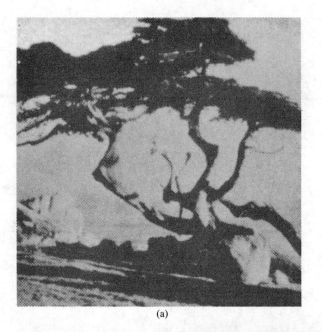

(a)

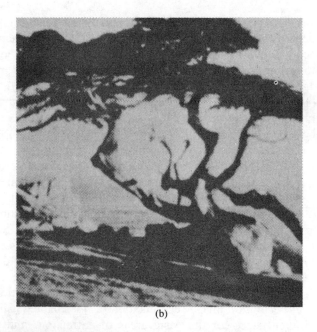

(b)

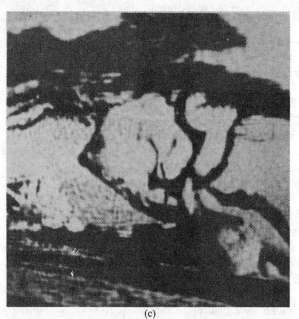

(c)

Fig. 2. Examples of images reconstructed using a finite set of two-dimensional Gabor EF's tessellating a Gabor sampling grid of 5 × 5. The original image (a) is decomposed using a finite scheme with ($|n_x|$, $|n_y|$ ≤ 19). The images in (b) and (c) are reconstructed using approximately 28 800, and 8000 coefficients, respectively.

required for image representation. However, as the example of Fig. 2 demonstrates, a relatively small number of coefficients suffices for good reconstruction. It should be noted that for $g(\cdot, \cdot)$ being a square window function (a nonbiological, nor optimal case), the resultant functions $\{f_{m_x n_x m_y n_y}\}$ are orthogonal and the functions $g(\cdot, \cdot)$ and $\gamma(\cdot, \cdot)$ are identical, thus simplifying the computational process. (For further details see [10] and [30].)

III. Texture Synthesis

It was previously shown that the perceived complexity of images generated by punctate spectra is related to the distribution of the frequency components [31]. In particular, it was demonstrated that a cluster of only 5–7 properly distributed frequency components of equal amplitude can generate a "chaotic" image in the sense of being at a first glance (preattentively [3]) indistinguishable perceptually from an image generated by a continuous two-dimensional bandlimited noise [32]. Here we extend the punctate spectra approach and investigate the structure of images synthesized using a smaller cluster of Gabor EF's.

Each of the images of Fig. 3 was generated using only six EF's of equal amplitude and random phase. As was stressed in the earlier study of Kronauer et al. [31], an

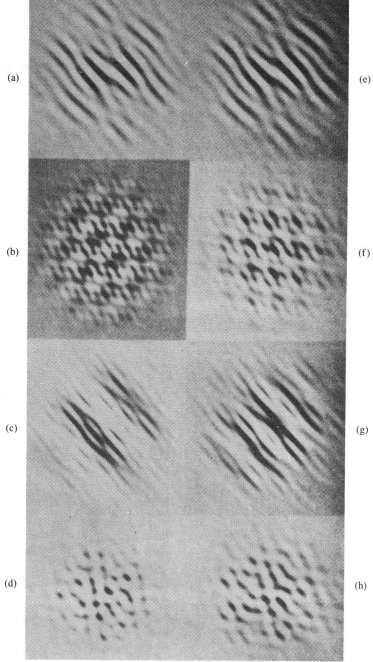

Fig. 3. Synthetic Gabor images. The set of Gabor coefficients generating the textural pattern of (a) is confined to a (radial) spatial frequency band of one octave and an orientation band of 30°. A 3 : 1 dilation of the Gabor cluster of (a) around its centroid generates the image of (b). The images of (c) and (d) are generated by dilating the Gabor cluster (3 : 1) either along the radial axis only or along the orientation axis. The sequence of images in (e)–(h) is similar to the one of (a)–(d) but with a scaling ratio of 4 : 1.

image such as shown in Fig. 3(a) is perceptually similar to the one generated by filtering of a two-dimensional random array of 512 × 512 Gaussian samples [32]. Both types of images are characterized by a salient frequency and orientation which appear as being modulated by noise. In both cases, the dominant frequency corresponds to the centroid (carrier) of the perceived band-limited noise. It is therefore important to stress that this perceived dominant frequency does not exist in the input space of Fig. 3(a), i.e., the cluster distributed over the frequency band does not include a component at the centroid. Furthermore, although the band-limited noise and the image gen-

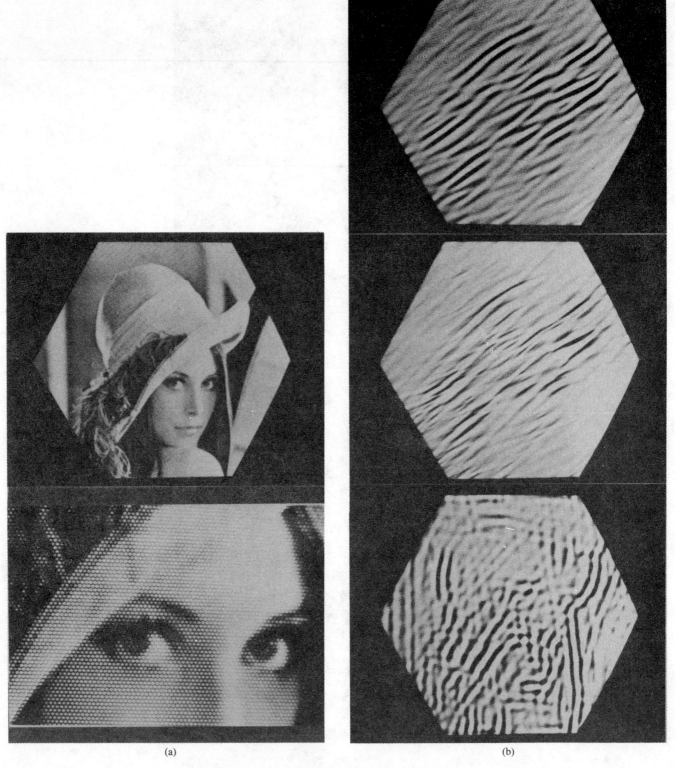

(a) (b)

Fig. 4. The perceived structure of images confined in their two-dimensional frequency band. A hexagonally sampled image (a) is broken down into components. The component shown in (b; top image) is confined to 30° × 1 octave. The centroid of its spectrum is clearly perceived. The percept of the centroid is lost once either the spatial (along the radial axis) or angular orientation bandwidth extends beyond the range characteristic of visual mechanisms (30° × 1 octave). The latter two cases are illustrated in the middle and bottom of (b), respectively [33].

268

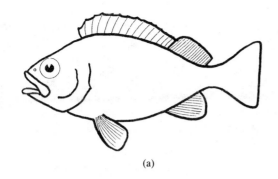

(a)

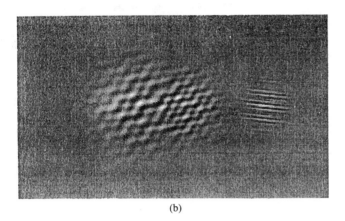

(b)

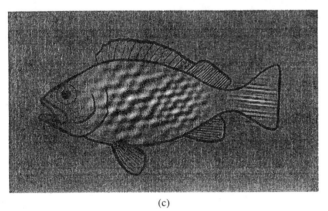

(c)

Fig. 5. Texturing images. The contoured (cartoon-like) image of (a) is textured using only eight localized Gabor EF's (b) to generate the image of (c).

erated by a cluster of EF's appear to induce the same perceptual complexity, the former image is characterized by its extremely high dimensionality whereas the latter is completely specified by the indexes of its six EF's.

The perceptual appearance of a carrier modulated by a band-limited noise disappears as the two-dimensional effective frequency band extends beyond the range characteristic of visual mechanisms [Fig. 3(b)–(d) and (f)–(h)]. In such circumstances, the global coherent (perceived) structure of the image is broken down into spatial frequencies and/or orientations of individual components which are presumably processed by independent visual mechanisms.

A similar observation is afforded by decomposition of

a natural image into components confined in their two-dimensional frequency band [33]. This is demonstrated in Fig. 4. The hexagonally sampled image [Fig. 4(a)] was extended into a hexagonally periodic one, and subsequently broken down into components characterized by two-dimensional spatial frequency bands of 30° × 1 octave. The image of Fig. 4(b) (top) represents such a component. As with the synthetic images, the percept of the spectral centroid is very vivid. This dominant component is lost, however, as either the spatial frequency (middle image) or the angular orientation bandwidth (bottom image) extends beyond the range of the support characteristic of visual mechanisms.

It is important to emphasize that the method of texture synthesis using Gabor EF's is integrated into more elaborative schemes of image generation, and as such provides a tool for texturing images. Manipulating both the spatial-frequency of the spectral component as well as its location over the image space incorporates the degrees of freedom necessary for accomplishing the task. This process of texturing contoured (cartoon-like) images [34] can provide a useful means for scene simulation [35]. It seems to be analogous to adding chromaticity to contoured images [36], in the sense that the contour induces the percept of well textured shape even when the contoured area is not textured precisely (Fig. 5). Other similarities of interaction between texture and contour as compared to the interaction between the achromatic channel and color will be discussed in detail elsewhere [37].

IV. TEXTURE ANALYSIS

Assuming that the primitives of natural textures are indeed localized frequency components in the form of Gabor EF's, texture analysis takes the form of inner product or correlation of such primitives with textured images. In addition to the positional information defined along the Gabor lattice in the combined position-frequency space, features characterizing texture are defined in relation to the EF parameters. In the following subsections we illustrate the application of the Gabor approach to texture analysis and synthesis using a set of Gabor EF's.

A. Feature Extraction

In our approach, six *localized* features are extracted from a given texture or image. The extraction is based on three primary features: spatial frequency along the preferred orientation, orientation of the spatial frequency, and intensity information. For each of these three features, the first and second moments are calculated to obtain a set of six features: dominant localized frequency (denoted by F), variance of the dominant localized frequency (VF), dominant orientation (T), variance of the dominant orientation (VT), mean of the localized intensity level (L) and variance of the localized intensity level (VL). These features are defined in the next paragraphs.

A textured image is first represented by its Gabor coefficients $\{a_{m_x n_x m_y n_y}\}$ where coefficients having common indexes of m_x and m_y represent the spectral components of an effective local area centered at the point $x = m_x D$, $y = m_y D$. The related spatial frequencies are determined by the harmonic numbers n_x and n_y, i.e., $\omega_x = n_x W$ and $\omega_y = n_y W$. Thus, according to this representation, the absolute value of a coefficient specified by indexes n_x, n_y is proportional to the power of the related spatial frequency components (ω_x, ω_y) over the effective area determined by m_x, m_y, and D. The two-dimensional frequency components (ω_x, ω_y) is conveniently expressed by separating the periodicity along the preferred orientation and its orientation, using a polar[2] coordinate representation.

It is assumed that the orientational parameter is fundamental to the definition of texture structure. This assumption is based on the observation that orientation is the most salient parameter characterizing the receptive field organization of cortical cells. It is further assumed that spatial frequency is an additional parameter characterizing the physiology of cortical cells [8], [19], [38]. The two parameters are expressed in the polar coordinates by the spatial frequency $\omega = \sqrt{\omega_x^2 + \omega_y^2}$ and orientation θ where $\tan(\theta) = \omega_y/\omega_x$.

The first feature, the dominant localized frequency (F) in the area designated by m_x, m_y is calculated according to

$$F_{m_x m_y} = \frac{\sum_{n_x=1}^{N-1} \sum_{n_y=1}^{N-1} |a_{m_x n_x m_y n_y}| \sqrt{n_x^2 + n_y^2}}{\sum_{n_x=1}^{N-1} \sum_{n_y=1}^{N-1} |a_{m_x n_x m_y n_y}|} \quad (4)$$

where the number of spectral components (along the frequency coordinates), N, is determined by the sampling rate of the digitized image. Note that the term $\sqrt{n_x^2 + n_y^2}$ represents the harmonic number of this spatial frequency ω related to n_x and n_y, and that (4) is reminiscent of a center of gravity. Since the power spatial frequencies is accounted for in this expression regardless of their orientations, this feature is inherently rotation-invariant [39] and generally insensitive to translation.[3] This is not true, however, for scaling, in which case the resultant feature is directly proportional to the scaling factor. Thus, the application of the dominant localized frequency is limited to cases where scaled versions of the same texture are considered different. The sensitivity of F to scaling is exploited in the definition of a scale invariant feature [expressed in (6)].

The second moment (variance) of the localized frequency VF is

$$VF_{m_x m_y} = \frac{\sum_{n_x=1}^{N-1} \sum_{n_y=1}^{N-1} |\sqrt{n_x^2 + n_y^2} - F_{m_x m_y}|}{N^2}. \quad (5)$$

This feature, which provides a measure of regularity of textures, represents the bandwidth of the localized spatial

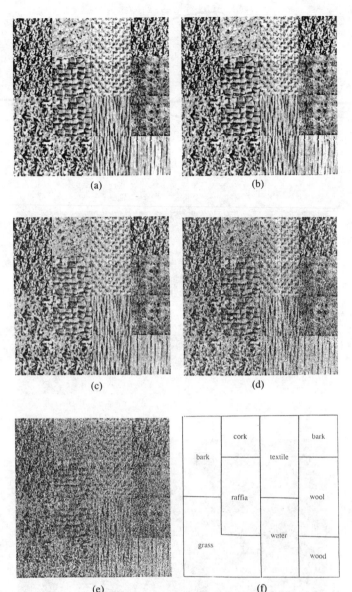

(a)   (b)

(c)   (d)

(e)   (f)

Fig. 6. (a) Image of eight textures: bark, wool, wood, textile, cork, grass, water, and raffia. The image is represented by 256×256 pixels, 8 bits per pixel. (b)–(e) are the same as in (a) but with additive Gaussian noise of zero mean and variances of 7, 15, 30, and 60, respectively.

frequency (in units of W). Since the bandwidth is affected when the whole texture is scaled, it is useful to normalize this feature by the respective scaling factor which appears implicitly in the dominant localized frequency F. The normalized second moment of the frequency, accordingly defined by the coefficient of variation

$$\widetilde{VF}_{m_x m_y} = \frac{VF_{m_x m_y}}{F_{m_x m_y}} \quad (6)$$

generates a scale invariant feature. Like the feature F, this one (VF or $\widetilde{VF}$) too is insensitive to rotation and/or translation by virtue of its definition. As will be demonstrated later, this feature is instrumental in the classification of textures such as shown in Fig. 6 where five of the eight textures are discriminated using this feature only.

Two additional features are determined by the orienta-

[2]Note that the preferred orientation defined in this paper is perpendicular to the one often used in neurophysiology cortical cells [7].

[3]This is approximately so as long as the spatial sampling interval (D) along the Gabor lattice is large compared to the texture periodicity.

tion characterizing the 2-D spatial frequencies. Since $\omega_x = n_x W$ and $\omega_y = n_y W$ one can express the orientation by either ω_y/ω_x or n_y/n_x. Defining the orientation $\theta(n_x, n_y)$, related to a Gabor function indicated by n_x and n_y (for certain m_x, m_y), as $\tan[\theta(n_x, n_y)] = (n_y/n_x)$ for $n_x \neq 0$ and $\tan[\theta(n_x, n_y)] = \pi/2$ for $n_x = 0$, the dominant local orientation is calculated according to the previous method of center of gravity, using the Gabor coefficients representing the effective area specified by m_x, m_y:

$$T_{m_x m_y} = \frac{\sum\limits_{n_x=1}^{N-1} \sum\limits_{n_y=1}^{N-1} |a_{m_x n_x m_y n_y}| \theta(n_x, n_y)}{\sum\limits_{n_x=1}^{N-1} \sum\limits_{n_y=1}^{N-1} |a_{m_x n_x m_y n_y}|} \quad (7)$$

and the variance of the local orientation is defined by

$$VT_{m_x m_y} = \frac{\sum\limits_{n_x=1}^{N-1} \sum\limits_{n_y=1}^{N-1} |\theta(n_x, n_y) - T_{m_x m_y}|}{N^2}. \quad (8)$$

The dominant local orientation is by its very nature sensitive to rotation, and as such is used in detection of edges (or contours) generated by rotations of the same texture. It should be pointed out, however, that the variance is a rotational-invariant feature, and that the dominant local orientation as well as its variance, are insensitive to scaling and/or translation.

The local mean intensity (L) is extracted to complete the set of features in order to characterize differences with respect to smoothness of localized areas that are similar according to the first four features. Clearly, smooth segments in the image, such as sky or a uniform wall for example, cannot be discriminated from each other using spatial-frequency information since they are represented by almost constant functions. In this case, the gray level information (or the color in the general case) is the only way to separate these regions. It appears as though these parameters are extracted in biological systems along channels other than those that are involved in Gabor-like processing (dc information is not mediated by X type retinal ganglion cells, but rather by the nonlinear Y cells [40]).

The locality of this feature is accomplished by multiplying the image with the two-dimensional window function $g(\cdot, \cdot)$. Then, by averaging the pixels in the resultant area we define

$$L_{m_x m_y} = \frac{1}{K} \sum_{x, y \in A(m_x m_y)} I(x, y) \quad (9)$$

where $A(m_x m_y)$ is the set of K pixels belonging to the area defined by the window function centered according to m_x, m_y, and $I(x, y)$ is the intensity function. As may be concluded, this feature is insensitive to rotation, translation, and scaling of the textures.

The last feature, the variance of the intensity level VL, is calculated to facilitate the discrimination of textures that appear to be similar according to the five features. This feature is in particular instrumental in cases of irregular textures that give insufficient (the extreme case of which is the white noise). This feature is calculated by

$$VL_{m_x m_y} = \frac{1}{K} \sum_{x, y \in A(m_x m_y)} |I(x, y) - L_{m_x m_y}| \quad (10)$$

where $A(m_x m_y)$ is defined as before. It is not related to the spatial-frequency (as may be easily demonstrated by the fact that the pixels designated by the area $A(m_x m_y)$ can be rearranged without affecting the variance) and as such provides extra information for the classification process.

These six features are calculated as the first stage of discrimination in order to obtain the feature vector. Note that the resultant vector $(F, VF, T, VT, L, VL)_{m_x m_y}$ is a position-dependent vector, indicated by m_x, m_y. Thus, for each localized area defined by m_x, m_y, a six-dimensional feature space is specified for which a classification scheme can be applied.

B. Classification Design and Results of Experiments

This section presents the resultant feature-vectors for images textured in a mosaic-like fashion in order to select the most efficient features in the classification scheme. The proposed features were tested using eight textures [Fig. 6(a)]. Noisy versions of these textures [Fig. 6(b)–(e)] were employed as input data for testing the stability of the features and the classification process in the presence of noise. In the first experiment, the features were calculated using square window functions of different sizes: 8×8, 16×16, and 32×32 pixels. Gray level representation of the features extracted by the above procedure [(4), (5), (7)–(10)] are shown in Fig. 7 where the results of each four neighboring squares are averaged to produce one number. The results show that each texture differs significantly from the others in at least one feature. However, the main conclusion to be drawn from these results is that considering the textures of Fig. 6 (including their noisy cases), the most informative features are VF and VL, and that these features alone can provide a reasonable discrimination for most of the tested textures. This observation motivates the following considerations, in which a two-dimensional feature space is spanned by these two features.

Discrimination by these features (VF, VL) is tested on rotated and translated versions of the textures shown in Fig. 6, using a square window function of 16×16 pixels. The results of the extracted features for the rotated versions of the textures are presented in Fig. 8. The features VF and VL were calculated for six of the textures[4] rotated in 49 different orientations (49×6 different samples in total). Every small square in Fig. 8(a) represents one point in the feature space VF versus VL, as calculated for one sample. Each group of samples belonging to the same tex-

[4]Using these only two features, the textures water and raffia are indistinguishable from the cork and the grass respectively. This problem is discussed later.

271

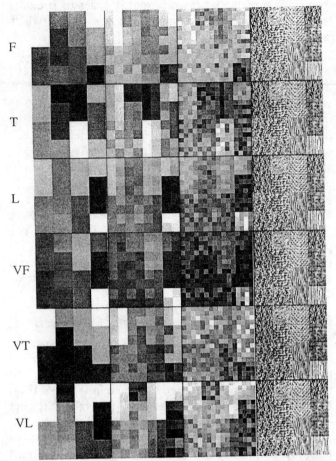

Fig. 7. Pyramidal gray level representation of the features extracted with 32 × 32 pixels squares (left column), 16 × 16 pixels (second column), and 8 × 8 pixels squares (third column). The original image is shown at the right column. Each row is a representation of one feature (according to the notations).

ture is indicated by the type of texture. The results obtained from noisy textures are presented in Fig. 8(b)-(e).

Inspecting these two-dimensional feature spaces, it becomes clear that a simple minimum-distance classifier should suffice for a classification since the groups of samples are well clustered (segregated). As can be expected, the spread of each cluster over the two-dimensional feature space is inversely proportional to the frequency of the dominant periodicity characteristic of the texture (compare, for example, the wood and grass texture patterns).

The effect of translation on the clustering is depicted by scatter diagrams obtained for 44 translated versions of each texture (Fig. 9). Since the window function employed in these computations is relatively small (16 × 16 pixels), the translated versions of each texture give rise to differences in the resultant feature vectors. The effect of translation becomes more significant when the texture has a less periodic nature, as may be observed in the wood clustering of the wood-texture patterns compared to the clustering of the other textures. However, the addition of noise hardly affects the clustering, although a shift toward higher values of VL and VF is observed for all groups as the noise level is increased.

Combination of translation and rotation of the texture

are tested and presented in Fig. 10(a). The results show that the 44 samples per texture are reasonably grouped together in the case of noise-free textures (Fig. 10), as well as the noisy images [Fig. 10(b)-(d)], even with both translation and rotation. Based on inspection of the resultant scatter one can expect good classification using a minimum distance classifier. The noisy image of Fig. 10(e) where the grouping seems to break down calls for a more sophisticated classifier, in cases where texture discrimination is required at such signal-to-noise levels [see Fig. 6(e)].

The above approach utilized in the context of a two-dimensional feature space is extended in a straight forward manner to a higher dimensional space. Whereas in the case of the two-dimensional feature space VL versus VF [Fig. 11(a)], we encountered difficulties in separating the water from the cork pattern and the grass from the raffia, all eight textures can be well separated in the three-dimensional feature space (VF, VL, T) regardless of translation [Fig. 11(c), (d)]. An example of using the dominant local orientation (T) instead of the feature VL, in which separation is achieved for these patterns (water, cork, grass, and raffia) is shown in Fig. 11(b).

As mentioned earlier, even a simple minimum-distance classifier is expected to produce good classification results. Such a classifier is tested using the two-dimensional feature space of VL and VF. The usual approach to evaluate a classifier performance is to create the so-called ''confusion matrix'' and consider the ratio of diagonal (correct classification) over off-diagonal (wrong classification) elements. The results presented in Table I are based on the samples of Fig. 8(a) (rotated versions of the textures) as the training samples, and the translated and rotated textures as the testing samples [Fig. 10(a)-(c)]. The accuracy obtained with these testing sets is indicated in the table for each texture. The main difficulty reflected in these matrices, is the poor discrimination between grass and bark in the presence of high noise levels. Interestingly, the human observer experiences the same difficulties (see Fig. 6).

V. DISCUSSION

As demonstrated in this paper by both synthesis and analysis of textures, the localized orientational wavelets in the form of two-dimensional Gabor EF's constitute a set of descriptors most suitable for texture processing and understanding. The advantage in using such a set relates to the universality of the representation in both of the mathematical and physical sense. As previously stressed in other studies [10], [25], [30], the set of Gabor EF's is complete and even overcomplete in certain senses [41], thus it is clear that any pattern, and textures as such, can be represented by Gabor EF's. However, any other complete set of two-dimensional functions also offers the universal property characteristic of the Gabor set. The difference between the Gabor set (and/or transform) and the other sets of functions can be appreciated once a finite representation is considered [26]. Also, a scheme based

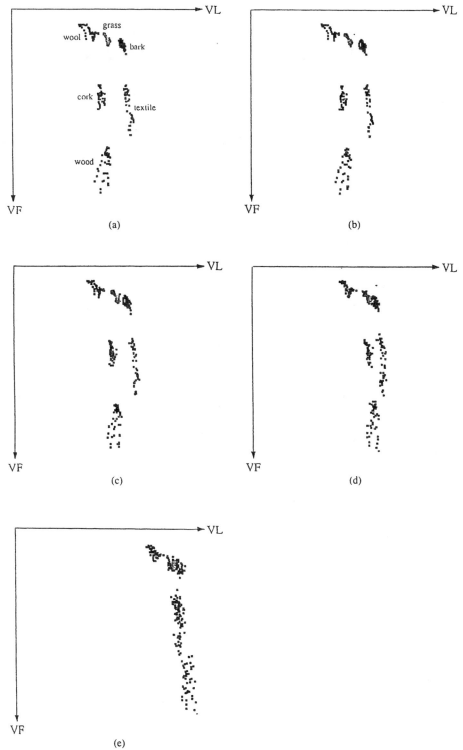

Fig. 8. (a) VF and VL feature-space for six textures of Fig. 6(a) as indicated. 44 samples were obtained per texture by generating rotated versions of the textures in 44 different orientations. (b)–(e) are the results in the presence of Gaussian noise with variances of 7, 15, 30, and 60 respectively.

on the localized characteristics of the Gabor space lends itself to direct implementation in image segmentation. The classification set obtained over each region is used in this case as a characteristic variable of a segmentation process (such as that proposed by Mumford and Shash, [42]).

Furthermore, since it appears as though the biological

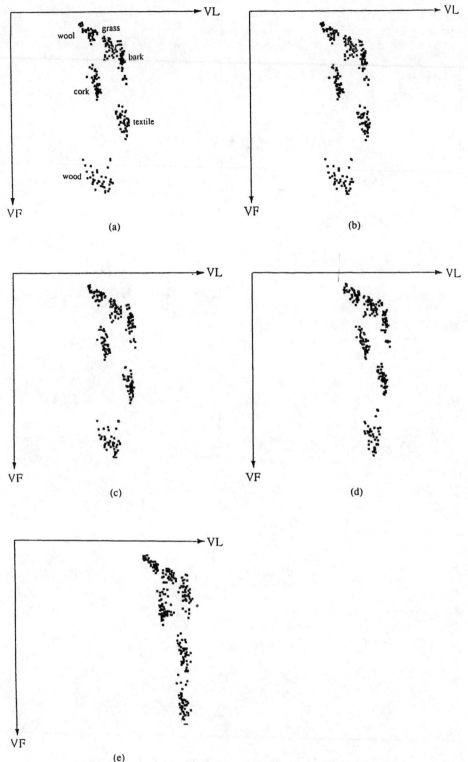

Fig. 9. (a) VF versus VL feature-space for the same six textures as in Fig. 8. 44 samples per texture were generated by taking segments of translated versions of each texture along the horizontal and/or the vertical directions. (b)–(e) are the results in the presence of Gaussian noise with variances of 7, 15, 30, and 60, respectively.

system utilizes such operators in extraction of image signatures, there are good reasons to believe that a mechanism or algorithm based on operation in the Gabor space should be efficient and robust. In fact, these observation motivated our general approach to image representation in the Gabor space [10]. Whereas, in the biological case

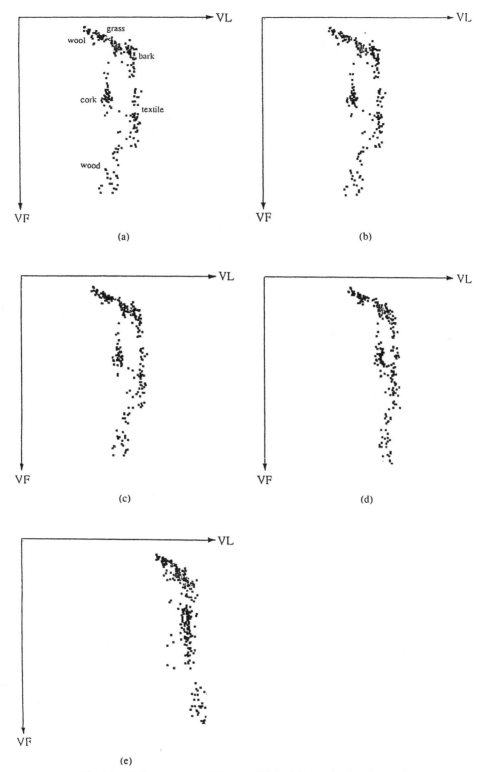

Fig. 10. (a) Feature space (VF versus VL) of 44 translated and rotated versions per texture for the six textures considered in Figs. 8 and 9. (b)–(e) are the results in the presence of Gaussian noise with variances of 7, 15, 30, and 60 respectively.

there seems to be hard wired schemes of tessellation of the Gabor space, a machine or scheme devised for a particular task of textured image analysis can be designed to

best match the task under consideration taking advantage of the degrees of freedom and tradeoffs inherent in the Gabor approach.

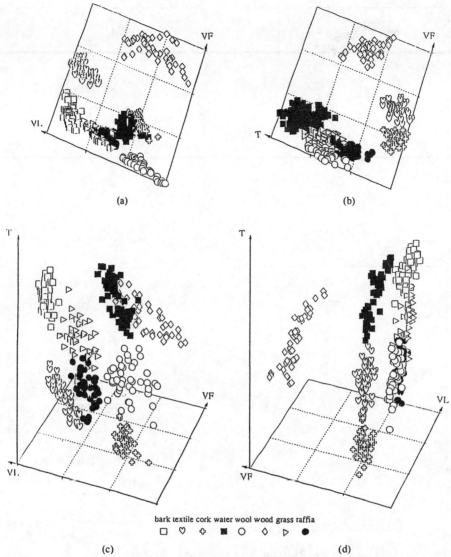

(a)

(b)

T

T

VF

VL

VF

VI.

bark textile cork water wool wood grass raffia

□   ♡   ✛   ■   ○   ◇   ▷   ●

(c)   (d)

Fig. 11. The feature space VL versus VF for the translated versions of all
eight textures of Fig. 6 is shown in (a) (i.e., the water and the raffia are
added to the other six textures). Note that the raffia and the grass are not
well separated and the same is true for the water and the cork. Better
separation is achieved in (b) where the feature T (dominant local orientation) is used instead of VL (variance of local intensity levels). Use of
these three features together (VF, VL, T) is one example of a 3-D feature space for discrimination of all the eight textures, as shown by the
two projections in (c) and (d).

Whereas our and other studies mentioned therein clearly demonstrate the advantages of Gaborian approach to vision as compared to the earlier global frequency (Fourier) approach, one should not overlook other possible representations in the combined space. Of these best known are the Wigner distribution [43] and the ambiguity-function [44]. Although these two representations seem to resemble the Gabor scheme in the sense of localized analysis and synthesis in the combined frequency-position space, they suffer mainly from the lack of linearity. Other types of "short distance" spectrogramic representation are endowed with the main features of the Gabor scheme (e.g.,

Hermit polynomials [45]), excluding the property of minimum uncertainty. The latter property which is uniquely characteristic of Gaborian functions necessitates, however, employing the complicated computations introduced by the $\gamma (\cdot)$ functions. This is one possible solution to the nonorthogonality. Gram's minimum distance calculation [46] is another (complicated) way to determine the set of coefficients $\{ a_{m_x n_x m_y n_y} \}$. In both cases without a special purpose hardware, the required computation of an image is quite intensive even on a powerful general purpose serial computer. Dedicated hardware can offer a solution to this computational problem [47].

276

TABLE I

CLASSIFICATION RESULTS BY THE FEATURES VF AND VL USING MINIMUM
DISTANCE CLASSIFIER. THE TRAINING SAMPLES ARE OF FIG. 8(a) (ROTATED
VERSIONS, NOISE FREE). THE RESULTS PRESENTED IN (a), (b) AND (c) ARE
ACHIEVED BY CLASSIFYING THE TESTING SAMPLES OF FIG. 10(a), (b), AND
(c), RESPECTIVELY, (TRANSLATED AND ROTATED VERSIONS OF THE
TEXTURES WITH NOISE LEVEL AS INDICATED).

	Noise free							
	bark	44	0	0	0	0	0	(100%)
	wool	0	43	0	0	0	1	(098%)
(a)	wood	0	0	38	5	1	0	(086%)
	textile	0	0	2	42	0	0	(095%)
	cork	0	0	0	0	43	1	(098%)
	grass	4	1	0	0	39		(088%)
	classification accuracy=94.2%

	Noise variance = 7							
	bark	44	0	0	0	0	0	(100%)
	wool	0	43	0	0	0	1	(098%)
(b)	wood	0	0	38	5	1	0	(086%)
	textile	0	0	2	42	0	0	(095%)
	cork	0	0	0	0	41	3	(093%)
	grass	8	0	0	0	0	36	(082%)
	classification accuracy=92.3%

	Noise variance = 15							
	bark	44	0	0	0	0	0	(100%)
	wool	0	39	0	0	0	5	(087%)
(c)	wood	0	0	37	7	0	0	(084%)
	textile	0	0	0	44	0	0	(100%)
	cork	2	0	0	0	41	1	(093%)
	grass	23	0	0	0	0	21	(048%)
	classification accuracy=85.8%

The results of texture discrimination presented in this paper should be considered only as an illustrative example of the Gabor approach. Texture discrimination using a simple classifier of minimum distance is found to be stable in the presence of additive noise, and degradation in the performance occurs only at high noise levels where the human visual system also starts to encounter discrimination problems. For a classification accuracy of about 90 percent, two features are found to be sufficient. It is expected that the addition of a third feature to the classification process, as well as the use of an improved classifier, would be a significant step towards more accurate and more stable (in the sense of noise effects) texture discrimination.

ACKNOWLEDGMENT

We wish to thank Dr. M. H. Loew and Dr. R. E. Kronauer for fruitful discussions.

REFERENCES

[1] R. M. Haralick, "Statistical and structural approaches to texture," *Proc. IEEE*, vol. 67, pp. 786–804, May 1979.
[2] H. Wechsler, "Texture analysis—A survey," *Signal Proc.*, vol. 2, pp. 271–282, 1982.
[3] B. Julesz and J. R. Bergen, "Texton, the fundamental elements in preattentive vision and perception of textures," *Bell Syst. Tech. J.*, vol. 62, pp. 1619–1645, 1983.
[4] S. Marcelja, "Mathematical description of the responses of simple cortical cells," *J. Opt. Soc. Amer.*, vol. 70, pp. 1297–1300, 1980.
[5] J. J. Kulikowski, S. Marcelja, and P. O. Bishop, "Theory of spatial position and spatial frequency relations in the receptive field of simple cells in the visual cortex," *Biol. Cybern.*, vol. 43, pp. 187–198, 1982.
[6] D. M. Mackay, "Strife over visual cortical function," *Nature*, vol. 289, pp. 117–118, 1981.
[7] David H. Hubel, "Exploration of the primary visual cortex, 1955–1978," *Nature*, vol. 299, pp. 515–524, 1982.
[8] D. A. Pollen and S. F. Ronner, "Visual cortical neurons as localized spatial frequency filter," *IEEE Trans. Syst., Man, Cybern.*, vol. SMC-13, pp. 907–916, May 1983.
[9] R. E. Kronauer and Y. Y. Zeevi, "Reorganization and diversification of signals in vision," *IEEE Trans. Syst., Man, Cybern.*, vol. SMC-15, pp. 91–101, Jan. 1985.
[10] M. Porat and Y. Y. Zeevi, "The generalized Gabor scheme of image representation in biological and machine vision," *IEEE Trans. Pattern Anal. Mach. Intell.*, vol. PAMI-10, pp. 452–468, 1988.
[11] J. P. Jones and L. A. Palmer, "The two-dimensional spatial structure of simple receptive fields in cat striate cortex," *J. Neurophysiol.*, vol. 58, no. 6, pp. 1187–1211, 1987.
[12] J. P. Jones, A. Stepnoski, and L. A. Palmer, "The two-dimensional spatial structure of simple receptive fields in cat striate cortex," *J. Neurophysiol.*, vol. 58, no. 6, pp. 1212–1232, 1987.
[13] J. P. Jones and L. A. Palmer, "An evaluation of the two-dimensional Gabor filter model of simple receptive fields in cat striate cortex," *J. Neurophysiol.*, vol. 58, no. 6, pp. 1233–1258, 1987.
[14] J. Y. Lettvin, H. R. Maturana, W. S. McCullough, and W. H. Pitts, "What the frog's eye tells the frog's brain," *Proc. IRE*, vol. 47, no. 11, pp. 1940–1951, 1959.

[15] J. E. Dowling, "Information processing by local circuits: The vertebrate retina as a model system," in *Neurosciences, Fourth Study Program*, F. O. Schmitt and F. G. Worden, Eds. Cambridge, MA: M.I.T. Press, 1979, pp. 163–181.

[16] F. W. Campbell and J. G. Robson, "Application of Fourier analysis to the visibility of gratings," *J. Physiol. (London)*, vol. 197, pp. 551–556, 1968.

[17] N. Graham and J. N. Nachmias, "Detection of grating pattern containing two spatial frequencies: A comparison of single-channel and multiple-channel models," *Vision Res.*, vol. 11, pp. 251–259, 1971.

[18] O. Braddick, F. W. Campbell, and J. Atkinson, "Channels in vision: Basic aspects," *Handbook of Sensory Physiology, Vol. VIII*, 1978.

[19] L. Maffei and A. Fiorintini, "The visual cortex as a spatial frequency analysis," *Vision Res.*, vol. 13, pp. 1255–1267, 1973.

[20] J. Daugman, "Uncertainty relation for resolution in space, spatial frequency, and orientation optimized by 2-D visual cortical filters," *J. Opt. Soc. Amer.*, vol. 2, no. 7, pp. 1160–1169, 1985.

[21] J. D. Cowan, "Some remarks on channel bandwidth for visual contrast detection," *Neurosci. Res. Prog. Bull.*, vol. 15, no. 3, 1977.

[22] A. B. Watson, H. B. Barlow, and J. G. Robson, "What does the eye see best?," *Nature*, vol. 302, pp. 419–422, 1983.

[23] D. J. Bennett and M. S. Banks, "Sensitivity loss in odd symmetric mechanism and phase anomalies in peripheral vision," *Nature*, vol. 326, pp. 873–876, 1987.

[24] Y. Y. Zeevi and M. Porat, "Combined frequency-position scheme of image representation in vision," *J. Opt. Soc. Amer.*, vol. 1, no. 12, p. 1248, 1984.

[25] D. Gabor, "Theory of communication," *J. Inst. Elec. Eng.*, vol. 93, p. 429–459, 1946.

[26] Y. Y. Zeevi and M. Porat, "Computer image generation using elementary functions matched to human vision," in *Theoretical Foundation of Computer Graphics*, R. A. Earnshaw, Ed. New York: Springer, 1988, pp. 1197–1241.

[27] A. Rosenfeld, Ed., *Multiresolution Image Processing and Analysis*. Berlin: Springer, 1984.

[28] A. B. Watson, "Detection and recognition of simple spatial forms," NASA Tech. Memo. 84353, Ames Res. Center, Moffett Field, CA, 1983.

[29] J. R. Higgins, *Completeness and Basis Properties of Sets of Special Functions*. Cambridge, England: Cambridge University, 1977.

[30] M. J. Bastiaans, "A sampling theorem for the complex spectrogram and Gabor expansion of a signal into Gaussian elementary signals," *Opt. Eng.*, vol. 20, no. 4, pp. 594–598, 1981.

[31] R. E. Kronauer, J. G. Daugman, and Y. Y. Zeevi, "Degree of disorder perceived in images with punctate spectra," in *Ann. Meet. Opt. Soc. Amer.*, Tucson, AZ, 1982.

[32] H. Mostafavi and D. J. Sakrison, "Structure and properties of a single channel in the human visual system," *Vision Res.*, vol. 16, pp. 957–968, 1976.

[33] E. Shlomot, Y. Y. Zeevi, and W. Pearlman, "On the importance of spatial frequency and orientation in image decomposition and coding," in *Proc. SPIE Cambridge Symp. Opt. Med. Visual Image Process.*, 1987.

[34] M. Kunt, A. Ikonomopoulos, and M. Kocher, "Second-generation image-coding techniques," *Proc. IEEE*, vol. 73, no. 4, pp. 549–574, 1985.

[35] Y. Y. Zeevi, M. Porat, and G. A. Geri, "Image generation for flight simulators: the Gabor approach," *J. Visual Comput.*, to be published.

[36] R. E. Kronauer, personal communication.

[37] R. E. Kronauer and Y. Y. Zeevi, "On texture and chromatic information processing in vision," to be published.

[38] K. K. DeValois, R. L. DeValois, and E. W. Yund, "Responses of striate cortical cells to grating and checkerboard patterns," *J. Physiol. London*, vol. 291, pp. 483–505, 1979.

[39] R. L. Kashyap and A. Khotanzad, "A model-based method for rotation invariant texture classification," *IEEE Trans. Pattern Anal. Mach. Intell.*, vol. PAMI-8, 1986.

[40] S. Hochstein and R. M. Shapley, "Linear and nonlinear sub units in Y cat retinal ganglion cells," *J. Physiol.*, vol. 262, pp. 265–284, 1976.

[41] A. Perelomov, *Generalized Coherent States and Their Applications*. New York: Springer, 1986.

[42] D. Mumford and J. Shah, "Boundary detection by minimizing functionals," in *Proc. IEEE Conf. Comput. Vis. Pattern Recogn.*, San Francisco, CA, 1985.

[43] E. Wigner, "On the quantum correction for thermodynamic equilibrium," *Phys. Rev.*, vol. 40, pp. 749–759, 1932.

[44] P. M. Woodward, *Probability and Information Theory, with Applications to Radar*. New York: McGraw-Hill, 1953.

[45] R. A. Young, "The Gaussian derivative theory of spatial vision: Analysis of cortical cell receptive field line-weighting profiles," General Motors Rep. GMR-4920, May 1985.

[46] I. Gohberg and S. Goldberg, *Basic Operator Theory*. Boston, MA: Birkhauser, 1981.

[47] P. D. Einziger and Y. Hertzberg, "On the Gabor representation and its digital implementation," EE Pub. 587, Technion, Haifa, 1986.

A Multitask Visual Information Processor with a Biologically Motivated Design

M. M. GUPTA AND G. K. KNOPF

Intelligent Systems Research Laboratory, College of Engineering, University of Saskatchewan, Saskatoon, Saskatchewan, Canada S7N OWO

Received January 25, 1991; accepted August 15, 1991

A biologically motivated design for a multitask visual information processor, called the Positive–Negative (PN) neural processor, is presented in this paper. The computational operations performed by the PN neural processor are loosely based upon the functional dynamics exhibited by certain nervous tissue layers found within the cortical and thalamic regions of the brain [31, 32]. The computational role of the PN neural processor extends beyond the scope of most existing artificial neural network models because it can be programmed to generate distinct steady-state and temporal phenomena in order to perform a variety of useful tasks such as storing, spatio-temporal filtering, and pulse frequency encoding two-dimensional time-varying signals. The PN neural processor is a plausible hardware visual information processor that can be applied toward the development of sophisticated neuro-vision systems for numerous engineering applications. In this context, the overall construction of a robust neuro-vision system involves both a parallel and a hierarchical architecture of numerous PN neural processors that are individually programmed to perform specific visual tasks. © 1992 Academic Press, Inc.

1. INTRODUCTION

The successful operation of any autonomous intelligent machine depends upon its ability to cope with a variety of unexpected events. These machines must independently perceive, memorize, and comprehend the constantly changing real-world environment in which they operate. By virtue of its remoteness from the physical scene and its diverse informative nature, vision is considered the richest of all the biological sensory processes. Our own visual experience is relatively quick, effortless, and highly robust. At present, this sophisticated form of perceptual vision is within the exclusive domain of higher-order biological organisms such as human beings. These basic attributes are absent in all existing computer vision algorithms and hardware systems which are developed for machine applications. In general, a machine vision system is not very robust because it is very slow and intolerant to stimulus variability.

Biological vision employs millions of very slow and largely unreliable processors called *neurons* to achieve complex computational operations that are far beyond the capabilities of even the most powerful digital computers in existence. A single neuron requires about 2 ms (or an equivalent bandwidth of about 500 Hz) to fire and transmit a response to all other interconnected neurons. Ironically, the entire process of recognizing a complex scene with these relatively slow neural processors takes only 70–200 ms [30]. In sharp contrast, the basic digital processor employed by a computer is up to a million times faster than a biological neuron, and yet a computer vision system takes several minutes, if not hours, to process a single static image. Furthermore, many aspects of early biological vision are achieved in only 18 to 46 transformation steps [29, 30], far fewer than the millions of transformation steps needed by a sequential algorithm implemented on a digital processor. Clearly, an understanding of the neural structures involved in biological vision will be of great help in designing more robust machine vision systems for industrial, medical science, and space applications.

The incredible speed and flexibility of human vision is both the necessary proof that robust vision is possible and the framework from which a comparable machine vision systems can be developed. From the perspective of a vision system engineer it is not necessary to emulate the precise electrophysiological behavior of biological vision. Rather, it is desirable to replicate some of the computational operations involved in storing and processing spatio-temporal visual information. In this way, the scientific principles derived from vision physiology are used to design and develop a more effective "engineered" machine vision system. The term *neuro-vision* is used to refer to any artificial or machine vision system that embodies the computational principles exhibited by biological neural circuits. The process of designing artificial neuro-vision systems based upon biological analogies is termed *reverse bioengineering* [18, 29, 30] or *inverse biomedical engineering* [13].

The objective of this paper is to introduce the computational architecture of a multifunctional neural informa-

Reprinted with permission from *Journal of Visual Communication and Image Representation*, vol. 3, no. 3, pp. 230–246, 1992.
(Copyright © 1992 by Academic Press, Inc.)

tion processor, called the Positive–Negative (PN)[1] neural processor, and examine briefly how it can be used to perform a variety of tasks associated with early vision. The computational operations employed by the PN neural processor are loosely based upon the functional dynamics exhibited by certain cortical and thalamic nervous tissue layers situated in the brain [31, 32]. The role of the PN neural processor extends beyond the scope of most existing artificial neural networks because it provides a plausible hardware structure for realizing diverse aspects of early vision. This neural processor can be programmed to generate various steady-state and temporal phenomena that may be employed for short-term visual memory (STVM), spatio-temporal filtering (STF), and pulse frequency modulation (PFM). In this context, a robust neuro-vision system may be constructed from a parallel and hierarchical architecture of numerous individually programmed PN neural processors.

2. THE COMPUTATIONAL ARCHITECTURE OF THE PN NEURAL PROCESSOR

The biological visual pathway is composed of numerous distinct anatomical regions such as the retina, lateral geniculate nucleus (LGN), primary visual cortex, secondary visual cortex, and other cortical regions of the brain. All visual information which is sensored by the eye is projected through these different anatomical regions such that the relative spatial and temporal relationships found to exist on the photoreceptive surface of the retina are maintained throughout each advancing region. Each anatomical region or subregion may, therefore, be envisioned as being a functionally two-dimensional nervous tissue layer. All aspects of neural information processing that occurs within such a nervous tissue layer exist as spatio-temporal patterns of neural activity.

The majority of neural network models described in the existing literature consider the behavior of a single neuron as the basic computing unit for describing neural information processing operations. Often each computing unit in the network is based on the concept of an *idealized* neuron. An ideal neuron is assumed to respond optimally to the applied inputs. However, experimental studies in neurophysiology show that the response of a biological neuron is a variable, and only by averaging many observations is it possible to obtain predictable results [10, 11, 25, 26, 31, 32]. This observed variability in the response of a neuron is a function of both the uncontrolled extraneous electrical signals that are being received from activated neurons in other parts of the nervous system and the intrinsic fluctuations of electrical membrane potential within the individual neuron.

In general, a biological neuron is an unpredictable mechanism for processing information. Mathematical analysis has shown that the random behavior of individual neurons can transmit reliable information if they are sufficiently redundant in numbers [32]. It is postulated, therefore, that the collective activity generated by large numbers of locally redundant neurons is more significant in a computational context than the activity generated by a single neuron [22, 25, 26, 31, 32].

Each nervous tissue layer may be conceptualized as being a two-dimensional array of radial columns, whereupon each column contains one or more classes of locally redundant neurons. The total neural activity generated within a radial column results from a spatially localized assembly of nerve cells called a *neural population*. Each neural population may be further divided into several coexisting *subpopulations*. A single subpopulation is assumed to contain a large class of similar acting neurons that lie in close spatial proximity. The individual synaptic connections within any subpopulation are random, but dense enough to ensure at least one mutual connection between any two neurons. Furthermore, these neurons within a subpopulation are assumed to receive a common input and exhibit a common output.

For analytical simplicity only two subpopulations are assumed to coexist within each radial column. The first subpopulation of this column contains only excitatory neurons which project a positive influence when they are active. The second subpopulation that coexists within this column contains only inhibitory neurons which project a negative influence when they are active. Each excitatory or inhibitory subpopulation may be further composed of one or more types of nerve cells.

The dynamic neural activities exhibited by a nervous tissue layer is a result of immense coupling interactions that occur among the radially and laterally distributed subpopulations. In this context, the basic neural computing unit for describing the functional operations performed by a nervous tissue layer corresponds to the total neural activity generated by an individual subpopulation. Two antagonistic neural computing units are assumed to coexist at each spatial location on the tissue layer surface. These positive (P) and negative (N) neural units reflect the activity generated within the respective excitatory and inhibitory subpopulations as illustrated in Fig. 1.

The computational architecture of a generalized nervous tissue layer, as shown in Fig. 2, is represented by a two-dimensional PN neural processor composed of densely interconnected antagonistic positive and negative neural units. Each neural unit receives inputs from an external source as well as all other neural units in the processor. All steady-state and temporal phenomena associated with neural information processing stem from the coupled interactions of these antagonistic neural

---

[1] P, Positive for the behavior of excitatory neurons. N, Negative for the behavior of inhibitory neurons.

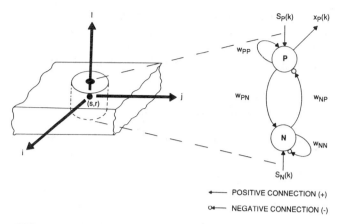

FIG. 1. A schematic diagram of the coupled interactions between a spatially isolated pair of positive and negative neural computing units.

units. The basic neural information processing element in the PN neural processor is, therefore, a spatially localized pair of antagonistic positive and negative neural computing units. A mathematical model of the PN neural processor is described in the following section.

3. THE MATHEMATICAL MODEL OF THE POSITIVE AND NEGATIVE NEURAL UNITS

The two state variables that describe the dynamic activity exhibited by the neural computing units at spatial location (s, r) are defined as the proportion of positive (excitatory) neurons active, $x_P(s, r, k)$, and the proportion of negative (inhibitory) neurons active, $x_N(s, r, k)$, at the spatio-temporal location (s, r, k). A neuron is assumed to be active if it is firing a sequence of action potentials and the measured axon potential at time k is greater than the rest potential. Since the response activities of the individual nerve cells in a neural unit are asynchronous, the proportion of neurons active at time k is composed of nonrefractory neurons that received new inputs and refractory neurons whose action potentials have not fully decayed.

The functional dynamics exhibited by a neural computing unit is defined by a first-order nonlinear state equation. For a discrete-time model of the neural unit dynamics, it is assumed that the sampling period is less than the time constant of the action potential generated by any constituent neuron. The state variables $x_P(s, r, k + 1)$ and $x_N(s, r, k + 1)$ generated at time $(k + 1)$ by the positive and the negative neural units at spatial location (s, r) of a two-dimensional PN neural processor are modeled as

$$x_P(s, r, k + 1) = \alpha x_P(s, r, k) + \beta y_P(s, r, k) \\ - \gamma x_P(s, r, k) \cdot y_P(s, r, k) \quad (1)$$

and

$$x_N(s, r, k + 1) = \alpha x_N(s, r, k) + \beta y_N(s, r, k) \\ - \gamma x_N(s, r, k) \cdot y_N(s, r, k) \quad (2)$$

The three most important factors that affect the dynamic properties of a neural unit are:

(i) The proportion of neurons active at time $(k + 1)$ that were active during the previous sampling period at time k. This factor is given by the term $\alpha x_\psi(s, r, k)$ in Eqs. (1) and (2), where the subscript ψ indicates either a positive (P) or a negative (N) state, and $\alpha < 1$ is the rate of decay in the proportion of neurons that are still active after one sampling period.

(ii) The proportion of neurons in the neural unit that is receiving inputs greater than an intrinsic threshold, $y_\psi(s, r, k)$. This factor is given by the term $\beta y_\psi(s, r, k)$, where β is the rate of growth in the proportion of neurons that become active during one sampling period. The rate of growth in neural activity is often assumed to be $\beta = 1 - \alpha$.

(iii) The proportion of neurons in the neural unit that are refractory but still receiving inputs greater than an intrinsic threshold is given by the expression $\gamma x_\psi(s, r, k) \cdot y_\psi(s, r, k)$. The rate of growth in refractory neurons during one sampling period is γ, where $\gamma \leq \beta$.

The proportion of neurons in a neural computing unit that receive inputs greater than a threshold value is given

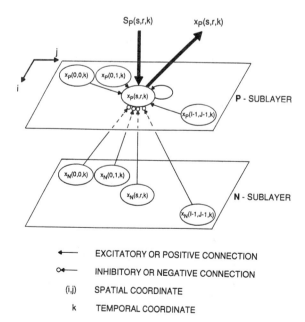

FIG. 2. A two-dimensional neural network structure with positive and negative neural computing units representing a PN neural processor. Connections are only shown to the positve neural unit at spatial location (s, r) and time k. The external stimulus applied to this neural unit is $S_P(s, r, k)$ and the corresponding external response is $x_P(s, r, k)$.

by a nonlinear function of the total applied inputs $u_\psi(s, r, k)$. This nonlinear input transformation function, $f_\psi(u_\psi(s, r, k))$, is related to the distribution of the neural thresholds, $g_\psi(u_\psi(s, r, k))$, within the neural unit. If the probability distribution of these neural thresholds about an aggregate value θ_ψ is given by a unimodal distribution, as shown in Fig. 3a, then the nonlinear input transformation is sigmoidal as shown in Fig. 3b. Thus, the proportion of neurons in a neural unit receiving inputs greater than an intrinsic threshold is given by the expression

$$y_\psi(s, r, k) = f_\psi(u_\psi(s, r, k))$$

$$= \int_{-\infty}^{u_\varphi(s,r,k)} g_\psi(u_\psi(s, r, k))du_\psi(s, r, k), \quad (3)$$

where the parameter pair (v_ψ, θ_ψ) determines the transformational properties of the function $f_\psi(\cdot)$. The parameter v_ψ is defined as the maximum slope of the sigmoidal relationship at the point of inflection given by the aggregate value θ_ψ. In other words, for a particular distribution of neural thresholds it is possible to determine the proportion of neurons receiving supra-threshold inputs by integrating the neural threshold distribution over the total applied inputs, Eq. (3).

The physiological significance of the sigmoidal curve in Fig. 3b is that for low levels of excitation most neurons within a neural unit will not be excited, whereas for very strong levels of excitation nearly all neurons become excited. An important assumption in deriving this function is that each neural unit is composed of only one "type" of neuron. This enables us to define the distribution of neural thresholds as a unimodal function, Fig. 3a. If more than one type of cell exists, then the nonlinear input

transformation function, $f_\psi(\cdot)$, becomes more complex. A unimodal threshold distribution is given as

$$g_\psi(u_\psi(s, r, k)) = \tfrac{1}{2} (v_\psi \operatorname{sech}^2(v_\psi(u_\psi(s, r, k) - \theta_\psi))) \quad (4)$$

and the corresponding monotonically increasing nonlinear input transformation function is

$$f_\psi(u_\psi(s, r, k)) = \tfrac{1}{2} [1 + \tanh(v_\psi(u_\psi(s, r, k) - \theta_\psi))], \quad (5)$$

where the subscript ψ is either P or N.

The input incident on a positive neural unit is defined as the proportion of neurons receiving supra-threshold inputs, and is given as

$$y_P(s, r, k) = f_P(u_P(s, r, k)). \quad (6)$$

Correspondingly, the input incident on the negative neural unit is given as

$$y_N(s, r, k) = f_N(u_N(s, r, k)). \quad (7)$$

The total inputs $u_P(s, r, k)$ and $u_N(s, r, k)$ applied to the corresponding neural unit at location (s, r) and time k are given by

$$u_P(s, r, k) = \omega_{PP} \sum_{i=0}^{I-1} \sum_{j=0}^{J-1} n_{PP}(i - s, j - r)x_P(i, j, k)$$

$$- \omega_{NP} \sum_{i=0}^{I-1} \sum_{j=0}^{J-1} n_{NP}(i - s, j - r)x_N(i, j, k)$$

$$+ S_P(s, r, k) \quad (8)$$

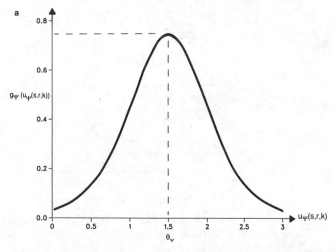
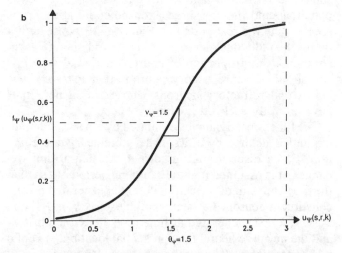

FIG. 3. Unimodal threshold distribution and the corresponding sigmoidal input transformation function for determining the proportion of neurons with total inputs, $u_\psi(s, r, k)$, greater than the threshold value. In this example $\theta_\psi = 1.5$ and $v_\psi = 1.5$, where the subscript ψ is either P or N. (a) A unimodal probability distribution $g_\psi(u_\psi(s, r, k))$ of the neural thresholds about θ_ψ. (b) The nonlinear sigmoidal function $f_\psi(u_\psi(s, r, k))$ arising from the neural threshold distribution given in (a).

and

$$u_N(s, r, k) = \omega_{PN} \sum_{i=0}^{I-1} \sum_{j=0}^{J-1} n_{PN}(i - s, j - r)x_P(i, j, k)$$

$$- \omega_{NN} \sum_{i=0}^{I-1} \sum_{j=0}^{J-1} n_{NN}(i - s, j - r)x_N(i, j, k)$$

$$+ S_N(s, r, k), \qquad (9)$$

where $S_P(s, r, k)$ and $S_N(s, r, k)$ are the external visual stimuli, $\omega_{\psi\psi'}$ is the mean synaptic weight of all the neural connections from the neural unit ψ to ψ', and $n_{\psi\psi'}(i - s, j - r)$ is a normalized spatial distribution function that describes the relative strength of the connections between the neurons in these different neural units with respect to the lateral distance $(i - s, j - r)$ which separates them.

If it is assumed that the spatial distribution function is isotropic, then the strength of the synaptic weights will decrease monotonically with distance from the origin at location (s, r). This condition of isotropy ensures that the relative strength of the connections between the neural units are

$$n_{\psi\psi'}(i - s, j - r) = n_{\psi\psi'}(p - s, q - r) \qquad (10)$$

for any ψ neural unit located at (i, j) or (p, q) of equal distance from the ψ' neural unit at location (s, r), regardless of direction.

The isotropic assumption enables the PN neural processor to exhibit the lateral excitatory on-center and inhibitory off-surround interactions commonly found in the nervous system. These neural interactions are most commonly defined as a circular receptive field [4, 10, 19–21] from which the inputs converge to a single sensory neuron. Neural network models with extensive lateral inhibition are often employed to describe these receptive field structures. However, a simple network model containing only lateral inhibition [10] is incapable of describing the complex computational operations associated with neural information processing because most nervous tissue layers, including those found in the visual cortex, contain densely interconnected populations of excitatory and inhibitory neurons. These more complex lateral on-center off-surround field structures are found in various nervous tissue layers associated with the hippocampus, neocortex, and cerebellum [12].

A normalized spatial distribution function incorporating this isotropic assumption is described as a two-dimensional Gaussian function written as

$$n_{\psi\psi'}(i - s, j - r)$$
$$= 1/(2\pi \sigma_{\psi\psi'}^2)\exp[-\{(i - s)^2 + (j - r)^2\}/(2\sigma_{\psi\psi'}^2)], \qquad (11)$$

where $\sigma_{\psi\psi'}$ is the standard deviation or spatial spread of the synaptic connections with respect to the lateral distance. A block diagram of Eqs. (1) to (11) for the spatially isolated antagonistic neural units is shown in Fig. 4.

A variety of spatial diffusion characteristics associated with neural field structures can be realized by employing different normalized spatial distribution functions. For example, if the spatial distribution function is assumed to be symmetric but directionally dependent, then the neural units will respond to regional orientations in the stimulus pattern. This response behavior is similar to the activity of the simple cells situated in the primary visual cortex [19, 21]. The numerous different possibilities for the spatial distribution functions are beyond the scope of the present paper, and therefore, this discussion is restricted to the isotropic case.

4. A QUALITATIVE DESCRIPTION OF THE PN NEURAL PROCESSOR DYNAMICS

The PN neural processor is not designed to emulate any specific anatomical region in the biological vision system. Rather, it represents a simplified mathematical model of a generalized nervous tissue layer. By modifying the parameters of the PN neural processor it is possible to generate a variety of different dynamical modes that can be correlated with biological neural activity [1–3, 22, 31, 32]. From a computational perspective, this neural processor is capable of generating a variety of steady-state and temporal phenomena that can be used to perform tasks such as STVM, STF, and PFM to name but a few.

The spatio-temporal stimulus, $S_P(k)$, used for the following simulation studies is defined as a scaled spatial pattern $b \cdot \lambda_P$ that varies with respect to a temporal function $\Phi(k)$ combined with a time-varying pseudo-random noise component $b \cdot \eta(k)$. Thus, the stimulus is written as

$$S_P(k) = b\{\lambda_P \cdot \Phi(k) + \eta(k)\}, \qquad (12a)$$

where

$$S_P(k) = \bigcup_{i=0}^{I-1} \bigcup_{j=0}^{J-1} \{S_P(i, j, k)\}, \qquad (12b)$$

b is a scalar that defines the upper bound of the stimulus intensity, $S_P(k)$, over the interval $[0, b]$ for $b \leq 1$, and $\bigcup$ is the union operation.

Unless it is stated otherwise, the spatial pattern λ_P is defined as a (200 $\times$ 200) pixel array with individual intensity values distributed over the range [0, 1.0] and is written as

$$\lambda_P = \bigcup_{i=0}^{I-1} \bigcup_{j=0}^{J-1} \{\lambda_P(i, j, k)\}, \quad I = J = 200. \qquad (13)$$

283

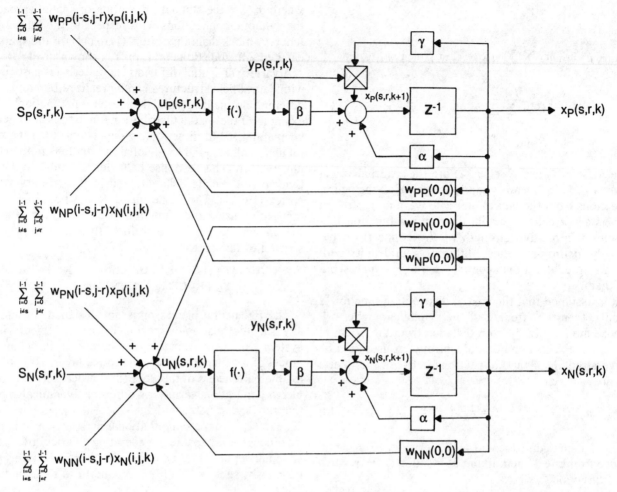

FIG. 4. A block diagram of Eqs. (1)–(11) for the coupled positive and negative neural units. The input and output response are shown for the neural units at spatial location (s, r).

The temporal function is defined as a pulse wave over the period $k \subset [k_a, k_b]$,

$$\Phi(k) = \begin{cases} 0 & \text{for } k < k_a, \ k > k_b \\ 1.0 & \text{for } k_a \leq k \leq k_b, \end{cases} \quad (14)$$

where k_a corresponds to the instant in time when the spatial pattern is suddenly applied to the PN neural processor and k_b is the instant when the pulse ceases.

The noise component $\eta(k)$ is a pseudo-random variable bounded over the range $[0, 0.2]$. This term is written as

$$\eta(k) = \bigcup_{i=0}^{I-1} \bigcup_{j=0}^{J-1} \{\eta(i, j, k)\}. \quad (15)$$

The stimuli for the negative neural units are zero; that is, $\mathbf{S}_N(k) = 0$, for all time k.

A direct analytical solution for determining the steady-state and temporal behavior exhibited by the PN neural processor is not possible because of the inherent nonlinearities in Eqs. (1) and (2). However, these nonlinear equations can be analyzed qualitatively by obtaining phase trajectories in the $x_P - x_N$ phase plane [9, 31]. These trajectories enable the system characteristics to be observed without solving the nonlinear equations. The locus of points where the phase trajectories have a given slope is called an *isocline curve*.

The steady-state activity exhibited by the various neural units of the PN neural processor is investigated by determining the isocline curves for $\Delta x_P(s, r) = 0$ and $\Delta x_N(s, r) = 0$ in the x_P–x_N phase plane. From Eqs. (1) and (2) these isocline curves are written as

$$\Delta x_P(s, r) \underline{\Delta} x_P(s, r, k + 1) - x_P(s, r, k) = 0 \quad (16a)$$

and

$$\Delta x_N(s, r) \underline{\Delta} x_N(s, r, k + 1) - x_N(s, r, k) = 0. \quad (16b)$$

From the assumption of an isotropic spatial distribution function, Eq. (11), the isocline curve for $\Delta x_P(s, r) = 0$ in terms of the state variable $x_N(s, r, k)$ is given by

$$x_N(s, r, k)$$

$$= \frac{2\pi\sigma_{NP}^2}{\omega_{NP}} \left\{ \omega_{PP} \sum_{i=0}^{I-1} \sum_{j=0}^{J-1} n_{PP}(i - s, j - r)x_P(i, j, k) \right.$$

$$- \omega_{NP} \sum_{\substack{i=0 \\ i \neq s}}^{I-1} \sum_{\substack{j=0 \\ j \neq r}}^{J-1} n_{NP}(i - s, j - r) \cdot x_N(i, j, k)$$

$$\left. - f_P^{-1}\left(\frac{(1 - \alpha)x_P(s, r, k)}{\beta - \gamma x_P(s, r, k)}\right) + S_P(s, r, k) \right\} \quad (17)$$

and the corresponding isocline curve for $\Delta x_N(s, r) = 0$ in terms of the state variable $x_P(s, r, k)$ is given by

$$x_P(s, r, k)$$

$$= \frac{2\pi\sigma_{PN}^2}{\omega_{PN}} \left\{ -\omega_{PN} \sum_{\substack{i=0 \\ i \neq S}}^{I-1} \sum_{\substack{j=0 \\ j \neq r}}^{J-1} n_{PN}(i - s, j - r)x_P(i, j, k) \right.$$

$$+ \omega_{NN} \sum_{\substack{i=0 \\ i \neq s}}^{I-1} \sum_{\substack{j=0 \\ j \neq r}}^{J-1} n_{NN}(i - s, j - r) \cdot x_N(i, j, k)$$

$$\left. + f_N^{-1}\left(\frac{(1 - \alpha)x_N(s, r, k)}{\beta - \gamma x_N(s, r, k)}\right) - S_N(s, r, k) \right\}. \quad (18)$$

In order to determine the shape of the isocline curves for $\Delta x_P(s, r) = 0$ and $\Delta x_N(s, r) = 0$ it is necessary to first

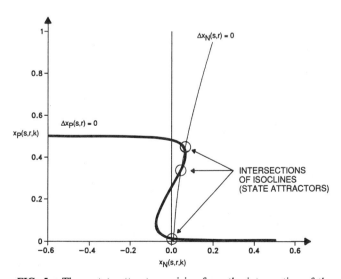

FIG. 5. Three state attractors arising from the intersection of the isocline curves for $\Delta x_P(s, r) = 0$ and $\Delta x_N(s, r) = 0$ in the x_P–x_N phase plane. The parameters used in this example are given in Table 1 and the stimulus intensity is $S_P(s, r, k) = 0$.

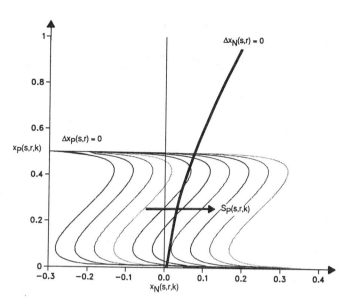

FIG. 6. The shift in the position of the isocline curve for $\Delta x_P(s, r) = 0$ due to an increase in the intensity of the stimulus $S_P(s, r, k)$. The parameters used in this figure are given in Table 1.

establish equilibrium conditions throughout the entire PN neural processor for a given stimulus pattern. A stimulus pattern with uniform intensity is used to initially determine the parameters necessary for a PN neural processor to generate a particular mode of response activity.

4.1. Multiple State Attractors: Short-Term Visual Memory

The intersections arising from the isoclines for $\Delta x_P(s, r) = 0$ and $\Delta x_N(s, r) = 0$, Fig. 5, represent the steady-state values known as *state attractors*. For neural units with only one type of positive or negative neuron, the number of state attractors is generally one or three. If more than one intersection exists then these state attractors alternate between regions of stability and instability [22, 31]. Linearized stability analysis about each state attractor can be used to determine local stability properties [22]. The effect of changing the magnitude of the external stimulus, $S_P(s, r, k)$, is to translate the isocline curve for $\Delta x_P(s, r) = 0$ parallel to the $x_N -$ axis, thereby altering the position and possibly even the number of state attractors. This effect is shown in Fig. 6. Typical parameters that are used to generate three state attractors for STVM are given in Table 1.

The observation that the position and the number of state attractors can be altered by a stimulus, $S_P(s, r, k)$, suggests that multiple attractors may generate a hysteresis loop over a specific range of stimulus intensities as shown Fig. 7. An important property of this hysteresis phenomena is that in order for the state activity, $x_P(s, r, k)$, to switch from a rest state to an excited state requires

TABLE 1
Typical Parameters Used to Generate Three State Attractors for
Short-Term Visual Memory (STVM)

$\alpha = 0.9$	$\beta = 0.1$	$\gamma = 0.1$	
$v_P = 1.5$	$\theta_P = 1.5$	$v_N = 1.5$	$\theta_N = 1.5$
$\omega_{PP} = 5$	$\omega_{NP} = 4$	$\omega_{PN} = 2$	$\omega_{NN} = 4$
$\sigma_{PP} = 0.4$	$\sigma_{NP} = 0.8$	$\sigma_{PN} = 0.8$	$\sigma_{NN} = 0.4$

the stimulus intensity to be greater than some upper threshold value, $S_P(s, r, k) > \Omega_H$. Similarly, the state activity can return to its original rest state by a future stimulus with an intensity less than a lower threshold value, $S_P(s, r, k) < \Omega_L$. The hysteresis phenomenon exhibits an important noise immunity characteristic beneficial for storing features from a noisy stimulus [5, 14, 15, 17, 22, 27, 31]. The inherent upper and lower thresholds prevent small perturbations or fluctuations within the applied stimulus pattern from drastically altering the PN neural processor steady-state activity. A stimulus that varies significantly from its prior value is required to alter the neural unit response activity.

A PN neural processor with neural units that exhibit localized hysteresis phenomena can function as a form of STVM [14–17, 22, 31]. This type of memory is the result of ongoing neural activity that is maintained by the dense excitatory feedback which exists among the various neural units. The neural activity will reverberate or circulate within the closed-loop neural circuitry of the PN neural processor such that the overall output response activity will remain constant, even after the stimulus pattern is removed. In this way any recipient information can be recalled while this reverberation occurs, and it will continue to occur until a strong inhibitory influence destroys the reverberating activity. Figure 8 is an example of STVM where the individual neural units of the PN neural processor exhibit a single hysteresis loop. A paper describing a PN neural processor exhibiting multiple hysteresis phenomena is being prepared by the authors. Any additional complexities introduced by these neural units are compensated for by the overall simplicity in the network's performance. For example, changes to the contents of visual memory occur without any physical modifications to the strength of the synaptic connections.

4.2. Temporal Phenomena: Transient Behavior and Limit Cycle Oscillations

The temporal behavior generated by a neural unit with multiple steady-state characteristics is primarily the switching action between different stable attractors. However, there are two classes of temporal responses generated by a PN neural processor which are very useful for information processing. Both classes of temporal

behavior are generated around single attractors in the x_P–x_N phase plane.

4.2.1. *Transient behavior: Spatio-temporal filtering.* A stimulus applied to a nervous tissue layer results in the formation of spatio-temporal patterns of neural activity. These patterns of neural activity arise from the nervous tissue time constants and the laterally distributed feedback that exist among the constituent neurons. This response behavior implies that the various neural units, or subpopulations, of a nervous tisue layer will simultaneously process the neural signals in both space and time [8, 10, 23, 32]. By integrating both spatial and temporal components into the same neural response activity, a nervous tissue layer will respond strongly to contiguous and coherent attributes in the stimulus and not to the random fluctuations contained therein.

One important task of early biological vision is to reduce the noise and unwanted details in the visual stimulus pattern without significantly degrading the embedded information. This role of visual information processing can be summarized as reducing the ambiguities inherent in the stimulus pattern while enhancing local discontinuities in an effort to better partition the stimulus pattern into coherent regions for additional analysis by the higher cortical levels. Although the visual stimulus pattern is initially received via the retina by a two-dimensional array of independent photoreceptors, the information contained within this pattern is visually perceived by humans as cohesive surfaces, boundaries, colors, and movements, and not as random variations in the incident inten-

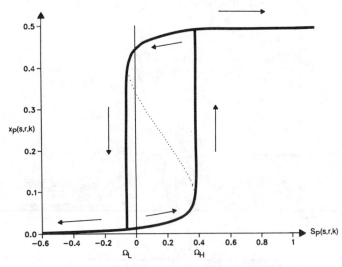

FIG. 7. The hysteresis loop arising from the isocline curves for $\Delta x_P(s, r) = 0$ and $\Delta x_N(s, r) = 0$ when the stimulus intensity is varied over the range [−1.0, 1.0]. The term Ω_L is the lower threshold intensity and the term Ω_H is the upper threshold intensity necessary for the neural activity to switch states. For the parameters given in Table 1 these thresholds are $\Omega_L = -0.05$ and $\Omega_H = +0.4$.

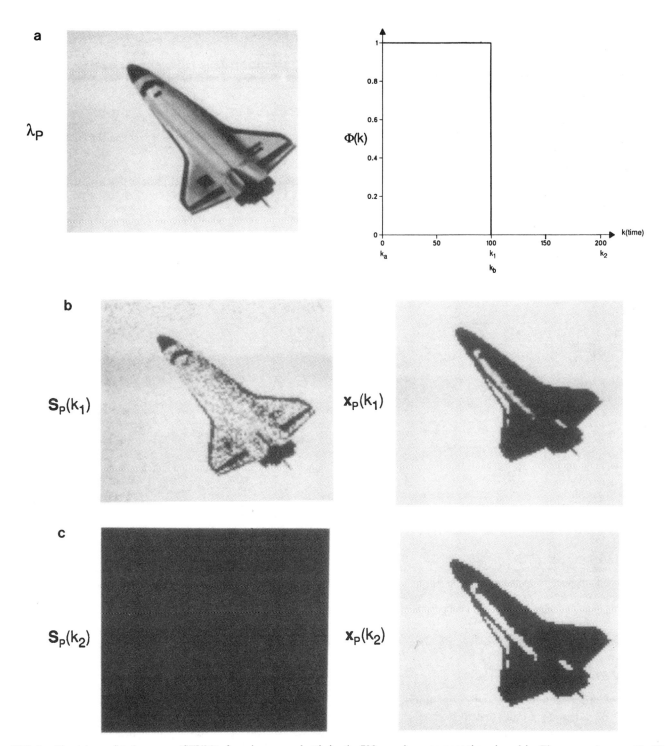

FIG. 8. Short-term visual memory (STVM) of a noisy space shuttle by the PN neural processor at times k_1 and k_2. The parameters used in this example are given in Table 1. The PN neural processor responses, $x_P(k_1)$ and $x_P(k_2)$, exhibit the important spatio-temporal noise suppression properties associated with the multiple state attractors. (a) The spatial pattern, λ_P, and the temporal component, $\Phi(k)$, of the visual stimulus. The upper bound of the stimulus intensity is $b = 0.5$. (b) The stimulus, $S_P(k_1)$, and the PN neural processor response, $x_P(k_1)$, at time k_1. (c) The stimulus, $S_P(k_2)$, and PN neural processor response, $x_P(k_2)$, at time k_2.

sities. Two simultaneous psychophysical manifestations of this neural information processing property mechanism that are commonly found throughout the early stage of human vision are *constancy* and *contrast*. Constancy is summarized as the grouping of similar spatio-temporal stimuli into a common response, whereas contrast is the segregation of dissimilar spatio-temporal stimuli.

Spatial constancy and contrast can be maintained in a

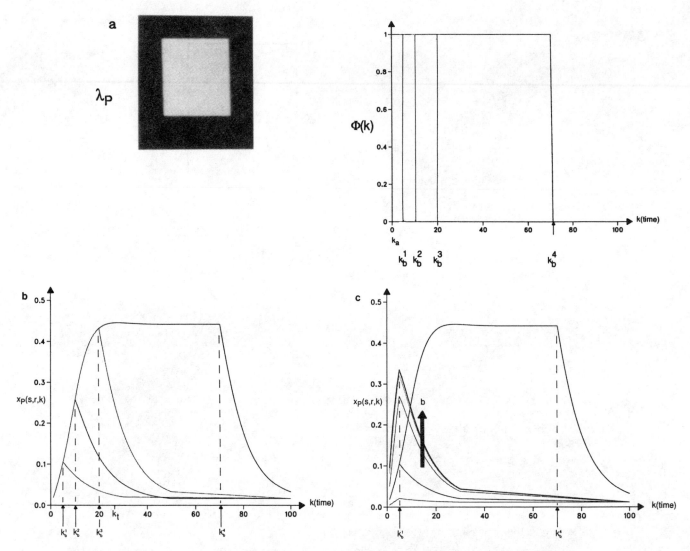

FIG. 9. Temporal properties of the spatio-temporal threshold associated with transient behavior arising from the parameters given in Table 2. In (b) the stimulus will generate a strong response only if it is applied for a duration of time greater than a temporal threshold, $k_b^i > k_t$. Even if the applied stimulus intensity is increased for a short temporal duration, as shown in (c), it will fail to generate a strong response. (a) The spatial pattern, λ_P, and the temporal component, $\Phi(k)$ of the stimulus. The upper bound of the stimulus intensity is $b = 1.0$. The spatial pattern used in this example is a (100×100) pixel array. (b) The temporal response of the positive neural unit at spatial location (s, r) to different temporal profiles [k_a, k_b^i] of the stimulus, where $i = 1, 2, 3$, and 4. (c) The temporal response of the positive neural unit at spatial location (s, r) to a stimulus with an increasing intensity, $b = 0.5, 1.0, 1.5, 2.0, 2.5$, and 3.0, but applied for a short temporal duration from k_a to k_b^1.

PN neural processor through the dense lateral feedback between the various spatially distributed neural units that generate localized transient behavior. Correspondingly, the temporal constancy and contrast are sustained by these same neural units responding in a dynamic fashion to both the stimulus and the lateral feedback inputs. The neural cells located in many of the sensory and cortical nervous tissue layers associated with biological vision are organized in such a way that the stimulation of a given neural unit will inhibit the activity of the neurons located in the neighboring neural units [4, 10, 19, 21]. The effect of this *lateral inhibition* is to enable the neurons to

discriminate the information contained in the neural signals being received and processed.

The effect of interdependent spatial and temporal components of visual information processing is illustrated in Figs. 9 and 10. If a stimulus pattern occurs too briefly then the PN neural processor will exhibit a very weak response regardless of the stimulus intensity. For neurovision system applications this inherent spatio-temporal threshold will suppress any time-varying spatially distributed random intensity fluctuations associated with pixel noise. By suppressing these local disturbances the PN neural processor enforces regional constancy on the out-

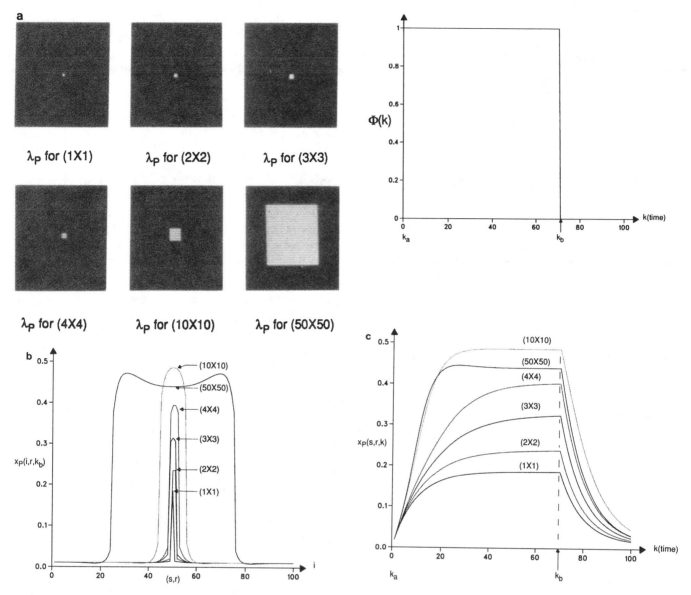

FIG. 10. The effect of the spatial dimensions of a stimulus on the steady-state response for a positive neural unit centered at (s, r). In this example the spatial spread values are $\sigma_{PP} = \sigma_{NN} = 3$ and $\sigma_{PN} = \sigma_{NP} = 6$. A very narrow stimulus applied for a time duration greater than the temporal threshold will still fail to trigger a strong steady-state response. The stimulus pattern of dimension (50×50) generates a lower steady-state response than (10×10) because of contrast effects at the boundaries. (a) The spatial patterns, λ_P, and the temporal component, $\Phi(k)$, of the stimuli. The upper bound of the stimulus intensity is $b = 1.0$. The various spatial patterns used in this example are (100×100) pixel arrays. (b) The cross-sectional profiles at instant k_b for the stimulus patterns given in (a). (c) The temporal response of the positive neural unit at spatial location (s, r) to inputs with different spatial dimensions.

put of each neural unit. Typical parameters that enable the neural processor to generate transient behavior for STF are given in Table 2.

An important attribute of any visual information processor is its sensitivity to the intensity contrast within the stimulus pattern. The sensitivity of the human visual system to the spatial spacing of a set of contrasting areas is known as *contrast sensitivity* [4, 19–21]. The input used

TABLE 2
Typical Parameters Used to Generate Transient Behavior for
Spatio-Temporal Filtering (STF)

$\alpha = 0.9$	$\beta = 0.1$	$\gamma = 0.1$	
$v_N = 1.5$	$\theta_N = 1.5$	$v_P = 1.5$	$\theta_N = 1.5$
$\omega_{PP} = 4$	$\omega_{NP} = 4$	$\omega_{PN} = 4$	$\omega_{NN} = 4$
$\sigma_{PP} = 0.75$	$\sigma_{NP} = 1.5$	$\sigma_{PN} = 1.5$	$\sigma_{NN} = 0.75$

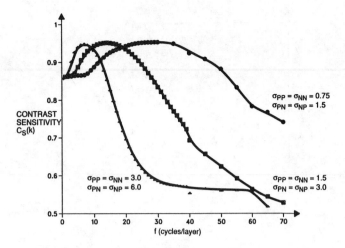

FIG. 11. Three different contrast sensitivity functions generated by the PN neural processor when employing different spatial spread values for the synaptic connections, $\sigma_{\psi\psi'}$, given in Eq. (11). The maximum peak-to-trough amplitude taken over the full dimension of the neural processor is given as the contrast sensitivity.

to determine contrast sensitivity is often given as a bar grating pattern in which the intensity along the horizontal profile varies in a sinusoidal manner. The units of spatial frequency of the bar grating patterns are expressed as cycles/millimeter. The contrast of the output pattern, $C_S(k)$, is measured by the maximum peak to minimum trough amplitude over the entire PN neural processor and is given by

$$C_S(k)$$

$$= \left| \bigvee_i^I \bigvee_j^J \{x_P(i, j, k)\} - \bigwedge_i^I \bigwedge_j^J \{x_P(i, j, k)\} \right|,$$

(19)

where $\bigvee$ and $\bigwedge$ are the maximum and minimum operations, respectively. The spatial frequency of the PN neural processor response is given in terms of cycles/layer. This contrast sensitivity function, $C_S(k)$, enables the response of the visual information processor to be described as a function of different spatial frequencies.

The three contrast sensitivity curves shown in Fig. 11 illustrate that the PN neural processor can be *tuned* to different spatial frequencies by adjusting the spatial spread values used for the synaptic connections, $\sigma_{\psi\psi'}$. The attenuation of both low and high spatial frequencies in the PN neural processor response is consistent with the contrast sensitivity observed in human vision [4, 19, 20].

The spatial and the temporal properties generated within a highly interconnected network of neural units which exhibit transient behavior can provide a plausible explanation for a variety of psychophysical observations.

In terms of visual perception, a sharp change in the contrast between an object and its background will cause two thin parallel bands of intensity to be perceived along the object contour. These bands are not physically present in the stimulus pattern but are caused by the neurons of the various nervous tissue layers inhibiting the activity of their neighboring nerve cells. This perceived enhancement of contrast is called the Mach Band effect [20]. The reflected light intensity of each strip in Fig. 12a is uniform over its entire width and differs from its neighbors by a constant amount. Pseudo-random noise is superimposed on the stimulus pattern. The visual appearance or *perception* of these gray scales is such that each strip is darker along its right side than its left. Figure 12b is a recreation of this Mach Band effect by the PN neural processor when it is programmed with the parameters in Table 2.

4.2.2. *Limit Cycle Oscillations: Pulse Frequency Modulation.* The second important temporal phenomenon that can be generated by the PN neural processor is limit cycle oscillations. The limit cycle oscillations are observed in response to a constant stimulation as shown in Fig. 13. There exists a threshold value, Ω_L, for the stimulus intensity which must be exceeded in order to evoke such oscillatory behavior. This lower threshold Ω_L is regarded as a necessary characteristic for low-level noise immunity. For a supra-threshold stimulus the frequency of the oscillations is a monotonic function of intensity as illustrated in Fig. 14. For extremely large intensities the limit cycle activity is extinguished because the neural units become saturated with positive or excitatory activity. Thus, there also exists an upper threshold, Ω_H, for generating limit cycle oscillations. Typical parameters that enable the PN neural processor to generate spatially localized limit cycle oscillations are given in Table 3.

The capability of generating limit cycle behavior enables the PN neural processor to uniquely encode the intensities of the analog visual information. Engineers know from communication theory that pulse frequency-modulated signals are less susceptible to channel noise than are amplitude-modulated (AM) signals and are, therefore, the preferred method of transmitting information over long distances.

TABLE 3

Typical Parameters Used to Generate Limit Cycle Oscillations for Pulse Frequency Modulation (PFM)

$\alpha = 0.9$	$\beta = 0.1$	$\gamma = 0.1$	
$v_N = 1.5$	$\theta_N = 2.0$	$v_P = 1.5$	$\theta_N = 1.5$
$\omega_{PP} = 8$	$\omega_{NP} = 8$	$\omega_{PN} = 8$	$\omega_{NN} = 0.1$
$\sigma_{PP} = 0$	$\sigma_{NP} = 0$	$\sigma_{PN} = 0$	$\sigma_{NN} = 0$

290

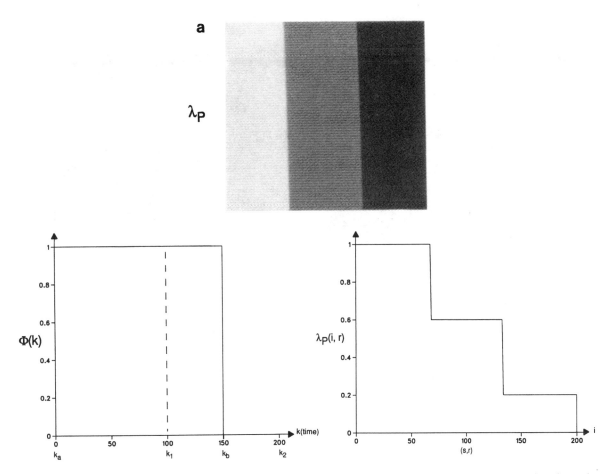

FIG. 12. A recreation of the Mach Band effect using the PN neural processor. The neural processor response at time k_1, $\mathbf{x}_P(k_1)$, exhibits simultaneous noise suppression and boundary enhancement phenomena. (a) The spatial pattern, $\boldsymbol{\lambda}_P$, and the temporal component, $\Phi(k)$, of the stimulus. The upper bound of the stimulus intensity is $b = 1.0$. (b) The applied stimulus, $\mathbf{S}_P(k_1)$, and the PN neural processor response, $\mathbf{x}_P(k_1)$ at time k_1.

However, for PFM applications it is necessary that the pulse-decoded response be a near duplicate of the original stimulus pattern. In order to prevent spatial diffusion characteristics from corrupting the frequency of limit cycle oscillations generated by the PN neural processor it is necessary to assume that the spatial spread of the synaptic connections is zero; that is, $\sigma_{\psi\eta\psi'} = 0$. In this way each spatially localized pair of antagonistic positive and negative neural units uniquely encodes the recipient stimulus intensity. If the physiological aspects of neural information processing are to be investigated [10, 32] then the spatial diffusion characteristics are included in the PN neural processor such that $\sigma_{\psi\eta\psi'} > 0$.

Once a PFM signal is received at its destination it may be decoded back into an analog or AM signal for additional processing as shown in Fig. 15. A simple peak detector can be used to convert the limit cycle oscillations to pulses at the transmitter, and then a time-limited pulse counter with a nonlinear signal enhancer, Fig. 16, can be used to reconstruct the image at the receiver.

Figure 17 is an example of a stimulus pattern that is converted to limit cycle behavior by the PN neural processor and then reconstructed using the simple pulse frequency-to-analog converter described above.

5. THE PN NEURAL PROCESSOR: A RETROSPECT

The goal of this paper was to outline the computational capabilities of a multitask visual information processor, called the Positive–Negative neural processor, that may be incorporated into a real-time on-line robust neurovision system for engineering applications. The PN neural processor extended beyond the scope of most specialized networks in that it could perform a variety of diverse tasks associated with early biological vision. The PN neural processor was programmed to generate distinct steady-state and temporal phenomena in order to perform computational tasks such as storing, spatio-temporal filtering, and pulse frequency encoding two-dimensional time-varying signals. This paper did not address

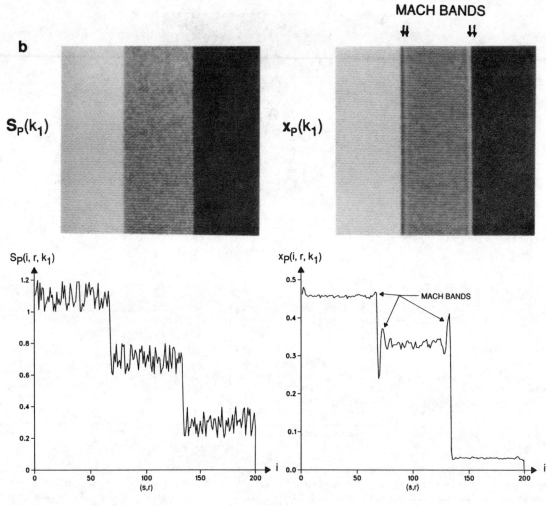

FIG. 12—*Continued*

the applicability of the PN neural processor to higher-level cognitive functions such as associative memory, learning, recognition, and reasoning. However, many of these computational operations may be possible because of the highly parallel and densely interconnected structure of this neural network. It was further postulated that this versatile network could simplify the design, development, and programmability of robust neuro-vision systems that must operate effectively in real-time.

In Section 2 the biological basis of information processing by nervous tissue layers was presented. The biological vision system was conceptualized as a shallow hierarchy of several distinct anatomical regions. Each anatomical region was assumed to be represented by one or more two-dimensional nervous tissue layers. A dynamic neural network model of a generic nervous tissue layer was proposed. This model was loosely based on a mathematical theory for describing the functional dynamics exhibited by cortical and thalamic nervous tissue layers as proposed by Wilson and Cowan [31, 32].

The fundamental neural design and structure of a nervous tissue layer was generalized in the form of a PN neural processor. This dynamic neural processor was described as a two-dimensional array of densely interconnected positive and negative neural computing units. A neural computing unit was assumed to contain a large class of similar neurons that lie in close spatial proximity. Each neural unit was mathematically represented by a nonlinear first-order difference equation. The coupling interaction between individual positive and negative neural units resulted in a variety of dynamic activities which were associated with neural information processing.

These distinct modes of dynamic neural activity were interpreted in Section 4 in terms of storing, filtering, and pulse frequency encoding visual information. This qualitative analysis was used to demonstrate the viability of the PN neural processor as a generic visual information processor for performing certain tasks of early vision. A PN neural processor with neural units that exhibited multiple steady states were shown to temporarily retain at-

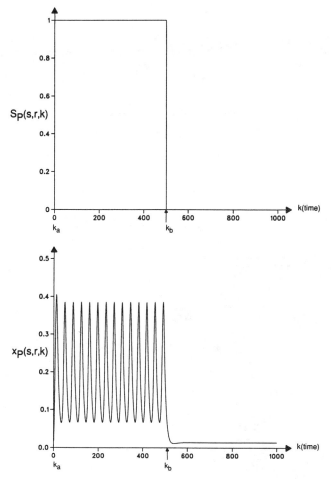

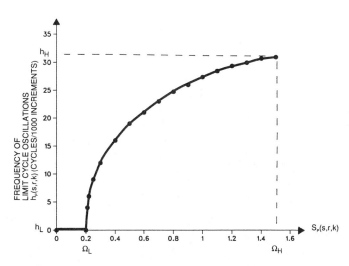

FIG. 13. Temporal response of a positive neural unit at spatial location (s, r) to a stimulus with constant intensity. The parameters used in this simulation are given in Table 3.

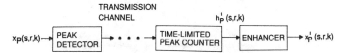

FIG. 15. The block diagram of a pulse frequency-to-analog converter.

tributes of the visual stimulus through the process of neural reverberation [21]. That is, the activity from all neural units circulated throughout the processor such that the overall response activity remained constant. No physical changes were imposed upon the synaptic weights that existed between the different neural units.

Psychophysiological experiments have shown that many perceptual aspects of early vision may be associated with transient neural activity. In this role, a PN neural processor was able to suppress small perturbations that corresponded to neural noise by simultaneously diverging and converging the neural activity in both space and time. Global manifestations of this process were given by the principles of constancy and contrast.

Finally, the ability of the PN neural processor to generate limit cycle oscillations suggested that it could also function as a pulse frequency encoder of the stimulus intensity. From practical considerations certain neurovision systems require that the information be transmitted over long distances through noisy channels. In this capacity, the pulse frequency-modulated signals are less

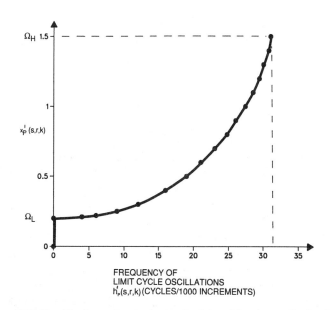

FIG. 16. Nonlinear signal enhancer for determining the amplitude of the signal, $x_P'(s, r, k)$, for different frequencies of limit cycle oscillations, $h_P'(s, r, k)$. The parameters are given in Table 3. The axes of Fig. 14 are inverted in the diagram.

FIG. 14. The frequency of limit cycle activity, $h_P(s, r, k)$, as a function of different constant values for the stimulus intensity $S_P(s, r, k)$. The parameters are given in Table 3.

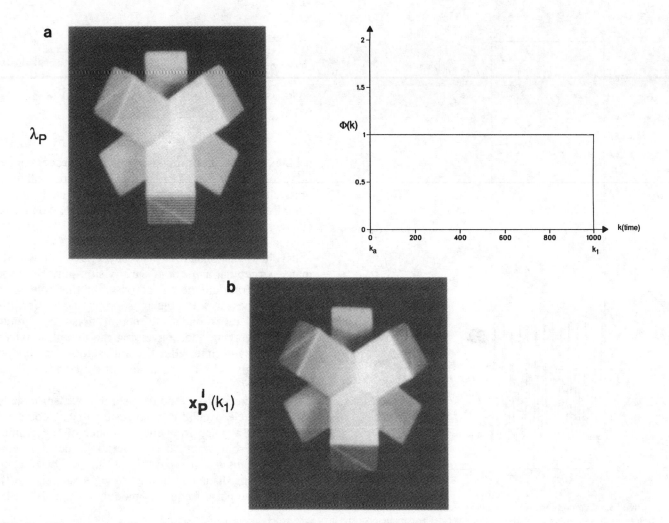

FIG. 17. The reconstructed image of a geometric figure from the frequency of the limit cycle oscillations generated by a PN neural processor programmed with the parameters given in Table 3. (a) The spatial pattern, λ_P, and the temporal component, $\Phi(k)$, of the noise-free stimulus. The upper bound of the stimulus intensity is $b = 1.0$. (b) The pulse frequency-to-analog converter response, $\mathbf{x}_P(k_1)$, at time k_1.

susceptible to channel noise then are analog or amplitude-modulated signals.

6. CONCLUSIONS

The process of early vision must occur in milliseconds and not the minutes or hours it takes all existing digital computer-based vision algorithms. To achieve these capabilities it is necessary to draw on our present knowledge of biological vision physiology in order to aid in the design and development of a more effective machine vision system. Within this framework a multitask visual information processor based loosely on a mathematical theory of the functional dynamics of cortical and thalamic nervous tissue [13–15, 22, 31, 32] was discussed. This neural processor was programmed to store, filter, and pulse frequency encode spatio-temporal visual information. Real-time perceptual vision may be possible by constructing a shallow parallel and hierarchical architecture from numerous PN neural processors that preprocess and store the visual information prior to performing high-level decision operations.

ACKNOWLEDGMENTS

This work has been supported in part by the Network of Centre of Excellence on Neuro-Vision Research (IRIS) and the Natural Sciences and Engineering Research Council of Canada. The authors are grateful to the reviewers for their helpful comments.

REFERENCES

1. S. Amari, Mathematical foundations of neurocomputing, *Proc. IEEE* **78,** 1990, 1443–1462.
2. S. Amari, Dynamic stability of formation of cortical maps, in *Neural Networks: Models and Data* (M. A. Arbib and S. Amari, Eds.), pp. 15–34, Springer-Verlag, New York, 1989.
3. S. Amari, Dynamics of pattern formation in lateral-inhibition type neural fields, *Bio. Cybernet.* **27,** 1977, 77–87.

4. V. Bruce and P. R. Green, *Visual Perception: Physiology, Psychology and Ecology,* Lawrence Erlbaum Assoc., London, 1985.

5. B. G. Cragg and H. N. Y. Temperley, Memory: The analogy with ferromagnetic hysteresis, *Brain* **78,** 1955, 304–316.

6. F. Crick, Memory and molecular turnover, *Nature* **312,** 1984, 101.

7. F. Crick, The recent excitement about neural networks, *Nature* **337,** 1989, 129–132.

8. H. Dinse and J. Best, Receptive field organization of the cat's visual cortex exhibit strong spatio-temporal interactions, *Neurosci. Lett.* **18,** 1984, S75.

9. O. I. Elgerd, *Control Systems Theory,* McGraw–Hill, New York, 1967.

10. W. J. Freeman, *Mass Action in the Nervous System,* Academic Press, New York, 1975.

11. W. J. Freeman, Why neural networks don't yet fly: Inquiry into neurodynamics of biological intelligence, in *Proceedings, IEEE International Conference on Neural Networks, San Diego, CA, July 24–27, 1988,* Vol. II, pp. 1–7.

12. S. Grossberg, Contour enhancement, short-term memory and constancies in reverberating neural networks, *Stud. Appl. Math.* **52,** 1973, 231–257.

13. M. M. Gupta, Biological basis for computer vision: Some perspectives, in *Proceedings, SPIE'S Advances in Intelligent Robotics, Philadelphia, PA, Nov. 5–10, 1989,* pp. 505–516.

14. M. M. Gupta and G. K. Knopf, A neural network with multiple hysteresis capabilities for short-term visual memory (STVM), in *Proceedings, International Joint Conference on Neural Networks, Seattle WA, July 8–12, 1991,* pp. 671–676.

15. M. M. Gupta and G. K. Knopf, A dynamic neural network for visual memory, in *Proceedings, SPIE's Conference on Visual Communications and Image Processing, Lausanne, Switzerland, Oct. 2–4, 1990,* pp. 1044–1055.

16. M. M. Gupta and G. K. Knopf, A multi-task neural network for vision systems, in *Proceedings, SPIE's Advances in Intelligent Systems, Boston, MA, Nov. 4–9, 1990,* pp. 60–73.

17. G. W. Hoffman, Neurons with hysteresis? in *Computer Simulation in Brain Science* (R. Coterill, Ed.), pp. 74–87, Cambridge Univ. Press, Cambridge, 1988.

18. J. J. Hopfield and D. W. Tank, Computing with neural circuits: A model, *Science* **233,** 1986, 625–633.

19. D. H. Hubel, *Eye, Brain and Vision,* W. H. Freeman and Co., New York, 1988.

20. L. H. Hurvich, *Color Vision,* Sinauer Assoc., Sunderland, MA, 1981.

21. E. R. Kandel and J. H. Schwartz, *Principles of Neural Science,* North-Holland, New York, 1985.

22. G. K. Knopf, *Theoretical Studies of a Dynamic Neuro-Vision Processor with a Biologically Motivated Design,* Ph.D. dissertation, University of Saskatchewan, 1991.

23. G. Krone, M. Mallot, G. Palm, and A. Schuz, Spatio-temporal receptive fields: A dynamical model derived from cortical architectonics, *Proc. Soc. London B* **226,** 1986, 421–444.

24. D. S. Levine, Neural population modeling and psychology: A review, *Math. Biosci.* **66,** 1983, 1–86.

25. R. G. MacGregor and E. R. Lewis, *Neural Modeling: Electrical Signal Processing in the Nervous System,* Plenum, New York, 1977.

26. A. C. Scott, *Neurophysics,* Wiley, New York, 1977.

27. P. Stolorz and G. W. Hoffmann, Learning by selection using energy functions, in *Systems with Learning and Memory Abilities* (J. Delacour and J. C. S. Levy, Eds.), pp. 437–452, North-Holland, New York, 1988.

28. D. J. Tolhurst and J. A. Movshon, Spatial and temporal contrast of striate cortical neurons, *Nature* **257,** 1975, 674–675.

29. L. Uhr, Psychological motivation and underlying concepts, in *Structured Computer Vision* (S. Tanimoto and A. Klinger, Eds.), pp. 1–30, Academic Press, New York, 1980.

30. L. Uhr, Highly parallel, hierarchical, recognition cone perceptual structures, in *Parallel Computer Vision* (L. Uhr, Ed.), pp. 249–292. Academic Press, New York, 1987.

31. H. R. Wilson and J. D. Cowan, Excitatory and inhibitory interaction in localized populations of model neurons, *Biophys. J.* **12,** 1972, 1–24.

32. H. R. Wilson and J. D. Cowan, A mathematical theory of the functional dynamics of cortical and thalamic nervous tissue, *Kybernetik* **13,** 1973, 55–80.

Analysis of Visual Motion by Biological and Computer Systems

SHIMON ULLMAN

MIT ARTIFICIAL INTELLIGENCE LABORATORY

Analysis of motion plays a central role in biological visual systems. Sophisticated mechanisms for observing, extracting, and utilizing motion exist even in simple animals. For example, the frog has efficient "bug detection" mechanisms that respond selectively to small, dark objects moving in its visual field.[1] The ordinary housefly can track moving objects and discover the relative motion between a target and its background, even when the two are identical in texture—and therefore indistinguishable in the absence of relative motion.[2]

In higher animals, including primates, the analysis of motion is "wired" into the visual system from the earliest processing stages. Some species, such as the pigeon[3] and the rabbit[4] (see Grusser and Grusser-Cornehls[5] for other examples) perform rudimentary motion analysis at the retinal level. In other animals, including cats and primates, the first neurons in the visual cortex to receive input from the eyes are already involved in the analysis of motion: they respond well to stimuli moving in one direction, but little, or not at all, to motion in the opposite direction.[6,7]

The central role of motion perception in biological systems is not surprising, since motion reveals valuable information about the environment. The use of motion by biological systems—in particular the human visual system—demonstrates the feasibility of carrying out certain information processing tasks and helps to establish specific goals for computer analysis of time-varying imagery. The tasks examined in this article are the recovery of structure from motion and the interpretation of Johansson-type moving light displays.

Conversely, computational studies on the interpretation of time-varying imagery can provide insight into general principles that apply to and increase our understanding of biological visual systems.

This article is about the computational problems fundamental to the analysis of time-varying imagery. These problems fall under two broad categories: motion detection and measurement and the interpretation of visual motion.

Motion detection and measurement

The motion of elements and regions in an image is not given directly, but must be computed from more elementary measurements. The initial registration of light by the eye or by electronic image digitizers can be described as producing a two-dimensional array of time-dependent light intensity values $I(x,y,t)$. Motion in an image can be described in terms of a vector field $V(x,y,t)$ that gives the direction and speed of movement of a point with image coordinates (x,y) at time t. While $I(x,y,t)$ is given directly by the initial measurements, $V(x,y,t)$ is not. The first problem in analyzing motion is therefore the computation of $V(x,y,t)$ from $I(x,y,t)$. This computation is the measurement of visual motion.

In some cases, it is sufficient to detect only certain properties of the vector field $V(x,y,t)$, rather than measure it completely and precisely. For example, it might be desirable to respond quickly to a moving object. In such cases motion must be detected, but not necessarily measured.

The category of problems discussed here, however, are those in which both detection and measurement of motion are important. As research progressed, these problems proved to be considerably more difficult than initially anticipated. The search for efficient and reliable measurement methods is therefore an important research area in the analysis of time-varying imagery.

Reprinted from *IEEE Computer*, vol. 14, no. 8, pp. 57–69, 1981.

Discrete and continuous motion. Psychological studies of motion detection and measurement by the human visual system established two types of motion, discrete and continuous. For human observers to perceive motion, the stimulus need not move continuously across the visual field. The appropriate spatial and temporal presentation parameters—such as those of motion pictures—can give the impression of smooth, uninterrupted motion to sequential stimuli. The visual system can fill-in the gaps in the discrete presentation, even when the stimuli are separated by up to several degrees of visual angle and by long (400 msec[8]) temporal intervals. The resulting motion, termed *apparent* or *beta*, is perceptually indistinguishable from continuous motion.[9] Further, the filled-in positions are available to subsequent processes such as stereopsis.[10] Apparent motion mechanisms are probably innate in both humans[11] and lower animals.[12]

The apparent motion phenomena raise the question of whether discrete and continuous motion are registered by the same or separate mechanisms. The fact that the visual system can register both types of motion does not necessarily imply separate mechanisms, since a system registering discrete motion could, in principle, register continuous motion. Recent psychophysical evidence, however, supports the existence of two different mechanisms.[13-18] Braddick[15] suggested the terms *short range* and *long range* for the two mechanisms. The short range mechanism measures continuous motion or discrete displacements of about 15 minutes of arc (in the center of the visual field) and temporal intervals of less than about 60-100 msec. The long range mechanism processes larger displacements and temporal intervals. This terminology characterizes the distinction between the two mechanisms better than the discrete/continuous dichotomy, since discrete presentation with jumps of up to 15 minutes of visual arc are processed by the short range mechanism.

There is a more fundamental distinction between the two systems than their difference in range. They seem to perform their motion measurements at different processing stages, based on different motion primitives. In measuring visual motion, it is useful to draw a distinction between two main schemes. At the lowest level, motion measurements are based directly on the local changes in light intensity values; these are called *intensity-based* schemes. Alternatively, it is possible to first identify features such as edges, lines, blobs, or regions and then measure motion by matching these features over time and detecting their changing positions. Schemes of this type are called *token-matching* schemes. In the human visual system, it appears that the short range process is an intensity-based scheme and the long range process is a token-matching scheme.

These two modes of motion detection and measurement give rise to different computational problems, and consequently to different kinds of processes in biological as well as in computer vision systems.

Intensity-based schemes. A number of different intensity-based schemes have been advanced as models for motion measurement in biological systems. The various biological schemes can be divided into two main types: correlation techniques and gradient methods.

Correlation schemes. A simple motion detector can be constructed by comparing the outputs of two detectors to light increments at two adjacent positions. The output at position p_1 and time t is compared with that of position p_2 at time $t - \delta t$. Two variations of this approach—called the *delayed comparison* scheme—have been proposed as models for biological systems. The first is obtained by multiplying the two values, i.e., $D(p_1, t) \cdot D(p_2, t - \delta t)$, where D denotes the output of the subunits (Figure 1a). If a point of light moves from p_2 to p_1 in time equal to δt, it causes a light increment at p_1 and, after an interval of δt, a similar increment at p_2. Therefore, the above product is positive. In an array of such detectors, the average output is essentially equivalent to a cross-correlation of the inputs.[19] This scheme provides a successful model for the overall optomotor behavior of various insects in response to motion in their visual fields.

A similar method is the "And-Not" scheme proposed by Barlow and Levick[20] for the directionally selective units in the rabbit's retina and by Emerson and Gerstein[21] for the cat's visual cortex. These units are termed *directionally selective* because their response to stimuli moving in the so-called "preferred" direction is much stronger than their response to the same stimuli moving in the opposite, or "null," direction. Since Barlow and Levick found evidence for inhibitory interaction within the directionally selective mechanism, they proposed a model in which the motion detector computes the logical "And" of $D(p_1,t)$ and "Not" of $D(p_2,t - \delta t)$ (Figure 1b). In this scheme, a motion from p_2 to p_1 is "vetoed" by the delayed response from p_2, whereas motion from p_1 to p_2 produces a positive response.

Torre and Reichardt[22] have proposed a similar scheme for the visual system of the fly in which the delay is replaced by low-pass temporal filtering. Torre and Poggio[23] describe an elegant synaptic mechanism that implements these computations.

Some general properties of the delayed comparison schemes are worth observing. First, these detectors re-

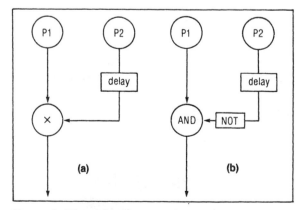

Figure 1. The delayed comparison motion detection scheme. P_1 and P_2 are detectors that respond transiently to a spot of light. (a) For a spot moving to the left at the appropriate speed, the responses of P_1 and P_2 coincide, yielding a positive output of the combined unit. (b) The veto scheme. Motion from P_2 to P_1 produces no response, since the delayed response from P_2 cancels the response from P_1.

spond selectively not only to continuous motion, but also to discrete jumps of the stimulus between positions p_1 and p_2. Second, they have some obvious limitations. For example, the speed of motion must lie within a certain range, determined by the delay (or the low-pass filtering) and the separation between the receptors. A range of velocities can be covered by a family of several detectors with different internal delays and interreceptor separations. Finally, motion measurement cannot be determined reliably from the output of a single detector of this type. For example, in a field of many moving elements, motion detectors of this type could be activated spuriously if the detector at p_1 is activated by one moving element and the detector at p_2 by a different element. To obtain accurate and reliable motion measurements, the outputs from an array of such detectors should be combined. (This combination problem is discussed below.)

Additional correlation techniques, such as the use of cross-correlation on the raw intensity values,[17,24] were proposed as models for motion measurement in the human visual system. Anstis[25] proposed a subtraction method in which two successive images are shifted and subtracted and displacements are indicated by minima in the resulting image. In general, no precise models were described for the biological implementation of these techniques, and there seems to be no compelling evidence for their existence in the human visual system.

Gradient schemes. A gradient scheme for the detection and measurement of motion by biological systems[26] has recently been proposed as a model for motion analysis by cortical simple cells. These cells, found in the primary visual cortex of the cat[6] and the monkey,[7] respond selectively to edges and bars of light. They are also selective for orientation and, often, for direction of motion. That is, to activate such a unit, the stimulus must have the orientation preferred by the unit and must move in the preferred direction. An analysis of the structure and function of simple cells therefore suggests mechanisms for the early detection and measurement of visual motion. These could, conceivably, be utilized in computer vision systems.

To understand the operation of simple cells, we need a brief description of the input they receive. This input is provided by the fibers of the optic nerve, coming from the eyes via an intermediate station called the LGN. The operations performed on the image by the retina and the LGN are neither direction nor orientation selective. What are these operations? How they are combined to measure the motion of visual stimuli?

Retinal operations on the image. The retinal structure serves two main functions. First, it registers the incoming light on an array of light-sensitive photoreceptors. Second, it performs the initial transformations of the registered image. The transformed image is then transmitted from the last layer of retinal cells (the ganglion cells layer) along about a million nerve fibers to the LGN, and from there to the visual cortex.

Retinal operations were studied experimentally using microelectrodes that measure the electrical activity of ganglion cells in response to light stimulation. Using this technique, the pioneering studies of Hartline,[27] Barlow,[28] and Kuffler[29,30] revealed two major properties of retinal ganglion cells. First, each ganglion cell responds to light stimulation falling within a limited retinal region, or *receptive field,* of the cell. Second, that the receptive field has a center-surround organization of two complementary types, called *on-center* and *off-center* cells. In on-center cells, activity is increased by light falling in the central region of the receptive field; light falling in a surrounding annulus inhibits activity. In the off-center cells, the roles of the center and surround are reversed. The organization of an on-center cell is shown in Figure 2a. Figure 2b is a cross-section through the middle of the field, where response to light is plotted against position in the receptive field. The response is maximal in the middle of receptive field, decreases as the light stimulus is moved outward, and becomes negative in the surround.

The shape of the receptive field can be described analytically as the difference of two gaussians,[31-34] or $\nabla^2 G$, where ∇^2 is the Laplacian operator and G is a two-dimensional gaussian. The retinal operation on the image I can then be described mathematically as $(\nabla^2 G) * I$, that is, the convolution of the image I with the retinal operator $\nabla^2 G$.

What can be derived from operating on the image with $\nabla^2 G$-shaped receptive fields? It is easier to consider this question in the one-dimensional case first; the extension to two dimensions then becomes straightforward. In the one-dimensional analog, the receptive field is described as $d^2 G/dx^2$, i.e., the second derivative of a one-dimensional gaussian G. The retinal operation is then the convolution $(d^2 G/dx^2) * I$.

The order of performing differentiation and convolution can be interchanged without affecting the result, as in

$$\left(\frac{d^2 G}{dx^2} \right) * I = \frac{d^2}{dx^2} (G * I)$$

We can thus view the retinal operation as a concatenation of two operations: gaussian filtering and a second derivative operation, both performed in a single stage.

The convolution $G * I$ is just a gaussian smoothing of the image. By controlling the size of the gaussian, it is possible to control the resolution at which the image is analyzed and to offset noise amplification introduced by the differentiation.

The second derivative operation that follows the gaussian smoothing is useful in locating sharp intensity

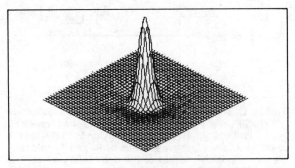

Figure 2. A plot of an on-center receptive field. This shape can be approximated by $\nabla^2 G$, where ∇^2 is the Laplacian operator and G is a two-dimensional gaussian.

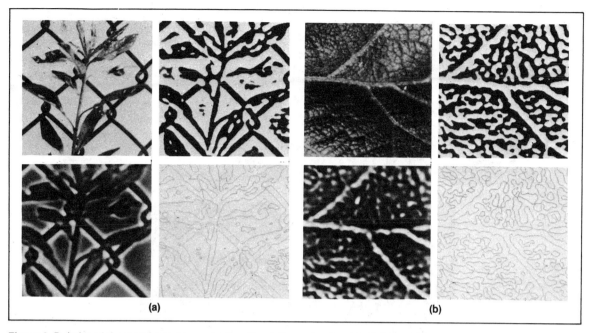

Figure 3. Results of the zero-crossing operation. Top left quadrants of both (a) and (b) show the original image. Lower left quadrants show the image convolved with $\nabla^2 G$. Top right quadrants: a binary image, where the positive convolution values are white and the negative black. Lower right quadrants: the zero-crossings in the convolved image.

changes. Steep intensity changes in the image correspond to peaks in the first derivative, or, equivalently, to zero-crossings in the second derivative. The second derivative has a further advantage: its two-dimensional analog, the Laplacian, is circularly symmetric (see Marr and Hildreth[34] for the two-dimensional case).

The conclusion is straightforward. Zero-crossings in the output of the retinal operation correspond to sharp intensity changes in the original image at the desired resolution, which is controlled in turn by the receptive field size. Figure 3 shows examples of the retinal operation and zero-crossing contours.

A zero-crossing detector can be thought of, roughly, as an edge detector. With the use of on-center and off-center units, it is simple to construct. Figure 4 shows the profile of $\nabla^2 G$ near a zero-crossing. The profile is positive on one side of the zero-crossing, and negative on the other. On-center units are activated in the positive region and off-center units in the negative region. The simultaneous activity of two adjacent units (one on-center and the other off-center) indicates a zero-crossing running between them.

Zero-crossings analysis and their use in edge detection are detailed in earlier work.[34,35] Comment here is restricted to the analysis of motion using the zero-crossings scheme.

The motion of a zero-crossing can be determined with use of one additional subunit. Let Z denote the current retinal position of the zero-crossing. It is clear from Figure 4 that the values of the convolution at position Z increase if the zero-crossing is moving to the right and decrease if the zero-crossing is moving to the left. Hence, by inspecting the sign of the time derivative of the convolution, i.e., of $d/dt\,(\nabla^2 G)*I$ at position Z, the direction of motion can be unambiguously determined. Furthermore, the time derivative and the slope of the zero-crossing determine the velocity in the direction between the on-center and off-center units. A motion measuring unit can thus be constructed by combining on-center, off-center, and time derivative units. In Marr and Ullman's biological model,[31,36] the time derivative is measured by Y-type cells, a subpopulation of the retinal ganglion cells.

In this scheme, motion is determined from the slope of the zero-crossing and the time derivative; it is therefore an intensity-based scheme that does not require the matching of elements over time. Motion in opposite directions is detected by different units, a view of human perception supported by psychological evidence.[37]

Details of the model[34] and an outline of its computer implementation[38] have been published. The computer implementation operates on a pair of images separated by a short time interval. The $\nabla^2 G$ operator is applied to the images; the zero-crossing contours are located in the output of the first image. The time derivative is approximated by subtracting the two convolved images and then used to determine the motion of the zero-crossing contours. Figure 5 shows an example of this analysis in which

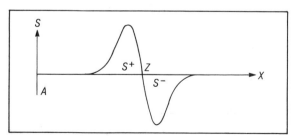

Figure 4. The convolution output (S) as a function of position (X) near a zero-crossing (Z). The zero-crossing is flanked by a positive lobe (S^+) and a negative one (S^-).

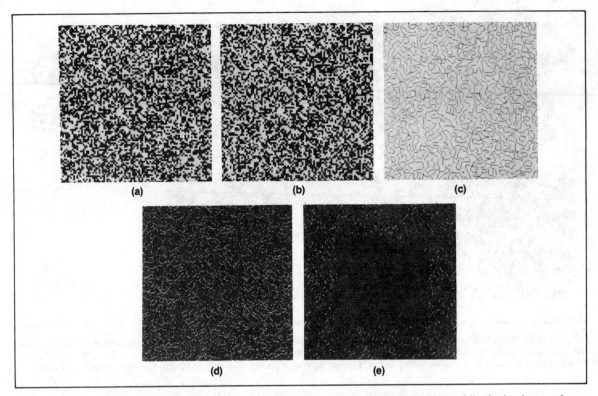

Figure 5. Random patterns. A central square in (a) is displaced slightly to the right in (b), while the backgrounds are uncorrelated. (c) The zero-crossing contours of (a) filtered through $\nabla^2 G$. The motion of the zero-crossings in (d) is in the direction of the light dots (motion assignments). (e) The central square is discovered on the basis of its motion alone. The light dots were removed from this area, except for isolated points where the directions assigned were incorrect.

an imbedded pattern is detected on the basis of its relative motion alone. A central square in Figure 5a is displaced slightly to the right in 5b. The backgrounds in the two images are uncorrelated. When the two patterns are presented in succession, human observers perceive a clearly delineated square moving against a background of uncorrelated noise. The zero-crossings of the first image filtered through $\nabla^2 G$ are shown in Figure 5c. Figure 5d represents the motion of the zero-crossings as determined by the time derivative. The small light dots attached to the contours indicate the direction of motion (the zero-crossing is moving toward the light dot). The central square was found to have a consistent common direction (to the right). Since the backgrounds are uncorrelated, no common motion exists in that region.

Using this scheme, motion measurements can be assigned to zero-crossing contours. However, neither the motion of these contours nor that of any other linear feature can be determined completely on the basis of purely local measurements due to the aperture problem illustrated in Figure 6. If motion is detected by a unit that is small compared to the overall contour, the only information that can be extracted is of the motion component perpendicular to the local orientation of the element. Motion along the element would be invisible. To determine the motion completely, a second stage must combine the local measurements, either in local neighborhoods or along the contour.[26,38]

The need for a combination stage is a general one: it does not depend on the particular zero-crossings scheme

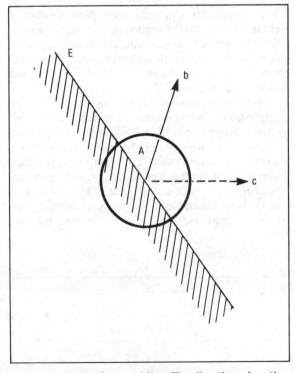

Figure 6. The aperture problem. The direction of motion of a one-dimensional profile cannot be recovered uniquely by a unit that is small in comparison to the moving element. Looking at the moving edge E through the aperture A, it is impossible to determine whether the actual motion is, e.g., toward b or toward c.

outlined above, but on the fact that no localized features are detected prior to motion measurement. Due to the aperture problem, the use of linear elements as primitives for the measurement would require a subsequent combination of the local measurement. A similar problem occurs in the intensity-based delayed comparison schemes described above. The activity of a single detector of this type is insufficient for determining the motion; a combination stage is required.

Intensity-based techniques in computer vision. A number of intensity-based schemes for motion detection and measurement have been considered for use in computer vision systems. One of them is the gray-level cross-correlation technique used for measuring motion in image pairs. This technique was applied, for example, to the measurement of cloud motion from satellite image data,[39,40] to traffic control,[41] and to the comparison of SLR images.[42] A related scheme, based on the comparison of intensity distributions over small image patches, was proposed.[43] Image subtraction methods were used for motion and change detection and for motion measurement.[44,45]

A fundamental problem of most cross-correlation and subtraction schemes is that they assume the image (or a large portion of it) moves as a whole between the two frames. Images containing independently moving objects and image distortions induced by the unrestricted motion of objects in space pose difficult—perhaps insurmountable—problems for these techniques.

Gradient schemes for motion detection have been proposed by several authors.[46-49] These methods are all based on the relation between the intensity gradient at a given point and the temporal intensity change produced at that point when the intensity pattern is moving. If $I(x,y)$ denotes the light intensity in the image, then

$$\frac{dI}{dt} = I_x u + I_y v$$

where dI/dt is the temporal intensity change at position (x,y); I_x and I_y represent the intensity gradient at that image point; and $u, v,$ are the local velocities in the x and y directions, respectively. Since dI/dt, I_x and I_y are all measurable, in principle, by the observer, a linear relation between u and v at the point in question can be determined by the above relation. However, uniquely determining the values of u and v requires more than a single measurement—it necessitates a combination stage using the local measurements. This, in turn, means that certain assumptions about the velocity field have to be made. The simplest is that u and v are constant over the image. Under such a condition, two independent measurements should suffice, but the applicability of the scheme will be restricted to uniform translations of the image.

The gradient methods outlined above (also see Thompson, pp. 20-28) and the zero-crossing scheme described previously are similar in several respects. Both use temporal change and image gradients to measure the local motion in the direction of the gradient. The method described by Fennema and Thompson[47] and that of Marr and Ullman[26] share another property—both are applied to the image after smoothing (i.e., at defocusing in the former and gaussian filtering at several resolutions in the latter).

Summary. The computation of the image velocity field using intensity-based techniques poses difficult and presently unresolved problems. Under general conditions (unrestricted motion, several objects), different parts of the image have different motions. Consequently, the preferred initial measurements are local. Such measurements are insufficient to determine the motion completely; therefore, the local measurements must be integrated in a subsequent stage. The integration stage is a major unresolved problem in both the understanding of biological systems and the construction of computer vision systems.

Token-matching schemes. In token-matching schemes for measuring motion, identifiable elements—tokens—are located and then matched over time. The apparent motion phenomena discussed above illustrate the capacity of the human visual system to establish motion by matching tokens over considerable spatial and temporal intervals. In perceiving continuous motion between successively presented elements, the visual system has to establish a *correspondence* between the elements of the two presentations. That is, a counterpart for each element in the first frame must be located in the second. A simple correspondence problem is illustrated in Figure 7. The filled circles in the figure represent the first frame, the open circles the second. There are two possible one-to-one matches between the elements of the two frames, leading to two possible patterns of perceived motion: horizontal (top) and diagonal (bottom).

In Figure 7 the match is only two-way ambiguous. In practice, each frame could contain many elements arranged in complex figures; a correspondence must then be

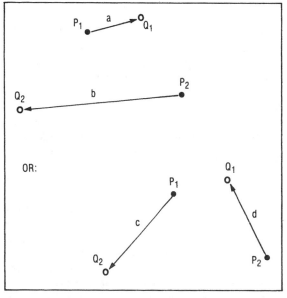

Figure 7. The correspondence problem. P_1 and P_2 are shown on the first frame, Q_1 and Q_2 on the next. Two one-to-one matches are possible, leading to two possible patterns of perceived motion.

established among them. The rules governing the correspondence process in human vision have been investigated in several studies,[17,50-57] but they are still far from being completely understood. A brief summary of some of the aspects of the correspondence process and a general discussion of problems relating to token-matching schemes is now in order.

When the elements participating in the motion are isolated dots alone (as in Figure 7), their correspondence is governed primarily by the distance between the dots. Other parameters being equal, each dot "prefers" to match its nearest neighbor in the subsequent frame.

If the elements in each frame are short line segments, additional rules apply. With line segments, correspondence depends not only upon the interelement distances, but upon their relative lengths and orientations. Other parameters being equal, a given line segment prefers to match another line of similar length and orientation. These results define an affinity metric between line segments that is a function of proximity, orientation, length, and contrast. Each element tends to match its highest-affinity neighbor. A simple and well-known example of this preference is the wagon wheel phenomenon in motion pictures, where the apparent rotation of a spoked wheel is opposite to its actual rotation. This phenomenon is a result of the visual system's preference to choose, from two competing motions, the one that involves minimal distance and angular change.

The correspondence between figures and groups of elements is not based on affinity alone. There are interactions that tend to map groups of elements on a one-to-one basis. As a result, an element might not match its highest-affinity neighbor because that neighbor already has a counterpart; two-to-one matches are ususally avoided.

Two general problems of token-matching schemes are relevant to both biological and machine motion analysis. The first concerns the level at which correspondence is established, that is, the degree of preprocessing and the complexity of the participating tokens. Matching can be established between simple tokens such as points, blobs, edge fragments, and short line segments. Alternatively, the matching process can operate on complex tokens such as structured forms, or even images of recognized objects. The use of complex tokens can simplify the correspondence process, since a complex token usually has unique counterpart in a subsequent frame. In contrast, a primitive token, such as a small edge fragment, usually has a number of competing possible matches. But the use of primitive tokens has two distinct advantages. The first is a reduced preprocessing requirement, which is of special importance in motion perception, where computation time is severely restricted. Second, primitive tokens allow the correspondence scheme to operate on arbitrary objects engaged in complex shape changes. This is because the correspondence between complex figures is established by matching the elementary blocks from which the figures are built. It seems, therefore, that the correspondence process should operate on the level of rather primitive elements, perhaps at the level of Marr's full primal sketch.[58]

The second general problem concerns the possible role of intensity-based and token-matching schemes in an integrated system for visual motion analysis. Intensity-based schemes tend to be fast and sensitive. The human visual system, for instance, can detect velocities as low as one minute of visual arc per second,[59,60] only four times the velocity of the sun across the sky. Directionally selective units in the cat's visual cortex respond reliably to displacements as small as 0.87 minutes of arc[61] (about 1mm at 4m); even smaller displacements can be detected by humans.[60] On the other hand, the ambiguity of the local measurements can make it difficult to recover the velocity field accurately with intensity-based schemes alone. A token-matching scheme can, in principle, track a sharply localized token (such as a line termination) over long distances, and thereby achieve a high degree of accuracy—at the price of more extensive processing to locate the tokens and solve the correspondence problem.

In light of the differences in their basic properties, the two motion measurement schemes could perform distinct visual tasks. The intensity-based system is useful as a peripheral, attention-attracting, "early warning" system and for separating moving objects from their background. Token-matching schemes might play an important role in the recovery of 3-D structure from motion, where accurate tracking over considerable distances is useful. Some recent psychophysical evidence[62] suggests that in the human visual system, the long range process is crucial to the recovery of structure from motion. A second possibility is that the two schemes interact to complement each other. For example, the computation of the long range correspondence could be guided by additional constraints supplied by the short range, intensity-based system.

Token-matching schemes in computer vision. Several token-matching schemes for motion detection have been investigated in the framework of computer vision research.[63,64] Motion is initially determined on the basis of matching edges or gray-level discontinuities. Velocity is assumed to be slow enough, with respect to the sampling rate, that the correspondence problem essentially disappears, and the discontinuities can be matched on the basis of proximity alone. For points not lying on the edges, motion is assigned on the basis of their distances from the edges, using specially constructed masks.

In another system,[65] region segmentation precedes motion detection. Motion is then established by matching regions, followed by cross-correlation on the objects' boundaries. Chow and Aggarwal[66] took a similar approach in analyzing the motion of planar figures, matching figures on the basis of shape descriptors. A more flexible scheme is described in other studies.[67-69] In these, matching is established not between complete figures, but between small fragments of the objects' boundaries. The use of small, primitive tokens overcame some of the difficulties in previous schemes. One such problem is object occlusion, which hinders the global matching of complete figures.

Taken together, psychophysical studies and computational considerations suggest that future research on token-matching schemes should explore, more extensively, the use of small, primitive tokens and study the integration of token-matching and intensity-based schemes.

The interpretation of visual motion

After motion has been detected and measured, it is used to recover properties of the visible environment. Three major uses, common to both biological and computer-based motion analysis systems, are listed below in order of increasing complexity:

(1) object-surround separation,
(2) recovery of three-dimensional shape, and
(3) motion-based recognition.

The following section illustrates and compares these three categories as they occur in human and computer vision systems.

Object-surround separation. The human visual system can separate a moving object from its surround on the basis of motion information alone. Figure 5 illustrates an example in which a moving subfigure is detected in a pair of random dot patterns shown in succession. The subfigure cannot be detected in either of the static frames, since it is defined solely by its frame-to-frame displacement. Experiments of this kind demonstrate that the visual system uses motion to delineate the boundaries of moving objects, even in the absence of intensity edges or texture changes at those boundaries.

In several studies,[64,65,70-72] visual motion was shown to provide useful cues for object-surround separation in computer vision systems. Reliable motion-based segmentation by computer systems proved, however, to be more difficult than anticipated. Some of these difficulties can be appreciated in light of the intensity-based schemes discussed above. In combining the results of the local measurements, continuity of the velocity field is often assumed. Therefore, considerable error can occur at object boundaries, where the continuity assumption is violated. Paradoxically, many intensity-based schemes would benefit if discontinuities in the velocity field were detected prior to the measurement of motion, rather than on the basis of the velocity measurement.

One way to cope with this difficulty is to use the fact that detection of motion discontinuities does not require precise measurements of the velocity field; rough estimates of direction and speed usually suffice. Consequently, it could prove profitable to carry out the local intensity-based motion measurements in two stages. In the first, rough estimates would be made and used to locate discontinuities in the velocity field. In the second, the velocity field would be established without propagating the smoothness constraint across discontinuity contours.

Three-dimensional structure from motion. The human visual system can recover the three-dimensional shape of moving objects even when the objects are unfamiliar and when each static view of the scene contains no 3-D information. The first systematic investigation of this remarkable capacity was carried out in the Wallach and O'Connell study of the kinetic depth effect.[73] In these experiments, an unfamiliar object was rotated behind a translucent screen, and the shadow of its orthographic projection observed from the other side of the screen. (In orthographic projection, the object is projected by parallel light rays that are perpendicular to the screen.) In most cases, the viewers were able to give a correct description of the hidden object's 3-D structure and motion in space, even when each static view was unrecognizable and contained no 3-D information. The original kinetic depth effect employed primarily wireframe objects which project as sets of connected lines. Later studies[56,74-77] established that 3-D structure can be perceived from displays consisting of unconnected elements in motion, and in continuous, as well as apparent, motion.

The computational problems underlying the recovery of 3-D structure from motion have been investigated in a number of studies. The main issues they explored were the conditions under which the structure-from-motion problem has a unique solution and the development of algorithms for the recovery of structure from motion. The main results of these studies are summarized in Table 1. As the table shows, both discrete and continuous versions of the problem have been investigated. The first formulation is discrete in both space and time. The computation is based on a number of discrete frames, or "snapshots," each of which contain a number of isolated points. It has been shown that a small number of frames and points are sufficient for a unique interpretation:[78] for a moving rigid object containing at least four noncoplanar points, the spatial motion and the 3-D coordinates of the points are determined by three frames.

The uniqueness proof is constructive, leading to a possible scheme for the recovery of structure from motion. The scene is divided into groups of about four elements each. The structure of each group is recovered independently (and therefore possibly in parallel), and, finally, the local results are combined in one additional step. This scheme is based on orthographic projection; perspective projection is treated by using the locality of the recovery scheme. That is, for four neighboring points, the two types of projections are similar. It is also possible to use perspective projection directly. There are indications[56] in the perspective case that two frames and

Table 1.
Main results of studies on the recovery of structure from motion.

DISCRETE POINTS AND VIEWS	DISCRETE POINTS, VELOCITIES	VELOCITY FIELD AND ITS DERIVATIVES
4 POINTS IN 3 ORTHOGRAPHIC VIEWS (ULLMAN, 1979)	5 POINTS AND THEIR VELOCITIES IN A SINGLE PERSPECTIVE VIEW (PRAZDNY, 1980)	UNIQUE SOLUTION FOR PURE TRANSLATION (CLOCKSIN, 1980)
5 POINTS IN 2 PERSPECTIVE VIEWS (ULLMAN, 1979)		UP TO 3 SOLUTIONS FOR GENERAL MOTION (LONGUET-HIGGINS AND PRAZDNY, 1980)

303

perhaps as few as five points are sufficient for a unique interpretation, but the proof of this case is not yet known.

Instead of considering the positions of the points in a number of discrete views, a single view indicating the positions, as well as the velocities of the points, can be taken as input (second column in Table 1). This might be considered a limiting case of the two-frame problem, as the time interval between the frames approaches zero. The problem then takes the following form: given the position and velocity of N points in the image, determine whether or not they belong to a single moving object and find the motion in space and their 3-D coordinates.

A preliminary theoretical problem is to determine the number N for which this recovery problem has a unique solution. Mathematically, this problem is still unresolved. A counting argument of equations and unknowns suggests that five points might suffice, an argument supported by a computer algorithm implemented by Prazdny.[79] Since the computer algorithm proved sensitive to errors in the input, especially when the viewed object was small, it seems that a robust recovery algorithm would require more than five points.

The third formulation of the problem uses velocities and spatial derivatives of the velocity field (third column of Table 1). This can be thought of as a limiting case of the previous formulation, as the distances between the points approaches zero. In a simplified version of this problem, the motion in space is restricted to pure translation.[80] Under this assumption, uniqueness of the solution is readily established. The surface orientation at each image point can be recovered from the velocity and the spatial derivatives of the velocity field at that point.

The more general case, in which the motion can contain rotation components, is considerably more complex. One analysis established that the velocity field at a point has, at most, three interpretations.[81] More precisely, it showed that for nonplanar surfaces (given the velocity and its first and second spatial derivatives at a point) there are, at most, three solutions to the surface orientation at that point. It also provided a scheme for computing the solution. The possible improvement of this result, in particular a determination of whether the solution is unique, poses an open question for future research.

Partial descriptors. The schemes described above aim at a full solution to the structure-from-motion problem. That is, they try to recover all motion parameters as well as the 3-D structure of the visible environment. In contrast to these comprehensive schemes, methods for partial descriptors seek to recover only selected parameters. For example, several mathematical and psychological studies attempted to isolate, in the image velocity field, variables that permit the separate and independent recovery of each of the rotation and translation components of the motion.[82-85] In general, such a decomposition of the problem is not possible, since the velocity field in the image is determined by the intricate interaction of all the motion parameters and the 3-D shape of the viewed objects. It therefore does not seem possible to isolate a variable in the motion field that directly determines, say, the rotation part of the motion independent of the translation components. Partial solutions do become tractable, however,

under restricted motion, such as pure translation with no rotation components. Four schemes have been proposed for partial descriptors under restricted motion.

Time to collision. A motion parameter that could be particularly useful for locomoting animals (or machines) is the time-to-collision variable proposed by Lee.[86,87] He argues that the absolute speed of an approaching observer toward an object and the absolute distance between objects cannot be recovered from the image velocity field. He does believe, however, that their ratio, which yields time to collision with the object, can be recovered from the rate of expansion of the image cast by the object. The simple relation between time to collision and image expansion holds, however, only for translatory motion. Under general conditions, it probably cannot be decoupled from the other parameters of motion and shape. Nevertheless, rate of expansion might be useful as a rough estimate of approaching speed. For animals, the fast detection of an approaching object is important, even if the computation is not entirely accurate. Psychophysical and physiological evidence for the existence of mechanisms that respond selectively to expanding stimuli were reported recently.[88,89] These reports could provide the mechanism for "looming" detection suggested by Lee.

Binocular looming detection. Motion in which the right eye sees motion to the left and the left eye sees motion to the right indicates a trajectory in space that is pointing between the two eyes. This can be used for the fast detection and avoidance of moving objects.[26,90]

Focus of the optical flow. Under pure translatory motion, all the points in the image are streaming toward a common vanishing point, which can lie outside the observer's field of view. The vector to this point gives the direction of the observer's motion (assuming a stationary environment).

Gibson[91] suggested that the center of expansion could be used in controlling locomotion. A later study[92] indicated that human observers, can, to a limited extent, locate the focus of expansion, even when it lies outside their field of view.[93] The focus of expansion of a perpendicular plane can be pointed at reliably only in the last 0.5 second prior to collision. It is unclear, therefore, whether this clue is in fact used by the human visual system.

Qualitative shape descriptions. Certain qualitative shape descriptions can be derived from local properties of the image velocity field. For example, Koenderink and van Doorn have shown that the sign of the gaussian curvature at a point is derived from the velocity field around it.[94] Other studies describe a simple scheme for locating depth boundaries in a changing image[95] and a scheme for edge classification (e.g., convex, concave, occluding) under the assumption of pure translatory motion.[80]

Summary on 3-D recovery. Many of the computational problems underlying the recovery of the 3-D structure of moving objects from the changing image are now well understood. In addition to consideration of the open questions, an important next step for machine application will be the development of efficient and robust recovery algorithms. Two major obstacles to such algorithms are:

- real-time computation constraints when the number of participating elements is large and
- robustness in the face of errors and deviations from perfect rigidity. Since measurement inaccuracies and some deformations of the viewed objects might occur, algorithms for the recovery of rigid structures should be able to perform even when perfectly rigid solutions are not available.

Motion-based recognition. Human observers can recognize certain objects solely on the basis of characteristic motion patterns. Powerful demonstrations of this capacity were provided by the studies of Johansson.[76,96] These demonstrations were created by filming human actors moving in the dark with small light sources attached to their main joints. Each actor is thus represented by up to 13 moving light dots. The resulting dynamic dot patterns create a vivid impression of the moving actors. Later studies[97,98] have demonstrated that male actors can often be distinguished from females, and sometimes familiar persons can be recognized on the basis of the moving light dots alone.

These motion-based recognition phenomena have attracted considerable interest among psychologists as well as workers in the field of computer vision. A number of computer-based systems have been constructed to study and simulate motion-based recognition.[99-103]

The general strategy in these studies has been to divide the problem into two stages, one for organizing and describing the motion patterns and another for comparing the resulting representations with similar descriptions stored in memory. The first stage is usually supposed to be autonomous, that is, guided by general organization principles rather than by knowledge of specific objects. The existence of such organizing principles in human perception has been demonstrated in a number of psychological studies,[76,104-106] but their details are still far from clear. Computer vision systems have primarily used spatial proximity and similarity of motion to group moving elements into higher-order units.[63,101,107] An approach recently proposed by Hoffman and Flinchbaugh[99] showed how, based on a planarity assumption, the motion of the limbs can be used to obtain a 3-D interpretation of moving light displays. When these principles are applied to the Johansson-type configurations, perhaps the organization principles will establish a connection between the main joints, yielding a moving stick-figure representation that can be analyzed in a subsequent stage, possibly using the scheme proposed by Marr and Nishihara.[108]

The study of motion-based recognition is only in its initial stages. It is an interesting and potentially useful research topic that combines the study of motion perception with a study of the higher cognitive functions involved in visual recognition and the organization of long-term memory. Experience has shown that advances in this area depend upon the cooperation of computational studies and empirical psychological research. ■

Acknowledgments

I thank E. Hildreth for invaluable comments. This report describes research done at the Artificial Intelligence Laboratory of the Massachusetts Institute of Technology. Support for the laboratory's artificial intelligence research is provided in part by the Advanced Research Project Agency of the Department of Defense under Office of Naval Research contract N00014-75-C-0643 and in part by National Science Foundation Grant MCS77-07569.

References

1. J. Y. Lettvin, H. R. Maturana, W. S. McCulloch, and W. H. Pitts, "What the Frog's Eye Tells the Frog's Brain," *Proc. IRE,* Vol. 47, 1959, pp. 1940-1951.

2. W. Reichardt and T. Poggio, "Figure-Ground Discrimination by Relative Movement in the Visual System of the Fly. Part I: Experimental Results," *Biology and Cybernetics,* Vol. 35, 1980, pp. 81-100.

3. H. R. Maturana and S. Frenk, "Directional Movement and Horizontal Edge Detectors in Pigeon Retina," *Science,* Vol. 142, 1963, pp. 977-979.

4. H. B. Barlow and R. N. Hill, "Selective Sensitivity to Direction of Movement in Ganglion Cells of the Rabbit Retina," *Science,* Vol. 139, 1963, pp. 412-414.

5. O-J. Grusser and U. Grusser-Cornehls, "Neuronal Mechanisms of Visual Movement Perception and Some Psychophysical and Behavioral Correlation," In *Handbook of Sensory Physiology,* R. Jung, ed., Vol. VII/3A, 1973, pp. 333-429.

6. D. H. Hubel and T. N. Wiesel, "Receptive Fields, Binocular Interaction, and Functional Architecture in the Cat's Visual Cortex," *J. Physiology* (London), Vol. 160, 1962, pp. 106-154.

7. D. H. Hubel and T. N. Wiesel, "Receptive Fields and Functional Architecture of Monkey Striate Cortex," *J. Physiology* (London), Vol. 195, 1962, pp. 215-243.

8. W. Neuhaus, "Experimentelle Untersuchung der Scheinbewegung," *Arch. Ges. Psychol.,* Vol. 75, 1930, pp. 315-348.

9. M. Wertheimer, "Experimentelle Studien über das Sehen von Bewegung," *Zeitschrift für Psychologie,* Vol. 61, 1912, p. 382.

10. M. J. Morgan, "Pulfrich Effect and the Filling-In of Apparent Motion" *Perception,* Vol. 5, 1976, pp. 187-195.

11. E. S. Tauber and S. Koffler, "Optomotor Response in Human Infants to Apparent Motion: Evidence of Innateness," *Science,* Vol. 152, 1966, p. 382.

12. I. Rock, E. S. Tauber, and D. P. Heller, "Perception of Stroboscopic Movement: Evidence for Its Innate Basis," *Science,* Vol. 147, 1964, pp. 1050-1052.

13. S. M. Anstis and B. J. Rogers, "Illusory Reversal of Visual Depth and Movement During Changes of Contrast," *Vision Research,* Vol. 15, 1975, pp. 957-961.

14. S. M. Anstis, "The Perception of Apparent Motion," *Philosophical Trans. Royal Soc. London,* Vol. B, No. 290, 1980, pp. 153-168.

15. O. J. Braddick, "A Short-Range Process in Apparent Motion," *Vision Research,* Vol. 14, 1974, pp. 519-527.

16. O. J. Braddick, "Low-Level and High-Level Processes in Apparent Motion," *Philosophical Trans. Royal Soc. London,* Vol. B, No. 290, 1980, pp. 137-151.

17. A. J. Pantle and L. Picciano, "A Multistable Display: Evidence for Two Separate Motion Systems in Human Vision," *Science,* Vol. 193, Aug. 6, 1976, pp. 500-502.

18. J. T. Petersik, K. I. Hicks, and A. J. Pantle, "Apparent Movement of Successively Generated Subjective Patterns," *Perception,* Vol. 7, 1978, pp. 371-383.

19. B. Hassenstien and W. Reichardt, "Systemtheoretische Analyse der Zeit-, Reihenfolgen-und Vorzeichenauswertung bei der Bewegungs-Perzeption der Russelkafers," *Chlorophanus. Z. Naturf.,* Vol. IIb, 1956, pp. 513-524.

20. H. B. Barlow and R. W. Levick, "The Mechanism of Directionally Selective Units in Rabbit's Retina," *J. Physiology* (London), Vol. 173, 1965, pp. 377-407.

21. R. C. Emerson and G. L. Gerstein, "Simple Striate Neurons in the Cat. II. Mechanisms Underlying Directional Asymmetry and Directional Selectivity," *J. Neurophysiology,* Vol. 40, No. 1, 1977, pp. 136-155.

22. T. Poggio and W. Reichardt, "Visual Control of Orientation Behavior in the Fly. Part II. Towards the Underlying Neural Interactions," *Quarterly Rev. Biophysics,* Vol. 9, 1976, pp. 377-438.

23. V. Torre and T. Poggio, "A Synaptic Mechanism Possibly Underlying Directional Selectivity to Motion," *Proc. Royal Soc. London,* Vol. B, No. 202, 1978, pp. 409-416.

24. H. H. Bell and J. S. Lappin, "Sufficient Conditions for the Discrimination of Motion," *Perception and Psychophysics,* Vol. 14, No. 1, 1973, pp. 45-50.

25. S. M. Anstis, "Phi Movement As a Subtraction Process," *Vision Research,* Vol. 10, 1970, pp. 1411-1430.

26. D. Marr and S. Ullman, "Directional Selectivity and Its Use in Early Visual Processing," *Proc. Royal Soc. London,* Vol. B, No. 211, 1981, pp. 151-180; available also as MIT A.I. Memo 524, MIT, Cambridge, Mass., 1979.

27. H. K. Hartline, "The Response of Single Optic Nerve Fibers of the Vertebrate Eye to Illumination of the Retina," *Am. J. Physiology,* Vol. 121, 1938, pp. 400-415.

28. H. B. Barlow, "Summation and Inhibition in the Frog's Retina," *J. Physiology* (London), Vol. 119, 1953, pp. 69-88.

29. S. W. Kuffler, "Neurons in the Retina: Organization, Inhibition and Excitation Problems," *Cold Spring Harbour Symp. Quantifiable Biology,* Vol. 17, 1952, pp. 281-292.

30. S. W. Kuffler, "Discharge Patterns and Functional Organization of Mammalian Retina," *J. Neurophysiology,* Vol. 16, 1953, pp. 37-68.

31. C. Enroth-Cugell and J. D. Robson, "The Contrast Sensitivity of Retinal Ganglion Cells of the Cat," *J. Physiology* (London), Vol. 187, 1966, pp. 517-522.

32. R. W. Rodieck, "Quantitative Analysis of Cat Retinal Ganglion Cell Responses to Visual Stimuli," *Vision Research,* Vol. 5, 1965, pp. 583-601.

33. R. W. Rodieck and J. Stone, "Analysis of Receptive Fields of Cat Retinal Ganglion Cells," *J. Neurophysiology,* Vol. 28, 1965, pp. 833-849.

34. D. Marr and E. Hildreth, "Theory of Edge Detection," *Proc. Royal Soc. London,* Vol. B, 1980, pp. 187-217.

35. E. C. Hildreth, *Implementation of a Theory of Edge Detection,* MIT A.I. Technical Report AI-TR-579, MIT, Cambridge, Mass., 1980.

36. G. Cleland, M. W. Dubin, and W. R. Levick, "Sustained and Transient Neurons in the Cat's Retina and LGN," *J. Physiology* (London), Vol. 217, 1971, pp. 473-496.

37. R. Sekuler and E. Levinson, "The Perception of Moving Targets," *Sci. Am.,* Vol. 236, No. 1, 1977, pp. 60-73.

38. J. Batali and S. Ullman, "Motion Detection and Analysis," In *ARPA Image Understanding Workshop,* L. S. Bauman, ed., Science Application Inc., Arlington, Va., pp. 69-75.

39. J. A. Leese, C. S. Novak, and V. R. Taylor, "The Determination of Cloud Pattern Motion from Geosynchronous Satellite Image Data," *Pattern Recognition,* Vol. 2, 1970, pp. 279-292.

40. E. A. Smith and D. R. Phillips, "Automated Cloud Tracking Using Precisely Aligned Digital ATS Pictures," *IEEE Trans. Computers,* Vol. 21, 1972, pp. 715-729.

41. K. Wolferts, "Special Problems in Interactive Image Processing for Traffic Analysis," *2nd Int'l Conf. on Pattern Recognition,* Vol. 1 and 2, 1974.

42. R. L. Lillestrand, "Techniques for Change Detection," *IEEE Trans. Computers,* Vol. C-21, 1972, pp. 654-659.

43. R. Jain, D. Militzer, and H.-H. Nagel, "Separating Non Stationary from Stationary Scene Components in a Sequence of Real-World TV Images," *Proc. 3rd Int'l Conf. Artificial Intelligence,* Aug. 1977, p. 612.

44. R. Jain and H.-H. Nagel, "On the Analysis of Accumulative Difference Picture from Image Sequences of Real World Scenes," *IEEE Trans. Pattern Analysis and Machine Intelligence,* Vol. 1, No. 2, 1979, pp. 206-214.

45. R. Jain, W. N. Martin, and J. K. Aggarwal, "Extraction of Moving Objects Images Through Change Detection," *Proc. 6th Int'l Conf. Artificial Intelligence,* 1979, pp. 425-428.

46. J. O. Limb and J. A. Murphy, "Estimating the Velocity of Moving Objects in Television Signals," *Computer Graphics and Image Processing,* Vol. 4, 1975, pp. 311-327.

47. C. L. Fennema and W. B. Thompson, "Velocity Determination in Scenes Containing Several Moving Objects," *Computer Graphics and Image Processing,* Vol. 9, 1979, pp. 301-315.

48. B. Hadani, G. Ishai, and M. Gur, "Visual Stability and Space Perception in Monocular Vision: Mathematical Model," *J. Optical Soc. America,* Vol. 70, No. 1, 1980, pp. 60-65.

49. B. K. P. Horn and B. G. Schunk, *Determining Optical Flow,* MIT A.I. Memo 572, MIT, Cambridge, Mass., 1980.

50. J. P. Frisby, "The Effect of Stimulus Orientation on the Phi Phenomenon," *Vision Research,* Vol. 12, 1972, pp. 1145-1166.

51. P. A. Kolers, *Aspects of Motion Perception,* Pergamon Press, New York, 1972.

52. A. J. Pantle, "Stroboscopic Movement Based Upon Global Information in Successively Presented Visual Patterns," *J. Optical Soc. America,* 1973, p. 1280.

53. J. Ternus, "Experimentelle Untersuchung Über Phanomenale Identitat," *Psychologische Forschung,* Vol. 7, 1926, pp. 81-136.

54. D. Navon, "Irrelevance of Figural Identity for Resolving Ambiguities in Apparent Motion," *J. Experimental Psychology, Human Perception and Performance,* Vol. 2, No. 1, 1976, pp. 130-138.

55. S. Ullman, "Two Dimensionality of the Correspondence Process in Apparent Motion," *Perception,* Vol. 7, 1978, pp. 683-693.

56. S. Ullman, *The Interpretation of Visual Motion,* MIT Press, Cambridge and London, 1979.

57. S. Ullman, "The Effect of Similarity Between Line Segments on the Correspondence Strength in Apparent Motion," *Perception,* Vol. 9, 1981, pp. 617-626.

58. D. Marr, "Early Processing of Visual Information," *Philosophical Trans. Royal Soc. London,* Vol. B, No. 275, 1976, pp. 483-524.

59. C. H. Graham, "Perception of Movement," In *Vision and Visual Perception,* C. H. Graham, ed., John Wiley and Sons, New York, 1965.

60. P. E. King-Smith, A. Riggs, R. K. Moore, and T. W. Butler, "Temporal Properties of the Human Visual Nervous System," *Vision Research,* Vol. 17, 1977, pp. 1101-1106.

61. A. W. Goodwin, G. H. Henry, and P.O. Bishop, "Direction Selectivity of Simple Striate Cells: Properties and Mechanism," *J. Neurophysiology,* Vol. 38, 1975, pp. 1500-1523.

62. J. T. Petersik, "The Effect of Spatial and Temporal Factors on the Perception of Stroboscopic Rotation Simulations," *Perception,* Vol. 9, 1980, pp. 271-283.

63. J. Potter, *The Extraction and Utilization of Motion in Scene Description,* PhD thesis, University of Wisconsin, Madison, Wis., 1974.

64. J. L. Potter, "Scene Segmentation Using Motion Information," *Computer Graphics and Image Processing,* Vol. 6, 1977, pp. 558-581.

65. H.-H. Nagel, "Formation of an Object Concept by Analysis of Systematic Time Variation in the Optically Perceptible Environment," *Computer Graphics and Image Processing,* Vol. 7, 1978, pp. 149-194.

66. W. K. Chow and J. K. Aggarwal, "Computer Analysis of Planar Curvilinear Moving Images," *IEEE Trans. Computers,* Vol. C-26, 1977, pp. 179-185.

67. W. N. Martin and J. K. Aggarwal, "Dynamic Scene Analysis: The Study of Moving Images," Information Systems Research Lab, Electronic Research Center, Technical Report 184, University of Texas, Austin, Tex., 1979.

68. C. J. Jacobus, R. T. Chien, and J. M. Selander, "Motion Detection and Analysis by Matching Graphs of Intermediate-Level Primitives," *IEEE Trans. Pattern Analysis and Machine Intelligence,* Vol. 2, No. 6, 1980, pp. 465-510.

69. S. Tsuuji, M. Osada, and M. Yachida, "Three-Dimensional Movement Analysis of Dynamic Line Images," *Proc. 6th Int'l Conf. Artificial Intelligence,* 1979, pp. 876-901.

70. J. L. Potter, "Velocity as a Cue for Segmentation," *IEEE Trans. Systems, Man, and Cybernetics,* Vol. SMC-5, 1975, pp. 390-394.

71. J. M. Prager, *Segmentation of Static and Dynamic Scenes,* PhD thesis, University of Massachusetts, Amherst, Mass., 1979.

72. W. B. Thompson, "Combining Motion and Contrast for Segmentation," *IEEE Trans. Pattern Analysis and Machine Intelligence,* Vol. 2, No. 26, 1980, pp. 543-549.

73. H. Wallach and D. N. O'Connell, "The Kinetic Depth Effect," *J. Experimental Psychology,* Vol. 45, 1953, pp. 205-217.

74. B. F. Green, "Figure Coherence in the Kinetic Depth Effect," *J. Experimental Psychology,* Vol. 62, No. 3, 1961, pp. 272-282.

75. G. Johansson, "Perception of Motion and Changing Form," *Scandinavian J. Psychology,* Vol. 5, 1964, pp. 181-208.

76. G. Johansson, "Visual Motion Perception," *Sci. Am.,* Vol. 232, No. 6, 1975, pp. 76-88.

77. M. L. Braunstein, "Depth Perception in Rotation Dot Patterns: Effects of Numerosity and Perspective," *J. Experimental Psychology,* Vol. 64, No. 4, 1962, pp. 415-420.

78. S. Ullman, "The Interpretation of Structure from Motion," *Proc. Royal Soc. London,* Vol. B, No. 203, pp. 405-426.

79. K. Prazdny, "Egomotion and Relative Depth Map from Optical Flow," *Biology and Cybernetics,* Vol. 36, 1980, pp. 87-102.

80. W. F. Clocksin, "Perception of Surface Slant and Edge Lables from Optical Flow: A Computational Approach," *Perception,* Vol. 9, No. 3, 1980, pp. 253-269.

81. H. C. Longuet-Higgins and K. Prazdny, "The Interpretation of a Moving Retinal Image," *Proc. Royal Soc. London,* Vol. B, No. 208, pp. 385-397.

82. Erik Borjesson and Claes von Hofsten, "Spatial Determinants of Depth Perception in Two-Dot Motion Patterns," *Perception and Psychophysics,* Vol. 11, No. 4, 1972, pp. 263-268.

83. Erik Borjesson and Claes von Hofsten, "Visual Perception of Motion in Depth: Application of a Vector Model to Three Dot Motion Patterns," *Perception and Psychophysics,* Vol. 13, No. 2, 1973, pp. 169-179.

84. J. J. Gibson, "What Gives Rise to the Perception of Motion?" *Psychology Rev.,* Vol. 75, No. 4, 1968, pp. 335-346.

85. C. J. Hay, "Optical Motions and Space Perception – An Extention of Gibson's Analysis," *Psychological Rev.,* Vol. 73, 1966, pp. 550-565.

86. D. N. Lee, "A Theory of Visual Control of Braking Based on Information About Time to Collision," *Perception,* Vol. 5, 1976, pp. 437-459.

87. D. N. Lee, "The Optic Flow Field: The Foundation of Vision" *Philosophical Trans. Royal Soc. London,* Vol. B, No. 290, 1980, 169-179.

88. D. Regan and K. I. Beverly, "Looming Detection in the Human Visual Pathway," *Vision Research,* Vol. 18, 1978, pp. 415-421.

89. D. Regan, K. I. Beverly, and M. Cynader, "The Visual Perception of Depth," *Sci. Am.,* Vol. 241, 1979, pp. 122-133.

90. D. Regan, K. I. Beverley, and M. Cynader, "Stereoscopic Subsystem for Position in Depth and for Motion in Depth," *Proc. Royal Society London,* Vol. B, No. 204, 1979, pp. 485-501.

91. J. J. Gibson, "Visually Controlled Locomotion and Visual Orientation in Animals," *British J. Psychology,* Vol. 49, 1958, pp. 182-194.

92. R. Warren, "The Perception of Motion," *J. Experimental Psychology,* Vol. 2, 1976, pp. 448-456.

93. I. R. Johnston, G. R. White, and R. W. Cumning, "The Role of Optical Expansion Patterns in Locomotor Control," *Am. J. Psychology,* Vol. 86, 1973, pp. 311-424.

94. J. J. Koenderink and A. J. van Doorn, "Invariant Properties of the Motion Parallax Field Due to the Motion of Rigid Bodies Relative to the Observer," *Optica Acta,* Vol. 22, No. 9, 1975, pp. 773-791.

95. K. Nakayama and J. M. Loomis, "Optical Velocity Patterns, Velocity Sensitive Neurons, and Space Perception: A Hypothesis," *Perception,* Vol. 3, 1974, pp. 63-80.

96. G. Johansson, "Visual Perception of Biological Motion and a Model for Its Analysis," *Perception and Psychophysics,* Vol. 14, No. 2, 1973, pp. 201-211.

97. J. E. Cutting, and L. T. Kozlowski, "Recognizing Friends by Their Walk: Gait Perception Without Familiarity Cues," *Bull. Psychonometric Soc.,* Vol. 9, No. 5, 1977, pp. 353-356.

98. L. T. Kozlowski and J. E. Cutting, "Recognizing the Sex of a Walker from Dynamic Point-Light Displays," *Perception and Psychophysiology,* Vol. 21, No. 6, 1977, pp. 575-580.

99. D. D. Hoffman, and B. E. Flinchbaugh, *The Interpretation of Biological Motion,* MIT A.I. Memo 608, MIT, Cambridge, Mass., 1981.

100. J. O'Rourke and N. I. Badler, "Model-Based Image Analysis of Human Motion Using Constraint Propagation," *IEEE Trans. Pattern Analysis and Machine Intelligence,* Vol. 3, No. 4, 1980, pp. 522-537.

101. R. Rashid, *LIGHTS: A System for the Interpretation of Moving Light Displays,* PhD dissertation, University of Rochester, Rochester, N.Y., 1980.

102. N. I. Badler, "Temporal Scene Analysis: Conceptual Descriptions of Object Movements," Technical Report 80, Dept. of Computer Science, University of Toronto, Toronto, Canada, 1975.

103. J. K. Tsotsos, *A Framework for Visual Motion Understanding,* PhD dissertation, University of Toronto, Toronto, Canada, 1980.

104. K. Koffka, *Principles of Gestalt Psychology,* Harcourt, Brace, and World, New York, 1935.

105. D. R. Proffitt, J. E. Cutting, and D. M. Stier, "Perception of Wheel-Generated Motions," *J. Experimental Psychology,* Vol. 5, No. 2, 1979, pp. 289-302.

106. H. Wallach, "The Perception of Motion," *Sci. Am.,* Vol. 201, 1959, pp. 56-60.

107. B. E. Flinchbaugh and B. Chandrasekaran, "Early Visual Processing of Spatio-Temporal Information," *Proc. IEEE Workshop on Computer Analysis of Time-Varying Imagery,* Apr. 1979, pp. 39-41.

108. D. Marr and H. K. Nishihara, "Representation and Recognition of the Spatial Organization of Three-Dimensional Shapes," *Proc. Royal Soc. London,* Vol. B, No. 200, 1978, pp. 269-294.

Article 5.6

Visual Cortical Neurons as Localized Spatial Frequency Filters

DANIEL A. POLLEN AND STEVEN F. RONNER

Abstract—Receptive field profiles of simple cells in the visual cortex often resemble even-symmetric or odd-symmetric Gabor filters; i.e., their receptive field profiles can be described by the product of a Gaussian and either a cosine or sine function. Their spatial frequency tuning is of medium bandwidth (~ one octave) which is narrow enough for a cell to distinguish the third harmonic from the fundamental frequency for square-wave gratings of low spatial frequency. The responses of adjacent simple cells, tuned to the same spatial frequency, orientation, and direction, differ in their phase response to drifting sine-wave gratings by approximately either $90°$ or $180°$. This latter result makes it possible to consider two adjacent simple cell pairs as operating like paired Gaussian-attenuated sine and cosine filters or Gabor filters for restricted regions of visual space. The entire set of simple cells provides a complete representation of the visual scene, yet each simple cell is unique in its response properties. At the complex cell stage, the cell's mean firing rate appears to represent the amplitude of a local Fourier coefficient, but phase information is seldom conveyed with much precision in the action potential code. The relationship of these and other properties of striate neurons to current issues in spatial pattern recognition is discussed.

I. INTRODUCTION

THE PURPOSE of this paper is to relate the receptive field properties of neurons in the primary visual cortex, i.e., the striate cortex, to current issues in spatial visual information processing. This introduction will present general background information. Detailed discussion of many new results by ourselves and others may be found in two recent papers [1], [2].

Hubel and Wiesel [3] discovered two classes of orientation-selective cells in the visual cortex of the cat. The receptive fields of simple cells could be subdivided into two or three parallel excitatory or inhibitory regions which produced pure "ON" or pure "OFF" responses, respectively, when small spots or slits of light were flashed at appropriate positions. These cells were principally found in the middle cortical layers which receive direct input from lateral geniculate neurons. Simple cells with two principal subregions, one excitatory, the other inhibitory, were considered selectively responsive to an edge. Cells with a central ON or OFF region flanked on both sides by an antagonistic surround were considered selectively responsive to bar width.

Complex cells had larger receptive fields than simple cells at corresponding retinal eccentricities [3]. Their receptive fields could not be subdivided into pure ON or OFF regions, and flashed stimuli generally produced mixed ON-OFF responses over most of the field. These cells were found most frequently in the superficial and deep layers of the striate cortex.

Both simple and complex cells in the striate cortex, unlike neurons in the retina and lateral geniculate nucleus, are highly selective to the orientation at which elongated slit stimuli are presented [3]. The response to a slit of light commonly falls to half-maximal amplitude when the slit is tested at orientations $15°-25°$ away from the preferred orientation. Some cells prefer movement in one direction perpendicular to the preferred orientation; others respond equally well to movement in either perpendicular direction.

Campbell and Robson [4] demonstrated by psychophysical techniques that linearly operating independent detectors or "channels" exist within the human visual system which are selectively sensitive to a limited range of spatial frequencies. (Spatial frequency refers to the number of cycles/deg subtended on the retina by a sine-wave grating, i.e., a grating in which the luminosity across the width dimension is modulated sinusoidally.)

Campbell and Robson [4] also demonstrated that a square-wave grating was perceived as different from a sine-wave grating when the third harmonic of the square-wave reached its own threshold. (According to Fourier theory, a square wave can be considered as the sum of the sine waves at the fundamental frequency and all higher odd harmonics with the strength of each harmonic being inversely proportional to its frequency.) Blakemore and Campbell [5], on the basis of adaptation studies, demonstrated that these spatial frequency selective channels were also orientation-selective. This result implicated the visual cortex as the most proximal likely site for these channels because retinal and geniculate receptive fields are not, in general, highly orientation-selective.

Pollen *et al.* [6] believed that the psychophysical results [4], [5] implied that "...the brain has at its disposal the two-dimensional Fourier transform of the presented brightness distribution." They realized that a set of spatial frequencies across a requisite number of orientations was mathematically equivalent to a two-dimensional Fourier transform. Moreover, the data set available at the simple cell stage seemed mathematically similar to data sets which Taylor [7] had used following Bracewell [8] and others to

Manuscript received August 1, 1982; revised April 21, 1983. This work was supported by the U.S. Public Health Service under Grant EY03290 from the National Eye Institute.

D. A. Pollen is with the Department of Neurology, University of Massachusetts Medical Center, 55 Lake Ave. North, Worcester, MA 01605.

S. F. Ronner is with the Neurosurgical Service, Massachusetts General Hospital, Warren Building, Room 459, Boston, MA 02114.

Reprinted from *IEEE Trans. Syst. Man, Cybern.*, vol. SMC-13, no. 5, pp. 907–916, Sept./Oct. 1983.

reconstruct two-dimensional celestial brightness distributions from sets of one-dimensional scans using Fourier methods. Furthermore, Pollen *et al.* [6] realized that certain mathematical operations required for spatial pattern recognition could be carried out more easily in the spatial frequency domain than in the spatial domain. For example, Fourier transforms express spatial functions as either sums of sine and cosine functions or as the sums of products of Fourier amplitudes and complex exponential terms representing the spatial phase. The shift theorem of Fourier analysis states that when a spatial function is shifted in position (like a shift of an image across the retina), then the Fourier components are unchanged in amplitude although altered in phase. It was this latter property of the Fourier transform and the need to find a mechanism that would permit the detection of objects independently of the precise position of their image across the central retina that led Pollen *et al.* [6] to propose the Fourier transform hypothesis "... for a restricted region of visual space."

Although Pollen *et al.* [6] and Pollen and Taylor [9] also hypothesized a global Fourier transform in higher visual cortices, both papers explicitly stated that at the level of the striate cortex the initial analysis must necessarily be restricted by the receptive field sizes of the local neurons. For example, Pollen and Taylor [9] proposed that "... a neural population sufficient to specify two-dimensional spatial frequency decompositions of subsections of visual space exists at the complex cell output stage in the striate cortex."

Maffei and Fiorentini [10] proposed that the simple cells were the spatial frequency analyzers because these cells responded with a modulated response pattern to each cycle of a drifting sine-wave grating, whereas complex cells generally responded with an unmodulated increase in firing level. Moreover, in their cell sample, simple cells were more narrowly tuned than were complex cells. Robson [11] favored the view of Maffei and Fiorentini [10] and extended the theoretical development in two ways. He recognized that the receptive field profiles of the two types of simple cells could frequently be characterized as either even-symmetric or odd-symmetric functions. Robson also suggested that a spatial frequency analysis might be carried out by simple cells on a patch-by-patch basis in which patches of a constant common size are scanned by a number of different spatial frequencies. This model predicts that cells tuned to higher spatial frequencies would have more cycles within the patch than cells tuned to lower spatial frequencies. Thus the bandwidth of a cell would be inversely proportional to its center spatial frequency.

We shall now consider the recent experimental results on simple and complex cells and the interpretation of these results in terms of certain models of spatial information processing.

II. SIMPLE CELLS: RELATIONSHIP BETWEEN RECEPTIVE FIELD PROFILE AND SPATIAL FREQUENCY SELECTIVITY

Five groups of investigators [12]–[16] have independently shown that the receptive field profiles of many simple cells (i.e., the more narrowly tuned cells) have

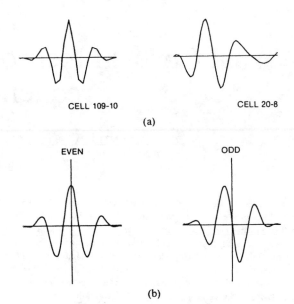

Fig. 1. Reconstructed receptive field profiles. (a) Simple cell with even-symmetric receptive field. (b) Odd-symmetric receptive field. (c) Photo of oscillographic representation of even-symmetric Gabor function with full bandwidth of about one octave. (d) Odd-symmetric Gabor function with bandwidth of about one octave. Both functions share *y* axis as their common axis of symmetry. In (c),(d), weak distant fringes of Gabor functions along the *x* axis are not shown. Note similarity of receptive field in (a) to even-symmetric Gabor signal in (c), and similarity of receptive field in (b) to odd-symmetric Gabor signal in (d). Examples in (a) and (b) were taken from unpublished and published illustrations, respectively from Andrews and Pollen [13]. Photos in (c) and (d) were prepared for us by John Daugman.

several additional sidebands or fringes in addition to the two or three central zones first described by Hubel and Wiesel [3]. Some, but not all, of the receptive field profiles closely approximate even- or odd-symmetric functions (Fig. 1(a),(b)).

Simple cells respond to spatial inputs in a reasonably linear manner [12], [13], and in a linear system the receptive field profiles and spatial frequency selectivity curves are Fourier transforms of each other (see especially [13]). The breadth of a spatial frequency tuning curve is usually defined by the full bandwidth at half-maximal amplitude. Bandwidths range from 0.6 to 2.0 octaves with an average of about 1.3 octaves [12], [13]. Estimates of the preferred spatial frequency are essentially independent of whether the sine-wave gratings tested were drifted across the receptive field at a constant velocity or at a constant temporal frequency [13]. Estimates of preferred spatial frequency and bandwidth also seem independent of test contrast [17].

Since spatial frequency bandwidth and the number of cycles within a receptive field are reciprocally related, it is impossible to define a receptive field profile which simultaneously provides sharp spatial frequency tuning and fine spatial localization of a signal. For example, a receptive field profile with more sidebands than are found for the simple cell would have sharper spatial frequency tuning but would provide less certain localization for a slit or spot. Conversely, a receptive field profile with fewer sidebands would provide improved spatial localization of a stimulus but greater uncertainty in the determination of its precise spatial frequency.

Gabor [19] had considered the analogous problem of defining signals in both the temporal frequency and time domain with a minimal uncertainty. He noted that Gaussian signals provide the best compromise of all waveforms because the product of their uncertainty in frequency and time has a minimal value. This same kind of relationship holds when a Gaussian is multiplied by a sine or cosine function. This multiplicative operation yields a periodic function attenuated by a Gaussian envelope in the time or space domain and shifts the Gaussian representing the tuning curve along the frequency axis in proportion to the frequency of the periodic function.

Marčelja [18] realized that even- or odd-symmetric receptive field profiles of simple cells (Fig. 1(a),(b)) closely approximated the elementary signals of Gabor [19] in the space domain (Fig. 1(c),(d)). He also realized that spatial frequency selectivity curves which approximated Gaussian envelopes had been found for simple cells in most of the reported studies. Thus the receptive field profile of the simple cell, to the extent that it matches a Gabor signal, represents a compromise such that the product of the uncertainty in defining the precise spatial frequency (Δf) and spatial position (Δx) of a signal is a minimum.

MacKay [20] has come to the same general conclusions as Marčelja. MacKay has expressed the uncertainty relationship as $\Delta x \cdot \Delta f \geqslant 1/2$ and noted that this relationship and the approximately one-octave bandwidth for simple cells implies that their respective fields "...seem to represent a near-optimal solution to the problem of sampling optical images in *both* the frequency and spatial domains."

Important extensions of these principles have been made by Kulikowski and Bishop [16] and by Kulikowski *et al.* [21]. Moreover, the extended relationship for joint optimization of resolution of a signal in space, spatial frequency, and orientation by two-dimensional filters has recently been developed by Daugman [22].

The Gabor functions, like sine and cosine functions, represent a complete mathematical set. The encoding of information is most efficient when these functions have a common axis of symmetry and are in a quadrature phase relationship (Fig. 1(c),(d)). In some cases actual receptive fields do not exactly resemble even- or odd-symmetric functions. However, such a deviation from the mathematical ideal is not an analytical problem as long as the two adjacent receptive fields are spatially overlapped with respect to each other so that their responses to drifting sine-wave gratings are 90° out-of-phase. The question of what phase relationships between adjacent simple cells actually exist in the visual cortex has recently been studied.

Pollen and Ronner [2] recorded from adjacent simple cell pairs in the striate cortex of the cat. They found 12 pairs in which the pair members had a common preference for spatial frequency, orientation, and direction. They then drifted gratings in the preferred spatial frequency range across the receptive field in the preferred direction and found that the responses of the two cells differed in spatial phase by approximately 90° (Fig. 2(a)).

Pollen and Ronner [2] used cross correlation techniques to estimate accurately these phase differences. Moreover, in several cases the phase shift across an extended range of the spatial frequency spectrum remained close to 90°. This finding indicates that the axes of the receptive field centers

must be the same and thus rules out the possibility that the two receptive field profiles are identical but simply shifted with respect to one another. The experimental results are, however, consistent with the possibility that the receptive fields are conjugate pairs—that is, one field with even symmetry and one with odd symmetry around the same axis.

Thus, experimental results indicate that adjacent simple cells can be considered to represent paired sine and cosine filters or Gabor functions with respect to their processing of afferent information. The problem is slightly more complicated for signals representing the output of simple cells because their responses are often truncated at the spontaneous firing level which is close to zero. A second sine and cosine pair of simple cells with receptive field polarities opposite to the first pair would be required to preserve the information that would otherwise be lost by truncation [2].

Very recently, Foster *et al.* [23] found four such pairs of simple cells with phase offsets within 10° of 180°. Analysis of the responses of these same cells to moving light and dark bars indicated that pair members had odd-symmetric receptive fields of opposite polarity sharing a common axis of symmetry. We had previously found simple cells with either on-center or off-center even-symmetric receptive fields paired with one or the other polarity of odd-symmetric receptive fields [2]. Thus four elemental receptive field functions of differing symmetry and polarity scan a common subdomain of visual space at each preferred orientation, direction, and spatial frequency [23] as previously predicted [2]. These four cells suffice to specify the spatial frequency, orientation, and direction over the receptive field region.

However, from a single microelectrode placement, we have not yet found a cell with an on-center symmetric receptive field paired with an off-center symmetric field. Such cells with such differing receptive field centers might be present in different cortical sublaminae just as on-center and off-center ganglion cells are stratified in different sublaminae in the retina [24].

There is anatomic evidence suggesting that the "on-center," "off-center" sampling dichotomy originates in the retina. Wässle *et al.* [25] recently reported that the population of beta-type ganglion cells (the *x* cells or "linear" cells of the physiologist [26]) in the retina divide into two regular independent mosaics, one for the on-center cells and one for the off-center cells. They also cite evidence that in some cases the on- and off-lattices may have identical sampling points.

III. SPATIAL FREQUENCY SELECTIVITY OF SIMPLE CELLS

The bandwidth (~ one octave) of simple cells is broad compared to that of an ideal Fourier filter. Nevertheless, when tested with square-wave gratings at a fundamental frequency of one-third the preferred spatial frequency, the more narrowly tuned of the simple cells respond three times to the passage of each cycle of the square-wave grating (Fig. 2(b)) [1]; that is, these cells are responding to each cycle of the third harmonic. The selectivity of simple

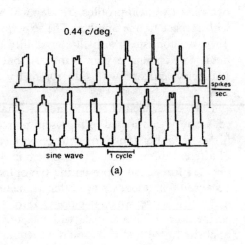

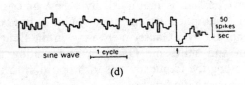

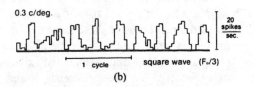

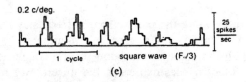

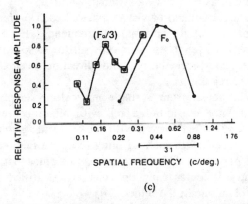

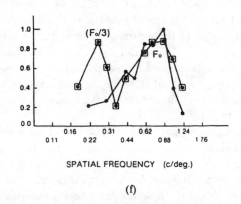

Fig. 2. (a) The averaged response histograms for two adjacent simple cells tuned to same spatial frequency and orientation. Visual stimulus for both simultaneously recorded neurons was drifting a sine-wave grating close to preferred spatial frequency. Note that the two sets of responses are about 90° out of phase with respect to each other. (b) Response of a simple cell to drifting square-wave grating at one-third preferred spatial frequency (F_0). (c) Response amplitudes of simple cell are plotted for drifting sine-wave gratings (closed circles) and drifting square-wave gratings (open squares). Peak of spatial frequency selectivity curve for sine-wave gratings has been normalized at 1.0 at preferred frequency (F_0). (d) Response of a complex cell to drifting sine-wave grating at preferred spatial frequency. Note that the response is essentially an increase in unmodulated level of activity, unlike the case for simple cells in (a). (e) Response of complex cell to a drifting square-wave grating at one-third the preferred spatial frequency. (f) Response amplitudes of complex cell are plotted for drifting sine-wave gratings (closed circles) and drifting square-wave gratings (open squares). Peak of spatial frequency selectivity (F_0) curve has been normalized to 1.0 as in (c).

cells to the third harmonic of a drifting square-wave grating may also be demonstrated by plotting the mean response amplitude as a function of the fundamental frequency of the sine-wave and square-wave gratings tested (Fig. 2(c)). At one-third the preferred spatial frequency, the mean response to a square-wave grating shows a secondary peak. Thus the simple cell can resolve the third harmonic from the fundamental frequency of the square-wave gratings. However, the bandwidths are not narrow enough so that the cells can resolve any harmonics above the third [1].

We now return to the issue of whether bandwidth is reciprocally related to the preferred spatial frequency as in Robson's model [11]. Kulikowski et al. [21] consider another model in which the receptive field size would be inversely proportional to the center frequency. In this latter case, the relative bandwidth in octaves would be a constant independent of the preferred spatial frequency. The experimental evidence shows that neither system is solely in operation. For example, although a definite tendency exists for relative bandwidth to narrow with increasing spatial frequency, considerable scatter occurs in the bandwidths found at any given spatial frequency [16], [27], [28]. Kulikowski and Bishop [16] find that the slope of the linear regression line between the logarithm of the bandwidth and the logarithm of the spatial frequency is only -0.3 for visual cortical neurons in the cat. DeValois et al. [28, Fig. 7] show a regression line with a slope of about -0.14 for striate neurons in the macaque monkey. These values fall far short of the value of -1.0 predicted by the equal patch model. Kulikowski et al. [21] consider that an intermediate system with scatter and redundancy may actually be in operation. Thus cells with narrower tuning might more advantageously sample periodic stimuli, whereas more broadly tuned cells, with their more spatially restricted receptive fields, would more effectively localize nonperiodic detail in the visual scene.

The actual range of preferred spatial frequencies represented in the primary visual cortex of the cat and the macaque monkey span a range of four to five octaves. In the cat the center frequencies range from 0.2 to 2.8 cycles/deg [10], [12], [13], whereas values for the macaque monkey range from 0.5 to 16.0 cycles/deg [28].

The preceding discussion has assumed that simple cells can be treated as approximately linear and independent filters. Even apart from the issue of truncation of the output [13], [29], which probably can be dealt with satisfactorily [1], several other problems must be considered. First, evidence exists that spatial frequency channels may not be entirely independent. For example, recent psychophysical [30] and neurophysiological [31] work suggests that the presence of higher spatial frequencies may inhibit the response to a lower test frequency and that the presence of lower frequencies [30] may actually facilitate the response to a higher test frequency. Furthermore, the "unresponsive" regions beyond the classically mapped receptive fields of cortical neurons may have either suppressive or facilatory effects upon the responsiveness of visual neurons which may modify estimates of bandwidth for both the orientation and spatial frequency selectivity [32]. Finally, the present discussion has not addressed the important contribution of temporal frequency selectivity upon neuronal responsiveness which has been considered elsewhere for the cat [12], [33] and macaque monkey [34], [35].

IV. ARE THE RESPONSE PROPERTIES OF EACH SIMPLE CELL UNIQUE?

Within each subsection of visual space as viewed by a single eye, response specificities can be ascribed to ocular dominance, preferred orientation, preferred direction, spatial frequency, position, and spatial phase. In our studies on simple cells over the past decade, we cannot find a single example when two adjacent or nearby simple cells had identical response properties. For example, when nearby cells shared a common ocular dominance and orientation column, some unidirectionally selective cells preferred one direction whereas other cells preferred the other direction. When all three response properties were

identical, nearby simple cells often differed with respect to the preferred spatial frequency by one-half octave or more. When the preceding response properties were virtually identical, adjacent cells differed incrementally in spatial phase by 90° in their response to drifting sine-wave gratings. Thus although neighboring cells may overlap in some response properties, at least one response characteristic always distinguishes one neuron from its neighbors. (When both eyes view the world, binocular cells might also differ with respect to retinal disparity, and in a trichromatic animal adjacent cells may differ in hue specificity.)

Hence we are led to a conjecture that the response properties of each simple cell may be unique. The cell biologist Edelman [36], on the basis of an analogy to the molecular biology of the synthesis of antibodies, proposed just such a scheme for a brain in which some redundancy of function would exist but never complete overlap among members of neuronal sets. Such a concept would have implications for pattern recognition theory, brain development, and above all, for a specificity of genetic coding that might permit both uniqueness in each member of a cell class and a complete representation of the visual scene by the entire cell set!

V. COMPLEX CELLS: RECEPTIVE FIELD PROPERTIES, SPATIAL FREQUENCY SELECTIVITY, AND THE PROBLEM OF PHASE REPRESENTATION

The definition of the simple cell depends upon finding purely excitatory and purely inhibitory zones at different positions across the receptive field [3]. On the contrary, complex cells are generally excited by either an increase or a decrease in the luminance of a properly oriented slit or edge placed anywhere within the receptive field [3].

An early attempt to resolve the substructure of the receptive field of the deep-layered complex cell was made by Rybicki et al. [37] who tested cell response as the spatial interval between two stationary test slits of light was varied. The response strength was found to be systematically dependent upon the spacing between the paired slits, and their data suggested that complex cells might be tuned to sine-wave gratings of such a frequency that one to one and one-half full cycles of the grating would cover the receptive field. Movshon et al. [38] greatly extended this type of analysis based upon varying the interslit spacing and found that the complex cell behaved as if it received inputs from cells that had line weighting profiles similar to those of simple cells. Movshon et al. [12] also convincingly showed that the range of preferred spatial frequencies for complex cells and their bandwidths are essentially the same as for simple cells. Earlier reports noting broader tuning for complex cells [10] may have been based upon sampling a higher proportion of neurons from the deeper cortical layers which are more broadly tuned for both orientation and spatial frequency.

Although simple cells respond to drifting sine-wave gratings with a well-modulated response pattern (Fig. 2(a)), albeit one that is often half-wave rectified [13], [29], complex cells generally respond with only an increased level of activity (Fig. 2(d)) [10], [33], [39]. However, when special efforts were made to vary the temporal frequency over narrow ranges, Pollen *et al.* [40] could find, in about half of the cells so studied, a drift frequency at which a modulated as well as unmodulated level of activity was present. Kulikowski and Bishop [41] found generally similar results.

Glezer *et al.* [42] used masks to test the responses of different parts of the receptive field of complex cells and produced strongly modulated responses which were phase dependent upon the position of the mask. They suggested that complex cells receive individual inputs which are themselves well-modulated, but which sum in different phase relationships so as to produce variable levels of modulated and unmodulated activity when the entire receptive field is stimulated with an extended drifting sine-wave grating.

When tested with drifting square-wave gratings at one-third the preferred spatial frequency, complex cells respond with two broad response peaks per cycle. Had the spatial frequency tuning of complex cells been very narrow, then their responses to square-wave gratings at this frequency should have consisted of a steady level of activity. However, one can show that it is just the interaction of some residual fundamental frequency component with the third harmonic response that produces the two response zones shown in Fig. 2(e) (see Section VIII). This pattern can be explained by a model that assumes that each complex cell receives information from two simple cell pairs tuned to the same spatial frequency and orientation. One such pair would be like the truncated sine and cosine pair shown in Fig. 2(a), and the second pair would selectively respond during the silent periods of the first pair; that is, their receptive field profiles would be inverted with respect to the first pair. Thus the relative phase offset between the fundamental and third harmonic of a square-wave grating could be preserved even though the absolute phase information to a single drifting sine-wave grating may frequently be lost.

Cavanagh [43] has noted that absolute phase information need not be of great importance in spatial pattern recognition, whereas "...the relative phase offset between components together with their amplitudes are sufficient to uniquely specify the pattern." Thus the breadth of the spatial frequency selectivity of visual neurons may actually be advantageous in permitting some interaction of adjacent spatial frequency components.

VI. Harmonic Analysis by Complex Cells

Evidence that the complex cells are actually responding to the third harmonic can be shown by testing these cells to both sine-wave and square-wave gratings and plotting the mean firing level as a function of the fundamental frequency. Just as in the case of the simple cell (Fig. 2(c)), the complex cell has a second relative maximum at one-third the preferred spatial frequency (Fig. 2(f)). Cells with these properties included the superficial cells generally and some

complex cells in the deep layers. The superficial complex cells project forward to higher cortical areas unlike certain deeper layer complex cells which project to the lateral geniculate or superior colliculus. Some cells in the deeper layers respond especially well to drifting textures [44] and may have different functional properties than the complex cells we have studied.

The superficial complex cells behave as if they received input from simple cells in a serial processing manner as Hubel and Wiesel first suggested [3]. However, it is disconcerting that the precision shown at the simple cell stage with respect to the presence of both amplitude and phase information is seldom seen in the complex cell stage. However, the rather steady or unmodulated level of activity of the complex cell frequently recorded in response to a drifting sine-wave grating is characteristic of a Fourier amplitude that is invariant for a spatially limited, but perhaps a functionally significant translational displacement of the stimulus. Thus the complex cell may convey information about a spatial frequency amplitude over a restricted region of visual space [1], [6].

VII. Anatomic Localization of Neurons as a Function of Their Selectivity for Orientation, Spatial Frequency, and Phase Within the Striate Cortex

The striate cortex is a three-dimensional structure, and one may ask how neurons selective for orientation, spatial frequency, and phase may be arranged within a volume of cortex. Hubel and Wiesel [3] first established that neurons selective to the same orientation had a columnar organization perpendicular to the cortex surface. More recently, they demonstrated [45] that the "columns" subserving constant preferred orientation are better described as parallel sheets or thin slabs running perpendicular to the cortical surface.

Maffei and Fiorentini [46] then reported that cells within a single orientation column represented a wide range of preferred spatial frequencies, whereas cells within the same cortical layer or sublayer have, of course, different preferred orientations as orientation columns are crossed but have virtually the same spatial frequency over an expanse of cortex. Their concept was challenged on the basis of 2-deoxyglucose autoradiographic studies by Silverman *et al.* [47] and others who believed that their data supported a contrary view that orientation columns existed within which neurons were selective to a single spatial frequency band. However, recent electrophysiological work by Berardi *et al.* [48] further supports the original proposal of Maffei and Fiorentini [46] that neurons with common optimal spatial frequencies are aligned along a direction orthogonal to the orientation columns. Berardi *et al.* [48] discuss reasons why the autoradiographic studies may not have had the resolution to bring out the same detail found in the electrophysiological studies. Tolhurst and Thompson [49] concurred with Berardi *et al.* [48] that neurons responsive to similar spatial frequencies tended to be anatomically aggregated, but the degree of ordering found by Tolhurst and Thompson was not high. They suggested "...that the unit of organization for optimal spatial frequency is neither columnar nor laminar; neurons are likely to have similar optima only if they lie within about 200 μ in the plane either of the columns or the laminae."

Whether or not the bands of common spatial frequencies are restricted to sublamina or to localized clusters, a third directional axis remains that can be defined as perpendicular to both the orientation axis and the axis of common preferred spatial frequencies. Kronauer has suggested that the 90° phase increments found for adjacent simple cells may define the orthogonal processing function along each sheet. At the simple cell level, the 90° phase pairs may constitute subsets of a much longer continuous cortical sequence. For example, progressive shifts in phase of 90° would imply a uniform stepwise translation of receptive fields over the retina that could be extended in a long sequence across the cortex. An analogous principle might hold for complex cells, in which case the "coordinates" of the receptive field center might be specified along this "phase" axis.

VIII. A MODEL FOR THE SYNTHESIS OF THE COMPLEX CELL RECEPTIVE FIELD

In Section III we noted that two pairs of simple cells, with the requisite quadrature phase relationship within each pair, could specify the amplitude and phase information at one spatial frequency, orientation, and direction for a subsection of visual space. We then wondered to what extent a "model complex cell" receiving input from four such simple cells would predict the response patterns of actual complex cells to various stimuli. The four-cell model we illustrate (Fig. 3) assumes a 1.3-octave bandwidth for both the on-center even-symmetric (Fig. 3(a)) and odd-symmetric (Fig. 3(b)) receptive field profiles.

The two receptive field profiles comprise one simple cell pair with a common vertical axis of symmetry. The second simple cell pair (not shown) would consist of an off-center even-symmetric cell and another odd-symmetric cell. The receptive field profile of the off-center cell would be the mirror image of the on-center receptive field profile (Fig. 3(a)) simply inverted around the horizontal axis which represents the zero firing level. The fourth receptive field profile would simply be the mirror image around the horizontal axis of the odd-symmetric field profile in Fig. 3(b).

If a complex cell received an input from each of these four cells, then a slit of light or dark bar tested at the preferred orientation anywhere across the receptive field would product both an ON and an OFF response, just as is the case for real complex cells, because each stimulus would necessarily stimulate part of the ON region of at least one cell and part of the OFF region of another.

Moreover, a narrow slit of light drifting across the receptive field of such a complex cell would successively excite the ON regions of successive simple cells and produce a field profile for a complex cell of the type shown in Fig. 3(c). This profile shows a series of periodically spaced peaks riding above an increase in the mean firing level. This profile resembles that of the "periodic complex cells" described by Pollen and Ronner [50] in response to a narrow slit moving across the receptive field. In this, as in subsequent tests, we assume that only the excitatory component of the simple cell response is conveyed to the complex cell. Note that the periodic component in Fig. 3(c), which represents inputs from successive ON regions, actually has a "spatial periodicity" which is four times the spatial frequency of the constituent simple cells (Fig. 3(a), (b)), whereas the preferred spatial frequency for the complex cell as tested with sine-wave gratings would be identical to that of its simple cell inputs.

Pollen and Ronner [1] found little functional difference in the responses of periodic and nonperiodic complex cells to drifting sine-wave and square-wave gratings. Any difference in the shape of the receptive field profiles of complex cells probably simply results from the degree of spatial overlap in the contributions from successive ON regions of precedent neurons.

Finally, we would like to test this complex cell model for a square-wave grating at one-third the preferred fundamental frequency. This is a key test because Pollen and Ronner [1] found that when square-wave gratings were tested at this spatial frequency, two distinct response zones existed for each full cycle of the square-wave grating (see [1, fig. 8]). Just such a result occurs (Fig. 3(d)) when the test square-wave grating (Fig. 3(e)) is convolved with each of the four simple cell receptive fields and their excitatory contributions are summated. The high peak response for each half-cycle of the square-wave grating occurs because the cell's spatial frequency bandwidth is broad enough to permit some contribution from both the fundamental frequency and the third harmonic. The relative minimum between each response zone occurs because a position exists at which each half-cycle of the low-frequency square-wave grating almost fully covers the receptive field of precedent neurons so that these cells then give a "null" or weak response.

Cavanagh [51] recently proposed a model in which several classes of complex cells would exist, but each class would behave as if it received inputs from only one type of simple cell. For example, he proposes that one class of complex cell could receive inputs from adjacent partially overlapping families of "light–dark" odd-symmetric simple cells, whereas a second class could receive inputs from only "dark–light" such cells and so on for the two varieties of even-symmetric cells. The important consequence of this model is that the complex cells would preserve a specificity to the relative phase offsets of components within their frequency bandpass. The formulation of these models is welcomed as they may help stimulate a more refined analysis of the substructure of the complex cell's receptive field.

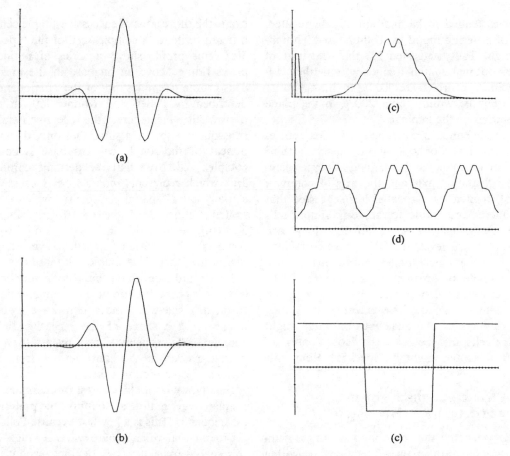

Fig. 3. (a) One-dimensional even-symmetric receptive field profile for hypothetical On-center simple cell with full bandwidth of 1.3 octaves. This function and all subsequent waveforms were digitalized into 65 values (bins). Function represented is $y = (2\sqrt{\pi} F_0 / 1.9712) e^{-(\pi x F_0/1.9712)^2} \cos 2\pi F_0 x$ for normal spatial frequency, F_0 value of 1 cycle/deg. (b) Odd-symmetric receptive field profile for hypothetical simple cell with same full bandwidth of 1.3 octaves is similarly digitized for the function: $y = (2\sqrt{\pi} F_0 / 1.9712) e^{-(\pi x F_0/1.9712)^2} \sin 2\pi F_0 x$. (c) Average response histogram calculated for a model complex cell as a narrow (two bin wide) hypothetical slit of light is drifted across the receptive field profile of the four precedent neurons described in text, two of which are shown in (a) and (b). (d) Calculated response of model complex cell to a low-frequency square-wave grating drifting across its "receptive field." Spatial frequency of square-wave grating is represented by waveform in (e). Note in (d) that one strong response zone exists for each half-cycle of drifting low spatial frequency square-wave grating. See text for other details.

IX. HIGHER LEVELS OF THE VISUAL SYSTEM: A LOOK AHEAD

It appears reasonable to suppose that one analytic function of the striate cortex has been to decompose the neural image locally into subsets of cells selectively sensitive to orientation, direction, spatial frequency, and, for the simple cells, the phase as well. Thus we do have "... two-dimensional spatial frequency decompositions of subsections of visual space" [9] for which the positional localization of each subsection remains an essential aspect of the description [18]. We do not, however, know how the information pertaining to spatial frequency selectivity and spatial localization is used at successively higher levels of the visual system.

Nevertheless, the more or less translationally invariant response of complex cells to drifting sine-wave gratings and slits of light may provide the basis for our ability to detect objects independently of the precise position of an image across the central retina [6]. Moreover, hypotheses based on Fourier models [52]–[54], with particular attention to the information inherent within the low spatial frequency portion of the transform, have had considerable success in explaining a number of psychological correlates of human vision. These results do not, of course, indicate that the brain actually utilizes Fourier analysis. Furthermore, the response characteristics of neurons in the striate cortex have not revealed how the visual system allows us to identify objects largely independent of their size and orientation. These tasks are presumably carried out in higher visual cortices. Several hypotheses have been made to resolve the issue of identification of objects independent of translation [6], of size and rotation [55], or all three [56]. The latter two hypotheses assume a final basis set consisting of members of the family of exponentially spaced concentric circles, rays, and logarithmic spirals. However, neurons in the next several extrastriate regions retain orientation-selectivity as a principal characteristic [57], a property that is not easily compatible with the buildup of sets of logarithmic spirals.

Yet there probably is a logical experimental approach to the extrastriate visual cortices. Beyond the striate cortex, receptive fields increase in successive higher visual areas reaching huge sizes in the inferotemporal cortex [58], [59]. Each subsection of these large fields must, therefore, be at least partially dependent upon the response properties of the preceding neurons in the striate cortex. We believe that the formulation of striate neurons as spatially localized, orientation-selective spatial frequency filters will facilitate analysis of the organization of the more spatially-extensive visual receptive fields found at higher cortical levels [60].

ACKNOWLEDGMENT

We wish to thank Drs. Richard Kronauer, Stjepan Marčelja, and John Daugman for their useful suggestions.

REFERENCES

[1] D. A. Pollen and S. F. Ronner, "Spatial computation performed by simple and complex cells in the visual cortex of the cat," *Vision Res.*, vol. 22, pp. 101–118, 1982.

[2] ——, "Phase relationships between adjacent cells in the visual cortex," *Sci.*, vol. 212, pp. 1409–1411, 1981.

[3] D. H. Hubel and T. N. Wiesel, "Receptive fields, binocular interaction and functional architecture in the cat's visual cortex," *J. Physiol.*, vol. 160, pp. 106–154, 1962.

[4] F. W. Campbell and J. G. Robson, "Application of Fourier analysis to the visibility of gratings," *J. Physiol.*, vol. 197, pp. 551–566, 1968.

[5] C. Blakemore and F. W. Campbell, "On the existence in the human visual system of neurons selectively sensitive to the orientation and size of retinal images," *J. Physiol.*, vol. 203, pp. 237–260, 1969.

[6] D. A. Pollen, J. R. Lee, and J. H. Taylor, "How does the striate cortex begin the reconstruction of the visual world?" *Sci.*, vol. 173, pp. 74–77, 1971.

[7] J. H. Taylor, "Two-dimensional brightness distributions of radio sources from lunar occultation observations," *Astrophys. J.*, vol. 150, pp. 421–426, 1967.

[8] R. N. Bracewell, "Strip integration in radio astronomy," *Australian J. Physics*, vol. 9, pp. 198–216, 1956.

[9] D. A. Pollen and J. H. Taylor, "The striate cortex and the spatial analysis of visual space," in *The Neurosciences*, *Third Study Program*, F. O. Schmitt and F. G. Worden, Eds. Cambridge, MA: MIT Press, 1974, pp. 239–247.

[10] L. Maffei and A. Fiorentini, "The visual cortex as a spatial frequency analyzer," *Vision Res.*, vol. 13, pp. 1255–1267, 1973.

[11] J. G. Robson, "Receptive fields: Neural representation of the spatial and intensive attributes of the visual image," in *Handbook of Perception*, E. C. Carterette and M. P. Friedman, Eds. New York: Academic, vol. 5, 1975, pp. 81–116.

[12] J. A. Movshon, I. D. Thompson, and D. J. Tolhurst, "Spatial and temporal contrast sensitivity of neurons in areas 17 and 18 of the cat's visual cortex," *J. Physiol.*, vol. 283, pp. 101–120, 1978.

[13] B. W. Andrews and D. A. Pollen, "Relationship between spatial frequency selectivity and receptive field profile of simple cells," *J. Physiol.*, vol. 287, pp. 163–176, 1979.

[14] K. K. De Valois, R. L. De Valois, and E. W. Yund, "Responses of striate cortex cells to grating and checkerboard patterns," *J. Physiol.*, vol. 291, pp. 483–505, 1979.

[15] L. Maffei, C. Morrone, M. Pirchio, and G. Sandini, "Responses of visual cortical cells to periodic and nonperiodic stimuli," *J. Physiol.*, vol. 296, pp. 24–47, 1979.

[16] J. J. Kulikowski and P. O. Bishop, "Fourier analysis and spatial representation in the visual cortex," *Experientia*, vol. 37, pp. 160–163, 1981.

[17] D. G. Albrecht and D. B. Hamilton, "Striate cortex of monkey and cat: contrast response function," *J. Neurophysiol.*, vol. 48, pp. 217–237, 1982.

[18] S. Marčelja, "Mathematical description of the responses of simple cortical cells," *J. Opt. Soc. Amer.*, vol. 70, pp. 1297–1300, 1980.

[19] D. Gabor, "Theory of communication," *J. Inst. Elec. Eng.*, vol. 93, pp. 429–459, 1946.

[20] D. M. MacKay, "Strife over visual cortical function," *Nature*, vol. 289, pp. 117–118, 1981.

[21] J. J. Kulikowski, S. Marčelja, and P. O. Bishop, "Theory of spatial position and spatial frequency relations in the receptive fields of simple cells in the visual cortex," *Biol. Cybern.*, vol. 43, pp. 187–198, 1982.

[22] J. Daugman, "Uncertainty relation for resolution in space, spatial frequency, and orientation optimized by two-dimensional visual cortical filters," *J. Opt. Soc. Am.*, in press.

[23] K. H. Foster, J. P. Gaska, S. Marčelja, and D. A. Pollen, "Phase relationships between adjacent simple cells in the visual cortex. II. 180° phase shifts," *J. Physiol.*, in press.

[24] R. Nelson, E. V. Famiglietti, Jr., and H. Kolb, "Intracellular staining reveals different levels of stratification for on- and off-center ganglion cells in the retina," *J. Neurophysiol.*, vol. 41, pp. 472–483, 1978.

[25] H. Wässle, B. B. Boycott, and R. B. Illing, "Morphology and mosaic of on- and off-beta cells in the cat retina and some functional considerations," *Proc. Roy. Soc.*, Ser. B., vol. 212, pp. 177–195, 1981.

[26] C. Enroth-Cugell and J. G. Robson, "The contrast sensitivity of the retinal ganglion cells of the cat," *J. Physiol.*, vol. 187, pp. 517–552, 1966.

[27] I. D. Thompson and D. J. Tolhurst, "Variations in the spatial frequency of neurons in the cat visual cortex," *J. Physiol.*, vol. 295, 33P, 1979.

[28] R. L. De Valois, D. G. Albrecht, and L. G. Thorell, "Spatial frequency selectivity of cells in macaque visual cortex," *Vision Res.*, vol. 22, pp. 545–559, 1982.

[29] J. A. Movshon and D. J. Tolhurst, "On the response linearity of neurones in cat visual cortex," *J. Physiol.*, vol. 249, pp. 56P–57P, 1975.

[30] Y. Y. Zeevi, R. E. Kronauer, and J. D. Daugman, "Spatiotemporal masking: asymmetry, non-separability and facilitation," *Invest. Ophthalmol. Visual Sci.*, Suppl., vol. 22, p. 252, 1982.

[31] K. K. De Valois and R. B. H. Tootell, "Spatial frequency-specific inhibition in cat striate cortex cells," *J. Physiol.*, vol. 336, pp. 359–376, 1983.

[32] J. Maffei and A. Fiorentini, "The unresponsive regions of visual cortical receptive fields," *Vision Res.*, vol. 16, pp. 1131–1139, 1976.

[33] H. Ikeda and M. J. Wright, "Spatial and temporal properties of 'sustained' and 'transient' neurons in area 17 of the cat's visual cortex," *Exp. Brain Res.*, vol. 22, pp. 363–383, 1975.

[34] K. H. Foster, J. P. Gaska, and D. A. Pollen, "Spatial and temporal selectivity of V1 neurons in the macaque monkey," *Invest. Ophthalmol. Visual Sci.*, Suppl., vol. 23, p. 228, 1983.

[35] J. P. Gaska, K. H. Foster, M. Nagler, and D. A. Pollen, "Spatial and temporal selectivity of V2 neurons in the macaque monkey," *Invest. Ophthalmol. Visual Sci.*, Suppl., vol. 23, p. 228, 1983.

[36] G. Edelman, "Group selection and phasic reentrant signaling: a theory of higher brain function," in *The Neurosciences: Fourth Study Program*, F. O. Schmitt and F. G. Worden, Eds. Cambridge, MA: MIT Press, 1979.

[37] G. B. Rybicki, D. M. Tracy and D. A. Pollen, "Complex cell response depends on interslit spacing," *Nature New Biology*, vol. 240, pp. 77–78, 1972.

[38] J. A. Movshon, I. D. Thompson, and D. J. Tolhurst, "Receptive field organization of complex cells in the cat's striate cortex," *J. Physiol.*, vol. 283, pp. 79–99, 1978.

[39] P. H. Schiller, B. L. Finlay, and S. F. Volman, "Quantitative studies of single-cell properties in monkey striate cortex. III. Spatial frequency," *J. Neurophysiol.*, vol. 39, pp. 1334–1351, 1976.

[40] D. A. Pollen, B. W. Andrews, and S. E. Feldon, "Spatial frequency selectivity of periodic complex cells in the visual cortex of the cat," *Vision Res.*, vol. 18, pp. 665–682, 1978.

[41] J. J. Kulikowski and P. O. Bishop, "Silent periodic cells in the cat striate cortex," *Vision Res.*, vol. 22, pp. 191–200, 1982.

[42] D. Glezer, T. A. Tscherbach, V. E. Gauselman, and V. M. Bondarko, "Spatio-temporal organization of receptive fields of the cat striate cortex," *Biol. Cybern.*, vol. 43, pp. 35–49, 1982.

[43] P. Cavanagh, "Functional size invariance is not provided by the cortical magnification factor," *Vision Res.*, vol. 22, pp. 1409–1412,

1982.

[44] P. Hammond and P. M. MacKay, "Differential responsiveness of simple and complex cells in cat striate cortex to visual texture," *Exp. Brain Res.*, vol. 30, pp. 275–296, 1977.

[45] D. H. Hubel and T. N. Wiesel, "Sequence regularity and geometry of orientation columns in the monkey striate cortex," *J. Comp. Neurol.*, vol. 158, pp. 267–293, 1974.

[46] L. Maffei and A. Fiorentini, "Spatial frequency rows in the striate cortex," *Vision Res.*, vol. 17, pp. 257–264, 1977.

[47] M. S. Silverman, R. B. Tootell, and R. L. De Valois, "Deoxyglucose mapping of orientation and spatial frequency in cat visual cortex," *Invest. Ophthalmol. Visual Sci., Suppl.*, vol. 19, p. 225, 1980.

[48] N. Berardi, S. Bisti, A. Cattaneo, A. Fiorentini, and L. Maffei, "Correlation between the preferred orientation and spatial frequency of neurons in visual areas 17 and 18 of the cat," *J. Physiol.*, vol. 323, pp. 603–618, 1982.

[49] D. J. Tolhurst and I. D. Thompson, "Organization of neurones preferring similar spatial frequencies in cat striate cortex," *Exp. Brain. Res.*, vol. 48, pp. 217–227, 1982.

[50] D. A. Pollen and S. F. Ronner, "Periodic excitability changes across the receptive fields of complex cells in the striate and parastriate cortex of the cat," *J. Physiol.*, vol. 245, pp. 667–697, 1975.

[51] P. Cavanagh, "Image transforms in the visual system," in *Figural Synthesis*, P. C. Dodwell and T. M. Caelli, Eds. Lawrence Erlbaum, 1983 (in press).

[52] M. Kabrisky, O. Tallman, C. M. Day, and C. M. Rodoy, "A theory of pattern recognition based on human physiology," in *Contemporary Problems in Perception*, A. T. Welford and L. H. Houssiadies, Eds. London: Taylor and Francis, 1970, pp. 129–147.

[53] A. P. Ginsburg, "Psychological correlates of a model of the human visual system," *IEEE Trans. Aerosp. Electron. Syst.*, vol. AES-7, pp. 283–290, 1971.

[54] A. P. Ginsburg, "Visual information processing based on spatial filters constrained by biological data," Ph.D. dissertation, Univ. of Cambridge, 1978.

[55] E. Schwartz, "Computational anatomy and functional architecture of striate cortex: a spatial mapping approach to perceptual coding," *Vision Res.*, vol. 20, pp. 645–669, 1980.

[56] P. Cavanagh, "Size and position invariance in the visual system," *Perception*, vol. 7, pp. 167–177, 1978.

[57] J. F. Baker, S. E. Petersen, W. T. Newsome, and J. M. Allman, "Visual response properties of neurons in four extrastriate visual areas of the owl monkey (*Aotus trivirgatus*): A quantitative comparison of medial, dorsomedial, dorsolateral, and middle temporal areas," *J. Neurophysiol.*, vol. 45, pp. 397–416, 1981.

[58] R. E. Weller and J. H. Kaas, "Cortical and subcortical connections of visual cortex in primates," in *Cortical Sensory Organization*; vol. 2, *Multiple Visual Areas*. Clifton, NJ: Humana Press, 1981, ch. 2, pp. 121–155.

[59] C. G. Gross, C. E. Rocha-Miranda, and D. B. Bender, "Visual properties of neurons in inferotemporal cortex of the macaque," *J. Neurophysiol.*, vol. 35, pp. 96–111, 1972.

[60] D. A. Pollen, M. Nagler, J. Daugman, R. Kronauer, and P. Cavanagh, "Use of Gabor signals to probe receptive field substructure of inferotemporal neurons in the owl monkey," *Invest. Ophthalmol. Visual Sci., Suppl.*, vol. 22, p. 282, 1982.

Part 6
Neuro-Vision Systems: Computational Architectures and Applications

Human vision is very perplexing: we see and recognize, we see but cannot recognize, and we do not see but can recognize.

HUMAN vision is robust in the sense that it can achieve maximum performance under a noisy situation even with partial and ambiguous visual information presented to it. When we gaze upon a scene—a scene that is only partially visible—the visual channels process and transmit this partial information to the brain. Our eyes try to capture visual information from different depths and angles, and the brain cooperatively combines this information and generates a globally consistent and unambiguous representation of form, color, and depth of the scene. If we can produce a neuro-vision system for robotic applications with only a partial duplication of human vision, our robots will be able to see and recognize patterns and perhaps perform visual tasks very quickly.

The processing power of biological vision lies in the large number of dynamic neurons that are linked by an enormous amount of synapses (interconnections). Currently available technology does not permit dense "biological-like" interconnections. However, biology has motivated the design of neuro-vision systems over the last decade and many new computational architectures have evolved with some exciting applications. After having presented the neurophysiology and the mathematical morphology of biological vision in the first five parts, in this part of the volume, we present some computational architectures of neuro-vision systems. Several of these architectures are general enough for a variety of vision applications, but most of these have been developed for specific applications.

S. Grossberg, E. Mingolla, and D. Todorovic present a general-purpose neural computational architecture for certain aspects of early or preattentive vision in article (6.1). This neural architecture uses two parallel channels for preattentive vision, one for the boundary contour system and the second for the feature contour system. At the higher level of processing, this information is fused together to generate information about form, color, and depth. Possible applications of this architecture are in the analysis of boundaries, textures, and smooth surfaces. The authors present some neurophysiological and psychophysical evidence for this network architecture.

Human vision is a dynamic process in which the eyes move through an evolving sequence of fixations in an effort to explore the visual world. In addition, the vision system selectively gathers the most relevant information for the task at hand. Neuro-vision systems must follow the inherent dynamic behavior of biological vision if they are to perform useful tasks in real time. One way to achieve this is to incorporate some intelligence in the process of seeing, thereby making efficient use of the limited computation resources.

In article (6.2), P. J. Burt presents a pyramid computational architecture for a vision machine. This architecture supports smart sensing and highly efficient computations. Key elements of this novel design are 1) hierarchical data structure for image representation, 2) fine-to-course algorithms for the fast generation of image measure, 3) course-to-fine search strategies that locate objects and events within a scene, and 4) high-level control mechanism that enables scene-data gathering to continue even as visual information is being processed. Several applications of such pyramid vision machines for industrial inspection, surveillance, and object recognition are reported.

F. W. Adams, Jr., H. T. Nguyen, R. Raghavan, and J. Slawny describe a parallel dynamical neural system designed to integrate model-based and data-driven approaches for image recognition in article (6.3). The authors provide a translation-invariant network using a probabilistic cellular automata, which combines feature detector outputs in order to collectively perform enhancement and recognition functions. The operation of the neural-network system is illustrated with examples derived from visual, infrared, and laser–radar imagery.

Most of the methods of pattern recognition, especially template matching, are sensitive to shifts in position and distortion in shape. In article (6.4), I. A. Rybak, A. V. Golovan,

319

V. I. Gusakova, N. A. Shevtsova, and L. N. Podladchikova present a parallel–sequential method that is invariant to position, rotation, and scale for processing gray-level images. The authors also describe some applications for recognizing gray-level images.

The early work (1960) of Widrow and Hoff on adaptive threshold logic units, called ADALINEs, provided an early impetus to the field of neural networks. In article (6.5), B. Widrow, R. G. Winter, and R. A. Baxter summarize the work they have done on ADALINEs for trainable pattern recognition problems. The proposed multilayered approach is insensitive to translation, rotation, changes in scale, and changes in perspective of the retinal input pattern. To adapt the ADALINE elements of the multilayered neural network, the authors introduce a new robust learning algorithm called MADALINE Rule II, or MRII, that uses the common sense principle of minimal disturbance. In summary, this rule can be stated as: "*give the responsibility to a group of neurons that can most easily assume it.*" In other words, do not rock the boat any more than necessary to achieve the desired training objective.

Another method for object recognition with invariant properties to scale, translation, and in-plane rotation is proposed by L. Spirkovska and M. B. Reid in article (6.6). The neural architecture, called higher-order neural network (HONN), does not need to learn invariances because they are built directly into the architecture. As a result, a smaller training set is required to distinguish the objects. This approach is different from the Neocognitron approach proposed by Fukushima in the next article.

In article (6.7), K. Fukushima and S. Miyake propose an algorithm that provides a robust solution to the problem of invariant pattern recognition. The network is called Neocognitron (this name was coined by Prof. Fukushima in the mid-seventies, and since then it has been used by him and many others in their theoretical and applied work). This article, which has appeared in various forms at various conferences and in scientific journals, takes a somewhat different point of view. The Neocognitron algorithm is motivated by the anatomy and physiology of the biological visual system as described by Hubel and Wiesel. The authors use a number of layers in cascade, which are driven by an initial retina of photoreceptors. The neural-network layers of the Neocognitron have strong self-organizing properties. The composition of Neocognitron is based on the S-cells (simple cells) and the C-cells (complex cells) in the primary visual cortex. The authors use this multilayered architecture in the recognition of handwritten characters with various shapes and distortions presented anywhere in the field of view of the system. There seems to be a large commercial potential for such an architecture that attempts to mimic the hardware in the brain.

Recent developments in neural networks have provided potential alternatives to traditional techniques used for object recognition. The inherent parallelism of neural nets enables many hypotheses to be pursued simultaneously, thereby resulting in high computation rates.

W.-C. Lin, F.-Y. Liao, C.-K. Tsao, and T. Lingutla propose a hierarchical approach to solving the surface and vertex correspondence problem in a multiview-based 3-D object-recognition system in article (6.8). They use a single-layer Hopfield neural network at each stage of the hierarchy. This scheme can be considered as a coarse-to-fine search process. The formulation of the network structure is simple and the matching process is reported to be easy to implement.

Vision seems to be an effortless process to the biological organism. We gaze around and we "see" and "perceive" the world in all its color, brightness, and motion. Flies, frogs, cats, and humans can all perceive motion and brightness in their visual world, yet there are great difficulties in endowing robots with similar abilities. Vision scientists face a challenging task in developing such human abilities for robotic applications. In this respect, we present two articles that deal with the problem of color.

Color constancy is the ability of the human visual system to judge, preattentively, the reflectance of objects in the visual scene under a range of different illuminations. Color constancy is not perfect. If the illuminant is strongly saturated (lacking in white), we make errors. However, for natural variations, such as changes in daylight conditions caused by varying cloud cover, humans do rather well. In article (6.9), A. Moore, J. Allman, and R. M. Goodman present a neural approach based on Land's retinex theory that addresses this problem of color constancy for video images. The approach was biologically motivated, and the authors present extensive simulation studies along with the VLSI implementation of the retinex algorithm.

Any color can be uniquely specified by its surface spectral-reflectance curve, known as its physical color attribute, which is defined as the fraction of incident irradiance that the surface reflects as a function of wavelength. However, the details of how the physiological system relates physical input to the psychological response are poorly understood. S. Usui, S. Nakauchi, and M. Nakano provide a wine-glass-type of five-layer neural network to generate an identity mapping of the surface spectral-reflection data of 1280 Munsell color chips in their article (6.10). This network seems to provide an interesting insight into the perception of color.

Stereo vision is a passive technique used to determine the depth of an object or a point in a scene using a pair of stereo images. In human vision, the brain receives similar images of a scene taken from two nearby points at the same horizontal level by means of the way our eyes are positioned and controlled. If the two objects are separated in depth from the viewer, the relative positions of their images will differ in the two eyes. The brain is capable of estimating this disparity and of using it to estimate depth.

In a brief article, (6.11), A. Khotanzad, A. Bokil, and Y.-W. Lee present a novel neural-network approach to stereopsis. The problem is formulated as a local nonlinear noniterative mapping problem. An important aspect of this approach is that it does not require a prior imposition of any scene-related constraints and will automatically tune itself to the constraints inherent in the problem, resulting in a flexible and more accurate model.

N. M. Nasrabadi and C. Y. Choo, in article (6.12), present an alternative optimization approach using a Hopfield neural network to solve the correspondence problem for a set of features extracted from a pair of stereo images.

The problem of restoring noisy-blurred images is very important for a large number of vision applications. Blurring is caused by many factors, such as motion, defocusing, atmospheric turbulence, and noisy instruments. Over the last three decades, various methods, such as the inverse filter, Wiener–Kalman filter, and many other model-based approaches, have been proposed for image restoration. In the last article, (6.13), Y. T. Zhou, R. Chellappa, A. Vaid, and B. K. Jenkins present a neural-network approach to the restoration of images degraded by a known shift-invariant blur function and adaptive noise. Although this article in image restoration does not provide a complete solution to the problem, this does indicate the various associated problems and directions for further work.

In this part of the volume, we have thus presented a set of thirteen representative articles dealing with neuro-vision computational architectures for various vision applications. In the next part, we will extend this presentation specifically to neuro-vision hardware implementations.

Further Reading

[1] D. Anastassiou, "Error diffusion coding for A/D conversion," *IEEE Trans. Circuits Syst.*, vol. 36, no. 9, pp. 1175–1186, 1989.

[2] R. Braham and J. O. Hamblen, "The design of a neural network with a biologically motivated architecture," *IEEE Trans. Neural Networks*, vol. 1, no. 3, pp. 251–262, 1990.

[3] G. A. Carpenter and S. Grossberg, "A massively parallel architecture for a self-organizing neural pattern recognition machine," *Comput. Vision, Graphics, Image Process.*, vol. 37, pp. 54–115, 1987.

[4] S. Connelly and A. Rosenfeld, "A pyramid algorithm for fast curve extraction," *Comput. Vision, Graphics, Image Process.*, vol. 49, pp. 332–345, 1990.

[5] N. H. Farhat, "Microwave diversity imaging and automated target identification based on models of neural networks," *Proc. IEEE*, vol. 77, no. 5, pp. 670–681, 1989.

[6] K. Fukushima, "A feature extractor for curvilinear patterns: A design suggested by the mammalian visual system," *Kybernetik*, vol. 7, pp. 153–160, 1970.

[7] K. Fukushima, "Neocognitron: A hierarchical network for visual pattern recognition," in *Fuzzy Computing: Theory, Hardware and Applications*, M. M. Gupta and T. Yamakawa, Eds., Amsterdam: North-Holland, pp. 53–69, 1988.

[8] K. Fukushima, "Selective attention in pattern recognition and associative recall," in *Fuzzy Computing: Theory, Hardware and Applications*, M. M. Gupta and T. Yamakawa, Eds., Amsterdam: North-Holland, pp. 71–88, 1988.

[9] S. Geman and D. Geman, "Stochastic relaxation, Gibbs distributions, and Bayesian restoration of images," *IEEE Trans. Pattern Anal. Machine Intell.*, vol. 6, pp. 721–741, 1984.

[10] A. D. Goltsev, "The neuronlike network for brightness picture segmentation," *Neural Networks World*, vol. 5, pp. 303–307, 1991.

[11] S. Grossberg and E. Migolla, "Neural dynamics of surface perception: Boundary webs, illuminants, and shape-from-shading," *Comput. Vision, Graphics, Image Process.*, vol. 37, pp. 116–165, 1987.

[12] N. G. Hatsopoulos and W. H. Warren, Jr., "Visual navigation with a neural network," *Neural Networks*, vol. 4, pp. 303–317, 1991.

[13] J. Hutchinson, C. Koch, J. Luo, and C. Mead, "Computing motion using analog and binary resistive networks," *IEEE Computer*, vol. 21, pp. 52–64, 1981.

[14] A. Khotanzad and J.-H. Lu, "Classification of invariant image representations using a neural network," *IEEE Trans. Acous., Speech, Signal Process.*, vol. 38, no. 6, pp. 1028–1038, 1990.

[15] G. K. Knopf and M. M. Gupta, "Design of a multitask neurovision processor," *J. Math. Imaging Vision*, vol. 2, pp. 233–250, 1992.

[16] R. Krishnapuram and L.-F. Chen, "Implementation of parallel thinning algorithms using recurrent neural networks," *IEEE Trans. Neural Networks*, vol. 4, no. 1, pp. 142–147, 1993.

[17] R. Krishnapuram and J. Lee, "Fuzzy-set-based hierarchical networks for information fusion in computer vision," *Neural Networks*, vol. 5, pp. 335–350, 1992.

[18] H. Marko, "Pattern recognition with homogeneous and space-variant neural layers," *Neural Networks World*, vol. 2, pp. 71–79, 1991.

[19] D. Marr and T. Poggio, "Cooperative computation of stereo disparity," *Science*, vol. 194, pp. 283–287, 1976.

[20] R. A. Messner and H. H. Szu, "An image processing architecture for real time generation of scale and rotation invariant patterns," *Comput. Vision, Graphics, Image Process.*, vol. 31, pp. 50–66, 1985.

[21] J. K. Paik and A. K. Katsaggelos, "Image restoration using a modified Hopfield network," *IEEE Trans. Image Process.*, vol. 1, no. 1, pp. 49–63, 1992.

[22] T. Poggio, E. B. Gamble, and J. J. Little, "Parallel integration of vision modules," *Science*, vol. 242, pp. 436–440, 1988.

[23] D. L. Standley, "An object position and orientation IC with embedded images," *IEEE J. Solid-State Circuits*, vol. 26, pp. 1853–1859, 1991.

[24] D. W. Tank and J. J. Hopfield, "Simple neural optimization networks: An A/D converter, signal decision circuit, and a linear programming circuit," *IEEE Trans. Circuits Syst.*, vol. 33, no. 5, pp. 533–541, 1986.

[25] D. Walters, "Selection of image primitives for general-purpose visual processing," *Comput. Vision, Graphics, Image Process.*, vol. 37, pp. 261–298, 1987.

[26] B. Widrow and M. A. Lehr, "30 Years of adaptive neural networks: Perceptron, Madaline and backpropogation," *Proc. IEEE*, vol. 78, no. 9, pp. 1415–1442, 1990.

[27] B. Widrow and R. Winter, "Neural nets for adaptive filtering and adaptive pattern recognition," *IEEE Computer*, vol. 21, no. 3, March, pp. 25–39, 1988.

[28] Y.-T. Zhou and R. Chellappa, *Artificial Neural Networks for Computer Vision*. New York: Springer-Verlag, 1992.

A Neural Network Architecture for Preattentive Vision

STEPHEN GROSSBERG, ENNIO MINGOLLA, AND DEJAN TODOROVIĆ

(Invited Paper)

Abstract—Recent results towards development of a neural network architecture for general-purpose preattentive vision are summarized. The architecture contains two parallel subsystems, the boundary contour system (BCS) and the feature contour system (FCS), which interact together to generate a representation of form-and-color-and-depth. Emergent boundary segmentation within the BCS and featural filling-in within the FCS are herein emphasized within a monocular setting. Applications to the analysis of boundaries, textures, and smooth surfaces are described, as is a model for invariant brightness perception under variable illumination conditions. The theory shows how suitably defined parallel and hierarchical interactions overcome computational uncertainties that necessarily exist at early processing stages. Some of the psychophysical and neurophysiological data supporting the theory's predictions are mentioned.

The Need for a General Purpose Preattentive Vision Machine

MANY AI algorithms for machine vision have been too specialized for applications to real-world problems. Such algorithms are often designed to deal with one type of information—for example, boundary, disparity, curvature, shading, or spatial frequency information. Moreover, such algorithms typically use different computational schemes to analyze each distinct type of information, so that unification into a single general-purpose vision algorithm is difficult at best. For such AI algorithms, other types of signals are often contaminants, or noise elements, rather than cooperative sources of ambiguity-reducing information. Unfortunately, most realistic scenes contain partial information of several different types in each part of a scene.

In contrast, when we humans gaze upon a scene, our brains rapidly combine several different types of locally ambiguous visual information to generate a globally consistent and unambiguous representation of form-and-color-in-depth. This state of affairs raises the question: what new computational principles and mechanisms are needed to understand how multiple sources of visual information cooperate automatically to generate a percept of three-dimensional form?

The Center for Adaptive Systems at Boston University

has been developing such a general purpose automatic vision architecture, and this paper reviews and integrates some of our recent work on its design. This architecture clarifies how scenic data about boundaries, textures, shading, depth, multiple spatial scales, and motion can be cooperatively synthesized in real-time into a coherent representation of three-dimensional form. Moreover, it has become clear through cooperative work with collegues at M.I.T. Lincoln Laboratory that the same processes which are useful to automatically process visual data from human sensors are equally valuable for processing noisy multidimensional data from artificial sensors, such as laser radars. These processes are called emergent segmentation and featural filling-in.

Why do We Bother to See? The Difference Between Seeing and Recognizing

The difficulties inherent in computationally understanding biological vision can be appreciated by considering a few examples. Fig. 1 depicts a type of visual image that has been named after L. Glass. When we view such a Glass pattern, we *see* and *recognize* many black dots on white paper, but we also *recognize* among the dots circular groupings that we do not *see*. For most individuals, these circular groupings do not generate brightnesses or colors that differ significantly from the background. Thus there is a profound difference between seeing and recognizing, and we can sometimes recognize groupings that we cannot see. This state of affairs raises the interesting question: if we can recognize things that we cannot see, then why do we bother to see?

The seriousness of this issue is illustrated by considering the image of a texture shown in Fig. 2, which was introduced by Beck [1]. Humans can very quickly, and without prior experience with that texture, distinguish its top-half from its bottom-half. One type of factor that we use to accomplish this are the long horizontal groupings which are generated perpendicular to the line ends in the top half of the texture. Although these emergent horizontal groupings, or segmentations, are critical in helping us to *recognize* that the bottom half is different from the top half, these horizontal segmentations are not *seen* in the traditional sense of generating a large brightness or color differences. Thus, perceptually invisible segmentations are critical in the recognition of visual form.

The other side of the coin is equally perplexing; namely, we can sometimes see things that are not in the image, as

Manuscript received January 29, 1988; revised July 5, 1988. This work was supported by the Air Force Office of Scientific Research Grants AFOSR F49620-86-C-0037, F49620-87-C-0018, and F49620-87-C-0018; the Army Research Office Grants DAAG-29-85-K-0095 and DAAG-29-85-K-0095; and the National Science Foundation Grant IRI-84-17756.

S. Grossberg and E. Mingolla are with the Center For Adaptive Systems, Boston University, Boston, MA 02215.

D. Todorović is with the Labroatoriha za Eksperimentalnu Psihologihu, Univerzitet u Beogradu, 11000 Beograd, Yugoslavia.

IEEE Log Number 8824418.

Reprinted from *IEEE Trans. Biomed. Eng.*, vol. 36, no. 1, pp. 65–84, Jan. 1989.

Fig. 1. A glass pattern: the emergent circular pattern is "recognized," although it is not "seen," as a pattern of differing contrasts. The text suggests how this happens.

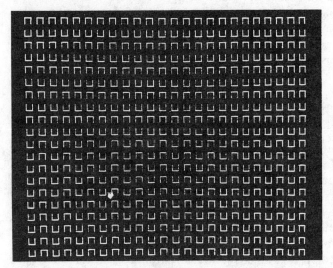

Fig. 2. Textural grouping supported by subjective contours: cooperation among end cuts induced perpendicular to the image line ends generates horizontal subjective contours in the top half of this figure. The text suggests how this happens.

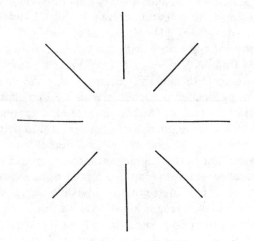

Fig. 3. An Ehrenstein figure: a bright circular disk is perceived even though all white areas are equally luminant. The text suggests how this happens.

in illusory figures. Thus, in viewing the Ehrenstein figure shown in Fig. 3, we can see a bright disk within the perpendicular lines, although the luminance across all white parts of the figure is the same.

THE HIERARCHICAL RESOLUTION OF UNCERTAINTY

In order to computationally understand such labile relationships between recognized emergent segmentations and seen brightnesses, it has been necessary to develop a qualitatively different type of vision theory [6], [10]–[13], [15]. Our theory holds that the seeming paradoxes of Figs. 1–3 can be understood by considering such figures to be probes of adaptive neural mechanisms which evolved as our ancestors coped with constantly changing visual environments. Specifically, our visual systems are designed to detect relatively invariant surface colors under variable illumination conditions, to detect relatively invariant object boundary structures amid noise caused by the eyes' own optics or occluding objects, and to recognize familiar objects or events in the environment. These three principle functions are performed by the three main subsystems of our theory, the feature contour system (FCS), the boundary contour system (BCS), and the object recognition system (ORS), respectively, as indicated in the macrocircuit of Fig. 4.

A unifying theme constraining the design of the theory's mechanisms is that there exist fundamental limitations of the visual measurement process—that is, uncertainty principles are just as important in vision as in quantum mechanics. For example, the computational demands placed on a system that is designed to detect invariant surface colors are, in many respects, complementary to the demands placed on a system that is designed to detect invariant boundary structures. That is why the FCS and BCS in Fig. 4 process the signals from each monocular preprocessing (MP) stage in parallel. This is not to say that the FCS and BCS are independent modules. Fig. 5 depicts in greater detail how levels of the FCS and BCS interact through multiple feedforward and feedback pathways to generate a visual representation at the final level of the FCS, which is called the binocular syncytium.

In addition to the complementary relationship between the FCS and the BCS, there also exist informational uncertainties at processing levels within each of these systems. As indicated below, the computations within the FCS which reduce uncertainty due to variable illumination conditions create new uncertainties about surface brightnesses and colors that are resolved at a higher FCS level by a process of featural filling-in. Likewise, the computations within the BCS which reduce uncertainty about boundary orientation create new uncertainties about boundary position that are resolved at a higher BCS level by a process of boundary completion.

The theory hereby describes how the visual system as a whole can compensate for such uncertainties using both parallel and hierarchical stages of neural processing. Thus the visual system is designed to achieve *heterarchical compensation for uncertainties of measurement*.

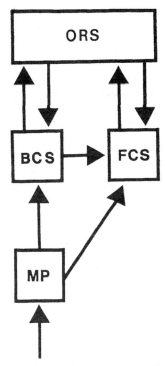

Fig. 4. A macrocircuit of processing stages: monocular preprocessed signals (MP) are sent independently to both the boundary contour system (BCS) and the feature contour system (FCS). The BCS preattentively generates coherent boundary structures from these MP signals. These structures send outputs to both the FCS and the object recognition system (ORS). The ORS, in turn, rapidly sends top–down learned template signals, or expectations, to the BCS. These template signals can modify the preattentively completed boundary structures using learned, attentive information. The BCS passes these modifications along to the FCS. The signals from the BCS organize the FCS into perceptual regions wherein filling-in of visible brightnesses and colors can occur. This filling-in process is activated by signals from the MP stage. The completed FCS representation, in turn, also interacts with the ORS.

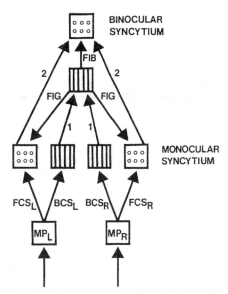

Fig. 5. Macrocircuit of monocular and binocular interactions within the boundary contour system (BCS) and the feature contour system (FCS): left and right monocular preprocessing stages (MP_L and MP_R) send parallel monocular inputs to the BCS (boxes with vertical lines) and the FCS (boxes with three pairs of circles). The monocular BCS_L and BCS_R interact via bottom-up pathways labeled 1 to generate a coherent binocular boundary segmentation. This segmentation generates output signals called filling-in generators (FIG's) and filling-in barriers (FIB's). The FIGs input to the monocular filling-in domains, or syncytia, of the FCS. The FIB's input to the binocular filling-in domains, or syncytia, of the FCS. Inputs from the MP stages interact with FIG's at the monocular syncytia where they select those monocular FC signals that are binocularly consistent. The selected FC signals are carried by the pathways labeled 2 to the binocular syncytia where they interact with FIB signals from the BCS to generate a multiple scale representation of form-and-color-in-depth within the binocular syncytia. The present article describes some monocular properties of the interactions from an MP stage through the first few BCS and FCS stages, namely those symbolized by the pathways labeled 1 and FIG.

One of the theory's most central and novel insights consists in the interactions which it posits between the BCS and the FCS. The division of labor described so far—the BCS to perform boundary segmentation and the FCS to detect veridical surface color—is not simply a partitioning for simplicity or convenience. Rather, the real-time computational demands of the two processes are intimately related and in specific ways. As shown below, BCS dynamics require oriented filtering operations followed by oriented cooperative–competitive feedback interactions because such an architecture can rapidly and in a context-sensitive manner perform the requisite boundary segmentation that the FCS itself needs in order to pool, or fill-in, its estimates of surface color among regions belonging to the same perceived objects. That pooling is a type of unoriented spatial averaging performed by a diffusion process which is described in a subsequent section. Were a diffusion of signals employed within the BCS itself, however, it could blur the very boundaries that it seeks to sharpen and thereby defeat both the BCS and FCS system goals. Accordingly, as shown in Fig. 4, the BCS processes occur separately of, and in parallel with, FCS processes, but send topographically matched signals to the FCS to organize the spatial structuring of FCS processes.

The theory's novelty is indicated by the types of para-

doxical statements that it makes computationally precise. Thus, not only are the circular and horizontal segmentations of Figs. 1 and 2 invisible, but also *all boundaries are invisible*. Not only are such apparent curiosities as the bright disk in Fig. 3 "illusory" percepts, but even rather mundane objects are "illusory" percepts. Indeed, as explained below, all line ends are illusory.

With this overview, we can now consider the dynamics of these two systems and their relationship to the ORS in greater detail.

Preattentive Visual Processing by the Boundary Contour System and Feature Contour System

The theory's general purpose capabilities depend upon its decomposition into BCS, FCS, and ORS subsystems. Both the BCS and FCS operate preattentively and automatically upon all images, whether or not these images have been experienced before. Unlike approaches based upon simulated annealing [8], [18], the BCS and FCS do not need to include specific information in the form of probability distributions about a limited class of expected images. Moreover, the BCS does not rely upon the independent manipulation of an external parameter, such as a temperature parameter, to regular convergence to an equilibrium determined by these predetermined probability distributions. Instead the BCS utilizes internal cooperative–competitive feedback interactions to regulate the real-time grouping and convergence of the system to one of a very large number of possible stable equilibria. Consequently, whereas stochastic relaxation techniques can, at best, sharpen expected properties of an image, the BCS can begin to simulate the key property of preattentive vision: the automatic discovery of emergent image groupings that may never have been experienced before.

Thus, the BCS is itself a general purpose device in the sense that it can generate an emergent 3-D boundary segmentation in response to a wide variety of image properties. For example, it is capable of detecting, sharpening, and completing image edges; of grouping textures; of generating a boundary web of boundary compartments that conform to the shape of smoothly shaded regions; and of carrying out a disparity-sensitive and scale-sensitive binocular matching process that generates fused binocular structures from disparate pairs of monocular images. The outcome of this 3-D boundary segmentation process is perceptually invisible within the BC System. Visible percepts are a property of the FC System.

A completed segmentation within the BC system elicits topographically organized output signals to the FC system. These completed BC signals regulate the hierarchical processing of color and brightness signals by the FC system (Fig. 5). Notable among FC system processes are the automatic extraction from many different types of images of color and brightness signals that are relatively uncontaminated by changes in illumination conditions—again a general purpose property. These feature contour signals interact within the FC system with the output signals from the BC system to control featural filling-in processes. These filling-in processes lead to visible percepts of color-and-form-in-depth at the final stage of the FC system, which is called the binocular syncytium (Fig. 5).

Such a theoretical decomposition of the vision process conforms to, and has in fact predicted, properties of a similar decomposition that governs the design of the mammalian visual cortex. For example, in the theory's analyses and predictions of neurobiological data, the monocular preprocessor stage (MP_L, MP_R) of Figs. 4 and 5 is compared with opponent cells of the lateral geniculate nucleus, the first stage of the BC system is compared with simple cells of the hypercolumns in area $V1$ of striate cortex, the first stage of the FC system is compared with cells of the cytochrome oxydase staining blobs of area $V1$ of striate cortex, the binocular syncytium is compared with cells of area $V4$ of the prestriate cortex, and the intervening BC system and FC system stages are compared with complex, hypercomplex, double opponent, and related cell types in areas $V1$, $V2$, and $V4$ of striate and prestriate cortex [10], [12]. Some of these neural interpretations are described in greater detail in subsequent sections.

INTERACTIONS BETWEEN PREATTENTIVE VISION AND POSTATTENTIVE LEARNED OBJECT RECOGNITION

The processes summarized in Figs. 4 and 5 are preattentive and automatic. These preattentive processes may,

however, influence and be influenced by attentive, learned object recognition processes. The macrocircuit depicted in Fig. 4 suggests, for example, that a preattentively completed boundary segmentation within the BCS can directly activate an object recognition system (ORS), whether or not this segmentation supports visible contrast differences within the FCS. In the Glass pattern of Fig. 1, for example, the circular groupings can be recognized by the ORS even though they do not support visible contrast differences within the FCS.

The ORS can, in turn, read out attentive learned priming, or expectation, signals to the BCS. Why the ORS needs to read out learned top-down attentive feedback signals is clarified elsewhere by results from adaptive resonance theory, which has demonstrated that learned top-down expectations help to stabilize the self-organization of object recognition codes in response to complex and unpredictable input environments [3]–[5]. In response to familiar objects in a scene, the final 3-D boundary segmentation within the BCS may thus be *doubly* completed, first by automatic preattentive segmentation processes and then by attentive learned expectation processes. This doubly completed segmentation regulates the featural filling-in processes within the FCS that lead to a percept of visible form. The FCS also interacts with the ORS in order to generate recognitions of color and surface properties.

The feedback interactions between the preattentive BCS and FCS and the attentive, adaptive ORS emphasize that these subsystems are not independent modules, and clarify why the distinction between preattentive and attentive visual processing has been so controversial and elusive in the vision literature. Indeed, while seminal workers such as Beck and Julesz have probed the preattentive aspects of textural grouping, no less distinguished work, using closely related visual images, has emphasized the attentive and cognitive aspects of vision, as in the ''unconscious inferences'' of Helmholtz and the ''cognitive contours'' of Gregory. The possibility that emergent segmentations within the BCS can be doubly completed, both by preattentive segmentations and attentive learned expectations, helps to unify these parallel lines of inquiry, and cautions against ignoring the influence of attentive feedback upon the ''preattentive'' BCS and FCS. In addition, the rules whereby such parallel inputs from the BCS and the FCS are combined within the ORS have recently been the subject of active experimental investigation, especially due to the excitement surrounding the discovery of ''illusory conjunctions'' [26], whereby form and color information may be improperly joined under suitable experimental conditions.

The functional distinction between the attentive learned ORS and the ''preattentive'' BCS and FCS also has a neural analog in the functional architecture of mammalian neocortex. Whereas the BCS and FCS are neurally interpreted in terms of data about areas $V1$, $V2$, and $V4$ of visual cortex, the ORS is interpreted in terms of data concerning inferotemporal cortex and related brain regions [23].

The present theory hereby clarifies two distinct types of

interactions that may occur among processes governing form and color perception: preattentive interactions from the BCS to the FCS (Fig. 5) and attentive interactions between the BCS and the ORS and the FCS and the ORS (Fig. 4). We now summarize the monocular model mechanisms whereby the BCS and the FCS preattentively interact. This foundation has elsewhere been used to derive the theory's binocular mechanisms [11].

DISCOUNTING THE ILLUMINANT: EXTRACTING FEATURE CONTOURS

One form of uncertainty with which the nervous system deals is due to the fact that the visual world is viewed under variable lighting conditions. When an object reflects light to an observer's eyes, the amount of light energy within a given wavelength that reaches the eye from each object location is determined by a product of two factors. One factor is a fixed ratio, or reflectance, which determines the fraction of incident light that is reflected by that object location to the eye. The other factor is the variable intensity of the light which illuminates the object location. Two object locations with equal reflectances can reflect different amounts of light to the eye if they are illuminated by different light intensities. Spatial gradients of light across a scene are the rule, rather than the exception, during perception, and wavelengths of light that illuminate a scene can vary widely during a single day. If the nervous system directly coded into percepts the light energies which it received, it would compute false measures of object colors and brightnesses, as well as false measures of object shapes. This problem was already clear to Helmholtz. It demands an approach to visual perception that points away from a simple Newtonian analysis of colors and white light.

Land [19] and his colleagues have sharpened contemporary understanding of this issue by carrying out a series of remarkable experiments. In these experiments, a picture constructed from overlapping patches of colored paper, called a McCann Mondrian, is viewed under different lighting conditions. If red, green, and blue lights simultaneously illuminate the picture, then an observer perceives surprisingly little color change as the intensities of illumination are chosen to vary within wide limits. The stability of perceived colors obtains despite the fact that the intensity of light at each wavelength that is reflected to the eye varies linearly with the incident illumination intensity at that wavelength. This property of color stability indicates that the nervous system "discounts the illuminant," or suppresses the "extra" amount of light in each wavelength, in order to extract a color percept that is invariant under many lighting conditions.

In an even more striking experimental demonstration of this property, inhomogeneous lighting conditions were devised such that spectrophotometric readings from positions within the interiors of two color patches were the same, yet the two patches appeared to have different colors. The perceived colors were, moreover, close to the colors that would be perceived when viewed in a homogeneous source of white light.

These results show that the signals from within the interiors of the colored patches are significantly attenuated in order to discount the illuminant. This property makes ecological sense since even a gradual change in illumination level could cause a large cumulative distortion in perceived color or brightness if it were allowed to influence the percept of a large scenic region. In contrast, illuminant intensities typically do not vary much across a scenic edge. Thus, the ratio of light signals reflected from the two sides of a scenic edge can provide an accurate local estimate of the relative reflectances of the scene at the corresponding positions. We have called the color and brightness signals which remain unattenuated near scenic edges FC signals.

The neural mechanisms which "discount the illuminant" overcome a fundamental uncertainty in the retinal pickup of visual information. In so doing, however, they create a new problem of uncertain measurement, which illustrates one of the classical uncertainty principles of visual perception. If color and brightness signals are suppressed except near scenic edges, then why do not we see just a world of colored edges? How are these local FC signals used by later processing stages to synthesize global percepts of continuous forms, notably of color fields and of smoothly varying surfaces?

FEATURAL FILLING-IN AND STABILIZED IMAGES

Our monocular theory has developed mechanisms whereby contour-sensitive FC signals activate a process of lateral spreading, or filling-in, of color and brightness signals within the FCS. This filling-in process is contained by topographically organized output signals from the BCS to the FCS (Fig. 5). Where no BC signals obstruct the filling-in process, its strength is attenuated with distance since it is governed by a nonlinear diffusion process. Our monocular model for this filling-in process was developed and tested using quantitative computer simulations of paradoxical brightness data.

Many examples of featural filling-in and its containment by BC signals can be cited. A classical example of this phenomenon is described in Fig. 6. The image in Fig. 6 was used by Yarbus [28] in a stabilized image experiment. Normally, the eye jitters rapidly in its orbit, and thereby is in continual relative motion with respect to a scene. In a stabilized image experiment, prescribed regions in an image are kept stabilized, or do not move with respect to the retina. Stabilization is accomplished by the use of a contact lens or an electronic feedback circuit. Stabilizing an image with respect to the retina can cause the perception of the image to fade. The adaptive utility of this property can be partially understood by noting that, in humans, light passes through retinal veins before it reaches the photosensitive retina. The veins form stabilized images with respect to the retina; hence, they are fortunately not visible under ordinary viewing conditions.

In the Yarbus display shown in Fig. 6, the large circular edge and the vertical edge are stabilized with respect to the retina. As these edge percepts fade, the red color outside the large circle is perceived to flow over and envelope

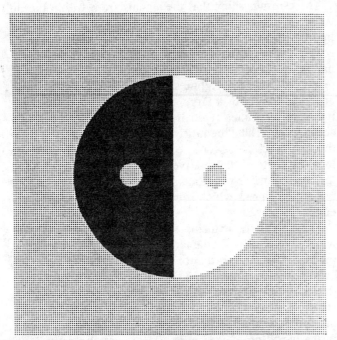

Fig. 6. A classical example of featural filling-in: when the edges of the large circle and the vertical line are stabilized on the retina, the red color (dots) outside the large circle envelopes the black and white hemidisks except within the small red circles whose edges are not stabilized [28]. The red inside the left circle looks brighter and the red inside the right circle looks darker than the enveloping red.

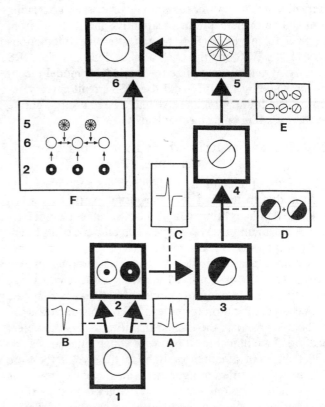

Fig. 7. Model of how the feature contour system discounts variable illuminants and regulates featural filling-in: The thick-bordered rectangles numbered from 1 to 6 correspond to the levels of the system. The symbols inside the rectangles are graphical mnemonics for the types of computational units residing at the corresponding model level. The arrows depict the interconnections between the levels. The thin-bordered rectangles coded by letters A through E represent the type of processing between pairs of levels. Inset F illustrates how the activity at level 6 is modulated by outputs from level 2 and level 5. This simplified model directly extracts boundaries from image contrasts, rather than generating emergent segmentations from image contrasts. The model's key elements concern how the level 2 network of shunting on-center off-surround interactions discounts variable illuminants while extracting feature contour signals, and how level 5 fills-in these signals via a nonlinear diffusion process within the compartments defined by boundary contour system output signals.

the black and white hemi-discs until it reaches the small red circles whose edges are not stabilized. This percept illustrates how FC signals can spread across, or fill-in, a scenic percept until they hit perceptually significant boundaries. Our neural network model of this process explains how filling-in occurs within the black and white regions, and why the left red disk appears lighter and the right red disk appears darker than the surrounding red region that envelopes the remainder of the percept.

This model is schematized in Fig. 7. It has been used to simulate a wide range of classical and recent phenomena concerning brightness perception which have not heretofore been explained by a single theory [15]. The equations defining the model are now defined.

A Model for Invariant Brightness Perception Under Variable Illumination Conditions

The equations underlying the Grossberg and Todorović [15] model are based on and extend work by Grossberg [9], Cohen and Grossberg [6], and Grossberg and Mingolla [13]. The exposition follows the description of levels in Fig. 7. Only the two-dimensional versions of the equations are presented. The one-dimensional forms can be derived by straightforward simplifications. The two-dimensional simulation in Fig. 9 below was performed on a 30 × 30 lattice and that in Fig. 10 on a 40 × 40 lattice. The one-dimensional simulations involve 256 units.

Level 1: Gray-Scale Image Description

Denote by I_{ij} the value of the stimulus input at position (i, j) in the lattice. In all simulations these values varied

between 1 and 9. In order to compute the spatial convolutions of level 2 cells without causing spurious edge effects at the extremities of the luminance profile, the luminance values at the extremities were continued outward as far as necessary.

Level 2: Shunting On-Center Off-Surround Network for Discounting Illuminants and Extracting FC Signals

The activity x_{ij} of a level 2 on-cell at position (i, j) of the lattice obeys a membrane equation, also called a shunting equation,

$$\frac{d}{dt} x_{ij} = -Ax_{ij} + (B - x_{ij})C_{ij} - (x_{ij} + D)E_{ij} \quad (1)$$

where $C_{ij}(E_{ij})$ is the total excitatory (inhibitory) input to x_{ij}. Each input C_{ij} and E_{ij} is a discrete convolution with Gaussian kernel of the inputs I_{pq}:

$$C_{ij} = \sum_{(p,q)} I_{pq} C_{pqij} \quad (2)$$

and

$$E_{ij} = \sum_{(p,q)} I_{pq} E_{pqij} \qquad (3)$$

where

$$C_{pqij} = C \exp \left\{ -\alpha^{-2} \log 2 \left[(p-i)^2 + (q-j)^2 \right] \right\} \qquad (4)$$

and

$$E_{pqij} = E \exp \left\{ -\beta^{-2} \log 2 \left[(p-i)^2 + (q-j)^2 \right] \right\}. \qquad (5)$$

The influence exerted on the level 2 potential x_{ij} by input I_{pq} diminishes with increasing distance between the two corresponding locations. Thus, the receptive fields have a circular shape. To achieve an on-center off-surround anatomy, coefficient C of the excitatory kernel in (4) is chosen larger than coefficient E of the inhibitory kernel in (5), but α, the radius of the excitatory spread at half strength in (4), is chosen smaller than β, its inhibitory counterpart in (5). In the simulations, this equation is solved at equilibrium. Then $(d/dt)x_{ij} = 0$, so that

$$x_{ij} = \frac{\sum_{(p,q)} (BC_{pqij} - DE_{pqij}) I_{pq}}{A + \sum_{(p,q)} (C_{pqij} + E_{pqij}) I_{pq}}. \qquad (6)$$

The denominator term normalizes the activity x_{ij}.

The output signal from level 2 is the nonnegative, or rectified, part of x_{ij}:

$$X_{ij} = \max (x_{ij}, 0). \qquad (7)$$

Levels 3–5 compute the boundary contour signals used to contain the featural filling-in process. These boundary contour signals do not include properties of emergent segmentation. The equations for the BCS may be appended to the model, as explained below, when emergent segmentation is required.

Level 3: Simple Cells

The potential y_{ijk} of the cell centered at position (i, j) whose oriented receptive field possesses orientation k obeys an additive equation

$$\frac{d}{dt} y_{ijk} = -y_{ijk} + \sum_{(p,q)} X_{pq} F_{pqij}^{(k)} \qquad (8)$$

which is computed at equilibrium:

$$y_{ijk} = \sum_{(p,q)} X_{pq} F_{pqij}^{(k)} \qquad (9)$$

in all our simulations. In order to generate an oriented kernel $F_{pqij}^{(k)}$ as simply as possible, let $F_{pqij}^{(k)}$ be the difference of an isotropic kernel G_{pqij} centered at (i, j) and another isotropic kernel $H_{pqij}^{(k)}$ whose center $(i + m_k, j + n_k)$ is

shifted from (i, j) as follows:

$$F_{pqij}^{(k)} = G_{pqij} - H_{pqij}^{(k)} \qquad (10)$$

where

$$G_{pqij} = \exp \left\{ -\gamma^{-2} [(p-i)^2 + (q-j)^2] \right\} \qquad (11)$$

and

$$H_{pqij}^{(k)} = \exp \left\{ -\gamma^{-2} [(p-i-m_k)^2 + (q-j-n_k)^2] \right\} \qquad (12)$$

with

$$m_k = \sin \frac{2\pi k}{K} \qquad (13)$$

and

$$n_k = \cos \frac{2\pi k}{K}. \qquad (14)$$

In the 2-D simulations, the number K is 12, whereas for the 1-D simulations it is 2.

The output signal from level 3 to level 4 is the non-negative, or rectified, part of y_{ijk}, namely

$$Y_{ijk} = \max (y_{ijk}, 0). \qquad (15)$$

Level 4: Complex Cells

Each level 4 potential z_{ijk} with position (i, j) and orientation k is made sensitive to orientation but insensitive to direction-of-contrast by summing the output signals from the appropriate pair of level 3 units with opposite contrast sensitivities; viz.,

$$z_{ijk} = Y_{ijk} + Y_{ij(k+K/2)}. \qquad (16)$$

An output signal Z_{ijk} is generated from level 4 to level 5 if the activity z_{ijk} exceeds the threshold L:

$$Z_{ijk} = \max (z_{ijk} - L, 0). \qquad (17)$$

Level 5: Boundary Contour Signals

A level 5 signal z_{ij} at position (i, j) is the sum of output signals from all level 4 units at that position; viz.,

$$Z_{ij} = \sum_k Z_{ijk}. \qquad (18)$$

Level 6 computes the filling-in process, which is regulated by feature contour inputs from level 2 and boundary contour inputs from level 5.

Level 6: Filling-In Process

Each potential S_{ij} at position (i, j) of the filling-in process obeys a nonlinear diffusion equation

$$\frac{d}{dt} S_{ij} = -MS_{ij} + \sum_{(p,q) \in N_{ij}} (S_{pq} - S_{ij}) P_{pqij} + X_{ij}. \qquad (19)$$

The diffusion coefficients that regulate the magnitude of cross influence of location (i, j) with location (p, q) depend on the boundary contour signals Z_{pq} and Z_{ij} as follows:

$$P_{pqij} = \frac{\delta}{1 + \epsilon(Z_{pq} + Z_{ij})}. \quad (20)$$

The set N_{ij} of locations comprises only the lattice nearest neighbors of (i, j):

$$N_{ij} = \Big\{ (i, j-1), (i-1, j), (i+1, j), (i, j+1) \Big\}. \quad (21)$$

At lattice edges and corners, this set is reduced to the set of existing neighbors. According to (19), each potential S_{ij} is activated by the feature contour output signal X_{ij} and thereupon engages in passive decay (term $-MS_{ij}$) and diffusive filling-in with its four nearest neighbors to the degree permitted by the diffusion coefficients P_{pqij}. At equilibrium, each S_{ij} is computed as the solution of a set of simultaneous equations

$$S_{ij} = \frac{X_{ij} + \sum_{(p,q) \in N_{ij}} S_{pq} P_{pqij}}{M + \sum_{(p,q) \in N_{ij}} P_{pqij}} \quad (22)$$

which is compared with properties of the brightness percept. See Grossberg and Todorović [15] for parameter choices.

Computer Simulations of Brightness Constancy, Contrast, and Assimilation

Fig. 8 depicts the results of four computer simulations with a single set of parameters using a one-dimensional version of the model to illustrate its responses to images which possess a one-dimensional symmetry. In such an image, each horizontal slice through the image possesses the same luminance profile, labeled stimulus in Fig. 8. Fig. 8(a) and (b) illustrate discounting the illuminant and brightness constancy; Fig. 8(c) illustrates discounting the illuminant and brightness contrast; and Fig. 8(d) illustrates brightness assimilation. Note that the feature contour patterns, labeled feature, are distributed activation patterns with positive baseline values, rather than zero crossings, binary edge patterns, or other classical objects. Comparison of the feature contour patterns of Fig. 8(a) and (b) illustrate how these patterns discount the illuminant. The theory also explains how a feature contour pattern triggers a filling-in, or diffusion, process within compartments bounded by a boundary contour pattern, labeled boundary, to generate the filled-in pattern, labeled output, on which the percept is based.

Visible Effects of Invisible Causes

The computer simulation summarized in Fig. 8(c) is of particular interest because it illustrates a visible effect of an invisible cause. The luminance gradient between the two equiluminant patches in the stimulus caused the different brightnesses of these patches in the output, but is

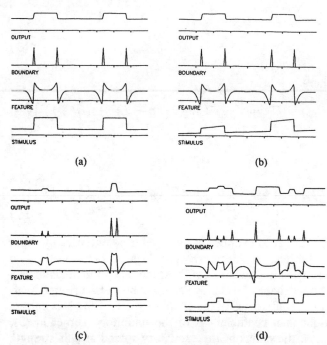

(a)　　(b)

(c)　　(d)

Fig. 8. Simulation of feature contour interactions in response to images with a one-dimensional symmetry: the luminance profile (stimulus) in (b) is tilted with respect to that in (a) due to an asymmetric light source, but the filled-in percept (output) is the same as that in (a), illustrating discounting of the illuminant and brightness constancy. Although the small patches have equal luminance in (c), their filled-in percepts are different, in the direction opposite to their backgrounds, illustrating brightness contrast. Although the small inner patches have equal luminance in (d), the filling-in percept of the right patch is darker than that of the left patch, in the direction of their surrounding patches, illustrating brightness assimilation.

itself rendered invisible in the output due to filling-in. Such a process helps to explain the percept of the Yarbus display in Fig. 6, which also includes a visible contrast due to an invisible filled-in image property.

Simulation of Craik–O'Brien Cornsweet and McCann Mondrian Percepts

Figs. 9 and 10 show the results of computer simulations using the full two-dimensional version of the model. These simulations suggest an explanation of two important visual phenomena which are partly due to featural filling-in: the Craik–O'Brien Cornsweet effect and a McCann Mondrian image in response to which humans perceive a brightness contrast effect that has not been explained by other computer vision theories. In Fig. 9, although the luminances are equal at the left and right sides of the image within the dark frame, the filled-in output on the left half of the image is more intense (''brighter'') than the output on the right. (Activation level is proportional to the size of the symbols at each location.) In Fig. 10, although the luminances are equal within the small square regions on the 135° diagonal in the upper-left and lower-right portions of the image, the filled-in output in the upper-left is more intense (''brighter'') than the output on the lower-right. Both of the effects simulated in Figs. 9 and 10 correspond to brightness judgments of human observers.

(a)   (b)

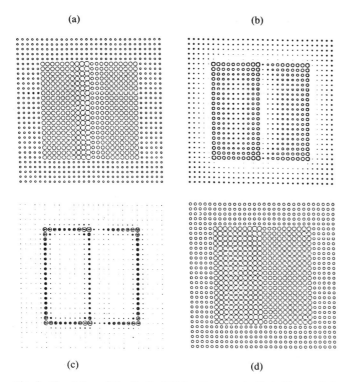

Fig. 9. Simulation of the Craik–O'Brien Cornsweet effect. The symbols of the units used in these simulations are introduced in Fig. 7. The size of the symbols codes the activity level of units at corresponding locations at different network levels. (a) The luminance distribution (stimulus). (b) The feature contour activity pattern that discounts the illuminant (feature). (c) The boundary segmentation (boundary). (d) The filled-in brightness profile (output).

a) STIMULUS   b) FEATURE

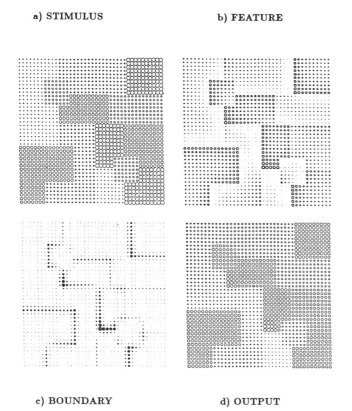

c) BOUNDARY   d) OUTPUT

Fig. 10. Simulation of a Mondrian image. The depicted network levels are the same as in Fig. 7. See text for details.

In summary, the uncertainty of variable lighting conditions is resolved by discounting the illuminant and extracting contour-sensitive FC signals. The uncertainty created within the discounted regions is resolved at a later processing stage via a featural filling-in process that is activated by the FC signals and contained within boundaries defined by BC signals.

THE BOUNDARY CONTOUR SYSTEM AND THE FEATURE CONTOUR SYSTEM OBEY DIFFERENT RULES

Fig. 11 provides another type of evidence that feature contour and boundary contour information is extracted by separate, but parallel, neural subsystems before being integrated at a later stage into a unitary percept. By now, the total body of evidence for this new insight takes several forms: the two subsystems obey different rules; they can be used to explain a large body of perceptual data that has received no other unified explanation; they can be perceptually dissociated; when they are interpreted in terms of different neural substrates (the cytochrome–oxydase staining blob system and the hypercolumn system of the striate visual cortex and their prestriate cortical projections), their rules are consistent with known cortical data and have successfully predicted new cortical data [10], [12].

Fig. 11 illustrates several rule differences between the BCS and FCS. The reproduction process may have weakened the percept of an "illusory" square, which is called a Kanizsa square. The critical percept is that of the square's vertical boundaries. The black-gray vertical edge of the top-left pac-man figure is, relatively speaking, a dark-light vertical edge. The white-gray vertical edge of the bottom-left pac-man figure is, relatively speaking, a light-dark vertical edge. These two vertical edges possess the same orientation but opposite directions-of-contrast. The percept of the vertical boundary that spans these opposite direction-of-contrast edges shows that the BCS is sensitive to boundary orientation but is indifferent to direction-of-contrast. This observation is strengthened by the fact that the horizontal boundaries of the square, which connect edges of like direction-of-contrast, group together with the vertical boundaries to generate a unitary percept of a square. Opposite direction-of-contrast and same direction-of-contrast boundaries both input to the same BCS.

The FCS must, on the other hand, be exquisitely sensitive to direction-of-contrast. If FC signals were insensitive to direction-of-contrast, then it would be impossible to detect which side of a scenic edge possesses a larger reflectance, as in dark-light and red-green discriminations. Thus the rules obeyed by the two contour-extracting systems are not the same.

The BCS and the FCS differ in their spatial interaction rules in addition to their rules of contrast. For example, in Fig. 11, a vertical illusory boundary forms between the boundary contours generated by a pair of vertically-oriented and spatially aligned pac-man edges. Thus, the process of boundary completion is due to an *inwardly* di-

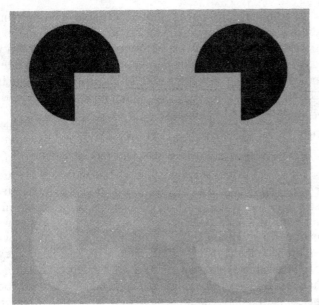

Fig. 11. A reverse-contrast Kanizsa square: an illusory square is induced by two black and two white pac-man figures on a grey background. Illusory contours can thus join edges with opposite directions-of-contrast. (This effect may be weakened by the photographic reproduction process.)

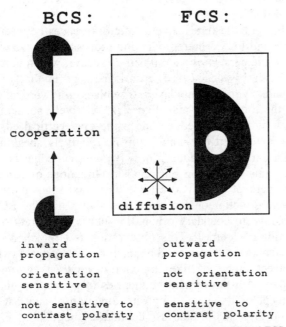

BCS: FCS:

cooperation

diffusion

inward propagation	outward propagation
orientation sensitive	not orientation sensitive
not sensitive to contrast polarity	sensitive to contrast polarity

Fig. 12. Some computational differences between the BCS and FCS: the outcome of a BCS interaction is independent of direction-of-contrast, oriented and induced by pairs, or larger numbers, of oriented inducers. The outcome of an FCS interaction is dependent upon direction-of-contrast, unoriented, and generated by individual inducers.

rected and *oriented* interaction whereby *pairs* of inducing BC signals can trigger the formation of an intervening boundary of similar orientation. In contrast, in the filling-in reactions of Figs. 8–10, featural quality can flow from each FC signal in all directions until it hits a boundary contour or is attenuated by its own spatial spread. Thus featural filling-in is an *outwardly* directed and *unoriented* interaction that is triggered by *individual* FC signals. These differences between the BCS and FCS rules are summarized in Fig. 12.

ILLUSORY PERCEPTS AS PROBES OF ADAPTIVE PROCESSES

The adaptive value of a featural filling-in process is clarified by considering how the nervous system discounts the illuminant. The adaptive value of a boundary completion process with properties capable of generating the percept of a Kanizsa square (Fig. 11) can be understood by considering other imperfections of the retinal uptake process. As noted above, light passes through retinal veins before it reaches retinal photoreceptors. Human observers do not perceive their retinal veins in part due to the action of mechanisms that attenuate the perception of images that are stabilized with respect to the retina.

Suppressing the perception of stabilized veins is insufficient, however, to generate an adequate percept. The images that reach the retina can be occluded and segmented by the veins in several places. Broken retinal contours need to be completed, and occluded retinal color and brightness signals need to be filled in. Holes in the retina, such as the blind spot or certain scotomas, are also not visually perceived due to a combination of boundary completion and filling-in processes. These completed boundaries and filled-in colors are illusory percepts, albeit illusory percepts with an important adaptive value. Observers are not aware which parts of such a completed figure are "real" (derived directly from retinal signals) or "illusory" (derived by boundary completion and featural filling-in). Thus, in a perceptual theory capable of understanding such completion phenomena, "real" and "illusory" percepts exist on an equal ontological footing. Consequently, we have been able to use the large literature on illusory figures, such as Figs. 1, 3, and 11, and filling-in reactions, such as in Figs. 8–10, to help us discover the distinct rules of BCS segmentation and FCS filling-in.

BOUNDARY CONTOUR DETECTION AND GROUPING BEGINS WITH ORIENTED RECEPTIVE FIELDS

Having distinguished the BCS from the FCS, the rules whereby boundaries are synthesized are now stated with increasing precision.

In order to effectively build up boundaries, the BCS must be able to determine the orientation of a boundary at every position. To accomplish this, the cells at the first stage of the BCS possess orientationally-tuned receptive fields, or oriented masks. Such a cell, or cell population, is selectively responsive to oriented contrasts that activate a prescribed small region of the retina, and whose orientations lie within a prescribed band of orientations with respect to the retina. A collection of such orientationally-tuned cells is assumed to exist at every network position, such that each cell type is sensitive to a different band of oriented contrasts within its prescribed small region of the scene, as in the hypercolumn model, which was developed to explain the responses of simple cells in area $V1$ of the striate cortex [17].

These oriented receptive fields illustrate that, from the very earliest stages of BCS processing, image contrasts

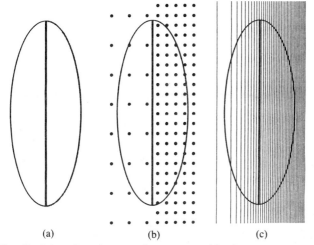

Fig. 13. Oriented masks respond to amount of luminance contrast over their elongated axis of symmetry, regardless of whether image contrasts are generated by (a) luminance step functions, (b) differences in textural distribution, or (c) smooth luminance gradients (indicated by the spacings of the lines).

are grouped and regrouped in order to generate configurations of ever greater global coherence and structural invariance. For example, even the oriented masks at the earliest stage of BCS processing regroup image contrasts. Such masks are oriented *local contrast* detectors, rather than edge detectors. This property enables them to fire in response to a wide variety of spatially nonuniform image contrasts that do not contain edges, as well as in response to edges (Fig. 13). In particular, such oriented masks can respond to spatially nonuniform densities of unoriented textural elements, such as dots. They can also respond to spatially nonuniform densities of surface gradients. Thus by sacrificing a certain amount of spatial resolution in order to detect oriented local contrasts, these masks achieve a general detection characteristic which can respond to boundaries, textures, and surfaces.

This general detection characteristic is achieved by using a relatively coarse weighted averaging and filtering of optical information at the earliest stages of the BCS. Such a coarse detection scheme obviates the need to proliferate a very large number of highly specialized detectors. In contrast, a vision system that postulated specialized dot, edge, angle, texture, shading, etc., detectors would be faced with a formidable problem of combining the data from each of these detectors. No less formidable is the problem that such specialized detectors often respond badly to other types of image statistics than the ones for which they are specialized. To overcome this problem, one would need an expert system to decide which type of detector should be applied to particular regions of a scene. Such a preprocessor would, however, have to solve the very problems that the vision system was supposed to solve. Thus, the reliance on highly specialized detectors leads to a formulation of the vision problem that does not work well on images whose properties are not narrowly defined, predictable, and controllable in advance.

On the other hand, the very properties of coarse sampling that lead to a general detection characteristic also imply a certain amount of informational uncertainty. From local estimates alone, such a detector cannot, for example, easily decide whether an edge, texture gradient, or shading gradient is present. The BCS thus accepts a certain amount of informational uncertainty at an early processing stage to ensure system versatility, and uses subsequent processing levels to help extract, sharpen, and complete from the spatial distribution of locally ambiguous signals those groupings which cohere into perceptually meaningful wholes.

In particular, the BCS is capable of automatically detecting and enhancing structures in a visual input by measuring inhomogeneities in the spatial distribution of local oriented contrasts against a statistical baseline that is determined by the input itself. This is done by a particular arrangement of short-range competition and long-range cooperation among orientation-sensitive nodes, following an initial stage of oriented-contrast filtering. Activations in groupings of nodes tuned to similar orientations that are approximately aligned in space receive a cooperative feedback advantage over randomly distributed network activations that arise from imaging noise. These random activations help to define the amount of aligned activity needed to be counted as signal. We now describe how this is done in greater detail.

AN UNCERTAINTY PRINCIPLE: ORIENTATIONAL CERTAINTY IMPLIES POSITIONAL UNCERTAINTY AT LINE ENDS AND CORNERS

The fact that the receptive fields of the BCS are *oriented* greatly reduces the number of possible groupings into which their target cells can enter. On the other hand, in order to detect oriented local contrasts, the receptive fields must be elongated along their preferred axis of symmetry. Then the cells can preferentially detect differences of average contrast across this axis of symmetry, yet can remain silent in response to differences of average contrast that are perpendicular to the axis of symmetry. Such receptive field elongation creates even greater positional uncertainty about the exact locations within the receptive field of the image contrasts which fire the cell. This positional uncertainty becomes acute during the processing of image line ends and corners.

Oriented receptive fields cannot easily detect the ends of thin scenic lines or scenic corners. This positional uncertainty is illustrated by the computer simulation in Fig. 14(a). The scenic image is a black vertical line (colored gray for illustrative purposes) against a white background. The line is drawn large to represent its scale relative to the receptive fields that it activates. In Fig. 14(a), each receptive field covers an area equivalent to 16 × 8 lattice points. The activation level of each oriented receptive field at a given position is proportional to the length of the line segment at that position which possesses the same orientation as the corresponding receptive field. The relative lengths of line segments across all positions encode the relative levels of receptive field activation due to different parts of the input pattern. We call such a spatial

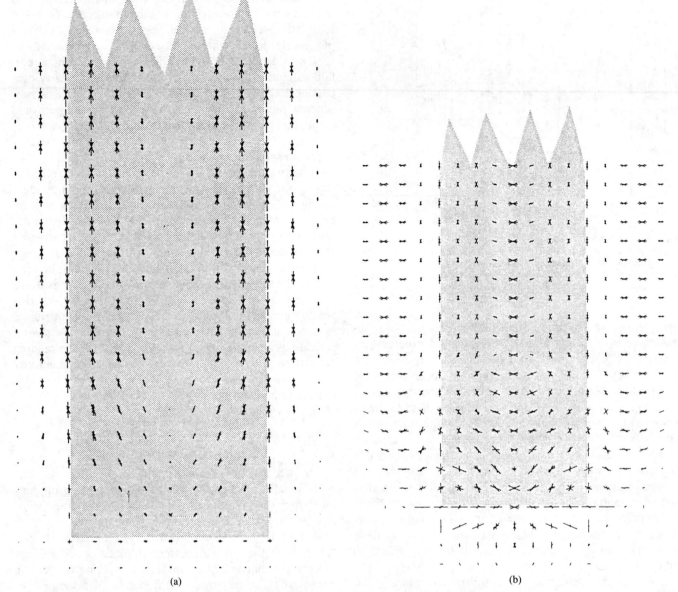

(a)   (b)

Fig. 14. (a) An orientation field: lengths and orientations of lines encode the relative sizes of the activations and orientations of the input masks at the corresponding positions. The input pattern, which is a vertical line end as seen by the receptive fields, correspond to the shaded area. Each mask has total exterior dimension of 16 × 8 units, with a unit length being the distance between two adjacent lattice positions. (b) Response of the second competitive stage, defined in (28) and Fig. 15, to the orientation field of Fig. 14(a): End cutting generates horizontal activations at line end locations that receive small and orientationally ambiguous input activations.

array of oriented responses an *orientation* field. An orientation field provides a concise statistical description in real-time of an image as seen by the receptive fields that it can activate. It models the responses of cortical simple cells in area $V1$ of the visual cortex [17].

In Fig. 14(a), a strong vertical reaction occurs at positions along the vertical sides of the input pattern that are sufficiently far from the bottom of the pattern. The contrast needed to activate these receptive fields was chosen low enough to allow cells with close-to-vertical orientations to be significantly activated at these positions. De-

spite the fact that cells were tuned to respond to relatively low contrasts, the cell responses at positions near the end of the line are very small. This result obtains in response to lines that are wider than lines which generate a continuous band of vertically-oriented responses throughout their interior, and are narrower than lines which generate a band of horizontally-oriented responses throughout their lowest extremity. Such a choice of lines always exist if the receptive field is elongated by a significant amount in a preferred orientation. Fig. 14(a) thus illustrates a basic uncertainty principle which says: orientational ''certainty'' implies positional ''uncertainty'' at the ends of scenic lines whose widths are neither too small nor too large with respect to the dimensions of the oriented receptive field. The next section shows that a perceptual disaster would ensue in the absence of hierarchical compensation for this type of informational uncertainty.

Boundary-Feature Tradeoff: A New Organizational Principle

The perceptual disaster in question becomes clear when Fig. 14 is considered from the viewpoint of the featural filling-in process that compensates for discounting the illuminant, as in Figs. 8-10. If no BC signals are elicited at the ends of lines and at object corners, then in the absence of further processing within the BCS, boundary contours will not be synthesized to prevent featural quality from flowing out of all line ends and object corners within the FCS. Many percepts would hereby become badly degraded by featural flow.

Thus, basic constraints upon visual processing seem to be seriously at odds with each other. The need to discount the illuminant leads to the need for featural filling-in. The need for featural filling-in leads to the need to synthesize boundaries capable of restricting featural filling-in to appropriate perceptual domains. The need to synthesize boundaries leads to the need for orientation-sensitive receptive fields. Such receptive fields are, however, unable to restrict featural filling-in at scenic line ends or sharp corners. Thus, orientational certainty implies a type of positional uncertainty, which is unacceptable from the perspective of featural filling-in requirements. Indeed, an adequate understanding of how to resolve this uncertainty principle is not possible without considering featural filling-in requirements. That is why perceptual theories which have not clearly distinguished the complementary computational requirements of the BCS and FCS have not adequately characterized how perceptual boundaries are formed. We call the complementary design balance that exists between BCS and FCS design requirements the *boundary-feature tradeoff*.

We now summarize how later stages of BC system processing compensate for the positional uncertainty that is created by the orientational tuning of receptive fields.

The Hierarchical Resolution of Orientation-Induced Uncertainty: All Line Ends are Illusory

Fig. 14(b) depicts the reaction of the BC system's next processing stages to the input pattern depicted in Fig. 14(a). Strong horizontal activations are generated at the end of the scenic line by these processing stages. These horizontal activations are capable of generating a horizontal boundary within the BCS whose output signals, as in Figs. 4 and 7, prevent flow of featural quality from the end of the line within the FCS. These horizontal activations form an ''illusory'' boundary, in the sense that this boundary is not directly extracted from luminance differences in the scenic image. The theory hereby suggests that the perceived ends of all such thin lines are generated by such ''illusory'' line end inductions, which we call *end cuts*. This conclusion is sufficiently remarkable to summarize it with a maxim: *all line ends are illusory*.

This seemingly paradoxical maxim can be understood as one manifestation of how the visual system overcomes, using multiple processing stages, the informational uncertainties that it cannot overcome at a single processing stage. In the present example, orientational tuning of receptive fields is needed to partially overcome the uncertainty of an image edge's orientation but in so doing renders uncertain the positions of the ends and corners of such edges. Later processing stages are needed to recover both the positional and orientational data that are lost in this way.

The OC Filter and the Short-Range Competitive Stages

The processing stages that are hypothesized to generate end cuts are summarized in Fig. 15. First, oriented-receptive fields of like position and orientation, but opposite direction-of-contrast, generate rectified output signals that summate at the next processing stage to activate cells whose receptive fields are sensitive to the same position and orientation as themselves, but are insensitive to direction-of-contrast. These target cells maintain their sensitivity to *amount* of oriented contrast, but not to the *direction* of this oriented contrast, as in our explanation of Fig. 12. Such model cells, which play the role of complex cells in area $V1$ of the visual cortex, pool inputs from receptive fields with opposite directions-of-contrast, which play the role of simple cells in area $V1$, in order to generate boundary detectors which can detect the broadest possible range of luminance or chromatic contrasts [7], [24]. These two successive stages of oriented contrast-sensitive cells are called the OC filter. Equations (8)–(16) above model simple cells and complex cells in our computer simulations of invariant brightness perception.

The rectified output from the OC filter activates a second filter which is composed of two successive stages of spatially short-range competitive interaction whose net effect is to generate end cuts (Fig. 15). First, a cell of prescribed orientation excites like-oriented cells corresponding to its location and inhibits like-oriented cells corresponding to nearby locations at the next processing stage. In other words, an on-center off-surround organization of like-oriented cell interactions exists around each perceptual location. This mechanism is analogous to the neurophysiological process of *end stopping*, whereby hypercomplex cell receptive fields are fashioned from interactions of complex cell output signals [16], [21]. The outputs from this competitive mechanism interact with the second competitive mechanism. Here, cells compete that represent different orientations, notably perpendicular orientations, at the same perceptual location. This competition defines a push–pull opponent process. If a given orientation is excited, then its perpendicular orientation is

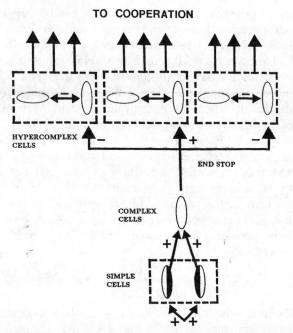

TO COOPERATION

Fig. 15. Early stages of boundary contour processing: at each position exist cells with elongated receptive fields (simple cells) of various sizes which are sensitive to orientation, amount-of-contrast, and direction-of-contrast. Pairs of such cells sensitive to like orientation but opposite directions-of-contrast (lower dashed box) input to cells (complex cells) that are sensitive to orientation and amount-of-contrast but not to direction-of-contrast (white ellipses). These cells, in turn, excite like-oriented cells (hypercomplex cells) corresponding to the same position and inhibit like-oriented cells corresponding to nearby positions at the first competitive stage. At the second competitive stage, cells corresponding to the same position but different orientations (higher-order hypercomplex cells) inhibit each other via a push–pull competitive interaction.

inhibited. If a given orientation is inhibited, then its perpendicular orientation is excited via disinhibition.

The combined effect of these two competitive interactions generate end cuts as follows. The strong vertical activations along the edges of a scenic line, as in Fig. 14(a), inhibit the weak vertical activations near the line end. These inhibited vertical activations, in turn, disinhibit horizontal activations near the line end, as in Fig. 14(b). Thus, the positional uncertainty generated by orientational certainty is eliminated at a subsequent processing level by the interaction of two spatially short-range competitive mechanisms which convert complex cells into two distinct populations of hypercomplex cells.

The properties of these competitive mechanisms have successfully predicted and helped to explain a variety of neural and perceptual data. For example, the prediction of the theory summarized in Fig. 14 predated the report by von der Heydt, Baumgartner, and Peterhans [27] that cells in prestriate visual cortex respond to perpendicular line ends, as in Fig. 14(b), whereas cells in striate visual cortex do not, as in Fig. 14(a). These cells properties also help to explain why color is sometimes perceived to spread across a scene, as in the phenomenon of neon color spreading [10], [12], [22], by showing how some BC signals are inhibited by boundary contour processes. An example of neon color spreading can be found on the cover of the journal *neural networks* where it is placed to em-

phasize how an emergent behavioral property can be induced by form-color interactions triggered across a whole scene. In that example, the red crosses in the image form the crosses of a cross-bar associative network. Such competitive interactions also clarify many properties of perceptual grouping, notably of the "emergent features" that group textures into figure and ground [1], [11], [12]. Such percepts can be explained by the end cutting mechanism when it interacts with the next processing stage of the BCS.

LONG-RANGE COOPERATION: BOUNDARY COMPLETION AND EMERGENT FEATURES

The outputs from the competition input to a spatially long-range cooperative process, called the *boundary completion* process. This cooperative process helps to build up sharp coherent global boundaries and emergent segmentations from noisy local boundary fragments. In the first stage of this boundary completion process, outputs from the second competitive stage from (approximately) like-oriented cells that are (approximately) aligned across perceptual space cooperate to begin the synthesis of an intervening boundary. For example, such a boundary completion process can span the blind spot and the faded stabilized images of retinal veins. The same boundary completion process is used to complete the sides of the Kanizsa square in Fig. 12. Further details about this boundary completion process can be derived once it is understood that the boundary completion process overcomes a different type of informational uncertainty than is depicted in Fig. 14.

This type of uncertainty is clarified by considering Fig. 16. The percept in Fig. 16(a), as well as those in Figs. 3 and 16(b), can be understood as a byproduct of four processes: within the BCS, perpendicular end cuts at the line ends [Fig. 14(b)] cooperate to complete a emergent boundary which separates the visual field into two domains. This completed boundary structure sends topographically organized boundary signals into the FCS (Fig. 7), thereby dividing the FCS into two domains. If different filling-in contrasts are induced within these domains due to the FC signals generated by the black scenic lines, then the illusory figure can become visible.

Fig. 16(a) shows that the tendency to form boundaries that are perpendicular to line ends is a strong one; the completed boundary forms sharp corners to keep the boundary perpendicular to the inducing scenic line ends. Fig. 16(b) shows, however, that the boundary completion process can generate a boundary that is not perpendicular to the inducing line ends under certain circumstances.

ORIENTATIONAL UNCERTAINTY AND THE INITIATION OF BOUNDARY COMPLETION

A comparison of Fig. 16(a) and (b) indicates the nature of the third problem of uncertain measurement that we have encountered. Fig. 16(a) and (b) show that boundary completion can occur within *bands* of orientations, which describe a type of real-time local probability distribution

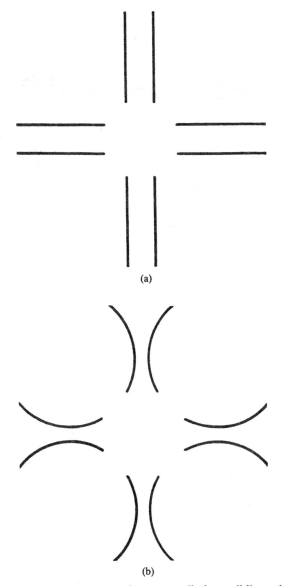

Fig. 16. (a) An illusory square forms perpendicular to all line ends. The global grouping confirms all the locally preferred perpendicular grouping orientations. (b) An illusory square forms almost perpendicular to all line ends. The global grouping amplifies grouping orientations that are not locally preferred and competitively inhibits the locally preferred perpendicular orientations. Both emergent segmentations (a) and (b) are sharp despite the fact that fuzzy bands of possible grouping orientations must exist.

for the orientations in which grouping can be initiated at each position. These orientations include the orientations that are perpendicular to their inducing line ends [Fig. 16(a)], as well as nearby orientations that are not perpendicular to their inducing line ends [Fig. 16(b)]. Fig. 14(b) illustrates how such a band of end cuts can be induced at the end of a scenic line. The existence of such bands of possible orientations increases the probability that spatially separated boundary segments can begin to group cooperatively into a global boundary. If only a single orientation at each spatial location were activated, then the probability that these orientations could precisely line up across perceptual space to initiate boundary completion would be vanishingly small. The (partial) orientational

uncertainty that is caused by bands of orientations is thus a useful property for the initiation of the perceptual grouping process that controls boundary completion and textural segmentation.

Such orientational uncertainty can, however, cause a serious loss of acuity in the absence of compensatory processes. If *all* orientations in each band could cooperate with *all* approximately aligned orientations in nearby bands, then a fuzzy band of completed boundaries, rather than a single sharp boundary, could be generated. The existence of such fuzzy boundaries would severely impair visual clarity. Fig. 16 illustrates that only a single sharp boundary usually becomes visible despite the existence of oriented bands of boundary inducers. How does the nervous system resolve the uncertainty produced by the existence of orientational bands? How is a single global boundary chosen from among the many possible boundaries that fall within the local oriented bandwidths?

Our answer to these questions suggests a basic reason why later stages of boundary contour processing must send nonlinear feedback signals to earlier stages of boundary contour processing. This cooperative feedback provides a particular grouping of orientations with a competitive advantage over other possible groupings by exploiting the competitive interactions described above.

BOUNDARY COMPLETION BY COOPERATIVE–COMPETITIVE FEEDBACK NETWORKS: THE CC LOOP

We assume, as is illustrated by Fig. 11, that pairs of similarly oriented and spatially aligned cells of the second competitive stage are needed to activate the intervening cooperative cells that subserve boundary completion (Fig. 17). These cells, in turn, feed back excitatory signals to like-oriented cells at the first competitive stage, which feeds into the competition between orientations at each position of the second competitive stage. Thus, in Fig. 16, positive feedback signals are triggered in pathway 2 by a cooperative cell if sufficient activation simultaneously occurs in both of the feedforward pathways labeled 1 from similarly oriented cells of the second competitive stage. Then both pathways labeled 3 can trigger feedback in pathway 4. This feedback exchange can rapidly complete an oriented boundary between pairs of inducing scenic contrasts via a spatially discontinuous bisection process.

Such a boundary completion process realizes a new type of real-time statistical decision theory. Each cooperative cell is sensitive to the position, orientation, density, and size of the inputs that it receives from the second competitive stage. Each cooperative cell performs like a type of statistical "and" gate since it can only fire feedback signals to the first competitive stage if both of its branches are sufficiently activated. We call such cooperative cells *bipole* cells. The existence of such bipole cells was predicted by our theory. Von der Heydt, Baumgartner, and Peterhans [27] reported the existence of such cells in the prestriate visual cortex, in the same report that confirmed the existence of prestriate cells which respond to perpen-

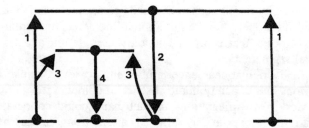

Fig. 17. A cooperative–competitive feedback exchange leading to boundary completion: cells at the bottom row represent like-oriented cells at the second competitive stage whose orientational preferences are approximately aligned across perceptual space. The cells in the top two rows are bipole cells in the cooperative layer whose receptive field pairs are oriented along the axis of the competitive cells. Suppose that simultaneous activation of the pair of pathways 1 activates positive boundary completion feedback along pathway 2. Then pairs of pathways such as 3 activate positive feedback along pathways such as 4. Rapid completion of a sharp boundary between the locations of pathways 1 can hereby be generated by a spatially discontinuous bisection process.

dicular line ends, as in Fig. 14(b). See [10] for a summary of these and related neurophysiological data. The entire cooperative–competitive feedback network is called the CC loop.

EQUATIONS FOR A MONOCULAR VERSION OF THE BOUNDARY CONTOUR SYSTEM

Fig. 18 depicts a BCS circuit that combines the OC filter and the CC loop. The following neural network equations represent a monocular, single-scale version of the OC filter and the CC loop. All processes, except the first competitive stage, are assumed to react so quickly that they can be represented at equilibrium as algebraic equations. This approximation speeds up the simulations, but does not influence the results. See Grossberg and Mingolla [13] for more complete definitions of these network processes. See Grossberg and Mingolla [14] for a modified version of this system.

As in (1)–(22), indexes (i, j) represent a cell position within a two-dimensional lattice and k represents an orientation.

OC FILTER

Oriented Filter: Complex Cell Receptive Fields

For simplicity, a different simple cell and complex cell model was used than in (8)–(16). Many variants are possible, including models based upon Gabor filters.

Letting X_{pq} equal the input to position (p, q),

$$J_{ijk} = \frac{[U_{ijk} - \alpha V_{ijk}]^+ + [V_{ijk} - \alpha U_{ijk}]^+}{1 + \beta(U_{ijk} + V_{ijk})} \quad (23)$$

where

$$U_{ijk} = \sum_{(p,q) \in L_{ijk}} X_{pq} \quad (24)$$

$$V_{ijk} = \sum_{(p,q) \in R_{ijk}} X_{pq} \quad (25)$$

and the notation $[p]^+ = \max(p, 0)$. In (23), the elongated receptive field is divided into a left-half L_{ijk} and a

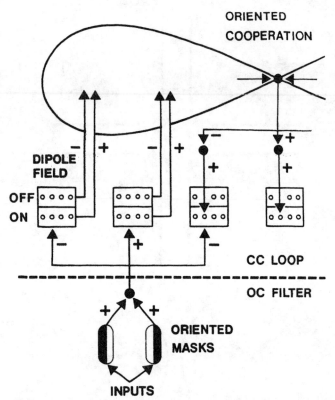

Fig. 18. Circuit diagram of the OC filter and CC loop of the BCS: the OC filter contains the simple cell and complex cell filter shown in Fig. 15. The CC loop contains the first and second competitive stages shown in Fig. 15, as well as the feedback interaction of these competitive stages with the cooperative bipole cells shown in Fig. 17. Additional BCS features are also here summarized: the hypercomplex cells of Fig. 15 are the on-cells of a dipole field. As in Fig. 15, on-cells at a fixed position compete among orientations. On-cells also inhibit off-cells which represent the same position and orientation. Off-cells at each position, in turn, compete among orientations. Both on-cells and off-cells are tonically active. As in Fig. 17, net excitation of an on-cell excites a similarly oriented cooperative bipole cell at a location corresponding to that of the on-cell. In addition, net excitation of an off-cell inhibits a similarly oriented cooperative bipole cell at a location corresponding to that of the off-cell. Thus, bottom-up excitation of a vertical on-cell, by inhibiting on-cell at that position, disinhibits the horizontal off-cell at that position, which in turn inhibits (almost) horizontally oriented cooperative bipole cells whose receptive fields include its position. Sufficiently strong net positive activation of both receptive fields of a cooperative bipole cell enables it to generate feedback via an on-center off-surround interaction among the like-oriented cells. On-cells which receive the most favorable combination of bottom-up signals and top-down signals generate the emergent perceptual grouping.

right-half R_{ijk}. The simple cell terms $U_{ijk} - \alpha V_{ijk}$ could be replaced by a Gabor filter, or a related oriented filter.

CC LOOP

First Competitive Stage: Hypercomplex Cells

$$\frac{d}{dt} w_{ijk} = -w_{ijk} + I + BJ_{ijk} + v_{ijk} - B \sum_{(p,q)} J_{pqk} A_{pqij}. \quad (26)$$

Second Competitive Stage: Higher-Order Hypercomplex Cells

$$O_{ijk} = C[w_{ijk} - w_{ijK}]^+ \quad (27)$$

$$y_{ijk} = \frac{EO_{ijk}}{D + O_{ij}} \qquad (28)$$

where K is the orientation perpendicular to k, and $O_{ij} = \Sigma_{k=1}^{n} O_{ijk}$.

Cooperation: Oriented And-Gates

$$z_{ijk} = g\left(\sum_{(p,q,r)} [y_{pqr} - y_{pqR}] F_{pqij}^{(r,k)} \right)$$

$$+ g\left(\sum_{(p,q,r)} [y_{pqr} - y_{pqR}] G_{pqij}^{(r,k)} \right) \qquad (29)$$

where

$$g(s) = \frac{H[s]^+}{K + [s]^+} \qquad (30)$$

and kernels $F_{pqij}^{(r,k)}$ and $G_{pqij}^{(r,k)}$ define the cell's two oriented receptive fields.

Cooperative Feedback to First Competitive Stage

$$v_{ijk} = \frac{h(z_{ijk})}{1 + \sum_{(p,q)} h(z_{pqk}) W_{pqij}} \qquad (31)$$

where

$$h(s) = L[s - M]^+. \qquad (32)$$

When a complete BCS is used to regulate the filling-in process described in (1)–(22), then the variables Z_{ijk} in (18) are replaced by y_{ijk} in (28).

The CC loop can generate a sharp emergent boundary from a fuzzy band of possible boundaries for the following reason. As in Fig. 16, certain orientations at given position are more strongly activated than other orientations. Suppose that the cells which encode a particular orientation at two or more approximately aligned positions can more strongly activate their target bipole cells than can the cells which encode other orientations. Then competitive cells of similar orientation at intervening positions will receive more intense excitatory feedback from these bipole cells. This excitatory feedback enhances the activation of these competitive cells relative to the activation of cells which encode other orientations. This advantage enables the favored orientation to suppress alternative orientations due to the orientational competition that occurs at the second competitive stage (Fig. 15).

A preattentive BCS representation emerges when CC loop dynamics approach a nonzero equilibrium activity pattern. The nonlinear feedback process whereby an emergent line or curve is synthesized need not even define a connected set of activated cells until equilibrium is approached. This process sequentially interpolates boundary components within progressively finer spatial intervals until a connected configuration is attained. Thus, *continuous boundaries are completed discontinuously.*

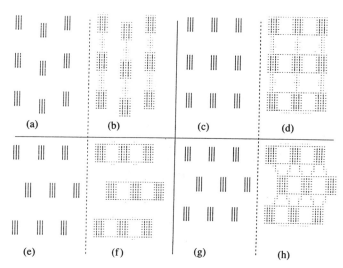

Fig. 19. Computer simulations of processes underlying textural grouping. The length of each line segment is proportional to the activation of a network node responsive to one of twelve possible orientations. Parts (a), (c), (e), and (g) display the activities of oriented cells which input to the CC loop. Parts (b), (d) (f), and (h) display equilibrium activities of oriented cells at the second competitive stage of the CC loop. A pairwise comparison of (a) with (b), (c) with (d), and so on indicates the major groupings sensed by the network. These simulations demonstrate that an emergent segmentation can form colinear to—as in (b) and (d),— perpendicular to—as in (d), (f), and (h), or diagonal to—as in (h), the inducing vertically oriented Lines by merely changing the relative positions of these lines. See text for details.

TEXTURAL GROUPING

Fig. 19 depicts the results of computer simulations which illustrate how these properties of the CC loop can generate a perceptual grouping or emergent segmentation of figural elements (as in Fig. 2). Fig. 19(a) depicts an array of nine vertically-oriented input clusters. Each cluster is called a Line because it represents a caricature of how a field of OC filter output cells respond to a vertical line. Fig. 19(b) displays the equilibrium activities of the cells at the second competitive stage of the CC loop in response to these Lines. The length of an oriented Line at each position is proportional to the equilibrium activity of a cell whose receptive field is centered at that position with that orientation. The input pattern in Fig. 19(a) possesses a vertical symmetry: triples of vertical Lines are colinear in the vertical direction, whereas they are spatially out-of-phase in the horizontal direction. The BCS senses this vertical symmetry, and generates emergent vertical boundaries in Fig. 19(b). The BCS also generates horizontal end cuts at the ends of each Line, which can trap the featural contrasts of each Line within the FCS. Thus, the emergent segmentation simultaneously supports a vertical macrostructure and a horizontal microstructure among the Lines.

In Fig. 19(c), the input Lines are moved so that triples of Lines are colinear in the vertical direction and their Line ends are lined up in the horizontal direction. Both vertical and horizontal boundary groupings are generated in Fig. 19(d). The segmentation distinguishes between Line ends and the small horizontal inductions that bound the sides of each Line. Only Line ends have enough sta-

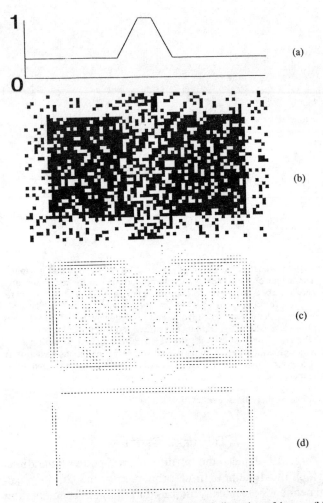

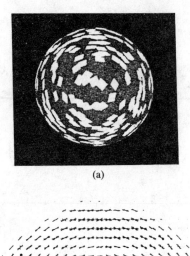

(a)

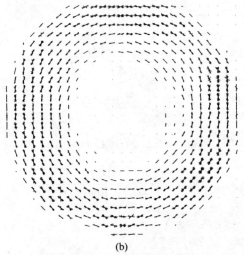

(b)

Fig. 20. (a) Distribution of noise in horizontal dimension of image; (b) binary image of a rectangle corrupted by noise whose distribution, as in (a), varies continuously; (c) responses of oriented contrast detectors to the image; (d) equilibrated responses of cooperative feedback cells of BC system. The rectangle is recovered and the ramped increase of noise in the middle of the figure is ignored.

Fig. 21. (a) A textured, curved surface (adapted from [25]). (b) Equilibrated response of cooperative feedback cells of the CC loop to the inputs from Fig. 21(a). The cooperative cells group the circular statistics of the parallelogram orientations near the figure's periphery, but suppress the discordant orientations near the center. A similar grouping process generates the circular segmentations induced by the Glass pattern in Fig. 1.

tistical inertia to activate horizontal boundary completion via the CC loop.

In Fig. 19(e), the input Lines are shifted to that they become noncolinear in a vertical direction, but triples of their Line ends remain aligned. The vertical symmetry of Fig. 19(c) is hereby broken. Consequently, in Fig. 19(f) the BCS groups the horizontal Line ends, but not the vertical Lines.

Fig. 19(h) depicts the emergence of diagonal groupings where no diagonals exist in the input pattern. Fig. 19(g) is generated by bringing the three horizontal rows of vertical Lines close together until their ends lie within the spatial bandwidth of the cooperative interaction. In Fig. 19(h), the BCS senses diagonal groupings of the Lines. Diagonally-oriented receptive fields are activated in the emergent boundaries, and these activations, as a whole, group into diagonal bands. Thus, these diagonal groupings emerge on both microscopic and macroscopic scales. The computer simulations illustrated in Fig. 19 show that the CC loop can generate large-scale segmentations without a loss of positional or orientational acuity.

The computer simulations of textural grouping in Fig. 19 do not deny that the two successive filters defined by the OC filter and the short-range competitive stages (Fig. 15) contribute to percepts of texture. Beck, Sutter, and Ivry [2] have provided recent experimental evidence supporting the role of these filters in texture segregation.

A number of other important properties of emergent segmentation have also been demonstrated through computer simulations of the BCS. Fig. 20 illustrates the BCS's ability to detect and complete sharp boundaries over long distances in the presence of severe noise, a type of capability useful in penetrating camouflage. This simulation illustrates the response of spatial scale large enough to group across individual image contrasts. Smaller spatial scales generate the boundaries of individual black and white compartments.

Fig. 21 illustrates the BCS's ability to detect form within a 2-D texture. Although the input is a pattern of discrete texture elements [Fig. 21(a)] the BCS can generate a dense *boundary web* of form-sensitive emergent groupings [Fig. 21(b)]. In a multiple scale version of the BCS, these boundary webs help to explain the percept of a smoothly curved 3-D surface. Todd and Akerstrom [25] have shown that the worst correlation between human psychophysical judgments of 3-D shape-from-texture and the theoretical predictions of such a multiple scale version of the BCS was 0.985. Meyer and Dougherty [20] have further shown that the theory is consistent with data about the effects of flicker-induced depth on chromatic subjective contours. The theory has also been able to analyze and predict many other perceptual and neural data that other vision theories cannot yet handle.

Thus, although a great deal of work remains to be done on further development of the BCS, the FCS, and their interactions, many promising results suggest that we are well along the way towards a better understanding of biologically-motivated vision systems which are equally at home in segmenting and filling-in the full range of visual phenomena—boundaries, textures, surfaces—from the discrete to the continuous.

References

[1] J. Beck, K. Prazdny, and A. Rosenfeld, "A theory of textural segmentation," in, *Human and Machine Vision*, J. Beck, B. Hope, and A. Rosenfeld, Eds. New York: Academic, 1983.

[2] J. Beck, A. Sutter, and R. Ivry, "Spatial frequency channels and perceptual grouping in texture segregation," Preprint, 1987.

[3] G. A. Carpenter and S. Grossberg, "A massively parallel architecture for a self-organizing neural pattern recognition machine," *Comput. Vis., Graph., Image Proc.*, vol. 37, pp. 54–115, 1987.

[4] —, "ART 2: Stable self-organization of pattern recognition codes for analog input patterns," *Appl. Opt.*, vol. 26, pp. 4919–4930, 1987.

[5] —, "The ART of adaptive pattern recognition by a self-organizing neural network," *Computer*, vol. 21, pp. 77–88, 1988.

[6] M. A. Cohen and S. Grossberg, "Neural dynamics of brightness perception: Features, boundaries, diffusion, and resonance," *Percep. Psychophys.*, vol. 36, pp. 428–456, 1984.

[7] R. L. DeValois, D. G. Albrecht, and L. G. Thorell, "Spatial frequency selectivity of cells in macaque visual cortex," *Vision Res.*, vol. 22, pp. 545–559, 1982.

[8] S. Geman and D. Geman, "Stochastic relaxation, Gibbs distribution, and the Bayesian restoration of images," *IEEE Pattern Anal. Mach. Intell.*, vol. PAMI-6, pp. 721–741, 1984.

[9] S. Grossberg, "The quantized geometry of visual space: The coherent computation of depth, form, and lightness," *Behavioral Brain Sci.*, vol. 6, pp. 625–657, 1983.

[10] —, "Cortical dynamics of three-dimensional form, color, and brightness perception, I: Monocular theory," *Percep. Psychophys.*, vol. 41, pp. 87–116, 1987.

[11] —, "Cortical dynamics of three-dimensional form, color, and brightness perception, II: Binocular theory," *Percep. Psychophys.*, vol. 41, pp. 117–158, 1987.

[12] S. Grossberg and E. Mingolla, "Neural dynamics of form perception: Boundary completion, illusory figures, and neon color spreading," *Psychol. Rev.*, vol. 92, pp. 173–211, 1985.

[13] —, "Neural dynamics of perceptual grouping: Textures, boundaries, and emergent segmentations," *Percep. Psychophys.*, vol. 38, pp. 141–171, 1985.

[14] —, "Neural dynamics of surface perception: Boundary webs, illuminants, and shape-from-shading," *Comput. Vis., Graph., Image Proc.*, vol. 37, pp. 116–165, 1987.

[15] S. Grossberg and D. Todorović, "Neural dynamics of 1-D and 2-D brightness perception: A unified model of classical and recent phenomena," *Percep. Psychophys.*, vol. 43, pp. 241–277, 1988.

[16] D. H. Hubel and T. N. Wiesel, "Receptive fields and functional architecture in two nonstriate visual areas (18 and 19) of the cat," *J. Neurophysiol.*, vol. 28, pp. 229–289, 1965.

[17] —, "Functional architecture of macaque monkey visual cortex," *Proc. Roy. Soc. London B*, vol. 198, pp. 1–59, 1977.

[18] S. Kirkpatrick, D. D. Gelatt, and M. P. Vecchi, "Optimization by simulated annealing," *Science*, vol. 220, pp. 671–680, 1983.

[19] E. H. Land, "The retinex theory of color vision," *Sci. Amer.*, vol. 237, pp. 108–128, 1977.

[20] G. E. Meyer and T. Dougherty, "Effects of flicker-induced depth on chromatic subjective contours," *J. Exp. Psych.: Human Percep. Perform.*, vol. 13, pp. 353–360, 1987.

[21] G. A. Orban, H. Kato, and P. O. Bishop, "Dimensions and properties of end-zone inhibitory areas in receptive fields of hypercomplex cells in cat striate cortex," *J. Neurophysiol.*, vol. 42, pp. 833–849, 1979.

[22] C. Redies and L. Spillmann, "The neon color effect in the Ehrenstein illusion," *Perception*, vol. 10, pp. 667–681, 1981.

[23] E. L. Schwartz, R. Desimone, T. Albright, and C. Gross, "Shape recognition and inferior temporal neurons," *Proc. Nat. Acad. Sci.*, vol. 80, pp. 5776–5778, 1983.

[24] H. Spitzer and S. Hochstein, "A complex-cell receptive field model," *J. Neurophysiol.*, vol. 53, pp. 1266–1286, 1985.

[25] J. T. Todd and R. A. Akerstrom, "Perception of three-dimensional form from patterns of optical texture," *J. Exp. Psych.: Human Percep. Perform.*, vol. 13, pp. 242–255, 1987.

[26] A. Treisman and H. Schmidt, "Illusory conjunctions in the perception of objects," *Cognitive Psych.*, vol. 14, pp. 107–141, 1982.

[27] R. von der Heydt, E. Peterhaus, and G. Baumgartner, "Illusory contours and cortical neuron responses," *Science*, vol. 224, pp. 1260–1262, 1984.

[28] A. L. Yarbus, *Eye Movements and Vision*. New York: Plenum, 1967.

Smart Sensing within a Pyramid Vision Machine

PETER J. BURT, MEMBER, IEEE

Invited Paper

In human vision, sensing is a distinctly dynamic process: the eyes move through an evolving sequence of fixations to explore the visual world, and to selectively gather information critical to the task at hand. Computer vision systems must follow similar smart sensing strategies if they are to perform useful tasks in real time. Through intelligent selection of data at an early analysis stage, systems can reduce the overall computational cost by orders of magnitude.

Through smart sensing a vision system makes efficient use of limited computing resources. We have built a machine, based on a pyramid architecture, that supports smart sensing and related highly efficient processing. Key elements of the design are a) hierarchical data structures for image representation, b) fine-to-coarse algorithms for the fast generation of image measures, c) coarse-to-fine search strategies that rapidly locate objects or events within a scene, and d) high level control mechanisms that guide data gathering even as visual information is being interpreted. This system, known as the Pyramid Vision Machine, achieves high performance at modest cost. Design considerations and several applications are described here.

I. Introduction

Images contain vast amounts of information, enough to challenge the capabilities of the most powerful computers. Yet only a small fraction of this information may be relevant to a given vision task. Thus it is expedient, often essential, that a vision system avoid or discard excessive detail at the earliest stages of analysis. It is equally important that analysis be performed with algorithms that are structured to be highly efficient, and that can be performed effectively on the system's computing hardware. Thus issues of computational efficiency are central to the design of an effective vision system. The designer must ask: given that computing resources will necessarily be limited, how should a system be organized and controlled to make most effective use of those resources?

Here we describe an approach to computer vision that makes careful use of selective analysis and fast algorithms to achieve efficiency. Together these techniques are called *smart sensing*. While vision tasks vary considerably in the information they must extract from a scene, smart sensing

may be based on relatively few generic techniques. For example, selective gathering of scene information requires mechanisms for locating regions of interest and for selectively processing these regions. Locating strategies can be based on broad area measures comparable to peripheral alerting in humans, and coarse-to-fine search comparable to foveation. Selective processing can be based on multiresolution techniques that match the resolution of image data being analyzed to that of information being extracted.

The techniques of smart sensing are analogous in a number of experts to aspects of human vision, such as search based on peripheral alerting and foveal analysis. But the motivations for these techniques can be given strictly in terms of computational efficiency. Smart sensing techniques are also related to those of 'active vision' [1], [2] described in this issue by Bajcsy [3].

The multiresolution image pyramid provides a natural framework for implementing a vision system based on smart sensing. We have built a computer vision system, the Pyramid Vision Machine (PVM), that implements such techniques. We illustrate smart sensing and the PVM with applications to industrial inspection, surveillance, and object recognition.

II. The Elements of Smart Sensing

Smart sensing may be defined as the selective, task oriented gathering of information from the visual world. It is a distinctly active process in which the viewer, be it man or machine, probes and explores the visual environment to extract information for the task at hand.

Many aspects of smart sensing are familiar from our own visual experience. Imagine, for example, the driver of a car traveling on a country road. His visual task is to locate and follow the road, observe oncoming traffic, read appropriate road signs, and avoid any objects in the road. To perform this task he does not examine the world in uniform detail. Rather he moves his eyes to fixate in turn certain critical points in the visual field, the road, an oncoming car, a sign. Two or three such fixations per second suffice to drive the car, yet he 'sees' only a minute fraction of the world before his eyes.

The eye is capable of gathering detailed scene infor-

Manuscript received December 31, 1987; revised March 14, 1988.

The author is with the David Sarnoff Research Center, Princeton, NJ 08543-5300, USA.

IEEE Log Number 8822796.

Reprinted from *Proc. IEEE*, vol. 76, no. 8, pp. 1006–1015, 1988.

mation only in the small region centered on its fovea. Its resolving power falls rapidly outside this region, toward peripheral vision. Thus while the driver fixates on the road he hardly notices individual leaves, or even trees by the side of the road, or objects in the fields beyond. But what is most remarkable is the skill with which his visual system locates and extracts just that information required to drive the car, while it ignores the vast flow of information not relevant to this task.

The same behavior is evident when humans perform an industrial vision task. Objects to be inspected during manufacturing, for example, may be large and intricate, but a human inspector quickly locates just those points that need close examination. As machines are designed to perform challenging vision tasks, such as automated vehicle navigation or industrial inspection, it will be imperative that they also implement smart sensing strategies.

What are the basic elements of smart sensing? In the case of human vision three such elements are apparent in the driver example. First is the marked concentration of resolving power within the fovea of the eye. This serves at once as a probe by which the visual system can explore the world, and as a mechanism by which it can limit the amount of detailed information it must process at any moment in time. Second is the broad field of view provided by peripheral vision. This serves alerting and guidance functions. While sensing the world at much reduced resolution peripheral vision can detect unexpected objects or events, and can direct the fovea for close examination.

A third element of smart sensing evident in the driver's behavior is the high level cognitive control of eye movements. As a viewer performs a task such as driving, he understands its requirements and moves his eyes to gather the specific information needed for the task. This aspect of natural vision is most remarkable, and most unlike present day computer vision systems. It reveals a tight coupling and dynamic interplay between high and low levels of visual analysis. Even as the low level system gathers pieces of scene information through the sequence of foveations, the high level system is attempting to interpret the world based on this partial data. In effect the high level system continually forms and reforms hypotheses about objects in the scene, and directs the eyes to gather additional information to confirm or reject these hypotheses.

These same mechanisms, selective foveal examination, broad area alerting and guidance, and high level control, are key elements of smart sensing in computer vision as well [4].

III. A COMPUTATIONAL FRAMEWORK

The image pyramid provides a computational framework that appears uniquely well suited for implementing smart sensing techniques. As a spatially organized, multiresolution image representation it provides a direct means for controlling the resolution at which data is represented for analysis and the domain over which that analysis is performed. As a hierarchical structure it supports a wide variety of fast, robust algorithms.

The image pyramid has been studied extensively in the past decade [5]–[7]. A pyramid organized SIMD architecture is described by Cantoni and Levialdi [8] in this issue. Since the pyramid will be the basis for defining the vision algo-

rithms presented here, a brief review of basic pyramid techniques will be useful.

Definitions

An image pyramid is a sequence of copies of an original image in which resolution and sample density are decreased in regular steps. An example low pass, or Gaussian pyramid is shown in Fig. 3(a). Here G_0 is the original image. This is convolved with a low pass filter w, then subsampled by discarding every other row and column to form G_1. G_1 is then filtered and subsampled to form G_2, and so on. In general, for $\ell > 0$,

$$G_\ell(i, j) = \sum_{m,n=-K}^{K} w(m, n) G_{\ell-1}(i - m2^{\ell-1}, j - n2^{\ell-1}).$$

This can be stated more concisely in terms of a convolution operator:

$$G_\ell = [w * G_{\ell-1}]_{\downarrow2}.$$

Here the notation $[\cdot]_{\downarrow2}$ indicates the image contained within brackets is subsampling by a factor of 2 in each spatial dimension.

The filter w is called the *generating kernel*. In practice this is chosen to be small and separable, so that the computation cost of the filter convolution is kept to a minimum. Subsampling means that, in effect, the generating kernel doubles in size relative to the original image with each interaction. As a result the band limit of pyramid levels decreases in octave, or power of two, steps. Pyramid construction is a fast algorithm that generates a·full set of filtered images at a cost typically less than 10 operations per pixel of the original image.[1]

The analytic properties of the Gaussian pyramid are best stated in terms of the *hierarchical kernel*, W_ℓ. This represents the net effect of the ℓ convolutions with w that generate pyramid level G_ℓ. To define W_ℓ it is convenient to imagine that pyramid construction steps are reordered so that all filter operations are performed before subsampling. In this case the generating kernel must explicitly double in size with each iteration. Let w_ℓ be an *expanded kernel* in which taps are separated by a distance $2^{\ell-1}$:

$$w_\ell(m, n) = \begin{cases} w\left(\dfrac{m}{2^{\ell-1}}, \dfrac{n}{2^{\ell-1}}\right), & \text{for } m \text{ and } n \text{ multiples of } 2^{\ell-1} \\ 0, & \text{otherwise.} \end{cases}$$

Then W_ℓ is the cascaded convolutions of expanded kernels w_1 to w_ℓ:

$$W_\ell = w_\ell * w_{\ell-1} * \cdots * w_1.$$

G_ℓ can now be expressed as a single convolution of W_ℓ followed by subsampling of 2^ℓ:

$$G_\ell = [W_\ell * G_0]_{\downarrow2^\ell}.$$

Although the hierarchical kernels are never explicitly computed in pyramid image processing, they concisely summarize the effect of repeated convolutions used in pyramid construction. For example, hierarchical kernels double in size with each iteration, but for a given generating

[1] In all examples given here w is a 5 by 5 separable kernel with binomial coefficients: $w(m, n) = \hat{w}(m) \hat{w}(n)$, and $\hat{w} = [1, 4, 6, 4, 1]\frac{1}{16}$. The computation cost is 7 operations per image pixel to build a full pyramid.

kernel, their shape is fixed. The 5 by 5 generating kernel used in examples in this paper results in hierarchical kernels that resemble the Gaussian density function. Thus the Gaussian pyramid represents the result of convolving an original image with a set of Gaussian kernels that differs in size by multiples of 2. The sample rate decreases with band limit, but it approximates the Nyquist limit so does not result in information loss, or otherwise alter the images.

A second pyramid type, the band pass, or Laplacian, is commonly used as the basis for multiresolution analysis in computer vision [6], [9], [10]. Roughly speaking, levels of the Laplacian pyramid are formed as difference images between successive levels of the Gaussian. See Fig. 3(b). If G_ℓ is the ℓth level of a Gaussian pyramid, then the corresponding Laplacian level L_ℓ is given by

$$L_\ell = G_\ell - w * G_\ell.$$

The Laplacian pyramid has a number of properties that recommend it for computer vision. It is, first of all, a complete image representation: the original image can be recovered exactly from its Laplacian pyramid representation through a simple inverse transformation. Furthermore, it is a compact representation, and one that tends to enhance important features of an image, such as edges. Features are further separated over levels of the pyramid according to their scale. These properties also make the Laplacian pyramid well suited for image compression and computer graphics [11], [12].[2]

Match to Resolution and Scale

Important aspects of smart sensing and efficient analysis may now be defined within the pyramid structure. First, we consider mechanisms for selecting resolution and scale.

The resolution required to perform a given vision task is not fixed, but may vary from moment to moment and from region to region over a scene. In some cases only coarse pattern structure needs to be measured over a relatively broad area of the visual field; in other cases details are required in small patches of the field. In computer vision it is essential that the scale and resolution of analysis operations be matched to that of salient information within the scene. Not to do so can mean orders of magnitude increase in the cost of analysis, or even in failure to perform the desired task, as the vision system becomes lost in irrelevant detail, 'missing the forest for the trees'.

As a simple but telling demonstration of the importance of scale and resolution, consider the problem of locating a target pattern T within an image I. If the target measures M by M samples, and the image measures N by N, then the cost of a correlation search is order M^2N^2. Next suppose we wish to search for the same target but increased in scale by a factor s. Two approaches may be considered. In the first a larger copy of the target pattern is constructed, and the search is repeated as before. The cost is now order $s^2M^2N^2$. In the second approach, the image is decreased in scale by s and correlation is repeated. In this case the cost is decreased to order M^2N^2/s^2. Provided the target is repre-

sented in sufficient detail to permit identification, the two methods will yield the same results. The cost of computations of the first approach, exceeds that of the second by a factor s^4. This can indeed be large for scale changes of 10 or more that are common in vision tasks!

While correlation may not be the method chosen for pattern matching in computer vision, the relation between cost and pattern scale is quite general. It means that image and target information must be represented at near the minimal resolution sufficient for the analysis task. In practice the penalty for failing to match analysis to the resolution of salient information is often worse than this. It can be shown that when searching for targets over a range of scales and orientations the cost is proportional to the 6th power of the target dimensions. Again, the importance of performing analysis at minimum size and resolution is clear.

Image resolution and scale can be controlled directly within the pyramid by selecting the appropriate level and region for analysis. While scales are represented only at discrete powers of 2 by the pyramid levels, this is generally adequate for vision applications, and is convenient for many hierarchical algorithms. In some cases it may be necessary to examine a resolution intermediate between those represented by the pyramid levels. Since the pyramid is a complete representation, data for intermediate resolutions can be obtained through standard interpolation techniques.

Fast Feature Generation

Hierarchical structures form the basis for implementing fast analysis algorithms. These may be divided into two classes: fine-to-coarse algorithms used in feature generation, and coarse-to-fine algorithms used in search. In either case the benefits of structuring an algorithm in a hierarchical format can be several orders of magnitude reduction in computation cost. It can also significantly reduce required arithmetic precision, and can simplify the hardware used to implement the algorithm.

Gaussian pyramid construction is itself a fast fine-to-coarse algorithm: convolutions with large kernels are obtained very efficiently as simple weighted sums of convolutions with smaller kernels. In combination with other standard image processing operations, such as feature selective convolutions and point operations, pyramid processing can generate a remarkable variety of image measures with the same high efficiency [14].

A generic computation of this type is shown in Fig. 1(a). This may be used, for example, to compute sets of local texture energy measures. A source image I is first decomposed into a set of bandpass components through Laplacian pyramid construction. Each band is then convolved with the filter f that is selective for a particular feature, or pattern characteristic, indicative of the texture measure of interest. The result is a *feature pyramid*. Next, levels of the pyramid are squared on a sample by sample basis (a point operation). Finally, a Gaussian pyramid is constructed for each of the feature pyramid levels. This has the effect of integrating the squared values to form local energy measures. Samples at level ℓ of such an *integration pyramid* represent a weighted average within a local neighborhood defined by the hierarchical kernel W_ℓ. The process of pyramid construction efficiently generates integrated measures in windows of many sizes. The result is a set of energy images, $\{E_{k\ell}\}$, where k indicates feature scale and ℓ indicates the integration win-

---

[2]The Laplacian pyramid can also be generated by applying a discrete Laplacian operator ∇^2 to levels of the Gaussian pyramid. Thus the Laplacian pyramid may be regarded as a discrete implementation of the ∇^2G operator introduced by Marr and Hildreth [13]. The construction is defined in such a way that exact reconstruction is possible through the inverse pyramid transform.

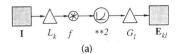

(a)

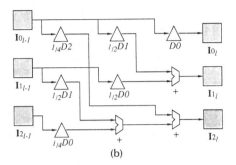

(b)

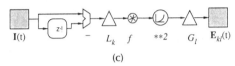

(c)

Fig. 1. Basic algorithms for generating image feature sets. (a) Texture measure. (b) Moments. (c) Change energy measure.

dow size. Energy measures of this form are ubiquitous in computer vision, and will be illustrated in the examples described below.

A second example of fine-to-coarse computation is the hierarchical generation of local image moments. These are useful, for example, in defining orientation or scale invariant features, or as the first steps in the fitting of polynomial patches to image data [15].

Let $Ip_\ell(i)$ be a normalized local image moment of order p centered at point i:

$$Ip_\ell(i) = \frac{1}{2^p} \sum_m W_\ell(m) I(i + m) m^p.$$

(The definition is given in one dimension to simplify notation.) Here again the hierarchical kernel W_ℓ serves as a window function and defines the local neighborhood in which the moment is computed. The *moment image* Ip_ℓ is formed by evaluating the moment with the window centered at each sample point i. It can be shown that the pth moment in window W_ℓ can be computed as a simple combination of p and lower order moments in window $W_{\ell-1}$:

$$Ip_\ell = \frac{1}{2^p} \sum_{q=0}^{P} \binom{p}{q} wr * Iq_{\ell-1}.$$

Here wr is a *moment generating kernel* which combines a moment arm with the standard Gaussian generating kernel

$$wr(m) = w(m)m^r.$$

In the above equation $r = p - q$.

The computation of zero, first and second order moment images at pyramid level ℓ is shown as an image flow diagram in Fig. 1(b). Here the pyramid operations labeled Dp are the same filter and subsample operations used in standard Gaussian pyramid construction except that moment generating kernels are used.

This example demonstrates the source of computational efficiency in fine-to-coarse algorithms. Complex measures within large windows are computed as combinations of simpler measures within smaller windows, and these are obtained in turn as combinations of still simpler measures. Intermediate results of the computation are thus used multiple times in forming later results.

Iterative Refinement and Coarse-to-Fine Search

Coarse-to-fine techniques are commonly used in computer vision. Coarse-to-fine search strategies, for example, provide a fast means for locating target patterns within an image (e.g., [16]–[18]). Such strategies play a key role in applications described here to surveillance and object recognition. In other applications it is not the location of selected patterns but the precision of results that is improved in coarse-to-fine fashion. This is the case, for example, in algorithms for estimating displacement vectors for stereo and motion [19], [20].

In general, coarse-to-fine algorithms achieve their efficiency through iterative refinement: approximate results are first obtained with the image represented as low resolution, then are refined in a sequence of steps while moving to progressively higher image resolution. Cost is minimized at low resolution by representing data at low sample density, and minimized at successively higher resolutions by using results at each processing step to guide processing at the next.

IV. BLEMISH DETECTION AND A MODEL OF HUMAN VISION

As a first application of smart sensing and related pyramid processing we consider the problem of detecting surface blemishes in manufactured products. This can be a particularly challenging problem in industrial inspection because blemishes are cosmetic in nature, and are significant only to the degree that they can be seen by humans. The computer vision system must therefore model human perception.

Fig. 2(a) shows a portion of a CRT screen that must be inspected for irregularities in the deposition of a phosphor coating in the manufacturing of TV sets. A diffuse flaw of a type known as a water mark is present. While the flaw is relatively easy for human inspectors to locate, it can be quite difficult for computers. Flaws of this type have low contrast, here only 4 gray levels, or 2 percent relative to the surrounding regions. And other features of the CRT image tend to mask the flaw, including a fine grain texture and a gradual but significant gradation in brightness over the CRT screen. The presence of these background characteristics precludes the use of simple thresholds, or other pixel resolution operations.

However the flaw can be detected quite readily on the basis of local spectral energy. This is apparent in Fig. 2(b). Here texture energy $E_{2,3}$ has been computed as Fig. 1(a), by squaring Laplacian level 2 then integrating to Gaussian level 3. The filter stage is omitted in this case. Frequency band 2 is well matched to the particular flaw shown, while other types of flaws may be detected in other bands. Still it remains to be determined how visible such patterns are to humans.

Over the past two decades there has been a concerted effort in the perceptual psychology research community to measure the ability of humans to detect and discriminate

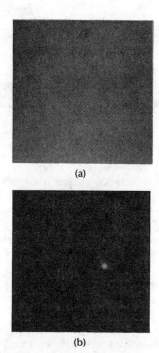

(a)

(b)

Fig. 2. Surface flaw inspection. (a) Original with water mask. (b) Flaw revealed by local energy measure.

patterns, and to infer from such abilities how visual information is represented and processed within the human visual system. This work has led to the formulation of models of human vision in terms of multiple spatial frequency tuned 'channels' (e.g., [21], [22]). Roughly speaking, such channels are analogous to levels of a Laplacian pyramid. Carlson and Cohen [23] have shown that the visibility of a pattern to humans can be predicted from a weighted sum of its energy within a set of octave wide spatial frequency bands, such as those in the pyramid. Weights are based on measurements of the sensitivity of human vision in these bands.

Thus the pyramid provides an elegantly direct method for modeling human vision for the purpose of flaw inspection. Laplacian pyramid construction decomposes the image into appropriate frequency bands, then squaring and local integration through Gaussian construction completes the computation of energy measures. These are weighted and summed to obtain estimates of visibility to humans.

V. Smart Surveillance and Mechanisms of Alerting and Foveation

It is often assumed that multiresolution techniques are not applicable to many of the most challenging vision tasks, such as the analysis of satellite images, because critical features are very small and are lost if the image resolution is even slightly reduced. In fact such fine pattern details can often be represented at low resolution through conversion to *integrated feature measures*. These record the presence of small features within the image, but represent their positions with reduced precision.

The steps required in generating integrated feature measures are the same as with local texture energy, Fig. 1(a). The source image is first decomposed into bandpass components through Laplacian pyramid construction. A selected high frequency band is then convolved with a filter f that enhances critical features. Features are 'detected' through application of a nonlinear point operation, such as a square or threshold. Finally, Gaussian pyramid construction is used to integrate, or group, elements within neighborhoods of various sizes.

An integrated feature measure is analogous to an array of complex cells in the human visual system. An individual complex cell becomes active if the particular pattern for which it is selective, such as an oriented line element, occurs anywhere within an extended receptive field. Cell activity represents the fact that the pattern has occurred but only specifies its location roughly, as being somewhere within the cell's receptive field. In the same way, a positive value of an integrated measure indicates that a selected feature occurs somewhere within a corresponding integration window.

Integrated measures provide a powerful basis for alerting and guidance. A system can monitor a wide field of view at low resolution yet be sensitive to events or features no larger than a single pixel. This is illustrated in the following application to 'smart surveillance'.

Suppose that an automated surveillance camera is required to provide security around a building. It must detect certain types of activity, such as people or cars moving in a parking lot, while ignoring other activity, such as the movement of leaves, birds, and clouds. Furthermore, detection and discrimination must be carried out continuously, in real time, on full rate video (e.g., 30 frames per second). The system should be low cost, which means only modest computing resources can be included, such as a microprocessor. Special hardware is assumed that can construct a pyramid for each frame at video rates (as in DSRC's Pyramid Vision Machine, described in Section VII).

An alerting procedure based on 'change energy' is well suited for this task [24]. The computation is shown schematically in Fig. 1(c). A difference image is first formed between successive frames of a video sequence. This is nonzero only where changes are taking place in the scene. The difference image is decomposed into a set of bandpass components, filtered, squared, and integrated, as in the standard procedure for integrated measures. Spectral energy will fall into different frequency bands depending on the size and surface pattern of moving objects and their velocity of motion. For example, small objects such as moving leaves, appear predominantly in the highest frequency band, while changes in illumination due to passing clouds appear in low frequency bands. Objects of interest may have predominant energy in an intermediate band.

Successive steps in the computation are shown in Fig. 3. The source image is a frame from a video sequence in which a car is moving in the background. Gaussian and Laplacian pyramids constructed from a single frame are shown in Fig. 3(a) and (b). Fig. 3(c) shows the Laplacian pyramid formed from the difference image between successive frames. The car has only moved slightly between frames, so change due to motion is most apparent in the highest spatial frequency pyramid level. The amplitude of the change falls rapidly with frequency, and it cannot be detected in the lower frequency levels of this pyramid. However, if the highest frequency band of the difference image is squared, then integrated, as in Fig. 4(d), then the motion remains clearly detectable even at the lowest frequency pyramid level. This demonstrates the power of the integrated measure to cap-

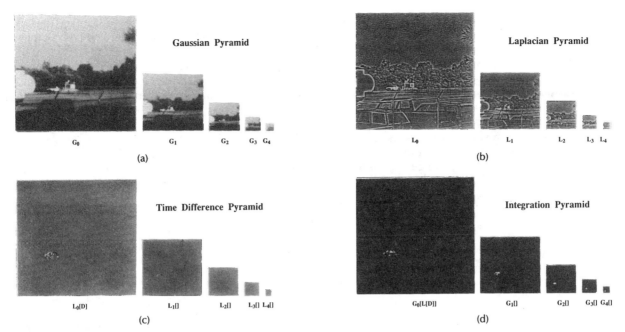

Fig. 3. Steps in computing 'change energy' measures for smart surveillence.

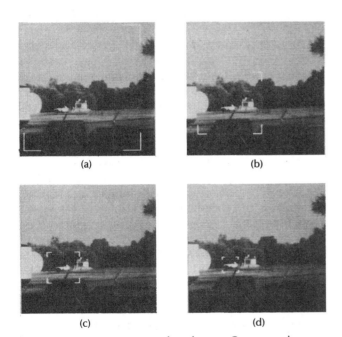

Fig. 4. Homing process over four frames. Corner marks indicate the image region examined each frame time. The region becomes smaller, but represents higher resolution, as analysis moves between pyramid levels.

ture even small image details and represent these at low resolution.

All levels of the integrated pyramid are made available to a microprocessor for analysis. Because the microprocessor has limited computing power it has time to examine only a small region of the change energy pyramid each frame time. Suppose, in particular, that a 16 by 16 array is analyzed. In the normal mode of operation, the microprocessor examines only the 16 by 16 low resolution pyramid level. Any change in the scene with the appropriate characteristics can be detected by the microprocessor at this level, even changes in single pixels, if these are deemed inter-

esting. If a possible event is detected, the system 'foveates' the corresponding region of the visual field through a homing process. This is a coarse-to-fine search over a sequence of frames: after detection within a 16 by 16 window at level ℓ in one frame time, the system shifts in the next frame time to examine a 16 by 16 analysis region at level $\ell - 1$. The analysis region is centered on the location of the detected level ℓ, and at each step represents a smaller area of the scene at higher resolution. The homing process is illustrated over 4 frames in Fig. 4.

In this example a single integrated measure has been used to guide 'foveal' analysis. More generally a vision system will base alerting and guidance on a set of different integrated measures. Through appropriate combinations of these measures the system can be made selective for a very limited class of events or a broad range of events, as required.

VI. Fast Object Recognition

Humans have a remarkable ability to direct their eyes to those regions of the visual field where important information is likely to exist. This is evident in the example of the automobile driver who moves his eyes from road to oncoming car to traffic sign. Such purposeful gathering of scene information must be guided by the viewer's understanding of the visual world and the objects that may be within it. In effect, his visual system anticipates, or hypothesizes what objects are present, and where they are located. Eye movements then serve as information gathering probes, designed to test and refine these hypotheses. The sequence of eye movements evolves dynamically, as new information is gathered and new hypotheses are formed. Thus in human vision there is a continuous interplay between the 'low level' information gathering processes and the 'high level' interpretation processes.

This hypothesis-test aspect of smart sensing is the most challenging to implement within a computer vision system. Information gathering processes must be model directed,

347

and control decisions must be made rapidly on the basis of partial information. The system designer must develop a structure for representing knowledge about objects and the scene that can be quickly updated as new information is gathered, and he must devise reasoning strategies that use this information to quickly determine where to direct the next step in selective gathering of scene information.

A rudimentary, but useful format for specifying such object models is provided by a *pattern tree*. This representation combines a compact description of the object with a description of a fast search strategy to guide object recognition.

Motivation for the pattern tree structure begins with the observation that even complex objects can often be identified on the basis of just a few distinctive features. These may be large scale patterns indicative of overall object shape, or small details that distinguish between otherwise similar objects. In general, large patterns can be specified at reduced resolution, while small patterns are represented at higher resolution. Thus the data required to specify a pattern within an object model is independent of its size. However, small features are more difficult to locate within a scene. Therefore when performing an object recognition task, it is expedient to search for large features first, within a low resolution representation of the scene, then proceed to search for progressively more detailed features using the locations of previously found features to direct the search, in a coarse-to-fine fashion.

A pattern tree model for a particular object consists of a set of nodes and links. Each node represents a particular object feature, while links represent the relative positions of these features. Generally speaking, features that are larger in scale are nearer the root of the tree. An example pattern tree description of a playing card is shown in Fig. 5. Boxes drawn over the pattern, Fig. 5(a), show regions represented as features within the tree. In this case such features are assumed to be encoded simply as sample arrays, or templates. Here all arrays measure 8 by 8 samples, so larger boxes correspond to lower resolution features in the tree. The tree itself is shown in Fig. 5(b). Fig. 5(c) shows the pattern information actually included in this tree, obtained by summing its features.

Object recognition is implemented as a search process that begins, typically, at the root of the tree. When a given node is found, a search is undertaken for branch nodes. The search continues until a sufficient number of features have been found to unambiguously identify the object. As a search proceeds, the system will need to periodically gather additional information from the scene. These sensing steps are guided by the pattern tree: it indicates the image region and resolution at which the next feature is likely to be found relative to previously located features. In this way the tree includes both an object description and a search strategy, and it supports rapid high level decisions about where to look next. The search thus follows a sequence of image probes similar to eye movements in human vision.

While the object model based on a pattern tree outlined here is relatively simple, it illustrates several powerful techniques that are also appropriate for more sophisticated object models. It was observed earlier that the cost of searching for a pattern over a range of positions, orientations, and scales is proportional to the sixth power of the size of the pattern (in sample intervals). This means there

is a very significant computational advantage to breaking a large complex pattern into smaller and less complex patterns, and these into still smaller patterns. By organizing these component patterns within a tree, the model provides a basis for additional computational efficiency through the coarse-to-fine search. The representation also provides flexibility in the object description: while component features may be specified in detail, a degree of variability in the relative positions of these features can be allowed. In this way, a description accommodates variability in shape of objects of a given type, as well as tolerance to variations in object size and orientation. And, finally, it provides a natural basis for recognizing objects that are partially occluded: recognition is possible when a number of characteristic features are in view, corresponding to a branch of the tree, even though most features of the object may not be visible.

VII. An Implementation, The PVM

A computer vision machine has been designed and built at David Sarnoff Research Center to perform pyramid based processing [25]. Called the Pyramid Vision Machine, or PVM, the system supports the smart sensing techniques described here, and performs many useful vision tasks in real time.

The overall architecture of the PVM is shown schematically in Fig. 6, while the machine itself is shown in Fig. 7. It consists of three (512 by 512) memory modules and two clustered processing modules, interconnected by a limited switching network. One processing module includes a multiplier, an ALU, and a shifter. The second is a custom-built component for performing pyramid operations at video rates. A host computer (not shown) controls data flow and computations, and performs higher level vision functions. The host can access data in any of the memory modules. While the PVM generates various feature images rapidly, in a fine-to-coarse fashion, the host explores this data to locate information of interest through coarse-to-fine search strategies. The PVM has been run with several different hosts, but most development has been with an IBM/AT.

The PVM is designed to run continuously on images obtained directly from a video camera. It is capable of constructing full Gaussian and Laplacian pyramids for 256 by 240 images frames at the rate of 30 per second. The pyramid module performs a five by five separable convolution, and handles boarders automatically (very important in a multiresolution system). The pyramid module includes its own microprogrammable controller, as well as look-up tables for performing point operations on pyramid levels as they are generated.

The components of the PVM are implemented as pipeline modules: a pyramid or other image operation is performed as data flows from a memory module, through one or more computing modules, and back to memory. This general architecture can be readily expanded to accommodate much larger images and more complex real time processing. Particularly high throughput and efficiency can be obtained with a network of such modules arranged as a *lattice pipeline* [26]. This consists of multiple pipelines running in parallel, possibly with merging and diverging data paths, but without loops.

The PVM and extended lattice pipeline architectures are

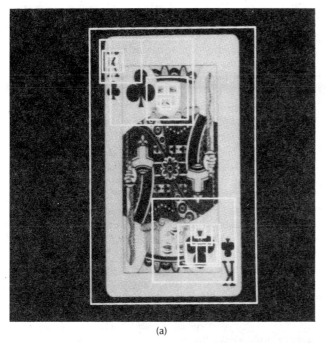

(a)

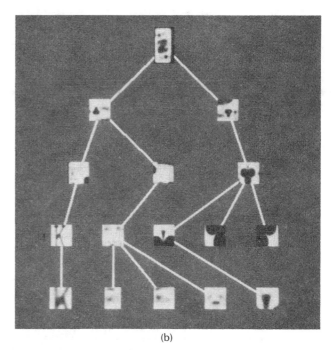

(b)

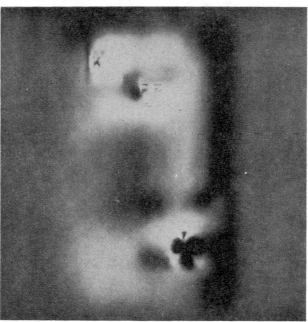

(c)

Fig. 5. Pattern tree representation of a playing card. (a) The original image with outlined regions indicating pattern components included in the tree representation. (b) The tree structure. (c) A composite image showing the information represented in the tree.

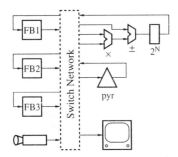

Fig. 6. A schematic representation of the Pyramid Vision Machine.

designed to support multiresolution processing, and readily accommodate both changes in sample density and in analysis region. It may be observed that other, more familiar forms of parallel architectures, such as SIMD designs, cannot efficiently handle such changes, and are therefore not well suited for vision applications based on smart sensing.

VIII. Summary and Discussion

It is the nature of the physical world that objects of interest are localized in space and events are localized in time. In computer vision it is expedient, therefore, to focus anal-

Fig. 7. The Pyramid Vision Machine.

ysis just on those regions of the visual field that carry salient information, and to move the analysis region dynamically as events unfold.

It is the nature of many computations in early vision that basic operations are repeated over extended regions and scales. Although such operations may be relatively simple, computations are data intensive and can therefore be extremely demanding. However, it is often possible to structure these computations as fast algorithms, that achieve efficiency by generating extended sets of such measures at once.

The image pyramid provides a computational framework for both selective analysis and fast algorithms. For example, it provides a natural structure for implementing 'alerting' and 'foveation' strategies for selective analysis, and hierarchical object models for fast high level control. The Pyramid Vision Machine, built at DSRC, was designed to support multiresolution processing and smart sensing. While this machine has relatively modest size, it can perform sophisticated tasks in real time.

It is interesting to note that the two approaches to efficiency outlined here, fast feature generation and selective analysis, represent complementary techniques. In procedures of the first type, efficiency is achieved by performing simple operations over an extended domain and repeatedly recombining results in a fine-to-coarse fashion. In the latter type it is obtained by restricting analysis to specific regions of interest, and by arranging the processing as sequences of analysis steps, with the results of each guiding the next in coarse-to-fine fashion. We refer to techniques of the first type as *generate-and-select* strategies, since extended sets of measures are generated, then just a few are selected for further analysis. We refer to the latter type as *selective-generation* strategies, since only the required measures are computed.

The distinction between generate-and-select and selective-generation strategies is similar to that traditionally made between pre-attentive and attentive vision in humans. Low level generation of feature sets tends to be global and parallel, while high level pattern analysis is focused and sequential. The former is associated with fine-to-coarse feature generation algorithms, and the latter with coarse-to-fine search and analysis. Ultimately the choice between strategies for performing a particular computation is one of efficiency and responsiveness. If fast algorithms exist for generating a particular measure, and results are required quickly and are likely to be required over several positions or resolutions, then a generate-and-select strategy is followed. If no fast generation algorithm exists, or only isolated measures will be required, then a selective-generation strategy is preferred.

We have stressed the role of smart sensing strategies in achieving computational efficiency. It may be asked, finally, how important it is to consider such efficiency issues in the overall design of a computer vision system. In the past there has been a tendency to regard efficiency as secondary in importance; it is an implementation issue rather than a fundamental aspect of the system design. However, as we have observed, fast algorithms and smart control can provide many orders of magnitude reduction in computation cost and response time. This represents not just the difference between a practical implementation and one that is interesting though impractical, but often the difference between a system that 'works' and one that does not. Furthermore, as we have seen, efficient analysis techniques are supported by major features of the architecture itself, such as multiresolution data structures, and foveal organization. In short, efficiency is of primary importance in the design of a vision system. To a large extent, it is the requirements of efficient techniques that dictate the basic architecture of such a system.

ACKNOWLEDGMENT

The author wishes to thank G. van der Wal and J. Sinniger for their design and construction of the Pyramid Vision Machine, and C. Anderson, M. Clark, and R. Kolczynski for work in developing algorithms and applications. C. Carlson has provided overall program guidance and continued encouragement.

REFERENCES

[1] J. Aloimonos, I. Weiss, and A. Bandyopadhyay, "Active vision," in *1st International Conf. on Computer Vision* (London, England), pp. 35–54, 1987.
[2] D. H. Ballard, "Eye movements and visual cognition," in *Proceedings of the Workshop on Spatial Reasoning and Multi-Sensor Fusion*, (St. Charles, IL), pp. 188–200, 1987.
[3] R. Bajcsy, "Active perception," this issue.
[4] P. J. Burt, "Smart sensing," in *Machine Vision, Algorithms, Architectures and Systems*, H. Freeman, Ed. New York, NY: Academic Press, 1988.
[5] S. L. Tanimoto and T. Pavlidis, "A hierarchical data structure for picture processing," *Computer Graphics and Image Processing*, vol. 4, pp. 104–109, 1975.
[6] P. J. Burt, "Fast filter transforms for image processing," *Comp. Graphics and Image Processing*, vol. 16, pp. 20–51, 1981.
[7] A. Rosenfeld, Ed., *Multiresolution Image Processing and Analysis*. New York, NY: Springer-Verlag, 1984.
[8] V. Cantoni and S. Levialdi, "Multiprocessor computing for images," this issue.
[9] J. L. Crowley and R. M. Stern, "Fast computations for the difference of low-pass transform," *IEEE Trans. Pattern Anal. Machine Intell.*, vol. 6, pp. 212–221, 1984.
[10] C. H. Anderson, "An alternative to the Burt pyramid algorithm," RCA internal correspondence, 1984.
[11] P. J. Burt and E. H. Adelson, "The Laplacian algorithm as a compact image code," *IEEE Trans. Commun.*, vol. 31, pp. 532–540, 1983.
[12] ——, "A multiresolution spline with application to image mosaics," *ACM Transaction on Graphics*, vol. 2, pp. 217–236, 1983.

[13] D. Marr and H. Hildreth, "Theory of edge detection," *Proc. Roy. Soc. London*, vol. B207, pp. 187–217, 1980.

[14] P. J. Burt, "Fast algorithms for estimating local image properties," *Comp. Vision, Graphics, and Image Processing*, vol. 21, pp. 368–382, 1983.

[15] ——, "Moment images, polynomial fit filters, and the problem of surface interpolation," in *Proceeding of the Computer Vision and Pattern Recognition Conf.*, (Ann Arbor, MI), pp. 144–152, 1988.

[16] M. D. Kelly, "Edge detection in pictures by computer using planning," in *Machine Intelligence*, B. Meltzer and D. Michie, Eds. Edinburgh, VI: Edinburgh Univ. Press, 1971, pp. 397–409.

[17] A. Rosenfeld and G. J. VanderBurg, "Coarse-fine template matching," *IEEE Trans. Syst., Man, Cybern.*, pp. 104–107, 1977.

[18] Y. Luo, R. T. Chin, and C. R. Dyer, "2-D object recognition using hierarchical boundary segments," in *Proc. IEEE Conf. on Computer Vision and Pattern Recognition*, pp. 426–428, 1985.

[19] L. H. Quam, "Hierarchical warp stereo," in *Proc. DARPA Image Understanding Workshop* (New Orleans, LA), pp. 149–155, 1984.

[20] J. R. Bergen and E. H. Adelson, "Hierarchical, computationally efficient motion estimation algorithm," *J. Opt. Soc. Am. A*, vol. 4, p. 35, 1987.

[21] H. R. Wilson and J. R. Bergen, "A four mechanism model for threshold spatial vision," *Vision Res.*, vol. 19, pp. 19–32, 1979.

[22] A. B. Watson, "The cortex transform: Rapid computation of simulated neural images," *Computer Vision, Graphics, and Image Processing*, vol. 39, pp. 311–327, 1987.

[23] C. R. Carlson and R. W. Cohen, "A simple psychophysical model for predicting the visibility of displayed information," in *Proceedings of the SID*, vol. 21, pp. 229–246, 1980.

[24] C. H. Anderson, P. J. Burt, and G. S. van der Wal, "Change detection and tracking using pyramid transform techniques," in *Proc. SPIE Conference on Intelligent Robots and Computer Vision*, (Boston, MA), pp. 72–78, 1985.

[25] G. S. van der Wal and J. O. Sinniger, "Real time pyramid transform architecture," in *SPIE Proc. Intelligent Robots and Comp. Vision*, (Boston, MA), pp. 300–305, 1985.

[26] P. J. Burt and G. van der Wal, "Iconic image analysis with the Pyramid Vision Machine (PVM)," in *IEEE Workshop on Computer Architecture for Pattern Analysis and Machine Intelligence*, (Seattle, WA), pp. 137–144, 1987.

A Parallel Network for Visual Cognition

Frank W. Adams, Jr., H. T. Nguyen, Raghu Raghavan, *Member, IEEE,* and Joseph Slawny

Abstract—This paper describes a parallel dynamical system designed to integrate model-based and data-driven approaches to image recognition in a neural network, and studies one component of the system in detail. That component is the translation-invariant network of probabilistic cellular automata (PCA's), which combines feature-detector outputs and collectively performs enhancement and recognition functions. Recognition is a novel application of the PCA. Given a model of the target object, conditions on the PCA weights are obtained which must be satisfied for object enhancement and noise rejection to occur, and "engineered" weights are constructed. For further refinement of the weights, a new training algorithm derived from optimal control theory is proposed. System operation is illustrated with examples derived from visual, infrared, and laser-radar imagery.

I. Introduction

THIS paper, which is a continuation of work first reported in [1], describes a multilayer, parallel feedback network that iteratively improves inferences regarding the presence of a target pattern in a scene. The network synthesizes model-based and data-driven approaches to recognition in a translation-invariant neural network. Structure imposed on the connections of the network embodies the model, while learning performed within that structure adjusts the network to the data. To accomplish iterative improvement, probabilistic cellular automata (PCA's) are introduced to suppress noise and enhance image features consistent with the target object. The purpose of the PCA network is to produce a "goal configuration" from image data. The goal configuration is defined as a configuration with a "1" where there is an object or a feature arising from the object of interest and a "0" everywhere else.

The primary focus of the paper is the PCA: what it is, how it is used for recognition, how its parameters reflect the model, and how to train it. Networks of CA's have long been a subject of image-processing research, especially in the literature on morphological methods [2]. However, both the motivation and the mathematical developments needed for the applications reported here are distinct from the earlier studies of CA's in image recognition. The statistical-physics literature on PCA's (see e.g., [3]) also has a different flavor, for there the primary concern is to construct the stationary measure characterizing

Manuscript received February 3, 1990; revised October 3, 1991. This work was supported by the Lockheed Independent Research Program under projects RDD504 and RDD506.

F. W. Adams, Jr., and H. T. Nguyen are with the Lockheed Palo Alto Research Laboratory, 9740/202, 3251 Hanover St., Palo Alto, CA 94304.

R. Raghavan was with the Lockheed Palo Alto Research Laboratory when this work was performed. He is now with the Institute of Systems Science, National University of Singapore, Kent Ridge, Singapore 0511.

J. Slawny is with the Center for Transport Theory and Mathematical Physics, Virginia Polytechnic Institute and State University, Blacksburg, VA 24060.

IEEE Log Number 9105995.

the long-time behavior, while for recognition the short-time behavior is most important.

It is almost a truism that a thoroughgoing systems approach is necessary for recognizing and categorizing images. In accord with this observation, much of the work reported here has been motivated by the attempt to incorporate prior knowledge in a recognition system based on a neural network. The system concept is briefly discussed in Section II. An example illustrating some of the system concepts is found in subsection V-A. Conference proceedings [1], [4] may also be consulted for a more complete description.

Section III defines the PCA and chooses a specific parameterization of it for further discussion. To aid interpretation of the parameters, limiting cases of the PCA are displayed. Section IV then develops the relationship between PCA parameters and the target model, and obtains from the model inequalities restricting the parameters. When the model is good, the PCA parameters so obtained can dramatically shorten learning time. Section V discusses some image recognition examples. Both visual imagery and multisensor laser radar and infrared images are used for demonstration. Section VI discusses learning in the PCA network and introduces new learning algorithms. The concluding section includes a brief comparison with other closely related methods.

II. System Operation

Before the neural-network explosion, image-processing literature could be roughly divided into studies of data-driven procedures for low-level vision and of model-based methods for high-level vision [6]. There are several reasons for this, of which we single out one. Low-level vision can use universal characteristics, such as statistical properties, to delimit boundaries of distinct regions, but restricting attention to universal characteristics is inherently limiting when the goal is recognition. In this application, it is advantageous to incorporate prior knowledge about the object and the context.

The structure of our system embodies an attempt to integrate model-based and data-driven approaches to learning. We structure the system data flow according to a hierarchical model of the object to be recognized but implement functions within the hierarchy in a data-driven manner. As in other neural nets, these functions can be learned from examples.

In this section, we discuss the system operating in its recognition mode, a block diagram of which is shown in Fig. 1. The issue of learning will be taken up in Section VI.

A. Model-Based Feature Detection

We begin with a model of the object to be recognized, and its decomposition into features. To recognize a tank, for example,

Reprinted from *IEEE Trans. Neural Networks*, vol. 3, no. 6, pp. 906–922, Nov. 1992.

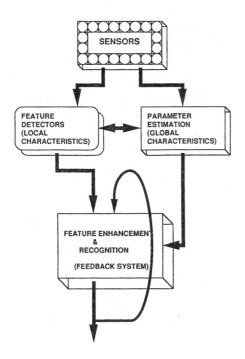

Fig. 1. Image recognition system. The interaction of the local and global characteristics to define a covariant feature detector system is shown as a schematic data flow diagram.

represents information at multiple resolutions.

The right half of Fig. 1 emphasizes that we have chosen a covariant rather than invariant method of feature detection, primarily because invariant methods of feature detection appear to lack the sensitivity needed for the more ambitious recognition tasks. By "covariant method" we mean that global parameters such as range, aspect, brightness, and contrast direct the construction of the feature detectors. For example, the range determines the sizes of the features being searched for. To elaborate the example, consider a perceptronlike feature detector (that is, a weighted sum of inputs followed by a sigmoid). The contrast in the image may determine how sharp the sigmoid can be, while the average brightness in a region of the image determines a bias or threshold. Thus, an important part of the recognition system is the independent extraction of these global parameters from the image, so as to accommodate variability of the features arising from aspect, range, motion, and illumination.

The collection of feature detectors at a particular hierarchical level provides, at each image point for that level, a set of numbers which constitutes an initial assignment for the object features. At a single point, more than one feature may be assigned a nonzero value. For convenience, we suppose all feature strengths lie between 0 and 1.

B. Feature Enhancement and Recognition

We now need to resolve ambiguities and conflicts among these initial assignments by combining and propagating information that originates at different image points. The bottom box of Fig. 1 represents the step in which ambiguities and conflicts among the detected features are resolved; the iterative nature is explicitly indicated. That box is the principal subject of the present paper. To combine evidence, we presently use a PCA, which involves Markovian dynamics with a spatial locality property and translation-invariant couplings. The PCA may be regarded as a feedback neural network with a probabilistic transition rule. By proper choice of inference weights and other parameters of the dynamical system, we hope to ensure that a few iterations will enhance the target's features and suppress features not belonging to it, yielding the correct goal configuration. The system is used dynamically, not asymptotically: it is designed for a short first-passage time to the neighborhood of the goal configuration and a long sojourn time in its neighborhood, rather than for long-time, or asymptotic, convergence to the goal.

Although the object model is organized hierarchically for optimum locality of inferences, the PCA feedback network may operate in a state space containing features from more than one hierarchical level. If so, and if the transition rules for lower-level features can depend on the values of higher-level features, then a question of synchrony arises from the differing spatial scales of the features. First consider a transition rule involving only the values of features at a single hierarchical level: in this case the PCA can operate in a completely parallel, or "synchronous," way. Then each time step of the dynamical system may be thought of as bringing in information to affect the value of a particular feature from a distance determined by the neighborhood of

we could use the decomposition of a tank into the component features shown in Fig. 2. The corresponding feature detectors are local in the sense that they are defined as translation-invariant window operators with windows of a limited size. That is, they examine a local region (window) of the image, the size of the window being determined by the scale of the feature. Thus the feature detectors are *not* scale invariant. We shall discuss this further below.

Locality is preserved for complex objects by hierarchical, multiresolution decomposition. The hierarchy reflects the natural hierarchy of the object's structure, namely the different spatial scales for the different features. Thus at the smallest scale, edge detectors are used, while at higher levels, we employ more sophisticated feature detectors whose spatial scale (measured in pixels) is larger. The consequent rescaling of lengths between hierarchical levels allows local inferences at a high level of the hierarchy to relate distant parts of a complex, extended object.

Fig. 2 shows this hierarchical decomposition of the example tank model. Sometimes this decomposition connects a level only to the ones directly above or below it. For example, we felt that a long line can be determined directly from a sequence of (short) edges. Sometimes, however, this connection between levels can be of longer range. For example, we found it necessary to have corner detectors examine inputs not only from the edges that may combine to make up the corner, but also from the original image as well. The reason is that the corner is almost at the same spatial scale as the edges and does require more information from a finer scale than the edges can provide. In each set of problems, the experience of the practitioners will determine the hierarchy, and this places no restriction on the dynamical system proposed in this paper. The superimposed spatial grid in Fig. 2 shows how the approach

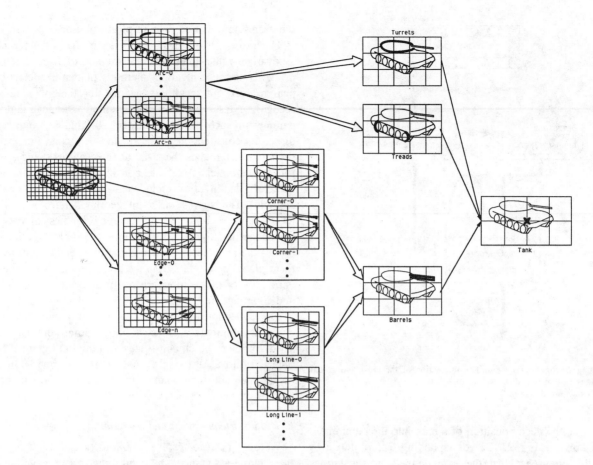

Fig. 2. Multiple-resolution hierarchical decomposition of tank into constituent features. Features of similar spatial scales are on the same level; the size of the features increases toward the bottom. The expansion of the spatial scale is indicated by the spacing of the grids.

direct connections. But when higher-level features are also involved, each will typically contain information from a larger region than the lower-level features do. In that case it is appropriate to iterate any portion of the network that is entirely confined to the lower level until it has collected information from a comparable region, before activating transition rules that update lower-level features according to the values of higher-level ones. The tank example of Section V mixes hierarchical levels in its PCA; our other examples are completely synchronous. Our theoretical development in subsection III-D assumes synchronous operation, but other results, in particular, the inequalities of subsection IV-A, are independent of synchrony.

This concludes our descriptive overview of the system operating in recognition mode. We now turn to the PCA itself.

III. THE PCA DYNAMICAL SYSTEM

In this section, we describe the PCA dynamics used for object enhancement and recognition. After introducing notation for the basic concepts, we give the PCA transition rule and present a parameterization which we shall use in all further discussion.

A. Definition of the PCA

The PCA is a transformation rule operating on a state space whose elements describe the image in terms of model features.

"Cellular" refers to the pixellated structure of the configuration space. The transformation rule is a Markov process having two additional properties: translation invariance and spatial locality. This subsection develops notation required to specify the PCA transformation rule.

The function of the PCA in the recognition system is to replace a noisy, ambiguous set of (static) feature data, representing a single static image, with a less noisy, less ambiguous set representing the same image. The second set is obtained from the first by iteratively applying the PCA transformation rule. The coordinate distinguishing successive iterates of the transformation rule is conventionally called time, to emphasize the fact that the transformation rule specifies a dynamical system; however, it has no relation to physical time or to the succession of input data in time.

At each hierarchical level of the model, image information is divided spatially into discrete cells, which we shall loosely call pixels, although (because of rescaling between hierarchical levels) only at the lowest level of the hierarchy will they necessarily correspond to the pixels of image data. Cells are indexed by a set Λ with elements i. Image information is represented in terms of a set Ω of features. We denote the strength of feature α at pixel i as C_i^α, $i \in \Lambda$, $\alpha \in \Omega$, and suppose that C_i^α assumes discrete values in the range $[0, 1]$. That is, for some integer $1/q$ (where q is called the quantum),

$$C_i^\alpha \in \{0, q, 2q, \cdots, 1\}. \tag{1}$$

The set of configurations C such that each component satisfies (1) is the state space C^q of the PCA dynamics. For practical purposes, $1/q$ is best chosen to be fairly small (say 10), but in the following discussion we shall consider both continuous ($q \to 0$) and binary ($q = 1$) variables.

To express the idea of locality, let N denote a subset of Λ consisting of neighbors of pixel 0. To emphasize translation invariance, we will use the additive notation $i + N$ for neighbors of pixel i. For convenience, we consider a pixel to be a neighbor of itself, that is, $0 \in N$. Whenever needed, we shall assume that $d \in N$ implies $0 \in d + N$. The restriction of the configuration C to the neighborhood $i + N$ is $C_{i+N} \in C_{i+N}^q$, where C_{i+N}^q is the restriction of the space C^q to the neighborhood $i + N$.

The PCA dynamics is defined on configurations $C \in C^q$ by a Markov process with transition probability $T(C, C')$ giving the probability of configuration C' at "time" $t + 1$ when the configuration at "time" t is known to be C. We require T to be spatially local and translation-invariant. In this paper we shall assume that the transition probabilities are independent of the "time" variable t, as implied by our notation, so that the Markov process is homogeneous; however, this assumption is not necessary. ("Time"-dependent transition probabilities are considered in Section VI.) A convenient representation of T with these properties is

$$T(C, C') = Z(C)^{-1} \exp[-\beta H(C, C')] \qquad (2)$$

where

$$H(C, C') = \sum_{i \in \Lambda} \phi(C_{i+N}, C_i') \qquad (3)$$

and

$$
\begin{aligned}
Z(C) &\equiv \sum_{C' \in \mathbf{C}^q} \exp[-\beta H(C, C')] \\
&= \prod_{i \in \Lambda} \sum_{C' \in \mathbf{C}_i^q} \exp[-\beta \phi(C_{i+N}, C')].
\end{aligned} \qquad (4)
$$

The factorization of $Z(C)$ in (4) follows from (3).[1] Translation invariance is enforced by using the same function ϕ for each $i \in \Lambda$. Throughout this work, we shall use what we consider to be the simplest useful form for ϕ, namely a sum of linear and bilinear interactions and a quadratic term:

$$
\begin{aligned}
\phi(C_{i+N}, C_i') = &-\sum_{\alpha \in \Omega} \mu^\alpha C_i'^\alpha - \sum_{d \in N} \sum_{\alpha, \gamma \in \Omega} C_i'^\alpha J_d^{\alpha\gamma} C_{i+d}^\gamma \\
&+ \lambda \sum_{\alpha \in \Omega} (C_i^\alpha - C_i'^\alpha)^2.
\end{aligned} \qquad (5)
$$

We refer to λ, μ^α, and $J_d^{\alpha\gamma}$ as the PCA weights; in addition, we sometimes use the terms "couplings" for the bilinear

[1] With (3) and (4), (2) becomes a product over the lattice points $i \in \Lambda$, with each factor depending only on the neighborhood N. Thus (2) defines a parallel, translation-invariant, local Markov process. Although the notation $H(C, C')$ is standard in the PCA literature [3], H is not an energy function (Hamiltonian), and PCA dynamics differs from the dynamics defined from an energy function by the Metropolis ("Monte-Carlo") algorithm. Setting $q = 1$ in (1) and $\lambda = \mu = 0$ in (5) reduces the PCA transition rule to Little dynamics; Peretto [6] relates this case to other neural-network transition rules and clarifies the relation to Gibbs states.

weights $J_d^{\alpha\gamma}$, "biases" for the linear weights μ^α, and "memory coefficient" for λ. Because of the normalization factor, an arbitrary function of the prior variable C_{i+N} may be added to $\phi(C_{i+N}, C_i')$ without changing the transition probabilities. This allows (5) to be rewritten in a convenient equivalent form:

$$\phi(C_{i+N}, C_i') = \lambda \sum_{\alpha \in \Omega} \left[C_i'^\alpha - C_i^\alpha - \frac{1}{2\lambda} V^\alpha(C_{i+N}) \right]^2 \qquad (6)$$

where

$$V^\alpha(C_{i+N}) = \mu^\alpha + \sum_d \sum_{\gamma \in \Omega} J_d^{\alpha\gamma} C_{i+d}^\gamma. \qquad (7)$$

Thus the most probable value(s) of $C_i'^\alpha$ are the values permitted by (1) which lie closest to the minimum of (6) considered as a continuous function of $C_i'^\alpha$.

B. The Large-β "Deterministic" Limit

Since our aim is to be able to integrate prior knowledge, it is important to interpret the PCA weights. To aid us in that, we develop the large-β and large-λ limits of the transformation rule defined by (2) to (5) and interpret those parameters.

For large β ("low temperature"), the Markov chain defined by (2) evolves for most of the time along trajectories minimizing H at each time step, i.e., C' evolves from C such that

$$H(C, C') = E(C) \equiv \min_{C' \in \mathbf{C}^q} H(C, C'). \qquad (8)$$

If we regard H as a cost function, this observation implies that the dynamical system tries to improve the configuration in the sense determined by H. To prove (8), let the set of "ground" states belonging to C be defined as

$$
\begin{aligned}
\mathbf{G}(C) &\equiv \left\{ C' \in \mathbf{C}^q : H(C, C') = E(C) \right\} \\
&= \Bigg\{ C' \in \mathbf{C}^q : \sum_{i \in \Lambda} \sum_{\alpha \in \Omega} \\
&\qquad \left[C_i'^\alpha - C_i^\alpha - \frac{1}{2\lambda} V^\alpha(C_{i+N}) \right]^2 \text{ is minimal} \Bigg\},
\end{aligned} \qquad (9)
$$

where the second characterization follows from (6). Since the configuration space is finite for $q > 0$, there is a strictly positive gap $\Delta(C)$ between the ground states and other "excited" states. By expanding in powers of $\exp[-\beta\Delta(C)]$, we find that, for $\beta \to \infty$,

$$T_\infty(C, C') = \begin{cases} |\mathbf{G}(C)|^{-1}, & C' \in \mathbf{G}(C) \\ 0, & \text{otherwise,} \end{cases} \qquad (10)$$

where $T_\infty(C, C') = \lim_{\beta \to \infty} T(C, C')$, and $|X|$ is the number of points in X. Thus the limiting process with transition matrix T_∞ minimizes H at each time step, choosing each of the equivalent minimizing configurations with equal probability. Although (10) is still probabilistic when $G(C)$ contains more than one element, we shall refer to it as the deterministic limit of the corresponding probabilistic dynamics.

C. The Large-λ Continuous-"Time" Limit

When $q \rightarrow 0$, so that the configuration variables C_i^α become continuous, then also $\Delta(C) \rightarrow 0$, and the above argument breaks down. However, a result of the same form holds when $q = 0$. In this case,[2] we take $\lambda \rightarrow \infty$ before $\beta \rightarrow \infty$ to determine a continuous-time process whose transition probability for small time intervals approximates the large-λ limit of $T(C, C')$. This is accomplished by computing from the large-λ limit of $T(C, C')$ the coefficients of the differential backward equation [7] for the continuous-time process. The stochastic differential equation corresponding [8] to this differential backward equation turns out to be

$$dC_i^\alpha = V^\alpha(C_{i+N})dt + \beta^{-1/2}dW. \qquad (11)$$

Because the backward equation is subject to reflecting boundary conditions on $[0, 1]^{|\Lambda||\Omega|}$ (the range of the continuous configuration variable C), solutions to (11) cannot be constructed in the usual way [8]. In the limit $\beta \rightarrow \infty$, however, the noise process W disappears, taking this difficulty with it, and a formal solution of the remaining ordinary differential equation for the limiting trajectories is easily obtained.

Equations (9) and (10) evidently give a discrete approximation to the large-β limit of (11), with the identification $dt \leftrightarrow (2\lambda)^{-1}$. Note that all PCA parameters except β remain in the $\beta \rightarrow \infty$ limiting form (9), and all but β and λ remain in (11). The deterministic $\beta \rightarrow \infty$ limit therefore contains a significant part of the relationship between PCA behavior and PCA weights.

D. Special Case: Symmetric Couplings

When the couplings are symmetric in the sense that

$$J_d^{\alpha\gamma} = J_{-d}^{\gamma\alpha} \qquad (12)$$

then $V(C)$ is a gradient. Using vector notation $V_i^\alpha(C) = V^\alpha(C_{i+N})$ we have $V(C) = -\nabla_C h(C)$, where

$$h(C) = -\sum_{i \in \Lambda} \sum_{\alpha \in \Omega} \left[\mu^\alpha C_i^\alpha + \frac{1}{2} \sum_{d \in N} \sum_{\gamma \in \Omega} C_i^\alpha J_d^{\alpha\gamma} C_{i+d}^\gamma \right] \qquad (13)$$

and H can be written

$$H(C, C') = C' \cdot \nabla_C h(C) + \lambda|C - C'|^2 \qquad (14)$$

(up to an additive function of the prior configuration C). According to (9) and (10), when $\beta \rightarrow \infty$ the final states C' are "ground states" in $G(C)$, i.e., the element(s) of C^q closest to

$$C' = C + \frac{1}{2\lambda}V(C) = C + \frac{1}{2\lambda}\nabla_C h(C), \qquad (15)$$

where (13) is used to obtain the second form of (15) from the first. Consequently, when (12) holds, the Markov process is specified by (14) and performs an approximate gradient descent on h for large β, with larger λ corresponding to smaller steps. Observe that (12) is required in order to characterize the process as gradient descent.

---

[2] The large-λ limit gives a very different continuous-time process when $q > 0$.

For finite β, the PCA makes unfavorable steps with nonzero probability, which can help avoid local minima of $h(C)$ when (12) holds. An analogous advantage is also to be expected from a probabilistic transition rule when (12) does not hold.

IV. RELATION OF PCA WEIGHTS TO A MODEL

Practical use of a dynamical system for recognition means applying the transformation rule a small number of times and accepting the resulting configuration as output. Consequently, the dynamical system must develop rapidly from its initial state to the neighborhood of a state representing a recognized object (or the absence thereof), and the probability must be low that it leaves the neighborhood before its configuration is examined. In the language of Markov processes, the first-passage time to the neighborhood of a goal configuration must be short, and the sojourn time in that neighborhood must be long.

In this section, we relate PCA weights to the object model from both short-time and long-time points of view. In subsection A, we obtain relations among PCA weights which can be used to determine their magnitudes by requiring correct short-time behavior when the PCA starts from prior configurations for which that behavior is known. In our treatment of this approach, the model takes the form of a set of ideal goal configurations demonstrating how features in Ω arrange themselves to represent the object. This result is quite general, but it relates such a large number of parameters that, without special assumptions, it can only be exploited numerically. In subsection B we use such special assumptions to construct a set of weights to which the inequalities can be applied (at least for toy problems) analytically. We start from a static model expressed as a set of feature-pairing rules. Such rules allow us to exploit special assumptions to construct an energy landscape whose minima represent goal configurations consistent with the model. The special assumptions include couplings that satisfy the symmetry condition (12) in order to take advantage of the results of subsection III-D. We consider the energy landscape to be related to long-time behavior in the sense that over long time intervals, energy minima should be the most likely configurations of a PCA constructed from an energy landscape. We will not attempt to make this intuition more precise or extend it to PCA's that do not possess an energy landscape. Applying the inequalities of subsection IV-A then puts bounds on the remaining free parameters to determine a set of PCA weights which may be used, for example, to start a learning procedure from prior knowledge. An explicit example of the synthesis is given for a toy problem in subsection IV-C.

The development of subsections A–C does not lead to complete understanding of the PCA weights. In particular, the construction of PCA weights in subsection B is carried out in a very restrictive framework; many other sets of weights will be approximately equivalent for the recognition application. Relaxing the symmetry condition (12) permits adjustments which give the PCA superior short-time behavior without changing sojourn times to a degree significant for this application; some heuristic arguments for this point will be found in subsection D. The significance of the simplifications of subsection B is the availability of a starting point which needs only the model, and not any presentation of examples. Subsequent learning procedures may therefore be sped up considerably.

A. Prior Information and Short-Time Behavior

If we know the desired short-term PCA behavior—say that feature α ought to increase or decrease at the origin—for some configuration C_N given in a neighborhood N of the origin, then we also know something about the weights of a PCA that has the desired behavior. Let Δ^α be a minimum change in the correct direction, i.e., $|\Delta^\alpha| = q$. According to (3),

$$\phi(C_N, C_0 + \Delta^\alpha) - \phi(C_N, C_0) < 0 \qquad (16)$$

is required to favor this change over no change. Substituting (6), we obtain

$$\lambda q < \text{sign}(\Delta^\alpha) V^\alpha(C_N). \qquad (17)$$

For $q < 1$ it may also make sense to limit the magnitude of the change to less than some value p, $q < p$, so that not too much initial information is discarded in a single step. Setting $|\Delta^\alpha| = p$ and reversing the inequality in (16) then gives an upper limit:

$$\lambda p \geq \text{sign}(\Delta^\alpha) V^\alpha(C_N). \qquad (18)$$

If we have a model of the target object, then we do know the desired behavior at least for configurations which are close to the model, and we should be able to use (17) and perhaps also (18) to capture this knowledge in terms of the PCA weights. We shall formalize this idea for later use in relating PCA weights to the model.

Suppose our prior knowledge consists of (small set of) "tinkertoy" construction(s) representing the target, whose components are features in Ω. Since the weights are translation invariant, it suffices to consider only a neighborhood N of the origin. By translating N over all points of the construction(s), we obtain a complete set $I_N \subset C_N^1$ of ideal configurations whose components C_d^α are all either 0 or 1. Let

$$\mathbf{I}_N^\alpha = \{C \in \mathbf{I}_N : C_0^\alpha = 1\} \qquad (19)$$

denote the set of ideal configurations consistent with α, and let $F_N^\alpha = I_N - I_N^\alpha$ denote those inconsistent with α. Let a star denote the doubled sets where each configuration is duplicated by another which is the same except that $C_0^\alpha = 0$. Applying (17) and (18), we obtain

$$\lambda q < \min_{C \in \mathbf{I}_N^{\alpha *}} \{V^\alpha(C_N)\} \leq \max_{C \in \mathbf{I}_N^{\alpha *}} \{V^\alpha(C_N)\} \leq \lambda p$$
$$-\lambda p \leq \min_{C \in \mathbf{F}_N^{\alpha *}} \{V^\alpha(C_N)\} \leq \max_{C \in \mathbf{F}_N^{\alpha *}} \{V^\alpha(C_N)\} < -\lambda q.$$
$$(20)$$

These relations are the weakest possible, in the sense that only ideal model goal configurations are examined. Intuitively, at least (17) should hold for any configuration sufficiently close to an ideal configuration, e.g., for $C + D$, $C \in I_N^{\alpha *}$,

$D \in C_N^q$, $|D| < b$. One can easily show that requiring (17) to hold also when each configuration in I_N grows into a ball of radius b (only one quadrant of which actually lies within C_N^q) is equivalent to replacing λq by $\lambda q + b|J^\alpha|$ in (20).

Relations (20) must hold whenever the short-time behavior of the PCA is consistent with the model given by I_N. They relate the memory coefficient λ to the quantum q, the maximum step p, and the PCA weights. In the example of subsection IV-C we shall use these relations to evaluate PCA weights explicitly for a simple model.

B. Prior Information and Energy Landscape

If we want the PCA to have a long sojourn time in the neighborhood of a goal configuration, a reasonable first approach is to construct couplings satisfying (12) such that the minimum-energy configurations for the corresponding energy function $h(C)$ are exactly the goal configurations. Such couplings may not be optimal, in the sense that there may exist couplings not satisfying (12) with superior short-time behavior, but symmetric couplings may offer a good starting point.

To carry out this program, specify the feature pairings permitted in a particular target model by a matrix[3] $E_d^{\alpha\gamma}$, $\alpha, \gamma \in \Omega$, $d \in N$:

$$E_{j-i}^{\alpha\gamma} = \begin{cases} 1, & \alpha \text{ at site } i \text{ allowed with } \gamma \text{ at site } j \\ 0, & \text{otherwise} \end{cases} \qquad (21)$$

with the convention that $E_0^{\alpha\alpha} = 1$. Define a "goal configuration" as a configuration of zeros and ones which is completely consistent with the model (21):

$$\mathbf{I}' = \{C \in C^1 : C_i^\alpha (E_d^{\alpha\gamma} - 1) C_{i+d}^\gamma = 0$$
$$\forall \alpha, \gamma \in \Omega, i \in \Lambda, d \in N\}. \qquad (22)$$

That I' be nonempty is a consistency requirement on all models. Set $\mu^\alpha = 0$ and with $\rho > 0$ let[4]

$$J_d^{\alpha\gamma} = \rho(E_d^{\alpha\gamma} - 1). \qquad (23)$$

Because the model is static, E and therefore J are symmetric in the sense of (12). According to (14), PCA time development in the large-β limit approximates gradient descent to a (possibly local) minimum of $h(C)$ defined by (13). Evidently the global minimum of h in C^1 is zero, and it is attained at all configurations in I'.

However, the set I' is too big, because couplings (23) treat the absence of a feature anywhere as consistent with the model.

---

[3] For more complicated objects, such that E is not easy to write down immediately, we may use an automated procedure that produces E from a clear or synthesized image. Given the model decomposition into features and a simplified drawing of the target object, we form the correlations

$$K_d^{\alpha\gamma} = \sum_i C_{i+d}^\alpha C_i^\gamma$$

by applying the given feature detectors to the model image. A matrix of the form (21) is obtained by thresholding $K_d^{\alpha\gamma}$. Alternatively, to start a learning procedure one can use initial PCA couplings $J_d^{\alpha\gamma} = K_d^{\alpha\gamma}$ directly.

[4] In this paper, we discuss only bilinear couplings. Often, inference rules are in the form, for example, that feature α occurs only in conjunction with both features γ and δ in appropriate positions. The most direct way to incorporate these would be with trilinear and higher order couplings. An alternative would be to have hidden units, but keep the couplings bilinear (see [9]).

In the extreme case, an isolated feature, which for recognition purposes is noise, is considered consistent with the model as long as no other feature is present to contradict it. We need to remove isolated features and partial targets from I' in order to make it agree with the notion of the model used in subsection IV-A. For this purpose we impose additional structure on the configuration space. First let us partition the feature set Ω into disjoint subsets Θ_k, $k = 1, \cdots, M$, such that only one feature of each Θ_k can "really" be present at a single pixel. For each Θ_k we introduce a "null feature" n_k representing the absence of all features in Θ_k, and set $\hat{\Theta}_k = \Theta_k \cup \{n_k\}$, $\hat{\Omega} = \hat{\Theta}_1 \cup \cdots \cup \hat{\Theta}_M$. (In the extreme case where all features may be present at the same pixel, we have doubled the feature set.) We write $\hat{C}^q$ for the augmented configuration space. To enforce the mutual exclusiveness of the features in each Θ_k, we (temporarily) impose on $\hat{C}^q$ the constraint

$$\sum_{\alpha \in \hat{\Theta}_k} C_i^\alpha = 1, \qquad k = 1, \cdots, M \qquad \forall i \in \Lambda, \qquad (24)$$

which is in addition to (1). For $q = 1$, (24) implies that exactly one configuration variable of each Θ_k at a given pixel has value 1, and the rest vanish: this expresses mutual exclusiveness within the feature sets Θ_k.

Now we can distinguish between a complete target and an obscured one by adding entries to E that forbid certain null–nonnull feature pairings. To permit the complete absence of targets we must have $E_d^{n'n''} = 1$ for all d and all pairs of null features n', n''. Relying on the constraint (24), we set $E_0^{\alpha\gamma} = 1$ for $\alpha, \gamma \in \Theta_k$, $k = 1, \cdots, M$, so that nonzero self-couplings $J_0^{\alpha\gamma}$ occur only for $\alpha \in \Theta_{k'}$, $\gamma \in \Theta_k$, $k' \neq k$. After this augmentation we should be able to characterize the ideal configurations of subsection IV-A as

$$\mathbf{I} = \Bigg\{ C \in \hat{C}^1 : \sum_{\alpha \in \hat{\Theta}_{k'}} \sum_{\gamma \in \hat{\Theta}_{k''}} C_i^\alpha E_d^{\alpha\gamma} C_{i+d}^\gamma = 1$$

$$\forall k', k'' \in \{1, \cdots, M\}, i \in \Lambda, d \in N \Bigg\}. \qquad (25)$$

Evidently (25) specifies the global minima of $h(C)$ in the space $\hat{C}^1$ subject to (24). By adding to $h(C)$ penalty terms

$$\frac{1}{2} f \sum_{i \in \Lambda} \sum_{\alpha \in \hat{\Omega}} C_i^\alpha (1 - C_i^\alpha) + \frac{1}{2} \sum_{i \in \Lambda} \sum_{k=1}^M g_k \left(1 - \sum_{\alpha \in \hat{\Theta}_k} C_i^\alpha \right)^2, \qquad (26)$$

where f and all g_k are positive, we can extend the assertion to the space $\hat{C}^q$ without the constraint (24). These additional terms can be included in the form (13) by setting the bias to

$$\mu^\alpha = -\frac{1}{2} f + g_k, \qquad \alpha \in \hat{\Theta}_k \qquad (27)$$

and adding extra self-couplings $J_0^{\alpha\gamma} \to J_0^{\alpha\gamma} + K^{\alpha\gamma}$, where

$$K^{\alpha\gamma} = \begin{cases} f - g_k, & \alpha = \gamma \in \hat{\Theta}_k \\ -g_k, & \alpha, \gamma \in \hat{\Theta}_k, \alpha \neq \gamma \\ 0 & \text{otherwise.} \end{cases} \qquad (28)$$

Now the global minima of h are exactly those configurations consistent with the model. The null features can be eliminated by means of (24), changing h by an additive constant. The couplings simplify to

$$\check{K}^{\alpha\gamma} = \begin{cases} 2f, & \alpha = \gamma \\ f, & \alpha \neq \gamma, \, \alpha, \gamma \in \Theta_k \\ 0, & \text{otherwise} \end{cases}$$

$$\check{J}_d^{\alpha\gamma} = J_d^{\alpha\gamma} - J_d^{\alpha n} - J_d^{n'\gamma} + J_d^{n'n},$$
$$= \rho \left[E_d^{\alpha\gamma} - E_d^{\alpha n} - E_d^{n'\gamma} + E_d^{n'n} \right]$$

$$\text{where } \alpha, n' \in \hat{\Theta}_{k'}, \qquad \gamma, n \in \hat{\Theta}_k. \qquad (29)$$

The biases become

$$\check{\mu}^\alpha = \mu^\alpha - \mu^{n'}$$
$$+ \sum_{k=1}^M \left[K^{\alpha n_k} - K^{n'n_k} + \sum_{d \in N} \left(J_d^{\alpha n_k} - J_d^{n'n_k} \right) \right],$$
$$\alpha, n' \in \hat{\Theta}_{k'}$$

$$= -f + \rho \sum_{k=1}^M \sum_{d \in N} [E_d^{\alpha n_k} - 1], \qquad (30)$$

where the second forms for $\check{J}$ and $\check{\mu}$ depend on (23) for J and (27) for μ. The energy function $h(C)$ defined from these biases and couplings contains only the parameters f and ρ.

C. Example: Two-Dimensional "Wheels"

In subsection IV-B we have constructed an energy function, $h(C)$, whose minima are the goal configurations of a target model specified by feature-pairing rules. Our intent in doing so was to use $h(C)$ to obtain PCA transition probabilities via (14) which would have long sojourn times in the neighborhood of goal configurations. Application of the PCA to recognition imposes an additional requirement: that the first goal configuration visited be the "correct" one corresponding to the starting configuration. To ensure this requires adjusting the parameters of $h(C)$ such that conditions (20), which were obtained by considering short-time behavior, are satisfied. In general these inequalities would have to be solved numerically because the number of configurations to examine could be quite large. In this subsection, we do it explicitly for a model simple enough to be analytically tractable and show that the PCA so obtained operates as expected.

This success does not, however, imply that our understanding of the PCA weights is complete or that learned weights will necessarily be similar to those constructed by this procedure. In fact, learned weights do not necessarily approach those constructed here. What this demonstration shows is that a model-based starting point for learning procedures is available.

Our simple model is the two-dimensional "wheel" shown in Fig. 3. It lives on the white squares of a checkerboard (the black squares being deleted) and consists of eight "arcs" of different orientations, which we denote by eight points of the compass. The arcs are mutually exclusive, and the null feature is denoted n. Our example uses a 5×5 neighborhood containing 13 white (undeleted) cells, with the automaton

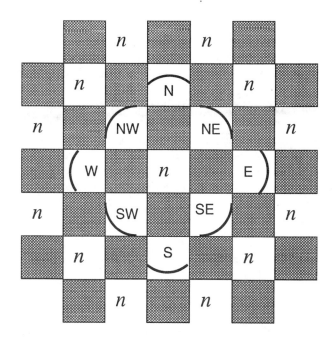

Fig. 3. Two-dimensional "wheel" model. Each of 12 white squares around the central one contains a point of the compass for one of eight arcs; "n" indicates no arc.

n	n, S	n			n	$n, W,$ SW, S	$n, W,$ SW, S
n	$n, W,$ $SW, S,$ SE, E, N	n			N	$n, NW,$ $W, SW,$ S, SE	$n, W,$ SW, S
NW	n	NE			NE	E	n
		N	n	n			
		NW	$n, W,$ $SW, S,$ NE	n			
		n	SE	E			
NW	N	NE			NE	n	n
W	n	E			n	$n, NW,$ $N, W, S,$ SW, E	n, W
SW	S	SE			SE	n	n

Fig. 4. Diagrammatic representation of $E_d^{\alpha\gamma}$ for two-dimensional "wheels." Only the northeast quadrant of the neighborhood is represented here. The automaton (center of the neighborhood) occupies the "home cell" in the lower left corner of this diagram. Bold entries in subsquares of the home cell specify the posterior-configuration arc associated with that subsquare of every cell; in other cells, subsquare entries specify the prior-configuration arcs of that cell which may pair with that subsquare's posterior-configuration arc located in the home cell.

$(d = 0)$ located in the center cell. Rather than tabulate $E_d^{\alpha\gamma}$, we show diagrammatically in Fig. 4 the nonzero elements corresponding to the northeast quadrant of the neighborhood; other quadrants may be obtained by symmetry. Because alternate squares of the checkerboard are missing, blank cells in Fig. 4 do not exist. The final-configuration features at the automaton location are shown bold in subsquares of the lower-left-corner cell, in positions corresponding to their location in the complete wheel. The prior variables that may pair with each are listed in the corresponding subsquares of the neighbor cells. These entries give the nonzero elements of $E_d^{\alpha\gamma}$. For example, n in the top left corner indicates that the null feature is the only "arc" that may be in the nearest cell due north of an NW arc; the NW two subsquares to the south of it is the only arc of that cell that may pair with SW to the south.

In Appendix I we evaluate the bounds (20) using special properties of this E matrix and determine permissible values for the parameters q, λ, and ρ. Fig. 6 gives the result of operating with that PCA on a wheel from the clear infrared image shown in Fig. 5. Before applying the feature detectors, the image was corrupted with Gaussian noise and by obscuration, which is more representative of streaks from clutter. The simulation actually includes two noncommunicating PCA's—a second on the black squares of Fig. 3—but the ideal wheel before corruption occupies only one sublattice. The performance in this case compares favorably with that with learned weights.

D. Nonsymmetric Couplings

A model-based recognizer infers the presence of an object from that of its components. This is an inductive process, in which the frequency of occurrence of a feature in the model is as significant as its geometric relationship with other features. For example, a null feature will have many more

Fig. 5. Original infrared image for example of Fig. 6.

valid pairings than will nonnull features, so that there will be many more ways that a null feature can be produced in the final configuration. Similarly, a corner (in a vehicle model like that of subsection V-A) much more strongly implies a neighboring long line than a line implies a corner, since clutter in an image often occurs as streaks. Another way to look at it is as follows. In deductive logic, the proposition $\sim b \Rightarrow \sim a$ is strictly equivalent to $a \Rightarrow b$, but because prior probabilities of occurrence must be considered in inductive inference, the confidence with which one infers $\sim a$ from $\sim b$ may differ from one's confidence in b on the evidence of a. For example, on leaving a building one may infer from dry pavement with fair confidence that it has not rained in the last half hour, but damp pavement could indicate irrigation as well as precipitation. Our intuition of such context-sensitive frequencies of occurrence is naturally expressed as strengths of the inferences. Since the PCA—unlike energy-landscape methods such as simulated annealing—is sensitive to asymmetry in the couplings, asymmetry of the couplings provides a natural way for the PCA to capture this intrinsic directionality of inductive inference.

In relation to the development of subsection IV-B, what we are contemplating is to add an antisymmetric part to the symmetric couplings of (22) such that, for example, a corner in the prior state causes a neighboring long line in the final state

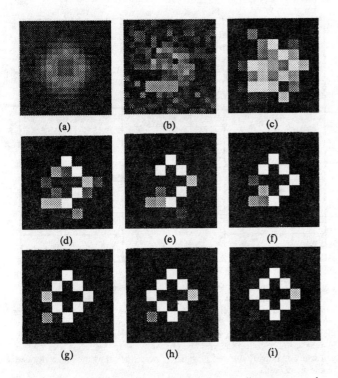

(a)   (b)   (c)

(d)   (e)   (f)

(g)   (h)   (i)

Fig. 6. Noisy "wheel" clarified by PCA using couplings constructed as described in the text. (a) One wheel from Fig. 5. (b) Same with added Gaussian noise and two rectangular obscurations. (c) Composite image of feature-detector outputs. (d)–(i) Composite images of PCA configuration after one to six iterations.

with greater probability than a prior long line implies a final neighboring corner. This method is intuitive and introduces free parameters to help adjust PCA behavior in the desired way. However, it is not yet clear to us whether asymmetry is *required* for this purpose, that is, whether an equivalent symmetric set of PCA weights can always be found. One theoretical difficulty is to determine a notion of equivalence for the PCA in this application. In subsection IV-B, we considered energy landscapes that had the same minimum-energy states to be equivalent, but this definition is not restrictive enough for the PCA. In particular, one can easily construct two sets of weights with the same ground states, one set satisfying and the other violating the inequalities (20); for recognition purposes the sets are not equivalent. On the other hand not every small change in the weights will be significant in the small number of iterations used for recognition. What we do know from experience is that when we have trained PCA's, even starting from a symmetric set of weights, the trained couplings are asymmetric. The following example gives a concrete illustration of these intuitive arguments.

Example: One-Dimensional "Wheels": Imaging a line drawn through the center of a circle. What the line "knows" of the circle is essentially the two intersections of the circle with the line. We shall imagine that the left and right intersections are distinguishable, and model a "wheel" in one dimension as a left arc "(" adjacent to a right arc ")"; the null feature we represent by the symbol "-." The configuration variables at each point i of the one-dimensional lattice constitute a triplet $C_i = (l_i, r_i, n_i)$ of numbers in $[0, 1]$. The phase space of this system is the set of $q^{-3|\Lambda|}$ possible configurations, where $|\Lambda|$ is the number of cells in the line Λ.

In addition to defining a wheel as adjacent left and right arcs, we impose the requirement that wheels be separated by at least one "empty" cell. An example of a valid configuration is the following, which we might imagine as representing a pair of four-wheeled vehicles:

```
----------()-()-()-()--------------()-()-()-()----------
```

On the other hand, both nonnull groups of the following example are forbidden:

```
--------()()-----))--------------
```

If we use a three-point neighborhood, $N = \{-1, 0, 1\}$, E is then as given in Table I. The first 1 in the table is $E_{-1}^{(}$, which indicates that "(" is permitted at i when "-" is at $i-1$ in the prior configuration, i.e., "-(" is permitted. The zero below it indicates that "-)" is not permitted.

To visualize configurations, we display only one of these symbols whenever that variable dominates the others. In case more than one is important at a point of the lattice, we display "$*$"; and where none are we show a period. (In the goal configuration the latter two symbols will not appear.) For our initial configuration, we use (31), shown at the bottom of the page, where the numbers below the symbolic display give the initial feature values. We display symbolically the first few iterations of the cellular automaton using weights $J_d^{\alpha\gamma} = 2E_d^{\alpha\gamma} - 1$ and *no* biases or memory term ($\lambda = 0$, $\mu = 0$):

```
---)---(*--
--**---(*--
--**----**--
```

A goal configuration is not reached. We argue however that there should be completed wheels at both locations where the stars are, in particular at the third and fourth points. This is because, given the strong right arc at the fourth point, the weak left arc at the third is "unlikely" to be noise. In other words, we must discount the evidence for no arcs, if there is even somewhat weak evidence for arcs. If we introduce an asymmetry by lowering the positive couplings for prior state "-" at neighbor sites ($d \neq 0$) from 1 to 0.8, the dynamical system develops to --()----()-- as desired. Reducing also the couplings for prior "-" at the same site ($d = 0$) speeds the development yet more. Further reducing the neighbor

	-	-	-	)	-	-	-	-	(	*	-	-	
(	0.00	0.00	0.45	0.00	0.00	0.10	0.00	0.00	1.00	0.00	0.00	0.00	(31)
)	0.00	0.00	0.00	0.70	0.00	0.00	0.00	0.00	0.00	1.00	0.00	0.00	
-	1.00	1.00	0.85	0.50	1.00	1.00	1.00	1.00	0.50	0.80	1.00	1.00	

TABLE I
PAIRINGS FOR ONE-DIMENSIONAL "WHEELS"

Final	Left Neighbor			Self			Right Neighbor		
	(	)	-	(	)	-	(	)	-
(	0	0	1	1	0	0	0	1	0
)	1	0	0	0	1	0	0	0	1
-	0	1	1	0	0	1	1	0	1

couplings with both prior and posterior feature equal to "-" also speeds development to the goal.

Inequalities analogous to (20) can also be derived for models with $\lambda = 0$ if we assume a specific form for the same-site $(d = 0)$ couplings; we find that couplings of the form $\rho E_d^{\alpha\gamma} - \sigma$ with $\rho = 2$, $\sigma = 1$, as used above, do not satisfy these inequalities. If we set $\sigma = -0.75$, $\rho = 2.5$ to satisfy the inequalities (still with no bias or memory term), the goal reached from (31) is --------( )--. Thus symmetric weights of a simple form do better than a matrix of ± 1's and worse than an asymmetric set of weights. By introducing a memory term and ensuring inequalities (17) are satisfied, one can obtain the correct goal without asymmetric couplings. However, in all cases we have studied, permitting asymmetry gives faster arrival at a goal configuration without causing premature departure from that neighborhood. That this can happen is not surprising, for the total number of PCA iterations is in practice not large. We have also determined couplings by training with new methods, and asymmetry then occurs naturally.

V. IMAGE RECOGNITION EXAMPLES

In subsection IV-C we gave a recognition example based on real infrared imagery. The image was relatively clean and the pattern very symmetrical. For further illustration of PCA behavior, we briefly discuss two more examples, one based on laser-radar range and infrared images of a tank and the other based on a catalog photograph of a touchtone telephone.

A. Tank Image Data and Models

The tank image data are shown in parts (a) and (b) of Fig. 7, which are respectively a laser-radar range image and an infrared image. For this exercise, we ignore the reflectivity and velocity (Doppler) information from laser radar. Fig. 7(a) cannot show the precision of the available range information, since the display has 8-bit precision while the data contain 16 bits. Evidently different information is available from the two sources. For example, wheels are frequently clearly visible in infrared images but not in laser-radar images, and so can potentially be used in recognition with the former but not the latter.

For this exercise we use the decomposition of a tank into component features shown in Fig. 2. This model was constructed ad hoc and not from study of model-based tank recognition; it is designed for easy conceptualization rather than superior recognition performance. As such, it is suited to the present purpose of illustrating the interaction of model and PCA dynamics in the process of recognition. Because

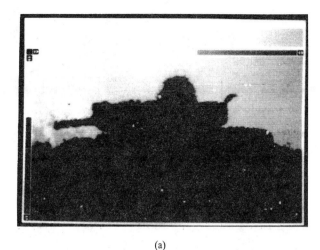

(a)

(b)

Fig. 7. (a) High-resolution laser-radar image of tank. (b) Simultaneous infrared image of the same.

recognition performance should depend on model details, the example should be examined not for bottom-line performance, but for the relationship of intermediate results to the model and to the eventual interpretation.

To highlight this relationship, we concentrate on one typical portion: combination of corners and long lines to form the barrel. Fig. 8 shows more details of this portion of the hierarchical model. The PCA state space consists of corners ($crnn$) and the leftmost points of long lines ($bllnn$); to construct these, edges ($edgen$) and long lines ($llnn$) are also required. These features are initially identified by perceptronlike detectors [10], trained on completely synthetic features by a standard backpropagation technique. Any other convenient method could be used, including standard image processing techniques; however, it is important that the outputs of the detectors be coded in a form suitable for use by the dynamical system. This means that the outputs be numbers in the range from 0 to 1 (or any other suitable range), where high numbers indicate the presence of the indicated feature and low numbers its absence. When we choose a simple perceptronlike form for the feature detectors (i.e., a weighted sum followed by a nonlinear transformation), we must deal with the covariance problems discussed in subsection II-A. For example, the initial setting of the bias is determined by the average brightness in the region

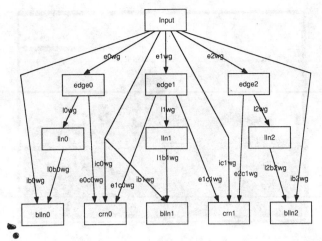

Fig. 8. Detail of laser-radar tank-barrel model. The highest-level features are at the bottom.

of the object. The scale of the features is determined by the relative sizes of the model elements and by an independent estimate of the size of the object in the field of view. Use of image processing methods for this scaling was discussed in [11].

The result of using these one-pass feature detectors on images of Fig. 7 is shown in Fig. 9. As "recognition" of the tank it is unsatisfactory. For example, there are multiple matches when only one "true" feature is present; the strongest matches are not necessarily where the barrel is and the corners corresponding to the barrel cannot yet be identified. This state of affairs is a desirable start for illustrating recognition with PCA dynamics, for it is the intended function of the dynamical system to resolve such conflicts and ambiguities.

B. Recognition of Laser-Radar Range Image

We first discuss use of the PCA to enhance only the laser-radar range data. Fig. 10 shows the couplings $J^{\alpha\gamma}$ of the PCA network as directed lines from γ to α. For example, the upper edge of the barrel (blln0) has both possible PCA couplings with the appropriate corner (crn0). These couplings were determined by learning with the update rules of Section VI; the training images used were obtained from a model. That model consists of a synthetic image that includes a barrel of the appropriate dimension. Before presenting the outcome of PCA action, we briefly discuss the learned weights in relation to the development of Section IV.

Feature lln0 is a horizontal line segment of fixed length whose location is (arbitrarily) represented at its left end. A long line, such as the top of a barrel, consists of a chain of segments lln0 terminated on the left by corner crn0: its right end and therefore its length are undetermined. Thus the barrel edge can extend indefinitely to the right of crn0. To illustrate (23) for this feature pair, we present a neighborhood image of $J_d^{\alpha\gamma}$ determined from (23) with $\rho = 1$:

$$
\begin{matrix}
-1 & -1 & -1 & -1 & -1 \\
-1 & -1 & -1 & -1 & -1 \\
-1 & -1 & 0 & 0 & 0 \\
-1 & -1 & -1 & -1 & -1 \\
-1 & -1 & -1 & -1 & -1
\end{matrix}
\tag{32}
$$

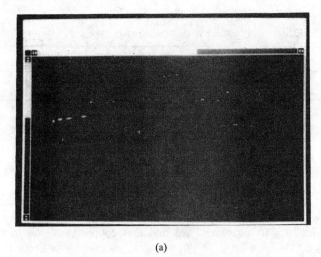

(a)

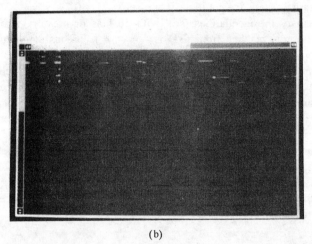

(b)

Fig. 9. (a) Output of one-pass barrel detector for Fig. 7(a). More evidence will be required to identify the barrel unambiguously. (b) Output of barrel detection applied to infrared image, Fig. 7(b). It is clear that this output does not assist in barrel recognition; however, it must not destroy the strong evidence from the laser-radar image.

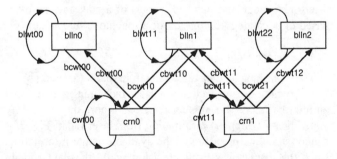

Fig. 10. PCA feedback net for corners and long lines of the tank barrel.

In this image, the initial state lln0 and final state crn0 are fixed while the neighbor index d varies. The location of crn0, $d = 0$, is shown in the center, and other neighbors $d \neq 0$ are placed in their proper position relative to that. The numbers are the values of model $J^{\text{crn0,lln0}}$ at the corresponding neighbor. Thus crn0 is at the center, and the long line, a chain of lln0 features, is imagined extending to the right. Only the right half of the middle cone contains lln0 positions consistent with corner crn0 at the center. If we round the corresponding learned couplings to the nearest integer we obtain a very similar neighborhood image that bears out the basic intuition:

$$
\begin{array}{ccccc}
-1 & -1 & -1 & -1 & -1 \\
-1 & -1 & 0 & -1 & -1 \\
-1 & -1 & 0 & 0 & 0 \\
0 & -1 & -1 & 0 & -1 \\
-1 & -1 & -1 & -1 & -1
\end{array}
\qquad (33)
$$

The rounded neighborhood image for $J^{lln0,crn0}$ (i.e., the long line is the final state and the corner is initial state) looks somewhat different:

$$
\begin{array}{ccccc}
-2 & -1 & -1 & -1 & -2 \\
-2 & -1 & -2 & -1 & -2 \\
1 & 3 & 4 & 0 & 0 \\
-2 & -2 & 2 & 0 & 0 \\
-2 & -2 & -1 & -1 & -1
\end{array}
\qquad (34)
$$

With this pairing the directionality of the PCA dynamics becomes evident. As anticipated, pairings such that corner crn0 is to the left of line segment lln0 are most favored. The rarity of initial feature crn0 compared with lln0 has resulted in stronger couplings than the preceding, reflecting the intuition that the overall frequency of the initial feature is related to the information contained in the fact of its presence: knowing that lln0 is present in the initial state does not precisely determine the location of the corresponding corner crn0, while knowing that crn0 is present strongly implies the presence of lln0 at the same location and more weakly implies other lln0 to the right. The neighborhood images (33) and (34) are consistent with this intuition, and consequently the symmetry rule (12) is not satisfied by them, although the basic pattern of allowed and forbidden pairings is as predicted by (23).

When the PCA with (unrounded) coupling constants obtained by learning is applied to the feature images of Fig. 9, it resolves the ambiguities and correctly identifies the tank and the unique location of each of its features. For example, the upper edges arising from the barrel are retained, while those from background are suppressed. The final result for each feature is a single point marking the position of that feature in the tank. We have found that successful recognition can be achieved with fully synchronous operation of the PCA on features of all levels of the model hierarchy. The enhanced interlevel feedback afforded by synchronous operation seems to help achieve a correct consensus, in the sense that model levels cannot be completely decoupled without causing extreme sensitivity to the strengths of the PCA couplings.

C. Fusion of Infrared and Laser-Radar Images

The simplest method to fuse data from two sources is to include features from both sources in each cell of the PCA network. In this way we have been able to enhance features selected from infrared and laser-radar sources by weighting the laser-radar evidence at least three times the infrared evidence. That is, if the laser radar indicates a barrel while the infrared indicates only background, the connections in the network are such as to favor the barrel as the final interpretation. We believe that the need for this post-hoc weighting results from the limitations of our tank model, which was constructed to allow detailed study of our proposed system rather than for

real-world data fusion. In particular, only geometry was used to construct the model, and no phenomenological information about infrared or laser-radar imagery. Models accounting for differing source characteristics will be required for effective fusion of multiple-sensor data.

D. Telephone Dialer

We use the second example, a touchtone telephone dialer, to illustrate what is meant by "recognition" using the PCA. A hierarchical model of its dialer array is shown in Fig. 11. The telephone shown in the source photograph also has a control array next to the dialer, details of which are omitted. To reduce dependence on contrast and brightness variations, we chose to define the lowest-level features of the model, namely the "vertical" and "horizontal" edges, from an image preprocessed by a standard Sobel edge detector. These edges, which are oriented obliquely in the test image, are paired elements of a family of edges related by rotation. We trained feedforward neural nets to detect edges of these orientations, using small portions of the test image as a training set. Because dialer buttons are small, a button is modeled as four appropriately placed and oriented edges (without corners); again the corresponding feature detector is implemented as a feedforward neural net. Fig. 12 shows the Sobel edge image and the products of these three feedforward nets. A third feedforward net assigns the detected buttons to positions in the dialer array. At each step up the hierarchy the resolution is coarsened by a factor of 2. A PCA whose configuration space consists of the individual button assignments then resolves conflict, but because the test image is the same that was used to train the feature detectors, there is little conflict to resolve.

Our experiment is to create conflict for the PCA, but not for the feature detectors, by translating the original image diagonally toward the corner of the field of view and so out of sight. For this experiment, PCA weights were trained by the Boltzmann-machine method (see Section VI), using as a training set the untranslated test image corrupted by added Gaussian noise and small, randomly placed obscurations. The results are shown in Fig. 13. The upper row shows the feature input to the PCA, and the lower shows PCA configuration after three iterations. The feedforward feature detectors continue to identify individual buttons of the array, weakening somewhat right at the edge of the picture. The PCA, which puts each button in the context of its neighbors, continues to give strong responses for all visible buttons until more than half of the dialer has left the field of view. Then all buttons abruptly disappear from the PCA output.

VI. Learning

In the context of data-driven recognition, "learning" is used to mean an improvement of system performance through a method involving the presentation of examples. The fundamental theory of learning is an active research topic [12], but has not yet led to practical applications. We develop some learning rules in this section, without any attempt to obtain rigorous bounds on sample or time complexity. In evaluating the learning rules from limited experiments, we make the usual assumption that the training examples are presented

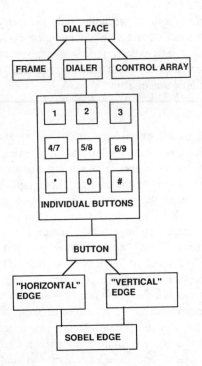

Fig. 11. Hierarchical model of touchtone telephone dialer. Input data are at the bottom.

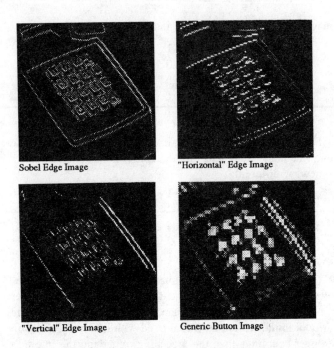

Fig. 12. Input data and feature-detector outputs for touchtone telephone dialer.

according to the same probability distribution under which the system is to be tested. In this section, we shall present some control-theory learning algorithms, emphasizing some novelties to which the PCA system leads us. We shall only describe learning the couplings. Another mode of learning would attempt to learn the model in question [4].

A. Learning for the Probabilistic Dynamics

The most widely used method for learning in a probabilistic dynamical system is the Boltzmann-machine method. This employs the relative entropy to measure the deviation of a trial distribution from a specified one:

$$D[P_0|P_1] \equiv \sum_C P_0(C) \, \ln[P_0(C)/P_1(C)]. \quad (35)$$

We assume that P_1 and P_0 are discrete and that P_1 has no zeros where P_0 is nonzero (see [9] for a detailed discussion). For our case, we choose P_1 to be the distribution obtained from a given starting distribution after a number of iterations, while P_0 is a known singular distribution, i.e., the distribution concentrated on the goal configuration belonging to an initial starting configuration. This is why we have written $D[P_0|P_1]$ and not $D[P_1|P_0]$: with the latter (which is the usual choice) we will be unable to avoid infinities in the definition of D.

The Boltzmann-machine learning method uses (35) for learning by performing gradient descent with respect to the couplings to be learned. Reference [9] analyzes in detail the conditions under which gradient descent will reach the minimum of the relative entropy, i.e., reach the set of states on which $P_1 = P_0$. For bilinear couplings of the form (5), the resulting formula for an update of the coupling coefficients is easily calculated. If we require the PCA to approximate the

target distribution in a single iteration, the learning rule is

$$\Delta J_d^{\alpha\gamma}(n+1) = \eta[C_i'^{\alpha} - I_i^{\alpha}]C_{i+d}^{\gamma} \quad (36)$$

where I is the ideal configuration belonging to the starting configuration $C(0)$, and η is a "convergence parameter." The updates are then cumulated over several samples of C', keeping $C(0)$ fixed, and then over several different $C(0)$. Translation invariance is restored by averaging over lattice sites or guaranteed by training with one window (a single receptive field for each feature). Reference [9] may be consulted for the formulas that obtain when the goal is to be attained in, say, $\tau > 1$ iterations: basically $C_i'^{\alpha}$ is the feature value after τ steps.

We have emphasized that performance is to be measured by first-passage times to goal configurations from perturbed ones, and also by sojourn times in the vicinity of the goals. The theory of control suggests itself for optimizing PCA parameters for good first-passage times. However, the general formulas for first-passage times in a Markov chain [7] are rather intractable for learning. Furthermore, while methods are available in the literature [13] for controlling passage times and sojourn times from the stochastic differential equation (SDE) obtained in the continuum limit of a Markov process, these methods cannot be directly applied to the SDE (12) for the PCA. The reason is the reflecting boundary conditions on the faces of the hypercube which is the configuration space. Current work in control theory may yield progress in this direction. In Appendix II, we briefly describe an alternative control-theory technique for driving an initial configuration along a trajectory that approaches the desired states as closely as possible, not in the shortest possible time, but in a given amount of time. After simplifications specified in the Appendix, the update rule for

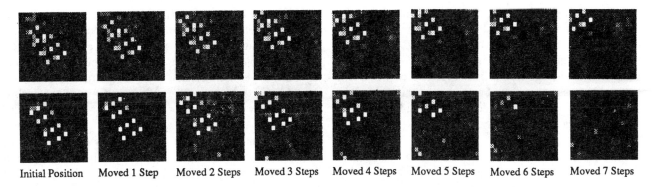

| Initial Position | Moved 1 Step | Moved 2 Steps | Moved 3 Steps | Moved 4 Steps | Moved 5 Steps | Moved 6 Steps | Moved 7 Steps |

Fig. 13. Behavior of PCA under translation of input image. Top row: composite of individual-button features input to PCA. Bottom row: PCA configuration after three iterations, shown as composite of individual-button features.

the couplings is

$$\Delta J_d^{\alpha\gamma} = \eta \sum_C T(C, I) \Pr\{C(0) = C\}$$
$$\cdot (I_i^\alpha - E\{C_i'^\alpha | C\}) C_{i+d}^\gamma \qquad (37)$$

where T is the transition probability. We see that this formula is similar to (36), although with an additional weighting by the transition probability from the current configuration to the goal.

B. Simulation Results

Simulations were run on both artificial one-dimensional patterns and real two-dimensional corrupted images. We discuss only the one-dimensional results. We also omit discussion of the relation between the weights so obtained and those determined by the model.

We refer to subsection IV-D for an explanation of the one-dimensional model. Let us choose the following allowed configuration as the ideal:

$$----(\,)-----------(\,)--- \qquad (38)$$

We select the following distortion of (38) as an initial image to be corrected:

$$--((\,)---)(---(---(\,)--- \qquad (39)$$

That (39) is a distortion of (38) is of course our arbitrary choice, and does not reflect any understanding of "natural" distortions occurring in real images. The configurations have been chosen only for illustrating the learning algorithm.

We first illustrate the speed of a "successful learning run" in Fig. 14. This we define as a run in which the final state is within 10% (i.e., the quantum q of subsection III-A) of the target state for *every* component of the configuration, or more precisely, $\sup_{i,\alpha} |C_i'^\alpha - I_i^\alpha| \leq 0.1$, where the final state is $C_i'^\alpha$. The number of learning steps is equated with the number of updates of the dynamics required, not with the complexity of the computation required at each update. In other words, we are measuring the *sample* complexity of the learning procedure, not the *time* complexity. It should also be noted that we are not yet discussing even trivial capabilities in performance or generalization, but only the speed with which the correct response was arrived at, given the desired goal as well as the starting configuration and an

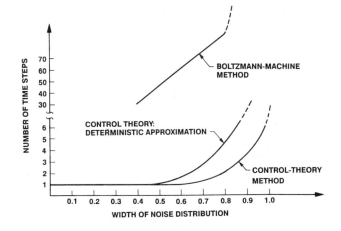

Fig. 14. Sample complexity of learning procedures derived from optimal control theory, compared with Boltzmann-machine method.

initial set of weights. For these experiments, the starting set of weights is the simplest consistent with model requirements, namely +1 for reinforcing features and −1 for contradictory features. We have used time-dependent weights in the control-theory procedures. The x axis is the width of noise distributed uniformly about an average of 0.5. The noise is added to the starting configuration displayed in (39). The results in Fig. 14 show clearly that both the full control-theory method and a deterministic approximation are significantly faster than the Boltzmann machine method when the objective is to steer a trajectory toward a desired goal. The behavior of the learned weights, i.e., a fixed set of weights operating on essentially new configurations (but still chosen with the same distribution used in the learning phase), is a separate matter, which we shall now discuss.

We have found that time-invariant weights determined by both control-theory methods are very similar to those obtained from the Boltzmann machine method, so that the behaviors of the three sets of learned weights on newly presented configurations are also similar. However, during the learning phase, the control-theory methods can steer wildly varying configurations toward a particular desired goal. This might seem to imply that the range of applicability of the control-theory methods is larger. This is not so; the final set of weights so learned is *not* effective in restoring highly perturbed configurations. This is an indication that the dynamics of the

365

weights are crucial here, and that the time dependence of the weights cannot simply be turned off during the recognition phase. If, for a particular number of time steps T, we average the results over samples at each particular time step t of the PCA but do not average the weights over t, then we obtain improved robustness over any of the other methods. In other words, it pays to have time-dependent weights, and the control-theory approach can provide increased robustness, at increased cost of processing and memory.

If we take the control-theory point of view even more seriously, then goals must continue to be generated during the recognition phase as well. These goals must come from the internal memory of the system. The PCA dynamics, augmented in this fashion, would become a truly dynamical system for both the configurations and the weights. This is an interesting conclusion, which Edelman arrives at from entirely different considerations (see [14] and his discussion on the "self versus nonself distinction"). We have not yet explored the consequences of this approach.

VII. Conclusions

We have shown that a multilayer, parallel feedback network of probabilistic cellular automata can iteratively improve inferences regarding the presence of a target pattern in a scene, and we have illustrated PCA operation with examples based on visible, infrared, and laser-radar images. We have also shown how prior information, in the form of a model of the target object, can be used to construct a set of PCA weights. For training the PCA, we have proposed a novel learning algorithm derived from optimal control theory.

The network was designed to incorporate prior knowledge in the form of local inference rules. Accordingly, we have everywhere assumed that a hierarchical model of the target object can be constructed such that network connections remain local. One may view our work as an exploration of how global consistency can be achieved with purely local dependencies, which is a traditional theme in statistical mechanics and has been studied by Waltz in the context of artificial intelligence [15]. Locality is also advantageous for an implementation on parallel hardware. However, the resulting network may not be equivalent to globally connected networks. In analyzing how to incorporate prior knowledge in the PCA itself we found an explicit null feature to be useful in formalizing the model, and we have shown how to eliminate it when its job is done. Given a model, we have shown how to construct an energy landscape whose minima are the goal configurations, and we have combined this energy function with inequalities derived from dynamic considerations to construct PCA weights. Such "engineered" weights, which satisfy a symmetry condition, should be most useful as a starting point for training, for our experience to date suggests that shorter first-passage times can usually be attained with nonsymmetric weights.

Throughout our work translation invariance has been strictly enforced, so that the object may appear anywhere within the field of view. A consequence of translation invariance is that strict probabilistic methods such as Bayesian inference networks [16] cannot be efficiently applied because the inference network is multiply connected (many loops). Like

other feedback schemes, the PCA method compounds these loops by iterating. Therefore, unlike a Bayesian network, the network of automata does not compute a probability that the target object is present but collectively combines data to make a yes–no decision. For recognition this behavior should be advantageous. The collective nature of the decision is particularly important, for it means that high precision is not required of individual elements, and high tolerance of noise and clutter should be attainable. As illustrated by our examples, feature detectors can be relatively crude, and more than one feature detector may respond to a single input pattern, without preventing effective recognition.

The collective nature of the decision is shared by other methods inspired by statistical mechanics. Statistical mechanics has given PCA theory a body of results on asymptotic states and invariant measures [3]. For recognition, on the other hand, the short-time behavior is most important. The same observation applies to methods such as the Metropolis algorithm and simulated annealing, which sample a Gibbs state. Because it explicitly concerns itself with dynamics, we have found optimal control theory to be more helpful.

Optimal control theory has led to the novel learning algorithm we propose in Section VI. As we observed there, the ideal learning technique would minimize first-passage time to the goal configuration, but the theory does not presently offer means to do this for configuration variables confined to the interval $[0, 1]$. A theoretical advance in this direction could result in an improved learning algorithm.

Appendix I

We work out a set of couplings for the two-dimensional wheels model of subsection IV-C. It is convenient to separate out the extra self-couplings $K^{\alpha\gamma}$. Substituting (29) for $K^{\alpha\gamma}$ and recalling that these are the only nonzero $d = 0$ couplings within a single set of mutually exclusive features, $V(C)$ may be written for the PCA without explicit null feature as

$$V^\alpha(C_N) = \mu^\alpha + f\left\{C_0^\alpha + \sum_{\gamma \in \Omega} C_0^\gamma\right\}$$

$$+ \left[\sum_{\gamma \in \Omega} \sum_{\substack{d \in N \\ d \neq 0}} J_d^{\alpha\gamma} C_d^\gamma\right]. \tag{A1}$$

The starred sets in (20) must be interpreted slightly differently for mutually exclusive features: instead of merely doubling the initial sets I_N^α by allowing $C_0^\alpha = 0$ as well as $C_0^\alpha = 1$, we must vary all features in the mutually exclusive subset Θ that contains α so as to satisfy (24). This means setting each arc and the null feature in turn to 1, the others all to 0. The factor in braces in (A1) is evidently maximized for $C_0^\alpha = 1$ and minimized for $C_0^n = 1$ (meaning that all the nonnull features vanish). The remaining problem is the double sum in brackets.

The E matrix of this model has special properties that make it possible to evaluate the bounds of that sum by hand. When a given arc may pair with more than one partner at a particular neighbor location, then one of the possible partners is the null feature. Furthermore, two arcs that can pair with the null feature at a particular neighbor location either both can, or both cannot pair with a given nonnull feature at that location. Using notation $L_{\mathbf{X}}^{\alpha}(U_{\mathbf{X}}^{\alpha})$ for lower (upper) bounds over $\mathbf{X}_N^{\alpha}$ of the bracketed sum in (A1), and substituting (29) for $J_d^{\alpha\gamma}$, we obtain, after some calculation using these special properties,

$$U_I^{\alpha} = L_I^{\alpha} = 2\rho \sum_{d \in N} [1 - E_d^{\alpha n}] = -2(\tilde{\mu}^{\alpha} + f) \quad \text{(A2)}$$

$$U_{\mathbf{F}}^{\alpha} = \rho \max_{\alpha' \neq \alpha} \left\{ \sum_{d \in N} [1 - E_d^{\alpha n}][1 - E_d^{\alpha' n}] \right\}. \quad \text{(A3)}$$

The second form of (A2) uses (30). To evaluate $L_{\mathbf{F}}^{\alpha}$, replace "max" by "min" in (A3). Equation (A2) counts the neighbors d at which the null feature cannot pair with the given feature α. Similarly, (A3) is the maximum over $\alpha' \neq \alpha$ of the count of neighbors d where neither α nor α' can pair with the null feature. Using the E-matrix of Fig. 4 we obtain $L_I^{SW} = 10\rho$, $L_I^{W} = 8\rho$, $U_{\mathbf{F}}^{SW} = U_{\mathbf{F}}^{W} = 2\rho$, $L_{\mathbf{F}}^{SW} = \rho$ and $L_{\mathbf{F}}^{W} = 0$. The bounds (20) then combine to give

$$\lambda p \geq 5\rho + f$$
$$\lambda q \leq 2\rho - f \quad \text{(A4)}$$

which determine the allowable range of ρ and f for given λ, p, q. As the first of these represents the strongest case for or against any feature, it is sensible to set $p = 1$ and demand that it hold as an equality. The second then implies

$$\frac{f}{\rho} \leq \frac{2 - 5q}{1 + q} \quad \text{(A5)}$$

which allows $f > 0$ for $q < 1/3$ and $f \geq \rho$ for $q \leq 1/6$. Accordingly, we may use $q = 0.1$, $2f = \rho = \lambda/6 = 1$, and $\beta = 10$. Since the norm of J^{α} can be computed (using the same special properties) to be $\sqrt{61}\rho$ for $\alpha = W$ and $\sqrt{63}\rho$ for $\alpha = SW$, these parameter values give a ball radius $b \approx 0.12$ around the ideal configurations within which (17) is satisfied.

Appendix II

This appendix outlines the derivation of the control-theory formula (37) for learning. We define the goal distribution as p_T, and our goal is to maximize the probability that the distribtuion P_T of final configurations after T PCA steps will equal p_T, constraining each iteration to be "close" to p_T and the weights to be finite. In our first application, the goal distribution, p_T, is trivial in that it is concentrated on the goal configuration I. The methods are, however, general. We want to minimize

$$S = -P_T(I) - \sum_{t=0}^{T-1} \kappa(t) P_t(I) \quad \text{(A6)}$$

subject to the constraint that the probabilities obey the Markov dynamics given by (1) to (3). We regard the couplings J as the objects to be controlled. Following the usual procedure [17], we introduce Lagrange multipliers χ, and define a Hamiltonian, H, at each time:

$$H(t+1, P, J, \chi) \equiv \kappa(t+1)P_{t+1}(I) + \sum_{C'} \chi(t+1, C')$$
$$\cdot \sum_{C} T_t(C, C')P_t(C). \quad \text{(A7)}$$

The PCA transition probabilities, T_t, are written with an explicit time index t since we shall implement time-dependent J's immediately below. If we follow variational calculus, or Pontryagin's principle, we get an extremal for S if

$$\delta S / \delta J_d^{\alpha\gamma} = \sum_{t=0}^{T} H(t+1) \quad \text{(A8)}$$

is minimal as a function of J (see [17] for details). Equation (A8) is satisfied if $\chi(t, C) = \partial H(t+1, P, J, \chi)/ \partial P(t, C)$ and the Markov dynamics for P (as discussed in Section III) holds. The final-value condition is $\chi(T, X) = \delta(X, I)$ (where δ is the Kronecker delta; i.e. $\delta(X, I) = 1$ if $X = I$, and 0 otherwise).

We have several options at this point. (i) The first (conventional) option is to assume that the couplings J are *not* time-varying, and to perform gradient descent with respect to J on the right-hand side of (A8). This guarantees that the change in S is nonpositive, since by (A8) it will be proportional to $-[\delta S/\delta J_d^{\alpha\gamma}]^2$. One might hope to find the minimum of S this way. In this case "time" is not PCA iteration time, but simply gradient descent iteration steps. (ii) Another is to allow time-varying J's and to start with a term proportional to $\|J\|^2 \equiv \sum_{d,\alpha,\gamma} (J_d^{\alpha\gamma})^2$ added to (A6). In this case (A8) has an added term proportional to $J(t)$, so that $J(t)$ can be set to $\partial H(t)/\partial J_d^{\alpha\gamma}$ at each PCA step. (iii) To obtain a time-invariant J, we may modify the second method by averaging the resulting expression for $J(t)$ over time. All three methods may be subsumed under the formula

$$J_d^{\alpha\gamma}(t+1) = \eta J_d^{\alpha\gamma}(t) + \eta' \Delta J_d^{\alpha\gamma}(t) \quad \text{(A9)}$$

where

$$\Delta J_d^{\alpha\gamma}(t) \equiv \delta H(t)/\delta J_d^{\alpha\gamma} = \beta \sum_{C'} \chi(t+1, C') \sum_{C} T_t(C, C')$$
$$\cdot P_t(C)(C_i'^{\alpha}(t+1) - E\{C_i'^{\alpha}|C(t)\})C_{i+d}^{\gamma}(t) \quad \text{(A10)}$$

where η and η' are convergence parameters which can be made time dependent for improved convergence. E means expected value. When we used these formulas in our experiments, the multipliers χ were set to their final-time values at all times. We can "justify" time-independent χ by a heuristic self-consistency argument: when the couplings are "good", the transition probabilities are large toward the goal configuration, and small away from it. In the limit where $T(I, C)$ can be neglected when $C \neq I$, so can the time dependence of χ. We can also add counterterms to S in (A6) to make χ time-independent [18]. However, our main motivation is to use simple formulas, and not attempt to solve the two-point boundary value problem usually encountered in control theory.

With the replacement of $\chi(t, X)$ by $\chi(T, X) = \delta(X, I)$ the formula (37) results. In the graph of the experimental results, we also show the performance of the learning rule obtained by taking the deterministic limit of the stochastic DE (11), and requiring that the goal configuration I be approached as closely as possible in T steps. By following the same procedure as outlined, we find (A9), with (A10) replaced by

$$\Delta J_d^{\alpha\gamma}(t) = \beta \sum_i I_i^\alpha C_{i+d}^\gamma(t) \tag{A11}$$

which can be seen to be a time-dependent modification of the Hopfield rule.

ACKNOWLEDGMENT

R. Raghavan wishes to express his gratitude to O. Farotimi, then of Stanford University, for exposing him to control-theory methods. Joint work with him on additional details of this approach is in preparation.

REFERENCES

[1] M. Brady, R. Raghavan, and J. Slawny, "Probabilistic cellular automata in pattern recognition," in *Proc. Int. Joint Conf. Neural Networks*, vol. 1, 1989, pp. 177–182.

[2] K. Preston, Jr., and M. J. B. Duff, *Modern Cellular Automata, Theory and Applications."* New York: Plenum Press, 1984.

[3] J. L. Lebowitz, C. Maes, and E. R. Speer, "Statistical mechanics of probabilistic cellular automata," *J. Stat. Phys.*, vol. 59, pp. 117–170, 1990.

[4] R. Raghavan, F. W. Adams, Jr., H. T. Nguyen, and J. Slawny, "Image recognition and learning in parallel networks," in *Proc. SPIE, Nonlinear Image Processing,* vol. 1247, 1990, pp. 258–273.

[5] K. Ikeuchi and T. Kanade, "Automatic generation of object recognition programs," *Proc. IEEE*, vol. 76, p. 1016, 1988.

[6] P. Peretto, "Collective properties of neural networks: A statistical physics approach," *Biol. Cybern.*, vol. 50, pp. 51–62, 1984.

[7] W. Feller, *An Introduction to Probability Theory and Its Applications*, vol. 2. New York: Wiley, 1966.

[8] C. W. Gardiner, *Handbook of Stochastic Methods for Physics, Chemistry and the Natural Sciences.* New York: Springer-Verlag, 1983.

[9] H. J. Sussmann, "On the convergence of learning algorithms for Boltzmann machines," Rep. SYCON-88-03, Rutgers Center for System and Control, Aug. 1988.

[10] D. E. Rummelhart and J. L. McClelland, Eds., *Parallel Distributed Processing: Explorations in the Microstructure of Cognition,* vol. 1. Cambridge, MA: MIT Press, 1986, ch. 8.

[11] H. T. Nguyen, R. Raghavan, and J. Slawny, "Telling wheels from tracks," Contract Report, DARPA contract on Statistical Pattern Recognition, Oct. 1987.

[12] B. K. Natarajan, *Machine Learning: A Theoretical Approach.* San Mateo, CA: Morgan Kaufmann, 1991. (See also the proceedings of the annual conferences on Computational Learning Theory.)

[13] S. M. Meerkov and T. Runolfsson, "Residence time control," *IEEE Trans. Automat. Contr.*, vol. 33, pp. 323–332, 1988.

[14] G. Edelman, *The Remembered Present.* New York: Basic Books, 1989.

[15] P. H. Winston and R. H. Brown, *Artificial Intelligence: An MIT Perspective.* Cambridge, MA: MIT Press, 1979.

[16] J. Pearl, *Probabilistic Reasoning in Intelligent Systems: Networks of Plausible Inference.* San Mateo, CA: Morgan-Kaufmann, 1988.

[17] A. Bryson and Y.-C. Ho, *Applied Optimal Control.* New York: Hemisphere Publishing, 1975.

[18] O. Farotimi, A. Dembo, and T. Kailath, "A general weight matrix formulation using optimal control," *IEEE Trans. Neural Networks*, vol. 2, pp. 378–394, May 1991.

A NEURAL NETWORK SYSTEM FOR ACTIVE VISUAL PERCEPTION AND RECOGNITION

I. A. Rybak, A. V. Golovan, V. I. Gusakova, N. A. Shevtsova and L. N. Podladchikova*)

Abstract

A method for parallel-sequential processing of grey-level images and their representation which is invariant to position, rotation, and scale, is developed. The method is based on the idea that an image is memorized and recognized by way of consecutive fixations of moving eyes on the most informative image fragments. The method provides the invariant representation of the image in each fixation point and of spatial relations between the features extracted in neighboring fixations. The applications of the method to recognition of grey-level images are considered.

1. Introduction

It would be difficult to understand and to explain the remarkable features of living recognition systems on the basis of neurophysiological data only without findings of visual psychology and psychophysics. For the same reason, most of the classical neural network paradigms cannot be directly used for analysis and invariant recognition of grey-level visual images. So, on the one hand, it is necessary to develop adequate neural network models of preattentive vision including preprocessing visual information and extraction of primary features of visual images. Progress in this direction has already taken place due to the remarkable research of S. Grossberg and E. Mingolla [4, 5], J. Daugman [3], M. Porat and Y. Zeevi [7], J. Buchmann and Chr. von der Malsburg [1], and some others. On the other hand, it is necessary to develop methods and algorithms for transformation of extracted primary features of grey-level images into invariant features which can be used as input signals for classical neural networks. In this case the neural networks would successfully realize the functions of classifier and associative memory of visual images. An example of the successful application of a similar approach was given by S. Troxel, S. Rogers, and M. Kabrisky [8]. They used the transformation of the image into the magnitude of the Fourier transform with log radial and angle axis, $|F(Lnr, \Theta)|$, feature space, on the low-er-level and the multilayer perceptron neural network using a back propagation algorithm on the upper-level of the recognizing system. But, it is interesting to find an adequate invariant transform and representation of the image on the basis of data and ideas of vision psychophysiology.

It is widely known that in the process of visual perception and image recognition human eyes move and consequently fixate on the most informative points of the image [9]. In accordance with the concept of Smart Sensing [2] (intelligent sensory perception), they actively accomplish a selective and problem-oriented collection of information from the visible world. The main principles of the Smart Sensing theory [2] are as follows:

(i) The eye is able to get exact information from a small area of the visual field only. The sharpness of perception decreases quickly from the fovea to the periphery of the retina. It provides the local processing in the areas of the fixation points and reduces the information processed in parallel.

(ii) The peripheral vision is of lower resolution but it excites and directs the gaze to shift to the next fixation point.

(iii) The high-level structures control eye movements for collecting information which is necessary for verification of hypotheses formed and reformed in the process of image recognition.

In 1971, D. Noton and L. Stark [6] carried out research devoted to comparing individual trajectories ("scanpaths") of human eye movements in two phases: when an object was being memorized (learning phase) and when it was being recognized (recognition phase). They have shown that these scanpaths are topologically similar and have suggested that an individual trajectory (a specific scanpath) is formed while the object is being viewed. As a result of this process, the object has been memorized and stored as an alternating sequence of sensory and motor memory traces, recording alternately the feature of the object and the eye movement required to reach the next feature. When the object is being recognized (when a hypothesis on the object is being verified), the reproduction of the successive eye movement memories and verification of the successive feature memories take place.

To realize the ideas described above in a concrete model, it is necessary to also develop the following aspects: 1. to realize primary transforms imitating

*) I. A. Rybak, A. V. Golovan, V. I. Gusakova, N. A. Shevtsova, and L. N. Podladchikova
Institute of Neurocybernetics at Rostov State University 194/1 Stachka Avenue, Rostov-on-Don 344104, USSR

Reprinted with permission from *Neural Networks World*, vol. 4, pp. 245–250, 1991.

a decrease in the resolution of visual field perception from the fovea to the retinal periphery; 2. to choose the set of primary features and to realize their extraction and encoding; 3. to develop algorithms for invariant representation of the image fragment in the fixation point and of spatial relations between the fragments in neighbor fixation points; 4. to develop algorithms of interactions between lower and higher levels of the system in operation modes of object memorizing, search, and recognition.

2. Primary Transform

The primary transform of an initial image $I = \{x_{ij}\}$ in the model developed forms the retinal image $I'(n) = \{x'_{ij}(n)\}$ in each n-th fixation point. The position of this point $(io(n), jo(n))$ and the resolution level $lo(n)$ in the round area rounding the point are considered as the initial parameters for the point. Three concentric circles with the center in the point $(io(n), jo(n))$ divide the raster into four areas. The radii of the circles are

$$Ro(lo) = 3 \cdot 2^{lo-1},$$
$$Ri(lo) = 3 \cdot 2^{lo}, \qquad (2.1)$$
$$Rz(lo) = 3 \cdot 2^{lo-1}.$$

Within the central round area, the image is represented on the resolution level $l = lo(n)$. Within the first ring area, it is represented with lower resolution (on the next resolution level $l = lo(n) + 1$). Within the second ring, it is represented on the resolution level $l = lo(n) + 2$.

Figure 1. Test image.

Figure 2. Retinal image in one fixation point.

To represent some part of the image $I = \{x_{ij}\}$ $((i,j) \in D)$ on the resolution level l the recurrent procedure of computation of the Gauss convolution in each point of the part D has been used:

$$x_{ij}^{(1)} = x_{ij},$$
$$x_{ij}^{(2)} = \sum_{p,q} G_{pqij} x_{pq}^{(1)}, \qquad (2.2)$$
$$\vdots$$
$$x_{ij}^{(l)} = \sum_{p,q} G_{pqij} x_{pq}^{(l-1)},$$

where $G_{pqij} = -\exp\left\{-v^2\left[(p-i)^2 + (q-j)^2\right]\right\}$, (2.3)

v is the coefficient $(v > 0)$ and i, j and p, q are the coordinates of image pixels.

Thus, the retinal image in the n-th fixation point $I'(n) = \{x'_{ij}(n)\}$ is formed from $I = \{x_{ij}\}$ in the following way:

$$x'_{ij}(n) = \begin{cases} x_{ij}^{(lo(n))} & \text{if } p_{ij}(n) \leq Ro(lo), \\ x_{ij}^{(lo(n)-1)} & \text{if } Ro(lo) < p_{ij}(n) \leq R_1(lo), \\ x_{ij}^{(lo(n)-2)} & \text{if } Ri(lo) < p_{ij}(n) \leq R_2(lo), \\ x_{ij}^{(lo(n)+3)} = \overline{x}_{ij} & \text{if } p_{ij}(n) > R_2(lo), \end{cases}$$

$$(2.4)$$

where $\overline{x}_{ij}$ is the averaged intensity of $I = \{x_{ij}\}$ and

$$p_{ij}(n) = \sqrt{(i - io(n))^2 + (j - jo(n))^2}. \quad (2.5)$$

Fig. 2 shows the retinal image in one fixation point

(marked by the cross sign) for the initial test image (*Fig. 1*). *Fig. 3* shows that a few fixation points seem to be sufficient for image recognition.

3. Extraction of Primary Features

As primary features (image elements) we have considered the oriented edge segments extracted with different resolutions depending on their positions in the retinal image. Although it seems more prospective and adequate to extract primary image elements by the use of the Gabor transform [1, 3, 7], for the present we have used a slightly modified algorithm of S. Grossberg and his colleagues [5]. Orientation tuning of a neuron is determined by its receptive field which is formed as the difference of two Gauss convolutions with spatially shifted centers.

The magnitude of the input signal to a neuron (i, j) tuned to the edge segment orientation α is calculated in the following way:

$$Y_{ij\alpha} = \sum_{p, q} x'_{pq} \left(G'_{pqij\alpha} \times G''_{pqij\alpha} \right), \qquad (3.1)$$

where

$$G'_{pqij\alpha} = -\exp\left\{ -\gamma^2 \left[(p - i - m_\alpha)^2 + (q - j - m_\alpha)^2 \right] \right\}, \qquad (3.2)$$

$$G''_{pqij\alpha} = -\exp\left\{ -\gamma^2 \left[(p - i + m_\alpha)^2 + (q - j + m_\alpha)^2 \right] \right\}.$$

The step of orientation tuning of a neuron was 22.5° and it was taken to be the unit of angle measure

Figure 3. United result of primary transforms of the test image in 11 fixation points.

$(\alpha = 0, 1, 2, \ldots, 15)$. The parameters m_α and n_α depend on the neuron orientation tuning α:

$$m_\alpha = d(l) \cos (2\pi\alpha/16),$$
$$n_\alpha = d(l) \sin (2\pi\alpha/16), \qquad (3.3)$$

where $d(l)$ defines the Gauss convolution center distances from the center of the receptive field (i, j) and depends on the resolution level l at the point (i, j) of the retinal image $I' = \{x'_{ij}(n)\}$:

$$d(l) = \max (2^{l-2}, 1) \qquad (3.4)$$

Sixteen neurons corresponding to each point i, j, but tuned to different edge orientations (different directions of brightness gradients) interacted competitively owing to the strong reciprocal inhibiting connections. The interactions between the neurons are described as follows:

$$\begin{cases} \tau \dfrac{d}{dt} U_{ij\alpha} = -\Theta_{ij\alpha} + Y_{ij\alpha} - B \sum_{k=0}^{15} Z_{ijk} - h, \\ Z_{ij\alpha} = f[U_{ij\alpha}], \quad \alpha = 0, 1, 2, \ldots, 15 \end{cases} \qquad (3.5)$$

where $U_{ij\alpha}$, $Z_{ij\alpha}$ and $Y_{ij\alpha}$ designate respectively the membrane potential, output and input signals of the neuron (i, j) tuned to the orientation α; B is the coefficient characterizing the reciprocal inhibitory interactions $(B > 1)$; h is the threshold, and τ is the time constant. f[U] is the nonlinear function

$$f[U] = \begin{cases} U \text{ if } U \geq 0, \\ 0 \text{ if } U < 0. \end{cases} \qquad (3.6)$$

The solution of the system passes to the state of equilibrium in which either all $Z_{ij\alpha} = 0$ (if all $Y_{ij\alpha} < h$) or only one $Z_{ij\alpha} = Y_{ij\alpha} - h > 0$ when $\alpha = \psi_s$ (for which $Y_{ij\alpha}$ is maximum), and the others $Z_{ij\alpha} = 0$ if $\alpha \neq \psi_s$. In the first case, it is considered that there is no oriented edge segments in the point (i, j). In the second case, it is considered that there is the edge segment in the point with the orientation $\alpha = \psi_s$ and with the corresponding contrast value as $Z_{ij\alpha}$.

In each fixation, the oriented edge segments are extracted in the fixation point $(io(n), jo(n))$ (the basic edge segment) and in 48 context points lying on intersections of 16 radiating lines differing 22.5° and of three concentric circles with exponentially increasing radii 2^{lo}, 2^{lo+1}, and 2^{lo+2} (*Fig. 4*). The oriented edge segments corresponding to the first (the smallest) circle are extracted with the same resolution as the basic one. The resolutions $lo(n)$ which the other edge segments were extracted with were determined by their position in the $I'(n) = \{x'_{ij}(n)\}$. The basic edge segment and context edge segments for one fixation point (the same as in *Fig. 2*) are shown in *Fig. 5* as the doubled white and black segments whose lengths are greater the lower the resolution.

371

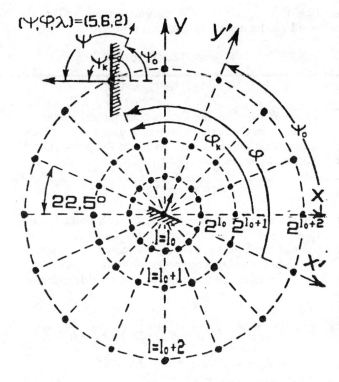

$(\Psi, \varphi \lambda) = (5, 6, 2)$

22,5°

2^{l_o} 2^{l_o+1} 2^{l_o+2}

$l = l_0$

$l = l_0 + 1$

$l = l_0 + 2$

Figure 4. Positions of the basic edge segment and context edge segments in fixation point.

4. Invariant Representation of the Image

Each context segment can be invariantly encoded in a given fixation point by the relative orientation ψ, the relative angle position φ, and the relative decrease of the resolution level λ (see in *Fig. 4*). These parameters for each context segment are calculated in the following way

$$\psi = \mathrm{mod}_{16}(\psi_k - \psi_o + 16),$$

$$\varphi = \mathrm{mod}_{16}(\varphi_k - \psi_o + 4),$$

$$\lambda = l - lo, \qquad (4.1)$$

$$\varphi, \psi \in \{0, 1, 2, \ldots, 15\},$$

$$\lambda \in \{0, 1, 2\},$$

where ψ_k and ψ_o are the orientations of the basic segment and the corresponding context one. φ_k is the angle position of the context segment in the coordinate system XOY, and l is the resolution level on which the context segment is extracted.

In this case, the image can be invariantly represented in each fixation point by the points on the surfaces of three tori each of which is formed by cyclic changing ψ and φ and corresponds to the definite value λ. This representation is shown in *Fig. 6* (for the same fixation point as in *Fig. 5*) as the black points in three coordinate systems on the evolvents of three tori (the abscissa and ordinate axes are the ψ and φ axes, respectively. Such representation of a grey-level imagage (or its fragment) in each fixation point is invar-

iant with respect to position, rotation, and size. Besides, it is appropriate to the application of a classical neural network classifier for memorizing, storing and recognition of image fragments.

It is most natural and suitable that the next fixation point be chosen from the set of context points. In our model, in the memorizing mode, the choice of each next fixation point could be accomplished by a supervisor or automatically. In the latter case the choice is defined by the contrast values of the segments. The invariant encoding of image fragments in fixation points is a necessary but insufficient condition for invariant representation of the whole image. In addition, it is necessary to encode invariant spatial relations between neighboring fragments of a scanpath. In the model, it is provided by encoding the position of the basic edge segment in the next $(n + 1)$-th fixation point in the coordinate system (X′OY′) joint with the basic edge segment in the previous n-th fixation point (by parameters $\Delta\psi_o(n + 1)$ and $\Delta\varphi_o(+ 1)$) and by encoding the relative change of resolution levels when the "gaze" is shifted from one fixation point ($\Delta lo(n + 1)$) to another (the position of the next fixation point is marked in *Fig. 6* by a circle). The parameters $\Delta\psi_o(n + 1)$, $\Delta\varphi_o(n + 1)$, and $\Delta lo(n + 1)$ are:

$$\Delta\psi(n + 1) = \mathrm{mod}_{1\sigma}(\psi_o(n + 1) - \psi(n) + 16),$$

$$\Delta\varphi_o(n + 1) = \varphi_k^*(n), \qquad (4.2)$$

$$\Delta lo(n + 1) = lo(n + 1) - lo(n),$$

where $\varphi_k^*(n)$ is the relative angle position of the context point (in the coordinate system joint with the n-th

Figure 5. The extracted basic and context segments in one fixation point.

372

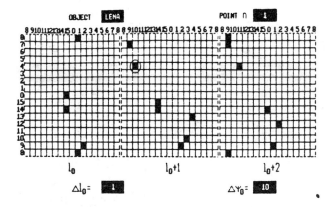

Figure 6. Invariant representation of one fragment (the same as in Fig. 5) as the black points in three coordinate systems on the evolvents of three tori.

fixation point) which is chosen as the next fixation point.

5. Object Memorizing, Search, and Recognition

The functional schema of the model of a visual neurocomputer is shown in *Fig. 7*. The model is to function in the following manner. In the mode of object memorizing, the image is processed in consecutively chosen points of fixation. In *Fig. 8a, b* the intermediate and final stages of sequential viewing of the object in the mode of memorizing are shown. In each fixation point, the set of oriented edge segments (the basic and several context ones) is extracted from the image fragment Then, the set is transformed into the form of three invariant patterns (as in *Fig. 6*). These patterns are memorized in the Neural Network playing the role of the Associative Memory for Fragment Storing. As a result of the memorizing mode, the fragments have been memorized in the Neural Network, and invariant relations between neighboring fragments have been memorized in the Motor Memory. In the mode of object search, the raster is scanned until a fragment similar to some memorized fragment of some object is found in some fixation point. When such a fragment is found, a hypothesis on the object is generated and the system turns to recognition. In the mode of recognition, consecutive fixations (controlled from the Motor Memory) and a consecutive verification of similarity of fragments (processed in the fixation points and represented in the invariant form) with the fragments stored in the Recognizing Neural Network take place. (A scanpath of viewing in the recognition mode ought to consequently reproduce the scanpath of viewing in the memorized mode). If a series of coincidences occurs, the decision is made that the object has been recognized. If it does not, the system turns to the mode of object search.

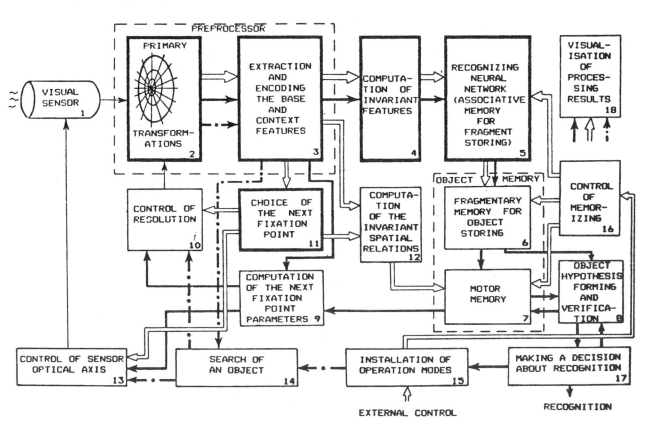

Figure 7. Functional scheme of the visual neurocomputer model. The interactions between functional blocks are depicted by arrows. The white, dot-dash, and black arrows relate to the modes of object momorizing, of object search, and of object recognition, respectively.

Figure 8. Intermediate (a) and final (b) stages of sequential viewing of the image.

6. References

[1] J. Buhmann, J. Lades. Chr. von der Malsburg, "Size and distortion invariant object recognition by hierarchical graph matching", *Proc. of the Int. Joint. Conf. on Neural Networks (IJCNN-90), San-Diego*, vol. II, pp. II—411—II—416, 1990.

[2] P. J. Burt, "Smart sensing within a pyramid vision machine", *Proc. of the IEEE*, vol. 76, pp. 1006—1015, 1988.

[3] J. Daugman, "Complete discrete 2-D Gabor transform by neural networks for image analysis and compression", *IEEE Trans. on Acoustic, Speech, and Signal Processing*, vol. 36, pp. 1169—1179, 1988.

[4] S. Grossberg, E. Mingolla, "A neural theory preattentive visual information processing: emergent segmentation, cooperative-competitive computation, and parallel memory storage", *Proc. of Int. Symp. "Struct. and Dyn. Nucl. Acids, Proteins, and Membranes, Riva del Garda, Aug. 31—Sept. 5, 1986"*, pp. 355—401, 1986.

[5] S. Grossberg, E. Mingolla, D. Todorovic, "A neural network architecture for preattentive vision", *IEEE Trans. on Biomedical Engineering*, vol. 36, pp. 65—84, 1989.

[6] D. Noton, L. Stark, "Scanpaths in eye movements during pattern recognition", *Science*, vol. 171, pp. 72—75, 1971.

[7] M. Porat, Y. Zeevi, "The generalized Gabor scheme of image representation in biological and machine vision", *IEEE Trans. on Pattern Analysis and Machine Intelligence*, vol. 10, pp.452—468, 1988.

[8] S. E. Traxel, S. K. Rogers, M. Kabrisky, "The use of neural networks in PSRI target recognition", *Proc. of the IEEE Int. Conf. on Neural Networks (ICNN-88), San Diego*, vol. I, pp. I—593—I—600, 1988.

[9] A. L. Yarbus, *Eye movements and vision*, Plenum Press, New York, 1967.

Article 6.5

Layered Neural Nets for Pattern Recognition

BERNARD WIDROW, FELLOW, IEEE, RODNEY G. WINTER, AND ROBERT A. BAXTER

Abstract—Adaptive threshold logic elements called ADALINES can be used in trainable pattern recognition systems. Adaptation by the LMS (least mean squares) algorithm is discussed. Threshold logic elements only realize linearly separable functions. To implement more elaborate classification functions, multilayered ADALINE networks can be used.

A pattern recognition concept involving first an "invariance net" and second a "trainable classifier" is proposed. The invariance net can be trained or designed to produce a set of outputs that are insensitive to translation, rotation, scale change, perspective change, etc., of the retinal input pattern. The outputs of the invariance net are scrambled, however. When these outputs are fed to a trainable classifier, the final outputs are descrambled and the original patterns are reproduced in standard position, orientation, scale, etc. It is expected that the same basic approach will be effective for speech recognition, where insensitivity to certain aspects of speech signals and at the same time sensitivity to other aspects of speech signals will be required.

The entire recognition system is a layered network of ADALINE neurons. The ability to adapt a multilayered neural net is fundamental. A new adaptation rule is proposed for layered nets which is an extension of the MADALINE rule of the 1960's. The new rule, MRII, is a useful alternative to the back-propagation algorithm.

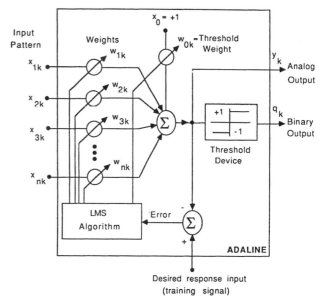

Fig. 1. An adaptive linear neuron (ADALINE).

INTRODUCTION

NETWORKS of neural elements can be utilized to construct trainable decision-making systems. The basic building block is the "adaptive linear neuron," or ADALINE [1], shown in Fig. 1. This is an adaptive threshold logic element. In a digital implementation, this element has at time k an input signal vector or input pattern vector $X_k = [x_0 x_{1k} x_{2k} \cdots x_{nk}]^T$ whose components are weighted by a set of coefficients. The weight vector is $W_k = [w_{0k} w_{1k} w_{2k} \cdots w_{nk}]^T$. The element produces an analog output, the inner product $y_k = X_k^T W_k = W_k^T X_k$. The bias weight w_{0k} is connected to a constant input, $x_0 = +1$, and it controls the threshold level. The element also produces a binary output, q_k. Decisions are made by a 2-level quantizer. The binary ± 1 output is $q_k = \text{SGN}(y_k)$.

The "desired response" is a special input signal used to train the neuron. During the training process, input patterns and corresponding desired responses are fed to this element. An adaptation algorithm automatically adjusts the weights so that the output responses to the input patterns will be as close as possible to their respective desired responses. Often this is done by adjusting the weights in accord with a least squares adaptation algorithm (the LMS algorithm [1], often called the Widrow-Hoff Delta Rule [2]). This algorithm minimizes the sum of the squares of the errors over the training set, where the error is defined as the difference between the desired response and the analog output.

The desired response and the components of X_k could be analog or binary. In neural networks, however, inputs and outputs are often binary and are preferred to be ± 1 rather than the unsymmetrical 0, 1. The weights are essentially continuously variable, and can take on negative as well as positive values.

Once the weights are adjusted and the neuron is trained, its responses can be tested by applying various input patterns. If the neuron responds correctly, with high probability, to input patterns that were not included in the training set, it is said that generalization has taken place. The capability of generalization is a highly significant attribute of neural nets.

Although the LMS algorithm originated in the field of neural nets, its greatest impact today is in the field of adaptive signal processing [3]. Commercial applications are in the field of telecommunications, adaptive equalizers [4] for high-speed digital modems, and adaptive echo cancellers [5] for long-distance telephone circuits and satellite channels. The LMS algorithm is widely used in adaptive signal processing and telecommunications.

Manuscript received February 22, 1988.

B. Widrow and R. A. Baxter are with the Department of Electrical Engineering, Stanford University, Stanford, CA 94305.

R. G. Winter is with the U.S. Air Force and the Department of Electrical Engineering, Stanford University, Stanford, CA 94305.

IEEE Log Number 8821364.

Reprinted from *IEEE Acoust., Speech, Signal Processing*, vol. 36, no. 7, pp. 1109–1118, 1988.

With n binary inputs and one binary output, a single neuron of the type shown in Fig. 1 is capable of implementing certain logic functions. There are 2^n possible input patterns. A general logic implementation would be capable of classifying each pattern as either $+1$ or -1, in accord with the desired response. Thus, there are 2^{2^n} possible logic functions connecting n inputs to a single output. A single neuron is capable of realizing only a small subset of these functions, known as the linearly separable logic functions [6]. These are the set of logic functions that can be obtained with all possible settings of the weight values.

In Fig. 2, a two-input neuron is shown. In Fig. 3, all possible binary inputs for a two-input neuron are shown in pattern vector space. In this space, the coordinate axes are the components of the input pattern vector. The neuron separates the input patterns into two categories, depending on the values of the input-signal weights and the bias weight. A critical thresholding condition occurs when the analog response y equals zero:

$$y = x_1 w_1 + x_2 w_2 + w_0 = 0 \qquad (1)$$

$$\therefore x_2 = -\frac{w_0}{w_2} - \frac{w_1}{w_2} x_1. \qquad (2)$$

This linear relation is graphed in Fig. 3. It comprises a separating line which has slope and intercept of

$$\text{slope} = -\frac{w_1}{w_2}; \quad \text{intercept} = -\frac{w_0}{w_2}. \qquad (3)$$

The three weights determine slope, intercept, and the side of the separating line that corresponds to a positive output. The opposite side of the separating line corresponds to a negative output.

As sketched in Fig. 3, the binary inputs are classified as follows:

$$(+1, +1) \rightarrow +1$$
$$(+1, -1) \rightarrow +1$$
$$(-1, -1) \rightarrow +1$$
$$(-1, +1) \rightarrow -1. \qquad (4)$$

This is an example of a linearly separable function. An example of a nonlinearly separable function with two inputs is the following.

$$(+1, +1) \rightarrow +1$$
$$(+1, -1) \rightarrow -1$$
$$(-1, -1) \rightarrow +1$$
$$(-1, +1) \rightarrow -1. \qquad (5)$$

No single line exists that can achieve this separation of the input patterns.

With two inputs, almost all possible logic functions can be realized by a single neuron. With many inputs, how-

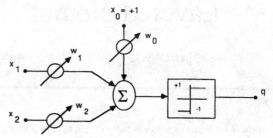

Fig. 2. A two-input neuron.

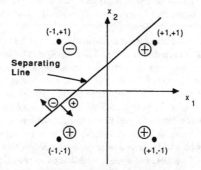

Fig. 3. Separating line in pattern space.

ever, only a small fraction of all possible logic functions are linearly separable. Since the single neuron can only realize linearly separable functions and generally cannot realize most functions, combinations of neurons or networks of neurons can be used to realize nonlinearly separable functions.

Before discussing networks of neurons, a simple means for achieving nonlinear separability with a single neuron with nonlinearities in its input signal path is shown next.

NONLINEAR SEPARABILITY—NONLINEAR INPUT FUNCTIONS

Nonlinear functions of the inputs applied to the single neuron can yield nonlinear decision boundaries. Consider the system illustrated in Fig. 4. The threshold condition is

$$y = w_0 + x_1 w_1 + x_1^2 w_{11} + x_1 x_2 w_{12}$$
$$+ x_2^2 w_{22} + x_2 w_2 = 0. \qquad (6)$$

With proper choice of the weights, the separating boundary in pattern space can be established as shown, for example, in Fig. 5. The nonlinearly separable function (5) can be realized by this configuration. Of course, with suitable choice of the weight values, all of the linearly separable functions are also realizable. The usage of such nonlinearities can be generalized for more inputs than two and for higher degree polynomial functions and cross product functions of the inputs. One of the first works in this area was done by Specht [7], [8] at Stanford in the 1960's, and later by Ivankhnenko [9] in the 1970's.

NONLINEAR SEPARABILITY—MADALINE NETWORKS

Another approach to the implementation of nonlinearly separable logic functions was initiated at Stanford by Hoff

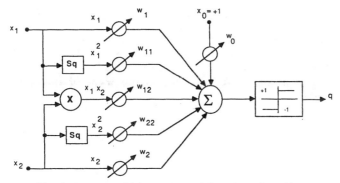

Fig. 4. A neuron with inputs mapped through nonlinearities.

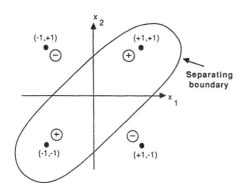

Fig. 5. An elliptical separating boundary for nonlinearly separable function realization.

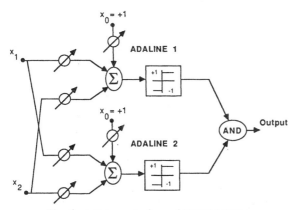

Fig. 6. A two-neuron form of MADALINE.

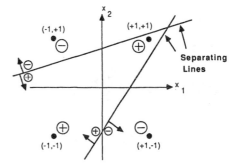

Fig. 7. Separating boundaries for MADALINE of Fig. 6.

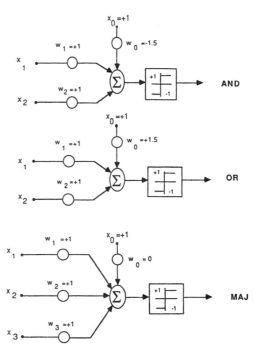

Fig. 8. Neuronal implementation of AND, OR, and MAJ logic functions.

various fixed logic devices in the second layer such as AND, OR, and MAJority vote-taker. These three functions are in themselves threshold logic functions, as illustrated in Fig. 8. The weights given will implement these functions, but the weight choices are not unique.

LAYERED NEURAL NETS

The MADALINES of the 1960's had adaptive first layers and fixed threshold functions for the second (the output) layers. The neural nets of the 1980's have many layers, and all layers are adaptive. The best-known multilayer work is by Rumelhart *et al.* [2]. A 3-layer adaptive network is illustrated in Fig. 9.

It is a simple matter to adapt the neurons in the output layer, since the desired responses for the entire network (which are given with each input training pattern) are the desired responses for the corresponding output neurons. Given the desired responses, adaptation of the output layer can be a straightforward exercise of the LMS algorithm. The fundamental difficulty associated with adaptation of a layered network lies in obtaining desired responses for

[10] and Ridgway [11] in the early 1960's. Retinal inputs were connected to adative neurons in a single layer. Their outputs in turn were connected to a fixed logic device providing the system output. Methods for adapting such nets were developed at that time. An example of such a network is shown in Fig. 6. Two ADALINES are connected to an AND logic device to provide an output. Systems of this type were called MADALINES (many ADALINES). Today such systems would be called neural nets.

With weights suitably chosen, the separating boundary in pattern space for the system of Fig. 6 would be as shown in Fig. 7. This separating boundary implements the nonlinearly separable logic function (5).

MADALINES were constructed with many more inputs, with many more neurons in the first layer, and with

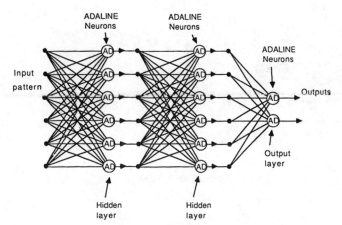

Fig. 9. A three-layer adaptive neural network.

the neurons in the layers other than the output layer. The back-propagation algorithm (reported earliest by Werbos [12] then discovered by Parker [13], and again discovered by Rumelhart *et al.* [2]) is one method for establishing desired responses for the neurons in the "hidden layers," those layers whose neuronal outputs do not appear directly at the system output (refer to Fig. 9).

Generalization in layered networks is a key issue. The question is: how well do multilayered networks perform with inputs that were not specifically trained in? Most of the work in the field deals with learning the training patterns. The question of generalization will be important and some good examples are being developed where useful generalizations take place. Many different algorithms may be needed for the adaptation of multilayered networks to produce required generalizations. Without generalization, neural nets will be of little engineering significance. Merely learning the training patterns can be accomplished by storing these patterns and their associated desired responses in a look-up table.

The layered networks of Parker and Rumelhart *et al.* utilize neuronal elements like the ADALINE of Fig. 1, except that the quantizer or threshold device is a soft limiting "sigmoid" function rather than the hard limiting "signum" function of the ADALINE. The various back-propagation algorithms for adapting layered networks of neurons require differentiability along the signal paths of the network, and cannot work with the hard limiter of the ADALINE element. The sigmoid function has the necessary differentiability. However, it presents implementational difficulties if the neural net is to be ultimately constructed digitally. For this reason, a new algorithm was developed for adaptation of layered networks of ADALINE neurons with hard limiting quantizers. The new algorithm is an extension of the original MADALINE adaptation rule [14], [15] and is called MADALINE rule II or MRII. The idea is to adapt the network to properly respond to the newest input pattern while minimally disturbing the responses already trained in for the previous input patterns. Unless this principle is practiced, it is difficult for the network to simultaneously store all of the required pattern responses.

LMS or Widrow–Hoff Delta Rule for the Single Neuron

The LMS algorithm applied to the adaptation of the weights of a single neuron embodies a minimal disturbance principle. A self-normalizing form of this algorithm can be written as

$$W_{k+1} = W_k + \frac{\alpha}{|X_k|^2} \epsilon_k X_k, \qquad (7)$$

where W_{k+1} is the next value of the weight vector, W_k is the present value of the weight vector, X_k is the present input pattern vector, and ϵ_k is the present error (i.e., the difference between the desired response and the analog output before adaptation). With binary ± 1 input vectors, $|X_k|^2$ equals the number of weights.

With each adapt cycle, the above recursion formula is applied, and the error is reduced as a result by the fraction α. This can be demonstrated as follows. At the kth interaction cycle, the error is

$$\epsilon_k = d_k - X_k^T W_k. \qquad (8)$$

The error is changed (reduced) by changing the weights.

$$\Delta \epsilon_k = \Delta(d_k - X_k^T W_k) = -X_k^T \Delta W_k. \qquad (9)$$

In accord with the LMS rule (7), the weight change is

$$\Delta W_k = W_{k+1} - W_k = \frac{\alpha}{|X_k|^2} \epsilon_k X_k. \qquad (10)$$

Combining (9) and (10), we obtain

$$\Delta \epsilon_k = -X_k^T \frac{\alpha}{|X_k|^2} \epsilon_k X_k$$

$$= -X_k^T X_k \frac{\alpha}{|X_k|^2} \epsilon_k$$

$$= -\alpha \epsilon_k. \qquad (11)$$

Therefore, the error is reduced by a factor of α as the weights are changed while holding the input pattern fixed. Putting in a new input pattern starts the next adapt cycle. The next error is then reduced by a factor of α, and the process continues. The choice of α controls stability and speed of convergence. Stability requires that

$$2 > \alpha > 0. \qquad (12)$$

Making α greater than 1 generally does not make sense, since the error would be overcorrected. Total error correction comes with $\alpha = 1$. A practical range for α is

$$1.0 > \alpha > 0.1. \qquad (13)$$

Fig. 10 gives a geometric picture of how the LMS rule works. W_{k+1} equals W_k plus ΔW_k in accord with (10), and ΔW_k is parallel with the input pattern vector X_k also in accord with (10). By (9), the change in the error will be equal to the negative dot product of X_k with ΔW_k. Since the LMS algorithm selects ΔW_k to be collinear with X_k,

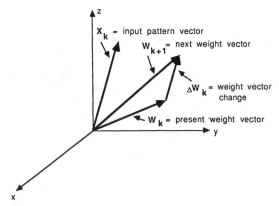

Fig. 10. Weight correction by the LMS rule.

the needed error correction is achieved with the smallest magnitude of weight vector change. When adapting to respond properly to a new input pattern, the responses to previous training patterns are therefore minimally disturbed, on the average. The algorithm also minimizes mean square error [3], for which it is best known.

ADAPTATION OF LAYERED NEURAL NETS BY THE MRII RULE

The minimal disturbance principle can be applied to the adaptation of the layered neural network of Fig. 9 in the following way. Present a retinal pattern vector and its associated desired response vector. The training objective is to reduce the number of output errors (the Hamming distance between the net's actual output and desired response vectors) to as low a level as possible. Accordingly, when the first training pattern is presented to the neural network, the first layer will be adapted as required to reduce the number of response errors at the final output layer. In accord with the minimal disturbance principle, the first-layer neuron whose analog response is closest to zero is given a trial adaptation in the direction to reverse its binary output. When the reversal takes place, the second layer inputs change, the second layer outputs change, and consequently the network outputs change. A check is made to see if this reduces the number of output errors. If so, the trial change is accepted. If not, the weights are restored to their previous values and the first-layer neuron whose analog response is next closest to zero is trial adapted, reversing its response. If this reduces the number of output errors, the change is accepted. If not, the weights are restored and one goes on to adaptively switch the neuron with an analog response next closest to zero, and so on, disturbing the neurons as little as possible. After adapting all of the first-layer neurons whose output reversals reduced the number of network output errors, neurons are then chosen in pair combinations and trial adaptations are made which can be accepted if output errors are reduced. After adapting the first-layer neurons in singles, pairs, triples, etc., up to a predetermined limit in combination size, the second layer is adapted to further reduce the number of network output errors. The method of choosing the neurons to be adapted in the second layer

is the same as that for the first layer. If further error reduction is needed, the output layer can be adapted. This is straightforward, since the output-layer desired responses are the desired responses for the network. After adapting the output layer, the responses will be correct. The next input pattern vector and its associated desired response vector are then applied to the neural network and the adaptive process resumes.

When training the network to respond correctly to the various input patterns, the "golden rule" is: *give the responsibility to the neuron or neurons that can most easily assume it*. In other words, *don't rock the boat* any more than necessary to achieve the desired training objective. This minimal-disturbance MRII algorithm has been tested extensively, and appears to converge and behave robustly. It appears to be a very useful algorithm and does not require differentiability throughout the net. A great deal of effort will be required to derive its mathematical properties. To simulate it and make it work is straightforward. Simulation gives insight into its behavioral characteristics. A parallel effort is contemplated: a) to analyze the algorithm mathematically, and b) to improve it and explore its application to practical problems on an empirical basis.

APPLICATION OF LAYERED NETWORKS TO PATTERN RECOGNITION

It would be useful to devise a neural net configuration that could be trained to classify an important set of training patterns as required, but have these responses be invariant to left–right, up–down translation within the field of view, and to be invariant to rotation and scale change. It should not be necessary to train the system with the specific training patterns of interest in all combinations of translation, rotation, and scale.

The first step is to show that a neural network exists having these properties. The next step is to obtain training algorithms to achieve the desired objectives.

INVARIANCE TO UP–DOWN, LEFT–RIGHT PATTERN TRANSLATION

Fig. 11 shows a planar network configuration (a "slab" of neurons) that could be used to map a retinal image into a single-bit output such that, with proper weights in the neurons of the network, the response will be insensitive to left–right translation and/or up–down translation. The same slab structure can be replicated, with different weights, to allow the retinal pattern to be independently mapped into additional single-bit outputs, all insensitive to left–right, up–down translation.

The general idea is illustrated in Fig. 12. The retinal image having a given number of pixels can be mapped through an array of slabs into a different image that could have the same number of pixels or possibly more or fewer pixels, depending on the number of slabs used. In any event, the mapped image would be insensitive to up–down, left–right translation of the original image. The

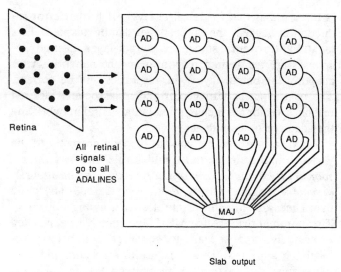

Fig. 11. One slab of a left–right, up–down translation invariant network.

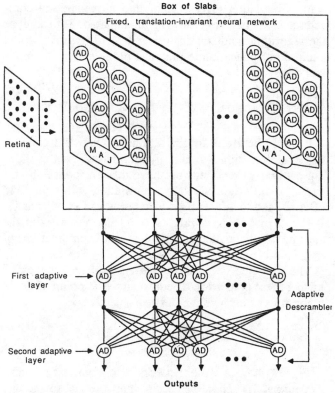

Fig. 12. A translation-invariant neural network and an adaptive two-layer descrambler network.

mapped image in Fig. 12 is fed to a set of ADALINE neurons that can be easily trained to provide output responses to the original image as required. These output responses would classify the original input images and would at the same time be insensitive to their left–right, up–down translations.

In the systems of Figs. 11 and 12, the elements labeled "AD" are ADALINES. Those labeled "MAJ" are majority vote-takers. (If the number of input lines to MAJ is even and there is a tie vote, these elements are biased to give a positive response.) The AD elements are adaptive

neurons and the MAJ elements are fixed neurons, as in Fig. 8.

How the weights are structured in the system of Fig. 11 to cause the output to be insensitive to left–right and up–down translation needs some further explanation. Our purpose here is to show that sets of weights exist that will achieve this function. How to adaptively obtain such weights is a separate issue. Consider the diagram of Fig. 13. This system is insensitive to up–down translation. Let the weights of each ADALINE in Fig. 13 be arranged in a square array. Let the corresponding retinal pixels also be arrayed in a square pattern. Let the array of weights of the topmost ADALINE be designated by the square matrix (W_1). Let the array of weights of the next lower ADALINE be $T_{D1}(W_1)$. The operator T_{D1} represents "translate down one." This set of weights is the same as that of the topmost ADALINE, except that they are en masse translated down by one pixel. The bottom row is wrapped around to comprise the top row. The patterns on the retina itself are wrapped around on a cylinder when they undergo translation. The weights of the next lower ADALINE are $T_{D2}(W_1)$, and those of the next lower ADALINE are $T_{D3}(W_1)$. As the input pattern is moved up or down on the retina, the roles of the various ADA-LINES interchange. Since the outputs of the four ADA-LINES are all equally weighted by the MAJ element, translating the input pattern up–down on the retina will have no effect on the MAJ element output.

The network of ADALINES of Fig. 13 is replicated on the slab of Fig. 11. Let the first column of weights in Fig. 11 be chosen like the weights of the column in Fig. 13. Let the second column of weights be chosen as

$$
\begin{array}{|c|}
\hline
T_{R1}(W_1) \\
T_{R1}T_{D1}(W_1) \\
T_{R1}T_{D2}(W_1) \\
T_{R1}T_{D3}(W_1) \\
\hline
\end{array}
\qquad (14)
$$

The topmost weights of this column are the weights (W_1) translated right one pixel. The next lower set of weights are translated right one, translated down one, and so forth. The pattern of weights for the entire array of ADALINES of Fig. 11 is given by

$$
\begin{array}{|cccc|}
\hline
(W_1) & T_{R1}(W_1) & T_{R2}(W_1) & T_{R3}(W_1) \\
T_{D1}(W_1) & T_{R1}T_{D1}(W_1) & T_{R2}T_{D1}(W_1) & T_{R3}T_{D1}(W_1) \\
T_{D2}(W_1) & T_{R1}T_{D2}(W_1) & T_{R2}T_{D2}(W_1) & T_{R3}T_{D2}(W_1) \\
T_{D3}(W_1) & T_{R1}T_{D3}(W_1) & T_{R2}T_{D3}(W_1) & T_{R3}T_{D3}(W_1) \\
\hline
\end{array}
\qquad (15)
$$

From column to column, the weight patterns are translated left–right. From row to row, the weight patterns are translated up–down. Since the outputs of all of the ADA-LINE units are equally weighted and dealt with symmetrically by the output MAJ element, it is clear that the out-

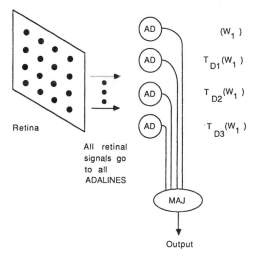

Fig. 13. Training insensitivity to up-down translation.

put of this system will be insensitive to both left–right and up–down translation.

The set of weights (W_1) could be randomly chosen. Once chosen, they can be translated according to (15) to fill out the array of weights for the system of Fig. 11. This array of weights can be incorporated as the weights for the first slab of ADALINES shown in Fig. 12. The weights for the second slab would require the same translational symmetries, but be based on a different randomly chosen set of weights (W_2) rather than (W_1). The mapping function achieved by the second slab would therefore be distinct from that of the first slab.

The translational symmetries in the weights called for in the system of Fig. 11 could be manufactured in and fixed, or the ADALINE elements could arrive at such symmetries as a result of a training process. If one knew

net. This system can be expanded to incorporate rotational invariance in addition to translational invariance.

Suppose that all input patterns can be presented in "normal" vertical orientation, approximately centered within the field of view of the retina. Suppose further that all input patterns can be presented when rotated by 90° from normal, and 180° and 270° from normal. Thus, each pattern can be presented in all four rotations and in addition, in all possible left–right, up–down translations. The number of combinations would typically be large. The problem is to design a neural net preprocessor that is invariant to translation and to rotation by 90°.

Refer to Fig. 11, which shows a single slab of ADALINE elements. This slab produces a majority output which is insensitive to translation of the input pattern on the retina. Refer next to Fig. 14, which shows four such slabs whose majority outputs feed into a single majority element. In the first slab, the matrix of weights of the ADALINE in the upper left-hand corner is designated by (W_1). The matrices of weights of all ADALINES in the first slab are shown in (15). In the second slab of Fig. 14, the weight matrix of the upper left-hand corner ADALINE corresponds to the weight matrix in the first slab, except rotated clockwise 90°. This can be designated by $R_{C1}(W_1)$. The corresponding upper left-hand corner ADALINE weight matrix of the third slab can be designated by $R_{C2}(W_1)$, and of the fourth slab $R_{C3}(W_1)$. Thus, the weight matrices of the upper left-hand corner ADALINES begin with (W_1) in the first slab, and are rotated clockwise by 90° in the second slab, by 180° in the third slab, and by 270° in the fourth slab. The weight matrices of all of these slabs are translated right and down, starting with the upper left-hand corner ADALINES. For example, the array of weight matrices for the second slab is represented by (16).

$$
\begin{array}{cccc}
R_{C1}(W_1) & T_{R1}R_{C1}(W_1) & T_{R2}R_{C1}(W_1) & T_{R3}R_{C1}(W_1) \\
T_{D1}R_{C1}(W_1) & T_{R1}T_{D1}R_{C1}(W_1) & T_{R2}T_{D1}R_{C1}(W_1) & T_{R3}T_{D1}R_{C1}(W_1) \\
T_{D2}R_{C1}(W_1) & T_{R1}T_{D2}R_{C1}(W_1) & T_{R2}T_{D2}R_{C1}(W_1) & T_{R3}T_{D2}R_{C1}(W_1) \\
T_{D3}R_{C1}(W_1) & T_{R1}T_{D3}R_{C1}(W_1) & T_{R2}T_{D3}R_{C1}(W_1) & T_{R3}T_{D3}R_{C1}(W_1)
\end{array}
\tag{16}
$$

when designing a pattern recognition system for a specific application that translational invariance would be a required property, it would make sense to manufacture the appropriate symmetry into a fixed weight system, leaving only the final output layers of ADALINES of Fig. 12 to be plastic and trainable. Such a preprocessor would definitely work, would provide a very high speed response without requiring scanning and searching for the pattern location and alignment, would be an excellent application of neural nets, and would be a useful practical product.

INVARIANCE TO ROTATION

The system represented in Fig. 12 is designed to preprocess retinal patterns with a translational invariant fixed neural net followed by a two-layer adaptive descrambler

Presenting a pattern to the retina causes an immediate response from the output majority element in Fig. 14. It is clear that this response will be unchanged by translation of the pattern on the retina. Rotation of the pattern by 90° causes an interchange of the roles of the slabs in making their responses, but since they are all weighted equally by the output majority element, the output response is unchanged by 90° rotation and translation.

If one wished to have insensitivity to 45° rotation, the system of Fig. 14 would need eight slabs, and the upper left-hand corner ADALINES would have weight matrices rotated by 45° relative to corresponding neighbors. In each slab, the weight matrices would be left–right, up–down translated. Rotation insensitivity can be achieved for much smaller angular increments by increasing the

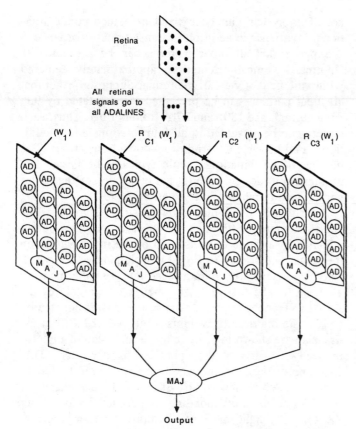

Fig. 14. A network for translational and rotational invariance.

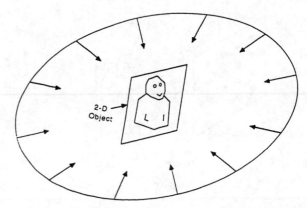

Fig. 15. Two-dimensional perspectives of a two-dimensional object.

Fig. 15 being photographed from various vantage points indicated by the arrows. Each two-dimensional photo will be of a certain perspective relative to the original object. The photos could be spatially quantized and provided as retinal inputs to a recognition system. The recognition problem requires first an insensitivity to perspective. The requirement is similar to insensitivity to scale, except that the vertical scale is fixed and the horizontal scale is variable. The method of approach is similar to that for insensitivity to scale, rotation, and translation.

Speech Recognition

The idea of an invariance net followed by a trainable classifier can, it is believed, be used effectively for speech recognition. Speech could be spectrally analyzed and sampled over time in each of a set of bandpass ranges, or it could be encoded by adaptive linear prediction and the LPC coefficients could be sampled over time, or some other form of preprocessing could be practiced to obtain input patterns for a speech classifier. Speech recognition requires insensitivity to certain aspects of speech and, at the same time, sensitivity to other aspects. Trainable sensitivity and insensitivity is needed. The system structure of Fig. 12 will have the proper attributes for this application. This will soon be tested and reported.

Simulation Experiments

The system of Fig. 12 was computer simulated. The training set consisted of 36 patterns each arranged on a 5 × 5 pixel retina in "standard" position. Twenty-five slabs, each with twenty-five ADALINES, having weights fixed in accord with the symmetry patterns of (15), were used in the translation-invariant preprocessor. The preprocessor output represented a scrambled version of the input pattern. The nature of this scrambling was determined by the choice of the upper-left ADALINE weight matrices (W_1), $\cdots$, (W_{25}). These weights were chosen randomly, the only requirement being that the input pattern to preprocessor output map be one-to-one. (This choice of weights produced a very noise intolerant mapping. Methods of training-in these weights using MRII to customize them to the training set are being investigated.)

MRII was used to train the descrambler. The descram-

number of slabs. Rotation of the weight matrices by small angular increments can only be done with large retinas having high resolution. All of this involves neural networks having large numbers of weights.

A complete neural network providing invariance to rotation and translation would involve the structures of both Figs. 12 and 14. Each slab of Fig. 12 would need to be replaced by the multiple slab and majority element system of Fig. 14.

Invariance to Scale

The same principles can be used to design invariance nets to be insensitive to scale or pattern size. Establishing a "point of expansion" on the retina so that input patterns can be expanded or contracted with respect to this point, two ADALINES can be trained to give similar responses to patterns of two different sizes if the weight matrix of one were expanded (or contracted) about the point of expansion like the patterns themselves. The amplitude of the weights must be scaled in inverse proportion to the square of the linear dimension of the retinal pattern. Adding many more slabs, the invariance net can be built around this idea to be insensitive to pattern size as well as translation and rotation.

Invariance to Perspective

Insensitivity to change in perspective is a difficult attribute to attain for three-dimensional objects. The following is a simpler problem. Consider the flat object of

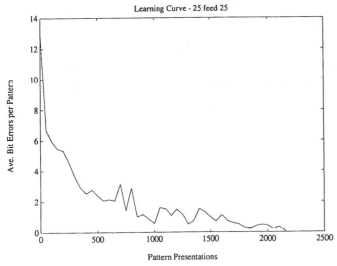

Fig. 16. Learning curve for 2-layer 25 by 25 adaptive descrambler.

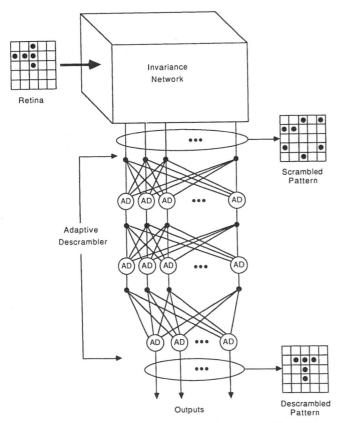

Fig. 17. A MADALINE system for pattern recognition.

scrambler is shown in Fig. 16. The graph shows the number of incorrect pixels at the output, averaged over the training set, every 50 pattern presentations.

Much work on MRII remains to be done, including detailed studies of its convergence properties and its ability to produce generalizations. Preliminary results are very encouraging. Applying the algorithm to problems will lead to insights that will hopefully allow a mathematical analysis of the algorithm.

Summary

A general concept for pattern recognition is described involving the use of an invariance net followed by a trainable classifier. The key ideas are illustrated in Fig. 17. The invariance net can be trained or designed to produce a set of outputs that are insensitive to translation, rotation, scale change, perspective, etc., of the retinal pattern. These outputs are scrambled, however. The adaptive layers can be trained to descramble the invariance net outputs and to reproduce the original patterns in ''standard'' position, orientation, scale, etc. The reader is referred once again to Fig. 17.

Multilayer adaptation algorithms are essential to making such a scheme work. A new MADALINE adaptation rule (MRII) has been devised for such a purpose, and preliminary experimental results indicate that it works and is effective.

References

[1] B. Widrow and M. E. Hoff, Jr., ''Adaptive switching circuits,'' in *IRE WESCON Conv. Rec.*, pt. 4, 1960, pp. 96–104.
[2] D. E. Rumelhart and J. L. McClelland, *Parallel Distributed Processing*, Vol. I and II. Cambridge, MA: M.I.T. Press, 1986.
[3] B. Widrow and S. D. Stearns, *Adaptive Signal Processing*. Englewood Cliffs, NJ: Prentice-Hall, 1985.
[4] R. W. Lucky, ''Automatic equalization for digital communication,'' *Bell Syst. Tech. J.*, vol. 44, pp. 547–588, Apr. 1965.
[5] M. M. Sondhi, ''An adaptive echo canceller,'' *Bell Syst. Tech. J.*, vol. 46, pp. 497–511, Mar. 1967.
[6] P. M. Lewis, II, and C. L. Coates, *Threshold Logic*. New York: Wiley, 1967.
[7] D. F. Specht, ''Vectorcardiographic diagnosis using the polynomial discriminant method of pattern recognition,'' *IEEE Trans. Biomed. Eng.*, vol. BME-14, pp. 90–95, Apr. 1967.
[8] ——, ''Generation of polynomial discriminant functions for pattern recognition,'' *IEEE Trans. Electron. Comput.*, vol. EC-16, pp. 308–319, June 1967.
[9] A. G. Ivakhnenko, ''Polynomial theory of complex systems,'' *IEEE Trans. Syst., Man, Cybern.*, vol. SMC-1, pp. 364–378, Oct. 1971.
[10] M. E. Hoff, Jr., ''Learning phenomena in networks of adaptive switching circuits,'' Ph.D. dissertation, Stanford Electron. Labs. Rep. 1554-1, Stanford Univ., Stanford, CA, July 1962.
[11] W. C. Ridgway, III, ''An adaptive logic system with generalizing properties,'' Ph.D. dissertation, Stanford Electron. Labs. Rep. 1556-1, Stanford Univ., Stanford, CA, Apr. 1962.
[12] P. Werbos, ''Beyond regression: New tools for prediction and analysis in the behavioral sciences,'' Ph.D. dissertation, Harvard Univ., Cambridge, MA, Aug. 1974.
[13] D. B. Parker, ''Learning logic,'' Tech. Rep. TR-47, Center for Comput. Res. Econ. and Manage. Sci., Mass. Inst. Technol., Cambridge, Apr. 1985.
[14] B. Widrow, ''Generalization and information storage in networks of adaline 'neurons,''' in *Self-Organizing Systems 1962*, M. C. Yovitz, G. T. Jacobi, and G. D. Goldstein, Eds. Washington, DC: Spartan Books, 1962, pp. 435–461.
[15] N. Nilsson, *Learning Machines*. New York: McGraw-Hill, 1965.

bler was a 2-layer system with 25 ADALINES in each layer. The initial weights of the descrambler were chosen randomly. (All random weights in the system were chosen independently, identically distributed uniformly on the interval $(-1, +1)$.) Patterns were presented in random order, each pattern being equally likely of being the next presented. The desired response used was the training pattern in standard position. The system as a whole would then recognize any trained-in pattern in any translated position on the input retina and reproduce it in standard position at the output. A typical learning curve for the de-

Article 6.6

Coarse-Coded Higher-Order Neural Networks for PSRI Object Recognition

Lilly Spirkovska and Max B. Reid, *Member, IEEE*

Abstract—A higher-order neural network (HONN) can be designed to be invariant to changes in scale, translation, and in-plane rotation. Invariances are built directly into the architecture of a HONN and do not need to be learned. Consequently, fewer training passes and a smaller training set are required to learn to distinguish between objects. The size of the input field is limited, however, because of the memory required for the large number of interconnections in a fully connected HONN. By coarse coding the input image, the input field size can be increased to allow the larger input scenes required for practical object recognition problems.

We describe a coarse coding technique and present simulation results illustrating its usefulness and its limitations. Our simulations show that a third-order neural network can be trained to distinguish between two objects in a 4096×4096 pixel input field independent of transformations in translation, in-plane rotation, and scale in less than ten passes through the training set. Furthermore, we empirically determine the limits of the coarse coding technique in the object recognition domain.

I. INTRODUCTION

THE objective in the position, scale, and rotation invariant (PSRI) object recognition domain is to recognize an object despite changes in the object's position in the input field, size, or in-plane rotation, as shown in Fig. 1. Various techniques have previously been applied to achieve this objective including a number of neural network methods. Three of the more successful neural network methods are first-order backward-error propagation (backprop) trained networks [1], the neocognitron [2], and higher-order networks [5]–[8]. In this paper, we will focus on the higher-order neural networks (HONN) approach. However, for comparison purposes, we will first briefly review results using the backprop algorithm as well as the neocognitron.

Backprop-trained first-order networks are the most popular methods used in neural network-based object recognition. The training process consists of applying input vectors sequentially and adjusting the network weights using a gradient descent learning rule until the input vectors produce the desired output vectors within some predetermined error. For a first-order network to learn to distinguish between a set of objects independent of their position, scale, or in-plane rotation, the network must be trained on a large subset of transformed views. The desired effect of including transformed views into the training set is that the hidden layers will extract the necessary invariant features and the network will generalize

Manuscript received January 15, 1991; revised February 25, 1992.

The authors are with the NASA Ames Research Center, Mountain View, CA.

IEEE Log Number 9202045.

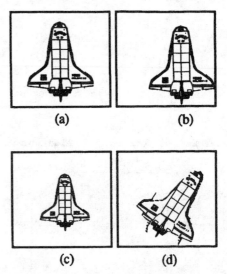

(a)   **(b)**

(c)   **(d)**

Fig. 1. In the PSRI (position, scale, and rotation invariant) object recognition domain, all four of these objects would be classified as a single object. Three transformations of the prototype in (a) are shown. The object in (b) is a translated view, (c) is scaled, and (d) is rotated in-plane.

the input vectors so that it can also recognize transformed views that are not part of the training set. Such generalization has been demonstrated in numerous simulations, including Rumelhart's T/C problem [3]. Typically, because first-order networks do not take advantage of predefined relationships between the input nodes, they require a large number of training passes to generalize the concepts behind the transformations. Also, even after extensive training with a large training set, they usually achieve only 80%–90% recognition accuracy on novel examples [3], [4].

A different approach to neural-based object recognition is the neocognitron. The human visual system is believed to be organized in a hierarchical structure in which first simple features are extracted and then combined into more complicated features. Moreover, a neuron in a higher stage of the hierarchy generally receives signals from a wide area of the preceding stage, thus correcting for small positional errors in the input. The neocognitron is based on this model of the human visual system.

Like the visual system, the neocognitron is arranged as a hierarchy of layers. The first stage is the input layer—a two-dimensional array of receptor cells. Each successive stage consists of two layers: "S-cells" followed by "C-cells." S-cells are feature extracting cells. The S-cells in the lower stages of the hierarchy extract local features such as lines in a particular orientation, whereas S-cells in higher stages extract

Reprinted from *IEEE Trans. on Neural Networks*, vol. 4, no. 2, pp. 276–283, March 1993.

global features such as substructures of the training pattern. Within each stage, a C-cell receives signals from a group of S-cells that extract the same feature, but from a slightly different position. Thus the C-cells desensitize the model to the exact position of the input. For a mathematical analysis of the training process, see Fukushima [2].

Following training, the neocognitron can recognize a pattern independent of its position in the input field, a slight change in size, or a slight deformation. Though deformations can include small rotations (up to a few degrees), the neocognitron has not been demonstrated for rotation invariance over a wider range [2].

The neocognitron has at least two limitations. First, the number of cells in the model increases almost linearly with the number of objects it is required to learn to distinguish. This makes the training process very slow. Also, as for first-order networks, the weights are pattern specific and thus the network must be completely retrained for each new set of patterns.

In contrast to these two approaches, in a HONN, known relationships are exploited and the desired invariances are built directly into the architecture of the network. Building such domain specific knowledge into the network's architecture results in a network which is "pretrained" and does not need to *learn* invariance to transformations. For each new set of training objects, a HONN only needs to learn to distinguish between the training objects; it does not need to generalize the concept behind the invariances. Therefore, training time is reduced significantly and HONN's need to be trained on just one view of each object, not on numerous transformed views. Moreover, 100% recognition accuracy is guaranteed for noise-free images characterized by the built-in transformations.

In this paper, we will discuss how known relationships can be exploited and desired invariances built into the architecture of higher-order neural networks, explain the limitations of using HONN's with higher resolution images, mention previous work on increasing the resolution by using partial connectivity strategies, and describe how coarse coding can be applied to HONN's to increase the input field size for use with practical object recognition problems. Furthermore, we discuss the problems associated with scale invariance and present empirical results determining the limits of the coarse coding technique.

II. HIGHER-ORDER NEURAL NETWORKS

The output of a node, denoted by y_i for node i, in a general higher-order neural network is given by

$$y_i = \Theta(\Sigma_j w_{ij} x_j + \Sigma_j \Sigma_k w_{ijk} x_j x_k + \Sigma_j \Sigma_k \Sigma_l w_{ijkl} x_j x_k x_l + \ldots) \quad (1)$$

where Θ is a nonlinear threshold function, the x_j's are the excitation values of the input nodes, and the interconnection matrix elements, w_{ij}, determine the weight that each input is given in the summation. As proposed by Giles *et al.* [5], [6], these higher-order terms can be used to build transformation invariance directly into the architecture of the network by using information about relationships expected between the input nodes. For instance, a strictly third-order network can be used to build simultaneous invariance to translation, scale, and in-plane rotation. The output for a strictly third-order network is given by the function

$$y_i = \Theta(\Sigma_j \Sigma_k \Sigma_l w_{ijkl} x_j x_k x_l). \quad (2)$$

As shown in Fig. 2, in a third-order network the input pixels are first combined in triplets and then the output is determined from a weighted sum of these products. These triplets of input pixels represent triangles with some included angles (α, β, γ). In order to build invariance to all three transformations into the architecture of the network, the weights are constrained such that all combinations of three pixels which define similar triangles are connected to the output with the same weight. That is

$$w_{ijkl} = w_{imno} \quad (3)$$

if the ordered included angles of the triangle formed by connecting pixels (j, k, l) are equal to the ordered included angles of the triangle formed by connecting pixels (m, n, o). The included angles are ordered such that the smallest angle is listed first and the next two angles are listed in the order they would be encountered if visited in a clockwise direction. Thus the three triangles represented by the included angles (30 60 90), (60 90 30), and (90 30 60) are all connected to the output node with the weight associated with (30 60 90), whereas the three triangles with included angles (30 90 60), (90 60 30), and (60 30 90) are all connected to the output node with the weight associated with (30 90 60). This in effect extracts all triangles which are geometrically similar. These similar triangle features are invariant to all geometric transformations which do not change the included angles including translation and in-plane rotation, as shown in Fig. 3. Similar triangles are also invariant to partial changes in scale. Unlike translation and in-plane rotation changes where an object and a transformed view of the same object contain exactly the same number of each possible triangle precluding the system from distinguishing between the two views, scaling an object introduces new triangles. We alleviate this problem and build partial scale invariance into the network in two ways. First, we limit the resolution to which the included angles are calculated, thereby decreasing the possible number of unique triangles. Second, we use edge-only images, thus reducing the number of new triangles introduced. To further alleviate the problem, the network can also be trained on scaled views of each object in order for it to be able to determine the relative content of triangles in scaled views of one object versus scaled views of the other objects. The amount of scale invariance automatically built into the network depends on the objects the network needs to distinguish between. In our work, we have achieved scale invariance up to a factor of four without including scaled views in the training set.

Note that the connections for similar triangles and equivalence of weights are established before any images are drawn in the field. Since these invariances are contained in the network architecture before any input vectors are presented, the network needs to learn to distinguish between just one view of each object, not numerous transformed views.

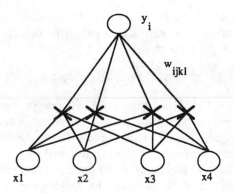

Fig. 2. A third-order network with 4 inputs and 1 output. Inputs are first multiplied together (at **X**) and then multiplied by a weight before being summed.

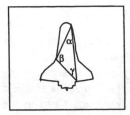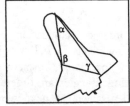

Fig. 3. Because the included angles are invariant over scale, rotation, or translation, invariance is built into the network by using the same weight for all similar triangles formed by input pixel triplets.

Consequently, fewer training passes and a smaller training set are required to learn to distinguish between the objects.

The most severe limitation of HONN's is that the number of possible triplet combinations increases as the size of the input field increases. In an $N \times N$ pixel input field, combinations of three pixels can be chosen in N^2-choose-3 ways. Thus for a 9×9 pixel input field, the number of possible triplet combinations is 81-choose-3 or 85 320. Increasing the resolution to 128×128 pixels increases the number of possible interconnections to 128^2-choose-3 or 7.3×10^{11}, a number too great to store on most machines. Furthermore, this number of interconnections is far too large to allow a parallel implementation in any hardware technology that will be commonly available in the foreseeable future.

To circumvent this limitation, in previous research we evaluated various strategies of connecting only a subset of input pixel triplets to the output node [8]. In particular, we evaluated regional connectivity in which triplets of pixels are connected to the output node only if the distances between all of the pixels composing the triplet fell within a set of preselected regions. Using this strategy, the input field size was increased to 64×64 while still retaining many of the advantages shown previously, such as a small number of training passes, training on only one view of each object, and successful recognition invariant to inplane rotation and translation. However, using regional connectivity, we were unable to recognize images invariant to changes in scale. Also, as the input field size increased, the amount of time for each pass on a sequential machine increased dramatically. The 64×64 pixel input field network took on the order of days on a Sun 3/60 to learn to distinguish between two objects. This is despite the fact that the number of interconnections was

greatly reduced from the fully connected version. The number of comparisons required was still huge.

In the following section, we will describe a coarse coding algorithm which allows a third-order network to be used with an input field size practical for object recognition problems while still retaining its ability to recognize images which have been scaled, translated, or rotated in-plane in an input field of at least 4096×4096 pixels. Training takes just a few passes and training time is on the order of minutes, instead of days for regionally connected networks.

III. COARSE CODING

The coarse coding representation presented is a variation of a distributed representation described by Hinton [9]. A distributed representation is a memory scheme in which each feature is represented by a pattern of activity over many units [10]. By using units which are very coarsely tuned, a network requires few units to encode many features accurately. The maximum number of features is determined by the density and degree of overlap of the units' receptive fields [11].

The coarse coding algorithm we use involves overlaying fields of coarser pixels in order to represent an input field composed of smaller pixels. This is analogous to the overlapping retinal fields which permit hyperacuity. To illustrate, refer to Fig. 4. Fig. 4(a) shows an input field of size 10×10 pixels. In Fig. 4(b), we show two offset but overlapping fields, each of size 5×5 "coarse" pixels. In this case, each coarse field is composed of pixels which are twice as large (in both dimensions) as in Fig. 4(a). To reference an input pixel using the two coarse fields requires two sets of coordinates. For instance, pixel $(x = 7, y = 6)$ on the original image would be referenced as the set of coarse pixels $((x = D, y = C)$ and $(x = III, y = III))$, assuming a coordinate system of (A, B, C, D, E) for coarse field one and (I, II, III, IV, V) for coarse field two. This is a one-to-one transformation. That is, each pixel on the original image can be represented by a unique set of coarse pixels.

Coarse coding can also be thought of as a variation of the general concept of a scale space [12] in which image data is simultaneously represented at differing levels of scale or resolution. Although in coarse coding the image is represented as a set of images at a fixed coarse scale, combining these low resolution images produces a progressively higher resolution image. Combining all of the low resolution images produces the original image. Note that the images are combined using the intersection of fields, not summation. Unlike scale space representations, however, where edge details may appear as the resolution increases, in coarse coding the gross shape of the object becomes apparent as lower resolution images are combined but this shape is not completely filled in and its bounding box is swollen.

The above transformation of an image to a set of smaller images can be used to greatly increase the resolution possible in a higher-order neural network. For example, a fully connected third-order network for a 10×10 pixel input field requires 10^2-choose-3 or 161 700 interconnections. Using 2 fields of 5×5 coarse pixels requires just 5^2-choose-3 or 2300 inter-

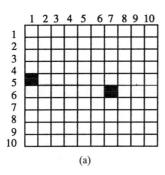

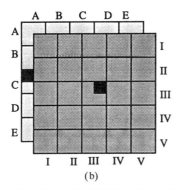

Fig. 4. (a) A 10×10 pixel input field. (b) Two fields of 5×5 coarse pixels.

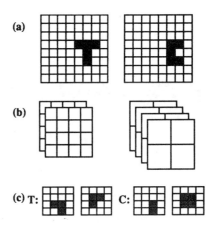

Fig. 5. (a) Two training images in an 8×8 pixel input field. (b) Two possible configurations of coarse pixels to represent the input field shown in (a). (c) Coarse coded representation of the training images shown in (a) using two layers of 4×4 coarse pixels.

connections. Thus the number of required interconnections is reduced by a factor of ~ 70. For a larger input field, the savings are even greater. For instance, for a 100×100 pixel input field, a fully connected third-order network requires 1.6×10^{11} interconnections. If we represent this field as 10 fields of 10×10 coarse pixels, only $161\,700$ interconnections are necessary. Thus the number of interconnections is decreased by a factor of $\sim 100\,000$.

One aspect of coarse coding which needs to be addressed is how the part of the image which is not intersected by all coarse fields is handled. That is, how is pixel (1,5) in the original image shown in Fig. 4(a) represented using the two fields in Fig. 4(b). There are at least two ways to implement coarse coding: 1) with wraparound or 2) by using only the intersection of the fields. If coarse coding is implemented using wraparound, pixel (1,5) could be represented as the set of coarse pixels ((A,C) & (V,II)). On the other hand, if coarse coding is implemented as the intersection of the coarser fields, the two fields shown in Fig. 4(b) would be able to uniquely describe an input field of 9×9 pixels, not 10×10.

Using wraparound, the relationship between input field size (IFS), coarse field size (CFS), and the number of coarse fields (n) in each dimension is given by

$$\text{IFS} = (\text{CFS}^{*}n). \qquad (4)$$

On the other hand, using the intersection of fields implementation, the relationship between input field size, number of coarse fields, and coarse field size in each dimension is given by

$$\text{IFS} = (\text{CFS}^{*}n) - (n-1). \qquad (5)$$

The effective input field size, IFS, is not significantly different with either implementation for small n.

IV. COARSE CODING AND HONN'S

As discussed in the previous section, coding an image as a set of coarser images greatly increases the size of the input field possible in a higher-order neural network. As an example of how coarse coding can be applied to HONN's, refer to Fig. 5. In order to train the network to distinguish between a "T" and a "C" in a 8×8 pixel input field, we could either train the network on the two images shown in Fig. 5(a) directly or apply coarse coding. Previous simulations [7] have demonstrated the first option. With coarse coding implemented with wraparound, as explained previously, there are two possible combinations which will provide an effective input field of 8×8 pixels: 2 fields of 4×4 coarse pixels or 4 fields of 2×2 pixels. Both possibilities are shown in Fig. 5(b).

Applying coarse coding by using 2 fields of 4×4 coarse pixels, the two images shown in Fig. 5(a) are transformed into the four images shown in Fig. 5(c). The network is then set up to associate the first two images with one output value and the second two images with a different output value. That is, the network is trained on the vectors:

$$(0000000001100010, 1)$$
$$(0000011001000000, 1)$$
$$(0000000000100010, 2)$$
$$(0000011001100000, 2)$$

where the first sixteen components represent the input pixel values and the last component represents the desired output value. Training of the network then proceeds in the usual way: the training vectors are applied and the weights modified until the network produces the desired output values. The output is determined using a hard limiting transfer function given by

$$\begin{aligned} y &= 1, \quad \text{if}\{\Sigma_n (\Sigma_j \Sigma_k \Sigma_l w_{jkl} x_j x_k x_l)\} > 0, \\ y &= 0, \qquad \text{otherwise,} \end{aligned} \qquad (6)$$

where $j, k,$ and l range from one to the number of coarse pixels, n ranges from one to the number of coarse fields, the x's represent coarse pixel values, and w_{jkl} represents the weight associated with the triplet of inputs (j, k, l). Moreover, since HONN's are capable of providing nonlinear separation

387

using only a single layer [7], the network can be trained using a simple perceptron-like rule of the form:

$$\Delta w_{ijkl} = (t_i - y_i) x_j x_k x_l \qquad (7)$$

where the expected training output, t, the actual output, y, and the inputs, x, are all binary.[1]

During testing, an input image is again transformed into a set of coarse images. Each of these "coarser" vectors are then presented to the network and an output value determined using (6).

V. SIMULATION RESULTS

We evaluated the coarse coding technique using an expanded version of the T/C problem. As explained in Rumelhart [3], in the T/C problem, both objects are constructed of 5 squares, as illustrated in Fig. 5(a), and the problem is to discriminate between them independent of translation or rotation. In our version of the problem, we use edge-only characters and the network is required to discriminate between the two objects independent of scale transformations, as well as translation and in-plane rotation.

A Sun 3/60 with 30 megabytes of swap space was used for simulations. Within this amount of memory, approximately 6.3 million (integer) interconnections can be stored. Thus for a third-order network, the size of the input field is limited to at most 18×18 pixels unless partial connectivity or coarse coding is used.

Implementing coarse coding using the intersection of fields, we have been able to increase the input image resolution for the T/C problem to 127×127 pixels using 9 fields of 15×15 coarse pixels. The network was trained on just two images: the largest "T" and "C" possible within the input field, as shown in Fig. 6. Training took just five passes.

A complete test set of translated, scaled, and one degree rotated views of the two objects in a 127×127 pixel input field consists of $\sim$135 million images. Assuming a test rate of 200 images per hour, it would take about 940 computer-months to test all possible views. Accordingly, we limited the testing to a representative subset consisting of four sets:

1) all translated views, but with the same orientation and scale as the training images;
2) all views rotated in-plane at 1° intervals, centered at the same position as the training images but only 60% of the size of the training images;
3) all scaled views of the objects, in the same orientation and centered at the same position as the training images;
4) a representative subset of approximately 100 simultaneously translated, rotated, and scaled views of the two objects.

The network achieved 100% accuracy on all test images in sets 1) and 2). Furthermore, the network recognized, with 100% accuracy, all scaled views, from test set 3), down to 38% of the original size. Objects smaller than 38% were all classified as C's. Finally, for test set 4), the network correctly recognized all images larger than 38% of the original size, regardless of the orientation or position of the test image.

[1] For efficiency, each unique weight is updated only once per pass.

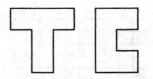

Fig. 6. A binary edge-only representation of a T and a C.

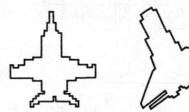

Fig. 7. A binary edge-only image of an F-18 aircraft and Space Shuttle orbiter.

A third-order network also learned to distinguish between practical images in a 127×127 pixel input field including a Space Shuttle Orbiter versus and F-18 aircraft (Fig. 7), shuttle versus X-29 aircraft, shuttle versus VW Bug, X-29 versus VW, etc. In the shuttle/F-18 case, training took just six passes through the training set, which consisted of just one (binary edge-only) view of each aircraft. As for the T/C problem, the network achieved 100% recognition accuracy of translated and in-plane rotated views of the two images. Additionally, the network recognized images scaled to almost half the size of the training images, regardless of their position or orientation. Results for the other training pairs were similar.

VI. COARSE CODING AND SCALE INVARIANCE

As the above examples illustrate, the amount of scale invariance a network achieves is not constant. As previously shown [7], invariance to scale is affected by the resolution to which the angles α, β, and γ in (4) are calculated. Briefly, as the resolution of the input field is increased, the resolution to which $\alpha, \beta,$ and γ are calculated can also be increased, generally increasing scale invariance. Angle resolutions of either 5°, 10°, or 20° were used in all the simulations presented below.

In addition, scale invariance varies with the coarse field size (CFS) as well as the number of coarse fields (n) used. In this section, we will discuss these two relationships in more detail.

In order to determine how CFS and n affect scale invariance, we simulated three scenarios using a third-order network trained on the T/C problem.

1) For a given CFS, we varied n.
2) For a given n, we varied CFS.
3) For a given input field size (IFS), we varied both CFS and n.

Table I shows the values for n, CFS, and IFS used for scenario one along with the scale invariance attained. The metric given for invariance is the ratio of the size of the training images, which were the largest scale "T" and "C" which could be drawn in the given IFS, to the size of the smallest test images correctly identified. Using a coarse field size of 10×10 pixels, we increased the number of fields,

TABLE I

VALUES USED FOR DETERMINING THE RELATIONSHIP BETWEEN THE NUMBER OF COARSE FIELD (n) AND SCALE INVARIANCE, ASSUMING THE COARSE FIELDS SIZE (CFS) REMAINS CONSTANT. SCALE INVARIANCE IS THE RATIO OF THE SIZE OF THE TRAINING IMAGES, WHICH WERE THE LARGEST VIEWS OF THE TWO OBJECTS WHICH COULD BE DRAWN IN THE GIVEN IFS, TO THE SIZE OF THE SMALLEST TEST IMAGES CORRECTLY IDENTIFIED. ALSO SHOWN IS THE EFFECTIVE INPUT FIELD SIZE (IFS).

CFS × CFS	n	IFS × IFS	Scale invariance
10 × 10	1	10 × 10	1.00
	2	19 × 19	1.49
	3	28 × 28	1.79
	4	37 × 37	1.72
	5	46 × 46	1.67
	6	55 × 55	1.64
	7	64 × 64	1.75
	8	73 × 73	1.72
	9	82 × 82	1.70
	10	91 × 91	1.75
	11	100 × 100	1.72
	12	109 × 109	1.79
	13	118 × 118	1.79
	14	127 × 127	1.75

TABLE II

VALUES USED FOR DETERMINING THE RELATIONSHIP BETWEEN THE COARSE FIELD SIZE (CFS) AND SCALE INVARIANCE, ASSUMING THE NUMBER OF COURSE FIELDS (n), REMAINS CONSTANT. ALSO SHOWN IS THE EFFECTIVE INPUT FIELD SIZE (IFS).

n	CFS × CFS	IFS × IFS	Scale invariance
5	4 × 4	16 × 16	1.00
	5 × 5	21 × 21	1.16
	6 × 6	26 × 26	1.14
	7 × 7	31 × 31	1.43
	8 × 8	36 × 36	1.20
	9 × 9	41 × 41	2.63
	10 × 10	46 × 46	1.67
	11 × 11	51 × 51	1.70
	12 × 12	56 × 56	1.49
	13 × 13	61 × 61	1.67
	14 × 14	66 × 66	1.81
	15 × 15	71 × 71	1.92
	16 × 16	76 × 76	1.67
	17 × 17	81 × 81	2.27
	18 × 18	86 × 86	2.33

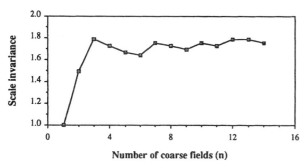

Fig. 8. Scenario one. The relationship between scale invariance and the number of coarse fields used in coarse coding an image. The coarse field size is constant.

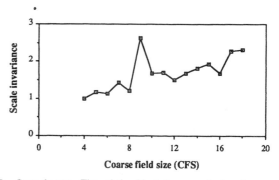

Fig. 9. Scenario two. The relationship between scale invariance and the coarse field size used in coarse coding an image. The number of coarse fields is constant.

TABLE III

VALUES USED FOR DETERMINING THE RELATIONSHIP BETWEEN THE COARSE FIELD SIZE (CFS), THE NUMBER OF FIELDS (n), AND SCALE INVARIANCE ATTAINED. ALSO SHOWN IS THE EFFECTIVE INPUT FIELD SIZE (IFS).

CFS × CFS	n	IFS × IFS	Scale invariance
3 × 3	63	127 × 127	1.00
4 × 4	42	127 × 127	1.20
5 × 5	31	125 × 125	1.18
6 × 6	25	126 × 126	1.14
7 × 7	21	127 × 127	1.14
8 × 8	18	127 × 127	1.27
9 × 9	16	129 × 129	1.35
10 × 10	14	127 × 127	1.75
11 × 11	13	131 × 131	1.43
12 × 12	12	133 × 133	2.00
13 × 13	11	133 × 133	2.56
14 × 14	10	131 × 131	2.38
15 × 15	9	127 × 127	2.63
16 × 16	9	136 × 136	1.72
17 × 17	8	129 × 129	2.70
18 × 18	8	137 × 137	3.45

thereby increasing the effective input field size up to 127×127 pixels. As Fig. 8 illustrates, the amount of scale invariance attained did not vary considerably relative to the number of coarse fields used.[2]

Similarly, Table II shows the values for n, CFS, IFS, and scale invariance attained for scenario two. Using five coarse fields, we increased the coarse field size up to the maximum possible (18×18 pixels, as will be discussed in the following section). As illustrated in Fig. 9, as the coarse field size is increased, the amount of scale invariance attained generally increases.

Finally, for scenario three, we designed a third-order network to solve the T/C problem in an input field as close to 127×127 pixels as possible using the intersection of fields implementation. Table III shows the values for n, CFS, and IFS used in simulations, as well as the scale invariance attained. As illustrated in Fig. 10, the amount of scale invariance attained generally increases as the coarse field size increases.

Alternatively, scale invariance increases as the number of fields decreases.

In general, a larger coarse field size yields greater scale invariance. However, the learning time also increases as the coarse field size increases, as illustrated in Fig. 11. Thus if

[2] For $n = 1$ and CFS $= 10 \times 10$, test images smaller than the training images could not be drawn, and the network was limited to scale invariance of 1. For $n = 2$ and CFS $= 10 \times 10$, three scales of T and C could be drawn giving three possibilities for scale invariance: 1, 1.5, or 2.1.

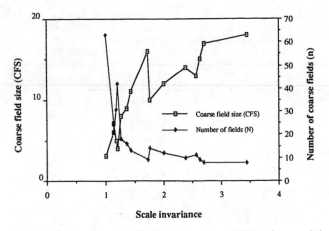

Fig. 10. Scenario three. The relationship between scale invariance and the coarse field size and number of coarse fields. Both coarse field size and number of coarse fields are allowed to vary while the input image size is held approximately constant.

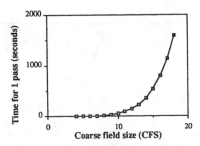

Fig. 11. The relationship between learning time and coarse field size. The input field size was held approximately constant at 127 pixels and the number of passes required to learn to distinguish between the training objects did not vary significantly relative to the coarse field size.

less scale invariance can be tolerated, a desired input field size can be represented with a smaller coarse field size and greater number of coarse fields. Even if speed is not critical, scale invariance can be increased but is still limited by the coarse field size. In the next section, we examine this limit as well as some of the other limits of coarse coding.

VII. LIMITS OF COARSE CODING

This section will discuss some of the limitations of the coarse coding technique including the minimum and maximum coarse field size, the minimum and maximum number of fields which can be used and still achieve transformation invariant recognition, and the maximum input field resolution possible.

The minimum possible coarse field size is determined by the training images. The network is unable to distinguish between the training images when the size of each coarse pixel is increased to the point where the training images no longer produce unique coarse coded representations. As an example, for the T/C problem, the minimum coarse field size which still produces unique representations is 3×3 pixels.

In contrast, the maximum limit is determined by the HONN architecture and the memory available for its implementation, and not by the coarse coding technique itself. As discussed previously, the number of possible triplet combinations in a third-order network is N^2-choose-3 for an $N \times N$ pixel input field. Given the memory constraints of our Sun 3/60, the

maximum possible coarse field size is therefore 18×18 pixels [8].

Regarding the number of coarse fields which can be used and still achieve PSRI object recognition, the minimum is one field whereas the maximum has not yet been reached. A minimum of one coarse field represents the non coarse-coded HONN case discussed in [5]–[8]. In order to determine the limit for the maximum number of fields possible, we ran simulations on the T/C problem coded with a variable number of 3×3 coarse pixels. A third-order network was able to learn to distinguish between the two characters in less than ten passes in an input field size of up to 4095×4095 pixels using 2047 fields.[3] Increasing the number of fields beyond this was not attempted because 4096×4096 is the maximum resolution available on most image processing hardware which would be used in a complete HONN-based vision system. Also, each object in such a large field requires 16 megabytes of storage space. It takes only a few such objects to fill up a disk.[4]

Finally, as with the maximum number of coarse fields, the maximum input field resolution possible with coarse coded HONN's has not been delimited. As discussed above, we trained a third-order network on the T/C problem in up to a 4096×4096 pixel input field. We expect a resolution of 4096×4096 is sufficient for most object recognition tasks. Notwithstanding, we also expect a greater resolution is possible.

VIII. CONCLUSIONS

The most important advantage of the HONN architecture is that invariance to geometric transformations, such as translation, scale, or in-plane rotation, can be incorporated into the network and does not need to be learned. Because the network weights are constrained by this domain specific knowledge, fewer training passes and a smaller training set are required to learn the desired concepts. However, because of the memory required for the large number of interconnections in a fully connected HONN, the size of the input field is limited. Using offset but overlapping fields of coarse pixels, we demonstrated that a larger input field is easily obtained.

In simulations, a third-order network was able to learn to distinguish between two objects in a 4096×4096 pixel input field using 273 fields of 16×16 coarse pixels. Compared with previous work on increasing the resolution of a HONN by using partial connectivity strategies, training time was reduced significantly. Also, using partial connectivity strategies, HONN's were unable to learn full in-plane rotation, translation, and scale invariance. In particular, a partially connected network was unable to distinguish between two objects independent of changes in scale. In comparison, using coarse coding, we demonstrated not only invariance to transformations in translation and in-plane rotation, but also scale up to a factor of over three.

[3] An input field resolution of 4096×4096 was also achieved by using 273 fields of 16×16 coarse pixels.

[4] Note that this is not a limitation of the coarse-coding scheme itself. If a 4096×4096 pixel image could be stored on disk, using the intersection of fields approach to coarse coding, we could represent it as 228 fields of 18×18 coarse pixels, requiring only 5.6 megabytes of memory.

Furthermore, we discussed the limitations of the coarse coding technique. We determined that the minimum coarse field size is dependent on the training images and can not be decreased to the point where the training images no longer produce unique coarse-coded representations, whereas the maximum is determined by the HONN architecture itself and the memory available for its implementation. Given our memory constraints of 30 megabytes, the maximum coarse pixel size cannot exceed 18×18 pixels. In addition, the minimum number of coarse fields is 1, representing the non coarse-coded HONN, whereas a maximum number of coarse fields has not been reached. The network successfully learned to distinguish between a T and a C using up to 2047 coarse fields, each of 3×3 coarse pixels, for an effective input field size of 4095×4095 pixels. And finally, the maximum input field resolution was also not reached. We trained a third-order network on the T/C problem in up to a 4096×4096 pixel input field. Though we expect this resolution is adequate for most object recognition tasks, we also expect a greater resolution is possible.

REFERENCES

[1] D. E. Rumelhart, G. E. Hinton, and R. J. Williams, "Learning internal representations by error propagation," in *Parallel Distributed Processing.* Cambridge, MA: MIT Press, 1986, vol. 1, ch. 8.

[2] K. Fukushima, "Analysis of the process of visual pattern recognition by the neocognitron," *Neural Networks,* vol. 2, pp. 413–420, 1989.

[3] D. E. Rumelhart, *Neural Networks,* vol. 2, pp. 348–352, 1989.

[4] S. E. Troxel, S. K. Rogers, and M. Kabrisky, "The use of neural networks in PSRI recognition," in *Proc. Joint Int. Conf. Neural Networks,* San Diego, CA, July 24–27, 1988, pp. 593–600.

[5] G. L. Giles and T. Maxwell, "Learning, invariances, and generalization in high-order neural networks," *Appl. Opt.,* vol. 26, pp. 4972–4978, 1987.

[6] G. L. Giles, R. D. Griffin, and T. Maxwell, "Encoding geometric invariances in higher-order neural networks," *Neural Information Processing Systems,* American Institute of Physics Conference Proceedings, pp. 301–309, 1988.

[7] M. B. Reid, L. Spirkovska, and E. Ochoa, "Simultaneous position, scale, and rotation invariant pattern classification using third-order neural networks," *Int. J. Neural Networks,* vol. 1, pp. 154–159, 1989.

[8] L. Spirkovska and M. B. Reid, "Connectivity strategies for higher-order neural networks applied to pattern recognition," in *Proc. Joint Int. Conf. Neural Networks,* San Diego, CA, June 18–21, 1990, pp. 121–126.

[9] G. E. Hinton, J. L. McClelland, and D. E. Rumelhart, "Distributed representations," in *Parallel Distributed Processing.* Cambridge, MA: MIT Press, 1986, vol. 1, ch. 3.

[10] R. Rosenfeld and D. S. Touretzky, "A survey of coarse-coded symbol memories," in *Proc. 1988 Connectionist Models Summer School,* Carnegie Mellon University, Pittsburgh, PA, June 17–26, 1988, pp. 256–264.

[11] J. Sullins, "Value cell encoding strategies," Tech. Rep. TR-165, Computer Science Department, University of Rochester, Rochester, NY, 1985.

[12] A. P. Witkin, "Scale-space filtering," in *Proc. 8th Int. Joint Conf. AI,* Karlsruhe, West Germany, August 8–12, 1983, pp. 1019–1022.

Article 6.7

NEOCOGNITRON: A NEW ALGORITHM FOR PATTERN RECOGNITION TOLERANT OF DEFORMATIONS AND SHIFTS IN POSITION

Kunihiko Fukushima and Sei Miyake

NHK Broadcasting Science Research Laboratories, 1-10-11, Kinuta, Setagaya, Tokyo 157, Japan

(*Received* 15 *May* 1981; *in revised form* 27 *October* 1981; *received for publication* 23 *December* 1981)

Abstract—Suggested by the structure of the visual nervous system, a new algorithm is proposed for pattern recognition. This algorithm can be realized with a multilayered network consisting of neuron-like cells. The network, "neocognitron", is self-organized by unsupervised learning, and acquires the ability to recognize stimulus patterns according to the differences in their shapes: Any patterns which we human beings judge to be alike are also judged to be of the same category by the neocognitron. The neocognitron recognizes stimulus patterns correctly without being affected by shifts in position or even by considerable distortions in shape of the stimulus patterns.

Visual pattern recognition	Deformation-resistant	Position-invariant
Unsupervised learning	Self-organization	Multilayered network
Neural network model	Visual nervous system	Simulation

1. INTRODUCTION

Most of the methods for pattern recognition, especially template matching techniques, are oversensitive to shifts in position and distortions in shape of the stimulus patterns, and it is necessary to normalize the position and the shape of the stimulus pattern beforehand. A good method for normalization, however, has not been developed as yet. Therefore, the finding of an algorithm for pattern recognition which can cope with shifts in position and distortions in shape of the stimulus patterns has long been desired.

In this paper, we propose a new algorithm* which gives an important solution to this problem. The new algorithm proposed here can be realized with a multilayered network consisting of neuron-like cells.

The network is called a "neocognitron". It is self-organized by unsupervised learning and acquires the ability for correct pattern recognition.

Historically, the three-layered perceptron proposed by Rosenblatt[4] is a famous example of networks of neuron-like cells capable of pattern recognition. For some time after the perceptron was first proposed, great hope was felt for its capability for pattern

recognition and a great deal of research was done on it. With the progress of this research, however, it was gradually revealed that the capability of the perceptron was not so great as had been expected.[5]

The perceptron consists of only three layers of cells, but it is well known that the capability of a multi-layered network can be greatly enlarged if the number of layers is increased. The algorithm of self-organization employed in the perceptron, however, cannot be successfully applied for the self-organization of a multilayered network. The three-layered perceptron is trained by supervised learning, a "learning-with-a-teacher" process, and only the deepest-layer cells have their input interconnections reinforced on instructions from a "teacher": the "teacher" knows the category to which each of the training patterns should be classified, and teaches each of the deepest-layer cells what its desired output is. If we want to train a multilayered network, in which not only the deepest-layer cells but also the intermediate-layer cells should have their input interconnections reinforced, the conventional training method used for the perceptron is not suited. This is because we do not know how the "teacher" should give instructions to the intermediate-layer cells, whose desired responses cannot simply be determined only from the information about the category to which the stimulus pattern should be classified.

One of the authors, Fukushima, formerly proposed a new algorithm for self-organization which can be effectively applied even to a multilayered network. This algorithm is based on the principle that only maximum-output cells have their input intercon-

---

* The basic idea of the new algorithm proposed here was first reported by one of the authors as a neural network model for a mechanism of visual pattern recognition in the brain.[1,2] In this paper, we discuss the problem from an engineering point of view, and concentrate our discussion on the application of the algorithm in pattern recognition and learning. Part of this paper was reported at the 5th ICPR[3] by the authors, and the results of a computer simulation were presented as a movie.

nections reinforced, and no instructions from a "teacher" are necessary. The "cognitron"[6,7] is a multi-layered network, in which this algorithm is employed. The self-organization of the cognitron is performed by unsupervised learning, a "learning-without-a-teacher" process. A computer simulation demonstrated that the cognitron had a much higher capability for pattern recognition than the three-layered perceptron.

However, the cognitron, as with the three-layered perceptron, does not have the capability to correctly recognize position-shifted or shape-distorted patterns: the same pattern presented at a different position is usually recognized as a different pattern by the conventional cognitron.

The "neocognitron", which will be discussed in this paper, is an improved version of the conventional cognitron and has the capability to recognize stimulus patterns correctly, even if the patterns are shifted in position or distorted in shape.

The self-organization of the neocognitron is also performed by unsupervised learning: only repetitive presentation of a set of stimulus patterns is necessary for the self-organization of the neocognitron and no information about the categories to which these patterns should be classified is needed. The neocognitron acquires the ability to classify and correctly recognize these patterns by itself, according to the differences in their shapes: any pattern which we human beings judge to be alike are also judged to be of the same category by the neocognitron. The neocognitron recognizes stimulus patterns correctly without being affected by shifts in position or even by considerable distortions in shape of the stimulus patterns.

The neocognitron has a hierarchical structure. The information of the stimulus pattern given to the input layer of the neocognitron is processed step by step in each stage of the multilayered network: a cell in a deeper stage generally has a tendency to respond selectively to a more complicated feature of the stimulus patterns and, at the same time, has a larger receptive field* and is less sensitive to shifts in position of the stimulus patterns. Thus, each cell in the deepest stage responds only to a specific stimulus pattern without being affected by the position or the size of the stimulus patterns.

2. CELLS EMPLOYED IN THE NEOCOGNITRON

Before discussing the structure of the neocognitron, let us discuss the characteristics of the cells employed in it.

All the cells employed in the neocognitron are of analog type: i.e., the input and output signals of the cells take non-negative analog values. Each cell has

characteristics analogous to a biological neuron, if we consider that the output signal of the cell corresponds to the instantaneous firing frequency of the actual biological neuron.

In the neocognitron, we use four different kinds of cells, i.e., S-cells, C-cells, V_S-cells and V_C-cells. As a typical example of these cells, we will first discuss the characteristics of an S-cell.

As shown in Fig. 1, an S-cell has a lot of input terminals, either excitatory of inhibitory. If the cell receives signals from excitatory input terminals, the output of the cell will increase. On the other hand, a signal from an inhibitory input terminal will suppress the output. Each input terminal has its own interconnecting coefficient whose value is positive. Although the cell has only one output terminal, it can send signals to a number of input terminals of other cells.

An S-cell has an inhibitory input which causes a shunting effect.[6,7] Let $u(1)$, $u(2)$, ..., $u(N)$ be the excitatory inputs and v be the inhibitory input. The output w of this S-cell is defined by

$$w = \varphi \left[\frac{1 + \sum_{v=1}^{N} a(v) \cdot u(v)}{1 + b \cdot v} - 1 \right], \qquad (1)$$

where $a(v)$ and b represent the excitatory and inhibitory interconnecting coefficients, respectively. The function $\varphi[\ ]$ is defined by the following equation:

$$\varphi[x] = \begin{cases} x & (x \geqq 0) \\ 0 & (x < 0) \end{cases}, \qquad (2)$$

Let us further discuss the characteristics of this cell. Let e be the sum of all the excitatory inputs weighted with the interconnecting coefficients and h the inhibitory input multiplied by the interconnecting coefficient; i.e.,

$$e = \sum_{v=1}^{N} a(v) \cdot u(v), \qquad (3)$$

$$h = b \cdot v. \qquad (4)$$

Equation (1) can now be written as

$$w = \varphi \left[\frac{1+e}{1+h} - 1 \right] = \varphi \left[\frac{e-h}{1+h} \right]. \qquad (5)$$

When the inhibitory input is small ($h \ll 1$), we have $w \doteq \varphi[e - h]$, which coincides with the characteristics

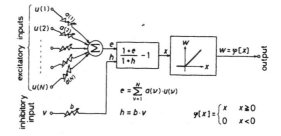

Fig. 1. Input-to-output characteristics of an S-cell: A typical, example of the cells employed in the neocognitron.

---

* The "receptive field" of a cell is defined as an area on the input layer such that a stimulus presented there gives some effect on the response of the cell. In other words, it is the area from which some information is transmitted, either directly or indirectly, to the cell.

of the conventional analog-threshold-element.[8] For a system like the neocognitron, where the interconnecting coefficients $a(v)$ and b increase unboundedly as learning progresses, the employment of elements such as analog-threshold-elements is not suitable because their outputs may increase without bound. In the cell employed here, however, if the interconnecting coefficients increase and we have $e \gg 1$ and $h \gg 1$, equation (5) reduces approximately to $w \doteq \varphi[e/h - 1]$, where the output w is determined by the ratio e/h and not by the difference $e - h$. Therefore, even if the interconnecting coefficients increase with learning, the output of the cell approaches a certain value without divergence, so long as both the excitatory interconnecting coefficients $a(v)$ and the inhibitory interconnecting coefficient b increase at the same rate.

Let us observe the input-to-output relation of the cell in the case where the excitatory and inhibitory inputs vary in proportion. If we write

$$e = \varepsilon x, \quad h = \eta x,$$

and if $\varepsilon > \eta$ holds, equation (5) can be transformed as

$$w = (\varepsilon - \eta)\frac{x}{1 + \eta x}$$

$$= \frac{\varepsilon - \eta}{2\eta}\left\{1 + \tanh\left(\frac{1}{2}\log \eta x\right)\right\}. \quad (6)$$

This input-to-output relation coincides with the logarithmic relation expressed by Weber-Fechner's low on which an S-shaped saturation, expressed by tanh is superposed. The same expression is often used as an empirical formula in neurophysiology and psychology to approximate the nonlinear input-to-output relations of the sensory systems of animals.

The cells other than S-cells also have characteristics similar to those of S-cells. The input-to-output characteristics of a C-cell are obtained from equation (5) if we replace $\varphi[\ ]$ with $\psi[\ ]$, where $\psi[\ ]$ is a saturation function defined by

$$\psi[x] = \begin{cases} \dfrac{x}{\alpha + x} & (x \geqq 0) \\ 0 & (x < 0). \end{cases} \quad (7)$$

The parameter α is a positive constant which determines the degree of saturation of the output. In the computer simulation discussed in Section 6, we chose $\alpha = 0.5$.

S-cells and C-cells are excitatory cells, i.e., the output terminals of these cells are connected only to excitatory input terminals of other cells.

On the other hand, V_S-cells and V_C-cells are inhibitory cells, whose output terminals are connected only to inhibitory input terminals of other cells. A V_s-cell has only excitatory input terminals and the output of the cell is proportional to the sum of all the inputs weighted with the interconnecting coefficients. That is, a V_S-cell yields an output proportional to the (weighted) arithmetic mean of its inputs.

A V_C-cell also has only excitatory input terminals,

but its output is proportional to the (weighted) root-mean-square of its input. Let $u(1), u(2), \ldots, u(N)$ be the inputs to a V_C-cell and $c(1), c(2), \ldots, c(N)$ be the interconnecting coefficients of its input terminals. The output w of this V_C-cell is defined by

$$w = \sqrt{\sum_{v=1}^{N} c(v) \cdot u^2(v)}. \quad (8)$$

3. STRUCTURE OF THE NETWORK

As shown in Fig. 2, the neocognitron consists of a cascade connection of a number of modular structures preceded by an input layer U_0. Each of the modular structures is composed of two layers of cells, namely a layer U_S consisting of S-cells, and a layer U_C consisting of C-cells*. In the neocognitron, only the input interconnections to S-cells are variable and modifiable and the input interconnections to other cells are fixed and unmodifiable.

The input layer U_0 consists of a photoreceptor array. The output of a photoreceptor is denoted by $u_0(\mathbf{n})$ where $\mathbf{n}$ is the two-dimensional co-ordinates indicating the location of the cell.

S-cells or C-cells in any single layer are sorted into subgroups according to the optimum stimulus features of their receptive fields. Since the cells in each subgroup are set in a two-dimensional array, we call the subgroup a "cell-plane". We will also use the terminology S-plane and C-plane, representing cell-planes consisting of S-cells and C-cells, respectively.

It is determined that all the cells in a single cell-plane have input interconnections of the same spatial distribution and only the positions of the preceding cells from which their input interconnections come are shifted in parallel. This situation is illustrated in Fig. 3. Even in the process of learning, in which the values of the input interconnections of S-cells are varied, the variable interconnections are always modified under this restriction.

We will use the notation $u_{Sl}(k_l, \mathbf{n})$ to represent the output of an S-cell in the k_l-th S-plane in the l-th module, and $u_{Cl}(k_l, \mathbf{n})$ to represent the output of a C-cell in the k_l-th C-plane in that module, where $\mathbf{n}$ is the two-dimensional co-ordinates representing the position of these cells' receptive fields on the input layer.

Figure 4 is a schematic diagram illustrating the interconnections between layers. Each tetragon drawn with heavy lines represents an S-plane or a C-plane and each vertical tetragon drawn with thin lines, in which S-

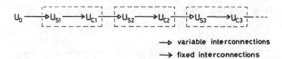

Fig. 2. The hierarchical structure of the neocognitron.

---

* S-cells and C-cells are named after simple cells and complex cells in physiological terms, respectively.

planes or C-planes are enclosed, represents an S-layer or a C-layer.

In Fig. 4, for the sake of simplicity, only one cell is shown in each cell-plane. Each of these cells receives input interconnections from the cells within the area enclosed by the ellipse in its preceding layer. All the other cells in the same cell-plane have input interconnections of the same spatial distribution and only the positions of the preceding cells, to which their input terminals are connected, are shifted in parallel from cell to cell. Hence, all the cells in a single cell-plane have receptive fields of the same function but at different positions.

Since the cells in the network are interconnected in a cascade as shown in Fig. 4, the deeper the layer is, the larger becomes the receptive field of each cell of that layer. The density of the cells in each cell-plane is so determined as to decrease in accordance with the increase in the size of the receptive fields. Hence, the total number of the cells in each cell-plane decreases with the depth of the cell-plane in the network. In the deepest module, the receptive field of each C-cell becomes so large as to cover the whole input layer and each C-plane is so determined as to have only one C-cell.

As mentioned in Section 2, the S-cells and C-cells are excitatory cells. Although it is not shown in Fig. 4, we also have inhibitory cells, namely, V_S-cells in S-layers and V_C-cells in C-layers.

Here we will describe the outputs of the cells in the network with numerical expressions.

As was discussed in Section 2, S-cells have inhibitory inputs with a shunting mechanism. The output of an S-cell of the k_l-th S-plane in the l-th module is given by

$$u_{Sl}(k_l, \mathbf{n}) = r_l \cdot \varphi \left[\frac{1 + \sum_{k_{l-1}=1}^{K_{l-1}} \sum_{v \in S_l} a_l(k_{l-1}, v, k_l) \cdot u_{Cl-1}(k_{l-1}, \mathbf{n} + v)}{1 + \frac{r_l}{1 + r_l} \cdot b_l(k_l) \cdot v_{Cl-1}(\mathbf{n})} - 1 \right]. \qquad (9)^*$$

where $\varphi[\ \ ]$ is a function defined by equation (2) before. In the case of $l = 1$ in equation (9), $u_{Cl-1}(k_{l-1}, \mathbf{n})$ stands for $u_0(\mathbf{n})$ and we have $K_{l-1} = 1$.

Here, $a_l(k_{l-1}, v, k_l)$ and $b_l(k_l)$ represent the values of the excitatory and inhibitory variable interconnecting coefficients, respectively. As described before, all the S-cells in the same S-plane have an identical set of input interconnections. Hence, $a_l(k_{l-1}, v, k_l)$ and $b_l(k_l)$ do not contain any argument representing the position $\mathbf{n}$ of the receptive field of the cell $u_{Sl}(k_l, \mathbf{n})$.

Parameter r_l in equation (9) controls the intensity of the inhibition. The larger the value of r_l is, the more selective becomes the cell's response to its specific feature. A more detailed discussion on the response of S-cells will be given in Section 4.2.

The inhibitory cell $v_{Cl-1}(\mathbf{n})$, which is sending an inhibitory signal to cell $u_{Sl}(k_l, \mathbf{n})$, receives its input

interconnections from the same cells as $u_{Sl}(k_l, \mathbf{n})$ does, and yields an output proportional to the weighted root-mean-square of its inputs:

$$v_{Cl-1}(\mathbf{n}) = \sqrt{\sum_{k_{l-1}=1}^{K_{l-1}} \sum_{v \in S_l} c_{l-1}(v) \cdot u_{Cl-1}^2(k_{l-1}, \mathbf{n} + v)}. \qquad (10)$$

The values of fixed interconnections $c_{l-1}(v)$ are determined so as to decrease monotonically with respect to $|v|$ and to satisfy

$$\sum_{k_{l-1}=1}^{K_{l-1}} \sum_{v \in S_l} c_{l-1}(v) = 1. \qquad (11)$$

The size of the connecting area S_l of these cells is set to be small in the first module and to increase with the depth l.

The interconnections from S-cells to C-cells are fixed and unmodifiable. As illustrated in Fig. 4, each C-cell has input interconnections leading from a group of S-cells in the S-plane preceding it (i.e., in the S-plane with the same k_l-number as that of the C-cell). This means that all of the S-cells in the C-cell's connecting area extract the same stimulus features but from slightly different positions on the input layer. The values of the interconnections are determined in such a way that the C-cell will be activated whenever at least one of these S-cells is active. Hence, even if a stimulus pattern which has elicited a large response from the C-cell is shifted a little in position, the C-cell will still keep responding as before, because another neighboring S-cell in its connecting area will become active instead of the first. In other words, a C-cell responds to the same stimulus feature as the S-cells preceding it, but is less sensitive to a shift in position of the stimulus feature.

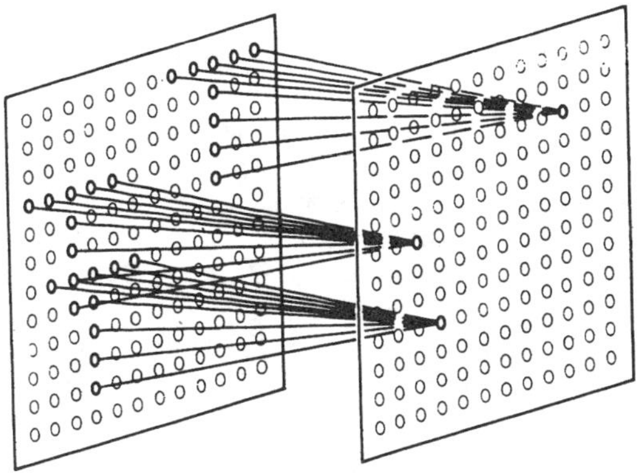

Fig. 3. Illustration showing the input interconnections to the cells of an arbitrary cell-plane.

---

*The notation $b_l(k_l)$ in this paper corresponds to $2b_l(k_l)$ in the previous papers by Fukushima.[1-3]

395

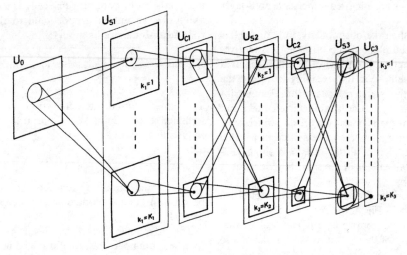

Fig. 4. Schematic diagram illustrating the interconnections between layers in the neocognitron.

Quantitatively, the output of a C-cell of the k_l-th C-plane in the l-th module is given by

$$u_{Cl}(k_l, \mathbf{n}) = \psi \left[\frac{1 + \sum_{v \in D_l} d_l(v) \cdot u_{Sl}(k_l, \mathbf{n} + v)}{1 + v_{Sl}(\mathbf{n})} - 1 \right], \quad (12)$$

where $\psi[\quad]$ is a function defined by equation (7).

The inhibitory cell $v_{Sl}(\mathbf{n})$, which sends inhibitory signals to this C-cell and makes up the system of lateral inhibition, yields an output proportional to the (weighted) arithmetic mean of its inputs:

$$v_{Sl}(\mathbf{n}) = \frac{1}{K_l} \sum_{k_l=1}^{K_l} \sum_{v \in D_l} d_l(v) \cdot u_{Sl}(k_l, \mathbf{n} + v). \quad (13)$$

In equations (12) and (13), the values of fixed interconnections $d_l(v)$ are determined so as to decrease monotonically with respect to $|v|$, as with $c_l(v)$. The size of the connecting area D_l is set to be small in the first module and to increase with the depth l.

4. SELF-ORGANIZATION OF THE NETWORK

4.1. *Reinforcement of variable interconnections*

The self-organization of the neocognitron is performed by means of unsupervised learning, "learning without a teacher". During the process of self-organization, the network is repeatedly presented with a set of stimulus patterns to the input layer, but it does not receive any other information about the category of the stimulus patterns.

As was discussed in Section 3, all the S-cells in a single S-plane should always have input interconnections of the same spatial distribution but from different positions. In order to modify the variable interconnections always keeping this restriction, we use the following procedure.

At first, several "representative" S-cells are chosen from each S-layer every time that a stimulus pattern is presented. The representatives are chosen from among those S-cells which have yielded large outputs, but the number of the representatives is so restricted that more than one representative should not be chosen from any single S-plane. The detailed procedure for choosing the representatives is given in Section 4.2.

For a representative S-cell, only the input interconnections through which non-zero signals are coming are reinforced. With this procedure, the representative S-cell becomes selectively responsive only to the stimulus feature which is now presented. A detailed discussion on S-cell response will appear in Section 4.3. All the other S-cells in the S-plane, from which the representative is chosen, have their input interconnections reinforced by the same amounts as those for their representative. These relations can be quantitatively expressed as follows.

Let cell $u_{Sl}(\hat{k}_l, \hat{\mathbf{n}})$ be chosen as a representative. The variable interconnections $a_l(k_{l-1}, v, \hat{k}_l)$ and $b_l(\hat{k}_l)$ which are incoming to the S-cells of this S-plane, are reinforced by the amount shown below:

$$\Delta a_l(k_{l-1}, v, \hat{k}_l) = q_l \cdot c_{l-1}(v) \cdot u_{Cl-1}(k_{l-1}, \hat{\mathbf{n}} + v), \quad (14)$$

$$\Delta b_l(\hat{k}_l) = q_l \cdot v_{Cl-1}(\hat{\mathbf{n}}), \quad (15)$$

where q_l is a positive constant which determines the speed of increment.

The cells in the S-plane from which no repre-

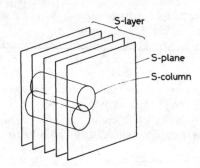

Fig. 5. Relation between S-planes and S-columns within an S-layer.

396

sentative is chosen, however, do not have their input interconnections varied at all.

The choice of initial values of the variable interconnections has little effect on the performance of the neocognitron, provided that they are small and are determined in such a way that each S-plane has a different set of initial values for its input interconnections. In the computer simulation discussed in Section 6, the initial values of the excitatory variable interconnections $a_l(k_{l-1}, v, k_l)$ are set to be small positive values in such a way that each S-cell has a very weak orientation slectivity and that its preferred orientation differs from S-plane to S-plane. That is, the initial values of these variable interconnections are given by a function of v, (k_l/K_l) and $|k_{l-1}/K_{l-1} - k_l/K_l|$, but they do not have any randomness. The initial values of inhibitory variable interconnections $b_l(k_l)$ are set to be zero.

4.2. *Choosing the representatives*

The procedure for choosing the representatives is as follows. First, in an S-layer we pick up a group of S-cells whose receptive fields are situated within a small area on the input layer. If we arrange the S-planes of an S-layer in the manner shown in Fig. 5, such a group of S-cells constitutes a column in an S-layer. Accordingly, we call the group an "S-column". An S-column contains S-cells from all the S-planes, i.e. an S-column contains various kinds of feature-extracting cells in it, but the receptive fields of these cells are situated almost at the same position. There are a lot of such S-columns in a single S-layer. Since S-columns overlap with each other, there is a possibility that a single S-cell is contained in two or more S-columns.

From each S-column, every time that a stimulus pattern is presented, the S-cell which is yielding the largest output is chosen as a candidate for the representative. Hence, there is a possibility that a number of candidates appear in a single S-plane. If two or more candidates appear in a single S-plane, only the one which is yielding the largest output among them is chosen as the representative from that S-plane. In case only one candidate appears in an S-plane, the candidate is unconditionally determined as the representative from that S-plane. If no candidate appears in an S-plane, no representative is chosen from that S-plane.

Since the representatives are determined in this manner, each S-plane becomes selectively sensitive to one of the features of the stimulus patterns and there is no possibility of the formation of redundant connections such that two or more S-planes are used for the detection of one and the same feature. Incidentally, representatives are chosen from only a small number of S-planes at a time, the rest of the S-planes producing representatives when other stimulus patterns are presented.

4.3. *Response of an S-cell*

In this section, we discuss how each S-cell comes to

respond selectively to differences in stimulus patterns*.

Since the structure between two adjoining modules is similar in all parts of the network, we observe the response of an arbitrary S-cell $u_{S1}(k_1, \mathbf{n})$ as a typical example. Figure 6 shows the interconnections converging on such a cell. For the sake of simplicity, we will omit the suffixes S and $l = 1$ and the arguments k_l and $\mathbf{n}$ and represent the response of this cell simply by u. Similarly, we will use the notation v for the output of the inhibitory cell $v_{C0}(\mathbf{n})$, which sends inhibitory signals to cell u. For the other variables, the arguments k_l and $\mathbf{n}$ and suffixes S, C, l and $l - 1$ will also be omitted.

Let $p(v)$ be the response of the cells of layer U_0 situated in the connectable area of cell u, so that

$$p(v) = u_0(\mathbf{n} + v). \tag{16}$$

In other words, $p(v)$ is the stimulus pattern (or feature) presented to the receptive field of cell u.

With this notation equations (9) and (10) can be written:

$$u = r \cdot \varphi \left[\frac{1 + \sum_v a(v) \cdot p(v)}{1 + \frac{r}{1 + r} \cdot b \cdot v} - 1 \right], \tag{17}$$

$$v = \sqrt{\sum_v c(v) \cdot p^2(v)}. \tag{18}$$

When cell u is chosen as a representative, the increments of the variable interconnections are derived from equations (14) and (15), i.e.,

$$\Delta a(v) = q \cdot c(v) \cdot p(v), \tag{19}$$

$$\Delta b = q \cdot v. \tag{20}$$

Let s be defined by

$$s = \frac{\sum_v a(v) \cdot p(v)}{b \cdot v}. \tag{21}$$

Then equation (17) reduces, approximately, to

$$u \doteqdot r \cdot \varphi \left[\frac{r + 1}{r} s - 1 \right], \tag{22}$$

provided that $a(v)$ and b are sufficiently large.

Let us suppose that cell u has been chosen N-times as a representative for the same stimulus pattern $p(v)$

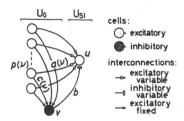

Fig. 6. Interconnections converging to an S-cell.

---

*The analysis for the conventional r.m.s.-cognitron[7] can be applied to our neocognitron with a small modification.

$= P(v)$. We also suppose that no other cell has been chosen as a representative from the S-plane in which cell u is located. Assuming that the initial values of the variable interconnections are small enough to be neglected, we obtain

$$a(v) = Nq \cdot c(v) \cdot P(v). \qquad (23)$$

$$b = Nq \sqrt{\sum_v c(v) \cdot P^2(v)}. \qquad (24)$$

Substituting equations (18), (23) and (24) into equation (21), we obtain

$$s = \frac{\sum_v c(v) \cdot P(v) \cdot p(v)}{\sqrt{\sum_v c(v) \cdot P^2(v)} \cdot \sqrt{\sum_v c(v) \cdot p^2(v)}}. \qquad (25)$$

If we regard $p(v)$ and $P(v)$ as vectors, equation (25) can be interpreted as the (weighted) inner product of the two vectors normalized by the norms of both vectors. In other words, s gives the cosine of the angle between the two vectors $p(v)$ and $P(v)$ in the multidimensional vector space. Therefore, we have $s = 1$ only when $p(v) = P(v)$ and we have $s < 1$ for all patterns such that $p(v) \neq P(v)$. This means that s becomes maximum for the learned pattern and becomes smaller for any other pattern.

Consider the case when N is so large that $Nq \gg 1$. In this case, equation (22) holds.

When an arbitrary pattern $p(v)$ is presented, if it satisfies $s > r/(r + 1)$, we have $u > 0$ by equation (22). Conversely, for a pattern which makes $s \leq r/(r + 1)$, cell u does not respond. We can interpret this by saying that cell u judges the similarity between patterns $p(v)$ and $P(v)$ using the criterion defined in equation (25), and that it responds only to patterns judged to be similar to $P(v)$. Incidentally, if $p(v) = P(v)$, we have $s = 1$ and consequently $u \doteq 1$.

Roughly speaking, during the self-organization process, patterns $p(v)$ which satisfy $s > r/(r + 1)$ are taken to be of the same class as $P(v)$ and patterns $p(v)$ which make $s \leq r/(r + 1)$ are assumed to be of different classes from $P(v)$.

The patterns which are judged to be of different classes will possibly be extracted by the cells in other S-planes.

Since the value $r/(r + 1)$ tends to 1 with increase of r, a larger value of r makes the cell's response more selective to one specific pattern or feature. In other words, a large value of r endows the cell with a high ability to discriminate patterns of different classes. However, a higher selectivity of the cell response is not always desirable, because it decreases the ability to tolerate the deformation of patterns. Hence, the value of r should be determined at a point of compromise between these two contradictory conditions.

In the Appendix we will give some numerical examples and further explain how the selectivity of the cell is controlled by parameter r.

In the above analysis, we supposed that cell u is trained only for one particular pattern $P(v)$. However, this does not necessarily mean that the training pattern sequence should consist of the repetition of only one pattern $P(v)$. Once the self-organization of the network progresses a little, each cell in the network becomes selectively responsive to one particular pattern. Hence, even if patterns other than $P(v)$ appear in the training pattern sequence, they usually do not elicit any response from cell u unless they closely resemble $P(v)$. Hence, they do not have any effect on the reinforcement of the input interconnections of u. Thus, among many patterns in the training-pattern sequence, only pattern $P(v)$ effectively works for the training of cell u.

In the above discussion we also assumed that the stimulus pattern is always presented at the same position in the input layer and consequently that the representative from an arbitrary S-plane, if any, is always the same cell. Actually, however, this restriction is not necessary for our discussion. We have the same results even if the position of presentation of the stimulus pattern varies each time. We can explain this as follows. If the stimulus pattern is presented at a different position, another cell in that S-plane will become the representative, but the position of the new representative relative to the stimulus pattern will usually be kept as before. On the other hand, according to the algorithm of self-organization discussed in Section 4.1, all the S-cells in that S-plane have their input interconnections modified in the same manner as their representative of the moment. Hence, the shift in position of the stimulus pattern does not affect the result of self-organization of the network.

The above discussion is not restricted to S-cells of layer U_{S1}. Each S-cell in succeeding modules shows a similar type of response, if we regard the response of the C-cells in their connectable area in the preceding layer as its input pattern.

4.4. The temporal progress of self-organization

In order to help the understanding of the algorithm of self-organization we will give a simple example and explain how the reinforcement of the network progresses "without-a-teacher".

As is seen from the discussions in the above sections, the fundamental rule for self-organization of the neocognitron, as with that of the conventional cognitron, lies in the principle that only maximum-output cells have their input interconnections reinforced. We will first explain this principle using a simplified network.

Let us consider the network shown in Fig. 7[a]. This network consists of only nine photoreceptor cells, one inhibitory cell and three S-cells. These S-cells are named A, B and C. The structure of the interconnections converging to each of the three S-cells are identical to the network of Fig. 6. We will explain how the self-organization progresses if three training patterns, say vertical, horizontal and diagonal lines as shown in Fig. 7[b] (i)–(iii), are presented by turns. The excitatory variable interconnections have very small positive initial values, while the initial values of the

398

inhibitory interconnections are zero. Hence, if the vertical line shown in Fig. 7[b] (i) is first presented to the photoreceptor array, all the S-cells yield very small but non-zero positive outputs. Among these three S-cells we choose the one which is yielding the maximum output. Let this cell be, say, cell A. Cell A has its input interconnections reinforced according to equations (19) and (20), i.e., the interconnections from cells p_2, p_5, p_8 and v, through which non-zero input signals are coming to cell A, are reinforced. It should be noticed that not only the excitatory interconnections but also the inhibitory interconnection is reinforced. If the value of parameter q in equations (19) and (20) is large enough, compared to the initial values of the variable interconnections, cell A acquires, after only this single training, selective responsiveness to this vertical line.

Next, let a horizontal line shown in Fig. 7[b](ii) be presented. Since cell A has already come to respond selectively to a vertical line, it does not respond to the horizontal line, provided the value of parameter r is not too small. Only cells B and C yield non-zero output this time. Let the maximum-output cell among these be, say, cell C. This time, cell C has its input interconnections reinforced according to equations (19) and (20) and acquires selective responsiveness to the horizontal line.

Let the next training pattern be the diagonal line shown in Fig. 7[b](iii). Since cells A and C have already become selectively responsive to vertical and horizontal lines, respectively, the rest of the cells, i.e., cell B, yields a non-zero output to the diagonal line. Hence, cell B has its input interconnections reinforced and becomes selectively responsive to the diagonal line.

If the next training pattern be, say, a horizontal line again, only cell C, which has once been reinforced to the horizontal line, is activated. Hence, cell C has its input interconnections reinforced to the horizontal line again and the selectivity to the horizontal line becomes more stable.

In the above example, we assumed that the training patterns were presented in the sequence order, vertical, horizontal, diagonal, ... We obtain the same result for self-organization, even if the identical training pattern appears successively in the training sequence, say vertical, vertical, horizontal, ... Let cell A be the maximum output cell and let it be chosen to be reinforced on the first presentation of a vertical line. It is a matter of course that cell A again yields the maximum output among the three when the vertical line is again presented as the second training pattern. Hence, the same cell A is again reinforced to the vertical line. In other words, there is no possibility that two or more cells could be reinforced to the same training pattern, even if the same training pattern is successively presented to the network.

If the number of different training patterns is four or more, none of the S-cells yield a positive output to the fourth training pattern, because cells A, B and C have already been reinforced and have acquired selective responsiveness to the first three training patterns.

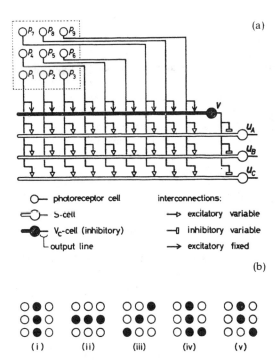

Fig. 7. Illustrations for the progress of self-organization. (a), Simplified network explaining the algorithm of self-organization. (b), Some examples of the stimulus pattern used to train the network of (a).

Consequently, no S-cell can be reinforced to the fourth training pattern in a network which has only three S-cells. Hence, in designing a network such as Fig. 7[a] we have to prepare a greater number of S-cells than the number of different training patterns to be recognized. In designing the whole system of the neocognitron, the number of S-planes in layer U_{S1} should be larger than the number of different stimulus features contained in the stimulus patterns to be recognized. This will be further discussed in Section 5. In the computer simulation discussed in Section 6, the number of S-planes in layer U_{S1} is 24.

As can be seen from the above examples, once an S-cell has been trained to one particular pattern the cell usually does not respond to any other patterns which are judged to be different from the former one by the criterion defined in Section 4.3 and the Appendix. Consequently, the cell usually cannot be reinforced to a new pattern and will preserve the same response characteristics. In a special situation, however, it is possible to make the cell come to respond to a completely new pattern. This can be performed if we change its response characteristics little by little as shown in the next example.

Suppose cell A is first reinforced to pattern (i) in Fig. 7[b]. It is assumed that the value of parameter r is chosen in such a way that cell A responds also to pattern (iv) but not to pattern (v). (Further discussions on the choice of the value of r appear in the Appendix). Hence, if training pattern (iv) is presented next, cell A yields a small but non-zero output. If no other cell has yet been trained to pattern (iv), cell A is probably the maximum-output cell and consequently is reinforced to pattern (iv). If we repeat the presentation of pattern (iv) many times, the response of cell A to pattern (iv) gradually increases and becomes larger than that to pattern (i). When the response to pattern (iv) becomes large enough, after repeated reinforcement, cell A now comes to yield a non-zero output to pattern (v) because pattern (v) has only one missing element compared to pattern (iv) (See Appendix). Hence, cell A can now be reinforced to pattern (v), to which cell A did not respond at the beginning. Thus, we can gradually change the response characteristics of a cell so as to make it respond to a considerably different pattern, if the speed of variation of the training pattern is slow enough. This situation resembles the phenomenon which we experience in recognition of a human face: the face of a person gradually changes with time but we scarcely perceive the change if we see him every day.

We have explained how the self-organization is performed by means of the principle that only maximum output cells have their input interconnections reinforced. In the neocognitron, this principle is applied only to the "representative cells" and the other cells mimic their representatives. Let us compare the network of Fig. 7 and that of the neocognitron. The photoreceptor cells in Fig. 7 correspond to cells of layer U_0 in the neocognitron and cells A, B and C correspond to S-cells of layer U_{S1}, which have receptive fields at the same position but belong to different S-planes. Actually, in the neocognitron, each S-plane has many S-cells in parallel, each of which should have input interconnections of the same spatial distribution as those of cell A, B or C.

Concerning the network of Fig. 7, we have just explained the case in which the positions of the receptive fields of cells A, B and C coincide exactly and the training patterns are always presented at the same position in these receptive fields. In the real situation of self-organization, however, the position of training-pattern presentation is not fixed. Nevertheless, the result of self-organization is not affected at all. Assume the case where a training pattern which can elicit a maximum response from cell A, is not presented to the receptive field of cell A but to the receptive field of, say, cell A', which belongs to the same S-plane as cell A. In this case, cell A' yields a larger output than cell A and cell A' is chosen as the representative instead of cell A. Since all the cells in the S-plane in which cells A and A' are situated have their input interconnections reinforced in the same manner as their representative, we have the same result of reinforcement without it being affected by whether the training pattern is presented to the receptive field of cell A or A'.

In the above explanation, we assumed that each training pattern contains only one stimulus feature. However, each training pattern usually contains many different stimulus features in it. Hence, in order to perform an effective self-organization, it is necessary to choose numbers of representatives from each S-layer at a time. Therefore, the technique discussed in Section 4.2 is employed to choose the representative; i.e., each S-plane is divided into many subgroups and maximum-output cells are individually chosen from these subgroups as candidates for the representatives and the representatives are chosen from these candidates.

When the reinforcement of the input interconnections of layer U_{S1} progresses to a certain extent and the response of layer U_{S1} to each training pattern becomes large and stable, the output from layer U_{C1}, which is directly driven by the output from layer U_{S1}, now begins to trigger the reinforcement of the variable interconnections between $U_{C1} \rightarrow U_{S2}$. Incidentally, during the initial state of reinforcement when the response characteristics of layer U_{S1} are still unstable and fluctuating, the output of layer U_{S1} is kept very small because the input interconnections to the cells of this layer are still very small and, consequently, the reinforcement of the interconnections between $U_{C1} \rightarrow U_{S2}$ scarcely progresses. On the other hand, when the response characteristics of layer U_{S1} become stable after a certain degree of progress in learning, the peaks of the response of layer U_{S1} become large and approach to value 1.0 and, consequently, the reinforcement of the interconnections between $U_{C1} \rightarrow U_{S2}$ begins to make rapid progress.

Thus, it is important in the self-organization of a hierarchical multilayered network to retard the reinforcement of the interconnections to the succeeding layers until the response characteristics of the preceding layers become stable. What would occur if the network were not designed in such a way? If some cells of layer U_{S1} happen to yield strange outputs during the initial stage of training, some cells of layer U_{S2} will be reinforced so as to detect this strange response. If this strange response does not appear in layer U_{S1} afterwards, these U_{S2}-cells which detect this strange response become useless and wasteful. In the neocognitron, however, this defect is avoided, because the progress of self-organization of each layer in the network is optimally controlled by the employment of analog cells with shunting inhibition and by the optimum choice of parameter q.

It can be seen from the above discussions that parameter q, which determines the speed of reinforcement, should be chosen as follows. When we want to reinforce a network which has only one layer of S-cells, we can choose a large value of q, by which self-organization of the network can be completed with only a single presentation of each training pattern. On the other hand, in the neocognitron which has many stages of modifiable layers (c.f. in the computer simulation in Section 6, we consider the network with three modifiable layers), the value of q should be small enough to retard the build up of the outputs of the cells of each layer until the response characteristics of all the cells in the layer become stable. Furthermore, during the stage of self-organization all the training patterns should be evenly presented with a certain number of repetitions, otherwise a decrease in value of q

becomes of little avail. Thus, self-organization of the neocognitron progresses step by step from the front layer, in the order U_{S1}, U_{S2}, U_{S3}.

5. A ROUGH SKETCH OF THE WORKING OF THE NEOCOGNITRON

In order to help with the understanding of the principles by which the neocognitron performs pattern recognition, we will make a rough sketch of the working of the network in the state after completion of self-organization. The description in this Section, however, is not so strict, because the purpose of this Section is only to show an outline of the working of the network.

First, let us assume that the neocognitron has been self-organized with repeated presentations of a set of stimulus patterns such as "A", "B", "C" and so on. In the state when self-organization has been completed, various feature-extracting cells are formed in the network, as shown in Fig. 8. (It should be noted that Fig. 8 shows only an example. It does not mean that exactly the same feature extractors as shown in this figure are always formed in the network.)

If pattern "A" is presented to the input layer U_0, the cells in the network yield outputs as shown in Fig. 8. For instance, the S-plane with $k_1 = 1$ in layer U_{S1} consists of a two-dimensional array of S-cells which extract $\wedge$-shaped features. Since the stimulus pattern "A" contains a $\wedge$-shaped feature at the top, an S-cell near the top of this S-plane yields a large output as shown in the enlarged illustration in the lower part of Fig. 8.

A C-cell in the succeeding C-plane (i.e., the C-plane in layer U_{C1} with $k_1 = 1$) has interconnections from a group of S-cells in this S-plane. For example, the C-cell shown in Fig. 8 has interconnections from the S-cells situated within the thin-lined circle and it is activated whenever at least one of these S-cells yields a large output. Hence, the C-cell responds to a $\wedge$-shaped feature situated in a certain area in the input layer and its response is less affected by the shift in position of the stimulus pattern than that of the preceding S-cells. Since this C-plane consists of an array of such C-cells, several C-cells which are situated near the top of this C-plane respond to the $\wedge$-shaped feature of the stimulus pattern "A". In layer U_{C1}, besides this C-plane, we also have C-planes which extract features with shapes like $\vdash$, $\diagdown$ and so on.

In the next module, each S-cell receives signals from all the C-planes of layer U_{C1}. For example, the S-cell of layer U_{S2} shown in Fig. 8 receives signals from C-cells within the thin-lined circles in layer U_{C1}. Its input interconnections have been reinforced in such a way that this S-cell responds only when $\wedge$-shaped, $\vdash$-shaped and $\diagdown$-shaped features are presented in its receptive field with configuration like $\overset{\wedge}{\vdash\diagdown}$. Hence, pattern "A" elicits a large response from this S-cell, which is situated a little above the center of this S-plane. Even if the positional relation of these three features is changed a little, this cell will still keep

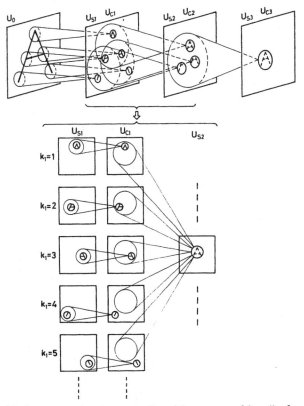

Fig. 8. An example of the interconnections between cells and the response of the cells after completion of the self-organization.

401

responding, because the preceding C-cells are not so sensitive to the positional error of these features. However, if the positional relation of these three features is changed beyond some allowance, this S-cell stops responding. This S-cell also checks the condition that other features such as ends-of-lines, which are to be extracted in S-planes in layer U_{S1} with $k_1 = 4, 5$ and so on, are not presented in its receptive field. The inhibitory V_C-cell, which makes inhibitory interconnections to this S-cell of layer U_{S2}, plays an important role in checking the absence of such irrelevant features.

Since operations of this kind are repeatedly applied through a cascade connection of modular structures of S- and C-layers, each individual cell in the network comes to have a wider receptive field in accordance with the increased number of modules before it and, at the same time, becomes more tolerant of shift in position and distortion in shape of the input pattern. Thus, in the deepest layer, each C-cell has a receptive field large enough to cover the whole input layer and is selectively responsive only to one of the stimulus patterns, say to "A", but its response is not affected by shift in position or even by considerable distortion in shape of the stimulus pattern. Although only one cell which responds to pattern "A" is drawn in Fig. 8, cells which respond to other patterns, such as "B", "C" and so on, have also been formed in parallel in the deepest layer.

From these discussions, it might be felt that an enormously large number of feature-extracting cell-planes becomes necessary with an increase in the number of input patterns to be recognized. However, this is not the case. With an increase in the number of input patterns, it becomes more and more probable that one and the same feature is contained in common in more than two different kinds of stimulus pattern. Hence, each cell-plane, especially the one near the input layer, will generally be used in common for feature extraction not from only one pattern but from numerous kinds of patterns. Therefore, the required number of cell-planes does not increase so much, in spite of an increase in the number of patterns to be recognized.

We can summarize the discussion in this Section as follows. The stimulus pattern is first observed within a narrow range by each of the cells in the first module and several features of the stimulus pattern are extracted. In the next module, these features are combined by observation over a slightly larger range and higher-order features are extracted. Operations of this kind are repeatedly applied through a cascade connection of a number of modules. In each stage of these operations, a small amount of positional error is tolerated. The operation by which positional errors are tolerated little by little, not at a single stage, plays an important role in endowing the network with an ability to recognize even distorted patterns.

6. COMPUTER SIMULATION

6.1. Parameters for the simulation

The network proposed here was simulated on a digital computer. In the computer simulation we considered a seven layered network: $U_0 \rightarrow U_{S1} \rightarrow U_{C1} \rightarrow U_{S2} \rightarrow U_{C2} \rightarrow U_{S3} \rightarrow U_{C3}$. In other words, the network has three stages of modular structures preceded by an input layer. The number of cell-planes K_l is equally 24 for all layers, $U_{S1}-U_{C3}$. The other parameters are listed in Table 1.

As can be seen from Table 1, the total number of C-cells in the deepest layer U_{C3} is 24, because each C-plane has only one C-cell.

The number of cells contained in a connectable area S_l is always 5×5 for every S-layer. Hence, the number of excitatory input interconnections* to each S-cell is 5×5 in layer U_{S1} and $5 \times 5 \times 24$ in layers U_{S2} and U_{S3}, because layers U_{S2} and U_{S3} are preceded by C-layers consisting of 24 cell-planes each. Although the number of cells contained in S_l is the same for every S-layer, the size of S_l, which is projected to and observed at layer U_0, increases with the depth of the S-layer, because of the decrease in the density of the cells in a cell-plane.

6.2. Recognition of five numerals

During the stage of learning in the first experiment, five training patterns, "0", "1", "2", "3" and "4" (shown

---

* It does not necessarily mean that all of these input interconnections actually grow up and become effective. In usual situations, only a part of these interconnections come to have large values, and the rest of them remain with small values.

Table 1. Parameters for the simulation

Layer	No. of exc. cells	No. of exc. input inter-connections per cell	Size of an S-column (No. of cells per S-column)	r_l	q_l
U_0	16×16				
U_{S1}	$16 \times 16 \times 24$	5×5	$5 \times 5 \times 24$	4.0	1.
U_{C1}	$10 \times 10 \times 24$	5×5			
U_{S2}	$8 \times 8 \times 24$	$5 \times 5 \times 24$	$5 \times 5 \times 24$	1.5	16.
U_{C2}	$6 \times 6 \times 24$	5×5			
U_{S3}	$2 \times 2 \times 24$	$5 \times 5 \times 24$	$2 \times 2 \times 24$	1.5	16.
U_{C3}	24	2×2			

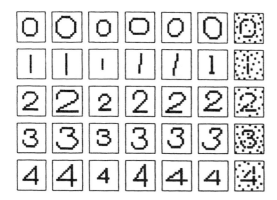

Fig. 9. Some examples of the stimulus patterns which the neocognitron recognized correctly. The neocognitron was first trained with the patterns shown in the leftmost column.

in the leftmost column in Fig. 9) were presented repeatedly to the input layer U_0. The positions of these training patterns were randomly shifted at every presentation. It does not matter, of course, if the training patterns are presented always at the same position. On the contrary, self-organization generally becomes easier if the position of pattern presentation is stationary rather than if it is shifted at random. Thus, experimental results under more difficult conditions are shown here.

The learning was performed without-a-teacher and the neocognitron did not receive any information about the categories of the training patterns.

After repeated presentations of these five training patterns, the neocognitron gradually acquired the

ability to classify these patterns by itself, according to the difference in their shape. In this simulation, each of the five training patterns was presented 20 times. By that time, self-organization of the network was almost completed.

Figure 10 collectively shows how the individual cells in the network came to respond to the five training patterns. In each of the pictures in Fig. 10, out of the seven cell-layers constituting the neocognitron we display only four layers, namely the input layer U_0 and C-cell-layers U_{C1}, U_{C2} and U_{C3}, arranging them vertically in order. In the deepest layer U_{C3}, which is displayed in the bottom row of each picture, it is seen that a different cell responds to each stimulus pattern "0", "1", "2", "3" and "4". This means that the neocognitron correctly recognizes these five stimulus patterns.

We will see, next, how the response of the neocognitron is changed by a shift in the position of presentation of the stimulus patterns. Figure 11 shows how the individual cells of layers U_0, U_{C1}, U_{C2} and U_{C3} respond to stimulus pattern "2" presented at four different positions. As can be seen in this figure, the responses of the cells in the intermediate layers, especially the ones near the input layer, vary with a shift in position of the stimulus pattern. However, the deeper the layer is, i.e., the lower in each of the four pictures the layer is, the smaller is the variation in response of the cells in it. Thus, the cells of the deepest layer U_{C3} are not affected at all by a shift in position of the stimulus pattern. This means that the neocognitron correctly recognizes the stimulus patterns irrespective of their positions.

The neocognitron recognizes the stimulus patterns

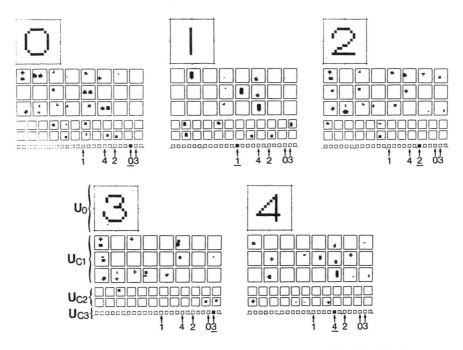

Fig. 10. Response of the cells of layers U_0, U_{C1}, U_{C2} and U_{C3} to each of the five stimulus patterns.

403

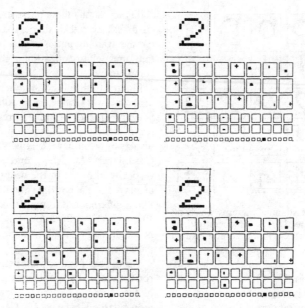

Fig. 11. Response of the cells of layers U_0, U_{C1}, U_{C2} and U_{C3} to the same stimulus pattern "2" presented at four different positions.

correctly, even if the stimulus patterns are distorted in shape or contaminated with noise. Figure 9 shows some examples of distorted stimulus patterns which the neocognitron recognized correctly. All the patterns in each row elicited the same response from the cells of the deepest layer U_{C3}. Even though a stimulus pattern was increased or diminished in size or was skewed in shape, the response of the cells of the deepest layer was not affected. Similarly, the stimulus patterns were correctly recognized even if they were stained with noise or had some parts missing.

As an example of the feature extracting cells formed in this network, Fig. 12 displays the receptive fields of the cells of each of the 24 S-planes of layer U_{S1}. In this figure, the excitatory parts of the receptive fields are indicated by the darkness of the cells in the picture. The arrangement of these 24 receptive fields in Fig. 12 is the same as that of the C-cells of layer U_{C1} in Figs 10 and 11. Hence, in each display of Figs 10 and 11 it is understood, for example, that the upper left C-plane of layer U_{C1} extracts the horizontal line components from the stimulus pattern.

6.3. Some other experiments

In order to check whether the neocognitron can acquire the ability for correct pattern recognition, even

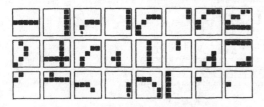

Fig. 12. Receptive fields of the cells of each of the 24 S-planes of layer U_{S1}, which has finished learning.

for a set of stimulus patterns resembling each other, another experiment was carried out. In this experiment, the neocognitron was trained using four stimulus patterns, "X", "Y", "T" and "Z". These four patterns resemble each other in shape: the upper parts of "X" and "Y" have an identical shape and the diagonal lines in "Z" and "X" have an identical inclination, and so on. After repetitive presentation of these resembling patterns, the neocognitron acquired the ability to discriminate between them correctly.

In a third experiment, the number of the training patterns was increased and ten different patterns, "0", "1", "2",..., "9", were presented during the process of self-organization. Even in the case of ten training patterns, it *is* possible to self-organize the neocognitron so as to recognize these ten patterns correctly, provided that various parameters in the network are properly adjusted and that the training patterns are skillfully presented during the process of self-organization. In this case, however, a small deviation of the values of the parameters or a small change in the sequence of pattern presentation has a critical influence upon the ability of the self-organized network. This means that the number of cell-planes in the network (i.e., 24 cell-planes in each layer) is not sufficient for the recognition of ten different patterns. If the number of cell-planes was further increased, the neocognitron would steadily, correctly recognize these ten patterns, or even a much greater number of patterns. A computer simulation for the case of more than 24 cell-planes in each layer, however, has not yet been carried out, because of the lack of memory capacity on our computer.

7. DISCUSSION

The "neocognitron" proposed in this paper has an

ability to recognize stimulus patterns without being affected by shifts in position or by considerable distortions in shape of the stimulus patterns. It also has a function of self-organization, which progresses by means of "learning-without-a-teacher". If a set of stimulus patterns is repeatedly presented to it, it gradually acquires the ability to recognize these patterns. It is not necessary to give any information about the categories to which these stimulus patterns should be classified. The performance of the neocognitron was demonstrated by computer simulation.

One of the greatest, and long-standing, difficulties in designing a pattern-recognizing machine was the problem of how to cope with shifts in position and distortions in shape of the input patterns. The neocognitron proposed in this paper gives an important solution to this difficulty. We would be able to vastly improve the performance of pattern recognizers if we introduced this algorithm into the design of the machines. The same principle could also be applied to auditory information processing, such as speech recognition, if the spatial pattern (the envelope of the vibration) generated on the basilar membrane in the cochlea is considered as the input signal to the network.

In this paper, we have demonstrated that the neocognitron can be realized with a multilayered network. When we want to build a neocognitron with hardware, however, the multilayered network is not the only method for realization. There are a variety of methods for constructing hardware working with this same algorithm. For instance, the use of digital filters combined with television-like scanning is one of the easily realizable methods.

SUMMARY

Suggested by the structure of the visual nervous system, a new algorithm is proposed for pattern recognition. This algorithm can be realized with a multilayered network consisting of cells of analog type. The network, which is called a "neocognitron", is self-organized by unsupervised learning: only repetitive presentations of a set of stimulus patterns are necessary for the self-organization of the network and no information about the categories to which these patterns should be classified is needed. The neocognitron by itself acquires the ability to recognize stimulus patterns according to the differences in their shapes: any patterns which we human beings judge to be alike are also judged to be of the same category by the neocognitron. The neocognitron recognizes stimulus patterns correctly without being affected by shifts in position or even by considerable distortions in shape of the stimulus patterns.

The neocognitron is a multilayered network with a hierarchical structure. Specifically, it consists of an input layer (photoreceptor array) followed by a cascaded connection of a number of modular structures,

each of which is composed of a layer of "S-cells" followed by a layer of "C-cells".

S-cells have variable input interconnections. With the progress of learning, these variable interconnections are modified and the S-cells develop into feature extractors.

Each C-cell has excitatory fixed interconnections leading from a group of S-cells. All the S-cells in the group extract the same feature but from different positions on the input layer and the C-cell is activated if at least one of these S-cells is active. Hence, the C-cell responds to the same feature as the S-cells preceding it but is less sensitive to a shift in position of the feature.

In the network consisting of a cascaded connection of these modules, the stimulus pattern is first observed within a narrow range by each of the cells in the first module and several features of the stimulus pattern are extracted. In the next module, these features are combined by observation over a little larger range and higher order features are extracted. Operations of this kind are repeatedly applied through a cascaded connection of a number of modules.

In each of these stages of feature extraction, a small amount of positional error is tolerated. The operation by which positional errors are tolerated little by little, not at a single stage, plays an important role in endowing the network with an ability to recognize even distorted patterns.

When a stimulus pattern is presented at a different position or is distorted in shape, the responses of the cells in intermediate layers, especially the ones near the input layer, vary with the shift in position or the deformation of the stimulus pattern. However, the deeper the layer is, the smaller become the variations in the response of the cells. Thus, the response of the cells in the deepest layer is entirely unaffected by shifts in position or by deformations of the stimulus pattern.

The ability of the neocognitron was demonstrated by a computer simulation.

REFERENCES

1. K. Fukushima, Neural network model for a mechanism of pattern recognition unaffected by shift in position—neocognitron—, *Trans. Inst. electronics commun. Engrs Japan* **62-A**, 658–665 (1979). (In Japanese.)
2. K. Fukushima, Neocognitron: a self-organizing neural network model for a mechanism of pattern recognition unaffected by shift in position, *Biol. Cybernet.* **36**, 193–202 (1980).
3. K. Fukushima and S. Miyake, Neocognitron: self-organizing network capable of position-invariant recognition of patterns, *Proc. 5th Int. Conf. Pattern Recognition,* Vol. 1, pp. 459–461 (1980).
4. F. Rosenblatt, *Principles of Neurodynamics.* Spartan Books, Washington, DC (1962).
5. M. Minsky and S. Papert, Perceptrons, *An Introduction to Computational Geometry.* MIT Press, Cambridge, Mass. (1969).
6. K. Fukushima, Cognitron: a self-organizing multilayered neural network, *Biol. Cybernet.* **20**, 121–136 (1975).
7. K. Fukushima, Cognitron: a self-organizing multilayered neural network model, NHK Technical Monograph No. 30 (1981).

8. K. Fukushima, Visual feature extraction by a multi-layered network of analog threshold elements, *IEEE Trans. Syst. Sci. Cybernet.* **SSC-5,** 322–333 (1969).

APPENDIX

Numerical examples for selectivity control

Using a concrete example, we will further explain how the selectivity of the S-cell shown in Fig. 6 is controlled by parameter r. We use the same notation as in Section 4.3. For the sake of simplicity, we will consider the case where the value of $c(v)$ is chosen to be a constant and to be independent of v. It is also assumed that both $P(v)$ and $p(v)$ consist of elements whose values are either 1 or 0. Let N be the number of active elements (i.e., the elements of value 1) in the training pattern $P(v)$. Let us make an elementwise comparison between the stimulus pattern $p(v)$ and the training pattern $P(v)$. Let n_1 be the number of elements which have value zero in $P(v)$ but are active in $p(v)$. Similarly, let n_0 be the number of elements which are active in $P(v)$ but have value zero in $p(v)$. Under these conditions, equation (25) reduces to the following equation:

$$ s = \frac{1 - \dfrac{n_0}{N}}{\sqrt{1 + \dfrac{n_1 - n_0}{N}}}. \tag{26} $$

As was discussed in Section 4.3, iff parameter r is in the range $s > r/(r+1)$, i.e., in the range

$$ \frac{1 - \dfrac{n_0}{N}}{\sqrt{1 + \dfrac{n_1 - n_0}{N}}} > \frac{r}{r+1}, \tag{27} $$

the S-cell, which has been reinforced to the training pattern $P(v)$, yields a positive output also to pattern $p(v)$.

We will give some numerical examples. First, let us consider the case which appeared in the example in Section 4.4. Let the training pattern $P(v)$ be the one shown in Fig. 7[b](i). We want to design a network in such a way that the S-cell which has been reinforced to $P(v)$ responds also to pattern (iv) of Fig. 7[b] but not to pattern (v). Since pattern (i) has three active elements, we have $N = 3$. Comparing pattern (i) with (iv) and (v), we have $(n_1, n_0) = (1, 0)$ and $(1, 1)$, respectively. Hence, in order to make equation (27) hold for $(n_1, n_0) = (1, 0)$ but not for $(1, 1)$, parameter r should be in the interval $2.00 < r < 6.46$. When parameter r is in this interval, we can easily see that the cell which is reinforced to pattern (iv) responds also to pattern (v): in this case we have $N = 4$ and $(n_1, n_0) = (0, 1)$ and equation (27) is satisfied when parameter r is in the range $r < 6.46$.

We will give another numerical example. Consider an S-cell of layer U_{S1}, which appeared in the computer simulation of Section 6. The S-cell has a receptive field consisting of 5×5 photoreceptor cells. Let the training pattern be, say, a vertical line of length 5 in the 5×5 array. In this case, we have $N = 5$. The pairs of n_1 and n_0 which satisfy equation (27) can easily be calculated. If we take $r = 4.0$, such pairs are only $(n_1, n_0) = (1, 0), (0, 1)$ and $(2, 0)$. Incidentally, for these pairs, we have $s = 0.91, 0.89$ and 0.85, respectively. This means that a vertical line which has one or two excessive elements or has one missing element is judged to be of the same class as $P(v)$. On the other hand, a vertical line with two missing elements, for example, a vertical line consisting of only three active elements, is judged to be of a different class from the training pattern $P(v)$. Incidentally, for a vertical line consisting of only three active elements, we have $s = 0.77$.

If we want to increase the selectivity and to design a network in such a way that the S-cell should yield output only when $(n_1, n_0) = (1, 0)$ and $(0, 1)$, parameter r should be in the interval $5.46 < r < 8.47$.

A Hierarchical Multiple-View Approach to Three-Dimensional Object Recognition

Wei-Chung Lin, *Member, IEEE*, Fong-Yuan Liao, *Member, IEEE*, Chen-Kuo Tsao, and Theresa Lingutla

Abstract—This paper proposes a hierarchical approach to solving the surface and vertex correspondence problems in multiple-view-based three-dimensional object recognition systems. The proposed scheme is a coarse-to-fine search process and a Hopfield network is employed at each stage. Compared with conventional object matching schemes, the proposed technique provides a more general and compact formulation of the problem and a solution more suitable for parallel implementation. At the coarse search stage, the surface matching scores between the input image and each object model in the database are computed through a Hopfield network and are used to select the candidates for further consideration. At the fine search stage, the object models selected from the previous stage are fed into another Hopfield network for vertex matching. The object model that has the best surface and vertex correspondences with the input image is finally singled out as the best matched model. Experimental results are reported using both synthetic and real range images to corroborate the proposed theory.

I. INTRODUCTION

THREE-DIMENSIONAL (3-D) object recognition is the process of matching an object to a scene description to determine the object's identity and/or its pose (position and orientation) in space [1]–[3]. Any system capable of recognizing its input image must in some sense be model-based. The problem of object recognition can be separated into two closely related subproblems—that of model building and that of recognition. There are different approaches to both these subproblems, and the procedure used for recognition will have a strong impact on the kind of model that will be required and vice versa.

The multiple-view approach to 3-D object recognition [4]–[10] models an object by collecting all its topologically different 2-D projections from various viewing angles. In the model database, each 2-D projection is topologically different from the others and is referred to as a *characteristic view* (CV) [4], [5]. In [11], we have proposed a computer system to automatically construct multiple-view model database for polyhedral objects. The database is organized as a graph in which a node represents a characteristic view and an arc represents the transformation between two characteristic views. It is also referred to as a CV library (or aspect graph [7], [9], [10]).

Although the redundancy of the model database has been reduced to the largest extent in the CV library generation process, the size of the library is still large if the target object is complex in shape. This makes the subsequent recognition process very time-consuming if a traditional sequential matching scheme is adopted. Generally, the bottleneck of the recognition process is to establish the correspondence relationships between the contents of the image and the object model.

In this paper, we propose a coarse-to-fine strategy to solve the correspondence problem in 3-D object recognition based on Hopfield networks [12], [13]. Compared with the conventional object matching schemes, the proposed technique provides a more general and compact formulation of the problem and a solution more suitable for parallel implementation. The rest of the paper is organized as follows. In the next section, the continuous Hopfield network model used in the development of our theory is introduced. Then, the processes to establish surface and vertex correspondences using this type of networks are described in Sections III and IV, respectively. This is followed by the presentation of experimental results using both synthetic and real images in Section V. Finally, in Section VI, the performances of the discrete and continuous Hopfield networks are compared. The issue of parallel implementation is also briefly addressed.

II. HOPFIELD NETWORKS FOR IMAGE MATCHING

A Hopfield net is built from a single layer of neurons, with feedback connections from each unit to every other unit (although not to itself). The weights on these connections are constrained to be symmetrical. Generally, a problem to be solved by a Hopfield net can be characterized by an energy function E. Through minimizing the energy function, an optimal (or near optimal) solution is ultimately reflected in the outputs of the neurons in the network. The applications of the Hopfield net are multifarious. In [14], object recognition is based on subgraph matching. The graph matching technique is formulated as an optimization problem where an energy function is minimized. The optimization problem is then solved by a discrete Hopfield network. In [15], a Hopfield network realizes a constraint satisfaction process to match visible surfaces of 3-D objects. In [16], the object recognition problem is casted as an inexact graph matching problem and then formulated in terms of constrained optimization. In [17], the problem of constraint satisfaction in computer vision is mapped to a network where the nodes are the hypotheses and the links are the constraints. The network is then employed to select the optimal subset of hypotheses which satisfy the given constraints.

In this paper, the Hopfield net for image matching is in the form of a two-dimensional array. The rows of the array represent the features of an input image, and the columns represent the features of an object model. The output of a neuron reflects the degree of similarity between two nodes, one from the image and the other from the object model. The matching process can

Manuscript received February 28, 1990; revised June 8, 1990.

The authors are with the Department of Electrical Engineering and Computer Science, Northwestern University, Evanston, IL 60208.

IEEE Log Number 9038253.

Reprinted from *IEEE Trans. on Neural Networks*, vol. 2, no. 1, pp, 84–92, 1991.

be characterized as minimizing the following energy function [14]:

$$E = -\sum_i \sum_k \sum_j \sum_l C_{ikjl} V_{ik} V_{jl} + \sum_i \left(1 - \sum_k V_{ik}\right)^2$$

$$+ \sum_k \left(1 - \sum_i V_{ik}\right)^2 \tag{1}$$

where V_{ik} is an output variable which converges to 1.0 if the ith node in the input image matches the kth node in the object model; otherwise, it converges to 0. The first term in (1) is a compatibility constraint. The second and third terms are included for enforcing the uniqueness constraint so that each node in the object model eventually matches only one node in the input image and the summation of the outputs of the neurons in each row or column is equal to 1. The major component of the compatibility measure C_{ikjl} (or strength of interconnection) between a neuron in row i column k and a neuron in row j column l is expressed in terms of a function F defined as follows:

$$F(x, y) = \begin{cases} 1, & \text{if } |x - y| < \theta \\ -1, & \text{otherwise} \end{cases} \tag{2}$$

where θ is a threshold value and x and y are features pertaining to row and column nodes, respectively. In this paper, two different sets of features and relations will be used for surface and vertex matching, and they will be detailedly described in Sections III and IV, respectively. In general, C_{ikjl} can be expressed as

$$C_{ikjl} = \sum_n W_n \times F(x_n, y_n) \tag{3}$$

where x_n is the nth feature of the node in row i column k, y_n is the nth feature of the node in row j column l, and the summation of the weighting functions W_n's is equal to 1 (i.e., $\sum_n W_n = 1$). Equation (1) can be simplified and fit into the energy function form of a Hopfield network [12] as follows:

$$E = -\frac{1}{2} \sum_i \sum_k \sum_j \sum_l T_{ikjl} V_{ik} V_{jl} - \sum_i \sum_k I_{ik} V_{ik} \tag{4}$$

where $I_{ik} = 2$, and

$$T_{ikjl} = C_{ikjl} - \delta_{ij} - \delta_{kl} \tag{5}$$

where $\delta_{ij} = 1$, if $i = j$, and $\delta_{ij} = 0$ otherwise.

Matching can be considered as a constraint satisfaction process. The global information extracted from the image provides positive or negative supports for local feature matching. According to Hopfield and Tank [14], the strength of the connection between each neuron pair can be derived from the energy function. Based on these connections, the equation of motion for state u_{ik} of a neuron at position (i, k) can be derived as follows:

$$du_{ik}/dt = \sum_j \sum_l C_{ikjl} V_{jl} - \sum_l V_{il} - \sum_j V_{jk} - u_{ik}/\tau + I_{ik} \tag{6}$$

where

$$V_{ik} = g(u_{ik}) = \left[1 + \exp\left(-2u_{ik}/u_0\right)\right]^{-1}. \tag{7}$$

Since the sum of V_{ik} on all the neurons at initialization is constrained to be equal to the number of the final desired output, i.e.,

$$\sum_i \sum_k V_{ik} = N \tag{8}$$

where N is either the number of rows or the number of columns of the array depending on which one is smaller, we can derive the initial condition for u_{ik} from (7) and (8) as follows:

$$u_{init} = -\frac{u_0}{2} \ln (N - 1). \tag{9}$$

In order to prevent the system from being trapped in an unstable equilibrium in which the voltage of each neuron is equal, a certain amount of noise must be added to this initial value. We can rewrite the initial conditions as follows:

$$u_{ik}^0 = u_{init} + \delta \tag{10}$$

and

$$V_{ik}^0 = g(u_{ik}^0) \tag{11}$$

where δ is a random number uniformly distributed between $-0.1u_{init}$ and $+0.1u_{init}$.

The algorithm for matching, based on the continuous Hopfield network model, is summarized as follows.

Algorithm

Input: A set of neurons arranged in a two-dimensional array with initial values V_{ik}^0, where $0 \leq i \leq row\_max - 1$, $0 \leq k \leq column\_max - 1$, and row_max and $column\_max$ are the numbers of rows and columns in the array, respectively.

Output: A set of stabilized neurons with output values V_{ik}, where $0.0 \leq V_{ik} \leq 1$ for $0 \leq i \leq row\_max$ and $0 \leq k \leq column\_max$.

Method:

1) Set the initial conditions using (10) and (11).
2) Set index = 1 and limit = n.
3) Randomly pick up a node (i, k).
4) Update the value of u_{ik}. In order to simulate (6), the fourth order Runge-Kutta method [25] is used. That is,

$$u_{ik}^{t+1} = u_{ik}^t + \frac{1}{6}(k_1 + 2k_2 + 2k_3 + k_4) \tag{12}$$

where

$$k_1 = hf(u_{ik}^t),$$

$$k_2 = hf(u_{ik}^t + \tfrac{1}{2}k_1),$$

$$k_3 = hf(u_{ik}^t + \tfrac{1}{2}k_2),$$

$$k_4 = hf(u_{ik}^t + k_3),$$

$f(\cdot)$ is the right-hand side of (6), and h is a constant.

5) Calculate the new output of neuron (i, k) as follows:

$$V_{ik} = g(u_{ik}).$$

6) Increment index by 1.
7) If index $< n$, then go to (3), else stop and output the final values of all the neurons based on the following rule:

$$V_{ik} = \begin{cases} 1, & \text{if } V_{ik} > \theta 1 \\ 0, & \text{otherwise} \end{cases}$$

where $\theta 1$ is a threshold value.

In the actual implementation, N is replaced by a value N_+ which is greater than N. This is to adjust the neutral positions of neurons. The coefficient τ is 1 and u_0 is 0.002. The constant h for the Runge-Kutta approximation is 0.0001. The instability problem of the Hopfield neural network has been extensively studied [21]-[23]. It is well known that the optimal solution is not always found. In the algorithm, two termination strategies are used to handle different situations. The freeze strategy is adopted whenever the outputs of all the neurons in the network are convergent. When a small number of neurons are not convergent after a long period of time, the time-out strategy is adopted to force the system to stop.

III. HOPFIELD NETWORKS FOR SURFACE CORRESPONDENCE ESTABLISHMENT

In this section, a Hopfield net is designed to establish the surface correspondences between an unknown object and an object model in the database. It is assumed that the unknown object is in the form of line drawings which are obtained by segmenting the original image and each object model is a 2-D projection of a 3-D object whose identity and pose are to be determined. The features for surface matching are firstly described. This is followed by the introduction of row-column assignment. Then, the strength of interconnection C_{ikjl} is defined. A method for quantitatively evaluating the degree of match between the input image and the object model is presented. Finally, the characteristics of the networks are discussed. Since regions (in 2-D) are the projections of surfaces (in 3-D), we use the two terms interchangeably in this paper.

A. Feature Selection and Row-Column Assignments

Before establishing surface correspondence, each object model or image has to be preprocessed. We first label all the regions in the image or model in order from left to right and top to bottom. This labeling scheme provides the basis for subsequent row-column assignment process. An example of labeled image is shown in Fig. 1. During the labeling process for each region, the area is calculated and the boundary traced for locating high curvature (or corner) points [19]. The original image is then converted to a set of polygons with vertices numbered in a certain order. The centroid of each polygon is then computed. For each polygon, two features are extracted for surface matching. One is a local feature, which is the area of the polygon. The other is a relational feature, which is defined as a set of distances originated from its centroid to all the centroids in other polygons of the image. An example demonstrating both features of a polygon is shown in Fig. 1. Since these two features are not scale invariant, a normalization process is performed to compensate this effect. This process starts with selecting the longest distance from the set of intercentroid distances in the input image. Then, based on the ratio between the longest intercentroid distance in the input image and the longest intercentroid distance in the object model, all the distances in the input image are divided by this ratio for normalization. The area of each polygon in the input image is normalized by dividing it by the square of this ratio.

The labels of the polygons in an input image or an object model is derived during the labeling process. In order to perform matching, each polygon in the input image is assigned a row index and each polygon in the object model is assigned a column index. An example is shown in Fig. 2.

B. C_{ikjl} for Surface Matching

At the stage of surface correspondence establishment, C_{ikjl} is expressed as follows:

$$C_{ikjl} = W_1 \times F(I_i, M_k) + W_2 \times F(I_j, M_l)$$
$$+ W_3 \times F(d_{I_i I_j}, d_{M_k M_l}) \qquad (13)$$

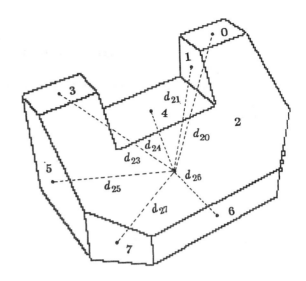

local feature : area of polygon 2

relational features : $\{d_{20}, d_{21}, d_{23}, d_{24}, d_{25}, d_{26}, d_{27}\}$

Fig. 1. A 2-D projection of a slotted wedge with its polygons labeled and the feature set of polygon 2.

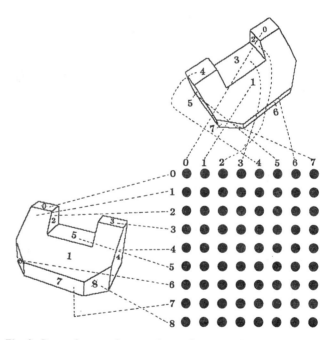

Fig. 2. Row-column assignment for surface correspondence establishment.

where I_x represents the (normalized) area of the xth polygon in the input image, M_y the area of the yth polygon in the object model, $d_{I_i I_j}$ the (normalized) distance between the centroids of the ith and the jth polygons in the input image, and $d_{M_k M_l}$ the distance between the centroids of the kth and the lth polygons in the object model. The values of W_i's reflect the importance of each term. They can be adjusted as long as the sum equals to 1. For the symmetric terms, the associated weights should be set equal (e.g., $W_1 = W_2$). The weight of the relational feature (W_3) is more important than the other two and is thus set with higher value.

C. Similarity Measure from Surface Matching

After the states of the Hopfield net for surface matching are stabilized, we can count the number of active neurons in the network and use it to measure the degree of match (or similarity) between the object model and the input image. The procedure consists of the following four steps.

Step 1: Initialize both *row_match* and *column_match* to be 0.

Step 2: Count the number of 1's in each row. If there is no 1 in a row, skip to the next row and leave *row_match* unchanged. If there is only one 1 in a row, add 1 to *row_match*. If there are n 1s ($n > 1$) in a row, then add $1/n$ to *row_match*. Repeat this for all the rows.

Step 3: Do the same calculation for all the columns and update *column_match*.

Step 4: Pick up the larger one from *row_match* and *column_match*, divide it by the number of rows, and take the result as the similarity measure.

Given an input image and a large number of object models (which is usually the case in a multiple-view approach), the degree of match between the input image and different object models can be derived by comparing the input image and each of the object models in the final state of the Hopfield net. Ideally, there should be at most one active neuron in each row or column. However, due to the influence of the first term in the right-hand side of (1), it is possible to have more than one candidate in the same row or column in the final state of the network. As far as matching is concerned, this situation should be considered as unfavorable and hence decreases the degree of match. This is the reason why $1/n$ is added to the degree of match (row or column) instead of 1 when there are n 1s simultaneously existing in the same row or column. When there is no 1 in a row (or column), it means a surface in the input image (or object model) does not have a corresponding surface in the object model (or input image). This does not contribute to the degree of match between the input image and the object model and thus the degree of match is left unchanged. For a model-based 3-D object recognition system using multiple-view approach, a set of 2-D object models are in the model database. To derive their degrees of match with the input image in the Hopfield net, we associate the input image with row indexes and object models column indexes. This arrangement allows us to compare all the object models simultaneously with the input image, provided that the dimension of the neuron array is large enough. This also explains why the number of rows is used as the denominator in the derivation of similarity measure.

D. Discussion

The proposed Hopfield net for surface matching has a flexible structure and is able to solve the surface correspondence problem even if the numbers of polygons in the input image and the object model are different. In other words, the two-dimensional neuron array may have different numbers of rows and columns and an inexact matching [24] can be performed in this net. Furthermore, based on the outputs of the neurons in the network, a similarity measure between any object model and the input image can be derived even if they contain a different number of surfaces.

This similarity measure is used to reduce the search space. Based on the proposed simple features, a set of object models most similar to the input image is selected from the database. This process can be considered as a coarse search step because

"good" candidates as well as some "bad" candidates are selected due to roughness of the feature set. However, this process discards a large number of object models in the database and significantly reduces the search space.

IV. Hopfield Networks for Vertex Correspondence Establishment

After the surface correspondences between the unknown object and the object model are confirmed, the next step is to apply Hopfield networks to establish the vertex correspondences. In this section, the features for vertex correspondence establishment are first described. This is followed by the introduction of row-column assignment. Next, the strength of interconnection C_{ikjl} is defined. Then, a technique for systematically deriving the best vertex correspondence is presented. Finally, the characteristics of the networks are discussed.

A. Feature Selection and Row-Column Assignments

Before we start establishing the vertex correspondences, the order of all the vertices in each polygon must be determined. This is usually achieved at the preprocessing stage by selecting the vertex of a polygon with minimum x coordinate as the starting vertex (oth vertex). If two vertices happen to possess the same minimum x coordinate, the one with smaller y coordinate is selected as the starting vertex. The subsequent vertices are numbered sequentially in a clockwise direction. The reason for making this ordering is to facilitate the subsequent row-column assignment process. A useful feature for vertex correspondence establishment is the *shape number* proposed in [20]. This feature is invariant to rotation, translation, and scaling in 3-D space. The method of deriving the shape number for each detected vertex is as follows. Consider a polygon in Fig. 3 which has a clockwise edge sequence of $(E_i E_{i+1} E_{i+2} \cdots)$ and a vertex sequence of $(N_i N_{i+1} N_{i+2} \cdots)$. Point I_i is the intersection of vector $\overrightarrow{N_i N_{i+2}}$ with vector $\overrightarrow{N_{i+1} N_{i+3}}$. Then, the ratio (distance from N_i to I_i)/(distance from N_i to N_{i+2}) which is assigned to vertex N_i of this polygon remains constant for any positioning of the surface in 3-D space.

For the general case, consider a polygon of n edges with a clockwise edge sequence of $(E_1 E_2 \cdots E_{n-1} E_n)$. Edge E_i has a clockwise orientation of N_i to $N_{(i+1)_n}$ where

$$(i + k)_n = \begin{cases} i + k, & \text{if } i + k \leq n \\ i + k - n, & \text{otherwise} \end{cases} \quad (14)$$

and

$$i + k \leq 2n.$$

Let $[A \quad B]$ be the distance from point A to point B. Then, the shape number for vertex N_i can be expressed as

$$Sh_i = \frac{[N_i \quad I_i]}{[N_i \quad N_{(i+2)_n}]} \times 100, \quad 1 \leq i \leq n \quad (15)$$

where I_i is the intersection of vector $\overrightarrow{N_i N_{(i+2)_n}}$ with vector $\overrightarrow{N_{(i+1)_n} N_{(i+3)_n}}$. For a nonconvex polygon, the intersection of the two vectors may be outside the contour or may not occur at all. This means that some Sh_is may be greater than 100 and some may not exist. An upper limit of 100 is placed on the calculation for those shape numbers which are over 100 and 0s are assigned to those Sh_is which do not exist.

To establish vertex correspondences, we associate a local

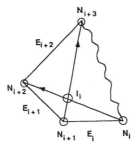

Fig. 3. A surface patch.

feature and a relational feature with each vertex. The local feature is its corresponding angle value and the relational feature is its shape number. In order to perform vertex matching, we select a reliable (i.e., number of edges greater than four) and matched polygon pair obtained from the surface matching process. Each vertex of the matched polygon in the input image is assigned a row index identical to its label. Similarly, each vertex of the matched polygon in the object model is assigned a column index identical to its label. The attributes of each row or column include the local and relational features of its corresponding vertex. An example of this assignment is shown in Fig. 4.

B. C_{ikjl} for Vertex Correspondence Establishment

For vertex correspondence establishment, C_{ikjl} can be expressed by an equation as follows:

$$C_{ikjl} = w_1 \times F(I_i, M_k) + w_2 \times F(I_j, M_l)$$
$$+ w_3 \times F(II_i, MM_k) + w_4 \times F(II_j, MM_l) \quad (16)$$

where I_x represents the shape number of the xth vertex of a polygon in the input image, M_y the shape number of the yth vertex of the corresponding polygon in the object model, II_x the angle of the xth vertex in a polygon of the input image, and MM_y the angle of the yth vertex in the corresponding polygon of the object model. The two selected polygons, one from the image and the other from the object model, have been matched at the previous stage. As to the weights (w_i's) on the right-hand side of (16), the following restrictions must be satisfied, i.e., $w_1 = w_2$, $w_3 = w_4$, and $\Sigma_{i=1}^{4} w_i = 1$. In general, the weights assigned to the relational features (w_3 and w_4) are higher than those of the local features (w_1 and w_2).

C. Deriving the Best Vertex Correspondences

Based on the row-column assignment mentioned in Section IV-A, the vertex labels of a matched polygon in the input image are arranged as the row indexes and the vertex labels of its corresponding polygon in the object model are arranged as the column indexes. Because of this particular assignment, the vertex correspondence problem can be analyzed in a systematic manner.

Before we proceed, we will define some terminologies which will be frequently used in the sequel. Let P represent an n-sided polygon whose vertices are sequenced clockwise as ($p_0 p_1 \cdots p_{n-1}$). If polygon P is rotated clockwise by m-vertex ($m < n$) into a new polygon P', then the vertex sequence is updated from ($p_0 p_1 \cdots p_{n-1}$) to ($p_m p_{(m+1)n} p_{(m+2)n} \cdots p_{n-1} p_0 \cdots p_{m-2} p_{m-1}$). Let A and B be two n-sided polygons with clockwise vertex sequences ($a_0 a_1 \cdots a_{n-1}$) and ($b_0 b_1 \cdots b_{n-1}$), respectively. Suppose the original vertex correspondences be-

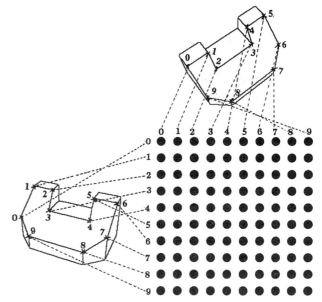

Fig. 4. Row-column assignment for vertex correspondence establishment.

tween A and B is $a_0 \rightarrow b_0$, $a_1 \rightarrow b_1$, $\cdots$, $a_{n-1} \rightarrow b_{n-1}$. If polygon A is rotated clockwise by m-vertex distance into A', then a new vertex correspondences between A' and B is $a_m \rightarrow b_0$, $a_{(m+1)n} \rightarrow b_1$, $a_{(m+2)n} \rightarrow b_2$, $\cdots$, $a_{m-2} \rightarrow b_{n-2}$, $a_{m-1} \rightarrow b_{n-1}$.

The simplest way to determine the correspondences between the vertices of two polygons is to fix one of them, rotate the other in 2-D space each time by 1-vertex (either clockwise or counterclockwise) and calculate the total error by accumulating the differences between all the corresponding node pairs. The comparison continues until the rotated polygon is brought back to the original position. For two n-sided polygons, there are n sequential comparisons to be performed. By using a Hopfield network, the comparisons can be executed concurrently and the results shown explicitly in the network.

Given two n-sided polygons with vertex labels prearranged as described before, we can construct a Hopfield network in the form of an $n \times n$ neuron matrix in which the row and column indexes correspond to the vertex labels of the two polygons, respectively. The two polygons will be referred to as row polygon and column polygon, respectively. Let $neuron(i, j)$ represent a neuron at position (i, j). Because the vertex orders of a polygon is preserved under rotation in 2-D space, the degree of match between a fixed polygon and each of the n rotated instances of the other polygon can be analyzed systematically as follows. Suppose we rotate the row polygon clockwise k-vertex ($k \neq 0$) and fix the column polygon. Then, the degree of match between the column polygon and the rotated row polygon can be computed from the following set of neurons:

$$\{ neuron(i, j) \mid \text{where } i = (j - k) \bmod n,$$
$$0 \leq i, j < n, 1 \leq k < n \} \quad (17)$$

where

$$(j - k) \bmod n = \begin{cases} j - k, & \text{if } j \geq k \\ j - k + n, & \text{otherwise.} \end{cases} \quad (18)$$

The degree of match between the fixed column polygon and the rotated row polygon can be determined by counting the number of active neurons (after the network stabilizes) in the neuron set represented in (17). Generally, the set of neurons in (17) with different k values can be represented by the union of neurons in two diagonals parallel to the main diagonal of the matrix. Using the main diagonal as basis, the upper-right diagonal starts from $neuron(0, k)$ and ends at $neuron(n - k - 1, n - 1)$. The lower-left diagonal starts from $neuron(n - k, 0)$ and ends at $neuron(n - 1, k - 1)$. When $k = 0$, only one diagonal starting from $neuron(0, 0)$ and ending at $neuron(n - 1, n - 1)$ exists. This happens if neither row nor column polygon is rotated. Based on this arrangement, the degree of match between the fixed column polygon and each of the n instances of the rotated row polygon can be determined concurrently in the network.

Let a_{ij} represent the output of the neuron at position (i, j), where $0 \leq i, j < n$. The best match out of the n comparisons can be determined by the following procedures.

Step 1: Calculate the number of active neurons from each of the n comparisons by the following equation:

$$Match(k) = \sum_{i=0}^{n-1} \sum_{j=0}^{n-1} \delta_{(i+k) \bmod n, j} a_{ij}, \qquad 0 \leq k < n. \quad (19)$$

Step 2: Determine the best match by

$$Max\_Match(m) = \max \left[Match(k) \right], \qquad 0 \leq k < n.$$

Step 3: If the best match measure $Max\_Match(m)$ is larger than a threshold ϵ, then the original vertex correspondence matrix is updated to a best vertex correspondence matrix as follows:

$$a_{ij} = \begin{cases} 1, & \text{if } i = (j - m) \bmod n \\ 0, & \text{otherwise} \\ 0 \leq i, j < n \text{ and } 0 \leq m < n. \end{cases} \quad (20)$$

In the first step, (19) is used to calculate the number of active neurons in each of the n comparisons. In the second step, the results derived from Step 1 are compared and the one that contains the largest number of active neurons is selected. In the third step, it is intended to generate the best vertex correspondence matrix by removing all ambiguities. All the neurons corresponding to the best match are activated by applying (17). Those neurons irrelevant to the activated neuron set are then inactivated.

D. Discussion

Being designed as a constraint satisfaction network, the Hopfield net may encounter problems such as multiple active neurons in a row or column after it is stabilized. This is because the given set of constraints is not adequate for singling out the optimal solution. However, a procedure which takes advantage of the fact that the vertex ordering of a polygon is preserved under any rotation in 2-D space is designed to determine the best vertex correspondences. This procedure is valid even if some intermediate vertices are not matched due to distortion caused by changing viewpoints.

We have mentioned that, at the surface correspondence stage, a set of object models are selected from the model database due to higher surface matching measures. The vertex correspondence establishment can be considered as a fine search process. At this stage, we eliminate those object models unable to establish any consistent vertex correspondence with the input image. The discarded object models may include the following: 1) those which are actually the projections of different objects but were accidentally picked up; and 2) those which are projections of the same object but are quite different from the input image. They were mistakenly selected due to the roughness of the features for surface matching. Among the object models whose vertices of the kernel region match those of the input image, the one with the highest surface matching score and the largest number of vertex correspondences is finally selected as the best matched model. Since the pose of the viewpoint where the best matched object model is visualized is predetermined in the modeling phase, the pose of the unknown object can be obtained by computing a 2-D rotation which brings the vertices in the input image to align with their corresponding vertices in the best matched object model.

V. EXPERIMENTAL RESULTS

A series of experiments have been conducted to corroborate the proposed theory. In this paper, only three objects are used to generate the model database. They are a pivot block, a slotted wedge, and a polyhedral object. In constructing the model database, each object is viewed from different angles and a set of topologically different characteristic views are obtained [11]. The overall model database is the collection of these three sets of characteristic views. In Fig. 5(a), a synthetic image is generated by viewing a pivot block from an unknown distance and angle. For illustration, only a few object models [Fig. 5(b)–(d)] are retrieved from the model database and compared with the input image. The surface matching scores s between the input image and the retrieved object models are also printed in Fig. 5(b)–(d), respectively. This number indicates the degree of match between the input image and each of the object models. The object model in Fig. 5(d) has the highest surface matching score with the image in Fig. 5(a). It is noted that the degree of match between the input image and the object models obtained from the projections of other objects [e.g., Fig. 5(b)] are relatively low. This means that even a large set of projections of different objects are in the database, the chance that these projections are mistakenly selected is small. Another experimental result used a slotted wedge. The three object models which are slotted wedges have matching scores s of 0.87, 0.75, and 0.62. The pivot block has a matching score of 0.37, and the polyhedron object has a matching score of 0.25. Fig. 6(a)–(b) shows the input image and the object model which are best matched in Fig. 5. Each polygon is labeled with a number obtained at the preprocessing stage. The neuron matrix showing the surface correspondences between the input image and the best matched object model using the continuous Hopfield network model is shown in the bottom part of Fig. 6(c). The top part of Fig. 6(c) shows the neuron matrix after the first iteration. From the matrix in Fig. 6(c), some matched surface pairs (with number of vertices greater than four) are selected to establish the vertex correspondences. For example, after checking the matrix in Fig. 6(c), it is found that surface 4 in the input image and surface 0 in the object model is a matched pair that contains more than four vertices. This surface pair is then fed into the Hopfield net to check their vertex correspondences. Fig. 6(d) and (e) shows the ordered vertices of surface 4 in the input image and the vertices of surface 0 in the best matched object model, respectively. Based on the method proposed in Section IV-C, the best vertex correspondences between surface 4 in the input image and surface 0 in the best matched object model can be derived and the results are: $0 \rightarrow 6$, $1 \rightarrow 7$, $2 \rightarrow 0$, $3 \rightarrow 1$, $4 \rightarrow 2$, $5 \rightarrow 3$, $6 \rightarrow 4$, $7 \rightarrow 5$. For another kernel surface pair, surface 2 in

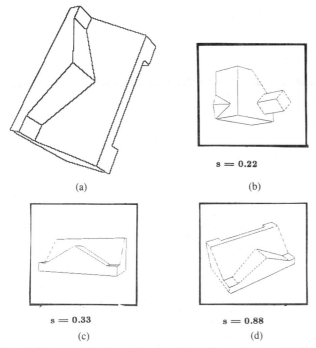

s = 0.22

(a)   (b)

s = 0.33   s = 0.88

(c)   (d)

Fig. 5. (a) A synthetic image of a pivot block. Three object models in the database: (b) Object model 1; (c) Object model 2; (d) Object model 3. "*s*" represents the surface matching score.

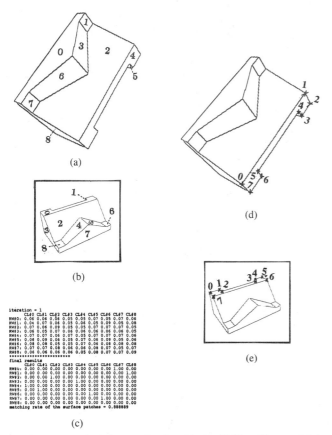

Fig. 6. (a) A synthetic image of a pivot block. (b) The object model that has the highest surface matching score with the input image. (c) The neuron matrix after the first iteration and the final neuron matrix that reflects the surface correspondences between (a) and (b). (d) Surface 4 of the input image in (a) and its vertices numbered in a clockwise direction. (e) Surface 0 of the object model in (b) and its vertices numbered in a clockwise direction.

Fig. 6(a) and surface 2 in Fig. 6(b), the results of the derived best vertex correspondences are: $0 \to 2$, $1 \to 3$, $2 \to 4$, $3 \to 5$, $4 \to 6$, $5 \to 0$, $6 \to 1$.

At the current stage, we use only a software simulator running on an ENCORE MULTIMAX model 320 to conduct experiments. For both surface and vertex correspondence establishment processes, the convergence time of the network varies. In general, if the freeze strategy is finally adopted, the convergence time ranges from 1 to several CPU min. Of course, the convergence time of the network depends on the complexity of the input image, the object models, and the features used to perform the matching task. If a small number of neurons are not convergent after a long period of time, the time-out strategy is used to terminate the algorithm. Under the circumstances, the convergence time ranges from ten min to one h CPU times (provided that 500 steps is used as the time-out limit). Since the features adopted in the vertex correspondence establishment process is more complicated than those of the surface correspondence process, the convergence time of the former is usually longer than that of the latter.

VI. CONCLUSIONS AND DISCUSSIONS

In this paper, we use Hopfield networks to solve both the surface and vertex correspondence problems for 3-D object recognition. The proposed scheme can be considered as a coarse-to-fine search process. In a 3-D object recognition system adopting multiple-view approach, the database is usually a set of 2-D projections which are topologically different. By calculating the surface matching score between the input image and each object model in the model database, a set of 2-D models with higher surface matching score is selected. This phase can be considered as a coarse search process. The object models selected from the first stage are then fed into the Hopfield net for establishing the vertex correspondences between the input image and each of these models. This phase is the fine search process. The object model that has the best vertex and surface correspondences with the input image is finally selected. Once an object model is identified, we can use the model coordinate frame as the reference frame to derive the pose of the unknown object.

Some researchers have used the discrete Hopfield networks [14] to solve the 3-D matching problems. For comparison purposes, we tried both the discrete and continuous models. The neuron matrix that reflects the surface correspondences between the input image in Fig. 6(a) and the object model in Fig. 6(b) using the discrete Hopfield network model is shown in Fig. 7. By comparing the neuron matrices shown in Fig. 6(c) and Fig. 7, we find that the performance of the continuous model is superior to that of the discrete model. In Fig. 7, the discrete model generates two mismatches: one is the mismatch between surface 1 in Fig. 6(a) and surface 6 in Fig. 6(b), and the other is the mismatch between surface 7 in Fig. 6(a) and surface 8 in Fig. 6(b). This is due to the approximation mechanism adopted by the discrete model. For the vertex correspondence problem, the performance of the continuous model is still better than that of the discrete model. However, the degradation caused by using the discrete model can be made up by applying the technique proposed in Section IV-C. In our experiments, both the continuous and the discrete models are comparable in solving vertex correspondence problems.

In case the results of image segmentation are such that some surfaces are fragmented, merged, or missing, the number of

```
row # 0 : 0000000010
row # 1 : 0000000100
row # 2 : 0010000000
row # 3 : 0000100000
row # 4 : 1000000000
row # 5 : 0100000000
row # 6 : 0000001000
row # 7 : 0000000001
row # 8 : 0000000100
```

Fig. 7. The neuron matrix describing the surface correspondences between Fig. 6(a) and (b) resulting from the discrete Hopfield network model.

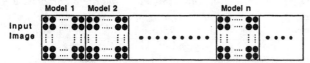

Fig. 8. Parallel implementation of object recognition.

rows in the neuron matrix at the surface matching stage may increase or decrease. This may have some effect on the calculation of the surface matching score. Experiments have been conducted to check the robustness of the proposed method in case of poor segmentation results. In our experiments, the good candidates are still "good enough" to be selected for further scrutiny. This shows that even though some minor parts of an image are missing, an object model similar to the scene image can still be selected with the proposed method. The problem created by missing parts is that the search space is expanded due to the smaller amount of information. It is understandable that if the missing parts are kernel surfaces in the image, it may be difficult to derive a good match. In other words, the loss of the crucial information for object recognition usually makes the task impossible. In sum, the existence of missing parts slows down the performance of the proposed system but does not affect the correctness of the final decisions. In case of oversegmentation or undersegmentation, the proposed method is also robust enough to generate accurate results.

Another merit of the proposed scheme is that it is suitable for parallel processing. For all the experiments we have conducted, the contents of the input image correspond to the row elements while the contents of the object model correspond to the column elements. This kind of arrangement can perform only one comparison between the input image and one of the object models. However, the potential of the Hopfield network can be fully exploited by employing the structure as shown in Fig. 8. By expanding the columns of the Hopfield network, a large number of the object models in the database can be fed into the network and processed simultaneously. The degrees of match between the input image and all the object models in the database can thus be obtained concurrently in the expanded Hopfield networks.

In comparison with conventional methods, there are several advantages in using Hopfield nets for image matching. Image matching can be regarded as a process of finding homomorphisms between two relational structures and is basically an NP-complete problem. In the worst case, its time complexity is expected to be exponential. In order to speed up the performance, several methods adopting look-ahead [27] or relaxation [28]–[30] schemes have been proposed. However, in general, it takes more effort to manage a look-ahead table or devise a relaxation algorithm. A Hopfield network takes advantage of its massively parallel structure to deal with matching problems in an elegant and systematic manner and quantitatively reflects the degree of similarity in the final states of the neurons. The formulation of

the network structure is simple and the matching process is easy to implement.

ACKNOWLEDGMENT

The authors wish to thank the reviewers of this paper for their many valuable suggestions on the preparation of this manuscript.

REFERENCES

[1] P. J. Besl and R. C. Jain, "Three-dimensional object recognition," *ACM Comput. Surveys*, vol. 17, no. 1, pp. 75–145, Mar. 1985.
[2] M. Oshima and Y. Shirai, "Object recognition using three-dimensional information," *IEEE Trans. Pattern Anal. Machine Intell.*, vol. PAMI-5, no. 4, pp. 353–361, July 1983.
[3] R. T. Chin and C. R. Dyer, "Model-based recognition in robot vision," *ACM Comput. Surveys*, vol. 18, no. 1, pp. 67–108, Mar. 1986.
[4] I. Chakravarty and H. Freeman, "Characteristic views as a basis for three-dimensional object recognition," in *Proc. Soc. Photo-Opt. Instr. Engrs*, vol. 336, pp. 37–45, 1982.
[5] H. Freeman and I. Chakravarty, "The use of characteristic views in the recognition of three-dimensional objects," E. Gelsema and L. Kanal, Eds., *Pattern Recognition in Practice*. Amsterdam: The Netherlands, North-Holland, pp. 277–288, 1980.
[6] I. Chakravarty, "The use of characteristic views as a basis for recognition of three-dimensional objects," Ph.D. Dissertation, Dept. of Computer and Systems Engineering, Rensselaer Polytechnic Institute, 1982.
[7] Z. Gigus, J. Canny, and R. Seidel, "Efficiently computing and representing aspect graphs of polyhedral objects," *IEEE 2nd Int. Conf. Computer Vision*, Tampa, FL, Dec. 5–8, 1988, pp. 30–39.
[8] M. R. Korn and C. R. Dyer, "3-D multiview object representations for model-based object recognition," *Pattern Recognition*, vol. 20, no. 1, pp. 91–103, 1987.
[9] J. Stewman and K. Bowyer, "Creating the perspective projection aspect graph of polyhedral objects," *IEEE 2nd Int. Conf. Computer Vision*, Tampa, FL, Dec. 5–8, 1988, pp. 494–500.
[10] L. Stark, D. Eggert, and K. Bowyer, "Aspect graphs and nonlinear optimization in 3-D object recognition," *IEEE 2nd Int. Conf. Computer Vision*, Tampa, FL, Dec. 5–8, 1988, pp. 501–507.
[11] W.-C. Lin and F.-Y. Liao, "An automated procedure to construct minimum aspect graphs for 3-D object recognition," submitted for publication.
[12] J. J. Hopfield and D. W. Tank, "Neural computation of decisions in optimization problems," *Biolog. Cybernet.*, vol. 52, pp. 141–152, 1985.
[13] ——, "Computing with neural circuits: A model," *Science*, vol. 233, pp. 625–633, 1986.
[14] W. Li and M. Nasrabadi, "Object recognition based on graph matching implemented by a hopfield-style neural network," *Int. J. Conf. Neural Networks*, II, Washington, DC, June 18–22, 1989, pp. 287–290.
[15] B. Parvin and G. Medioni, "A constraint satisfaction network for matching 3D objects," *Int. J. Conf. Neural Networks*, II, Washington, DC, June 18–22, 1989, pp. 281–286.
[16] E. Mjolsness, G. Gindi, and P. Anandan, "Optimization in model matching and perceptual organization," *Neural Computation*, vol. 1, pp. 218–229, 1989.
[17] R. Mohan, "Application of neural constraint satisfaction networks to vision," *Int. J. Conf. Neural Networks*, II, Washington, DC, June 18–22, 1989, pp. 619–620.
[18] P. J. Besl and R. C. Jain, "Segmentation through variable-order surface fitting," *IEEE Trans. Pattern Anal. Machine Intell.*, vol. PAMI-10, no. 2, pp. 167–192, Mar. 1988.
[19] S.-Y. Chen and M.-Y. Chern, "Flexible corner detection based on a single-parameter control," *Proc. of SPIE*, vol. 848, pp. 108–114, 1987.
[20] S. A. Underwood and C. L. Coates, Jr., "Visual learning from multiple views," *IEEE Trans. Comput.*, vol. C-24, no. 6, pp. 651–661, 1975.
[21] G. V. Wilson and G. S. Pawley, "On the stability of the travell-

ing salesman problem algorithm of Hopfield and Tank," *Biolog. Cybernet.*, vol. 58, pp. 63–70, 1988.

[22] G. W. Davis, "Sensitivity analysis in neural net solutions," *IEEE Trans. Syst., Man, Cybernet.*, vol. 19, no. 5, pp. 1078–1082, Sept./Oct. 1989.

[23] P. Floreen and P. Orponen, "Counting stable states and sizes of attraction domains in Hopfield nets is hard," *Int. J. Conf. Neural Networks, I*, Washington, DC, June 18–22, 1989, pp. 395–399.

[24] L. G. Shapiro and R. M. Haralick, "Structural description and inexact matching," *IEEE Trans. Pattern Anal. Machine Intell.*, vol. PAMI-3, pp. 504–515, 1981.

[25] H. R. Schwarz, *Numerical Analysis: A Comprehensive Introduction.* New York, NY: Wiley, pp. 384–392, 1980.

[26] W.-C. Lin, F.-Y. Liao, C.-K. Tsao, and T. Lingutla, "A connectionist approach to multiple-view based 3-D object recogni-tion," *Int. J. Conf. Neural Networks*, San Diego, CA, June 17–21, 1990.

[27] L. G. Shapiro, J. D. Moriarty, and R. M. Haralick, "Matching three-dimensional objects using a relational paradigm," *Pattern Recognition*, vol. 17, no. 4, pp. 385–405, 1984.

[28] R. M. Haralick and L. G. Shapiro, "The consistent labeling problem: Part I," *IEEE Trans. Pattern Anal. Machine Intell.*, vol. PAMI-1, no. 2, pp. 173–184, Apr. 1979.

[29] ——, "The consistent labeling problem: Part II," *IEEE Trans. Pattern Anal. Machine Intell.*, vol. PAMI-2, no. 3, pp. 193–203, May 1980.

[30] R. M. Haralick and J. S. Kartus, "Arrangements, homomorph-isms, and discrete relaxation," *IEEE Trans. Syst., Man, Cybern.*, vol. SMC-8, pp. 600–612, Aug. 1978.

Article 6.9

A Real-Time Neural System for Color Constancy

Andrew Moore, *Student Member, IEEE*, John Allman, and Rodney M. Goodman, *Member, IEEE*

Abstract—This paper presents a neural network approach to the problem of color constancy. Various algorithms based on Land's retinex theory are discussed, with an eye on neurobiological parallels, computational efficiency, and suitability for VLSI implementation. The efficiency of one algorithm is improved by the application of resistive grids and is tested in computer simulations; the simulations make clear the strengths and weaknesses of the algorithm. A novel extension to the algorithm is developed to address its weaknesses. An electronic system based on the original algorithm was built, using subthreshold analog CMOS VLSI resistive grids, that operates at video rates. The system displays color constancy abilities and qualitatively mimics aspects of human color perception.

I. Introduction

ANYONE who has tried to take a picture of a friend or of a vase of flowers under different lighting conditions has realized that our present technology for capturing images is flawed. While the color of skin or of a rose may look the same to us at high noon or at sunset, a film or video camera just does not see it that way. Color constancy is the ability of the human visual system to judge, preattentively, the reflectance of objects in the visual world under a range of different illuminants. Color constancy is not perfect: if the illuminant is strongly saturated (lacking in white), we make errors. However, for natural variations, such as changing daylight conditions caused by varying cloud cover, we do rather well.

While the problem of color constancy has been recognized for some time (Helmholtz commented on it [1]), the computational essence of the problem has been grappled with only recently. In this paper, we present a system that addresses this problem for video images. The idea for the system originated in consideration of mammalian neurophysiology and human psychophysics; its validity was tested in computer simulations and it was implemented using analog VLSI. The electronic system is the first real-time instantiation of Land's retinex theory of color constancy for video imaging.

In the following, we first describe the neurobiological and computational aspects of the problem. Next we describe various manifestations of Land's retinex algorithm, improve on one of them by applying resistive grids, and propose a novel one. Results of computer simulations of the improved Land algorithm and the new algorithm are presented. Finally we describe an electronic system which performs the improved algorithm at video rates.

Manuscript received August 13, 1990; revised November 21, 1990. This work was supported (via fellowships to A. Moore) by the Parsons Foundation and the Pew Charitable Trust and (via research assistantships) by the Office of Naval Research, the Joint Tactical Fusion Program, and the Center for Research in Parallel Computation.

The authors are with the Computation and Neural Systems Program at the California Institute of Technology, Pasadena, CA 91125.

IEEE Log Number 9042027.

II. Neurobiological and Computational Issues in Color Constancy

A. Neural Computation of Color

The only system which, at present, is capable of approximating color constancy in real time is the nervous system. As such, all algorithms for color constancy should be judged in comparison with the CNS. The following is a necessarily simplified sketch of the neurobiology of color vision, a subject of continuing extensive research.

We sense light with three classes of receptors, the cones (rod vision is not considered here). The three classes of cones have different spectral band-pass properties. They are called long, medium, and short (from the spectral bands that they are sensitive to), or colloquially, red, green, and blue. At the level of retinal ganglion cells, the output cells of the retina, the image has been transformed from three arrays of band-pass signals to three arrays of combinations of those signals. One set of outputs codes along the black–white axis of the color space, and the other two code along the red–green and yellow–blue axes.

Cortical visual area V4, many synapses "upstream" from the retina, receives inputs from lower visual areas that work with color difference signals. In early investigations V4 was dubbed the color area [2] because the cells could only be excited with color. (This view is now modified, as it is known that V4 cells can also respond to orientation and binocular disparity [3]. Here, only the spectral properties of V4 cells are considered.) Cortical neurons in this visual area are especially interesting since they seem to be responsive to perceived color, rather than wavelength; that is, they are "color constant" according Zeki's informal study [4], [5]. An example of his work is as follows. With white illumination, he centered a cell's receptive field on one colored patch from a large field of many colored patches. A given cell responded only to a red patch, for example—yellow or green patches produced no cell firing under white light. Next he centered the cell receptive field on a yellow patch, turned off the white light, and carefully constructed a new illuminant such that *the spectrum of light coming from the yellow patch was the same for this illuminant as the spectrum from the red patch under the white illuminant*. To a human observer, the yellow patch still looked yellow, not red. Zeki found that the V4 cell did not fire when presented with the yellow patch which reflected red light, and so had discounted the illuminant. In contrast, he found that cells in the first visual area are sensitive to wavelength alone and so responded like a photometer, firing identically to a red patch under white light and a yellow patch under red light.

· Desimone and his colleagues [6] obtained results from V4 cells that are in a sense supportive of Zeki's observations. In a study of the "nonclassical" receptive fields of extrastriate visual neurons, they found that V4 cells respond to white, and to many wavelengths, but have a maximal response at some wave-

Reprinted from *IEEE Trans. on Neural Networks*, vol. 2, no. 2, pp. 237–247, March 1991.

416

length "analogous to a broad-band color filter, such as a piece of colored glass." They found that V4 cells are suppressed by stimuli in a large (30° or greater) "silent surround"; the suppression is maximum at the wavelength most effective in exciting the cell center, and falls off as the surround stimulus wavelength is moved away from the most effective center stimulus wavelength.

By comparing the color in the center of the receptive field with the color in a large area outside of the center, V4 cells judge *relative color*. This is the presumed basis for color constancy. If the illuminant is red, for example, a reddish cast is added to all parts of the scene. Though the cell center may see red, its surround does as well, and so it will not respond. Thus the cell discounts the illuminant and contributes to color constancy.

B. The Computational Essence of Color Constancy

Under normal variations (e.g., noon versus sunset or clear versus overcast sky), the spectrum of daylight varies somewhat. The variation is limited enough that is can be represented with three spectral basis functions [7]. A wide range of naturally occurring object reflectances can also be described with only three basis functions [8]. The light reaching a point on the retina, i.e., the set of three cone *quantum catches*, is just the product of the illuminant and the reflectance at a point in the world, to a first approximation (this is refined below). Thus, six unknowns determine the light impinging on each point of the retina, and only three data values, the quantum catches of the three cone classes, are available for further processing by the visual system. Yet we seem to be able to discount the illuminant and perceive the object reflectance [9]-[14]. *This is the computational problem of color constancy: How do we solve three equations in six unknowns?*

Various models of color constancy exist in the literature [15]-[23]. Several authors [9], [16]-[18] have shown that if the three basis functions for reflectance, illumination, and cone absorption are different, a color constancy algorithm must solve a tensor transformation from six unknowns to three knowns in order to find the reflectance from the cone signals with varying illumination. Each model makes assumptions to simplify the problem more or less. Here, we focus on Land's models since, through a powerful set of simplifying assumptions, he reduces the computational complexity of the color constancy problem tremendously [24], perhaps more than any other model.

III. Land's Retinex Theory

Land's assumptions and various versions of color constancy algorithms based on them are discussed in this section. For each algorithm, the biological basis, computational complexity, and suitability for VLSI implementation are noted.

A. Three Separate Lightnesses

One of Land's basic premises is that color constancy can be achieved by the computation of three separate *designators* or lightness values at each point, in three separate systems called retinexes. (Since he was not sure at first whether the computation took place in the retina or in the cortex, he coined the term *retinex*.) Further, he emphasizes the ability of the nervous system to perceive reflectance even though the illuminant is varying (albeit slowly) in space.

The three lightness signals are assumed to be independent;

Land does not state how this may occur, but Hurlbert and Poggio offer a derivation [24]. With this assumption, the color constancy tensor relation collapses to three independent equations. Within each channel i, the lightness l_i is the product of the illuminant m_i and reflectance p_i:

$$l_i(x) = m_i(x)\, p_i(x). \tag{1}$$

The log is taken to form a sum:

$$l_i'(x) = \log l_i(x) = \log m_i(x) + \log p_i(x)$$
$$= m_i'(x) + p_i'(x). \tag{2}$$

Once the two variables that make up the color signal are separated, the second of the three main assumptions of retinex theory is applied, namely, that the illumination is slowly varying in space but the reflectance signal varies mostly at sharp edges. Implementations of retinex theory work with this assumption by removing the slowly varying component $m'(x)$ to produce an image that depends only on reflectance $p'(x)$. Homomorphic filtering algorithms also use the logarithm to separate the components of the color signal in this way [25], [26]. The slowing varying component (the illuminant) is then separated by low-pass filtering via Fourier techniques. Retinex algorithms, in contrast, perform all operations in the spatial domain. Three implementations are presented.

B. Early Implementations

Land's original scheme [19], [20] considers the color signal at a point in one color plane of an image relative to a spatial average signal computed along a set of paths from other points in the image to the point in question. The starting point of a particular path is chosen randomly, and the logarithms of the ratio of color signals at transitions encountered along the path are accumulated if the transition represents a reflectance change versus a change in shading. A threshold operation is used to make this distinction. This procedure is repeated for many paths and the resulting values are averaged. The resulting average of logs is the log of the lightness of the point divided by a measure of the spatially averaged lightness. For an infinite number of paths and no thresholding, this measure of the spatial average is the geometric mean [27]. Land claims that he gets good results with 200 paths. Finally, the reported lightness is normalized to the lightest point in the image for this color plane.

The division by the average lightness and subsequent normalization imply the third main assumption of Land's theory, that the spatial average reflectance in each lightness channel is constant for all images. The retinex algorithm, then, operates under a *gray world assumption*. It is possible to defeat the algorithm by placing a strongly colored patch in a very simple scene so that the average reflectance is not gray [27].

This algorithm and variants of it can produce nice results (see, for example McCann's images in [28]). However, the procedures are cumbersome and it is difficult to see how the nervous system could carry them out. Further, the computational complexity, though reduced by assuming three separate lightness channels, is still daunting. For each point in the image, much of the rest of the image must be traversed by one of the paths to obtain the correct lightness. In other words, for an $N \times N$ image, on the order of N^4 calculations are required. In a VLSI implementation, each pixel would have to be connected with many other pixels.

Horn [15], [22] utilizes the Laplacian operator to compare lightness across edges. The Laplacian of the image is then thresholded, to remove the slowly varying illuminant. Finally, the inverse Laplacian is performed. Analytically, this is done by convolving with the Green's function for the Laplacian, $(1/2\pi) \log(r)$. In a resistive grid framework, the Laplacian is inverted via a feedback network. In a digital implementation, the Poisson equation is solved iteratively via Gauss-Siedel elimination. Several variants of this implementation exist in the literature (e.g., [23] and [29]).

Marr [30] has proposed a scheme in which the nervous system may carry out this implementation, and the resistive grid framework is suitable for analog VLSI implementation since only nearest-neighbor connections between pixels are required. The undesirable spatial connectivity of the previous implementation is converted to the time domain. That is, the time required for the feedback network to settle is sufficient for information to cross the entire image space through the nearest-neighbor connections. To our knowledge, no one has attempted to build chips based on this algorithm.

C. Recent Implementations

In 1986, Land published an alternative to the algorithm described above [21]. This implementation involves computing an average weighted by distance from the point in question, and subtracting the log of this average from the log of the lightness of the point in question. This idea came from Land after his collaboration with Livingstone and Hubel [31] and Zeki [2] and has a strongly biological flavor to it. That is, the operator he uses looks like a cortical "nonclassical" receptive field, with a narrow center and a huge surround [6], [32].

In practical terms, the algorithm corresponds to subtracting from an image a blurred version of itself. The distance weighting (type of blurring) Land proposes varies as $1/r^2$, so the operation is a center minus surround operation, where the surround is the center convolved with a $1/r^2$ kernel:

$$l'_{\text{out},i}(x, y) - \log\left(l_i(x, y) \otimes \frac{1}{r^2}\right), \quad r \neq 0. \quad (3)$$

Hurlbert arrived at the same sort of operation analytically [24] with a Gaussian kernel:

$$l'_{\text{out},i}(x, y) = l'_i(x, y) - l'_i(x, y) \otimes e^{-r^2/\sigma} \quad (4)$$

where σ is large enough that the kernel extends across most of the image. Except for the different kernels, the only difference between the two procedures is that Hurlbert's involves taking the log of the lightness of the surrounding points before rather than after averaging. She claims that in practice there is little difference between the two procedures [33].

This type of retinex algorithm, then, has a biological basis and sound computational underpinnings. But the complexity is too great. Since the required surround is so large, such a convolution across an $N \times N$ pixel image entails on the order of N^4 operations. On a chip, this corresponds to explicit connections from each pixel to most if not all other pixels.

A similar operation can be carried out much more efficiently

by switching from a convolution to a resistive grid calculation. The operations are similar since the weighting of neighboring points (Green's function) in a resistive grid decreases in the limit as the exponential of the distance from a given location on a resistive grid. With this type of kernel, the operation in each retinex (color channel) is

$$l'_{\text{out},i}(x, y) = l'_i(x, y) - l'_i(x, y) \otimes e^{-|r|/\lambda} \quad (5)$$

where λ is the length constant or extent of weighting in the grid [34]. Since the calculation is purely local, the complexity is reduced dramatically from $O(N^4)$ to $O(N^2)$. On a chip, a local computation corresponds to connections only between nearest-neighbor pixels. So, in this novel retinex implementation, since a resistive grid is used to form the spatial average (i.e., to blur the image for subtraction from the original), the complexity is reduced to tractable levels, and the algorithm is appropriate for implementation in analog VLSI.

IV. SIMULATION RESULTS

A. Simulations of the Retinex Algorithm

Tools for simulating Land's most recent algorithm were developed and used to process both black and white images and color images. First, Hurlbert's results for one-dimensional black and white images were confirmed. A large spatial sample was obtained around each pixel by convolving with a filter whose weights drop off exponentially as the distance from the center pixel. This surround value was subtracted from the center pixel value. As Hurlbert and Poggio report [33], this scheme handily removes illumination gradients. Next, the simulation was extended to two dimensions with similar results and tremendous increase in run time, owing to the $O(N^4)$ complexity of the Gaussian convolution needed to form the spatial average for subtraction. For 128×128 pixel black and white images, the simulation took over an hour on a Sun 4 workstation.

Next, the same results were arrived at much more efficiently by switching from a convolution to a resistive grid calculation. The resistive grid simulation runs in a minute rather than an hour, since the calculation is purely local. With resistive grid code, color images were simulated next (Fig. 1(a) and (b)).

Specifically, in color simulations of the Land algorithm, 512×512 pixel images are subsampled to 128×128 resolution. Our frame grabber captures 8 bits each of R, G, and B. Within a color plane, the 8 bit pixel values are converted to floating point numbers and the log is taken. These values are then treated as input currents to a resistive grid; Kirchhoff's current law is used in local calculations to simulate the spread of the input across the grid. Several iterations are usually required for the voltages to settle down. (We stop the simulation when the difference in the node voltages across the grid between two iterations is less than one tenth of 1% of the maximum pixel value. About one hundred iterations are usually sufficient to meet this criterion.) Next the settled net values are subtracted from the log of the input values. Finally, the minimum of the corrected values in the three planes is found and subtracted from all values in the three planes, and all values are scaled up so that the maximum of all values in the three planes is set to the maximum value of our frame buffer, 255:

$$R_{\text{out}}(x, y) = 255 \cdot \frac{R_0(x, y) - \min(\min(R), \min(G), \min(B))}{\max(\max(R), \max(G), \max(B)) - \min(\min(R), \min(G), \min(B))} \quad (6)$$

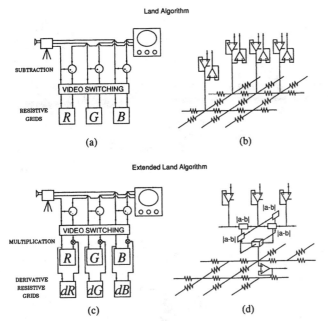

(a)   (b)

Extended Land Algorithm

(c)   (d)

Fig. 1. (a) The Land algorithm. The three color camera outputs are smoothed on three separate resistive grids, labeled R, G, and B. The smoothed signal is subtracted from the camera output. (b) Resistive grid for smoothing images. (c) Extended Land algorithm. The magnitude of the local spatial derivative is smoothed for each color channel on the resistive grids labeled dR, dG, and dB and used to modulate the strength of the smoothed image before subtraction from the original. (d) The scheme for computing edginess. The average of the magnitudes of the local derivatives serves as the input to a resistive grid.

This last step is a form of gain control and is crucial; without it, all colors would tend to gray since the subtraction of the blurred image is a compressive operation. Note that it is the only step that requires operations across the three color planes. All prior steps proceed independently within each color plane. We go to this trouble since there are some images in which there is little or no information in a given channel. For example, in forest scenes there is not much signal in the blue channel. Normalizing independently in each channel for such a scene would artificially expand the pixel values in the blue channel, causing noise to be accentuated and generally changing the image color globally in the wrong way.

Fig. 2 shows the results of simulations of the Land algorithm. At top are three images obtained directly from the video camera. For images (a) and (b) the color output controls of the video camera were adjusted to match skin color and a color card fairly well under ordinary fluorescent illumination. One image (top left, (a)) was captured under this illuminant; it will be called the (camera) corrected or fluorescent image. The fluorescent lights were then turned off, and the same subject was illuminated with incandescent light. A second image (middle top, (b)) was captured without correcting the camera color settings under this new illuminant; it will be called the uncorrected or incandescent image. While colors in the scene looked a bit shifted to the red to us in the room when the second image was taken, they were not as bad as those captured by the camera—the second image is unacceptable. The skin color is too red, the background is lost in darkness, and the shadows are very deep. Unfortunately, in these respects it resembles many amateur video images taken indoors.

The middle row of images in Fig. 2 show the result of applying the retinex operation to the original images. The corrected image (middle left, (d), corresponding to (a) above it) is somewhat improved in terms of contrast enhancement. Note, for example, the highlights in the hair that are not visible in the original. The color is less saturated (i.e. less pure, more washed out, more gray) but hue is well preserved. The uncorrected image is strikingly improved (center image, (e), corresponding to (b)). Skin color is more muted, the shadows across the face are softened, and detail is visible in the background. While color correction is not perfect, it is significant. The contrast enhancement inherent in this algorithm is at least as significant.

One drawback of this algorithm, however, is apparent in these images, namely, color induction across edges. Close examination of image (e) of Fig. 2 reveals that the (black) border of the CIE diagram poster has been tinged with red above and to the right of the horseshoe-shaped diagram and tinged green below the diagram. The discoloration decreases with distance from the edge of the diagram. The unwanted color, overlaid on the black border, is the complementary color of the area on the other side of the edge: induced red abuts the green region on the right and induced green abuts the red region on the bottom. Red and green are complementary colors. From these facts one may conclude that color induction across abrupt edges is inherent in the algorithm. Consider, for example, a point in the black border area just adjacent to the CIE diagram on the right side of the poster. Its surround is strongly weighted green by the nearby region of the color diagram. This (mainly green) surround is subtracted from the black center to yield black plus green's complement, red. (Along with the red value, the blue value is raised over the green channel in this region. So in this sense, it could be said that green's complement is red plus blue. What we perceive, however, is mostly the complement to green, which is more red than blue.) A black border point further from the color edge is less induced to red since the green area is further away, and thus weighted less in forming the surround. Image (d) is similarly distorted but the distortion is less noticeable by inspection. This effect is quantified below.

Color induction is not mentioned in any of the studies of retinex theory except the most recent one by Land [21]. In this paper, he notes induction in terms of *Mach bands*, a well-known phenomenon in psychophysics. Fig. 5 of that paper shows how "spill-over" of the surround is responsible for a relatively dark region in the light region adjacent to a dark–light edge and a complementary, relatively light region in the dark area near the edge. Normally one hears only of Mach bands along the achromatic (black–white) lightness axis. Whether color Mach bands are visible is controversial. However, it suffices to say that we do not perceive effects as strong as the effects produced by the Land algorithm with video camera inputs; we do not see, for example, a green halo surrounding a red ball placed against a gray background.

Another limitation of the Land algorithm is revealed by the images in the right column of Fig. 2. At top (image (c)) is the output of a video camera shot of a still life in which a large portion of the scene is composed of just one color. This is a common situation; often half of an image is filled with sky or foliage. The scene was deliberately captured under dim illumination, to study the contrast enhancement capabilities of this algorithm. At middle right (image (f)) is the result of retinex processing. Although the shadows were softened considerably, much of the image is gray, not green. This illustrates how the gray world assumption can go wrong. Since we are subtracting a blurred version of the image from the original image, in this case we are subtracting green from green, leaving gray.

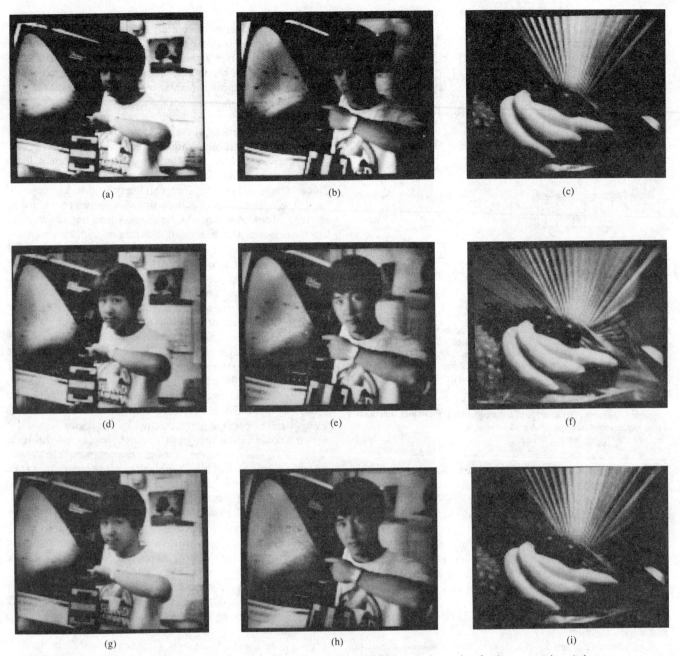

Fig. 2. Results of simulations. At top are the original images. In the middle row are the results of retinex processing. At bottom are the results after applying the extension to the retinex algorithm.

The upshot of all of this is that the Land model is too simple in at least two ways. First, it embodies but a simplification of a static aspect of visual processing that psychophysicists call *simultaneous contrast* [14], [35]–[37]. (In this sense it could also be called the Cornsweet model, the Jameson and Hurvich model, or even the Mach model as all of these researchers have pointed to simultaneous contrast as a mechanism for color constancy.) Land's model of simultaneous contrast is insufficient in that it ignores edge information and thus suffers from induction across borders. While retinex proponents point to cortical visual area V4 as being a site of surround suppression in color processing, they do not cope with the fact that V4 cells respond well to edges [3], [6]. Second, the model suffers from overreliance on the gray world assumption. As we shall see below, edge information can also help with this problem.

B. An Extension to the Retinex Algorithm

A modification of the retinex algorithm was applied next to the same color images (bottom row of Fig. 2). The magnitude of the spatial derivative is smoothed on a second resistive grid, to yield a measure of "edginess"; this measure is used to weight the surround before subtraction from the center (parts (c) and (d) of Fig. 1). In other words, while for a retinex simulation we have

$$\text{output} = \text{center} - \text{surround} \qquad (7)$$

$$l'_{\text{out},i}(x, y) = l'_i(x, y) - l'_i(x, y) \otimes e^{-r/\lambda} \qquad (8)$$

to ameliorate induction effects and lessen reliance on the gray world assumption, we need to modify the surround weight from point to point. In particular, if edginess is given a value close to 0 in homogeneous regions such as the black border of the poster in the left images, and is given a value close to 1 in more detailed regions such as the colored shirt, we have a better formulation as follows:

$$\text{output} = \text{center} - \text{surround} \cdot \text{edginess}. \qquad (9)$$

In this relation, the surround is effectively zeroed in smooth areas before it is subtracted, so that induction is diminished—more of the original color is retained.

Parts (c) and (d) of Fig. 1 show how edginess is computed and used. The 512×512 image is again sampled at a low resolution. The magnitude of the first spatial derivative, labeled $|a - b|$, is computed between points; the average of the absolute value of the four local spatial derivatives are fed as a current into each node of the grid. The output voltage of this resistive grid is multiplied with the surround value read out from the first resistive grid. This modified surround is then subtracted from the camera output, to yield a color-corrected signal. Signifying the averaged magnitude of local spatial derivatives as $|\partial l'_i(x, y)|$, the mathematical expression for the resistive grid smoothing of that quantity is the convolution of it with an exponential distance weighting function, so the complete expression for the extended algorithm is

$$l'_{\text{out}, i}(x, y) = l'_i(x, y) - l'_i(x, y) \otimes e^{-r/\lambda}$$
$$\cdot |\partial l'_i(x, y)| \otimes e^{-r/\lambda}. \qquad (10)$$

The bottom figures of Fig. 2 show images processed with this extended retinex algorithm. The color induction is much less noticeable upon inspection in the middle and left images, and color is returned to the palm frond at bottom right. The extended algorithm effectively varies, point by point, the degree of subtraction of the blurred version of the image from the original. In detailed areas, edginess is high, so the subtraction is carried out as for the original algorithm. In smooth areas, however, the degree of correction (weight of surround subtracted) varies as the distance from the nearest edgy area. In smooth areas, more of the original image "passes through," and so there is less color correction. Color constancy will be worse for such areas. For example, in Fig. 2(h) the skin tone is redder than in Fig. 2(e). The extended algorithm, then, is a working compromise between color constancy via strict application of the gray world assumption and no color constancy at all.

Some of these results are quantified in Fig. 3. A horizontal and a vertical line through the images in places that show induction artifacts were selected (Fig. 3(a) and (b)). The green intensity at each pixel in each line was subtracted from the red intensity at the pixel to show the value of the red–green axis of color at the pixel in the original images, in the images processed with the retinex algorithm, and in the images processed with the extended retinex algorithm. Concentrating on the black border area of the poster, note that for the original images (thick lines) the pixel value is zero in these regions—red and green are balanced in the achromatic, black region. A shift from zero here results from induction. At the top of the poster border, red is strongly induced in the retinex-processed image (dashed line at pixels 10–30 of plots (e) and (f) of Fig. 3). It is induced by the neighboring green area (pixels 30–50). The extended retinex algorithm produces less induction (thin line). Similarly, green is induced in a black region next to the reddish face area after retinex processing in a region crossed by the horizontal line (pixels 50–70 of plot (d)). The extended algorithm (thin line)

is not much better than the original retinex algorithm (dashed line) in this instance.

Other resistive grid methods for color correction have been explored in simulation. If at each point of input to a grid computing the surround for subtraction, the input resistance is modulated by the local spatial derivative, a surround is formed that consists of areas "filled in" or interpolated between edgy regions. Here the local spatial derivatives form an input confidence [38], [39]. Mach bands are lessened in this algorithm in comparison with the Land algorithm, but the degree of smoothing required to form good surrounds varies from image to image, so the algorithm is not as robust as the extension detailed above. We have also tried varying the lateral resistances according to local spatial derivatives, with disastrous results; variation of the lateral resistances strongly disturbs current flow in the grid, segmenting the image into discrete areas [40], [41]. As a result, subtraction of the grid outputs leads to patches of gray in most smooth areas of the input image. In other words, variation of the lateral resistance by local values is more appropriate for segmentation than for normalization. We have not tried to vary the input or lateral resistances according to smoothed edginess, though it may be more comparable to the extended method discussed above.

These results are anecdotal and limited in nature, but they show the strengths and weaknesses of Land's algorithm and allow us to see ways to improve the algorithm. The extension explored, modulation of the surround by a measure of edginess calculated by smoothing the magnitude of the spatial derivative on a second resistive grid, is easy to implement in VLSI.

V. VLSI IMPLEMENTATION OF THE RETINEX ALGORITHM

From the simulation results, it appears that the Land algorithm and simple extensions to it may be effective in color correction. We have implemented the Land algorithm in analog CMOS VLSI. Fig. 1(a) shows the outline of a system of video camera color correction based on Land's algorithm. The three color outputs of a video camera (labeled red, green, and blue here) are fed onto three separate resistive grids built from subthreshold analog CMOS VLSI. Each 48 by 47 node resistive grid was built using 2 μm design rules and contains about 60 000 transistors.

Since a single chip can contain only a small grid (roughly 50 by 50), the 525×525 video image must be sampled at a low resolution with appropriate video switching and sample-and-hold circuitry. Perhaps the most novel aspect of this design is in its sample-and-hold architecture. A horizontal line of NTSC video is about 50 μs in duration; 48 horizontal pixels must be fed with the video input averaged onto a capacitor over 1 μs. However, the data must be held for input to the resistive grid for the field duration, which is about 16 ms for NTSC video. Thus the sample time and the hold time differ by over four orders of magnitude. The crucial design feature of these chips is that a two-stage sample-and-hold scheme is used. At the bottom of the chip, 48 capacitors are charged up at the line rate. Followers broadcast these voltages into the array, where the currently selected row of nodes reads the 48 values and integrates them into a second sample-and-hold circuit. This second circuit is a follower-connected transconductance amplifier, set to run in the subthreshold range, feeding a capacitor. Five video lines

421

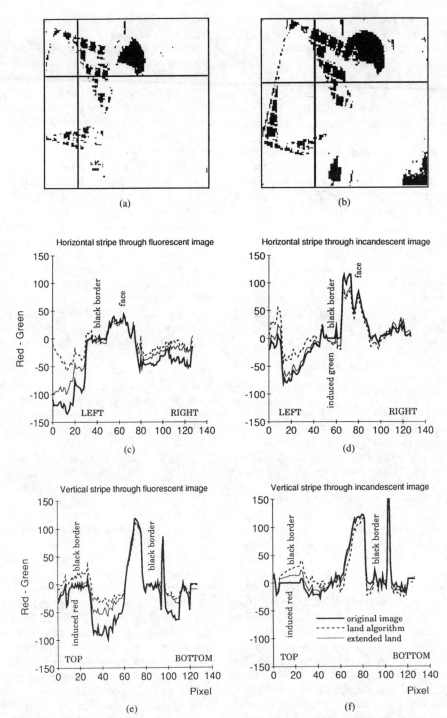

(a)

(b)

Horizontal stripe through fluorescent image

Horizontal stripe through incandescent image

(c)

(d)

Vertical stripe through fluorescent image

Vertical stripe through incandescent image

Pixel

Pixel

(e)

(f)

Fig. 3. Quantification of simulation results. At top ((a) and (b)) are binary representations of the images in the left two columns of Fig. 2. As in Fig. 2, the fluorescent-illuminated image is at left (a) and the incandescent-illuminated image is at right (b). A horizontal and vertical line of pixels was selected through each image, in areas where the color induction effects of the color correction algorithms are notable. At bottom ((c)–(f)) are plots of the red pixel value minus the green pixel value along the selected lines for the original image (Fig. 2(a) and (b), thick line), the retinex-processed images (Fig. 2 (d) and (e), dashed line), and the images processed with the extended Land algorithm (Fig. 2(g) and (h), thin line). See text for details.

are integrated by each of the 47 rows of the resistive grid in each field of the video frame [42].

The circuit details within each pixel are similar to those of the analog retina [34]. A current proportional to the node sample-and-hold capacitor voltage is injected into the grid with a follower-connected transconductance amplifier run in the subthreshold range. The grid consists of n-type transistors interconnecting the input nodes; a "horizontal resistor" bias circuit at each node sets the gate bias of the interconnect transistors so that the resistance is linear regardless of the transistor source voltage. These bias circuits are also set to run in the subthreshold range. The output of each node is a follower-connected transconductance amplifier, run above threshold, which produces a current proportional to the node voltage. This current is sensed and transformed to a voltage by an off-chip current sensing amplifier. Current steering identical to that used in the analog retina directs one node output at a time to the sense amp.

Fig. 4 shows the ability of the system to correct skin color under a common variation in lighting. At top are the two original images. At left is an image under fluorescent lights, with the camera corrected for this illuminant; skin color looks normal. In the right image, the illuminant is incandescent light, but the camera is still set up for fluorescent light; the skin color is too red. At bottom are the outputs of the system after a smoothed version of the image is subtracted. Though the image at bottom right is more red than the one at bottom left, the color difference is less between the bottom images than between the top images. The system-corrected images are of a poorer quality than the camera images, because of switching noise, cross-talk, etc. The point is that the color is more constant for the processed images than for the camera.[1]

Conventional methods are capable of this level of correction. Many video cameras have an ambient light sensor attachment, which is used to sense the illuminant; a global subtraction of the global value corrects skin color as well as our system. In fact, simply averaging the red, green, and blue signal over a video frame and subtracting this average will work with richly colored scenes such as these (i.e., with scenes for which the gray world assumption is valid). The strength of this algorithm and its value as a model of the biology lie in its use of a spatially varying average for subtraction. This feature enables it to enhance contrast, soften shadows, and reproduce color shifts that are observed by humans. Our electronic system is not very good at shadow softening and contrast enhancement, for three reasons. First, we are not taking the log of the video signal before processing, so we are not taking advantage of as much of the signal as we are in the simulations. Second, the noise in the surrounds produced by nonidealities in the analog CMOS fabrication technology distorts the image in dark areas. Third, the resolution of the surround is much lower than the resolution of the original image (50×50 versus 512×512). However, we are able to reproduce one aspect of human color perception with this electronic system, an aspect that illustrates the spatially varying nature of the color normalization: color darkening in light regions of a scene and color lightening in dark regions, as shown in Fig. 5.

Fig. 5 shows three set of images of color bars. At top are the video camera outputs under fluorescent light, fluorescent and blue light, and fluorescent and green light. The middle row of images shows the corrected system output for identical lighting conditions as the top three images. The bottom row of images are the direct output of the resistive grids, with no smoothing. The color constancy among images in the middle row is impressive compared with the top and bottom rows. These images also show the spatial aspect of the color correction. The red bars in these images are cut from the same piece of paper. Note that in the top row the red bar next to the white bar looks darker

than the red bar next to the black bar. When the red bars are examined in isolation the color is identical. This is easiest to see by cutting two holes in a piece of paper so that one hole lies over the top red bar, and the other hole lies over the bottom red bar. In isolation the colors are identical, but the perception is influenced by nearby colors; this is simultaneous contrast [14], [35]–[37]. In the color-corrected images of the second row, the red bar in the light region appears darker than the red bar in the dark region, even when viewed in isolation. This demonstrates that the system is using local information to perform the correction; this is the first system to show these color effects with video images.

The bottom row of Fig. 5 shows images of the same color bars taken from the resistive grid outputs, under the same lighting conditions as the top two rows. (The smoothing is set to zero here, to show the bars clearly; for correction, the image is smoothed greatly, so that the resistive grid outputs are an uninteresting blur.) As expected, the color varies as the lighting is changed just as in the video camera images (top row). The two-hole test described above reveals that the top and bottom red bars in this row of images are identical in color.

In summary, our real-time system, which forms a blurred version of the image on resistive grids for subtraction from the original, demonstrates color constancy and simultaneous contrast effects. Other effects produced by Land's retinex algorithm, such as color Mach bands, have been observed with the electronic system, but are not shown here.

VI. Conclusion

Land's retinex theory is a model for our natural ability to see color as roughly constant as the lighting varies widely. The neurobiology and psychophysics of color constancy support the plausibility of his model; computational analysis of the problem shows that his is an elegant solution. We have applied resistive grid processing to his model, greatly reducing its complexity. Through computer simulations we have explored the strengths and weaknesses of the retinex theory; we have developed an extension of it that lessens its weakness. Impressed with its strengths, we have implemented the retinex algorithm using analog VLSI. The system, based on three resistive grids, is capable of color correction and displays color shifts that qualitatively mimic those of human perception. The system operates at video rates, and as such is the first of its kind. With further development, systems such as this, designed to implement the retinex algorithm and simple extensions to it, would be useful in a variety of video applications.

Is this system a neural network? Even though there are no weights, thresholds, energy surfaces, or the like in its architecture and operation, we feel that it is. We were led to this problem after exploring the nonclassical receptive fields of cortical cells that process visual motion [32]. We turned to psychophysics to understand the problem and to computational theory to understand the models proposed to solve it. Finally, after computer simulation, we had the confidence to build the system. It is neural in the sense that it is a realization of the premier model of how the brain accomplishes color constancy. In the introduction, we pointed out that our present technology for capturing images is flawed—it is too simple. By studying the brain we have been able to build a system that does it better.

Acknowledgment

The authors are grateful to many of our colleagues at Caltech and elsewhere for discussions and support in this endeavor: G.

[1]In preparing the final images for Fig. 4, the *scene dependence* of color constancy was discovered. In order to obtain the level of constancy of Fig. 4(d), the subject had to be placed between a dark region and a bright region. By accident rather than design, this is how the subject was arranged in parts (b), (e), and (h) of Fig. 2. This further weakness of the Land algorithm may not have been discovered without a real-time system. For further details, see [43].

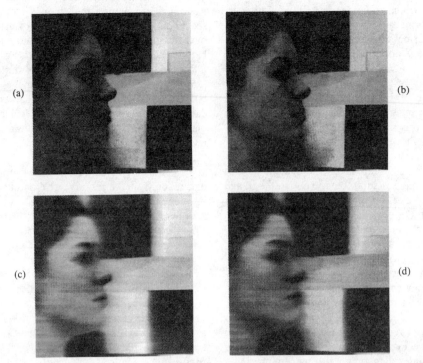

Fig. 4. Skin color correction with an electronic implementation of the Land algorithm. At top are the camera outputs under (a) fluorescent and (b) incandescent light. The camera was adjusted to report colors well under fluorescent light. The bottom images show the output of the color correction system for (c) fluorescent and (d) incandescent illuminants. The skin tone in the bottom images changes less for the two conditions than the camera images.

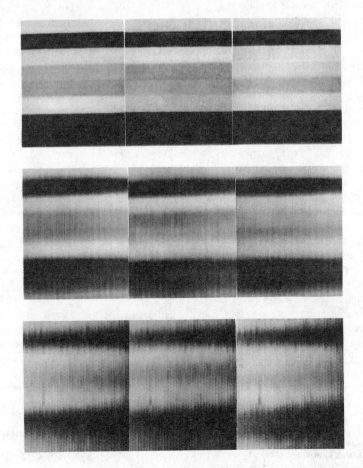

Fig. 5. Color constancy results from the electronic system. The top images are the video camera outputs, the middle images are the color-corrected outputs, and the bottom images are the outputs from the three resistive grids with no smoothing. The color bars are lit with fluorescent light in the left column. Narrow-band blue light is added in the middle column, and narrow-band green light is added in the right column.

Fox, F. Perez, and S. Shein for discussions about color constancy; M. Mahowald, C. Mead, and M. Sivilotti, inventors of the original silicon retina, for systems and VLSI discussions; J. Harris, J. Luo, and C. Koch for discussions about resistive grids; D. Lyon, M. Mahowald, and S. Ryckebush for discussions about sample-and-hold circuitry; J. Lazzaro for discussions on systems issues; and S. Chascsa, T. Horiuchi, and F. Perez for assistance with photography. The authors express their gratitude to DARPA for MOSIS fabrication services, and to Hewlett Packard for computing support in the Mead Lab.

REFERENCES

[1] H. von Helmholtz, *Treatise on Physiological Optics*, vol. 2, 3rd ed., J.P.C. Southall, Ed. New York: Dover, 1962.
[2] S. M. Zeki, "The representation of colours in the cerebral cortex," *Nature*, vol. 284, p. 412, 1980.
[3] E. A. DeYoe and D. C. Van Essen, "Concurrent processing streams in monkey visual cortex," *Trends Neurosci.*, vol. 11, p. 219, 1988.
[4] S. M. Zeki, "Colour coding in the cerebral cortex: The reaction of cells in the monkey visual cortex to wavelengths and colours," *Neurosci.* vol. 9, 1983.
[5] S. M. Zeki, "Colour coding in the cerebral cortex: The responses of wavelength-selective and colour-coded cells in monkey visual cortex to changes in wavelength composition," *Neurosci.*, vol. 9, 1983.
[6] R. Desimone, S. J. Schein, J. Moran, and L. G. Ungerleider, "Contour, color, and shape analysis beyond the striate cortex," *Vision Res.*, vol. 25, p. 441, 1985.
[7] D. B. Judd, D. L. MacAdam, and G. Wysecki, "Spectral distribution of typical daylight as a function of color temperature," *J. Opt. Soc. Amer.*, 1031, 1964.
[8] L. T. Maloney, "Evaluation of linear models of surface spectral reflectance with small numbers of parameters," *J. Opt. Soc. Amer.*, A3, p. 1673, 1986.
[9] M. D'Zmura and P. Lennie, "Mechanisms of color constancy," *J. Opt. Soc. Amer.*, vol. A3, p. 1662, 1986.
[10] K. T. Blackwell and G. Buchsbaum, "Quantitative studies of color constancy," *J. Opt. Soc. Amer.* vol. A5, p. 1772, 1988.
[11] L. Arend and A. Reeves, "Simultaneous color constancy," *J. Opt. Soc. Amer.*, vol. A3, p. 1743, 1986.
[12] J. A. Worthey, "Limitations of color constancy," *J. Opt. Soc. Amer.*, vol. A2, p. 1014, 1985.
[13] D. Ingle, "The goldfish as a retinex animal," *Science*, vol. 227, p. 651, 1985.
[14] T. N. Cornsweet, *Visual Perception*. New York: Academic Press, 1970.
[15] B. K. P. Horn, *Robot Vision*. New York: McGraw-Hill, 1985.
[16] G. Buchsbaum, "A spatial processor model for colour perception," *J. Franklin Inst.*, vol. 310, no. 1, 1980.
[17] L. T. Maloney, "Computational approaches to color constancy," Ph.D. thesis, Stanford University, 1984.
[18] L. T. Maloney and B. A. Wandell, "Color constancy: A method for recovering surface spectral reflectance," *J. Opt. Soc. Amer.* vol. A3, p. 29, 1986.
[19] E. H. Land and J. J. McCann, "Lightness and retinex theory," *J. Opt. Soc. Amer.*, vol. 61, p. 1, 1971.
[20] E. H. Land, "Recent advances in retinex theory and some implications for cortical computations: color vision and the natural image," *Proc. Nat. Acad. Sci. U.S.*, vol. 80, p. 5163, 1983.
[21] E. H. Land, "An alternative technique for the computation of the designator in the retinex theory of color vision," *Proc. Nat. Acad. Sci. U.S.* vol. 83, p. 3078, 1986.
[22] B. K. P. Horn, "Determining lightness from an image," *Comput. Graph. Image Proc.*, vol. 3, p. 277, 1974.
[23] B. Funt and M. Drew, "Color constancy computations in near-Mondrian scenes using a finite-dimensional linear model," *Proc. IEEE Conf. Comp. Vis. Patt. Rec.*, June 1988.
[24] A. Hurlbert, "Formal connections between lightness algorithms," *J. Opt. Soc. Amer.*, vol. A3, p. 1684, 1986.
[25] A. V. Oppenheim, R. W. Shafer, and T. G. Stockham, Jr., "Nonlinear filtering of multiplied and convolved signals," *Proc. IEEE*, p. 1264, 1968.
[26] O. D. Faugeras, "Digital color image processing within the framework of a human visual model," *IEEE Trans. Acoust., Speech, Signal Process.*, vol. ASSP-27, p. 380, 1979.
[27] D. H. Brainard and B. A. Wandell, "Analysis of the retinex theory of color vision," *J. Opt. Soc. Amer.*, vol. 3A, p. 1611, 1986.
[28] M. La Brecque, "Retinex: Physics and the theory of color vision," *Computers in Physics*, Nov/Dec 1988.
[29] A. Blake, "Boundary conditions for lightness computation in mondrian world," *Comp. Vis. Graph. Image Proc.*, vol. 32, 1985.
[30] D. Marr, "The computation of lightness by the primate retina," *Vision Res.*, vol. 14, p. 1377, 1974.
[31] M. S. Livingstone and D. H. Hubel, "Anatomy and physiology of a color system in primate primary visual cortex," *J. Neurosci.*, vol. 4, p. 309, 1984.
[32] J. Allman, F. Miezin, and E. McGuinness, "Direction- and velocity-specific responses from beyond the classical receptive field in the middle temporal visual area (MT)," *Perception*, vol. 14, p. 105, 1985.
[33] A. Hurlbert and T. Poggio, "Learning a color algorithm from examples," MIT AI Memo 909, 1987.
[34] C. A. Mead, *Analog VLSI and Neural Systems*. Reading, MA: Addison-Wesley, 1989.
[35] L. M. Hurvich, *Color Vision*. Sunderland, MA: Sindauer Associates, 1981.
[36] O. Creutzfeldt, B. Lange-Malecki, and K. Wortmann, "Darkness induction, retinex, and cooperative mechanisms in vision," *Exp. Brain Res.*, vol. 67, p. 270, 1987.
[37] P. Lennie and M. D'Zmura, "Mechanisms of color vision," *CRC Crit. Rev. Neurobiol.*, vol. 3, p. 333, 1988.
[38] S. Grossberg and E. Mingolla, "Neural dynamics of form perception: Boundary completion, illusory figures, and neon color spreading," *Psych. Rev.*, vol. 92, 1985.
[39] J. Hutchinson, C. Koch, J. Luo, and C. Mead, "Computing motion using analog and binary resistive networks," *IEEE Computer*, vol. 21, 1988.
[40] P. Perona and J. Malik, "Scale-space and edge detection using anisotropic diffusion," *IEEE Trans. Pattern Anal. Mach. Intell.*, vol. 12, 1990.
[41] J. Harris, C. Koch, and J. Luo, "A two-dimensional analog VLSI circuit for detecting discontinuities in early vision," *Science*, vol. 248, 8 June 1990.
[42] A. Moore and R. Goodman, "Image smoothing at video rates with analog VLSI," in *Proc. IEEE Conf. Syst., Man, Cybern.*, Nov. 1990.
[43] A. Moore, G. Fox, J. Allman, and R. Goodman, "A VLSI neural network for color constancy," in *Advances in Neural Information Processing 3*, D. S. Touretzky and R. Lippman, Eds. San Mateo, CA: Morgan Kauffmann, 1991 (in press).

Article 6.10

Reconstruction of Munsell color space by a five-layer neural network

Shiro Usui, Shigeki Nakauchi, and Masae Nakano

Department of Information and Computer Sciences, Toyohashi University of Technology,
Tempaku, Toyohashi 441, Japan

Received April 22, 1991; revised manuscript received November 5, 1991; accepted November 7, 1991

We have constructed a wine-glass-type five-layer neural network and generated an identity mapping of the surface spectral-reflectance data of 1280 Munsell color chips, using a backpropagation learning algorithm. To achieve an identity mapping, the same data set is used for the input and for the teacher. After the learning was completed, we analyzed the responses to individual chips of the three hidden units in the middle layer in order to obtain the internal representation of the color information. We found that each of the three hidden units corresponds to a psychological color attribute, that is, the Munsell value (luminance), red–green, and yellow–blue. We also examined the relationship between the internal representation and the number of hidden units and found that the network with three hidden units acquires optimum color representation. The five-layer neural network is shown to be an efficient method for reproducing the transformation of color information (or color coding) in the visual system.

INTRODUCTION

Any color can be uniquely specified by its surface spectral-reflectance curve, known as its physical color attribute, which is defined as the fraction of the incident irradiance that the surface reflects as a function of wavelength. Psychologically, color is identified by three basic qualities of appearance: hue, value (luminance), and chroma. These attributes can be arranged on orthogonal scales that geometrically span a three-dimensional cylindrical space. Hues are arranged in equal angular spacing around the black–white axis (the Munsell value axis), and the chroma is represented by the radial distance from the central axis. The perceived colors form the Munsell color solid (Fig. 1), which is obtained by ordering the color chips according to the perceptual distances among them.

Recent physiological studies of the visual system have revealed portions of the neural circuitry and of the neural-response characteristics of the visual system. For example, the light that is received by three types of photoreceptor (red, green, and blue cones) in the retina is coded into the opponent color signals at the outer-plexiform layer.[1] It is also known that in the lateral geniculate nucleus, which directly receives the retinal signal, there are red–green-, yellow–blue-, and white–black-type neurons.[2-4] The information-processing mechanism in the visual system must play a key role in linking the physical color attributes to the psychological color attributes. However, the details of how the physiological system relates to the physical input and the psychological response are poorly understood.

Because Munsell color chips are selected on the basis of visual appearance criteria, the surface spectral-reflectance data of these chips must in some way reflect the color representation in the visual system. Therefore an analysis of the surface spectral-reflectance data of the Munsell color chips may provide clues to elucidate the internal color representation and the color-coding mechanism in the visual system.

To gain an understanding of color representation in a visual system, many studies on multispectral analysis of Munsell color have been conducted, for example, principal-component analysis by the Karhunen–Loève (KL) expansion.[5] These surface spectral reflectances can be represented by a linear combination of the KL basis function $S_k(\lambda)$,

$$R^i(\lambda) = \sum_{k=1}^{n} \sigma_k{}^i S_k(\lambda),$$

where $R^i(\lambda)$ and $\sigma_k{}^i$ are the surface spectral reflectance and the characteristic parameter of the ith color, respectively. Cohen[6] first analyzed the surface spectral reflectance of 433 randomly selected Munsell color chips by the KL expansion method. He concluded that surface spectral-reflectance data can be described by this linear model using three or four parameters (i.e., $n = 3$ or 4) and discussed the results in terms of trichromatic color vision. Maloney[7] extended Cohen's analysis to 462 Munsell color chips and concluded that the linear KL model fit the data when five to seven parameters are used. Sobagaki[8] and Parkkinen et al.[9,10] analyzed 1257 Munsell color chips and concluded that seven or eight of these linear parameters are required.

The purpose of these analyses was to find the most efficient basis set, from the statistical point of view, for a given color set by using KL basis functions. Comparing the results with physiological data showed interesting similarities.[11] However, because accuracy depends on the number of parameters that are chosen, Cohen's linear model does not afford a reasonable approach to understanding color representation in the visual system. We therefore seek a nonlinear model.

To this end, we constructed a wine-glass-type five-layer neural network and generated an identity mapping of surface spectral-reflectance data of 1280 Munsell color chips, using a backpropagation (BP) learning algorithm. The network is divided into two parts: an encoder and a

Reprinted with permission from S. Usui, S. Nakauchi, and M. Nakano, *J. Opt. Soc. Am.*, vol. 9, no. 4, pp. 516–520, April 1992.

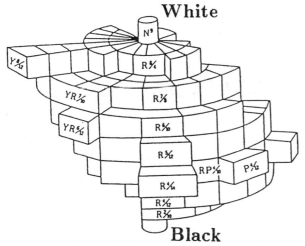

White

Fig. 1. Munsell color solid for specifying colors on scales of hue, value, and chroma. The hues are arranged with equal angular spacing around the central axis. The vertical columns specify the levels of value. The chroma is represented by the distance from the central axis.

decoder. The surface spectral-reflectance data are transformed nonlinearly in each part. After the identity mapping was established, we analyzed the response pattern of the three hidden units in the middle layer to various color chip inputs in order to obtain the internal representation of the color information.

METHODS

Feature Extraction by a Wine-Glass-Type Neural Network

Artificial neural networks have been used for feature extraction in a variety of fields.[12,13] In this application, the network is constrained to perform an identity mapping through a narrow channel (the middle layer is much smaller than either the input or the output layer, i.e., a wine-glass-type network).

The network consists of two subnetworks, an encoder and a decoder. In this study, each of these subnetworks consists of a three-layer neural network with (1) an input layer, (2) a hidden layer with a sigmoid function, and (3) an output layer with a linear function. (We follow the notation of counting the input layer as layer 1 rather than as layer 0.) We assemble the complete network by placing two such three-layer networks in a cascade, so that they share the third (linear) layer, as shown in Fig. 2. The network maps the input data nonlinearly to a feature space with reduced dimensionality in the middle layer and also provides nonlinear inverse mapping from the feature space. The network therefore is forced to encode the given data set efficiently, and the feature-space coordinates can be extracted from the middle layer of the five-layer network through the network learning. We can also change the number of units in the middle layer to vary the dimensions of the feature space. The performance of such five-layer neural networks is described below.

Network Learning

Figure 3 shows the structure of the network. The available data consist of the surface spectral-reflectance curves of 1569 different Munsell color chips sampled at 81 wavelengths from 380 to 780 nm (5-nm intervals).

The network's total of 81 input–output units corresponds to this number of data points. We first fixed the number of units in the middle (third) layer at three to match the number of psychological color attributes and changed it to two or four later to test the optimality of the internal representation in the feature space. The choice of 10 units for the second and the fourth layers was arbitrary. The data from the 1569 chips were divided into 1280 sets for training and 289 sets for testing. We used a BP learning

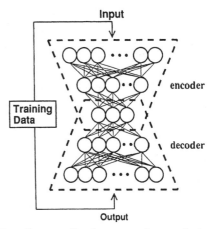

Fig. 2. Wine-glass-type five-layer neural network that performs an identity mapping. The encoder and decoder each consist of a three-layer neural network. The same data are used for the input and for the teacher, to train the network.

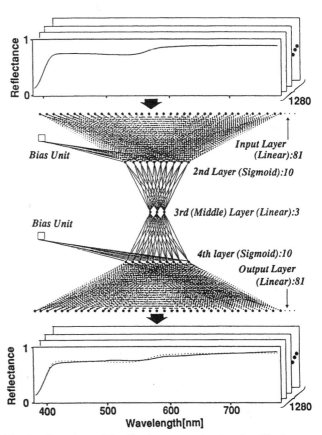

Fig. 3. Structure of the five-layer neural network. The layers consist of 81, 10, 3, 10, and 81 units, respectively. The numbers of input and output units correspond to the data points of the spectral reflectance. The number of middle-layer units is three, which corresponds to the fundamental number in color vision.

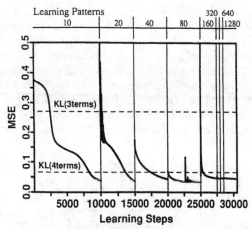

Fig. 4. Change in the MSE during BP learning. The horizontal lines show errors by the KL expansion with three and four terms for comparison. Note that the error increases when the training data are doubled.

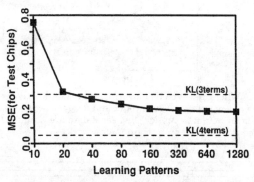

Fig. 5. MSE for test chips at each learning phase. The dotted lines show errors by the KL expansion with three and four terms for comparison. The average error for test data is considerably lower than that of the KL expansion with three terms. According to this criterion, the network was fairly well trained after the presentation of a small training set, such as 40 to 80 examples.

algorithm[14] to adjust the network weights. The method is as follows:

Step 1: Train the network, using 10 chips randomly selected from the training set.

Step 2: After the network has learned sufficiently well, add another randomly selected set of training chips of equal size and train the network with this doubled set.

Step 3: Repeat step 2 until all the data in the training set have been used.

RESULTS

Accuracy of the Reconstruction

The change in the mean-square error (MSE) during BP learning and, for purposes of comparison, the residual errors of the KL expansion with three and four eigenvectors are shown in Fig. 4; the MSE is defined as

$$\text{MSE} = \frac{1}{N} \sum_{i=1}^{N} \sum_{j=1}^{81} [\hat{R}^i(\lambda_j) - R^i(\lambda_j)]^2,$$

where $R^i(\lambda_j)$ is the original reflectance data (training data), $\hat{R}^i(\lambda_j)$ is the reconstructed reflectance value (output of the network), and N is the number of the data set. The height of the jumps in the error curve when the training-

set size is doubled decreases as the size of the training set increases. This shows that the network has learned and is able to generalize the surface spectral-reflectance data of the Munsell color chips.

After each learning phase, we evaluated the network with the 289 test chips to determine the ability of the network to generalize. Figure 5 shows the MSE for 289 test chips at each learning phase. The MSE for the test chips was considerably lower than that of the KL expansion with three terms. By this criterion, the network is fairly well trained after the presentation of a small training set (40 to 80 examples). This suggests that, if the data can be described by a small number of parameters, the network

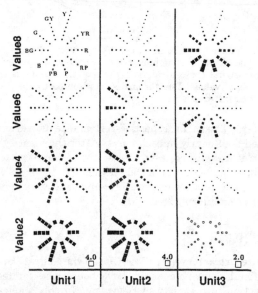

Fig. 6. Responses of the units in the middle layer on the constant-value plane. The size of a square shows the absolute value of the response. The open and the filled squares show the positive and the negative values, respectively.

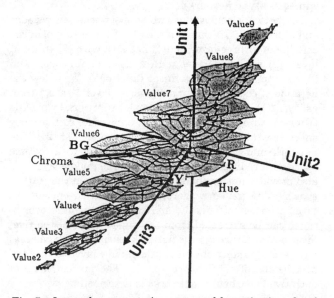

Fig. 7. Internal representation expressed by activation of each unit in the middle layer. The three axes of space are the responses of the units in the middle layer. Each grid shows unit 1, unit 2, and unit 3 outputs for Munsell colors of constant value. Note that unit 1 responds to the value axis and that both unit 2 and unit 3 represent the chromaticity of input surface spectral-reflectance data.

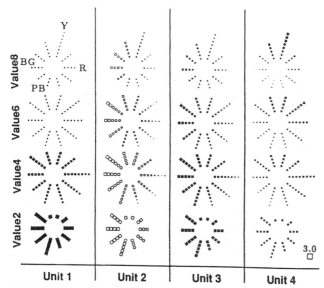

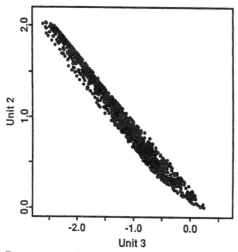

Fig. 8. Responses of the units in the middle layer on the constant-value plane in a network with four hidden units. The responses of unit 2 and unit 3 have similar properties with opposite signs. The open and the filled squares show the positive and the negative values, respectively.

Fig. 9. Response correlation of unit 2 and unit 3 of a network with four hidden units. The responses of these units are highly anticorrelated ($r = -0.991$).

can extract the features of the training set after the presentation of a relatively small number of training chips.

Analysis of Feature Space
After training with the full training set, we analyzed the patterns of response of the three units in the middle layer to the surface spectral-reflectance data of the individual chips. The responses of the three units in the Munsell constant-value plane are shown in Fig. 6. It was found that unit 1 is selectively responsive to the value but is virtually nonresponsive to changes in the hue and the chroma. The responses of unit 2 and unit 3 appear to be tuned to red versus green and blue versus yellow, respectively.

We also analyzed how the surface spectral-reflectance data of the 1569 color chips are represented in the feature space defined by the responses of the three hidden units. Figure 7 shows the acquired internal representation based on the activity of each middle-layer unit. Each

grid shows unit 1, unit 2, and unit 3 outputs for Munsell colors of constant values. It was found that unit 1 corresponds to a value and that unit 2 and unit 3 represent the opponent responses to input surface spectral-reflectance data. The unit 2 axis corresponds to red (reddish-purple)–green (bluish-green), and the unit 3 axis corresponds to yellow (greenish-yellow)–purplish-blue. These relationships are consistent with the evidence from physiological color-opponent studies.[1-4] That is, the Munsell color solid, organized according to psychological attributes, is reconstructed from the surface spectral-reflectance data by the feature space of the hidden units.

We also examined the relationship between the internal representation and the number of hidden units. Figure 8 displays the responses of the network with four hidden units and shows that unit 2 and unit 3 have similar response properties. Figure 9 shows the correlation of these units and demonstrates that the responses of unit 2 and unit 3 are highly anticorrelated ($r = -0.991$). Therefore either unit 2 or unit 3 is redundant.

Figure 10 shows the internal representation of the network with only two hidden units. The responses of the hidden units to different colors now overlap, and thus these colors cannot be discriminated by the network with only two hidden units. The undiscriminated colors are yellow and blue. In other words, this representation lacks a blue–yellow axis; that is, the network with two hidden units appears to exhibit tritanopia dichromacy.

We confirmed that the internal representation does not depend on the initial weight values of the network. Consequently, we concluded that the network with three hidden units acquires an optimum color representation through BP learning of the identity mapping.

DISCUSSION

The neural network method described above may provide a new approach to color-feature extraction. Cottrel and Munro[12] previously applied a three-layer wine-glass-type neural network to image compression. However, it has

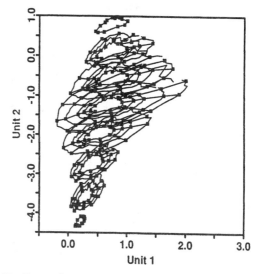

Fig. 10. Internal representation of a network with two hidden units. The responses of the hidden units to colors between yellow and blue overlap. The network with two hidden units thus exhibits tritanopia dichromacy.

been shown[15] that the accuracy of the identity mapping achieved with a three-layer neural network with linear output units is less than that of a linear analysis method such as KL expansion. In a three-layer wine-glass-type network, the encoder and the decoder each consist of a two-layer neural network. Because each two-layer network can create only a linear mapping, such a three-layer wine-glass network behaves as if it consisted of two independent single-layer perceptrons. Thus the accuracy depends on the number of hidden units corresponding to terms in the KL expansion.

However, any continuous mapping can be realized approximately by a three-layer neural network.[16] Therefore the five-layer wine-glass-type neural network, which is created by placing two three-layer networks back to back, is adequate for the nonlinear mapping required for the transformation from physical to psychological color coordinates.

CONCLUSION

We have generated an identity mapping of the surface spectral reflectance of 1569 Munsell color chips by using a five-layer neural network and have shown that the network can generalize from a relatively small number of training examples. We analyzed the three-dimensional feature space acquired by learning and found that one of three units represents the value and that the other two units represent the two chromaticity axes. That is, the Munsell color solid was reconstructed from physical data. A network with four hidden units produces a redundant internal representation, and a network with two hidden units cannot effectively discriminate some color combinations. We conclude that the surface spectral-reflectance curves of the Munsell color chips can be compressed into three-dimensional space and that the nonlinear feature extraction by a five-layer neural network is adequate to reproduce the transformation from the physical to the psychological representation of color in the neural system.

ACKNOWLEDGMENTS

We are grateful to G. Kawakami and H. Sobagaki for supplying the surface spectral-reflectance data of standard color chips conforming with Japanese Industrial Standard (JIS) Z8721. We also thank T. P. Vogl for his helpful and important discussions. This study was supported by a Grant-in-Aid (02255107) for Scientific Research on Priority Areas from the Ministry of Education, Science and Culture of Japan.

REFERENCES

1. S. Usui, S. Saruyama, G. Mitarai, M. Sakakibara, and T. Yagi, "Image-sensing mechanisms in the vertebrate retina," *Biomechanism* (U. Tokyo Press, Tokyo, 1984), Vol. 7, pp. 41–49.
2. T. N. Wiesel and D. H. Hubel, "Spatial and chromatic interactions in the lateral geniculate nucleus of the rhesus monkey," J. Neurophysiol. **29**, 1115–1156 (1966).
3. R. L. De Valois, I. Abramov, and G. H. Jacobs, "Analysis of response patterns of LGN cells," J. Opt. Soc. Am. **56**, 966–977 (1966).
4. A. M. Derrington, J. Krauskopf, and P. Lennie, "Chromatic mechanisms in lateral geniculate nucleus of macaque," J. Physiol. **357**, 241–265 (1984).
5. E. Oja, *Subspace Methods of Pattern Recognition* (Research Studies, Letchworth, England, 1983).
6. J. Cohen, "Dependency of the spectral reflectance curves of the Munsell color chips," Psychonomic Sci. **1**, 369–370 (1964).
7. L. T. Maloney, "Evaluation of linear models of surface spectral reflectance with small numbers of parameters," J. Opt. Soc. Am. A **3**, 1673–1683 (1986).
8. H. Sobagaki, "New approach to the colorimetric standardization for object colors," Bull. Electrotechnical Lab. Jpn. **48**, 785–792 (1984).
9. J. P. S. Parkkinen, J. Hallikaineln, and T. Jaaskelainen, "Characteristic spectra of Munsell colors," J. Opt. Soc. Am. A **6**, 318–322 (1989).
10. J. P. S. Parkkinen and T. Jaaskelainen, "Color vision: machine and human," in *Visual Communications and Image Processing IV*, W. A. Pearlman, ed., Proc. Soc. Photo-Opt. Instrum. Eng. **1199**, 1184–1192 (1989).
11. R. A. Young, "Principal-component analysis of macaque lateral geniculate nucleus chromatic data," J. Opt. Soc. Am. A **3**, 1735–1742 (1986).
12. G. W. Cottrell and P. Munro, "Principal component analysis of image via back propagation," in *Visual Communications and Image Processing '88: Third in a Series*, T. R. Hsing, ed., Proc. Soc. Photo-Opt. Instrum. Eng. **1001**, 1070–1076 (1988).
13. H. Bourlard and Y. Kamp, "Auto-association by multilayer perceptrons and singular value decomposition," Biol. Cybern. **59**, 291–294 (1988).
14. D. E. Rumelhart and J. L.McClelland, *Parallel Distributed Processing* (MIT Press, Cambridge, Mass., 1986).
15. K. Funahashi, "On the approximate realization of identity mappings by three-layer neural networks," Inst. Electron. Inform. Commun. Eng. Trans. **J73-A**, 139–145 (1990).
16. B. Irie and S. Miyake, "Capabilities of three-layered perceptrons," IEEE Int. Conf. Neural Networks **1**, 641–648 (1988).

Stereopsis by Constraint Learning Feed-Forward Neural Networks

Alireza Khotanzad, Amol Bokil, and Ying-Wung Lee

Abstract— This paper presents a novel neural network (NN) approach to the problem of stereopsis. The correspondence problem (finding the correct matches between pixels of the epipolar lines of the stereo pair from amongst all the possible matches) is posed as a noniterative many-to-one mapping. Two multilayer feed-forward NN's are utilized to learn and code this nonlinear and complex mapping using the back-propagation learning rule and a training set. The first NN is a conventional fully connected net while the second one is a sparsely connected NN with a fixed number of hidden layer nodes. Three variations of the sparsely connected NN are considered. The important aspect of this technique is that none of the typical constraints such as uniqueness and continuity are explicitly imposed. All the applicable constraints are learned and internally coded by the NN's enabling them to be more flexible and more accurate than the existing methods. The approach is successfully tested on several random-dot stereograms. It is shown that the nets can generalize their learned mappings to cases outside their training sets and to noisy images. Advantages over the Marr–Poggio algorithm are discussed and it is shown that the NN's performances are superior.

I. Introduction

Human vision is stereoscopic in that two images are taken of the world from horizontally separated vantage points. These separate images are analyzed in the visual cortex and provide information about the three-dimensional properties of the objects being viewed. Stereoscopic vision has been studied for over a century and much is known about the way biological organisms process and use stereoscopic information. Despite such successes, building a computational model of the stereopsis has proven to be a difficult problem. Often, a set of simplifying assumptions in the form of imposed constraints are considered in order to develop a computationally feasible model. These constraints always involve some assumptions about the form of the underlying scene. Consequently, such models have had limited success as an accurate characterization of biological stereopsis.

The computational problem of depth from stereopsis has generally been considered as a two-part process. First, features in the left and the right eye images are matched to one another, and second, the disparity between the locations of corresponding features in the two eyes is used to calculate the three-dimensional location of the features. While the calculation of depth from disparity is straightforward, the matching

Manuscript received March 1, 1992; revised July 7, 1992.

The authors are with the Image Processing and Analysis Laboratory, Electrical Engineering Department, Southern Methodist University, Dallas, TX.

IEEE Log Number 9203735.

of the features in the two eyes has proven itself to be a very difficult problem. For this reason, all computational models have concentrated on solving the first part of the process, or the *correspondence problem*, as it has been called. Stereopsis is an "ill-posed" problem in that there are an infinite number of three-dimensional surface solutions consistent with any pair of two-dimensional images. The goal of the computations, thus is to arrive at a unique solution which consists of the most likely true correspondences. From these true correspondences, a depth map is calculated.

There have been many computational approaches to solving the correspondence problem. A review of some of these approaches can be found in [1] and [2]. As mentioned before, common to all such techniques is the employment of a set of simplifying assumptions in the form of imposed constraints in order to develop a computationally feasible model. Prominent among the constraints are those originally proposed by Marr and Poggio [8] namely; 1) uniqueness—that any feature in one image of a stereo pair can have at most one match in the other image, and 2) smoothness—that three-dimensional surface depths change smoothly with abrupt changes happening at few places such as object boundaries. These constraints are often implemented as strict rules that are fixed *a priori*. Unfortunately, psychophysical evidence of human stereopsis suggests that the appropriate constraints are more complex and more flexible than can be characterized by simple fixed rules.

In this paper, we present a neural-network approach to the stereo correspondence and disparity computation problems. The problem is formulated as a local nonlinear, noniterative mapping problem. Two kinds of multilayer feed-forward back-propagation neural networks (NN) are used to learn and generalize this mapping. An important aspect of this approach is that it does not require *a priori* imposition of any scene-related constraints and will automatically tune itself to the constraints inherent in the problem resulting in a flexible and more accurate model.

This technique assumes an epipolar stereo imaging paradigm. This involves a pair of imaging devices (cameras) with their optical axes mutually parallel and separated by a horizontal distance denoted as the baseline. The cameras have their optical axes perpendicular to the stereo baseline, and their image scan-line parallel to the baseline. Therefore, the projection of a point in a three-dimensional plane onto the image plane of the two cameras falls on the same scan-line (row) of both images with differing column locations. Such an epipolar imaging geometry helps limit the search space in

Reprinted from *IEEE Trans. on Neural Networks*, vol. 4, no. 2, pp. 332–342. March 1993.

the correspondence problem to the epipolar (same) rows in the stereo pair.

The proposed approach attempts to find matches at the pixel level. We work with binary random dot stereograms which are discussed later. Binary images are commonly encountered in many other stereo approaches. For example, in the feature-based techniques which try to match features (e.g., edges), the utilized feature images are typically binary indicating the presence or absence of a feature at a pixel location.

II. Previous Neural Net Approaches To Stereopsis

The formulation of the correspondence problem is well-suited to computation by a neural-like network. The iterative algorithm developed by Marr and Poggio [8] can be regarded as a crude neural network approach with no embedded learning. Due to the resemblance of the initial set-up of our approach to that adopted by Marr-Poggio, more details about their algorithm are provided in the next section. However, the later stages of the two algorithms are quite distinct with ours involving a learning process and noniterative operation in a local neighborhood. In [4], an exact neural implementation of the Marr-Poggio algorithm involving no learning is discussed.

Qian and Sejnowski [13] developed an iterative approach for stereopsis using a recurrent neural network. They took advantage of translational invariance of the problem to model the process by a single net. Although they try to learn the uniqueness and smoothness constraints, they end up placing restrictions on the weights by making them identical in prescribed neighborhoods. This makes their model very similar to that of Marr-Poggio's.

A rather different approach is to formulate the correspondence problem as an optimization task followed by utilization of a neural net to perform the optimization. This is the approach adopted by Zhou and Chellappa [16] and Nasrabadi and Choo [9].

O'Toole [10] proposed a computational model of structure from stereo that developed smoothness constraints naturally by associative learning of a large number of example mappings from disparity data to surface depth data. One important aspect of her model is that it computes local depth change from point to point across the image, rather than finding absolute depth at these points. Thus outputs of the computations are local and stringing them together yields a global percept.

Sun *et al.* [15] used an iterative associate memory type NN to perform stereopsis. Using Hebbian rule, they set the weights and show that the neurons in the same layer excite each other while the ones on different layers are inhibitory. The large size of their proposed net makes its use rather impractical.

III. Formulation of Correspondence Problem as a Mapping Problem

The initial phase of our procedure involves casting the correspondence problem as a many-to-one mapping problem. The process starts by identifying all potential matches through forming an "initial match matrix" (IMM) between each of the epipolar rows of the two images of the stereo pair. The IMM

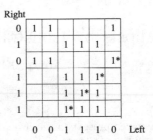

Fig. 1. The initial match matrix (IMM) for left and right rows of two six pixel wide images. 1 represents a match. The correct matches are starred.

is the same as the "compatibility matrix" used in Marr-Poggio algorithm. Construction of this matrix is illustrated by an example shown in Fig. 1 involving epipolar rows of six pixels wide binary images. The pixel value of the left and the right images are placed at the bottom and to the left of this matrix, respectively. The $(i, j)th$ element of the matrix is then computed by performing Exclusive NOR operation between the pixel values to the left of the ith row and the bottom of the jth column. This generates a 1 when both pixels are the same (a match) and a 0 otherwise. Thus the IMM includes all the possible matches of which only some are correct. Correct matches are those that consist of left-right feature pairs that originate at the same point in three-dimensional space. The correct matches in Fig. 1 are starred.

Operating on the IMM, the main task of a computational model is to separate the correct matches from the many possible matches in the IMM. To do so, Marr and Poggio imposed the uniqueness and smoothness constraints on the problem. The uniqueness constraint requires that only one element of the IMM retain a value of 1 along each line of sight, i.e., along each row or column of the matrix. The second constraint translates into a tendency for the correct matches to spread along the 45° directions (iso-disparity contours). These constraints are implemented through weighted connections between IMM elements. The uniqueness constraint is modeled by inhibitory weights (negative feedback) along the horizontal/vertical lines of sight. The continuity constraint gives rise to excitatory weights (positive feedback) along 45° lines. All excitatory feedbacks are assumed to be equal to a positive number α while inhibitory feedbacks are equal to a negative number β. To reduce computations, such feedbacks are only considered from IMM elements within a prescribed neighborhood of the considered element. Marr and Poggio showed that after a number of iterations of the IMM with such feedbacks, the majority of the false matches are suppressed while most of the correct ones are retained. When the elements of the matrix converge to a stable state, the obtained result is taken as the "final match matrix" (FMM). Ideally, the FMM should have zeros everywhere except at locations corresponding to correct matches signified by 1 s.

A major issue in using Marr-Poggio algorithm is finding the optimal values for the positive and negative feedbacks, i.e., α and β. In this work, we developed a gradient descent approach for this task. This algorithm is a modification of the one developed by Pineda [11] and used in [13] for learning in recurrent NN's. The modification involves replacement of nonlinear processing units with linear ones. Also, unlike Marr–Poggio method, Pineda's algorithm allows all the feedbacks to change freely. However, to be consistent with the idea of Marr–Poggio, additional constraints were placed on the feedbacks forcing all the feedbacks in the excitatory region (α) to be identical and those in the inhibitory region (β) to be identical.

The view that we take is that the described correspondence solving task can be posed as a mapping operation. In the Marr–Poggio algorithm, each element of the IMM iteratively evolves based on the feedbacks that it receives from elements in its excitatory and inhibitory regions. What actually takes place is that the IMM is transformed into the FMM. Such a transformation can be considered as a one-shot (noniterative) mapping in a local neighborhood from the initial matches to the final ones. Through this mapping, each IMM element is assigned a final state of 0 (no match) or 1 (match) based on the initial states of the elements in its neighboring region. If m neighbors of an element are considered, this will be a mapping of an $(m + 1)$ bit long string into one bit (0 or 1). Such a mapping is a complex nonlinear relationship which is very difficult to model by conventional methods. However, a neural net can learn, and more importantly generalize it.

Note that in this framework, there is no longer a need to label the neighbors as excitatory/inhibitory. The NN will automatically learn the appropriate function of the neighbors thus relaxing the uniqueness and continuity constraints. Although in this study we use the same neighborhood topology as prescribed by Marr and Poggio, there is no restrictions on the topology of neighborhood that could be used in our method.

The described row wise matching does not consider the vertical dependency of pixels in two-dimensional images. To account for inter-row relationships, the procedure is extended as follows. First, for each pair of epipolar rows of the two images, the two-dimensional IMM is computed as explained before. These IMM's are then stacked on top of each other resulting in a three-dimensional "initial match volume" (IMV), as shown in Fig. 2. The neighboring region of an element in the interior of this volume is also extended to a three-dimensional region. If a Marr–Poggio type neighborhood is considered, an excitatory region which supports inter-row dependence is a circular disc while the inhibitory region remains on the two-dimensional plane of the row-wise match. Fig. 3 shows such a neighborhood for an excitatory disc of radius 2 and inhibitory lines of three elements on each side.

Thus the correspondence problem can be formulated as a mapping problem from the three–dimensional IMV to the three-dimensional final match volume (FMV) on an element by element basis. Each element of the IMV along with m of its three-dimensional neighbors constitute an $(m + 1)$ string which is mapped into a final state (0 or 1) in the FMV. The task to be performed by the neural net is to learn this complex mapping, which embodies any appropriate constraints as well.

IV. Solving Correspondence Mapping By Neural Networks

After setting up the IMV, the task is to learn the mapping that can be applied to each element of IMV to correctly

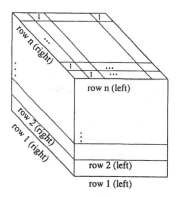

Fig. 2. Schematic of the initial match volume (IMV) constructed by stacking up row wise IMM's on top of each other.

transform it to its FMV value. This mapping is taken to be a function of the value of the underlying element in IMV and those of its neighbors in a neighborhood S around it in the match volume. Formally,

$$\mathrm{fmv}(x_1, x_2, x_3) = F(\mathrm{imv}(a, b, c) | (a, b, c) \epsilon S(x_1, x_2, x_3))$$

where

$\mathrm{fmv}(x_1, x_2, x_3)$	the FMV value of the IMV element at coordinate (x_1, x_2, x_3)
F	the nonlinear mapping function
$\mathrm{imv}(a, b, c)$	the IMV value of the IMV element at coordinate (a, b, c)
$S(x_1, x_2, x_3)$	a set of three-dimensional coordinates including (x_1, x_2, x_3) and those of its neighbors in a specified neighborhood

In such a formulation, the goal of the utilized NN is to learn and code the function F. Again note that this function is very complex and hard to derive analytically. Furthermore, no constraints is imposed since no *a priori* excitatory/inhibitory assignments are made. Only a unified concept of a neighboring region, S, which influences the disparity computation is adopted. The influence of the elements in S on the solution is learned by the NN. This means that all the appropriate constraints are automatically learned.

This NN formulation allows us to consider any shape or size for the neighborhood, S. In discussions in the next sections we use a neighborhood similar to the one used by Marr and Poggio [8] so as to be able to compare our results with theirs. The considered neighborhood is shown in Fig. 3.

Based on the above discussions then, the general form of the NN calls for the inputs to be the value of an element in the IMV along with those that affect its final value, i.e., elements in S. The output should be the value of the corresponding element in the FMV.

In this study, we use two topologically different multilayer feed-forward neural nets for carrying out the task of learning the outlined mapping. One is a conventional "fully connected" net and the other is a "sparsely connected" one. The main task in utilizing each of these nets is to teach them the mapping between initial matches and final ones. This is done by constructing a training set which consists of several IMV's along with their corresponding FMV's. Several stereo pairs

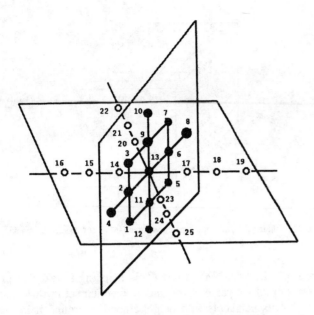

Fig. 3. An example of a neighborhood structure in the three-dimensional match volume. If used in Marr–Poggio algorithm, the filled and unfilled circles represent excitatory and inhibitory regions, respectively.

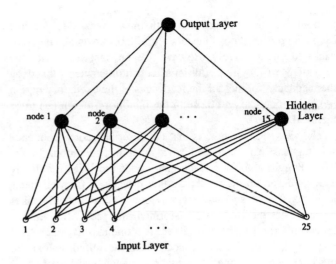

Fig. 4. The topology of the fully connected neural network if the neighborhood shown in Fig. 3 is considered.

whose correct disparity maps are known can serve as a good training set. The "error back-propagation" (BP) learning algorithm [14] is used throughout to teach the utilized NN's.

A. The Fully Connected Neural Net

The first kind of NN used for this study is a conventional multilayer feed-forward NN. This network consists of an input layer, an output layer, and one hidden layer. Connections within the same layer or from upper layer to lower layer are not allowed. The input nodes have a transfer function of unity. The hidden layer nodes and the output node have sigmoid nonlinearity transfer function. Therefore if the output of the jth node is represented by y_j

$$y_j = \frac{1}{1 + \exp\left(- \sum_i y_i w_{ij}\right)}$$

where w_{ij} is the connection weight from node i in the layer below to node j.

The inputs to this net consist of the value of an IMV element along with those in its neighborhood S. For instance, if a Marr–Poggio neighborhood as shown in Fig. 3 is to be used, 25 input nodes (one for the considered element, 12 for its neighbors in the 45° vertical plane, and 12 for those in the horizontal plane), one output node, and an undecided number of hidden nodes are required. Fig. 4 shows this net for such a neighborhood.

To train this net one must find proper weights for all of its connections as well as thresholds associated with the nodes. This is carried out by the back-propagation learning algorithm. Unfortunately, there is no specific rule for the selection of the optimal number of hidden layer nodes. Their number must not be too large such that its many weights could not be reliably estimated or too small to learn the necessary mapping.

B. The Sparsely Connected NN with Augmented Inputs

In this section, we develop another net which does not suffer from the ad hoc selection of its number of hidden nodes. Again let us use the neighborhood shown in Fig. 3 to illustrate the idea. In this case, each element in the IMV gets affected by 24 other elements as shown in Fig. 3. Our suggested network for such an S is shown in Fig. 5. It has 625 inputs, 25 hidden nodes and one output node. Each hidden node is only connected to one set of 25 input nodes. The 625 inputs consist of 25 sets of 25 elements of the IMV. Let us denote these sets by $I_1, I_2, \ldots, I_{25}$, respectively. The first set of 25 inputs consists of the value of the element of the IMV whose final state is sought along with those of its 24 neighbors. Let us denote this node and its neighbors by t and $S^t = s_1^t, s_2^t, \ldots, s_{24}^t$ respectively. Then $I_1 = \{t, S^t\}$. The second set is composed of the same type of information for neighbor s_1^t. In other words $I_2 = \{s_1^t, S^{s_1^t}\}$. $I_3, \ldots, I_{25}$ are made similarly. So in general

$$I_j = \left\{ s_j^t, S^{s_j^t} \right\}, j = 2, 3, \ldots, 25.$$

Therefore, the status of the considered element in the IMV along with those of its neighbors, and neighbors of neighbors, make up the 625 inputs for the computation of the final state of the considered element. Note that there is a good degree of overlap among these 625 inputs. However, these redundant inputs are processed separately in the hidden layer as explained later. Due to the structure of this input, it is referred to as "augmented input."

The hidden layer consists of 25 nodes, each of which is connected to only one of the 25 sets of inputs through weights to be learned. Thus each node of the hidden layer processes the result of evolution of one of the 25 input sets. The effects of processing these 25 evolved sets would then be integrated at the single output node through the connection weights between the hidden nodes and the output node. The output node then computes the corresponding final state of the considered initial match element.

In the suggested topology the number of hidden layer nodes is always equal to the number of elements in S. This removes

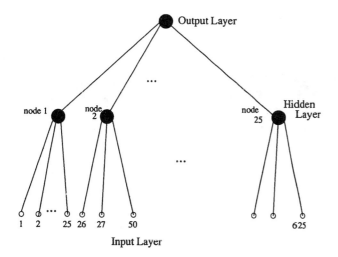

Fig. 5. The topology of the sparsely connected neural network with augmented inputs if the neighborhood shown in Fig. 3 is considered.

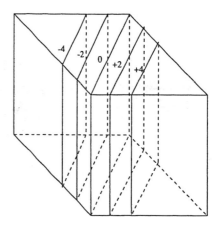

Fig. 6. The loci of constant disparity levels (in pixels) in the match volume.

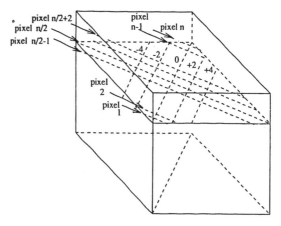

Fig. 7. Illustration of the process of assigning proper disparity levels to one of the "n" pixel wide rows of the disparity map image.

the requirement for ad hoc selection of the number of hidden nodes as in the case of fully connected net.

Three variations of the sparsely connected NN is considered in this study. The topology of all these are the same but they differ in the procedure used for weight adjustment during BP training. The first NN (version V1) utilizes the BP in the standard form, i.e., all the weights receive random initial values and are allowed to change freely during the training process. The second and third variations take note of the structure of I_j s. Since each I_j has a similar topology which consist of an element in IMV along with its S neighbors, it is reasonable to expect a uniform effect from neighbors in the same location. Thus in the second variation (version V2) of the net, we impose a weight similarity constraint on the input to hidden layer weights. This means that instead of starting with 625 different weights, we only use 25 distinct weights which are randomly selected. The neighbors with similar relative position in each set receive the same initial weight in all the 25 considered sets. Therefore, if $w_i(I_j)$ represent the connection weight from the ith input node of I_j, $i,j = 1,2,...,25$, we start with

$$w_i(I_1) = w_i(I_2) = \ldots = w_i(I_{25}), \quad i = 1,2,...,25.$$

In the second variation, this constraint of similar weights is forced throughout the BP training. During each pass of the training stage, the required change for each of the above weights is computed individually using the standard BP method. These changes are then averaged for each ith input and this average is used as a common weight change for all $w_i(I_j)$s, i.e.,

$$w_i^{(k+1)}(I_j) = w_i^{(k)}(I_j) + \Delta w_i(I_j)$$

$$\Delta w_i(I_j) = \frac{1}{25} \sum_{j=1}^{25} \delta w_i(I_j), \quad i,j = 1,2,...25$$

where the superscript indicates iteration number and $\delta w_i(I_j)$ represents required changes computed by BP. Therefore, the

second variation of the model deals with only 25 distinct weights for the input to hidden layer.

The third variation (version V3) of the model starts the same as the second variation but does not enforce the concept of shared weights throughout the training process. Therefore, it starts with a set of 25 randomly selected shared weights for the input to hidden layer and allows these weights to change freely during the BP training ultimately yielding 625 different weights for this layer.

V. Construction of The Disparity (Depth) Map

After the correspondence problem is solved, the result is used to construct a "disparity map" which is a two-dimensional image of the same size of the stereo pair. This map can also be considered a depth map because depth and disparity are monotonically related. Each pixel of the disparity map is assigned the disparity level (in pixels) computed between the two images at that pixel. Fig. 6 shows the loci of the constant disparity elements in the match volume. They are 45° oriented vertical planes. Fig. 7 illustrates how a disparity value is assigned to one of the n pixels of the jth row of the disparity map. The FMV values at the intersection of the arrow corresponding to the nth pixel with each of the disparity

Left   Right   2-d   3-d

Fig. 8. A RDS pair with two-dimensional and three-dimensional schematics of the image perceived when the pair is observed through a stereoscope.

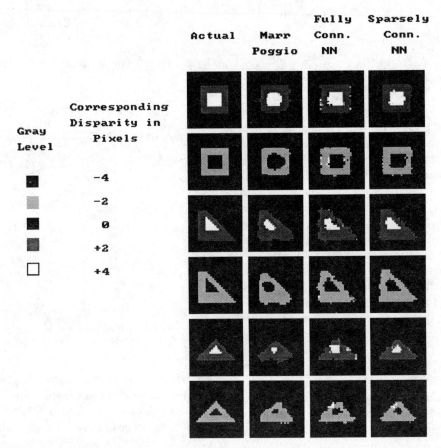

Fig. 9. The results of disparity computation for six 50% dense RDS's whose actual disparity maps are used to train the neural networks.

planes are compared. The disparity value of the one with the maximum value is then assigned to this nth pixel.

VI. EXPERIMENTAL STUDY

The performance of the proposed neural network approach is tested on several computer-generated random-dot stereograms (RDS) which are a popular kind of imagery for testing computational models of stereopsis. A random dot stereogram consists of a pair of similar structural images filled with randomly generated black and white dots, with some regions of one of the images shifted to either left or right relative to the other image. When viewed through a stereoscope, a human can perceive the shifted structures as either floating upward or downward (i.e., different depth levels) according to their relative disparities. An example of a RDS along with

its perceived fused image is shown in Fig. 8. The fused image is perceived as a three-layer structure with each square region (shown with a different intensity) being perceived as floating above the background. Thus each intensity level actually represents a depth level. Depth perception in such images (which do not possess any physical cues) indicate that human stereo fusion does not depend on shape or familiarity with physical appearance of objects. An accurate model of stereopsis should therefore be able to solve RDS's and is thus used for testing the performance of our approach.

The actual disparity maps of six 32×32 RDS's with varying disparities as shown in Fig. 9 are used to teach the network. Initially, RDS's with 50% density (i.e., half black (0 s) and half white (1 s)) are used. Each stereogram contains three different depth levels (disparity regions) represented by different gray levels. Therefore, six three-dimensional IMV's and their six

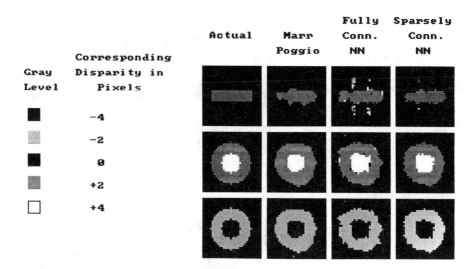

Gray Level	Corresponding Disparity in Pixels
■	-4
▨	-2
■	0
▨	+2
□	+4

Fig. 10. The results of disparity computation for 50% dense RDS's whose disparity region shapes are different from those in the training set.

TABLE I
NUMBER OF ERROR PIXELS (OUT OF A TOTAL OF 1024 PIXELS) IN THE COMPUTED DISPARITY MAPS. 50% DENSE RDS'S USED IN BOTH TRAINING AND TESTING

	Row	Marr & Poggio	Fully Conn. NN	Sparsely Connected NN		
				V1	V2	V3
Training (See Fig. 9)	1st	27	33	12	16	10
	2nd	25	38	23	25	22
	3rd	48	56	27	41	19
	4th	46	44	24	35	30
	5th	35	38	17	28	14
	6th	34	37	22	37	19
Testing (See Fig. 10)	1st	70	69	50	48	54
	2nd	41	74	33	37	45
	3rd	41	67	39	41	48

corresponding FMV's comprise the training set for the NN. Each IMV and its corresponding FMV contains 32^3 input-output pairs. Since six stereograms are considered, a total of 6×32^3 input-output pairs are available for training. In all the following examples, 60 passes over the training data are performed. 15 hidden nodes are used for the fully connected NN. The selected parameters for the back-propagation algorithm are: learning rate = 0.2, momentum = 0.7.

After the nets are trained, their performances are tested on several RDS's as outlined next. The obtained results are shown both in pictorial and numerical form. The numerical values are the number of pixels assigned incorrect disparity levels in the output disparity map. In the case of pictorial results for the sparsely connected NN, only the best result among the three possible variations is shown. The testing is performed on the following RDS's.

1) The same RDS's that the nets are trained with. The results are shown in Fig. 9 and Table I.

2) RDS's with disparity regions whose shapes are different from those used in training (testing set). The results are shown in Fig. 10 and Table I.

3) Another bigger size (64×64) RDS with both different shape regions and different disparity levels than those used in training. The results are shown in Fig. 11 and Table II.

4) Noisy RDS's where 3%, 9%, and 12% noise is added to the right image of the stereo pair. Two cases are shown in Figs. 12, 13, and Table III. The image containing squares (Fig. 12) is a case where the noiseless stereo pair is in the training set while the other (Fig. 13) is new to the nets.

5) RDS's with a lower density. 30% density (i.e., 30% white (1 s), 70% black (0 s)) RDS's are generated and tested. Fig. 14 depicts the results for 30% RDS's, the 50% counterparts of which are used for training the network, while Fig. 15 illustrates the results of disparity computation for 30% RDS's (testing set), the 50% counterparts of which are not used in the training of the network. Numerical results for both the above cases are enumerated in Table IV.

In each case, the results obtained using the Marr–Poggio algorithm are also shown for comparison. The utilized parameters for Marr–Poggio method are $\alpha = 31.509$, $\beta = -0.044$. These parameters were obtained by applying the described gradient descent approach to the six training RDS's. In general, it can be seen that the NN's outperform Marr–Poggio in terms of pixels with correct disparity levels in the computed disparity map (see the Tables). Also note that the sparsely connected net consistently does better than the fully connected one. This could be due to the fact that the architecture of the sparsely connected net takes into account more neighborhoods allowing a sort of local averaging (smoothing) operation to be performed, whereas for the fully connected net, a single neighborhood is considered. Numerically, i.e., in terms of error pixels, the three versions of sparsely connected NN are very similar in their performance although version one seems to

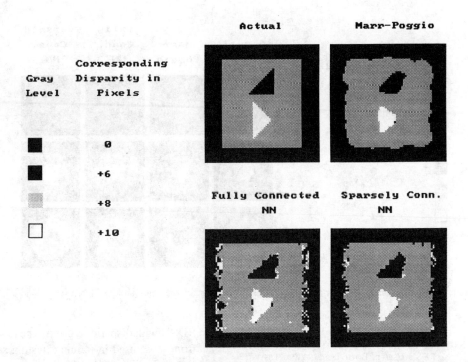

Fig. 11. The results of disparity computation for a (64 × 64) RDS (50% dense) whose disparity levels and disparity region shapes are different from those in the training set.

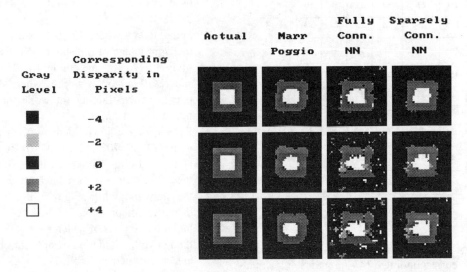

Fig. 12. The results of disparity computation for noisy 50% dense RDS. 3% (top row), 9% (middle row), and12% (bottom row) noise is added to the right images of RDS. Note that the noiseless stereo pair of the above type is in the training set.

TABLE II

NUMBER OF ERROR PIXELS (OUT OF A TOTAL OF 4096 PIXELS) IN THE COMPUTED DISPARITY MAPS FOR A RDS OF A LARGER SIZE (64 × 64) WITH BOTH DIFFERENT SHAPE REGIONS AND DIFFERENT DISPARITY LEVELS THAN THOSE USED FOR TRAINING. PICTORIAL RESULTS ARE SHOWN IN FIG. 11.

Marr & Poggio	Fully Conn. NN	Sparsely Connected NN		
		V1	V2	V3
260	332	261	268	269

yield the best results in majority of cases. The performance of the fully connected NN tends to deteriorate slightly in case of noisy RDS's while the deterioration effect is not significant in the performance of the sparsely connected NN. Although, the performance level tends to decline when the lower density RDS's are considered, the percentage of pixels assigned correct disparity levels in the computed disparity map still remains in the high 90%'s.

Table V lists the learned weights for the second version (V2) of the sparsely connected NN which is the one with the least number of parameters among the three. Interpretation of the reported weights in a direct manner is inappropriate because of the nonlinearities (sigmoid) involved as transfer functions of hidden and output nodes. Also the effect of the Bias increases the difficulty of offering a direct interpretation for the learned

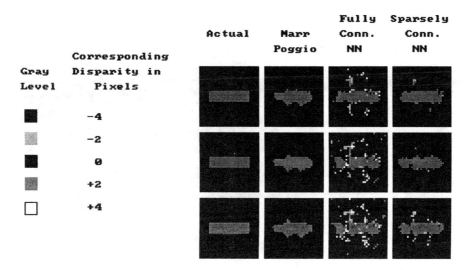

Fig. 13. The results of disparity computation for noisy 50% dense RDS. 3% (top row), 9% (middle row), and 12% (bottom row) noise is added to the right images of RDS. Note that the noiseless stereo pair of the above type is not in the training set.

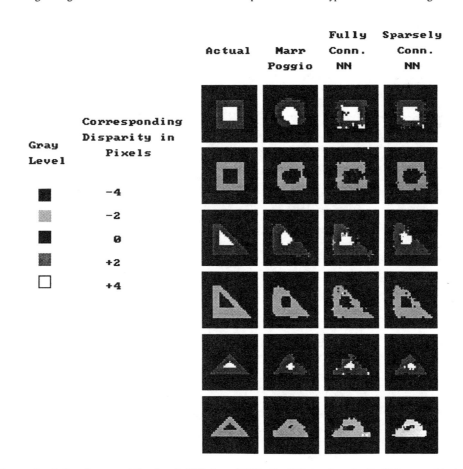

Fig. 14. The results of disparity computation for six 30% dense RDS's, the 50% counterparts of which are used to train the net.

weights. The general comment that can be made is that the appropriate constraints are coded in a distributive manner in these weights.

Overall, the obtained results are good indications of generalization capabilities of NN's. They show that the learned mapping can be generalized to previously unseen situations such as noise, different disparity levels and shapes, and different densities.

VII. CONCLUSION

In this paper, a neural network approach to the problem of stereopsis is discussed. Two multilayer feed-forward nets are used to learn the mapping that retains the correct matches between pixels of the epipolar lines of the stereo pair from amongst all the possible matches. The only constraint that is explicitly imposed is the "epipolar" constraint. All the other

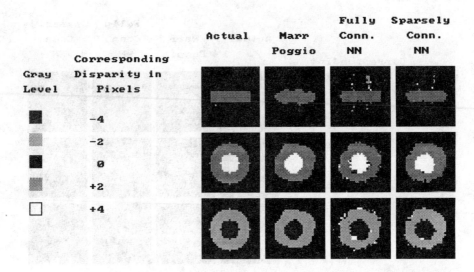

Fig. 15. The results of disparity computation for a testing set comprising of 30% dense RDS's.

TABLE III
NUMBER OF ERROR PIXELS (OUT OF A TOTAL 1024 PIXELS) IN THE COMPUTED DISPARITY MAPS FOR A TRAINING SET AND A TESTING SET SAMPLE (RDS) WITH 50% DENSITY AND NOISE ADDED TO THE RIGHT IMAGE OF THE RDS.

	Amount Of Noise Added	Row	Marr & Poggio	Fully Conn. NN	Sparsely Connected NN		
					V1	V2	V3
(See Fig. 12)	3%	1st	35	56	22	30	21
	9%	2nd	41	111	39	51	46
	12%	3rd	41	152	56	63	60
(See Fig. 13)	3%	1st	75	85	56	48	52
	9%	2nd	70	133	68	58	69
	12%	3rd	81	148	77	73	74

TABLE IV
NUMBER OF ERROR PIXELS (OUT OF A TOTAL OF 1024 PIXELS) IN THE COMPUTED DISPARITY MAPS. 30% DENSE RDS'S USED FOR TESTING.

	Row	Marr & Poggio	Fully Conn. NN	Sparsely Connected NN		
				V1	V2	V3
(See Fig. 14)	1st	64	58	49	47	46
	2nd	38	48	34	38	35
	3rd	51	69	44	46	47
	4th	53	51	38	43	38
	5th	46	33	36	37	23
	6th	34	37	30	31	30
(See Fig. 15)	1st	67	65	48	52	48
	2nd	52	76	55	47	54
	3rd	52	76	53	44	48

TABLE V
LEARNED WEIGHTS FOR THE SECOND VERSION (V2) OF THE SPARSELY CONNECTED NN

Node Number	Learned weights	
	From Input to Hidden	From Hidden to Output
1	0.43	-3.52
2	-0.81	-3.77
3	0.25	-3.05
4	-1.57	-3.60
5	0.08	-2.25
6	-0.90	-2.65
7	0.29	-3.50
8	-1.25	-2.74
9	-0.75	-2.58
10	-1.29	-2.12
11	-0.50	-2.79
12	-1.24	-2.07
13	1.96	-5.74
14	0.27	-0.38
15	-0.04	0.47
16	-0.09	0.02
17	-0.13	0.06
18	-0.07	-0.47
19	-0.11	0.11
20	0.01	0.03
21	0.02	0.07
22	-0.12	0.48
23	-0.05	0.51
24	0.23	-1.20
25	0.13	-0.11
BIAS	-0.78	-10.09

appropriate constraints are learned and coded in the nets in a distributed fashion. One network is a fully connected net with one input layer, one hidden layer, and one output layer.

The other net has the same structure but is sparsely connected. Three variations of the sparsely connected NN are considered. The pattern of connections is decided by the topology of a neighborhood used in deciding the correct matches. The number of the hidden nodes in the second net is also decided based on the topology of this neighborhood. The nets learn by examples of stereo pairs and their corresponding depth maps. The back-propagation learning rule is used in both cases. The procedure is tested on several random-dot stereograms and the performance of the NN found to be quite good. It is shown that they can successfully generalize their learning to disparity levels, shapes, and densities not seen during the training stage. They are also capable of handling moderate levels of noise. The net performances are compared to those of the Marr–Poggio algorithm and are found to be superior.

REFERENCES

[1] S. T. Barnard and M. A. Fischler, "Computational stereo," *Computing Surveys*, vol. 14, no. 4, pp. 553-572, Dec. 1982.

[2] U. R. Dhond and J. K. Aggarwal, "Structure from stereo—A review," *IEEE Trans. Syst., Man, Cybern.*, vol. 19, Nov./Dec. 1989.

[3] M. Drumheller and T. Poggio, "On parallel stereo," in *Proc. IEEE Intl. Conf. on Robotics and Automation*, 1986, vol. 3, pp. 1439-1448.

[4] A. F. Gmitro and G. R. Gindi, "Optical neurocomputer for implementation of the Marr–Poggio stereo algorithm," in *Proc. IEEE First Int. Conf. on Neural Networks*, San Diego, CA, June 1987, pp. 599-606.

[5] A. Khotanzad and Y. W. Lee, "Depth perception by neural networks," *IEEE Midcon/90 Conf. Record*, Dallas, TX, Sept. 11-13, 1990, pp. 424-427.

[6] A. Khotanzad and Y. W. Lee, "Stereopsis by a neural network which learns the constraints," in *Advances in Neural Information Processing Systems 3*, R. P. Lippmann, J. E. Moody, and D. S. Touretzky, Eds. San Mateo, CA: Morgan Kaufmann, 1991, pp. 327-335.

[7] R. P. Lippmann, "An introduction to computing with neural nets," *IEEE ASSP Mag.*, pp. 4-22, Apr. 1987.

[8] D. Marr and T. Poggio, "Cooperative computation of stereo disparity," *Science*, vol. 194, pp. 283-287, Oct. 1976.

[9] N. M. Nasrabadi and C. Y. Choo, "Hopfield network for stereo vision correspondence," *IEEE Trans. Neural Networks*, vol. 3, Jan. 1992.

[10] Alice J. O'Toole, "Structure from stereo by associative learning of the constraints," *Perception*, vol. 18, pp. 767-782, 1989.

[11] F. J. Pineda, "Generalization of back-propagation to recurrent neural networks," *Phys. Rev. Lett.*, vol. 59, pp. 2229–2232, 1987.

[12] T. Poggio, "Vision by man and machine," *Sci. Amer.*, vol. 250, pp. 106-116, Apr. 1984.

[13] N. Qian and T. J. Sejnowski, "Learning to solve random-dot stereograms of dense and transparent surfaces with recurrent backpropagation," in *Proc. 1988 Connectionist Models*, Summer School, Carnegie Mellon University, Pittsburgh, PA, June 17-26, 1988, pp. 435-443.

[14] D. E. Rumelhart, G. E. Hinton, and R. J. Williams, "Learning internal representations by error propagation," in *Parallel Distributed Processing: Explorations in the Microstructure of Cognition*, D. E. Rumelhart and J. L. McClelland, Eds. Cambridge, MA: MIT Press, 1986, vol. 1.

[15] G. Z. Sun, H. H. Chen, and Y. C. Lee, "Learning stereopsis with neural networks," in *Proc. IEEE First Int. Conf. on Neural Networks*, San Diego, CA, June 1987, pp. 345-355.

[16] Y. T. Zhou and R. Chellappa, "Stereo matching using a neural network," in *Proc. IEEE Int. Conf. Acoustics, Speech, and Signal Processing, ICASSP-88*, New York, Apr. 11-14, 1988, pp. 940-943.

Hopfield Network for Stereo Vision Correspondence

Nasser M. Nasrabadi, *Member, IEEE,* and Chang Y. Choo, *Member, IEEE*

Abstract—An optimization approach is used to solve the correspondence problem for a set of features extracted from a pair of stereo images. A cost function is defined to represent the constraints on the solution, which is then mapped onto a two-dimensional Hopfield neural network for minimization. Each neuron in the network represents a possible match between a feature in the left image and one in the right image. Correspondence is achieved by initializing (exciting) each neuron that represents a possible match and then allowing the network to settle down into a stable state. The network uses the initial inputs and the compatibility measures between the matched points to find a stable state.

I. INTRODUCTION

STEREO vision is a passive technique used to determine the depth of an object or a point in a scene using a pair of stereo images [1]. The depth information is essential in many applications such as robotics, remote sensing, and medical imaging. The study of vertebrate binocular vision systems has revealed that the distance perceived by the binocular stereo vision system depends on the retinal disparity. The retinal disparity is the difference between the location of the retinal image points in the two eyes. Because of the different vantage points of the eyes, retinal points nearer to the observer will have larger disparity than retinal points farther away from the observer. The retinal images are fused in the visual cortex to produce perception of a single image. The neural mechanism as to how the brain fuses the two images is not yet fully understood by neurobiologists [2], [3]. However, it has been shown that there are binocular neurons that respond only when they are excited by the two eyes [4]. Julesz [5] has shown, by using computer-generated random-dot stereograms, that stereo fusion does not depend on shape or recognition of objects. Therefore, to fuse the two random dot stereograms with no structural information, cooperative interactions between neurons is essential in order to find the correct corresponding points.

There are several approaches for solving the correspondence problem: one is to match every point in the left image with that of the right image [6], [7]; another is to extract distinct

features from each image and try to match them [8], [9]. It is not clear if the human binocular system performs the stereo fusion cooperatively in a point-to-point manner or distinct features, such as edges, are matched first, followed by surface interpolation. However, it is well known that the receptive fields of the neurons in higher layers of the visual cortex have orientation selectivity [10].

In this paper, we are interested in solving the correspondence problem using the parallelism and the computational power offered by the neural networks. A feature-based stereo technique is introduced where the features are matched in parallel by a Hopfield network. For some robotics applications where dense depth information is not required, it is computationally more efficient to choose only a few distinct points to match than to try to match every point in the image. These distinct points should be features that represent the areas of high variance such as edges or corners of objects. We have chosen a feature extraction technique developed by Moravec [11], [12] called the interest operator to find points of high interest. The output of the interest operator comprises mostly corners or feature points with high variance, where variance is defined as the difference in the gray level values between successive pixels within a window. The Moravec operator was chosen because it is computationally very efficient to implement compared with more complicated corner detectors.

It is not an easy task to find the corresponding feature points between two images, especially when not all the feature points (interesting points) in one image are visible in the other image. Occlusion or shading caused by the light source may hide or displace some of the feature points in the second image. Therefore, only a number of points in the left image may find a correct match in the right image. However, the best solution should satisfy the uniqueness constraint; that is, each point in the left image can have only a unique match in the right image and vice versa [6].

One approach to obtaining an optimal solution is to use parallel matching techniques. There are several parallel stereo matching techniques, such as graph matching [13], [14] or relaxation techniques [15]–[17], where compatibility measures between matched features are used to find the best solution. One major problem with conventional graph matching techniques such as the clique finding [14] is the computational complexity involved in finding all the possible cliques. In the case of the relaxation technique the uniqueness constraint or any other constraint on the solution cannot be explicitly included in the algorithm. However, when using the neural network technique the matching problem can be formulated as minimization of a cost function (constrained optimization) where all the constraints on the solution can explicitly be

Manuscript received February 4, 1991; revised July 16, 1991. This work was supported in part by the National Science Foundation under Contract IRI-88-08523 and the Air Force Office of Scientific Research under Contract AFOSR-89-0037.

N. M. Nasrabadi was with the Department of Electrical Engineering, Worcester Polytechnic Institute, Worcester, MA. He is now with the Department of Electrical and Computer Engineering, State University of New York at Buffalo, Buffalo, NY 14260.

C. Y. Choo was with the Department of Electrical Engineering, Worcester Polytechnic Institute, Worcester, MA. He is now with the Department of Electrical and Computer Engineering, California State University at San Jose, San Jose, CA.

IEEE Log Number 9103357.

Reprinted from *IEEE Trans. on Neural Networks*, vol. 3, no. 1, pp. 5–13, Jan. 1992.

included in the cost function. Minimization of the cost function can then be performed by a distributed network such as a Hopfield network [18]–[20] or by a stochastic optimization technique such a simulated annealing [21]. Many vision tasks can be formulated as minimization of a cost function [22]–[29]. For example, in [25] an image restoration technique is developed where a cost function is minimized by a Hopfield network. In [26]–[28], feature matching is considered as subgraph isomorphism, which is implemented by a neural network.

A sparse depth map is obtained by the proposed algorithm. However, it is possible to obtain dense depth information by the technique proposed in [29], where a three-dimensional binary Hopfield network was used to obtain a dense depth map for a motion stereo sequence. This technique performs well on stereograms, but its performance is very poor on real stereo images, especially those having very large smooth areas. In these networks the number of processing elements is very large compared with the proposed network in this paper and computationally more complex.

II. FEATURE EXTRACTION AND THE INTEREST OPERATOR

The first step of the algorithm is to find points of high interest in both images. The points of high interest are salient points in the two images which can be more easily matched than any other point in the image. These points generally occur at the corners and edges of the object in the image.

To find these points a simple technique developed by Moravec [12] is used which locates all the points of high interest in the image. These points, called the interesting points, are defined as points in the image that have high variance in all directions. The operator used is called the interest operator [12], which finds the variance in the horizontal, vertical, and both diagonal directions for each point in the image. The minimum of these values is then chosen as the variance for that point. Fig. 1 shows how the variance is found. The variance equations for each direction are given below:

$$\text{horizontal displacement } (HD) = \sum_{x=0}^{4} \sum_{y=0}^{3}$$
$$\cdot \left[f(x,y) - f(x,y+1) \right]^2 \quad (1)$$

$$\text{vertical displacement } (VD) = \sum_{x=0}^{3} \sum_{y=0}^{4}$$
$$\cdot \left[f(x,y) - f(x+1,y) \right]^2 \quad (2)$$

$$\text{diagonal displacement } (DD - 135°) = \sum_{x=0}^{3} \sum_{y=0}^{3}$$
$$\cdot \left[f(x,y) - f(x+1,y+1) \right]^2 \quad (3)$$

$$\text{diagonal displacement } (DD - 45°) = \sum_{x=0}^{3} \sum_{y=1}^{4}$$
$$\cdot \left[f(x,y) - f(x+1,y-1) \right]^2. \quad (4)$$

The function $f(x,y)$ refers to the gray level value at that point

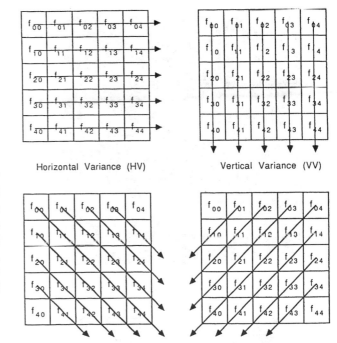

Fig. 1. The directional variances calculated by the interest operator. The minimum of these is chosen as the interest operator value.

in the image. The smallest value of VD, HD, $DD - 45°$, and $DD - 135°$, called the interest operator value, is taken as the variance for that point.

Usually at regions of high variance a large number of interesting points are found in a cluster. To reduce the number of interesting points and to have distinct features scattered over the whole image, the point having the local maxima variance in each local region (a window of size 20×20) is chosen as the interesting point. Fig. 2 shows a stereo pair with several objects at different disparities with the interesting points marked by a + superimposed onto the original images.

III. ENERGY MINIMIZATION BY A HOPFIELD NEURAL NETWORK

In this section, it is shown that the stereo correspondence problem can be formulated as an optimization task where a cost function (energy equation) representing the constraints on the stereo solution is minimized [22]–[27]. It is also shown that the minimization problem can be mapped onto a Hopfield neural network [18]–[20] such that the cost (energy) function is the same as the Lyapunov function of the network, with the synaptic interconnection weights between the neurons representing the constraints imposed by the correspondence problem. The Lyapunov function represents the collective behavior of the network. When the network is at its stable state the energy function is said to be at its local minimum. The basic principle of the neural networks is to make a cooperative decision based on the simultaneous input of a whole community of neurons in which each neuron receives information from and gives information to every other neuron. This information is used by each neuron to force the network to converge to a stable state in order to make a decision.

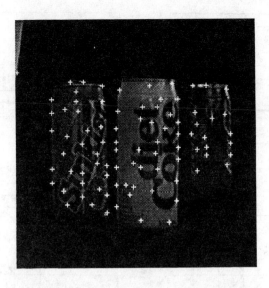

(a)

(b)

Fig. 2. Original stereo images with the interesting points marked by a + symbol overlapped onto the original images. (a) Left image. (b) Right image.

A two-dimensional binary Hopfield network is used to find the correspondence between the interesting points in the left and right images. The network is represented as an $N_l \times N_r$ array of neurons, where N_l and N_r are the total number of interesting points in the left and the right image, respectively. The state of each neuron (on or off) in the network represents a possible match between an interesting point in the left image with one in the right image. Fig. 3 shows the 2-D network and the connection weights between its neurons.

The Lyapunov function for a two-dimensional binary (two-state) Hopfield network [18] is given by

$$E = -(1/2) \sum_{i=1}^{N_l} \sum_{k=1}^{N_r} \sum_{j=1}^{N_l} \sum_{l=1}^{N_r} T_{ikjl} V_{ik} V_{jl} - \sum_{i=1}^{N_l} \sum_{k=1}^{N_r} I_{ik} V_{ik} \tag{5}$$

where V_{ik} and V_{jl} represent the binary states of ik and jl neurons, respectively, which can be either 1 (active) or 0 (inactive), $T_{ikjl} (= T_{jlik})$ is the interconnection strength

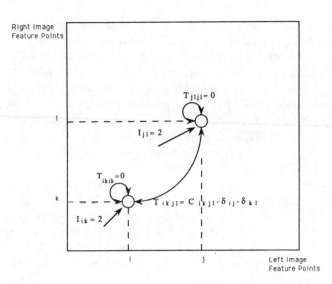

Fig. 3. The 2-D Hopfield network with its neurons interconnections.

between the two neurons, the self-feedback to each neuron is $T_{ikik} = 0$, and I_{ik} is the initial input to each neuron. A change in the state of neuron ik by ΔV_{ik} will cause an energy change of ΔE_{ik}:

$$\Delta E_{ik} = - \left[\sum_{j=1}^{N_l} \sum_{l=1}^{N_r} T_{ikjl} V_{jl} + I_{ik} \right] \Delta V_{ik}. \tag{6}$$

The above equation describes the dynamics of the network which was shown by Hopfield to be always negative with a stochastic updating rule

$$V_{ik} - \rightarrow 0 \quad \text{if} \quad \left[\sum_{j=1}^{N_l} \sum_{l=1}^{N_r} T_{ikjl} V_{jl} + I_{ik} \right] > 0$$

$$V_{ik} - \rightarrow 1 \quad \text{if} \quad \left[\sum_{j=1}^{N_l} \sum_{l=1}^{N_r} T_{ikjl} V_{jl} + I_{ik} \right] < 0$$

$$\text{no change} \quad \text{if} \quad \left[\sum_{j=1}^{N_l} \sum_{l=1}^{N_r} T_{ikjl} V_{jl} + I_{ik} \right] = 0. \tag{7}$$

To solve the stereo correspondence problem, the cost function given below is minimized:

$$E = - \sum_{i=1}^{N_l} \sum_{k=1}^{N_r} \sum_{j=1}^{N_l} \sum_{l=1}^{N_r} C_{ikjl} P_{ik} P_{jl} + \sum_{i=1}^{N_l} \left(1 - \sum_{k=1}^{N_r} P_{ik} \right)^2$$

$$+ \sum_{k=1}^{N_r} \left(1 - \sum_{i=1}^{N_l} P_{ik} \right)^2 \tag{8}$$

The first term in (8) represents the degree of compatibility of a match between a pair of points (i, j) in the left image and a pair of points (k, l) in the right image, while the second and third terms tend to enforce the uniqueness constraint where the probabilities (states of neurons) in each row or column should add up to 1. Each probability represents a measure of match between a feature point in the left image and that of the right image. Equation (8) can be rearranged (as shown in the Appendix) to get

$$E = -(1/2)\sum_{i=1}^{N_l}\sum_{k=1}^{N_r}\sum_{j=1}^{N_l}\sum_{l=1}^{N_r}(C_{ikjl} - \delta_{ij} - \delta_{lk})P_{ik}P_{jl}$$

$$-\sum_{i=1}^{N_l}\sum_{k=1}^{N_r}2P_{ik} \qquad (9)$$

where $\delta_{ij} = 1$ if $i = j$, otherwise 0; similarly $\delta_{lk} = 1$ if $l = k$, otherwise 0. This cost function can be shown to be equivalent to the Lyapunov function of a Hopfield network with states of the neurons defined as $V_{ik} = P_{ik}$ and $V_{jl} = P_{jl}$, and the input to each neuron set to $I_{ik} = 2$ (see the Appendix). The synaptic connection weight between two neurons is defined as $T_{ikjl} = (C_{ikjl} - \delta_{ij} - \delta_{kl})$, where the compatibility measure is given by

$$C_{ikjl} = \frac{2}{[1 + e^{\lambda(X-\theta)}]} - 1 \qquad (10)$$

where X is

$$X = [W_1|\Delta d| + W_2|\Delta D|]. \qquad (11)$$

Equation (11) shows that the compatibility is based on two types of comparisons for the two matched point pairs. The first comparison, Δd, is the difference in the disparities of the matched points pairs (i, k) and (j, l). If the points belong to the same object, then the disparity difference should be very small, owing to the object rigidity and surface smoothness. The other comparison, ΔD, is the difference between the distance from i to j and the distance from k to l, which is small when the feature points are correctly matched. $W_1 = 0.4$ and $W_2 = 0.6$ are constants which weigh these comparisons appropriately and satisfy the relationship $W_1 + W_2 = 1$. More weight was assigned to ΔD since its value is more stable than Δd.

The nonlinear function used in (10) scales the compatibility measure smoothly between $+1$ and -1. Fig. 4 shows this nonlinear function for several values of λ, where λ is a parameter that sets the slope of the function. A very large value of λ will result in a step function for the compatibility measure with possible values of $+1$ or -1. If a very small value of λ is used, the function will smoothly switch from $+1$ to -1, with possible compatibility values between. The parameter θ controls the position where the nonlinear function crosses the X axis. This parameter is chosen such that a compatibility of $+1$ is obtained for a good match ($X = 0$); a mutual compatibility of 0 for a match when the X value is not exactly zero, allowing a tolerance for noise and distortion; and a compatibility of -1 for a bad match ($X \gg 0$). From the experimental tests the best values for these parameters were found to be $\lambda = 1$ and $\theta = 10$.

A state change in a neuron will result in an energy change of ΔE_{ik}, given by

$$\Delta E_{ik} = -\left[\sum_{j=1}^{N_l}\sum_{l=1}^{N_r}(C_{ikjl} - \delta_{ij} - \delta_{kl})P_{jl} + 2\right]\Delta P_{ik}. \qquad (12)$$

This expression is equivalent to the motion equation of the Hopfield network (eq. (6)), which is always negative if the

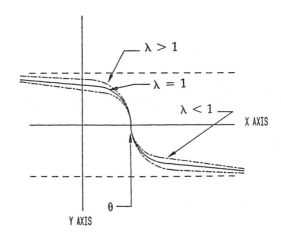

Fig. 4. Graph of the nonlinear function used to obtain the compatibility.

state of each neuron is updated randomly and asynchronously according to the Hopfield updating rule given below:

$$P_{ik}- \rightarrow 0 \quad \text{if} \quad \left[\sum_{j=1}^{N_l}\sum_{l=1}^{N_r}(C_{ikjl} - \delta_{ij} - \delta_{kl})P_{jl} + 2\right] < 0$$

$$P_{ik}- \rightarrow 1 \quad \text{if} \quad \left[\sum_{j=1}^{N_l}\sum_{l=1}^{N_r}(C_{ikjl} - \delta_{ij} - \delta_{kl})P_{jl} + 2\right] > 0$$

$$\text{no change} \quad \text{if} \quad \left[\sum_{j=1}^{N_l}\sum_{l=1}^{N_r}(C_{ikjl} - \delta_{ij} - \delta_{kl})P_{jl} + 2\right] = 0$$

$$(13)$$

The optimal solution is when the Hopfield network is at its minimum energy. However, the network could settle down into one of many locally stable states. The discrete (binary output) Hopfield network was chosen rather than the continuous (graded output) Hopfield network because of its simplicity in computational complexity. However, using a continuous Hopfield network, a number of local minima may be avoided owing to the smoothness of the surface of the energy function.

It is important to note that, in the above summations, i is selected randomly from all the features in the left image. The neighboring feature points within a window opened around i are taken as the j's for that comparison; all the other points are assumed to have zero compatibility contributions because they are too far and probably belong to another object in the scene. Each feature k is also chosen randomly out of a window (40×40) opened around i's (x, y) locations offset by an estimated disparity in the right image. The window is used to eliminate the possibility of choosing k points that have no chance of being a candidate for a match.

IV. EXPERIMENTAL RESULTS

Results are presented for running the algorithm on several pair of stereo images. Images were acquired by a single camera at two different positions such that each scan line in the left image corresponds approximately to the same scan line in the right image. Therefore, each feature point in the left image is almost on the same scan line in the other image but shifted to the right by its corresponding disparity value. Fig. 5 shows a pair of stereo images of a Renault part with interesting points detected and labeled. The numbers of interesting points found in the left and right images are $N_l = 53$ and $N_r = 52$, respectively. This clearly indicates that there will not be a match for every point in the left image, since some points in the right image are missing or occluded.

A two-dimensional binary Hopfield network consisting of $N_l \times N_r$ neurons is implemented where the state of each neuron P_{ik} is modified by the updating rule given by (13). This updating is simulated by randomly choosing an interesting point i in the left image and opening a window of size 40×40 in the right image. This window in the right image is centered at the location of the point i shifted by a horizontal offset (an initial estimated disparity). Every feature point k in this window is considered a possible match by assigning an initial probability of $P_{ik} = 1$ to each of them. This technique uses a modified epipolar constraint since only the feature points that lie within the window are considered as possible matching candidates. The window size was chosen large enough to include the largest disparity in the stereo images. Also, a window of size 40×40 is opened around the point i in the left image and all the other points in this window are considered as the j's for the summation in (13). The updating procedure is iterated until the network reaches a stable state. The network is said to be at its stable state (minimum energy) when there is no change in the states of neurons. The network is then stopped after several iterations. The network usually settles down after 1000 iterations. It should be pointed out that the final state of the Hopfield network depends on the initial state of the network. However, experimentally it was found that only a few feature points are matched differently when the network is started with a different initial condition.

After running the Hopfield network, some of the matched points will still have multiple matches. To find a single match for these interesting points, the vertical disparity (Y disparity) of each multiple match is compared with an average Y disparity obtained from all the single matched points. The candidate whose Y disparity is within a prespecified threshold of the average Y disparity is chosen as the correct match and other matches are deleted. Our assumption is that the Y disparity should be approximately the same for all the correctly matched points. Ideally the interesting points should have no vertical shift since stereo images were obtained with a parallel-axis camera setup. Any vertical shift occurring is probably due to the relation camera's orientation and the difference in shading and illumination between the two images.

In Fig. 5 the interesting points with a single match are denoted by a square around them. The points with multiple matches are surrounded by a smaller square, provided if they found a single match after going through the Y disparity comparison. The Y disparity comparison was found to be very effective in changing the multiple matches to good single matches. For example, in Fig. 5 the interesting point $\#7_{(106,66)}$ in the left image matches two points $\#1_{(92,52)}$ and $\#7_{(98,64)}$ in the right image, but after Y disparity only one correct match $\#7$ is chosen. However, for some multiple matches the ambiguity in mismatches is not resolved. Consider

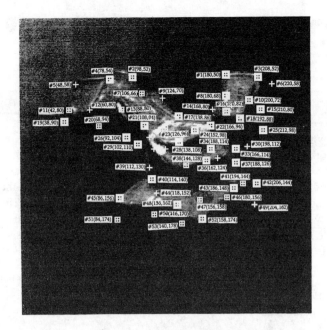

(a)

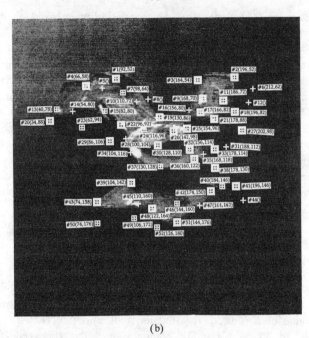

(b)

Fig. 5. Stereo images with the interesting points labeled. The large squares are the output of the matched points with a single match; the small squares are the matched points whose multiple matches are resolved by the Y-disparity comparison. (a) Left image. (b) Right image.

the feature point $\#6_{(220,58)}$ in the left image, which matches two points $\#2_{(196,52)}$ and $\#6_{(212,62)}$ in the right image. Since the Y disparity was not satisfied no match was assigned to this point, although one of the matches was the correct one. The matched points that are displayed are not necessarily all one-to-one correct matches; as shown in Table I, there are three mismatches. One way to resolve this ambiguity is to perform the matching from left to right and right to left and only retain the interesting points that have a one-to-one match in both directions. Fig. 6 shows another pair of stereo images with their matched feature points labeled. Table II shows all these one-to-one matches where five feature points are mismatched.

TABLE I
The Matched Feature Points for the Stereo
Images of a Renault Part as Shown in Fig. 5

Matched feature points with their corresponding disparity						
Left feature points			Right feature points			
Curve-#	X_l	Y_l	Curve-#	X_r	Y_r	Disparity
1	180	50	3	164	54	16
2	98	52	1	92	52	6
3	208	52	2	196	52	12
4	78	54	4	66	58	12
7	106	66	7	98	64	8
8	180	68	9	168	70	12
10	200	72	11	186	72	14
11	42	80	13	40	78	2
13	88	80	15	82	80	6
15	210	80	18	196	82	14
16	180	82	17	166	82	14
17	138	86	19	130	86	8
18	192	88	21	178	88	14
19	38	90	20	34	88	4
20	68	94	23	62	94	6
21	108	94	22	96	92	12
22	166	94	25	154	96	12
23	126	96	24	116	96	10
24	152	98	26	142	98	10
25	212	98	27	202	98	10
26	92	104	29	86	106	6
28	138	108	30	128	110	10
29	102	110	29	86	106	16 (mismatch)
33	166	114	32	156	114	10
34	188	114	33	178	114	10
36	162	124	36	160	122	2 (mismatch)
37	188	126	38	178	130	10
38	144	128	37	130	128	14
40	114	140	39	104	142	10
41	194	144	40	184	146	10
42	206	144	41	196	146	10
43	186	148	42	174	150	12
45	86	156	43	74	158	12
46	180	156	42	174	150	6 (mismatch)
47	156	158	46	144	160	12
48	136	162	48	122	164	14
50	116	170	49	106	172	10
51	84	174	50	74	176	10
52	158	174	51	144	176	14
53	140	178	52	126	180	14

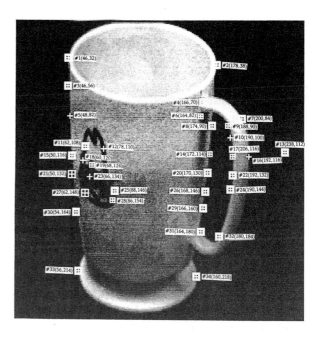

(a)

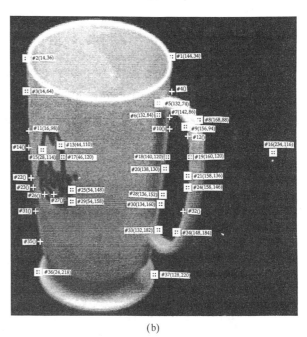

(b)

Fig. 6. A pair of stereo images with their matched interesting points. (a) Left image. (b) Right image.

Another pair of stereo images used in our experiment, shown in Fig. 7, contains three objects (cans) each at a different distance from the camera, thus resulting roughly in three different possible disparity values for the feature points. Running the Hopfield network resulted in 49 interesting points having a single match and five interesting points having multiple matches. Fig. 8 shows a histogram of the disparities obtained by tabulating only the disparities of the interesting points with a single match. From the peaks in the histogram it is clearly obvious that there are three objects with approximate disparities of 10, 26, and 38 pixels. Also from the histogram it is seen that not all the 49 single matches are correct one-to-one matches since there are more than three peaks in the histogram.

V. Conclusions

In this paper, the stereo correspondence problem is formulated as a minimization of a cost function. It is then mapped onto a two-dimensional binary Hopfield neural network with appropriate connection weights between neurons to minimize a cost function representing the dynamics of the network. This cost function is at its minimum when the system is at its equilibrium or stable state. The cost function is designed such that it is at its minimum when the conditions on the stereo solution as well as the uniqueness constraint are satisfied. The proposed stereo technique uses the salient feature points extracted by Moravec's interest operator as a base for matching. This simple feature extraction technique turned out to be a very effective way of bringing out enough important feature points in the scene to allow a quick and effective solution to the correspondence problem. The major computational cost

TABLE II
THE MATCHED FEATURE POINTS FOR THE
STEREO IMAGES OF A CUP AS SHOWN IN FIG. 6

Matched feature points with their corresponding disparity						
Left feature points			Right feature points			
Curve-#	X_l	Y_l	Curve-#	X_r	Y_r	Disparity
1	46	32	2	14	36	32
2	178	38	1	144	64	34
3	46	56	3	14	64	32
4	166	70	5	132	74	34
7	200	84	8	168	88	32
8	174	90	9	156	94	18 (mismatch)
11	62	108	13	44	110	18 (mismatch)
13	238	112	16	234	116	4
14	172	114	18	140	120	32
15	50	116	15	28	114	22 (mismatch)
16	192	116	19	160	120	32
19	68	124	17	46	120	22 (mismatch)
20	170	130	20	138	130	32
22	192	132	21	158	136	34
24	190	144	24	158	146	32
25	88	146	25	54	148	34
26	168	146	28	136	152	32
29	166	160	30	134	160	32
30	54	164	29	54	158	0 (mismatch)
31	164	180	33	132	182	32
32	180	184	34	148	184	32
33	56	214	36	24	218	32
34	160	218	37	128	220	32

in this algorithm is the Moravec interest operator but it can easily be implemented by a parallel digital processor. The Hopfield neural network is computationally very efficient if implemented in an analog form. The advantage of using a neural network is that a global match is automatically achieved because all the neurons (processors) are interconnected in a feedback loop and the output of one affects the input of all the others. Although each individual neuron is very slow, the network as a whole will be very powerful, owing to the fact that the neurons in the network are operating simultaneously.

VI. APPENDIX
DERIVATION OF EQUATION (9)

The goal is to prove that the cost function represented by (9) is equivalent to the Lyapunov function (eq. (5)) of a Hopfield network. The cost function is given by

$$E = -\sum_{i=1}^{N_l}\sum_{k=1}^{N_r}\sum_{j=1}^{N_l}\sum_{l=1}^{N_r} C_{ikjl} P_{ik} P_{jl} + \sum_{i=1}^{N_l}\left(1 - \sum_{k=1}^{N_r} P_{ik}\right)^2$$
$$+ \sum_{k=1}^{N_r}\left(1 - \sum_{i=1}^{N_l} P_{ik}\right)^2. \quad (A1)$$

Let us simplify the last two terms:

$$\sum_{i=1}^{N_l}\left(1 - \sum_{k=1}^{N_r} P_{ik}\right)^2 = \sum_{i=1}^{N_l}(1) + \sum_{i=1}^{N_l}\left(\sum_{k=1}^{N_r} P_{ik}\right)^2$$
$$- 2\sum_{i=1}^{N_l}\sum_{k=1}^{N_r} P_{ik} \quad (A2a)$$
$$= \sum_{i=1}^{N_l}(1) + \sum_{i=1}^{N_l}\left(\sum_{k=1}^{N_r}\sum_{l=1}^{N_r} P_{ik} P_{il}\right)$$

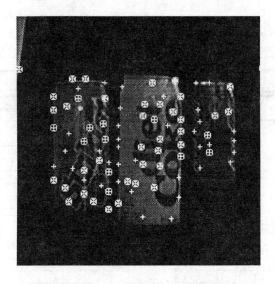

(a)

(b)

Fig. 7. A pair of stereo images consisting of three objects at different depths, with the matched interesting points represented by squares. (a) Left image. (b) Right image.

$$- \sum_{i=1}^{N_l}\sum_{k=1}^{N_r} 2 P_{ik} \quad (A2b)$$
$$= N_l + \sum_{i=1}^{N_l}\sum_{k=1}^{N_r}\sum_{l=1}^{N_r} P_{ik} P_{il}$$
$$- \sum_{i=1}^{N_l}\sum_{k=1}^{N_r} 2 P_{ik}. \quad (A2c)$$

Substitute for $P_{ik} P_{il} = P_{ik} P_{jl}\delta_{ij}$ in (A2c):

$$\sum_{i=1}^{N_l}\left(1 - \sum_{k=1}^{N_r} P_{ik}\right)^2 = N_l + \sum_{i=1}^{N_l}\sum_{k=1}^{N_r}\sum_{j=1}^{N_l}\sum_{l=1}^{N_r} P_{ik} P_{jl}\delta_{ij}$$
$$- \sum_{i=1}^{N_l}\sum_{k=1}^{N_r} 2 P_{ik}. \quad (A3)$$

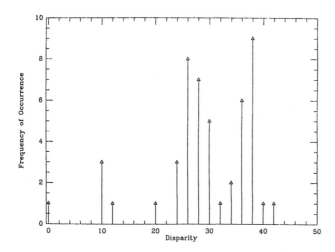

Fig. 8. Histogram of the disparities of the matched points.

the states of the neurons.

Similarly, the third term in (A1) can be simplified to

$$\sum_{k}^{N_r} \left(1 - \sum_{i=1}^{N_l} P_{ik}\right)^2 = N_r + \sum_{i=1}^{N_l}\sum_{k=1}^{N_r}\sum_{j=1}^{N_l}\sum_{l=1}^{N_r} P_{ik}P_{jl}\delta_{kl}$$
$$- \sum_{i=1}^{N_l}\sum_{k=1}^{N_r} 2P_{ik}. \quad (A4)$$

Therefore, (A1) can be rewritten as

$$E = (N_l + N_r) + \sum_{i=1}^{N_l}\sum_{k=1}^{N_r}\sum_{j=1}^{N_l}\sum_{l=1}^{N_r}(C_{ikjl} - \delta_{ij} - \delta_{lk})P_{ik}P_{jl}$$
$$- \sum_{i=1}^{N_l}\sum_{k=1}^{N_r} 4P_{ik} \quad (A5)$$

or

$$\frac{E - (N_l + N_r)}{2} = - (1/2)\sum_{i=1}^{N_l}\sum_{k=1}^{N_r}\sum_{j=1}^{N_l}\sum_{l=1}^{N_r}$$
$$\cdot (C_{ikjl} - \delta_{ij} - \delta_{lk})P_{ik}P_{jl}$$
$$- \sum_{i=1}^{N_l}\sum_{k=1}^{N_r} 2P_{ik}. \quad (A6)$$

The above expression is equivalent to the Lyapunov function of a Hopfield network:

$$\frac{E - (N_l + N_r)}{2} = - (1/2)\sum_{i=1}^{N_l}\sum_{k=1}^{N_r}\sum_{j=1}^{N_l}\sum_{l=1}^{N_r}(T_{ikjl} - V_{ik} - V_{jl})$$
$$- \sum_{i=1}^{N_l}\sum_{k=1}^{N_r} I_{ik}V_{ik}. \quad (A7)$$

where N_l and N_r represent the numbers of nodes in the network. The input to each neuron is $I_{ik} = 2$; the interconnection between two neurons is given by $T_{ikjl} = (C_{ikjl} - \delta_{ij} - \delta_{kl})$; and $P_{ik} = V_{ik}$ and $P_{jl} = V_{jl}$ represent

REFERENCES

[1] U. R. Dhond and J. K. Aggarwal, "Structure from stereo—A review," *IEEE Trans. Syst., Man, Cybern.*, vol. 19, pp. 1489–1510, Nov. 1989.
[2] E. R. Kandel and J. H. Schwartz Eds., *Principles of Neural Science.* New York: Elsevier Science Publishing, 1982.
[3] W. S. Kuffler, G. J. Nicholls, and R. A. Martin, *From Neurons to Brain.* Boston, MA: Sinauer, 1984.
[4] P. O. Bishop, "Neurophysiology of binocular single vision and stereopsis," in *Handbook of Sensory Physiology* (vol. 7, part 3A: Central Processing of Visual Information), R. Jung, Ed. Berlin: Springer, 1973, pp. 255–305.
[5] B. Julesz, *Foundation of Cyclopean Perception.* Chicago: University of Chicago Press, 1971.
[6] D. Marr and T. Poggio, "Cooperative computation of stereo disparity," *Science*, vol. 194, pp. 283–287, 1976.
[7] K. Prazdny, "Detection of binocular disparity," *Biol. Cybern.*, vol. 52, pp. 93–99, 1985.
[8] W. E. L. Grimson, "Computational experiments with a feature based stereo algorithm," *IEEE Trans. Pattern Anal. Mach. Intell.*, vol. PAMI-7, pp. 17–34, 1985.
[9] G. Medioni and R. Nevatia, "Segment based stereo matching," *Comput. Vision Image Processing*, vol. 31, pp. 2–18, 1985.
[10] D. H. Hubel and T. N. Wiesel, "Receptive fields, binocular interaction and functional architecture in the cats visual cortex," *J. Physiol.*, vol. 166, pp. 106–154, 1962.
[11] H. Moravec, "Obstacle avoidance and navigation in the real world by a seeing robot rover," Ph.D. thesis, Stanford Artificial Intell. Lab., AIM-340, Sept. 1980.
[12] H. Moravec, *Robot Rover Visual Navigation.* Ann Arbor, MI: U.M.I. Research Press, 1981.
[13] N. M. Nasrabadi and Y. Liu, "Stereo vision correspondence using a multichannel graph matching technique," *Image and Vision Computing*, vol. 7, no. 4, pp. 237–245, Nov. 1989.
[14] R. Nevatia, *Machine Perception.* Englewood Cliffs, NJ: Prentice-Hall, 1979.
[15] A. Rosenfeld, R. Hummel, and S. Zucker "Scene labeling by relaxation operations," *IEEE Trans. Syst., Man, Cybern.*, vol. SMC-6, pp. 420–453, June 1976.
[16] S. Barnard and W. Thompson, "Disparity analysis of images," *IEEE Trans. Pattern Anal. Mach. Intell.*, vol. PAMI-2, pp. 333–340, July 1980.
[17] N. M. Nasrabadi, "A stereo vision technique using curve-segments and relaxation matching," *IEEE Trans. Pattern Anal. Mach. Intell.*, vol. 13, Nov. 1991.
[18] J. Hopfield, "Neural networks and physical systems with emergent collective computational abilities," *Proc. Nat. Acad. Sci.*, vol. 79, pp. 2554–2558, Apr. 1982.
[19] J. Hopfield, "Neurons with graded response have collective computational properties like those of two-state neurons," *Proc. Nat. Acad. Sci.*, vol. 81, pp. 3088–3092, May 1984.
[20] J. Hopfield and D. W. Tank, "'Neural' computation of decisions in optimization problems," *Biol. Cybern.*, vol. 52, pp. 141–152, 1985.
[21] S. Kirkpatrick, C. D. Gellatt, Jr., and M. P. Vecchi, "Optimization by simulated annealing," *Science*, vol. 220, no. 4598, pp. 671–680, May 1983.
[22] M. Bertero, T. A. Poggio, and V. Torre, "Ill-posed problems in early vision," *Proc. IEEE*, vol. 76, pp. 869–889, Aug. 1988.
[23] G. Sperling, "Binocular vision: A physical and neural theory," *Amer. J. Psychol.*, vol. 83, no. 4, pp. 461–534, Dec. 1970.
[24] N. M. Nasrabadi, S. P. Clifford, and Y. Liu, "Integration of stereo vision and optical flow by using an energy minimization approach," *J. Opt. Soc. Amer. A*, vol. 6, no. 6, pp. 900–907, June 1989.
[25] Y.-T. Zhou, R. Chellappa, A. Vaid, and B. K. Jenkins, "Image restoration using a neural network," *IEEE Trans. Acoust., Speech, Signal Process.*, vol. 36, no. 7, July 1988.
[26] C. Von der Malsburg, "Pattern recognition by labeled graph matching," *Neural Networks*, vol. 1, no. 2, pp. 141–148, 1988.
[27] N. M. Nasrabadi and W. Li, "Object recognition by a Hopfield neural network," *IEEE Trans. Syst., Man, Cybern.*, vol. 21, 1991.
[28] W.-C. Lin, F.-Y. Liao, C.-K. Tsao, and T. Lingutla, "A hierarchical multiple-view approach to three-dimensional object recognition," *IEEE Trans. Neural Networks*, vol. 2, pp. 84–92, Jan. 1991.
[29] Y.-T. Zhou and R. Chellappa, "Neural network algorithms for motion stereo," in *Proc. IEEE Int. Joint Conf. Neural Networks*, vol. 2, June 1989, pp. 251–258.

Article 6.13

Image Restoration Using a Neural Network

YI-TONG ZHOU, STUDENT MEMBER, IEEE, RAMA CHELLAPPA, SENIOR MEMBER, IEEE, ASEEM VAID, AND B. KEITH JENKINS, MEMBER, IEEE

Abstract—A new approach for restoration of gray level images degraded by a known shift-invariant blur function and additive noise is presented using a neural computational network. A neural network model is employed to represent a possibly nonstationary image whose gray level function is the simple sum of the neuron state variables. The restoration procedure consists of two stages: estimation of the parameters of the neural network model and reconstruction of images. During the first stage, the parameters are estimated by comparing the energy function of the network to a constrained error function. The nonlinear restoration method is then carried out iteratively in the second stage by using a dynamic algorithm to minimize the energy function of the network. Owing to the model's fault-tolerant nature and computation capability, a high-quality image is obtained using this approach. A practical algorithm with reduced computational complexity is also presented. Several computer simulation examples involving synthetic and real images are given to illustrate the usefulness of our method. The choice of the boundary values to reduce the ringing effect is discussed, and comparisons to other restoration methods such as the SVD pseudoinverse filter, minimum mean-square error (MMSE) filter, and modified MMSE filter using the Gaussian Markov random field model are given. Finally, a procedure for learning the blur parameters from prototypes of original and degraded images is outlined.

I. INTRODUCTION

RESTORATION of a high-quality image from a degraded recording is an important problem in early vision processing. Restoration techniques are applied to remove 1) system degradations such as blur due to optical system aberrations, atmospheric turbulence, motion, and diffraction; and 2) statistical degradations due to noise. Over the last 20 years, various methods such as the inverse filter [1], Wiener filter [1], Kalman filter [2], SVD pseudoinverse [1], [3], and many other model-based approaches have been proposed for image restorations. One of the major drawbacks of most of the image restoration algorithms is the computational complexity, so much so that many simplifying assumptions such as wide sense stationarity (WSS), availability of second-order image statistics have been made to obtain computationally feasible algorithms. The inverse filter method works only for extremely high signal-to-noise ratio images. The Wiener filter is usually implemented only after the wide sense stationary assumption has been made for images. Furthermore, knowledge of the power spectrum or correlation

matrix of the undegraded image is required. Often times, additional assumptions regarding boundary conditions are made so that fast orthogonal transforms can be used. The Kalman filter approach can be applied to nonstationary image, but is computationally very intensive. Similar statements can be made for the SVD pseudoinverse filter method. Approaches based on noncausal models such as the noncausal autoregressive or Gauss Markov random field models [4], [5] also make assumptions such as WSS and periodic boundary conditions. It is desirable to develop a restoration algorithm that does not make WSS assumptions and can be implemented in a reasonable time. An artificial neural network system that can perform extremely rapid computations seems to be very attractive for image restoration in particular and image processing and pattern recognition [6] in general.

In this paper, we use a neural network model containing redundant neurons to restore gray level images degraded by a known shift-invariant blur function and noise. It is based on the method described in [7]–[9] using a simple sum number representation [10]. The image gray levels are represented by the simple sum of the neuron state variables which take binary values of 1 or 0. The observed image is degraded by a shift-invariant function and noise. The restoration procedure consists of two stages: estimation of the parameters of the neural network model and reconstruction of images. During the first stage, the parameters are estimated by comparing the energy function of the neural network to the constrained error function. The nonlinear restoration algorithm is then implemented using a dynamic iterative algorithm to minimize the energy function of the neural network. Owing to the model's fault-tolerant nature and computation capability, a high-quality image is obtained using this approach. In order to reduce computational complexity, a practical algorithm, which has equivalent results to the original one suggested above, is developed under the assumption that the neurons are sequentially visited. We illustrate the usefulness of this approach by using both synthetic and real images degraded by a known shift-invariant blur function with or without noise. We also discuss the problem of choosing boundary values and introduce two methods to reduce the ringing effect. Comparisons to other restoration methods such as the SVD pseudoinverse filter, the minimum mean-square error (MMSE) filter, and the modified MMSE filter using a Gaussian Markov random field model are given using real images. The advantages of the method developed in this paper are: 1) WSS assumption is not required

Manuscript received February 22, 1988. This work was supported in part by AFOSR Contract F-49620-87-C-0007 and AFOSR Grant 86-0196.

The authors are with the Signal and Image Processing Institute, Department of Electrical Engineering—Systems, University of Southern California, Los Angeles, CA 90089.

IEEE Log Number 8821366.

Reprinted from *IEEE Trans. Acoust., Speech, Signal Processing*, vol. 36, no. 7, pp. 1141–1151, July 1988.

for the images, 2) it can be implemented rapidly, and 3) it is fault tolerant.

In the above, the interconnection strengths (also called weights) of the neural network for image restoration are known from the parameters of the image degradation model and the smoothing constraints. We also consider learning of the parameters for the image degradation model and formulate it as a problem of computing the parameters from samples of the original and degraded images. This is implemented as a secondary neural network. A different scheme is used to represent multilevel activities for the parameters; some of its properties are complementary to those of the simple sum scheme. The learning procedure is accomplished by running a greedy algorithm. Some results of learning the blur parameters are presented using synthetic and real image examples.

The organization of this paper is as follows. A network model containing redundant neurons for image representation and the image degradation model is given in Section II. A technique for parameter estimation is presented in Section III. Image generation using a dynamic algorithm is described in Section IV. A practical algorithm with reduced computational complexity is presented in Section V. Computer simulation results using synthetic and real degraded images are given in Section VI. Choice of the boundary values is discussed in Section VII. Comparisons to other methods are given in Section VIII. A procedure for learning the blur parameters from prototypes of original and degraded images is outlined in Section IX, and conclusions and remarks are included in Section X.

II. A Neural Network for Image Representation

We use a neural network containing redundant neurons for representing the image gray levels. The model consists of $L^2 \times M$ mutually interconnected neurons where L is the size of image and M is the maximum value of the gray level function. Let $V = \{ v_{i,k}$ where $1 \le i \le L^2, 1 \le k \le M \}$ be a binary state set of the neural network with $v_{i,k}$ (1 for firing and 0 for resting) denoting the state of the (i, k)th neuron. Let $T_{i,k;j,l}$ denote the strength (possibly negative) of the interconnection between neuron (i, k) and neuron (j, l). We require symmetry:

$$T_{i,k;j,l} = T_{j,l;i,k} \quad \text{for } 1 \le i, j \le L^2 \text{ and}$$

$$1 \le l, k \le M.$$

We also allow for neurons to have self-feedback, i.e., $T_{i,k;i,k} \neq 0$. In this model, each neuron (i, k) randomly and asynchronously receives inputs $\Sigma T_{i,k;j,l} v_{j,l}$ from all neurons and a bias input $I_{i,k}$:

$$u_{i,k} = \sum_{j}^{L^2} \sum_{l}^{M} T_{i,k;j,l} v_{j,l} + I_{i,k}. \tag{1}$$

Each $u_{i,k}$ is fed back to corresponding neurons after thresholding:

$$v_{i,k} = g(u_{i,k}) \tag{2}$$

where $g(x)$ is a nonlinear function whose form can be taken as

$$g(x) = \begin{cases} 1 & \text{if } x \ge 0 \\ 0 & \text{if } x < 0. \end{cases} \tag{3}$$

In this model, the state of each neuron is updated by using the latest information about other neurons.

The image is described by a finite set of gray level functions $\{ x(i, j)$ where $1 \le i, j \le L \}$ with $x(i, j)$ (positive integer number) denoting the gray level of the pixel (i, j). The image gray level function can be represented by a simple sum of the neuron state variables as

$$x(i, j) = \sum_{k=1}^{M} v_{m,k} \tag{4}$$

where $m = (i - 1) \times L + j$. Here the gray level functions have degenerate representations. Use of this redundant number representation scheme yields advantages such as fault tolerance and faster convergence to the solution [10].

By using the lexicographic notation, the image degradation model can be written as

$$Y = HX + N \tag{5}$$

where H is the "blur matrix" corresponding to a blur function, N is the signal independent white noise, and X and Y are the original and degraded images, respectively. Furthermore, H and N can be represented as

$$H = \begin{bmatrix} h_{1,1} & h_{1,2} & \cdots & h_{1,L^2} \\ h_{2,1} & h_{2,2} & \cdots & h_{2,L^2} \\ \vdots & \vdots & \cdots & \vdots \\ h_{L^2,1} & h_{L^2,2} & \cdots & h_{L^2,L^2} \end{bmatrix} \tag{6}$$

and

$$N = \begin{bmatrix} N_1 \\ N_2 \\ \vdots \\ N_L \end{bmatrix} = \begin{bmatrix} n_1 \\ n_2 \\ \vdots \\ n_{L^2} \end{bmatrix},$$

$$N_i = \begin{bmatrix} n(i, 1) \\ n(i, 2) \\ \vdots \\ n(i, L) \end{bmatrix} = \begin{bmatrix} n_{(i-1) \times L + 1} \\ n_{(i-1) \times L + 2} \\ \vdots \\ n_{i \times L} \end{bmatrix} \tag{7}$$

respectively. Vectors X and Y have similar representations. Equation (5) is similar to the simultaneous equations solution of [10], but differs in that it includes a noise term.

The shift-invariant blur function can be written as a convolution over a small window, for instance, it takes

451

the form

$$h(k, l) = \begin{cases} \frac{1}{2} & \text{if } k = 0, l = 0 \\ \frac{1}{16} & \text{if } |k|, |l| \le 1, (k, l) \ne (0, 0); \end{cases}$$

(8)

accordingly, the "blur matrix" H will be a block Toeplitz or block circulant matrix (if the image has periodic boundaries). The block circulant matrix corresponding to (8) can be written as

$$H = \begin{bmatrix} H_0 & H_1 & 0 & \cdots & 0 & H_1 \\ H_1 & H_0 & H_1 & \cdots & 0 & 0 \\ \vdots & \vdots & \vdots & \cdots & \vdots & \vdots \\ H_1 & 0 & 0 & \cdots & H_1 & H_0 \end{bmatrix}$$

(9)

where

$$H_0 = \begin{bmatrix} \frac{1}{2} & \frac{1}{16} & 0 & \cdots & 0 & \frac{1}{16} \\ \frac{1}{16} & \frac{1}{2} & \frac{1}{16} & \cdots & 0 & 0 \\ \vdots & \vdots & \vdots & \cdots & \vdots & \vdots \\ \frac{1}{16} & 0 & 0 & \cdots & \frac{1}{16} & \frac{1}{2} \end{bmatrix},$$

$$H_1 = \begin{bmatrix} \frac{1}{16} & \frac{1}{16} & 0 & \cdots & 0 & \frac{1}{16} \\ \frac{1}{16} & \frac{1}{16} & \frac{1}{16} & \cdots & 0 & 0 \\ \vdots & \vdots & \vdots & \cdots & \vdots & \vdots \\ \frac{1}{16} & 0 & 0 & \cdots & \frac{1}{16} & \frac{1}{16} \end{bmatrix}$$

(10)

and $\mathbf{0}$ is null matrix whose elements are all zeros.

III. ESTIMATION OF MODEL PARAMETERS

The neural model parameters, the interconnection strengths, and bias inputs can be determined in terms of the energy function of the neural network. As defined in [7], the energy function of the neural network can be written as

$$E = -\frac{1}{2} \sum_{i=1}^{L^2} \sum_{j=1}^{L^2} \sum_{k=1}^{M} \sum_{l=1}^{M} T_{i,k;j,l} v_{i,k} v_{j,l} - \sum_{i=1}^{L^2} \sum_{k=1}^{M} I_{i,k} v_{i,k}.$$

(11)

In order to use the spontaneous energy-minimization process of the neural network, we reformulate the restoration problem as one of minimizing an error function with constraints defined as

$$E = \frac{1}{2} \| Y - H\hat{X} \|^2 + \frac{1}{2} \lambda \| D\hat{X} \|^2$$

(12)

where $\| Z \|$ is the L_2 norm of Z and λ is a constant. Such a constrained error function is widely used in the image restoration problems [1] and is also similar to the regu-

larization techniques used in early vision problems [11]. The first term in (12) is to seek an $\hat{X}$ such that $H\hat{X}$ approximates Y in a least squares sense. Meanwhile, the second term is a smoothness constraint on the solution $\hat{X}$. The constant λ determines their relative importance to achieve both noise suppression and ringing reduction.

In general, if H is a low-pass distortion, then D is a high-pass filter. A common choice of D is a second-order differential operator which can be approximated as a local window operator in the 2-D discrete case. For instance, if D is a Laplacian operator

$$\nabla = \frac{\partial^2}{\partial i^2} + \frac{\partial^2}{\partial j^2}$$

(13)

it can be approximated as a window operator

$$\frac{1}{6} \begin{bmatrix} 1 & 4 & 1 \\ 4 & -20 & 4 \\ 1 & 4 & 1 \end{bmatrix}.$$

(14)

Then D will be a block Toeplitz matrix similar to (9).

Expanding (12) and then replacing x_i by (4), we have

$$\begin{aligned} E &= \frac{1}{2} \sum_{p=1}^{L^2} \left(y_p - \sum_{i=1}^{L^2} h_{p,i} x_i \right)^2 + \frac{1}{2} \lambda \sum_{p=1}^{L^2} \left(\sum_{i=1}^{L^2} d_{p,i} x_i \right)^2 \\ &= \frac{1}{2} \sum_{i=1}^{L^2} \sum_{j=1}^{L^2} \sum_{k=1}^{M} \sum_{l=1}^{M} \sum_{p=1}^{L^2} h_{p,i} h_{p,j} v_{i,k} v_{j,l} \\ &\quad + \frac{1}{2} \lambda \sum_{i=1}^{L^2} \sum_{j=1}^{L^2} \sum_{k=1}^{M} \sum_{l=1}^{M} \sum_{p=1}^{L^2} d_{p,i} d_{p,j} v_{i,k} v_{j,l} \\ &\quad - \sum_{i=1}^{L^2} \sum_{k=1}^{M} \sum_{p=1}^{L^2} y_p h_{p,i} v_{i,k} + \frac{1}{2} \sum_{p=1}^{L^2} y_p^2. \end{aligned}$$

(15)

By comparing the terms in (15) to the corresponding terms in (11) and ignoring the constant term $\frac{1}{2} \Sigma_{p=1}^{L^2} y_p^2$, we can determine the interconnection strengths and bias inputs as

$$T_{i,k;j,l} = -\sum_{p=1}^{L^2} h_{p,i} h_{p,j} - \lambda \sum_{p=1}^{L^2} d_{p,i} d_{p,j}$$

(16)

and

$$I_{i,k} = \sum_{p=1}^{L^2} y_p h_{p,i}$$

(17)

where $h_{i,j}$ and $d_{i,j}$ are the elements of the matrices H and D, respectively. Two interesting aspects of (16) and (17) should be pointed out: 1) the interconnection strengths are independent of subscripts k and l and the bias inputs are independent of subscript k, and 2) the self-connection $T_{i,k;i,k}$ is not equal to zero which requires self-feedback for neurons.

From (16), one can see that the interconnection strengths are determined by the shift-invariant blur function, differential operator, and constant λ. Hence, $T_{i,k;j,l}$ can be computed without error provided the blur function

452

is known. However, the bias inputs are functions of the observed degraded image. If the image is degraded by a shift-invariant blur function only, then $I_{i,k}$ can be estimated perfectly. Otherwise, $I_{i,k}$ is affected by noise. The reasoning behind this statement is as follows. By replacing y_p by $\sum_{i=1}^{L^2} h_{p,i} x_i + n_p$, we have

$$
\begin{aligned}
I_{i,k} &= \sum_{p=1}^{L^2} \left(\sum_{i=1}^{L^2} h_{p,i} x_i + n_p \right) h_{p,i} \\
&= \sum_{p=1}^{L^2} \sum_{i=1}^{L^2} h_{p,i} x_i h_p + \sum_{p=1}^{L^2} n_p h_{p,i}.
\end{aligned}
\tag{18}
$$

The second term in (18) represents the effects of noise. If the signal-to-noise ratio (SNR), defined by

$$
\text{SNR} = 10 \log_{10} \frac{\sigma_s^2}{\sigma_n^2}
\tag{19}
$$

where σ_s^2 and σ_n^2 are variances of signal and noise, respectively, is low, then we have to choose a large λ to suppress effects due to noise. It seems that in the absence of noise, the parameters can be estimated perfectly, ensuring exact recovery of the image as error function E tends to zero. However, the problem is not so simple because the restoration performance depends on both the parameters and the blur function when a mean-square error or least square error such as (12) is used. A discussion about the effect of blur function is given in Section X.

IV. Restoration

Restoration is carried out by neuron evaluation and an image construction procedure. Once the parameters $T_{i,k;j,l}$ and $I_{i,k}$ are obtained using (16) and (17), each neuron can randomly and asynchronously evaluate its state and readjust accordingly using (1) and (2). When one quasi-minimum energy point is reached, the image can be constructed using (4).

However, this neural network has self-feedback, i.e., $T_{i,k;i,k} \neq 0$. As a result, the energy function E does not always decrease monotonically with a transition. This is explained below. Define the state change $\Delta v_{i,k}$ of neuron (i, k) and energy change ΔE as

$$
\Delta v_{i,k} = v_{i,k}^{\text{new}} - v_{i,k}^{\text{old}} \quad \text{and} \quad \Delta E = E^{\text{new}} - E^{\text{old}}.
$$

Consider the energy function

$$
E = -\frac{1}{2} \sum_{i=1}^{L^2} \sum_{j=1}^{L^2} \sum_{k=1}^{M} \sum_{l=1}^{M} T_{i,k;j,l} v_{i,k} v_{j,l} - \sum_{i=1}^{L^2} \sum_{k=1}^{M} I_{i,k} v_{i,k}.
\tag{20}
$$

Then the change ΔE due to a change $\Delta v_{i,k}$ is given by

$$
\begin{aligned}
\Delta E = &- \left(\sum_{j=1}^{L^2} \sum_{l=1}^{M} T_{i,k;j,l} v_{j,l} + I_{i,k} \right) \Delta v_{i,k} \\
&- \frac{1}{2} T_{i,k;i,k} (\Delta v_{i,k})^2
\end{aligned}
\tag{21}
$$

which is not always negative. For instance, if

$$
v_{i,k}^{\text{old}} = 0, \quad u_{i,k} = \sum_{j=1}^{L^2} \sum_{l=1}^{M} T_{i,k;j,l} v_{j,l} + I_{i,k} > 0
$$

and the threshold function is as in (3), then $v_{i,k}^{\text{new}} = 1$ and $\Delta v_{i,k} > 0$. Thus, the first term in (21) is negative. But

$$
T_{i,k;i,k} = - \sum_{p=1}^{L^2} h_{p,i}^2 - \lambda \sum_{p=1}^{L^2} d_{p,i}^2 < 0
$$

with $\lambda > 0$, leading to

$$
-\frac{1}{2} T_{i,k;i,k} (\Delta v_{i,k})^2 > 0.
$$

When the first term is less than the second term in (21), then $\Delta E > 0$ (we have observed this in our experiment), which means E is not a Lyapunov function. Consequently, the convergence of the network is not guaranteed [12].

Thus, depending on whether convergence to a local minimum or a global minimum is desired, we can design a deterministic or stochastic decision rule. The deterministic rule is to take a new state $v_{i,k}^{\text{new}}$ of neuron (i, k) if the energy change ΔE due to state change $\Delta v_{i,k}$ is less than zero. If ΔE due to state change is > 0, no state change is affected. One can also design a stochastic rule similar to the one used in stimulated annealing techniques [13], [14]. The details of this stochastic scheme are given as follows.

Define a Boltzmann distribution by

$$
\frac{p_{\text{new}}}{p_{\text{old}}} = e^{-\Delta E / T}
$$

where p_{new} and p_{old} are the probabilities of the new and old global state, respectively, ΔE is the energy change, and T is the parameter which acts like temperature. A new state $v_{i,k}^{\text{new}}$ is taken if

$$
\frac{p_{\text{new}}}{p_{\text{old}}} > 1 \quad \text{or if} \quad \frac{p_{\text{new}}}{p_{\text{old}}} \leq 1 \text{ but } \frac{p_{\text{new}}}{p_{\text{old}}} > \xi
$$

where ξ is a random number uniformly distributed in the interval $[0, 1]$.

The restoration algorithm is summarized as below.
Algorithm 1:
1) Set the initial state of the neurons.
2) Update the state of all neurons randomly and asynchronously according to the decision rule.
3) Check the energy function; if energy does not change, go to step 4); otherwise, go back to step 2).
4) Construct an image using (4).

V. A Practical Algorithm

The algorithm described above is difficult to simulate on a conventional computer owing to high computational complexity, even for images of reasonable size. For instance, if we have an $L \times L$ image with M gray levels, then $L^2 M$ neurons and $\frac{1}{2} L^4 M^2$ interconnections are required and $L^4 M^2$ additions and multiplications are needed at each iteration. Therefore, the space and time complexities are $O(L^4 M^2)$ and $O(L^4 M^2 K)$, respectively, where K, typically 10–100, is the number of iterations. Usually, L and M are 256–1024 and 256, respectively. However, simplification is possible if the neurons are sequentially updated.

In order to simplify the algorithm, we begin by reconsidering (1) and (2) of the neural network. As noted earlier, the interconnection strengths given in (16) are independent of subscripts k and l and the bias inputs given in (17) are independent of subscript k; the M neurons used to represent the same image gray level function have the same interconnection strengths and bias inputs. Hence, one set of interconnection strengths and one bias input are sufficient for every gray level function, i.e., the dimensions of the interconnection matrix T and bias input matrix I can be reduced by a factor of M^2. From (1), all inputs received by a neuron, say the (i, k)th neuron, can be written as

$$u_{i,k} = \sum_{j}^{L^2} T_{i,\cdot;j,\cdot} \left(\sum_{l}^{M} v_{j,l} \right) + I_{i,\cdot}$$

$$= \sum_{j}^{L^2} T_{i,\cdot;j,\cdot} x_j + I_{i,\cdot} \qquad (22)$$

where we have used (4) and x_j is the gray level function of the jth image pixel. The symbol "$\cdot$" in the subscripts means that the $T_{i,\cdot;j,\cdot}$ and $I_{i,\cdot}$ are independent of k. Equation (22) suggests that we can use a multivalue number to replace the simple sum number. Since the interconnection strengths are determined by the blur function, the differential operator, and the constant λ as shown in (16), it is easy to see that if the blur function is local, then most interconnection strengths are zeros and the neurons are locally connected. Therefore, most elements of the interconnection matrix T are zeros. If the blur function is shift invariant taking the form in (8), then the interconnection matrix is block Toeplitz so that only a few elements need to be stored. Based on the value of inputs $u_{i,k}$, the state of the (i, k)th neuron is updated by applying a decision rule. The state change of the (i, k)th neuron in turn causes the gray level function x_i to change:

$$x_i^{\text{new}} = \begin{cases} x_i^{\text{old}} & \text{if } \Delta v_{i,k} = 0 \\ x_i^{\text{old}} + 1 & \text{if } \Delta v_{i,k} = 1 \\ x_i^{\text{old}} - 1 & \text{if } \Delta v_{i,k} = -1 \end{cases} \qquad (23)$$

where $\Delta v_{i,k} = v_{i,k}^{\text{new}} - v_{i,k}^{\text{old}}$ is the state change of the (i, k)th neuron. The superscripts "new" and "old" are for after and before updating, respectively. We use x_i to represent the gray level value as well as the output of M neurons representing x_i. Assuming that the neurons of the network are sequentially visited, it is straightforward to show that the updating procedure can be reformulated as

$$u_{i,k} = \sum_{j}^{L^2} T_{i,\cdot;j,\cdot} x_j + I_{i,\cdot} \qquad (24)$$

$$\Delta v_{i,k} = g(u_{i,k}) = \begin{cases} \Delta v_{i,k} = 0 & \text{if } u_{i,k} = 0 \\ \Delta v_{i,k} = 1 & \text{if } u_{i,k} > 0 \\ \Delta v_{i,k} = -1 & \text{if } u_{i,k} < 0 \end{cases} \qquad (25)$$

$$x_i^{\text{new}} = \begin{cases} x_i^{\text{old}} + \Delta v_{i,k} & \text{if } \Delta E < 0 \\ x_i^{\text{old}} & \text{if } \Delta E \geq 0. \end{cases} \qquad (26)$$

Note that the stochastic decision rule can also be used in (26). In order to limit the gray level function to the range 0–255 after each updating step, we have to check the value of the gray level function x_i^{new}. Equations (24), (25), and (26) give a much simpler algorithm. This algorithm is summarized below.

Algorithm 2:

1) Take the degraded image as the initial value.

2) Sequentially visit all numbers (image pixels). For each number, use (24), (25), and (26) to update it repeatedly until there is no further change, i.e., if $\Delta v_{i,k} = 0$ or energy change $\Delta E \geq 0$; then move to the next one.

3) Check the energy function; if energy does not change anymore, a restored image is obtained; otherwise, go back to step 2) for another iteration.

The calculations of the inputs $u_{i,k}$ of the (i, k)th neuron and the energy change ΔE can be simplified furthermore. When we update the same image gray level function repeatedly, the input received by the current neuron (i, k) can be computed by making use of the previous result

$$u_{i,k} = u_{i,k-1} + \Delta v_{i,k} T_{i,\cdot;i,\cdot} \qquad (27)$$

where $u_{i,k-1}$ is the inputs received by the $(i, k-1)$th neuron. The energy change ΔE due to the state change of the (i, k)th neuron can be calculated as

$$\Delta E = -u_{i,k} \Delta v_{i,k} - \tfrac{1}{2} T_{i,\cdot;i,\cdot} (\Delta v_{i,k})^2. \qquad (28)$$

If the blur function is shift invariant, all these simplifications reduce the space and time complexities significantly from $O(L^4 M^2)$ and $O(L^4 M^2 K)$ to $O(L^2)$ and $O(M L^2 K)$, respectively. Since every gray level function needs only a few updating steps after the first iteration, the computation at each iteration is $O(L^2)$. The resulting algorithm can be easily simulated on minicomputers for images as large as 512 × 512.

VI. COMPUTER SIMULATIONS

The practical algorithm described in the previous section was applied to synthetic and real images on a Sun-3/160 Workstation. In all cases, only the deterministic decision rule was used. The results are summarized in Figs. 1 and 2.

Fig. 1 shows the results for a synthetic image. The original image shown in Fig. 1(a) is of size 32 × 32 with three gray levels. The image was degraded by convolving with a 3 × 3 blur function as in (8) using circulant boundary conditions; 22 dB white Gaussian noise was added after convolution. A perfect image was obtained after six

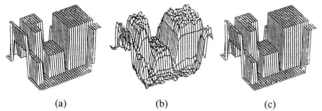

Fig. 1. Restoration of noisy blurred synthetic image. (a) Original image.
(b) Degraded image. (c) Result after six iterations.

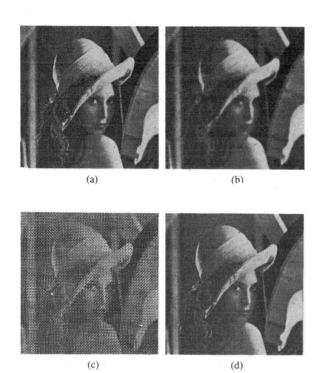

Fig. 2. Restoration of noisy blurred real image. (a) Original girl image.
(b) Image degraded by 5 × 5 uniform blur and quantization noise. (c)
The restored image using inverse filter. (d) The restored image using our
approach.

iterations without preprocessing. We set the initial state of all neurons to equal 1, i.e., firing, and chose λ = 0 due to the well conditioning of the blur function.

Fig. 2(a) shows the original girl image. The original image is of size 256 × 256 with 256 gray levels. The variance of the original image is 2797.141. It was degraded by a 5 × 5 uniform blur function. A small amount of quantization noise was introduced by quantizing the convolution results to 8 bits. The noisy blurred image is shown in Fig. 2(b). For comparison purpose, Fig. 2(c) shows the output of an inverse filter [15], completely overridden by the amplified noise and the ringing effects due to the ill-conditioned blur matrix H. Since the blur matrix H corresponding to the 5 × 5 uniform blur function is not singular, the pseudoinverse filter [15] and the inverse filter have the same output. The restored image by using our approach is shown in Fig. 2(d). In order to avoid the ringing effects due to the boundary conditions, we took 4 pixel wide boundaries, i.e., the first and last four rows and columns, from the original image and updated the interior region (248 × 248) of the image only. The noisy

blurred image was used as an initial condition for accelerating the convergence. The constant λ was set to zero because of small noise and good boundary values. The restored image in Fig. 2(d) was obtained after 213 iterations. The square error (i.e., energy function) defined in (12) is 0.02543 and the square error between the original and the restored image is 66.5027.

VII. CHOOSING BOUNDARY VALUES

As mentioned in [16], choosing boundary values is a common problem for techniques ranging from deterministic inverse filter algorithms to stochastic Kalman filters. In these algorithms, boundary values determine the entire solution when the blur is uniform [17]. The same problem occurs in the neural network approach. Since the 5 × 5 uniform blur function is ill conditioned, improper boundary values may cause ringing which may affect the restored image completely. For example, appending zeros to the image as boundary values introduces a sharp edge at the image border and triggers ringing in the restored image even if the image has zero mean. Another procedure is to assume a periodic boundary. When the left (top) and right (bottom) borders of the image are different, a sharp edge is formed and ringing results even though the degraded image has been formed by blurring with periodic boundary conditions. The drawbacks of these two assumptions for boundary values were reported in [16], [2], [18] for the 2-D Kalman filtering technique. We also tested our algorithm using these two assumptions for boundary values; the results indicate the restored images were seriously affected by ringing.

In the last section, to avoid the ringing effect, we took 4 pixel wide borders from the original image as boundary values for restoration. Since the original image is not available in practice always, an alternative to eliminate the ringing effect caused by sharp false edges is to use the blurred noisy boundaries from the degraded image. Fig. 3(a) shows the restored image using the first and last four rows and columns of the blurred noisy image in Fig. 2(b) as boundary values. In the restored image, there still exists some ringing due to the naturally occurring sharp edges in the region near the borders in the original image, but not due to boundary values. A typical cut of the restored image to illustrate ringing near the borders is shown in Fig. 4. To remove the ringing near the borders caused by naturally occurring sharp edges in the original image, we suggest the following techniques.

First, divide the image into three regions: border, subborder, and interior region as shown in Fig. 5. For the 5 × 5 uniform blur case, the border region will be 4 pixels wide due to the boundary effect of the bias input $I_{i,k}$ in (17), and the subborder region will be 4 or 8 pixels wide. In fact, the width of the subborder region will be image dependent. If the regions near the border are smooth, then the width of the subborder region will be small or even zero. If the border contains many sharp edges, the width will be large. For the real girl image, we chose the width

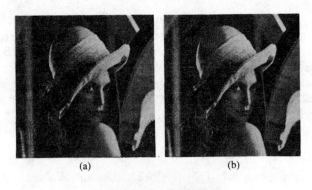
(a)   (b)

(c)

Fig. 3. Results using blurred noisy boundaries. (a) Blurred noisy boundaries. (b) Method 1. (c) Method 2.

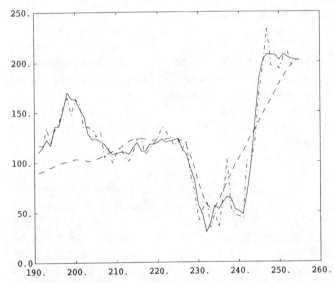

Fig. 4. One typical cut of the restored image using the blurred noisy boundaries. Solid line for original image, dashed line for blurred noisy image, and dashed and dotted line for restored image.

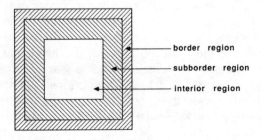

Fig. 5. Border, subborder, and interior regions of the image.

of the subborder region to be 8 pixels. We suggest using one of the following two methods.

Method 1: In the case of small noise, such as quantization error noise, the blurred image is usually smooth. Therefore, we restricted the difference between the restored and blurred image in the subborder region to a certain range to reduce the ringing effect. Mathematically, this constraint can be written as

$$\|\hat{x}_i - y_i\| \leq T \quad \text{for } i \in \text{subborder region} \quad (29)$$

where T is a threshold and $\hat{x}_i$ is the restored image gray value. Fig. 3(b) shows the result of using this method with $T = 10$.

Method 2: This method simply sets λ in (12) to zero in the interior region and nonzero in the subborder region, respectively. Fig. 3(c) shows the result of using this method with $\lambda = 0.09$. In this case, D was a Laplacian operator.

Owing to checking all restored image gray values in the subborder region, Method 1 needs more computation than Method 2. However, Method 2 is very sensitive to the parameter λ, while Method 1 is not so sensitive to the parameter λ. Experimental results show that both Methods 1 and 2 reduce the ringing effect significantly by using the suboptimal blurred boundary values.

VIII. COMPARISONS TO OTHER RESTORATION METHODS

Comparing the performance of different restoration methods needs some quality measures which are difficult to define owing to the lack of knowledge about the human visual system. The word ''optimal'' used in the restoration techniques usually refers only to a mathematical concept, and is not related to response of the human visual system. For instance, when the blur function is ill conditioned and the SNR is low, the MMSE method improves the SNR, but the resulting image is not visually good. We believe that human objective evaluation is the best ultimate judgment. Meanwhile, the mean-square error or least square error can be used as a reference.

For comparison purposes, we give the outputs of the inverse filter, SVD pseudoinverse filter, MMSE filter, and modified MMSE filter using the Gaussian Markov random field (GMRF) model [19], [5].

A. Inverse Filter and SVD Pseudoinverse Filter

An inverse filter can be used to restore an image degraded by a space-invariant blur function with high signal-to-noise ratio. When the blur function has some singular points, an SVD pseudoinverse filter is needed; however, both filters are very sensitive to noise. This is because the noise is amplified in the same way as the signal components to be restored. The inverse filter and SVD pseudoinverse filter were applied to an image degraded by the 5×5 uniform blur function and quantization noise (about 40 dB SNR). The blurred and restored images are shown in Fig. 2(b) and (c), respectively. As we mentioned before, the outputs of these filters are completely overridden by the amplified noise and ringing effects.

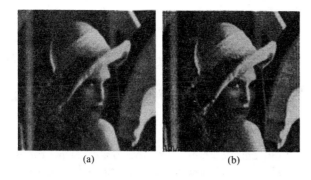

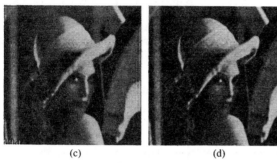

(a)   (b)

(c)   (d)

Fig. 6. Comparison to other restoration methods. (a) Image degraded by 5 × 5 uniform blur and 20 dB SNR additive white Gaussian noise. (b) The restored image using the MMSE filter. (c) The restored image using the modified MMSE filter. (d) The restored image using our approach.

B. MMSE and Modified MMSE Filters

The MMSE filter is also known as the Wiener filter (in the frequency domain). Under the assumption that the original image obeys a GMRF model, the MMSE filter (or Wiener filter) can be represented in terms of the GMRF model parameters and the blur function. In our implementation of the MMSE filter, we used a known blur function, unknown noise variance, and the GMRF model parameters estimated from the blurred noisy image by a maximum likelihood (ML) method [19]. The image shown in Fig. 6(a) was degraded by 5 × 5 uniform blur function and 20 dB SNR additive white Gaussian noise. The restored image is shown in Fig. 6(b).

The modified MMSE filter in terms of the GMRF model parameters is a linear weighted combination of a Wiener filter with a smoothing operator (such as a median filter) and a pseudoinverse filter to smooth the noise and preserve the edge of the restored image simultaneously. Details of this filter can be found in [5]. We applied the modified MMSE filter to the same image used in the MMSE filter above with the same model parameters. The smoothing operator is a 9 × 9 cross shape median filter. The resulting image is shown in Fig. 6(c).

The result of our method is also shown in Fig. 6(d). The D we used in (12) was a Laplacian operator as in (13). We chose $\lambda = 0.0625$ and used 4 pixel wide blurred noisy boundaries for restoration. The total number of iterations was 20. The improvement of mean-square error between the restored image and the original image for each method is shown in Table I. In the table, the "MMSE (o)" denotes that the parameters were estimated from the

TABLE I
MEAN-SQUARE ERROR IMPROVEMENT

Method	MMSE	MMSE (o)	Modified MMSE	Neural Network
Mean-square error	1.384 dB	2.139 dB	1.893 dB	1.682 dB

original image. The restored image using "MMSE (o)" is very similar to Fig. 6(a). As we mentioned before, the comparison of the outputs of the different restoration methods is a difficult problem. The MMSE filter visually gives the worst output which has the smallest mean-square error for the MMSE (o) case. The result of our method is smoother than that of the MMSE filter. Although the output of the modified MMSE filter is smooth in flat regions, it contains some artifacts and snake effects at the edges due to using a large sized median filter.

IX. PARAMETER LEARNING FOR LINEAR IMAGE BLUR MODEL

Apart from fine-grain parallelism, fast (and preferably automatic) adaptation of a problem-solving network to different instances of a problem is a primary motivation for using a network solution. For pattern recognition and associative memory applications, this weight training is done by distributed algorithms that optimize a distance measure between sample patterns and network responses. However, in feedback networks, general problems that involve learning higher order correlations (like the exclusive OR) or combinatorial training sets (like the Traveling Salesperson problem) are difficult to solve and may have exponential complexity. In particular, techniques for finding a compact training set do not exist.

A. Learning Model

For model-based approaches to "neural" problem solving, the weights of the main network are computed from the parameters of the model. The learning problem can then be solved by a parallel, distributed algorithm for estimating the model parameters from samples of the inputs and desired outputs. This algorithm can be implemented on a secondary network. An error function for this "learning" network must be constructed, which will now be problem-dependent.

For the linear shift-invariant blur model (5), the problem is that of estimating the parameters corresponding to the blur function in a $K \times K$ small window centered at each pixel. Rewrite (5) as

$$y(i, j) = z(i, j)^t h + n(i, j) \qquad i, j = 1, 2, \cdots, L \tag{30}$$

where t denotes the transpose operator and $z(i, j)$ and h are $K^2 \times 1$ vectors corresponding to original image samples in a $K \times K$ window centered at (i, j) and blur function, respectively.

For instance, for $K = 3$, we have

$$\mathbf{h} = \begin{bmatrix} h_1 \\ h_2 \\ h_3 \\ \vdots \\ h_9 \end{bmatrix} = \begin{bmatrix} h(-1, -1) \\ h(-1, 0) \\ h(-1, 1) \\ \vdots \\ h(1, 1) \end{bmatrix} \quad (31)$$

and

$$\mathbf{z}(i, j) = \begin{bmatrix} z(i, j)_1 \\ z(i, j)_2 \\ z(i, j)_3 \\ \vdots \\ z(i, j)_9 \end{bmatrix} = \begin{bmatrix} x(i - 1, j - 1) \\ x(i - 1, j) \\ x(i - 1, j + 1) \\ \vdots \\ x(i + 1, j + 1) \end{bmatrix}. \quad (32)$$

We can use an error function for estimation of $\mathbf{h}$, as in the restoration process, because the roles of data $\{x(i, j)\}$ and parameter $\mathbf{h}$ are simply interchanged in the learning process. Therefore, an error function is defined as

$$E = \sum_{(i,j) \in S} [y(i, j) - \mathbf{h}'\mathbf{z}(i, j)]^2 \quad (33)$$

where S is a subset of $\{(i, j), i, j = 1, 2, \cdots, L\}$ and $y(i, j)$ and $\mathbf{z}(i, j)$ are training samples taken from the degraded and original images, respectively. The network energy functions is given by

$$E = -\sum_{k=1}^{K^2} \sum_{l=1}^{K^2} w_{kl} h_k h_l - \sum_{k=1}^{K^2} \theta_k h_k \quad (34)$$

where h_k are the multilevel parameter activities and w_{kl} and θ_k are the symmetric weights and bias inputs, respectively. From (33) and (34), we get the weights and bias inputs in the familiar outer-product forms:

$$w_{kl} = -\sum_{(i,j) \in S} z(i, j)_k z(i, j)_l \quad (35)$$

$$\theta_k = 2 \sum_{(i,j) \in S} z(i, j)_k y(i, j). \quad (36)$$

A greedy, distributed neural algorithm is used for the energy minimization. This leads to a localized multilevel number representation scheme for a general network.

B. Multilevel Greedy Distributed Algorithm

For a K^2 neuron second-order network, we choose Γ discrete activities $\{f_i, i = 0, 1, \cdots, \Gamma - 1\}$ in any arbitrary range of activities (e.g., $[0, 1]$) where we shall assume without loss of generality that $f_i > f_{i-1}$ for all i. Then, between any two activities f_m and f_n for the kth neuron, we can locally and asynchronously choose the one which results in the lowest energy given the current state

of the other neurons because

$$E_{h_k = f_m} - E_{h_k = f_n} = [\theta_k - \zeta_k - (f_m + f_n)w_{k,k}]$$
$$\cdot [f_m - f_n] \quad (37)$$

where

$$\zeta_k = \sum_{i, i \neq k}^{K^2} w_{i,k} h_i$$

is the current weighted sum from the other neuron activities. Thus, we choose level m over n for $m > n$ if

$$\zeta_k > \theta_k - (f_m + f_n)w_{k,k}. \quad (38)$$

Some properties of this algorithm follow.

1) Convergence is assured as long as the number of levels is not decreasing with time (i.e., assured if coarse to fine).

2) Self-feedback terms are included as level-dependent bias input terms.

3) The method can be easily extended to higher order networks (e.g., based on cubic energies). Appropriate lower order level-dependent networks (like the extra bias input term above) must then be implemented.

The multilevel lowest energy decision can be implemented by using variations of feedforward min-finding networks (such as those summarized in [20]). The space and time complexity of these networks are, in general, $O(\Gamma)$ and $O(\log \Gamma)$, respectively. However, in the quadratic case, it is easy to verify from (38) that we need only implement the decision between all *neighboring* levels in the set $\{f_i\}$; this requires exactly Γ neurons with level-dependent inputs. The best activity in the set is then proportional to the sum of the Γ neuron outputs so that the time complexity for the multilevel decision can be made $O(1)$. This means that this algorithm is similar in implementation complexity (e.g., the number of problem-dependent global interconnects required) to the simple sum energy representation used in [10] and in this paper. Also, in the simple sum case, visiting the neurons for each pixel in sequence will result in conditional energy minimization. Otherwise, from the implementation point of view, the two methods have some properties that are complementary. For example, we have the following.

1) The simple sum method requires asynchronism in the update steps for each pixel, while the greedy method does not.

2) The level-dependent terms arise as *inputs* in the greedy method as compared to *weights* in the simple sum method.

C. Simulation Results

The greedy algorithm was used with the weights from (35) and (36) to estimate the parameters from original and blurred sample points. A 5×5 window was used with two types of blurs: uniform and Gaussian. Both real and synthetic images were used, with and without additive Gaussian noise.

TABLE II
RESULTS FOR PARAMETER LEARNING. THE NUMBER Γ OF DISCRETE ACTIVITIES IS 256 FOR ALL TESTS. *A*:
ARBITRARY CHOICE OF PIXELS FROM IMAGE. *L*: PIXELS CHOSEN FROM THRESHOLDED LAPLACIAN

Image	Noise	Blur	Samples	Methods	Iterations	MSE
Synthetic		Gaussian	68	*A*	49	0.000023
Synthetic		Uniform	100	*A*	114	0.000011
Real		Uniform	50	*A*	94	0.00353
Real		Uniform	100	*L*	85	0.00014
Real	20 dB	Uniform	100	*A*	72	0.00232
Real	20 dB	Uniform	100	*L*	83	0.00054

The estimated parameters for all types of blur matrices were numerically very close to the actual values when synthetic patterns were used. The network took longest to converge with a uniform blur function. The levels chosen for the discrete activity set $\{f_i\}$ were 128–256 equally spaced points in $[0, 1]$ with 50–100 sample points from the image. Results for various cases are summarized in Table II.

When the sample pixels were randomly chosen, the errors increased by two orders of magnitude for a real image [Fig. 2(b)] as compared to synthetic ones. This is due to the smooth nature of real images. To solve this problem, sample points were chosen so as to lie close to *edges* in the image. This was done by thresholding the Laplacian of the image. Using sample points above a certain threshold for estimation improved the errors by an order of magnitude. The results were not appreciably degraded with 20 dB noise in the samples.

X. Conclusion

This paper has introduced a new approach for the restoration of gray level images degraded by a shift-invariant blur function and additive noise. The restoration procedure consists of two steps: parameter estimation and image reconstruction. In order to reduce computational complexity, a practical algorithm (Algorithm 2), which has equivalent results to the original one (Algorithm 1), is developed under the assumption that the neurons are sequentially visited. The image is generated iteratively by updating the neurons representing the image gray levels via a simple sum scheme. As no matrices are inverted, the serious problem of ringing due to the ill-conditioned blur matrix H and noise overriding caused by inverse filter or pseudoinverse inverse filter are avoided by using suboptimal boundary conditions. For the case of a 2-D uniform blur plus small noise, the neural network-based approach gives high-quality images compared to some of the existing methods. We see from the experimental results that the error defined by (12) is small, while the error between the original image and the restored image is relatively large. This is because the neural network decreases energy according to (12) only. Another reason is that when the blur matrix is singular or ill conditioned, the mapping from *X* to *Y* is not one to one; therefore, the error measure (12) is not reliable anymore. In our experiments, when the window size of a uniform blur function is 3 × 3, the ringing effect was eliminated by using blurred noisy boundary values without any smoothing constraint. When the window size is 5 × 5, the ringing effect was reduced with the help of the smoothing constraint and suboptimal boundary conditions. We have also shown that a smaller secondary network can effectively be used for estimating the blur parameters; this provides a more efficient learning technique than Boltzman machine learning on the primary network.

References

[1] H. C. Andrews and B. R. Hunt, *Digital Image Restoration*. Englewood Cliffs, NJ: Prentice-Hall, 1977.
[2] J. W. Woods and V. K. Ingle, "Kalman filtering in two dimensions: Further results," *IEEE Trans. Acoust., Speech, Signal Processing*, vol. ASSP-29, pp. 188–197, Apr. 1981.
[3] W. K. Pratt, *Digital Image Processing*. New York: Wiley, 1978.
[4] R. Chellappa and R. L. Kashyap, "Digital image restoration using spatial interaction models," *IEEE Trans. Acoust., Speech, Signal Processing*, vol. ASSP-30, pp. 461–472, June 1982.
[5] H. Jinchi and R. Chellappa, "Restoration of blurred and noisy image using Gaussian Markov random field models," in *Proc. Conf. Inform. Sci. Syst.*, Princeton Univ., Princeton, NJ, 1986, pp. 34–39.
[6] N. H. Farhat, D. Psaltis, A. Prata, and E. Paek, "Optical implementation of the Hopfield model," *Appl. Opt.*, vol. 24, pp. 1469–1475, May 15, 1985.
[7] J. J. Hopfield and D. W. Tank, "Neural computation of decisions in optimization problems," *Biol. Cybern.*, vol. 52, pp. 141–152, 1985.
[8] J. J. Hopfield, "Neural networks and physical systems with emergent collective computational abilities," *Proc. Nat. Acad. Sci. USA*, vol. 79, pp. 2554–2558, Apr. 1982.
[9] S.-I. Amari, "Learning patterns and pattern sequences by self-organizing nets of threshold elements," *IEEE Trans. Comput.*, vol. C-21, pp. 1197–1206, Nov. 1972.
[10] M. Takeda and J. W. Goodman, "Neural networks for computation: Number representations and programming complexity," *Appl. Opt.*, vol. 25, pp. 3033–3046, Sept. 1986.
[11] T. Poggio, V. Torre, and C. Koch, "Computational vision and regularization theory," *Nature*, vol. 317, pp. 314–319, Sept. 1985.
[12] J. P. LaSalle, *The Stability and Control of Discrete Processes*. New York: Springer-Verlag, 1986.
[13] N. Metropolis *et al.*, "Equations of state calculations by fast computing machines," *J. Chem. Phys.*, vol. 21, pp. 1087–1091, 1953.
[14] S. Kirkpatrick *et al.*, "Optimization by stimulated annealing," *Science*, vol. 220, pp. 671–680, 1983.
[15] W. K. Pratt *et al.*, "Visual discrimination of stochastic texture fields," *IEEE Trans. Syst., Man, Cybern.*, vol. SMC-8, pp. 796–814, Nov. 1978.
[16] J. W. Woods, J. Biemond, and A. M. Tekalp, "Boundary value problem in image restoration," in *Proc. Int. Conf. Acoust., Speech, Signal Processing*, Tampa, FL, Mar. 1985, pp. 692–695.
[17] M. M. Sondhi, "The removal of spatially invariant degradations," *Proc. IEEE*, vol. 60, pp. 842–853, July 1972.
[18] J. Biemond, J. Rieske, and J. Gerbrand, "A fast Kalman filter for images degraded by both blur and noise," *IEEE Trans. Acoust., Speech, Signal Processing*, vol. ASSP-31, pp. 1248–1256, Oct. 1983.
[19] R. Chellappa and H. Jinchi, "A nonrecursive filter for edge preserving image restoration," in *Proc. Int. Conf. Acoust., Speech, Signal Processing*, Tampa, FL, Mar. 1985, pp. 652–655.
[20] R. P. Lippmann, "An introduction to computing with neural nets," *IEEE ASSP Mag.*, pp. 4–22, Apr. 1987.

459

Part 7
Neuro-Vision Systems:
Hardware Implementations

Biological neurons have inspired scientists to generalize the neuronal mathematical notion and the neurons' intricate connectivity within the central nervous system. This has further spurred the interest of engineers to develop new neural computing architectures and their hardware implementations.

THE emulation of biological vision and other functions of our central nervous system (CNS) presents numerous challenges that are theoretical, algorithmic, technological, and implementational in nature. Let us look briefly at the computational aspects of our CNS. There is a widespread myth that the CNS is a poorly designed computing machine that is slow, built out of slimy stuff, and uses ionic currents instead of the flow of electrons. When the Whirlwind computer was first built almost half a century ago at MIT, a movie named *Faster than Thought* was produced. The Whirlwind did less computation than a five-dollar digital wrist watch that one can buy today. Over the past five decades, since the appearance of the Whirlwind, we have added a computational power by a factor of over 10^7, yet we still cannot begin to do even the simplest computations that can be done by the brain of a house fly, let alone handle the tasks routinely performed by the human CNS.

What is it that makes biological information processing so efficient and effective compared to the information-processing approaches used by the digital technology of today? C. Mead, in article (7.1), argues that biological information-processing systems operate on completely different computational principles from those familar to engineers. For many problems, particularly those in which the input data are ill conditioned or the necessary computations must be specified in a *relative* manner, the biological solutions are many orders of magnitude more effective than those we have been able to implement using digital methods. This advantage can be attributed principally to the use of elementary physical phenomena as computational primitives, and to the representation of information by the relative values of analog signals, rather than by the absolute value of digital signals. Although the author of this article does not mention it, it is worth pointing out to readers that biological information processing is based on relative grades inherent to fuzzy logic. Perhaps this is the reason why humans may take several seconds in performing a numerical

computation (for example, 315.618 × 5.245), but require only a fraction of a second to recognize complex patterns. This article lays a basic philosophical background for the hardware aspects of neuronal computing.

Biological systems can routinely perform computations, such as pattern recognition and visual motion, that baffle our most powerful computers. J. C. Lee, B. J. Sheu, W. C. Fang, and R. Chellappa exploit the massively parallel computational power of the neural networks and present a system design of a locally connected competitive neural network for video motion detection in article (7.2). By using compact analog circuit design for the neuron and synaptic connections, the authors show that highly parallel computations on the pixel level can be achieved. A (1.5 × 2.8)-cm^2 chip in 1.2-μm CMOS technology can accommodate 64 velocity selective neural processors. Each chip can achieve 83.2 giga-connections per second. The intrinsic speed-up factor over a SUN 4/75 workstation is claimed to be around 180, a very impressive number. In addition to these two articles, (7.1) and (7.2), readers are directed to the book *Analog VLSI and Neural Systems* (1989) by Carver Mead, published by Addison-Wesley.

Hardware capable of sensing two-dimensional signals and processing them in real-time is of great importance in robotic vision systems. In article (7.3), H. Kobayashi, J. L. White, and A. A. Abidi describe an architecture using an active resistive mesh containing both positive and negative resistors to implement a Gaussian convolution for two-dimensional images. The width of the convolutions are constantly under the user's control. D. L. Standley describes a CMOS VLSI chip that determines the position and orientation of an object against a dark background in article (7.4). This chip operates in a continuous-time analog fashion, with a response time as short as 200 μs and power consumption under 50 mW.

In the next set of articles, we present some VLSI hardware for various general-purpose neural-network applications. To take full advantage of the state-of-the-art VLSI and related technologies, artificial neural networks must adapt to efficient all-digital implementations. In article (7.5), B. A. White and M. I. Elmasry describe a digital approach to neural-network hardware that is in contrast to the analog approach proposed by Mead and his colleagues in (7.1). In this article, the Neocognitron architecture is reviewed and its digital implementation is presented. This digital model of Neocognitron is used in a character-recognition problem.

A. M. Chiang and M. L. Chuang describe a charge-coupled device (CCD)-based image processor that performs 2-D filtering on a gray-level image with 20 programmable 8-bit (7×7) spatial filters in the next article, (7.6). This device is also suitable for neural networks with local connections and replicated weights. This CCD processor has also been used for the implementation of Neocognitron architecture.

In (7.1) to (7.4), we presented articles involving analog VLSI technology; in (7.5), we examined the digital VLSI technology; and in (7.6), we looked at CCD processors for the implementation of neural circuits. In the next two articles, we present optical and holographical implementations of neural-network architectures.

In article (7.7), H. J. Caulfield, J. Kinser, and S. K. Rogers present an optical implementation of a neural-network architecture. Optical implementation of neural networks is another hardware solution that seems to have a great future. Specifically, electronics can provide a neural structure with a small number of neurons ($< 10^4$) and a small number of synaptic connections ($< 10^8$), whereas in optics, one can implement a large amount of neurons ($10^3 \sim 10^6$) and a large amount of synaptic connections ($10^6 \sim 10^{12}$). However, these numbers are very small compared to those of the human brain whose number of neurons are of the order 10^{11} and number of synaptic connections are of the order of 10^{14}.

In the final article (7.8), K. Y. Hsu, H. Y. Li, and D. Psaltis describe an optical implementation of a Hopfield neural-network architecture. The basic implementation and experimental results on the recognition of stored images are also discussed by the authors in this article.

In this part, we have presented eight representative articles that deal with a variety of VLSI, CCD, and optical implementations of neural networks for different engineering applications. Hopefully, this brief presentation along with bibliographical material will provide further insights into the hardware-implementation aspects of neural networks.

Further Reading

[1] A. J. Agranat, C. F. Neugebauer, R. D. Nelson, and A. Yariv, "The CCD neural processor: A neural network integrating circuit with 65536 programmable analog synapses," *IEEE Trans. Circuits Syst.*, vol. 37, no. 8, pp. 1073–1075, 1990.

[2] D. Z. Anderson, "Optical systems that imitate human memory," *Comput. Phys.*, vol. 3, no. 2, March/April, pp. 19–25, 1989.

[3] O. Barkan, W. R. Smith, and G. Persky, "Design of coupling resistor networks for neural network hardware," *IEEE Trans. Circuits Syst.*, vol. 37, no. 6, pp. 756–765, 1990.

[4] K. A. Boahen, P. O. Pouliquen, A. G. Andreou, and R. E. Jenkins, "A heteroassociative memory using current-mode MOS analog VLSI circuits," *IEEE Trans. Circuits Syst.*, vol. 36, no. 5, pp. 747–755, 1989.

[5] B. E. Boser, E. Sackinger, J. Bromley, Y. Le Cun, and L. D. Jackel, "An analog neural network processor with programmable topology," *IEEE J. Solid-State Circuits*, vol. 26, no. 12, pp. 2017–2025, 1991.

[6] D. Casasent, "Multifunctional hybrid neural net," *Neural Networks*, vol. 5, pp. 361–370, 1992.

[7] H. P. Graf, L. D. Jackel, and W. E. Hubbard, "VLSI implementation of a neural network model," *IEEE Computer*, vol. 21, no, 3, pp. 41–49, 1988.

[8] S. Kemeny, H. Torbey, H. Meadows, R. Bredthauer, M. La Shell, and E. Fossum, "CCD focal-plane image recognization processors for lossless image compression," *IEEE J. Solid-State Circuits*, vol. 27, pp. 398–405, 1992.

[9] M. K. Habib and H. Akel, "A digital neuron-type processor and its VLSI design," *IEEE Trans. Circuits Syst.*, vol. 36, no. 5, pp. 739–745, 1989.

[10] B. Hochet, V. Peiris, S. Abdo, M. J. Declerq, "Implementation of a learning Kohonen neuron based on a new multilevel storage technique," *IEEE J. Solid-State Circuits*, vol. 26, no. 3, pp. 262–267, 1991.

[11] H. Li and C. H. Chen, "Simulating a function of visual peripheral processes with an analog VLSI network," *IEEE Micro*, vol. 11, pp. 8–15, 1991.

[12] M. A. Maher, S. P. Deweerth, M. A. Mahowald, and C. A. Mead, "Implementing neural architectures using analog VLSI circuits," *IEEE Trans. Circuits Syst.*, vol, 36, no. 5, pp. 643–653, 1989.

[13] M. A. Mahowald and C. Mead, "The silicon retina," *Sci. Amer.*, vol. 264, no. 5, May, pp. 76–82, 1991.

[14] C. Mead, *Analog VLSI and Neural Systems*. Reading MA: Addison-Wesley, 1989.

[15] A. N. Michel, J. A. Farrell, and H. Sun, "Analysis and synthesis techniques for Hopfield type synchronous discrete time neural networks with application to associative memory," *IEEE Trans. Circuits Syst.*, vol. 37, no. 11, pp. 1356–1366, 1990.

[16] A. F. Murray, D. Del Corso, and L. Taraaenko, "Pulse-stream VLSI neural networks mixing analog and digital techniques," *IEEE Trans. Neural Networks*, vol. 2, no. 2, pp. 193–204, 1991.

[17] D. Psaltis, D. Brady, X. Gu, and K. Hsu, "Optical implementation of neural computers," in *Optical Processing and Computing*, H. H. Arsenault, T. Szoplik, and B. Macukow, Eds., Boston: Academic Press, pp. 251–276, 1989.

[18] M. Sabourin and A. Mitiche, "Optical character recognition by a neural network," *Neural Networks*, vol. 5, pp. 843–852, 1992.

[19] S. W. Tsay and R. W. Newcomb, "VLSI implementation of ART1 memories," *IEEE Trans. Neural Networks*, vol. 2, no. 2, pp. 214–221, 1991.

[20] D. E. van den Bout and T. K. Miller, "A digital architecture employing stochasticism for the simulation of Hopfield neural nets," *IEEE Trans. Circuits Syst.*, vol. 36, no. 5, pp. 732–738, 1989.

Neuromorphic Electronic Systems

CARVER MEAD

Invited Paper

Biological information-processing systems operate on completely different principles from those with which most engineers are familiar. For many problems, particularly those in which the input data are ill-conditioned and the computation can be specified in a relative manner, biological solutions are many orders of magnitude more effective than those we have been able to implement using digital methods. This advantage can be attributed principally to the use of elementary physical phenomena as computational primitives, and to the representation of information by the relative values of analog signals, rather than by the absolute values of digital signals. This approach requires adaptive techniques to mitigate the effects of component differences. This kind of adaptation leads naturally to systems that learn about their environment. Large-scale adaptive analog systems are more robust to component degredation and failure than are more conventional systems, and they use far less power. For this reason, adaptive analog technology can be expected to utilize the full potential of wafer-scale silicon fabrication.

Two Technologies

Historically, the cost of computation has been directly related to the energy used in that computation. Today's electronic wristwatch does far more computation than the Eniac did when it was built. It is not the computation itself that costs—it is the energy consumed, and the system overhead required to supply that energy and to get rid of the heat: the boxes, the connectors, the circuit boards, the power supply, the fans, all of the superstructure that makes the system work. As the technology has evolved, it has always moved in the direction of lower energy per unit computation. That trend took us from vacuum tubes to transisitors, and from transistors to integrated circuits. It was the force behind the transition from n-MOS to CMOS technology that happened less than ten years ago. Today, it still is pushing us down to submicron sizes in semiconductor technology.

So it pays to look at just how much capability the nervous system has in computation. There is a myth that the nervous system is slow, is built out of slimy stuff, uses ions instead of electrons, and is therefore ineffective. When the Whirlwind computer was first built back at M.I.T., they made a movie about it, which was called "Faster than Thought." The Whirlwind did less computation than your wristwatch

Manuscript received February 1, 1990; revised March 23, 1990.
The author is with the Department of Computer Science, California Institute of Technology, Pasadena, CA 91125.
IEEE Log Number 9039181.

does. We have evolved by a factor of about 10 million in the cost of computation since the Whirlwind. Yet we still cannot begin to do the simplest computations that can be done by the brains of insects, let alone handle the tasks routinely performed by the brains of humans. So we have finally come to the point where we can see what is difficult and what is easy. Multiplying numbers to balance a bank account is not that difficult. What is difficult is processing the poorly conditioned sensory information that comes in through the lens of an eye or through the eardrum.

A typical microprocessor does about 10 million operations/s, and uses about 1 W. In round numbers, it cost us about 10^{-7} J to do one operation, the way we do it today, on a single chip. If we go off the chip to the box level, a whole computer uses about 10^{-5} J/operation. A whole computer is thus about two orders of magnitude less efficient than is a single chip.

Back in the late 1960's we analyzed what would limit the electronic device technology as we know it; those calculations have held up quite well to the present [1]. The standard integrated-circuit fabrication processes available today allow us to build transistors that have minimum dimensions of about 1 μ (10^{-6} m). By ten years from now, we will have reduced these dimensions by another factor of 10, and we will be getting close to the fundamental physical limits: if we make the devices any smaller, they will stop working. It is conceiveable that a whole new class of devices will be invented—devices that are not subject to the same limitations. But certainly the ones we have thought of up to now—including the superconducting ones—will not make our circuits more than about two orders of magnitude more dense than those we have today. The factor of 100 in density translates rather directly into a similar factor in computation efficiency. So the ultimate silicon technology that we can envision today will dissipate on the order of 10^{-9} J of energy for each operation at the single chip level, and will consume a factor of 100–1000 more energy at the box level.

We can compare these numbers to the energy requirements of computing in the brain. There are about 10^{16} synapases in the brain. A nerve pulse arrives at each synapse about ten times/s, on average. So in rough numbers, the brain accomplishes 10^{16} complex operations/s. The power dissipation of the brain is a few watts, so each operation costs only 10^6 J. The brain is a factor of 1 billion more efficient than our present digital technology, and a factor of

Reprinted from *Proc. IEEE*, vol. 78, no. 10, pp. 1629–1636, Oct. 1990.

10 million more efficient than the best digital technology that we can imagine.

From the first integrated circuit in 1959 until today, the cost of computation has improved by a factor about 1 million. We can count on an additional factor of 100 before fundamental limitations are encountered. At that point, a state-of-the-art digital system will still require 10 MW to process information at the rate that it is processed by a single human brain. The unavoidable conclusion, which I reached about ten years ago, is that we have something fundamental to learn from the brain about a new and much more effective form of computation. Even the simplest brains of the simplest animals are awesome computational instruments. They do computations we do not know how to do, in ways we do not understand.

We might think that this big disparity in the effectiveness of computation has to do with the fact that, down at the device level, the nerve membrane is actually working with single molecules. Perhaps manipulating single molecules is fundamentally more efficient than is using the continuum physics with which we build transistors. If that conjecture were true, we would have no hope that our silicon technology would ever compete with the nervous system. In fact, however, the conjecture is false. Nerve membranes use *populations* of channels, rather than individual channels, to change their conductances, in much the same way that transistors use populations of electrons rather than single electrons. It is certainly true that a single channel can exhibit much more complex behaviors than can a single electron in the active region of a transistor, but these channels are used in large populations, not in isolation.

We can compare the two technologies by asking how much energy is dissipated in charging up the gate of a transistor from a 0 to a 1. We might imagine that a transistor would compute a function that is loosely comparable to synaptic operation. In today's technology, it takes about 10^{-13} J to charge up the gate of a single minimum-size transistor. In ten years, the number will be about 10^{-15} J—within shooting range of the kind of efficiency realized by nervous systems. So the disparity between the efficiency of computation in the nervous system and that in a computer is primarily attributable not to the individual device requirements, but rather to the way the devices are used in the system.

Where Did the Energy Go?

Where did all the energy go? There is a factor of 1 million unaccounted for between what it costs to make a transistor work and what is required to do an operation the way we do it in a digital computer. There are two primary causes of energy waste in the digital systems we build today.

1) We lose a factor of about 100 because, the way we build digital hardware, the capacitance of the gate is only a very small fraction of capacitance of the node. The node is mostly wire, so we spend most of our energy charging up the wires and not the gate.

2) We use far more than one transistor to do an operation; in a typical implementation, we switch about 10 000 transistors to do one operation.

So altogether it costs 1 million times as much energy to make what we call an operation in a digital machine as it costs to operate a single transistor.

I do not believe that there is any magic in the nervous system—that there is a mysterious fluid in there that is not defined, some phenomenon that is orders of magnitude more effective than anything we can ever imagine. There is nothing that is done in the nervous system that we cannot emulate with electronics if we understand the principles of neural information processing. I have spent the last decade trying to understand enough about how it works to be able to build systems that work in a similar way; I have had modest success, as I shall describe.

So there are two big opportunities. The first factor-of-100 opportunity, which can be done with either digital or analog technology, is to make algorithms more local, so that we do not have to ship the data all over the place. That is a big win—we have built digital chips that way, and have achieved a factor of between 10 and 100 reduction in power dissipation. That still leaves the factor of 10^4, which is the difference between making a digital operation out of bunches of AND and OR gates, and using the physics of the device to do the operation.

Evolution has made a lot of inventions, as it evolved the nervous system. I think of systems as divided into three somewhat arbitrarily levels. There is at the bottom the *elementary functions*, then the *representation of information*, and at the top the *organizing principles*. All three levels must work together; all three are very different from those we use in human-engineered systems. Furthermore, the nervous system is not accompanied by a manual explaining the principles of operation. The blueprints and the early prototypes were thrown away a long time ago. Now we are stuck with an artifact, so we must try to reverse engineer it.

Let us consider the primitive operations and representations in the nervous system, and contrast them with their counterparts in a digital system. As we think back, many of us remember being confused when we were first learning about digital design. First, we decide on the information representation. There is only one kind of information, and that is the bit: It is either a 1 or a 0. We also decide the elementary operations we allow, usually AND, OR, and NOT or their equivalents. We start by confining ourselves to an incredibly impoverished world, and out of that, we try to build something that makes sense. The miracle is that we can do it! But we pay the factor of 10^4 for taking all the beautiful phyics that is built into those transistors, mashing it down into a 1 or a 0, and then painfully building it back up, with AND and OR gates to reinvent the multiply. We then string together those multiplications and additions to get more complex operations—those that are useful in a system we wish to build.

Computation Primitives

What kind of computation primitives are implemented by the device physics we have available in nervous tissue or in a silicon integrated circuit? In both cases, the state variables are analog, represented by an electrical charge. In the nervous system, there are state variables represented by chemical concentrations as well. To build a nervous system or a computer, we must be able to make specific connections. A particular output is connected to certain inputs and not to others. To achieve that kind of specificity, we must be able to isolate one signal on a single electrical node, with minimum coupling to other nodes. In both electronics and the nervous system, that isolation is achieved by building an energy barrier, so that we can put some charge on an electrical node somewhere, and it does not leak over to some other node nearby. In the nervous system, that energy barrier is built by the difference in the dielectric constant between fat and aqueous solutions. In electonics, it is built by the difference in the bandgap between silicon and silicon dioxide.

We do basic aggregation of information using the conservation of change. We can dump current onto an electrical node at any location, and it all ends up as charge on the node. Kirchhoff's law implements a distributed addition, and the capacitance of the node integrates the current into the node with respect to time.

In nervous tissue, ions are in thermal equilibrium with their surroundings, and hence their energies are Boltzmann distributed. This distribution, together with the presence of energy barriers, computes a current that is an exponential function of the barrier energy. If we modulate the barrier with an applied voltage, the current will be an exponential function of that voltage. That principle is used to create active devices (those that produce gain or amplification in signal level), both in the nervous system and in electronics. In addition to providing gain, an individual transistor computes a complex nonlinear function of its control and channel voltages. That function is not directly comparable to the functions that synapses evaluate using their presynaptic and postsynaptic potentials, but a few transistors can be connected strategically to compute remarkably competent synaptic functions.

Fig. 1(a) and (b) shows the current through a nerve membrane as a function of the voltage across the membrane. A plot of the current out of a synapse as the function of the voltage across the presynaptic membrane is shown in (c). The nervous system uses, as its basic operation, a current that increases exponentially with voltage. The channel current in a transistor as a function of the gate voltage is shown in (d). The current increases exponentially over many orders of magnitude, and then becomes limited by space charge, which reduces the dependence to the familiar quadratic. Note that this curve is hauntingly similar to others in the same figure. What class of computations can be implemented efficiently using exponential functions as primitives? Analog electronic circuits are an ideal way to explore this question.

Most important, the nervous system contains mechanisms for long-term learning and memory. All higher animals undergo permanent changes in their brains as a result of life experiences. Neurobiologists have identified at least one mechanism for these permanent changes, and are actively pursuing others. In microelectronics, we can store a certain quantity of charge on a floating polysilicon node, and that charge will be retained indefinitely. The floating node is completely surrounded by high-quality silicon dioxide—the world's most effective known insulator. We can sense the charge by making the floating node the gate of an ordinary MOS transistor. This mechanism has been used since 1971 for storing digital information in EPROM's and similar devices, but there is nothing inherently digital about the charge itself. Analog memory comes as a natural consequence of this near-perfect charge-storage mechanism. A silicon retina that does a rudimentary form of learning and long-term memory is described in the next section [2]. This system uses ultraviolet light to move charge through the oxide, onto or off the floating node. Tunneling to and from the floating node is used in commercial EEPROM devices. Several hot-electron mechanisms also have been employed to transfer charge through the oxide. The ability to learn and retain analog information for long periods is thus a natural consequence of the structures created by modern silicon processing technology.

The fact that we can build devices that implement the same basic operations as those the nervous system uses leads to the inevitable conclusion that we should be able to build entire systems based on the organizing principles used by the nervous system. I will refer to these systems generically as *neuromorphic systems*. We start by letting the device physics define our elementary operations. These functions provide a rich set of computational primitives, each a direct result of fundamental physical principles. They are not the operations out of which we are accustomed to building computers, but in many ways, they are much more interesting. They are more interesting than AND and OR. They are more interesting than multiplication and addition. But they are very different. If we try to fight them, to turn them into something with which we are familiar, we end up making a mess. So the real trick is to invent a representation that takes advantage of the inherent capabilities of the medium, such as the abilities to generate exponentials, to do integration with respect to time, and to implement a zero-cost addition using Kirchhoff's law. These are powerful primitives; using the nervous system as a guide, we will attempt to find a natural way to integrate them into an overall system-design strategy.

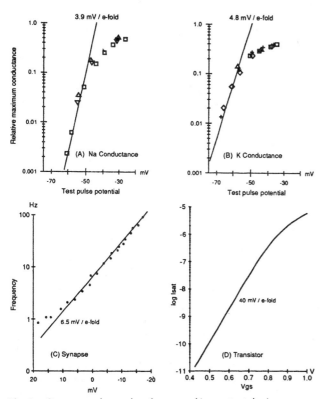

Fig. 1. Current–voltage plots for several important devices, each showing the ubiquitous exponential characteristic. Curves *A* and *B* show the behavior of populations of active ion channels in nerve membrane. Curve *C* illustrates the exponential dependence of the arrival rate of packets of the neurotransmitter at the postsynaptic membrane on the presynaptic membrane potential. Curve *D* shows the saturation current of a MOS transistor as a function of gate voltage.

I shall use two examples from the evolution of silicon retinas to illustrate a number of physical principles that can be used to implement computation primitives. These examples also serve to introduce general principles of neural computation, and to show how these principles can be applied to realize effective systems in analog electronic integrated-circuit technology.

In 1868, Ernst Mach [3] described the operation performed by the retina in the following terms.

The illumination of a retinal point will, in proportion to the difference between this illumination and the average of the illumination on neighboring points, appear brighter or darker, respectively, depending on whether the illumination of it is above or below the average. The weight of the retinal points in this average is to be thought of as rapidly decreasing with distance from the particular point considered.

For many years, biologists have assembled evidence about the detailed mechanism by which this computation is accomplished. The neural machinery that performs this first step in the chain of visual processing is located in the outer plexiform layer of the retina, just under the photoreceptors. The lateral spread of information at the outer plexiform layer is mediated by a two-dimensional network of cells coupled by resistive connections. The voltage at every point in the network represents a spatially weighted average of the photoreceptor inputs. The farther away an input is from a point in the network, the less weight it is given. The weighting function decreases in a generally exponential manner with distance.

Using this biological evidence as a guide, Mahowald [4], [5] reported a silicon model of the computation described by Mach. In the silicon retina, each node in the network is linked to its six neighbors with resistive elements to form a hexagonal array, as shown in Fig. 2. A single bias circuit

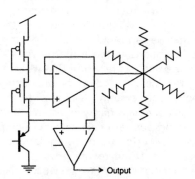

Fig. 2. Schematic of pixel from the Mahowald retina. The output is the difference between the potential of the local receptor and that of the resistive network. The network computes a weighted average over neighboring pixels.

associated with each node controls the strength of the six associated resistive connections. Each photoreceptor acts as a voltage input that drives the corresponding node of the resistive network through a conductance. A transconductance amplifier is used to implement a unidirectional conductance so the photoreceptor acts an effective voltage source. No current can be drawn from the output node of the photoreceptor because the amplifier input is connected to only the gate of a transistor.

The resistive network computes a spatially weighted average of photoreceptor inputs. The spatial scale of the weighting function is determined by the product of the lateral resistance and the conductance coupling the photoreceptors into the network. Varying the conductance of the transconductance amplifier or the strength of the resistors changes the space constant of the network, and thus changes the effective area over which signals are averaged.

From an engineering point of view, the primary function of the computation performed by a silicon retina is to provide an automatic gain control that extends the useful operating range of the system. It is essential that a sensory system be sensitive to changes in its input, no matter what the viewing conditions. The structure executing this level-normalization operation performs many other functions as well, such as computing the contrast ratio and enhancing edges in the image. Thus, the mechanisms responsible for keeping the system operating over an enormous range of image intensity have important consequences with regard to the representation of data.

The image enhancement performed by the retina was also described by Mach.

Let us call the intensity of illumunation $u = f(x, y)$. The brightness sensation v of the corresponding retinal point is given by

$$v = u - m\left(\frac{d^2u}{dx^2} + \frac{d^2u}{dy^2}\right)$$

where m is a constant. If the expression in parentheses is positive, then the sensation of brightness is reduced; in the opposite case, it is increased. Thus, v is not only influenced by u, but also its second differential quotients.

The image-enhancement property described by Mach is a result of the receptive field of the retinal computation, which shows an antagonistic center-surround response. This behavior is a result of the interaction of the photoreceptors, the resistive network, and the output amplifier. A transconductance amplifier provides a conductance through which the resistive network is driven towards the photoreceptor potential. A second amplifier senses the voltage difference across that conductance, and generates an output proportional to the difference between the photoreceptor potential and the network potential at that location. The output thus represents the difference between a center intensity and a weighted average of the intensities of surrounding points in the image.

The center-surround computation sometimes is referred to as a Laplacian filter, which has been used widely in computer vision systems. This computation, which can be approximated by a difference in Gaussians, has been used to help computers localize objects; this kind of enhancement is effective because discontinuities in intensity frequently correspond to object edges. Both of these mathematical forms express, in an analytically tractable way, the computation that occurs as a natural result of an efficient physical implementation of local normalization of the signal level.

In addition to its role in gain control and spatial filtering, the retina sharpens the time response of the system as an intrinsic part of its analog computation. Effective temporal processing requires that the time scale of the computation be matched to the time scale of external events. The temporal response of the silicon retina depends on the properties of the horizontal network. The voltage stored on the capacitance of the resistive network is the temporally as well as spatially averaged output of the photoreceptors. Because the capacitance of the horizontal network is driven by a finite conductance, its response weights its input by an amount that decreases exponentially into the past. The time constant of integration is set by the bias voltages of the wide-range amplifier and of the resistors. The time constant can be varied independently of the space constant, which depends on only the difference between these bias voltages, rather than on their absolute magnitude. The output of the retinal computation is thus the difference between the immediate local intensity and the spatially and temporally smoothed image. It therefore enhances both the first temporal and second spatial derivatives of the image.

Adaptive Retina

The Mahowald retina has given us a very realistic real-time model that shows essentially all of the perceptually interesting properties of early vision systems, including several well-known optical illusions such as Mach bands. One problem with the circuit is its sensitivity to transistor offset voltages. Under uniform illumination, the output is a random pattern reflecting the properties of individual transistors, no two of which are the same. Of course, biological retinas have precisely the same problem. No two receptors have the same sensitivity, and no two synapses have the same strength. The problem in wetware is even more acute than it is in silicon. It is also clear that biological systems use adaptive mechanisms to compensate for their lack of precision. The resulting system performance is well beyond that of our most advanced engineering marvels. Once we understand the principles of adaptation, we can incorporate them into our silicon retina.

All of our analog chips are fabricated in silicon-gate CMOS technology [6]. If no metal contact is made to the gate of a particular transistor, that gate will be completely surrounded by silicon dioxide. Any change parked on such a floating gate will remain for eons. The first floating-gate experiments of which I am aware were performed at Fairchild Research Laboratories in the mid-1960's. The first product to represent data by charges stored on a floating gate was reported in 1971 [7]. In this device, which today is called an EPROM, electrons are placed on the gate by an avalanche breakdown of the drain junction of the transistor. This injection can be done selectively, one junction at a time. Electrons can be removed by ultraviolet light incident on the chip. This so-called erase operation is performed on all devices simultaneously. In 1985, Glasser reported a circuit in which either a binary **1** or a binary **0** could be stored selectively in each location of a floating-gate digital memory [8]. The essential insight contributed by Glasser's work was that there is no fundamental asymetry to the current flowing through a thin layer of oxide. Electrons are excited into the conduction band of the oxide from both electrodes. The direction of current flow is determined primarily by the direction of the electric field in the oxide. In other words, the application of ultraviolet illumination to a capacitor with a silicon-dioxide dielectric has the effect of shunting the capacitor with a very small leakage conductance. With no illumination, the leakage con-

ductance is effectively zero. The leakage conductance present during ultraviolet illumination thus provides a mechanism for adapting the charge on a float gate.

Frank Werblin suggested that the Mahowald retina might benefit from the known feedback connections from the resistive network to the photoreceptor circuit. A pixel incorporating a simplified version of this suggestion is shown in Fig. 3 [2]. In this circuit, the output node is the

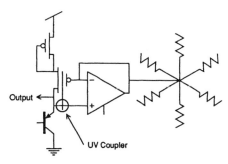

Fig. 3. Schematic of a pixel that performs a function similar to that of the Mahowald retina, but can be adapted with ultraviolet light to correct for output variations among pixels. This form of adaptation is the simplest form of learning. More sophisticated learning paradigms can be evolved directly from this structure.

emitter of the phototransistor. The current out of this node is thus set by the local incident-light intensity. The current into the output node is set by the potential on the resistive network, and hence by the weighted average of the light intensity in the neighborhood. The difference between these two currents is converted into a voltage by the effective resistance of the output node, determined primarily by the Early effect. The advantage of this circuit is that small differences between center intensity and surround intensity are translated into large output voltages, but the large dynamic range of operation is preserved. Retinas fabricated with this pixel show high gain, and operate properly over many orders of magnitude in illumination. The transconductance amplifier has a hyperbolic-tangent relationship between the output current and the input differential voltage. For proper operation, the conductance formed by this amplifier must be considerably smaller than that of the resistive network node. For that reason, when a local output node voltage is very different from the local network voltage, the amplifier saturates and supplies a fixed current to the node. The arrangement thus creates a center-surround response only slightly different from that of the Mahowald retina.

To reduce the effect of transistor offset voltages, we make use of ultraviolet adaptation to the floating gate that has been interposed between the resistive network and the pull-up transistor for the output node. The network is capacitively coupled to the floating node. The current into the output node is thus controlled by the voltage on the network, with an offset determined by the charge stored on the floating node. There is a region where the floating node overlaps the emitter of the phototransistor, shown inside the dark circle in Fig. 3. The entire chip is covered by second-level metal, except for openings over the phototransistors. The only way in which ultraviolet light can affect the floating gate is by interchanging electrons with the output node. If the output node is high, the floating gate will be charged high, thereby decreasing the current into the output node. If the output node is low, the floating gate will be charged low, thereby increasing the current into the output node. The feedback occasioned by ultraviolet illumination is thus negative, driving all output nodes toward the same potential.

ADAPTATION AND LEARNING

The adaptive retina is a simple example of a general computation paradigm. We can view the function of a particular part of the nervous system as making a prediction about the spatial and temporal porperties of the world. In the case of the retina, these predictions are the simple assertions that the image has no second spatial derivative and no first temporal derivative. If the image does not conform to these predictions, the difference between expectation and experience is sent upward to be processed at higher levels. A block diagram of the essential structure is shown in Fig. 4.

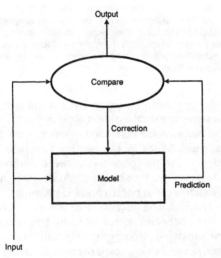

Fig. 4. Conceptual arrangement of a single level of a neural processing system. The computation consists of a prediction of the input, and a comparison of that prediction to the actual input. When the model accurately predicts the input, no information is passed to the next level, and no correction is made to the model. When the model fails to predict the input, the difference is used to correct the model. Random differences will cause a continued small ''random walk'' of the model parameters around that required for correct prediction. Systematic differences will cause the model to center itself over the true behavior of the input. Most routine events are filtered out to low level, reserving the capabilities of higher centers for genuinely interesting events.

The box labeled ''model'' is a predictor, perhaps a crude one; in the case of the retina, the model is the resistive network. We give the predictor the input over time, and it computes what is likely to happen next, just before the actual input arrives. Then, when that input materializes, it is compared to the prediction. If the two values are the same, no new information is produced; the system already knew what was about to happen. What happened is what was expected; therefore, no information is sent up to the next level of processing. But when something unexpected has occurred, there is a difference, and that difference is transferred on up to the next level to be interpreted. If we repeat this oper-

ation at each level of the nervous system, the information will be of higher quality at each subsequent level because we process only the information that could not be predicted at lower levels.

Learning in this kind of system is provided by the adaptation feedback from the comparator to the model. If the model is making predictions that are systematically different from what happens in nature, the ongoing corrections based on the individual differences will cause the model to learn what actually happens, as well as can be captured at its level of representation. It is only those events that are truly random, or that cannot be predicted from this level and therefore appear random, that will cancel out over all experience. The system parameters will undergo a local random walk, but will stay nearly centered on the average of what nature is providing as input. The retina is presented with a wide variety of scenes; it sees white edges and black edges. But every pixel in the retina sees the same intensity, averaged over time. Corrections towards this average constantly correct differences in photoreceptor sensitivity and variation in the properties of individual neurons and synapses. All other information is passed up to higher levels. Even this simple level of prediction removes a great deal of meaningless detail from the image, and provides a higher level of representation for the next level of discrimination.

That a system composed of many levels organized along the lines of Fig. 4 can compute truly awesome results is perhaps not surprising: each level is equipped with a model of the world, as represented by the information passed up from lower levels. All lower level processing may, from the point of view of a given level, be considered preprocessing. The most important property of this kind of system is that the same mechanism that adapts out errors and mismatches in its individual components also enables the system to build its own models through continued exposure to information coming in from the world. Although this particular example of the adaptive retina learns only a simple model, it illustrates a much more general principle: this kind of system is *self-organizing* in the most profound sense.

NUERAL SILICON

Over the past eight years, we have designed, fabricated, and evaluated hundreds of test chips and several dozen complete system-level designs. All these adaptive analog chips were fabricated using standard, commercially available CMOS processing, provided to us under the auspices of DARPA's MOSIS fabrication service. These designs include control systems, motor-pattern generators, retina chips that track bright spots in an image, retina chips that focus images on themselves, and retina chips that perform gain control, motion sensing, and image enhancement. We have made multiscale retinas that give several levels of resolution, stereo-vision chips that see depth, and chips that segment images. A wide variety of systems has been designed to process auditory input; most of them are based on a biologically sensible model of the cochlea. There are monaural chips that decompose sound into its component features, binaural chips that compute horizontal and vertical localization of sound sources, and Seehear chips that convert a visual image into an auditory image—one where moving objects produce sound localized in the direction of the object.

This variety of experiments gives us a feeling for how far we have progressed on the quest for the nine order of magnitude biological advantage. The retina described in the preceding section is a typical example; it contains about 10^5 devices, performs the equivalent of about 10^8 operations/s, and consumes about 10^{-3} W of power. This and other chips using the same techniques thus perform each operation at a cost of only about 10^{-11} J compared to about 10^{-7} J/operation for a digital design using the same technology, and with 10^6 J/operation for the brain. We are still five orders of magnitude away from the efficiency of the brain, but four orders of magnitude ahead of that realized with digital techniques. The real question is how well the adaptive analog approach can take advantage of future advances in silicon fabrication. My prediction is that adaptive analog techniques can utilize the potential of advanced silicon fabrication more fully than can any other approach that has been proposed. Today (1990), a typical 6 in diameter wafer contains about 10^8 devices, partitioned into several hundred chips. After fabrication, the chips are cut apart and are put into packages. Several hundred of these packages are placed on a circuit board, which forms interconnections among them.

Why not just interconnect the chips on the wafer where they started, and dispense with all the extra fuss, bother, and expense? Many attempts by many groups to make a digital wafer-scale technology have met with abysmal failure. There are two basic reasons why wafer-scale integration is very difficult. First, a typical digital chip will fail if even a single transistor or wire on the chip is defective. Second, the power dissipated by several hundred chips of circuitry is over 100 W, and getting rid of all that heat is a major packaging problem. Together, these two problems have prevented even the largest computer companies from deploying wafer-scale systems successfully. The low-power dissipation of adaptive analog systems eliminates the packaging problem; wafers can be mounted on edge, and normal air convection will adequately remove the few hundred milliwatts of heat dissipated per wafer. Due to the robustness of the neural representation, the failure of a few components per square centimeter will not materially affect the performance of the system: its adaptive nature will allow the system simply to learn to ignore these inputs because they convey no information. In one or two decades, I believe we will have 10^{10} devices on a wafer, connected as a complete adaptive analog system. We will be able to extract information from connections made around the periphery of the wafer, while processing takes place in massively parallel form over the entire surface of the wafer. Each wafer operating in this manner will be capable of approximately 10^{13} operations/s. At that time, we will still not understand nearly as much about the brain as we do about the technology.

Scaling Laws

The possibility of wafer-scale integration naturally raises the question of the relative advantage conveyed by a three-dimensional neural structure over a two-dimensional one. Both approaches have been pursued in the evolution of animal brains so the question is of great interest in biology as well. Let us take the point of view that whatever we are going to build will be a space-filling structure. If it is a sheet, it will have neurons throughout the whole plane; if it is a volume, neurons will occupy the whole volume. If we allow every wire from every neuron to be as long as the dimensions of the entire structure, we will obviously get an explosion in the size of the structure as the number of neurons increases. The brain has not done that. If we compare our brain to a rat brain, we are not noticeably less efficient in our use of wiring resources. So the brain has evolved a *mostly local* wiring strategy to keep the scaling from getting out of hand. What are the requirements of a structure that keep the fraction of its resources devoted to wire from exploding as it is made larger? If the structure did not scale, a large brain would be all wire and would have no room for the computation.

First, let us consider the two-dimensional case. For the purpose of analysis, we can imagine that the width W of each wire is independent of the wire's length L, and that the probability that a wire of length between L and $L + dL$ is dedicated to each neuron is $p(L) \, dL$. The expected area of such a wire is the $WL \, p(L) \, dL$. The entire plane, of length and width L_{max}, is covered with neurons, such that there is one neuron per area A. Although the wires from many neurons overlap, the total wire from any given neuron must fit in area A. We can integrate the areas of the wires of all lengths associated with a given neuron, assuming that the shortest wire is of unit length:

$$\int_1^{L_{max}} WL \, p(L) \, dL = A.$$

The question is then: What are the bounds on the form of $p(L)$ such that the area A required for each neuron does not grow explosively as L_{max} becomes large? We can easily see that if $p(L) = 1/L^2$, the area A grows as the logarithm of L_{max}— a quite reasonable behavior. If $p(L)$ did not decrease at least this fast with increasing L_{max}, the human brain would be much more dominated by wire than it is, compared to the brain of a rat or a bat. From this argument, I conclude that the nervous system is organized such that, on the average, the number of wires decreases no more slowly than the inverse square of the wire's length.

We can repeat the analysis for a three-dimensional neural structure of extent L_{max}, in which each neuron occupies volume V. Each wire has a cross-sectional area S, and thus has an expected volume $SL \, p(L)$. As before, the total wire associated with each neuron must fit in volume V:

$$\int_1^{L_{max}} SL \, p(L) \, dL = V.$$

So the three-dimensional structure must follow the same scaling law as its two-dimensional counterpart. If we build a space-filling structure, the third dimension allows us to contact more neurons, but it does not change the basic scaling rule. The number of wires must decrease with wire length in the same way in both two and three dimensions.

The cortex of the human brain, if it is stretched out, is about 1 m/side, and 1 mm thick. About half of that millimeter is wire (white matter), and the other half is computing machinery (gray matter). This basically two-dimensional strategy won out over the three-dimensional strategies used by more primitive animals, apparently because it could evolve more easily: new areas of cortex could arise in the natural course of evolution, and some of them would be retained in the genome if they conveyed a competitive advantage on their owners. This result gives us hope that a neural structure comprising many two-dimensional areas, such as those we can make on silicon wafers, can be made into a truly useful, massively parallel, adaptive computing system.

CONCLUSION

Biological information-processing systems operate on completely different principles from those with which engineers are familiar. For many problems, particularly those in which the input data are ill-conditioned and the computation can be specified in a relative manner, biological solutions are many orders of magnitude more effective than those we have been able to implement using digital methods. I have shown that this advantage can be attributed principally to the use of elementary physical phenomena as computational primitives, and to the representation of information by the relative values of analog signals, rather than by the absolute values of digital signals. I have argued that this approach requires adaptive techniques to correct for differences between nominally identical components, and that this adaptive capability leads naturally to systems that learn about their environment. Although the adaptive analog systems build up to the present time are rudimentary, they have demonstrated important principles as a prerequisite to undertaking projects of much larger scope. Perhaps the most intriguing result of these experiments has been the suggestion that adaptive analog systems are 100 times more efficient in their use of silicon, and they use 10 000 times less power than comparable digital systems.

It is also clear that these systems are more robust to component degradation and failure than are more conventional systems. I have also argued that the basic two-dimensional limitation of silicon technology is not a serious limitation in exploiting the potential of neuromorphic systems. For these reasons, I expect large-scale adaptive analog technology to permit the full utilization of the enormous, heretofore unrealized, potential of wafer-scale silicon fabrication.

REFERENCES

[1] B. Hoeneisen and C. A. Mead, "Fundamental limitations in microelectronics—I. MOS technology," *Solid-State Electron.*, vol. 15, pp. 819–829, 1972.
[2] C. Mead, "Adaptive retina," in *Analog VLSI Implementation of Neural Systems*, C. Mead and M. Ismail, Eds. Boston, MA: Kluwer, 1989, pp. 239–246.
[3] F. Ratliff, *Mach Bands: Quantitative Studies on Neural Networks in the Retina*. San Francisco, CA: Holden-Day, 1965, pp. 253–332.
[4] M. A. Mahowald and C. A. Mead, "A silicon model of early visual processing," *Neural Networks*, vol. 1, pp. 91–97, 1988.
[5] ——, "Silicon retina," in C. A. Mead, *Analog VLSI and Neural Systems*. Reading, MA: Addison-Wesley, 1989, pp. 257–278.
[6] C. A. Mead, *Analog VLSI and Neural Systems*. Reading, MA: Addison-Wesley, 1989.
[7] D. Frohman-Bentchkowsky, "Memory behavior in a floating-gate avalanche-injection MOS (FAMOS) structure," *Appl. Phys. Lett.*, vol. 18, pp. 332–334, Apr. 1971.
[8] L. A. Glasser, "A UV write-enabled PROM," in *Proc. 1985 Chapel Hill Conf. VLSI*, H. Fuchs, Ed. Rockville, MD: Computer Science Press, 1985, pp. 61–65.

VLSI Neuroprocessors for Video Motion Detection

Ji-Chien Lee, *Member, IEEE*, Bing J. Sheu, *Senior Member, IEEE*,
Wai-Chi Fang, *Member, IEEE*, and Rama Chellappa, *Fellow, IEEE*

Abstract—The system design of a locally connected competitive neural network for video motion detection is presented. The motion information from a sequence of image data can be determined through a two-dimensional multiprocessor array in which each processing element consists of an analog neuroprocessor. Massively parallel neurocomputing is done by compact and efficient neuroprocessors. Local data transfer between the neuroprocessors is performed by using an analog point-to-point interconnection scheme. To maintain strong signal strength over the whole system, global data communication between the host computer and neuroprocessors is carried out in a digital common bus. A mixed-signal very large scale integration (VLSI) neural chip that includes multiple neuroprocessors for fast video motion detection has been developed. Measured results of the programmable synapse, and winner-take-all circuitry are presented. Based on the measurement data, system-level analysis on a sequence of real-world images was conducted. A 1.5×2.8-cm^2 chip in a 1.2-μm CMOS technology can accommodate 64 velocity-selective neuroprocessors. Each chip can achieve 83.2 giga connections per second. The intrinsic speed-up factor over a Sun-4/75 workstation is around 180.

I. INTRODUCTION

RAPID advances in a very large scale integration (VLSI) technologies have made possible the integration of multiple-million transistors on a single chip. In 1992, the feature size for computer memory technologies is around 0.4 μm [1]. The use of VLSI circuits can greatly reduce the physical size and enhance the performance and reliability of microelectronic systems. In the microprocessor domain, continuous progress on reduced instruction set computers (RISC) enables the introduction of the Intel-i860 chip [2], the SPARC chip from Sun Microsystems, Inc. [3], and the 400-MIPS Alpha chip from Digital Equipment Corporation [4]. In the digital signal processing domain, the TMS-320C40 chip from Texas Instruments, Inc. [5] includes six communication ports to facilitate various data communication schemes. In the dedicated neural computing domain, the 11-million-transistor CNAPS chip from Adaptive Solutions, Inc. and Inova Microelectronics, Inc. [6] includes 64 digital processors for general-purpose neural network execution.

A desirable configuration for an integrated information processing system is shown in Fig. 1. A powerful multimedia data-fusion machine is equipped with several smart interface units to communicate with the analog signals in the real world. These analog signals contain information with some degree of fuzziness [7]. The image acquisition/understanding

Manuscript received July 5, 1991; revised April 23, 1992.

The authors are with the Department of Electrical Engineering (Electrophysics and Systems), Signal and Image Processing Institute, University of Southern California, Los Angeles, CA 90089–0271.

IEEE Log Number 9201749.

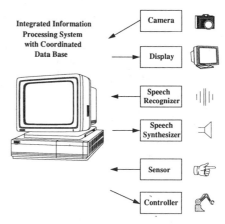

Fig. 1. An integrated information system. Information can be transferred between the system and the real world in multimedia format.

and advanced display units are used to process visual information. The speech recognizer and synthesizer units are used to process audio information [8]. The microsensor [9] and controller units are used to perform physical actions. Such an intelligent system can be used in offices, factories, and autonomous vehicles. VLSI neural chips can be effectively used in the construction of the interface units.

Various design approaches are applicable for the construction of neural chips. The analog circuit approach is quite attractive in terms of hardware size, power consumption, and speed [10]. Analog neural networks were used as sensory devices to preprocess the real-world data, as reported by Mead *et al.* [11], [12] and Abidi *et al.* [13]. In addition, many other analog VLSI neural chips have been reported [14]–[16]. One unique feature of a purely analog neural network is the limited computational precision for complex problems. To enhance the performance of analog VLSI neurocomputing, extra analog switching circuits can be used to facilitate the reconfigurability and scalability of analog neural networks [17]. The digital circuit approach offers greater flexibility, scalability, and accuracy than the analog circuit approach. By using logic and memory, a large problem can be partitioned and processed by the digital neural networks. Some general-purpose digital VLSI neural chips were reported [18]–[20].

In this paper, a mixed-signal design approach is used to exploit the massively parallel computational power of the neural network architecture for video motion detection. To solve low-level vision processing problems, multiple neurons and synapses can be clustered together to function as one pixel processing element. By using compact analog circuit design for the neuron and synapse cells, highly parallel computation on the pixel level can be achieved.

Reprinted from *IEEE Trans. on Neural Networks*, vol. 4, no. 2, pp. 178–191, March 1993.

II. System Architecture

Motion information extracted from a sequence of time-varying images plays a key role in the image understanding and automated control processes. The requirement of an enormous amount of computational power for analyzing image sequences is always a major barrier to real-world applications of most vision-processing algorithms. By using multiprocessor-based VLSI design, the parallelism embedded in low-level vision processes can be fully explored. The single instruction multiple data (SIMD) architecture is a good example [21], [22]. Two specific multiprocessor-based neural engines based on the SIMD architecture have been reported. The CNAPS machine, from Adaptive Solutions, Inc. [18], consists of an array of processing nodes (PN's). Each PN is an arithmetic processor with its own local memory. The array is sequenced by a system controller. Thus every PN executes the same instruction at a given clock period. The input data and control commands are broadcast to all PN's through the common bus. The output data of the PN's are transmitted through the data bus by the time-multiplexing scheme. A local digital data link exists between adjacent PN's to allow quick data transfer. Due to the simplicity of the broadcast scheme, no complex routing networks are required. The systolic/cellular array processors (SCAP) system, from Hughes Research Lab. in Malibu, CA [23], consists of a 16×16 processor array, a dual-port array memory, and a system controller. The mesh-connection architecture is used. The boundary columns are connected via the wrap-around scheme, and the top and bottom rows are connected to the two ports of the system memory. Data communication can be conducted in the paralleled format or in the pipelined format.

In our design, a mesh-connected two-dimensional neuro-processor array is used for high-speed video motion detection. Each processoring element can extract the velocity information for one pixel. Interprocessor communication is done by dedicated analog point-to-point interconnections. Data communication between the host computer and array processors is carried out through the digital common bus to preserve signal strength and to achieve simple network scalability. By using this efficient communication among processors, a high computational power per unit silicon area can be achieved.

III. Motion Detection Algorithm

Many features from the images such as points, lines, curves, and optical flow, can be used to estimate motion parameters. Optical flow is the apparent motion of the brightness patterns. Generally, the optical flow corresponds to the motion field [24], and provides important information about the spatial arrangement of the objects, the rate of change of this arrangement in a given scene, and also the perceiver's own movements. Optical flow can thus be used for deriving relative depth of points [25], [26], segmenting images into regions [27], and estimating the object motion in the scene [28].

According to the nature of the measured primitives, existing approaches to optical flow computing can be divided into two types: the image intensity based approach and the token based approach. The intensity based approach relies on the assumption that changes in intensity are strictly due to the motion of the object and uses the image intensity values and their spatial and temporal derivatives to compute the optical flow. By expanding the intensity function into a first-order Taylor series, Horn and Schunck [29] derived an optical flow equation using the brightness constancy assumption and spatial smoothness constraints. An iterative method for solving the resulting equation was also developed. The token based approach is to consider the motion of tokens such as edges, corners, and linear features in an image. The key advantage of the token based approach is that tokens are less sensitive to variations of the image intensity. The token based approach provides the information of the object motion and shape at edges, corners, and linear features. An interpolation procedure has to be included when dense data are required.

Recently, several researchers used neural networks to conduct optical flow computing [30], [31]. To prevent the smoothness constraint from taking effect across strong velocity gradients, a line process has been incorporated into the optical flow equation [31]. The resulting equation is nonconvex and includes the cubic and some higher terms. Instead of using an annealing algorithm which is very time consuming, a deterministic algorithm was used to obtain a near-optimal solution. Convergence of such a network was obtained within a few iteration cycles. Basically, the mixed analog/digital neural network approach is to first use Horn's optical flow equation to find a smoothest solution and then to update the line process by lowering the energy function of the network repeatedly. In the hardware implementation, the resistive network is quite susceptible to device variation effects from the silicon CMOS fabrication processes.

In order to obtain a dense flow field, the intensity based approach is preferable. However, the intensity value may be corrupted by noise appeared in natural images and partial deviatives of the intensity value are sensitive to rotation. It is difficult to detect the rotational objects in natural images based on such measurement primitives. Under the assumption that changes in intensity are strictly due to the motion of the object, Zhou et al. [32], [33] use the principal curvatures of the intensity function to compute the optical flow because they are rotation-invariant. The intensity values and their principal curvatures are estimated by using a polynomial fitting technique. Under the assumption of local rigid motion and the smoothness constraint, a self-organizing neural network [34]–[36] was developed to compute the optical flow. A deterministic decision rule was used for the updating of neuron states.

Let the velocity field consist of two components k and l. A set of $(2D_k + 1)(2D_l + 1)$ modules of neurons are used to represent the optical flow field, where D_k and D_l are the maximum values of velocity components in k and l directions, respectively. For the implementation purposes, the velocity component range is sampled using bins of size Q. As shown in Fig. 2, each module corresponds to a velocity value and contains $N_r \times N_c$ neurons if the images are of size $N_r \times N_c$. All neurons in the same module are self-connected and locally interconnected with other neurons in a neighborhood of size $\Gamma \times \Gamma$. Every pixel is represented by $(2D_k + 1)(2D_l + 1)$

mutually exclusive neurons which form a hypercolumn for velocity selection. When the neuron at the point (i, j) in the (k, l)th module is one, the actual velocities in the k and l directions at the point (i, j) are kQ and lQ, respectively.

Let $V = \{v_{i,j,k,l}, 1 \leq i \leq N_r, 1 \leq j \leq N_c, -D_k \leq k \leq D_k, -D_l \leq l \leq D_l\}$ be a binary set of the neural network with $v_{i,j,k,l}$ denoting the state of the (i, j, k, l)th neuron which is located at point (i, j) in the (k, l)th module, $T_{i,j,k,l;m,n,k,l}$ be the synaptic interconnection strength from neuron (i, j, k, l) to neuron (m, n, k, l), and $I_{i,j,k,l}$ be the bias input.

At each step, the neuron (i, j, k, l) synchronously receives signals from itself, neighboring neurons, and a bias input

$$u_{i,j,k,l} = \sum_{(m-i, n-j) \in S_0} T_{i,j,k,l;m,n,k,l} v_{m,n,k,l} + I_{i,j,k,l} \quad (1)$$

where S_0 is an index set for all neighbors in a $\Gamma \times \Gamma$ window centered at point (i, j). The $u_{i,j,k,l}$ is then processed by the winner-take-all circuitry to determine the velocity of the pixel

$$v_{i,j,k,l} = g(u_{i,j,k,l}) \quad (2)$$

where $g(x_{i,j,k,l})$ is the winner-take-all function:

$$g(x_{i,j,k,l}) = \begin{cases} 1 & \text{if } x_{i,j,k,l} = \max(x_{i,j,p,q}; -D_k \leq p \leq D_k, \\ & \quad -D_l \leq q \leq D_l). \\ 0 & \text{otherwise.} \end{cases} \quad (3)$$

The network operation will be terminated if the network converges; i.e., the energy function of the network defined by

$$E = -\frac{1}{2} \sum_{i=1}^{N_r} \sum_{j=1}^{N_c} \sum_{k=-D_k}^{D_k} \sum_{l=-D_l}^{D_l}$$
$$\cdot \left(\sum_{(m-i, n-j) \in S_0} T_{i,j,k,l;m,n,k,l} v_{i,j,k,l} v_{m,n,k,l} \right.$$
$$\left. + I_{i,j,k,l} v_{i,j,k,l} \right), \quad (4)$$

reaches a minimum.

Two important features of the network should be noted:

i) The synaptic interconnection strength between neurons on different modules are zeros because only the neurons in the same module are connected, i.e.

$$T_{i,j,k,l;m,n,p,q} = 0, \quad \text{for } (k, l) \neq (p, q),$$
$$\text{if } (i, j) \neq (m, n). \quad (5)$$

ii) A maximum evolution function is used to ensure that only one neuron which has the maximum excitation is fired and the other $(2D_k + 1)(2D_l + 1) - 1$ neurons are turned off.

As reported in [32], a smoothness constraint is used for obtaining a smooth optical flow field and a line process is employed for detecting motion discontinuities. The line process consists of vertical and horizontal lines, L^v and L^h, respectively. Each line can be in either one of the two states: 1 for being active and 0 for being idle. The error function for

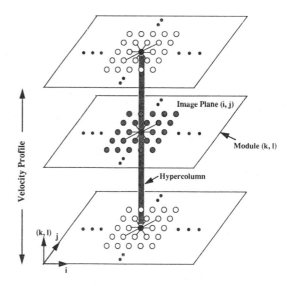

Fig. 2. A competitive neural network is used for optical flow computing. The neurons are arranged in modules according to their velocity selectivity. Indexes i and j denote the image coordinates. (k, l) denotes the velocity coordinate. Each hypercolumn represents the velocity selectivity of one image pixel.

computing the optical flow from a pair of image frames can be expressed as

$$E = \sum_{i=1}^{N_r} \sum_{j=1}^{N_c} \sum_{k=-D_k}^{D_k} \sum_{l=-D_l}^{D_l} \left[\left\{ A[k_{11}(i, j) - k_{21}(i+k, j+l)]^2 \right. \right.$$
$$+ A[k_{12}(i, j) - k_{22}(i+k, j+l)]^2$$
$$+ [g_1(i, j) - g_2(i+k, j+l)]^2 \Big\} v_{i,j,k,l}$$
$$+ \left\{ \frac{B}{2} \sum_{s \in S} \left(v_{i,j,k,l} - v_{(i,j)+s,k,l}\right)^2 \right.$$
$$+ \frac{C}{2} \left[\left(v_{i,j,k,l} - v_{i+1,j,k,l}\right)^2 \left(1 - L^h_{i,j,k,l}\right) \right.$$
$$\left. \left. \left. + \left(v_{i,j,k,l} - v_{i,j+1,k,l}\right)^2 \left(1 - L^v_{i,j,k,l}\right) \right] \right\} \right] \quad (6)$$

where $k_{11}(i, j)$ and $k_{12}(i+k, j+l)$ are the principal curvatures of the first image, $k_{21}(i, j)$ and $k_{22}(i+k, j+l)$ are the principal curvatures of the second image, $g_1(i, j)$ and $g_2(i+k, j+l)$ are the intensity values of the first and second images, respectively. Here, $S = S_0 - (0, 0)$ is an index set excluding $(0, 0)$. A, B, and C are empirical constants.

The principal curvatures are defined as [37]

$$k_1(i, j) = M + \left(M^2 - G\right)^{1/2} \quad (7)$$

and

$$k_2(i, j) = M - \left(M^2 - G\right)^{1/2} \quad (8)$$

where $k_1(i, j)$ and $k_2(i, j)$ are the principal curvatures, G and M are the Gaussian and mean curvatures given by

$$G = \frac{\partial^2 g(i, j)}{\partial i^2} \cdot \frac{\partial^2 g(i, j)}{\partial j^2} - \left[\frac{\partial^2 g(i, j)}{\partial i \partial j}\right]^2 \quad (9)$$

and

$$M = \frac{1}{2}\left[\frac{\partial^2 g(i,j)}{\partial j^2} + \frac{\partial^2 g(i,j)}{\partial j^2}\right]. \tag{10}$$

A polynomial fitting technique can be used to estimate the derivatives. The k_{11}, k_{21}, k_{12}, and k_{22} values are calculated from the images by the host computer and sent to the neuroprocessor for network evaluation.

In (6), the first term is to find velocity values such that all points of two images are matched as closely as possible in a least-squares sense. The second term, which is weighted by B, is the smoothness constraint on the solution and the third term, which is weighted by C, is a line process to weaken the smoothness constraint and to detect motion discontinuities. The constant A in the first term determines the relative importance of the intensity values and their principal curvatures to achieve the best results. The line process weakens the smoothness constraints by changing the smoothing weights, resulting in space-variant smoothing weights. For example, if all lines are on, the weights will be $B/2$. If all lines are off, the weights at the four nearest neighbors of the center point are increased by $C/2$.

By choosing the interconnection strengths and bias inputs as

$$
\begin{aligned}
T_{i,j,k,l;m,n,k,l} = &-[48B + C(4 - L^h_{i,j,k,l} - L^h_{i,j+(-1),k,l}\\
&- L^v_{i,j,k,l} - L^v_{i+(-1),j,k,l})]\delta_{i,m}\,\delta_{j,n}\\
&+ C[(1 - L^h_{i,j,k,l})\delta_{i,m}\,\delta_{j+1,n}\\
&+ \left(1 - L^h_{i,j+(-1),k,l}\right)\delta_{i,m}\,\delta_{j+(-1),n}\\
&+ (1 - L^v_{i,j,k,l})\delta_{i+1,m}\,\delta_{j,n}\\
&+ (1 - L^v_{i+(-1),j,k,l})\delta_{i+(-1),m}\,\delta_{j,n}]\\
&+ 2B\sum_{s\in S}\delta_{(i,j),(m,n)+s}
\end{aligned}
\tag{11}
$$

and

$$
\begin{aligned}
I_{i,j,k,l} = -A\{&[k_{11}(i,j) - k_{21}(i+k,j+l)]^2\\
&+ [k_{12}(i,j) - k_{22}(i+k,j+l)]^2\}\\
&- [g_1(i,j) - g_2(i+k,j+l)]^2
\end{aligned}
\tag{12}
$$

where $\delta_{a,b}$ is the Dirac delta function, the error function in (6) is mapped into the energy function of the neural network in (4). Notice that the interconnection strengths consist of constants and line process only. The bias inputs contain all the information from images. When the network reaches a stable condition, the optical flow field is determined by the neuron states. The size of a typical smoothing window is 5×5.

Since the first and second terms in (6) do not contain the line process, the updating of the line process is prior to the updating of neuron states. Let $L^{v;\text{new}}_{i,j,k,l}$ and $L^{v;\text{old}}_{i,j,k,l}$ denote the new and old states of the vertical line $L^v_{i,j,k,l}$, respectively. Let $\Psi_{i,j,k,l}$ be the potential of the vertical line $L^v_{i,j,k,l}$ given by

$$\Psi_{i,j,k,l} = \frac{C}{2}\left(v_{i,j,k,l} - v_{i+1,j,k,l}\right)^2. \tag{13}$$

Then, the new state is determined by

$$L^{v;\text{new}}_{i,j,k,l} = \begin{cases} 1 & \text{if } \Psi_{i,j,k,l} > 0\\ 0 & \text{otherwise.} \end{cases} \tag{14}$$

Whenever the states of neurons $v_{i,j,k,l}$ and $v_{i+1,j,k,l}$ are

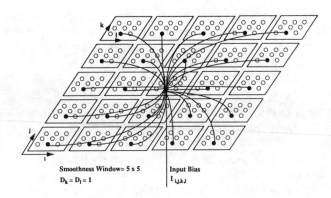

Fig. 3. An artificial neural network. Each small frame denotes a hypercolumn. The neurons in a hypercolumn are uniformly distributed on a plane. In addition to an external bias input, each neuron has a self-feedback, and receives inputs from similar directionally selective neurons at the neighboring hypercolumns.

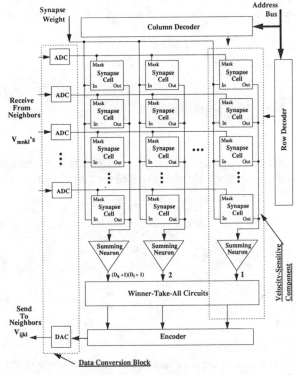

Fig. 4. Functional diagram of one neuroprocessor. It contains a velocity-sensitive component array and data conversion block. The velocity of one image pixel can be determined by one neuroprocessor.

different, the vertical line $L_{i,j,k,l}$ will be active provided that the parameter C is greater than zero. If $C = 0$, then all lines are inactive, which means that no line process exists in the network operation. The choice of C is closely related to selecting the smoothness parameter B in (6). A similar updating scheme is also used for the horizontal lines. In the prototype neural chip design, computation for the terms which are weighted by the parameter C is not included.

The state of each neuron is synchronously evaluated and updated according to (1) and (2). The initial states of the neurons are set as

$$
v_{i,j,k,l} = \begin{cases} 1 & \text{if } I_{i,j,k,l} = \max(I_{i,j,p,q;} - D_k \le p \le D_k,\\ & \quad -D_l \le q \le D_l)\\ 0 & \text{otherwise} \end{cases}
\tag{15}
$$

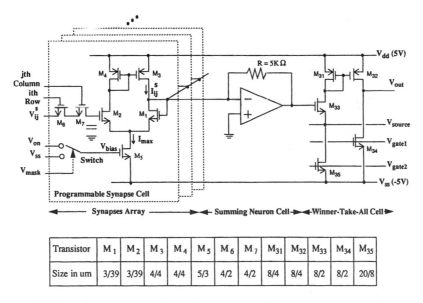

Transistor	M_1	M_2	M_3	M_4	M_5	M_6	M_7	M_{31}	M_{32}	M_{33}	M_{34}	M_{35}
Size in um	3/39	3/39	4/4	4/4	5/3	4/2	4/2	8/4	8/4	8/2	8/2	20/8

Fig. 5.   Circuit schematic of the velocity-sensitive component. It contains a programmable synapse array, a summing neuron, and a winner-take-all cell.

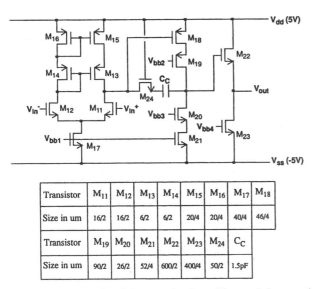

Transistor	M_{11}	M_{12}	M_{13}	M_{14}	M_{15}	M_{16}	M_{17}	M_{18}
Size in um	16/2	16/2	6/2	6/2	20/4	20/4	40/4	46/4
Transistor	M_{19}	M_{20}	M_{21}	M_{22}	M_{23}	M_{24}	C_C	
Size in um	90/2	26/2	52/4	600/2	400/4	50/2	1.5pF	

Fig. 6.   Circuit schematic of the operational amplifier used for summing neuron.

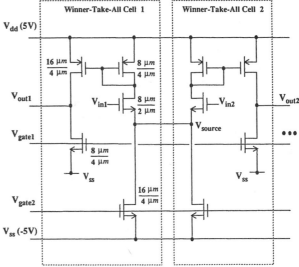

Fig. 7.   Two winner-take-all cells are connected as a differential operational amplifier.

where $I_{i,j,k,l}$ is the bias input. The initial conditions are completely determined by the bias inputs. If there are two maximal bias inputs at point (i, j), then only the neuron corresponding to the smaller velocity is initially set to 1 and the other one is set to 0. This is consistent with the minimal mapping theory [38]. In the updating scheme, the minimal mapping theory is also used to handle the case of two neurons having the same largest inputs.

IV. THE NEURAL-BASED NEUROPROCESSOR DESIGN

A. VLSI Architecture

To implement the electronic neural network processor, a VLSI architecture has been developed which maps the three-dimensional neural network configuration onto a two-dimensional plane. As shown in Fig. 3, each small frame represents one velocity-selective hypercolumn which

contains $(2D_k + 1)(2D_l + l)$ velocity-sensitive components. Each hypercolumn is locally interconnected with the $\Gamma \times \Gamma - 1$ neighboring hypercolumns. The hypercolumn is designed as a neuroprocessor within which the velocity selectivity of an image pixel can be conducted. Mixed analog/digital design technologies are utilized for the neuroprocessor design to achieve compact and programmable synapses and neurons for massively paralleled neural computation [39].

To simplify the two-dimensional interconnection design for computation of optical flow, the analog point-to-point interconnection for local communication and the digital common bus for global communication are used. Since velocity information of one pixel is affected by its neighbors, each neuroprocessor receives information from the neighboring neuroprocessors during the network operation. Data communication between these locally interconnected neuroprocessors is one key factor on the overall system performance. There are three different methods to accomplish the local data communication with trade-offs on the operation speed and silicon area.

The first method is to use the digital bit-parallel point-to-point interconnection. The $(2D_k + 1)(2D_l + 1)$-bit $v_{i,j,p,q}$'s, where $-D_k \leq p \leq D_k, -D_l \leq q \leq D_l$, are transmitted using the word-wide point-to-point interconnections. The data transfer speed is very fast. However, the total number of interconnection lines for each neuroprocessor is as large as $(2D_k + 1)(2D_l + 1)(\Gamma \times \Gamma)$. The silicon area for the interconnection routing is large. The required large pin count becomes a major constraint for hardware implementation.

The second method is to use the digital bit-serial point-to-point interconnection. The $v_{i,j,p,q}$'s are sent in a bit-serial order by using a time-multiplexing technique. The total number of interconnection lines is reduced by a factor of $(2D_k + 1)(2D_l + 1)$. However, the time required for data transfer increases with the same factor [40]. In addition, the required hardware overhead for time-multiplexing includes a one-bit latch for each synapse cell, the multiplexing control signals, and the associated decoding circuitry.

The third method is to use the analog bit-parallel point-to-point interconnection. The $v_{i,j,p,q}$'s are converted to an analog value, and then sent to the neighboring neuroprocessors. The $v_{i,j,p,q}$'s are converted back into digital values at the receiving sites. The required hardware overhead includes the digital/analog converter or analog/digital converter at the two ends of interconnection wire. Both the analog interconnection method and the multiplexing digital interconnection method are suitable in the neural network processor design. For applications with large D_k and D_l values, the multiplexing digital interconnection method is preferred.

A functional diagram of the velocity-selective neuroprocessor is shown in Fig. 4. It includes a velocity-sensitive component array, and a data conversion block. The array has $(2D_k + 1)(2D_l + 1)$ velocity-sensitive components which are laterally connected through the winner-take-all circuit. The velocity of the neuroprocessor is determined by competition which is performed by the winner-take-all circuit. Only one velocity component which has the maximum excitation will be the winner to represent the velocity of that pixel. The data conversion block is used for the analog point-to-point interprocessor interconnection.

As shown in Fig. 5, the velocity-sensitive component is constructed with one synapse array, one summing neuron, and one winner-take-all cell. The synapse array contains $\Gamma \times \Gamma + 1$ programmable synapses. The synapse weights $T_{i,j,k,l;m,n,k,l}$ are stored as charge packets on capacitors and must be refreshed periodically [17], [41]. The binary outputs $v_{m,n,p,q}$ from the neighboring neuroprocessors are routed to the corresponding mask ports of the synapse cells to conduct the network operation. A summing neuron functions as a parallel current-mode adder. Each summing neuron with its associated programmable synapse array perform a complete inner-product computation. The binary outputs of the winner-take-all circuit represent the velocity status.

The synapse weights and bias inputs are calculated by the host computer or a digital coprocessor and stored in a digital static-RAM. The 8-bit digital/analog converter transforms the

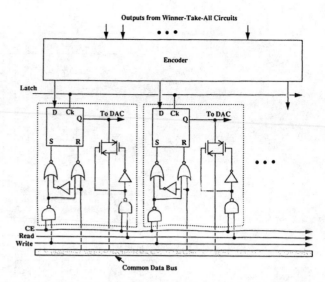

Fig. 8. The data latch is used to store the final results of the image pixels. The contents of latch can be read/write by host computer through the common data bus.

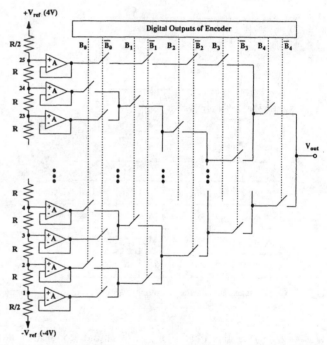

Fig. 9. A voltage-scaling digital-to-analog converter. The unity-gain followers are used to buffer the resistor string from loading.

digital representation of the synapse weights into analog values for charging the weight-storage capacitances of the synapse matrix. A two-port static-RAM and differential amplifier-based synapse design allows network retrieving and learning processes to occur concurrently.

B. Detailed Circuit Design

In Fig. 5, a transconductance amplifier consisting of transistors M_1-M_5 produces synapse output current $I_{i,j}^s$ according to mask voltage V_{mask} and weight voltage $V_{i,j}^s$. The bias voltage V_{bias} controls the dynamic range of synapse cells by adjusting the bias current in the transconductance amplifiers. When the V_{mask} is a logic 1, the V_{bias} is connected to V_{on}

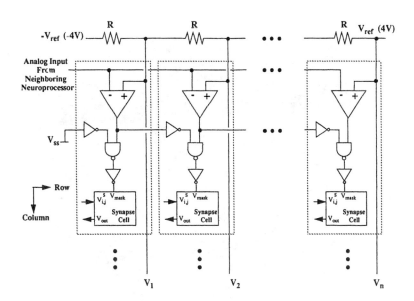

Fig. 10. A parallel and distributed analog-to-digital converter. One common reference voltage and one scaling resistor-chain are used. The comparators and associated digital decoding circuits are distributed to each synapse cell.

to provide the amplifier with a specific bias current I^{max}. When the V_{mask} is at logic 0, the V_{bias} is connected to the negative power supply so that no synapse output current is produced. Therefore, the V_{mask} performs a masking operation on the synapse weight voltage $V_{i,j}^s$. The mask voltage of each synapse cell is directly related to the value of the $v_{m,n,k,l}$ which represents the velocity information of the neighboring pixels. The maximum synapse conductance is decided by device sizes of the differential pair and the bias current I^{max}, while the minimum synapse conductance is determined by the resolution of the weight value on the MOS capacitance. The synapse output currents are summed up and converted to the voltage format at the summing neuron. This compact synapse circuit performs a two-quadrant multiplication. The polarity of the synapse output depends on the value of weight voltage $V_{i,j}^s$. An 8-bit resolution can be easily supported in the DRAM-style synapse cell. The required refreshing time is around 100 ms. Recently, detailed design of four quadrant Gilbert multiplier for synapse cells were reported [17], [42]. Multiple differential pairs and current-mirror circuits make the wide-range operation possible. If more than 8-bit resolution is required for the synapse function, large-geometry MOS transistors, and shorter refreshing time will be needed. In the EEPROM-style synapse cell [43], [44], at least a 6-bit resolution can be obtained.

The summing neuron functions as a current-to-voltage converter and is realized by using a two-stage operational amplifier and a feedback resistor. Circuit schematic diagram of the two-stage operational amplifier is shown in Fig. 6. Transistors M_{13} and M_{14} form an improved cascode stage to increase the voltage gain and M_{24} operates as a resistor for proper frequency compensation. The amplifier voltage gain of 100 dB can be achieved.

The outputs of the winner-take-all circuit are binary values. Only one winner cell with the maximum input voltage will have the logic-1 output value. The other cells will have the logic-0 output value. The winner-take-all circuitry functions

as a multiple-input parallel comparator. Fig. 7 shows the circuit schematic diagram of two winner-take-all cells. The high-resolution and expandability of this winner-take-all circuit makes it suitable for many competitive learning neural networks [45]–[48]. Winner-take-all circuits with transistors biased in the subthreshold region were reported in the literature. Such low-power winner-take-all circuits [49], [50] have slower speed response and are suitable for special applications if the power consumption is crucial.

After the winner-take-all circuit, the $(2D_k + 1)(2D_l + 1)$ binary outputs represent the velocity information of one image pixel. Combinational logic gates are used to encode these $(2D_k + 1)(2D_l + 1)$ binary signals and to store the result into a data latch. Fig. 8 shows digital circuits of the data latch with the associated read/write control logic. The final velocity result is read by the host computer from the data latches through the digital common bus.

Fig. 9 shows a voltage-scaling digital-to-analog converter [51] which is used to convert the encoded binary code to the analog value and send it to the neighboring neuroprocessors. The voltage-scaling converter uses a series of resistors connected between V_{ref} and $-V_{\mathrm{ref}}$ to provide intermediate voltage values. For an N-bit converter, the resistor string would have $2^N + 1$ resistor segments. In Fig. 9, a total of 26 resistor segments are used. The resistor is implemented in the P-well diffusion layer of the MOS fabrication process. The sheet resistance of the P-well layer is around 2 KΩ/$\square$ from the MOSIS 1.2-μm CMOS P-well process [52], [53]. Unity-gain followers are used to buffer the resistor string from conductive loading. Each tap is connected to a switching tree whose switches are controlled by the bits of the digital word. Each switch is implemented by a CMOS transmission gate.

When the analog velocity information from the neighboring neuroprocessors is received, a total of $\Gamma \times \Gamma - 1$ analog-to-digital converters are used to convert these analog values back to the binary values with $(2D_k + 1)(2D_l + 1)$ bits.

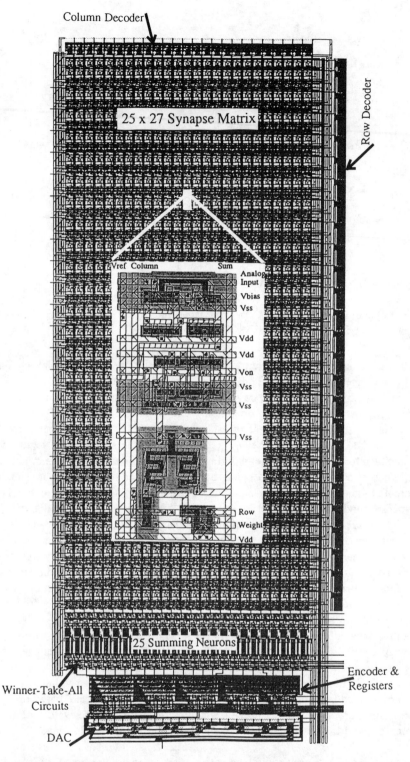

Fig. 11. The layout of one velocity-selective neuroprocessor. It contains 25 neurons, 25 × 27 synapse matrix and is able to detect the moving object with 25 different velocities. It occupies $2482 \times 5636\lambda^2$ silicon area. The synapse cell is shown in the insert.

Only one of these bits is logic-1 and the others are logic-0. To achieve high-speed performance and a compact silicon area, a parallel and distributed analog-to-digital converter has been designed. One voltage scaling resistor-chain is used. As shown in Fig. 10, the comparators and the associated digital decoding circuitries are distributed into the synapse cells. The comparators included in the same velocity-sensitive component use the same reference voltage provided by the resistor-chain. The distributed decoding circuitries make sure that only one of $(2D_k + 1)(2D_l + 1)$ binary outputs is logic 1 and the others are inhibited to logic 0.

V. EXPERIMENTAL RESULTS

In the prototype neuroprocessor chip design, $D_k = D_l = 2$ and a size of 5×5 smoothing window are used. The

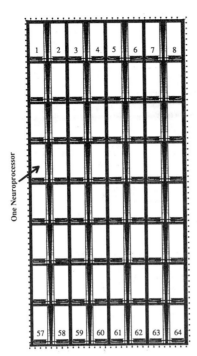

Fig. 12. The layout of VLSI neural chip. It consists of 64 neuroprocessors and occupies 1.5×2.8 cm^2 silicon area.

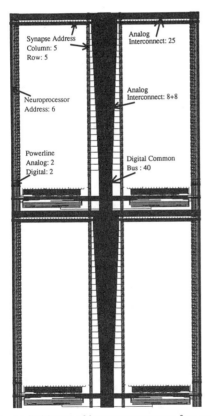

Fig. 13. The detailed layout of interconnects among four neuroprocessors.

TABLE I
PERFORMANCE COMPARISON OF TWO INTERCONNECT METHODS

Performance	Design Approach	
	Using Bit-Parallel Analog Interconnect Method	Using Bit-Parallel Digital Interconnect Method
Chip Size (cm^2)	1.5×2.8	1.5×2.8
Number of Neuro-processors	64	12
Interconnection Routing Area (%)	23	85
Pin count	178	3,250
Network Ineration Time (ns)	522	250
Speed Performance (connection/second)	8.03×10^{10}	2.08×10^{10}

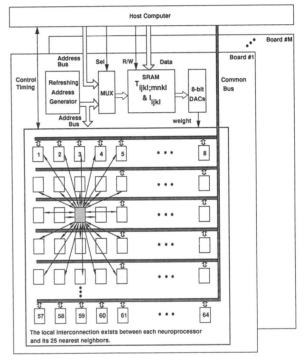

Fig. 14. The system diagram for high-speed motion detection using multiple VLSI neural chips. Each VLSI neural chips can accommodate 64 neuroprocessors with 1.2 μm CMOS technology and 1.5×2.8 cm^2 chip area. Each neuroprocessor in the VLSI neural chip can communicate with its neighbors through the analog point-to-point interconnections. The standard IC parts such as SRAM and 8-bit DAC are used for refreshing of synapse weights.

physical layout of the velocity-selective neuroprocessor for one image pixel using the scalable CMOS design rules is shown in Fig. 11. It occupies an area of $2,482 \times 5,636\lambda^2$ and contains 25 neurons, 25×27 synapse cells, and is able to detect the moving object with 25 different velocities. In the hardware implementation, two rows of synapses are used to increase the resolution of synapse weights coming from the bias inputs and also to enhance the fault tolerance of the network. With an advanced 1.2-μm CMOS technology, 64 neuroprocessors can be accommodated into one VLSI neural chip of 1.5×2.8 cm^2 in size. The chip layout is shown in Fig. 12. It requires a 178-pin PGA package. The analog interprocessor data communication requires 128 pins. The detailed layout of interconnects among four neuroprocessors is shown in Fig. 13. The interconnection routing area occupies 23% of the chip area. A performance comparison against the digital bit-parallel point-to-point interconnection method is listed in Table I. In the digital bit-parallel method, each data link requires 25 lines. Only 12 neuroprocessors can be

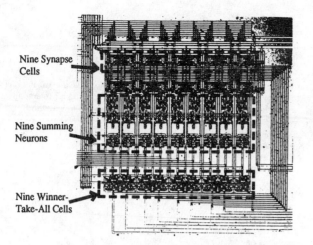

Fig. 15. The layout of the test module which includes key circuit blocks.

Nine Synapse Cells

Nine Summing Neurons

Nine Winner-Take-All Cells

TABLE II
CIRCUIT RESPONSE TIME

	Measured Results
Analog-to-Digital Conversion	73 ns
Synapse Multiplication	120 ns
Neuron thresholding	20 ns
Winner-Take-All Operation	38 ns
Encoder & Data Latch	8 ns
Digital-to-Analog Conversion	84 ns+, 263 ns*
Total	343 ns+, 522 ns*

Note: $T_{ox} = 202$ Å in MOSIS 1.2-um CMOS technology.
+ with an output loading of 5 pF
* with an output loading of 50 pF

TABLE III
PERFORMANCE OF VLSI MOTION ESTIMATION SYSTEM

Synapse Weight Loading Time (into SRAM)	2,080 us (50 ns per write)
Network Execution Time (for 36 iterations)	18.792 us
Neuron State Read Out Time	409.6 us (50 ns per read)
Total Processing Time	2.509 ms

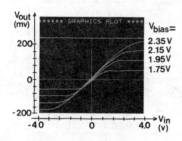

Fig. 16. Measured results of programmable synapse characteristics. A big bias voltage can provide a large dynamic range.

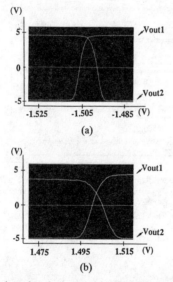

(a)

(b)

Fig. 17. Measured results of winner-take-all circuits. (a) one input as indicated in the x-axis changes linearly from −1.53 V to −1.48 V, the second input is connected to 1.5 V, and the other seven inputs are kept at −1.525 V. (b) one input as indicated in the x-axis changes linearly from 1.47 V to 1.52 V, the second input is connected to 1.5 V, and the other seven inputs are kept at 1.475 V.

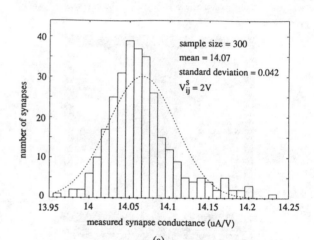

(a)

sample size = 300
mean = 14.07
standard deviation = 0.042
$V_{ij}^{s} = 2V$

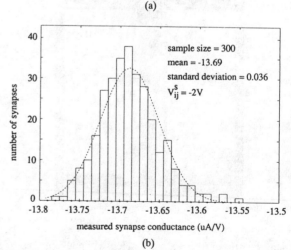

(b)

sample size = 300
mean = -13.69
standard deviation = 0.036
$V_{ij}^{s} = -2V$

Fig. 18. The statistical distribution of measured synapse output conductances. (a) The synapse conductances can be described by a Gaussian distribution with a mean value of 14.07 μA/V and a standard deviation of 0.042 μA/V at weight voltage $V_{i,j}^{s} = 2$ V. (b) The synapse conductances can be described by a Gaussian distribution with a mean value of −13.69 μA/V and a standard deviation of 0.036 μA/V at weight voltage $V_{i,j}^{s} = -2$ V.

accommodated in the same chip area and 85% of chip area will be used for the interconnection routing purpose.

With 128 VLSI neural chips and many supporting standard IC parts such as SRAM's and 8-bit DAC's for storing the weight information and dynamically refreshing of the synapse cells, computation of optical flow from an image with 64×128

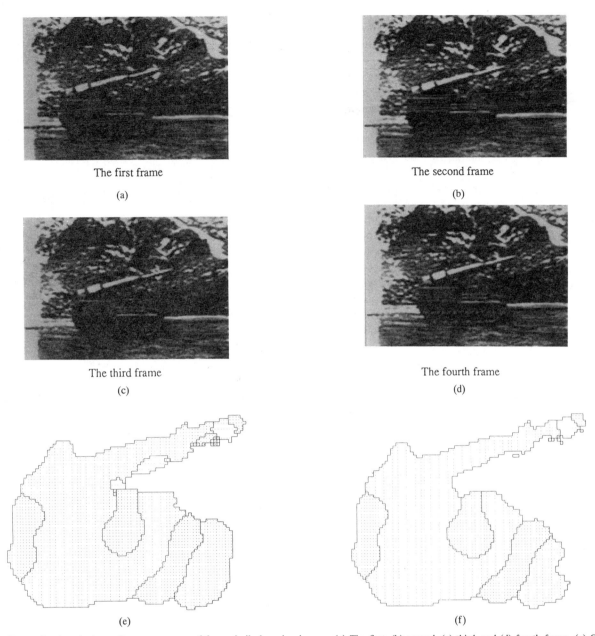

Fig. 19. System-level analysis result on a sequence of four missile launcher images. (a) The first, (b) second, (c) third, and (d) fourth frame. (e) Obtained result using the parameters $A = 4$, $B = 850$, $C = 0$, $D_k = 7$, $D_l = 1$, and after 36 iterations. The effects of process variation on synapse weights are included through the Gaussian function. (f) Obtained result using same parameters as those in 19(e) except that the effects of process variation on synapse weights are not included.

pixels and 256 gray levels can be performed at a rate of 30 frames per second. The proposed system set-up for fast motion detection using multiple VLSI neural chips is shown in Fig. 14.

To obtain the electrical properties of the basic circuit blocks, a test structure containing key circuit components was fabricated with a 2-μm CMOS process from Orbit Semiconductor, Inc. through the MOSIS Service of USC/Information Sciences Institute at Marina del Ray, CA and tested. The picture of the test structure is shown in Fig. 15. Measured transfer curves of the synapse cell with different bias voltages are shown in Fig. 16. The dynamic range of the synapse cell is controlled by the bias voltage. Experimental data on the winner-take-all circuit are shown in Fig. 17. The circuit consists of nine

winner-take-all cells. Two experiments were conducted. In Fig. 17(a), one input sweeps linearly from -1.53 to -1.48 V, the second input is connected to -1.5 V, and the other seven inputs are kept at -1.525 V. In Fig. 17(b), one input sweeps linearly from 1.47 to 1.52 V, the second input is connected to 1.5 V, and the other seven inputs are kept at 1.475 V. The winner-take-all function is successfully implemented with a resolution of 15 mV.

The processing time for one network iteration is around 522 ns. Each iteration cycle includes synapse multiplication, neuron summing, winner-take-all operation, data storage on latches, digital/analog and analog/digital conversion, and interprocessor data transfer. SPICE [54] simulation results on various circuit blocks are listed in Table II. The large response time of the synapse multiplication is due to the significant capacitance loading on the current-summation line. For the digital/analog conversion simulations, 5 pF and 50 pF effective capacitance loadings are estimated for interchip data communication and off-chip data communication, respectively. The major delay will come from the off-chip interprocessor data communication. The total computing power of 8.32×10^{10} connections per second can be achieved by using one VLSI neural chip containing 1600 neurons, 41 600 synapses cells, and operated at a master clock rate of 2 MHz. Based on the results of Table II the speed comparison of a system using 128 VLSI neural chips with a Sun-4/75 SPARC workstation is listed in Table III. The speedup factor is very large.

System-level analysis has been conducted to illustrate the performance of the motion detection chip. The mismatch effect of analog synapse components has been included. Fig. 18 shows the statistical distribution of measured synapse output conductances. A total of 300 synapses was measured. In Fig. 18(a), the synapse conductances can be described by a Gaussian distribution with a mean value of 14.07 μA/V and a standard deviation of 0.042 μA/V at weight voltage $V_{i,j}^s = 2$ V. In Fig. 18(b), the synapse conductances can be described by a Gaussian distribution with a mean value of -13.69 μA/V and a standard deviation of 0.036 μA/V at weight voltage $V_{i,j}^s = -2$ V. During computer analysis, the effects of process variation on synapse weights are included through the use of Gaussian function.

A set of four successive image frames directly produced by a Sony XC-77 CCD camera was used as the input data. Fig. 19(a)-(d) shows four successive image frames of a mobile missile launcher moving from left to right against a stationary background. The size of each image frame is 130×160 pixels. The maximum displacement of the mobile missile launcher between the time-varying image frame is 7 pixels. To estimate the principle curvatures and intensity values, a 5×5 window and a third order polynomial was used for all frames. By setting $A = 4, B = 850, C = 0, D_k = 7$, and $D_l = 1$, the velocity field was obtained after 36 iterations. The parameter A is set to 4, because four successive image frames are used. The parameter B is chosen by using trial-and-error method. The parameter C is set to 0 in the prototype design to simplify the neuron-state updating scheme of the network. Fig. 19(e) shows the final result of using synapse weights obtained by including the effects of process variation. Comparing with the result in Fig. 19(f), which the effects of process variation are not included, the motion information of the moving object still can be successful detected.

VI. Conclusion

A mixed-signal two-dimensional mesh-connected architecture for high-speed motion detection has been presented. A compact and efficient VLSI neuroprocessor which including 25 neurons and 25×27 synapse cells is able to estimate the motion of each pixel with 25 different velocities. Multiple neuroprocessors can be connected as a two-dimensional mesh to fully exploit the massively parallel computational power of neural networks. In this architecture, the local computation is processed in analog neuroprocessor and the local data communication is performed in parallel. Each 1.5×2.8-cm^2 VLSI neural chip from a 1.2-μm CMOS technology can operate at a rate of 83.2 giga connections per second.

Acknowledgment

Discussions with Dr. Y.-T. Zhou on artificial neural networks, and Dr. B. W. Lee on neural circuit design are highly appreciated. J. Choi provided detailed information on winner-take-all circuit design. The authors would like to thank the reviewers for valuable comments and suggestions.

References

[1] H. Koike et al., "A 30 ns 64 Mb DRAM with built-in self-test and repair function," in Tech. Dig. IEEE Int. Solid-State Circ. Conf., San Francisco, CA, Feb. 1992, pp. 150–151.
[2] L. Kohn and N. Margulis, "Introducing the Intel i860 64-bit microprocessor," IEEE Micro Mag., vol. 9, no. 4, pp. 15–30, Aug. 1989.
[3] SPARC Architecture Manual, Sun Microsystems, Inc., Mountain View, CA, 1987.
[4] D. Dobberpuhl et al., "A 200MHz 64b dual-issue CMOS microprocessor," in Tech. Dig. IEEE Int. Solid-State Circ. Conf., San Francisco, CA, Feb. 1992, pp. 106–107.
[5] Second-Generation TMS 320 User's Guide, Texas Instruments, Inc., Dallas, TX, 1990.
[6] M. Griffin, G. Tahara, K. Knorpp, R. Pinkham, and B. Riley, "An 11-million transistor neural network execution engine," in Tech. Dig. IEEE Int. Solid-State Circ. Conf., San Francisco, CA, Feb. 1991, pp. 180–181.
[7] L. A. Zadeh, "Fuzzy sets as a basis for a theory of possibility," Fuzzy Sets and Systems, vol. 1, pp. 3–28, 1978.
[8] R. W. Brodersen, "Low-power design of a wireless multimedia terminal," in Proc. Elec. Eng. Dep. Res. Symp., University of California, Los Angeles, Feb. 1992.
[9] C. H. Mestrangelo and R. S. Muller, "A thermal absolute-pressure sensor with on-chip digital front-end processor," in Tech. Dig. IEEE Int. Solid-State Circ. Conf., San Francisco, CA, Feb. 1991, pp. 188–189.
[10] Y. Tsividis, "Analog MOS integrated circuits—certain new ideas, trends, and obstacles," IEEE J. Solid-State Circ., vol. 22, pp. 317–321, June 1987.
[11] M. Mahowald and C. Mead, "Silicon retina," in Analog VLSI and Neural Systems, C. Mead, Ed. Reading MA: Addition-Wesley Publishing Company 1989.
[12] R. Lyon and C. A. Mead, "An analog electronic cochlea," IEEE Trans. Acoust. Speech, Signal Processing, vol. 36, pp. 1119–1134, July 1988.
[13] H. Kobayashi, J. White, and A. Abidi, "An analog CMOS network for Gaussian convolution with embedded image sensing," in Tech. Dig. IEEE Int. Solid-State Circ. Conf., San Francisco, CA, Feb. 1990, pp. 216–217.
[14] B. Boser and E. Sackinger, "An analog neural network processor with programmable network topology," in Tech. Dig. IEEE Int. Solid-State Circ. Conf., San Francisco, CA, Feb. 1991, pp. 184–185.
[15] T. Morishita, Y. Tamura, and T. Otsuki, "A BiCMOS analog neural network with dynamically updated weights," in Tech. Dig. IEEE Int. Solid-State Circ. Conf., pp. 142–143, San Francisco, CA, Feb. 1990.
[16] J. Van der Spiegel, P. Mueller, D. Blackman, P. Chance, C. Donham, R. Etienne, and P. Kinget, "An analog neural computer with modular architecture for real-time dynamic computations," IEEE J. Solid-State Circuits, vol. 27, no. 1, pp. 82–92, Jan. 1992.
[17] S. Satyanarayana, Y. P. Tsividis, and H. P. Graf, "A reconfigurable VLSI neural network," IEEE J. Solid-State Circuits, vol. 27, pp. 67–81, Jan. 1992.
[18] D. Hammerstrom, "A VLSI architecture for high-performance, low-cost, on-chip learning," IEEE/INNS Proc. Int. Joint Conf. Neural Networks, vol. II, San Diego, CA, 1990, pp. 537–544.
[19] D. A. Orrey, D. J. Myers, and J. M. Vincent, "A high performance digital processor for implementing large artificial neural networks," Proc. IEEE Custom Integrated Circuits Conf., San Diego, CA, May 1991, pp. 16.3.1–16.3.4.
[20] B. J. Sheu, "VLSI Neurocomputing with analog programmable chips and digital systolic array chips," presented at the Int. Symp. Circuits and Systems (invited paper), Singapore, June 1991.
[21] K. S. Fu and T. Ichikawa, Special Computer Architectures for Pattern Recognition. Boca Raton, FL: CRC Press, 1982.

[22] K. Hwang and F. Briggs, *Computer Architecture and Parallel Processing.* New York: McGraw Hill: 1984.

[23] K. Przytula, W. Lin, and V. Kumar, "Partitioned implementation of neural networks on mesh connected array processors," in *VLSI Signal Processing IV*, H. Moscovitz, K. Yao, and R. Jain, Eds. Piscataway, NJ: IEEE Press, 1991.

[24] B. Horn, *Robot Vision.* Cambridge, MA: The MIT Press, 1986.

[25] K. Prazdny, "Egomotion and relative depth map from optical flow," in *Biological Cybernetics.* Berlin, Germany: Springer-Verlag, 1980, vol. 36, pp. 87–102.

[26] W. Simpson, "Depth discrimination from optical flow," *Perception*, vol. 17, pp. 497–512, 1988.

[27] G. Adiv, "Determining three-dimensional motion and structure from optical flow generated by several moving objects," *IEEE Trans. Patt. Anal. Mach. Intell.*, vol. 17, pp. 384–401, July 1985.

[28] B. Ballard and O. Kimbal, "Rigid body motion from depth and optical flow," in *Computer Graphics and Image Processing.* New York: Academic Press, 1983, vol. 22, pp. 95–115.

[29] B. Horn and B. Schunck, "Determining optical flow," in *Artificial Intelligence.* Amsterdam, Netherlands: North-Holland Publishing Co., 1981, vol. 17, pp. 185–203.

[30] N. Grzywacz and A. Yuille, "Massively parallel implementations of theories for apparent motion," *Tech. Rep. AI Memo 888, CBIP Memo 016*, MIT Artificial Intelligence Lab. and Center for Biological Information Processing, June, 1987.

[31] J. Hutchinson, C. Koch, J. Luo, and C. Mead, "Computing motion using analog and binary resistive networks," *IEEE Computer Mag.*, pp. 52–63, Mar., 1988.

[32] Y. Zhou and R. Chellappa, "Computation of optical flow using a neural network," in *IEEE Proc. Int. Conf. Neural Networks*, San Diego, CA, 1988, vol. 2, pp. 71–78.

[33] Y.-T. Zhou and R. Chellappa, "A network for motion perception," in *Proc. IEEE/INNS Int. Joint Conf. Neural Networks*, San Diego, CA, June 1990, vol. II, pp. 875–884.

[34] T. Kohonen, "The self-organizing map," *Proc. IEEE*, vol. 78, pp. 1464–1480, Sept. 1990.

[35] T. Kohonen, *Self-Organization and Associative Memory, 2nd ed.* New York: Springer-Verlag: 1988.

[36] S. Grossberg, "Competitive learning: from interactive activation to adaptive resonance," *Cognitive Science*, vol. 11, pp. 23–63, 1987.

[37] B. O'Neil, *Elementary Differential Geometry.* New York: Academic Press: 1966.

[38] S. Ullman, *The Interpretation of Visual Motion.* Cambridge, MA: The MIT Press, 1979.

[39] B. W. Lee and B. J. Sheu, *Hardware Annealing in Analog VLSI Neurocomputing.* Boston, MA: Kluwer Academic Publishers, 1991.

[40] P. Denyer and D. Renshaw, *VLSI Signal Processing: A Bit-Serial Approach.* Reading, MA: Addison-Wesley, 1985.

[41] B. W. Lee and B. J. Sheu, "A compact and general-purpose neural chip with electrically programmable synapses," in *Proc. IEEE Custom Integrated Circuits Conf.*, Boston, MA, May 1990, pp. 26.61–26.6.4.

[42] B. J. Sheu, J. Choi, and C.-F. Chang, "An analog neural network processor for self-organizing mapping," *Tech. Dig. IEEE Int. Solid-State Circuits Conf.*, San Francisco, CA, Feb. 1992, pp. 136–137, 266.

[43] M. Holler, S. Tam, H. Castro, and R. Benson, "An electrically trainable artificial neural network (ETANN) with 10240 "floating gate" synapses," *IEEE/INNS Proc. Int. Joint Conf. Neural Networks*, Washington, DC, 1989, vol. 2, pp. 191–196.

[44] B. W. Lee, B. J. Sheu, and H. Yang, "Analog floating-gate synapses for general-purpose VLSI neural computation," *IEEE Trans. Circuits Syst.*, vol. 38, June 1991.

[45] J. Dayhoff, *Neural Network Architectures.* New York: Van Nostrand Reinhold, 1990, pp. 97–114.

[46] D. Rumelhart and D. Zipser, "Feature discovery by competitive learning," in *Parallel Distributed Processing*, D. Rumelhart and J. McClelland, Eds. and PDP Group. Cambridge, MA: MIT Press 1986, pp. 151–193.

[47] R. Hecht-Nielsen, *Neurocomputing.* Reading, MA: Addison-Wesley, 1990, pp. 64–70.

[48] J. Choi, B. J. Sheu, and S. M. Gowda, "Analog VLSI neural network implementations of hardware annealing and winner-take-all functions," presented at the *34th Midwest Symp. Circuits and Syst. (invited paper)*, Monterey, CA, May 1991.

[49] J. Lazzaro, S. Ryckebush, M. A. Mahowald, and C. A. Mead, "Winner-take-all network of O(N) complexity," *Advances in Neural Information Processing Systems—I.* San Mateo, CA: Morgan Kauffman 1989, pp. 703–711.

[50] A. G. Andreou, K. A. Boahen, P. O. Pouliquen, A. Pavasovic, R. E. Jenkins, and K. Strohbehn, "Current-mode subthreshold MOS circuits for analog VLSI neural systems," *IEEE Trans. Neural Networks*, vol. 2, pp. 205–213, Mar. 1991.

[51] A. B. Grebene, *Bipolar and MOS Analog Integrated Circuit Design.* New York: Wiley 1984.

[52] G. Lewicki, "Foresight: A fast turn-around and low cost ASIC prototyping alternative," presented at the *IEEE ASIC Conf. Exhibit*, Rochester, NY, Sept. 1990, pp. 6.8.1–6.8.2.

[53] C. Tomovich, "MOSIS—A gateway to silicon," *IEEE Circuits and Devices Mag.*, vol. 4, no. 2, pp. 22–23, Mar. 1988.

[54] B. Johnson, T. Quarles, A. R. Newton, D. O. Pederson, and A. Sangiovanni-Vincentelli, *SPICE3 Version 3E1 Users Guide*, Department of Electrical Engineering and Computer Sciences, University of California, Berkeley, Apr. 1991.

An Active Resistor Network for Gaussian Filtering of Images

Haruo Kobayashi, Joseph L. White, *Student Member*, *IEEE*, and Asad A. Abidi, *Member*, *IEEE*

Abstract —The architecture of an active resistive mesh containing both positive and negative resistors to implement a Gaussian convolution in two dimensions is described. With an embedded array of photoreceptors, this may be used for image detection and smoothing. The convolution width is continuously variable by 2:1 under user control. Analog circuits implement a 45×40 mesh on a 2-μm CMOS IC, and perform an entire convolution in 20 μs on applied images.

I. INTRODUCTION

HARDWARE capable of sensing an input in two dimensions and processing it in parallel to obtain results in real time is of great interest in applications such as low-power compact image recognition systems. In digital signal processors today, a 2D input from a sensor is first scanned and quantized, and subsequently processed using pipelined parallel algorithms to obtain a fast throughput rate [1]. The data at each grid point in the 2D input, corresponding to one pixel in the case of a sampled image, serially enter this signal processor and flow through it at some usually fast clock rate. A substantial increase in throughput may be obtained over this signal flow rate by using *simultaneous* processing *per pixel*, particularly if the signal fan-out is eliminated by not digitizing the input but retaining it as an analog quantity. This is how signal processing takes place in natural biological systems [2]–[4].

Much of signal processing consists of data reduction and the extraction of high-level content for purposes such as identification, classification, or storage. The hardware to accomplish this will very often implement an algorithm derived from a study of physical or biological systems, which naturally perform a similar task. In a programmable digital signal processor, an explicit algorithm is entered as a sequence of instructions, or as their hardwired equivalent in a dedicated processor. Analog hardware, on the other hand, cannot be programmed as

digital operations may be, and is almost always hardwired: a circuit must be constructed in which Kirchhoff's laws and the terminal characteristics of the components together embody the desired algorithm. Insofar as this synthesis is guided by experience, ingenuity, and taste, the approach is ad hoc and limited in its generality; but when successfully executed, it may offer a savings in power and enhancement in speed by orders of magnitude over the digital approach [5]. The input to an analog signal processor is some current or voltage, the output some other voltage or current determined by the laws of physics governing the circuit. The early analog computers were built on this principle, but being composed of building blocks with quite general functions, they were not very efficient in hardware for massively parallel tasks. Translinear integrated circuits are one well-known example of an efficient use of hardware to embody complex nonlinear algorithms, although usually for scalar or one-dimensional array inputs. They achieve hardware efficiency by exploiting transistor device physics rather than from complex building blocks such as operational amplifiers; they are also hardwired to accomplish a specific task [6], [7]. Our work deals with a class of circuits suited to simultaneous signal processing in two dimensions also using processing at the transistor level.

II. IMAGE SMOOTHING USING SIMULTANEOUS 2D SIGNAL PROCESSING

This section will discuss the algorithm and architecture of a particular image processing function we have implemented for potential use in compact machine vision systems [8].

A. Smoothing Images by a Gaussian Operation

Many electronic image recognition systems tend to replicate the hierarchy from low- to high-level processing found in biological organisms. A raw image is usually smoothed to suppress noisy features; its outline is then obtained with some form of edge-enhancement operation, and the outline after normalization and rotation is compared with stored templates. While the quantity of data might reduce along this chain, the complexity of the operations increases significantly. Our work relates to the lowest level of image processing, the smoothing of raw

Manuscript received September 27, 1990; revised January 25, 1991. This work was supported by the Office of Naval Research under Contract N00014-89-J-1282, Rockwell International, TRW, and the State of California MICRO Program. This paper was first presented at the 1990 International Solid-State Circuits Conference (ISSCC).

H. Kobayashi was with the Integrated Circuits and Systems Laboratory, Electrical Engineering Department, University of California, Los Angeles, CA 90024-1594 on leave from Yokogawa Electric Corporation, Tokyo, Japan.

J. L. White and A. A. Abidi are with the Integrated Circuits and Systems Laboratory, Electrical Engineering Department, University of California, Los Angeles, CA 90024-1594.

IEEE Log Number 9143314.

Reprinted from *IEEE J. Solid-State Circuits*, vol. 26, no. 5, pp. 738–748, May 1991.

image data with a Gaussian convolution function of variable width.

There is broad evidence suggesting that a noisy image is best smoothed by a Gaussian convolution kernel prior to edge enhancement. This corresponds to the defocusing action of a lens, and is inherent in many biological systems. The defocusing blurs the small sharp features characteristic of visual noise, which are extraneous to important objects in the field of view. Unless the image is properly smoothed beforehand, differentiating the intensity map of the image to enhance the edges will also accentuate the sharp noisy features. Theoretical work has proven that a noisy image is best smoothed by a Gaussian convolution kernel to obtain the largest signal-to-noise ratio after differentiation [9], [10].

The optimal width, or extent, of the convolution used to smooth a particular image depends on the spatial standard deviation of the noise, and also on the scale of the objects which is usually not known in advance. The width of the Gaussian smoothing must therefore be variable under the control of the user. Adaptive methods such as scale space filtering [11] rely on this capability. Our experiments suggest that a Gaussian with a width variable by a factor of 2 is adequate to smooth the noise in many simple images sampled at a resolution of 50 by 50 pixels.

We set about after these considerations to implement one analog integrated circuit capable of sampling an image at a resolution of 50 pixels on a side, smoothing it by a Gaussian in about 5 μs, and giving the user the flexibility of continuously varying the Gaussian width by a factor of 2:1. This speed of operation is orders of magnitude faster than digital implementations of this convolution function, which in addition to the requirements of image buffering also require the image to be circulated several times through a filter to obtain the property of variable width.

B. Computation in 2D Using Resistive Meshes

Resistor networks were used as analog computers in the past to solve complex boundary value problems in electromagnetics [12]–[15]. These were later replaced by numerical simulation on digital computers, primarily because of the ease of programmability. Digital computation, however, could neither surpass the low power dissipation nor the speed of analog computers, because when the latter solve complex 2D problems, the currents and voltages could attain their final values within a very short RC relaxation time. This high speed is the main attraction of analog computation for 2D real-time signal processing, in that the number of calculations unlike digital computation does not grow proportionally to the resolution, but more as the square root. The use of this concept for similar applications has also been noted elsewhere [16].

Unlike a resistive sheet subject to a potential difference between two edges, where the resulting lateral equipotential contours solve electrostatic or magnetostatic field

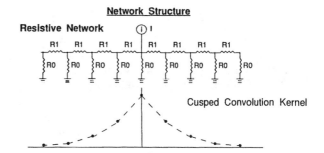

Fig. 1. 1D mesh with leakage resistors to ground, and its convolution kernel.

problems, the contours in a sheet which also has a continuous *leakage* to ground will decay in a characteristic fashion in response to a voltage applied at a single point. The spatial rate of decay depends on the leakage conductivity to ground relative to the lateral conductivity. This decay function may be thought of as the spatial impulse response of the leaky resistive sheet, or, equivalently, its convolution kernel; the potential contours in response to multiple-point stimuli will then be determined by linear superposition. Consider, for example, a one-dimensional discrete version of the leaky resistive sheet composed of a uniform linear mesh of resistors R_1 with resistors R_0 from every node to ground (Fig. 1). In response to a current excitation at one node, the resulting voltage distribution on the mesh decays n nodes away from the excitation according to an exponential function $\exp(-nR_1/R_0)$ [16]. This convolution kernel differs from a Gaussian in two important ways: it has a slower decay at its tails, and the exponentials on either side of the excitation meet at the center to produce a cusp (Fig. 1). The discontinuity in derivative at this point would produce undesirable results when this function is applied to a noisy image and then followed by edge enhancement. The mesh must therefore be modified to produce a characteristic function which better resembles the flat-topped Gaussian at the point of excitation. Obtaining a practical realization of this mesh was one of the key contributions of our work.

C. An Active Resistive Mesh Implementing Gaussian Convolution

We first qualitatively examine why the resistive mesh in the previous example produces a cusped convolution kernel, and how it must be modified. An indirect procedure for synthesizing the desired network is then described, followed by methods to extend it to two dimensions.

The spatial derivative of voltage at a point in a resistive sheet or discrete mesh specifies the potential gradient or the electric field there. According to the point form of Ohm's law, $J = \sigma E$, a current injected at a point (assuming the point has nonzero extent, so that the current density there is not infinite) on a resistive sheet with leakage to ground will produce some nonzero electric field (E) there, and therefore a nonzero potential gradient. A nonzero J may produce a zero E only if $\sigma \to \infty$, which implies that the sheet must appear perfectly conductive at the point of injection. If a negative resistance is introduced to locally neutralize the dissipation in the sheet, while maintaining the dissipation across the large scale, a convolution function may be obtained with a flat top and decaying tails. It is plausible to achieve this in a discrete resistive mesh by introducing negative resistors not between every node, because that would simply modify the value of R_1, but between every other node, or perhaps even straddling several nodes. Investigating this numerically, we found that a mesh implementing a convolution of the desired shape could be obtained using negative resistors of a certain value connecting nodes with their *second nearest* neighbors. We also came upon an alternative procedure to synthesizing the same mesh, based on the theoretical work relating to the optimal smoothing of images. This is now described.

Poggio *et al.* [9] have analyzed how to smooth samples V_j, $-\infty < j < \infty$, of a noisy function to best estimate the derivative if the noise were not present. They seek a fitting function $U(x)$ with continuous first derivative which interpolates the sample points V_j with a least-mean-square difference, but with the constraint that the derivatives of $U(x)$ are not allowed to fluctuate excessively to obtain the least noisy estimate of the actual derivatives of the sampled function. This is expressed as the problem of minimizing an energy functional E, defined as the mean square difference between the interpolating function and the samples, subject to a penalty on excessively large second derivatives. The strength of the penalty is controlled by a parameter λ, called the regularization parameter:

$$E = \sum_j \left(U(x=j) - V_j \right)^2 + \lambda \int \left(\frac{d^2 U}{dx^2} \right)^2 dx. \quad (1)$$

It is shown that the $U(x)$ minimizing E in (1) is obtained by convolving V_j with an almost exactly Gaussian kernel, and the width of this kernel increases with λ. We may use this result by exploiting a fundamental connection between the minimum of an energy functional and the operating point of a circuit. It is known from circuit theory that Kirchhoff's laws and the constituent relations of the components drive a network to a state of minimum energy dissipation, so it is reasonable to construct a network whose energy dissipation is described by (1). The network equations may be obtained directly by setting the derivative of the right-hand side of (1) to zero.

Using a discrete estimate of the second derivative in (1), we get

$$E = \sum_j \left(U_j - V_j \right)^2 + \lambda \sum_j \left(U_{j+1} + U_{j-1} - 2U_j \right)^2 \quad (2)$$

where $U_j = U(x=j)$. This is a quadratic form, and therefore has a unique minimum where $\partial E / \partial U_j = 0$ for all j, so

$$0 = 2\left(U_j - V_j \right) + \lambda \frac{\partial}{\partial U_j} \sum_i \left(U_{i+1} + U_{i-1} - 2U_i \right)^2 \quad \text{for all } j. \quad (3)$$

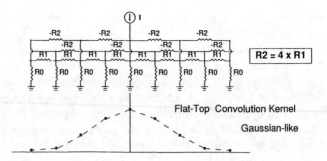

Fig. 2. 1D mesh with negative resistors between second nearest neighbors produces a convolution with a flat top.

Differentiating the terms in the sum and noting that $\partial U_i / \partial U_j = 0$ if $i \neq j$,

$$0 = \left(U_j - V_j \right) + \lambda \left(6U_j - 4\left(U_{j-1} + U_{j+1} \right) + \left(U_{j-2} + U_{j+2} \right) \right). \quad (4)$$

This describes the node equations of a one-dimensional mesh [17] consisting of positive resistors (R_1) connecting nearest-neighbor nodes (i.e., $j-1, j$ and $j, j+1$), negative resistors ($-R_2 = -4R_1$) connecting second nearest neighbors, and resistors $R_0 = \lambda R_1$ to ground from every node, which are the leakage resistors described previously in the qualitative model (Fig. 2). The V_j correspond to voltage excitations in series with the leakage resistors. The network will produce as an array of node voltages (U_j) the convolution of the array of excitation voltages (V_j) with a Gaussian kernel whose width is controlled by λ. If $\{V_j\}$ were a set of photovoltages consisting of samples along a scan line through an image, the output set of voltages produced by the network would be the smoothed scan line.

The desired smoothing in an image, however, must take place across two dimensions. To obtain this, samples of a 2D image as a matrix of photovoltages should drive a *two-dimensional* mesh to obtain the desired result. The one-dimensional prototype of a Gaussian convolution mesh must then be extended to implement the kernel with circular symmetry in two dimensions. Noting, for instance, that a two-dimensional Gaussian function $G(x, y)$ is separable, that is, $G(x, y) = G(x) \cdot G(y)$, the desired 2D convolution may be obtained by driving an array of 1D meshes parallel to the y axis with the matrix of sampled photovoltages, and an identical array of 1D meshes along the x axis with the matrix of *buffered* outputs from the first array. This is not very efficient in hardware, because each mesh must have independent active circuits to produce the negative resistances, and an intermesh buffer must be used at every node.

Another possible implementation on a 2D rectangular grid is to connect every node to its *four* nearest neighbors oriented 90° apart with resistors R_1, and the *four* second nearest neighbors at the same orientations with resistors $-R_2$. The simulated spatial impulse response of this network decayed more rapidly along the diagonals than axially, producing an unacceptably large deviation from

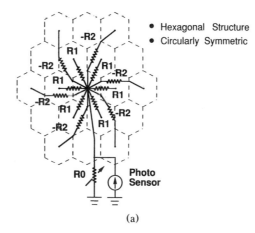

- Hexagonal Structure
- Circularly Symmetric

(a)

- **2D Gaussian-like**

- **Good Circular Symmetry**

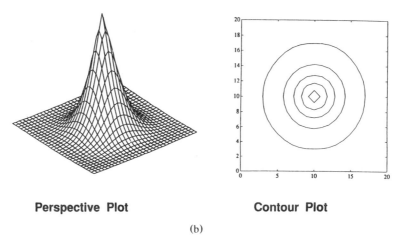

Perspective Plot　　　　　**Contour Plot**

(b)

Fig. 3. (a) Extension of the mesh to 2D on a hexagonal grid produces (b) the best circular symmetry in the convolution kernel.

circular symmetry. A better circular symmetry was obtained by adding similar positive and negative resistive connections along the four diagonal directions, but weighted four times larger in magnitude. It became evident that a large number of components would be required to contrive circular symmetry on a rectangular grid, but not so on a hexagonal grid which inherently possesses a circular symmetry. The image must also be sampled on a hexagonal grid for compatibility with the mesh, which now consists of equal resistive connections 60° apart in orientation to nearest and second nearest neighbors. A hexagonal grid affords the greatest spatial sampling efficiency in the sense that the least photoreceptor sites will attain a desired coverage of the image [18], and the fewest network elements will yield the desired circular symmetry (Fig. 3(a)). The latter was verified in the simulated convolution kernel of this 2D network (Fig. 3(b)).

We required the kernel width to be variable by a factor of 2 under user control. That the convolution width depends on the ratio R_0/R_1 was known from the synthesis procedure, but the strength of this dependence was not. Simulations of the network showed a weak dependence (Fig. 4)

$$\text{Convolution width} \propto \left(\frac{R_0}{R_1}\right)^{1/4} \qquad (5)$$

It was simplest in terms of implementation to keep R_1 and R_2 fixed to preserve the Gaussian shape, and make R_0 alone variable by 16:1 to obtain the desired 2:1 variation in smoothing width.

Several aspects of this design procedure and simulated results invite analysis. Is there a systematic way to generalize a 1D mesh prototype with circular symmetry to 2D? Is the characteristic function of this combination of positive and negative resistors stable in space (i.e., does it decay rather than oscillate indefinitely)? Stable in time? Can the network be generalized to other convolution functions? What is the analytical relation between the width of the convolution function and the network elements? We have answered some of these questions elsewhere [19].

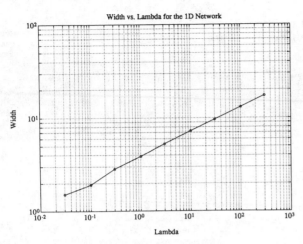

Fig. 4. The width of the convolution kernel increases as the 1/4th power of the grounded resistor.

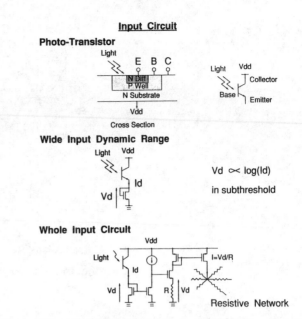

Fig. 5. The vertical bipolar transistor in a CMOS well produces logarithmic compression at the gate voltage by a MOSFET in subthreshold. A transconductance buffer drives the network.

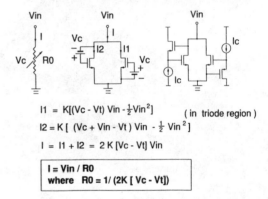

$$I1 = K[(Vc - Vt) \, Vin - \tfrac{1}{2} Vin^2]$$ (in triode region)
$$I2 = K[\, (Vc + Vin - Vt) \, Vin - \tfrac{1}{2} Vin^2]$$
$$I = I1 + I2 = 2K [Vc - Vt] \, Vin$$

$$I = Vin / R0$$
$$\text{where} \quad R0 = 1/ (2K [\, Vc - Vt])$$

Fig. 6. The linearized variable resistor, with implementation of gate bias.

III. CIRCUIT DESIGN

The practicality of implementing this signal processing technique depends greatly on whether it is realizable on a standard (digital) CMOS IC process. We discuss now the circuit design of the required components, including the photosensors, and the special considerations for layout of this highly interconnected 2D network as a monolithic integrated circuit.

A. Logarithmic Photoreceptor

An image focused on the chip surface may be sampled by a matrix of photoreceptors, one at every node of the network. The intensity across a simple image may vary by two to three orders of magnitude in a laboratory environment, more in natural backgrounds, so a linear photoreceptor, which converts the intensity to a proportional voltage or current, would drive the active circuits in the network into saturation. A logarithmic photoreceptor is therefore required, and as studies on image processing have shown, perfectly adequate for the task on hand [3]. Photosensing is most economically obtained using the parasitic vertical bipolar in a CMOS well as a phototransistor, whose collector current becomes proportional to the light intensity incident on the collector junction along the well boundary. This may be compressed into a logarithmic voltage by a diode-connected MOSFET biased in the subthreshold region by the small photocurrent density produced under room lighting conditions. A compact logarithmic photoreceptor is in this way obtained with a two-transistor circuit [20], [21] (Fig. 5).

Although the stimulus to the prototype network in the discussion above was a voltage source in series with the variable resistor R_0, the circuits for the photosensor output and R_0 (described below) are naturally grounded on one end, so the Norton transformation must be invoked to convert the stimulus into a parallel combination of a grounded current source and a shunt resistor. A transconductance photoreceptor buffer was used, consisting a level-shift PMOS driving a resistively degenerated NMOSFET, which appears to the photoreceptor as a voltage-controlled current source (Fig. 5).

B. Variable Resistor

The width of the convolution kernel is set by a resistor R_0, whose value should ideally be continuously variable under user control. A single MOSFET operating in triode region used as a variable resistor would introduce an undesirable parabolic nonlinearity in the I–V characteristics. Two MOSFET's in parallel obeying the simplified square law equations, however, can exactly cancel each other's parabolic nonlinearity in the triode region of operation if their gate biases are applied in a particular way, and the resulting linearized resistance is controlled by the bias. We used this as the variable resistor (Fig. 6). The floating-gate bias voltages were obtained as the V_{GS} of source-follower FET's carrying a control current.

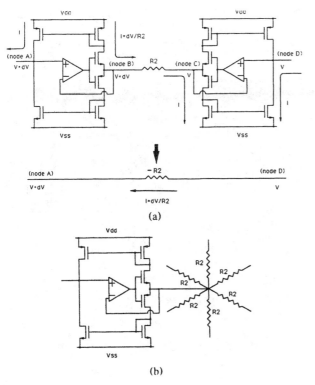

Fig. 7. (a) An NIC inverts the polarity of a resistor. (b) One NIC serves all resistors converging on a node.

The mean network voltage at a given level of photosensor illumination will change with the convolution width: for example, when the convolution width is decreased by making all R_0 large, the mean voltage will also increase because the buffered photocurrents will flow into larger resistors. This will impose the unnecessary demand of a large common-mode range of operation in active circuits such as R_0. We used a scheme to normalize the network inputs by slaving the buffer transconductance of the logarithmic photoreceptor proportionally to R_0, so as to maintain a constant mean network voltage at all illuminations.

C. Network Resistors

The 5-kΩ resistors for the nearest-neighbor internode connections in the network were implemented using p-well diffusions. A Gaussian convolution kernel would be obtained in spite of tolerances in the p-well resistivity as long as the relative magnitude of the positive and negative resistors remains 1:4. To make this ratio on the chip depend only on geometry, both R_1 and R_2 were implemented in the same material, p-well diffusion, and a negative impedance converter (NIC) was attached to R_2 to invert its polarity.

Our NIC implementation (Fig. 7) consists of the combination of a voltage follower and current inverter. The op-amp-based followers at each end of R_2 impose across it the potential difference at their inputs, and the resulting current flow, forced through the Class-B type output

stages, is sourced from or sunk into the positive or negative power supply. Current mirrors in series then apply the same current at the input leads of the followers, inverting the sense of current flow as perceived at the network nodes. A negative resistance $-R_2$ is presented to the network.

Six negative resistors converge on every node in this hexagonal mesh. Six different NIC's are, however, not required at each node; instead, a single NIC placed at the node *after* the confluence of the resistors will simultaneously make them all negative (Fig. 7(b)). The dc gain in a simple five-FET op amp was large enough to obtain accurate inversion of the resistor $I-V$ characteristics and eliminate the crossover nonlinearity in the Class-B stage. The NIC at every node thus contained only 11 FET's.

D. Layout Considerations

A key concern in the implementation of this network as an IC is whether the usual two layers of metal and one of polysilicon can implement the starlike fan-out of interconnections emanating from every node. We proved to ourselves at the outset of this work that this was possible. A hexagonal grid was obtained by horizontally staggering successive rows of cells, and their interconnections implemented on a Manhattan geometry (Fig. 8(a)). All three available layers of interconnect were used to create abuttable cells. The power, ground, control, and output rails ran parallel to these rows from edge to edge of the chip.

A unit cell, including its portion of interconnect, measured 170×200 μm in 2-μm CMOS (Fig. 8(b)). The area of the photoreceptor collector–base junction, the blank rectangle in the cell layout at the lower left, measured 56×24 μm. No wires were allowed to traverse the photosensor because metal would absorb the incident light. Parasitic photocurrents generated in the source/drain junctions of other active circuits would have negligible effect on the voltages at the low-impedance nodes there. We observe finally that the active circuits occupied only 57% of the cell area, a measure of the toll exacted by the richness of interconnect in this circuit.

E. Output Means

This convolution network accepts a 2D input in the form of an incident image, does 2D signal processing across the resistive mesh, but on a standard IC is restricted to *1D output* at the pins along the periphery. The output therefore must be read at the pins (Fig. 9) by accessing one row of nodes at a time, and, at least in this implementation, becomes the bottleneck to the throughput rate. Addressable MOS switches were used to connect every node to output lines, and on-chip vertical bipolar transistors connected as emitter followers served as analog buffers at the pads. The speed of signal processing was determined by the relaxation time of this unclocked network, but a clock was introduced at the output to scan out the rows. To relieve this bottleneck, one can

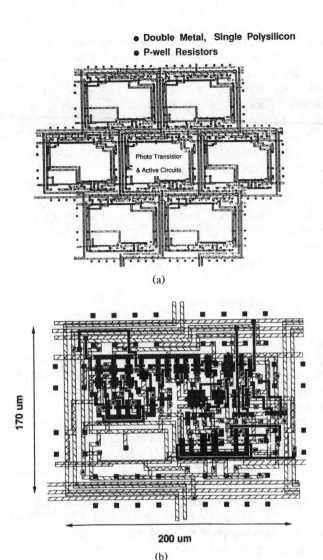

● Double Metal, Single Polysilicon
● P-well Resistors

Photo Transistor
& Active Circuits

(a)

170 um

200 um

(b)

Fig. 8. (a) The layout of interconnects among a cluster of seven cells on a hexagonal grid; the blank areas contain the photoreceptor and associated active circuits in each cell. (b) Unit cell layout.

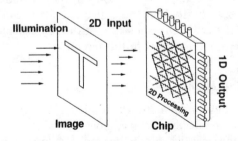

Fig. 9. Output mechanism. The network has 2D input, accomplishes 2D signal processing, but is forced to output results in 1D.

envisage connecting several 2D computational IC's performing a cascade of low-level vision tasks, with micro solder balls joining together matrices of pads on their surfaces, or through via holes on the back sides of the chips. This technique, originally developed for "flip-chip" mounting, is used at very high densities today to mate 2D focal plane array sensors to active substrates [22]. Once the desired data reduction has taken place at the output

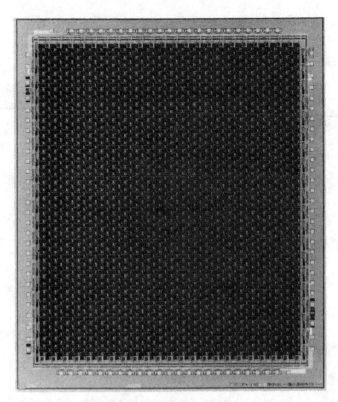

Fig. 10. Chip photograph.

of the such a cascade of chips, a few high-level outputs containing image features could be scanned out in parallel on pins with no loss in throughput speed.

IV. EXPERIMENTAL RESULTS

We were able to fit a 45×40 array of unit cells on a 7.9×9.2-mm die, the largest die size available to us through the MOSIS foundry service. Power supplies of $+5$ and -5 V were used, mainly for convenience in circuit design; the circuits could be modified with a minor effort for operation on a single 5-V supply. The fabricated chip (Fig. 10) contained more than a 100 000 transistors and was fully functional.

The network response to optical input was measured by shining light on the exposed chip, and reading the outputs using a specially developed interface board under control of a personal computer. An array of analog column voltages along an addressed row were digitized and stored, and the smoothed output image reconstructed on the computer screen after all rows had been scanned.

A. Component Characteristics

Test circuits were included to independently verify operation of some of the key building blocks in the network. The log compression FET and the transconductance buffer following the photosensor gave the desired log-linear relationship across 2.5 decades of photocurrent (Fig. 11(a)). The variable resistor could be changed by the control current by a factor of $16:1$ in magnitude, from 20 to 320 kΩ (Fig. 11(b)). The network simulations described

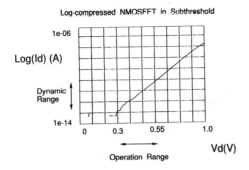

Input Dynamic Range = 2.5 Decades

(a)

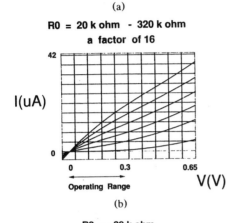

(b)

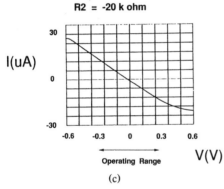

(c)

Fig. 11. Measured characteristics of the component circuits: (a) logarithmic compression at the photoreceptor output (V_d) versus photocurrent; (b) the variable resistor, which becomes nonlinear when one FET goes from triode to saturation; and (c) the negative resistor.

previously predict that this would yield the desired 2:1 variation in convolution width. A strong nonlinearity in the I–V characteristics appeared for voltages larger than 0.3 V, but we had designed the range of the network voltages not to exceed this value under normal illumination. A negative resistor of the desired value was also obtained (Fig. 11(c)), with very little observable nonlinearity at applied voltages of 0.3 V of either polarity.

B. Response to Optical Inputs

The network function was characterized with two simple incident images, a pinhole excitation representing a spatial impulse, and the character "T." The images were produced on the chip surface by light transmitted through

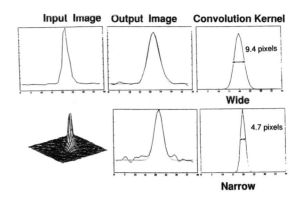

Fig. 12. Measured convolution kernel of the network. The measured network stimulus is deconvolved from the output. Dashed lines superimposed on output show the numerical smoothing used.

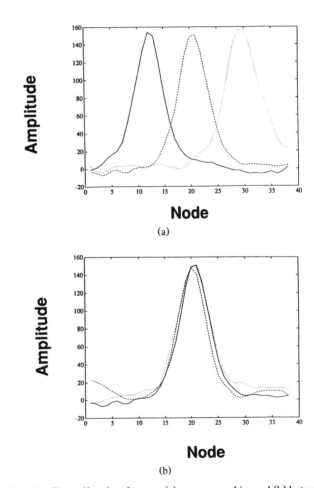

Fig. 13. The uniformity of output (a) across one chip, and (b) between three chips.

a mask used in place of the lid on the cavity of the ceramic PGA package. We had also made provision on the IC to measure the actual compressed signal driving the network, so that the true network function could be obtained by deconvolving it from the measured output.

The convolution kernel was thus deduced from measurements of the network input and output (Fig. 12). It was difficult at this sampling resolution to accurately

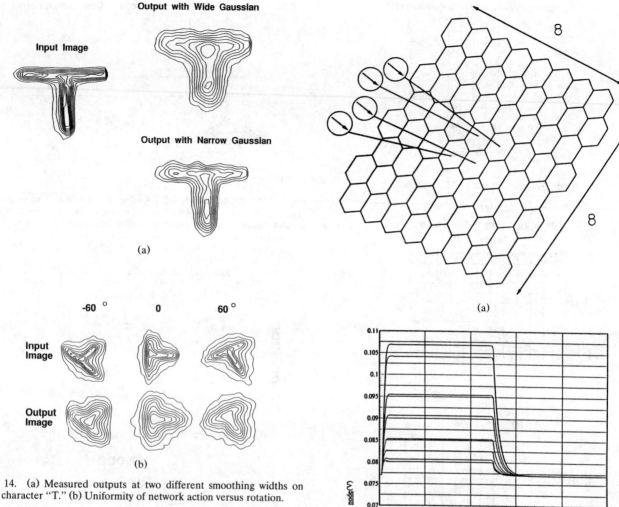

Fig. 14. (a) Measured outputs at two different smoothing widths on character "T." (b) Uniformity of network action versus rotation.

Fig. 15. (a) An 8×8 subnetwork simulated at the transistor level on SPICE, and (b) at various distances away from excitation, showing settling within 2 μs.

ascertain that it was a Gaussian function, but the characteristic inflection in the function as it approaches the peak value was evident. This would not appear unless the network contained negative resistors. We were able to change the full width at half maximum of the kernel by a factor of 2, from 4.7 to 9.4 pixels wide, by changing R_0 across its full span with the control current. The network output was most noisy at its tails at minimum R_0, and we had to use smoothing in the sense of a least-mean-square fit to deduce the kernel function. Light through the pinhole nominally sampled only a small neighborhood on the chip; we moved the pinhole to points on the chip either side of the center, and found an acceptable uniformity in the response (Fig. 13(a)), which is determined here by MOSFET matching across the extent of the chip surface [23]. The slight uptilt of the output at the ends of the measured response was caused by the edge effect when the network terminates at the chip boundary. The uniformity across three chips was also acceptable at this sampling resolution (Fig. 13(b)), except for one chip where a particularly large uptilt appears.

The smoothing effected by the network on a character "T" was also measured (Fig. 14(a)), and its symmetry after rotations relative to the chip axis verified (Fig. 14(b)). Both were satisfactory.

Precautions were required in making the measurement to compensate for the effects of the 2-W power dissipation when no heat sink was mounted on the package. This large power dissipation produced a thermal gradient across the IC, peaked at the center with circularly symmetric isotherms spreading out towards the chip boundary. We deduced this from a corresponding pattern in photoreceptor dark currents, which appeared as a stimulus to the network in the absence of an optical input. This had to be calibrated and subtracted from all measurements to obtain the true optical response. We emphasize that this relatively large power dissipation was not fundamental to the network; 75% of it was due to an unnecessarily large bias current in one building block, the control circuit for the variable resistor. A further reduction in quiescent power could be obtained by devising a voltage drive to the network nodes, because the current sources in the present implementation produce some steady power dissipation through R_0, even when the chip is not illumi-

TABLE I
Electrical Characteristics

Photosensor sites	45×40
Sampling geometry	Hexagonal
Area per pixel	$170 \times 200 \ \mu m$
Rise time of network (10–90%)	$2 \ \mu s$
Rise time of photosensors	$20 \ \mu s$
Width of convolution (FWHM)	4.7–9.4 pixels
Chip size	7.9×9.2 mm
Technology	2-μm CMOS, single poly, double metal
Power dissipation	2 W (75% in one function block)

nated. The power dissipation could be made even smaller by scaling down all the currents in the IC, but at a trade-off of longer relaxation times.

The settling time of the entire network in response to a step input from the photoreceptors determined the 2D computational speed. For all practical purposes, a step change in a photoreceptor has only to propagate a few nodes away before the decay in the convolution function will swamp it out, and the voltages at nodes farther away will remain relatively unchanged. We simulated an 8×8 subnetwork at the transistor level on SPICE, and the results indicated settling in less than $2 \ \mu s$ in response to a step in photocurrent (Fig. 15). However, a settling time of $20 \ \mu s$ was experimentally observed in response to illumination from a light chopper, which we surmise was dominated by the slow response of the phototransistors [20]. The graceful settling in the transient SPICE simulation verified the stability of the network response in time. A similar waveform of the settling of node voltages was also observed experimentally.

The electrical performance of the Gaussian convolution IC is summarized in Table I.

V. Conclusions

Parallel processing of images per pixel will offer the highest possible speed in functions related to low-level vision. This is indeed the present trend in real-time hardware for digital image processing. We have described a single-chip *analog* implementation of this concept to perform a Gaussian convolution with the use of an active mesh. Although it may be argued that a variable focus lens also effects this function, there are two significant differences: the active resistive mesh may be extended to many different convolution functions, including orientation selective ones [19], most of which cannot be simply implemented with geometric optics; furthermore, no mechanical system could attain the physical compactness and microsecond control of the convolution functions. The difference in output of two independent meshes on the same chip, for example, could implement the much sought after difference of Gaussian function in image processing [3]. In short, the notion of an active mesh opens many new opportunities for realizing application-specific analog signal processors. Digital signal processors have as advantages an immunity to component noise and mismatches, more ready programmability, and shorter development times, but tend to be considerably larger chips than their analog equivalents. On the other hand, inaccuracies in analog computation may not be limitations in low-level vision functions, but much more of a detriment in high-level classification tasks. This leads us to believe that compact hardware with the least power dissipation to implement real-time image recognition and classification may ultimately consist of a judicious mix of analog computation of the type described here, and conventional digital signal processing.

Acknowledgment

The formulation of the network was influenced in the early stages by B. Mathur and H. T. Wang of Rockwell International Science Center, and by our colleague R. L. Baker. A. Nahidipour designed and constructed the interface board used to measure the chip response. B. Furman contributed to simulations of the network action on complex images. Transient simulations of the network were carried out at the University of California at San Diego Supercomputer Center with support from the National Science Foundation.

References

[1] P. A. Ruetz and R. W. Brodersen, "Architectures and design techniques for real time image processing ICs," *IEEE J. Solid-State Circuits*, vol. SC-22, pp. 233–250, Apr. 1987.

[2] J. Dowling, *The Retina: An Approachable Part of the Brain.* Cambridge, MA: Harvard University Press, 1987.

[3] D. Marr, *Vision.* San Francisco, CA: W. H. Freeman, 1982.

[4] C. A. Mead and M. A. Mahowald, "A silicon model of early visual processing," *Neural Networks*, vol. 1, pp. 91–97, 1988.

[5] E. A. Vittoz, "Future of analog in the VLSI environment," in *Proc. ISCAS* (New Orleans, LA), May 1990, pp. 1372–1375.

[6] B. Gilbert, "Translinear circuits: A proposed classification," *Electron. Lett.*, vol. 11, pp. 14–16, 1975.

[7] B. Gilbert, "A monolithic 16 channel analog array normalizer," *IEEE J. Solid-State Circuits*, vol. SC-19, pp. 954–963, Dec. 1984.

[8] H. Kobayashi, J. L. White, and A. A. Abidi, "An analog CMOS network for Gaussian convolution with embedded image sensing," in *ISSCC Dig. Tech. Papers* (San Francisco, CA), Feb. 1990, pp. 216–217.

[9] T. Poggio, H. Voorhees, and A. Yuille, "A regularized solution to edge detection," Mass. Inst. Technology, Cambridge, MA, AI Memo, May 1985.

[10] T. Poggio, V. Torre, and C. Koch, "Computational vision and regularization theory," *Nature*, vol. 317, pp. 314–319, Sept. 1985.

[11] J. Babaud, A. P. Witkin, M. Baudin, and R. O. Duda, "Uniqueness of the Gaussian kernel for scale-space filtering," *IEEE Trans. Pattern Anal. and Mach. Intell.*, vol. PAMI-8, pp. 26–33, Jan. 1986.

[12] T. K. Hogan, "A general experimental solution of Poisson's equation for two independent variables," *J. Inst. Eng. (Australia)*, vol. 15, pp. 89–92, Apr. 1943.

[13] G. Liebmann, "Solution of partial differential equations with a resistance network analogue," *Brit. J. Appl. Phys.*, vol. 1, pp. 92–103, Apr. 1950.

[14] G. W. Swenson, Jr. and T. J. Higgins, "A direct current network analyzer for solving wave equation boundary value problems," *J. Appl. Phys.*, vol. 23, pp. 126–131, Jan. 1952.

[15] J. R. Hechtel and J. A. Seeger, "Accuracy and limitations of the resistor network used for solving Laplace's and Poisson's equations," *Proc. IRE*, vol. 49, pp. 933–940, May 1961.

[16] C. A. Mead, *Analog VLSI and Neural Systems.* Reading, MA: Addison Wesley, 1989.

[17] T. Poggio and C. Koch, "Ill-posed problems in early vision: From computational theory to analogue networks," *Proc. Roy. Soc. London*, vol. B-226, pp. 303–323, 1985.

493

[18] D. Dudgeon and R. Mersereau, *Multidimensional Signal Processing*. Englewood Cliffs, NJ: Prentice Hall, 1984.

[19] J. L. White and A. A. Abidi, "Analysis and design of parallel analog computational networks," in *Proc. Int. Symp. Circuits Syst.* (Portland, OR), June 1989, pp. 70–73.

[20] S. G. Chamberlain and J. P. Y. Lee, "A novel wide dynamic range silicon photodetector and linear imaging array," *IEEE J. Solid-State Circuits*, vol. SC-19, pp. 41–48, Feb. 1984.

[21] C. Mead, "A sensitive electronic photoreceptor," in *Proc. 1985 Chapel Hill Conf. VLSI* (Chapel Hill, NC), 1985, pp. 463–471.

[22] S. B. Stetson, D. B. Reynolds, M. G. Stapelbroek, and R. L. Stermer, "Design and performance of blocked impurity band detector focal plane arrays," in *Proc. SPIE*, vol. 686 (San Diego, CA), Aug. 1986, pp. 48–65.

[23] M. J. M. Pelgrom, A. C. J. Duinmaijer, and A. P. G. Welbers, "Matching properties of MOS transistors," *IEEE J. Solid-State Circuits*, vol. 24, no. 5, pp. 1433–1440, Oct. 1989.

Article 7.4

An Object Position and Orientation IC with Embedded Imager

David L. Standley, *Member, IEEE*

Abstract —A CMOS VLSI chip that determines the position and orientation of an object against a dark background is described. The chip operates in a continuous-time analog fashion, with a response time as short as 200 μs and power consumption under 50 mW. A self-contained phototransistor array acquires the image directly, and the output is a set of eight currents from which the position and orientation can be found. Orientation is determined to within ± 2° or better for moderately sized and sufficiently elongated objects. Chip dimensions are 7900 μm × 9200 μm.

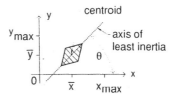

Fig. 1. Example of object centroid and axis of least inertia.

I. INTRODUCTION

AN ANALOG VLSI chip that determines the position and orientation of an object against a dark background is described. The implemented algorithm is based on finding the first and second moments of the object's spatial intensity distribution [1]. These moments allow the centroid (an indicator of position) and the axis of least inertia (an indicator of orientation) to be computed (Fig. 1). The chip has a self-contained 29 × 29 array of phototransistors, which are available in CMOS [2], so that the input is acquired by focusing the scene directly onto the chip surface. Each cell in the array occupies a 190-μm × 190-μm area. Using a novel scheme proposed by Horn [3], the moments are computed using a uniform grid of linear resistors. Only eight measurements per frame are required (in the particular architecture implemented). Resistive sheets have been used in earlier systems to determine the position of objects [4], [5], e.g., a small, bright spot. Also, the analog VLSI chip by DeWeerth and Mead [6] finds the centroid of an object, though using a different method. Yet neither performs the orientation task. There are digital chips that compute first-, second-, and higher order moments, e.g., [7]. However, these require input data in digital form; there is a significant A–D conversion overhead for real-time system operation. The chip presented here is a continuous-time analog imager and moment computer that performs both the position and orientation tasks. The output can be sampled at up to 5000 frames/s, and there is a greatly reduced A–D conversion requirement (per frame) for real-time interfacing with a digital system.

The work reported here was done in collaboration with Horn [8], [9], and a brief overview appeared in [10]. In this paper, transistor-level circuit design is given more emphasis. Complete details are in the dissertation by the author [11].

II. ALGORITHM

Consider an image (in continuous space) having brightness $B(x, y)$ in a field where $0 \leqslant x \leqslant x_{\max}$ and $0 \leqslant y \leqslant y_{\max}$. At each location, the brightness is assigned a weighting

$$m(x, y) \triangleq f(B(x, y)) \tag{1}$$

where

$$f(B) \triangleq \begin{cases} 0, & 0 \leqslant B \leqslant B_{\mathrm{thr}} \\ B - B_{\mathrm{thr}}, & B > B_{\mathrm{thr}} \end{cases} \tag{2}$$

and B_{thr} is a threshold value. This piecewise-continuous *brightness conditioning function* $f(B)$, shown in Fig. 2, removes a dim scene background while essentially retaining the gray-level character of the image.

A. Moment Definitions

The first moments of the weighting $m(x, y)$ are

$$M_x \triangleq \int_0^{x_{\max}} \int_0^{y_{\max}} x m(x, y) \, dx \, dy \tag{3}$$

$$M_y \triangleq \int_0^{x_{\max}} \int_0^{y_{\max}} y m(x, y) \, dx \, dy. \tag{4}$$

Manuscript received May 9, 1991; revised July 31, 1991. This work was supported by the National Science Foundation and the Defense Advanced Research Projects Agency under Contract MIP-8814612 and by DuPont Corporation. Manuscript preparation was supported in part by Rockwell International Corporation.

The author was with the Department of Electrical Engineering and Computer Science, Massachusetts Institute of Technology, Cambridge, MA 02139. He is now with the Imaging Devices Department, Rockwell International Science Center, Thousand Oaks, CA 91358.

IEEE Log Number 9103299.

Reprinted from *IEEE J. Solid-State Circuits*, vol. 26, no. 12, pp. 1853–1859, Dec. 1991.

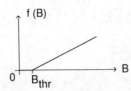

Fig. 2. This brightness conditioning function shows the image data weighting versus the brightness. Thresholding is included to completely remove a dim background.

Similarly, the second moments are

$$M_{xy} \triangleq \int_0^{x_{\max}} \int_0^{y_{\max}} xy\, m(x,y)\, dx\, dy \qquad (5)$$

$$M_{x^2} \triangleq \int_0^{x_{\max}} \int_0^{y_{\max}} x^2 m(x,y)\, dx\, dy \qquad (6)$$

$$M_{y^2} \triangleq \int_0^{x_{\max}} \int_0^{y_{\max}} y^2 m(x,y)\, dx\, dy. \qquad (7)$$

The zeroth moment M_0 is simply

$$M_0 \triangleq \int_0^{x_{\max}} \int_0^{y_{\max}} m(x,y)\, dx\, dy. \qquad (8)$$

B. Position and Orientation from Moments

The centroid $(\bar{x}, \bar{y})$, which indicates the position, is given by the normalized first moments

$$\bar{x} = M_x / M_0 \qquad (9)$$

and

$$\bar{y} = M_y / M_0. \qquad (10)$$

The angle of the axis of least inertia, which indicates the orientation, can be found by first calculating the quantities

$$a' \triangleq M_{x^2} - M_0(\bar{x})^2 \qquad (11)$$

$$b' \triangleq M_{xy} - M_0(\overline{xy}) \qquad (12)$$

and

$$c' \triangleq M_{y^2} - M_0(\bar{y})^2. \qquad (13)$$

Then the angle of the axis of least inertia, as shown in Fig. 1, is given by

$$\theta = \frac{1}{2}\arctan(2b', a' - c') \qquad (14)$$

where $\arctan(v, u)$ for any $(v, u) \neq (0,0)$ is the unique angle $\phi \in [0°, 360°)$ such that

$$u = \sqrt{u^2 + v^2}\, \cos\phi$$

and

$$v = \sqrt{u^2 + v^2}\, \sin\phi.$$

Note that certain objects, such as a square, will not have a unique axis of least inertia, and hence orientation is not defined by this method. Yet many objects, e.g., uniform elongated ones, will have an orientation angle. Also note that the three second moments are not needed separately; only M_{xy} and the difference $M_{x^2} - M_{y^2}$ are required.

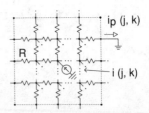

Fig. 3. Uniform resistor grid is grounded around the perimeter. A 2-D array of current (corresponding to the image data) is injected into the grid, and currents leaving around the perimeter contain the information needed to compute the required first and second moments.

III. RESISTIVE GRID SCHEME

The resistive grid scheme proposed by Horn [3] is essentially processing by dimensional reduction of data. In the continuous image field case, a uniform resistive sheet can be used to reduce the double integrals in the above moment formulas to a single integral; this can be thought of as a 2-D to 1-D reduction. For simplicity we assume a square image field, i.e., $x_{\max} = y_{\max}$. In the discrete image case (i.e., with pixels), which is implemented, each corresponding weighted sum (which replaces an integral) over an $N \times N$ image array can be reduced to an equivalent sum over $4N$ quantities with a resistor grid. These, in turn, can be reduced to eight quantities with resistor lines [11]. Fig. 3 shows a uniform resistor grid, which is grounded around the perimeter. Each *internal* node corresponds to a pixel (j, k) in the 2-D array, for $j = 1, 2, \cdots, N$ and $k = 1, 2, \cdots, N$, and a current $i(j, k)$ (proportional to the weighting $m(j, k)$ at the pixel) is injected into the grid. The $4N$ currents flowing out of the perimeter contain enough information to extract the moments. In particular,

$$\sum_{j=1}^{N}\sum_{k=1}^{N} h(j,k)i(j,k) = \sum_{(j,k) \in P} h(j,k)i_p(j,k) \qquad (15)$$

where P is the set of all nodes *on the perimeter* (i.e., with $j = 0, N+1$ and $k = 0, N+1$), $i_p(j, k)$ is the current flowing out of the grid at each perimeter node, and $h(j, k)$ is any *harmonic* function (i.e., the Laplacian of $h(j, k)$ vanishes identically) [11, ch. 2]. In the continuous case the required spatial weightings are $h(x, y) = 1$, x, y, xy and $x^2 - y^2$; to within a scale factor, these correspond to discrete weightings of $h(j, k) = 1$, j, k, jk, and $j^2 - k^2$, respectively, which are all harmonic. Thus, (15) shows that the 2-D weighted sum over the image array can be converted to an equivalent 1-D weighted sum around the perimeter of the grid. The resistor lines, at the periphery of the grid, reduce the 1-D data array to a fixed number of quantities, independent of the array size N. The lines operate as current dividers. The following section describes the setup more specifically; algebra is omitted for brevity (see [11, ch. 2] for complete details).

IV. ARCHITECTURE

Figs. 4 and 5 show the chip architecture. The resistor grid and *photoreceptor cell array* (Fig. 4) occupy most of the active chip area. The grid is a 30×30 array of 3-kΩ

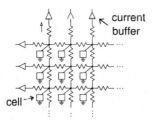

Fig. 4.   Resistor grid and photoreceptor cell array.

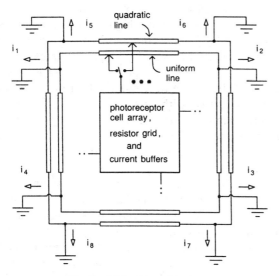

Fig. 5.   Main chip architecture.

polysilicon resistors, which is driven by a 29×29 array of photoreceptor cells. Each photoreceptor cell contains a phototransistor together with other circuitry to implement the brightness conditioning function of Fig. 2; i.e., the incident brightness is converted to a current proportional to $m(j, k)$, which is injected into the grid. (Note that effective subpixel resolution is available if the image is blurred slightly to avoid aliasing resulting from the finite sampling grid.) Around the perimeter of the grid are the *current buffers*, which hold each perimeter node at a common dc voltage (effectively ground) and convey the currents flowing out of the grid into uniform and quadratic resistor lines at the periphery (Fig. 5). The buffer outputs can be simultaneously steered to either the uniform or quadratic lines, and the corresponding sets of output currents, $i_1 - i_4$ and $i_5 - i_8$, respectively, are measured. Each uniform line simply gives a linear weighting of the buffered grid currents as a function of position (or array index) on a side of grid. Each quadratic line weights the currents according to the square of the normalized distance along the line, where the origins are at the left and the bottom for the horizontally and vertically oriented lines, respectively. (This is accomplished by making the resistor values linearly graded as a function of the appropriate position index.) The resistors in the lines are polysilicon, and each resistor in each quadratic line is made by connecting certain other resistors (selected from a set of "primitives") in series. The ends of the lines are

held at a virtual ground by *external* op-amp circuits (not shown) that convert the currents flowing out of the chip into voltages. The total resistance of each line is about 4.5 kΩ.

The following formulas give normalized moments from which the position and orientation can be found [11, pp. 157–158]. We assume a 100×100 image field, or $x_{\max} = y_{\max} = 100$. The centroid coordinates are given by

$$\bar{x} = 100 \left(\frac{(i_2 + i_3)}{i_1 + i_2 + i_3 + i_4} \right) \qquad (16)$$

and

$$\bar{y} = 100 \left(\frac{(i_1 + i_2)}{i_1 + i_2 + i_3 + i_4} \right). \qquad (17)$$

The quantities $2b'$ and $a' - c'$, normalized by the zeroth moment M_0, are given by

$$\frac{2b'}{M_0} = \frac{2(i_2 i_4 - i_1 i_3) \times 10^4}{(i_1 + i_2 + i_3 + i_4)^2} \qquad (18)$$

and

$$\frac{a' - c'}{M_0} = \frac{(i_7 - i_5) \times 10^4}{(i_5 + i_6 + i_7 + i_8)}$$
$$+ \frac{(i_1 + 2i_2 + i_3)(i_1 - i_3) \times 10^4}{(i_1 + i_2 + i_3 + i_4)^2}. \qquad (19)$$

Note that while the sums of $i_1 - i_4$ and $i_5 - i_8$ are equal ideally, a small discrepancy is present in the real system due to nonideal effects such as current buffer output conductance. These sums, which appear in the denominators of the above formulas, are distinguished to provide some cancellation of these errors [11, chs. 2 and 4].

V. CIRCUITRY AND FABRICATION

Chips have been fabricated using a 2-μm double-metal CMOS process. Fig. 6 shows a die photo. Total dimensions are 7900 μm $\times$ 9200 μm, including the pad frame. The cell array occupies a 5500-μm $\times$ 5500-μm area. There are 841 photoreceptor cells (in the 29×29 array) and 116 current buffers. The photoreceptor cell and current buffer circuits are now discussed.

A. Photoreceptor Cell Circuitry

Fig. 7 shows the schematic of a photoreceptor cell, together with bias sources on global buses. These sources are realized by diode-connected PFET's driven by external current sources. Transistors $M1 - M3$ form the thresholding current source i_{th}, which subtracts from the photocurrent i_p of $Q1$. The gate of output transistor $M4$ is held at about 3.0 V above ground. The drain of $M4$ is the cell output, which is connected to the resistor grid. In normal operation, the grid voltage is at most 3.0 V, and thus $M4$, which is either cut off or in saturation, acts like a diode in the sense that current can flow in only one direction. It also serves as a cascode transistor, which

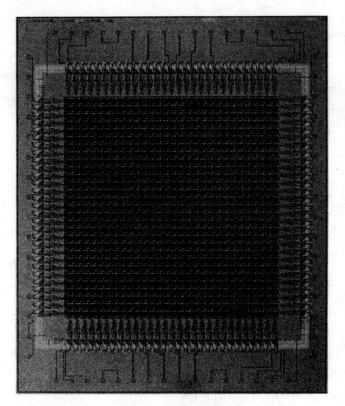

Fig. 6. Die photograph.

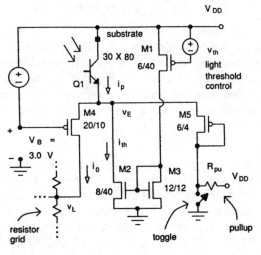

Fig. 7. Circuit for photoreceptor cell. All sizes are in micrometers. Voltage sources and the toggle are on global buses.

gives a higher output resistance than if $M4$ were simply diode connected. If the incident light level is below the threshold, i.e., if $i_p < i_{th}$, the output current $i_o = 0$. If the light level is above the threshold, i.e., $i_p > i_{th}$, then $i_o = i_p - i_{th}$. The result is a continuous, piecewise-linear dc response curve, ideally like $f(B)$ of Fig. 2. Diode-connected PFET $M5$ is connected to a bus normally held high, so it is cut off. Grounding this toggle bus forces i_o to zero for all the cells. By measuring the final outputs with all cells "shut off," the net effects of offset errors in the system are measured and thus cancellable; this was done in all experiments. Typical operating currents are $i_p = 0.1$

to 1.0 μA and $i_{th} = 0.2$ μA, though i_p may be as high as 5 μA and i_{th} as high as 1 μA for normal operation. The supply voltage (V_{DD}) is 5.5 V. The cell dimensions are about 160 μm $\times$ 160 μm, not including the grid resistors. Total area for each cell and its associated pair of grid resistors is 190 μm $\times$ 190 μm.

The source for i_{th} uses a ratioed current mirror ($M2$, $M3$) to get relatively good matching at low currents. Note that $M2$ is made long and narrow. Transistor $M1$, which is driven by a global bus, is also long and narrow. The fact that $M1$ supplies a current of $5i_{th}$ means that $M1$ can operate with a comparatively higher drive above threshold than $M2$ would if $M2$ were simply connected to a global bus. This "two-stage" source design mitigates the effect of transistor threshold voltage gradients across the chip. Note that if the design were modified for higher threshold currents, a source with less area for a given accuracy could be designed. However, the area of $Q1$ would need to be increased, a brighter image would be needed, or i_p would need to be amplified. Power dissipation would also increase.

The speed of the cell and of the entire system is limited by $Q1$, in particular by its large equivalent collector–emitter capacitance (in the open-base configuration) together with the resistance of $M4$ as seen by $Q1$. Large-signal effects can limit the speed. The dc emitter voltage v_E is at least 4 V when the light is above threshold. If the light goes below threshold for a significant length of time, v_E can drop to a few tenths of a volt above ground. This causes a long response delay when the light level goes above threshold, as v_E must rise to about 4 V again. To overcome this effect, a special scheme, which consists of shining light pulses on the chip, can be used. These pulses have a short duty cycle; they keep v_E from falling far below 4 V (or the turn-on threshold of $M4$). The output is sampled shortly before the beginning of each pulse; i.e., during the OFF period, the cells are settling from an ON state in which $M4$ is conducting. For a falling brightness step input (to zero), settling time to $i_o = 0$ from an initial $i_o = 2$ μA is about[1] 200 μs at a threshold current $i_{th} = 200$ nA [11, ch. 5].

B. Current Buffer Circuitry

The current buffer described here is somewhat different from standard followers and conveyors [12], [13]. Fig. 8 shows a diagram of the buffer in a mixed circuit-block form. The input is connected to a test *voltage* source v_s; this allows a feedforward description of the dc operation. For simplicity, first assume $i_{off} = 0$. A global bus provides a bias of 2.5 V to the negative input of the transconductance amplifier (or "transamp"), which is common to all buffers. The difference $v_{in} = v_s - v_{B1}$ at the transamp

---

[1] If the brightness falls to a value just slightly below the threshold, instead of zero, the settling time will certainly be longer. Yet for an allotted settling period, incomplete settling for such cases can be thought of as a *complete* settling with a *smaller effective value* of i_{th}, or as a distortion of the conditioning function $f(B)$.

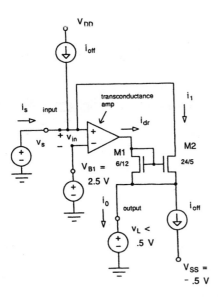

Fig. 8. Current buffer in a mixed circuit-block representation.

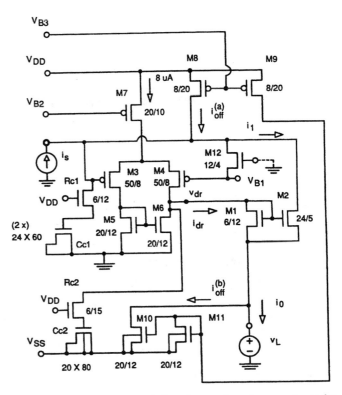

Fig. 9. Schematic of current buffer. Sources i_s and v_L are shown for performance characterization.

input causes a driver current i_{dr} to flow into mirror $M1$, $M2$, and the resulting current i_1 flows into the buffer input from the source v_s (i.e., $i_s = i_1$ because $i_{\text{off}} = 0$). The output current is $i_o = i_1 + i_{dr}$, or

$$i_o = K i_1 \qquad (20)$$

where

$$K \triangleq 1 + \frac{i_{dr}}{i_1}. \qquad (21)$$

To first order, K is constant. The measured mirror ratio i_1 / i_{dr} is about 12, so that (21) gives

$$K \cong 1.08. \qquad (22)$$

Thus the circuit is a nearly unity-gain buffer. The transamp has $g_m \cong 25\ \mu\text{S}$, so that the input conductance of the buffer is about $g_m(i_1/i_{dr}) \cong 300\ \mu\text{S}$, which corresponds to an input resistance (as seen from the grid) of about

$$R_{\text{in}} \cong 3\ \text{k}\Omega. \qquad (23)$$

The buffer is designed for a maximum i_1 of 20 μA, though $i_1 < 10\ \mu$A in most imaging cases. The transamp never runs near the saturation region of its transfer curve, and thus the input resistance is quite linear. The load voltage (i.e., the voltage on the resistor lines around the perimeter) must be 0.5 V or less for proper operation.

The circuit requires positive values of i_1 for normal operation. But on the chip, all the buffers are connected to the same grid; because of (random) input offset voltage mismatches between buffers, some buffers can be cut off (i.e., $i_1 = 0$) while others conduct. To ensure that all buffers are conducting (and hence presenting a low input resistance to the grid), there is a current source i_{off} at the input and a corresponding opposite current source at the output of each buffer. Nominally $i_{\text{off}} = 4\ \mu$A is used; this ensures that $i_1 > 2\ \mu$A for input offset voltage mismatches (between adjacent buffers) of 25 mV [11, ch. 3].

Fig. 9 shows a schematic of the buffer, now driven by a test current source i_s. Transistors $M3$–$M7$ form the transamp, which is biased at 8 μA nominally. The offsetting current sources are formed by $M8$–$M11$; $M10$ and $M11$ are connected to a negative supply V_{SS} of -0.5 V so that $M10$ remains in saturation if the load voltage v_L is near zero. Frequency compensation elements R_{C1}, C_{C1}, R_{C2}, and C_{C2} are used to make the buffer appear as a dynamically passive element from the grid,[2] for stability against oscillation. Under typical current values, specifically i_s of 1 to 10 μA and $i_{\text{off}} = 4\ \mu$A, the measured output resistance for a fixed current input is over 5 MΩ. While the grid feeding the buffers is certainly not a stiff current source, the effect of the grid conductance as seen from the buffer is manifested in the reverse voltage gain of the buffer, i.e., the change in the input voltage in response to v_L. This reverse gain $\Delta v_{\text{in}} / \Delta v_L$ is measured at 0.007 or less under typical conditions, i.e., $i_1 > 1\ \mu$A.

VI. Results

Accuracy measurements were made using stationary white planar objects against a dark background, mounted on metered translation and rotation stages [11, ch. 5]. The scene lamp was mounted on the same unit, so that the

---

[2]This is based on a small-signal analysis [11, ch. 3]. In the design of such a chip, *large-signal* sustained oscillations are still a potential problem. Pass transistor $M12$ can be turned on to short the grid to the bias bus V_{B1}, to act as a damper if such oscillations are suspected. This was not necessary here.

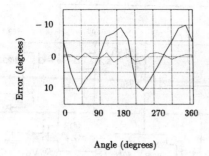

Fig. 10. Orientation angle error versus object angle (for diamond). Solid and dashed lines are for the uncalibrated and calibrated cases, respectively.

image would remain consistent under movement; i.e., any error component from nonuniform illumination would remain constant. The brightness threshold was set to completely remove the background. Ideally, one would measure the absolute accuracy of the chip by using test objects with an accurately known centroid and orientation, together with a precisely calibrated optical system. The relative accuracy measurements in this work, on the other hand, are not sensitive to object and optical system uncertainties (to first order); yet they can still indicate how accurately a specific system using the chip can be calibrated.

Position error is characterized by how closely a least-squares fit line matches a plot of the chip centroid output (in each direction) versus the translation stage position. The position of a 25×25 square (on a 100×100 image field) is determined to within $\pm 0.3\%$ of the usable range (i.e., the range for which the object remains completely in the image field) when referenced to the linear least-squares fit line.

Orientation error is characterized by measuring the chip system output angle (including final digital calculations) for a set of uniformly spaced angles of the rotation stage, typically at $0°, 15°, 30°, \cdots, 345°$. The mean of the errors over this set of angles is then subtracted from each error measurement, to leave only the variation about the mean (so that uncertainty in the object's absolute orientation is removed). This variation is typically within $\pm 2°$ for elongated and moderately sized objects, e.g., a diamond of diagonal dimensions 25×50 (on a 100×100 field). This result is based on adding calibration constants to the quantities given in (18) and (19), which are found by averaging these quantities over one set of angles (one complete rotation). Ideally, this average would be zero because of the uniformly spaced angle samples and sinusoidal dependence on the angle. While the chip introduces offsets due to component mismatches, etc., the calibration constants cancel much of this error.[3] Without

the constants, the error is $\pm 10°$, though it is smoothly varying as a function of the orientation angle. Fig. 10 shows a plot of the error for both cases, i.e., with and without the calibration. Measurements were made for several other objects. Larger objects generally give less error and smaller objects give significantly larger error. Of the position and orientation tasks, the latter is more sensitive to error in the chip output, especially for small objects. Chip power consumption was under 50 mW for all objects tested.

Acknowledgment

The author acknowledges Prof. B. Horn at the Massachusetts Institute of Technology (M.I.T.) as a collaborator, who proposed the resistive grid scheme. The author also wishes to thank Prof. H. Lee, Prof. C. Sodini, and Prof. J. Wyatt at M.I.T., together with the reviewers, for several helpful comments. This work was performed at the Research Laboratory of Electronics at M.I.T., and further work is continuing at Rockwell.

References

[1] B. K. P. Horn, *Robot Vision*. Cambridge, MA: M.I.T. Press (New York: McGraw-Hill), 1986, pp. 48–57.

[2] C. Mead, "A sensitive electronic photoreceptor," in *Proc. 1985 Chapel Hill Conf. VLSI*, pp. 463–471.

[3] B. K. P. Horn, Artificial Intelligence Lab., Mass. Inst. Technol., Cambridge, MA, A.I. Memo 1071, Dec. 1988, pp. 31–34.

[4] G. P. Petersson and L. Lindholm, "Position sensitive light detectors with high linearity," *IEEE J. Solid-State Circuits*, vol. SC-13, no. 3, pp. 392–399, June 1978.

[5] D. J. W. Noorlag and S. Middelhoek, "Two-dimensional position-sensitive photodetector with high linearity made with standard i.c.-technology," *Inst. Elec. Eng.: J. Solid-State Electron Devices*, vol. 3, no. 3, pp. 75–82, May 1979.

[6] S. P. DeWeerth and C. A. Mead, "A two-dimensional visual tracking array," in *Proc. 1988 MIT Conf. VLSI*. Cambridge, MA: M.I.T. Press, pp. 259–275.

[7] M. Hatamian, "A real-time two-dimensional moment generating Algorithm and its single chip Implementation," *IEEE Trans. Acoust., Speech, and Signal Processing*, vol. ASSP-34, no. 3, pp. 546–553, June 1986.

[8] D. L. Standley and B. K. P. Horn, "An object position and orientation IC with embedded imager," in *ISSCC Dig. Tech. Papers* (San Francisco, CA), Feb. 13–15, 1991, pp. 38–39.

[9] D. L. Standley and B. K. P. Horn, "Analog CMOS IC for object position and orientation," *SPIE Proc.*, vol. 1473, pp. 194–201, Mar. 1991.

[10] J. L. Wyatt, Jr., D. L. Standley, and W. Yang, "The MIT vision chip project: Analog VLSI systems for fast image acquisition and early vision processing," in *Proc. 1991 IEEE Int. Conf. Robotics Automation*, Apr. 1991, pp. 1330–1335.

[11] D. L. Standley, "Analog VLSI implementation of smart vision sensors: Stability theory and an experimental design," Ph.D. dissertation (Part 2), Dept. Elec. Eng. Comput. Sci., Mass. Inst. Technol., Cambridge, MA, Jan. 1991.

[12] A. S. Sedra and G. W. Roberts, "Current conveyor theory and practice," in *Analogue IC Design: the Current-Mode Approach*, C. Toumazou, F. J. Lidgey, and D. H. Haigh, Eds. London: Peter Peregrinus, 1990, pp. 93–126, ch. 3.

[13] C. Toumazou and F. J. Lidgey, "Universal current-mode analog amplifiers," in *Analogue IC Design: the Current-Mode Approach*, C. Toumazou, F. J. Lidgey, and D. H. Haigh, Eds. London: Peter Peregrinus, 1990, pp. 139–146, ch. 4.

[3]The constants themselves depend on the object, and thus cancellation is not as good when using the same values over a variety of objects. Further work could investigate other error cancellation schemes, such as using near-unity correction factors on the measured output currents.

The Digi-Neocognitron: A Digital Neocognitron Neural Network Model for VLSI

Brian A. White, *Member, IEEE,* and Mohamed I. Elmasry, *Fellow, IEEE*

Abstract—For artificial neural networks (ANN's) to take full advantage of state-of-the-art VLSI and ULSI technologies, they must adapt to an efficient all-digital implementation. This is because these technologies, at higher levels of integration and complexity, are mainly a digital implementation medium, offering many advantages over analog counterparts. This paper illustrates this thesis by adapting one of the most complicated ANN models, the neocognitron (NC), to an efficient all-digital implementation for VLSI. The new model, the digi-neocognitron (DNC), has the same pattern recognition performance as the NC. The DNC model is derived from the NC model by a combination of preprocessing approximations and the definition of new model functions, e.g., multiplication and division are eliminated by conversion of factors to powers of 2, requiring only shift operations. In this paper, the NC model is reviewed, the DNC model is presented, a methodology to convert NC models to DNC models is discussed, and the performances of the two models are compared on a character recognition example. The DNC model has substantial advantages over the NC model for VLSI implementation. The area–delay product is improved by two to three orders of magnitude, and I/O and memory requirements are reduced by representation of weights with 3 bits or less and neuron outputs with 4 bits or 7 bits.

I. INTRODUCTION

IN recent years, there has been a great deal of research activity on artificial neural networks (ANN) in the area of simulation and hardware implementations [1]–[6]. Because of the special features offered by ANN's, such as the capability to learn from examples, adaptation, parallelism, fault tolerance, and noise resistance, they have been applied to a number of real-world problems, including image and speech processing [3], [6]–[9]. To enhance the impact of ANN's and broaden the area of applications, it is imperative that ANN's benefit from state-of-the-art VLSI and ULSI implementation technologies. Because these technologies are basically a digital implementation medium, ANN's must be adapted to an all-digital implementation approach. To illustrate this thesis, the research work reported in this paper offers a practical example of adapting an ANN model to an all-digital VLSI implementation.

An all-digital ANN VLSI implementation offers several advantages over its analog counterpart.

Manuscript received March 12, 1991; revised July 31, 1991. This work was supported in part by NSERC and MICRONET research grants.

B. A. White was with the VLSI Research Group, University of Waterloo, Waterloo, Ontario, Canada. He is now with New Vista Technology Inc., 165 Manitou Way, Ancaster, Ontario, Canada L9G 1X9.

M. I. Elmasry is with the VLSI Research Group, Department of Electrical and Computer Engineering, University of Waterloo, Waterloo, Ontario, Canada N2L 3G1.

IEEE Log Number 9103359.

1) In most real-world applications, ANN's are embedded in existing *digital* hardware/software systems [10]. An all-digital ANN VLSI implementation solves the compatibility problem.

2) Real-world applications require *large* neural networks of more than 10 000 neurons and synapses [8]. Digital VLSI/ULSI is more appropriate at this level of complexity, whereas analog VLSI/ULSI suffers from noise susceptibility and difficulties in fabricating high-precision resistors and capacitors.

3) Larger ANN's are most likely implemented in a multichip set, and the analog implementation would make it more difficult to transfer signals from chip to chip, and also to match board-level capacitive loads and time constants [11].

4) At any given time, digital VLSI technology is always more mature than its analog counterpart in terms of fabrication technology and simulation and design automation tools. It also offers a wide range of fabrication technologies, including such technologies as field programmable gate arrays [12] for rapid prototyping.

5) Real-world examples may suffer from I/O bottlenecks [9], which are best addressed by digital techniques such as input buffers, shift registers, and pipelining. Moreover, power dissipation reduction techniques, such as dynamic logic and complementary operation, can be used.

6) Digital implementation offers a homogeneous implementation environment between the processing elements and the on-chip or external memory storage.

Other advantages of digital VLSI implementation apply specifically to the neocognitron ANN [13]–[15] that is considered here. The neocognitron has a locally connected network with *repetitive* use of the *same* weights; this fits well with time division multiplexing of digital hardware [8], [9]. For *temporally sparse* (only a small subset of inputs actually take part in the computation) ANN's such as the neocognitron (as shown in Section IV), fully parallel analog multipliers look less attractive and a digital shared resource approach is again more suitable [16]. The neocognitron model also uses a variety of complex functions, not just a single activation function. It is easier to implement these functions digitally in lookup tables than to attempt to design a number of appropriate analog elements.

There are also certain shortcomings of digital VLSI that must be resolved in order to implement ANN's. Most ANN neuron calculations involve a weighted sum of the neuron in-

Reprinted from *IEEE Trans, on Neural Networks*, vol. 3, no. 1, pp. 73–85, Jan. 1992.

puts, and the multiplier required for this multiply–accumulate operation is slow and consumes large area in a digital VLSI implementation. However, if the neural network model is carefully modified to approximate all multiplying factors by powers of 2 (to replace a multiplier by a shifter), this problem can be eliminated, as shown in Section III, and an all-digital implementation becomes very attractive.

It is also important to indicate why the neocognitron neural network model, possibly the most complicated network ever developed [3], was investigated for all-digital VLSI implementation in this work, rather than a simpler model. Our approach was to select a real-world application area (optical character recognition) and let the application dictate the selection of the ANN. Realistic two-dimensional image recognition systems require position, scale, and rotation invariance, as well as tolerance of noise and distortions. The neocognitron uses a hierarchical type of network to produce outputs invariant to position, size, and small distortions and is capable of complex character recognition [3], [6]. Its architecture of neurons organized in two-dimensional planes, local interconnections, and repeated weights also matches the general features required [8], [9] for successful optical character recognition by ANN's. Section II describes the neocognitron model in detail.

This paper proposes a new neural network model called the digi-neocognitron (DNC), described in Section III, which has the same pattern recognition performance as the neocognitron (NC) but is better suited for digital VLSI implementation. The DNC model is derived from the NC model by a combination of preprocessing approximations and definition of new model functions. Multiplication and division are eliminated by conversion of factors to powers of 2, requiring only shifts. Bit widths are restricted, and complex functions are implemented with lookup tables, carefully tailored to retain performance. A methodology for conversion of a particular NC model to a DNC model is described; this procedure utilizes the neocognitron learning capability and fault tolerance to compensate for approximations. Since the learning procedure uses the NC model, it is performed off-line.

Section IV reports on the simulation results of a character recognition example, which proves the feasibility of this approach. The NC model is trained on centered versions of the input patterns, which are alphanumeric characters in a 12 by 12 pixel array [17], and the conversion methodology is followed to derive a DNC model. Both neural networks are tested on translations of the original patterns with varying levels of added random noise; this quantifies recognition performance, translation invariance, and noise tolerance. Both ANN's have very good recognition rates in the presence of large amounts of noise, and the DNC model has no deterioration from NC performance. Both ANN's can also classify input patterns as unknown, which significantly reduces the undetectable error rate (wrong classifications); this is very important for commercial applications [18].

Section V reports on the advantages of the DNC model relative to the NC model for VLSI implementation. The area–delay product for implementation of the multiplication in the weighted sum calculation is improved by two to three orders of magnitude. I/O and memory requirements are substantially reduced by representation of weights with 3 bits or less and neuron outputs with 4 bits or 7 bits.

II. NEOCOGNITRON NEURAL NETWORK MODEL

The neocognitron, proposed by Fukushima [13]–[15], is an artificial neural network model for visual pattern recognition. It has generated interest owing to its capabilities for shift-invariant and deformation-resistant pattern recognition, and has been applied to character recognition tasks [3], [14], [19]–[21]. The neocognitron has some similarities to the human visual system, and is self-organizing; i.e., it performs unsupervised learning, or learning without a teacher. We focus our attention, as in [22], on the more popular unsupervised learning model, although a supervised learning version also exists [19].

The basic architecture of the neocognitron neural network model is shown in Fig. 1. There are four different kinds of neurons, called S cells, C cells, Vs cells, and Vc cells. All of the cells have nonnegative outputs. The Vc cells and Vs cells provide inhibitory inputs to suppress outputs of S cells and C cells, respectively. The neocognitron is a multilayer neural network, with two-dimensional input layer connected to a cascade of layers consisting of planes of S cells and planes of C cells. S cells can be interpreted as feature detectors, and C cells tolerate position errors by averaging S-cell outputs in a small area. Only interconnections to S cells have modifiable weights, determined during learning; other interconnection weights are fixed, but are adjustable architectural parameters that influence learning and recognition performance. Typically, each S-cell plane develops weights that look for a different type of feature, and the number of planes can be different for each level. There is spatially local interconnect, with interconnection weights to a given neuron defined only in a small connection area, indicated by the circles in Fig. 1. These weights are also constrained to be translationally invariant, with the same set of weights applying at all two-dimensional positions within a cell plane. These features give the neocognitron capabilities for toleration of translations and deformations. At higher levels, cells respond to more complicated features, and the effective receptive field becomes larger. The number of neurons in a cell plane reduces at higher levels, until at the final (recognition) level there is only one neuron per plane, each representing a recognition class.

The neocognitron neural network model can be described mathematically as follows [14]. The S-cell output is

$$u_{Sl}(k, \underline{n})$$

$$= r_l \phi \left[\frac{1 + \sum_{\kappa=1}^{K_{Cl-1}} \sum_{\underline{v} \in A_l} a_l(\kappa, \underline{v}, k) u_{Cl-1}(\kappa, \underline{n} + \underline{v})}{1 + \frac{r_l}{1+r_l} b_l(k) v_{Cl}(\underline{n})} - 1 \right] \tag{1}$$

where the nonlinear activation function is

$$\phi[x] = \max(x, 0). \tag{2}$$

Here $u_{Sl}(k, \underline{n})$ describes the output of an S cell at two-

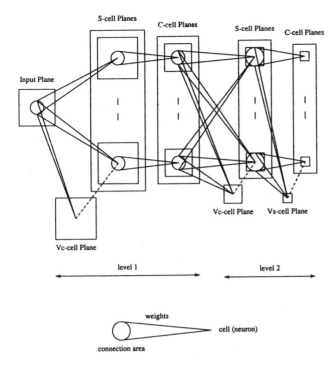

Fig. 1. Architecture of the neocognitron neural network.

S-cell Planes C-cell Planes S-cell Planes C-cell Planes

Input Plane

Vc-cell Plane Vs-cell Plane

Vc-cell Plane

level 1   level 2

weights

cell (neuron)

connection area

and this then requires division by the sum

$$csum = \sum_{\kappa=1}^{K_{Cl-1}} \sum_{\underline{v} \in A_l} c_l(\underline{v}) \tag{5}$$

to obtain the same result for $v_{Cl}(\underline{n})$. This normalization process does not change the Vc-cell and S-cell outputs and is not necessary for the neocognitron. It is necessary for the digi-neocognitron model, as it provides a consistent range of values for the c_l fixed weights, which aids the approximations discussed in Section III.

Interconnections from the S cells to the C cells have fixed weights, which are adjustable in the model architecture but are not modified by learning. The C-cell output is given by

$$u_{Cl}(k, \underline{n}) = \Psi \left[\frac{1 + \sum_{\underline{v} \in D_l} d_l(\underline{v}) u_{Sl}(k, \underline{n} + \underline{v})}{1 + v_{Sl}(\underline{n})} - 1 \right] \tag{6}$$

where the saturation function is

$$\Psi[x] = \frac{x}{\alpha_l + x}, \qquad x \geq 0$$
$$= 0, \qquad x < 0 \tag{7}$$

with saturation parameter α_l. This function limits response to the interval $[0, 1]$. The excitation summation is over a single small connection area D_l, with the previous level S-cell outputs (for the same plane only) multiplied by d_l fixed weights, which are taken as a two-dimensional Gaussian with variance σ_d. Optionally, there may exist inhibitory Vs cells in the architecture, which provide a form of lateral inhibition, with nonzero C-cell output only if the excitation sum is greater than the inhibitory term. The Vs-cell output is given by

$$v_{Sl}(\underline{n}) = \frac{1}{K_{Sl}} \sum_{\kappa=1}^{K_{Sl}} \sum_{\underline{v} \in D_l} d_l(\underline{v}) u_{Sl}(\kappa, \underline{n} + \underline{v}). \tag{8}$$

This is a weighted average of activity in the connection area, but now taken across all K_{Sl} preceding level S-cell planes.

The unsupervised learning rules for the neocognitron will not be covered in much detail, except to indicate the modification required by our change of c_l normalization. In the learning process, *representative* S cells with the strongest output in columns (centered on connection areas) through the S-cell planes are selected, at most one per S-cell plane. Interconnection weights over the connection area are reinforced in proportion to the input activities and then replicated to all positions in the plane.

The rules as originally stated by Fukushima are, for *representative* $u_{Sl}(K, \underline{N})$,

$$\Delta a_l(\kappa, \underline{v}, K) = q_l c_l(\underline{v}) u_{Cl-1}(\kappa, \underline{N} + \underline{v}) \tag{9}$$

$$\Delta b_l(K) = q_l v_{Cl}(\underline{N}) \tag{10}$$

where q_l is a reinforcement parameter which affects the speed of weight development and the type of feature detectors that

dimensional coordinate $\underline{n}$ in the kth plane in level l. The excitation weighted sum in the numerator sums the modifiable weight a_l multiplied by the previous level C-cell outputs, but only over the small connection area A_l. The sum is over all K_{Cl-1} planes in the previous level; this degenerates to the single input layer plane for level 1 S cells (see Fig. 1). The a_l weights are developed in the learning process; note that they are not a function of position $\underline{n}$. The inhibitory term in the denominator has a nonlinear effect on the output, and involves the modifiable weight b_l developed during learning (represented by the dotted line in Fig. 1), the Vc-cell output, and the selectivity parameter r_l. The selectivity is very important in the learning process; a larger r_l causes S cells to be more selective in their response, owing to more inhibition, but also less tolerant of distortions. The S-cell output is nonzero only if the excitation sum is greater than the inhibitory term; the inhibitory cells suppress output when irrelevant features are presented.

The inhibitory Vc-cell output is given by a weighted rms average of the previous level C-cell outputs over the same connection area A_l:

$$v_{Cl}(\underline{n}) = \left[\frac{1}{csum} \sum_{\kappa=1}^{K_{Cl-1}} \sum_{\underline{v} \in A_l} c_l(\underline{v}) u_{Cl-1}^2(\kappa, \underline{n} + \underline{v}) \right]^{1/2}. \tag{3}$$

The c_l are fixed weights, which are usually [23] taken as a two-dimensional Gaussian with adjustable variance σ_c. Here we have changed the normalization (from Fukushima) such that

$$c_l(0) = 1 \tag{4}$$

emerge. With the renormalization to $c_l(0) = 1$, the first learning rule becomes

$$\Delta a_l(\kappa, \underline{v}, K) = q_l \frac{c_l(\underline{v})}{csum} u_{Cl-1}(\kappa, \underline{N} + \underline{v}). \quad (11)$$

As discussed above, this normalization change is not necessary for the neocognitron model and yields the same results as the neocognitron. It is necessary for the digi-neocognitron model.

III. DIGI-NEOCOGNITRON: A DIGITAL NEURAL NETWORK MODEL FOR VLSI

A. Approach to VLSI Implementation

The need for VLSI implementation is considered at the highest level of abstraction possible, namely the neural network model itself. The neocognitron (NC) neural network model functions and weight values are changed to facilitate a digital VLSI circuit implementation, and this results in a new neural network, which we call the digi-neocognitron (DNC).

Multiplications and divisions are replaced by simple shifts by conversion of multiplying or dividing factors to powers of 2; shifters have a simple hardware implementation which substantially reduces the silicon area and propagation delays compared with multipliers. Bit ranges are restricted as much as possible. Complex functions are replaced by lookup tables, which can be implemented by simple combinatorial logic or memory arrays, owing to the reduced bit ranges.

Bit range restrictions in the DNC model start from decisions (tested by simulation) on the representation of the different types of cell outputs. Vc-cell and C-cell outputs are in the interval [0,1] and are reasonably represented with 4 b (4 binary places to the right of the binary point). There is no explicit range constraint on neocognitron S-cell outputs, but in principle the output is in the interval [0,1], as discussed by Fukushima [15]. However, the DNC model approximation of modifiable weights as powers of 2 (discussed below) can result in S-cell outputs greater than 1 if excitatory weights are rounded up and inhibitory weights rounded down. In our simulations the DNC S-cell outputs have been less than 2, but a representation of 7 b (with 4 binary places) is used to provide a practical safety margin (represent outputs up to 8).

The following sections describe the DNC neural network model, including preprocessing approximations that would always be done in a DNC simulator, and model functions that would be implemented in VLSI hardware. The model is described functionally, including necessary bit widths; for more details see [24]. Detailed VLSI architectural issues are addressed in [25].

B. Power-of-2 Representations

In digital circuit implementations, the multiplication (or division) of binary numbers requires large chip area and causes speed deterioration; a method for reducing this hardware complexity approximates binary numbers by the sum of a limited number of signed power-of-2 terms [26], [27]. Multiplication or division by a power of 2 is a shift operation, with a simple hardware implementation, which reduces the silicon area and propagation delays, as shown in Section V. Note that a power of 2 in the range 2^{-m} to 2^n has only

$(n + m + 1)$ distinct values, so the number of bits required for input is also reduced considerably.

The DNC model uses single-term power-of-2 approximations in all cases except one, which requires a two-term expansion. The description of the DNC model uses the following notation, similar to [27] but modified for the case of positive numbers and fractional parts.

Denote a particular single-term power-of-2 space (set of admissible values in the representation) as

$$P_{m,n} = \left\{ 2^m, 2^{m+1}, \cdots, 2^{n-1}, 2^n \right\}$$

where m and n are integers, with $m \leq n$. Define

$$\langle x \rangle_{2^m, 2^n; b} \quad (12)$$

to denote rounding x to the nearest term belonging to the representation $P_{m,n}$, with bias $b \in [0,1]$ to rounding up. If x is outside the range of the representation, the appropriate endpoint of the representation is used as the approximation.

Bias 0.0 selects the power of 2 that is less than or equal to the binary number, bias 1.0 selects the power of 2 that is greater than or equal to the number, and bias 0.5 selects the closest power of 2. We can simply denote these as

$$\langle x \rangle_{2^m, 2^n; le} \doteq \langle x \rangle_{2^m, 2^n; 0.0} \qquad \langle x \rangle_{2^m, 2^n; ge} \doteq \langle x \rangle_{2^m, 2^n; 1.0}$$
$$\langle x \rangle_{2^m, 2^n} \doteq \langle x \rangle_{2^m, 2^n; 0.5} \quad (13)$$

Extending this concept to the one case where two terms are required, denote a particular two-term power-of-2 space (set of admissible values in the representation) as

$$P^2_{m,n} = \left\{ y \mid y = 2^p + s2^k, y > 0 \right\}$$

where m and n are integers, with $m \leq n$, $p, k \in \{m, m+1, \cdots, n-1, n\}$, and $s \in \{-1, 0, 1\}$.
Define

$$\langle\langle x \rangle\rangle_{2^m, 2^n} \quad (14)$$

to denote rounding x to the nearest term belonging to the representation $P^2_{m,n}$.

C. Digi-Neocognitron: Inhibitory Vc Cells

1) Preprocessing: Equation (3) describes the inhibitory Vc-cell output function of the NC model. The normalization change of (4) provides a consistent range of values for c_l that allows approximation by values c_l restricted to 0 and simple powers of 2, as shown in Table I. The normalization sum of the fixed weights in (5) is now

$$C_{\Sigma} = \sum_{\kappa=1}^{K_{Cl-1}} \sum_{\underline{v} \in A_l} \overline{c_l(\underline{v})}. \quad (15)$$

To replace the division in (3) by a shift operation, a power-of-2 approximation of equation (15) is done as follows for level l:

$$\overline{C_{\Sigma}} = \langle C_{\Sigma} \rangle_{1, 2048; le}, \qquad l = 1$$
$$= \langle C_{\Sigma} \rangle_{1, 2048; ge}, \qquad l > 1. \quad (16)$$

The representation accommodates architectures having a c_l mask size (connection area A_l) up to 7 by 7 and a number of preceding planes K_{Cl-1} up to 128. At level $l = 1$, le rounding

TABLE I
PREPROCESSING OF FIXED WEIGHTS

Fixed Weight c_l, d_l Interval	Fixed Weight $\overline{c_l}, \overline{d_l}$ Approximation	Interpretation
[0.0, 0.1)	0	force 0
[0.1, 0.4)	1/4	shift 2 R
[0.4, 0.75)	1/2	shift 1 R
[0.75, 1.0]	1	shift 0

is used to increase the inhibit output to suppress noise in the S-cell plane outputs; at higher levels ge rounding is used to decrease the inhibit (noise is already suppressed by level 1) to allow S cells to be activated more easily.

2) DNC Model Functions: With the preprocessing approximations, the DNC model Vc-cell output is

$$\overline{v_{Cl}(\underline{n})} = \left[\frac{1}{\overline{C_\Sigma}} \sum_{\kappa=1}^{K_{Cl-1}} \sum_{\underline{v} \in A_l} \overline{c_l(\underline{v})} \, \overline{u_{Cl-1}(\kappa, \underline{n} + \underline{v})}^2 \right]^{1/2} \quad (17)$$

which is implemented as shown in Fig. 2. The inputs $\overline{u_{Cl-1}}$ are lower level C-cell outputs or the input layer pattern, represented with 4 b; on the input layer a 0 pixel is input as 0.0000 binary and a 1 pixel as 0.1111 binary for consistency of hardware implementation. Multiplication by c_l is implemented by forcing 0 or shifting 0–2 right, per Table I; results are truncated to 4 b. To implement the squaring of $\overline{u_C}$ without a multiplier, a power-of-2 approximation of $\overline{u_C}$ is used to control shifting. This is defined in Table II, and can be implemented in digital hardware with a simple combinatorial circuit. Results of the shift are truncated to 4 b. Note that the *output* of the shifter is not restricted to powers of 2.

Summation over connection areas in (17) requires a 16 b accumulator (adder plus register). Note that we are describing the DNC model functions, not the VLSI architectural implementation, which could have parallel shifters feeding into pipelined carry-save adders, for instance. Division by $\overline{C_\Sigma}$ is implemented with a shift. The square root in (17) is approximated with a lookup table as shown in Table III; this can be implemented with simple combinatorial logic. The first four entries increase the inhibit at low activity levels for S-cell output noise suppression and to compensate for truncations. The final $\overline{v_C}$ output is 4 b.

Note that a shift operation is used to implement the squaring of $\overline{u_C}$, rather than a lookup table as used for the square root. The square root calculation is only done once per $\overline{v_C}$ calculation, whereas the $\overline{u_C}$ squaring is done for every term in the summation. In the VLSI implementation, it is likely that many summation terms will be calculated in parallel in identical pipelined systolic cells, so it is important to reduce the area and delay of the squaring circuit. In this model, as shown in Fig. 2, only the shifter delay appears on the critical path, with shift control determined in parallel. This achieves a critical path delay significantly less than a lookup table approach, and also uses less area. The accuracy of this shift implementation is the same as a lookup table for inputs up to and including 0.1000 binary. For larger inputs the output is

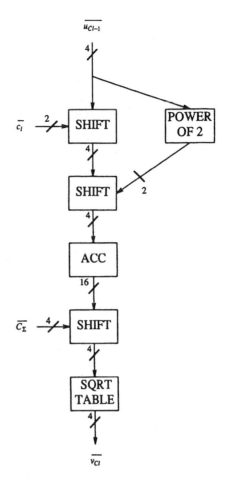

Fig. 2. Digi-neocognitron Vc-cell block diagram, with bit widths indicated.

TABLE II
POWER OF 2 APPROXIMATION FOR SQUARING C-CELL OUTPUT

Input $\overline{u_C}$ (binary)	Power of 2 ($\overline{u_C}$) Shift Control
0000	Force 0
0001	Force 0
0010	Force 0
0011	Shift 2 R
0100	Shift 2 R
0101	Shift 1 R
0110	Shift 1 R
0111	Shift 1 R
1000	Shift 1 R
1001	Shift 0
1010	Shift 0
1011	Shift 0
1100	Shift 0
1101	Shift 0
1110	Shift 0
1111	Shift 0

greater than for an "accurate" lookup table, but it was found in simulation that this provided better results for $\overline{v_C}$ when combined with other truncations and approximations in the DNC model.

D. Digi-Neocognitron S Cells

1) Preprocessing: Equation (1) describes the S-cell output function of the neocognitron. Modifiable weights a_l and b_l

505

TABLE III
SQUARE ROOT TABLE FOR Vc-CELL OUTPUT

Input (decimal)	Input (binary)	Output (binary)	Output (decimal)
0.0	0.0000	0.0100	0.25
0.0625	0.0001	0.0110	0.375
0.125	0.0010	0.0111	0.4375
0.1875	0.0011	0.1000	0.5
0.250	0.0100	0.1000	0.5
0.3125	0.0101	0.1001	0.5625
0.375	0.0110	0.1010	0.625
0.4375	0.0111	0.1011	0.6875
0.5	0.1000	0.1011	0.6875
0.5625	0.1001	0.1100	0.75
0.625	0.1010	0.1101	0.8125
0.6875	0.1011	0.1101	0.8125
0.75	0.1100	0.1110	0.875
0.8125	0.1101	0.1110	0.875
0.875	0.1110	0.1111	0.9375
0.9375	0.1111	0.1111	0.9375

(actually $r_l b_l/(1 + r_l)$) are approximated by powers of 2 as described below. For fine-tuning, all the a_l and b_l weights can be scaled by a factor f_l to improve alignment with the power-of-2 representation; this is specified on an input file to the DNC model simulator, as shown in the Appendix. For f_l close to 1.0 this is justifiable since a *small* change in all weight values is equivalent to using a different value of reinforcement q_l in the neocognitron learning equations (10) and (11).

Our experience with real examples is that the critical factor in emulating the neocognitron with the digi-neocognitron is the inhibition term in the S cells, i.e., the Vc-cell output and the $r_l b_l/(1 + r_l)$ weight factor; this agrees with the conclusions of a fault tolerance analysis of the neocognitron [28]. A power-of-2 approximation of $r_l b_l/(1 + r_l)$ consequently uses one or *two* power-of-2 terms (as specified on the input file to the DNC model simulator shown in the Appendix):

$$\overline{r_l b_l(k)/(1 + r_l)} = \langle f_l r_l b_l(k)/(1 + r_l) \rangle_{1,64} \qquad (18)$$

or

$$\overline{r_l b_l(k)/(1 + r_l)} = \langle\langle f_l r_l b_l(k)/(1 + r_l) \rangle\rangle_{1,64}. \qquad (19)$$

One term is sufficient on lower levels but two terms are needed on higher levels.

A power-of-2 approximation of the modifiable weight a_l, after scaling by f_l, is done as follows. If $f_l a_l$ is less than half the smallest division in the representation (1/16), it is approximated as 0 to avoid rounding up and increasing the output from irrelevant feature detectors. Otherwise, the approximation is

$$\overline{a_l} = \langle f_l a_l \rangle_{1/8,8} \qquad (20)$$

selecting the closest power of 2 in the range. This results in eight possible values, which can be encoded in 3 b; in fact, the encoding is compatible with the control signals required to implement the shifting. To summarize this very important result, *the weights a_l can be approximated with 3 b*.

The power-of-2 approximation of r_l is (applying to the r_l multiplying the ϕ function)

$$\overline{r_l} = \langle r_l \rangle_{1,16;2/3}. \qquad (21)$$

This selects the closest power of 2 in the range, with a bias of 2/3 to rounding up; i.e., if r_l is in the upper two thirds of the range it is rounded up, in the lower one third of the range it is rounded down. The bias is used to preferably increase rather than decrease S-cell output, once inhibition is properly handled as above.

2) DNC Model Functions: With the preprocessing approximations applied to the NC model S-cell output equation (1), the DNC model S-cell output is

$$\overline{u_{Sl}(k, \underline{n})} = \overline{r_l} \phi \left[\frac{E - IC}{1 + IC} \right], \qquad \phi[x] = \max(x, 0) \qquad (22)$$

where the excitation sum is

$$E = \sum_{\kappa=1}^{K_{Cl-1}} \sum_{\underline{v} \in A_l} \overline{a_l(\kappa, \underline{v}, k)} \, \overline{u_{Cl-1}(\kappa, \underline{n} + \underline{v})} \qquad (23)$$

and the inhibitory term is

$$IC = \overline{r_l b_l(k)/(1 + r_l)} \, \overline{v_{Cl}(\underline{n})}. \qquad (24)$$

The inhibit (IC) portion is implemented as shown on the left of Fig. 3. If $r_l b_l/(1 + r_l)$ is represented by a sum or difference of two powers of 2, the multiplication is a sum or difference of two shifts, implemented by the sign input to the accumulator to add or subtract. The DNC model approximates the $1/(1 + IC)$ inhibit function in (22) by a function of the form $1/IC2$, where IC2 is a power of 2, to enable implementation by another shift operation. With this approximation, the S-cell output function is

$$\overline{u_{Sl}(k, \underline{n})} = \overline{r_l} \left[\frac{E - IC}{IC2} \right], \qquad E > IC$$
$$= 0 \qquad \text{otherwise.} \qquad (25)$$

The IC2 approximation is defined as shown in Table IV in decimal format; this can be implemented by simple combinatorial logic.

The rest of the model is implemented as shown on the right of Fig. 3. The same accumulator is used for the excitation sum (23) and the $E - IC$ subtraction in (25). To implement the ϕ function, the hardware must also detect $E - IC < 0$, and generate a force 0 signal to the following shifter.

E. Digi-Neocognitron: Inhibitory Vs Cells

Note that the presence of Vs cells in the neural network model is an architectural option. Typically Vs cells are not used on the lower levels but are used on the final level to give a form of lateral inhibition.

1) Preprocessing: Equation (8) describes the inhibitory Vs-cell output function of the NC model. The fixed weights d_l are a two-dimensional Gaussian with variance σ_d and normalization $d_l(0) = 1$, and the same approximation (Table I) as for c_l is used. The number K_{Sl} of previous level S-cell planes, assumed to be less than 128, is approximated as a

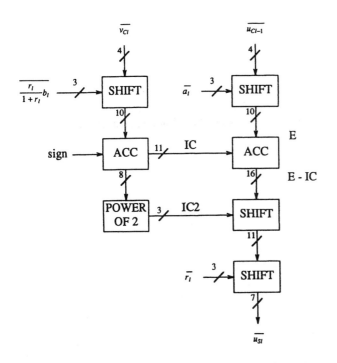

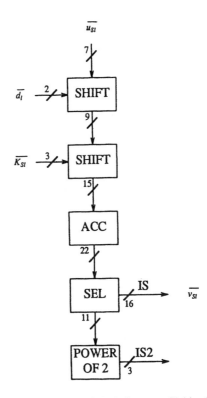

Fig. 3. Digi-neocognitron S-cell block diagram, with bit widths indicated.

Fig. 4. Digi-neocognitron Vs-cell block diagram, with bit widths indicated.

TABLE IV
POWER OF 2 APPROXIMATION FOR $1/(1+I)$ INHIBIT FUNCTION

IC, IS Interval	IC2, IS2 Approximation	Interpretation
<0.5	1	shift 0
[0.5, 2.0)	2	shift 1 R
[2.0, 4.5)	4	shift 2 R
[4.5, 10.0)	8	shift 3 R
[10.0, 21.0)	16	shift 4 R
≥ 21.0	32	shift 5 R

The le rounding is used to increase rather than decrease C-cell outputs.

2) DNC Model Functions: With the preprocessing approximations applied to the NC model C-cell output equation (6), the DNC model C-cell output is

$$\overline{u_{Cl}(k,\underline{n})} = \Psi\left[\frac{E - \text{IS}}{\text{IS2}}\right], \qquad E > \text{IS}$$
$$= 0 \qquad \text{otherwise} \qquad (29)$$

where the saturation function Ψ is defined in (7). The excitation sum and the inhibitory term are

$$E = \sum_{\underline{v} \in D_l} \overline{d_l(\underline{v})}\, \overline{u_{Sl}(k, \underline{n} + \underline{v})} \qquad \text{IS} = \overline{v_{Sl}(\underline{n})} \qquad (30)$$

and the $1/(1 + \text{IS})$ inhibit function is approximated by $1/\text{IS2}$. This is implemented as shown in Fig. 5. The final step in the DNC model involves approximation of the Ψ function in (7) in order to evaluate (29):

$$\overline{\Psi[x]} = \frac{z}{1+z}, \qquad z = x/\overline{\alpha_l}. \qquad (31)$$

power of 2 to replace the division in equation (8) by a shift operation:

$$\overline{K_{Sl}} = \langle K_{Sl} \rangle_{1,64;le} \qquad (26)$$

2) DNC Model Functions: With the preprocessing approximations, the DNC model Vs-cell output is

$$\overline{v_{Sl}(\underline{n})} = \frac{1}{\overline{K_{Sl}}} \sum_{\kappa=1}^{K_{Sl}} \sum_{\underline{v} \in D_l} \overline{d_l(\underline{v})}\, \overline{u_{Sl}(\kappa, \underline{n} + \underline{v})} \qquad (27)$$

which is implemented as shown in Fig. 4. The final block approximates the $1/(1 + \text{IS})$ inhibit function which occurs in the C-cell calculation (next section), by a function of the form $1/\text{IS2}$, with IS2 a power of 2 (Table IV).

F. Digi-Neocognitron: C Cells

1) Preprocessing: Equation (6) describes the C-cell output function of the NC model. The fixed weights d_l are approximated as before (Table I). The saturation parameter α_l in (7) is approximated as

$$\overline{\alpha_l} = \langle \alpha_l \rangle_{1/32,1;le}. \qquad (28)$$

This is implemented by a shift to transform approximately to z, followed by a table lookup implementation of the $z/(1 + z)$ function, as defined in Table V. The critical decision region for the saturation function (31) is from $z = 1/3$, where the output is 0.25, to $z = 3$, where the output is 0.75. This allows defining the lookup table primarily to cover this range well, which only requires a 4 b input plus an overflow bit.

507

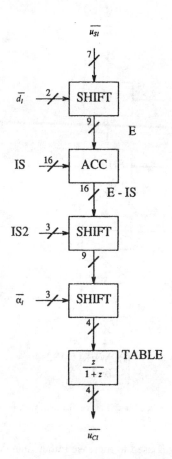

Fig. 5. Digi-neocognitron C-cell block diagram, with bit widths indicated.

TABLE V
$Z/(1 + Z)$ Table for C-Cell Output

Input (decimal)	Input (binary)	Output (binary)	Output (decimal)
0.0	00.00	0.0000	0.0
0.25	00.01	0.0011	0.1875
0.5	00.10	0.0101	0.3125
0.75	00.11	0.0111	0.4375
1.0	01.00	0.1000	0.5
1.25	01.01	0.1001	0.5625
1.5	01.10	0.1010	0.625
1.75	01.11	0.1010	0.625
2.0	10.00	0.1011	0.6875
2.25	10.01	0.1011	0.6875
2.5	10.10	0.1011	0.6875
2.75	10.11	0.1100	0.75
3.0	11.00	0.1100	0.75
3.25	11.01	0.1100	0.75
3.5	11.10	0.1100	0.75
3.75	11.11	0.1101	0.8125
>	>	0.1111	0.9375

G. Methodology for Conversion from NC Model to DNC Model

The procedure for conversion of an NC model to a DNC model utilizes the inherent NC fault tolerance characteristics [28] and unsupervised learning capability to compensate for inaccuracies introduced by the implementation approximations, and consists of the following steps.

1)` Do unconstrained simulation (including learning) with the NC model, in order to get something that works for the particular problem. If there is not already an existing NC model, also incorporate the following step.

2) Change the NC model to use approximate fixed weights, as in Table I. If feasible, also use appropriate powers of 2 for the selectivity r_l and saturation α_l parameters. This recognizes that some of the DNC model preprocessing approximations can be treated as just another set of NC model parameters. Repeat simulation (including learning) with the NC model, and also tailor the number of training iterations to develop weights that are appropriate for the DNC representations, as in (18), (19), and (20).

3) Preprocess level 1 to create level 1 DNC model approximations.

4) Run the DNC model simulator on level 1 for all input patterns in the training set, and compare with level 1 NC model outputs.

5) Repeat (if necessary) steps 2, 3, and 4 in order to obtain good weight approximations, trying different scaling factors or changing the amount of training.

6) Use the level 1 outputs from the DNC model to *retrain* level 2 of step 2 in the NC model. This is a very important step. The level 2 feature detectors *must* be developed (learned) with inputs from the lower levels that are representative of what will be seen in the DNC model. Otherwise, there will not be enough similarity between lower-level outputs and higher-level feature detectors to have a robust conversion of the NC model pattern recognition capabilities to the DNC model.

7) Preprocess level 2 to create level 2 DNC model approximations.

8) Repeat this process for all levels in the architecture; e.g., if there are three or more levels, next run the DNC simulator on level 2, and use these outputs to retrain level 3 in the NC model.

9) Use the DNC model to check final level outputs for all input patterns using all levels in the neural network.

IV. Character Recognition Example

This section reports simulation results on a character recognition example which proves the feasibility of the DNC model. It involves recognizing 7 by 12 pixel characters *A* through *E* left-justified on a 12 by 12 pixel array [17]. The NC model is trained on *centered* versions of the input patterns (left side of Fig. 6), both for generality and to test translation invariance in recognizing the left-justified patterns. The conversion methodology is followed to derive a DNC model, and both ANN's are tested on translations of the original patterns with varying levels of added random noise.

A. NC and DNC Model Solutions

The architecture and parameters of an NC model that provides a solution to this character recognition problem are described on the input file to the NC model simulator, as shown in the Appendix. Only two levels of S-cell and C-cell planes are required, as shown in Fig. 1. The input plane is 12 by 12, and the 20 level 1 S-cell planes are oversized to 14 by 14, in order not to lose feature detector outputs when patterns are

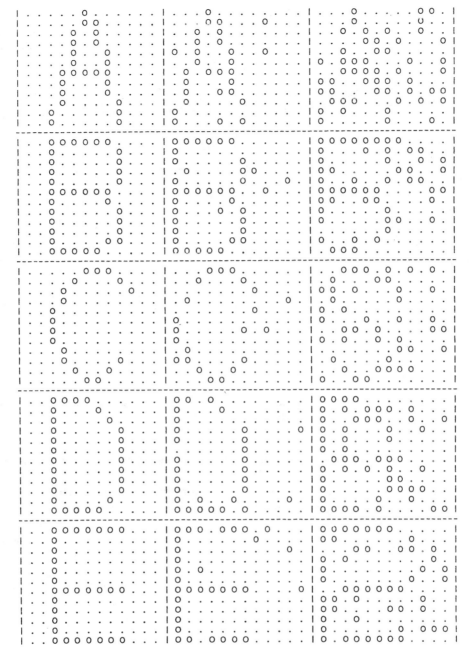

Fig. 6.   Character recognition example input patterns of 12 × 12 pixels: (*left*) centered *A* through *E* used for training; (*middle*) typical edge-translated *A* through *E* with 5% noise; (*right*)typical edge-translated *A* through *E* with 30% noise.

translated to an edge of the input plane. The number of neurons in the level 1 C-cell planes is thinned out by a 2:1 ratio (with oversizing) to 8 by 8, skipping every other C cell since they carry nearly the same information owing to *smearing* of the S-cell outputs through the 5 by 5 receptive field averaging. The five level 2 S-cell planes are thinned out, by dropping periphery locations which carry less information, to 6 by 6, and level 2 C cells consist of one output neuron per pattern class. Vs-cell inhibition is used at level 2; this serves to sharpen distinctions between outputs but does not necessarily cause only one output neuron to be activated. In order to have good noise tolerance, it is necessary that more than one output neuron be activated for the noiseless version of some patterns, with output level in proportion to the strength of the

recognition of the pattern; e.g., consider the pattern *E* which is *part of* the pattern *B* in Fig. 6.

This neural network architecture contains 5762 neurons and 181 509 possible interconnections, with 2800 unique weights possible (many may be zero). Training details are not presented here; there were only 7 iterations at level 1 and 14 iterations at level 2. When the NC model learning process is complete, only 910 (33%) of the possible 2810 unique weights are nonzero. The NC model simulator also determines how many of the neurons and interconnections are active (nonzero) when a particular input pattern is processed; an interconnect is termed active if the weight is nonzero and the input neuron's activity is nonzero. For the five centered patterns *A* through *E*, the number of active neurons ranges from 321 (5.6%) to 539 (9.4%).

509

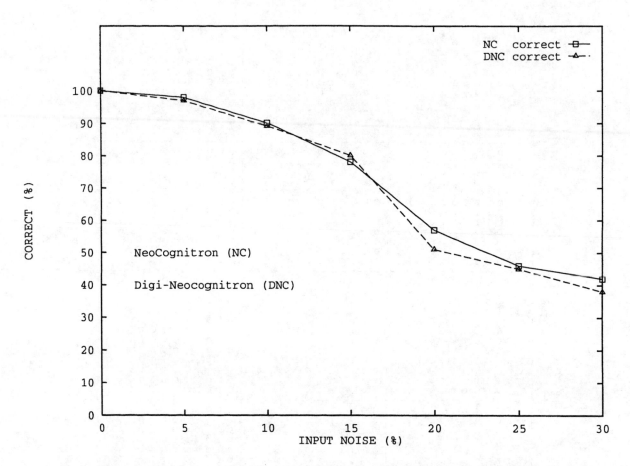

Fig. 7. Neocognitron and digi-neocognitron character recognition: correct identifications as a function of input noise.

The number of active connections ranges from 10 054 (5.5%) to 19 616 (10.8%). This is the basis for concluding that the neocognitron is *temporally sparse* [16], as mentioned earlier.

The DNC model is derived from the NC model following the methodology outlined previously. The preprocessing parameter file for the DNC model, shown in the Appendix, uses a level 1 weight scaling factor of 0.991 to fine-tune the approximation, and represents the inhibitory weight factor with a single-term power-of-2 approximation. Level 1 of the DNC model is then run for all of the training patterns, and these outputs are used to repeat the level 2 NC model learning. Level 2 is then preprocessed using a scaling factor of 0.949 and a two-term power-of-2 approximation for the inhibitory weight factors. The DNC model is then run on all patterns as a test. A final adjustment was done manually to slightly reduce the inhibitory weight factors for the B and C pattern S cells since their level 2 C-cell outputs were low.

B. Results

Both ANN's are tested on translations of the original patterns with varying levels of random noise added; this quantifies recognition performance, translation invariance, and noise tolerance and allows for a meaningful comparison of the NC and DNC models. As in [17], the original patterns are translated to the left edge, a fixed percentage of random pixel noise is added, and the noisy image is presented to the ANN for recognition. This test procedure is repeated 100 times at each noise level, in 5% increments ranging from 0% to 30%. Note

that this random noise percentage is defined as a percent of the total number of pixels in the input plane, not in the pattern. At 5% noise, or a Hamming distance of 7 (i.e., seven pixels are reversed), the patterns are still recognizable, as shown by the examples in the middle part of Fig. 6. At 30% noise, or a Hamming distance of 43 (greater than the total number of pixels in any pattern), the patterns are not very recognizable, as shown by the examples in the right part of Fig. 6.

The correct recognition rate as a function of noise added is shown in Fig. 7. Both ANN's have excellent recognition rates in the presence of large amounts of noise, and the DNC model has no deterioration from NC performance. The NC model recognition rate falls to 78% at 15% noise and is 42% when there is 30% noise; the DNC model recognition rate is 80% at 15% noise and 38% at 30% noise. These ANN's are also coping with translation and edge effects at the same time.

Both ANN's can also classify input patterns as unknowns or rejects, indicated by all C-cell outputs at zero or below a threshold, or by more than one near-equal maximum C-cell output. This significantly reduces the undetectable error rate (wrong classifications) and is very important for commercial applications [18]. The reject rate as a function of noise added is shown in Fig. 8, and incorrect recognition rate as a function of noise added is shown in Fig. 9. The NC model reject rate gradually rises, up to 11% at 15% noise and 38% at 30% noise. As a result, the incorrect recognition rate is less than 22% (occurs at 20% and 25% noise) and is only 20% at 30% noise. The DNC model reject rate is 11% at 15% noise and

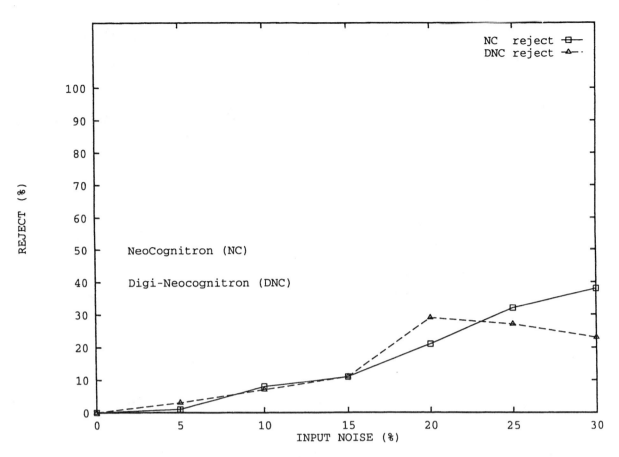

Fig. 8. Neocognitron and digi-neocognitron character recognition: rejects as a function of input noise.

NeoCognitron (NC)

Digi-Neocognitron (DNC)

TABLE VI
VLSI ADVANTAGE OF DIGI-NEOCOGNITRON MODEL

Modelm	NC	DNC	DNC
Calculation	$c_l u_C$ or $a_l u_C$	$c_l u_C$	$a_l u_C$
Implementation	multiplier	shifter	shifter
FPGA: Area (#modules) Delay (ns)	176 253	4 10	23 19
CMOS gate array: Area (# cells) Delay (ns)	810 61	31 3	133 5

23% at 30% noise; the incorrect recognition rate is less than 39% (occurs at 30% noise). The NC and DNC model incorrect recognition rates are lower than Brown [17] at all input noise percentages. The ANN's were also tested on the shifted and original patterns, which were correctly recognized.

V. ADVANTAGES FOR VLSI IMPLEMENTATION

Table VI illustrates the advantages of the DNC model over the NC model for VLSI implementation of the multiplication in the weighted sum calculations. An 8 bit parallel (array) multiplier is assumed for implementation of the NC model; this is formed from 48 full adders, eight half adders, and 64 AND gates, and has a worst-case delay of 17 times the worst-case adder delay [29]. The DNC model implementation is as presented in Section III.

The ACTEL ACT I family [30] is used as the field-programmable gate array (FPGA) technology example. The multiplier for the NC model requires 176 logic modules and has a worst-case delay of 253 ns. The DNC model power-of-2 shift circuit to implement $c_l u_C$ ($a_l u_C$) is designed using ACTEL MX4 4:1 multiplexer macros; it requires 4 (23) logic modules and has a worst case delay of 9.9 (19.2) ns.

The gate array technology example is Texas Instruments TGC100 1 μm CMOS gate arrays [31]. The multiplier for the NC model requires 810 gate array cells (adding 35% for routing) and has a worst-case delay of 60.8 ns. The DNC model power-of-2 shift circuit to implement $c_l u_C$ ($a_l u_C$) is designed using gate array macros such as 2:1 and 4:1 MUX's, and requires (31) 133 cells, assuming only 10% for routing since this is a much simpler circuit than the multiplier, and has a worst-case delay of 2.6 (4.6) ns.

The area-delay product is *improved by two to three orders of magnitude,* and this does not even consider the elimination of division and other complex functions. A custom CMOS implementation could achieve even better ratios by using a transmission gate implementation (barrel shifter) of the shift circuit. In addition, the restriction of the bit widths in the DNC model, such as 3 bit or less representation of weights, and representation of neuron outputs with 4 or 7 bits, substantially reduces the I/O and memory requirements.

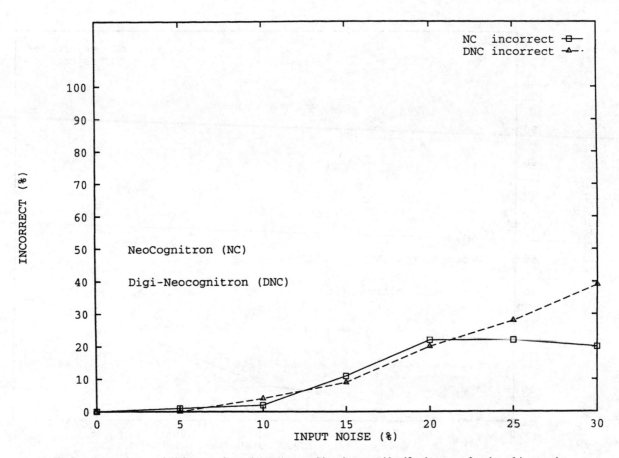

Fig. 9. Neocognitron and digi-neocognitron character recognition: incorrect identifications as a function of input noise.

VI. CONCLUSIONS

This paper has presented a new artificial neural network model, the digi-neocognitron (DNC), which adapts the neocognitron (NC) neural network model to an efficient all-digital implementation for VLSI. It was shown how the DNC model is derived from the NC model by a combination of preprocessing approximations and a definition of new model functions. For example, multiplication and division operations are eliminated by conversion of factors to powers of 2, so that only shift operations are required. A methodology for conversion of NC models to DNC models was presented. The feasibility of this approach was demonstrated on a character recognition example. The DNC model had the same pattern recognition performance as the NC model when tested on translated and noisy input patterns. The DNC model has substantial advantages over the NC model for VLSI implementation. The area–delay product is improved by two to three orders of magnitude, and I/O and memory requirements are reduced by representation of weights with 3 bits or less and neuron outputs with 4 bits or 7 bits.

APPENDIX

Architectural Description File for NC Model

    lmax 2
    layer U0 12 12

    layer US1 14 14 20 nothin
    selectivity 5.0
    reinforcement 1.0
    connection area 3 3 approx
    sigmac 3.0

    layer UC1 8 8 20 thin normal
    saturation 0.25
    connection area 5 5 approx
    sigmad 2.5

    layer US2 6 6 5 thinper
    selectivity 1.0
    reinforcement 24.0
    connection area 5 5 approx
    sigmac 5.0

    layer UC2 1 1 5 thinper inhibit
    saturation 0.4
    connection area 6 6 approx
    sigmad 8.0

Preprocessing Parameter File for DNC Model

    wscale 1 0.991
    wscale 2 0.949

    brpow2 1 1
    brpow2 2 2

REFERENCES

[1] D. E. Rumelhart and J. L. McClelland, *Parallel Distributed Processing,* vol. 1, *Foundations.* Cambridge, MA: MIT Press, 1986.

[2] R. P. Lippmann, "An introduction to computing with neural nets," *IEEE ASSP Magazine,* vol. 4, pp. 4–22, Apr. 1987.

[3] R. Hecht-Nielsen, "Neurocomputing: Picking the human brain," *IEEE Spectrum,* vol. 25, pp. 36–41, Mar. 1988.

[4] *IEEE Trans. Neural Networks,* 1990, issues.

[5] L. E. Atlas and Y. Suzuki, "Digital systems for artificial neural networks," *IEEE Circuits and Devices Magazine,* pp. 20–24, Nov. 1989.

[6] P. Treleaven *et al.* "VLSI architectures for neural networks," *IEEE MICRO Magazine,* pp. 8–27, Dec. 1989.

[7] *Proc. IEEE IJCNN,* (San Diego, CA), 1990.

[8] R. E. Howard *et al.,* "Optical character recognition: A technology driver for neural networks," in *Proc. IEEE ISCAS,* 1990, pp. 2433–2436.

[9] L. D. Jackel *et al.,* "Hardware requirements for neural-net optical character recognition," in *Proc. IEEE IJCNN,* (San Diego, CA), 1990, vol. II, pp. 855–861.

[10] D. Hammerstrom, "A VLSI architecture for high-performance, low-cost, on-chip learning," in *Proc. IEEE IJCNN,* (San Diego, CA), 1990, vol. II, pp. 537–544.

[11] M. S. Tomlinson *et al.,* "A digital neural network architecture for VLSI," in *Proc. IEEE IJCNN,* (San Diego, CA), 1990, vol. II, pp. 545–550.

[12] A. El Gamal *et al.,* "An architecture for electrically configurable gate arrays," *IEEE J. Solid-State Circuits,* vol. 24, pp. 394–398, Apr. 1989.

[13] K. Fukushima, "Neocognitron: A self-organizing neural network model for a mechanism of pattern recognition unaffected by shift in position," *Biol. Cybern.,* vol. 36, pp. 193–202, 1980.

[14] K. Fukushima and S. Miyake, "Neocognitron: A new algorithm for pattern recognition tolerant of deformations and shifts in position," *Pattern Recognition,* vol. 15, no. 6, pp. 455–469, 1982.

[15] K. Fukushima, "Analysis of the process of visual pattern recognition by the neocognitron," *Neural Networks,* vol. 2, pp. 413–420, 1989.

[16] D. Hammerstrom and E. Means, "System design for a second generation neurocomputer," in *Proc. IEEE IJCNN,* Jan. 1990, vol. II, pp. 80–83.

[17] H. K. Brown *et al.,* "Orthogonal extraction training algorithm," in *Proc. IEEE IJCNN,* Jan. 1990, vol. I, pp. 537–540.

[18] C. L. Wilson *et al.,* "Self-organizing neural network character recognition on a massively parallel computer," in *Proc. IEEE IJCNN,* (San Diego, CA), 1990, vol. II, pp. 325–329.

[19] K. Fukushima, S. Miyake, and T. Ito, "Neocognitron: A neural network model for a mechanism of visual pattern recognition," *IEEE Trans. Syst. Man, Cybern.,* vol. SMC-13, pp. 826–834, Sept. 1983.

[20] Y. Lee *et al.,* "Hangul recognition using neocognitron," in *Proc. IEEE IJCNN,* Jan. 1990, vol. I, pp. 416–419.

[21] S. Wang and C. Pan, "A neural network approach for Chinese character recognition," in *Proc. IEEE IJCNN,* (San Diego, CA), 1990, vol. II, pp. 917–923.

[22] E. Barnard and D. Casasent, "Shift invariance and the neocognitron," *Neural Networks,* vol. 3, pp. 403–410, 1990.

[23] K. Johnson *et al.,* "Feature extraction in the neocognitron," in *Proc. IEEE IJCNN,* 1988, vol. II, pp. 117–126.

[24] B. A. White and M. I. Elmasry, "Digi-Neocognitron: A neocognitron neural network model for VLSI," Report No. UW/VLSI 91–01, VLSI Group, University of Waterloo, Waterloo, Ontario, Jan. 1991.

[25] B. A. White and M. I. Elmasry, "VLSI architecture of the digi-neocognitron neural network," to be published.

[26] Y. C. Lim *et al.,* "VLSI circuits for decomposing binary integers into signed power-of-two terms," in *Proc. IEEE ISCAS,* 1990, pp. 2304–2307.

[27] M. Marchesi *et al.,* "Multi-layer perceptrons with discrete weights," in *Proc. IEEE IJCNN,* (San Diego, CA), 1990, vol. II, pp. 623–630.

[28] Q. Xu *et al.,* "A fault tolerance analysis of a neocognitron model," in *Proc. IEEE IJCNN,* Jan. 1990, vol. II, pp. 559–562.

[29] N. H. E. Weste and K. Eshraghian, *Principles of CMOS VLSI Design: A Systems Perspective.* Reading: Addison-Wesley, 1985, p. 344.

[30] *ACT 1 Family Gate Arrays Design Reference Manual,* ACTEL Corporation, 1989.

[31] Texas Instruments, "TGC100 Series 1-micron CMOS Gate Arrays," May 1990.

A CCD Programmable Image Processor and its Neural Network Applications

Alice M. Chiang, *Senior Member, IEEE*, and Michael L. Chuang, *Student Member, IEEE*

Abstract —A CCD-based image processor that performs 2-D filtering of a gray-level image with 20 programmable 8-b 7×7 spatial filters is described. The processor consists of an analog input buffer, 49 multipliers, and forty-nine 8-b 20-stage local memories in a 29-mm^2 chip area. Better than 99.999% charge transfer efficiency and greater than 42-dB dynamic range have been achieved by the processor, which performs one billion arithmetic operations per second and dissipates less than 1 W when clocked at 10 MHz. The device is also suited for neural networks with local connections and replicated weights. Implementation of a specific neural network, the neocognitron, based on this CCD processor has been simulated. The effect of weight quantization imposed by use of this CCD device on the performance of the neocognitron is presented.

I. INTRODUCTION

A PROGRAMMABLE image processor that can be used as a multiple-template two-dimensional FIR filter for signal conditioning such as noise reduction, and enhancing and/or skeletonizing an input image is reported here. The device can also be used to detect features in the input image. For this reason, we will henceforth call this device an image-feature extractor, or IFE. Clocked at 10 MHz, the IFE performs one billion arithmetic operations per second and dissipates less than 1 W. The processor was developed based on charge-coupled device (CCD) technology. The architecture, design consideration, and performance of this device will be described in this paper.

The IFE is ideally suited for implementation of multilayer neural networks (NN's) that are characterized by local connectivity patterns and groups of nodes constrained to have the same weights on their input lines. Such networks can be described as a hierarchical collection of replicated feature detectors and have been applied successfully to tasks ranging from handwritten character recognition to phoneme extraction in speech preprocessing [1], [2]. Simulation of a neocognitron [3], a neural network for feature extraction and pattern recognition, implemented using the IFE has been performed. The effect on the neocognitron of weight quantization, which would be imposed by use of the IFE, is presented.

Manuscript received April 30, 1991. This work was supported by DARPA, the Office of Naval Research, and the Department of the Air Force.

The authors are with Lincoln Laboratory, Massachusetts Institute of Technology, Lexington, MA 02173.

IEEE Log Number 9103256.

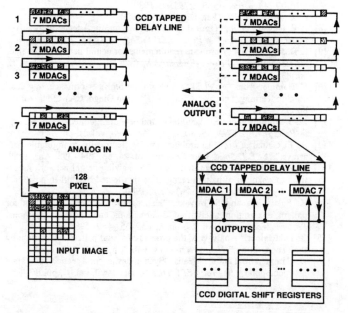

Fig. 1. Layout arrangement and data flow of the CCD image feature extractor. The pattern in the CCD delay line at the upper right occurs one clock period after that shown at the upper left.

II. DEVICE ARCHITECTURE

A block diagram of the IFE is shown in Fig. 1. The chip is designed to perform multiple template two-dimensional 7×7 FIR filtering on a serially scanned input image 128 columns wide. The number of rows in the input is essentially arbitrary, though we generally will assume that the input is 128×128 pixels. Conceptually, the IFE slides a 7×7 window over the input image. At each window position, inner products of the stored weight templates (of which there may be up to 20) and the windowed portion of the input are computed. The input pixels are serially read into the IFE line by line and the task of reformatting the input and selecting the appropriate pixels for windowing is performed on chip. As can be seen from Fig. 1, the IFE consists of two major functional blocks: processing elements and input buffer elements. The processing elements consist of 49 multipliers and forty-nine 20-stage CCD digital shift-register memories for storing the templates. The input buffer memory is a 775-stage CCD tapped delay line that provides the functions of shifting and holding input pixels, reformatting the serially scanned inputs to achieve the appropriate windowing of pixels,

Reprinted from *IEEE J. Solid-State Circuits*, vol. 26, no. 12, pp. 1894–1901, Dec. 1991.

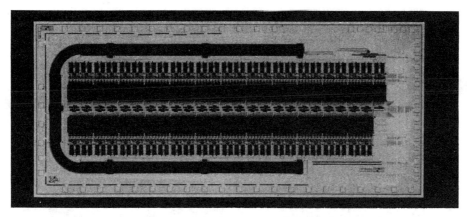

Fig. 2. Photomicrograph of a CCD IFE.

and applying this windowed portion of the input to the processing elements. The multipliers are implemented using 8-b CCD four-quadrant multiplying D-to-A converters (MDAC's) with the digital word represented in two's complement notation [4]. Digital cyclic shift registers are used to store the weights so that each set of weights can be applied to the windowed pixels before shifting the input data. The digital memory read-and-write architecture is the same as reported in [4]. As described in [4], a low-power, high-packing-density CCD digital shift register was employed in this memory design. Use of the normally volatile CCD device was possible in this case because a feedback enable switch has been incorporated at each bit of the memory to permit the digital data to be refreshed as needed by being read and rewritten into the memory again.

The IFE's 775-stage tapped delay line holds six 128-pixel lines of the input image plus an additional seven pixels. The input values are represented in the tapped delay line by analog charge packets that are sensed nondestructively using floating-gate taps. The taps are placed at the first seven of every 128 stages of the delay line so that the values sensed from the one-dimensional line correspond to those that would be covered by a two-dimensional 7×7 window. This is shown in Fig. 1. (The actual tapped delay line is implemented as a U-shaped structure, but is depicted in Fig. 1 as a serpentine structure to show the relationship of the window to the image.) The values sensed from the tapped delay line are multiplied in parallel by 8-b digital weights using MDAC's. The resulting charge-domain partial products are summed in a common output node; this allows a complete inner-product computation to be performed on each clock. Shifting the contents of the tapped delay line by one position corresponds to moving the window over the image by one pixel.

Operation of the IFE is shown in Fig. 1 and described as follows. A 2-D image is continuously loaded into the processor line by line. After a latency equal to the time required to load the first six lines and the first six pixels of line 7 of an image into the device, inner products of the input image and the weight templates are sequentially computed after each of the subsequent load-data clocks.

After 121 such load-data-then-compute cycles, the sliding window has moved to the upper right-hand corner of the input image. On the next six clock cycles, only load-data clocks are used; this moves the window down one row and back to the left-hand side of the input image. After the first seven elements of line 8 are loaded into the device, the device is ready to compute the inner products of lines 2 through 8 of the input image and the 7×7 templates. The procedure continues until the inner products of the templates and the last seven lines of the image are computed and the complete feature information of the input image is extracted. Although the operation of the IFE is most easily visualized as sliding a window over an input image, in reality the pixels of the image are read into the device raster fashion. Clocked at 10 MHz, the IFE can process a 128×128-pixel input image to produce 20 filtered output images or "feature maps" in 32 ms.

III. DEVICE DESIGN AND PERFORMANCE

A. IFE Design and Performance

A photomicrograph of the IFE is shown in Fig. 2. The chip area is 29 mm^2 and the device was fabricated with a double-polysilicon, double-metal, buried-channel CCD/CMOS process. The design rules are 3 μm for the second poly and second metal layers, 2.5 μm for the first metal layer, and 2 μm for all the other layers. Design considerations and test results are described next.

In a CCD, the time required for free charge to transfer from a potential well under one gate to a receiving well under an adjacent gate can be calculated by solving the current equation and continuity equation. It has been shown in [5] that the charge transfer inefficiency, which is the ratio of the amount of charge $Q(t)$ remaining in the delivering well at time t to the initial charge Q_0, can be expressed as

$$\frac{Q(t)}{Q_0} = \frac{e^{-t/\tau_f}}{1 + \dfrac{Q_0 \tau_f}{Q_{th} \tau_{th}}(1 - e^{-t/\tau_f})}$$

515

Fig. 3. Detail of the U-shaped portion of the CCD tapped delay line.

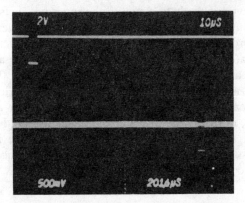

Fig. 4. Input and output signals of the CCD tapped delay line demonstrating better than 0.99999 transfer efficiency at 10-MHz clock rate.

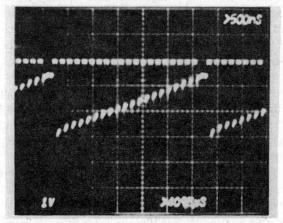

Fig. 5. Test result demonstrating uniformity of CCD MDAC's.

where

$$\tau_f \approx \left(\frac{4}{\tau_{th}} + \frac{\mu^2 E_f^2}{4 D_n} \right)^{-1}$$

$$\tau_{th} = \frac{4 L^2}{\pi^2 D_n}$$

and E_f is the minimum electric fringing field due to the externally applied potentials on the gate electrodes, L is the gate length, and $Q_{th} = 2kT / qLC_{\text{eff}}$, where C_{eff} is the effective gate capacitance. Based on the above expression, 99.999% charge transfer between two adjacent gates can be achieved in less than 6 ns, so long as the electrode length is kept shorter than 5 μm. There are four transfers per stage of delay in a two-phase CCD shift register, therefore, a high-speed buffer capable of shifting charge at more than 20 MHz can be achieved.

In order to minimize the chip area, the 775-stage CCD line buffer was designed as a U-shaped structure, which is shown in Fig. 2. Fig. 3 is a photomicrograph of a corner of

the U-shaped CCD buffer; note that care was taken to keep the transfer gate less than 4 μm wide. Evaluation of the transfer efficiency of the CCD delay line is shown in Fig. 4. The test was carried out at a 10-MHz clock rate. The top trace shows an input step function; the bottom trace shows the output from the device after 775 stages of delay, or 77.5 μs later. At this clock rate, no transfer loss was observed after 3100 transfers, indicating that the transfer efficiency is better than 99.999%.

It can also be seen in Fig. 3 that extra design effort was taken to minimize the chip area of an MDAC. In the IFE processor, an 8-b four-quadrant CCD MDAC has been realized in a 200×220-μm^2 chip area. The uniformity of the MDAC's is evaluated next. In this test, the 20 templates of the device are programmed as follows. In the first template, 40 of the digital weights are set to their largest positive value (the corresponding MDAC's are said to be "fully turned on"), while the other nine weights are set to zero. The second template has 38 MDAC's fully

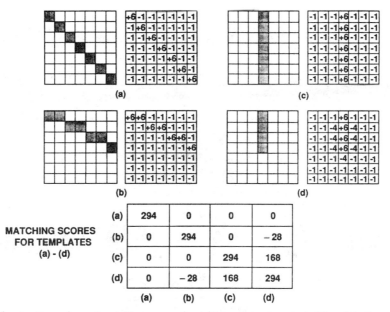

(a)

(b)

(c)

(d)

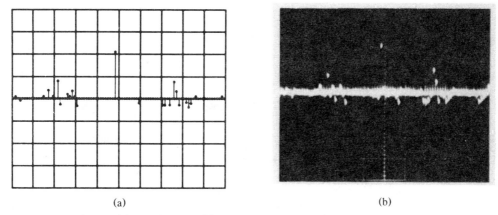

MATCHING SCORES FOR TEMPLATES (a) - (d)	(a)	294	0	0	0
	(b)	0	294	0	− 28
	(c)	0	0	294	168
	(d)	0	− 28	168	294
		(a)	(b)	(c)	(d)

Fig. 6. Examples and matching scores of weight templates for oriented line detection.

(a)

(b)

Fig. 7. (a) Calculated and (b) measured correlation output of the CCD IFE.

turned on, with the remaining 11 weights set to zero, and so forth, until the 20th template has two MDAC's fully turned on. When a uniform gray-level image is applied to the device, the 20 outputs corresponding to each window position should be a linear-ramped waveform proportional to the number of MDAC's turned on in each template. As shown in Fig. 5, the output waveform computed by the processor demonstrates the uniformity among the MDAC's.

Experiments using the IFE processor to extract feature information from an input image are reported next. The processor is programmed to detect line segments of different orientations. The feature templates contain both positive and negative weight values, and the weights were selected so that cross-correlations between template i and a feature corresponding to template j produce a near zero output when $i \neq j$ and a large output when $i = j$. Examples of the weights selected and matching scores between different templates are shown in Fig. 6. Fig. 7 shows both the calculated outputs expected when each of the templates is applied to an input image containing a

feature corresponding to one of the stored patterns, as well as the actual correlation outputs computed by the device. These result demonstrate the computational accuracy offered by the processor. Test results indicate that more than 42-dB dynamic range has been achieved by this device. In the next experiment, the processor is programmed to detect 20 features, such as oriented line segments. The feature templates are shown at the top of Fig. 8. Trace (a) of Fig. 8 is a portion of an input image that contains a feature corresponding to the pattern stored in template 5. Trace (b) shows the correlation outputs computed by the device when each of the templates is applied to the input shown in trace (a). The correlation outputs indicate that the input feature has been detected. In trace (c) of Fig. 8, the same input image is embedded in Gaussian noise with SNR = 2; trace (d) shows the correlation of the noisy input with the stored templates as computed by the IFE, indicating that the processor has extracted the correct feature from the noisy input.

To demonstrate the computational power offered by the IFE processor, a technology comparison of this pro-

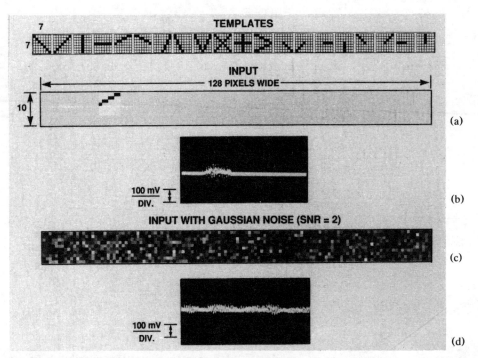

Fig. 8. Performance of the CCD NN feature extractor.

TABLE I
TECHNOLOGY COMPARISON FOR IMAGE FEATURE EXTRACTORS

	LL IMAGE PROCESSOR	MATSUSHITA IMAGE PROCESSOR
On-Chip Line Buffer	YES	NO
On-Chip Template Store	20 7×7 templates	one 5×5-template
Processor Elements	49	4
MPY Accuracy	ANALOG×8 b	12×13 b
Throughput Rate	1.0 BOPS	0.2 MOPS
Chip Area	29 mm^2	197 mm^2
Design Rules	2–3-μm CCD/CMOS	1.2-μm CMOS

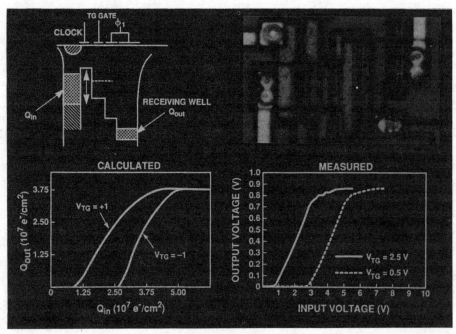

Fig. 9. Calculated and measured performance of a CCD charge-domain sigmoidal nonlinear detection circuit.

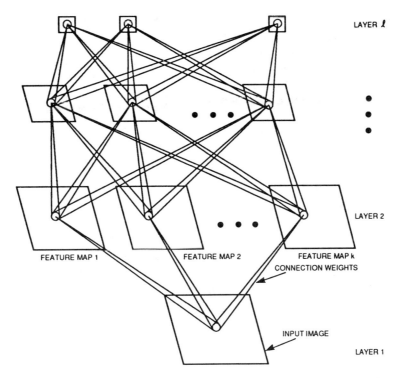

Fig. 10. Schematic of a multilayer hierarchical RWNN with local connectivity patterns and groups of nodes constrained to have the same weights.

cessor with a recently reported state-of-the-art image processor [6] is shown in Table I.

B. Charge-Domain Nonlinear Detection Circuit

As stated before, the IFE is ideally suited for NN applications. In general, computational elements or nodes used in neural net models are nonlinear. The simplest node sums weighted inputs and passes the result through a nonlinear output function. One commonly used nonlinear function is a sigmoid. A sigmoidal charge-domain nonlinear detection circuit (see Fig. 9) has been designed and is reported here. The device design is based on the ability to calculate the charge transfer efficiency from an n^+ diffusion region over a bias gate to a receiving well as a function of device parameters [7]. For certain operating conditions there is a sigmoidal nonlinear dependence between the input and output charge. We can see from Fig. 9 that if the incoming weighted-sum signal charge is below a given threshold level set by the transfer gate voltage V_{TG}, no output charge will be transferred to the output port; therefore, the incoming signal will be ignored. On the other hand, if the weighted-sum signal charge is above the threshold level, the amount of charge transferred to the output port is the difference of the weighted-sum charge input and the threshold level. Therefore, this circuit has a programmable threshold level; the amount of charge transferred to the receiving well is controlled by the amplitude of the transfer gate voltage. In addition, the maximum charge can be limited by the size and gate voltage of the receiving well, which in turn determines the maximum output generated by the device.

The predicted and measured nonlinear responses of this circuit for two different threshold levels are also shown in Fig. 9. The area of this circuit is only 40×80 μm^2, which clearly demonstrates the computational power offered by the CCD technology. This circuit can be used together with the IFE chip to perform both the weighted sum and output nonlinearity computations of a neural network node.

IV. APPLICATIONS OF THE IFE AS A NN PROCESSOR

A multilayer neural network that has only local connections and groups of nodes that have the same weights on their input lines is a collection of replicated feature detectors. Neural networks with local connections and identically weighted nodes will be referred to in this paper as replicated-weight neural networks (RWNN's), and groups of identically weighted nodes will be called "node planes." Such RWNN's have been applied successfully to a variety of tasks, including handwritten character recognition and phoneme extraction in speech preprocessing. In the latter case, delayed copies of the input are presented to the network in addition to the actual input, and the weights should be thought of as temporally replicated.

A schematic of a multilayer RWNN is shown in Fig. 10. Such an RWNN can be used as a classifier for small images, such as preprocessed (e.g., thinned, segmented, size normalized) handwritten characters, or to generate feature maps from large complex images. The idea in both cases is to use the first layer of the network to break up the image into collection of simple features, such as

519

oriented line segments. Higher layers put the pieces back together into successively more complex features. If the network is to be used as a classifier, then the output layer consists of a small number of nodes where each node corresponds to a single learned category. A handwritten-digit classifier, for example, would have ten output nodes [1]. The output of a feature map-generating RWNN consists of one or more vectors that are feature maps of the input image [8].

A. Implementation of Replicated-Weight Neural Networks

The description of the first level of an RWNN as a collection of spatially replicated feature detectors with overlapping receptive fields indicates that this structure is amenable to implementation using the CCD IFE. The mapping of the first layer onto an IFE device is fairly straightforward. Suppose we have an RWNN that accepts an $N \times N$-pixel image as input. Let the nodes of the first layer of the network by divided into k node planes with $n \times n$ receptive fields. This implies that the first layer will have k sets of weights. These weights can be stored on chip in n^2 k-stage digital shift registers. An $[N(n-1)+n]$-stage CCD input buffer will serve to hold and shift input pixels. Taps are placed at the first n of every N stages along the delay line to simulate an $n \times n$ window corresponding to the receptive fields of the nodes. At each window position, k inner products of the stored weights and the windowed pixels are performed. Each inner product, which can be passed through an on-chip nonlinear output circuit such as the sigmoidal circuit described above, is a node output. Fig. 10 depicts the node planes of the first layer as k feature maps generated from the input. With the window initially over the upper left-hand corner of the input image, node outputs $x_1, x_2, \cdots, x_k, y_1, y_2, \cdots, y_k$, are generated in order as shown in Fig. 11.

The mapping of higher layers onto IFE devices is somewhat more involved. The input buffer of the IFE must be modified to implement a pipelined architecture. A simple modification of the tapped delay line buffer can be incorporated so that inner-product computations are performed on previously loaded input, while a new input is being loaded into the IFE. The modification consists of inserting an extra switch between each tap output and its corresponding MDAC input. The switch is off while the data are being loaded into the delay line and is turned on to parallel-load data into the MDAC's. With this modified input double-buffered IFE, no time is lost in loading the input buffer. Now suppose that the second layer of our network is also partitioned into k node planes and that each second-layer node has a compound receptive field that covers the same coordinates in every first-layer feature map. This second layer structure can be implemented using k IFE devices as shown in Fig. 11. A single device, labeled IFE(1, 1), performs the first-layer computations, both the dot product and the output nonlinearity. The second-layer computations are divided up among the

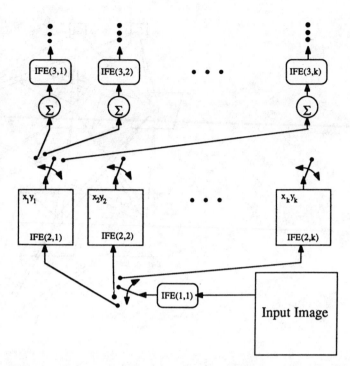

Fig. 11.   Implementation of multilayer network using IFE devices.

k devices labeled IFE$(2,1), \cdots,$ IFE$(2, k)$. Each output value from IFE$(1, 1)$ is sent to exactly one of the second-layer devices, and each second-layer device receives an output once every k clocks. Outputs of the second layer are not generated directly by a single second-layer IFE since each output node of the second layer has a receptive field over every first-layer node plane. The output of IFE$(2, 1)$ generated from a given input-window position is only a portion of the complete output of the first node plane of layer 2. To this output must be added the output of IFE$(2, 2)$ on through the output of IFE$(2, k)$ generated from the same input window position. As can be seen in Fig. 11, this can be achieved by summing the output of IFE$(2, 1)$ at time t_i and the output of IFE$(2, 2)$ at time $t_i + t_c$ on through the output of IFE $(2, k)$ at time $t_i + (k-1)t_c$, where $t_c = 1/f_c$, and f_c is the computation rate of the IFE's. This operation can be realized by accumulating these partial outputs at the input of each third-layer IFE's buffer before the total summed charge is transferred into the tapped delay line. After an initial delay (required to load the first-layer delay line), every processor is busy performing useful computations all of the time.

It is important to note that with this parallel pipelined system architecture, a real-time multilayer RWNN can be realized. In general, an l-layer RWNN with k planes in each hidden layer that accepts an $N \times N$ input image can be implemented with $(l-2) \times k + 1$ IFE's and one additional chip for top-layer output nodes. The time required to process an $N \times N$-pixel image for this l-layer RWNN is $[N \times (n-1) + (N - n + 1) \times (N - n + 1) \times k + (N - n + 1) \times (n-1) + (l-2) \times k]t_c$. For example, 22 chips can be used to realize a four-layer RWNN that processes an 128×128 input image with ten node planes in each of the

TABLE II
PERCENTAGE OF CORRECTLY RECOGNIZED INPUTS RELATIVE TO
NETWORK USING FLOATING-POINT ARITHMETIC

Precision	Original	Modified
floating-point	100.0%	100.0%
10 b	97.2%	98.6%
9 b	94.3%	98.6%
8 b	89.4%	96.0%
7 b	74.5%	91.9%

dure was developed to minimize the effect of quantization on the performance of the network. A network trained using the modified procedure has a slightly lower (approximately three percent reduction) recognition capability when floating-point arithmetic is used, but performs significantly better when quantized weights and lower precision arithmetic is used. The results are also shown in Table II.

two hidden layers. With a 10-MHz clock rate, the processing time for each image on this four-layer net is only 15.036 ms and images can be continuously loaded into this pipelined system.

ACKNOWLEDGMENT

The authors wish to thank J. LaFranchise for laying out the chip and assisting in the device testing, and Orbit Semiconductor, Inc. for fabricating the CCD device reported here.

B. Simulation Results of the Neocognitron

The neocognitron is a multilayer feedforward RWNN for feature extraction and pattern recognition that was first proposed by Fukushima et al. in the early 1980's [3]. It has a structure similar to the hierarchical model of the early visual system proposed by Hubel and Wiesel [9]. The network consists of a cascaded connection of many layers of cells. The information in a stimulus pattern presented to the input layer is processed step by step in each stage of the multilayered network. Cells in lower layers respond to simple features such as oriented line segments, while higher layers respond selectively to more complicated features, and are less sensitive to shifts in position of the stimulus patterns than cells in a lower layer. The multilayer system can be implemented by using several CCD IFE's in a parallel pipelined form. A three-layer neocognitron was implemented in software on a SPARCstation1 and training to recognize the four capital letters A, P, S, and T [10]. The letters were represented as 20×20-pixel binary images. The test set consisted of 80 examples of each letter for a total of 320 test characters. The neocognition was first implemented using floating-point arithmetic for all calculations. The program was then modified to simulate the effect of quantized weights and low-precision arithmetic. The results are shown in Table II. As can be seen in Table II, the ability of the trained neocognitron to identify characters correctly decreased with arithmetic precision. A modified weight-update training proce-

REFERENCES

[1] Y. LeCun et al., "Handwritten digit recognition with a back-propagation network," in Advances in Neural Information Processing Systems 2. San Mateo, CA: Morgan Kaufmann, pp. 396–404, 1989.
[2] A. Waibel, T. Hanazawa, G. Hinton, K. Shikano, and K. Lang, "Phoneme recognition using time-delay neural networks," IEEE Trans. Acoust., Speech, Signal Process., vol. 37, no. 3, pp. 328–339, 1989.
[3] K. Fukushima, S. Miyake, and T. Ito, "Neocognitron: A neural network model for a mechanism of visual pattern recognition," IEEE Trans. Syst., Man, Cybern., vol. SMC-13, no. 5, pp. 826–834, 1983.
[4] A. M. Chiang, "A CCD programmable signal processor," IEEE J. Solid-State Circuits, vol. 25, no. 6, pp. 1510–1517, 1990.
[5] Y. Daimon, A. Mohsen, and T. C. McGill, "Final stage of the charge-transfer process in charge-coupled devices," IEEE Trans. Electron Devices, vol. ED-21, p. 266, 1974.
[6] M. Maruyama et al., "A 200 MIPs image signal multiprocessor on a single chip," in ISSCC Dig. Tech. Papers, Feb. 1990, pp. 122–123.
[7] K. K. Thornber, "Incomplete charge transfer in IGFET bucket-brigade shift registers," IEEE Trans. Electron Devices, vol. ED-18, pp. 941–950, 1971.
[8] R. L. Harvey, P. N. DiCaprio, K. G. Heinemann, M. L. Silverman, and J. M. Dugan, "A neural architecture for Potentially Classifying Cytology Specimens by Machines," in Symp. Computer Applications Medical Care Proc., Nov. 1990, pp. 539–543.
[9] D. Hubel and T. Wiesel, "Sequence regularity and geometry of orientation columns in the monkey striate cortex," J. Comp. Neur., vol. 158, pp. 267–294, 1974.
[10] M. L. Chuang, "A study of the neocognitron pattern recognition algorithm," Master's thesis, Dept. EECS, Mass. Inst. Technol., Cambridge, 1990.

Optical Neural Networks

H. JOHN CAULFIELD, SENIOR MEMBER, IEEE, JASON KINSER, AND
STEVEN K. ROGERS, MEMBER, IEEE

Invited Paper

Classical optical information processing and classical neural networks can be mutually adapted to create optical neural networks which offer significant and fundamental advantages over electronic neural networks in various well-defined cases. We offer here a systematic morphology of optical neural networks, a discussion of special problems they create, an indication of the state of the art in their implementation, and some supportable speculations on their future.

I. INTRODUCTION

Optical neural networks are the offspring of two parents: optical information processing and neural network theory. While the balance of this special issue deals with optical computing, a brief overview of neural networks is in order, to introduce the basic concepts to readers who may be unfamiliar with them.

That brains and digital computers function very differently is obvious to all who pose the question. Digital computers are ideal for numerical solution of equations, numerical processing by iterative algorithms, sorting, formal logic, and probability calculation—in short, algorithmically derived problems. Human brains tend to do those tasks slowly and poorly. Formal reasoning is hard, but inspired guessing is easy. Biological brains are especially adept at very complex pattern recognition, generalization, abduction, intuition, problem finding, and language. These differences represent more than just a measure of the current limited state of computer development. It may also seem that brain-like architecture and function is much better adapted to these "characteristically biological" tasks than are digital computers. Neural networks, at present, are brain-inspired processors which utilize a very small number and only a very few of the types of structural components we find in brains, appropriately adapted for tech-

nological (electronic or optical) implementation. In contrast to conventional computers they are not necessarily algorithmically programmed with code but are adaptive, plastic, and may learn, although they can have "system algorithms" to make them function.

The basic component (cell) of a brain is a neuron. While biological neurons are very complicated, certainly more complicated than we now understand, artificial or technological neurons are very simple. Fig. 1 shows such an arti-

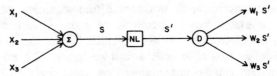

Fig. 1. A highly simplified neuron used for technological implementation.

ficial neuron symbolically. The components are

- input signals, $\{x_i\}$
- a summer, Σ
- a nonlinear operator, $NL(\cdot)$
- a distributer, D.

The summer produces a signal

$$s = \Sigma \, x_i. \tag{1}$$

The nonlinear operator produces a signal

$$s' = NL(s). \tag{2}$$

Usually $NL(\cdot)$ gives $s' = 0$ for low s, a fixed (saturated) s' for high enough s, and a monotonic transition region. The distributer sends signal $w_j s'$ to neuron j, etc. Thus $w_j s'$ becomes an input x to neuron j. Normally $1 > s' > 0$ and w_j can be either positive (excitatory to neuron j) or negative (inhibitory to neuron j).

Biological and technological neural networks are usually arranged in layers. A very simple feedforward, single-layer neural network is shown in Fig. 2. Such units can be connected in a forward direction from one layer to the next or backward or even laterally. The outputs of one layer become the inputs of another or, sometimes, the final outputs. Interconnect weights of zero are allowed. We can view the

Manuscript received May 23, 1989; revised June 2, 1989. This work was supported primarily by the Department of the Navy under Contract N00014-86-K-0591.

H. J. Caulfield is with the Center for Applied Optics, University of Alabama, Huntsville, AL 35899, USA.

J. Kinser is with Teledyne Brown Engineering, PO Box 070007, Huntsville, AL 35807-7007, USA.

S. K. Rogers is with the Department of Electrical Engineering, Air Force Institute of Technology, Wright Patterson Air Force Base, OH 45433, USA.

IEEE Log Number 8930389.

Reprinted from *Proc. IEEE*, vol. 77, no. 10, pp. 1573–1583, 1989.

522

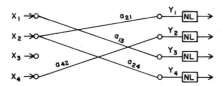

Fig. 2. Most neural networks (biological and technological) are arranged in layers or slabs. Shown here is a very simple layered system. The input vector $\vec{x} = (x_1, x_2, x_3, x_4)^T$ multiplies a matrix A (nonzero components a_{13}, a_{21}, a_{24}, and a_{42} shown in this oversimplified example) to obtain an output vector $\vec{y} = (y_1, y_2, y_3, y_4)^T$. Each $\vec{y}$ component is then acted upon by a nonlinear operator.

input set as a vector $\vec{x}$. Each output neuron produces a sum

$$y_i = \sum_j a_{ij} x_j. \qquad (3)$$

We can view the y_i's as components of a vector $\vec{y}$ and a_{ij} as a component of a matrix A. Then we have

$$\vec{y} = A\vec{x}. \qquad (4)$$

The nonlinear operation works on each y_i, giving

$$y_i' = NL(y_i). $$

In many neural networks, the system is far more complicated. Multiple layers, feedback, and feed lateral operations occur. A bias may be added to effectively vary the threshold. Multiplicative as well as additive elements can occur. These are dealt with in Section IV-C as higher order neural networks. They also include "shunting" operations. In short, neurons need not be simple.

Neural networks carry out several types of operations. First, the network can learn (by itself or with a teacher). Learning here means adjusting the strengths of the interconnections so that, to some degree, each input leads to the proper output. This operation is sometimes called Long-Term Memory or simply LTM. Second, the network can apply what it has learned to new inputs by flowing them through the system to the output layer. In biology, Short-Term Memory (STM) is a dynamic reverbatory pattern within the network which recalls previously stored patterns. In artificial neural systems, STM is sometimes used to mean use of the stored (LTM) patterns. In biology, these functions occur in the same system of hardware or "wetware." In technological neural networks, we can choose to use separate hardware for LTM and STM.

It is easy to show that digital computers and neural networks can each embody the other. From the beginning, it was realized that Boolean operations could be performed by neurons. Likewise, since 1936 it has been widely believed (Church's thesis) that anything which can be calculated by any means (such as a neural network) can be calculated digitally by a "Universal Turing Machine." In this sense, digital computers and neural networks are "formally equivalent." The neural network paradigm, however, often proves a useful one for associative memory, pattern classification, innovation, robustness, etc. It seems a natural fit for biology. We know of no biological Boolean operation. As we will see, it is also a "natural" application for optics.

Optical neural networks are made possible by adaptation of three other fields: "classical" neural networks (the "connectionist model"), optical computing, and optical com-

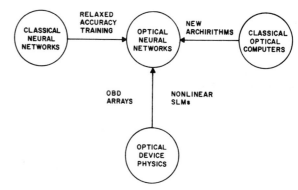

Fig. 3. Optical neural networks require adaptations of concepts and components from three other fields as noted symbolically here.

ponents. The needed adaptations of each are sketched in Fig. 3 and elaborated somewhat below.

A few general references can be recommended for readers who want to learn more about neural networks [1]–[3].

This is a vast and growing field. We will attempt a fair and balanced overview of the field but certainly not a complete literature survey. We have omitted many important papers because they were not necessary to the exposition.

II. WHY OPTICS?

There are sound reasons for using optics rather than electronics for implementing at least some neural networks. We will elaborate on some of these in Section III. In this section, we want to make a few general observations.

The key ingredient of neural networks is the interconnection of neurons. There may be many neurons per layer with each neuron having high fan-in (number of input signals) and high fan-out (number of distributed signals). Very large fan-in/fan-out (10^3–10^6) is quite impractical for VLSI technology because it uses a unique discrete channel for each input or output. The space and power penalties in VLSI for these large fan-in/fan-out values are prohibitive. Most optical neural networks use unconfined or free-space interconnections which avoid these problems by allowing freely crossing and overlapping interconnection paths. Thus large numbers of neurons and interconnections are the natural domain of optics. A quantitative analysis of these advantages is shown in Section III.

Power consumption is often a major advantage of optics. Most electronic digital computers use around 10^8 kT per fan-in and fan-out. Here k is the Boltzmann constant, T is the absolute temperature, and kT is the ambient thermal energy. Many optical processors operate at around 10^4 kT. Because coherent optics allow each photon to effectively perform the full fan-in of up to 10^6, the energy per fan-in can be much less than kT [4].

Of course, the general advantages and disadvantages of optics relative to electronics in computing apply here as well. These have to do with easy three-dimensional (3D) interconnection (with no soldering), natural parallelism, insensitivity to electromagnetic interference, and other advantages detailed elsewhere in this issue.

As we will seek to show, optics is sometimes but not always preferable to electronics for implementing neural networks. It is *a* solution, not *the* solution to the problem of implementing neural networks.

III. Neural Network Morphology

A. Introduction

It is convenient to survey the field of optical neural networks on the systematic basis of some sort of morphology. While these morphologies reflect real properties of neural networks, they are far from unique. The intent is to define the morphology well enough so that when all of the morphological choices are made, the resulting neural network will be fairly well defined.

B. Interconnection Constraints

In electronics, connections are necessarily made through prescribed discrete paths (wires, channels, etc.). In optics we can use discrete paths; paths constrained in one dimension only, or unconstrained ("free-space") interconnections. As we pass toward unconstrained interconnections, we embrace more and more of the unique advantages of optics and lose more and more of the unique advantages of electronics. With fully constrained optical interconnections, optical fibers replace wires, so advantages must be sought in cost, fan-out/fan-in, etc. Fiber-optic-based neural networks abandon the advantages of free-space interconnections but still claim some advantages over electronics. First, it is straightforward to accomplish a fan-in and fan-out of about 1000 by either butt-coupling many small fibers into a large one or by using some more advanced couplers. Second, optical fibers need no soldering and are, thus, easier and more reliably assembled. Optical fiber interconnects are often more light-efficient than optical free-space interconnects. As we move to partially constrained integrated optics we gain a measure of flexibility unavailable in electronics. Finally, when we move into unconstrained, free-space interconnection, we gain a tremendous advantage in the number of neurons per layer which can be fully interconnected.

If the interconnections are only confined in one dimension, as is the case in many integrated optics systems, then holograms in the plane of the waveguide can be used to program the interconnections [5].

Another approach might be to use optically programmed electronic interconnections among electronic neurons [6]. Various interconnection patterns can be stored in holograms and called forth at will. If Page Oriented Holographic Memories are used, somewhere between 10^4 and 10^6 patterns can be stored (depending on pattern complexity). These can affect electronic interconnections via photoconductivity. Of course, such reconfigurability is beyond electronics. Although multilayer switching arrays can do arbitrary rearrangements, in principle, they are very expensive and unsuitable for various fan-in/fan-out geometries.

There are a variety of optical methods for fully interconnecting an $N \times N$ input array with an $N \times N$ output array with N^4 interconnections. For large N, say, $N = 10^3$, this amounts to 10^{12} interconnections. Only optics can do full interconnects in this way. By using far more neurons with much smaller fan-in/fan-out, biological neural networks can have far more interconnections.

For many reasons, fan-in/fan-out in VLSI or VHSIC technology is even more limited than in biological neural networks. Electronics is ideal for two-dimensional (2D) arrays of somewhat locally connected neurons. Fig. 4 shows one

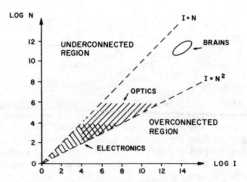

Fig. 4. In a single-layer system with N neurons per layer, we can connect each input to a single output with $I = N$ interconnections. To connect each input to every output requires N^2 interconnections. Even in more complex systems, useful interconnection patterns among N neurons tend to use I interconnects with $N \leq I \leq N^2$. Brains dominate the high-N/high-I region. There are regions of moderate-N/moderate-I which appear uniquely accessible to optics.

way of plotting these relations. Suppose we have two N-neuron layers. If the fan-in/fan-out is 1, the number of interconnections I is N. If the fan-in/fan-out is N, then $I = N^2$. For $I < N$, the system is underconnected. For $I > N^2$, the system is overconnected. Although any neural networks are far more complex than this simple example, most useful neural networks satisfy

$$N \leq I \leq N^2. \qquad (5)$$

What is evident from Fig. 4 is that there are regions of high N and high I that are uniquely accessible to optics. For regions accessible both to electronics and optics, optics must seek advantages in flexibility, power consumption, fan-in/fan-out, etc.

C. Scaling Laws

The first optical neural networks had a linear input array connected to a linear output array through a square interconnection array [7]. Let us call this an $N:N^2:N$ system.

In thick hologram systems, a great deal of crosstalk can occur if we try to interconnect an $N \times N$ input to an $N \times N$ output. Using a fractal mask to achieve an effective $N^{3/2}:N^3:N^{3/2}$ system avoids the problem and can achieve good results [8] at the expense of underusing available space–bandwidth product of input–output devices.

The crosstalk problem is described in [9] and a possible solution is described in [10]. This would restore the full N^4 interconnection capability to photorefractive thick holograms.

There are, however, many schemes for achieving an $N^2:N^4:N^2$ system.

The middle term (the scaling of the interconnection) is vital to those seeking an advantage over electronics in numbers of interconnections. For all of these systems, N is unlikely to be much larger than 1000. Thus the approximate bounds for optical systems are as follows:

System Scaling	Approximate I_{max}
$N:N^2:N$	10^6
$N^{3/2}:N^3:N^{3/2}$	10^9
$N^2:N^4:N^2$	10^{12}

D. Interconnection Methods

The following optical interconnection methods comprise an essentially complete set of methods suggested to date:

- fiber-optic fan-in/fan-out [11],
- holographic in-plane connection in integrated optics [5],
- optical parallel matrix–vector multipliers [7],
- lenslet-array multiple imaging [12],
- thick holographic associative networks [8],
- fixed hologram arrays [13]–[16].

Of these methods, the last two offer the greatest number of parallel interconnections. We will concentrate our attention on them.

From the very early days of holography, the value of thick holograms as associative memories has been known [17]. Wavefronts representing paired 2D patterns are interfered in a 3D recording medium. If one wavefront is incident on the hologram, the other wavefront is reconstructed (approximately). Multiple pairs of wavefronts can be stored in this way. The various pairs must be recorded separately. If there are M pairs, each can use only $1/M$ of the dynamic range of the recording medium. This leads to a $1/M$ signal-to-noise ratio decrease for each hologram relative to the $M = 1$ case [18]. What has changed recently is the use of photorefractive crystals as hologram recording materials [8]–[10]. These have several advantages over photographic media:

- They can be millimeters rather than micrometers thick and thus offer very good selectivity and discrimination.
- These materials are reusable in "real time" and hence lead to continuous learning.
- Since only spatial differences in patterns cause refractive index changes, bias buildup is not a problem.

On the other hand, old recorded pairs fade as new ones are added. Furthermore, even readout records the readout beam and weakens the previously recorded memories.

Thus while there are many new promises and opportunities in photorefractive associate networks, additional research will be needed to optimize this approach.

Another holographic method which dates from the early days of holography is the Page-Oriented Holographic Memory or POHM [19]. The basic idea of the POHM is to store many holograms side by side on the same substrate. The holograms are made in such a way that they have a common 2D output plane. By deflecting a laser beam toward any hologram in the POHM, we cause the corresponding 2D "page" of data to appear in the output plane.

To use the POHM in neural networks, only two major changes are required: address all of the holograms in parallel and (sometimes) place the "write plane" of an optically addressable Spatial Light Modulator (SLM) in the common output plane. Fig. 5 shows one of many such configurations. Let the holograms be indexed by subscripts i and j. Since the output plane is an image of the hologram plane (through the transmissive SLM), it too is indexed by i and j. The input is a 2D SLM whose picture elements or "pixels" are indexed by k and l. Let the amplitude of light from the i, j hologram toward the k, l pixel be called T_{ijkl}. If the transmission of that pixel is a_{kl}, then the light contributed to the i, j output from the k, l input is T_{ijkl}. Of course, all inputs contribute to that output which can be written

$$b_{ij} = \sum_{k,l} T_{ijkl} a_{kl}. \tag{6}$$

We can also write this in the form

$$\vec{b} = T\vec{a} \tag{7}$$

where $\vec{a}$ is a 2D input vector, $\vec{b}$ is a 2D output vector, and T is a four-dimensional (4D) matrix or tensor. Since i, j, k, and l can all run from 1 to N, N^4 independent T_{ijkl}'s (interconnections) can be generated in parallel. Currently available components limit N to "only" 256, although $N = 1024$ (roughly 10^{12} parallel interconnections) appear feasible [20]. Of course, this is well beyond the capability of current or foreseeable electronics.

The "problem," which we will show later can be viewed as an advantage, of this approach is that the interconnect strengths are fixed. Once they are fixed, these neural networks cease to learn (or forget!). As we will show below, fixed holographic memories are ideal for this situation because they can store vast numbers of interconnections and because they are readily and accurately copied (cloned).

E. Data Insertion

The object of the neural network is to perform operations on received data. There are two ways that data can be inserted into an optical neural network. First, they can be inserted as a pattern of light modulated by electrical signals. An array of modulators is, of course, a Spatial Light Mod-

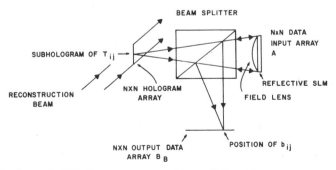

Fig. 5. Shown here is a way the i, j hologram in 2D hologram array can address all elements (indexed by k, l) of a 2D input array and be recollected by a lens onto the i, j position of a 2D output array. This allows full interconnect of a 2D input with a 2D output. In effect, the interconnect is 4D. This is the type of system which allows optics to occupy the moderate-N/moderate-I region of Fig. 4.

ulator (SLM). SLMs can modulate either the reflected or the transmitted light. On the other hand, information can be inserted into the system directly as a modulated pattern of light. That pattern of light can be derived from an array of sources or from possibly spatially separated sources and be brought together as an input via optical fibers. It is best to avoid as many optics-to-electronics and electronics-to-optics steps as possible, and therefore to use optical insertion in multilayer systems would be preferred.

F. On-Line versus Off-Line Learning

In biological neural networks, learning (LTM) and processing (STM) take place in the same wetware. One consequence is the ability, in principle, for brains to continue to learn. In technological neural networks we can choose to do the learning off-line, in a digital computer, for example, or on-line in the neural network itself. That choice has immediate and profound consequences. To change its repertoire of behaviors, we must store new fixed interconnection strengths, after which the neural network will again cease to learn.

Is it important that the neural network continue to learn? Not always. If the neural network is to be an assistant to or, eventually, a replacement of a human being performing an evolving, complex task, continued learning is essential. A very limited kind of learning may be useful even in "fixed interconnect" systems to adjust to a priori unpredictable component variations. Thus the bulk of the computation could be made with the fixed system and "corrections" could be learned on-line. The fixed (nonlearning) network is preferable when many identical neural networks are required. A general wants predictable soldiers who are not independently evolving and implementing their own theory of the battle.

A direct consequence of off-line learning is that the task of the optical neural network is greatly simplified. This results in almost inevitable advantages in speed, size, power consumption, and cost.

G. Adaptivity

Adaptivity is not the same as learning. Obviously, a system that learns adapts. Nonlearning systems can also vary their outputs in a way that reflects changing input conditions. This is what we normally mean by the word "adaptive." A nonlearning adaptive system will adapt the same way to a given situation each time, except for noise. Usually this is not important, but there may be "chaotic" situations where this noise is dominant. A learning system may adapt differently next time.

The adaptivity of fixed interconnect systems can arise from either of two means. First, neural networks are adaptive in the sense given above. Second, high-threshold nonlinearities can be rendered sensitive (likely to respond to significant input) or insensitive by controlling an external optical bias which can itself be controlled by a portion of the neural network. This allows an assembly of specialized neural network modules to be brought into play. The modules would compete for dominance in each situation [21]. There is circumstantial evidence that human brains are organized in a similar manner [22]. Likewise, it is possible to give neural networks changeable predispositions and thus make them "attentive" to user desires [23].

H. Generality

Many optical neural networks are designed to embody a particular neural network architecture and training method. A good example is a neural network designed to exploit the wavelength associativity of thick holograms. Indeed, to our knowledge, all optical neural networks which embody on-line learning do so at some significant loss of generality. As a rule, the fixed interconnect methods are more readily adaptable to networks of diverse types.

There are a variety of "hybrid" neural network concepts which operate optically under control of an electronic computer. These achieve a combination of some of the advantages of off-line processing with flexible operation.

I. Interconnect Matrix Character

Most of the holographic neural networks permit full interconnect (every input to every output) and thus follow full rank matrices. In off-line training it is sometimes convenient to arbitrarily preset many of these to zero. This can lead to sparse matrices which are easier to train and may still give satisfactory results. Particularly simple implementations of rank one matrices with 10^{12} or more components can be made. These permit a small but useful number of applications [24]. Diagonal matrices correspond to the more conventional spatial filtering.

IV. SPECIAL ISSUES

A. Accuracy

The optical neural network methods just described are analog in magnitude representation. While analog optical dynamic range can be many orders of magnitude, the predictability and repeatability is inherently poor. A 10-percent accurate optical interconnection would require elaborate methods and very good optical procedures. Thus the low accuracy of optics must be mitigated in some way. Many popular learning methods require high accuracy in the learning but lead to weights that can be very coarsely quantized a posteriori. It is not clear if analog neural network learning requires high accuracy if we learn in the system we eventually use.

B. Accuracy Mitigation

To some extent, the on-line learning methods are more forgiving in this regard. Repeatable "inaccuracies" are automatically taken into account in the training. It is not clear, though, to what extent these inaccuracies restrict system performance. With analog recurrent networks, some of the accuracy problems may be avoided or canceled out.

In off-line training, it is possible to adapt the conventional approaches such as backward error propagation to quantize the interconnect strengths into two (0 and 1,) three (-1, 0, 1), or a few levels [25]. A 10-percent error still allows minimum confusion between 1 and 0. To achieve results equivalent to, say, 16-bit accurate interconnects, requires more interconnections and more neurons in the hidden layers (between input and output layers, more hidden layers, etc.) This analysis applies for feedforward networks only.

C. Finding Uses

Optical neural networks, according to the arguments presented above, will have as their most obvious applications those which involve truly large numbers of neurons and interconnections. What applications are those?

Higher order neural networks [26] deliberately increase (usually roughly square) the input dimensionality. Thus a 100-component vector leads to about 5000 independent two-component products. Outer product learning of two such vectors gives 2.5×10^7 interconnections. This would be very hard to implement electronically.

By partitioning the input, output, and interconnection matrix we can store multiple-layer neural networks in a single-layer optical neural network [27]. By simple extension, many independent small modules may be implemented in such a system and adaptively interconnected as suggested in Section III-G.

Direct storage neural networks, which store numerous representor vectors of various classes and access them in parallel, will also require optics [28].

D. Space Invariance of Interconnections

Suppose the output at position x_i, y_j is

$$O(x_i, y_j) = \sum_{k,l} a_{ijkl} i(\xi_k, \eta_l) \tag{8}$$

where ξ_k and η_l are input coordinates and, for all $ijkl$,

$$a_{ijkl} = a(x_i - \xi_k, y_j - \eta_l). \tag{9}$$

This interconnection pattern is said to be space-invariant, since a_{ijkl} does not depend on x_i, y_j, ξ_k, and η_l directly but only on their relative displacements. Such interconnections are readily implemented in Fourier optics. All other cases (the vast majority of neural networks) do not satisfy (9) and are thus called "space-variant." Higher order neural networks can be configured to have geometrical invariances by making use of their greater number of degrees of freedom [26].

E. Handling Real Numbers

Implicitly assumed so far is the ability of optics to represent real as opposed to simply nonnegative numbers. There are two ways of doing this.

First, and far more commonly, we represent a real number r as two nonnegative numbers p and n. Thus

$$r = p - n. \tag{10}$$

Ideally, at least one of p and n is zero. Multiplying reals requires four nonnegative multiples, i.e.,

$$(p_1 - n_1)(p_2 - n_2) = (p_1 p_2 + n_1 n_2)$$
$$- (p_1 n_2 + p_2 n_1). \tag{11}$$

We usually represent p and n either by two orthogonal polarization or phase states or by spatially separate pixels. In either case, electronics is usually necessary. In typical sums and products both the p and the n parts will be positive. The smaller must be subtracted from the larger to return the result to the useful economical form where one of the pair is zero.

Second, we can use interference. This is done automatically in the thick hologram systems where relative phase patterns have profound effects. It can also be built into polarization or phase representation systems involving fixed holograms. In a broader sense, all holographic neural networks are based on interference. It is still possible in those cases, however, to encode the reals either spatially or by interference.

V. Optical Neural Network Experiments

In this section we wish to explore the results obtained from those optical neural network architectures. Naturally, we cannot provide detailed descriptions or include all of the innovative designs, but we hope to provide a basic understanding of the progress in this area.

These architectures display the associative properties of the neural network. The network consists of a memory matrix M which is multiplied by an input vector $\vec{x}$ and, after thresholding, produces an output vector $\vec{y}$. However, it should be noted that all machines that perform associations are not neural networks, but all neural networks (in a sense) perform associations. Sections VI, VII, and VIII describe architectures which are based on simple vector–matrix multiplication schemes of neural network models. In this fashion, input and output neurons are interconnected by weighted lines.

The performance of an optical neural network can be measured by several parameters. Perhaps the two most important parameters are P, the number of associations the system is able to recall, and N, the number of elements in these vectors. $\dot{P}$, the number of associations per second, is also vital. Since optics is especially advantageous in applications which require large P, $\dot{P}$, and N, these numbers become important.

Another parameter of importance is how well the system performs with noisy inputs. This has been discussed in only a few references [7], [29] so we are not able to deal with this parameter in detail.

The differing architectures are divided into four categories: 2D interconnections, 3D interconnections, 4D interconnections, and Fourier transforms. We will give a general description of each category and give some of the results.

VI. Two-Dimensional Interconnects

A typical 2D interconnect design is shown in Fig. 6. [7], [30]. The matrix M is stored in an SLM, and the vector $\vec{x}$ is presented to the SLM as a series of LED, or Bragg cells.

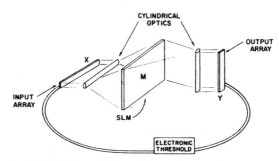

Fig. 6. Typical 2D optical neural network.

Through cylindrical optics the elements in $\vec{x}$ are multiplied by the proper elements in M and the results are summed at the detector array $\vec{y}$. The results are electronically read from the detectors and after a threshold are fed back to $\vec{x}$.

Farhat [7] performed neural network operations with the

design. This architecture recalled three associations ($P = 3$) with each vector of length 32 ($N = 32$). This method provides the advantage of easily changing the matrix values, which is equivalent to "teaching" the neural network.

Unfortunately, this system will eventually reach a physical limit. It is very difficult to conceive of this design reaching even $N = 10^3$. Another restriction is the dynamic range offered by the SLM. The range required of any element of the matrix is P (or $2P$ for a bipolar case) using a simple outer product learning scheme. A "clipped" matrix may be used (all matrix elements are either $+1$ or -1) and 0s on the diagonals. This clipping will reduce the total number P allowed by the system of size N.

VII. THREE-DIMENSIONAL INTERCONNECTS

Optics allows the use of a third spatial dimension that electronics cannot use. When this is employed the N can increase dramatically.

Fig. 7 shows a simple 3D design where the volume hologram provides the interconnections. The input and out-

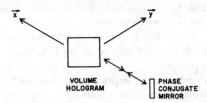

Fig. 7. Simple 3D interconnect design.

put vectors $\vec{x}$ and $\vec{y}$ are presented to the volume hologram in one and a half ($1\frac{1}{2}$) dimensions each.

Perhaps the $1\frac{1}{2}$-dimensional vector representation needs to be explained. It is easy to rearrange the elements of a 1D vector into a 2D array in order to compact the information. If both $\vec{x}$ and $\vec{y}$ are in 2D then the interconnection would be 4D. A volume hologram allows clean interconnections with only three dimensions. Therefore, only some of the elements in the 2D input and output arrays are available. The dimensionalities of $\vec{x}$ and $\vec{y}$ cannot sum to greater than 3. Examples of $1\frac{1}{2}$D to $1\frac{1}{2}$D (fractal) vector representation are shown in Fig. 8(a)-(c). Fig. 8(d) shows a 2D-to-1D mapping which can also be made since the required interconnects do not surpass three dimensions. Note that Owechko [10] has found a possible way to utilize the *full* areas of the input and output.

Several researchers [13], [25], [31]-[33], have employed the hologram-PCM design in Fig. 7. The thick holograms are recorded in "real time" in photorefractive crystals. In these designs, the inputs and outputs are continuous images so N is effectively given by the space-bandwidth product, or simply the resolution of the input-output devices. These experiments have stored and recalled from 1 to 4 associations ($P = 4$).

These 3D designs offer advantages over other designs in that they contain dynamic memories. The photorefractive crystals used in storing the volume holograms can be allowed somewhat to change the associations stored in memory.

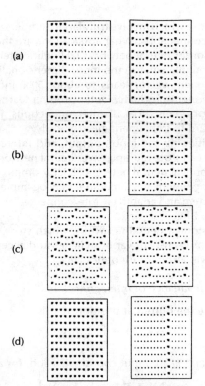

Fig. 8. Typical $\vec{x}$ and $\vec{y}$ patterns allowed by a 3D volume hologram interconnect scheme [31].

VIII. FOUR-DIMENSIONAL FIXED INTERCONNECTS

Machines have been built that use the full dimensionality available to optics to create fixed 4D interconnected neural networks [16], [35], [36]. Fig. 9 shows a typical 4D intercon-

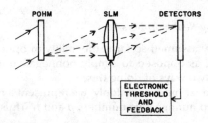

Fig. 9. Typical 4D interconnection scheme. Two different holograms in the POHM are seen addressing the full array of the SLM and the information collecting at individual detectors.

nect design. Several patterns are stored in a page-oriented holographic memory (POHM). All of these patterns are simultaneously multiplied by the input written on an SLM. The multiplications are summed to a detector array.

The POHM may be thought of as a 4D interconnection since it contains a 2D array of 2D fully interconnected patterns. In this fashion, every pixel on the 2D SLM can be independently connected to any detector in the 2D detector array.

The results of this type of design are in line with other architectures: $N = 16$, $P = 2$ [16]; $N = 6$, $P = 4$ [35]; and $N = 49$, $P = 4$ [36].

Theoretically, these designs can also scale up to very large N and P. There is also no restriction in using continuous images rather than pixelated 2D vectors [35], [36].

Using present POHM would mean that the interconnections cannot be altered. There are designs to correct this problem but, so far as we know, none has been built.

IX. Fourier Transform Associative Memories

Finally, associative memories have been built using the Fourier Transform property of lenses [16], [32], [38], [39]. Fig. 10 shows the basic design of one of these machines.

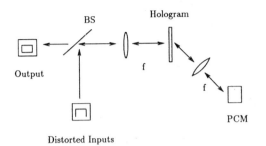

Fig. 10. The single-iteration associative memory.

The Fourier mask contains all of the Fourier transforms of the stored patterns, each stored with a different reference beam angle. The strongest of the reconstructed reference beam is nonlinearly amplified and fed back through the same or/and identical hologram to reconstruct the corresponding stored pattern.

This is then a good associative memory of 2D continuous images. As many as 70 [40] patterns have been stored at one time. However, an argument continues as to whether this design is a neural network or just an associative memory.

The Fourier transform holographic memory is an all-optical content-addressable memory capable of recalling complete objects from a distorted or partial input. Fig. 10 shows the basic design of one of these machines. The memory can be either a thin Fourier transform hologram (film) or a photorefractive crystal acting as a volume hologram. The particular crystal used as the memory can be tailored to allow for faster access times or longer retention of the memories. The self-pumped phase conjugate mirror acts as a nonlinear thresholding device. Specifically, the phase conjugate mirror processes the multiple correlation peaks amplifying and returning only the reference that most closely matches the input. The phase conjugate return is used to re-address the holographic memory. This process is analogous to the previous neural network equations. Using the outer product associative artificial neural network model of McCulloch and Pitts [41] and later popularized by Grossberg [42] and again by Hopfield [43]

$$y_{ij} = NL\left(\sum_{kl} a_{ijkl} x_{kl}\right). \tag{12}$$

By multiplying the Fourier transforms and then again transforming them through a lens on the way to the phase conjugate mirror, the optical system has accomplished the weighted sum of the neural network equation. The self-pumped phase conjugate mirror only reflects those correlation peaks above a threshold [37]. The beam splitter then breaks off the output which is the complete memory most closely approximating the input. There are several interesting modifications that can be made to this system. For example, parts of it could be done electrically [9]. The use of electronics allows for the most direct implementation of the classical neural network paradigms.

Many optical information processing algorithms require feedback to perform iterative processing. The recurrent neural network algorithms exemplify this requirement. Another candidate for an optical associative memory would consist of a resonator, photorefractive crystals, and holographic plates. Anderson [44] has investigated the results of using photorefractive crystals within resonators. A resonator similar in concept to Anderson's is a design by Stoll and Lee [45]. Fig. 11 shows the design which uses two BaTiO$_3$ crystals, planar mirrors for feedback, two fixed holograms, and a set of pinholes. The input is sent through crystal C1 and is projected onto hologram T1 which acts as a VanderLugt filter. The correlation term is Fourier transformed by lens L1. The correlations are spatially filtered by the pinholes and amplified by crystal C2 to become reference beams for hologram T2. The recalled object from hologram T2 is fed back to crystal C1 where it is added

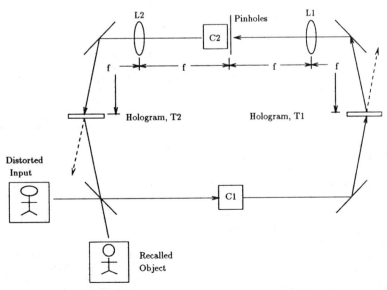

Fig. 11. Northrop's associative memory. The pump beams for the two-wave coupling within the BaTiO$_3$ crystals are not pictured.

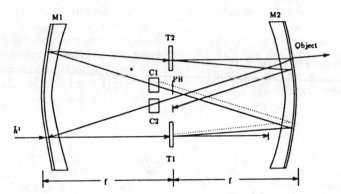

Fig. 12. Optical associative memory in confocal resonator.

coherently with the input. The system then resonates until a steady-state solution is found. The operation of the crystals within this associative memory is critical. Crystal C2 operates as a linear amplifier to compensate for losses within the resonator. However, crystal C1 is operating as a nonlinear gain mechanism in which the gain is dependent on the intensity of the input beam (commonly called the probe beam in optical two-wave mixing) compared to the pump beam—the larger the input, the lower the gain. Two wave mixing within the photorefractive crystals allows the transfer of energy from one of the beams, the pump beam, into the other, the probe beam. This is accomplished by gratings being formed within the crystal by the interference between the two beams. Within neural network terminology, crystal C1 operates as a node in which the nonlinear summation occurs. There is then competition between the stored objects for the available gain within the resonator with the mode, the memory, that most closely matches the input winning the competition. An alternate architecture has been designed by Wilson [46]. The differences with the Stoll and Lee design are the feedback system used and the use of the two crystals. The feedback system used is a confocal resonator which allows for compactness of design with two Fourier and two image planes. The greatest difference is in the use of the crystals. Both of the Northrop's crystals (z cuts) are used for amplification. Therefore, there is only competition for the gain within the resonator between stored objects. In the Wilson work a 45° cut crystal is used for linear amplification and a z cut crystal is used as a nonlinear attenuator. This combination allows for competition for the available gain while suppressing the weaker objects competing for the gain with the nonlinear attenuation. Fig. 12 shows the design.

X. Conclusions

A useful criterion of the youth of a field is the simplicity of its important new concepts. As a field matures, most of the important new concepts become highly technical and highly complex. Innovators come to be called "genius." Fields in their youth produce important advances through ideas which, in retrospect, look obvious. As a consequence, almost simultaneous inventions proliferate and progress is rapid. Our first observation is that, by this criterion, optical neural networks is a young field.

Historically, products tend to arise during the youth of a field. These will build the technical and financial bases for later development of even more successful products. Are there already commercializable optical neural network systems? It is hard to say with certainty. The simplest to build also has the most available interconnections: the rank one N^4 system. The problem with this is that the only well-developed algorithm for such a system is the outer product approach popularized by Hopfield [43]. Other approaches to "program" these remain largely untested. In general, the most sophisticated systems are the most promising in the long run. These are also the furthest from commercialization. If the field progresses logically, simple commercial systems could appear by the early-to-mid-1990s with the currently most sophisticated systems becoming available by the end of the century. Of course, major fields never advance "logically." It seems likely that the youth of this field will provide us with heretofore unforeseen approaches significantly superior to what we have outlined here. Indeed, our hope is that this paper will interest enough clever readers to assure that outcome.

Acknowledgment

The authors wish to thank Dr. B. Soffer for a careful reading of the manuscript. No blame, but some real credit is due to his efforts.

References

[1] D. E. Rumelhart, J. L. McClelland, and G. Hinton, "The appeal of parallel distributed processing," in *Parallel Distributed Processing: Explorations in the Microstructure of Cognition,* D. E. Rumelhart, J. L. McClelland, and the PDP Research Group, vol. 1. Cambridge, MA: MIT Press, 1986.

[2] R. P. Lippman, "An introduction to computing with neural nets," *IEEE Acoust., Speech, Signal Process. Mag.,* vol. 4, no. 2, pp. 4-22, Apr. 1987.

[3] S. Grossberg, "Nonlinear neural networks: Principles, mechanisms and architectures," *Neural Networks,* vol. 1, pp. 17-61, 1988.

[4] H. J. Caulfield and J. Shamir, "Wave particle duality considerations in (optical) computing," *Appl. Opt.,* vol. 28, no. 12, pp. 2184-2186, June 15, 1989. Elements of this work were presented at the Optical Society of America meeting on Optical Computing, Salt Lake City, UT, Feb.-Mar. 1989.

[5] M. R. Feldman, S. C. Esener, C. C. Guest, and S. H. Lee, "Comparison between optical and electrical interconnects based on power and speed considerations," *Appl. Opt.,* vol. 27, pp. 1742-1751, 1988.

[6] A. Agranat, C. F. Neugebauer, and A. Yariv, "Parallel optoelectronics realization of neural network models using CID technology," *Appl. Opt.,* vol. 27, pp. 4354-4355, 1988.

[7] N. H. Farhat, D. Psaltis, A. Prata, and E. Park, "Optical implementation of the Hopfield model," *Appl. Opt.,* vol. 24, pp. 1469-1475, 1985.

[8] D. Psaltis, J. Yu, X. G. Gu, and H. Lee, "Optical neural nets implemented with volume holograms," in *Proc. OSA 2nd Topical Meet. on Optical Computing*, p. 129.

[9] Y. Owechko, B. H. Soffer, and G. J. Dunning, "Optoelectronic neural networks based on holographically interconnected image processors," *Proc. SPIE*, vol. 882 (*Neural Network Models for Optical Computing*), 1988.

[10] Y. Owechko, "Self-pumped optical neural networks," presented at the Optical Society of America meeting on Optical Computing, Salt Lake City, UT, Feb.–Mar. 1989.

[11] R. Arathoon, private communication to H. J. Caulfield, 1987.

[12] N. H. Farhat, S. Miyahara, and K. S. Lee, "Optical analog of two-dimensional neural networks and their application in recognition of radar targets," in *Neural Networks for Computing*. New York, NY: Amer. Inst. Phys., 1986, pp. 146–152.

[13] H. J. Caulfield, "Parallel N^4 weighted optical interconnections," *Appl. Opt.*, vol. 26, pp. 4039–4040, 1987.

[14] R. Clark, C. Hester, and P. Lindberg, "Mapping sequential processing algorithms onto parallel distributed processing architectures," *Proc. SPIE*, vol. 880, 1988.

[15] H. J. White, N. B. Aldridge, and I. Lindsay, "Digital and analogue holographic associative memories," *Opt. Eng.*, vol. 27, pp. 30–37, 1988.

[16] J. S. Jang, S-W Jung, S-Y Lee, and S-Y Shin, "Optical implementation of the Hopfield model for two-dimensional associative memory," *Opt. Lett.*, vol. 13, pp. 248–250, 1988.

[17] R. J. Collier and K. S. Pennington, "Ghost imaging in holograms formed in the near field," *Appl. Phys. Lett.*, vol. 8, pp. 44–46, 1966.

[18] H. J. Caulfield, Sun Lu, and J. L. Harris, "Biasing for single-exposure and multiple-exposure holography," *J. Opt. Soc. Amer.*, vol. 58, p. 1003, 1968.

[19] F. M. Smits and L. E. Gallaher, "Design considerations for a semipermanent optical memory," *Bell Syst. Tech. J.*, vol. 46, p. 1267, 1967.

[20] J. Shamir, H. J. Caulfield, and R. B. Johnson, "Massive holographic interconnection networks and their limitations," *Appl. Opt.*, vol. 28, pp. 311–324, 1989.

[21] H. J. Caulfield, "An optical society of mind," post paper presented at the Int. Neural Network Soc. Conf., Boston, MA, 1988. Also available as Neural Networks Paper 89-8, Center for Applied Optics, Univ. of Alabama in Huntsville.

[22] M. Minsky, *The Society of Mind*. New York, NY: Simon and Schuster, 1986.

[23] R. Athale, C. Friedlander, and B. Kushner, "Attentive associative architectures and their implementations," *Proc. SPIE*, vol. 625, no. 11, pp. 179–188, 1986.

[24] H. J. Caulfield, "Variable and fixed rank 1 N^4 interconnects," paper submitted to Int. Joint Conf. on Neural Networks, 1989.

[25] E. Fiesler, A. Choudry, and H. J. Caulfield, "Weight discretization in backward error propagation neural networks," submitted to *IEEE Trans. Syst. Man Cybern.*

[26] T. Maxwell, C. L. Giles, Y. Lee, and H. H. Chen, "Transformation invariance using high order correlations in neural net architectures," in *Proc. IEEE Int. Conf. on Systems, Man, and Cybernetics* (Atlanta, GA, Oct. 14–17, 1986) pp. 627–632.

[27] N. H. Farhat, "Architectures for optoelectronic analogs of self organizing neural networks," *Opt. Lett.*, vol. 12, pp. 6–8, 1987.

[28] B. Montgomery and V. Kumar, "Nearest-neighbor non-iterative error correcting optical associative memory processor," *Proc. SPIE*, vol. 638, pp. 83–90, 1986.

[29] S. H. Song and S. S. Lee, "Properties of holographic associative memory prepared by the polarization encoding process," *Appl. Opt.*, vol. 27, pp. 3149–3154, 1988.

[30] A. D. Fisher, W. L. Lippincott, and N. N. Lee, "Optical implementations of associative networks with versable adaptive learning capability," *Appl. Opt.*, vol. 26, pp. 5039–5054, 1987.

[31] D. Psaltis, lectures delivered at 31st Scottish Summer School in Physics, NATO Advanced Study Institute, Optical Computing, Aug. 19–26, 1988.

[32] B. H. Soffer, G. J. Dunning, Y. Owechko, and E. Marom, "Associative holographic memory with feedback using phase-conjugative mirrors," *Opt. Lett.*, vol. 11, pp. 118–120, 1986.

[33] K. Wagner and D. Psaltis, "Multilayer optical learning networks," *Appl. Opt.*, vol. 26, pp. 5067–5076, 1987.

[34] H. J. White, "Experimental results from an optical network using photorefractive crystals," *Appl. Opt.*, vol. 27, pp. 1752–1759, 1988.

[35] ——, "Experimental results from an optical implementation of a simple neural network," draft.

[36] J. M. Kinser and H. J. Caulfield, "Extension and network of the direct storage neural network for optical implementation," submitted to *Appl. Opt.*, 1988. Also available as Neural Networks Paper 89-9, Center for Applied Optics, Univ. of Alabama in Huntsville.

[37] J. M. Kinser, H. J. Caulfield, and J. Shamir, "Design for a massive all-optical bidirectional associative memory: The big BAM," *Appl. Opt.*, vol. 27, pp. 3992–3999, 1988.

[38] Y. Owechko, "Optoelectronic resonator neural networks," *Appl. Opt.*, vol. 26, pp. 5104–5111, 1987.

[39] G. Dunning, B. Soffer, and Y. Owechko, "Optical associative memory incorporating holography and phase conjugation," *Optic News*, pp. 17–19, Dec. 1987.

[40] D. A. Gregory and H. K. Liu, "Large-memory real-time multichannel multiplexed pattern recognition," *Appl. Opt.*, vol. 23, pp. 4560–4570, 1984.

[41] W. S. McCulloch and W. Pitts, "A logical calculus of ideas immanent in nervous activity," *Bull. Math. Biophys.*, vol. 5, p. 115, 1943.

[42] S. Grossberg, "On learning and energy-entropy dependence in recurrent and nonrecurrent signed networks," *J. Stat. Phys.*, vol. 1, p. 319, 1969.

[43] J. J. Hopfield, "Neural networks and physical systems with emergent collective computational abilities," *Proc. Nat. Acad. Sci. U.S.*, vol. 79, pp. 2554–2558, 1982.

[44] D. Z. Anderson, "Coherent optical eigenstate memory," *Opt. Lett.*, vol. 11, pp. 56–58, 1986.

[45] H. M. Stoll and L. S. Lee, "A continuous time optical neural network," in *Proc. IEEE Int. Conf. on Neural Networks*, vol. 2, pp. 373–384, 1988.

[46] J. A. Wilson, "Optical information processing in a confocal Fabry–Perot resonator," M.S. thesis, AFIT GEO 88D-2, School of Engineering, Air Force Institute of Technology (AU), Wright-Patterson AFB, OH, 1988.

Article 7.8

Holographic Implementation of a Fully Connected Neural Network

KEN-YUH HSU, HSIN-YU LI, AND DEMETRI PSALTIS, MEMBER, IEEE

Invited Paper

This paper describes an optical implementation of a fully connected neural network similar to the Hopfield network. Experimental results which demonstrate its ability to recognize stored images are given, followed by a discussion of its performance and analysis based on a proposed model for the system.

I. INTRODUCTION

In this paper we present a holographic implementation of a fully connected neural network [1], [2]. This model has a simple structure and is relatively easy to implement while its operating principles and characteristics can be extended to other types of networks, since any architecture can be considered as a fully connected network with some of its connections missing. In the following sections, the basic principles of the fully connected network are reviewed. The optical implementation of the network is presented in Section III and its experimental results are presented in Section IV. Special attention is focused on the dynamics of the feedback loop and the trade-off between distortion tolerance and image-recognition capability of the associative memory. Mathematical modeling and analysis of the system are presented in Section V.

II. THE HOPFIELD MEMORY

The basic structure of the network is shown in Fig. 1. It is a single-layer network with feedback. There are two main components: the neurons and the interconnections. The neurons are distributed in the neural plane. The neurons receive inputs, perform nonlinear thresholding on the received input, provide gain, and re-emit the output patterns. The output of each unit is connected to the input of all other neurons to form a feedback network.

Manuscript received September 25, 1989; revised April 12, 1990. This work is supported by DARPA and in part by the Air Force Office of Scientific Research.
K.-Y. Hsu was with the Department of Electrical Engineering, California Institute of Technology, Pasadena, CA 91125, USA. He is now with the Institute of Electro-Optical Engineering, National Chiao Tung University, Hsin-Chu 30050, Taiwan, ROC.
H.-Y. Li and D. Psaltis are with the Department of Electrical Engineering, California Institute of Technology, Pasadena, CA 91125, USA.
IEEE Log Number 9039181.

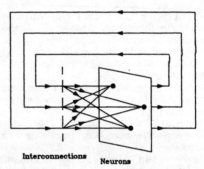

Interconnections Neurons

Fig. 1. Two dimensional fully connected network.

There are two phases in the operation of the network: learning and recall. In the learning phase, the information to be stored is recorded according to the outer product scheme [1], [2]. This storage specifies the interconnection strengths between the neurons. In the recall phase, an external input is presented to the system. The state of the system then evolves according to the correlation between the input and the stored data. M N-bit binary words are stored in a matrix $\omega_{i,j}$ according to

$$\omega_{i,j} = \begin{cases} \sum_{m=1}^{M} v_i^m v_j^m, & \text{if } i \neq j; \\ 0, & \text{otherwise,} \end{cases} \quad (1)$$

where $v_i^m = \pm 1$, $i = 1, \cdots, N$, is the ith bit of the m0th memory. Suppose, for example, that v^{m0}, the mth stored vector, is presented to the system in the recall phase. This vector is multiplied by the matrix $w_{i,j}$, giving the output of the first iteration:

$$\hat{v}_i^{m0} = sgn \left\{ \sum_{j=1}^{N} w_{i,j} v_j^{m0} \right\}, \quad (2)$$

where $sgn\{\cdot\}$ is the thresholding function,

$$sgn\{x\} = \begin{cases} 1, & \text{if } x \geq 0; \\ -1, & \text{if } x < 0. \end{cases} \quad (3)$$

The thresholded result of the first iteration is then fed back to the system as input for the next iteration, and so on.

Reprinted from *Proc. IEEE*, vol, 78, no. 10, pp. 1637–1645, Oct. 1990.

There are three operations performed by the system: vector-matrix multiplication, thresholding, and feedback. A network of this type using optoelectronics was first implemented by Psaltis, Farhat, and their colleagues [3], [4]. They used a computer-generated transparency to provide the interconnection matrix. A 1-D array of 32 photodiode pairs followed by electronic thresholding plus a 1-D array of 32 LEDs was used to simulate 32 neurons. In this paper the optical implementation of such a system for 2-D images uses holograms. The design and implementation of this system are presented in the following section.

III. Optical Implementation

The interconnection pattern for 2-D images is described by the following equation:

$$\omega(x, y; \xi, \eta) = \sum_{m=1}^{M} f_m(x, y) f_m(\xi, \eta), \qquad (4)$$

where $f_m(x, y)$ is the mth image, and M is the total number of images to be stored. Note that $\omega(x, y; \xi, \eta)$ is a four dimensional kernel and cannot be implemented directly using a single transparency since a 2-D optical system has only two spatial coordinates. The system described in this paper is based on a method for implementing this 4-D kernel that uses a 2-D array of spatial frequency multiplexed holograms [3], [5], [6]. Jang et al. used a 2-D array of $N \times N$ diffused holograms to obtain the 4-D interconnection [7], [8]. Other approaches to this problem include the use of spatial multiplexing [9] and volume holograms [10]–[13].

In the recall phase, the output of the system is described by the equation

$$\hat{f}(x, y, t) = g\left\{\int\int \omega(x, y; \xi, \eta) f(\xi, \eta, t)\,d\xi\,d\eta\right\}, \qquad (5)$$

where $g\{\cdot\}$ represents the nonlinear thresholding of the neurons, $f(x, y, t)$ is the input to the system at time t, and $\hat{f}(x, y, t)$ is the output of the system. Substituting the expression for $\omega(x, y; \xi, \eta)$ into this equation, and rearranging the order of integration and summation, we obtain

$$\hat{f}(x, y, t) = g\left\{\sum_{m=1}^{M} f_m(x, y)\left[\int\int f_m(\xi, \eta)\right.\right.$$
$$\left.\left.\cdot f(\xi - x, \eta - y, t)\,d\xi\,d\eta\right]_{x=0, y=0}\right\}. \qquad (6)$$

From (6) we see that the implementation of the 2-D associative memory can be achieved in three steps [6]. First the 2-D correlation between the input image f and each of the memories f_m is calculated, and then the correlation function is evaluated at the origin to obtain the inner product values. Second, each inner product is multiplied by the associated stored memory. Third, these products are summed over all memories and thresholded by the neurons.

The implementation of the system will be explained with the aid of Fig. 2. Here four images are spatially separated and stored as the reference images in each of two correlators. When one of the stored patterns A is presented at plane P_1 of the system, the first correlator produces the auto-correlation along with three cross-correlations of plane P_2. The pinhole array at P_2 samples these correlation functions at the center of each pattern where the inner products

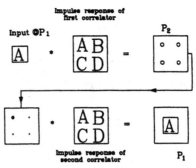

Fig. 2. Block diagram of the operations performed by the optical loop.

between the input and each of the stored images form. Each of the four signals that pass through the pinholes act as delta functions, reconstructing from the second correlator the four images that are stored there. These reconstructed images are spatially translated according to the position of each pinhole and superimposed at plane P_1. At the center of the output plane of the second correlator we obtain the superposition of the four stored images. The stored image that is most similar to the input pattern gives the strongest correlation signal, hence the brightest reconstructed image. In Fig. 2 we show only the image that is reconstructed by the strongest auto-correlation peak. The weak read-out signal that is due to cross-correlations is suppressed by the thresholding operation of the neurons. The output from the plane of neurons becomes the new input image for the next iteration. In this way the stable pattern that is established in the loop is typically the stored image that is most similar to the original input.

The optical implementation makes use of the Vander Lugt correlator [14] shown in Fig. 3. If we place a hologram at the

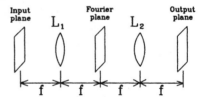

Fig. 3. Vander Lugt correlator.

Fourier plane of the system in Fig. 3 whose transmittance function is the complex conjugate of the Fourier transform of a second, reference image, then it can be shown that the output is the 2-D correlation function between the input and reference images [15]. In our system, the reference image in each of two correlators is a composite of four images that are spatially separated. A transparency is prepared containing the four images and the Fourier transform of this pattern is formed with a lens. A hologram of the Fourier transform of the composite pattern is then formed by recording its interference with a plane wave reference. The holograms that are formed in this manner are placed at the intermediate planes of two Vander Lugt correlators that are cascaded to form the optical memory loop.

The schematic diagram of the overall optical architecture is shown in Fig. 4, and a photograph of the experimental apparatus is shown in Fig. 5. The first correlator consists of the liquid crystal light valve (LCLV) at P_1, the beam splitter

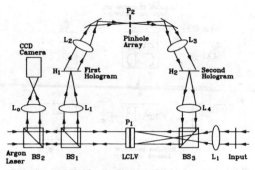

Fig. 4. Schematic diagram of the optical loop.

Fig. 5. Photograph of the optical loop.

Fig. 6. Stored images. (a) The original images. (b) Images reconstructed from H_1. (c) Images reconstructed from H_2.

cube BS_1, the lenses L_1, L_2, and the hologram H_1. The LCLV here functions as a 2-D array of neurons. It consists of a dielectric mirror sandwiched between a light-sensing layer and a light-modulation layer. The light-sensing layer is a CdS photoconductor which acts as a photosensor, whereas the light-modulation layer is a thin layer (a few microns) of nematic liquid crystal. When light strikes the photosensor, its conductance changes, which in turn changes the voltage across the liquid crystal on the other side. When a reading light beam across the liquid crystal layer is reflected off the light-modulating side, its polarization state is modulated in proportion to the voltage across the liquid crystal layer.

The second correlator consists of P_2, L_3, H_2, L_4, BS_3, and P_1 shown in Fig. 4. The input pattern is imaged onto the LCLV by lens L_i and through beam splitter BS_3. A collimated argon laser beam illuminates the read-out side of the LCLV through beam splitters BS_2 and BS_1. A portion of the reflected light from the LCLV that propagates straight through BS_1, is diverted by BS_2, and it is imaged by lens L_0 onto a CCD television camera through which we monitor the system. The portion of light reflected by BS_1 into the loop is Fourier transformed by lens L_1 and illuminates hologram H_1. The correlation between the input image and each of the stored images is produced at plane P_2. The spacing of the pinhole array at P_2 corresponds to the spatial separation between the stored images. The remainder of the optical system from P_2 back to the neural plane P_1 is essentially a replica of the first half, with hologram H_2 storing the same set of images as H_1.

The holograms in this system are thermoplastic plates, with an area of 1 in^2 and 800 lines/mm resolution. The hologram H_1 is made with a high-pass characteristic for edge enhancement to improve discrimination. H_2 on the other hand is broadband so that the feedback images have high fidelity with respect to the originals. We use a diffuser to

achieve this when making H_2. Fig. 6(a) shows the four original images. Fig. 6(b) shows the images reconstructed from the first hologram H_1, and Fig. 6(c) shows the images reconstructed from the second hologram H_2.

The pinhole array at P_2 samples the correlation signal between the image coming from the LCLV and the images stored in hologram H_1. The pinhole diameter used in these experiments ranges from 45 μm to 700 μm. If the pinholes are too small, the light passing through to reconstruct the feedback image is too weak to be detected by the LCLV. On the other hand, large pinholes introduce excessive blurring and cross-talk and make the reconstructed images unrecognizable. The pinhole size also affects the shift invariance of the loop. In order to be recognized, the autocorrelation peak from an external image should stay within the pinhole. Larger pinholes allow more shift in the input image. The system performance under different selections of pinhole diameters is discussed in the next section. As the optical signal goes through the loop, it is attenuated because of the small diffraction efficiency of the Fourier transform holograms and the losses from pinholes, lenses, and beam splitters. To compensate for this loss, we use an image intensifier at the photoconductor side of the LCLV. The microchannel plate of the image intensifier is sensitive to a minimum incident intensity of approximately 1 nW/cm^2 and reproduces the input with an intensity 10^4 times brighter (10 μW/cm^2), sufficient to drive the LCLV. If we use a beam with intensity equal to 10 mW/cm^2 to read the LCLV, then the intensity of the output light is approximately 1 mW/cm^2. Thus, the combination of the image intensifier and the LCLV provides an optical gain up to 10^6. It turns out that the setting of the gain is the key parameter that mediates the trade-off between distortion invariance and the discrimination capability of the loop. This will also be discussed in the next section.

IV. Experimental Results

The optical associative loop of Fig. 4 can be lumped into the simplified blocks shown in Fig. 7(a). The LCLV is represented as the component **Gain** in Fig. 7(a). The other parts of the loop are all lossy, linear components and are represented by the component **Loss** in Fig. 7(a).

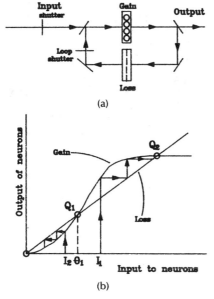

Fig. 7. (a) The gain and loss components of the loop. (b) The stable states of the loop.

The dynamics of the recall process can be understood by using the iteration map shown in Fig. 7(b). In the figure the gain curve represents the input–output response of the neurons, whereas the straight line gives the loop loss due to the holograms, and pinholes, etc. The intersection point Q_1 is the threshold level, and the intersection point Q_2 gives a stable point. If the initial condition is above the threshold level θ_1, the signal (I_1) grows in successive iterations until it arrives and latches at Q_2. On the other hand, if the initial condition is below θ_1, the signal (I_2) decays to zero. The number of iterations (convergence time) depends on the initial condition. This of course is only a simplified picture of what goes on in the loop. A more precise analysis will be given in Section V.

The loop dynamics were measured by controlling the two shutters shown in Fig. 7(a). An example of the temporal response of the loop to an input pattern is shown in Fig. 8. The lower trace represents the intensity of the external input image and the upper trace represents the corresponding light intensity detected at the loop output. Before time t_1, both shutters are closed and the response is low. At time t_1 the input shutter is opened (with the loop shutter still closed) and the lower trace becomes high. The upper trace shows the corresponding response of the neurons to the external input. At time t_2 the loop shutter is opened and the loop is closed. The feedback signal arrives at the neurons as an additional input and iteration begins. It takes about two seconds in this case for the loop to reach a stable state. At time t_3 the input shutter is closed and the lower trace becomes low. However, the loop remains latched to a stable state, which is one of the stored images. We get similar results with reduced input intensity. It takes longer to reach a stable state when the input is weak, but the final state remains the same.

Since the external input does not affect the shape of the final state, but only selects which state is produced, there is a certain degree of invariance in the system since a distorted version of a stored image can recall the stored image. The effect of distortions such as scale, rotation and shift,

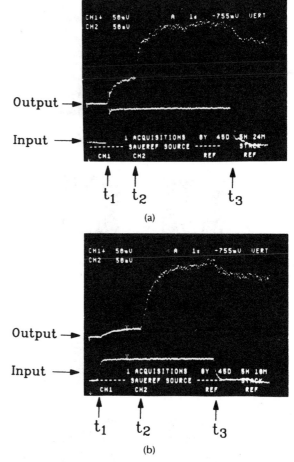

Fig. 8. Temporal response of the loop. (a) Strong input. (b) Weak input. Timing: t_1 = Input ON, t_2 = Feedback ON, t_3 = Input OFF.

is to decrease the initial intensity level of the loop. However, as long as the initial condition is above the threshold (θ in Fig. 7(b)), the loop still converges to a memory state. The strength of the initial condition is determined by the degree of distortion of the input, while the threshold is determined by the neural gain and loop loss.

The images stored in the loop are the four faces shown in Fig. 6(a). Fig. 9(a) shows the response of the system when a partially blocked face is presented to the system with the loop shutter closed. This sets the initial condition. The loop shutter is then opened to close the feedback path, and the state of the system evolves. After some time the loop reaches stable state and a complete face appears. The time for this process ranges from less than one second to several seconds, depending on the initial condition and the system parameters. The complete image remains latched in the loop when the external input is removed. Fig. 9(b) shows the system output at the moment the loop shutter is closed. We see that the feedback image is superimposed on the input. Fig. 9(c) to (e) shows the evolution of the output after the feedback loop is closed. The complete image obtained 2 seconds after the loop is closed is shown in Fig. 9(e). Fig. 9(f) shows that after the external input is removed, the recalled image stays latched. The same situation occurs when other partially blocked faces are used.

In a separate experiment, a rotated version of each of the faces was used as input. Fig. 10(a) shows the output of the

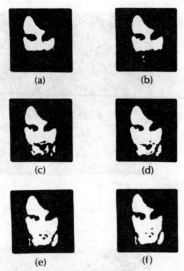

Fig. 9. Retrieval of the complete image from the partial input. (a) The partial input at $t = 0$. (b) $t = 0^+$ (loop closed). (c) $t = 400$ *ms*. (d) $t = 800$ *ms*. (e) $t = 2$ sec. (f) Input OFF.

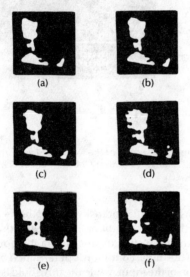

Fig. 10. Retrieval of the complete image from the rotated input. (a) The input at $t = 0$. (b) $t = 0^+$ (loop closed). (c) $t = 1.8$ sec. (d) $t = 3.6$ sec. (e) $t = 4.8$ sec. (f) Input OFF.

system when a rotated version (by 6°) of one of the faces is presented to the system with the loop shutter closed. Fig. 10(b) shows the memory output immediately after the feedback loop is closed. The evolution of the system towards the original unrotated image is shown in Fig. 10(c) to Fig. 10(e).

In Fig. 11(a) the upper curve is the intensity of the final image and the lower curve is the convergence time, both plotted as functions of rotation angle. The larger the rotation angle, the longer it takes to converge. However, once the loop reaches stable state, the output intensity is always the same regardless of the initial rotation. The output intensity drops to zero when the angle is more than 8°. This means that the initial condition is below threshold and the rotated image does not elicit a response. One way to increase tolerance to rotation is by increasing the neural gain so that it can detect weaker feedback signals. It is found that with the gain set 10 times higher, the tolerance increases to 16°.

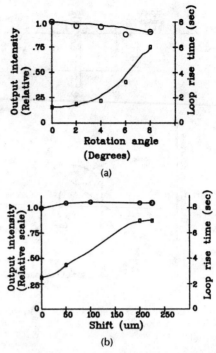

Fig. 11. (a) Loop response to rotated inputs. (b) Loop response to shifted inputs. (Optical gain = 10^4; ○: Output intensity. □: Loop rise time.)

However, although we can obtain more tolerance by increasing the gain, this enhances crosstalk and may cause the loop to converge to the wrong image. Similar experiments were carried out to measure the ability of the system to tolerate scale changes. The results were similar, with tolerance in the range of 7% to 9%, depending on the gain.

This system has very small tolerance to position errors at the input, i.e., it is not shift invariant. When the input image is translated, the entire correlation pattern in the intermediate plane P_2 shifts also. The autocorrelation peak that is normally aligned with the pinhole is blocked. A small degree of shift invariance exists due to the finite width of the pinhole and the correlation peak. In the experimental system, the pinhole diameter was 90 μm. Fig. 11(b) shows the strength of the final state and the rise time versus the amount of shift in the input from its nominal position. A larger pinhole yields more shift invariance. But as the pinhole diameter increases, the reconstruction from the second hologram is blurred because the output becomes the convolution of the stored image with its autocorrelation pattern. This results in a loss in correlation strength in subsequent iterations, and can result in insufficient gain for maintaining a stable state.

The experimental results shown above demonstrate the distortion-invariance capability of the associative loop. By raising the neural gain sufficiently high, the loop can always be made to produce an image as a stable state no matter how much we distort the input image. But the ability to reliably produce correct associations between initial and final states degrades as the gain increases. If there is too much gain, then just shining a flashlight at the input of the system can cause it to converge to one of its stable states. If the gain is set too low, the slightest distortion of the stored images renders it unrecognizable. If the gain is set even lower, no input can cause the loop to latch on a stable state. Fig. 12

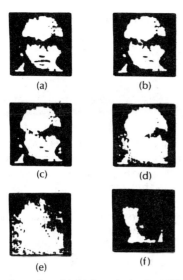

Fig. 12. Loop dynamics with high optical gain. (a) The input at $t = 0$. (b) $t = 0^+$ (loop closed). (c) $t = 1.2$ sec. (d) $t = 1.8$ sec. (e) The input is OFF. (f) Stable state.

shows an example of the behavior obtained when the gain is set too high. An unfamiliar input initially produces an unrecognizable state. When the external input is removed, the system latches erroneously to one of the stored images.

V. A NETWORK MODEL FOR THE OPTICAL LOOP

The optical associative memory presented in this paper is very similar to a Hopfield network, but it is not quite the same. The neurons are simulated by the LCLV, which responds to light intensity, which is the magnitude squared of the light amplitude, the quantity that is modulated by the output stage of the LCLV and multiplied by the weights. Consequently, the input signal to the neurons is first squared before being thresholded and as a result the neural gain is unipolar instead of bipolar (as in the Hopfield model). The interconnection weights are bipolar quantities (actually they can be complex since they are holographic gratings). As mentioned before, the first correlator contains a high pass version of the stored memories. In our analysis we will assume that the high pass filtering operation subtracts the mean value of each image, thus transforming the unipolar initial images into their bipolar versions. Since in the optical system the outer product needed to specify the interconnection matrix is formed as a cascade of two correlators, the resulting weight is the outer product between bipolar and unipolar versions of the stored images. These differences give us characteristics that are distinct from the Hopfield model, such as a ground state (which the Hopfield model does not have) and a dependence of the stable states on the gain the system (in the optical system an increase in gain transforms the shape of the stable states). Thus although the Hopfield model has been analyzed extensively, all the results can not be applied directly to our system, and further analysis is necessary.

In the following, we present a model for the optical associative-memory loop described above. For simplicity we will revert in the subsequent analysis to 1-D, discrete notation. Let x_i^m denote the i-th bit of the mth unipolar (0 or 1) memory. The interconnection matrix that is implemented by the optics is

$$w_{ij} = \sum_{m=1}^{M} (x_j^m - a_m)x_i^m, \qquad (7)$$

where $a_m = 1/N \sum_{j=1}^{N} x_j^m$ is the mean value of the mth memory. A neuron is optically simulated by one pixel of the LCLV, which is modeled as shown in Fig. 13. Let x_i denote the out-

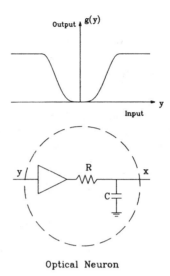

Optical Neuron

Fig. 13. Model for the LCLV and the gain function.

put of the ith neuron (or equivalently the reflectivity of a pixel on the LCLV). Then

$$\frac{dx_i}{dt} = -x_i + g\left(\sum_{j=1}^{N} w_{ij}x_j\right), \qquad i = 1 \cdots N \qquad (8)$$

where g is a nonlinear function describing the neuron response. Note that g is an even function instead of an odd (sigmoid-like) function, as is usually assumed.

In the above equation the response of each pixel is coupled to all other pixels and depends on all the memories stored in w_{ij}. To gain some understanding about what the stable states are and how they are related to the patterns we attempt to store in the system, we introduce a change of variables.

Assume that the stored images $x^1, x^2, \cdots, x^M$ are linearly independent. We decompose the vector space R^N into two subspaces, V_1 and V_2, where V_1 is the vector space spanned by the stored images and V_2 is normal to V_1. We define a basis $\beta_1 = \{y^1, y^2, \cdots, y^M\}$ for V_1, such that

$$y^i \cdot x^j = \delta_{ij} \qquad i, j = 1, \cdots, M \qquad (9)$$

and we select an orthonormal basis $\beta_2 = \{y^{M+1}, \cdots, y^N\}$ for V_2. We then have $\beta = \beta_1 \cup \beta_2 = \{y^1, \cdots, y^N\}$ which forms a basis for R^N.

Consider the vector u whose jth component is $(x_j - 1/N\sum_{k=1}^{N} x_k)$. (We will call u the bipolar version of x.) Let c_l be the lth component of u expanded in terms of the basis β. Using (9), a set of differential equations can be found for the c_l's:

$$\frac{dc_l}{dt} = -c_l + \sum_{i=1}^{N} (x_i^l - a_l)g\left(\sum_{m=1}^{M} c_m x_i^m\right),$$

$$l = 1, \cdots, M, \qquad (10)$$

$$\frac{dc_l}{dt} = -c_l + \sum_{i=1}^{N} (y_i^l - b_l)g\left(\sum_{m=1}^{M} c_m x_i^m\right),$$

$$l = M + 1, \cdots, N \qquad (11)$$

where

$$b_l = \frac{1}{N}\sum_{j=1}^{N} y_j^l. \qquad (12)$$

We also have

$$\sum_{j=1}^{N} w_{ij}x_j = \sum_{m=1}^{M} c_m x_i^m. \qquad (13)$$

In general, when the state of the system approaches the lth stored pattern, the variable c_l becomes large. In particular, if the stored memories x^m were orthogonal (no overlapping) then c^l would simply be the inner product between the bipolar version u of the state of the system and the lth stored memory. The lth equation of (10) has a driving force which is the inner product between the bipolar version of the lth memory and the output of the neurons. If the state of the system starts to approach one of the stored memories then the corresponding c^l will tend to grow thus providing the system with a tendency to be attracted to that state. Setting $d/dt = 0$ in (9) and using (10), we get the following expression for the equilibrium states of the system:

$$x_i = g\left(\sum_{m=1}^{M} c_m x_i^m\right). \qquad (14)$$

If one of the c_m's becomes dominant, then the stable state of the system resembles the corresponding stored pattern. Note, however, that the neurons will also pick up some cross-correlation components. This is a property observed in our experiments where increase of the gain led to the distortion of the stable states and eventually to the creation of unrecognizable mixture states.

Note that $c_1, \cdots, c_M$ are coupled together in (10), but the driving terms of the equations for $c_{M+1}, \cdots, c_N$ (11) depend only on $c_1, \cdots, c_M$. Thus once the steady states of $c_1, \cdots, c_M$ are known, so will those of $c_{M+1}, \cdots, c_N$. Therefore we need only consider the l coupled equations in (10).

To gain some insight of how the system behaves, we introduce a geometrical method to illustrate how the system evolves to a stable state, and how it is influenced by the parameters such as gain and initial conditions. In order to illustrate the concept, we will consider the case where only two images, x^1 and x^2, are stored in the memory. As we shall see, the two-image case contains all the salient features of the dynamics. Similar arguments can be made to extend the results to the general case of multiple stored images.

Equation (10) is reduced to two equations:

$$\frac{dc_1}{dt} = -c_1 + \sum_{i=1}^{N} (x_i^1 - a_1)g(c_1 x_i^1 + c_2 x_i^2) \qquad (15)$$

$$\frac{dc_2}{dt} = -c_2 + \sum_{i=1}^{N} (x_i^2 - a_2)g(c_1 x_i^1 + c_2 x_i^2). \qquad (16)$$

Recall that a_1 and a_2 are the average levels of the input images x^1 and x^2. Let $h_1(c_1, c_2)$ represent the driving term in (15), and $h_2(c_1, c_2)$ the summation term in (16). For simplicity, assume that x^1 and x^2 have no overlapping nonzero components. Thus x_i^1 can be nonzero only when $x_i^2 = 0$, and vice versa.

In this case, the driving forces can be written as

$$h_1(c_1, c_2) = \sum_{x_i^1 \neq 0}^{N} (x_i^1 - a_1)g(c_1 x_i^1) - a_1 \sum_{x_i^2 \neq 0} g(c_2 x_i^2) \qquad (17)$$

$$h_2(c_1, c_2) = \sum_{x_i^2 \neq 0}^{N} (x_i^2 - a_2)g(c_2 x_i^2) - a_2 \sum_{x_i^1 \neq 0} g(c_1 x_i^1) \qquad (18)$$

There are two parts in each of the driving forces. Consider $h_1(c_1, c_2)$. The first term comes from the correlation between the neuron state $g(c_1 x^1)$ and the bipolar version of stored image x^1, and the second term results from the coupling between c_1 and c_2 through the dc level a_1. Since a_1 and the gain function $g(x)$ are always positive, the second term gives a negative contribution to the driving force. This means that the coupling pulls the system away from x^1. The same description also applies to c_2. We plot $h_1(c_1, c_2)$ against c_1 for $c_2 = 0$ and $c_2 \neq 0$ in Fig. 14(a).

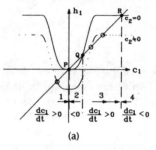

(a)

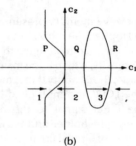

(b)

Fig. 14. The driving force and the dynamics of the loop. (a) The driving force for the first stored image. (b) The boundary lines of the equilibrium states of the first image.

In the figure, the solid curve represents the case $c_2 = 0$, and the dashed curve represents the case for $c_2 \neq 0$. We also plot the line $h(c_1) = c_1$ in the same figure. It is seen that there are three intersections, P, Q, and R, between the straight line and the solid curve $h_1(c_1, c_2)$ (for $c_2 = 0$). As we increase the value of c_2 from 0 to a positive or negative value, the curve $h_1(c_1, c_2)$ changes due to the second summation term in (18), as shown in Fig. 14(a). The intersection points P, Q, and R then also change. As c_2 increases, the points Q, and R will typically merge together and then vanish. If we plot out the values of c_1 corresponding to P, Q, and R for different c_2 values in the (c_1, c_2) plane, they will trace out three curves. An example is shown in Fig. 14(b) (here the curves by Q, and R merge to become a closed loop). We will call these the boundary lines (of c_1).

Consider the three intersection points for a particular c_2 as shown in Fig. 14(a). The c_1 axis is divided into four regions, designated as 1 to 4. In regions 1 and 3, c_1 is smaller than $h_1(c_1, c_2)$ and $dc_1/dt > 0$. Thus, in these regions the system state evolves in the direction of increasing c_1. This is rep-

538

resented by the arrows pointing to the right in the figure. On the other hand, in regions 2 and 4, $dc_1/dt < 0$; thus, the system evolves toward decreasing c_1. The corresponding situation is shown in the (c_1, c_2) plane in Fig. 14(b). Here the regions 2 and 4 merge. The arrows again denote the direction that c_1 changes.

By going through the same procedure, we can obtain similar boundary lines for c_2. We then plot the two groups of boundary lines in the same (c_1, c_2) plane to obtain the phase diagram for (15) and (16). An example is shown in Fig. 15.

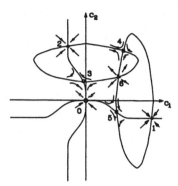

Fig. 15. Phase flow of the two-image auto-associative memory. States 0, 1, 2 are stable. States 3, 4, 5 are unstable (saddle points). State 6: Source state. (unstable)

We see that there are 7 equilibrium points; one source, three sinks, and three saddles. The three sinks represent the null state (no image) and the two stored images. Point 1 represents the stable state corresponding to stored image x^1, since at that position c_1 is large and c_2 is small. On the other hand, at point 2 c_1 is small and c_2 is large, and this represents the stable state corresponding to stored image x_2. It can be seen from the figure that if we start from an initial state that is close to one of the stored states, the system will converge to that state. Otherwise, it will decay to zero.

From the phase diagram we see that the stable state is always a mixture state of the stored memories. The extent of mixture can be reduced by reducing the neural gain. However, if the gain is too small, then the system will not be able to sustain the stored memories. To see why this is so, consider the three intersection points in Fig. 14(a). Reducing the gain shrinks the $h_1(c_1, c_2)$ curve, so that the points Q, and R merge at a lower value of c_2 in Fig. 14(b). If we lower the gain further, the intersection points Q, and R will disappear altogether, and there will be only one boundary line in Fig. 14(b). Thus in Fig. 15, as the gain decreases, the intersection points 4 and 6 will first disappear as the two closed loops (boundary lines) shrink. As the gain decreases further, the loops disappear, and with it the intersection points 1, 2, 3, and 5. In this case, there will be only one equilibrium state, viz., the null state at the origin. No matter where the initial state is, the system always decays to zero.

On the other hand, suppose the neural gain is set very high. In this case the loops in Fig. 15 will become larger, and two more equilibria points can appear, as shown in Fig. 16. The state m is a strongly mixed state of x^1 and x^2. We also see that m has a large region of attraction. Thus it is important that the gain is not set too high.

Next consider the case where the stored memories have

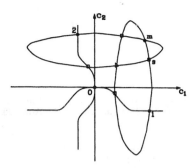

Fig. 16. The dynamics of the loop at high gain. Two new equilibrium states are generated: M is a mixture state and s is a saddle point.

some slight overlap. In principle we can still plot out corresponding boundary lines for this case. The shape and position of these lines will be altered somewhat from the nonoverlapping case. However, since the neural gain function is continuous the general features of the system will be the same if the overlap is small. As the overlap between the stored states increases, the boundary lines in the phase diagram become distorted. In computer simulations, the stable points that ought to resemble the vectors we attempt to store in the memory, become a mixture of all the stored states and the system performance degrades. We do not yet have a prediction for the amount of overlap that is tolerated in this system.

It is interesting to use the method described above to investigate the effect of using an all-pass hologram instead of a high-pass hologram in the first correlator of our system. Note that in this case, the interconnection matrix w_{ij} will be symmetric. We expand here x instead of u, and consider the components c_i of x expanded in basis β. Equations (15) and (16) then become

$$\frac{dc_1}{dt} = -c_1 + \sum_{i=1}^{N} x_i^1 g(c_1 x_i^1 + c_2 x_i^2) \qquad (19)$$

$$\frac{dc_2}{dt} = -c_2 + \sum_{i=1}^{N} x_i^2 g(c_1 x_i^1 + c_2 x_i^2) \qquad (20)$$

By going through similar arguments, we can draw the boundary lines and the phase diagram for this system. Fig. 17 shows one example. It is seen that there are four stable states: two memory states, 1 and 2, one null state 0, and one mixture state m. If we decrease the neural gain, then the points 1, 2, s_1, and s_2, may disappear. However, the mixture state m always exists. This shows why a high-pass hologram

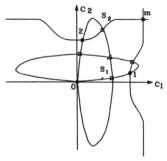

Fig. 17. The dynamics of the loop without the high pass hologram. There are four stable states: 1 and 2 are the stored states, O is the null state. m is a mixture state. The other states are unstable.

is crucial for good performance of the memory loop, a fact confirmed by the experimental system.

REFERENCES

[1] J. J. Hopfield, "Neural networks and physical systems with emergent collective computational abilities," *Proc. Natl. Acad. Sci. USA*, vol. 79, pp. 2554–2558, Apr. 1982.

[2] J. A. Anderson, J. W. Silverstein, S. A. Ritz, and R. S. Jones, "Distinctive features, categorical perception, and probability learning: some applications of a neural model," *Psychological Review*, vol. 84, pp. 413–451, 1977.

[3] D. Psaltis and N. Farhat, "Optical information processing based on an associative-memory model of neural nets with thresholding and feedback," *Opt. Lett.*, vol. 10, pp. 98–100, 1985.

[4] N. H. Farhat, D. Psaltis, A. Prata, and E. Paek, "Optical implementation of the Hopfield Model," *Appl. Opt.*, vol. 24, pp. 1469–1475, 1985.

[5] Y. S. Abu-Mostafa and D. Psaltis, "Optical neural computers," *Scientific American*, vol. 256, no. 3, pp. 88–95, 1987.

[6] E. G. Paek and D. Psaltis, "Optical associative memory using Fourier transform holograms," *Opt. Eng.*, vol. 26, no. 5, pp. 428–433, May 1987.

[7] J. S. Jang, S. W. Jung, S. Y. Lee, and S. Y. Shin, "Optical implementation of the Hopfield model for two-dimensional associative memory," *Opt. Lett.*, vol. 13, pp. 248–250, 1988.

[8] J. S. Jang, S. Y. Shin, and S. Y. Lee, "Optical implementation of quadratic associative memory with outer-product storage," *Opt. Lett.*, vol. 13, pp. 693–695, 1988.

[9] N. H. Farhat and D. Psaltis, "Optical implementation of associative memory based on models of neural networks," in *Optical Signal Processing* Chap. 2.3, J. L. Horner, Ed. San Diego, CA: Academic Press, 1987.

[10] L. S. Lee, H. M. Stoll, and M. C. Tackitt, "Continuous-time optical neural associative memory," *Opt. Lett.*, vol. 14, p. 162, 1989.

[11] B. H. Soffer, G. J. Dunning, Y. Owechko, and E. Maron, "Associative holographic memory with feedback using phase-conjugate mirrors," *Opt. Lett.*, vol. 11, pp. 118–120, 1986.

[12] D. Psaltis, D. Brady, and K. Wagner, "Adaptive optical networks using photorefractive crystals," *Appl. Opt.*, vol. 27, pp. 1752–1759, 1988.

[13] D. Psaltis, D. Brady, X.-G. Gu, and S. Lin, "Holography in artificial neural networks," *Nature*, vol. 343, no. 25, pp. 325–330, 1990.

[14] A. B. Vander Lugt, "Signal Detection by Complex Spatial Filtering," *IEEE Trans. Inform. Theory*, vol. IT-10, no. 2, pp. 139–145, 1964.

[15] J. W. Goodman, *Introduction to Fourier Optics*, Chap. 2, New York: McGraw Hill, 1968.

Author Index

A

Abidi, A. A., 484
Adams, Jr., F. W., 352
Ahumada, Jr., A. J., 220
Alexandre, F., 209
Allman, J., 416
Amari, S. -I., 118
Anderson, J. A., 101

B

Baxter, R. A., 375
Bokil, A., 431
Burnod, Y., 209
Burt, P. J., 342

C

Caulfield, H. J., 522
Changeux, J. -P., 149
Chellappa, R., 450, 471
Chiang, A. M., 514
Choo, C. Y., 442
Chuang, M. L., 514
Churchland, P. S., 39, 44

D

Daugman, J. G., 233
Dehaene, S., 149

E

Elmasry, M. I., 501

F

Fang., W. -C., 471
Fukushima, K., 392

G

Golovan, A. V., 198, 369
Goodman, R. M., 416
Granrath, D. J., 52
Grossberg, S., 323
Gupta, M. M., 279
Gusakova, V. I., 369
Guyot, F., 209

H

Haton, J. -P., 209
Hopfield, J. J., 140
Hsu, K. -Y., 532
Hubel, D. H., 163, 177

J

Jenkins, B. K., 450

K

Kalil, R. E., 90
Kandel, E. R., 80
Khotanzad, A., 431
Kinser, J., 522
Knopf, G. K., 279
Kobayashi, H., 484
Koch, C., 44
Kohonen, T., 126
Koruga, D., 153
Kronauer, R. E., 187

L

Lee, J. -C., 471
Lee, Y. -W., 431

541

Subject Index

P

packing, in molecular network, 154–159
parallelism
    in artificial neural network, 127
    in biological vision, 187, 210
    in CNNs, 32
    in matrix/vector associative models, 106
    neurobiological explanation of, 99, 101–117, 103–104
    psycho-physical, 138
    stereo correspondence and, 442–449
    video motion detection and, 471–483
parallel network, for visual cognition, 352–368
parvocellular system
    in biological vision, 178–185
    magno system and, **183**
    in monkey, **41**
pattern recognition
    algorithm for, 392–406
    by learned responses, 134–135
    for characters, 217
    feed-forward networks for, 140
    layered neural networks and, 375–383
    MADALINE network for, **383**
    neocognition and, 385
    neocognitron and, 396–406
    neural computing and, 129–130, 144
    visual systems for, 185
    See also learning
patterns
    activity patterns from single dot, **108**
    discrimination of by house fly, 46
    dot patterns, **108–109**
    Glass pattern, 323, **324**
    grating pattern, **12**
    prototype dot pattern with distortion, **107**
    random, **300**
    signature for, 12
    stimulus pattern and neocognitron, **403, 404**
    trigger feature and, 7
    See also dot pattern
PCA. *See* probalistic cellular automata
PE. *See* neuronal processing elements
peptide hormones, 82
perception
    artificial, 129–130
    color vision and, 40–41
    computational neuroscience and, 44
    in human vision, 52
    neural network system for, 369–374
    scientific understanding of, 35
    See also recognition
perspective, invariance to, 382
PFM. *See* pulse frequency modulation
pharmacological agents
    affect of on cortical inhibition, 48
    See also chemical processes
photoreceptor
    cell circuitry for, 497–498
    logarithmic, 488
    in retina, 3, 45, 187, 188–191
planes, neurons and, 31, 42
position, scale, rotation invariant (PSRI) object recognition, 384–391
positive-negative (PN) neural processor, 279–295
    block diagram of equations for, **284**
    computational architecture of, 280–281
    Mach Band effect recreation using, **291–292**

    mathematical model of, 281–283
    neural processor dynamics description, 283–291
    temporal phenomena and, 286–290
    temporal response of, **293**
postattentive learned object recognition, preattentive vision and, 326–327
postsynaptic potential (PSP), 6
potentiation (long-term), NMDA receptors effect on, **97**
preattentive vision
    neural network architecture for, 323–341
    postattentive learned object recognition and, 326–327
primary transform, perception and, 370–371
primary visual cortex
    in biological visual pathway, **8**
    cerebral cortex and, 163–164, **165**
    columnar neuronal structure of, **10**
    domain model for, 198–208
    hexagonal orthogonal-oriented pyramid model of, 220–230
    hypothetical pattern of activity in, **175, 176**
    neuronal process in, 102
    neuron of in cat, **69**
    ocular-dominance columns in, **164**
    orientation in, **174**
    orientation selectivity in, 47–49
    in parallel-hierarchical architecture of vision, **4**
    role of in vision, 3, 7, 9, 280
    segment of in cat, **95**
    visual field in area of, in cat, **103**
probalistic cellular automata (PCA)
    defined, 354–356
    relationship of to model, 356–361
    visual cognition and, 352–368
problem solving. *See* decision making
processing
    in computational network, 216–217
    image processing, 52–61, 220–221
    levels of, 39–40
    macro-circuit of, **325**
programming of biological network, 127–128
PSP. *See* postsynaptic potential
PSRI. *See* position, scale, rotation invariant
psychic concepts, in neural computing, 137
psychological computation, with neural models, 101–117
psychology
    color display and, 60
    color vision and, 40–41
psychophysics, multichannel models in, 245–247
pulse frequency modulation (PFM), 280
    limit cycle oscillations and, **290**
pyramid
    band pass (Laplacian), 344
    hexagonal orthogonal-oriented quadrature (HOP), 220–230, **224**
    pyramid vision machine, smart sensing and, 342–351
pyramid vision machine (PVM), 348–**349**

R

receptive field
    bandwidth and, **12**
    boundary contour system and, 332–333
    of cell, 393, **404**
    characteristics of, 7, **9**, 49, 189–**190**, 221
    color vision and, **178**, 180
    comparisons of, **169**
    cortical, **227**
    divisions of, **48**

video, Land's retinex theory and, **419**–423
video motion detection, VLSI neuroprocessor for, 471–483
vision
  brain mechanisms of, 163–176
  in human beings, 35, 36
  localized texture processing in, 264–278
  physiology of in multichannel models, 245–247
  preattentive, 323–341
  seeing vs. recognizing, 323–324
vision system. *See* biological vision
visual cognition
  parallel network for, 352–368
  See also cognitive computation
visual cortex. *See* primary visual cortex
visual neurophysiology, biological vision and, 161–230
visual pathway
  in biological system, 7–10, **8**, 166–**167**, **245**
  in cat, development of, **94**
  in cat, simulated, **49**
  human, side view of, **3**
  nervous system and, **5**
  organization of, 187–197
  primate, **179**
  simulation of in cat, **49**
  See also biological vision

visual patterns
  trigger feature and, 7
  See also patterns
visual receptive field structures, 10–14
visual receptor fields, functional role of, 1
VLSI. *See* very large scale integration

W

wavelet transform, 250–253
  applications of, 259–260
  in two dimensions, 253–254
wheel model
  one-dimensional, **360**–361
  two-dimensional, **359**, 366
window Fourier transform, 248–250
wiring
  of motion analysis, 296
  underlying orientation selectivity, **48**
  See also hardware

Z

zero crossings
  motion detection and, **299**–300
  multi-frequency channel decomposition and, 260–261

Editors' Biographies

Madan M. Gupta (fellow: IEEE and SPIE) received the B. Eng. (Hons.) and the M.Sc. in Electronics-Communications Engineering, from the Birla Engineering College (now the BITS), Pilani, India, in 1961 and 1962, respectively. He received the Ph.D. degree from the University of Warwick, United Kingdom, in 1967 in adaptive control systems. Dr. Gupta is currently Professor of Engineering and the Director of the Intelligent Systems Research Laboratory and the Centre of Excellence on Neuro-Vision Research at the University of Saskatchewan, Canada.

He was elected Fellow of IEEE for his contributions to the theory of fuzzy sets and the adaptive control systems, and the advancement of the diagnosis of cardiovascular disease. He was also elected Fellow of SPIE for his contributions to the field of neuro-vision, neuro-control, and neuro-fuzzy systems.

Dr. Gupta has served the engineering community worldwide in various capacities through societies such as IEEE, IFSA, IFAC, SPIE, NAFIP, UN, CANS-FINS, and ISUMA. He has been elected as a visiting professor and a special advisor, in the areas of high technology, to the European Centre for Peace and Development (ECPD), University for Peace, which was established by the United Nations.

In addition to publishing over 400 research papers, Dr. Gupta has co-authored two books on fuzzy logic with Japanese translation, and has edited fourteen volumes in the field of adaptive control systems, fuzzy logic/computing, neuro-vision, and neuro-control systems.

Dr. Gupta's present research interests are expanded to the areas of neuro-vision, neuro-control and integration of fuzzy-neural systems, neuronal morphology of biological vision systems, intelligent and cognitive robotic systems, cognitive information, new paradigms in information processing, and chaos in neural systems. He is also developing new architectures of computational neural networks (CNNs), and computational fuzzy neural networks (CFNNs) for applications to advanced robotic systems.

George Karl Knopf received the B.A. degree in the humanities and the B.E. degree in mechanical engineering in 1984, and the M.Sc. and Ph.D. degrees in machine vision in 1987 and 1991, respectively, from the University of Saskatchewan.

Dr. Knopf is currently with the Faculty of Engineering Science at the University of Western Ontario. He was previously a research associate with the Intelligent Systems Research Laboratory at the University of Saskatchewan. This position was sponsored by the Institute for Robotic and Intelligent Systems (IRIS), a research network within the government of Canada's Networks of Centres of Excellence program.

Dr. Knopf has co-authored numerous technical papers on neuro-vision system architectures, and the application of fuzzy set theory to image processing and control. His major research interests include active vision system architectures, neural networks, robotics, fuzzy approximate reasoning methods for ill-defined systems, and biological paradigms for engineering applications.